Encyclopedia of Information Ethics and Security

Marian Quigley
Monash University, Australia

INFORMATION SCIENCE REFERENCE

Hershey · New York

Acquisitions Editor:	Kristin Klinger
Development Editor:	Kristin Roth
Senior Managing Editor:	Jennifer Neidig
Managing Editor:	Sara Reed
Assistant Managing Editor:	Diane Huskinson
Copy Editor:	Maria Boyer
Typesetter:	Sara Reed
Cover Design:	Lisa Tosheff
Printed at:	Yurchak Printing Inc.

Published in the United States of America by
Information Science Reference (an imprint of IGI Global)
701 E. Chocolate Avenue, Suite 200
Hershey PA 17033
Tel: 717-533-8845
Fax: 717-533-8661
E-mail: cust@igi-pub.com
Web site: http://www.igi-pub.com/reference

and in the United Kingdom by
Information Science Reference (an imprint of IGI Global)
3 Henrietta Street
Covent Garden
London WC2E 8LU
Tel: 44 20 7240 0856
Fax: 44 20 7379 0609
Web site: http://www.eurospanonline.com

Library of Congress Cataloging-in-Publication Data

Encyclopedia of information ethics and security / Marian Quigley, Editor.
    p. cm.
  Topics address a wide range of life areas affected by computer technology, including: education, the workplace, health, privacy, intellectual property, identity, computer crime, cyber terrorism, equity and access, banking, shopping, publishing, legal and political issues, censorship, artificial intelligence, the environment, communication.
  Summary: "This book is an original, comprehensive reference source on ethical and security issues relating to the latest technologies. It covers a wide range of themes, including topics such as computer crime, information warfare, privacy, surveillance, intellectual property and education. It is a useful tool for students, academics, and professionals"--Provided by publisher.
  Includes bibliographical references and index.
  ISBN 978-1-59140-987-8 (hardcover) -- ISBN 978-1-59140-988-5 (ebook)
  1. Information technology--Social aspects--Encyclopedias. 2. Information technology--Moral and ethical aspects--Encyclopedias. 3. Computer crimes--Encyclopedias. 4. Computer security--Encyclopedias. 5. Information networks--Security measures--Encyclopedias. I. Quigley, Marian.
  HM851.E555 2007
  174'.900403--dc22
                        2007007277

British Cataloguing in Publication Data
A Cataloguing in Publication record for this book is available from the British Library.

All work contributed to this encyclopedia set is new, previously-unpublished material. The views expressed in this encyclopedia set are those of the authors, but not necessarily of the publisher.

Editorial Advisory Board

List of Contributors

Contents

Preface

We create technology and choose to adopt it. However, once we have adopted a technological device, it can change us and how we relate to other people and our environment. (Quinn, 2006, p. 3)

...the computer profoundly shapes our ways of thinking and feeling...computers are not just changing our lives but our selves. (Turkle, 2000, p. 129)

Alongside the examination of technological advancements and the development of new computer software and hardware, an increasing number of scholars across a range of disciplines are researching and writing about the ethical dilemmas and security issues which the world is facing in what is now termed the Information Age. It is imperative that ordinary citizens as well as academics and computer professionals are involved in these debates, as technology has a transformative effect on all of our daily lives and on our very humanness. The *Encyclopedia of Information Ethics and Security* aims to provide a valuable resource for the student as well as teachers, researchers, and professionals in the field.

The changes brought about by rapid developments in information and communication technologies in the late twentieth century have been described as a revolution similar in impact to the Industrial Revolution of the nineteenth century. The development of the personal computer in the 1980s and the creation of the World Wide Web (WWW) in the early 1990s, followed by the development of low-cost computers and high-speed networks, have resulted in dramatic changes in the way humans communicate with one another and gain information. Today, more than 600 million people have e-mail accounts (Quinn, 2006, p. 2). Communication via cell phone and the Internet is now regarded as commonplace, if not indeed, essential by Westerners, yet there remain many groups both in developing countries and within developed countries who do not have access to these technologies or who lack the skills to use them. Technology has thus helped to create social divisions or to reinforce existing ones based on socio-economic and educational differences. These divisions are often described as the gap between the 'information rich' and the 'information poor.'

Technology can bring harm as well as benefit. It can undermine basic human rights and values, and challenge established social or cultural norms and legal practices. While the home PC with an Internet connection may provide us with ready access to a wealth of information, it also makes us potential victims of cyber crime or subject to invasions of our privacy. Some members of society may enthusiastically embrace the new opportunities offered by new technologies, while others such as the elderly or disabled may become increasingly marginalized by the implementation of these technologies in the public domains of commerce, banking, and education.

It is important to remember that no technical invention is conceived or used in complete isolation or without repercussions which impact on others, therefore we need to study technological developments and their ramifications within their social and cultural contexts. As Raymond Williams noted as far back as 1981 in his seminal text *Contact: Human Communication and History,* "a technology is always, in a full sense, social. It is necessarily in complex and variable connection with other social relations and institutions...' (p. 227). It is therefore rewarding to see that particular ethical or security issues concerning local cultures and institutions or developing nations are addressed by a number of the encyclopedia's contributors.

Although the technologies may be new, many of the moral dilemmas they give rise to are longstanding. Consequently, knowledge of history is an essential accompaniment to our knowledge of current ethical issues and new technological developments. This is demonstrated by several contributors to this volume who, in addressing ethical problems, draw upon the writings of earlier moral philosophers such as Aristotle and Immanuel Kant. Similarly, articles such as those by Christopher Walker concerning ancient methods of document security remind us that information security is not merely a twenty-first-century issue, but rather one to which computers have given an added dimension.

Although the area of Information Ethics is gaining increasing credence in the academic community, the recent study by Jordan, Rainer, and Marshall, which is included in this volume, reveals that there are still relatively few articles devoted to ethics in information systems journals compared with those devoted to security management. The *Encyclopedia of Information Ethics and Security* addresses this gap by providing a valuable compilation of work by distinguished international researchers in this field who are drawn from a wide range of prominent research institutions.

This encyclopedia contains 95 entries concerning information ethics and security which were subjected to an initial double-blind peer review and an additional review prior to their acceptance for publication. Each entry includes an index of key terms and definitions and an associated list of references. To assist readers in navigating and finding information, this encyclopedia has been organized by listing all entries in alphabetical order by title.

Topics covered by the entries are diverse and address a wide range of life areas which have been affected by computer technology. These include:

- education
- the workplace
- health
- privacy
- intellectual property
- identity
- computer crime
- cyber terrorism
- equity and access
- banking
- shopping
- publishing
- legal and political issues
- censorship
- artificial intelligence
- the environment
- communication

These contributions also provide an explanation of relevant terminology and acronyms, together with descriptions and analyses of the latest technological developments and their significance. Many also suggest possible solutions to pressing issues concerning information ethics and security.

Apart from providing information about current and possible future technological developments, this volume contains much thought-provoking material concerning the social and moral implications of information and communication technologies which is of immense importance to us all. Hopefully, it will enable us to make considered and cautious decisions in our adoption and use of new technologies in order to support human flourishing.

In the current era of globalization which has been enabled by the revolution in communications, the renowned ethicist, Peter Singer, suggests that the developed nations should be adopting a global approach to the resolution of ethical and security issues—issues which, he argues, are inextricably linked. As he explains: "For the rich nations not to take a global ethical viewpoint has long been seriously morally wrong. Now it is also, in the long term, a danger to their security" (Singer, 2004, p. 15).

REFERENCES

Quinn, M. (2006). *Ethics for the Information Age* (2nd ed.). Boston: Pearson.

Singer, P. (2002). *One world: The ethics of globalisation.* Melbourne: Text Publishing.

Turkle, S. (2000). Who am we? In Baird et al. (Eds.), *Cyberethics: Social and moral issues in the computer age* (pp. 129-141). New York: Prometheus.

Williams, R. (1981). Communications technologies and social institutions. In R. Williams (Ed.), *Contact: Human communication and its history.* London: Thames and Hudson.

Dr. Marian Quigley
Monash University
Berwick, Victoria, Australia
May 2007

Acknowledgment

I wish to thank all of those involved in the collation and review process of this encyclopedia, without whose support the project could not have been satisfactorily completed.

As well as providing articles for this volume, most of the authors also served as referees for other submissions. Additional reviews were undertaken by my colleagues at Monash University: Mark Szota, Grace Rumantir, Tom Chandler, Joachim Asscher, and by Tim van Gelder of Melbourne University and Allison Craven at James Cook University. Thanks go to all for their constructive and comprehensive reviews.

I am also indebted to Bianca Sullivan, Cheryl Ely, Carmel Dettman, Michelle Jones, and Melanie Smith of the Berwick School of Information Technology, Monash University, who assisted with collating the final submissions and assembling the final document at a time which, due to unforeseen circumstances, was a particularly trying period for me.

Special thanks also go to the publishing team at IGI Global for their invaluable assistance and guidance throughout the project, particularly to Michelle Potter and Kristin Roth, who promptly answered queries and kept the project on track, and to Mehdi Khosrow-Pour for the opportunity to undertake this project.

This has been a mammoth task, but one which I have found most rewarding. I am particularly grateful to the authors for their excellent contributions in this crucial and growing area of research and to the Editorial Advisory Board members who, in addition to their contributions as reviewers and authors, helped to promote interest in the project.

Dr. Marian Quigley
Monash University
Berwick, Victoria, Australia
May 2007

About the Editor

Marian Quigley, PhD (Monash University); B.A. (Chisholm Institute of Technology); Higher Diploma of Teaching Secondary (Art and Craft) is a former senior lecturer in the Faculty of Information Technology, Monash University, Australia. Her research interests include the social effects of technology and animation. Her recent publications include the books *Women Do Animate: Interviews with 10 Australian Animators* (Insight Publications, 2005) and *Information Security and Ethics: Social and Organizational Issues* (IRM Press, 2004).

3D Avatars and Collaborative Virtual Environments

3D

Koon-Ying Raymond Li
e-Promote Pty. Ltd., Australia

James Sofra
Monash University, Australia

Mark Power
Monash University, Australia

INTRODUCTION

With the exponential growth in desktop computing power and advancements in Web-based technologies over the past decade, the virtual community is now a reality. The latest derivative of the virtual community, made possible by 3D avatars, is called the collaborative virtual environment (CVE). These CVEs often provide "fantasy-themed online worlds" for participants to socially interact. Instead of placing emphasis on team-playing, the sharing of information, and collaborative activities, a CVE focuses on social presence and communication processes. Unlike virtual environments which allow participants to discuss what is going on in the real world, the participants' experiences of the virtual world provided by the CVE are often the main topics for discussion. These CVEs, just like their real counterparts, have their own issues and problems. This article will analyze the potential benefits of avatars, helping to build virtual communities and explore the possible issues that are associated with the CVE.

A virtual community (VC) is a computer-mediated communication environment that exhibits characteristics of a community. Unlike the physical community, the participants in a virtual community are not confined to a well-defined physical location or to having distinctive characteristics. Members of most VCs (for example, the Final Fantasy game community or a newborn baby support group) are often bounded only by a common interest.

A VC can be a simple message board with limited or no visual identifiers for its users to utilize when posting and sharing their text messages with others. Conversely, it can also be a sophisticated 3D environment with interactive objects and fully detailed human-oid character animations. The ARPANET, created in 1978 by the U.S. Department of Defense's Advanced Research Projects Agency, is often said to be the first virtual community (Rheingold, 2000). Other significant landmarks in the evolution of VCs, as noted by Lu (2006), are: Multi-User Domain/Dungeon (MUD) (1979), Internet Relay Chat (IRC) (1988), America On-Line (AOL) (1989), Doom (online games) (1993), ICQ (instant messaging) (1996), Everquest (Massively Multi-player Online Role-Playing Game (MMORPG)) (1999), and Friendster (social networks) (2003). While the earlier VCs emphasized team-playing, the sharing of information, and collaborative activities, the latest ones (the social networks) focus on social presence and communication processes (Kushner, 2004).

These social networks may be referred to as collaborative virtual environments (Brown & Bell, 2004). They provide a "fantasy-themed online world" for participants to socially interact and collaborate. There is also a distinctive difference between the two types of VCs in terms of the contents of their discussion: the earlier VCs provide an online media to allow participants to discuss what is going on in the real world, while the inhabitants' experiences within the virtual world are the main topics for conversations in a CVE.

Anonymity of its members is one of the important features of VCs. Avatars are often employed by their members to identify each other. The word 'avatar' comes from ancient Sanskrit and means "a manifestation of the divine in human form or reincarnation" (Parrinder, 1982). In other words, it is the earthly manifestation of God. The term 'avatar' is now used to describe a person's alter ego in a virtual world. Avatars, such as those used in an online chat environment like ICQ, are 2D image based. The users in these environments select a name or a 2D image so other members may identify them.

Avatars can also be 3D. With 3D avatars, users can project a certain amount of their own personality through the appearance of the avatars chosen to represent them, while remaining anonymous. A majority of the current 3D avatars are humanoid in form and many allow for gestures and facial expressions.

This article focuses only on 3D avatars and their 3D virtual worlds. The benefits of 3D avatars helping to build virtual communities will be explored and the associated issues, particularly those relating to CVE, will be analyzed and discussed.

3D AVATARS AND THE VIRTUAL WORLD

Users can use their 3D avatars' appearance to project their chosen personalities and characteristics to others within a virtual world (see Figure 1) and, at the same time, can maintain their chosen degree of anonymity. Anonymity helps open communication channels, encourages users to voice more freely, and removes social cues. As such, avatars can help to promote the better sharing of information. With the freedom of choice in both representation and anonymity, users will acquire a more comfortable version of themselves, which would help them to increase their levels of confidence in dealing with others. According to Brown and Bell (2004), anonymity encourages interactions between strangers which do not happen in the real world. Avatars can also be used to help businesses and large corporations conduct successful meetings (Exodus,

Figure 1. Avatar's eyelashes shape and fingernail color can be customized (Source: www.There.com)

2003). Avatars, including the text- and 2D-based types, can help to remove human inequalities, such as racism and sexism, as well as biases against mental deficiencies and handicaps (Castronova, 2004). Victims who are troubled by "issues of secrecy, hyper vigilance, sexuality and intimacy" can now gain comfort from other virtual world inhabitants and online therapists. Victims, having been physically or sexually abused, who feel ashamed to discuss their situations, can use their avatars to enter the virtual world to commence treatment (Fenichel et al., 2002).

In text-based chat virtual environments, meanings are sometimes lost due to lack of supporting cues such as body language and facial expression. Emoticons, such as smileys ( ), can help to partially solve this issue. 3D avatars in humanoid form can now provide gestures, postures, body languages, as well as facial expressions. Gestures include handshakes, nodes, and even dancing with joy. According to Brown and Bell (2004), "emotional communication enhances communication." 3D avatars can help to express emotions through facial expressions and gestures, thus enhancing the communication process. They help to provide a better environment for collaborative activities.

In text-based virtual communication, posted messages are often not specific for a particular participant. Conversations within a 3D avatar world, however, can be targeted at a particular audience, similar to what is happening in the real world. 3D avatars' gestures and gazes can assist in the communication process within a crowded virtual room and identify who is currently engaged in a conversation. It also helps to identify those who are in private communication and thus allows conversations to remain undisturbed (Salem & Earle, 2000).

Besides being more aesthetically appealing to users, 3D avatars can be more engaging as the users can have a choice in their perspective: a *first-* or *third-person* view of the virtual world. These avatars not only represent the presence of their users in a virtual space, but also display the users' orientations and locations (Salem & Earle, 2000). The users can now interact with other objects or avatars within the virtual world similar to what is happening in the real world. Some 3D virtual worlds are now enhanced with 3D sound (with distance attenuation and stereo positioning) to provide feedback as to the spatial positioning of other participants and elements within the virtual world. As such, 3D avatars do not only have the potential to assist

Figure 2. VC inhabitants can interact as if in real life in virtual environments, such as this 3D dance club or shopping for virtual goods (Source: www.There. com)

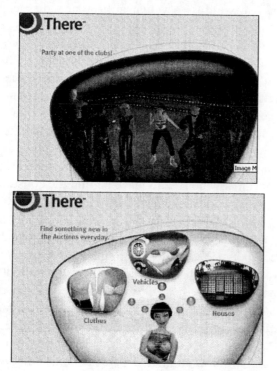

in building and reinforcing virtual communities; they can also motivate and encourage all users to enter a VC for a longer period of time.

3D avatars provide compelling experiences to users by transforming VCs from the traditional environment for collaborative/competing activities and sharing information, into fantasy-theme-based online hangout spots (Kushner, 2004). 3D avatars now enable millions to experience life in a digital landscape and allow them to engage in novel experiences (see Figure 2).

A CVE inhabitant can now experience what it is like to have another career. He or she can now take on the opposite gender. This would allow him or her to explore the ways in which one gender interacts with the other and learn to appreciate the opposite sex. Socialization and experience within the virtual world take precedence over the discussion of real-world issues. "The virtual world feeds upon itself, providing shared experiences that its inhabitants can chat about" (Kushner 2004). For example, *a glitch in the system* provides exciting news within a virtual world for its inhabitants to be excited for a few days (Brown & Bell, 2004).

Avatars can now be customized with extra virtual items to reflect the chosen status of the persons they represent. Users of virtual worlds can now use real monies to purchase real-life fashion-branded (for example, Nike and Levi) virtual items. This helps to create a virtual economy that ultimately will consolidate and provide further growth to the virtual communities (Kushner, 2004).

POTENTIAL PROBLEMS

An avatar allows its user to retain a chosen degree of anonymity. Therefore, no one can be assured as to whether the user is disclosing his or her true identity. An avatar's appearance and name can easily be changed by its user, and therefore, consistency in identification can never be assured (Taylor, 1999). This removes accountability for ones' actions and can thus prompt users to behave badly and rudely or to act irresponsibly (Sulers, 1997). Users may even commit offences that they would not otherwise do in the real world. There are already reported cases of *rape in cyberspace*. For example, the owner of a male avatar used some coding trick to control female avatars and then sodomized them in a public room in front of a large "crowd." It was also reported that some of these victims felt that they had been violated personally, despite the fact that the events were virtual; they carried such feelings over to the real world (Dibbell, 1993)! Cyber bullying, online harassment, and cyber stalking are other examples of offences. Countermeasures such as user IP tracking and possible prosecution in the real world are being developed. Nevertheless, the incidence of these offences are on the rise (ABC, 2006).

Anonymity may keep users of virtual communities motivated to participate, but can also lead to *identity deception*: the use of avatars allows participants in a virtual world to conceal their true identities and to claim to be someone that they are not. A member of a virtual community can deliberately have as many avatars or identities as he or she sees fit, with the intention to deceive others. The identity deceptions may be in the form of gender, race, or qualification. While real-world evidence of a person's credibility is reasonably easy to determine, such assurance may not be offered in the virtual world. In the real world we are better equipped to ascertain whether what we are being told is fact or lie. Taking advice within a virtual world is therefore dangerous. In fact, it is important to bear in mind that "the best, busiest experts are probably the least likely ones to bother registering with any kind of expert locator service" (Kautz & Selman, 1998). With the ease in changing avatar at will, it is almost impossible to ban any users who have violated their privileges. Identity deception can easily lead to virtual crimes, such as hacking into others' accounts and selling of a virtual house and other properties to another person for real money.

Assuming a person's gender from his or her avatars is impossible. In VC where *chimeras* and *cyborgs* are available as the choice for avatars, gender identity is often blurred. A user can also impersonate an opposite sex. In fact, many male users log onto the VCs as women because they enjoy the sexually suggestive attention they received from other avatars. Gender blurring and gender impersonation with an intention to deceive others can be a big issue (Kaisa, Kivimaki, Era, & Robinson, 1998).

The ability to propagate ideas to individuals across the globe with probable anonymity can be alarming. Social behaviors, especially for the youth, can easily be shaped by media through propaganda and promotions. Behavior molding is now easy when the youths are actually "living" out their experiences through their avatars (Winkler & Herezeg, 2004, p. 337).

Because of the lack of facts about a VC member's identity, respect and trust between members can be issues. Lack of respect and trust of others may introduce problems into the real world when some of the VC members carry their behaviors over to the real world.

In an online forum, it is generally accepted that those who participate are actually who they purport to be and have the desire to maintain their individuality consistently. The motivation behind this may be that a user needs to use his or her avatar's position as a 'status symbol' for dissimulating his knowledge, or may merely stem from his or her wish for instant recognition by fellow members. However, within a 3D-avatar-based virtual environment, in particular the CVE, it is generally accepted as fact that an avatar is a fabrication of a user's imagination. As such, many users of VC treat "other players impersonally, as other than real people" (Ludlow, 1996, p. 327) and may carry these molded unwelcome behaviors over to the real world.

As virtual spaces can be accessed simultaneously, a user will, therefore, have the ability to take on various identities within multiple CVEs. They can also take on various identities within one virtual world. They can exert different personalities behind their avatars simultaneously. Such a behavior would be considered in the real world as a psychiatric disorder—dissociative identity disorder.

Addiction to CVEs is an issue. 3D avatars make one feel that one is really 'there'. CVE has the elements of suspense and surprise that can be experienced in the real world—one will not know what is around the corner or the reactions from others in the shared virtual spaces. Those who endure loneliness, alienation, and powerlessness in the real world will look to the virtual world for comfort (Bartle, 2003; Cooper, 1997). They can now be free to leave behind the constraints of the real world and play a role in the community that they feel is more comfortable to them. They may even abandon the real world and continue to hang out at the cyber spots. CVE is also an attraction to teenagers who may have found that they can acquire their perfect self and interact with those who can only be found in their imagination. Despite the fact that some of the larger virtual worlds already have mechanisms in place for detection and prevention, a user can hop from one virtual world to another to satisfy their addiction to VC, refusing to live in the real world.

As the realism in the CVE improves, some users may find it difficult to differentiate the real world from the virtual world. Illusion of being in the cyber world while in the real world can be a problem. CVEs bring people of different cultures together. Different ethnic or national cultures, as well as religions or religious attitudes may have variations in their definitions of acceptable behaviors. These differences in perceptions about acceptable actions and behaviors can create tensions within the virtual world. The worst case scenario would be the lowering of the community norm to the common denominator and ultimately alter the norms in the real world.

In many CVEs, avatars are owned by the virtual world creators, but users can customize their avatars to represent them. In addition to minor alterations to appearance, such as fingernail colors or hair highlights, users can now purchase virtual items for their avatars with real money. There are already reported cases of teenagers committing real-world crimes to finance their purchases of the branded items just so that they can improve the "social" status of "themselves" in the virtual world (Lee, 2004).

CONCLUSION

Avatar technology helps to build virtual communities and makes CVEs a reality. It brings compelling experiences to VC users and encourages more users to enter virtual worlds for longer periods. Just like any other emerging technology, avatars benefit humankind but also bring some negatives. Addiction to CVEs, abandonment of the real world, the blurring between the real world and the virtual world, crimes commission in the pursuance of the finance of virtual items, virtual rape, gender impersonation, and personality disorders are just some of the issues. If unchecked, these problems will likely cause significant detriment to our real-world community in the future. Currently, solutions such as user-IP tracking, laws against virtual crimes and bullying, and rules of some virtual world creators forbidding users from performing certain acts (such as lying down, removing clothing from avatars, and touching without consent) have been developed to tackle some of the issues. However, due to anonymity and the fact that users can change their avatars at will, it would be difficult, if not impossible, to address all of the relevant issues. Significant cooperation efforts at the global level between the virtual world creators, law reinforcing agencies, computer security and networking experts, user groups, and virtual community organizers are needed in the next few years to develop countermeasures and to stop problems at their roots. Above all, there should be a global agent that will oversee the conduct of virtual world creators, virtual world organizers, and users, and prosecute those who have abused their privileges within the virtual world.

REFERENCES

ABC. (2006). Cyber bullying on the rise, say experts. *ABC News - Good Morning America,* (February 2).

Bartle, R.A. (2003). *Designing virtual worlds.* New Riders Publishing.

Brown, B., & Bell, M. (2004). Social interaction in 'there'. *CHI, 24*(19).

Castronova, E. (2004, February 10). The future of cyberspace economics. *Proceedings of the O'Reilly Emerging Technology Conference,* San Diego, CA.

Cooper, S. (1997). Plenitude and alienation: The subject of virtual reality. In D Holmes (Ed.), *Virtual politics: Identity and community in cyberspace* (pp. 93-106). London: Sage.

Dibbell, J. (1993). A rape in cyberspace. *The Village Voice,* (December 21).

Exodus. (2003). *Avatar-based conferencing in virtual worlds for business purposes.* Retrieved February 2, 2006, from http://www.exodus.gr/Avatar_Conference/pdf/Avatar_leaflet.pdf

Fenichel, M., Suler, J., Barak, A., Zelvin, E., Jones, G., Munro, K., Meunier, V., & Walker-Schmucker, W. (2002). Myths and realities of online clinical work. *CyberPsychology & Behavior, 5*(5), 481-497.

Heim, M. (2000). *Some observations on Web-art-writing.* Retrieved February 2, 2006, from http://www.fineartforum.org/Backissues/Vol_14/faf_v14_n09/text/feature.html

Lu, K.Y. (2006). *Visual identity and virtual community.* Retrieved January 31, 2006, from http://www.atopia.tk/eyedentity/netid.htm

Kaisa, K., Kivimaki, A., Era, T., & Robinson, M. (1998, November 2-5). Producing identity in collaborative virtual environments. *Proceedings of VRST'98.*

Kautz, H., & Selman, B. (1998). *Creating models of real-world communities with ReferalWeb.* Retrieved September 6, 2005, from http://citeseer.csail.mit.edu/kautz98creating.html

Kushner, D. (2004). My avatar, my self. *Technology Review, 107*(3).

Lee, O. (2004). Addictive consumption of avatars in cyberspace. *CyberPsychology & Behavior, 7*(4).

Ludlow, P. (1996). *High noon on the electronic frontier: Conceptual issues in cyberspace.* Massachusetts Institute of Technology, USA.

Paniaras, I. (1997). Virtual identities in computer mediated communication. *SIGGROPT Bulletin, 18*(2).

Parrinder, G. (1982). *Avatar and incarnation: A comparison of Indian and Christian beliefs.* New York: Oxford University Press.

Power, M. (1997). *How to program a virtual community.* Macmillan Computer Publishing.

Rheingold, H. (2000). *The virtual community: Homesteading on the electronic frontier.* Cambridge, MA: The MIT Press.

Salem, B., & Earle, N. (2000). Designing a non-verbal language for expressive avatars. *Proceedings of CVE 2000.*

Suler, J. (1997). *The psychology of cyberspace.* Retrieved September 4, 2005, from http://www.rider.edu/~suler/psycyber/psycyber.html

Taylor, T.L. (1999). *Life in virtual worlds: Plural existence, multimodalities.* Retrieved October 23, 2005, from http://www.cts.cuni.cz/~konopas/liter/Taylor_life%20in%20Virtual%20Worlds.htm

Winkler, T., & Herezeg, M. (2004). Avatars—can they help developing personality among students in school? *Proceedings of IEEE 2004.*

KEY TERMS

Avatar: A graphical symbol used by virtual community members in order to represent themselves in the virtual environment.

Collaborative Virtual Environment: A virtual community usually represented in the form of a 3D environment where individuals are afforded a high degree of interaction via their avatar with other individuals and objects within the environment.

Dissociative Identity Disorder: A psychiatric disorder of an individual projecting more than one distinct identity into his or her environment.

Emoticon: Image icon used in a text-based chat environment to communicate emotional expression, for example, happy, sad, laughing.

First-Person View: Where visual information is presented to the individual as though being perceived through the eyes of his or her avatar.

Message Board: A Web-hosted communication tool in which individuals can correspond via the posting of text messages.

Social Network: A social structure that provides a platform where individuals may extend their personal contacts or attain personal goals.

Third-Person View: Where visual information is presented to the individual from a perspective external to his or her 3D avatar.

Virtual Community: An environment where the principal communication between groups of individuals is computer mediated.

Access Control for Healthcare

Yifeng Shen
Monash University, Australia

INTRODUCTION

Thanks to the rapid development in the field of information technology, healthcare providers rely more and more on information systems to deliver professional and administrative services. There are high demands for those information systems that provide timely and accurate patient medical information. High-quality healthcare services depend on the ability of the healthcare provider to readily access the information such as a patient's test results and treatment notes. Failure to access this information may delay diagnosis, resulting in improper treatment and rising costs (Rind et al., 1997).

Compared to paper-based patient data, computer-based patient data has more complex security requirements as more technologies are involved. One of the key drivers to systematically enhance the protection of private health information within healthcare providers is compliance with the healthcare information system security standard framework and related legislation. Security standards and legislation of the healthcare information system are critical for ensuring the confidentiality and integrity of private health information (Amatayakul, 1999). Privacy determines who should have access, what constitutes the patient's rights to confidentiality, and what constitutes inappropriate access to health records. Security is embodied in standards and technology that ensure the confidentiality of healthcare information and enable health data integrity policies to be carried out.

Based on the investigation of security standard and legislation, we can analyze and create basic security requirements for the healthcare information system. To meet the security requirements, it is necessary to deploy an appropriate access control policy and system within the organization. As discussed elsewhere (Sandhu, Coyne, Feinstein, & Youman, 1996), role-based access control (RBAC) is a promising technology for managing and enforcing security in a large-scale distributed system. In the healthcare industry, RBAC has already been adopted by the Health Level Seven (HL7) organization as a key access control standard (Blobel & Marshall, 2005).

HL7 was established in 1987 to develop standards for the electronic interchange of clinical, financial, and administrative information among independent healthcare-oriented computer systems. In June of 1994, HL7 was designated by the American National Standard Institute (ANSI) as an ANSI-accredited standards developer. HL7, in its draft Security Service Framework (Kratz et al., 2005) categorizes healthcare information security exposures in the following manner:

- **Disclosure:** Exposure, interception, inference intrusion
- **Deception:** Masquerade, falsification, repudiation
- **Disruption:** Incapacitation, corruption, obstruction
- **Usurpation:** Misappropriation

Although RBAC has been introduced to the latest version of HL7 (version 3) for strengthening the security features, it only includes those basic functions. Due to the complexity of the healthcare process, RBAC with only basic functions may not be sufficient. More context constraints need to be processed in addition to traditional RBAC operations.

The major contributions we have made in this article are:

- Illustrating the detailed design of a flexible and securer RBAC model for a healthcare information system based on HL7 standard;
- Introducing the basic elements of HL7 v3 and RBAC, which are necessary for us to realize our proposed model; and
- Analyzing the potential weakness of current HL7 standard and the basic RBAC model in terms of security and flexibility.

The rest of the article is organized as follows. The next section provides a general introduction and basic analysis of HL7 version 3. We then explain the RBAC concept model and describe our major work, and finish with our conclusion and future work.

HL7 VERSION 3

What is HL7?

Health Level Seven is one of several American National Standards Institute-accredited Standards Developing Organizations (SDOs) operating in the healthcare arena. Most SDOs produce standards (sometimes called specifications or protocols) for a particular healthcare domain such as pharmacy, medical devices, imaging, or insurance (claims processing) transactions. HL7's domain is clinical and administrative data (HL7, 2005).

HL7 is also a non-profit volunteer organization. Its members are the providers, vendors, payers, consultants, and government groups who have an interest in the development and advancement of clinical and administrative standards for healthcare services. In its achievements so far, HL7 has already produced HL7 Version 2 (HL7 v2) specifications (HL7, 2005), which are in wide use as a messaging standard that enables disparate healthcare applications to exchange key sets of clinical and administrative data. However, the newer specification HL7 Version 3 (HL7 v3), still under development, pertains to all aspects of clinical and administrative data in health services. Unlike its older version, HL7 v3 specifications are completely based upon the extensible markup language (XML) standards, and so have potential to win an instant acceptance by developers and vendors alike.

The target system during our research is based on HL7 v3, so only HL7 v3 will be described in this article.

The lack of data and process standards between both vendor systems and the many healthcare provider organizations present a significant barrier to design application interfaces. With HL7 v3, vendors and providers will finally have a messaging standard that can provide solutions to all of their existing problems.

HL7 v3 is based on a reference information model (RIM). Although RIM is not stabilized yet, once it is stabilized, it will be the most definitive standard to date for healthcare services. The following section will highlight some key components of RIM.

Reference Information Model

RIM is the cornerstone of the HL7 Version 3 development process. An object model created as part of the Version 3 methodology, RIM is a large pictorial representation of the clinical data (domains) and identifies the lifecycle of events that a message or groups of related messages will carry. It is a shared model between all the domains and as such is the model from which all domains create their messages. RIM comprises six main classes (Beeler et al., 2005):

1. **Act:** Represents the actions that are executed and must be documented as health care is managed and provided.
2. **Participation:** Expresses the context for an act in terms such as who performed it, for whom it was done, where it was done, and so forth.
3. **Entity:** Represents the physical things and beings that are of interest to and take part in health care.
4. **Role:** Establishes the roles that entities play as they participate in health care acts.
5. **ActRelationship:** Represents the binding of one act to another, such as the relationship between an order for an observation and the observation event as it occurs.
6. **RoleLink:** Represents relationships between individual roles.

Three of these classes—Act, Entity, and Role—are further represented by a set of specialized classes or sub-types.

RIM defines all the information from which the data content of HL7 messages are drawn. It follows object-oriented modeling techniques, where the information is organized into classes that have attributes and that maintain associations with other classes. RIM also forms a shared view of the information domain used across all HL7 messages, independent of message structure.

HL7 v3 Security

The focus of HL7 security needs analysis on how systems communicate information using HL7 message. It is expected that healthcare application systems that implement HL7 v3 will be required to have significantly more functionalities to protect the confidentiality of patient information and to authenticate requests for services than has been common in the past. The new functions may include, but are not limited to, limiting the right to view or transfer selected data to users with specific kinds of authorization, and auditing access to patient data, electronic signature, and authentication of users based on technologies more advanced than passwords. Version 3 will seek out and reference standards such as X.500 (Weider, Reynolds, & Heker, 1992) and RFC 1510 to support conveying the necessary information from one healthcare application system to another, so that these systems may perform the authorization and authentication functions. Version 3 will also seek out and adopt industry security standards that support conveying the necessary information from one healthcare application system to another, so that these systems may perform the confidentiality functions.

To meet the security goals, the HL7 Secure Transaction Special Group has created a security service framework for HL7 (Kratz et al., 2005). According to the scope of the framework, HL7 must address the following security services: authentication, authorization and access control, integrity (system and data), confidentiality, accountability, availability, and non-repudiation. The HL7 security service framework uses case scenarios to illustrate all the services mentioned above. All those case scenarios can help the readers to understand those services in a very direct way. However case scenarios are not detailed enough to be an implementation guide for the security services.

In this article we are going to design a flexible model for one key security service—access control. This model will extend the case scenarios to a very detailed level which can be directly used as an implementation guide for HL7 v3.

ROLE-BASED ACCESS CONTROL

RBAC has became very popular in both research and industry. RBAC models have been shown to be "policy-neutral" in the sense that by using role hierarchies and constraints (Chandramouli, 2003), a wide range of security policies can be expressed. Security administration is also greatly simplified by the use of roles to organize access privileges. A basic RBAC model will be covered in this section, as well as an advanced model with context constraints.

Basic RBAC Model

The basic components of the RBAC model are *user, role,* and *permission* (Chen & Sandhu, 1996). The user is the individual who needs access to the system. Membership to the roles is granted to the user based on his or her obligations and responsibilities within the organization. All the operations that the user can perform should be based on the user's role.

Role means a set of functional responsibilities within an organization. The administrator defines roles, a combination of obligation and authority in organization, and assigns them to users. The user-role relationship represents the collection of users and roles.

Permission is the way for the role to access more than one resource.

As shown in Figure 1, the basic RBAC model also includes *user assignment* (UA) and *permission assignment* (PA) (INCITS359, 2003).

The user assignment relationship represents which user is assigned to perform what kind of role in the organization. The administrator decides the user assignment relationship. When a user logs on, the system UA is referenced to decide which role it is assigned to. According to the object that the role wants to access, the permission can be assigned to the role referenced by the permission assignment relationship.

The set of permissions (PRMS) is composed of the assignments between operations (OPS) and objects (OBS).

UA and PA can provide great flexibility and granularity of assignment of permissions to roles and users to roles (INCITS359, 2003). The basic RBAC model has clearly illustrated the concept about how role-based access control works within an organization. However it may not be dynamic enough when the business process becomes very complex. Thus the idea of context constraints is introduced to make the RBAC model more useful.

RBAC Model with Context Constraints

Traditional RBAC supports the definition of arbitrary constraints on the different parts of a RBAC model (Sandhu et al., 1996). With the increasing interest in RBAC in general and constraint-based RBAC in particular, research for other types of RBAC constraints has gained more attention (Bertino, Bonatt, & Ferrari,

Figure 1. Core RBAC

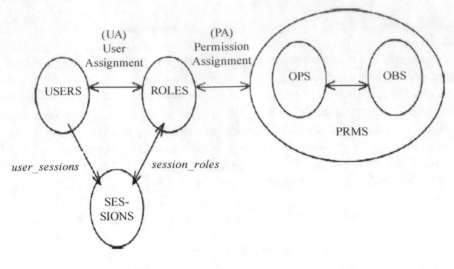

Figure 2. RBAC permissions with context constraints

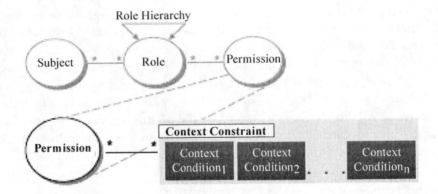

2001). In this section we describe the context constraints in an RBAC environment.

A context constraint is an abstract concept. It specifies that certain context attributes must meet certain conditions in order to permit a specific operation. As authorization decisions are based on the permissions a particular subject/role possesses, context constraints are associated with RBAC permissions (see Figure 2).

The context constraint is defined through the terms context attribute, context function, and context condition (Strembeck & Neumann, 2004):

- A *context attribute* represents a certain property of the environment whose actual value might change dynamically (like time, date, or session-data, for example) or which varies for different

instances of the same abstract entity (e.g., location, ownership, birthday, or nationality). Thus, context attributes are a means to make context information explicit.

- A *context function* is a mechanism to obtain the current value of a specific context attribute (i.e., to explicitly capture context information). For example, a function *date*() could be defined to return the current date. Of course, a context function can also receive one or more input parameters. For example, a function *age*(*subject*) may take the subject name out of the *subject*, *operation*, *object_* triple to acquire the age of the subject, which initiated the current access request, for example, the age can be read from some database.

- A *context condition* is a predicate that consists of an operator and two or more operands. The first operand always represents a certain context attribute, while the other operands may be either context attributes or constant values. All variables must be ground before evaluation. Therefore, each context attribute is replaced with a constant value by using the corresponding context function prior to the evaluation of the respective condition.

- A *context constraint* is a clause containing one or more context conditions. It is satisfied if and only if (iff) all context conditions hold. Otherwise it returns false.

A context constraint can be used to define conditional permissions. Based on the terms listed above, the conditional permission is a permission associated with one or more context constraints, and grants access iff each corresponding context constraint evaluates as "true."

As we can see, a context constraint can help the organization provide more flexible and securer control for the RBAC model.

Design a RBAC Model with Context Constraints for the Healthcare Information System Based on HL 7 Version 3

The access control model we are going to describe is a method to control access on a healthcare information system. It is developed to enhance the security and flexibility of traditional access control systems. The resource to be accessed in this article is limited to a patient's electronic health record (EHR).

The primary purpose of the EHR is to provide a documented record of care that supports present and future care by the same or other clinicians. This documentation provides a means of communication among clinicians contributing to the patient's care. The primary beneficiaries are the patient and the clinician(s) (ISO/TC-215 Technical Report, 2003).

System design will include two major phases:

1. **Components design:** Describes all the necessary elements that make up the system.
2. **Data flow design:** Describes all the processes that make the whole system work.

Components Design

As described in the previous section, the RBAC system must include the basic elements such as user, role, permission, user-role assignment, and role-permission assignment. All those elements will be associated with real values in our system design. Figure 3 illustrates the overall structure of the system.

- **User:** Anybody with authenticated identity can act as the user in the system. For example, after Tom successfully logs into the hospital's computer system with his user ID 19245678, he becomes the user of our system.

- **Role:** The set of roles can be retrieved from those functional roles that already exist in the current healthcare information system such as physician, pharmacist, registered nurse, and so forth. As the number of roles is limited in our system, we can store all the role information by simply using an XML file instead of a database. This file is named "Common Role File.xml."

- **Permission:** The scope of the permissions in our design will focus on those system operations (create, read, update, delete, execute, etc.). Similar to role information, we use another XML file with the name "Common Permission File.xml" to represent all the permission information.

As shown in Figure 3, the user, role, and permission file can be used as the basic input for the whole system. To generate user-role assignment and role-permission assignment relationship, we introduce the *administration function* module. This module is designed to create and maintain the user role assignment file and role permission assignment file.

The rules of user role assignment and role permission assignment are referenced from the security section of HL7 v3 standard (HL7 Security Technical Committee, 2005).

In addition to the administration function module, we also designed another two function modules: *support function* module and *review function* module. The support function module provides the core function of the system. It receives the access request from the user and makes judgment based on the input from different sources to decide whether the access can be granted. The detailed process will be described in the next section.

Figure 3. Flexible RBAC model for HL7 v3-based healthcare information system

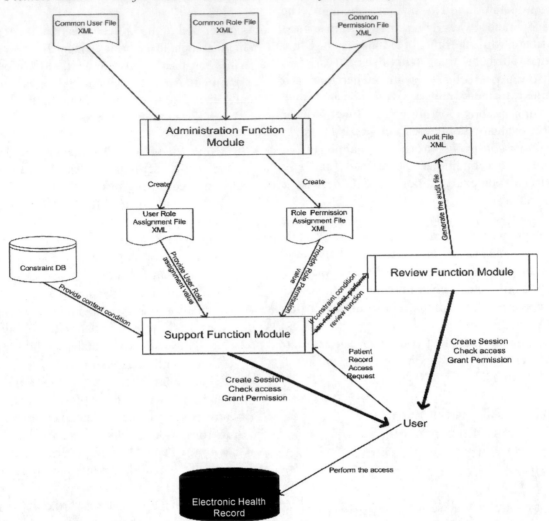

The review function module is an extension of the support function module. It is used for exceptional scenarios, such as emergent circumstances that do not satisfy the constraint condition. Every time the review function module is initiated, an audit file will be created to record all the necessary information of the exceptional case. In our system, the audit file is saved in XML format with the name " Audit File.xml."

The ultimate object the users want to access is the EHR. The existing database that stores all the EHRs can be used directly by our system.

Another database included in this system is the constraint database, which stores all the context attributes and context conditions. The context attributes and context conditions can be used as input for the support function module during the access control decision process.

In summary, the components can be categorized into three types based on the design:

- **Type 1 – Basic elements:** Role, User, Permission, User Role Assignment, Role Permission Assignment, Audit File. All these basic elements are represented in XML format.

- **Type 2 – System functional modules:** Administration Function Module, Support Function Module, Review Function Module. All these modules provide the core functions of the system and are represented in real program.

- **Type 3 – Database:** EHR database and constraint database.

Data Flow Design

After all the components are defined, we will design the proper data flows to make the system work. The data flow design is based on the three functional modules previously discussed. Thus, we introduce three kinds of data flow in this article:

- data flow for administration function module,
- data flow for support function module, and
- data flow for review function module.

Data flow for administration function module

1. Administration function module reads the common user file, common role file, and common permission file. Those files contain all the user information, role information, and permission information respectively.
2. Based on the pre-defined user-role relationship/role-permission relationship, the administration function module creates a user role assignment file and a role permission assignment file in XML format.

Data flow for support function module

1. The user sends an access request to the support function module.
2. The support function module requests and receives role information about the user from the user assignment file.
3. The support function module requests and receives the permission which is assigned to the role. This can be retrieved from the permission assignment file.
4. Get context attributes and context condition information from the constraints database.
5. The support function module performs the "check access" function then grants the access permission to the user.
6. The user can retrieve the information from the EHR database.

Data flow for review function module

1. Sometimes the context condition cannot be met, however all the other conditions (permission assignment, user assignment) can be met and the user really wants to access the resource because of emergency. In this case, all authentication information will be forwarded to the review function module.
2. The review function module records all the necessary information and generates an audit file, then grants conditional access permission to the user.
3. The user can retrieve the information from the EHR database.

All the steps listed above for the data flow just give a brief description. More detailed steps are necessary when it comes to the system implementation phase.

CONCLUSION AND FUTURE WORK

Clinical information sharing between different healthcare information systems is the key factor to improve the quality of service. Health Level Seven is the data exchange standard for clinical information. In this article we first introduce the basic concept of Health Level Seven and role-based access control. Then we illustrate how to design a flexible role-based access control model for a healthcare information system based on Health Level Seven version 3. The design utilizes the existing access control feature of Health Level Seven version 3 and integrates context constraints to make the system more secure and more flexible.

In the future, the major work will be the development of those function modules and applying this model to a real healthcare information system to see how the security access control can be improved.

REFERENCES

Amatayakul, M. (1999). *Chapter three, section 5.0: Standards, processes and organizations: Setting standards in health care information.* Computer-Based Patient Record Institute.

Beeler, G., Case, J., Curry, J., Hueber, A., Mckenzie, L., Schadow, G., et al. (2005, July 31). *HL7 reference information model 2006.*

Bertino, E., Bonatt, P.A., & Ferrari., E. (2001). TRBAC: A temporal role-based access control model. *ACM Transactions on Information and System Security, 4*(3).

Blobel, B., & Marshall, G. (2005). Role based access control (RBAC) role engineering overview. *HL7® Version 3 Standard.*

Chandramouli, R. (2003, July 27-30). Specification and validation of enterprise access control data for conformance to model and policy constraints. *Proceedings of the World Multiconference on Systems, Cybernetics and Informatics,* Orlando, FL.

Chen, F., & Sandhu, R.S. (1996). Constraints for role based access control. *Proceedings of the ACM RBAC Workshop.*

HL7. (2005). *About_HL7.* Retrieved April 2006 from http://www.hl7.org

HL7 Security Technical Committee. (2005). *Role based access control (RBAC) healthcare permission catalog version 2.*

INCITS359. (2003). *Role based access control.* American National Standard Institute.

ISO/TC-215 Technical Report. (2003). *Electronic health record definition, scope, and context.*

Kratz, M., Humenn, P., Tucker, M., Nolte, M., Wagner, S., Wilson, W. et al. (2005). *HL 7 Security framework.* Retrieved April 2006 from http://www.hl7.org/library/committees/secure/HL7_Sec.html

Rind, D.M., Kohane, I.S., Szolovits, P., Safran, C., Chueh, H.C., & Barnett, G.O. (1997). Maintaining the confidentiality of medical records shared over the Internet and the World Wide Web. *Annals of Internal Medicine, 127*(2), 138-141.

Sandhu, R.S., Coyne, E.J., Feinstein, H.L., & Youman, C.E. (1996). Role-based access control models. *IEEE Computer, 29*(2), 38-47.

Strembeck, M., & Neumann, G. (2004). An integrated approach to engineer and enforce context constraints in RBAC environments. *ACM Transactions on Information and System Security (TISSEC), 7*(3), 392-427.

Weider, C., Reynolds, J., & Heker, S. (1992). *Technical overview of directory services using the X.500 protocol.* Retrieved May 5, 2006, from http://www.ietf.org/rfc/rfc1309.txt

KEY TERMS

Electronic Health Record (HER): A longitudinal electronic record of patient health information generated by one or more encounters in any care delivery setting.

Extensible Markup Language (XML): A W3C initiative that allows information and services to be encoded with meaningful structure and semantics that computers and humans can understand.

Health Level Seven (HL7): One of several American National Standards Institute (ANSI)-accredited Standards Developing Organizations (SDOs) operating in the healthcare arena.

Permission Assignment (PA): Assigns permission to an authorized role.

Reference Information Module (RIM): The cornerstone of the HL7 Version 3 development process and an essential part of the HL7 v3 development methodology. RIM expresses the data content needed in a specific clinical or administrative context, and provides an explicit representation of the semantic and lexical connections that exist between the information carried in the fields of HL7 messages.

Role-Based Access Control (RBAC): A system of controlling which users have access to resources based on the role of the user.

User Assignment (UA): Assigns a role to a user.

Advertising in the Networked Environment

Savvas Papagiannidis
University of Newcastle upon Tyne, UK

Michael Bourlakis
Brunel University, UK

INTRODUCTION

Advances in technology, in particular the Internet and mobile/wireless devices, have significantly affected business operations. As technology changes, communicating and interacting with customers could not be left untouched; the dot.com era saw many new forms of marketing emerge on the electronic landscape.

In this article, we discuss the possible marketing implications of the convergence of electronic media focusing on the delivery of advertising messages. We acknowledge the profound impact of information technology on marketing channels (Leek, Turnbull, & Naude, 2003) and use examples of various technologies to present changes that occurred in existing channels to illustrate the future potential of emerging channels. For each of the above, we provide examples of applications that can potentially be integrated to deliver advertising convergence.

PERVASIVE AND UBIQUITOUS ADVERTISING IN THE NETWORKED ENVIRONMENT

Personalization

Personalization is a critical factor when it comes to a successful campaign. Despite the technological advances of the last decade, a holistic approach to delivering personalized messages and keeping track of the process is still too cumbersome. In fact it is not often possible to identify the customer at all. For example, watching a television broadcast does not require people to log in to the TV channel.

Perhaps, the only real exception is the World Wide Web. Online users create accounts and profiles to access services that are used to personalize them and provide a platform for the delivery of targeted advertising. Even when profiles are not available, the users' interaction with an online service, such as a search facility, provides a plethora of opportunities to deliver targeted messages. In more complex cases, targeted advertising is achieved by looking at group profiles, with Amazon's technique, "users who bought this item were interested in this item as well," probably being the most famous example of all. Other techniques can be used and related to business logic rules. The following list gives an idea of possible personalization techniques (van Amstel, van der Eijk, Haasdijk, & Kuilman, 2000):

- rules-based matching (club members, frequent visitors, etc.);
- matching agents (established profile can be matched with other profiles displaying similar purchasing behavior);
- feedback and learning (fields of interest);
- community ratings (others help define good from bad);
- attribute searches (all books with reduced prices);
- full-text search (personalization based on keywords used for the search); and
- collaborative filtering (feedback on products and services defines groups of individuals with similar interests).

Personalization techniques for targeted advertising delivery, although powerful, have been mainly limited by the virtual boundaries of the Internet and the physical boundaries of the areas where the computers were placed. With the constant introduction of more powerful mobile devices and the ability to get everything online cheaply, they could soon be widely available on-the-move, allowing for a whole new host of applications and, in this case, targeted personalized advertising.

Mobile Marketing and Location-Based Services

As technology is about to change, future advertising messages will be delivered intelligently anywhere at any time. Advertising messages are currently confined within the narrow boundaries of the medium they were created to serve. The next generation Internet will change this; everything could be easily and cheaply connected and serve as a potential advertising channel. When visiting the mall, shoppers could end up constantly being greeted by automated marketing 'bots' that tirelessly try to convince them of the great value that their products offer. Perhaps the intelligence planet that Kaku (1998) envisioned may become frustratingly intelligent! Unrealistic as this may sound, one has only to look at the proliferation of spam (unsolicited messaging) to realize that such a scenario is not that difficult to be realized.

Interestingly, personalization often does not need personal information. Knowledge of the location and time can be enough to increase the value of the delivered message substantially. New generation mobile phone services have promised to deliver location-based services, which they do deliver already to a certain degree. Popular mobile portals such as Vodafone Live! can approximately locate a phone's position and offer relevant information. In the future, localized wireless technologies like Bluetooth may be able to provide more precise location positioning services.

Perhaps, however, even more important than locating someone carrying a mobile device is that he is carrying and using it most of the time. In 2003, seven out of ten (67%) of the 'young communicators' in the UK said they could not live without their mobile phones (Mori, 2002). This renders mobile devices, especially mobile phones, an invaluable tool:

While it is undoubtedly an effective one-to-one communications channel that can be easily personalized, it is also an invaluable conduit for pulling together strands of any multimedia marketing and/or marketing campaign. It is a ubiquitous and immediate point of convergence that has an enviable reach if used responsibly and effectively. (Kerckhove, 2002)

Permission-Based Advertising

Location-based services can be a 'blessing' for marketers but a 'curse' for customers as they may end up becoming the constant recipients of advertising messages for nearby services and goods. This would bring spamming, which so far has been limited to e-mails, to a completely new level of frustration. For channels that have more or less been left untouched by spamming, there is always the fear that this may change at any time. For example, "although some research has suggested that teen mobile users often welcome unsolicited SMS messages, there is a growing fear that the rise in unwanted commercial text messages could jeopardize the whole future of mobile marketing" (Haig, 2001).

Of far more concern is that "the possibility of processing very precise location data should not lead to a situation where mobile users are under permanent surveillance with no means to protect their privacy other than not using mobile communications services at all" (Worthy & Graham, 2002). Different pieces of legislation and codes of conduct, like the Directive on Privacy Electronic Communications, have been introduced to regulate different forms of communications (Crichard, 2003).

As can be seen from Table 1, an implicit (in the form of an opt-out option or a 'soft opt-in' based on a prior relationship) or explicit (i.e., when the customer volunteers to opt-in and consents to his details becoming available for a specific purpose, usually marketing related) consent is required before addressing a potential customer. However, if no implicit consent is available, how will companies manage to reach new customers proactively? Obtaining permission from the customer to contact him again means that there has already been a contact. This gives the company the opportunity to lock the customer, if it can manage the communication channels effectively. What is going to happen with everybody else who does not have a previous contact?

Direct mailing could be used, if the details of the customer are known, as direct mailing, even when unsolicited, is not considered to be 'spamming'. Perhaps, though, what is needed in the context of a networked economy are more innovative uses of existing relationships that could be employed to create new soft opt-ins. For example, "the fact that mobile phones are essentially peer-to-peer communication tools provides

Table 1. Communication and type of consent per recipient (Adopted from Crichard, 2003)

Type of Recipient	Communication Method	Type of 'Consent' Required
Individual	Fax Automated calling systems (no human intervention)	Prior consent ('opt-in') required
Individual	E-mail/SMS	Prior consent ('opt-in') required, except where there is a prior relationship (in which case the 'soft opt-in' rules may apply)
Individual	Telephone	Left to member states. The government is expected to maintain the existing 'opt-out' regime (including registration through the Telecoms Privacy Directive)
Corporates	Telephone/Fax	Left to member states. The government is expected to extend existing 'opt-out' regime to both fax and telephone.
Corporates	E-mail/SMS	Left to member states. The government is not expected to extend opt-out or opt-in rights to this area.

yet another advantage, and means the possibilities for viral marketing are almost limitless" (Haig, 2001).

Hence, the connections between agents can have a serious effect on how a message is distributed. Viral marketing refers to a message that 'infects' a market and is spread from node to node in the network. In viral marketing, although the content has to be of interest for each node to pass it to the next level, the connections among the nodes are equally important. These connections are not just the means for the advertising message to go from A to B, but also act as a filtering and a profiling system; the recipient of the advert implicitly decides to whom the message is relevant and forwards it. As viral marketing is based on digital messages, these may go around the network for a very long time with very little resource from the marketer's side. Once the message is released, there is no way to get it confined until its effects fade off.

Profiling and Convergence

Proactive delivery of advertising messages would require a permission-based framework, which may be inclusive instead of exclusive. The customers will define their interests and the kind of messages they want to receive; everything else will get filtered. With advanced profiling now being possible as there is adequate space to store data and enough computational power intelligibly to retrieve and make sense out of the data in real time, this naturally leads to a profile-oriented solution.

In addition, one of the promised deliverables for technology has always been the convergence of media. On one hand convergence can allow one to reach multiple audiences through many different media. On the other hand, this requires synchronization, additional resources, time and effort, and a good understanding of each medium. As convergence of media occurs, profiling will become easier. For example, most of the technologies mentioned in the next section are native Internet technologies and could potentially be delivered through a common mechanism that will identify and track individual users. This could be based on an identification system similar to the Microsoft Passport service, which aims to authenticate users among different services. Each of these services could contribute to the customer's profile. In exchange, they would gain access to the parts of the profile contributed by the other services. As a result, convergence could allow delivery of targeted and relevant personalized advertising across multiple channels and the numerous applications that will run on them.

Figure 1. A mechanism to converge the electronic advertising delivery

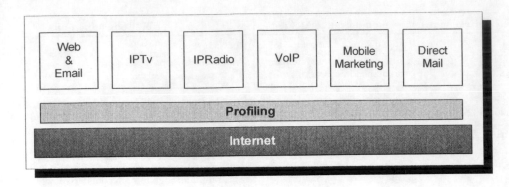

The Internet and the Promise of Channel Convergence

"Business interactions and relationships do not occur in a vacuum: the environment in which they take place influences them" (Leek et al., 2003). Advertising—engaging the customer to inform him about the company's products and services—relies heavily on the environment where it takes place and the channels available. In this section we discuss how the Internet could be used as the common ground for advertising convergence by presenting examples of how existing channels have been or could be migrated on it and converge into one delivery mechanism.

Web/E-Mail

Everyone who has been on the Web or has an e-mail address will have almost certainly come across advertising banners and will almost certainly receive unsolicited e-mails (spam). Still, it would be hard to deny that Web and e-mail advertising have revolutionized advertising. This is primarily due to the interactivity that the Internet can offer. When a user comes across an advertisement, a simple click is enough to find out more about the product. This cannot be compared to watching a TV advertisement, which requires the viewer to take much more time-consuming action. Still, banner ads and commercial e-mails have been traditionally restricted to text and pictorial representations of the message to be delivered, although recently this has started changing. One may now come across

an animation or occasionally a video clip. The availability of faster connections will support the rationale behind including such multimedia advertising messages on the Web and even e-mails, in order to make them more appealing.

IPTv

Television has traditionally been a medium that required significant investment in order to reach its viewers. The Internet is now about to change this. Broadcasters have looked for ways to exploit the potential of narrowcast for a long time, but conventional narrowcast models have been hindered by the geographical and technological limitations in reaching audiences big enough to be economically viable. This is something that the Internet can address, as it is naturally disposed toward one-to-one communications and high levels of interactivity (Papagiannidis, Berry, & Li, 2006a). For example, Microsoft and BT announced BT's intention to use the Microsoft TV Internet Protocol Television (IPTv) Edition software platform to deliver TV over broadband in the United Kingdom:

Unlike most conventional pay-TV delivery systems in consumer homes today, the Microsoft TV platform allows network operators to integrate the delivery of pay-TV services with other broadband services delivered to PCs, telephones, game consoles, mobile devices and other devices in the home using a common set of back-office and network systems. (Microsoft, 2005)

Equally importantly, the reduction in cost of broadcasting represented by the technology behind IPTV means that it is no longer impossible for smaller, special interest groups to create their own strand of programming, with content and format most likely to attract viewers of similar interests (Papagiannidis et al., 2006a). This is very similar to the proliferation of independent Web sites for news and opinions; anyone can now have a private Web site or blog. In the future, it will be possible, and there are already examples (e.g., podcasting or vodcasting), for everyone to be able to create audiovisual content and post it on the Internet to effectively become a broadcaster.

The above two changes will result in a plethora of new channels, many of which will be controlled by smaller broadcasters. The fragmentation of interest may also result in fragmentation of advertising.

IPRadio

Similarly to IPTv, IPRadio could provide a conduit for marketers to push their products and services. In fact, audio broadcasting over the Internet is very common, and many thousands of streams already exist. Among them, there are many commercial 'traditional' radio station broadcasts that are usually restricted to broadcasting shows, as they would have normally been. These could be complemented by value-adding services that could provide additional information to the listeners and encourage them to take certain actions. For example, the above mentioned service could be extended by simply providing a link to a music store where the listener could buy the song currently playing. The same could apply to all advertisements and other announcements.

One could argue that when listening to the radio, listeners do not visually engage with the radio device itself, hence such messages may go unnoticed. Although this may be true to a great extent, listeners often come across a message that they would have liked to have somehow captured, in order to find more information. For example, if one listens to an advertisement about an offer for a product of interest, one could look at the radio player and use the displayed information, instead of waiting for the next time the spot will be played.

Narrowcasting (e.g., in the form of podcasting) could reach audiences that traditionally were extremely difficult or very expensive to target. With listeners coming from all over the world, it would be possible to market globally digital products and services that could be distributed and accessed via the Internet. Potentially, the marketing of physical products could benefit as well from this level of exposure.

VoIP

Voice over IP (VoIP) has the potential not only to replace 'traditional' telephony, but also extend it, providing new opportunities to telemarketers. In VoIP it does not matter where one is as long as one is connected to the Internet. As a result it does not matter where calls are made from and where they are destined. The calls cost much less than normal, especially when it comes to international calls. In fact, many calls may even be free. VoIP will have a number of implications for marketers. As phone costs will be minimized, advertising campaigns could potentially be much cheaper and reach a wider audience.

Mobile/SMS/Mobile Marketing

For electronic advertising to become totally ubiquitous and pervasive, it had to find a means of escaping the boundaries of the Internet. This was made possible by mobile-based services, for example, using mobile phones, which provided a natural extension to the Internet. "Mobile phone ownership in the UK is all pervasive—it spans all genders, ages and social classes. What was once the toy of the young and rich, often the size of a 'brick', is now the 'thing' that people, along with their keys, never fail to pick up when they leave the house" (Papagiannidis, Carr, & Li, 2006b). As a result, the responder can be reached at almost any time. This creates a number of issues ranging from timeliness, message format, location, reaching sensitive consumer groups (e.g., children), interactivity (immediate response), and so forth.

The main point of interest, though, is that mobile phones can easily be reached from the Internet and vice versa. Mobile marketing—what Scharl, Dickinger, and Murphy (2005) define as using a wireless medium to provide consumers with time- and location-sensitive, personalized information that promotes goods, services, and ideas—can be the natural extension of Internet-based marketing. The mobile phone is hence treated as just another Internet device, with SMS and multimedia messages playing the role that e-mails play.

Direct Mail

Traditional direct mailing has a number of challenges such as the high cost of short runs, problems with obsolescence, often high time to market and accountability issues, among others. Collateral fulfillment, that is, short-run print on demand via the Web, can address challenges like the above (Papagiannidis & Li, 2005). This is achieved by harnessing the power of professional digital print devices through a Web interface. These devices can produce customized documents of very high print and finishing quality. Such documents are of high value as they can deliver a personalized message to the customer, maximizing the advertising impact the message has. This minimizes management costs while it allows for greater flexibility. Direct mailing, although it may not be an electronic medium, in its new form could not have been possible without advances in communication technologies and profiling techniques; the Internet is to collateral fulfillment what ink is to printing.

Ethical Implications

The previous analysis has highlighted the issue of media convergence anticipated to happen in the near future. It also begs a range of questions related to the ethical aspects for consumers emanating from that convergence. Specifically, is there a provision for the development of a regulatory body that will act as a controlling mechanism overseeing the responsible use of these exchanges and at the same time protecting consumers' interests? A key fact may be that consumers will become increasingly annoyed by the continuous bombardment of messages that will also impinge on their privacy. On the other hand, "although personalization and privacy seem to be in conflict the bottom line is that personalization benefits all involved: company, customer, supplier" (Cannon, 2002).

The creation of a relevant body will be of pivotal importance for consumers and other stakeholders (e.g., firms involved) and will increase their credibility and legitimacy, guaranteeing the fair use of these mediums. It will also harmonize and standardize an environment that is used to operating under an ad hoc manner, and will install processes that will minimize any adverse and negative impacts on consumers. For example, such a body could apply systems monitoring the messages sent to consumers—for example, check whether messages sent to the targeted audience were appropriate and whether sensitive groups, such as children and teenagers, are protected from possible exploitation. "Children are a vulnerable group and the immediacy and freedom of the Internet make it difficult for companies to insure children's protection on kid-based Internet sites" (Austin & Reed, 1999). Perhaps it may not be surprising that the second 'stickiest' site on the Internet is NeoPets.com (Kushner, 2005). On average, users (four out of five Neopians are under age 18, and two out of five are under 13) spend 6 hours and 15 minutes per month on the site during which a seamless interweaving of marketing and entertainment takes place (Kushner, 2005). Phenomena like this prompted Moore (2004) to suggest that the blurring of advertising and entertainment targeted at children is a social, political, and ethical issue that deserves our collective attention. Convergence and profiling makes this requirement for all stakeholders a more demanding one.

In addition, have all consumer segments been given equal opportunities to join these services, and hence, is possible consumer social exclusion minimized? Equally, will these consumers have the chance to provide their consent to receive these services, or will an unnecessary bombardment of messages take place?

Another concern is associated with the cost of that service and the overall financial implications. Who is going to be ultimately responsible for such a service? The consumer may not be charged initially, especially when a trial period or promotional launch takes place. Nevertheless, part of the cost of a new service or technology is almost always included in the final price of the product or service used by the consumer at some point. Again, will sensitive groups be protected, and subsequently, will specific groups bear the cost (e.g., affluent consumers) or will a one-price policy be applied?

These are some of the ethical issues that need to be addressed. We could suggest that there are three overarching levels when tackling any ethical issues related to media convergence: at the micro level, we are dealing with pure consumer issues; at the meso level, we are dealing with the firms and resultant systems involved, while at the macro level, we are dealing with governments and regulatory bodies that will oversee the fair use of these systems and will guarantee to consumers the responsible use of the above. To maximize consumer welfare, continuous dialogue and interaction between these three levels is required, while the launch of a specific regulatory body would send the right signals to stakeholders about the importance and significance of these issues.

CONCLUSION

The developments in information technology continue apace and will continue to impact on business interactions. Face-to-face contact is likely to decrease as full use is made of intranets, extranets, and the Internet. The majority of the new methods of communication remove both visual cues and physical presence cues so companies may move away from trusting, open, committed, cooperative relationships as face-to-face interaction decreases. At the moment, companies are not making full use of information technology capabilities, which suggests that in the near future relationships will still require considerable face-to-face interaction, be informal and close, trusting, and cooperative. However, in the future, they may become increasingly impersonal and formal, and more difficult to manage as technological developments continue and filter through to companies.

Similarly, the increased Internet penetration rates suggest that we could certainly envisage "access to the Internet" becoming as ubiquitous as access to the telephone and television—at least in the developed countries" (Fortin, Dholakia, & Dholakia, 2002), resulting in a range of further implications. One implication is related to the possible media convergence enabling businesses to provide complete customer relationship management. For example, companies may not necessarily have the complete picture of a customer, but they contribute their information to a common profiling database, after the customer has given his consent. A good example is the use of free e-mail services where, in exchange for the free e-mail services provided, they scan e-mails for information that could help them deliver targeted advertisements.

At the same time, there are many serious implications for consumers where the ethics of these exchanges can be questioned; the previous section shed light on these, and it is envisaged that further work in the future will address the issues posed.

REFERENCES

Austin, M.J., & Reed, M.L. (1999). Targeting children online: Internet advertising ethics issues. *Journal of Consumer Marketing, 16*(6), 590-602.

Cannon, D.A. (2002). The ethics of database marketing. *The Information Management Journal,* (May/June), 42-44.

Crichard, M. (2003). Privacy and electronic communications. *Computer Law & Security Report, 19*(4), 299-303.

Fortin, D.R., Dholakia, R.R., & Dholakia, N. (2002). Emerging issues in electronic marketing: Thinking outside the square. *Journal of Business Research, 55*(8), 623-627.

Haig, M. (2001). Talking to the teen generation. *Brand Strategy,* (December), 30.

Kaku, M. (1998). *Visions.* Oxford: Oxford University Press.

Kerckhove, A.D. (2002). Building brand dialogue with mobile marketing. *International Journal of Advertising & Marketing to Children, 3*(4), 37.

Kushner, D. (2005). *The Neopets addiction.* Retrieved July 19, 2006, from http://www.wired.com/wired/archive/13.12/neopets.html

Leek, S., Turnbull, P.W., & Naude, P. (2003). How is information technology affecting business relationships? Results from a UK survey. *Industrial Marketing Management, 32*(2), 119-126.

Microsoft. (2005). *BT selects Microsoft TV as software platform for TV over broadband in the United Kingdom.* Retrieved July 22, 2005, from http://www.microsoft.com/tv/content/Press/BT_2005.mspx

Moore, E.S. (2004). Children and the changing world of advertising. *Journal of Business Ethics, 52,* 161-167.

Mori. (2002). *The British mobile communications survey.* Retrieved January 29, 2005, from http://www.mori.com/polls/2002/pdf/vodafone.htm

Papagiannidis, S., Berry, J., & Li, F. (2006a). Well beyond streaming video: IPv6 and the next generation television. *Technical Forecasting and Social Change, 73*(5), 510-523.

A

Papagiannidis, S., Carr, J., & Li, F. (2006b). M-commerce in the UK. In N. Dholakia, M. Rask, & R. Dholakia (Eds.), *M-commerce in North America, Europe and Asia-Pacific*. Hershey, PA: Idea Book Publishing.

Papagiannidis, S., & Li, F. (2005). Management and delivery of digital print via the Web: A case study of Gaia Fulfilment. *International Journal of Cases of Electronic Commerce, 1*(1), 1-18.

Scharl, A., Dickinger, A., & Murphy, J. (2005). Diffusion and success factors of mobile marketing. *Electronic Commerce Research and Applications, 4*(2), 159-173.

van Amstel, P., van der Eijk, P., Haasdijk, E., & Kuilman, D. (2000). An interchange format for cross-media personalized publishing. *Computer Networks, 33*(1-6), 179-195.

Worthy, J., & Graham, N. (2002). Electronic marketing: New rules for electronic marketing – an obstacle to m-commerce? *Computer Law & Security Report, 18*(2), 106-108.

KEY TERMS

Collateral Fulfillment: Short-run print on demand via the Web.

Convergence (Technological): When a number of technologies come together, forming a new platform that addresses many of the shortcomings of the individual technologies and providing new functions that none of the technologies could provide alone.

IPTv: Transmission of television over the Internet of other IP-based networks.

Mobile Marketing: Marketing specifically aiming at mobile devices, such as mobile phones, PDAs, and so forth. The attributes and characteristics of these devices have created new opportunities and posed new challenges for practitioners.

Personalization: Configuring a product or service, often in real time, based on the consumer's profile.

Podcasting: Distribution of multimedia files using a syndication format, for example, RSS. Podcasts could also be made available as direct downloads from a Web site. Perhaps the most frequent use of podcasts is to deliver radio shows that are either stand-alone creations or even regular productions. The files can be reproduced by a number of different devices, such as multimedia players and computers.

Vodcasting: Similar to podcasting, but refers to feeds that include video. A form of video-on-demand.

VoIP: Transmission of voice and telephony services over the Internet or other IP-based networks.

Anonymous Peer-to-Peer Systems

Wenbing Zhao
Cleveland State University, USA

INTRODUCTION

A peer-to-peer (P2P) system refers to a distributed system in which the role played by each member is roughly equivalent, that is, a member both consumes and provides services to other members. Therefore, a member in such a system is often referred to as a *peer*. The primary design goal of P2P systems is to facilitate sharing of resources, including files, processing power, and network bandwidth.

A Brief History of P2P Systems

The first major P2P system, Napster (Taylor, 2004), was introduced in 1999. Since then, P2P systems have evolved very rapidly. The first generation of P2P systems, represented by Napster, used a centralized index server to provide peer and resource discovery. This design makes the systems vulnerable to attacks on the central server. The second-generation P2P systems, such as Gnutella, avoided such problems by adopting a fully decentralized design (Taylor, 2004). However, these systems do not provide anonymity to their users, in that a resource owner is exposed to its requester, and vice versa. A user's activities are also easily observable by the neighboring nodes. The privacy concerns triggered the development of the third generation of P2P systems (Rossi, 2006; Rohrer, 2006). These systems followed a variety of strategies to achieve anonymity, which will be discussed in detail in this article. Even though most of such systems are in the early development phase, we believe they will soon take over the second generation of P2P systems.

Why Should We Care About Anonymous P2P Systems?

First of all, P2P systems have become an essential part of the Internet, as evidenced by the fact that P2P traffic constitutes more than 40% of the total TCP traffic and it is still growing (Saroiu, Gummadi, Dunn, Gribble, & Levy, 2002). P2P systems have revolution-ized the Internet by enabling direct communication and resource sharing among the end users operating inexpensive PCs. The security and ethical use of such systems are crucial to the health of the Internet and the commerce of many sectors, especially the music and movie industries.

Secondly, by allowing anonymous information flow, anonymous P2P systems protect users' privacy and freedom of speech. It allows one to voice unpopular opinions, to report misconduct of one's superiors, or simply to discuss freely on controversial issues, without being threatened. As an end user, to select the best P2P system that protects users' rights, one needs to know how anonymity is achieved in such systems.

Thirdly, from the government and copyright owners' perspective, we need to understand the anonymity techniques to devise an effective surveillance method for illegal activities in P2P systems. Indeed, existing P2P systems are commonly used for trading copyrighted materials. It is also a legitimate concern that such systems might aid terrorism and many other illegal activities. Virtually every practical anonymity technique has its limitations. Such limitations offer the possibility for surveillance.

BACKGROUND

Put simply, *anonymity* means the state of not being identified. To avoid confusion, anonymity must be said with respect to some observing entity. Whether a subject can remain anonymous depends on how much effort the observing entity spends to uncover the identity of the subject. Unfortunately, such contextual information is often omitted or not clearly stated (Chothia & Chatzikokolakis, 2005).

In P2P systems, the main subjects of concern related to anonymity are the peer that initiated a request (i.e., *requester,* also termed as sender or initiator) and the peer that responded to the request (i.e., *responder,* also referred to as receiver or recipient). For a requester (responder), the observing entity could be the responder (requestor), or some other entity within or external to the P2P system.

If the observing entity has the intention to remove the anonymity of the subject, we call such an entity an attacker, or an *adversary*. An adversary is not restricted to a single node. It can consist of multiple nodes that may *observe* part or all communications coming in and out of a subject. A more powerful adversary may compromise or introduce malicious nodes into the system and consequently be able to *control* part or all network traffic.

Consequently, we can categorize adversaries into *local* and *global* adversaries, based on the scale of network traffic they can observe or control, and also into *passive* and *active* adversaries, based on if they actively compromise nodes in the system and/or generate network traffic to help uncover the identity of the subject.

In P2P systems, there exist several forms of anonymity:

- *Requester anonymity* means that the system can hide the requester's identity from the responder and some adversaries.
- *Responder anonymity* refers to the fact that the responder's identity is hidden from the requester and some adversaries.
- If the system ensures that neither the requester nor the responder knows with whom it is communicating, we have achieved a form of *mutual anonymity*.
- It is also possible that the relationship between a requester and a responder needs to be hidden from some observers, although the requester and the responder themselves might be seen to have made requests and responses. We call this type of anonymity *unlinkability of requester and responder*.

We should note that with respect to a determined local or global adversary, *absolute anonymity* is often not achievable (unless a subject never communicates with others). Therefore, in practice, anonymity is described in terms of probabilistic metrics and relative to other peers in the system (Reiter & Rubin, 1998). A more appropriate term perhaps is pseudonymity rather than anonymity in the context of P2P systems.

ANONYMOUS COMMUNICATION IN P2P SYSTEMS

There have been a large number of proposals for anonymous communication in P2P systems. These approaches can be roughly classified into three categories: (1) using a pre-determined indirect path from a requester to a responder with layered encryption; (2) mixing a new request (or response) with relayed traffic; and (3) using transient pseudo identities and multi-path routing. All three approaches depend, to different degrees, on the strength of cryptography. In general, the more honest the peers that join the communication, the higher the degree of anonymity that can be achieved. We do not include multicast-based approaches (Chaum, 1988; Dolev & Ostrovsky, 2000) because they are not practical in large-scale P2P systems.

Indirect Path with Layered Encryption

Mixes (Chaum, 1981), *onion routing* (Reed, Syverson, & Goldschlag, 1998), and many of their derivatives belong to this category. The strategy is to set up an indirect path between the requester and the responder, so that: (1) the relationship between the requester and the responder is hidden, and (2) the requester is made anonymous to the responder.

Mixes are proposed by Chaum (1981). The idea is to use one or more computers to serve as intermediaries to relay a requester's message to the destination. To defend against traffic analysis (Back, Moller, & Stiglic, 2001) that might link an input with its corresponding output, every computer batches and reorders its inputs. Hence, this method is referred to as mixes and so are the computers used for that purpose.

As shown in Figure 1, each message is signed by the requester and recursively encrypted using the public keys of the responder and the mixes on the path. When this message reaches the first mix P1, P1 decrypts the outermost layer of encryption using its private key, retrieves the next node on the path (P2) as chosen by the requester, and passes the remaining ciphertext to P2 after batching and reordering. This process continues until the message is relayed to the final destination B. The reply message is passed along the same path in reverse direction.

Because the path information, including the responder address, is directly encrypted in the message,

Figure 1. Message routing using layered encryption

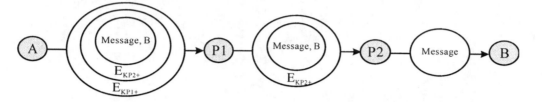

the anonymity of mixes is largely dependent on the strength of the cryptography used.

The original onion routing design is basically the same as mixes except that the requester does not sign the message and the routers do not perform batching and reordering (Reed et al., 1998). The aim is to support interactive communications that require low latency. The mixes design is more appropriate to support anonymous communications that can tolerant high latencies, such as e-mail exchanges.

The onion routing is later revised in Tor (Dingledine, Mathewson, & Syverson, 2004) to use symmetric encryption and virtual circuit. This second-generation onion routing requires an additional step before the actual anonymous communication takes place. In this step, the requester negotiates a (symmetric) session key with each node along the path and builds the virtual circuit incrementally. The use of session keys has many advantages. First, the symmetric-key-based encryption and decryption are much faster than the public-key-based operations. Second, if a session key is compromised, only the messages encrypted using that particular key can be interpreted. Third, a relay node can deny that it has relayed a message as soon as the virtual circuit is closed and the session key is removed from its memory. The node cannot enjoy the same deniability if long-term public keys are used.

The indirect-path-based methods can be adapted to support mutual anonymity by using some special proxy agents, or rendezvous points, to connect a hidden requester and a hidden responder together (Scarlata, Levine, & Shields, 2001; Xiao, Xu, & Zhang, 2003; Dingledine et al., 2004).

Mixing in a Crowd

This approach was first fully described by Bennett and Grothoff (2003) as part of the GNUnet project. The design philosophy is that by relaying messages coming from other peers in the system, a message initiated by a peer is virtually indistinguishable from the those relayed, consequently, even with respect to a passive global adversary, the requester (or responder) anonymity is preserved because the adversary cannot be certain that the peer has initiated a request (or reply). Therefore, the requester and responder anonymity can be achieved with respect to a wide range of adversaries.

In GNUnet, each request carries a source address in conjunction with the query itself. A flooding-based routing algorithm is used to propagate a request across the P2P network. If a peer has the resource requested, it may reply to the requester using the source address indicated in the request message. To defend against casual eavesdroppers, link-level encryption is used.

On receiving a request, a peer may decide to rewrite the source address in the request with its own address and forward the request to some other peers. Alternatively, the peer might simply forward the original message to its neighbors, or drop the message if it is too busy. Normally, a node is motivated to perform the source address rewriting. If it simply forwards a request without rewriting, the next peer that receives the forwarded message knows that it did not originate from this peer. Consequently, the number of messages this peer can utilize to bury its own messages into is reduced. An example of source address rewriting is shown in Figure 2.

We should note that the reply does not necessarily follow the same path, due to the possibility of relaying without source address rewriting. This allows the responder to send a reply directly to the requester without compromising the anonymity of either the requester or the responder, because either one of them could have been relaying the message for other peers.

A related, but less aggressive (in terms of anonymity goal) approach is *crowds* (Reiter & Rubin, 1998).

Figure 2. An example of source address rewriting in GNUnet. The new message generated by node C is mixed with relayed messages.

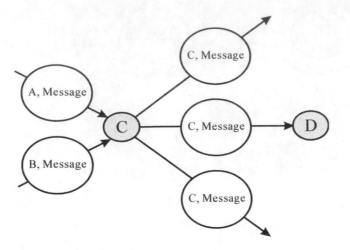

The crowds protocol assumes that the requester knows the identity of the responder. Consequently, the design goal is to achieve some form of requester anonymity with respect to the responder. In crowds, a requester selects a relay node in the system and sends the node its request. On receiving a request, the relay node decides randomly whether to forward the message to another randomly chosen relay node or to submit the request directly to the intended responder. The reply follows the same path in reverse direction.

In the original crowds design, a relay node does not generate any requests directly. A local adversary can tell easily if a node has generated a request. Therefore, crowds does not guarantee sender anonymity with respect to a local adversary. However, crowds can be trivially modified to provide such anonymity by requiring every requester to relay others' messages.

ARA Routing and Pseudo Identifier

Recent P2P systems, such as ANTsp2p (Rossi, 2006) and MUTE (Rohrer, 2006), adopted a multi-path, non-deterministic routing algorithm, called ARA (Gunes, Sorges, & Bouazzi, 2002). In ARA, the path is determined pseudo-randomly, with more weight given to the path that is used more frequently, as shown in Figure 3. Therefore, messages routed between the same source destination pair can automatically converge to the shortest path between the pair, while still allowing some to take a different path with certain probability.

This routing algorithm provides robust defense against disruptions introduced by an active adversary. For example, if a compromised node drops one or more reply messages, the probability for a message to be routed over a different path increases, and eventually the traffic converges to a different optimal path. Deterministic routing does not offer the same self-adaptability.

Peers in these new P2P systems use pseudo identifiers to enhance their anonymity. The pseudo identifiers are self-generated and are used to communicate with each other instead of the IP addresses, which can reveal one's ISP and eventually the user's identity. Furthermore, each pseudo identifier is used only for a brief period of time, after which a new one will be generated and used.

The biggest challenge, however, is how to minimize the linkability between a peer's pseudo identifier and its IP address. Obviously, if an adversary can observe the content of every input and output message, it can easily detect if the peer has generated a message. Since a peer's IP is always exposed to its neighbors (and other eavesdroppers), the linkability is exposed to the adversary in this case.

One solution is to implement link-level encryption so that the input and the output look differently for the same message (different keys are used to do encryption in different links). However, the link-level encryption is not adequate to defend against more powerful at-

Figure 3. *An example ARA routing*

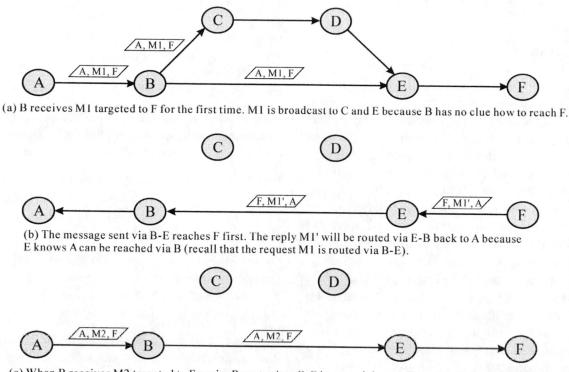

(a) B receives M1 targeted to F for the first time. M1 is broadcast to C and E because B has no clue how to reach F.

(b) The message sent via B-E reaches F first. The reply M1' will be routed via E-B back to A because E knows A can be reached via B (recall that the request M1 is routed via B-E).

(c) When B receives M2 targeted to F again, B routes it to B-E because it knows F can be reached via this route. If in the past, B has seen messages originated from F via C-B too, it will randomly select a route between B-C and B-E with more weight given to the route being used more frequently.

tacks such as timing-based analysis. For example, if a compromised peer relayed a request and receives a reply to this request immediately from one of its neighbors, it can infer with large certainty that this neighbor responded directly and consequently detects the linkability (Chothia & Chatzikokolakis, 2005).

FUTURE TRENDS

Being an open and anonymous P2P system, it is impossible to prevent an adversary to plant compromised peers into the system. Unfortunately, virtually none of the anonymous communication techniques described in the previous section can ensure the anonymity of a peer if it is completely surrounded by compromised nodes (i.e., the peer's neighbors are all compromised). Furthermore, many anonymous communication techniques would be weakened if there are a significant number of compromised nodes in a communication

path. Therefore, it is crucial to minimize the impact of compromised nodes. Also important is to detect and remove compromised nodes in a timely manner (Rennhard & Plattner, 2002).

Tarzan (Freedman & Morris, 2002) is one of the first systems that paid significant attention to these issues. It proposed a number of measures to minimize the impact of compromised nodes. Most notably, it introduced the domain concept that defines the scope in which an adversary can exercise its control. When choosing a peer as one's neighbor, at most one peer can be chosen from each domain. Furthermore, a peer must relay all messages through its neighbors (called *mimics*). Direct requester and responder connection is not allowed.

Another significant issue is the accountability of anonymous peers (Cornelli, Damiani, De Capitani, Paraboschi, & Samarati, 2002). The anonymity given to the peers in the P2P systems can be abused and often is. Anonymity may also make it easy to launch a variety of network-based attacks on the P2P system itself or other targets in cyberspace.

CONCLUSION

Anonymity is closely related to security. In particular, an anonymous P2P system warrants a user's privacy. Such systems can be used as valuable tools to protect the freedom of speech and civil liberty. On the other hand, they can also be used unethically, such as sharing copyrighted materials. Consequently, the use of P2P systems has been a subject of great controversy. Unfortunately, an easy resolution does not seem to exist. Nevertheless, there is no doubt that the development of anonymous P2P systems is an important step forward in computing and communication.

In this article, we provided a brief technical overview of anonymous P2P systems. As we stated earlier, it is important to understand the underlying anonymous communication techniques, both from a user's perspective to choose a system that best protects one's privacy, and from governmental and businesses' perspective to help design surveillance methods.

REFERENCES

Back, A., Moller, U., & Stiglic, A. (2001). *Traffic analysis attacks and trade-offs in anonymity providing systems* (pp. 245-257). Berlin: Springer-Verlag (LNCS 2137).

Bennett, K., & Grothoff, C. (2003). *GAP: A practical anonymous networking* (pp. 141-160). Berlin: Springer-Verlag (LNCS 2760).

Chaum, D. (1981). Untraceable electronic mail, return addresses, and digital pseudonyms. *Communications of the ACM, 4*(2), 84-90.

Chaum, D. (1988). The dining cryptographers problem: Unconditional sender and recipient untraceability. *Journal of Cryptology, 1*(1), 65-75.

Chothia, T., & Chatzikokolakis, K. (2005). *A survey of anonymous peer-to-peer file sharing* (pp. 744-755). Berlin: Springer-Verlag (LNCS 3823).

Cornelli, F., Damiani, E., De Capitani, S., Paraboschi, S., & Samarati, P. (2002). Choosing reputable servants in a P2P network. *Proceedings of the International World Wide Web Conference* (pp. 376-386). Honolulu: ACM Press.

Dingledine, R., Mathewson, N., & Syverson, P. (2004). Tor: The second-generation onion router. *Proceedings of the USENIX Security Symposium* (pp. 303-320). San Diego, CA.

Dolev, S., & Ostrovsky, R. (2000). Xor-trees for efficient anonymous multicast and reception. *ACM Transactions on Information and System Security, 3*(2), 63-84.

Freedman, M., & Morris, R. (2002). Tarzan: A peer-to-peer anonymizing network layer. *Proceedings of the 9th ACM Conference on Computer and Communications Security* (pp. 193-206). Washington, DC.

Gunes, M., Sorges, U., & Bouazzi, I. (2002). ARA—the ant-colony based routing algorithm for MANETS. *Proceedings of the IEEE International Workshop on Ad Hoc Networking* (pp. 79-85). Vancouver, Canada.

Reed, M., Syverson, P., & Goldschlag, D. (1998). Anonymous connections and onion routing. *IEEE Journal on Selected Areas in Communications, 16*(4), 482-494.

Reennhard, M., & Plattner, B. (2002). Introducing MorphMix: Peer-to-peer based anonymous Internet usage with collusion detection. *Proceedings of the ACM Workshop on Privacy in the Electronic Society* (pp. 91-102). Washington, DC.

Reiter, M., & Rubin, A. (1998). Crowds: Anonymity for Web transactions. *ACM Transactions on Information and System Security, 1*(1), 66-92.

Rossi, R. (2006). *ANTs P2P project.* Retrieved from http://antsp2p.sourceforge.net/ANtsProject.html

Rohrer, J. (2006). *MUTE project.* Retrieved from http://mute-net.sourceforge.net/

Scarlata, V., Levine, B., & Shields, C. (2001). Responder anonymity and anonymous peer-to-peer file sharing. *Proceedings of the IEEE International Conference on Network Protocols* (pp. 272-280). Riverside, CA.

Saroiu, S., Gummadi, K., Dunn, R., Gribble, S., & Levy, H. (2002). An analysis of Internet content delivery systems. *Proceedings of the USENIX Symposium on Operating Systems Design and Implementation* (pp. 315-328). Boston.

Taylor, I. (2004). *From P2P to Web services and grids: Peers in a client-server world.* Berlin: Springer-Verlag.

Xiao, L., Xu, Z., & Zhang, X. (2003). Low-cost and reliable mutual anonymity protocols in peer-to-peer networks. *IEEE Transactions on Parallel and Distributed Systems, 14*(9), 829-840.

KEY TERMS

Anonymous Communication: An entity can communicate with some other entity without being detected.

ARA Routing: This algorithm is inspired by the study of ant behavior. Messages routed using this algorithm can converge automatically to the shortest path between two communication parties. It is a non-deterministic, multi-path routing algorithm.

Domain: A block of continuous IP addresses with identical prefix of certain length. A domain defines the scope in which an adversary can exercise its control.

Mixes: A group of computers used to relay a requester's message to the destination. Every computer, called mix, batches and reorders input messages before relaying them. Each message is signed by the requester and recursively encrypted using the public keys of the responder and each of the mixes on the path.

Onion Routing: A message is wrapped within several layers of encryption before being routed along a pre-determined path. Each node in the path peels off a layer of encryption and forwards the remaining message to the next node. This process repeats until the destination is reached.

Peer-to-Peer System (Anonymous): A distributed system in which the role played by each member is roughly equivalent—that is, it both consumes and provides services to other members. An anonymous peer-to-peer system allows anonymous information flow among the members in the system.

Pseudo Identifier: A transient, self-generated identifier used to in peer-to-peer systems to increase the anonymity of each peer.

Session Key: A symmetric key that is used to encrypt and decrypt messages exchanged in a communication session. A session key should never be reused.

Argumentation and Computing

Ephraim Nissan
Goldsmiths College, University of London, UK

INTRODUCTION

Argumentation is usually thought of as a domain within philosophy, or rhetoric. Yet, it has made inroads in the works of computer scientists, especially, yet not only, the logicists among them. *Information Ethics and Security,* in the title of this encyclopedia, respectively belong in ethics (in general) and in the forensic sciences (security is both preventative and about discovering traces of perpetrators). Deontic logic—that is, logic for representing obligations and permissions (Åqvist, 2002; Abrahams & Bacon, 2002) being used, for example in databases or in security—has been an early (1970s) and conspicuous stream within "AI & Law," a domain in which models of argumentation have featured prominently since the 1990s (e.g., Ashley, 1990; Prakken & Sartor, 1996).

To ascertain (other than trivially) ethical status, or to make a point of law—or to persuade in politics (Atkinson, Bench-Capon, & McBurney, 2005) or to reach a negotiated settlement (Zeleznikow, 2002)—argumentation is paramount. Besides, natural-language generation makes use of argumentation at the rhetorical level, as do tutorial dialogues (Carenini & Moore, 2001). For organizing and handling arguments, there exist both general tools (e.g., *Carneades* – Gordon & Walton, 2006) and specialized ones: *MarshalPlan* is for law (Schum, 2001). There also is the category of graphic or multimedia tools for visualizing the relations among arguments (van den Braak, van Oostendorp, Prakken, & Vreeswijk, 2006); these include *Araucaria* (Reed & Rowe, 2004), *QuestMap* (Conklin & Begeman, 1988; Carr, 2003), *ArguMed* (Verheij, 1999), and *Room 5* (Loui et al., 1997).

In order to avoid this merely being an overview, we try to give readers some operational knowledge. This article should be read along with the next article, "Argumentation with Wigmore Charts, and Computing," which more specifically focuses on a given method. Notational variants exist (both in formulae and in graphs). There is a panoply of alternative computer tools and formal models, and it is not our purpose here to be exhaustive in listing them.

BACKGROUND

A concise, apt overview of achievements follows:

Potential for exploitation of research in the philosophical theory of argumentation, in informal logic, and in dialectics, have been recognised relatively recently by researchers in artificial intelligence, but already fruits of such cross fertilisation are beginning to ripen. Recent successes include agent system negotiation protocols that demonstrate higher levels of sophistication and robustness; argumentation-based models of evidential relations and legal processes that are more expressive; models of language generation that use rhetorical structures to produce effective arguments; groupwork tools that use argument to structure interaction and debate; computer-based learning tools that exploit monological and dialogical argument structures in designing pedagogic environments; decision support systems that build upon argumentation theoretic models of deliberation to better integrate with human reasoning; and models of knowledge engineering structured around core concepts of argument to simplify knowledge elicitation and representation problems. Furthermore, benefits have not been unilateral for AI, as demonstrated by the increasing presence of AI scholars in classical argumentation theory events and journals, and AI implementations of argument finding application in both research and pedagogic practice within philosophy and argumentation theory. (CMNA, 2006)

Computational models of argumentation come in three categories: logic based (highly theoretical), pragmatic *ad hoc* treatments which are not probabilistic, and probabilistic models of argument (the latter, not treated in this entry). Recent paper collections include, for example, Dunne and Bench-Capon (2005) and Reed and Norman (2003). Classics include the HYPO system (Ashley, 1990), which was continued in the CABARET project (Rissland & Skalak, 1991) and the CATO project (Aleven & Ashley 1997).

Arguments themselves come in different categories, such as deontological (in terms of right or wrong) or teleological (what acting or not acting in a given way may bring or not bring about) (MacCormick 1995, pp. 467-468). In a disputation with *adversary arguments,* the players do not actually expect to convince each other, and their persuasion goals target observers. ABDUL/ILANA simulated the generation of adversary arguments on an international conflict (Flowers, McGuire, & Birnbaum, 1982). *Persuasion arguments,* instead, have the aim of persuading one's interlocutor, too. Persuasive political argument is modeled in Atkinson et al. (2005). AI modeling of persuasion in court was discussed by Bench-Capon (2003).

For the class of such computational models of argument which are based on logic (neat, theoretical models), a good survey from which to start is Prakken and Sartor (2002):

Argumentation is one of the central topics of current research in Artificial Intelligence and Law. It has attracted the attention of both logically inclined and design-oriented researchers. Two common themes prevail. The first is that legal reasoning is defeasible, i.e., an argument that is acceptable in itself can be overturned by counterarguments. The second is that legal reasoning is usually performed in a context of debate and disagreement. Accordingly, such notions are studied as argument moves, attack, dialogue, and burden of proof. (p. 342)

Prakken and Sartor (2002) usefully:

...propose that models of legal argument can be described in terms of four layers. The first, logical layer defines what arguments are, i.e., how pieces of information can be combined to provide basic support for a claim. The second, dialectical layer focuses on conflicting arguments: it introduces such notions as 'counterargument', 'attack', 'rebuttal' and 'defeat', and it defines, given a set of arguments and evaluation criteria, which arguments prevail. The third, procedural layer regulates how an actual dispute can be conducted, i.e., how parties can introduce or

challenge new information and state new arguments. In other words, this level defines the possible speech acts, and the discourse rules governing them. Thus the procedural layer differs from the first two in one crucial respect. While those layers assume a fixed set of premises, at the procedural layer the set of premises is constructed dynamically, during a debate. This also holds for the final layer, the strategic or heuristic one, which provides rational ways of conducting a dispute within the procedural bounds of the third layer. (Section 1.2)

VARIOUS APPROACHES TO ARGUMENT STRUCTURE

A graphical notation for the relation among a multitude of arguments was proposed by a prominent American legal scholar, John Henry Wigmore (1863-1943). He introduced a complex graphical notation for legal argument structuring (Wigmore 1937). *Wigmore Charts* were usefully simplified in Anderson and Twining (1991, cf. Anderson, 1999). Schum (2001) used them in *MarshalPlan.* Prakken (2004) has adopted them as well, visualizing the argument structure by using *Araucaria* (Reed & Rowe, 2004). In the next article, "Argumentation with Wigmore Charts, and Computing," we teach how to use Wigmore Charts. Arguably, they deserve widespread use.

In computer science, for representing an argument, use of Toulmin's (1958) argument structure is relatively widespread, certainly more so than Wigmore Charts have been. A chart with Toulmin's argument components is given in Figure 1, whereas an example of application is given in Figure 2.

In Toulmin's model, an argument consists of a single premise ("Datum" or "Data"), of the Claim (which is the conclusion), of a Qualifier which states the probative value of the inference (e.g., *necessarily,* or *presumably*), of the Warrant—which is a kind of rule which supports the inference from the premise to the conclusion of the argument—and of the Backing (an additional piece of data which provides support for the warrant), as well as of a Rebuttal (which is an exception).

Gordon and Walton (2006) described a formal model, implemented in *Carneades,* using a functional programming language and Semantic Web technologies. In the model underlying this tool, instead of Toulmin's single datum, there is generally a set of prem-

Figure 1.

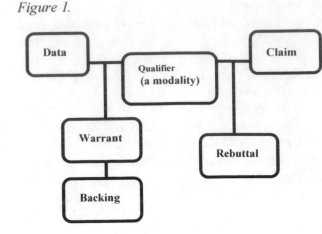

Figure 2.

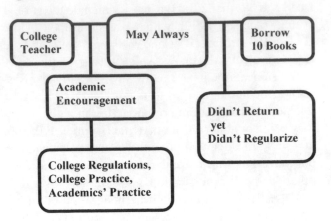

ises. A Rebuttal is modeled using a contrary argument. The Qualifier, which in Toulmin's approach indicates the probative weight of the argument, in *Carneades* is handled by means of a degree, out of a set of proof standards (see below). *Carneades* treats Warrant and Backing differently from Toulmin. In fact, *Carneades* does not directly allow arguments about other arguments, and the conclusion of an argument must be a statement. Therefore, with *Carneades* the equivalent of Toulmin's Warrant is to add a presumption for the warrant to the premises of an argument. "Backing, in turn, can be modeled as a premise of an argument supporting the warrant" (Gordon & Walton, 2006).

Gordon and Walton (2006) further define four proof standards: "If a statement satisfies a proof standard, it will also satisfy all weaker proof standards." The weakest is SE (scintilla of evidence): 'A statement meets this standard iff it is supported by at least one defensible pro argument'. The second weakest is PE (preponderance of the evidence): "A statement meets this standard iff its strongest defensible pro argument outweighs its strongest defensible con argument." A stronger standard is DV: "A statement meets this standard iff it is supported by at least one defensible pro argument and none of its con arguments is defensible." The strongest is BRD (beyond reasonable doubt: not necessarily in its legal meaning): "A statement meets this standard iff it is supported by at least one defensible pro argument, all of its pro arguments are defensible and none of its con arguments are defensible."

In Gordon and Walton's (2006) notation for argument graphs, a circle node is an argument, a box is a statement. The labels for the argument or the statement are inside the circle node or the box node. Arguments have boxes on both sides in the path: boxes and circles alternate in the path. Edges in the graph are labeled as follows: If there is a black-filled circle (which means *presumption*) at the end of an edge (—●), which touches an argument node, this indicates that the statement in the source node (a box) is a presumption, and as such it is a premise of that argument. If the circle is hollow, instead, then this edge (—○) stands for an exception, and the exception statement is a premise for the argument. If the edge had an arrow head (→), then the statement in its source is an ordinary premise.

In the formulae that accompany the argument graph within the same approach, each formula is labeled with an argument identifier, and each formula has a left-hand side (the set of premises), a right-hand side (a statement identifier, this being the conclusion), and an arrow from the left-hand side to the right-hand side. The arrow indicates this is a pro argument, but if its head is not an arrow head but rather a hollow circle, then this is a con (contrary) argument. The left-hand side of the rule is a list of premises, separated by commas. The premises may be statement identifiers with no circle prefix (then this is an ordinary premise), or a statement identifier prefixated with a black circle (a presumption), or a statement prefixated with a hollow circle (an exception). Examples of formulae are:

a1.	b, ○c	→	a
a2.	d, ●e	—○	a

These are two out of five formulae which in Gordon and Walton (2006) accompany their Figure 1, a reduced version of which (representing only the two formulae given above) appears here as Figure 3.

Not all computer tools handle argumentation in the same perspective, with the same theoretical foundations, or with a similar interface structure or protocol. Take *Convince Me* (Schank & Ranney, 1995), one of the tools reviewed in van den Braak et al. (2006). It is based on Thagard's Theory of Explanatory Coherence (e.g., Thagard, 2000), and the arguments consist of causal networks of nodes which can display either evidence or hypotheses, and the conclusion which users draw from them. *Convince Me* predicts the user's evaluations of the hypotheses based on the arguments produced, and gives feedback about the plausibility of the inferences the users draw.

Some tools envisage collaboration among users. *Reason!Able* (van Gelder, 2002) is not designed for collaboration: the intended primary usage is by one user per session. *Reason!Able* guides the user step by step through the process of constructing an argument tree, containing claims, reasons, and objections, the latter two kinds being complex objects which can be unfolded to see the premises. *Reason!Able* is intended for single-user instruction and learning of argumentation techniques, for which it is well suited.

Collaborative problem identification and solving is the purpose of IBIS, an Issue-Based Information System. Problems are decomposed into issues. *QuestMap* (Carr, 2003) is based on IBIS, mediates discussions, supports collaborative argumentation, and creates information maps in the context of legal education.

RECOMMENDED APPROACH

A specific recommendation: Wigmorean analysis deserves to be better known among computer scientists. Toulmin structure is best known, yet the approach in *Carneades* includes a corrective to Toulmin's somewhat redundant treatment of Warrant and Backing.

A general recommendation: it is convenient and neat to represent arguments explicitly. It adds flexibility and transparency. Decision support systems can greatly benefit. In particular, tools are conceivable for information ethics validation, and in these, representing argumentation clearly makes sense. Also tools for supporting computer security, for example, with diagnosis functions, or then for prescribing a course of action, can benefit from arguments being represented.

FUTURE TRENDS AND CONCLUSION

We have preferred to focus on a few nuggets of operational knowledge, rather than subject the reader to a flurry of citations of methods and tools. Future trends surely include even more theoretical work, in addition to the sophisticated extant logic-based approaches. They also include more *ad hoc* tools, a broader range of applications, and more information technologists realizing the potential of incorporating argument handling in architectures they design. Tools grounded in theory exist; they could be viewed as a black box. What most users, or even designers, of potential applications would see is an interface. The domain has attained both maturity and some variety of approaches. It is a resource to be tapped into.

Figure 3.

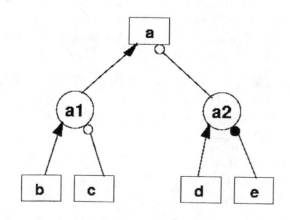

REFERENCES

Abrahams, A.S., & Bacon, J.M. (2002, May). The life and times of identified, situated, and conflicting norms. In A.J.I. Jones & J. Horty (Eds.), *Proceedings of ΔEON'02: The 6th International Workshop on Deontic Logic in Computer Science* (pp. 3-20). London.

Aleven, V., & Ashley, K.D. (1997). Evaluating a learning environment for case-based argumentation skills. *Proceedings of the 6th International Conference on Artificial Intelligence and Law* (pp. 170-179). New York: ACM Press.

Anderson, T.J. (1999). The Netherlands criminal justice system. In M. Malsch & J.F. Nijboer (Eds.), *Complex cases* (pp. 47-67). Amsterdam: THELA THESIS.

Anderson, T., & Twining, W. (1991). *Analysis of evidence.* London: Weidenfeld and Nicolson, 1991; Boston: Little, Brown & Co., 1991; Evanston, IL: Northwestern University Press, 1998.

Åqvist, L. (2002). Deontic logic. In D. Gabbay & F. Guenthner (Eds.), *Handbook of philosophical logic* (2nd ed., vol. 8). Dordrecht: Kluwer.

Ashley, K. (1990). *Modeling legal argument.* Cambridge, MA: The MIT Press.

Atkinson, K., Bench-Capon, T., & McBurney, P. (2005). Persuasive political argument. In F. Grasso, C. Reed, & R. Kibble (Eds.), *Proceedings of the 5th International Workshop on Computational Models of Natural Argument* (*CMNA 2005, at IJCAI 2005*), Edinburgh.

Bench-Capon, T.J.M. (2003). Persuasion in practical argument using value based argumentation frameworks. *Journal of Logic and Computation, 13*(3), 429-448.

Carenini, G., & Moore, J. (2001). An empirical study of the influence of user tailoring on evaluative argument effectiveness. *Proceedings of the 17th International Joint Conference on Artificial Intelligence* (IJCAI 2001), Seattle, WA.

Carr, C.S. (2003). Using computer supported argument visualization to teach legal argumentation. In P.A. Kirschner, S.J. Buckingham Shum, & C.S. Carr (Eds.), *Visualizing argumentation: Software tools for collaborative and educational sense-making* (pp. 75-96). London: Springer-Verlag.

CMNA. (2006, August). *Handouts of the 6th International Workshop on Computational Models of Natural Argument* (*CMNA '06, in concomitance with ECAI 2006*), Riva del Garda, Italy.

Conklin, J., & Begeman, M.L. (1988). IBIS: A hypertext tool for exploratory policy discussion. *ACM Transactions on Office Information Systems, 4*(6), 303-331.

Dunne, P.E., & Bench-Capon, T. (Eds.). (2005). *Argumentation in AI and law.* Nijmegen: Wolff Publishers (IAAIL Workshop Series 2).

Flowers, M., McGuire, R., & Birnbaum, L. (1982). Adversary arguments and the logic of personal attacks. In W. Lehnert & M. Ringle (Eds.), *Strategies for natural language processing* (pp. 275-294). Hillsdale, NJ: Lawrence Erlbaum.

Gordon, T.F., & Walton, D. (2006, August). The Carneades argumentation framework: Using presumptions and exceptions to model critical questions. *Proceedings of the 6th International Workshop on Computational Models of Natural Argument (in conjunction with CMNA, 2006).*

Loui, R.P., Norman, J., Alpeter, J., Pinkard, D., Craven, D., Lindsay, J., & Foltz, M. (1997). Progress on Room 5. *Proceedings of the 6th International Conference on Artificial Intelligence and Law (ICAIL 1997)* (pp. 207-214). New York: ACM Press.

MacCormick, N. (1995). Argumentation and interpretation in law. *Argumentation, 9,* 467-480.

Prakken, H., & Sartor, G. (Eds.). (1996). Logical models of legal argumentation. *Artificial Intelligence and Law, 5*(special issue), 157-372. Reprinted as *Logical models of legal argumentation,* Dordrecht: Kluwer.

Prakken, H., & Sartor, G. (2002). The role of logic in computational models of logic argument: A critical survey. In A. Kakas & F. Sadri (Eds.), *Computational logic* (LNCS 2048, pp. 342-380). Berlin: Springer-Verlag.

Prakken, H. (2004). Analysing reasoning about evidence with formal models of argumentation. *Law, Probability & Risk, 3,* 33-50.

Reed, C., & Norman, T.J. (Eds.). (2003). *Argumentation machines: New frontiers in argument and computation.* Dordrecht: Kluwer.

Reed, C.A., & Rowe, G.W.A. (2004). Araucaria: Software for argument analysis, diagramming and representation. *International Journal on Artificial Intelligence Tools, 14*(3/4), 961-980. (*Araucaria* can be downloaded from http://www.computing.dundee. ac.uk/staff/creed/araucaria/).

Rissland, E.L., & Skalak, D.B. (1991). CABARET: Statutory interpretation in a hybrid architecture. *International Journal of Man-Machine Studies, 34,* 839-887.

Schank, P., & Ranney, M. (1995). Improved reasoning with Convince Me. *Proceedings of CHI '95: Confer-*

ence Companion on Human Factors in Computing Systems (pp. 276-277). New York: ACM Press.

Schum, D. (2001). Evidence marshaling for imaginative fact investigation. *Artificial Intelligence and Law, 9*(2/3), 165-188.

Thagard, P. (2000). Probabilistic networks and explanatory coherence. *Cognitive Science Quarterly, 1,* 91-114.

Toulmin, S.E. (1958). *The uses of argument.* Cambridge, UK: Cambridge University Press (reprints: 1974, 1999).

van den Braak, S.W., van Oostendorp, H., Prakken, H., & Vreeswijk, G.A.W. (2006, August). A critical review of argument visualization tools: Do users become better reasoners? *Proceedings of the 6th International Workshop on Computational Models of Natural Argument* (in conjunction with *ECAI'06*), Riva del Garda, Italy.

van Gelder, T.J. (2002). Argument mapping with Reason!Able. *The American Philosophical Association Newsletter on Philosophy and Computers,* 85-90.

Verheij, B. (1999). Automated argument assistance for lawyers. *Proceedings of the 7th International Conference on Artificial Intelligence and Law (ICAIL 1999)* (pp. 43-52). New York: ACM Press.

Zeleznikow, J. (2002). Risk, negotiation and argumentation: A decision support system based approach. *Law, Probability and Risk: A Journal for Reasoning Under Uncertainty, 1*(1), 37-48.

KEY TERMS

Adversary Argument: "[N]either participant expects to persuade or be persuaded: The participants intend to remain adversaries, and present their arguments for the judgment of an audience (which may or may not actually be present). In these arguments, an arguer's aim is to make his side look good while making the opponent's look bad" (Flowers et al., 1982, p. 275). The ABDUL/ILANA program models such arguers.

Araucaria: A relatively widespread tool for visualizing arguments (Reed & Rowe, 2004). The software is freely available.

AI & Law: Artificial intelligence as applied to law, this being an established discipline both within legal computing and within artificial intelligence.

Argumentation: How to put forth propositions in support or against something. An established field in rhetoric; within AI & Law it became a major field during the 1990.

Carneades: A computer tool, implemented using a functional programming language and Semantic Web technology, based on a particular formal model of argumentation (Gordon & Walton, 206).

Deontic, Deontology: Pertaining to duty and permissibility. Deontic logic has operators for duty. Deontological arguments appeal to principles of right or wrong, ultimate (rather than *teleological*) principles about what must, or ought or must not or ought not to be or be done.

Generalization: One of a set of common-sense heuristic rules that apply to a given instance, a belief held concerning a pattern, and are resorted to when interpreting the evidence and reconstructing a legal narrative for argumentation in court. Also called background knowledge or empirical generalization.

Persuasion Argument: The participants in the dialogue are both willing to be persuaded as well as trying to persuade. This is relevant for computer tools for supporting negotiation.

Teleological: Of an argument (as opposed to *deontological* reasoning): a "reason given for acting or not acting in a certain way may be on account of what so acting or not acting will bring about...All teleological reasoning presupposes some evaluation" (MacCormick, 1995, p. 468).

Toulmin's Model: A widespread model of argument structure (Toulmin, 1958). It consists of the following parts: Data (the premises), Claim (the conclusion), Qualifier (the modality of how the argument holds), Warrant (support for the argument), Backing (support for the Warrant), and Rebuttal (an exception).

Wigmore Charts: A graphic method of structuring legal arguments, currently fairly popular among legal evidence scholars; originally devised in the early twentieth century.

Argumentation with Wigmore Charts and Computing

Ephraim Nissan
Goldsmiths College, University of London, England, UK

INTRODUCTION

In the previous article, "Argumentation and Computing," we provided an overview as well as some operational knowledge of this important, emerging intersection of *argumentation* (paramount as it is in philosophy, ethics, and law) and *computational models* or *computer tools*. In the present short entry, instead, we focus on providing operational knowledge about a particular graphical notation for argumentation, *Wigmore Charts*, quite valuable for legal scholars, yet which have deservedly come within the notice of computer scientists. Once you learn how to use Wigmore Charts, they may well be the handiest notation around. This is why we find it important to teach how to use them.

Whereas arguably *MarshalPlan* (Schum, 2001) is the principal computer tool to incorporate Wigmore Charts, also consider that at the interface level, Wigmore Charts can be used in any out of a number of argument visualization tools. *Araucaria* (Reed & Rowe, 2004), which is freely available, is a visualization tool in which use of Wigmore Charts has been reported in the literature (Prakken, Reed, & Walton, 2003).

It is important to realize that the name *Wigmore Charts* does *not* cover every visualization of complex argumentation in which propositions are nodes and evidential relations are links. The term has been (and should) be used for Wigmore's distinctive kind of argument diagrams, and the term *argument diagram* or *argument map* has been used for the more general class. There are several kinds of visualization of argument which have nothing to do with Wigmore Charts (or Wigmorean analysis). Yet, Wigmore's own original conventions for his diagrams were complex, and in recent decades, a few authors developed a simplified version for which they retained the name *Wigmore Charts*. This accounts for differences among a few visualizations that go by the name *Wigmore Charts*.

BACKGROUND

American legal scholar John Henry Wigmore (1863-1943) introduced a complex graphical notation for legal argument structuring (Wigmore, 1937). Wigmore Charts were usefully simplified in Anderson and Twining (1991, cf. Anderson, 1999). Schum (2001) used them in *MarshalPlan*. Wigmore's original notation was much more complex, for example, distinguishing whether a claim was made by the plaintiff or by the defendant. This is not strictly necessary for a notation for argumentation in law, let alone for argumentation for general purposes.

Let us consider a context of use of Wigmore Charts in a tool which also incorporates other formalisms. Hopefully, seeing things in context rather than just learning about Wigmore Charts in isolation will help the reader to better realize why this kind of diagram is meaningful.

MarshalPlan is a tool for marshalling the evidence and structuring the chronologies and the arguments by means of a formalism, based on Wigmore Charts, at pre-trial and trial within the American system of legal procedure (not only for criminal cases, but in civil cases as well). *MarshalPlan* is not available commercially (so many interesting tools developed by scholars are not), but it can be obtained from its developers (through Professor Peter Tillers at the Cardozo Law School in New York). It has been variously applied within legal, medico-legal, and legal didactic applications.

The formalism in *MarshalPlan* is organized as an algebra. Statistical processing can be added. *MarshalPlan* is intended to provide:

a. an environment allowing the development of a case-specific database of evidence and evidentiary details;
b. support for the development of lines of fact investigation;

c.   support and documentation of investigation protocols;

d.   organization of evidence relevant to given proposed hypotheses or scenarios;

e.   visual representation of the chronological relationships between facts according to hypothesized scenarios;

f.   visual representation of chronologies involved in the narrative and proceedings;

g.   visualization of argument structures;

h.   support and protocols for checking, testing, and evaluating evidence;

i.   temporal consistency checking; and

j.   a bridge to forensic disciplines such as forensic statistics.

Prakken et al. (2003), a paper on using argumentation schemes for reasoning on legal evidence, is mainly an exploration of applying *Araucaria* to an analysis in the style of Wigmore Charts. Prakken and Renooij (2001) explored different methods for causal reasoning, including argument-based reconstruction of a given case involving a car accident. The main purpose of Prakken (2004) "is to advocate logical approaches as a worthwhile alternative to approaches rooted in probability theory," discussing in particular logics for defeasible argumentation:

What about conflicting arguments? When an argument is deductive, the only possible attack is on its premises. However, a defeasible argument can be attacked even if all its premises are accepted...One way to attack it is to rebut it, i.e., to state an argument with an incompatible conclusion...A second way to attack the argument is to undercut it, i.e., to argue that in this case the premises do not support its conclusion. (Prakken, 2004, Section 3.2)

AN EXAMPLE OF WIGMOREAN ANALYSIS

Let us use Anderson's (1999) simplified notation in order to evaluate evidence in a "whodunit" context. Remember that common-sense generalizations (rules of thumb about behavior) are involved in such reasoning. Seeing things done is a powerful didactic tool. The intent of providing here a fully developed example is to show the reader how to develop an application in its entirety, and to give the reader the final satisfaction that we analyzed "a case," without the disappointment of just having done something extremely simple, which would be didactically dreary.

We are not going to analyze an actual courtroom case. Rather, we make an example out of a fairly routine situation of bringing up children. Mum is in the roles of the investigator, the prosecutor, and the judge, whereas Dad helps with the investigation and turns out to be the defense counsel. Grandma is a witness, called by the defendant (one of the children).

As per Anderson's (1999) conventions, let circles be claims or inferred propositions. Squares are testimony. An infinity symbol associated with a circle signals the availability of evidence whose sensory perception (which may be replicated in court) is other than listening to testimony. An arrow reaches the *factum probandum* (which is to be demonstrated) from the *factum probans* (evidence or argument) in support of it, or possibly from a set of items in support (in which case the arrow has one target, but two or more sources). A triangle is adjacent to the argument in support of the item reached by the line from the triangle. An open angle identifies a counterargument instead.

An example of such a Wigmore Chart is given in Figure 1. The numbered propositions follow next. Here is the story. A boy, Bill, is charged with having disobeyed his mother, by eating sweets without her permission. The envelopes of the sweets have been found strewn on the floor of Bill's room. Bill tries to shift the blame to his sister, Molly. The mother acts as both prosecutor and fact finder: it is going to be she who will give a verdict. Dad is helping in the investigation, and his evidence, which may be invalid, appears to exonerate Bill. This is based on testimony that Dad elicited from Grandma (Dad's mother), who is asked to confirm or disconfirm an account of the events given by Bill, and which involves Grandma giving him permission to eat the sweets and share them with Molly. Grandma's evidence is problematic, because Dad's approach to questioning her was confirmationist (i.e., such that would tend to confirm an assumption). Grandma has received from Dad a description of the situation. She may be eager to spare Bill punishment. Perhaps this is why she is confirming his account. Yet, for Mum to make a suggestion to that effect, that the truthfulness of her mother-in-law's testimony is questionable, is politically hazardous and potentially explosive.

Figure 1.

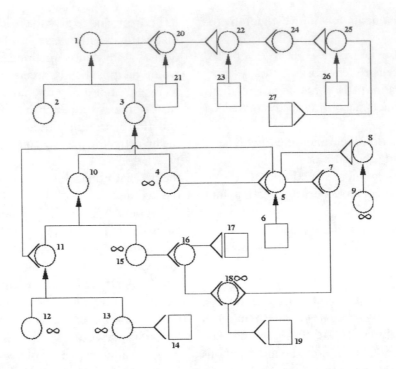

1. *Bill disobeyed Mum.*
2. *Mum had instructed her children, Bill and Molly, not to eat sweets, unless they are given permission. In practice, when the children are given permission, it is Mum who is granting it.*
3. *Bill ate the sweets.*
4. *Many envelopes of sweets are strewn on the floor of Bill's room.*
5. *It was Molly, not Bill, who ate the sweets whose envelopes were found in Bill's room.*
6. *Bill says it was Molly who ate the sweets and placed the envelopes in his room, in order to frame him.*
7. *Molly is very well-behaved.*
8. *Bill would not have left around such damning evidence, implicating him as being the culprit.*
9. *The envelopes were very conspicuously strewn on the floor of Bill's room.*
10. *Medical evidence suggests that Bill ate the sweets.*
11. *Bill's teeth are aching, the reason being that he ate the sweets.*
12. *Bill has bad teeth.*
13. *Bill's teeth are aching at the time the charge against him is being made.*
14. *Bill says that his teeth were already aching on the previous two days.*
15. *Mum is a nurse, and she immediately performed a blood test on Bill, and found an unusually high level of sugar in his blood-stream.*
16. *If there was a mix-up, then Molly is the culprit, not Bill.*
17. *Bill rang up Dad and claimed that Bill insisted with Mum to test also Molly's blood, not only Bill's blood, and that Mum did so, but must have mixed up the results of the two tests.*
18. *Mum tested both Bill and Molly for sugar in their bloodstream, and both of them tested positive.*
19. *Molly says she only ate sweets because Bill was doing so and convinced her to do likewise.*
20. *Bill was justified in eating the sweets.*
21. *Bill rang up Dad, related to him his version of the situation, and claimed to him that Grandma had come on visit, and while having some sweets herself, instructed Bill to the effect that both Bill and Molly should also have some sweets, and Bill merely complied.*
22. *Dad's evidence confirms that Bill had Grandma's permission.*
23. *Dad rang up Grandma, and she confirmed that she gave Bill the permission to take and eat the sweets.*
24. *Dad's evidence is not valid, because Dad told Grandma about Bill's predicament, and Grandma wanted to save Bill from punishment.*
25. *What Dad admitted confirms that his way of questioning Grandma may have affected whether she was being sincere.*
26. *Dad confirms that he told Grandma about Bill's predicament, and didn't just ask her whether she had come on visit first, and next, whether sweets were being had.*
27. *Dad: "How dare you question Grandma's sincerity?!"*

Proposing that exceeding benevolence and leniency for one's grandchildren is typical behavior for grandmothers is an example of commonsensical "background generalization." This could have been one more proposition in the list. "Children are fond of sweets" and "Children are less likely to resist temptation for something they crave" are other generalizations. "Molly is very well-behaved" is an example of character evidence and is related to a background generalization, "A person who on record is very well-behaved, is unlikely to be a perpetrator (if a suspect), or to be a perpetrator again (if guilt is proven, but extenuating circumstances are invoked)."

Bex, Prakken, Reed, and Walton (2003, Section 4.2) discuss such generalizations in the context of a formal computational approach to legal argumentation about a criminal case, as does Prakken (2004, Section 4). The latter (Section 4.2) lists four manners of attacking generalizations:

- "attacking that they are from a valid source of generalizations";
- "attacking the defeasible derivation from the source" (e.g., arguing that a given proposition is general knowledge indeed, but that "this particular piece of general knowledge is infected by folk belief");
- "attacking application of the generalisation in the given circumstances" ("this can be modelled as the application of applying more specific generalisations"); and
- "attacking the generalisation itself."

Note that Molly is not necessarily lying, even if Grandma actually gave Bill permission for both Bill and Molly, not in Molly's presence. Molly may simply have been suspicious of Bill's sincerity. It may be that she topped this up by littering his room with sweets envelopes, in order to have him ensconced as being the one responsible. Or then, Bill may have littered his room unthinkingly. Some inconsistency in Bill's reports is not necessarily fatal for his case. Dad's "How dare you question Grandma's sincerity?!" is an example of a political consideration about the evidence.

RECOMMENDED APPROACH

Such computer scientists who use diagrams for argument are likelier to use Toulmin's than Wigmore's. Wigmore's (in Anderson's simplified form) are handy, once you learn. Both Wigmore Charts and *Carneades* (Gordon & Walton 2006; see previous article, "Argumentation and Computing") do away with Toulmin's fixtures, the Warrant and the Backing. Yet, pure Wigmore Charts omit the probative value, whereas Toulmin allows one to indicate the strength of an argument in a Qualifier (a modality: e.g., *necessarily,* or *possibly*). Schum, among the main proponents of Wigmore Charts, incorporated a probabilistic model. See Schum (1993) on using probability theory with Wigmore Charts.

Computer scientists using software tools may be quite happy with a probabilistic model. Or then, probabilities or odds are too much for the cognition of most, which is why Gordon and Walton (2006) avoided such a formalism, in order to quantify the *defensibility* of arguments, rather than "prefer to use a simpler ordinal scale, since we are skeptical that users can estimate such weights with a greater degree of accuracy." There is no reason the same could not be used along with Wigmore Charts.

In particular, decision support systems could benefit from the incorporation of both an argument structuring component and a formalism for quantifying the strength of arguments. Depending on the purpose, the threshold of persuasion needs to be different. This is a point that deserves emphasis. For that purpose, and in line with our approach in this article of providing a context for Wigmore Charts, even when it does not directly shed light on that formalism itself, we examine how purpose affects the threshold of persuasion. This also dovetails with the article "Artificial Intelligence for Handling Legal Evidence" in this encyclopedia.

Let us consider how adjudication at courts of law has been formalized, according to whether it is a civil case or a criminal case. Convicting an innocent in a criminal case is something much more undesirable than in a civil case.

One theoretical approach to adjudication is in terms of utility (see Friedman, 1997, pp. 277-278; Lempert, 1977, pp. 1021, 1032-1041). Let there be two options:

A

plaintiff p wins, that is, the court finding for the plaintiff, or defendant d wins, that is, the finding is for d. It would seem wisest to select the option with the greater expected utility. The formulae are:

$$EU(p) = P(\Pi) \times U(p,\Pi) + P(\Delta) \times U(p,\Delta)$$

and

$$EU(d) = P(\Pi) \times U(d,\Pi) + P(\Delta) \times U(d,\Delta),$$

where EU(p) and EU(d) represent the expected utilities of judgments for the plaintiff and the defendant, respectively; P(Π) represents the probability that the facts are such that the plaintiff is entitled to judgment, and P(Δ) represents the comparable probability with respect to the defendant. (Friedman, 1997, p. 277)

Of the two arguments of the (social) utility function U, the first one represents the winner ("the party who receives the judgment"), and the second one stands for the party that in truth deserves to win ("the party who is in fact entitled to judgment").

Thus, for example, U(p,Δ) equals the social utility of a judgment for the plaintiff when the truth, if it were known, is such that the defendant should receive judgment. U(p,Π) and U(d,Δ) must each have greater utility than U(p,Δ) and U(d,Π); it is helpful to assume that the first pair has positive utility and the second pair has negative utility. (Friedman, 1997, pp. 277-278)

The *standard of persuasion* $O(\Pi)$ is the degree of confidence when:

$$EU(p) = EU(d)$$

The *plaintiff wins* is optimal "only if the fact-finder's degree of confidence in the plaintiff's case is at least as great as this level" (Friedman, 1997, p. 278), if it is a civil case.

$$O(\Pi) = P(\Pi)/(1-P(\Pi)) =$$
$$(U(d,\Delta)-U(p,\Delta))/(U(p,\Pi)-U(d,\Pi))$$

In contrast, in a criminal case the standard is *beyond a reasonable doubt*. The negative utility of wrongly convicting an innocent $U(p,\Delta)$ "far exceeds any of the other utilities in magnitude" (Friedman, 1997, p. 278).

In civil cases, the usual conception is that $U(p,\Pi) = U(d,\Delta)$ and that $U(p,\Delta) = U(d,\Pi)$:

This means that the standard of persuasion, expressed in odds, equals 1, or 0.5 expressed as a probability. This, of course, is the familiar 'more likely than not', or 'balance of probabilities' standard. (Friedman, 1997, p. 278)

It is useful to understand this, in order to appreciate the difference between merely *quantifying the strength of arguments,* and also setting a *threshold* (based on *purpose*) for a given strength to result in persuasion.

FUTURE TRENDS AND CONCLUSION

Wigmore Charts appear to be gaining popularity among some scholars. Their potential, however, roughly overlaps with the potential of argumentation representations within computing. In the previous article, "Argumentation and Computing," we proposed that argumentation offers large potential indeed. The technologies to support argumentation are growing. The tools available in 2007 were relatively rudimentary, and better tools are a *desideratum*. The field is active. As a referee remarked: "Promotion and dissemination should come (and will follow naturally) only when far better software has been developed."

REFERENCES

Anderson, T.J. (1999). The Netherlands criminal justice system. In M. Malsch & J.F. Nijboer (Eds.), *Complex cases* (pp. 47-67). Amsterdam: THELA THESIS.

Anderson, T., & Twining, W. (1991). *Analysis of evidence.* London: Weidenfeld and Nicolson, 1991; Boston: Little, Brown & Co., 1991; Evanston, IL: Northwestern University Press, 1998.

Bex, F.J., Prakken, H., Reed, C., & Walton, D.N. (2003). Towards a formal account of reasoning about evidence. *Artificial Intelligence and Law, 12,* 125-165.

Friedman, R. D. (1997). Answering the Bayesioskeptical challenge. In R. Allen & M. Redmayne (Eds.), *The International Journal of Evidence and Proof, Bayesianism and Juridical Proof, 1*(Special Issue),

276-291 (with a consolidated bibliography: pp. 354-360). London: Blackstone.

Gordon, T.F., & Walton, D. (2006, August). The Carneades argumentation framework: Using presumptions and exceptions to model critical questions. *Proceedings of the 6ᵗʰ International Workshop on Computational Models of Natural Argument* (held with ECAI'06), Riva del Garda, Italy.

Lempert, R. (1977). Modeling relevance. *Michigan Law Review, 75,* 1021ff.

Prakken, H. (2004). Analysing reasoning about evidence with formal models of argumentation. *Law, Probability & Risk, 3,* 33-50.

Prakken, H., & Renooij, S. (2001). Reconstructing causal reasoning about evidence: A case study. In B. Verheij, A.R. Lodder, R.P. Loui, & A.J. Muntjwerff (Eds.), *Legal Knowledge and Information Systems. Jurix 2001: The 14ᵗʰ Annual Conference* (pp. 131-137). Amsterdam: IOS Press.

Prakken, H., Reed, C., & Walton, D.N. (2003, June 24-28). Argumentation schemes and generalizations in reasoning about evidence. *Proceedings of ICAIL '03,* Edinburgh. New York: ACM Press.

Reed, C.A., & Rowe, G.W.A. (2004). Araucaria: Software for argument analysis, diagramming and representation. *International Journal on Artificial Intelligence Tools, 14*(3/4), 961-980. (*Araucaria* can be downloaded from http://www.computing.dundee.ac.uk/staff/creed/araucaria/).

Schum, D.A. (1993). Argument structuring and evidence evaluation. In R. Hastie (Ed.), *Inside the juror: The psychology of juror decision making* (pp. 175-191). Cambridge: Cambridge University Press.

Schum, D. (2001). Evidence marshaling for imaginative fact investigation. *Artificial Intelligence and Law, 9*(2/3), 165-188.

Wigmore, J.H. (1937). *The science of judicial proof as given by logic, psychology, and general experience, and illustrated judicial trials* (3ʳᵈ ed.). Boston: Little, Brown & Co.

KEY TERMS

AI & Law: Artificial intelligence as applied to law, this being an established discipline both within legal computing and within artificial intelligence.

Argumentation: How to put forth propositions in support or against something. An established field in rhetoric, within AI & Law it became a major field during the 1990s.

Carneades: A computer tool, implemented using a functional programming language and Semantic Web technology, based on a particular formal model of argumentation (Gordon & Walton, 2006).

Factum Probandum: That which is to be demonstrated by means of the *factum probans* (or of several *facta probantes*). Plural: *facta probanda.*

Factum Probans: Evidence in support of a *factum probandum.* Plural: *facta probantes.*

Generalization: One of a set of common-sense heuristic rules that apply to a given instance, a belief held concerning a pattern, and are resorted to when interpreting the evidence and reconstructing a legal narrative for argumentation in court. Also called background knowledge or empirical generalization.

MarshalPlan: A computer tool prototype (Schum, 2001) of David Schum and Peter Tillers, supporting the organization of the evidence, and combining Wigmore Charts, an algebraic approach, and hypertext. Appeared to be about to enter its fully operational phase around 2005, yet the project started in the early 1990s.

Weight (Evidential): The probative value of the evidence.

Wigmore Charts: One out of several diagrammatic methods of structuring legal arguments. It is currently fairly popular among legal evidence scholars; originally devised in the early twentieth century.

Artificial Intelligence Tools for Handling Legal Evidence

Ephraim Nissan
Goldsmiths College, University of London, UK

INTRODUCTION

This article is a concise overview of a field which until the late 1990s did not exist in its own right: computer and computational methods for modeling reasoning on legal evidence and crime analysis and detection. Yet, for various kinds of forensic tests, computer techniques were sometimes used, and statistical methods have had some currency in the evaluation of legal evidence. Until recently it would not have been possible to provide an overarching review such as the present one.

Until around 2000, legal evidence was a surprisingly inconspicuous subject within the field of artificial intelligence (AI) and law, which had been developing since the early 1970s and is more specific than legal computing. Within AI and law, with some seminal work from the end of the 1980s and then organically from the late 1990s, a new area has been developing which applies AI techniques to how to reason on legal evidence. This requires also capturing within a formal setting at least some salient aspects of the legal narrative at hand. It took a systematic, organic effort to promote evidence as a subdomain within AI and law. Editorial initiatives included Martino and Nissan (2001), Nissan and Martino (2001, 2003, 2004a), and MacCrimmons and Tillers (2002). Also see Nissan (2004).

The subdomain of AI and law that is mainly concerned with evidence is distinct from the application of computing in any of the multitude of individual forensic disciplines, for example, tools for chemistry or fluid dynamics (Nissan, 2003a), or computer imaging or computer graphic techniques within the pool of methods (Wilkinson, 2004) for reconstructing from body remains a set of faces in three dimensions, practically fleshing out a skull, which show what a dead person may have looked like (forensic facial reconstruction).

AI in general had been much concerned with evidentiary reasoning. Yet, it is no trivial matter to apply such results from AI: the status of quantitative, especially probabilistic models for judicial decision making in criminal cases (as opposed to civil cases) is a hotly disputed topic among legal scholars. AI practitioners need to exercise care, lest methodological flaws vitiate their tools in the domain with some legal scholars, let alone opponents in litigation. This is different from the situation of the police, whose aim is to detect crime and to find suspects, without having the duty of proving their guilt beyond a reasonable doubt, which is the task of the prosecutors.

BACKGROUND

Legal Scholars and Statisticians: Bayesians or Probabilists and Skeptics

Legal scholars and statisticians fiercely supporting or opposing Bayesianism, in handling probabilities in judicial contexts (Allen & Redmayne, 1997; Tillers & Green, 1988), continue a controversy that started in the early modern period (Nissan, 2001), with Voltaire being skeptical of probabilities in judicial decision making, whereas in the 19th century Boole, of Boolean algebra fame, believed in the formalism's potential applicability to law. Scholars in both camps of that controversy came to realize the desirability of models of plausibility, rather than of just (strictly) probability. Among the Bayesians, perhaps none is more so than Robertson and Vignaux (e.g., Robertson & Vignaux, 1995; cf. Aitken, 1995), whereas Ron Allen is prominent among the skeptics (see Allen, in Martino & Nissan, 2001, on his desiderata vis-à-vis AI modeling of the plausibility of legal narratives). Even skeptics praised Kadane and Schum's (1996) evaluation of the evidence in the Sacco & Vanzetti case from the 1920s, but in a sense the skeptics could afford to be generous, because that project had taken years to develop and therefore is of little "real-time" practical use in ongoing judicial settings. The statistics of identification of perpetrators from DNA samples is the one area in which the statisticians appear to prevail upon the skeptics. Not all probabilists are Bayesians. Some statistical tools are respected and accepted, including in court, depending on context. Information technologists entering the field need be careful.

Psychologists, Judicial Decision Making, and Jury Research

The descriptive modeling of the decision-making process of jurors is an active area of research in psychology in North America. Sometimes, computer tools have been involved in simulations. Models involve strong simplifications. Gaines, Brown, and Doyle (1996) simulated quantitatively how the opinion of a jury is shaped, and apparently this was the first such model to appear in an AI forum. Following the cognitive model in Hastie, Penrod, and Pennington (1983), Hastie (1993) is the standard reference about descriptive meter-models of juror decision making—that is, such quantitative models that are not concerned with specific narrative details. Compare Dragoni and Nissan (in Nissan & Martino, 2004), which applies a belief revision formalism to the dynamics of how judicial fact finders (judges or jurors) propend to either verdict; an architectural component modifies (by feedback) the credibility of the source from which an item of information comes, according to how the credibility of that item of information is currently faring.

The research in Hastie (1993) includes "four competing approaches represented" among behavioral scientists' descriptive models of decision making (p. 10), namely, those "based on probability theory, 'cognitive' algebra, stochastic processes, and information processing theory" (pp. 10-11). The excessive focus on juries is problematic: in many countries, there only are bench trials (i.e., without a jury), and bench trials also exist in the UK and United States.

The Year 1989 as a Watershed Date

Seminal works were published in 1989: Thagard (1989) on ECHO (cf. Thagard, 2004), Kuflik, Nissan, and Puni (1989) on Nissan's ALIBI, and Lutomski (1989) on an attorney's statistical automated consultant. In ECHO, neural computing is resorted to (each hypothesis and finding is a node) in order to model the reasoning of a jury.

In Thagard (1989), this was the California murder trial against Peyer. Eventually Josephson and colleagues reimplemented the Peyer case, using a different infer-

ence engine, PEIRCE-IGTT, for abductive reasoning (i.e., inference to the "best" explanation), which formed its conclusions quickly (Fox & Josephson, 1994). The Peyer case was also modeled in Ciampolini and Torroni (in Nissan & Martino, 2004), using abductive logic-based agents and their ALIAS multi-agent architecture in the LAILA language for expressing agent behavior.

ALIBI (Kuflik et al., 1989; Fakher-Eldeen et al., 1993) is an AI planner that impersonates a person who is being accused. Given an accusation, ALIBI decomposes it, computes effects and liability, and composes an alternative explanation, claiming exoneration or a lesser liability.

TOOLS FOR DOMAINS OR ASPECTS OF EVIDENCE

Oatley, Zeleznikow, and Ewart (2004), using data mining techniques, are concerned with assisting the police in detecting the perpetrators of burglary from homes. ADVOKATE (Bromby & Hall, 2002) is about the evaluation of the credibility of eyewitness evidence. Keppens and Zeleznikow's (2003) Dead Bodies Project has the goal of determining cause of death. Mugs are portraits of suspects: photographs, or sketch artist's renditions from verbal descriptions, or composites. Computerized systems, E-FIT, PROfit (CD-FIT), and Mac-A-Mug Pro, are old-fashioned vs. CRIME-VUs, which handles composites in three dimensions and uses morphing (Bruce & Hancock, 2002). In Caldwell and Johnston (1989), a genetic algorithm was used to track a criminal suspect through 'face-space'.

Crime Networks and Link Analysis

In criminal investigation, intelligence analysts oftentimes reason on criminal networks. Products for link analysis include: COPLINK (Hauck, Atabakhsh, Ongvasith, Gupta, & Chen, 2002; Chen et al., 2003a, 2003b, 2004), FinCEN (Goldberg & Wong, 1998) on money laundering, and the Link Discovery Tool (Horn, Birdwell, & Leedy, 1997) using shortest-path algorithms to link individuals.

In England, Richard Leary's FLINTS produces a graphical pattern of links between crimes and criminals. Leary, van den Berghe, and Zeleznikow (2003) described an application of the FLINTS model to financial fraud modeling. Another system has been tried by the Zurich police in Switzerland; it was developed by Olivier Ribaux.

Other Models

Papers in Nissan and Martino (2003) include, for example, Perloff's, showing how a modal logic of agency can be concretely applied in legal analysis, and Yovel's treatment, *MicroProlog* style, of the *relevance* of evidence. Approaches to the automated reasoning on other agents' beliefs were treated in Ballim et al. (in Nissan & Martino, 2001) and Barnden (in Martino & Nissan, 2001). Jøsang and Bondi (2000) apply a subjective logic, using probability theory, to legal evidence. Dragoni and Animali (in Nissan & Martino, 2003) used belief revision and the Dempster-Shafer statistical approach for representing inconsistencies among and inside witness assertions. Poole (in MacCrimmons & Tillers, 2002) applied to legal argumentation about evidence a formalism called independent choice logic (ICL), representing Bayesian belief networks. Shimony and Nissan (in Martino & Nissan, 2001) applied a probabilistic interpretation of Spohn's kappa calculus to Åqvist's logical theory of legal evidence. In MacCrimmons and Tillers (2002), Snow and Belis, as well as Levitt and Laskey, analyzed the Omar Raddad case from France, 1994. Snow and Belis structure credibility judgments as graphs and treat credibility assessments change. Levitt and Laskey (2002) apply Bayesian inference networks.

Legal Narratives

Important treatments of legal narratives are Bennett and Feldman (1981), Jackson (1988), and Wagenaar, van Koppen, and Crombag (1993). In the latter's *Theory of Anchored Narratives,* narrative (e.g., the prosecution's claim that John murdered his wife) is related to evidence (e.g., John's fingerprints on the murder weapon) by a connection, called *anchor,* to common-sense beliefs, which are generally accepted as true most of the time (see a critique in Jackson, 1996). Such common sense is termed *background generalizations* in the legal literature. Prakken (2004, Section 4.2) lists four manners of attacking generalizations (see the article, "Tools for Representing and Processing Narratives" in this encyclopedia). Nissan (2003b) applied a given

method of representation to legal and other narratives, involving individual or kind identification.

Computational Models of Legal Argumentation about Evidence

John Henry Wigmore (1863-1943) was a very prominent exponent of legal evidence theory (and of comparative law) in the United States. A particular tool for structuring argumentation graphically, called Wigmore Charts and first proposed by Wigmore (1913, 3rd ed. 1937), was resurrected in the 1980s (Anderson & Twining, 1991; Schum, 2001). See the two companion articles, "Argumentation and Computing" and "Argumentation with Wigmore Charts, and Computing" in this encyclopedia.

Schum first combined computing, legal evidence, and argumentation. Until Prakken (2001, 2004) turned to evidence, only Gulotta and Zappalà (2001) also combined the three: exploring two criminal cases by resorting to DART (Freeman & Farley, 1996) for argumentation, and other tools. This was when a body of published research started to emerge of AI techniques for dealing with legal evidence, mainly in connection with mostly separate organizational efforts by Nissan, Tillers, and Zeleznikow.

Procedural-Support Systems for Organizing the Evidence

Procedural-support systems are AI & Law programs that lack domain knowledge and thus cannot solve problems, but that instead help the participants in a dispute to structure their reasoning and discussion, thereby promoting orderly and effective disputes...When procedural-support systems are to be useful in practice, they should provide support for causal reasoning about evidence. (Prakken & Renooij, 2001)

Products of CaseSoft include the *CaseMap* case analysis software (for lawyers to organize the evidence for a trial), *TimeMap* chronology-graphing software, and the *NoteMap* outliner (the latter, upstream of a document-processor or of the generation of a slideshow presentation).

MarshalPlan (Schum, 2001) is a tool for marshalling the evidence and structuring the chronologies and the arguments by means of a formalism, based on Wigmore

Charts, at pre-trial and trial within the American system of legal procedure (not only for criminal cases, but in civil cases as well). The formalism is organized as an algebra. Statistical processing can be added.

Daedalus is a tool for the Italian *sostituto procuratore* (examining magistrate during investigation, and prosecutor at trial). In the late 1990s, it was adopted by magistrates in the offices of the judiciary throughout Italy (Asaro, Martino, & Nissan, in Nissan & Martino, 2001). A sequel project is *Itaca,* for the Cassations Court in Rome.

RECOMMENDED APPROACH

AI for legal evidence was bootstrapped into existence as a field in its own right, bringing together relevant scholars and techniques that formerly were scattered.

Various directions are worth pursuing. Commonsense is a challenge for AI, and therefore for automatically processing legal narratives. Newcomers from computing into legal evidence modeling need beware of misapplying statistics, debate on whose role in law is fierce anyway; in litigation, opponents look for vulnerable spots, including in method. One thing is enhancing the police's ability to detect suspect perpetrators; another thing is using as evidence in court an argument which depends on the acceptability of some computational technique.

CONCLUSION AND FUTURE TRENDS

There are different contexts of application of the tools we have been concerned with: crime detection, crime analysis, and crime prevention are in the remit of the police, whereas legal professionals will be interested in tools for marshalling and organizing the evidence.

There is a risk involved: will the spread of such tools empower the individual (the citizen, but possibly a foreign worker), or will it further empower rich corporations, or the institutions, against the impecunious? Arguably, both kinds of outcomes could result. It will be up to the developers of such tools to see to it that targeted user profiles are inclusive of private individuals with a small budget, or that the tools enhance their position in society, instead of only catering to the powerful so that the gap with ordinary people would further widen.

REFERENCES

Aitken, C. (1995). *Statistics and the evaluation of evidence for forensic scientists.* Chichester, UK: John Wiley & Sons.

Allen, R., & Redmayne, M. (Eds.). (1997). Bayesianism and juridical proof. *The International Journal of Evidence and Proof, 1*(Special Issue), 253-360.

Anderson, T., & Twining, W. (1991). *Analysis of evidence.* London: Weidenfeld & Nicolson, 1991; Boston: Little, Brown & Co., 1991; Evanston, IL: Northwestern University Press, 1998.

Bennett, W.L., & Feldman, M.S. (1981). *Reconstructing reality in the courtroom.* New Brunswick, NJ: Rutgers University Press/London: Tavistock.

Bex, F.J., Prakken, H., Reed, C., & Walton, D.N. (2003). Towards a formal account of reasoning about evidence. *Artificial Intelligence and Law, 12,* 125-165.

Bromby, M.C., & Hall, M.J.J. (2002). The development and rapid evaluation of the knowledge model of ADVOKATE. *Proceedings of JURIX 2002, the 15th International Conference* (pp. 143-152). Amsterdam: IOS.

Bruce, V., & Hancock, P. (n.d.). *CRIME-VUs: Combined recall images from multiple experts and viewpoints.* Department of Psychology, University of Stirling, Scotland. Retrieved 2002, from http://www.stir.ac.uk/Departments/HumanSciences/Psychology/crimevus/index.htm

Caldwell, C., & Johnston, V.S. (1989). Tracking a criminal suspect through 'face-space' with a genetic algorithm. *Proceedings of the 3rd International Conference on Genetic Algorithms* (pp. 416-421).

Chen, H., Zeng, D., Atabakhsh, H., Wyzga, W., & Schroeder, J. (2003a). COPLINK managing law enforcement data and knowledge. *Communications of the ACM, 46*(1), 28-34.

Chen, H., Schroeder, J., Hauck, R., Ridgeway, L., Atabakhsh, H., Gupta, H., Boarman, C., Rasmussen, K., & Clements, A. (2003b). COPLINK Connect. *Decision Support Systems, 34*(3), 271-285.

Chen, H., Chung, W., Xu, J.J., Wang, G., Qin, Y., & Chau, M. (2004). Crime data mining. *IEEE Computer, 37*(4), 50-56.

A

Fakher-Eldeen, F., Kuflik, T., Nissan, E., Puni, G., Salfati, R., Shaul, Y., & Spanioli, A. (1993). Interpretation of imputed behavior in ALIBI (1 to 3) and SKILL. *Informatica e Diritto* (Florence), year 19, 2nd series, *2*(1/2), 213-242.

Fox, R., & Josephson, J.R. (1994). Software: PEIRCE-IGTT. In J.R. Josephson & S.G. Josephson (Eds.), *Abductive inference* (pp. 215-223). Cambridge: Cambridge University Press.

Freeman, K., & Farley, A.M. (1996). A model of argumentation and its application to legal reasoning. *Artificial Intelligence and Law, 4*(3/4), 157-161.

Gaines, D.M., Brown, D.C., & Doyle, J.K. (1996). A computer simulation model of juror decision making. *Expert Systems with Applications, 11*(1), 13-28.

Goldberg, H.G., & Wong, R.W.H. (1998). Restructuring transactional data for link analysis in the FinCEN AI system. In D. Jensen & H. Goldberg (Eds.), *Artificial intelligence and link analysis. Papers from the AAAI Fall Symposium,* Orlando, FL.

Gulotta, G., & Zappalà, A. (2001). The conflict between prosecution and defense in a child sexual abuse case and in an attempted homicide case. *Information and Communications Technology Law, 10*(1), 91-108.

Hastie, R. (Ed.). (1993). *Inside the juror.* Cambridge: Cambridge University Press.

Hastie, R., Penrod, S.D., & Pennington, N. (1983). *Inside the jury.* Cambridge, MA: Harvard University Press.

Hauck, R.V., Atabakhsh, H., Ongvasith, P., Gupta, H., & Chen, H. (2002). COPLINK concept space. In *Digital Government,* special issue of *IEEE Computer, 35*(3), 30-37.

Horn, R., Birdwell, J.D., & Leedy, L.W. (1997, August 18-22). Link discovery tool. *Proceedings of the Counter-drug Technology Assessment Center's ONDCP/CTAC International Symposium,* Chicago.

Jackson, B. (1988). *Law, fact and narrative coherence.* Merseyside, UK: Deborah Charles.

Jackson, B. (1996). 'Anchored narratives' and the interface of law, psychology and semiotics. *Legal and Criminological Psychology, 1,* 17-45.

Jøsang, A., & Bondi, V.A. (2000). Legal reasoning with subjective logic. *Artificial Intelligence and Law, 8,* 289-315.

Kadane, J., & Schum, D. (1996). *A probabilistic analysis of the Sacco and Vanzetti evidence.* New York: John Wiley & Sons.

Keppens, J., & Zeleznikow, J. (2003). A model based reasoning approach for generating plausible crime scene scenarios from evidence. *Proceedings of the 9th Conference on Artificial Intelligence and Law,* Edinburgh, Scotland (pp. 51-59). New York: ACM Press.

Kuflik, T., Nissan, E., & Puni, G. (1989, September). Finding excuses with ALIBI. In *Proceedings of the International Symposium on Communication, Meaning and Knowledge vs. Information Technology,* Lisbon.

Leary, R.M., van den Berghe, W., & Zeleznikow, J. (2003). User requirements for financial fraud modeling. *Proceedings of BILETA 2003: British & Irish Law, Education & Technology Association 18th Annual Conference.*

Lutomski, L.S. (1989). The design of an attorney's statistical consultant. *Proceedings of the 2nd International Conference of Artificial Intelligence and Law* (pp. 224-233). New York: ACM Press.

MacCrimmons, M., & Tillers, P. (Eds.). (2002). *The dynamics of judicial proof.* Heidelberg: Physica-Verlag.

Martino, A.A., & Nissan, E. (Eds.). (2001). Formal approaches to legal evidence. *Artificial Intelligence and Law, 9*(2/3), 85-224.

Nissan, E. (2001). Can you measure circumstantial evidence? *Information and Communications Technology Law, 10*(2), 231-245.

Nissan, E. (2003a). Review of B.L. Murphy & R.D. Morrison (Eds.), *Introduction to environmental forensics* (San Diego: Academic Press, 2002). *Cybernetics and Systems, 34*(6/7), 571-579.

Nissan, E. (2003b). Identification and doing without it, parts I to IV. *Cybernetics and Systems, 34*(4/5), 317-358, 359-380; *34*(6/7), 467-500, 501-530.

Nissan, E. (2004). Legal evidence scholarship meets artificial intelligence (reviewing MacCrimmons & Tillers, 2002). *Applied Artificial Intelligence, 18*(3/4), 367-389.

Nissan, E., & Martino, A.A. (Eds.). (2001). Software, formal models, and artificial intelligence for legal evidence. *Computing and Informatics, 20*(6), 509-656.

Nissan, E., & Martino, A.A. (Eds.). (2003). Building blocks for an artificial intelligence framework in the field of legal evidence. *Cybernetics and Systems, 34*(4/5), 233-411; *34*(6/7), 413-583.

Nissan, E., & Martino, A.A. (Eds.). (2004). The construction of judicial proof: A challenge for artificial intelligence modeling. *Applied Artificial Intelligence, 18*(3/4), 183-393.

Oatley, G., Zeleznikow, J., & Ewart, B. (2004). Matching and predicting crimes. In A. Macintosh, R. Ellis, & T. Allen (Eds.), *Applications and innovations in intelligent systems XII* (pp. 19-32). Berlin: Springer-Verlag.

Prakken, H. (2001). Modelling reasoning about evidence in legal procedure. *Proceedings of the 8th International Conference on Artificial Intelligence and Law (ICAIL 2001)*, St. Louis, MO (pp. 119-128). New York: ACM Press.

Prakken, H. (2004). Analysing reasoning about evidence with formal models of argumentation. *Law, Probability & Risk, 3*, 33-50.

Robertson, B., & Vignaux, G.A. (1995). *Interpreting evidence*. Chichester, UK: John Wiley & Sons.

Schum, D. (2001). Evidence marshaling for imaginative fact investigation. *Artificial Intelligence and Law, 9*(2/3), 165-188.

Thagard, P. (1989). Explanatory coherence. *Behavioral and Brain Sciences, 12*(3), 435-467.

Thagard, P. (2004). Causal inference in legal decision making. *Applied Artificial Intelligence, 18*(3/4), 231-249.

Tillers, P., & Green, E. (Eds.). (1988). *Probability and inference in the law of evidence*. Boston: Kluwer.

Wagenaar, W.A., van Koppen, P.J., & Crombag, H.F.M. (1993). *Anchored narratives*. Hemel Hempstead, UK: Harvester Wheatsheaf/New York: St. Martin's Press.

Wigmore, J.H. (1937). *The science of judicial proof...* (3rd ed.). Boston: Little, Brown & Co..

Wilkinson, C. (2004). *Forensic facial reconstruction*. Cambridge: Cambridge University Press.

KEY TERMS

Abductive Inference: Inference to the "best" explanation. Not as constrained as deductive inference.

Anchored Narrative: For the prosecution's narrative to be comprehensively anchored, each individual piece of evidence need be not merely plausible, but safely assumed to be certain, based on common-sense rules which are probably true (Wagenaar et al., 1993). Also see *Generalization*.

Bayesian: A legal scholar of evidence or a forensic statistician who strongly supports the use of Bayes' theorem as a foundation for statistical analysis as applied to legal evidence. Opposed by the Bayesio-skeptics.

[Bayesio-] Skeptic: A legal scholar of evidence who has misgivings about the validity or desirability of Bayes' theorem, or even of other probabilistic or statistical formalisms, in the analysis of the evidence of given criminal cases (while not necessarily opposed to such use in civil cases).

Deontic, Deontology: Pertaining to duty and permissibility. Deontic logic has operators for duty.

Evidential Reasoning: A major area within artificial intelligence since the 1970s, as well as a prominent area within legal scholarship; yet within AI & Law, it only emerged as a conspicuous area around 2000.

Forensic Science: A set of scientific specialties (such as chemistry, areas within medicine, psychology, handwriting analysis, fingerprint analysis, geology, archaeology, palynology [pollen], pedology [soil], and so forth) when applied for the purposes of crime analysis and fact investigation.

Generalization: One of a set of common-sense heuristic rules resorted to when interpreting the evidence and reconstructing a legal narrative for argumentation in court. Also called background knowledge or empirical generalization.

Link Analysis: Its aim is to discover crime networks, to identify the associates of a suspect, to track financial transactions (possibly by data mining), to detect geographical patterns (possibly by kind of crime), and so forth.

Procedural: *Procedural,* as opposed to *substantive,* pertains to how to administer the judiciary process. For example, the order in which the parties and their witnesses testify belongs in procedure.

Procedural-Support System: A category of computer tools for assisting participants in a dispute in structuring their reasoning and discussion; for example, *CaseMap, MarshalPlan, Daedalus.*

Substantive: As opposed to *procedural,* pertains to the rules of right administered by a court, rather than to how to administer it.

Wigmore Charts: A graphic method of structuring legal arguments, currently fairly popular among legal evidence scholars; originally devised in the early twentieth century.

Barriers Facing African American Women in Technology

B

Jianxia Du
Mississippi State University, USA

George H. Pate
Mississippi State University, USA

Deneen Sherrod
Mississippi State University, USA

Wei-Chieh Yu
Mississippi State University, USA

INTRODUCTION

In technology education, African American women are normally in the minority. Contributing factors include the continuation of discrimination based on race and/or gender in American society, together with African American women's own self-perception, which is itself influenced by their history of discrimination. These factors in turn affect their access to technology and technology education.

BACKGROUND

According to Thomas, Witherspoon, and Speight (2004), for many individuals, race, gender, and social class—and their influence on identity—cannot be separated. The influence of multiple identity factors must be examined, particularly for groups that experience multiple sources of oppression, such as African American women (Thomas et al., 2004). Scon (2003) suggests that race, class, and gender affect the perceptions and the expectations of the viewing audience as well as the performance of the observed individuals.

To understand a group and issues that confront them, you must look at their history (Jeffries, 1995). Emancipation from slavery in 1863 and the beginning of reconstruction in 1865 brought freedom for African Americans, but sadly they were still treated unjustly and viewed in a subordinate and inferior fashion (Christensen, 2005). Just as the larger American society believed that women were responsible for so-

cializing children and men, and uplifting families and communities, those engaged in the process of creating an African American professional class also believed that the black woman alone had the power to uproot ignorance, break down prejudice, and solve the great race problem (Shaw, 2004).

African American women teachers who taught during the early days of desegregation experienced conflicts with colleagues, administrators, and white parents—the latter often challenging their competence as teachers solely on the basis of race (Foster, 1990). Though frustrated by conflicts with white parents, some teachers recognized that their presence and success forced white parents and students to confront their own feelings of superiority (Foster, 1990) and were determined to remain in education.

Research indicates that due to differences, the majority group creates boundaries that impose limits on how minority workers will be defined in the workplace (Mabokela & Madeson, 2003). European American colleagues failed to understand the differences in other ethnic groups and projected narrowly defined roles for African American teachers (Mabokela & Madeson, 2003). African American women educators feel that other groups lack certain awareness or have a lack of exposure to the perspectives of people of color, and they feel that they must be bicultural: operating not only in their own world, but in one created for them by others (Roberts & Winiarczyk, 1996).

Historically paid less than their white counterparts, rarely employed except to teach African American pupils, opposed by unions seeking to preserve seniority rights for their largely white constituencies, dismissed in large numbers following the *Brown v. Board of Education* decision, and denied access to teaching positions through increased testing at all levels, the lives and careers of African American teachers have been seriously affected by racism (Foster, 1990). African American women teachers in particular are often burdened with the extra pressure of having to prove their worth because their expertise is frequently questioned by their colleagues, as well as by their students and parents (Mabokela & Madeson, 2003).

Through being thought of as inferior teachers in their technology profession to having to prove themselves almost on a daily basis, African American women have remained a strong force in education despite the multiple barriers presented to their success.

BARRIERS FOR AFRICAN AMERICAN WOMEN IN TECHNOLOGY

Before entering technology education, African American women had reservations about a career involving technology, and according to a report by the American Association of University Women, there is a gender gap in technology education (Brunner, 2003). Girls are more ambivalent about technology than boys, who are more positive regarding technology (Brunner, 2003). Young girls are conditioned to believe that skills associated with technology are for boys, and therefore girls take fewer computer science and computer design courses than boys do (Pinkard, 2005). Due to society's increasing dependence on technological skills, the continued existence of the technological gender and cultural gap is a problem that must be addressed in order to ensure that the technological tools are equally accessible to women and children of color (Pinkard, 2005). The gender and cultural technology gap is also contributed to by the level of computer usage in the home, unequal access to technology in some communities, lack of female technologically literate role models, and the negative climate in higher education toward females and minorities (Pinkard, 2005).

Computer usage in the home is very important when it comes to a child's view of technology (Pinkard, 2005). If computer usage is at a high level in the home, the child will come to view technology as very important, but if usage is low, they may not view technology as important and shy away from technology courses completely. Also when placed in a technology class, children may have a feeling of failure because they are not as computer literate as the other students. In education it is important that every child, regardless of race, gender, or class, have access to technology in all levels of education.

Unequal access to technology in our schools is due once again to society's view of technology as an area that is dominated by males (Bush, Henle, Cohen, Jenkins, & Kossy, 2002). Counselors and parents play an important role in the selection of courses, and most young women are not encouraged to enroll in technical classes. Some educators feel that schools have unknowingly contributed to the limited enrollment of minorities and women in classes that would prepare them for high-tech careers (Brown, 2003). Career counselors should become more open to the technological potential of minorities and women, ensuring that they do not allow prejudicial thinking to keep them from offering appropriate career guidance (Brown, 2003). Those women and minorities that are in technology courses are generally there because they or their parents had to make a request to be there.

Lack of community resources is also a major factor restricting minorities and women to needed technology (Bush et al., 2002). Some African American communities may not have the funding to provide technical training for their citizens, and the only access to technology often may be what they have in the school system and the public library, but time constraints may limit the use of these resources. School districts should make it a priority for all students, regardless of race, gender, or parents' economic status, to be exposed to technology as part of their educational development.

Women of color are traditionally under-represented in technology careers as well as in most state-approved certificate and degree programs (Bush et al., 2002). One of the reasons is the lack of peer role models with technology backgrounds. Under-representation discourages African American women from entering technological careers because they do not see people like themselves (Bush et al., 2002). To remedy this situation, educational institutions should provide minority women with appropriate career information, support, and training, encouraging them to enter technology fields (Bush et al., 2002). Providing role models and mentors for African American girls would also help to engender their interest in technology careers (Brown, 2003).

BARRIERS FOR AFRICAN AMERICAN WOMEN IN TECHNOLOGY EDUCATION

African American women face many obstacles related to technology education in public schools. These obstacles are due not only to society's view of African American women, but also to lack of training, funding, equipment, software, supportive school administrators, and adequate support staff in the educational institutions. All of these barriers can also apply to other racial and/or gender groups. American society continues to question African American women and their ability to perform, especially when it comes to technology and education. This view is evident and is reflected in the lack of positions held by African American women in public education.

Training provided in public schools for educators is limited to after-school workshops or staff development training. Training sessions are short, and most teachers do not remember how to apply what they have learned due to insufficient time devoted to training. Most of the training encompasses the basic knowledge of software, and the training is provided to all teachers. Technology educators are already proficient in the software basics and are frequently called upon to facilitate the training. If technology educators need training beyond the basics or to stay abreast of new technology, they must look outside of their district. If there is money in the budget, the school district may pay for the training, but if there is not, the teacher must pay for the training or receive none.

Funding may be limited in public schools and technology classes may not be provided with the necessary resources to stay abreast of the latest technology. Technology educators must utilize the hardware and software provided and make the best of it even if it does not match the state framework for the course. The school administration's attitude toward technology directly influences what resources the technology educators receive. If the administration feels technology is important and funding is available, equipment and software for technology courses will be provided. However, if they feel academics are more important, technology courses may be last on the list for funding.

An adequate support staff is very important when there are problems involving technology. This is especially important when equipment has been in the school system for several years. Sometimes technical support personnel are slow to respond because they are responsible for assisting the entire school system. This delay hinders the technology teacher in the classroom because a particular piece of equipment may be needed for instruction and it is waiting for repair. Lack of available funds can also determine the number of people on the support staff, creating an overworked and underpaid group of employees.

When integrating technology into the classroom, African American women are also likely to face many barriers. One that is overly evident is how the students perceive the educator. The teacher, once again, must prove her skills and ability to instruct the class, for example, in how to use multimedia technology or e-learning platforms. Students are a product of their environment and are likely to be influenced by the discriminatory attitudes of their society or parents.

Once accepted by students, African American teachers must contend with students' attitudes about their self-image, gender, and resources outside of school as they relate to technology or computer use (Pinkard, 2005). Computers sometimes intimidate students due to lack of use or lack of technology in the home. Girls, in particular, may feel that they are not as capable because of prevailing attitudes that technology is for boys.

SUGGESTED SOLUTIONS

Research indicates that gender-stereotypical attitudes and behaviors by educators are influential in perpetuating these attitudes and expectations in their students (Reilly, 1992). Mabokela and Madeson (2003) suggest that administrators should be more supportive of their minority faculty and not place them in positions where their professional development and integrity are compromised by racially insensitive comments from students, parents, or other teachers.

Research on teachers has generally failed to include the experiences of African American educators (Foster, 1990). Their presence in education is crucial for Caucasian faculty members who need to interact with their African American colleagues in order to gain a better understanding of minority cultures (Patitu & Hinton, 2003). Racial and gender composition of schools strongly influences the options available for women to have positive experiences in both gender and racial identity (Jackson, 1998). Culturally astute educators are dynamic agents for social justice, precisely because they define themselves out of a sense of connection with

B

and a responsibility to the human struggle of minorities for freedom and justice (Beauboeuf, 1999). In order for change to occur, mutual respect and dialogue is necessary between African American women and members of different cultural groups. African American women are the primary source for how to overcome obstacles to technology education related to stereotypes of race and gender in their profession and should be utilized as important resources for setting standards.

CONCLUSION

There are many barriers involving equity and access that continue to plague African American women in technology education. Working with technology in public schools and integrating technology into the classroom is often not an easy task for African American women. Many improvements have been made in an attempt to remedy these challenges, although African American women are still plagued by the old stereotypes of our society depicting them as inferior educators.

In technology education, particularly where the majority of students are African American, there is a need for African American role models (Irvin, 1988). An increase in the number of African American women in technology education would enable female students to consider a career in technology.

In American society, race and gender are two major factors that impede access to technology and technology education. In the case of African American women, these factors are inextricably linked. Current educators can help to overcome this dilemma by using collaborative and cooperative learning environments to strategically promote learning through social interaction with other racial and gender groups (Brown, 2003). Interacting with others is a key technique in learning to see others in a non-stereotypical fashion and in eliminating racial and gender stereotyping within society.

REFERENCES

Beauboeuf, T. (1999, April). Politicized mothering: Evidence of a relational and extended self-concept among culturally relevant women educators. *Proceedings of the Annual Meeting of the American Educational Research Association,* Montreal, Quebec, Canada.

Brown, B.L. (2003, April). The appeal of high-tech careers. *Women's Educational Equity Digest.* Retrieved April 25, 2006, from http://www2.edc.org/womensequity/pdffiles/tech_dig.pdf

Brunner, C. (2003, April). Approaching technology. *Women's Educational Equity Digest.* Retrieved April 25, 2006, from http://www2.edc.org/womensequity/pdffiles/tech_dig.pdf

Bush, S., Henle, T., Cohen, S., Jenkins, D., & Kossy, J. (2002). *Recruiting lower-income women into information technology careers: Building a foundation for action.* Retrieved from http://web112.epnet.com/DeliveryPrintSave.asp?tb=1&_ug=sid+F564B66B-B1A2-41FF-A3

Christensen, L.M. (2005). Women who passed the torch of freedom. *Social Studies, 96*(3), 99-104.

Collison, M.N.-K. (1999). Race women stepping forward. *Black Issues in Higher Education, 16*(7), 24-27.

Foster, M. (1990). The politics of racism: Through the eyes of African-American teachers. *Journal of Education, 172*(3), 123-141.

Irvin, J.J. (1988). An analysis of the problem of the disappearing black educator. *Elementary School Journal, 88*(5), 503-514.

Jackson, L.R. (1998, April). Examining both race and gender in the experiences of African American college women. *Proceedings of the Annual Meeting of the American Educational Research Association,* San Diego, CA.

Jeffries, R.B. (1995). African American teaching and the matriarch performance. *Proceedings of the Critical Issues in Education for Pupil Service Personnel Forum Series,* Milwaukee, WI.

Jones, B.B. (1993, February). Working with the "only one" in the division. *Proceedings of the Annual International Conference for Community College Chairs, Deans, and Other Instructional Leaders,* Phoenix, AZ.

Logan, S.W. (1998, April). Late twentieth-century racial uplift work. *Proceedings of the Annual Meeting of the Conference on College Composition and Communication,* Chicago.

Mabokela, R.O., & Madsen, J.A. (2003). Crossing boundaries: African American teachers in suburban schools. *Comparative Education Review, 47*(1), 90-111.

Patitu, C.L., & Hinton, K.G. (2003). The experiences of African American faculty and administrators in higher education: Has anything changed? *New Directions for Student Services, 140,* 79-93.

Pinkard, N. (2005). How the perceived masculinity and/or femininity of software applications influence students' software preferences. *Journal of Educational Computing Research, 32*(1). Retrieved from http://web112.epnet.com/DeliveryPrintSave.asp?tb=1&_ug=sid+F564B66B-B1A2-41FF-A3

Reilly, L.B. (1992). *Study to examine impact of gender equity training programs on attitude expressed toward women in nontraditional roles.* Division of Adult and Occupational Education, New Jersey State Department of Education, Trenton.

Roberts, N.S., & Winiarczyk, E.J. (1996). Women in experiential education speak out: An anthology of personal stories across cultures. *Women's Voices in Experiential Education.*

Scon, K.A. (2003). My students think I'm Indian: The presentation of an African-American self to pre-service teachers. *Race, Ethnicity & Education, 6*(3), 211-226.

Shaw, S.J. (2004). We are not educating individuals but manufacturing levers: Creating a black female professional class during the Jim Crow era. *OAH Magazine of History, 18*(2), 17-21.

Thomas, A.J., Witherspoon, K.M., & Speight, S.L. (2004). Toward the development of the stereotypic roles for black women scale. *Journal of Black Psychology, 30*(3), 426-442.

KEY TERMS

Brown v. Board of Education: In 1954, the United States Supreme Court made an extremely important decision that definitively declared that racial segregation was illegal in all facilities in which public education occurred. "Separate but equal" public education that could not provide African Americans with the same educational standards as those available to white Americans was outlawed in this landmark decision.

E-Learning Platform: An information system that schools, universities, and institutions can use for teaching (only online or supporting traditional teaching) which can have the following features (altogether or individually): (a) be a content management system (CMS), guaranteeing the access to didactic materials for the students; (b) be a learning management system (LMS), where the use of learning objects makes easier the learning of a given topic; (c) be a computer-supported collaborative learning system (CSCLS), which makes easier the use of collaborative and situated teaching/learning strategies; and (d) be a virtual community of students, tutors, and professors built using knowledge management (KM) strategies.

Emancipation: On January 1, 1863, President Abraham Lincoln declared that all slaves were freed in the Confederate States of America. Lincoln based this proclamation on the war powers that the Constitution gave the President during war times such as the American Civil War taking place at that time.

Equity: Justice applied in circumstances covered by law yet influenced by principles of ethics and fairness. An equitable right or claim.

Gender Identity: Describes the gender with which a person identifies (i.e., whether one perceives oneself to be a man, a woman, or describes oneself in some less conventional way), but can also be used to refer to the gender that other people attribute to the individual on the basis of what they know from gender role indications (clothing, hair style, etc.).Gender identity may be affected by a variety of social structures, including the person's ethnic group, education, employment status, religion, or family.

Integrating Technology: Technology-connected activities should be based on ideas and concepts that you are teaching and materials that are of critical importance to what the students need to learn. Technology will become a tool for acquisition, organization, evaluation, and application of knowledge. The teacher and student are partners in constructing knowledge and answering essential questions.

Racial Identity: Identity is a series of stages everyone must go through to determine who they are as an individual. A sense of group or collective identity based on one's perception that he or she shares a common racial heritage with a particular racial group. Racial identity development theory concerns the psychological implications of racial-group membership—that is, a belief system that evolves in reaction to perceived differential racial-group membership.

Technology Education: An integrated, experience-based instructional program designed to prepare students to be knowledgeable about technology—its evolution, systems, technologies, utilization, and social and cultural significance. It results in the application of mathematics and science concepts to technological systems in areas such as, but not limited to: construction, manufacturing, communications, transportation, biotechnology, and power and energy. Students are challenged to discover, create, solve problems, and construct solutions by using a variety of tools, machines, computer systems, materials, processes, and technological systems.

B–POS Secure Mobile Payment System

Antonio Grillo
Università di Roma "Tor Vergata", Italy

Alessandro Lentini
Università di Roma "Tor Vergata", Italy

Gianluigi Me
Università di Roma "Tor Vergata", Italy

INTRODUCTION

The B-POS (Bluetooth Point of Sale) is the prototype of a secure, mobile macropayment system. Since heterogeneous wireless network technologies such as PANs, LANs, and WANs have well-known security weaknesses, it is mandatory to enforce security services, such as authentication, confidentiality, integrity, and non-repudiation. This article describes a Java-based macropayment system prototype featuring security and independence from an e-money third party acting as an intermediary. This system can rely on the existing financial network infrastructure (e.g., credit card, ATM networks).

BACKGROUND

Currently, most of m-payment (payment performed with a mobile device) systems rely upon mobile WAN (wide area network, e.g., GSM/GPRS/UMTS), enabling the customer to buy contents (by mobile carrier) or goods billed to the mobile phone contract account or to a prepaid card (in a business model called "walled garden"). The widespread diffusion of Bluetooth-enabled mobile phones, however, can possibly boost the deployment of new application paradigms based on personal area networks (PANs) and NFC (near field communications), enlarging the payment paradigm to financial and banking systems and circuits (e.g., EFC —electronic financial circuits), so achieving two major benefits: (1) to escape from the "walled garden," so acquiring the capability to buy every good and every service, not only those from the mobile carrier; and (2) collecting the payment capabilities in a personal trusted device (PTD, e.g., the smartphone) without dealing with

the ATM/credit cards in the wallets, supporting both micropayments and macropayments (Me, 2003).

There has been a considerable amount of research focusing on the adoption of mobile payments using a POS (Me & Schuster, 2005). Most of the research effort on usability led to description of the adoption factors influencing the consumer in the adoption of the payment solution (Dahlberg, Mallat, & Oorni, 2003; Mallat, 2004; Pousttchi, 2003; Zmijewska, Lawrence, & Steele, 2004). Other research has focused on finding the most critical factor of success and the different requirements of mobile payment systems (Hort, Gross, & Fleisch, 2002; Muller, Lampe, & Fleisch, 2004). Many more studies focused on the adoption intentions of the consumers and the merchants toward a new electronic payment system (Plouffe & Vandenbosch, 2001). Early local mobile payment systems (cash like, micropayments) were pioneered by Chaum CAFÉ-IR (www.chaum.com/CAFE_Project.htm) based on public-key encryption and the blind signature scheme of Ecash: this system uses a smartcard and an electronic prepaid "wallet" to complete transactions via the InfraRed technology. The work of Blaze, Ioannidis, and Keromytis (2001) on microchecks (over the InfraRed links) is (somewhat) similar to ours, except for (at least) its minor concerns with fraudulent transactions (due to their small amount). Another important difference is that the payer is not required to authenticate the merchant during a transaction. Several other e-check systems have been implemented during recent years, but they were never customized for mobile/local transactions (e.g., SET, echeque, First Virtual). The foremost e-check system, Kerberos based, was NetCheque (http://gost.isi.edu/info/NetCheque/).

Currently, several countries have adopted mobile payments: in the Asian market, Singapore, South

Korea, and Japan reached an advanced market stage, for example, the FeliCa contactless payment system, currently the de-facto standard method in Japan with over 20 million users, counts over six million FeliCa-enabled handsets and POS installed in all the major shop chains (www.sony.net/Products/felica). Europe is following close behind with successful m-payment services already launched in Austria, Croatia, and Norway, and in Italy, Telecom Italia Lab unveiled in December 2005 a contactless system called Z-SIM, where mobile phones can communicate with any terminal or object by very simple interaction. As a rule, a mobile payment system can be operator independent, where billing is based on an association between a credit card or bank account to the mobile phone (e.g., the Italian major credit card distributor CartaSi has recently launched its own mobile payment system).

MAIN FOCUS OF THE ARTICLE

B-POS aims to be a secure mobile macropayment system for local, contactless, and operator-independent payment systems, involving three different entities—bank, shop, and customer (smartphone)—communicating via secure channels, as shown in Figure 1. Due to well-known mobile vulnerabilities, especially regarding Bluetooth (Nichols & Lekkas, 2001, 402-415; Jacobson & Wetzel, 2001), it is mandatory to enforce security, firstly on wireless links. For this reason, the requirement of macropayment system security is met at the application layer, avoiding various communication layer vulnerabilities, (e.g. E3—electromagnetic environmental effects) or new, unpredictable vulnerabilities (e.g., wireless transport layer security (WTLS) gap in versions prior to WAP 2.0). This task is performed using an asymmetric keys schema for the authentication with a derived symmetric session key. A mutual authentication is implemented

among B-POS's communication parties, so the entities involved can trust each other.

The Bluetooth link connects the smartphone to the shop (1). Information exchanged between the shop and the bank happens on a secure channel. The customer refers to his own bank through a virtual private network (VPN), taking advantage of both these channels (3).

Since the end user trust should be placed into a customer-reliable authority, we centralized all the responsibilities into the bank, whose former task was to release and setup the BPOS mobile application on the customer device.

In order to achieve a widespread diffusion between customers, the prototype is suited for devices as PDAs and smartphones equipped with Kilo Virtual Machine (KVM). Former benefits in adoption of J2ME reside in advantages to use cross-platform code and embedded security mechanisms (safe box). Several further considerations suggest the J2ME platform as appropriate to support m-payments (Sun Microsystems, 2000a; Cervera, 2002):

- **Broad user experience:** The J2ME API provides enhanced possibilities to present GUI, for example, event handling and rich graphics.
- **Comprehensiveness:** The details of the machine architecture, operating system, and display environment are all handled transparently by the Java virtual machine (JVM). The same Mobile Information Device Profile (MIDP) m-payment client can run on all the MIDP-compliant devices (Sun Microsystems, 2000a, 2000b; Cervera, 2002). This allows the m-payment system providers to target a wider range of end-users.
- **Reduced network and server load:** The J2ME-based applications can operate when disconnected, and they only interact with a server when necessary. J2ME has its own runtime environment and the capability to store data in the mobile device.

Figure 1. BPOS architecture

The ease of use and the cheapness of further requirements led to a wireless point-to-point communication between the shop and the customer. For this reason, Bluetooth technology represents the most suitable alternative due to its limited range and the mobile phone market penetration (in Europe).

Money or virtual checks are not exchanged between entities, thus reducing fraud and stealing due to eavesdroppers. BPOS payments are performed in the bank context, where a customer authorizes the bank to commit a fund transfer from his or her personal bank account to the shop's.

Application's Schema Description

We divide the whole transaction in different phases (see Figure 2). Firstly, a former procedure is required, where the user physically interacts with the bank/CA, in order to install on his smartphone the BPOS application. He could request for this service from his trusted bank where he owns an account.

Setup Procedure

The BPOS Bank's portion code creates a symmetric key associated to a specific user that had requested the BPOS service. The key, stored into the BPOS application, will be installed on the user's personal device. The bank asks the user to turn on the application, forcing the user to select an application PIN, used to protect the system from unauthorized spawn of the application. Furthermore the customization of the application, needed for the individual payment, includes the storage of a specific certificate and an asymmetric key pair on the user device: this operation means that bank plays the role of CA. For further transactions, mutual authentication between the user personal device and the bank is no longer needed. Moreover the setup of the VPN guarantees the confidentiality of the exchanged information, avoiding spoofing attacks and repudiability, while a control acknowledge message prevents replay attacks.

Figure 2 shows the application schema, enlightening three different interactions between the involved entities:

Figure 2. BPOS application's schema

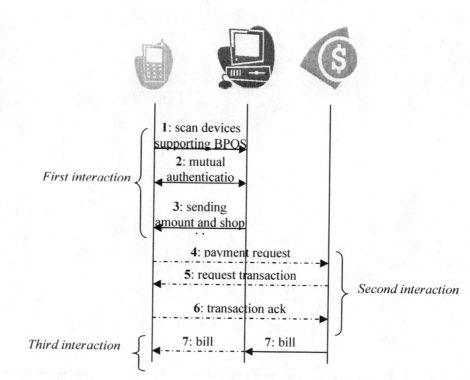

1. smartphone-shop (via Bluetooth),
2. smartphone-bank (via VPN), and
3. bank-shop-smartphone.

First interaction takes place on a Bluetooth connection and consists of three sub-steps: device discovery, (1) mutual authentication (2), and the payment amount dispatch (3). In the former phase, the user runs the BPOS application on his device, inserts his PIN, and starts the scan for devices. The scanning phase is filtered by the service presence in order to identify only the BPOS partner, then the user selects the shop where he is purchasing in a proposed list of shops.

The second sub-step of the user interaction with *shop* is the mutual authentication, achieving two different goals:

1. shop-customer, ensuring to the customer that the shop is the place where he is purchasing; and

2. customer-shop, ensuring to the shop that the ticket is addressed to the customer required to pay.

The latter authentication side is important because the ticket is the only method to identify the current paying customer.

After the successful mutual authentication phase, the shop (payer) and the smartphone (payee) agree on a session key, used by the shop to send to the client:

• the amount to be paid, and
• its unique ID registered to the bank.

Second interaction involves the user and the bank over a VPN (see Figure 2), via a three-step communication: smartphone sending request for payment (4), bank sending request for the transaction confirm (5), and smartphone transaction acknowledge (6).

Table 1. Notation

Mutual Authentication Protocol:
  i. $A \rightarrow B$: $Cert_A$
  ii. $A \leftarrow B$: $Cert_B$, $PK_A(C_B , R_B)$
  iii. $A \rightarrow B$: $SK_A(C_B)$, $PK_B(C_A , R_A)$
  iv. $A \leftarrow B$: $SK_B(C_A)$
  v. $A \rightarrow B$: AS

Symbol	Description
A	*Smartphone*
B	*Shop*
$Cert_A$	*Certificate of A*
$Cert_B$	*Certificate of B*
$PK_A(m)$	*Message "m" encrypted with the Public Key of A*
$PK_B(m)$	*Message "m" encrypted with the Public Key of B*
$SK_A(m)$	*Message "m" encrypted with the Private Key of A*
$SK_B(m)$	*Message "m" encrypted with the Private Key of B*
C_A	*Challenge of A for B*
C_B	*Challenge of B for A*
R_A	*Random number of A*
R_B	*Random number of B*
AS	*Arrangement of session key with HMAC-SHA256(R_A, R_B)*

The smartphone needs to send a request to the bank for payment, so it creates a packet containing:

- customer identification number, registered to the bank (not encrypted); and
- an embedded packet encrypted with the symmetric key shared with the bank containing:
  - shop ID registered to the bank, received from the shop in the previous step (Figure 2, step 3);
  - amount to be paid received from the shop in the previous step (Figure 2, step 3);
  - a nonce X.

Moreover, the bank, after processing the information received, accesses its database in order to find information about the entities involved in the transaction, and consequently sends a request for transaction confirm to the smartphone via the established VPN. Hence, the bank translates information recovered in a new packet and sends it back to the smartphone. Finally, the smartphone/customer sends a transaction acknowledge to the bank. The customer views all the previous information on the device's display, so he can decide whether to confirm or not the requested transaction. This step is crucial to unmask a malicious subject pretending to be the genuine shop. In order to avoid replay attacks, the protocol uses a transaction Ack to keep the session state. Ack is computed using random X combined by cod.op to random Y (these are produced in steps 4 and 5).

Third interaction involved the bank sending the transaction status (a virtual ticket) to other entities, which protects the latter one by the use of the VPN.

Technical Features

Since B-POS fulfills the security as central requirement, the system is based on a large, careful use of cryptographic technique. Due to the hardware device restriction, the crypto-primitives implementation relied on the BouncyCastle APIs (http://www.bouncycastle.org, http://java.sun.com/products/javacomm/index.jsp). The Elliptic Curve Integrated Encryption Scheme (ECIES) algorithm, with a 192-bit elliptic curve (EC), provides support for asymmetric key needs and symmetric encryption/decryption, and ensures packet integrity between the shop and the customer. The ECIES combines the EC asymmetric encryption with the Advanced Encryption Standard (AES, 128-bit key) and adds a SHA-1 hash for message authentication. In comparison to a 1024-bit RSA key, the ECC (Elliptic Curve Cryptography) provides shorter keys, shorter encrypted messages, and faster private key operations. The system relies on the Elliptic Curve Digital Signature Algorithm (ECDSA) to sign the transmitted data with additional 48-byte signature value, thus avoiding its unnoticed modification. In this PKI, the bank entity produces the certificate and the asymmetric keys for other system entities. The X.509 certificate stored on the mobile devices and shop is signed by a 1024-bit RSA public key of the bank, embedded in a PKCS12 envelop, which protects this information with a password. The mutual authentication phase between the shop and the smartphone could be performed in a secure way, exchanging the certificates guaranteed from the CA.

In a second phase of the application schema, the communications between the authenticated entities are protected by a session key. This key is derived from two random numbers R, derived from the challenge response authentication phase relying on a HMAC-SHA256(R1,R2) hash function. The message integrity is ensured via AES and a SHA-1 hash.

FUTURE TRENDS

The BPOS is suitable for the end user because of its ease of use, security, and independence from third parties; the overall time to complete the transaction is upper bounded at an acceptable two minutes. Further studies and field trials have to be carried on in environments with multiple Bluetooth devices running, since Bluetooth inquiry performances are currently not acceptable in terms of reliability of service.

CONCLUSION

In this article we proposed a local mobile payment system with respect to:

- **Security:** Communication sessions between principals are based on well-understood cryptographic techniques.
- **Traceability:** Transactions are not kept anonymous.

- **Usability and convenience:** Costs of deployment and management for all principals involved (consumers, merchants, and banks) are acceptable.
- **Portability and interoperability:** System design is based on "de facto" standards (hardware equipment and software modules).

In particular, the system does not rely on a third party because it makes use of the existing bank network infrastructure. This assumption, together with use of open software on smartphones, minimizes the impact (and costs) on merchants, customers, and banks.

Since current trends in mobile phone technology move towards a direction of miniaturization and higher computational and graphical performance, allowing the completion of the whole payment procedure in less than a minute, we believe that the BPOS prototype can help the development of new forms of payments, local payments, with very low impact on customers (payers), due to widespread diffusion of mobile phone and shops, allowing their reuse in the same financial network.

The final advantage consists of the avoidance of all the fraudulent activities dealing with ATM/credit cards.

REFERENCES

Blaze, M., Ioannidis, J., & Keromytis, A.D. (2001). Offline micropayments without trusted hardware. *Proceedings of Financial Cryptography 2001.* Retrieved from www.crypto.com/papers/knpay.pdf

Cervera, A. (2002). *Analysis of J2ME™ for developing mobile payment systems.* Retrieved from http://www.microjava.com/articles/Final01092002.pdf

Dahlberg, T., Mallat, N., & Oorni, A. (2003). Trust enhanced technology acceptance model: Consumer acceptance of mobile payment solutions. *Proceedings of the Stockholm Mobility Roundtable 2003.*

Hort, C., Gross, S., & Fleisch, E. (2002). *Critical success factors of mobile payment.* Technical Report, M-Lab.

Jacobson, M., & Wetzel, M. (2001). Security weaknesses in Bluetooth. *Topics in Cryptology-CT-RSA* (pp. 176-191). Retrieved from http://www.belllabs.com/user/markusj/bluetooth.pdf

Mallat, N. (2004). Theoretical constructs of mobile payment adoption. *IRIS27.*

Me, G., & Schuster, A. (2005, Fall). A secure and reliable local payment system. *Proceedings of IEEE VTC.*

Me, G. (2003). Security overview for m-payed virtual ticketing. *Proceedings of the 14th IEEE PIMRC* (pp. 844-848).

Muller, G.S., Lampe, M., & Fleisch, E. (2004). Requirements and technologies for ubiquitous payment. *Proceedings of Multikonferenz Wirtschaftsinformatik, Techniques and Applications for Mobile Commerce.*

Nichols, R.K., & Lekkas, P.C. (2001). *Wireless security: Model, threats and solutions* (pp. 402-415). New York: McGraw-Hill Telecom.

Plouffe, C.R., & Vandenbosch, M. (2001). Intermediating technologies and multi-group adoption: A comparison of consumer and merchant adoption intentions toward a new electronic payment system. *The Journal of Product Innovation Management, 18*(2), 65-81.

Pousttchi, K. (2003). Conditions for acceptance and usage of mobile payment procedures. *Proceedings of the 2nd International Conference on Mobile Business* (pp. 20-210).

Sun Microsystems. (2000a). *Connected, Limited Device Configuration (CLDC) specification, version 1.*

Sun Microsystems. (2000b). *Mobile Information Device Profile (MIDP) specification, version 1* (pp. 551-561).

Zmijewska, A., Lawrence, E., & Steele, R. (2004). Towards understanding of factors influencing user acceptance of mobile payment systems. *Proceedings of IADIS WWW/Internet 2004,* Madrid.

KEY TERMS

Bluetooth: A standard for cable-free, short-range connectivity between mobile phones, mobile PCs, handheld computers, and other peripherals developed by Bluetooth Special Interest Group (Ericsson, IBM, Intel, Nokia, and Toshiba Consortium, http://www.bluetooth.com). It uses short-range, low-power radio links in the 2.4 GHz Instrumentation Scientific and Medical (ISM) band.

Elliptic Curve Integrated Encryption Scheme (ECIES): One of the most popular ECC (Elliptic Curve Cryptography) schemes, defined in *ANSI X9.63-2002, Public Key Cryptography for the Financial Services Industry: Key Agreement and Key Transport Using Elliptic Curve Cryptography* and *IEEE P1363a: Standard Specifications for Public Key Cryptography: Additional Techniques (draft)*. ECC is based on arithmetic using elliptic curves, providing shorter key lengths, and under some conditions, improved performance over systems based on integer factorization and discrete logarithms.

Java2 Micro Edition (J2ME): A version of Java used to develop applications running on a consumer wireless device platform (like a smartphone or PDA). A MIDlet is a J2ME™ application, and the KVM Kilo Virtual Machine is the java virtual machine for mobile devices.

Macro/Micro-Payment: An electronic payment can be loosely categorized according to the amount of money conveyed from the payer (customer) to the payee (merchant): *macropayments* for transaction volumes exceeding $10 (10€) , *micropayments* for amounts less than $10 (10€).

Mobile Payment: An electronic payment can be defined as "the transfer of electronic means of payment from the payer to the payee through the use of an electronic payment instrument," where the electronic payment instrument is viewed as "a payment instrument where the forms are represented electronically and the processes to change the ownership of the means of payment are electronic" (Mobile Payment Forum, 2002). Mobile payments are a subset of electronic payments, where the payee device performs at least one payment step via a wireless link.

Point of Sale (POS): An electronic device used by a retail business (payer) to process credit/debit card transactions. The payee swipes or slides his credit/debit card through the machine, or in mobile POS, connects through radio network instead of swiping the card.

Public Key Cryptography Standards (PKCS12): A series of documents, published by RSA Data Security, defining standard protocols to enable compatibility among public key cryptography implementations. PKCS12 defines a file format commonly used to store private keys with accompanying public key certificates protected with a password-based symmetric key.

Smartphone: An electronic handheld device that integrates mobile phone capabilities, personal information management, short-medium range network capability (e.g., RFid, Bluetooth Wi-Fi), and resources to run ad-hoc application in the same device.

Virtual Private Network (VPN): A way to provide a confidential network through a public network. In IP-based networks, VPNs are defined by a network of secure links over a public IP infrastructure, for example, PPTP (Point-to-Point Tunneling Protocol), L2TP (Layer 2 tunneling protocol), and IP Security (IPSec).

X.509: An ITU-T standard for public key infrastructure (PKI). X.509 specifies standard formats for public key certificates and a certification path validation algorithm.

B

Building Secure and Dependable Information Systems

Wenbing Zhao
Cleveland State University, USA

INTRODUCTION

Information systems are essential building blocks in any business or institution. They can be used to automate most business processes and operations. In the Internet age, virtually all such systems are accessible online, and many of them are interconnected. This mandates that such systems be made highly secure and dependable.

A secure and dependable system has many desirable attributes, including confidentiality, integrity, availability, reliability, safety, and maintainability (Avizienis, Laprie, Randell, & Landwehr, 2004). Confidentiality means that only legitimate users can access its services and that the communication, both within the system and between the system and its users, is kept confidential. Integrity means that the services provided by the system are what the users expect and no one can corrupt the information without being detected. Availability means that the services provided by the system are available whenever legitimate users want to use them. Reliability is a metric of the continuity of a service. The safety means the system will not have catastrophic effect on its users and environment. The maintainability indicates the ability to use, upgrade, and repair the system.

Historically, the confidentiality and integrity-related issues have been the focus in the secure computing field, while the availability and reliability issues are central concerns in dependable (or fault-tolerant) computing (Avizienis et al., 2004). We have seen a trend for the two communities to work together to advance the state of the art in building information systems that are both highly secure and highly dependable. In the last decade, many exploratory secure and dependable systems have been designed and implemented. The demand for secure and dependable systems has also prompted many companies to take initiatives to increase the trustworthiness of their products (Charney, 2006).

BACKGROUND

Security refers to the state of being protected against the loss of valuable asset (Pfleeger & Pfleeger, 2002). A secure information system is one that guarantees confidentiality, integrity, and availability of information. The information can be transmitted over the network, processed in a computer system, and persisted in stable storage. The threats to an information system can be categorized into the following four types:

1. **Interception:** An adversary gains unauthorized access to the information, for example, by breaking into a system or by eavesdropping messages sent over the network.
2. **Interruption:** An adversary prevents authorized users from accessing the information. This can be done by destroying information or by disrupting the availability of the system that provides the information. Examples of the latter include crashing the system, or overloading the system and the networks. Attacks of this sort are often referred to as *denial-of-service* attacks.
3. **Modification:** An adversary not only gains access to the information, but modifies it as well.
4. **Fabrication:** An adversary introduces fake information into the system. This can take the form of inserting counterfeit records into the databases or sending fabricated messages to a system.

There are many countermeasures to defend against the above threats. The most fundamental method is *encryption*. Encryption is the process of scrambling a *plaintext* into unrecognizable *ciphertext,* often parameterized with a *key.* The same or a different key is needed to *decrypt* (i.e., unscramble) the ciphertext back into the original plaintext. The messages sent over the network should be encrypted so that an eavesdropper cannot interpret the content of the ciphertext. The information stored on disk can be encrypted as well.

Other countermeasures include better software design and implementation (including good *access control*), and better security-related policies and procedures to minimize the vulnerabilities in software systems and their operations.

In dependable computing, the vulnerability and threats to a system are often modeled as a variety of *faults*. A fault can leads to an *error* in the system, and eventually can cause a system *failure*. Consequently, the means to achieve dependability include fault avoidance, fault tolerance, fault removal, and fault forecast. Fault avoidance is achieved through good design in software and hardware. Virtually all security measures can be regarded as a form of fault avoidance. Fault tolerance is essential to achieve high availability and reliability. Fault tolerance involves hardware and software redundancy so that if one component fails, other replicated components can continue providing services. Fault removal consists of removing software bugs and faulty hardware components during the testing phase, and isolating, removing, or repairing faulty components during run time. Fault forecasting involves the evaluation of the system operations with respect to the possibility of failure occurrences.

SECURE AND DEPENDABLE SYSTEM DESIGN

To build secure and dependable systems, the traditional software engineering practice must be enhanced to explicitly address the security and dependability issues from the beginning of the project lifecycle. The first step is to model all the potential threats to the system. Once a threat model is developed, appropriate security and dependability techniques must be used to mitigate the threats. A set of test cases must also be developed according to the threat model and used to verify the implemented system.

In this section, we first enumerate some common threats to information systems. We subsequently discuss how to counter such threats, using state-of-the-art security and dependability techniques. Finally, we discuss the challenges in building secure and dependable systems.

Threat Model

An information system can be modeled as a system that stores, processes, and exchanges information with other systems. Normally, the system can be accessed only through a few well-defined entry points. It also has a few exit points where information can flow out of the system. Below are some common threats to an information system:

- Illegal access or modification of information: This can happen in a number of different ways:
  o An adversary eavesdrops the messages transmitted over the network to gain access to the information.
  o An adversary may gain access through undocumented backdoor entry points, or through *buffer-overflow attacks.*
  o An adversary accesses or modifies information via compromised communication channels with a system.
- Unauthorized access to confidential information by authenticated users: This can happen if an adversary successfully launches a privilege elevation attack, for example, a regular user gains root or administrator privilege.
- Confidential information leak through exit points, either explicitly or through covert channels.
- Corruption or deletion of information, application code, or even the operation system services and logs.
- Repudiation: A user might deny that he/she has requested some information from the system or has supplied some information to the system.
- Reduced service availability caused by denial-of-service (DoS) attacks: An adversary might overload or crash the system, by sending ill-formed requests to the system.
- Hardware failures, power outages, or other environmental disasters.
- Incorrect software execution may render the service unavailable, delete or corrupt information, or leak confidential information: This may be caused by bad design, implementation bugs, or intrusions from adversaries.
- Threats may also come from internal, e.g., from disgruntled employees, or corrupted system administrators: They may be able to bypass normal interface and security check to steal confidential

information from, destroy, or corrupt information of systems under their control.

Note that the threats listed above are no way exhaustive. For each system, application-specific threats must be carefully considered.

Security and Dependability Techniques

Encryption, Authentication, and Authorization

All communication over the network should be encrypted to defend against potential interception and modification threats. It is also desirable to encrypt the information persisted in stable storage. However, using encryption alone is inadequate. Before a user is allowed to read or modify confidential information, the user must first be authenticated—that is, the user's identity is verified.

Even though it is relatively straightforward to verify a local user that is physically collocated with the system, it is a lot harder to authenticate a remote user over an untrusted network. To get the job done, we need to run a carefully crafted authenticated protocol between the user and the system. The protocol can be constructed based on either symmetric-key (the same key is used for encryption and decryption) or public-key (different keys are used for encryption and decryption, and the public key is made public) cryptography. The symmetric-key-based approaches often rely on the existence of a trusted key distribution center and on a challenge-response protocol. An example symmetric-key-based protocol is Kerberos (Neuman & Tso, 1994). The public-key-based approaches require a public-key infrastructure (PKI) where there are multiple levels of certificate authorities so that a chain of trust can be established and verified on the ownership of a public key. The Secure Socket Layer (SSL) uses a public-key-based authentication protocol (Rescoria, 2001).

The repudiation threat can be mitigated by using the digital signature technique. The digital signature is produced by first hashing the message to be sent using a secure hash function, such as SHA1, and then by encrypting the hash using the sender's private key.

To preserve the integrity of messages sent over the network, messages can be digitally signed by the sender or by using the message authentication code (MAC). The code is produced by hashing on both the original message and a shared secret key. MAC is computationally less expensive than digital signature. So MAC is preferred if nonrepudiation is not needed.

To control what information an authenticated user can access or modify, all requests from the user should be mediated by an authorization process. The user's requests can contain an authorization token (issued by the information system) to indicate the user's role and privilege to help determine what permission can be granted to the user. It is wise to grant the user the least privilege possible.

Session keys are typically used to increase the robustness of secure communication. A session key is a symmetric key used to encrypt and decrypt messages exchanged in a single session. A session key should never be reused. Aside from the benefit of better efficiency, the use of session keys minimizes the impact of security breaches because only the messages encrypted using the compromised key can be interpreted by the adversary.

Fault Tolerance

Traditional security techniques discussed previously cannot mitigate all the threats. Most notably, we need additional techniques to ensure high availability despite hardware faults, software faults, DoS attacks, and intrusions from adversaries. Such techniques include fault tolerance and intrusion tolerance. They will be covered in this and the next subsections.

Fault tolerance is a technique that uses hardware and software redundancy to tolerate and mask benign faults. The most common fault model is the fail-stop fault. A fail-stop process stops immediately if it fails. Another fault model is a value fault. Such a faulty process might send some wrong value (consistently) to other processes. By running several replicas, the service will continue to be available even if a fault occurs, as long as there are enough healthy replicas (Schneider, 1990). The most common replication techniques include active replication and passive replication (Powell, 1991):

- **Active replication:** All replicas perform exactly the same actions in the same order, and all of them communicate their results. To cope with value fault, voting is necessary with at least three replicas deployed.
- **Passive Replication:** Only one replica (the primary) processes requests and sends replies. The

primary periodically transfers its state to the rest of the replicas (backups).

Except for stateless systems, the replicas must be made consistent with one another so that there is no service disruption when one replica fails and another takes over. To maintain replica consistency, it is necessary that incoming messages are delivered to each replica in the same order. This requirement is often satisfied by using a group communication system that ensures total ordering and virtual synchrony (Birman, 2005). Without virtual synchrony, requests might be delivered more than once and some requests might not be delivered at all, if fault occurs. In addition to the message ordering requirement, replica non-determinism caused by multithreading, location-dependent, and time-dependent operations must also be masked or sanitized.

Intrusion Tolerance

Tolerating non-benign faults, especially those caused by intrusions, is much more challenging. Such fault is often referred to as the Byzantine fault (Lamport, Shostak, & Pease, 1982). A Byzantine faulty replica might send conflicting information to other replicas in the same group or collude with a faulty client to leak confidential information out.

Several Byzantine fault tolerant systems have been proposed and implemented. Some, such as BFT (Castro & Liskov, 2002), use 3f+1 replicas to tolerate f Byzantine faulty replicas. An alternative approach requires the use of only 2f+1 replicas to tolerate f Byzantine faults, assuming the existence of a group of nodes dedicated to reaching Byzantine agreement on the order of messages (Yin, Martin, Venkataramani, Alvisi, & Dahlin, 2003). To prevent information leakage from a faulty replica, a technique called privacy firewall has been proposed (Yin et al., 2003). All reply messages sent by the replicas must traverse through the privacy firewall. Replies from faulty replicas are detected and suppressed by the privacy firewall.

An adversary often breaks into a system by exploiting software defects. If all replicas consist of identical software running on the same operating system, we risk the danger of all replicas being compromised. Consequently, intrusion tolerance encourages operating system and implementation diversity. One method is called n-version programming (Chen & Avizienis, 1978), where each replica is implemented using different programming languages based on distinct design (but with the same interface and functionality).

To further protect the system from internal threats (can be regarded as special form of intrusion threats), confidential information must be dispersed to several administrative domains. One such technique is called the fragmentation-redundancy-scattering (FRS) (Deswarte, Blain, & Fabre, 1991). The basic idea is that a file is first fragmented into a number of pieces, then each piece is replicated, and finally all pieces are scattered into multiple storage sites. A pseudo-random algorithm is used to decide which piece stores on which storage site. All pieces are encrypted to further enhance their confidentiality. Consequently, an adversary must collect a large number of pieces and break the encryption to steal confidential information. Similar techniques include Shamir's (1979) secret sharing scheme, and Rabin's (1989) information dispersal technique.

Challenges in Building Secure and Dependable Systems

One major challenge in building secure and dependable systems at present stage is to integrate security and dependability design into the software engineering process. Quite often, functionality and feature set are of primary concern, and security and dependability are only afterthoughts. Such an approach has proved to be inadequate.

The threat model for an information system must be comprehensive. Neglecting or underestimating some threats may cause security vulnerabilities. However, developing a comprehensive threat model is difficult because the system is typically highly complicated and there are many entry and exit points. To defend a system, all aspects of the system must be made secure. However, an adversary can cause serious damage by exploiting the weakest part of the system.

Comparing security, dependability is even less emphasized except for some most critical systems. High availability and reliability require redundancy in hardware and software. However, redundancy requires more investment in hardware, software, storage, power supply, and maintenance. This is especially true for n-version programming to tolerant software design fault and intrusion. Future research is needed to lower the cost of Byzantine fault tolerance to an acceptable level to gain wide acceptance in practical systems.

It is also important to know that a system will not be rendered secure and dependable just because some security and dependability techniques are used in the system. The right technique must be used in the right place when needed. For example, if message integrity is required but not confidentiality and nonrepudiation, then the MAC can be used without encryption and digital signature.

FUTURE TRENDS

Most existing research on secure and dependable information systems has focused on how to keep the services available to their clients despite being disrupted by benign or malicious faults. Many recent incidents, such as the break-in of CardSystems Solutions (Dash & Zeller, 2005) which exposed the confidential data of more than 40 million credit card holders, suggest that there is a strong need in intrusion-tolerant information systems. Such systems not only provide high availability and integrity, but high confidentiality as well.

An alternative, but complimentary approach is recovery-oriented computing (Brown & Patterson, 2001). In this approach, the main concern is how to reduce the recovery time if the system is brought down by a fault. By minimizing the recovery time, the system's availability can be improved with less complexity and cost.

CONCLUSION

Information systems have become indispensable in our life. These systems are expected to be secure and dependable. In this article, we have discussed the challenges and state-of-the-art techniques to build secure and dependable systems. We emphasize that security and dependability cannot be afterthoughts. They must be integrated into the whole lifecycle of any information system project, even though this may mean higher budget and longer development time.

REFERENCES

Avizienis, A., Laprie, J., Randell, B., & Landwehr, C. (2004). Basic concepts and taxonomy of dependable and secure computing. *IEEE Transactions on Dependable and Secure Computing, 1*(1), 11-33.

Birman, K. (2005). *Reliable distributed systems: technologies, Web services, and applications*. New York: Springer.

Brown, A., & Patterson, D.A. (2001). Embracing failure: A case for recovery-oriented computing. *Proceedings of the High Performance Transaction Processing Symposium,* Asilomar, CA.

Castro, M., & Liskov, B. (2002). Practical Byzantine fault tolerance and proactive recovery. *ACM Transactions on Computer Systems, 20*(4), 398-461.

Charney, S. (2006). *Momentum and commitment: Trustworthy computing after four years.* Retrieved from http://www.microsoft.com/mscorp/twc/2005review.mspx

Chen, L., & Avizienis, A. (1978). N-version programming: A fault-tolerance approach to reliability of software operation. *Proceedings of the IEEE International Symposium on Fault Tolerant Computing* (pp. 3-9). Toulouse, France.

Dash, E., & Zeller, T. (2005). MasterCard says 40 million files are put at risk. *New York Times,* (June 18).

Deswarte, Y., Blain, L., & Fabre, J. (1991). Intrusion tolerance in distributed computing systems. *Proceedings of the IEEE Symposium on Security and Privacy* (pp. 110-121). Oakland, CA.

Lamport, L., Shostak, R., & Pease, M. (1982). The Byzantine generals problem. *ACM Transactions on Programming Languages and Systems, 4*(3), 382-401.

Neuman, B., & Tso, T. (1994). Kerberos: An authentication service for computer networks. *IEEE Communications, 32*(9), 33-38.

Pfleeger, C., & Pfleeger, S. (2002). *Security in computing* (3rd ed.). Englewood Cliffs, NJ: Prentice Hall.

Powell, D. (1991). *Delta-4: A generic architecture for dependable distributed computing.* Berlin: Springer-Verlag.

Rabin, M. (1989). Efficient dispersal of information for security, load balancing and fault tolerance. *Journal of ACM, 36*(2), 335-348.

Rescoria, E. (2001). *SSL and TLS: Designing and building secure systems.* Boston: Addison-Wesley.

Schneider, F. (1990). Implementing fault-tolerant services using the state machine approach: A tutorial. *ACM Computer Survey, 22*(4), 299-319.

Shamir, A. (1979). How to share a secret. *Communications of the ACM, 22*(11), 612-613.

Yin, J., Martin, J., Venkataramani, A., Alvisi, L., & Dahlin, M. (2003). Separating agreement from execution for Byzantine fault tolerant services. *Proceedings of the ACM Symposium on Operating Systems Principles* (pp. 253-267). Bolton Landing, NY.

KEY TERMS

Authentication: Verification of the true identity of an entity.

Byzantine Fault: A component suffering from this fault may send conflicting information to other components in the system. A Byzantine fault is also referred to as a malicious fault or an arbitrary fault.

Dependability: The trustworthiness of a system. A dependable system has the following attributes: availability, reliability, integrity, safety, and maintainability.

Fault and Intrusion Tolerance: The ability to provide continuous service, even in the presence of faults and intrusion attacks. Fault and intrusion tolerance is provided by using replication, or redundancy, to mask faults.

Group Communication System: A system that provides reliable, ordered message delivery service, membership service, and virtual synchrony service.

Integrity: One can verify that the message received has not been modified during transmission. It also refers to the system state that has been maintained correctly.

Nonrepudiation: The mechanism that ensures that someone that has sent a message cannot later deny the sending of the message, and that a receiver cannot forge a message that is not sent.

Replication (Passive, Active): Multiple copies of a component are executed on different computers. In passive replication, only one replica, the primary replica, processes requests and sends replies, and it also transfers its state periodically to its backups. In active replication, all of the replicas process requests and send replies.

Security: Refers to the state of being protected against the loss of valuable asset. A secure system is one that guarantees confidentiality, integrity, and the availability of the system.

Threat: A scenario that might cause loss or harm. Threats can take the form of interception, interruption, modification, and fabrication of messages and system state.

Classifying Articles in Information Ethics and Security

Zack Jourdan
Auburn University, USA

R. Kelly Rainer Jr.
Auburn University, USA

Thomas E. Marshall
Auburn University, USA

INTRODUCTION

Practitioners and researchers have been working to develop information systems (IS) that are functional and yet secure from a variety of threats at a reasonable cost (Austin & Darby, 2003; Mercuri, 2003; Cavusoglu, Cavusoglu, & Raghunathan, 2004; Sipponen, 2005). *Information security* and *ethics* (ISS/E) research involves a number of diverse subjects, including networking protocols (Sedaghat, Pieprzyk, & Vossough, 2002), database management (Sarathy & Muralidhar, 2002), cryptography (Anderson, 1994), ethics (Tavani, 2004; Straub & Welke, 1998), coping with risk (Banerjee, Cronan, & Jones, 1998), end-user attitudes (Harrington, 1996), and passwords (Zviran & Haga, 1999).

This diverse body of research illustrates two related needs that provide the motivation for this article. The first is to identify critical *knowledge gaps,* which are content areas in ISS/E where little or no research has yet been done (Webster & Watson, 2002). The second is that research methodologies must be periodically evaluated to gain additional insights into a field of interest, which in our case is information security and ethics (Scandura & Williams, 2000).

We first identify the trends in the ISS/E literature pertaining to: (1) the number and distribution of ISS/E articles published in leading IS journals, (2) methodologies employed in ISS/E research, and (3) the research topics being published in ISS/E research. We then discuss these trends in past ISS/E research in order to provide directions for future research efforts in this important area.

BACKGROUND

We examined 15 information systems (IS) journals over the last 15 years. To determine which journals to search, we chose four relatively recent rankings for IS journals (Rainer & Miller, 2005; Lowry, Romans, & Curtis, 2004; Katerattanakul, Han, & Hong, 2003; Peffers & Ya, 2003). By choosing the top seven journals in each of these four rankings, we created a list of 15 journals.

We then used the ABI/INFORM database to find ISS/E research articles by searching the titles and abstracts of the 15 journals using the phrases "security," "computer security," "information security," and "ethics." Because we were looking only for research articles, we omitted book reviews, editorials, and studies of job security and financial securities. Our search yielded a total of 217 articles.[1]

MAIN FOCUS OF THE ARTICLE

From 1991 to 1995, the 15 journals published an average of eight articles per year. In 1996, 25 articles appeared. The years from 1997 to 2003 saw an average of 13 articles per year, followed by 2004 with 23 articles and 2005 with 36 articles. These numbers indicate that ISS/E issues are becoming increasingly important to practitioners and researchers. The spike of ISS/E articles in 1996 is interesting. We speculate that it may have been due to emergence of e-commerce (Borenstein, 1996) and the increasing availability of the Internet (Bhimani, 1996).

Table 1. ISS/E articles as a percentage of total articles

Journal Name	ISS/E	Articles/Year	Years	Total	%
Information & Management	34	32	15	480	7.1
Communications of the ACM	75	84	15	1260	6.0
Decision Support Systems	14	16	15	240	5.8
Journal of the ACM	20	30	15	450	4.4
IEEE Transactions on Software Engineering	30	48	15	720	4.2
Communications of the AIS	13	80	7	560	2.3
MIS Quarterly	5	20	15	300	1.7
Information Systems Research	4	24	15	360	1.1
European Journal of Information Systems	3	20	14	280	1.1
Journal of Management Information Systems	6	44	15	660	0.91
Decision Sciences	4	36	15	540	0.74
Harvard Business Review	4	90	15	1350	0.30
Artificial Intelligence	2	60	15	900	0.22
Management Science	3	120	15	1800	0.17
Human-Computer Interaction	0	15	15	225	0.00

To determine the degree to which leading IS journals are focusing on ISS/E topics, we calculated the percentage of ISS/E articles based on the total number of articles published in each journal over the 15-year timeframe. We eliminated editors' notes, book reviews, editorial pages, and other such journal material. (The *European Journal of Information Systems* was published for 14 of the 15 years, and *Communications of the AIS* was published for seven of the 15 years.) Table 1 shows the journals, ranked by percentage of ISS/E articles published. The low percentage of ISS/E articles published (7% or less), compared to the importance of information security and ethics, illustrates the variety of broad, wide-ranging topics in the information systems field.

Each research strategy is associated with certain trade-offs that researchers must make when designing a study. These trade-offs are inherent flaws that limit the conclusions that can be drawn from a particular design method. The trade-offs refer to: generalizability from the sample to the target population which relates to the issue of external validity; precision in measurement and control of behavioral variables which relates to internal and construct validity; and the issue of realism of context (see Scandura & Williams, 2000).

The three authors independently classified each article into one research strategy. Upon completion of the classification, we calculated the three pairwise intercoder reliabilities using Cohen's kappa (Cohen, 1960) for each pair. All three values were greater than .8, indicating an acceptable level of agreement among us. If two authors did not agree on how a particular article was coded, the third author arbitrated the discussion of how the disputed article was to be coded. This process resolved the disputes in all cases. Table 2 shows the number of ISS/E articles in each research strategy.

The three most widely used strategies are exploratory in nature and exhibit high generalizability to the target population (Scandura & Williams, 2000). The Theory and Literature Review strategy provides the foundation for future empirical studies by developing theoretical models. The Sample Survey strategy uses questionnaires whose items are derived from a review of relevant theory and literature. The computer simulation strategy is typically used to test research hypotheses when it is difficult to obtain an analytical solution to a problem.

To elicit the ISS/E topic categories, we independently examined the 217 articles and created a proposed list

Table 2. Number of articles per research strategy

Research Strategy	Number of Articles
Theory and Literature Review Summarizes the literature to conceptualize models for empirical testing	117
Sample Survey Neutralizes context by asking for behaviors unrelated to the context in which they are elicited	33
Computer Simulation Involves artificial data creation or simulation of a process	28
Field Study: Primary Data Investigates behavior in its natural setting	25
Field Study: Secondary Data Involves studies that use data collected by a person, agency, or organization other than the researchers	8
Laboratory Experiment Brings participants into an artificial setting that will not impact the results	3
Field Experiment Collects data in a field setting, but manipulates behavioral variables	3
Experimental Simulation Contrives situations where there is an attempt to retain realism with situations or scenarios	0
Judgment Task Participants judge or rate behaviors	0

of categories. Through a process of negotiation, we found 11 distinct ISS/E topic categories. We then independently classified each article into one topic category, following the same procedure that we used in classifying articles into research strategies. These 11 categories provided a subject-area classification for all 217 articles in our research sample. Table 3 displays the ISS/E categories with examples of topics relevant to each category.

Table 4 shows each category as it appears in each journal. The topic of security management is covered in almost every journal and is ranked first among number of articles per ISS/E category. This finding could be due to:

1. The fact that many leading IS journals are also business journals, targeted to business researchers and practitioners

Table 3. Number of articles per ISS/E category

Category	Number of Articles
Security Management Budgeting, Part of Larger IS, Policy, Risk, Strategies	47
Cryptography Technology Comparison, Key Escrow, Tutorials, Theory	32
E-Commerce Auctions, Trust, Payment, Privacy	25
Software Piracy Prevention, Protocols	24
Networking/Hardware Architecture, Frameworks, Protocols, Smartcards	23
Prevention Password, Spyware, Other Policies, User Attitudes	16
Database Architecture, Evaluating DB Security, Technology	13
Detection Hacking, Intrusion Detection Systems, Attach Types	13
Legal Intellectual Property Law, International Issues	13
Ethics Codes of Ethics, User Attitudes Toward Ethics	6
Innovation Diffusion Biometrics, TAM Related (Davis, 1989)	5

Table 4. ISS/E category vs. journal

	Cryptography	Database	Detection	E-Commerce	Ethics	Innovation Diffusion	Legal	Networking/ Hardware	Prevention	Security Management	Software	Total
AI	1								1			**2**
CACM	11	1	5	7	1	1	9	8	7	13	12	**75**
CAIS			1	2				1	1	8		**13**
DS		2	1							1		**4**
DSS	1	3		6				1		2	1	**14**
EJIS						1				2		**3**
HBR					1		1			2		**4**
HCI												**0**
I&M		2		8	1	2	2	1	5	12	1	**34**
IEEETSE	5	2	4	2				8	1	1	7	**30**
ISR		1	1		1					1		**4**
JACM	14							4			2	**20**
JMIS						1	1		1	2	1	**6**
MISQ			1		2					2		**5**
MS		2								1		**3**
Total	32	13	13	25	6	5	13	23	16	47	24	**217**

2. The possibility that it is easier to collect data from organizations on this specific ISS/E topic because it is not proprietary information (i.e., most organizations are investing in ISS/E and therefore have ISS/E budgets, policies, etc.)

3. The possibility that security management was used to categorize the more subjective topics within ISS/E research

For example, articles related to risk assessment (Rainer, Snyder, & Carr, 1991), budgeting (Lewis, Snyder, & Rainer, 1995), planning (Straub & Welke, 1998), strategy (Austin & Darby, 2003), and ISS/E as a component of a larger IS (Palvia & Basu, 1999) were put into the security management category if they were aimed at practitioners and were non-technical in nature. The e-commerce, prevention, legal, ethics, and innovation diffusion research categories also focused more on business managers, IS practitioners, and IS researchers in business schools.

On the other hand, the cryptography, software, networking/hardware, database, and detection categories are technical in nature. Articles in these categories have a target audience of computer scientists and engineers rather than practitioners and researchers. That is, these articles are written more for a technical professional who works with the technology than for business managers.

By plotting ISS/E category against research strategy (see Table 5), many of the gaps in ISS/E research are highlighted. While all the ISS/E research categories have numerous articles that use the Formal Theory/Literature Review research strategy, the more technical categories typically use the field study—primary data and computer simulation strategies. The more non-technical categories such

Table 5. ISS/E category vs. research strategy

	FT/LR	Survey	Lab Exp.	Exp. Sim.	Field-Pri.	Field-Sec.	Field Exp.	Judgment	Comp. Sim.	Total
Cryptography	27				3				2	32
Database	6								7	13
Detection	4				1	1	2		5	13
E-Commerce	9	6	2		6				2	25
Ethics	2	3			1					6
Innovation Diffusion	2	3								5
Legal	8	1				4				13
Networking/Hardware	17				4				2	23
Prevention	6	6	1		3					16
Security Management	22	13			3	2	1		6	47
Software	14	1			4	1			4	24
Total	117	33	3	0	25	8	3	0	28	217

as e-commerce, innovation diffusion, legal, ethics, and security management seem to rely heavily on sample surveys and field studies using both primary and secondary data.

The strategies that are most frequently employed are the most appropriate for the early stages of ISS/E research. In these exploratory stages, formal theory/literature reviews are appropriate to provide an overview of a field. Second, researchers in business schools often use sample surveys more than experimental simulation, judgment task, and computer simulation. In fact, computer scientists and computer engineers wrote the majority of the computer simulation articles found in our search, whereas business researchers wrote the majority of articles using sample surveys. Third, organizations are typically less likely to commit to certain strategies (i.e., primary and secondary field studies and field experiments) because these strategies are more expensive. These research strategies are labor intensive to the organization being studied because records will need to be examined, personnel will need to be interviewed, and senior managers will be required to devote at least some time to help facilitate the research project. Finally, as mentioned by Kotulic and Clark (2004), field studies are very difficult to set up when organizations are very secretive about their security practices.

FUTURE TRENDS

Future trends in ISS/E can occur in three areas: research topics, research strategies, and theoretical foundation. Based on our findings, the ISS/E field should increase research efforts on the topic of ethics. For example, the widespread misuse of copyrighted material, such as downloading music files and pirating software, suggests that ethics is a fruitful area for research. Other topics that should receive increased attention include prevention, detection, and legal issues. These three areas will increase in importance as the severity of attacks on information security continues to escalate.

For researchers to address important questions in ISS/E, they must employ a wider variety of research strategies. Our findings show that future research strategies might use the laboratory experiment and judgment task strategies. As many university students are experienced computer and Internet users, these two research strategies could use students as surrogates without losing external validity.

Most of the research in our sample does not attempt to relate ISS/E studies to any theories in academic disciplines such as information systems, management, psychology, or criminology, among others. The absence of coordinated theory development causes research in ISS/E to appear haphazard and unfocused. Future studies should have a theoretical base which will help ISS/E become a more coherent discipline.

CONCLUSION

Our objectives in this study were to identify: (1) the number and distribution of ISS/E articles published in leading IS journals, (2) the research strategies employed in ISS/E research, and (3) the research topics being published in ISS/E research. We found that, while relatively steady from 1997 to 2003, the number of ISS/E articles in leading IS journals increased markedly in 2004 and 2005. Further, *Information and Management, Communications of the ACM,* and *Decision Support Systems* published the largest percentage of ISS/E articles from 1991-2005. As for ISS/E research strategies, the majority of articles have utilized the Theory and Literature Review strategy. Finally, the top research topics in the ISS/E area are Security Management (22%), Cryptography (15%), E-Commerce (12%), Software (11%), and Networking/Hardware (11%).

Our study does have limitations. Future literature reviews could search a broader domain of research outlets. We deliberately did not search journals devoted solely to information system security and/or ethics.

Research in ISS/E may always prove difficult, because researchers may be hampered by organizations' reluctance to share their systems' strengths and weaknesses with researchers (Kotulic & Clark, 2004). However, the good news is that despite this organizational reluctance, many of the categories in ISS/E need research efforts. We hope that this analysis of the ISS/E literature has laid the foundation for efforts that will enhance the IS body of knowledge and theoretical progression in the ISS/E area.

REFERENCES

Anderson, R.J. (1994). Why cryptosystems fail. *Communications of the ACM, 37*(11), 32-40.

Austin, R.D., & Darby, C.A.R. (2003). The myth of secure computing. *Harvard Business Review, 81*(6), 120-126.

Banerjee, D., Cronan, T.P., & Jones, T.W. (1998). Modeling IT ethics: A study in situational ethics. *MIS Quarterly, 22*(1), 31-60.

Bhimani, A. (1996). Securing the commercial Internet. *Communications of the ACM, 39*(6), 29-35.

Borenstein, N.S. (1996). Perils and pitfalls of practical cybercommerce. *Communications of the ACM, 39*(6), 36-44.

Cavusoglu, H., Cavusoglu, H., & Raghunathan, S. (2004). Economics of IT security management: Four improvements to current security practices. *Communications of the AIS, 14,* 65-75.

Cohen, J. (1960). A coefficient of agreement for nominal scales. *Educational and Psychological Measurement, 20*(1), 37-46.

Davis, F.D. (1989). Perceived usefulness, perceived ease of use, and user acceptance in information technology. *MIS Quarterly, 13*(3), 319-340.

Harrington, S.J. (1996). The effect of codes of ethics on personal denial of responsibility on computer abuse judgments and intentions. *MIS Quarterly, 20*(3), 257-278.

Katerattanakul, P., Han, B., & Hong, S. (2003). Objective quality ranking of computing journals. *Communications of the ACM, 46*(10), 111-114.

Kotulic, A.G., & Clark, J.G. (2004). Why there aren't more information security research studies. *Information & Management, 41,* 597-607.

Lewis, B.R., Snyder, C.A., & Rainer, R.K. Jr. (1995). An empirical assessment of the information resource management construct. *Journal of Management Information Systems, 12*(1), 199-223.

Lowry, P., Romans, D., & Curtis, A. (2004). Global journal prestige and supporting disciplines: A scientometric study of information systems journals. *Journal of the Association for Information Systems, 5*(2), 29-75.

Mercuri, R.T. (2003). Analyzing security costs. *Communications of the ACM, 46*(6), 15-18.

Palvia, P.C., & Basu, C.S. (1999). Information systems management issues: Reporting and relevance. *Decision Sciences, 30*(1), 273-290.

Peffers, K., & Ya, T. (2003). Identifying and evaluating the universe of outlets for information systems research: Ranking the journals. *JITTA: Journal of Information Technology Theory and Application, 5*(1), 63-84.

Rainer, R.K. Jr., & Miller, M. (2005). Examining differences across journal rankings. *Communications of the ACM, 48*(2), 91-94.

Rainer, R.K. Jr., Snyder, C.A., & Carr, H.H. (1991). Risk analysis for information technology. *Journal of Management Information Systems, 8*(1), 129-147.

Sarathy, R., & Muralidhar, K. (2002). The security of confidential numerical data in databases. *Information Systems Research, 13*(4), 389-403.

Scandura, T.A., & Williams, E.A. (2000). Research methodology in management: Current practices, trends, and implications for future research. *Academy of Management Journal, 43*(6), 1248-1264.

Sedaghat, S., Pieprzyk, J., & Vossough, E. (2002). On-the-fly Web content integrity check boosts users' confidence. *Communications of the ACM, 45*(11), 33-37.

Sipponen, M.T. (2005). An analysis of the traditional IS security approaches: Implications for research and practice. *European Journal of Information Systems, 14*(3), 303-315.

Straub, D.W., & Welke, R.J. (1998). Coping with systems risk: Security planning models for management decision making. *MIS Quarterly, 22*(4), 441-469.

Tavani, H.T. (2004). *Ethics and technology: Ethical issues in an age of information and communication technology.* New York: John Wiley & Sons.

Webster, J., & Watson, R.T. (2002). Analyzing the past to prepare for the future: Writing a literature review. *MIS Quarterly, 26*(2), xiii-xxiii.

Zviran, M., & Haga, W.J. (1999). Password security: An empirical study. *Journal of Management Information Systems, 15*(4), 161-185.

KEY TERMS

Computer Simulation: Involves artificial data creation or simulation of a process.

Experimental Simulation: A situation contrived by a researcher in which there is an attempt to retain some realism of context through use of simulated (artificial) situations or scenarios.

Field Experiment: Collecting data in a field setting, but manipulating behavior variables.

Field Study (with Primary Data): Investigates behavior in its natural setting. Involves collection of data by researchers.

Field Study (with Secondary Data): Involves studies that use secondary data (data collected by a person, agency, or organization other than the researchers.)

Formal Theory/Literature Review: Summarization of the literature in an area of research in order to conceptualize models for empirical testing.

Judgment Task: Participants judge or rate behaviors. Sampling is systematic vs. representative, and the setting is contrived.

Laboratory Experiment: Participants are brought into an artificial setting, usually one that will not significantly impact the results.

Sample Survey: The investigator tries to neutralize context by asking for behaviors that are unrelated to the context in which they are elicited.

ENDNOTE

[1] For the full bibliography of the 217 articles, please contact Kelly Rainer at rainer@business.auburn.edu.

Computational Ethics

Alicia I. Ruvinsky
University of South Carolina, USA

INTRODUCTION

Computational ethics is the integration of computer simulation and ethics theory. More specifically, computational ethics is an agent-based simulation mechanism that takes a computational perspective to ethics theory. This approach uses computer modeling and multiagent systems to generate societies of agents capable of adopting various ethical principles. The principle adopted by an agent will dictate its moral action in response to a moral dilemma. By simulating the agents' application of ethical principles to moral dilemmas and observing the resulting moral landscape of a group of affected agents, we are better able to understand the social consequences of individual ethical actions.

Chung (2004) describes simulation modeling and analysis as "the process of creating and experimenting with a computerized mathematical model of a physical system" (pp. 1-2). A significant advantage to simulation modeling is that once developed, various configurations of the variables comprising the simulation may be explored without incurring the expense or disruption elicited by real-world experimentation (Banks, 1998). It is important to remember that simulations provide a *descriptive* assessment of the system under its current configuration, not a *prescriptive* one. Simulations give an understanding of how the system's configuration relates to the system's behavior, not how to set the configurations so that a certain behavior is elicited (Trick, 1996).

Ethics may be defined as individual principles of conduct or as societal guiding philosophies.[1] The difference between these definitions is a matter of granularity. Ethics as principles of conduct characterize the high granularity of individual agent actions. At a lower granularity, where individual actions are overshadowed by the society's behavior, ethics becomes a societal guiding philosophy. This dichotomy begs the question of how the ethics involved in a principle of conduct manifests itself in a guiding philosophy. Computational ethics attempts to model an ethical system with the intent of observing the dynamics of the system. Hence, in modeling and analyzing a system, computational ethics is exploring the relationship between individual ethical actions and their contributions to the evolution of a large-scale emergent ethic.

Axelrod (1997) gives an example of an emergent ethical system. During the trench warfare of World War I, both sides began to exhibit restraint in killing the enemy, only shooting in retaliation. This group-level behavior was a result of the entities' individual ethics of not wanting to kill the enemy and wanting to defend themselves. How did these individual ethics come about? How does an individual's ethical action affect its neighbors' ethics? How many members of the group must exhibit this ethic before a social ethic emerges? A computational ethics simulation inspired by this episode would assist in exploring these questions.

Computational ethics provides a mechanism for experimenting with and testing social ethical theory. As such a tool, computational ethics could significantly enable a means of facilitating quantitative research in ethics. These simulations may be configured to test proposed theoretical frameworks, allowing for a unique analysis of individual ethical principles and the moral interrelationships that may arise between an agent and its society. Computational ethics provides a mechanism for exploring the consequences of individual moral actions on the emerging social ethic. These consequences in turn may expose hidden ethical dilemmas not foreseen in the original analysis. Discovering the manifestation of secondary (or deeper) dilemmas while a society is attempting to resolve the original dilemma may provide insight into the nature of the particular ethical configuration of the society, namely the kinds of solutions this society generates (Surowiecki, 2004).

Computational ethics addresses the individual behavioral manifestations of an ethic, as well as the emerging social consequences to which individual actions contribute. Computational ethics can be used to explore how multiple individual agents interact with each other as well as the agent society with regard to a moral dilemma, thereby providing a means of analyzing the evolution of an emergent ethical system of the agent society. As Moss states (2001), "For the social simulator, the issue of how society can impact upon individual behavior is at least as important as how individuals impact on society" (p. 2). As an area of research, computational ethics provides invaluable mechanisms for studying the nature of computational worlds in which certain ethical principles prevail and other worlds in which these same principles may be extinguished. This article provides a background to the conceptualization of computational ethics, followed by a discussion of its implementations and future trends.

BACKGROUND

A natural inclination for human curiosity concerning ethics stems from the many varying and often contradicting moral stances that exist within any group of people, even among close associations such as families. This variance has elicited the exploration and definition of models of morality within the field of ethics theory. The systematizing of morality by defining mathematical models based on formal ethics theory models is useful in a computational sense. These moral systems may be represented computationally and simulated within a multiagent system. This is the backbone of computational ethics.

Ethics

In enabling an agent to adopt an ethic, various simulations may be generated to explore the effects of individual morality on a society. An ethic is a moral framework characterized by rights, liberties, and duties, which are parameters in an ethic model. A *right* may either be a *claim right,* in that it is an agent's opinion about another agent's behavior, or it may be a *liberty right,* which is a right that an agent uses to justify its own behavior. A claim right manifests itself as an external social pressure that an agent senses when making an ethical choice. An agent feels[2] judged by the claim rights of other agents. A liberty right would be used by an agent to justify its action as ethical, making the action immune to social coercion or criticism (Van Wyk, 1990).

Liberty is freedom or autonomy. In a computational agent world, liberty is the means by which an agent interprets the forces in its environment and in its society. If an agent has little liberty, then there exists a controlling entity, such as another agent or the society in social contract ethics. With a large amount of liberty, an agent is more independent[3] in its moral decision making. An ethical theory allows for various liberties, as well as denies other liberties to the agent[4] (Van Wyk, 1990).

A *duty* is either an obligation or responsibility. An *obligation* is when an agent has no moral alternative other than to perform the action represented by the obligation. Not to perform this action would be morally wrong. Obligations can be either directly or indirectly created. A directly created obligation is one in which the agent enters into the obligation at its own volition. For example, an agent has the directly created personal obligation to satisfy its own hunger. An indirectly created obligation results from exterior forces such as social pressure. When these exterior forces become too great, then the agent must behave in the obligated manner.

A *responsibility* is a duty to produce a desired result, or at least contribute to the eventual realization of that result. The agent is not required to perform any specific action, but simply to ensure that its actions contribute to the desired result. For example, Bob has the responsibility to eliminate world hunger. There is no specific action that is required of Bob by this responsibility; however, he reasons that feeding another hungry person will decrease hunger in the world, thereby contributing to the realization of his responsibility. Bob realizes that he "ought" to feed the hungry person, but he is not obligated to do so. If he is occupied in other actions, such as obligations (e.g., satisfying his own hunger), then he may not actually feed the hungry person, though he does acknowledge his responsibility to do so (Van Wyk, 1990).

Moral Dilemmas

With an ethical framework in place, we now consider the moral dilemmas facing the agents. The relationship between individual ethics and social ethics may be explored via moral dilemmas defined in the field of game theory. A prime example of such a moral dilemma is the *prisoner's dilemma* (PD), which can be seen as a moral conflict between duty to oneself and duty to another. The individual actions of rational agents are unable to establish an emergent cooperative ethic when playing PD (Axelrod, 1984). Yet, Kant's categorical imperative[5] provides a moral mechanism for establishing cooperation among agents playing PD. An agent cannot defect and at the same time desire that defection become a universal law. Yet, the agent can cooperate while desiring cooperation to become a universal law. Hence, the Kantian categorical imperative will facilitate cooperation in the Prisoner's Dilemma. This is an example of how a particular dilemma elicits different social ethics based on the ethical actions of the agents comprising the society.

In a computational ethics simulation, the moral dilemma is manifested in the agents' environment. All agents are able to perceive the dilemma. The agents adopt an ethic, and act with respect to that ethic in the game or dilemma being played. The simulation iterates such that the agent repeatedly analyzes its environment and reacts ethically, thus exposing aspects of the emergence of an ultimate social ethic.

A simulation allows us to observe the evolution of the society's *strategic equilibrium* via the individual interactions experienced by the agents in the system. This strategic equilibrium may be mapped to the society's ultimate social morality in order to give insight into the effects of various ethical principles within a society on its overall moral landscape.

COMPUTATIONAL ETHICAL MODELS

The social interactions of interest in computational ethics are invoked by agents in a simulated agent society. The agents in these simulations are invested with preconfigured *computational ethical models* composed of *computational beliefs* that map to ethical principles in real-world ethical theories. The agents' actions or behaviors must be a direct result of a logical execution of the agents' computational beliefs within the computational ethical model. In order to be simulated in this way, an ethical theory must be quantified. This quantification requires the delineation of notions describing an agent, such as physical existence, status of existence, behaviors, and motivations for behaviors, in terms of the ethical model in question.

Physical existence involves the life and death of an agent. The status of existence is defined as a range of states, from a failing state to a succeeding state. In entering a failing state, an agent has entered a configuration that has brought it dangerously close to death. This may

result when an agent chooses to give all its food to its neighbor altruistically, thereby causing the agent itself to have no food left to eat. Entering a failing state does not necessarily bring about death. The altruistic agent in this example may itself encounter another neighbor that chooses to share its food (for some ethical reason), thereby saving the altruistic agent.

The succeeding state of an ethical model is defined as the agent having entered a configuration that temporarily ensures its life. These states may result from multiple altruistic neighbors or hard work on the part of the agent or a reward bestowed upon the agent for an ethical action. Similar in a failing state, being in a successful state does not ensure continued success.

It is assumed that the agents in a simulation have a desire to remain alive. This desire for life may not necessarily be a subsuming quality. Yet, sacrificing life must be ethically justifiable within the agent's ethical boundaries. For example, a starving altruistic agent will not give its remaining food to a well-fed and amply-supplied fellow agent, despite its ethics of giving. Its desire to stay alive will, in this case, take precedence over performing a futile, self-sacrificial act.

The behaviors motivated by an ethical model must be logical consequents of the principles outlined in the model. This is imperative because it generates the transcendent relationship between belief and action that is essential for simulating the physical ramifications of a meta-physical theory. After all, ethics reside solely in intangible human thought, only perceivable once they are acted upon. An agent's behavior results from the ethical analysis of its world. Each individual behavior must result from an ethical analysis triggered by a motivation residing in the physical world. For example, a motivation for performing a pro-social act of charity may be the observance of a fellow agent in need (i.e., in a failing state).

The quantification of an ethical theory is established by identifying real-world beliefs in terms of rights, liberties, and duties, and the actions such beliefs elicit. These beliefs are translated into computational beliefs, and the consequential action is paired with the belief via rules within the computational ethical model. These rules will be triggered by environmental input, and the output will be ethically justified actions the agent may take. For example, within the divine command ethical model, there is the commandment or belief, "Thou shall not kill." The action motivated by this belief is the decision not to do anything that will lead to the demise of a fellow agent. A rule will enforce this relationship by establishing the effect of an action on the other agent as the consideration in deciding whether or not to take the action. If an agent with a Divine Command ethical model is starving and encounters a starving altruistic agent that offers its last morsel of food, then the Divine Command agent will not accept the food offered by the altruistic agent because of the likelihood that this action will result in the demise of the altruistic agent.

Once an ethical theory is quantified and implemented within a multiagent system, simulations are generated in order to further explore the social implications resulting from the simulated model. Similarly, once many ethical models are quantified in this way, a society of agents with heterogeneous ethical models may be simulated. These simulations are useful in considering emergent effects of distinct moral perspectives within a society. For example, what kind of social ethic would emerge in a simulation of the Prisoner's Dilemma in which half of the population adopts a Kantian ethical model while the other half adopts a rational agent model?

Computational ethics is characterized by configurable agent and environment settings, which enable the investigation of various combinations of ethical principles and moral dilemmas. The ultimate problem being exposed and explored by this flexibility is the relationship between individual ethics, societal ethics, and environment (or dilemma). For example, the ethical principle of the agents may be held constant, while the moral dilemma of the world is changed. This will expose the effectiveness of the same ethical principle in different moral dilemmas. Inverting the constancy of these variables, such that the agents' ethics are variable and the world's moral dilemma is static, will provide data for understanding the ramifications of different ethical principles in a specific moral dilemma.

By simulating various ethical theories within an agent society, researchers can study the effects of individual computationally moral actions within the society on the ultimate ethical equilibrium of the society. With quantified ethical theories in hand, a simulation can be implemented to explore the potential of this computational ethical model in a large society. The simulations will provide insight into ethical models, or ethical systems, resulting in a useful tool for considering the utility of the model or system, identifying potential weaknesses or flaws in the system, and comparing

multiple systems in order to identify unique ethical phenomena for a specific environment.

Limitations to Computational Ethics

There are limitations to computational ethics in as much as there are limitations to computer simulations of real-world complexity. In order to yield accurate results, the model must be correct. Yet, our understanding of nature is not complete, particularly the nature of human ethics, thereby impeding the correctness of our model. A person's ethical makeup is rarely pure and is ever changing. When this is modeled discretely to allow for computational simulation, many complexities are lost in translation.

Such a lost complexity is that of creative human reasoning which cannot be duplicated by a computer. Though sophisticated, state-of-the-art inference engines are still limited in the complexity of the reasoning they enable, and any reasoning on par with human creativity is beyond current capabilities. This motivates the simplification of an ethic to antecedent/consequent type axioms. An example is given by the following axiom for the ethics of reciprocity:[6]

If the agent would like the action to be done to it, then the agent may perform the action toward another agent.

This axiom can be used by an agent. The agent will consider the personal consequences of a particular action if the action were done to itself. If the action increases its own utility, then the ethics of reciprocity agent may invoke the action towards another agent.

FUTURE TRENDS

Computational ethics provides a useful perspective for ethics theory and other fields, such as political science or sociology. Politicians may use computational ethics to better understand public reaction to campaign platforms. Sociologists may use computational ethics to facilitate research in understanding social norms by exploring recursive effects of an agent on its society and a society on its agents.

Computational ethics may be used by evolutionary ethicists. This research explores human ethical models as ecological necessities (Corning, 1996). Formalizing and simulating these models will provide a tool for investigating how ethical characteristics such as cooperation can evolve (Axelrod et al., 1981). These researchers may use computational ethics to assist in supporting or refuting their claims.

Multiagent systems explore the interactions between agents within a society of agents. An example scenario in which these interactions are significant is an online auction where one agent is an auctioneer and other agents are bidders or sellers. A world is imaginable where each of us own computational agents responsible for enforcing our personal ethical ideals (or desired ethical ideals) in their interactions with other agents in the society. For example, we may ask our personal computational agents to buy a car for us. Our agent will interact with agents that represent car sellers to find the best deal for the car we want. In finding this deal, we do not want our agents to lie or cheat, but we also do not want our agents to be lied to or cheated. We want to ensure an ethical environment in which these agent interactions may productively occur. This would require a more intentional approach to social ethics than is described in this article. To create ethical environments for agents, there is a specific social ethic to promote within the society, such as fairness or cooperation. This would require investigating how to manipulate a society's ethics in light of a particular moral dilemma, such that the agents grow to want to elicit the ethic being cultivated.

CONCLUSION

Computational ethics is the simulation of ethical theories designed to explore individual behavioral manifestations of these theories, as well as the emerging social consequences to which these individual behaviors contribute. The simulations allow us to observe the evolution of a society's social ethic via the interactions experienced by the agents within the system.

The execution of a computational ethics simulation and the observation of its individual and social consequences provide useful tools in understanding the possible proximate and ultimate causes of the computational ethical model and its representative ethical theory. These simulations are a useful tool aiding in assessing the utility of an ethical theory or system. They may also be used in identifying weaknesses or flaws in an ethical theory or system when applied to

a moral dilemma, or comparing multiple theories or systems in order to identify the most ideal ethics for a specific moral dilemma.

Computational simulations for ethical models enhance our awareness of a large-scale ethical picture. In order to understand ourselves as a society, we must understand the consequences of our perceptions of right and wrong. These simulations allow us to investigate the influences we have on one another that ultimately generate our emergent group ethics.

ACKNOWLEDGMENT

Dr. Michael Huhns' participation as advisor and editor to this manuscript has been invaluable.

REFERENCES

Axelrod, R. (1997). *The complexity of cooperation.* Princeton: Princeton University Press.

Axelrod, R. (1984). *The evolution of cooperation.* New York: Basic Books.

Axelrod, R., & Hamilton, W.D. (1981). The evolution of cooperation. *Science, 211*(4489), 1390-1396.

Banks, J. (1998). *Handbook of simulation: Principles, methodology, advances, applications, and practice.* New York: John Wiley & Sons.

Chung, C. (2004). *Simulation modeling handbook: A practical approach.* Boca Raton: CRC Press.

Corning, P.A. (1996). Evolution and ethics...an idea whose time has come? *Journal of Social & Evolutionary Systems, 19*(3), 277-285.

Moss, S. (2001). Messy systems: The target for multi agent based simulation. In S. Moss & P. Davidsson (Eds.), *Multi-agent-based simulation* (pp. 1-14). Berlin: Springer-Verlag.

Surowiecki, J. (2004). *The wisdom of crowds.* New York: Doubleday.

Trick, M. (1996). *An Introduction to simulation.* Retrieved June 22, 2006, from http://mat.gsia.cmu.edu/simul

Van Wyk, R. (1990). *Introduction to ethics*. New York: St. Martin's Press.

KEY TERMS

Claim Right: An agent's ethically reasoned opinion about another agent's behavior, manifesting itself as an external social pressure.

Computational Belief: A model of an ethical principle. Computational beliefs comprise computational ethical models.

Computational Ethical Model: A model of an ethical theory. Computational ethical models consist of one or more computational beliefs.

Computational Ethics: The translation of an ethical model into computational terms enabling the model or the system of models to be simulated in a computational environment such as a multiagent system.

Computer Modeling: A computer program that simulates a model or system. Computer modeling is often used in simulating natural systems in fields like physics, biology, economics, and sociology.

Ethical Principle: A formal description of an ethical argument.

Ethical System: A society characterized by various ethical theories. A society of 100 agents with 40 altruists and 60 rationalists is a characterization of an ethical system.

Ethical Theory: An ethical stance consisting of multiple ethical principles.

Ethics Theory: The study of ethical theories.

Liberty: Freedom or autonomy.

Liberty Right: A right that an agent uses to justify its own behavior. An ethical action justified by a liberty right (e.g., the right to life) is immune to social coercion or criticism.

Moral Action: An action resulting from an ethical analysis of the environment.

Moral Dilemma: A situation arising from the conflict of simultaneous moral imperatives. No moral action may be taken without an immoral action also being taken.

Multiagent System: A collection of software agents that interact with each other as a single group or society.

Obligation: When an agent has no moral alternative other than to perform the action represented by the obligation. Not to perform this action would be morally wrong.

Prisoner's Dilemma: A social dilemma characterized by greed and fear. Two players, A and B, are presented with these choices:

a. Player A cooperates (getting one year in prison), while player B cooperates (getting one year)
b. Player A cooperates (getting five years), while player B defects (getting no years)
c. Player A defects (getting no years), while player B cooperates (getting five years)
d. Player A defects (getting three years), while player B defects (getting three years)

Each player knows that the other player was given the same information, but does not know the action the other player will take. Players A and B must decide independently whether to cooperate or defect (Axelrod, 1984).

Each player is better off defecting, despite what its opponent does. "The dilemma is that if both defect, both do worse than if both had cooperated" (Axelrod, 1984). Though the best action is for both criminals to cooperate, greed is tempting them to defect, while fear that their opponent will defect is keeping them from cooperating.

Responsibility: The duty to produce a desired result or contribute to the eventual realization of that result. The agent is not required to perform a particular action, but simply to ensure that its actions contribute to achieving the desired result.

Social Ethic: The emerging ethical landscape of a society resulting from the ethically motivated actions of individual agents in the society.

Strategic Equilibrium: The stabilized state of a simulated society where all agents are performing a particular action consistently and predictably.

ENDNOTES

[1] As defined by *The American Heritage® Dictionary of the English Language, Fourth Edition.*

[2] The act of "feeling" may be computationally simulated by establishing a sensitivity threshold in the agent. For example, the agent will "feel judged" when the number of claim rights exerted on this agent exceeds the agent's sensitivity threshold.

[3] Independence may be implemented as a high sensitivity threshold, such that the agent is not easily swayed by external forces such as social pressure.

[4] Liberty may be implemented as thresholds characterized by the degree the society and other external forces influence the agent's actions.

[5] "Act only on such a maxim through which you can at the same time will that it should become a universal law." This is taken from Kant's *Critique of Practical Reason and Other Works on the Theory of Ethics.*

[6] http://www.religioustolerance.org/reciproc.htm

Computer Ethics and Intelligent Technologies

Yefim Kats
Southwestern Oklahoma State University, USA

INTRODUCTION

This article is a survey of moral and social challenges related to the development of intelligent technologies and the emerging phenomenon of the Semantic Web. We explicate the ethical issues arising from the growing popularity of intelligent software agents and Web-based knowledge representation systems. In this context, we consider the growing technical capabilities of intelligent software tools vs. corresponding social and moral responsibilities. Moreover, the rapidly changing software engineering environment is reshaping the role of an educator in the design and development of computerized systems in general and intelligent tools in particular. From this perspective, the integrated approach to software engineering education is discussed and analyzed.

BACKGROUND: COMPUTER ETHICS AND SOFTWARE ENGINEERING

Computer ethics—rooted as a discipline in the established ethical frameworks of deontology, consequentialism, and virtue ethics—refers to the manner in which these standard ways of moral discourse are applied to design and use of information technology (Johnson, 2001; Ermann, Williams, & Shauf, 2002). At first sight such a discipline seems to be as viable and explicitly defined as any other traditional branch of applied ethics. However, due to the recent explosive growth of software products and the rapid changes in the corresponding design procedures, computer ethics may need further refinement in the definition of its problem area, especially in a view of the popular conjecture that in the near future computer ethics may disappear as a separate discipline.

The claim of computer ethics' disappearance is clearly articulated by Johnson: "As we come to presume computer technology as part of the world we live in, computer ethics as such is likely to disappear" (as cited by Maturano, 2002, p. 71). The idea behind this line of argument is that with time, the use and design of information technology would become as routine as the use and design of, say, television sets. In this respect, we would like to make a distinction between the moral issues related to *design and development* of information technology vs. those related primarily to *use* of information technology. Consequently, it may be helpful to distinguish between *design ethics* and *use ethics.*

The argument for computer ethics disappearance seems more applicable to the *users* of information technology rather than *designers*. Unlike TV sets, computers consist of the clearly distinguishable *hardware* and *software* components. From the *software* development perspective, computer ethics is becoming increasingly important. Hence, it is imperative to define the set of mature and socially sensitive design methods for software developers, enabling them to follow the procedures to be reflected in the appropriate professional standards such as the Institute of Electrical and Electronics Engineers (IEEE) standards and recommendations. Once ethical guidelines are embedded into such standards, many moral and legal challenges faced by software engineers would be gradually reduced to sheer professionalism.

From this perspective, it is difficult to overestimate the *software engineering* skills for information technology professionals. Johnson (2001) correctly emphasizes the importance of the Texas initiative to establish licenses for software engineers in the state of Texas (USA). Such a license should assume a high level of proficiency in the *socially responsible* software design methods, provided that the appropriate code of ethics is integrated into the standard design procedures. As a result, it would also help "the public to understand how to think about the products and services being provided by software engineers," and consequently to make right choices about such products (Johnson, 2001, pp. 66-67).

The key issue is whether all moral and social concerns related to information technology design and use could eventually be addressed in a framework of the appropriate standards and regulations, so that computer ethics (as Johnson suggested) would "disappear." The affirmative answer, which is essentially a form of *moral reductionism,* seems untenable, especially in view of the potentially unlimited variety of emerging software tools and the corresponding design procedures. First of all, we should take into consideration that software tools are increasingly created not only by the likes of Microsoft, but also by thousands and thousands of free-source software proponents. The popularity of the free-source phenomenon makes moral guidance in this area ever more important. Second of all, the importance of computer ethics is only emphasized by the explosive growth of intelligent technologies, such as intelligent agents and distributed knowledge representation systems. In the following sections we examine moral challenges related to the growing technical capabilities of increasingly popular forms of intelligent technologies.

INTELLIGENT TECHNOLOGIES AND MORAL RESPONSIBILITIES

In the current economic environment, the success of a business model is highly dependent on the information technology tools employed, especially for the emerging *e-commerce* businesses. At the same time, moral aspects of software design and use, such as data security and privacy, are directly related to the ability of businesses to attract and retain customers.

The problems related to business software have been aggravated due to the popularity of *intelligent agents* in e-commerce applications. Intelligent agents are often classified depending on the type of customer behavior they are supposed to support. The typical buying behavior pattern proceeds through the stages of need identification, product brokering, merchant brokering, negotiation, purchase, product service, and the follow-up evaluation of customer satisfaction. To give a few examples of the artificial agents assisting customers to carry out the aforementioned tasks, the monitors and notification agents are useful for need identification; intelligent agents like PersonaLogic and Tête-à-Tête are able to assist in product brokering; BargainFinder as well as Jango are used for the merchant brokering phase; agent systems such as AuctionBot and Kasbah provide help in the negotiation stage of a transaction (Maes, Guttman, & Moukas, 1999).

The mode of customer behavior determines the possible damage a particular agent technology can cause and the corresponding moral constraints to be imposed on such an agent. In this context, the benefits and the side effects of agent technologies are closely interrelated. The need identification procedures can be excessively intrusive, an issue especially important when dealing with underage potential customers. The current business practice in the 'consumer society' is often aimed at engineering the artificial needs and consequently creating the products to 'satisfy' them. Too often, humans and human rights are redefined by the corporations and politicians as consumers and consumer rights. We believe that this point carries on to intelligent technologies enabled and often intended to amplify the potentially abusive impact of intrusive business practices. The developers of such technologies should be taught to distinguish between support tool design vs. 'social engineering' tool design.

These considerations are especially relevant to the so-called mobile intelligent agents representing a form of distributed computing. Such agents are mostly involved in product brokering, merchant brokering, and negotiation. Although able to provide special technical benefits, in particular parallel processing and the efficient use of system resources, mobile agents pose new moral and legal challenges (Lange & Oshima, 1999; Mandry, Pernul, & Rohm, 2000; Turban & Wagner, 2002). In a most trivial sense, mobile agents act in a way similar to certain viruses such as Trojan Horses and may cause similar problems. The fact that they execute on the server side involves special security risks, including a potential unauthorized data access, data destruction, or abuse of host machine resources.

However, intelligent mobile agents are smarter than typical viruses and able to exhibit many more subtle patterns of malicious behavior. For example, negotiating agents may renege on their obligation to complete a transaction once they encounter a more promising opportunity. In general, taking into account that an agent may be required to make a decision dynamically, we have to consider the correlation between the ability to make a decision and the measure of moral responsibility for the decision taken—an issue especially important for mission-critical applications. A special concern is related to the emergence of the new cutting-edge technology, the *Semantic Web,* where agent-to-agent and agent-to-human interactions are closely linked to the ability to handle metadata rich with a variety of social connotations.

THE NEW WEB, THE NEW CHALLENGES

The term Semantic Web is a reflection of the conceptual shift, whereby the World Wide Web is viewed as a complex infrastructure involving multiple communities represented as a variety of semantic domains or *ontologies* intended to "provide a shared and common understanding of a domain that can be communicated between people and heterogeneous and widely spread application systems" (Fensel, 2003, p. 1). Moreover, due to the continuing *globalization* trend, increasingly involving communities from the developing countries, the ongoing Semantic Web project requires cooperation between the parties belonging to different social and economic domains, thus laying the ground for a more *humane* global communication environment.

The humane nature of the new Web is reflected in the interaction between the philosophical and technical aspects of information management process. In particular, the study of Web ontologies emphasizes the newly found interaction between the variety of disciplines such as philosophy, sociology, anthropology, and computer science. The multifaceted study of Web ontologies includes:

- *Philosophical* study of ontologies in a spirit of both *analytic* and *continental* traditions
- *Empirical* study of ontologies, including *sociological* and *psychological* analysis of Web communities
- Ontological studies in the context of *computer science* and *mathematics,* including formal ontologies, the 'mappings' between ontologies, and intelligent data search

The practical implementation of the Semantic Web is based on certain results in computer science and, in particular, on the development of new languages aimed at reshaping the Web as a hierarchy of ontologies representing different knowledge domains such as e-commerce, travel, art, politics, and so forth. The leading candidates for the future linguistic skeleton of the Semantic Web are XML-based languages such as RDF/S (resource description framework/schema),

DAML (DARPA agent markup language), OIL (ontology inference layer), and OWL (ontology Web language). In particular, the DAML project has been focused on developing "a language aimed at representing semantic relations in machine-readable ways that will be compatible with current and future Internet technologies" such as agent technologies (Hendler, 2001).

The integration of Web ontologies, Web services, and agent technologies would make a considerable impact on the development of efficient and scalable Web applications, while the heterogeneous ontology environment could also enhance availability of agent-to-agent Web interactions, leading eventually to the development of multiagent systems distributed over the global network. The more the agent technology is semantically enabled, the more autonomous can we expect the intelligent agents to be. Enabled to function in a heterogeneous environment, the autonomous intelligent agents would allow people to personalize their Web experience and speed up the decision-making processes. Consequently, the agents could be entrusted with all or most of the details of typical Web interactions. The issue of trust thus becomes an intrinsic layer of the Web-enabled communication environment (Kats, 2003).

Is a decision-making ability in a distributed Web environment sufficient to turn an *intelligent agent* into a *moral agent*? Giving this question a more technical turn, does passing the Turing test qualify an intelligent artificial agent as also a moral agent? Some researchers maintain that it is sensible and logical to assign to an artificial intelligent agent at least a status of a *moral patient* (Floridi & Sanders, 2004). Whether the last point is correct or not as a matter of principle, it is clear that the mobile intelligent agent technology represents a significant moral challenge, further erasing the boundaries between the 'computers and humanities'.

Another important issue is a close connection between Web technologies and natural language processing (NLP). Typical NLP applications, such as author/language identification or text categorization, are based on structured text analysis and could be applied to the study and design of ontologies. In particular, the entropy analysis could be used to capture highly subjective properties of text-based ontologies such as writer's affective state, strong cultural/political sentiment, and so forth. Such an approach could be applied to political or cultural polling evaluations and to finance.

At the same time, the latest developments in homeland security underline the growing concerns that data mining and NLP tools can be used or abused; sometimes it may be difficult to draw a line between, for example, a legitimate analysis of cultural and political preferences vs. using such an analysis in order to influence public opinion in a desired direction (and most importantly in an automated and dehumanizing way). As an interesting example, we would like to bring the reader's attention to the Russian project called VAAL. Admittedly, "VAAL is a system allowing to evaluate (and predict) the unconscious effects of textual information on groups, to compose texts intended to produce a certain psychological result, etc." (http://www.vaal.ru/). From this angle, the integration of technical and moral issues should become one of the main priorities in the software development cycle.

FUTURE TRENDS IN INFORMATION TECHNOLOGY EDUCATION

Software integration is a key element in the success story of many of the information technology companies, Microsoft included. We believe that integration is also a crucial factor in building the successful up-to-date educational environment in information technology. An integrated approach to both the software development process and the education of future software developers requires that the educational process for software engineers is structured around the major phases of the software development cycle: from the understanding of problem domain to the delivery of the final product. All educational modules, at all levels, have to be considered as reflecting the different facets of an integrated software engineering process as specified by IEEE and the international standards (IEEE, 1999).

In this context, Thayer (2002) correctly emphasizes the importance of every stage in the software development process: systems engineering, software systems engineering, and software engineering per se. First and foremost, the appropriate social and moral issues should be raised at the *systems engineering* stage, when the problem domain is examined and analyzed. Furthermore, the primary importance of software systems engineering "as a distinct and a powerful tool" lies in the fact that it is at this stage, or more precisely, during the phase of *software requirements analysis,* that all the issues related to social dimensions of future software products can be addressed (Thayer, 2002, p. 68). At the *architectural software design* phase, a developer has an opportunity to ensure that these issues are resolved one way or another.

The area of *systems analysis and design* deserves special attention as the first and the most important stage where information technology professionals encounter a *semantic* aspect of their work. Already the very first step—the analysis of business problem domain—must include the appropriate social and moral elements pertaining to a particular business model. The ethical issues related to the work of a systems analyst are multi-fold. As rightly indicated by Marakas (2001): "The systems analyst commonly has access to data and information that is of a highly sensitive and private nature"; moreover, the analyst often has an intimate knowledge of an enterprise "from a *design perspective*" (p. 10). The additional moral challenges facing the systems analyst are related to the recommended logical models and their physical implementation. As we saw, practically all the types of e-commerce supporting agents assume a far-reaching information-collection process; furthermore, they may be able to impose on the end user a potentially abusive interpretation model. All these and other related issues should be addressed by an educator, as well as embedded into the appropriate standards and regulations related to software engineering process in general, and the systems analysis and design phase in particular. The failure to accomplish these objectives can be costly, possibly contributing to still another crisis similar to the one the business world witnessed in the 1990s.

It is reasonable to expect that IEEE software engineering standards will address the vital social concerns related to security, privacy, and the overall behavior of mobile intelligent agents at the level of system as well as software architecture. The possible candidates for such requirements are IEEE Standards 1229-1998, 830-1998, 1012-1998, and 12207-1996/97; the ethical recommendations related to agent-to-agent and agent-to-human interactions would be especially important. Once the relevant social and moral considerations are incorporated into the standard software design procedures, thus becoming an integral component of the software engineering culture, they would help to reshape both the educational environment and the software development practice.

As each and every facet of the educational process is glued into one integrated whole, the educators should be able to convey the conceptual unity of their subject matter to the students; of course, *what it is* that constitutes this conceptual unity is the key question to be examined and reexamined as the information technology field evolves. The intrinsic dynamics of this question are driven by the long-standing tension between the industry and the academic community. In a sense, it brings us back to the old controversy between professional and academic education models. The choice between technological efficiency and moral responsibility is only an exemplification of this controversy. In this respect, an important question raised by a number of theorists is whether computer ethics principles should be based on the a priori moral foundation or if it is being continuously reshaped by the changing design environment. The answer to this question is inevitbaly linked to the status of an educator. Who is the most appropriate candidate to teach in this field—a philosopher or a software engineer? Let us answer with a motto: "Moral ontology recapitulates technology." The interaction between ethics and technology must be reciprocal and mutually beneficial.

CONCLUSION

We experience the deepening penetration of technology into the very fabric of our society. The revolutionary changes in information technology are transforming all aspects of social life—from entertainment to business, politics, and art. From this angle, it is difficult to overestimate the importance of interdisciplinary and *global* character of research efforts needed to successfully address the social and moral problems arising from ongoing radical changes in information technology. We have come to the point in history when the practical fields of business and politics find it important to team up with philosophy previously often treated as impractical or useless! This tendency towards the integration of philosophical and moral studies with business, politics, and technology brings hope to those who are looking to advance not only material prosperity, but also human values and intercultural understanding.

REFERENCES

Ermann, M.D., Williams, M.B., & Shauf, M.S. (Eds.). (2002). *Computers, ethics, and society.* New York: Oxford University Press.

Fensel, D. (2003) *Ontologies: A silver bullet for knowledge management and electronic commerce* (2nd ed.). New York: Springer-Verlag.

Floridi, L., & Sanders, J.W. (2004). On the morality of artificial agents. *Minds and Machines, 14*(3), 349-379.

IEEE. (1999). *IEEE software engineering standards collection* (pp. 1-4). Piscataway, NJ: IEEE Press.

Hendler, J. (2001). Agents and the Semantic Web. *IEEE Intelligent Systems, 16*(2), 30-37.

Johnson D. (2001). *Computer ethics* (3rd ed.). Upper Saddle River, NJ: Prentice Hall.

Kats, Y. (2003). Enabling intelligent agents and the Semantic Web for e-commerce. *Computing, 2*(3), 153-159.

Lange, D.B., & Oshima M. (1999) Dispatch your agents; shut off your machine. *Communication of the ACM, 42*(3), 88-89.

Maes, P., Guttman, R.H., & Moukas, A.G. (1999). Agents that buy and sell. *Communications of the ACM, 42*(3), 81-91.

Mandry, T., Pernul, G., & Rohm, A. (2000). Mobile agents on electronic markets. *International Journal of Electronic Commerce, 5*(2), 47-60.

Marakas, G.M. (2001). *Systems analysis and design: An active approach.* Upper Saddle River, NJ: Prentice Hall.

Maturano, A. (2002). The role of metaethics and the future of computer ethics. *Ethics and Information Technology, 4,* 71-78.

Project VAAL: Retrieved August 10, 2006, from http://www.vaal.ru/

Thayer, R.H. (2002). Software system engineering: A tutorial. *Computer,* (April), 68-73.

Turban, E., & Wagner, C. (2002). Are intelligent e-commerce agents partners or predators? *Communications of the ACM, 45*(5), 84-90.

KEY TERMS

Computer Ethics: Discipline engaged in the analysis of moral and social issues related to the design and use of computerized technologies.

Data Mining: Knowledge discovery methodology with a potential to compromise data privacy and security.

Intelligent Agent: Autonomous Web-based software module with information-collection and decision-making capabilities.

Semantic Web: Emerging World Wide Web infrastructure focused on explicit representation of data semantics.

Software Engineering: Protocol concerned with tools, methods, and procedures employed in software development.

Trust: In a framework of the Semantic Web, refers to a specific layer intended to enhance the security of information exchange and business transactions.

Web Ontology: Machine-readable form of knowledge representation for the Semantic Web, which can be easily integrated with intelligent agent technologies.

Computer Worms, Detection, and Defense

Robert J. Cole
The Pennsylvania State University, USA

Chao-Hsien Chu
The Pennsylvania State University, USA

INTRODUCTION

Since the first widespread Internet worm incident in 1988, computer worms have become a major Internet threat and a subject of increasing academic research. This worm, known as the *Morris Worm*, was written by Cornell University student Robert Morris. Morris's worm infected Sun Microsystems Sun 3 and VAX hosts running versions of 4 BSD UNIX by exploiting flaws in several standard services. Although there is no strong consensus as to the definition of a worm (Kienzle & Elder, 2003), the general notion of a worm can be understood by way of contrast with viruses. A virus is a program that can 'infect' another program through modification to include a copy of itself (Cohen, 1984). Worms, in contrast, are often characterized as not requiring another program for execution or another agent for activation—that is, a worm can execute and propagate itself autonomously (Spafford, 1988). This characterization of worms as malcode that does not require human intervention for propagation is, however, not universally accepted. For example, Kienzle and Elder (2003) define worms as malicious code that propagates over a network, either with or without human intervention. Such a definition includes e-mail-based mass-mailer viruses, a category that would be largely excluded if the need for human intervention is excluded from the definition of a worm.

In the years following the Morris Worm, many new worms have been observed. From a network security perspective, worms represent a special category of threat due to the fact that worms attack on large spatial and short temporal scales. For example, on July 19, 2001, more than 359,000 computers were infected by the Code Red worm in less than 14 hours (Moore, Shannon, & Brown, 2002). As rapid as this infection was, attacks on shorter temporal scales are possible, a point made theoretically by Staniford, Paxson, and Weaver (2002) and later demonstrated by the Slammer worm, which in 2003 infected 90% of vulnerable hosts within 10 minutes (Moore, Shannon, Voelker, & Savage, 2003). Such rapid attacks are too fast for human-mediated countermeasures, and thus have motivated the development of automated detection and defense systems.

This article presents a worm overview focused on detection and defense. For the reader with little background knowledge of worms, this article will be useful as a short survey of this important topic. Below, background material is presented, followed by a discussion of detection and defense methods, and future trends.

BACKGROUND

An understanding of worm behavioral characteristics is an essential prerequisite to understanding worm detection and defense. This section presents an overview of worm target discovery and epidemic modeling.

Worms use various technical means such as buffer overflow attacks to exploit vulnerabilities in victim machines, victims that are first discovered in a target discovery phase. Target discovery can occur in two forms: with or without a priori knowledge of vulnerable hosts. A worm instance with a priori knowledge of victims must possess a pre-established list of such victims, a list possibly prepared by an attacker well in advance of the start of the attack. Such a list of initial vulnerable hosts is termed a *hitlist*. Absent a hitlist, or following the exhaustion of the hitlist, the worm attack must transition to target discovery methods that use no a priori knowledge of vulnerable hosts. Such methods often use random scanning, in which a potential victim network address is selected randomly using one of several methods and the host is subsequently attacked through the transmission of the exploit payload to the target address. Below, target discovery methods are discussed in greater detail.

Due to the indiscriminate nature of random scanning, observation of attack traffic is readily accomplished using monitors called *network telescopes* (Moore, Shannon, Voelker, & Savage, 2004). Network telescopes monitor *dark address space,* sections of the current Internet IPv4 address space that are routable but contain no production hosts. Thus, traffic observed by network telescopes is anomalous by definition. Network telescopes are characterized by their size, which is denoted using /n notation, where n refers to the number of bits in the network portion of the 32-bit address. Large '/8' network telescopes can monitor 1/256th of the IPv4 address space.

Worm Behavior Modeling

Various models borrowed from epidemiology have been applied to model worm dynamics. The simple epidemic model (SEM) (Frauenthal, 1980), also known as the susceptible infectious (SI) model, characterizes hosts as transitioning from the susceptible to the infectious state. The SEM has been extended to include hosts recovering from infection and returning to the infectious state (SIS model) or being permanently removed from the vulnerable population (SIR). Both the SI and SIS models have nonzero equilibrium infected populations, whereas in the SIR model, the infected population can eventually reach zero. These models assume the *homogeneous mixing* condition, where every infected individual is assumed to be equally likely to infect any susceptible individual. Below, the SEM is explained in greater detail.

In the SEM, rate of change of the number of infected hosts I(t) is given by:

$$\frac{dI(t)}{dt} = \beta S(t)I(t) \tag{1}$$

where S(t) is the number of susceptible hosts at time t, and β is the pairwise infection rate given by the average number of contacts leading to a new infection per unit of time per infective per susceptible in the population (Frauenthal, 1980).

For a worm attack, a susceptible host is one that exhibits the particular vulnerability exploited by the worm. Under the assumption that the number of vul-

nerable hosts N is constant throughout the attack, the number of infected and susceptible hosts are related by I(t) + S(t) = N. In this case, (1) can be written as:

$$\frac{dI(t)}{dt} = AI(t) - BI^2(t) \tag{2}$$

where A = βN and B = β. For a worm attack using uniform random scan (see Target Discovery Methods section below), the pairwise infection rate β is given by the ratio of average individual targeting rate η and the IPv4 address space (Zou, Gong, Towsley, & Gao, 2005); thus $\beta = \eta/2^{32}$. Equation (2) is a special form of Bernoulli equation known as the Verhulst equation, which has the following solution (Kreyszig, 1999):

$$I(t) = \frac{I_0 A}{BI_0 + (A - BI_0)e^{-At}} \tag{3}$$

The solution to the Verhulst equation is known as the logistic law of population growth. The steady-state value of I, I_∞, can be found by setting dI(t)/dt to zero, which gives the solution I_∞ = A/B. Thus this type of growth is characterized by populations that monotonically increase or decrease to the limit A/B for any initial population size. In the case of the SEM, A/B = N; thus the limit of the number of infections is the vulnerable population size. Figure 1 shows I(t) for N = 360,000, I_0 = 1, and η = 6, 12, and 18. The parameters for the η = 6 curve are representative of the Code Red (Moore et al., 2002) attack; the η = 12 and η = 18 curves illustrate the impact of increasing the targeting rate.

Target Discovery Methods

A worm's method of target discovery is an important characteristic because it affects the virulence of the resulting epidemic and has associated behavioral invariants that may be exploited for detection purposes. Several important target discovery methods are described below.

Uniform Random Scan

Scanning refers to the process of attempting communication with a potential victim, using either TCP or UDP transport protocols. A worm without a priori knowledge of the location of vulnerable hosts can simply scan the entire IPv4 address space in a uniformly random

Figure 1. SI curves

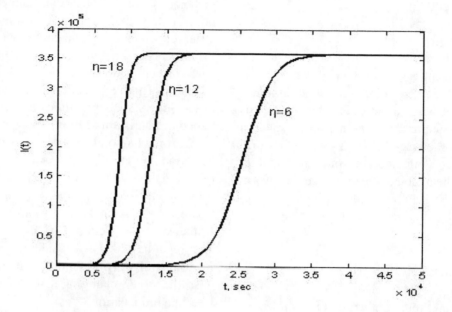

manner, using a pseudo random number generator to discover victims. Such a worm is known as a *uniform scan worm,* which can be modeled using the SEM with pairwise infection rate $\beta = \eta/2^{32}$ (Zou et al., 2005).

Local Preference Scan

When victim hosts are spread non-uniformly through the Internet or when an infected host is behind a firewall, a localized scanning strategy in which a worm scans local subnets with higher probability than other address ranges can result in faster propagation than a uniform scan. Such a scanning approach was used by Code Red version 2, which scanned the local '/16' network with probability 0.375, the local '/8' network with probability 0.5, and the whole Internet with probability 0.125 (Staniford et al., 2002).

Sequential Scan

In a sequential scan, a worm will scan incrementally either higher or lower from an initially selected IP address. An example of a sequential scan worm is Blaster, which began scanning at an address either based on the local address or a random address after which it sequentially scanned blocks of 20 addresses (Eeye, 2003).

Hitlist

A hitlist worm uses a list of vulnerable hosts prepared beforehand as an initial infected population. For instance, the Witty worm first infected a hitlist of known vulnerable hosts before initiating its scanning phase (Kumar, Paxson, & Weaver, 2005; Shannon & Moore, 2004).

Flash Scan

Staniford et al. (2002) introduce the concept of the *flash worm.* Such a worm begins with a hitlist of most or all of the extant vulnerable hosts and does not waste scans on invulnerable hosts. If the scan algorithm is implemented such that no vulnerable host is scanned more than once, optimal propagation is achieved, creating what Zou, Towsley, and Gong (2003a) call a *perfect worm.*

Routable Scan

Zou, Towsley, Gong, and Cai (2003b) introduce the concept of the routing worm. The routing worm optimizes its pairwise infection rate β through minimization of scanning address space. This is accomplished by using BGP routing information to construct an address space consisting of only allocated IP addresses, which in 2003 consisted of only 28.6% of the IPv4 address space (Zou et al., 2003b).

Permutation Scan

Permutation scanning (Staniford et al., 2002) is a mechanism to achieve coordination, which assumes a worm can detect when a target is infected. In this approach, worms share a common pseudo random sequence through the target address space. If a worm detects that a target is infected, it assumes that another worm is already ahead of it in the sequence. The worm responds by selecting a new random point in the sequence to minimize duplication of scanning effort.

DETECTION METHODS

Worm detection methods analyze data at either the local or global level to determine whether an outbreak is occurring. Data of interest include connection failures, scan rates, host-level behavioral changes, and address dispersion of connection attempts as well as DNS queries.

Connection failures, or attempts to make connections to non-existent hosts, are common for random scanning worms and provide a basis for anomaly-based worm detection. Because routers may send ICMP Type 3 messages to a source host when a destination is unreachable, Berk, Bakos, and Morris (2003) propose an ICMP-based detection scheme. In this architecture, routers, a central collector, and analyzers are used to collect and analyze packets to identify traffic patterns characteristic of worms, such as a sudden bloom of ICMP packets.

Network telescopes can be easily instrumented to capture scans to non-existent hosts and thus have become a standard Internet monitoring tool used to track the spread of worms. Epidemic detection via scan rate monitoring of network telescope data was proposed by Zou et al. (2005). They proposed the use of a malware warning center to monitor the number of infected hosts and use a Kalman filter to estimate the value of α, the per-host infection rate in the SEM. Simulations show that detection can be made at infection levels of between 1% and 2% of infected hosts for Code Red and Slammer worms.

Connection failures at the local level can also be used for detection. The threshold random walk algorithm (Jung, Paxson, Berger, & Balakrishnan, 2004) detects malicious sources by observing connection success and failure outcomes, and classifying a source based on the observed sequence of connection outcomes according to the theory of sequential hypothesis testing. Detection based on connection success is also possible under assumption of high connection fanout, an approach taken by the Superspreader method of Venkataraman, Song, Gibbons, and Blum (2005).

Worm behavioral invariants can also be used for detection. Gu et al. (2004) examined the correlation of destination and sources to flag suspicious activity characterized by a host sending and receiving a packet on the same port. A more general behavioral framework was proposed by Ellis, Aiken, Attwood, and Tenaglia (2004), who identify three behavioral invariants of worms: sending similar data from one host to another, changing a server into a client, and tree-like propagation.

Indirect measures of worm activity are also available at the local level, including simple mail transfer protocol (SMTP) and Domain Name System (DNS) activity. Wong, Bielski, McCune, and Wang (2004) note that volume and size of mail packets have been observed to change during a worm outbreak, suggesting the possibility of detection based on mail traffic analysis. DNS-based detection uses the observation that legitimate connections are typically preceded by DNS queries. Whyte, Kranakis, and Oorschot (2005) propose correlation of DNS queries with outbound connections to detect scanning worms since the network activity of random scanning worms will not generate DNS queries.

DEFENSE METHODS

Defense approaches attempt to minimize victim count and reduce the rate of epidemic spread to enable human-mediated responses. Defense approaches generally focus on containment, the process of blocking or limiting communication from infected hosts. Containment approaches include quarantine, rate limiting and content filtering.

Quarantine refers to isolating a host from the rest of the network. Blacklisting is a typical quarantine method achieved through access controls in network devices, such as firewalls. Rate limiting methods enforce a bound on connection rates in order to limit the rate at which a worm can spread. Williamson (2002) proposed rate limiting for new connection requests and empirically demonstrated that setting rate limits sufficiently low can significantly limit worm spread while having minimal effect on legitimate traffic. Rate limiting has been implemented in Windows XP Service Pack 2 by limiting the number of incomplete outbound TCP connection attempts (Microsoft, 2004).

Content filtering approaches, which block traffic using signatures of known malicious packet content, can be found in signature-based intrusion detection systems such as Snort (*http://www.snort.org*) or Bro (Paxson, 1999). Such methods are effective for known worms, but novel worms require methods of timely signature generation. Systems such as Earlybird (Singh, Estan, Varghese, & Savage, 2004) and Autograph (Kim & Karp, 2004) automatically generate worm signatures based on content prevalence, signatures that are robust against a degree of polymorphism.

FUTURE TRENDS

Worms represent a large-scale threat that has received significant attention in the academic research community. Previous studies have been predominately focused on modeling and understanding worm activation and propagation methods and behavior. Current attention has been centered on worm detection and defense. Global detection using network telescopes are often used; however the long-term viability of this approach is questionable. Richardson, Gribble, and Lazowska (2005) argue that global scan detection techniques will suffer, increasing degradation in detection latency due to a rise in Internet background noise levels. In light of this, they advocate local scanning and signature approaches for the long term.

Almost all worm research has assumed the present 32-bit IPv4 address space in which random scanning worms can successfully find targets. The 128-bit IPv6 address space is far too sparse for random scanning to be effective for target discovery. Thus under an IPv6 infrastructure, worm authors will be forced to invent new target discovery methods, such as DNS-based discovery (Kamra, Feng, Misra, & Keromytis, 2005). More research is needed to understand worm design options under IPv6, as well as new methods of detection and defense.

Another area of future research in worms is attack attribution, the process of identifying the host or hosts responsible for initiating a worm epidemic. Worm attribution is an important area of forensics that has received little attention to date. Similar to other security research, the development of a more systematic and defense-in-depth approach that considers multiple countermeasures such as prevention, detection, forensics, containment, and recovery can be expected.

CONCLUSION

Worms, by virtue of their ability to attack on broad spatial and short temporal scales, represent a significant threat to Internet security. This brief article has presented an overview of the worm problem with emphasis on detection and defense. The introduction presented here provides background on the current state of the art in these important areas. This background will enable the interested reader to perform further investigation in this area through the references below.

REFERENCES

Berk, V., Bakos, G., & Morris, R. (2003). Designing a framework for active worm detection on global networks. *Proceedings of the IEEE International Workshop on Information Assurance,* Darmstadt, Germany.

Cohen, F. (1984). Computer viruses theory and experiments. *Proceedings of the 2nd IFIP International Conference on Computer Security,* Toronto, Ontario, Canada.

Eeye. (2003). *Analysis: Blaster worm.* Retrieved from http://www.eeye.com/html/Research/Advisories/AL20030811.html

Ellis, D.R., Aiken, J.G., Attwood, K.S., & Tenaglia, S.D. (2004). A behavioral approach to worm detection. *Proceedings of the 2004 Workshop on Rapid Malcode (WORM'04).*

Frauenthal, J.C. (1980). *Mathematical modeling in epidemiology.* New York: Springer-Verlag.

Gu, G., Sharif, M., Qin, X., Dagon, D., Lee, W., & Riley, G. (2004). Worm detection, early warning and response based on local victim information. *Proceedings of the 20ᵗʰ Annual Computer Security Applications Conference.*

Jung, J., Paxson, V., Berger, A.W., & Balakrishnan, H. (2004). Fast portscan detection using sequential hypothesis testing. *Proceedings of the 2004 IEEE Symposium on Security and Privacy (S&P'04).*

Kamra, A., Feng, H., Misra, V., & Keromytis, A.D. (2005). The effect of DNS delays on worm propagation in an IPv6 Internet. *Proceedings of INFOCOM'05.*

Kienzle, D.M., & Elder, M.C. (2003). Recent worms: A survey and trends. *Proceedings of the Workshop on Rapid Malcode (WORM'03).*

Kim, H.-A., & Karp, B. (2004). Autograph: Toward automated, distributed worm signature detection. *Proceedings of the 13ᵗʰ USENIX Security Symposium.*

Kreyszig, E. (1999). *Advanced engineering mathematics* (8ᵗʰ ed.). Hoboken, NJ: John Wiley & Sons.

Kumar, A., Paxson, V., & Weaver, N. (2005). Exploiting underlying structure for detailed reconstruction of an Internet-scale event. *Proceedings of the Internet Measurement Conference (IMC'05).*

Microsoft. (2004). *Changes to functionality in Microsoft Windows XP Service Pack 2.* Retrieved from http://www.microsoft.com/technet/prodtechnol/winxppro/maintain/sp2netwk.mspx

Moore, D., Shannon, C., & Brown, J. (2002). Code-Red: A case study on the spread and victims of an Internet worm. *Proceedings of the Internet Measurement Workshop.*

Moore, D., Shannon, C., Voelker, G.M., & Savage, S. (2003). Internet quarantine: Requirements for containing self-propagating code. *Proceedings of INFOCOM 2003* (Vol. 3, pp. 1901-1910).

Moore, D., Shannon, C., Voelker, G.M., & Savage, S. (2004). *Network telescopes.* Technical Report No. TR-2004-04, Caida.

Paxson, V. (1999). Bro: A system for detecting network intruders in real-time. *Computer Networks, 31*(23-24), 2435-2463.

Richardson, D.W., Gribble, S.D., & Lazowska, E.D. (2005). The limits of global scanning worm detectors

in the presence of background noise. *Proceedings of the ACM Workshop on Rapid Malcode (WORM'05).*

Shannon, C., & Moore, D. (2004). The spread of the witty worm. *IEEE Security & Privacy Magazine, 2,* 46-50.

Singh, S., Estan, C., Varghese, G., & Savage, S. (2004). Automatic worm fingerprinting. *Proceedings of Operating Systems Design and Implementation (OSDI'04).*

Spafford, E.H. (1988). *The Internet worm program: An analysis.* No. CSD-TR-823, Department of Computer Science, Purdue University, USA.

Staniford, S., Paxson, V., & Weaver, N. (2002). How to own the Internet in your spare time. *Proceedings of the 11th USENIX Security Symposium,* San Francisco.

Venkataraman, S., Song, D., Gibbons, P.B., & Blum, A. (2005). New streaming algorithms for fast detection of superspreaders. *Proceedings of the Network and Distributed System Security Symposium (NDSS'05).*

Whyte, D., Kranakis, E., & Oorschot, P.C. (2005). DNS-based detection of scanning worms in an enterprise network. *Proceedings of the Network and Distributed System Security Symposium.*

Williamson, M.M. (2002). Throttling viruses: Restricting propagation to defeat mobile malicious code. *Proceedings of ACSAC-2002.*

Wong, C., Bielski, S., McCune, J.M., & Wang, C. (2004). A study of mass mailing worms. *Proceedings of the ACM Workshop on Rapid Malcode (WORM'04).*

Zou, C.C., Gong, W., Towsley, D., & Gao, L. (2005). The monitoring and early detection of Internet worms. *IEEE/ACM Transactions on Networking, 13*(5), 961-974.

Zou, C.C., Towsley, D., & Gong, W. (2003a). *On the performance of Internet worm scanning strategies.* No. TR-03-CSE-07.

Zou, C.C., Towsley, D., Gong, W., & Cai, S. (2003b). *Routing worm: A fast, selective attack worm based on IP address information.* No. TR-03-CSE-06, University of Massachusetts, Amherst, USA.

KEY TERMS

Containment: Refers to actions taken to block or limit network communication.

Flash Worm: A worm using an initial hitlist consisting of the majority of vulnerable hosts. Such worms are capable of achieving Internet-scale infection in tens of seconds.

Network Telescope: A system that monitors dark or unused addresses; has become a standard Internet monitoring tool.

Quarantine: A containment concept that refers to isolating an infected host from the rest of the network.

Rate Limiting: A containment concept that refers to enforcing a bound on the connection rate of a host.

Virus: A program that can 'infect' other programs by modifying them to include a possibly evolved copy of itself (Cohen, 1984).

Worm: A program that can run by itself and can propagate a fully working version of itself to other machines (Spafford, 1988).

Conflicting Value of Digital Music Piracy

Matthew Butler
Monash University, Australia

INTRODUCTION

The term MP3 conjures up a great many different thoughts and feelings. To some the creation and proliferation of the MP3 music file has meant the ability to transport a vast music collection on devices no bigger than a deck of cards. It has meant the ability to listen to music that until several years ago would have not been readily available to the average consumer. To others, the MP3 represents one of the biggest challenges in business models and retaining business revenue their industry has seen. To both collectives however, the MP3 has links to the topic of digital piracy.

Digital piracy in general represents the electronic duplication and illegal distribution (or sharing) of digital files, be they music or movies, games or business software. Although this has been an issue for almost two decades, the rise of audio and video encoding standards such as MP3 and DivX, the availability of high speed Internet access and other sharing mechanisms, and the popularity of portable devices capable of playing this content have shifted this issue to the forefront.

The music recording industry, along with the motion picture and gaming industries, is at the forefront of any discussion relating to this issue. Both industry bodies such as the Recording Industry Association of America (RIAA) and industry giants such as Sony and Universal Music have been quick to cast judgment on the new technologies and their users, damning any individual who illegally acquires copyrighted digital materials and claiming that these people are responsible for the industry losing "millions of dollars a day" (RIAA, 2003).

The purpose of this article is to take a different approach in examining the issues surrounding these record label concerns. A brief historical overview of the technologies in question will be provided in order to lay foundation for the discussion. Using this as a springboard, issues relating to digital piracy will be raised, primarily from a recording industry perspective, including an analysis of music sales figures. Of equal importance however are case studies of several

high-profile recording artists which serve to contradict this record label rhetoric, revealing how the advent of digital music has facilitated not only greater exposure for artists, but also greater sales. The MySpace phenomenon will also be raised as a contradiction to industry concerns. It must be noted that the intent of this piece is not necessarily to discredit industry concerns, but rather to raise questions as to the true nature of the existing problems, their documented impact, and exceptions to the perceived rule.

A HISTORICAL BACKGROUND OF DIGITAL MUSIC AND PIRACY

It was in 1991 that the seed of what would become the digital music standard was born: MPEG-1 Audio Layer 3, more commonly known as MP3 (Brandenburg, 1999). At a standard quality of 128 kbit/s, the size of a digital music file could be reduced to approximately 1 MB per minute of audio, enabling easier sharing of these files (Anonymous, 2000). Prior to this development, one minute of audio would be represented by over 11 MB of data.

Widespread adoption of this standard came with the availability of a number of PC-based applications for playing these files, however their popularity boomed with worldwide proliferation of high-speed Internet access such as ADSL. With faster data transmission on conventional phone lines, combined with software to facilitate ease of file sharing, the distribution of MP3 files has become simple for even the most novice PC user. The term MP3 has also become synonymous with music portability, thanks to mobile devices such as the iPod, mobile phones, and personal data assistants (PDAs). It has however become linked with the widely publicized issue of music piracy.

Digital piracy has been in existence for many years. The first targets of the copying and distribution of digital files were PC games and software. Thanks to affordable media (which in the late 1980s primarily consisted of floppy discs) and global PC networking technologies (such as bulletin boards), pirated games and "warez" were commonplace among computing students. Although acknowledged as a legitimate issue at the time, this was still primarily the domain of select groups who were computer savvy and part of a larger, dedicated community.

The MP3 arrived and began its proliferation, however it was a simple file-sharing utility called Napster that placed it well and truly within the piracy vernacular. Released in 1999, Napster facilitated sharing of music between individual computers; it was rapidly embraced by a music-loving community becoming increasingly disenfranchised with increasing CD costs and perceived lower quality of albums. Napster suddenly created the ability for users to acquire individual songs without buying a whole CD. It is important to acknowledge however that users were primarily trading copyrighted songs, illegal under copyright acts around the world. Recording labels were alerted and began to complain.

In 2000, the issue came to a head, with one of the world's largest recording artists, Metallica, filing suit against Napster for facilitating the illegal distribution of its recordings. This action, ultimately settled in 2001, was a call to arms for more than 20 million registered Napster users, who protested against the Napster lawsuit, showing that the music-listening community had evolved significantly (Anonymous, 2001). Thanks to Napster and the broader Internet, a significant shift in thought on the legalities of copyright had begun. The Internet was now being viewed as a place of free trade of ideas and data, particularly by teenage users. A new generation of music consumers with a different mindset had been born.

In the years since Napster's demise, illegal sharing of MP3 files has only strengthened. Similar file-sharing software such as Morpheus, eDonkey, and more recently Bit Torrent technologies have seen no slow down in this activity, now embracing Hollywood movies with arguably more vigor. It is difficult to obtain accurate statistics, given the reluctance of peer-to-peer (P2P) software companies to divulge account numbers, and the nature of the Bit Torrent technology. Data collected by Big Champagne Online Media Measurement, in conjunction with Nielsen Entertainment, indicates that the number of people logged on to P2P networks at the same time and at any point around the clock rose from approximately 5.6 million in December 2003, to approximately 7.6 million in December 2004,

and to approximately 9.6 million in December 2005 (Anonymous, 2006a).

It has been during this time that the major recording labels have also complained more strongly about the impact of this file sharing. In 2006, four major record labels dominate the recording market: Universal Music Group, Sony BMG Music Entertainment, EMI Group, and Warner Music Group (Lamb, 2006). All claim to be experiencing a drop in music sales, primarily citing the rise of digital piracy as the major reason.

Recording industry bodies such as the Recording Industry Association of America (RIAA) and Australian Recording Industry Association (ARIA) are also placing blame for lagging sales on piracy. Both association Web sites provide news and their response to the issue of piracy. The RIAA in particular provides many articles and editorials. One goes so far as to dramatically state: "Today's pirates operate not on the high seas but on the Internet, in illegal CD factories, distribution centers, and on the street" (Recording Industry Association of America, 2003). It must be asked, however, is the argument this clear-cut?

WHAT IS THE ACTUAL ISSUE?

Sales

Again, the RIAA, ARIA, and recording labels would have you believe that lagging sales are the direct result of digital piracy. Before further discussion, it must be acknowledged that many downloaders of digital music fit the RIAA profile, with substantial numbers of computer users today downloading music without any intent of purchasing the original recording. Importantly, however, anecdotal evidence suggests that most people who are downloading copyrighted music are individuals who would not normally buy the albums they have downloaded. The RIAA also discounts the many users who download in order to sample a recording before purchase. Although this practice is still by definition illegal, to simplify the argument as the RIAA has done is unproductive.

Simply on face value, figures from both the United States and Australia do paint the picture of a declining music industry. In the United States, total retail record sales have dropped from a high of 869.7 million in 1999 to 634.8 million in 2005: a drop of approximately 27% (RIAA, 2006). In Australia, the statistics tell a similar, though not as drastic, a story. Sales of 63.9 million in 2001 have dropped over 8% to 58.3 million units in 2005 (ARIA, 2006).

Although these figures indicate falling music sales, it is improper to consider them in isolation. To begin with, the rise of digital music sales from sites such as iTunes are regularly overlooked in record sales figures. Issues exist on how these sales should be recorded and analyzed, as a single-track download typically represents about one-tenth or less of an album sale (Barnes, 2004). Sales monitoring bodies such as RIAA and Billboard however are consolidating this. The RIAA reports that in 2005, there were 383.1 million digital sales. As explained, however, these are deemed "units" and are difficult to correlate directly with the retail sales figures quoted above.

It is also important to acknowledge that the average consumer does not have unlimited money to spend on other forms of entertainment, therefore it is more pertinent to consider record sales as part of the overall "entertainment" dollar. If we accept that music sales have indeed fallen, it is difficult to ignore the fact that sales of both DVDs and games for consoles such as PS2 and X-Box have increased, leading to higher "entertainment" expenditure than in the past. The *Age* newspaper in Australia reports:

According to market research company Inform, a record $180 million was spent on interactive games (in Australia) in December 2002 alone [and] CDs are also facing competition from within their own camp, from music video/DVD sales which increased more than 150 per cent last year (in Australia) to more than 2.45 million copies. (Kruger, 2003)

Exceptions to the "Rule"

Discussion of this issue continues, despite inconclusive sales figures that are subject to different interpretation. In fact it is the artists, not the record labels, that provide some of the most compelling evidence. Three differing cases are examined below in order to demonstrate the positive side of the download debate.

Radiohead is both a critically acclaimed and commercially successful band from Oxford, England. In the United States, however, it took the release of several of their albums before their records began to sell. In 2000, at the height of Napster's popularity, the band's fourth album, "Kid A," leaked into the file-sharing

domain several weeks before the formal release date, with millions of copies downloaded. On release, the album debuted at number 1 on the U.S. music charts, selling over 200,000 copies in the U.S. in its first week alone (Cohen, 2000). What makes this more important is that the band had not entered the U.S. Top 20 prior to this. It must be acknowledged that the band's previous album, "OK Computer," was universally acclaimed and had generated considerable hype for the band. What makes the sales even more remarkable is that "Kid A" represented a significant stylistic shift into a darker, more inaccessible domain.

Wilco is also a critically acclaimed band from Chicago. While not at the sales levels of Radiohead, they enjoy quite substantial record sales both at home and abroad. In 2001 their record label, Reprise Records, deemed their work "Yankee Hotel Foxtrot" to be unreleasable, and subsequently dumped the band from its roster. Without a label or distributor, Wilco took matters into their own hands and began streaming the album on their Web site, free for all. Word of mouth led to radio play and critical acclaim, and a resultant bidding war to acquire Wilco began, with Nonesuch obtaining rights. The album was commercially released and became their biggest-selling record up to that time. In keeping with this ethos, Wilco streamed their current work, "A Ghost Is Born," on their Web site several months before its official release in 2004. This has become their most commercially successful release to date.

Both these examples feature bands that lie within the domain of the music-o-philes, which, while enjoying commercial success, are still not representative of the more typical "pop" output of the singles charts (the focus of many downloaders). The major "exception" to the industry belief that downloading reduces sales can be found in the music phenomenon of 2005/2006, the Arctic Monkeys of Sheffield, England.

Arctic Monkeys began as little more than school friends learning to play musical instruments. After their first performances, the band began recording demos and burning them onto CDs to hand out at their live shows. They also put these songs onto file-sharing networks for people to download and distribute as they liked. The band began to gain a reputation in England during 2005, culminating in a performance at the Reading festival that had thousand of fans singing along to songs that had not been commercially released. When their debut album, "Whatever People Say I

Am, That's What I'm Not," was released in January 2006, it became the fastest-selling debut album in UK chart history, selling almost 400,000 in its first week (Anonymous, 2006b). It also debuted at number 1 in many countries around the world, including Australia. The BBC has described this outcome as a result of "not...record company hype, but good old fashioned word of mouth" (Dyson, 2005).

The approaches taken by these recording artists are not isolated cases. Bhattacharjee, Gopal, Lertwachara, and Marsden (2003) provide a thorough economic model of online music, considering five different pricing models that encompass not only traditional stores, but also online stores and subscription services. In their conclusion they found that "revenue-maximization strategies for the seller do not necessarily involve efforts to eliminate online music piracy" (p. 305).

The MySpace Phenomenon

MySpace (www.myspace.com) came into being in 2003 as a social networking Web site. In just over three years, over 100 million users have registered MySpace accounts. With the ability to have streaming audio files linked to a user's profile, it has quickly become the domain of bands across the world looking to spread their music to a wider audience. This can be done by exclusively streaming the song or also allowing download of the MP3 file.

The Wilco and Arctic Monkeys case studies discussed above allude to the power that a site such as MySpace can have on record sales. Two other recording artists also exemplify the ability for MySpace to generate artist awareness and sales in 2006: Lily Allen and Sandi Thom. Lily Allen used her MySpace profile to stream demos of tracks from her forthcoming album. In order to generate further awareness of her work by word of mouth, she began keeping a satirical blog in which she detailed the daily dramas of her life, along with amusing observations of British celebrities. Links to and copies of her tracks began circulating around Britain, with radio adding tracks to playlists and the music press reviewing the material before any official release. On commercial release, Lily's album debuted at number 2 in the UK, along with number 7 in Australia.

Sandi Thom provides a similar MySpace success story. Rather than launch a career from cyberspace, Sandi had already been signed to a record label, how-

ever her first single release was considered a failure. Things began to change in February 2006 when Sandi began streaming live performances from her flat in England. MySpace was used to notify her fans of the performances, and as with Lily Allen, word quickly spread, to the point where thousands of Internet users would "tune in" to her performances.

What MySpace demonstrates, among many other things, is that success and record sales can again stem from the free distribution of recorded works. Record companies are now embracing MySpace and its free streaming audio, with virtually all major label recording artists maintaining a MySpace site complete with streaming or downloadable audio. It is important for recording labels to consider the power of such sites as MySpace when considering the impact that downloading of music is having on their industry and sales. It appears that when it comes to record sales, recording labels are damning many of the same Internet users they are trying to draw in through these new avenues.

CONCLUSION

It is not the intent of this article to defend downloading of copyrighted material, nor solve problems of digital piracy. The primary purpose is to consider many of the arguments involved with digital music distribution, provide cases that highlight successes in the mediums, and identify future opportunities both for recording artists and labels.

It is clear that a shift in thinking by recording companies needs to take place in order to deal with the many ethical issues surrounding digital music and piracy. Success stories such as those discussed here show that the downloading of music can have an immense impact on record sales. Seemingly outdated business models in the industry must be examined to incorporate the advantages that sites like MySpace provide. Similarly, the psychology of music downloading must be examined in order to tap into how it can be used for artist success. Fetscherin (2006) discusses a detailed model of online music and consumer behavior, encompassing not only economics, but also willingness to pay, quality, security, and digital rights restrictions, and still acknowledges that "there might still be additional parameters which have been excluded" (p. 604).

If recording labels work closely with artists, along with sites such as MySpace, then legitimate models for working with digital music can be found. The members of Wilco continue to provide downloadable content on their Web site (www.wilcoworld.net) for those who have purchased their CDs. American band Weezer demoed their last album entirely on their Web site (www.weezer.com) for fans to comment on upcoming tracks, leading to immense record sales. Ultimately, file sharing can serve to promote music consumption, a fact that is not lost on the artists and therefore must be considered by the recording industry.

REFERENCES

Anonymous. (2000, November 17). *MPEG Audio Layer 3 (MP3) technical guide.* Retrieved September 9, 2006, from http://www.bbc.co.uk/dna/h2g2/A157178

Anonymous. (2001, July 13). *Napster settles Metallica lawsuit.* Retrieved September 9, 2006, from http://news.bbc.co.uk/1/hi/entertainment/new_media/1436796.stm

Anonymous. (2006a, January 11). *P2P file sharing is on the rise.* Retrieved September 9, 2006, from http://www.p2pnet.net/story/7570

Anonymous. (2006b, January 29). *Arctic Monkeys make chart history.* Retrieved September 9, 2006, from http://news.bbc.co.uk/1/hi/entertainment/4660394.stm

ARIA (Australian Recording Industry of Australia). (2006). *Australian sales by unit for the years ended 31 December: Physical music product.* Retrieved September 9, 2006, from http://www.aria.com.au/pages/documents/Table2.pdf

Barnes, K. (2006, January 4). *Album sales slump as digital downloads rise.* Retrieved September 9, 2006, from http://www.usatoday.com/life/music/news/2006-01-04-music-salesman_x.htm

Bhattacharjee, S., Gopal, R.D., Lertwachara, K., & Marsden, J.R (2003). Economics of online music. *Proceedings of the 5th International Conference on Electronic Commerce* (pp. 300-309).

Brandenburg, K. (1999). MP3 and AAC explained. *Proceedings of AES 17th International Conference on High Quality Audio Coding* (pp. 1-12).

Cohen, W. (2000, October 11). *With Radiohead's Kid A, Capitol busts out of a big time slump (thanks, Napster).* Retrieved September 9, 2006, from http://bigpicture.typepad.com/comments/2004/11/_i_n_s_i_d_e_wi.html

Dyson, M. (2005, August 30). *Review: Arctic Monkeys.* Retrieved September 9, 2006, from http://www.bbc.co.uk/berkshire/content/articles/2005/08/30/reading_festival_review_arctic_monkeys_feature.shtml

Fetscherin, M. (2006). Economics of online music and consumer behaviour. *Proceedings of the 8th International Conference on Electronic Commerce* (pp. 599-604).

Kruger, C. (2003, January 28). *Piracy not the burning issue in CD sales slide: ARIA.* Retrieved September 9, 2006, from http://www.theage.com.au/articles/2003/01/28/1043534039320.html

Lamb, B. (2006, January 9). *The big 4 record labels.* Retrieved September 9, 2006, from http://top40.about.com/b/a/207679.htm

RIAA (Recording Industry Association of America). (2003). *Anti-piracy.* Retrieved September 9, 2006, from http://www.riaa.com/issues/piracy/default/asp

RIAA (Recording Industry Association of America). (2006). *2005 year-end statistics.* Retrieved September 9, 2006, from http://www.riaa.com/news/newsletter/pdf/2005yrEndStats.pdf

KEY TERMS

Bit Torrent: A peer-to-peer file distribution protocol. Also the name of a popular software implementation of the protocol.

File Sharing: Making digital files on one's own computer available for other Internet users to download. This often refers to the practice of using peer-to-peer software to download digital audio and video from other users.

MP3: Short for MPEG-1 Audio Layer 3, this is a form of encoding and compressing of audio, reducing the amount of data required to represent the original audio.

MySpace: An Internet social networking Web site (www.myspace.com).

C

Napster: An Internet music service, originally a peer-to-peer file-sharing service.

Peer-to-Peer: A computer network that does not rely on dedicated servers, rather data is distributed and shared among participants' computers.

Streaming Audio: Audio files that are being delivered to the computer user while he or she is listening to it.

Content Filtering Methods for Internet Pornography

Jengchung V. Chen
National Cheng Kung University, Taiwan

ShaoYu F. Huang
National Cheng Kung University, Taiwan

INTRODUCTION

The Internet is widely recognized as an important information and communication medium. It has also become a useful tool for children's education, but since the Internet is an open environment, it contains much information unsuitable for the under aged. This article introduces several content-filtering methods that can assist parents and educators in protecting children from harmful material. However, it must be noted that these are of limited value unless they are supported by sex education and parental monitoring of children's Internet use.

BACKGROUND

As a number of researchers have noted, the Internet is becoming inundated with pornographic materials (Avgoulea, Bouras, Paraskevas, & Stathakopoulos, 2003; Panko & Beh, 2002; Wishart, 2004). A simple Net search using common Internet search engines such as Google with keywords "XXX and porn" is likely to provide more than 10 million Web documents. Furthermore, these pornographic sites usually group together to form huge adult networks, thus increasing their strength and visibility (Lim, Teo, & Loo, 2002). They are also one of the first few groups to employ the latest Internet technologies in their business and Web site implementation.

THE FOUR MAJOR CONTENT-FILTERING TECHNIQUES AND WEB RATING

This section first introduces four content-filtering approaches, followed by the Web rating system. The four content-filtering techniques are Platform for Internet Content Selection (PICS), URL blocking, keyword filtering, and intelligent content analysis (Lee, Hui, & Fon, 2002).

Platform for Internet Content Selection (PICS)

Not everyone needs to block reception of the same materials (Paul & James, 1996). The content-filtering software should consider at least three factors as follows:

1. **Supervisor:** Parenting styles differ, as do philosophies of management and government
2. **Recipient:** What's appropriate for one 15-year-old may not be for an 8-year-old, or even all 15-year-olds
3. **Context:** A game or chat room that is appropriate to access at home may be inappropriate at work or school

But in the traditional content-filtering software illustrated in Figure 1 (Paul & James, 1996), customers have limited abilities to set the software until Platform for Internet Content Selection appears. PICS is a set of specifications for content-rating systems. It lets Web publishers associate labels or metadata with Web pages to limit certain Web content to target audiences. Figure 2 shows the basic idea of flexible blocking. Parents can set the rating systems themselves.

The two most popular PICS content-rating systems are RSACi and SafeSurf. Created by the Recreational Software Advisory Council, RSACi (http://www.rsac.org/) uses four categories: harsh language, nudity, sex, and violence. For each category, it assigns a number indicating the degree of potentially offensive content, ranging from 0 (none) to 4. SafeSurf is a much more de-

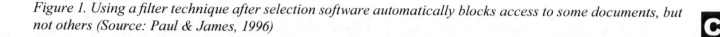

Figure 1. Using a filter technique after selection software automatically blocks access to some documents, but not others (Source: Paul & James, 1996)

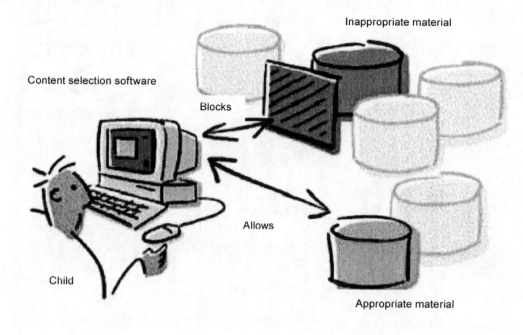

tailed content-rating system. Besides identifying a Web site's appropriateness for specific age groups, it uses 11 categories to describe Web content's potential offensiveness. Each category has nine levels, from 1 (none) to 9. Currently, Microsoft Internet Explorer, Netscape Navigator, and several content-filtering systems offer PICS support and can filter Web pages according to the embedded PICS rating labels. However, PICS is a voluntary self-labeling system, and each Web content publisher is totally responsible for rating the content. Consequently, content-filtering systems should use PICS only as a supplementary filtering approach.

URL Blocking

This technique restricts or allows access by comparing the requested Web page's URL (and equivalent IP address) with URLs in a stored list. Two types of lists can be maintained: a black list contains URLs of objectionable Web sites to block; a white list contains URLs of permissible Web sites. Most content-filtering systems that employ URL blocking use black lists. The chief advantages of this approach are speed and

efficiency. A system can make a filtering decision by matching the requested Web page's URL with one in the list even before a network connection to the remote Web server is made. However, this approach requires implementing a URL list, and it can identify only the sites on the list. Also, unless the list is updated constantly, the system's accuracy will decrease over time, owing to the explosive growth of new Web sites. Most content-filtering systems that use URL blocking employ a large team of human reviewers to actively search for objectionable Web sites to add to the black list. They then make this list available for downloading as an update to the list's local copy. This is both time consuming and resource intensive. Despite this drawback, the fast and efficient operation of this approach is desirable in a content-filtering system. Using sophisticated content analysis techniques during classification, the system can first identify the nature of a Web page's content. If the system determines that the content is objectionable, it can add the page's URL to the black list. Later, if a user tries to access the Web page, the system can immediately make a filtering decision by matching the URL. Dynamically updat-

Figure 2. Selection software blocks based on labels provided by publishers and third-party labeling services, and based on selection criteria set by the parent (Source: Paul & James, 1996)

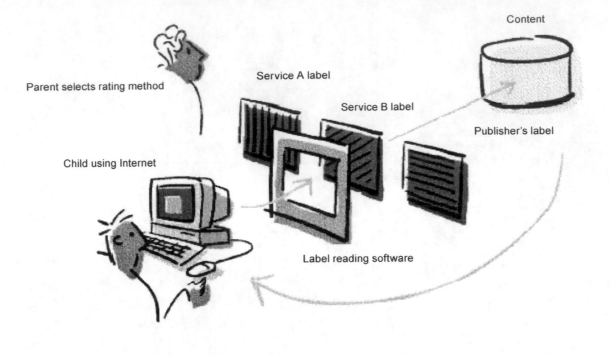

ing the black list achieves speed and efficiency, and accuracy is maintained provided that content analysis is accurate.

Keyword Filtering

This intuitively simple approach blocks access to Web sites on the basis of the occurrence of offensive words and phrases on those sites. It compares every word or phrase on a retrieved Web page against those in a keyword dictionary of prohibited words and phrases. Blocking occurs if the number of matches reaches a predefined threshold. This fast content analysis method can quickly determine if a Web page contains potentially harmful material. However, it is well known for overblocking—that is, blocking many Web sites that do not contain objectionable content. Because it filters content by matching keywords (or phrases) such as "sex" and "breast," it could accidentally block Web sites about sexual harassment or breast cancer, or even the homepage of someone named Sexton. Although the dictionary of objectionable words and phrases does not require frequent updates, the high overblocking rate greatly jeopardizes a content-filtering system's capability and is often unacceptable. However, a con-

tent-filtering system can use this approach to decide whether to further process a Web page using a more precise content analysis method, which usually requires more processing time.

As documents often have too many words to be processed, a data reduction process will be needed (Liu, Lu, & Lee, 2000; Singhal, Salton, Mitra, & Buckley, 1996). The scoring of individual features in a feature subset selection approach used on text data can be performed using some of the measures utilized in machine learning for feature selection during the learning process (Mladeni & Grobelnik, 2003). For instance, information gain used in decision tree induction can be used to score the features. In machine learning, several measures are known appropriate for different kinds of class and feature values. They are information gain, chi-square test, odd ratio, and TFxIDF (Li & Jain, 1998; Mladeni & Grobelnik, 2003; Salton & Buckley, 1988).

Intelligent Content Analysis

A content-filtering system can use intelligent content analysis to automatically classify Web content. One interesting method for implementing this capability is artificial neural networks (ANNs), which can learn and adapt according to training cases fed to them. Such a learning and adaptation process can give semantic meaning to context-dependent words such as "sex" which can occur frequently in both pornographic and non-pornographic Web pages. To achieve high classification accuracy, ANN training should involve a sufficiently large number of training exemplars, including both positive and negative cases. ANN inputs can be characterized from the Web pages, such as the occurrence of keywords and key phrases, and hyperlinks to other similar Web sites (Lee et al., 2002). Besides ANN, some researchers use the genetic algorithm to evaluate which characteristics are important (Arentz & Olstad, 2004; Atkinson-Abutridy, Mellish, & Aitken, 2004; Horng & Yeh, 2000).

Web Rating System

The Web rating system has several components: crawler, natural language processing (NLP), knowledge base construction, index generation, and k-nearest neighbors (KNNs).

Crawler Component

The crawler component is an autonomous WWW browser, which communicates with WWW servers using Hypertext Transfer Protocol (HTTP). It visits a given WWW site, traverses hyperlinks in a breadth-first manner, retrieves WWW pages, and extracts keywords and hyperlink data from the pages (Yuwono & Lee, 1996).

NLP Component

The NLP component is used to extract the keywords from HTML documents so that high-frequency function words (stop-words) such as "the," "a," "to," and "in" are excluded. Then a procedure called stemming is performed, which strips off word endings, reducing them to a common core or stem. For example, words such as "computer," "computers," "compute," "computing," "computed," "computation," and "computational" will be reduced to the basic form "comput" by a stemming algorithm. In comparison, in Chinese text, several segmentation methods such as PAT-tree are proposed (Chien, 1999).

Knowledge Base Construction Component

The knowledge base construction component builds a knowledge base of information that includes the Library of Congress (LCC) subject headings and their interrelationships, as well as other information during classification. At the same time, the vector space model method is used which represents a document as a vector. In the vector space model, there is one component in the document vector for every distinct term that appears in the document collection. The simplest way of constructing such a vector for a document is to use a binary representation: to put a "1" in the corresponding term position if this term appears, otherwise a "0." Because a document may contain too many terms, feature selection is necessary. As described in the previous section, there are several feature selection methods. By means of feature selection methods, a document can be reduced to a short list of features for the future.

Index Generation Component

The index construction component is used to give each test document an index (a category label). I can classify document by means of this knowledge base. Two useful methods are k-nearest neighbors (Kwon & Lee, 2000, 2003) and naïve bayes (Wang, Hodges, & Tang, 2003).

K-Nearest Neighbors

The KNN approach can be broken down into two steps. Given a test document, the first step is to find k-nearest samples among the training documents, using document-document similarity. The similarity score of each neighbor document to the test document is used as the weight of the categories pre-assigned to the training document. The second step is to estimate the likelihood of each category by summing the weight of the category of the k nearest documents.

INFORMATION ETHICS EDUCATION AT HOME

The above technical approaches to passively filter out unwanted information on the Internet are regarded by many researchers as having failed. These researchers suggest that we should focus more on information ethics education (Greenfield, 2004). According to Greenfield (2004), any forbidden rules never succeed. Consequently, parents should concentrate on the sexual education of their children by implementing the following methods:

1. Maintain an open family communication style
2. Remain open to discussions about sexual topics
3. Remember that communication about specific sexual topics is less important than developing and maintaining a warm and communicative parent-child relationship
4. Make sure that your child gets sex education
5. Use the Internet (and other media) with your child
6. Put the computer in a public place in your home, and if at all possible, do not let your children have a computer with Internet access in their room
7. If you have a child with antisocial tendencies, restrict use of the Internet, including file sharing, to supervised sessions

FUTURE TRENDS

As the age of children utilizing the Internet is decreasing, it becomes increasingly important for adults to monitor their actions online. Content filtration is useful not only for blocking out pornography, but it can be used for blocking pop-ups or filtering unwanted e-mail. New content-filtering techniques will be developed that will become more powerful and effective. But as they may never be powerful enough to block everything unwanted, education remains of primary importance. Education is a key factor for content filtering to fully function; as the technology of content-filtering improves, so should education.

CONCLUSION

This article highlights the importance of content-filtering methods that are not only widely adopted in fighting Internet pornography, but also are valuable for providing efficient Internet searching. Given the continued expansion of the Internet, the ability to filter out unwanted information plays an important role. This article introduces four methods to lay the foundation for a Web rating system. However, any technical means has its limitations and should be preceded by information ethics education in domestic and educational environments.

REFERENCES

Arentz, W.A., & Olstad, B. (2004). Classifying offensive sites based on image content. *Computer Vision and Image Understanding, 94*(1-3), 295-310.

Atkinson-Abutridy, J., Mellish, C., & Aitken, S. (2004). Combining information extraction with genetic algorithms for text mining. *Intelligent Systems, 19*(3), 22-30.

Avgoulea, M., Bouras, C., Paraskevas, M., & Stathakopoulos, G. (2003). Policies for content filtering in educational networks: The case of Greece. *Telematics and Informatics, 20*(1), 71-95.

Chien, L.F. (1999). PAT-tree-based adaptive keyphrase extraction for intelligent Chinese information retrieval. *Information Processing and Management, 35*(4), 501-521.

Greenfield, P.M. (2004). Inadvertent exposure to pornography on the Internet: Implications of peer-to-peer file-sharing networks for child development and families. *Journal of Applied Developmental Psychology, 25*(6), 741-750.

Horng, J.T., & Yeh, C.C. (2000). Applying genetic algorithms to query optimization in document retrieval. *Information Processing and Management, 36*(5), 737-759.

Kwon, O.W., & Lee, J.H. (2000). Web page classification based on k-nearest neighbor approach. *Proceedings of the 5th International Workshop on Information Retrieval with Asian Languages* (pp. 9-15). Hong Kong.

Kwon, O.W., & Lee, J.H. (2003). Text categorization based on k-nearest neighbor approach for Web site classification. *Information Processing and Management, 39*(1), 25-44.

Lee, P.Y., Hui, S.C., & Fong, A.C.M. (2002). Neural networks for Web content filtering. *Intelligent Systems, 17*(5), 48-57.

Li, Y., & Jain, A.K. (1998). Classification of text documents. *Proceedings of the 14ᵗʰ International Conference on Pattern Recognition* (Vol. 2, pp. 1295-1297). Brisbane, Australia.

Lim, V.K.G., Teo, T.S.H., & Loo, G.L. (2002). Internet abuse in the workplace: How do I loaf here? Let me count the ways. *Communications of the ACM, 45*(1), 66-70.

Liu, C.H., Lu, C.C., & Lee, W.P. (2000). Document categorization by genetic algorithms. *Proceedings of the IEEE International Conference on Systems, Man, and Cybernetics* (vol. 5, pp. 3868-3872). Nashville, TN.

Mladeni, D., & Grobelnik, M. (2003). Feature selection on hierarchy of Web documents. *Decision Support Systems, 35*(1), 45-87.

Panko, R.R., & Beh, H.G. (2002). Internet abuse in the workspace: Monitoring for the pornography and sexual harassment. *Communications of the ACM, 45*(1), 84-87.

Paul, R., & James, M. (1996). PICS: Internet access controls without censorship. *Communications of the ACM, 39*(10), 87-93.

Salton, G., & Buckley, C. (1998). Term weighting approaches in automatic text retrieval. *Information Processing and Management, 24*(5), 513-523.

Singhal, A., Salton, G., Mitra, M., & Buckley, C. (1996). Document length normalization. *Information Processing and Management, 32*(5), 619-633.

Wang, Y., Hodges, J., & Tang, B. (2003). Classification of Web documents using a naïve Bayes method. *Proceedings of the 15ᵗʰ IEEE International Conference on Tools with Artificial Intelligence* (pp. 560-564).

Wishart, J. (2004). Internet safety in emerging educational contexts. *Computers & Education, 43*(1-2), 193-204.

Yuwono, B., & Lee, D.L. (1996). Search and ranking algorithms for locating resources on the World Wide Web. *Proceedings of the 12ᵗʰ International Conference on Data Engineering* (pp. 164-171). New Orleans, LA.

KEY TERMS

Content Filtering: Text look-up and discard of unwanted information.

Cookie: A message that the Web server gives to the Web browser which is stored in a text file. This file is constantly updated; the main purpose is to identify users and possibly prepare a customized Web page for the user.

Information Ethics: The art and science that seeks to bring sensitivity and method to the discernment of moral values in information-related fields.

Internet: An electronic communications network that connects computer networks and organizational computer facilities around the world.

Keyword Filtering: Filtering of unwanted Web pages according to a certain keyword. You can choose the pages you do not want if it consists of a certain word you selected.

Pornography: Material (a book or a photograph) that depicts erotic behavior and is intended to cause sexual excitement.

URL Blocking: Saves the sites that you do not want in the black list and pages that you allow in the white list. This can prevent you from entering sites that you do not want to enter.

Web Surfing: Refers to switching between different Web sites simultaneously, similar to the term "TV channel surfin."

Cyber–Terrorism in Australia

Christopher Beggs
Monash University, Australia

INTRODUCTION

Cyber-terrorism has evolved as a new form of terrorism since the development of new information and communication technologies (ICTs) such as the Internet. It has become an issue of concern to the Australian government as well as a global issue since the impact of the September 11, 2001, tragedies, the Bali bombings in 2002, and the London bombings of 2005. Australia, together with other leading nations such as the U.S., currently faces the threat of conventional terrorism; however, we also now face the possibility of a new digital form of terrorism: cyber-terrorism. This article explores this new form of terrorism and provides examples of possible cyber-terrorism and closely related cases. It also highlights vulnerabilities within Australian computer systems and provides an overview of the future trends of this new emerging threat within the Australian context.

CYBER-TERRORISM DEFINED

There are varying definitions of cyber-terrorism. Dorothy E. Denning, during her appearance before the U.S. Special Oversight Panel on terrorism, described it as:

...the convergence of terrorism and cyber space. It is generally understood to mean unlawful attacks against computers, networks and the information stored therein when done to intimidate or coerce a government or its people in furtherance of political or social objections. Further, to qualify as cyber-terrorism, an attack should result in violence against persons or property, or at least cause enough harm to generate fear. (Denning, 2000)

Similarly, Sofaer (2000, p. 32) suggests that cyber-terrorism is the "international use or threat of use, without legally recognized authority, of violence, disruption, or interference against cyber systems, when it is likely that such use would result in death or injury of a person or persons, substantial damage to physical property, civil disorder or significant economic harm." Lewis (2002, p. 1) takes this definition one step further, claiming that cyber-terrorism is "the use of computer network tools to shut down critical infrastructure such as energy, transportation, government operations or to coerce or intimidate a government or civilian population."

The author defines cyber-terrorism as the use of ICTs to attack and control critical information systems with the intent to cause harm and spread fear to people, or at least with the anticipation of changing domestic, national, or international events (Beggs, 2005, p. 1). For example, penetrating a system controlling gas pressure in a gas plant by manipulating the pipeline and causing an explosion would be classified as cyber-terrorism.

It is important to note that cyber-terrorism is not the same as hacking, even though they are closely related. Hacking generally involves a hacker taking a delight in experimenting with system hardware, software, and communications systems in an attempt to gain unauthorized access into a computer system. Unlike the cyber-terrorist, a hacker does not spread fear or cause harm to people, rather he/she demonstrates his/her prowess, as well as revealing the fallibility of computer security (Warren, 1999). According to Warren (1999), both hackers and cyber-terrorists utilize an arsenal of techniques in order to breach the security of the targeted system. However, from a motivation perspective, a cyber-terrorist is different in that he/she operates with a specific political or ideological agenda to support his/her activities. For example, a cyber-terrorist may attack specific systems or infrastructures such as water, gas, and power in an attempt to cause or spread harm to innocent people.

Also it is important to note that cyber-terrorism is different from information warfare. Janczewski and Colarik (2005) suggest that information warfare attacks are planned by nations or by agents. These types of attacks are against information and computer systems, programs, or data that result in enemy losses.

The major difference between the two concepts is that cyber-terrorism is about causing fear and harm to anyone in the vicinity such as bystanders, while information warfare has a defined or declared target in a war. For example, if two nations launch cyber-based attacks against each other in efforts to destroy data or infrastructure, this type of attack would be classified as information warfare. On the other hand an attack against an infrastructure that spread fear and harm to innocent people within a community would be classified as cyber-terrorism.

CYBER-TERRORISM: POSSIBLE SCENARIOS

Rapid technological developments based on the Internet and other information infrastructures create an attractive environment for groups who cannot directly confront the Australian government, yet are willing to use death, destruction, and disruption to achieve their objectives. Increasingly, a cyber-terrorist (a person with malicious intent using ICT to spread fear or harm to civilians) can achieve impact in Australia from nearly anywhere around the globe. Terrorist groups such as Al-Qaeda can access global information infrastructures owned and operated by the government and corporations they want to target. Therefore digital attacks have a wide variety of means to cause disruption or destruction (Rattray, 2000). For example, the more developed a country becomes, the greater the vulnerability in the area of ICT. Terror attacks against communication systems are relatively easy to implement. The means required for these attacks are not particularly costly, and after the act the perpetrators are difficult to find (Schweitzer, 2003).

Cyber-terrorists can exploit vulnerabilities through achieving unauthorized access and control over a targeted system through a vast array of intrusive tools and techniques, commonly referred to as hacking. Means for successful intrusion range from comprised passwords to sophisticated software for identifying and exploiting known vulnerabilities in operating systems and application software. If control over a targeted computer or network is achieved, a cyber-terrorist could inflict a wide range of destruction. Possibilities could range from the changing of graphics on a Web page, to corrupting the delivery schedules for medical supplies or military equipment, or denying access to 000 (emergency) services, air traffic control data, or disrupting telecommunication networks. A main advantage of intrusion for cyber-terrorism is the ability of tight control over the timing of the attack (Rattray, 2000). For example, if a cyber-terrorist was to change the flight path of an aircraft, this change could be made with precision because of the electronic magnitude of the tools being used.

Cyber-space presents countless opportunities to commit acts that cause significant disruption to society without discreet loss of life, injury, or harm to material objects. For example, digital attacks might cause stock market disruptions by denying service to computer and communication systems. This analysis of cyber-terrorism includes both acts that involve physical violence and those causing significant social disruption based on attacking information systems and infrastructure (Rattray, 2000).

Collin (2000) highlights the following examples of potential cyber-terrorist acts:

- Attacking an aircraft control system, causing two planes to collide
- Altering the formulas of medication at pharmaceutical manufacture, causing several lethal dosages
- Changing the pressure in the gas lines causing a valve failure, resulting in an explosion
- Contaminating water supplies, causing many deaths
- Attacking the share market, causing economic chaos and disrupting the economy
- Attacking electrical power supplies, causing blackouts

There are many more possible examples of cyber-terrorism, however it should be noted that many cyber-terrorist attacks would generally aid conventional terrorism. For example, if a bomb was to be exploded in the Rialto building in Melbourne, Australia in conjunction with a cyber-attack such as blocking the emergency phone lines (000) and disabling power supplies in the CBD, the number of casualties would be increased, because rescue teams could not assist wounded casualties. Such an attack would support the terrorists' motives and goals.

Lewis (2005) claims that if cyber-terrorism occurred, it would be possible to coincide with a conventional attack. He claims that these types of multiple attacks cannot be ruled out. However, Denning (2005) argues that these types of attacks are not very likely, as there is no evidence to suggest that terrorists are planning such an attack involving cyber-tactics and conventional methods. Although these compound attacks are possible, realistically the likelihood of such attacks occurring is still questionable.

CYBER-TERRORISM-RELATED CASES

Gazprom 1999

In 1999, hackers broke into Gazprom, a gas company in Russia. The attack was collaborated with a Gazprom insider. The hackers were said to have used a Trojan horse to gain control of the central switchboard which controls gas flows in pipelines, although Gazprom, the world's largest natural gas producer and the largest gas supplier to Western Europe, refuted the report (Denning, 2000).

Queensland 2000

In November 2000, in Queensland, Australia, a man hacked into an industrial control system using the Internet, a wireless radio, and stolen control software, and consequently managed to release millions of liters of sewage into the river and costal waters of Maroochydore in Queensland, Australia (Lemos, 2002).

SQL Slammer 2003

In January 2003, an Internet-based worm called SQL Slammer was released. At the Davis Besse nuclear power plant in Ohio, the worm activity on the process control network blocked SCADA traffic, causing the operators to lose some degree of control of the system. As a consequence, the plant's safety parameter display system and plant process computer was disabled for four hours and fifty minutes and six hours and nine minutes respectively (ITSEAG, 2005).

These cases demonstrate the fallibility of ICT security, but more importantly highlight the possibility of cyber-terrorism occurring. The Queensland case most closely resembles cyber-terrorism because it demonstrates its ability to cause serious damage and to spread fear to the residents of Maroochydore.

VULNERABILITIES IN AUSTRALIAN COMPUTER SYSTEMS

Vulnerabilities within systems in Australia are being discovered daily and are occurring more frequently as technology is advancing. Donovan (2003), a managing director of Symantec, a world leading Internet security organization, claims that 2,524 new vulnerabilities were discovered in 2002—an increase of 81.5% over the prior six months. Approximately 60% of all new vulnerabilities could be easily exploited either because the vulnerability did not require the use of exploit code or because the required exploit code was widely available. However, of the subset of vulnerabilities that required the use of exploit code, only 23.7% actually had exploit code available in 2002 as compared with 30% in 2001. The malicious code trends in 2002 constitute the most frequently reported threat. These threats involved blends of two or more viruses, worms, Trojan horses and malicious code. Eighty percent of all malicious code submissions were caused by only three: Klez, Opaserv, and Bugbear. Although there were no real cases of cyber-terrorism cited within this report, it still highlights the vulnerability within systems and therefore the potential for a cyber-terrorist attack.

Likewise, Jenkins (2004) claims that, according to a recent report, Australia has jumped from 14th to 5th place in a global ranking of the sources of Internet attacks. The report, published by the Internet security company Symantec, shows that during the six months prior to December 2003, Australia accounted for 3% of all non-worm Internet security threats. This suggests that Australia is becoming more vulnerable to cyber attack by highlighting the weaknesses in our information systems.

However, Denning (2005) suggests that vulnerability has been increased due to the fact that there are more Internet users. Unfortunately, some of these users have malicious intent, which highlights the increase of malicious attacks from in the past. For example, there are now more hackers online who are orchestrating cyber-based attacks with financial incentive. These attackers are discovering new vulnerabilities as technology is advancing which still remains a concern for cyber-security.

POSSIBILITY OF A CYBER-TERRORIST ATTACK

Even though Denning (2001) claims cyber-terrorism is a real possibility, she also argues that digital attacks have several drawbacks. Systems are complex, so controlling an attack and achieving a desired level of damage may be harder than using physical weapons. Unless people are killed or badly injured, there is also less drama and emotional appeal.

However, Lewis (2005) claims that cyber-terrorism is possible, but he suggests that attacks on information systems or information warfare will be more likely. He argues that attacks on the integrity of data are more likely to be a threat than a cyber-terrorist attack. For example, if a terrorist was able to scramble the data of a customs database that would affect the response of security forces, this would have devastating effects. Lewis believes that these types of attacks will be more likely and effective than shutting down a power plant.

Furthermore, Quinn (2002) suggests that the most serious scenario facing any computer network is intrusion. Intrusion is the most difficult to accomplish, as a system can only be hacked along pre-existing paths of entry, and consequently hackers spend much of their time trying to be mistaken for someone else. He also claims that once a network has been breached, an intruder is awarded specific access to computers within it. Since infrastructures usually comprise many interconnected networks, getting into one part of the system does not mean it provides access to others. A hacker who compromises the accounts of an electronic plant will not automatically be able to shut down the turbines. Not all networks are interconnected: many organizations, particular government agencies, have unclassified public networks that are accessible from the Internet and a classified network that is not. If these two networks are not connected, there is no way a hacker can move from one system to another.

Similarly, Lewis (2002) argues that whereas many computer networks remain very vulnerable to attack, few critical infrastructures are equally vulnerable. He suggests that computer network vulnerabilities are an increasingly serious business problem, but the threat to national security is overstated. He also claims that critical infrastructure systems are more distributed, diverse, redundant, and self-healing. Cyber-terrorists would need to attack multiple targets simultaneously for a long period of time to create terror, achieve strategic goals, or have any noticeable effect. For most of the critical infrastructures, multiple sustained attacks are not a feasible scenario for terrorist groups. Cyber-attacks are less effective and less disruptive than physical attacks; their one advantage is that they are cheaper and easier to carry out. He also highlights a risk assessment from the Information Assurance Task-Force of the National Security Telecommunications Advisory Committee in the U.S. which claims that physical destruction is still the greatest threat facing the electric power infrastructure, compared with electronic intrusion which represents an emerging, but still relatively minor threat.

Schneier (2003) also claims that cyber-terrorist attacks are very difficult to execute. The software systems controlling Australia's infrastructure are filled with vulnerabilities, but they are generally not the kinds of vulnerabilities that cause catastrophic disruptions. The systems are designed to limit damage that occurs from errors and accidents. He suggests that they have manual overrides that have been proven to work. In 1999, a software bug knocked out a nationwide paging system for one day. Although the results were annoying and engineers spent days or weeks fixing the problem, the effect on the general population was minimal.

He also argues (in Berinato, 2002) that cyber-terrorism is not terrorism in cyberspace because there is no terror there. He distinguishes between the term cyber-terrorism and what he calls "cyberhooliganism," which would include viruses, Web site defacement, and so forth. Schneier claims that terrorism is like lightning. It takes the path of least resistance to its end, and right now it is easier to blow something up than to figure out how to damage it by hacking into and manipulating a computer system.

The Center for Strategic and International Studies points out that a cyber-terrorist cannot cause aircrafts to fly into each other because there are still pilots and air traffic controllers that do not depend on computers. The real risk of cyber-terrorism, however, lies in the potential to manipulate or gain access to valuable information. This is the area of greatest risk for users of computer networks rather than infrastructure attacks, and it is the area of cyber-security that should be emphasized (Unknown, 2003). Nonetheless, organizations are becoming increasingly dependent on technology to carry out business processes. In the future, this may well extend to include aircraft control systems.

FUTURE TRENDS FOR CYBER-TERRORISM

Cyber-terrorism will become a more likely threat to Australia in the future with the development and cross-fertilization of terrorist groups. Innovative terrorist groups will emerge with new cyber tactics, which could include cyber-terrorism as their arsenal. For example, hacking groups could merge within terrorist groups which could possibly create specialist cyber-terrorist groups specialized in the cyber-arena. More importantly, with ICTs continuing to advance, new technologies for terrorist groups are being developed to exploit vulnerabilities in critical infrastructure systems.

New cyber-security strategies and methods need to be developed to protect organizations from cyber-terrorism. These developments need to be orchestrated via a public and private sector partnership/model, and should focus on methods to reduce vulnerability and to improve information security. Terrorism is unfortunately here to stay, and as the physical and virtual worlds converge, cyber-terrorism will become more likely and could even be a preferred method of attack for terrorist groups.

CONCLUSION

Although cyber-terrorism has not yet occurred within the Australian context, it is established theoretically and provides terrorists with new methods to entice terror within the Australian security environment. This article has introduced the concept of cyber-terrorism and suggested possible scenarios for cyber-terrorism, as well as acknowledging vulnerabilities and weakness within Australian computer systems. The future for cyber-terrorism is unknown however; organizations need to be prepared for such attacks as cyber-terrorist groups will emerge with a new arsenal of technological weapons that could lead to death or even destruction of our society and our economy.

REFERENCES

Beggs, C. (2005). Cyber-terrorism: A threat to Australia? *Proceedings of the Information Resources Management Association Conference on Managing Modern Organization with Information Technology,* San Diego, CA.

Berinato, S. (2002). *The truth about cyber-terrorism.* Retrieved June 1, 2004, from http://www.cio.com/archive/031502/truth.html

Collin, B. (2000). *The future of cyber-terrorism.* Retrieved May 28, 2004, from http://afgen.com/terrorism1.html

Denning, D. (2000). *Cyber-terrorism: Testimony before the Special Panel on Terrorism Committee on Armed Services, U.S. House of Representatives.* Retrieved September 29, 2005, from http://www.cs.georgetown.edu/~denning/infosec/cyberterror.html

Denning, D. (2001). *Is cyber terror next?* Retrieved June 1, 2004, from http://www.ssrc.org/sep11/essays/denning.htm

Denning, D. (2005, May 22). Personal Communication.

Donovan, J. (2003). *Parliamentary Joint Committee on the Australian Crime Commission inquiry into cyber-crime.* Retrieved May 11, 2004, from http://www.aph.gov.au/Senate/committee/acc_ctte/cybercrime/submissions/sub13.pdf

ITSEAG (IT Security Expert Advisory Group). (2005). *Supervisory Control and Data Acquisition–SCADA security advice for CEOs.* Retrieved November 7, 2005, from http://www.tisn.gov.au

Janczewski, L., & Colarik, A. (2005). *Managerial guide for handling cyber-terrorism and information warfare.* Hershey, PA: Idea Group Inc.

Jenkins, C. (2004). *Australia jumps Net threat list.* Retrieved June 3, 2004, from http://australianit.news.com/articles/0,7102,8975723%5e16123%5e%5dnbv%5e,00.html

Lawler, J. (2005). *National Security Australia 2005.* Retrieved September 29, 2005, from http://ww.afp.gov.au/afp/page/Publications/Speeches/210205NatSecAust2005.htm

Lemos, R. (2002). *E-terrorism: Safety: Assessing the infrastructure risk.* Retrieved May 20, 2004, from http://news.com.com/2009-1001-954780.html

Lewis, J. (2002). *Assessing the risks of cyber-terrorism, cyber war and other cyber threats.* Retrieved May 28, 2004, from http://www.csis.org/tech/0211_lewis.pdf

Lewis, J. (2005, May 31). Personal Communication.

Quinn, T. (2002). *Opinions: Electro-paranoia.* Retrieved May 18, 2004, from http://www.ists.dartmouth.edu/ISTS/press_release/august29_02.htm

Rattray, J.G. (2000). *The cyber-terrorism threat.* Retrieved May 11, 2004, from http://www.usafa.af.mil/inss/terror/ch5.pdf

Schneier, B. (2003). *The risks of cyber-terrorism.* Retrieved June 1, 2004, from http://www.mail-archive.com/cybercrime-alerts@freelists.org/msg00250.html

Schweitzer, Y. (2003). *The globalization of terror.* New Brunswick, NJ: Transaction.

Shea, D. (2003). *Critical infrastructure: Control systems and the terrorist threat.* Retrieved June 1, 2004, from http://www.fas.org/irp/crs/RL31534.pdf

Sofaer, A. (2000). *Proposal for an international convention on cyber crime and terrorism.* Retrieved June 1, 2004, from http://iis-db.stanford.edu/pubs/11912/sofaergoodman.pdf

Terrorism Awareness and Protection. (2003). *TAP.* Retrieved March 10, 2004, from http://www.pa-aware.org/what-is-terrorism/pdfs/b-2.pdf

Unknown. (2003). *Cyber attacks missing in action.* Retrieved May 28, 2004, from http://www.csis.org/tech/0403_cyberterror.pdf

Warren, M.J. (1999). *Cyber-terrorism: The political evolution of the computer hacker.* Retrieved June 1, 2004, from http://www.cissr.com/whitepapers/cyberterrorism4.pdf

KEY TERMS

Critical Infrastructure: Involves the basic services and commodities that support key sectors within an economy or society.

Cyber-Terrorism: "The use of ICTs to attack and control critical information systems with the intent to cause harm and spread fear to people, or at least with the anticipation of changing domestic, national or international events" (Beggs, 2005, p. 1).

Hacking: Involves a hacker taking a delight in experimenting with system hardware, software, and communications systems in an attempt to gain unauthorized access into a computer system. Unlike the cyber-terrorist, a hacker does not spread fear or cause harm to people, rather he/she demonstrates his/her prowess, as well as revealing the fallibility of computer security (Warren, 1999).

Information Communication Technology (ICT): Technology used to transfer and communicate information between two parties.

Information Warfare: Attacks are planned by nations or by agents. These types of attacks are against information and computer systems, programs, or data that result in enemy losses. The major difference between the two concepts is that cyber-terrorism is about causing fear and harm to anyone in the vicinity such as bystanders, while information warfare has a defined or declared target in a war (Janczewsk & Colarik, 2005).

National Security: Involves human security safety from chronic threats and protection from sudden hurtful disruptions in the patterns of daily life (Lawler, 2005).

Terrorism: A premeditated, politically motivated violence perpetrated against non-combat targets by sub-national groups or clandestine agents, usually intended to influence an audience (Terrorism Awareness and Protection, 2003, p. 2).

Data Security and Chase

Zbigniew W. Ras
University of North Carolina at Charlotte, USA

Seunghyun Im
University of Pittsburgh at Johnstown, USA

INTRODUCTION

This article describes requirements and approaches necessary for ensuring data confidentiality in knowledge discovery systems. Data mining systems should provide knowledge extracted from their data which can be used to identify underlying trends and patterns, but the knowledge should not be used to compromise data confidentiality. Confidentiality for sensitive data is achieved, in general, by hiding them from unauthorized users in conventional database systems (e.g., data encryption and/or access control methods can be considered as data hiding). However, it is not sufficient to hide the confidential data in knowledge discovery systems (KDSs) due to Chase (Dardzinska & Ras, 2003a, 2003c). Chase is a missing value prediction tool enhanced by data mining technologies. For example, if an attribute is incomplete in an information system, we can use Chase to approximate the missing values to make the attribute more complete. It is also used to answer user queries containing non-local attributes (Ras & Joshi, 1997). If attributes in queries are locally unknown, we search for their definitions from KDSs and use the results to replace the non-local part of the query.

The problem of Chase with respect to data confidentiality is that it has the ability to reveal hidden data. Sensitive data may be hidden from an information system, for example, by replacing them with null values. However, any user in the KDS who has access to the knowledge base is able to reconstruct hidden data with Chase by treating them as incomplete or missing elements. For example, in a standalone information system with a partially confidential attribute, knowledge extracted from a non-confidential part can be used to reconstruct hidden (confidential) values (Im & Ras, 2005a). When a system is distributed with autonomous sites, knowledge extracted from local or remote information systems (Im, Ras, & Dardzinska, 2005b) may reveal sensitive data to be protected. Clearly, mechanisms that would protect against these vulnerabilities have to be implemented in order to build a security-aware KDS.

BACKGROUND

Security in KDS has been studied in various disciplines such as cryptography, statistics, and data mining. A well-known security problem in the cryptography area is how to acquire global knowledge in a distributed system while exchanging data securely. In other words, the objective is to extract global knowledge without disclosing any data stored in each local site. Proposed solutions are based primarily on the idea of secure multiparty protocol (Yao, 1996) that ensures each participant cannot learn more than its own input and outcome of a public function. Various authors expanded the idea to build secure data mining systems. Clifton and Kantarcioglou (2002) employed the concept to association rule mining for vertically and horizontally partitioned data. Du and Zhan (2002) and Lindell and Pinkas (2000) used the protocol to build a decision tree. They focused on improving the generic secure multiparty protocol for ID3 algorithm (Quinlan, 1993). All these works have a common drawback in that they require expensive encryption and decryption mechanisms. Considering that real-world systems often contain an extremely large amount of data, performance has to be improved before we apply these algorithms. Another research area of data security in data mining is called perturbation. A dataset is perturbed (e.g., noise addition or data swapping) before its release to the public, to minimize disclosure risk of confidential data while maintaining statistical characteristics (e.g., mean and variable). Muralidhar and Sarathy (2003) provided a theoretical basis for data perturbation in terms of data utilization and disclosure risks. In the

KDD area, protection of sensitive rules with minimum side effects has been discussed by several researchers. Oliveira and Zaiane (2002) suggested a solution to protecting sensitive association rules in the form of a "sanitization process" where protection is achieved by hiding selective patterns from the frequent itemsets. There has been another interesting proposal for hiding sensitive association rules. Saygin, Verykios, and Elmagarmid (2002) introduced an interval of minimum support and confidence value to measure the degree of sensitive rules. The interval is specified by the user, and only the rules within the interval are to be removed. In this article, we focus data security algorithms for distributed knowledge sharing systems. Previous and related works concentrated only on a standalone information system or did not consider knowledge sharing techniques to acquire global knowledge.

CHASE ALGORITHM

Suppose that we have an incomplete information system $S = (X, A, V)$ where X is a finite set of objects, A is a finite set of attributes (functions from X into V or relations over X×V), and V is a finite set of attribute values. An incomplete information system is a generalization of an information system introduced by Pawlak (1991). It is understood by having a set of weighted attribute values as a value of an attribute. In other words, multiple values can be assigned as an attribute value for an object if their weights (ω) are larger than a minimum threshold value (λ).

Chase requires two input parameters to replaces null or missing values: (1) knowledge and (2) existing data in an information system. The main phase of the Chase algorithm for S is the following:

1. Identify all incomplete attribute values in S
2. Extract rules from S describing these incomplete attribute values
3. Incomplete attribute values in S are replaced by values (with a weight) suggested by the rules
4. Steps 1-3 are repeated until a fixed point is reached

More specifically, suppose that a knowledge base $KB = \{(t \to v_c) \in D : c \in In(A)\}$ is a set of all rules extracted from S by $ERID(S, \lambda_1 \lambda_2)$, where $In(A)$ is the set of incomplete attributes in S and λ_1, λ_2 are thresholds for minimum support and minimum confidence, correspondingly. $ERID$ (Dardzinska & Ras, 2003b) is the algorithm for discovering rules from incomplete information systems and used as a part of Chase. Assuming that $Rs(x_i) \subseteq KB$ is the set of rules in which all of the conditional parts of the rules match with the attribute values in $x_i \in S$, and $d(x_i)$ is a null value, there are three cases for value replacements (Dardzinska & Ras, 2003a, 2003c):

1. $Rs(x_i) = \Phi$. $d(x_i)$ cannot be replaced.
2. $Rs(x_i) = \{r_1 = [t_1 \to d_1], r2 = [t_1 \to d_1], ... r_k = [t_k \to d_1]\}$. $d(x_i) = d_1$ because every rule implies a single decision attribute value.
3. $Rs(x_i) = \{r_1 = [t_1 \to d_1], r2 = [t_1 \to d_2], ... r_k = [t_k \to d_k]\}$. Multiple values can be assigned as d.

Clearly, the weight of predicted value is 1 for case 2. For case 3, the weight is calculated based on the confidence and support of rules used for the prediction (Ras & Dardzinska, 2005b). As defined, any predicted value with $\omega > \lambda$ is considered to be valid value.

Chase is an iterative process. An execution of the algorithm generates a new information system, and the execution is repeated until it reaches a state where no additional null value imputation is possible. Figure 1 shows the number of null value imputations at each execution for a sample data set describing the U.S. congressional voting (Hettich & Merz, 1998). In its first run, 163 null values are replaced. In the second run, 10 more attribute values are filled. The execution stops after the third iteration.

SECURITY PROBLEMS

Suppose that an information system S is part of a distributed knowledge discovery system (DKDS). Then, there are two cases in terms of the source of knowledge.

1. Knowledge is extracted from local site S.
2. Knowledge is extracted from remote site $S_i \in DKDS$, for $S_i \neq S$.

We examine confidential data disclosure for these two cases.

Figure 1. Execution of Chase algorithm

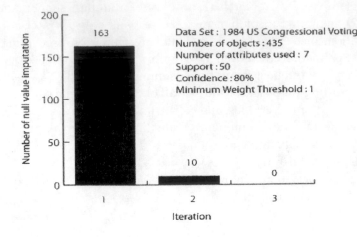

Table 1. Information system S

X	a	b	c	d
x_1	a_1	b_1	c_1	d_3
x_2	a_1	b_2	c_2	d_3
x_3	a_2	b_1	c_2	d_1
x_4	a_2	b_2	c_2	d_1
x_5	a_1	b_1	c_2	d_3
x_6	a_1	b_2	c_1	d_3

Scenario One: Disclosure by Local Knowledge

Consider a simple example that illustrates how locally discovered rules are revealing confidential data. Suppose that we have a set of confidential data $v_{conf} = \{d(x_1), d(x_2), d(x_3), d(x_4)\}$ in S (see Table 1). To protect v_{conf}, we construct $S_d = (X, A, V)$ as shown in Table 2. Now, we extract rules from S_d in terms of d using the remaining non-confidential data, as shown in Table 3. Since $r_1 = a_1 \rightarrow d_3$ is applicable to objects in $\{x_1, x_2\}$ by Chase, the execution returns the confidential data d_3 for x_1 and x_2.

It is possible that predicted values are not equal to the actual values. In general, there are three different cases.

1. $d_{S_d(x)} = d_{S(x)}$ and $w \geq \lambda$

2. $d_{S_d(x)} = d_{S(x)}$ and $w < \lambda$

3. $d_{S_d(x)} \neq d_{S(x)}$.

Clearly, confidential data can be correctly predicted in case 1. We may not need to take any action for case 2 and case 3.

Scenario Two: Disclosure by Distributed Knowledge

The principal of DKDS is that each site develops knowledge independently, and the independent knowledge is used jointly to produce global knowledge (Ras, 1994). The advantage of DKDS is that organizations are able

Table 2. Information system S_d

X	a	b	c	d
x_1	a_1	b_1	c_1	
x_2	a_1	b_2	c_2	
x_3	a_2	b_1	c_2	
x_4	a_2	b_2	c_2	
x_5	a_1	b_1	c_2	d_3
x_6	a_1	b_2	c_1	d_3

Table 3. Rules in KB

rid	rule	support	confidence	Source
r_1	$a_1 \rightarrow d_3$	20%	100%	Local

to share global knowledge without implementing complex data integrations. However, security problems may arise when knowledge is extracted from a remote site, because some of them can be used to reveal confidential data stored in local sites. For example, assume that an attribute d in an information system S (see Table 4) is confidential, and we hide d from S and construct $S_d = (X, A, V)$, where:

1. $a_S(x) = a_{Sd}(x)$, for any $a \in A - \{d\}$, $x \in X$
2. $d_{Sd}(x)$ is undefined, for any $x \in X$

In this scenario, no local rule for d is generated because all attribute values in d are completely hidden. Instead, rules are extracted from remote sites (e.g., r_1, r_2 in Table 5). Now, disclosure risks are similar to those encountered previously. For example, $r_1 = b_1 \rightarrow d_1$ supports objects $\{x_1, x_3\}$, and $r_2 = a_2 \cdot b_2 \rightarrow d_2$ supports object $\{x_4\}$. These confidential values can be reconstructed. In addition, we can see that a local rule $r_3 = c_1 \rightarrow a_1$ can be used to reconstruct a_1, which is involved in confidential value reconstruction by r_2. Therefore, we need to consider both local and remote rules.

Since rules are extracted from different information systems in DKDS, inconsistencies in semantics (if exists) have to be resolved before any null value imputation can be applied (Ras & Dardzinska, 2004a). There are two options:

1. A knowledge base at the local site is kept consistent (all inconsistencies have to be resolved before rules are stored in the knowledge base)
2. A knowledge base at the local site is inconsistent (values of the same attribute used in two rules extracted at different sites may be of different granularity levels and may have different semantics associated with them)

In general, we assume that the information stored in ontology (Guarino, 1995) and, if needed, in inter-ontologies (if they are provided) is sufficient to resolve inconsistencies in semantics of all sites involved in Chase. In other words, any meta-information in distributed information systems is described by one or more ontologies, and the inter-ontology relationships are used as a semantic bridge between autonomous information systems in order to collaborate and understand each other.

PROTECTION METHODS

Minimum Data Loss

Because some degree of data loss is almost inevitable to prevent the data reconstruction by Chase, protection algorithms should limit possible disclosure with the least amount of additional data loss to improve data

Table 4. Information system S_d

X	A	B	C	D
x_1	a_1	b_1	c_1	hidden
x_2	a_1	b_2	c_1	hidden
x_3	a_2	b_1	c_3	hidden
x_4	a_2	b_2	c_2	hidden
x_5	a_3	b_2	c_2	hidden
x_6	a_3	b_2	c_4	hidden

Table 5. Rules in KB

rid	rule	support	confidence	Source
r_1	$b_1 \rightarrow d_1$	20%	100%	Remote
r_2	$a_2 \cdot b_2 \rightarrow d_2$	20%	100%	Remote
r_3	$c_1 \rightarrow a_1$	33%	100%	Local

availability. This task is computationally intensive because Chase often builds up reclusive predictions as shown in the previous section. Several algorithms (Im & Ras, 2005a, 2005b) have been proposed to improve performance based on the discovery of Chase closure.

When we design a protection method, one promising approach is to take advantage of hierarchical attribute structure and replace the exact value with more generalized values at a higher level in the hierarchy (Im et al., 2005c). An information system represented in hierarchical attribute structures is a way to make an information system more flexible. Unlike a single-level attribute system, data collected with different granularity levels can be assigned into an information system with their semantic relations. For example, when the age of a person is recorded, the value can be 20 or *young*. In this system, we may show that a person is 'young' instead of '20 years old' if disclosure of the value 'young' does not compromise the privacy of the person. The advantage of this approach is that users will be able to get more explicit answers for their queries.

Minimum Knowledge Loss

Another aspect of loss to be considered is knowledge loss (in the form of rules). Clearly, when we start hiding data from an information system, some knowledge will be lost because some data have to be hidden or generalized. An important issue in developing a strategy for this problem is to determine the set of significant knowledge, because the notion of significance varies considerably from site to site and is often subjective (Silberschatz & Tuzhilin, 1996). For example, some sites value common sense rules, while others are interested in surprising or actionable rules. One way to measure the significance of rules in an objective way is to check their support and confidence. Clearly, certain rules provide better guidance to the overall trends and patterns of the information system than that of possible rules, and rules with higher support also reflect the overall figure of the information system better.

FUTURE TRENDS

Much work remains in the research and development to provide data security against Chase. For example, there is a trade-off between data security and data availability. As we add more security to confidential data against Chase, we have to hide (or modify) more data from an information system. A method of measuring the trade-off would help knowledge experts and security administrators to determine appropriate security levels for the information system. Another research direction is the study of data security in dynamic information systems. When information has to be updated, confidential data may be revealed by newly discovered rules even if protection has been applied. Integration of ontology into KDS is also important in order to more precisely identify Chase-applicable rules in a distributed knowledge discovery system.

CONCLUSION

The use of Chase may reveal confidential data in an information system. This article discussed disclosure risk and a few different approaches for reducing the risk. In general, additional data and/or knowledge loss is unavoidable to protect confidential data. If the objective is to minimize data loss, we have to hide the minimum set of additional attribute values that will prevent predictions by Chase. If an information system is represented in hierarchical attribute structures, the number of additional data hidings can be further reduced. If the objective is to achieve data confidentiality with minimum knowledge loss, the set of significant knowledge has to be determined before measuring the loss. The objective dimension of the significant rules can be measured by the most commonly used criteria, such as support and confidence of rules.

REFERENCES

Dardzinska, A., & Ras, Z. (2003a). Chasing unknown values in incomplete information systems. *Proceedings of the ICDM '03 Workshop on Foundations and New Directions of Data Mining.*

Dardzinska, A., & Ras, Z. (2003b). On rules discovery from incomplete information systems. *Proceedings of the ICDM '03 Workshop on Foundations and New Directions of Data Mining.*

Dardzinska, A., & Ras, Z. (2003c). Rule-based Chase algorithm for partially incomplete information sys-tems. *Proceedings of the 2nd International Workshop on Active Mining.*

Du, W., & Zhan, Z. (2002). Building decision tree classifier on private data. *Proceedings of the IEEE ICDM Workshop on Privacy, Security and Data Mining.*

Guarino, N., & Giaretta, P. (1995). Ontologies and knowledge bases, towards a terminological clarification. *Towards Very Large Knowledge Bases: Knowledge Building and Knowledge Sharing.*

Hettich, C.B., & Merz, C. (1998). *UCI repository of machine learning databases.*

Im, S., & Ras, Z. (2005a). Ensuring data security against knowledge discovery in distributed information system. *Proceedings of the 10th International Conference on Rough Sets, Fuzzy Sets, Data Mining, and Granular Computing,* Regina, Canada.

Im, S., Ras, Z., & Dardzinska, A. (2005b). Building a security-aware query answering system based on hierarchical data masking. *Proceedings of the ICDM Workshop on Computational Intelligence in Data Mining,* Houston, TX.

Im, S., Ras, Z., & Dardzinska, A. (2005c). SCIKD: Safeguring Classified Information against Knowledge Discovery. *Proceedings of the ICDM Workshop on Foundations of Data Mining,* Houston, TX.

Muralidhar, K., & Sarathy, R. (2003). A theoretical basis for perturbation methods. *Statistics and Computing,* 329-335.

Kantarcioglou, M., & Clifton, C. (2002). Privacy-preserving distributed mining of association rules on horizontally partitioned data. *Proceedings of the ACM SIGMOD Workshop on Research Issues in Data Mining and Knowledge Discovery.*

Lindell, Y., & Pinkas, B. (2000). Privacy preserving data mining. *Proceedings of the 20th Annual International Cryptology Conference on Advances in Cryptology.* London: Springer-Verlag.

Oliveira, S.R.M., & Zaiane, O.R. (2002). Privacy preserving frequent itemset mining. *Proceedings of the IEEE ICDM Workshop on Privacy, Security and Data Mining* (pp. 43-54).

Pawlak, Z. (1991). *Rough sets-theoretical aspects of reasoning about data.* Boston: Kluwer.

D

Quinlan, J.R. (1993). *C4.5: Programs for machine learning.*

Ras, Z. (1994). Dictionaries in a distributed knowledge-based system. *Concurrent engineering: Research and applications.* Pittsburgh, PA: Concurrent Technologies Corporation.

Ras, Z., & Dardzinska, A. (2004a). Ontology based distributed autonomous knowledge systems. *Information Systems International Journal, 29*(1), 47-58.

Ras, Z., & Dardzinska, A. (2004b). Query answering based on collaboration and Chase. *Proceedings of the 6th International Conference on Flexible Query Answering Systems,* Lyon, France.

Ras, Z., & Dardzinska, A. (2005). CHASE-2: Rule based Chase algorithm for information systems of type Lambda. *Proceedings of the 2nd International Workshop on Active Mining,* Maebashi City, Japan.

Ras Z., & Dardzinska, A. (2005b). Data security and null value imputation in distributed information systems. In *Advances in soft computing* (pp. 133-146). Berlin/London: Springer-Verlag.

Ras, Z., & Joshi, S. (1997). Query approximate answering system for an incomplete DKBS. *Fundamenta Informaticae Journal, 30*(3/4), 313-324.

Saygin, Y., Verykios, V., & Elmagarmid, A. (2002). Privacy preserving association rule mining. *Proceedings of the 12th International Workshop on Research Issues in Data Engineering.*

Silberschatz, A., & Tuzhilin, A. (1996). What makes patterns interesting in knowledge discovery systems. *IEEE Transactions on Knowledge and Data Engineering, 8,* 970-974.

Yao, A.C. (1996). How to generate and exchange secrets. *Proceedings of the 27th IEEE Symposium on Foundations of Computer Science.*

KEY TERMS

Chase: A recursive strategy applied to a database V, based on functional dependencies or rules extracted from V, by which a null value or an incomplete value in V is replaced by a new, more complete value.

Distributed Chase: A recursive strategy applied to a database V, based on functional dependencies or rules extracted both from V and other autonomous databases, by which a null value or an incomplete value in V is replaced by a new more complete value. Any differences in semantics among attributes in the involved databases have to be resolved first.

Intelligent Query Answering System: Enhancements of a query-answering system into a sort of intelligent system (capable of being adapted or molded). Such systems should be able to interpret incorrectly posed questions and compose an answer not necessarily reflecting precisely what is directly referred to by a question, but rather reflecting what the intermediary understands to be the intention linked with the question.

Knowledge Base: A collection of rules defined as expressions written in predicate calculus. These rules have a form of association between conjuncts of values of attributes.

Knowledge Discovery System: A set of information systems that is designed to extract and provide patterns and rules hidden from a large quantity of data. The system can be standalone or distributed.

Ontology: An explicit formal specification of how to represent objects, concepts, and other entities that are assumed to exist in some area of interest and relationships holding among them. Systems that share the same ontology are able to communicate about domain of discourse without necessarily operating on a globally shared theory. The system commits to ontology if its observable actions are consistent with the definitions in the ontology.

Semantics: The meaning of expressions written in some language, as opposed to their syntax, which describes how symbols may be combined independently of their meaning.

Defending against Distributed Denial of Service

Yang Xiang
Central Queensland University, Australia

Wanlei Zhou
Deakin University, Australia

WHAT IS THE DDOS ATTACK?

Recently the notorious Distributed Denial of Service (DDoS) attacks made people aware of the importance of providing available data and services securely to users. A DDoS attack is characterized by an explicit attempt from an attacker to prevent legitimate users of a service from using the desired resource (CERT, 2006). For example, in February 2000, many Web sites such as Yahoo, Amazon.com, eBuy, CNN.com, Buy. com, ZDNet, E*Trade, and Excite.com were all subject to total or regional outages by DDoS attacks. In 2002, a massive DDoS attack briefly interrupted Web traffic on nine of the 13 DNS "root" servers that control the Internet (Naraine, 2002). In 2004, a number of DDoS attacks assaulted the credit card processor Authorize. net, the Web infrastructure provider Akamai Systems, the interactive advertising company DoubleClick (left that company's servers temporarily unable to deliver ads to thousands of popular Web sites), and many online gambling sites (Arnfield, 2004). Nowadays, Internet applications face serious security problems caused by DDoS attacks. For example, according to CERT/CC Statistics 1998-2005 (CERT, 2006), computer-based vulnerabilities reported have increased exponentially since 1998. Effective approaches to defeat DDoS attacks are desperately demanded (Cisco, 2001; Gibson, 2002).

Figure 1 shows a hierarchical model of a DDoS attack. The most common attacks involve sending a large number of packets to a destination, thus causing excessive amounts of endpoint, and possibly transit, network bandwidth to be consumed (Householder, Manion, Pesante, Weaver, & Thomas, 2001). The attack usually starts from multiple sources to aim at a single target. Multiple target attacks are less common; however, there is the possibility for attackers to launch such type of attack.

In order to launch a DDoS attack, the attacker first scans millions of machines for vulnerable service and other weaknesses that permit penetrations, then gains access and compromises these machines' so-called handlers, and zombies or slaves. Malicious scripts—such as scanning tools, attack tools, root kits, sniffers, handler and zombie programs, and lists of vulnerable and previously compromised hosts, and so forth—are then installed, and the infected machines can recruit more machines. This propagation phase is quite like computer viruses.

Next the communication channels between the attacker and the handlers, and between the handlers and zombies are established. These control channels are designed to be secret from the public, in order to conceal the activity of the attacker. TCP, UDP, ICMP, or a combination of these protocols is used to perform the communication. Recently, some attack tools exploited the existing infrastructure of Internet Relay Chat (IRC) networks, which are not as easily discovered as earlier versions, because they do not present a new open port that could be found by a scan or audit scheme (Houle & Weaver, 2001).

Staying behind the scenes of attack, the real attacker sends a command to the handlers to initiate a coordinated attack. When the handlers receive the command, they transfer it to the zombies under their control. Upon receiving attack commands, the zombies begin the attack on the victim (Lau, Stuart, & Michael, 2000). The real attacker is trying to hide himself from detection, for example by providing spoofed IP addresses. It makes it difficult to trace the real source of the attacker and filter malicious packets from the legitimate traffic.

Figure 1. A hierarchical model of a DDoS attack

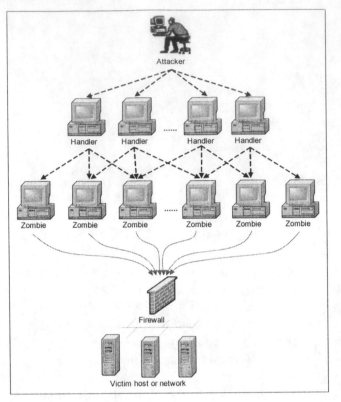

PASSIVE DEFENSE AGAINST DDOS ATTACKS

Passive Defense Cycle

We define passive defense as defense actions taken only after the DDoS attacks are launched. Hence, the target host or network is harmed to some certain extent before the attack source(s) can be located and handled. The traditional passive defense mechanism includes a protect-detect-react cycle (Householder et al., 2001). That is, after attack actions are detected, some reacting steps are taken, such as traffic limiting, blocking, and filtering. This method has advantages over the poor "lesson learned" experience, which responds to the attack only after the accident is over. However, it is far from enough. We need an active defense system with a surveillance-trace-control cycle, which will be presented in detail later in this article.

By deploying the passive defense system, an attack is usually detected by monitoring of inbound traffic volumes and other performance metrics. But ironically, the first signal of attack often comes from the external

customer's report that shows the service is no longer reachable, instead of the alarm of detection system. Then apparently it is too late to protect the victim from the attack.

Current Passive Defense Mechanisms

Passive defense mechanisms can be classified into two categories: one is the detecting mechanism, and the other is the reacting mechanism. The common detection method includes monitoring traffic volumes and source IP addresses, and resource accounting. However, usually simply monitoring the traffic volume cannot tell accurately the real attack, because sometimes Internet flash crowds also cause network congestion (Jung, Krishnamurthy, & Rabinovich, 2002). So this method cannot differentiate legitimate requests or malicious requests. According to the characteristic of IP spoofing techniques of DDoS attack, monitoring source IP addresses is a feasible measure to mitigate the attack.

After detecting the malicious actions of DDoS attacks, the passive defense system turns into reacting

Table 1. Summary of current passive defense mechanisms (Xiang, Zhou, & Chowdhury, 2004a)Technical Report

D

Defense Mechanism		Main Features	Advantages	Disadvantages
Detecting mechanism	Traffic volume monitoring	Detect attacks by monitoring the changes of traffic volume. Detectable features of traffic are required.	• Easy to deploy • Simple and fast algorithm	• Cannot differentiate flash crowd and the real attack • Ineffective when the DDoS attack does not have high traffic volume
	Source IP address monitoring	Detect attacks by monitoring the incoming packets' IP addresses.	• Can differentiate flash crowd and the spoofed IP addresses attack • To some degree it can detect the attack pattern using reflectors	• Invalid when the attacks come from real IP addresses • Less effective for the high traffic volume attacks
	Packet content analysis	Detect attacks by analyzing the features of packet content such as ramp up, spectral content, etc.	• Have good, logical, precise pertinence to some certain attack patterns	• Current coarse granularity analysis introduces errors. • The computation work may be too complex to deploy.
Reacting mechanism	Filtering	Dropping the unwanted packets in routers.	• Can filter out the spoofed IP packets • Potential to defend the highly distributed attacks	• Only effective when it is deployed globally • Cannot defend the attack using real IP addresses
	Congestion control	Regulate the traffic behaviors by analyzing flows. It is a method aiming at solving the congestion problem, instead of radically solving the DDoS problem.	• Can avoid overall network congestion • Not only DDoS can be controlled, but also other misbehaviors can be adjusted	• May have some unfairness effects • Ineffective when the attack is a low-bandwidth attack • Cannot detect the discontinuous attack flows • May block some legitimate traffic
	Replication	Prepare the spare resource for consuming of attacks, which is a typical passive method.	• It can absorb some attack flood and provide resources to legitimate users. • No computation burden	• Expensive installation of spare resources • The resources still may be exhausted by DDoS attacks.

stage. Filtering out the attack traffic stream is one of the simple and straightforward methods to counter DDoS attacks. It relies on an ingenious and sensitive detection system; otherwise it will drop the legitimate packets as well, and in that case it also falls in a denial of service. Reconfiguration (Mirkovic & Reiher, 2004) is another measure to defeat attacks. It changes the topology of the victim or the intermediate network to either add more resource to the victim or to isolate the attack machines.

An apparent feature of the DDoS attacks is network congestion. To alleviate the harm of DDoS attacks, network traffic rate limiting is a popular measure. Congestion control is a mechanism for a router to identify and restrict flows that are using a disproportionate share of bandwidth in times of congestion. The main features, advantages, and disadvantages of current passive defense mechanisms are listed in Table 1.

Limitation of Passive Defense

As we mentioned before, the passive defense mechanism includes a protect-detect-react cycle (Householder et al., 2001). The passive defense system just waits for the possible attacks, then after the attack actions are detected, the reacting steps such as traffic limiting, blocking, filtering, and traceback are taken. For more effective defense, today's passive defense architectures evolve toward those that are distributed and coordinated.

However, most of the current passive systems are not automated and often show high-detection false-positive. In industry, Cisco routers have some features to defend DDoS attacks, such as access lists, access list logging, debug logging, and IP accounting. However, it mainly describes how to detect the attack manually when the router is the ultimate target of Smurf attacks and SYN floods, or used as a Smurf reflector. So the main limitation of a passive defense system is that it can only detect and react after an attack is launched. Other limitations are listed as follows:

- Response is always lagging behind the attack, thus it is not a potent defense method inherently.
- It is hard to deploy an automated and intelligent passive system, because most of the methods rely on manual configuration and other defense actions.
- It cannot effectively avoid network congestion; since the flood has already arrived, congestion control can only be the rescue after the event.
- If attackers continue their attack for a limited time, being traced by the passive system becomes impossible.
- The "ultimate" source may in fact be a compromised computer, but not the real attacker, so passive traceback becomes less effective, because the huge number of sources could overwhelm the trace system.

ACTIVE DEFENSE AGAINST DDOS ATTACKS

Active Defense Cycle

We outline some key methods used before making an effective DDoS attack, for example, scanning, propagation, and communication. If we can block these basic

actions of scanning, propagation, and communication on the early stage of attacks, then we are able to minimize the damage as much as possible. Here we introduce the original idea of an active defense cycle, a surveillance-trace-control cycle.

In this active defense cycle, surveillance is one of the important chains. It is different from the passive monitoring actions, which is just waiting for the attack signals. Surveillance is to deploy distributed sensors throughout the protected network, which proactively surveys the possible attack signatures. Here attack signatures not only include some patterns which can be used to help distinguish malicious packets from normal traffic (Stone, 2000), but also the scanning signatures, propagation patterns, and communication patterns of the masters, agents, and zombies.

Traceback may be an effective method to find the real attacker. Passive traceback usually cannot locate the real attacker, but it detects thousands of attack zombies, which exhausts the capability of a defense system. The aim of active traceback is not just to find the zombies, but to dig out the wire-puller behind the curtain. Current traceback such as logging and packet marking can be applied in active DDoS defense systems.

The control stage of the active defense cycle is to block attack packets not only near the victim side, but also close to the attack source end. Pushback is a cooperative mechanism in which routers can ask adjacent routers to clog an aggregate upstream, in order to punish the source attacker.

Compared with the passive defense cycle, which is a protect-detect-react cycle, the active defense cycle has its features such as surveying in advance, active traceback, and source end control. We also acknowledge that the active defense cycle may not always be suitable for all kinds of DDoS attacks. In some situations, we should still need passive react, to assist the active system, or even degrade or shut down services, although this is the worst-case scenario.

Current Active Defense Mechanisms

Current active defense mechanisms include source end defense, active traceback which is classified into logging traceback and packet marking traceback, and protocol-based defense. In Table 2, the main features, advantages, and disadvantages of each method are analyzed. In the next section, we introduce an example of active DDoS defense.

Table 2. Summary of current active defense mechanisms (Xiang et al., 2004a) Technical Report

Defense Mechanism	Main Features	Advantages	Disadvantages
Source end defense	Both detection components and defeating components are deployed at the source end of attacking.	• Detect DDoS attack as soon as possible • Avoid overall network congestion	• Lack of coordination • Less sensitive to catch the attack signals • Liability problems
Logging traceback	Gather (sample) packets in the network to reconstruct the path of attack traffic	• Can find the source of attack packets even when there is only very a limited number of packets • Can be exploited to trace the real attacker who sends attack commands	• Large storage of logging data • Sometimes needs excessive processing time • Less scalability compared with other traceback methods
Packet marking traceback	Insert traceback data in to IP packet for marking the packet on its way through the various of routers	• No extra storage is needed since it puts a mark in IP header • Can also be used in packet filtering • May be suitable for distributed attacks	• Can only track back in a probabilistic manner • Encounters difficulties when the number of attack sources increases • The system must collect a minimum number of packets to perform the task.
Protocol-based defense	Modify current protocols or propose new protocols in order to solve the current security problems	• If the limitation of current network protocols can be fixed, the DDoS problem can be controlled fundamentally.	• Depends on the wide acceptance and deployment of new protocols

AN EXAMPLE OF ACTIVE DDOS DEFENSE

Overview of DADS

In this section we introduce an example of active DDoS defense. Our work is based on a series of projects on DDoS defense that aim to explore both practical and theoretical models of the Distributed Active Defense System (DADS) at Deakin University (*www.deakin.edu.au/~yxi/dads*). The outcome of our work is first, then we established a novel architecture of DADS that is deployable in a real network environment; second, we developed three refined sub-systems under this architecture including Intrusion Surveillance System (ISS) (Xiang & Zhou, 2006b), Active Traceback System (ATS) (Xiang, Zhou, & Rough, 2004b)FDPM, and Attack Control System (ACS) (Xiang & Zhou, 2006a, 2006c, 2006d)MADF. Finally, we implemented and tested the system in a large-scale simulation network environment with different real-case network topologies and a real local network environment.

Our work is based on an information infrastructure-level protection (Zhou, Xiang, & Shi, 2006) Elsevier, instead of local area network-level or host-level protection, although in some places of the text we also use network to refer to information infrastructure because it is actually a large-scale computer network system as well. Information infrastructures have become mission-critical for governments, companies, institutions, and millions of everyday users. Total stoppage or severe impairment of activity of information infrastructure and the nodes of it can result in causing nationally significant financial loss, damaging the economic well-being of the nation, seriously damaging public confidence on the information infrastructure, threatening life or public health, harming other critical infrastructures such as financial, energy, and transport systems, and threatening public order. It is very important to defense against DDoS attacks on the information infrastructure level. Some researchers argue that in terms of best detection, only the victim can distinguish between attack and legitimate traffic, but not others. However, according to the analysis of key phases of DDoS attacks and passive/active defense cycles, we found that if the protection is only performed by a single victim, it is very difficult to achieve a satisfied defense result. Moreover, we do prove that the attack can be well detected and filtered, not only by the victim, but by deploying a distributed defense system on the information infrastructure level (Xiang, 2006).

System Design

Figure 2 depicts the architecture of the Distributed Active Defense System, which is a scalable distributed architecture with nodes and sensors. We first proposed a similar active defense system in 2004 (Xiang et al., 2004a)Technical Report. This system shields the whole network, finds potential attacks as early as possible, traces sources of attacker, and blocks the attack traffic. Moreover, if DADS is deployed globally throughout the network, it can be exploited to combat against not only DDoS attacks, but also other cyber crimes such as viruses, spam, telecommunication fraud, and system penetration. DADS follows an active defense cycle, the surveillance-traceback-control cycle, which shields the entire network during the whole lifespan of DDoS attacks. A database is used to store security policies, rules, and configurations. With a management server and interface that are in charge of deployment of nodes, administrators can access this system remotely.

The main components in this system are nodes and sensors, which are autonomously managed. Here we define sensor as the lightweight software that performs simple functions. It can also be implemented as hardware that can be plugged into the network. Failure of the nodes or sensors will not affect the operation of the rest of the system, although a full capacity of defense

can be diminished. The sensors hold the promise of facilitating large-scale, real-time data processing in complex environments. The advantages of using sensors are that they are lightweight and low cost, thus are suitable to collect and analyze low-level data that require cooperation, aggregation, and coordination; they are fault-tolerant and running in an ad hoc fashion; and they can actively probe the surrounding environments. Admittedly, sensors themselves are vulnerable to DoS and DDoS attacks (Wood & Stankovic, 2002). Therefore, security should be carefully considered in the design of sensors, which will be one direction of our future work.

As the deployment is concerned, the best approach is the mixture deployment at both source end and victim end. The reason for this deployment is that first, the victim end aggregates the most information of the attack-launching phase of DDoS for the detection and can achieve high-detection, true, positive rates; second, by detecting preliminary attack signatures at source end allows the defense system to mitigate a DDoS attack at its initial phases; third, the source end traffic controlling can protect the network's availability to a maximum degree because not only the victim, but also the rest of network can be free of network flooding.

Innovations of the System

The outcomes of our research can be directly applied in building a dependable and secure national information infrastructure. The research will provide paradigms and standards of protecting critical infrastructures for both industry and academia in information security.

Figure 2. Architecture of DADS

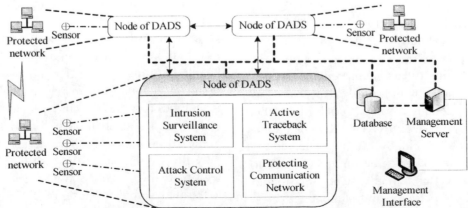

Compared to the traditional passive DDoS defense systems, the important and innovative characteristics of DADS are:

- **Comprehensive Protection:** DADS covers the whole lifespan of DDoS attacks, thus it can defend against attacks as early as possible, find out the real attacker, and control the overall network congestion. Unfortunately, most current defense systems operate at a very late stage of DDoS attacks and cannot respond in a timely manner.

- **Distribution and Interoperability:** DADS is a distributed DDoS defense system. Each node of DADS shares detection signatures with the others, and collaborates in attack control and traceback processes. However, in most current systems, their defense only resides in the sphere of victim end.

- **Low Resource Consumption:** The sensors and nodes of DADS are light- to medium-weight components, whereas other passive defense systems can overly consume resources such as CPU, memory, disk storage, and bandwidth. Additionally, DADS has an overload prevention mechanism to avoid the overload problems when it performs its functions.

- **Autonomy and Survivability:** The node in this architecture can be independently designed, constructed, and managed. Even if one of the nodes fails to perform its functions, the DADS system still can provide dependable protections to the protected networks.

- **Adaptability and Scalability:** Once the communication protocol is formalized, various defense systems can be smoothly integrated into it. In particular, it is also beneficial to defend against other large-scale attacks, such as the serious virus storms.

CONCLUSION AND CHALLENGES

Actually DDoS defense is much like other forms of defense. One extremely similar example is the National Missile Defense (NMD) system (Tsipis, 2000) to shield a country from a ballistic-missile attack. There are four phases of launching a typical intercontinental ballistic missile attack, which include boost phase (start flight), post-boost phase (speed up), mid-course phase (flight out of atmosphere), and re-entry phase (target locked, the missile re-enters atmosphere). The most advantageous time to defend against the missile attack is immediately after its start point—that is, in the first phase—and the most disadvantageous time is the last phase, because the target has been locked and will most likely to be attacked in a very short time.

The research on DDoS defense has grown rapidly in recent years, especially in the last year. Many have developed approaches similar to our innovative idea of distributed active defense, although there is still no other systematic work like we have done. For example, some collaborative approaches (Cai, Hwang, Kwok, Song, & Chen, 2005; Chen & Song, 2005) were proposed to achieve minimum damage caused by DDoS flooding or viruses and prevent the attacks in advance.

We envision the idea of distributed active defense will be widely accepted and more research on it will be carried out in the future. The way of detecting and suppressing the DDoS attack as early as possible and as close to the attacker as possible, but not just waiting and reacting, is much more effective than other traditional approaches. Here we list several potential research directions or topics that could further enhance the research on active DDoS defense:

- Reliable and secure communication is needed between different sub-systems and nodes. In our work, we proposed a Protecting Communication Network (PCN) sub-system to accomplish the task of communication and assumed the communication is perfectly reliable. No message will be lost or captured by the attackers. Although many current technologies will be able to fulfill this task, for example, peer-to-peer overlay networks, more research still needs to be done. The challenges could be the communication overhead, compatibility with existing protocols, and the encryption cost.

- Since our system is to protect the infrastructure level of a network against attacks, most of the functions are router based. The routing operation is a highly visible target that must be shielded against the attacks (Papadimitratos & Haas, 2002). Both internal and external attackers can acquire the topology knowledge by eavesdropping, and actively falsify the routing information and the knowledge of the network state by erasing, meaningfully altering, injecting, and replaying control and routing traffic. Therefore, securing the routers is essential to the robustness of the system because all the work a defense system can do totally relies on the routing infrastructure.

- Next is standardization of DDoS defense technologies: collaborative defense requires standardization. This work seems much more difficult because the assembly of current Internet protocols is still in a loose status, and most of the DDoS defense technologies are still immature. However, since both academia and industry will benefit from the standards, related patents, and affiliated products, all the research work will evolve towards this direction.

REFERENCES

Arnfield, R. (2004). *Credit-card processor hit by DDoS attack.*

Cai, M., Hwang, K., Kwok, Y.-K., Song, S., & Chen, Y. (2005). Collaborative Internet worm containment. *IEEE Security & Privacy, 3*(3), 25-33.

CERT. (2006). *Cert/CC statistics 1988-2005.*

Chen, S., & Song, Q. (2005). Perimeter-based defense against high bandwidth DDoS attacks. *IEEE Transactions on Parallel and Distributed Systems, 16*(6), 526-537.

Cisco. (2001). *Cisco QoS and DDoS engineering issues for adaptive defense network.*

Gibson, S. (2002). *Distributed reflection denial-of-service attacks.*

Houle, K.J., & Weaver, G.M. (2001). *Trends in denial of service attack technology.*

Householder, A., Manion, A., Pesante, L., Weaver, G.M., & Thomas, R. (2001). *Managing the threat of denial-of-service attacks.*

Jung, J., Krishnamurthy, B., & Rabinovich, M. (2002). Flash crowds and denial of service attacks: Characterization and implications for CDNs and Web sites. *Proceedings of the International World Wide Web Conference 2002.*

Lau, F., Stuart, R.H., & Michael, S.H. (2000). Distributed denial of service attacks. *Proceedings of the IEEE International Conference on Systems, Man, and Cybernetics.*

Mirkovic, J., & Reiher, P. (2004). A taxonomy of DDoS attack and DDoS defense mechanisms. *ACM Computer Communications Review, 34*(2), 39-53.

Naraine, R. (2002). *Massive DDoS attack hit DNS root servers.*

Papadimitratos, P., & Haas, Z.J. (2002). Securing the Internet routing infrastructure. *IEEE Communications, 40*(10), 60-68.

Stone, R. (2000). Centertrack: An IP overlay network for tracking DoS floods. *Proceedings of the 9th Usenix Security Symposium.*

Tsipis, K. (2000). Defense mechanisms. *The Sciences, 40*(6), 18-23.

Wood, A.D., & Stankovic, J.A. (2002). Denial of service in sensor networks. *IEEE Computer, 35*(10), 54-62.

Xiang, Y. (2006). *A distributed active defense system against DDoS attacks.*

Xiang, Y., & Zhou, W. (2006a). Classifying DDoS packets in high-speed networks. *International Journal of Computer Science and Network Security, 6*(2B), 107-115.

Xiang, Y., & Zhou, W. (2006b). An intrusion surveillance system to detect IRC-based DDoS attacks. *Proceedings of the International Multi-Conference on Computing in the Global Information Technology.*

Xiang, Y., & Zhou, W. (2006c). Protecting information infrastructure from DDoS attacks by mark-aided distributed filtering (MADF). *International Journal of High Performance Computing and Networking, 4*(3/4).

Xiang, Y., & Zhou, W. (2006d). Protecting Web applications from DDoS attacks by an active distributed defense system. *International Journal of Web Information Systems, 2*(1), 35-42.

Xiang, Y., Zhou, W., & Chowdhury, M. (2004a). *A survey of active and passive defence mechanisms against DDoS attacks.* Technical Report C04/02, School of Information Technology, Deakin University, Australia.

Xiang, Y., Zhou, W., & Rough, J. (2004b). Trace IP packets by flexible deterministic packet marking (FDPM). *Proceedings of the IEEE International Workshop on IP Operations & Management* (IPOM 2004).

Zhou, W., Xiang, Y., & Shi, W. (2006). Distributed defense to protect grid services against distributed denial-of-service attacks. In *Future generation computer systems.* Elsevier.

KEY TERMS

Active Defense Cycle: Active defense can defend against DDoS attacks before the attack is really launched. Active defense cycle is a surveillance-trace-control cycle.

Denial of Service: An attempt to make a computer resource unavailable to its legitimate users.

Distributed Denial of Service: A denial of service launched from multiple attacking sources.

Filtering: Dropping unwanted packets on the network routers.

Internet Relay Chat (IRC): A form of instant communication over the Internet. Mainly designed for group (many-to-many) communication in discussion forums called channels, but also allows one-to-one communication.

Passive Defense Cycle: Passive defense has defense actions that are taken only after the DDoS attacks are launched. A traditional passive defense mechanism includes a protect-detect-react cycle.

Traceback: Finding out the source of IP packets without relying on the Source IP Address field in the IP header.

Digital Divide Implications and Trends

Irene Chen
University of Houston – Downtown, USA

Terry T. Kidd
University of Texas Health Science Center, USA

INTRODUCTION

Within the past decade, a growing body of evidence supports the ever-widening technological gap among members of the society and world, in particular children and the elderly (NTIA, 1995, 1997, 1999). This "digital divide" has become a leading economic and civil rights issue. The digital divide is referred to as a social/political issue encompassing the socio-economic gap between communities that have access to computers, the Internet, and other information technology-related services and those that do not. The term also refers to gaps that exist between groups regarding their ability to use ICTs (information and communications technologies) effectively and the gap between those groups that have access to quality, useful digital content, and those that do not. Disparities in computer and information technology use can be found among individuals in rural, urban, and suburban locations, with the division drawn upon socio-economic lines. This trend indicates that those who have the means only become more information-rich, while those who are poor and of the working class are lagging even further behind. The groups identified who lack access to information and technological resources include: minorities specifically African American and Hispanic Americans, those who are poor and of the working class, individuals of low income, those who possess less than a high school level of education, children of single parents, residents of inner-cities and rural areas, and the elderly (NTIA, 1995, 1997, 1999). Despite, the current literature on this issue and the efforts of state and local government agencies, the current literature indicates that outside of a person's workplace, educational institutions are the second most frequent place where individuals have access to the Internet. Since many in society do not have adequate knowledge of technology to pass onto their society, community, or children, educational institutions will serve as the catalyst for preparing America's community for the age of technology. Since educational institutions are important for information and technology literacy and access, the federal government has arranged for funds to aid America's schools in purchasing technology infrastructure and professional developments. Educators, community development personnel, and technologists should be aware of the government initiative to help bridge the information and technological divide. With this in mind, the aim of this article is to discuss specific aspects of the digital divide and to provide strategies where educator, community development personnel, public policymakers, and the general citizenry can practice helping shrink this growing technology gap.

BACKGROUND

The "digital divide" is the phrase commonly used to describe the gap between those who benefit from new technologies and those who do not—or the digital "haves" and the digital "have-nots." The concept of the digital divide was originally popularized with regard to the disparity in Internet access between rural and urban areas of the United States. More importantly, the term deals with the socio-economic issues relating to information, communication, and technology access. In the mid-1990s, research on digital divide focused on *who is connected.* As we move further into the twenty-first century, the key question to be answered deals with the notion of *who is or who will be served.* The "digital divide" can be further explained in the concept of a division between those with access to new ICTs and those without, from a political, economic, social, and public policy standpoint. The "digital divide" has become a critical issue for countries, one that if left unchecked, threatens to increase economic inequality and sharpen social division.

The National Telecommunications and Information Administration (NTIA) in the U.S. Department of Commerce has released five reports examining this problem, all under the heading "Falling Through the Net" (NTIA, 1995, 1997, 1999, 2000). Each study has reached the same glaring conclusion: the digitally divided are becoming more divided. In its most recent report, the NTIA (1999) writes:

The data reveal that the Digital Divide—the disparities in access to telephones, personal computers (PCs), and the Internet across certain demographic groups—still exists, and in many cases, has widened significantly. The gap for computers and Internet access has generally grown larger by categories of education, income, and race.

Excerpts from 1999 NTIA report include the following information that reveals the disparity in the information, communication, and technology access and utilization in the following:

- income
- education and
- ethnicity, income, and race

Clearly, according to a variety of demographic indicators—income, education, race, and more—there are significant disparities in one's ability to access and use modern technologies. However, regardless of the social, economic, or racial characteristics one attributes to the digital divide, it is clear that there are two distinct groups that have emerged as a result of the information age: the digital "haves" and digital "have-nots," or the information "rich" and the information "poor." By defining the digital divide in these terms, one should draw attention away from the mere concepts of technology infrastructure and training, and move towards a more holistic conceptualization that looks at how new technologies can serve to empower individuals, families, and communities.

Foulger (2002) described the implications of the divide in regarding basic infrastructure, economy, literacy, information, and health:

- **The Basic Infrastructure Divide:** Production and distribution is only one of many areas in which the infrastructures of digital "have-not" countries or societies are an order of magnitude

or more behind digital "have" countries or societies.

- **The Economic Divide:** The countries that are least prepared to bridge the digital divide have average GDPs per capita that are more than an order of magnitude lower than the countries or societies that have already bridged the digital divide.
- **The Literacy Divide:** Literacy rates in some digital "have-not" countries or societies are less than 20%, but even countries that claim literacy rates as high as 100% may supply most citizens with two or three years of education.
- **The Information Divide:** All media, including newspapers, radio, and television, are in short supply in many digital "have-not" countries or societies.
- **The Health and Lifespan Divide:** The countries or societies that are least prepared to bridge the digital divide have average lifespans that are not much longer than might have been expected 2,000 years ago. They also have the highest infant mortality rates and the highest rates of HIV infection.

Barriers to Equity

Lack of access means more than inconvenience—it means lack of educational opportunities. Lack of access is considered challenges for equity and fairness by some population groups. For instance, those learners who are not able to grow up playing and learning with computers can be less comfortable using them and may develop feelings of helplessness or negative beliefs about technology. Many fields in the sciences and mathematics rely on computers or other technology, so when pupils reach upper levels in high school, they may not be comfortable enough to take courses that employ abundant technology. This reluctance in middle and high school, in turn, blocks access to similar classes in college and in the job market later.

Roblyer (2006) indicated that four groups do not enjoy equity regarding computer and technology use in schools, and thus, in time may not reap the benefits of a technology-based economy: pupils from low-income homes and schools, minority pupils, pupils with special needs, and girls. The result of not having equal access can be far-reaching for all of these groups.

In addition, issues of access include physical challenges affecting an individual's potential at equity. Potential students and instructors may have mobility, vision, hearing, speech, learning, and other disabilities that could influence their participation in courses as they are currently designed. Adaptive technologies for low-vision and blind users are available.

Gender bias is another concern when discussing the digital divide. Gender bias, like the literature of the past, may be evident when motivating software excludes girls in its programs. Stereotyping may send a message that women use computers for clerical jobs. Armitage (1993) described that parents may unintentionally contribute to the problem by more frequently locating computers in boys' rooms. Boys tend to spend more time on computers at home than girls, and this use remains level with age for boys but declines for girls. In education, how girls and women relate to technology is often devalued (Schrum & Gisler, 2003). A study conducted by the Pew Internet and American Life Project shows that women are catching up to men in most measures of online life (Fallows, 2005).

Existing studies of differential Internet access and use document inequalities among various segments of the population with particular attention to education, race, gender, age, income, and rural residence. Fulton and Sibley (2003) also laid out the framework of essential components necessary for full opportunity in the digital age. They are:

- access to up-to-date hardware, software, and connectivity
- access to meaningful, high-quality, and culturally responsive content, along with the opportunity to contribute to the knowledge base represented in online content
- access to educators who know how to use digital tools and resources effectively and
- access to systems sustained by leaders with vision and support for change through technology

Global Digital Divide

The global digital divide is a term used to describe "great disparities in opportunity to access the Internet and the information and educational/business opportunities tied to this access...between developed and developing countries" (Lu, 2001, p. 37). Unlike the traditional notion of the "digital divide" between social classes, the "global digital divide" is essentially a geographical division.

The "global digital divide" is distinguishable from the "digital divide." The international geographical context to the digital divide is well documented. The global divide refers to the divergence of Internet access between industrialized and developing societies (Ryder, 2006). This global divide is often described as falling along the so-called "north-south divide" of "northern" wealthier nations and "southern" poorer ones. Researchers noted that developed nations are reaping enormous benefits from the information age, while developing nations are trailing along at a much slower pace. The entry costs to acquire equipment and to set up services are beyond the means of most third-world communities when startup and maintenance costs of technology have to compete with resources needed for essential human survival. The most developed nations of the world (primarily Canada, the United States, Japan, and Western Europe) and the underdeveloped and developing countries (primarily Latin America, Africa, and Southeast Asia) are showing a widening of economic disparity due to different rates of technological progress (Norris, 2002). The poorer are those least likely to benefit from Internet access. Ryder (2006) made the similar observation that concentration of access to ICTs abounds in North America, Europe and the Northern Asia Pacific, while access is restricted in southern regions of the globe, most notably in Africa, rural India, and the southern regions of Asia.

The proposed solutions for developing countries are the provision of efficient communications within and among developing countries, so that citizens can effectively help each other solve their own problems. Sources of widespread public information such as television broadcasting, telephone services, educational institutions, and public libraries are taken for granted in developed countries. In developing countries, however, such infrastructure is seriously deficient, and this cripples the citizens' ability to gather information and coordinate with each other to solve their problems. Through its ability to promote the efficient dissemination of information, the Internet promises a quantum leap in improving internal communications in and among developing countries (Norris, 2002).

FUTURE RESEARCH

In the mid-1990s, research on digital divide focused on *who is connected*. As we move toward the twenty-first century, the key question to be answered deals with the notion of *who is or who will be served* (Ushering in the Second Digital Revolution, n.d.). There has been a series of studies examining the various implications of the digital divide.

The Democratic Divide

Within the online community, the democratic divide signifies the difference between those who do, and do not, use the panoply of digital resources to engage, mobilize, and participate in public life (Ryder, 2006). Research conducted by Norris (2000) focuses on the potential impact of the digital world on the distribution of power and influence in political systems. He pointed to the range of possibilities that the Internet provides for the involvement of ordinary citizens in direct democracy. This can manifest itself as a political chat room, electronic voting, mobilization of virtual communities, and the revitalizing of participation in public affairs. There is an unleashing of new inequalities of power and wealth, reinforcing a deeper division between the information rich and poor, and the activists and the disengaged. In sum, they generally agree that Internet politics will disproportionately benefit the elite (Plüss, n.d.).

The Social Divide

After 10 years of efforts to research the digital divide, researchers also indicate trends in the social aspect of the digital divide in relation to occupation, age, household type, group, and gender. The social divide concerns the gap between information rich and poor in each nation. Norris (2000) observed that "technological opportunities are often highly unevenly distributed, even in nations like Australia, the United States and Sweden at the forefront of the information society." Lower rates of Internet penetration are in the poorer households, among those with limited education and among certain ethnic groups such as the African Americans, Hispanics, rural communities, and among women and girls. Built on the foundation of previous research, Keniston (2003) further distinguishes four social divisions: (1) those who are rich and powerful, and those who are

not; (2) those who speak English and those who do not; (3) those who live in technically well-established regions and those who do not; and (4) those who are technically savvy and those who are not. Ryder (2006) also described the language barrier:

By the year 2000, only 20% of all Web sites in the world were in languages other than English, and most of these were in Japanese, German, French, Spanish, Portuguese, and Chinese. But in the larger regions of Africa, India, and south Asia, less than ten percent of people are English-literate while the rest, more than two billion, speak languages that are sparsely represented on the Web. Because of the language barrier the majority of people in these regions have little use for computers.

CONCLUSION

Digital technology can have an impact on the flow of investment, goods, and global services in the global marketplace. Researchers have also identified the specific interest stakeholders such as national governments, IT corporations, and investor institutions. The big multi-national investment banks in each emerging market are working closely with other commercial stakeholders, national governments, and IT corporations to define opportunities to investors, as technology moves ever closer to the village level.

The initiatives from both federal and private provide the means and methods to narrow this gap. Some researchers simply saw the digital divide issue as "an extension of the 50-year-old political warfare over the concept of 'universal service' in which governments and telephone companies quibbled about who should pay the additional costs of serving isolated rural folks" (Ushering in the Second Digital Revolution, n.d.). Norris (2002) observed that governments in Finland, Germany, Canada, and Sweden have all announced programs to address access inequalities. The British government has established a network of city learning centers and developed a national grid linking all public libraries to the Internet. Norris (2000, 2002) noted that the predominance of the United States on the Internet has gradually declined over time as more and more people have come online elsewhere, although still one-third of all users worldwide are American (106 out of 300 million users). Regionally, e-ASEAN and APEC-Tel, the telecommunications consortium of the Asia Pacific Economic Cooperation network, already provide structure through which government-to-government standards can be set to facilitate wireless diffusion into Asia. The EU prioritized social inclusion as one of the three key objectives when launching the e-Europe Action Plan in Lisbon in March 1999 (Norris, 2000).

Worldwide, the World Bank plays an active role in encouraging public policy integration so that each country has a chance to leap-frog over its competitors, taking skillful advantage of its distinct strengths (Ushering in the Second Digital Revolution, n.d.). The United Nations in 2001 called for "a bridge that spans the digital divide" (Hermida, 2003). The efforts continue until today. The public media also helps to raise public awareness of the issues on digital divide. For example, in the United States, PBS aired in the mid-1990s a whole series of programs that addressed the issues of the digital divide and technology as it affects the classroom, gender, race, and issues at work.

Many non-profit organizations such as the Alliance for Technology Access, Technology Access Foundation, and Black Family Network have been formed to make sure small groups, children, and individuals with disabilities were not left out in the efforts to bridge the digital divide. In the campaign for public awareness and support, corporate-level participants play an important role. Many hi-tech companies devoted products, service, and grants to feedback to the communities.

Public schools and higher education also contribute to the campaign. They team up with communities in the dialogue for solutions. Education and income appears to be among the leading determinants driving the digital divide today. Because these factors vary along racial and ethnic lines, minorities will continue to face a greater digital divide as we move into the next century.

In an effort to close the digital divide gap, members of society can consider the following suggestions:

- learn how technology reaches all parts of the future workforce and household affecting all generations, especially school children;
- demonstrate positive role models in effective uses of technology;
- create and/or expand programs that train and motivate youngsters and adults currently in the workforce to become the technological workforce of tomorrow;

- outline the educational needs in local communities, so students can learn and effectively compete in the future;
- improve existing educational programs to enhance math, science, and technology courses at all levels; and
- recognize the range of resources available locally, nationally, and through industry.

REFERENCES

Armitage, D. (1993). Where are the girls? Increasing female participation in computer, math, and science education. In D. Carey, R. Carey, D.A. Willis, & J. Willis (Eds.), *Technology and teacher education—1993* (pp. 19-24). Charlottesville, VA: Association for the Advancement of Computing in Education.

Fallows, D. (2005). *How women and men use the Internet*. Washington DC: Pew Internet & American Life Project.

Foulger, D. (2002). *Seven bridges over the global digital divide*. Retrieved February 20, 2006, from http://pages. prodigy.net/davis_foulger/articles/digitalDivide.htm

Fox, S. (2005). *Digital division*. Washington, DC: Pew Internet & American Life Project.

Fulton, K., & Sibley, R. (2003). Barriers to digital equity. In G. Solomon, N. Allen, & P. Resta (Eds.), *Toward digital equity: The challenges of bridging the educational digital divide*. Allyn & Bacon/Longman.

Hermida, A. (2003, December). *Nations wrestle with Internet age*. Retrieved February 20, 2006, from http://news.bbc.co.uk/1/hi/technology/3318371.stm

Keniston, K. (2004). Introduction: The four digital divides. In K. Keniston & D. Kumar (Eds.) *IT experience in India*. Delhi: Sage.

Lu, M.T. (2001). Digital divide in developing countries. *Journal of Global Information Technology Management, 4*(3).

NTIA. (1995). *Falling through the Net*. Retrieved February 20, 2006, from http://www.ntia.doc.gov/ntia-home/fallingthru.html

NTIA. (1997). *Falling through the Net II: New data on the digital divide.* Retrieved February 20, 2006, from http://www.ntia.doc.gov/ntiahome/net2/falling.html

NTIA. (1999). *Falling through the Net III: Defining the digital divide.* Retrieved February 20, 2006, from http://www.ntia.doc.gov/ntiahome/digitaldivide/

NTIA. (2000). *Falling through the Net: Toward digital inclusion.* Retrieved March 10, 2006, from http://www.ntia.doc.gov/ntiahome/digitaldivide/

NTIA. (2002). *A nation online: Internet use in America.* Retrieved March 10, 2006, from http://www.ntia.doc.gov/ntiahome/digitaldivide/

NTIA. (2004). *A nation online: Entering the broadband age.* Retrieved March 10, 2006, from http://www.ntia.doc.gov/ntiahome/digitaldivide/

Norris, P. (2000). *The worldwide digital divide: Information poverty, the Internet and development.* Cambridge, MA: Harvard University Press.

Norris, P. (2002). *Digital divide? Civic engagement, information poverty and the Internet in democratic societies.* New York: Cambridge University Press.

Plüss, M. (n.d.). *Geographical dimensions of the digital divide.* Retrieved February 20, 2006, from http://hsc.csu.edu.au/pta/gtansw/publications/itupdate/Digital%20Divide.htm

Roblyer, M.D. (2006). *Integrating educational technology into teaching* (4th ed.). Upper Saddle River, NJ: Merrill, Prentice Hall.

Ryder, M. (2006). *The digital divide.* Retrieved February 20, 2006, from http://carbon.cudenver.edu/~mryder/dig_div_este.html

Shrum, L., & Geisler, S. (2003). Gender issues and considerations. In G. Solomon, N. Allen, & P. Resta (Eds.), *Toward digital equity: The challenges of bridging the educational digital divide.* Allyn & Bacon/Longman.

KEY TERMS

Democratic Divide: Researchers investigate the issues of the democratic divide. Their focus is on the potential impact of the digital world on the distribution of power and influence in political systems.

Digital Divide: The phrase commonly used to describe the gap between those who benefit from new technologies and those who do not—or the digital "haves" and the digital "have-nots."

Global Digital Divide: A term used to describe the great disparities in opportunity to access the Internet and the information and educational/business opportunities tied to this access between developed and developing countries. Unlike the traditional notion of the "digital divide" between social classes, the "global digital divide" is essentially a geographical division.

Social Divide: Concerns the gap between information rich and poor in each nation. After 10 years of efforts on researching the digital divide, researchers indicate trends in the social aspect of the digital divide in relation to occupation, age, household type, group, and gender.

Digital Rights Management Metadata and Standards

Jo Anne Cote
Reginald J. P. Dawson Library, QC, Canada

Eun G. Park
McGill University, Canada

INTRODUCTION

In the digital world, several ways to organize and describe digital rights management (DRM) have been developed to enforce fairness and transparency in business trades. Metadata is beginning to serve this purpose as it attempts to address property rights, licensing, privacy, and confidentiality issues in a manner that ideally renders information or content easily accessible over a variety of platforms (Koenen, 2001). With the rise of security breaches and computer crimes such as identity theft, DRM is increasingly an issue for creators, content owners, purveyors, and consumers of all sorts of digital materials. This article defines what DRM is and explains how it is implemented into description and assessment in practical metadata schemes. DRM components are discussed, in particular those related to identification and rights expression. The two commonly used standards of describing DRM are discussed with Open Mobile Alliance and MPEG-21 (Rosenblatt, 2005). Issues and problems of metadata in DRM are also discussed for future implications.

BACKGROUND: CHARACTERISTICS OF DRM

DRM is a technology used to protect owners of content and services. It was first developed from concerns of security and encryption that protects the content and restricts its distribution and dissemination only to persons who are permitted or who paid (Martin et al., 2002). DRM is a relatively recent development, and only two generations have evolved to date (Rightscom, 2003; Krishna, 2004; Erickson, 2003). The first generation focused on security and encryption that restricted the content and its distribution to only those who paid, and the second generation, in effect, comprises the description, identification, trading, protection, monitoring, and tracking of rights usages over tangible and intangible rights assets including management of rights holder's relationships. Iannella (2001) emphasizes that DRM is the "digital management of rights" and not the "management of digital rights...DRM manages *all* rights, not just those applicable to permissions over digital content" (p. 1).

DRM COMPONENTS

DRM systems need to fulfill a range of functions for a variety of people, which are reflected in the following eight components: (1) secure containers; (2) right expressions; (3) content identification and description systems; (4) identification of people and organizations; (5) authentication of people or organizations; (6) authentication of content; (7) reporting events; and (8) payment systems (Rump, 2003). Secure containers make content inaccessible to users who are not authorized to access the content via cryptographic algorithms such as Data Encryption Standard or Advance Encryption Standard. Some examples include the Multimedia Protection Protocol and Digifile. Rights expressions communicate to whom access to content wrapped in secure containers is permitted. Complex expressions may use the Rights Expression Language (REL) of MPEG-21 (Mulligan & Burstein, 2002). Basic elements of rights expression languages are rights, asset, and party (Guth, 2003, p. 103). Content identification and description systems uniquely identify content (i.e., ISBN, Digital Object Identifier) and associate metadata with content (i.e., Society of Motion Picture and Television Engineers SMPT's Metadata Dictionary, MPEG's Rights Data Dictionary). Identification of people and organizations are expression of association of rights owner claim to content unique identification of consumer in order to limit access to content as required. Authentication of people or organizations involves cryptographic algorithms that may need an agency to issue "passports or certificates" (Trusted Third Party or TTP). Authentication of content persistently associates identifiers and other information with the content (MPEG-21 PAT). These technologies that may be used are watermarking or fingerprinting. Reporting events applies to the business model that allows event-based payments to proceed (i.e., pay-per-view), and it may be also of interest to organizations that collect royalties. Payment systems are enabled through reporting systems.

Metadata is used to manage these components. Metadata is data about data and can be used to describe discrete information objects. Metadata is used to describe content, context, and structure of an object to enhance access to these objects. It can certify the authenticity or degree of completeness of an information object. It is increasingly useful for digital rights management where identification of people or organizations or rights information is essential.

DIGITAL OBJECT IDENTIFIERS

One way to identify content objects in the digital environment is to use the *digital object identifier* (DOI). DOIs are names assigned to any entity for use on digital networks. They are used to provide current information, including where they (or information about them) can be found on the Internet (International DOI Foundation, 2001). DOIs can be applied to any piece of intellectual property (creation), but not to entities such as people and agreements. Information about a digital object may change over time, including where to find it, but its DOI will not change. The DOI system provides a framework for persistent identification, managing intellectual content and metadata, linking customers with content suppliers, facilitating electronic commerce, and enabling automated management of media. DOIs can be used for any form of management of any data, whether commercial or non-commercial. Using DOIs as identifiers makes managing intellectual property in a networked environment much easier and more convenient, and allows the construction of automated services and transactions (International DOI Foundation, 2005). The aim of the DOI data model is to enhance interoperability and improve the quality of administration of DOIs by Registration Agencies (International DOI Foundation, 2005).

Metadata provides the value of identifiers. Without information that may include names, identifiers, descriptions, types, classifications, locations, times, measurements, relationships, or any other kind of information related to a resource, the identified resource is of little use to either humans or computers (International DOI Foundation, 2005). An important component of the Digital Object Identifier system is the data dictionary. DOI has three metadata components for semantic definition that provide well-formed and interoperable metadata to support the use of DOIs: the Kernel Metadata Declaration; indecs Data Dictionary; and Resource Metadata Declaration (International DOI Foundation, 2005).

Rights Data Dictionary

Every rights expression language has a rights vocabulary that identifies the vocabulary permitted as well as its semantics in relation to each REL instance—that is, valid rights expressions (Mulligan & Burstein, 2002).

For example, in an REL instance the print, play or view vocabulary items may be used as granted permissions; the time, location and individual vocabulary items may be used to express a requirement to obtain a permission. Similar vocabulary definitions exist for requirements, constraints, and the context element. The condition element can be expressed by means of the requirements and constraints vocabulary. (Guth, 2003, pp. 104-105)

Rights data dictionaries define vocabulary applicable to every aspect of a digital object. Ideally they are designed to ensure maximum interoperability with existing metadata element sets; the framework allows the terms to be grouped in meaningful ways (DOI Application Profiles) so that certain types of DOIs all behave predictably in an application through association with specified services (International DOI Foundation, 2005). Metadata must use the terms of the appropriate data dictionary to adequately validate DOIs and RELs.

Rights Expression Language

Rights expression languages offer a way to convey use and access rights to assets (or digital objects/digital items). The two main factors in a language are its *syntax,* or the rules of grammar that apply to the vocabulary, and *semantics,* which refers to the meaning of 'valid sentences' in the language (Guth, 2003, p. 103). The grammar can be articulated by the rights language concept and the semantics of rights vocabulary by the rights data dictionary. The basic components of a rights expression language are *rights, asset,* and *party* (Guth, 2003, p. 103). *Rights* indicate expressions that grant usage or access permissions to digital goods or services; permissions specified in more detail are called prerequisites or restrictions. These restrictions can narrow the right granted by time, location, individual, and so forth. *Asset* indicates the digital goods or services to which the rights apply. An asset must be described by a non-ambiguous identifier such as a Digital Object Identifier (Paskin, 2003, p. 29). *Party* means any kind of party (from legal entity to physical person) that has a relationship to the DI (product or service). Examples of parties in contracts are rights holder, author, creator, content provider, consumer, administrator, and so forth.

Guth (2003) depicts "the rights language concept very clearly in her diagram of a subset of the Open Digital Rights Language (ODRL)" (p. 104). In this case, rights comprise the agreement/offer. ODRL identifies prerequisites as *requirements,* restrictions as *constraints,* and also provides for *conditions.* In addition, all rights expression languages in use today are expressed using XML, meaning that the language concept and the data dictionary are defined using XML schemas or data type definitions (DTD) documents (Guth, 2003, p. 109).

TWO METADATA STANDARDS OF DRM

Some of the standards most in use today include the Open Mobile Alliance (OMA) with its Download and DRM standards, and MPEG 21: REL.

Open Mobile Alliance

OMA was formed in June 2002 by nearly 200 companies that include mobile operators, device and network suppliers, information technology companies, and content and service providers; it aims to consolidate all specification activities in the service enabler space. According to Rosenblatt (2005), the OMA was the most successful DRM standards initiative in 2004, with many major European wireless carriers using OMA-compliant content services. OMA has a Content Management Licensing Authority, which is a compliance and licensing body, as well as a data dictionary. The Open Mobile Alliance has adopted subsets of the Open Digital Rights Language (ODRL) for its DRM standards. It offers forward lock, which stops the content from leaving the device thereby avoiding peer-to-peer distribution.

Content delivery in OMA controls content usage with the DRM message containing two objects, the content and a rights object. The rights object defines permissions and constraints for the use of content—for example, permission to play a tune only once, or using the content only for x number of days. Neither content nor the rights object can be forwarded from the target device (Open Mobile Alliance, 2003). Separate Delivery is another aspect of OMA and its purpose is to protect higher value content. It enables "super distribution," which permits the device to forward the content, but not the usage rights. This is achieved by delivering the media and usage rights through separate channels. The content is encrypted into DRM Content Format (DCF) using symmetric encryption. The DCF provides plaintext headers describing content type, encryption algorithm, and other useful information. The rights object holds the symmetric Content Encryption Key (CEK), which is used by the DRM User Agent in the device for decryption.

Using OMA Rights Expression Language (REL) creates the Rights Object. OMA Right Expression Language is a mobile profile of ODRL (Open Digital Rights Language) 1.1 (Open Mobile Alliance, 2003). ODRL is freely available and there are no licensing requirements (Martin, et al., 2002). To date the OMA is not used in the United States wireless services market (Rosenblatt, 2005). OMA is an open organization, and its digital rights management is narrower in scope than MPEG-21 (Rosenblatt, 2005).

MPEG-21

The other widely used DRM standard is MPEG-21, in particular its Rights Expression Language (MPEG REL), Rights Data Dictionary (RDD), and Intellectual Property Management and Protection (IPMP) elements. MPEG stands for the Moving Picture Experts Group; it was established in 1988. The working group for MPEG-21 began in 2000 in an effort to address the need for a multimedia framework. This standard can be expressed in XrML (eXtensible rights Markup Language), which is a general-purpose, XML-based specification grammar for expressing rights and conditions associated with digital content, services, or any digital resource. It was developed by the Xerox Palo Research Center in 1996, and is owned and maintained by ContentGuard (Krishna, 2004; ContentGuard, n.d.). XrML is supported by Microsoft and the Moving Picture Experts Group, and is under patent protection (Conry-Murray, 2004). MPEG-21 is much broader in scope than the ODRL adopted by the OMA, and its expression language XrML has been criticized for being overly complicated and difficult to use (Rosenblatt, 2005). Intellectual Property Management and Protection (IPMP) represents the DRM framework of MPEG-21 and provides consistent rights management to digital items via the mechanisms of MPEG REL and the MPEG Rights Data Dictionary, all realized in XML schema. The REL declares rights, conditions, and obligations in identifying and associating these rights with digital items. REL can declare rights and permissions using the terms defined in the RDD. XrML is a language that comprises three schemas: XrML core schema, XrML standard extension (sx) schema, and XrML content extension (cx) schema. Guth (2003) explains that XML namespace information is essential for the validation of XML instances (pp. 110-111).

The International Organization for Standardization approved MPEG REL in April 2004, as well as other standards bodies including Open eBook Forum, TV Anytime, and Content Reference Forum (Rosenblatt, 2005). Other initiatives in the field of rights expression language include the RealNetworks eXtensible Media Commerce Language (XMCL), and the IEEE Learning Technology Standards Committee (LTSC) Digital Rights Expression Language (DREL), which expresses digital rights in the field of education (Mooney, 2001). Also interesting is OASIS's v1.0 of the eXtensible Access Control Markup Language (XACML), which addresses access control policies for digital goods and services instead of usage rights; the "Rights Grammar" of the e-book industry, which hopes to provide interoperability among DRM systems in this field; and the Creative Commons, which "aims at defining licenses [through a metadata format] to support rights holders to assign the public domain specific rights to their creative works" (Guth, 2003, p. 107).

ISSUES

DRM is a confusing and greatly discussed topic in recent years. There are numerous issues that affect DRM with respect to metadata, for example, economics, ambiguities of identity and granularity, and interoperability.

Economics

Paskin (2003) states that "while there is general recognition of the advantages to create an infrastructure for DRM, there is a misconception that one can have a system at no cost" (p. 34). Assigning identifiers, making them actionable, and then managing their long-term viability (persistence and resolution) involves an unavoidable cost because of the need for human intervention as well as some form of regulation. The cost of adding value like metadata must be paid eventually and, depending on the situation, probably can be done at any stage of the value chain.

Another economic issue relates to the increased security provided by metadata expressing rights, licensing, access conditions, and so forth that may in fact act as a disincentive to legal commerce. Although the industry is striving for flexible licensing rules, a securely DRM-wrapped song is strictly *less* attractive and customers *will* be restricted in their actions if the system is to provide meaningful security. A vendor will probably make more money by selling unprotected objects than protected objects. As a result, the dark net is convenient and costs less than additional security (Biddle, England, Peinado, & Willman, 2002). It ends up, as Biddle et al. (2002) explain, an MP3 file sold on a Web site seems as useful as the version freely acquired from the dark net.

Ambiguities

Ambiguities between identity and sameness, and granularity are also significant. Automated DRM systems are not capable of making inferences from common knowledge or intuitive concepts and must have context clearly delineated. The word "same" can be used to represent similarity or qualitative sameness—it is a comparison of metadata and it is best to consider that, for example, A is the same as B in a defined context where sorted sets of metadata are relevant to particular applications (Paskin, 2003, p. 37). Recognizing granularity is related to identity and refers to the level of content detail identified. Again, this depends on context and may be arbitrary in a digital environment. Relational identification may be required which would add to the size and structure of the codes. If the licensing of an object is larger than the media itself and the attractiveness, viability and cost of such an item is significantly diminished. Resources can be viewed in an infinite number of ways.

Interoperability

At present there is no general standard in DRM and this greatly affects interoperability and information access. According to Hartung (2003), "it is hardly acceptable if an end-user can access content from content provider A only using device X, and content provider B only using device Y, but device Y cannot use content from A" (p. 140). Just like a common system of measurement, standardization in DRM would improve efficiency, cost, and market development. Certain standardizations, however, are beginning to emerge in specific domains, like mobile communications (OMA ODRL). Rightscom views the MPEG's Rights Expression Language as one of the cornerstones of MPEG-21 and feels that it is the key to technical interoperability between proprietary DRM systems (Rightscom, 2003, p. 9; Erickson, 2001). Interoperability is an important issue in DRM and is very relevant if communication between different networks or systems (proprietary or standardized) is to be established and maintained.

FUTURE TRENDS AND CONCLUSION

An examination of digital rights management, particularly how metadata is adopted and implemented, and a review of OMA (ODRL) and MPEG-21 (XrML) reveal various issues that affect future development. The relative newness of DRM and its dynamic evolution reflects the pressure of economics. It is likely that DRM will evolve according to the financial support behind it, market demands, the ease of use for everybody on the value chain, and the acceptance of consumers for e-content regulation that provides a balance between rights holders' interests and fair use access to materials. Problems of ambiguity regarding identification and granularity echo the same problems experienced by many catalogers and indexers. While standards

definitely help, a strong subject knowledge and, in the case of digital objects, knowledge of the user and opportunities (including restrictions) for use also play significant roles. Time interoperability is likely to be improved with increased technological capabilities and eventual growth towards a DRM standard. In the meantime crosswalks may be of use to bridge the standards that do exist today.

REFERENCES

Biddle, P., England, P., Peinado, M., & Willman, B. (2002). The Darknet and the future of content distribution. *Proceedings of the 2002 ACM Workshop on Digital Rights Management,* Washington, DC. Retrieved April 30, 2006, from *crypto.stanford.edu/DRM2002/darknet5.doc*

Conry-Murray, A. (2004). XrML: Defining digital rights. *Network Magazine,* (April 5). Retrieved April 30, 2006, from www.itarchitect.com/showArticle.jhtml?articleID=18900094

ContentGuard. (n.d.). *Extensible Rights Markup Language (XrML) 2.0 specification.* Retrieved April 30, 2006, from www.xrml.org

Dublin Core Metadata Initiative (2005). *DCMI Glossary.* Retrieved April 27, 2007 from http://dublincore.org/documents/usageguide/glossary.shtml#C

Erickson, J.S. (2003). Fair use, DRM, and trusted computing. *Communications of the ACM, 46*(4), 34-39.

Erickson, J.S. (2001). Information objects and rights management: A mediation-based approach to DRM interoperability. *D-Lib Magazine, 7*(4). Retrieved April 30, 2006, from www.dlib.org/dlib/april01/erickson/04erickson.html

Guth, S. (2003). Components of DRM systems: Rights expression languages. In *Digital rights management: Technological, economic, legal and political aspects* (pp. 101-112). Heidelberg, Germany: Springer-Verlag (LNCS 2770).

Hartung, F. (2003). Components of DRM systems: Mobile DRM. In *Digital rights management: Technological, economic, legal and political aspects* (pp. 138-149). Heidelberg, Germany: Springer-Verlag (LNCS 2770).

Iannella, R. (2001). Digital rights management (DRM) architectures. *D-Lib Magazine, 7*(6). Retrieved April 30, 2006, from www.dlib.org/dlib/june01/iannella/06iannella.html

International DOI Foundation. (2001, February). *The DOI handbook version 1.0.0*. Retrieved April 30, 2006, from www.doi.org/handbook_2000

International DOI Foundation. (2005, February 25). *The Digital Object Identifier system*. Retrieved April 30, 2006, from www.doi.org

Koenen, R. (2001, December). *From MPEG-1 to MPEG-21: Creating an interoperable multimedia infrastructure, Organisation Internationale de Normalization, ISO/IEC JTC1/SC29/WG1, coding of moving pictures and audio*. Retrieved April 30, 2006, from www.chiariglione.org/mpeg/from_mpeg-1_to_mpeg-21.htm

Krishna, A. (2004). Protection & security of your digital content with DRM, AIIM. *E-DocMagazine*, (July/August). Retrieved April 30, 2006, from www.edocmagazine.com/archives_articles.asp?ID=28507

Martin, M., Agnew, G., Kuhlman, D.L., McNair, J.H., Rhodes, W.A., & Tipton, R. (2002). Federated digital rights management: A proposed DRM solution for research and education. *D-Lib Magazine, 8*(7/8). Retrieved April 30, 2006, from www.dlib.org/dlib/july02/martin/07martin.html

Mooney, S. (2001). Interoperability: Digital rights management and the emerging e-book environment. *D-Lib Magazine, 7*(1). Retrieved April 30, 2006, from www.dlib.org/dlib/january01/mooney/01mooney.html

Mulligan, D., & Burstein, A. (2002). Implementing copyright limitations in rights expression languages. *Proceedings of the 2002 ACM Workshop on Digital Rights Management*, Washington, DC.

Open Mobile Alliance. (2003, December). Retrieved April 30, 2006, from www.openmobilealliance.org

Paskin, N. (2003). Components of DRM systems: Identification and metadata. In *Digital rights management: Technological, economic, legal and political aspects* (pp. 26-61). Heidelberg, Germany: Springer-Verlag (LNCS 2770).

Rightscom. (2003, July 14). *The MPEG-21 rights expression language: A white paper*. Retrieved April 30, 2006, from www.contentguard.com/whitepapers/MPEG21_REL_whitepaper_Rightscom.pdf

Rosenblatt, B. (2005, January 6). *2004 year in review: DRM standards*. Retrieved April 30, 2006, from www.drmwatch.com/standards/article.php/3455231

Rump, N. (2003). Digital rights management: Technological aspects: Definition, aspects, and overview. In *Digital rights management: Technological, economic, legal and political aspects* (pp. 3-15). Heidelberg, Germany: Springer-Verlag (LNCS 2770).

KEY TERMS

Authentication: The process of identifying an individual usually based on a username and password. Authentication merely ensures that the individual is who he or she claims to be, not the access rights of the individual.

Crosswalk: A key or legend that maps the relationships and equivalencies of different metadata schemes (Dublin Core Metadata Initiative, 2005).

Data Dictionary: A file of explaining the organization of a database, containing a list of all files in the database, the number of records in each file, and the names and types of each field, and so forth.

Digital Rights Management: A system for protecting the copyrights of data circulated via the Internet or other digital media by enabling secure distribution and/or disabling illegal distribution of the data.

Encryption: The translation of data into a secret code to achieve data security. To read an encrypted file, a secret key or password to decrypt is necessary.

Fair Use: A U.S. legal term for uses of content that are considered valid defenses to copyright infringement for criticism or educational purposes. This is often misapplied to the reasonable expectations of consumers that use purchased content on all owned devices.

Identifier: Same as name, usually referring to variable names.

License: A contract that grants a party explicit rights to use intellectual property; or a digital permit containing descriptions of rights that can be applied to one or more pieces of content.

Metadata: Data about data that describes how and when and by whom a particular set of data was collected, and how the data is formatted. Metadata is essential for understanding information stored in data warehouses and in XML-based Web applications.

Right: A legally recognized entitlement to do something to or with content.

Security: A set of techniques for ensuring that data stored in a computer is not used or read by any individuals without authorization.

Dilemmas of Online Identity Theft

Omer Mahmood
Charles Darwin University, Australia

INTRODUCTION

Identity theft is a rapidly growing problem in the electronic environment. It has been recognized as the most widespread and fastest growing crime in the United States (Ahern, 2003). It is of great concern to online users, online service providers, governments, and law enforcement agencies. Identity theft could happen as a result of highly specialized electronic attacks (Sweeney, 2005), bugs in the system of the service providers, physical theft, misplaced paperwork, or just because of human negligence. Victims of identity theft sometimes spend considerable time and money to fix the problem; however their personal loans, mortgage, credit cards, and car loans can still be refused (FTC, 2002). This is shattering the confidence of users, thus creating a distrustful environment while making it very hard for small and medium-sized online service providers to compete with both established online and physically present service providers.

Various governments and law enforcement agencies are introducing tougher data protection and data security breach notification acts. These are increasing the operational costs of small to medium-sized online businesses, so it is becoming hard for them to compete with eBay merchants, and online and international specialized sellers. Even though small and specialized merchants provide better economic benefits to users, they are restricted from materializing business goals due to lack of trust in their infrastructure and absence of privacy policies. In this article a conceptual model is proposed as the future direction to protect the end user from possible online identity theft. The proposed conceptual model is based on the notion of having a trusted third party in between the user and the seller.

IDENTITY THEFT

The Identity Theft and Assumption Act was passed by the U.S. Congress in 1998, making identity theft a federal crime in which one:

Knowingly transfers or uses, without lawful authority, a means of identification of another person with the intent to commit, or aid or abet, any unlawful activity that constitutes a violation of Federal law, or that constitutes a felony under any applicable State or local law. (U.S. Congress, 1998, p. 1)

The above definition by U.S. Congress clearly states that identity theft is directly related to unlawful use and exchange of personal information to commit any illegal activity.

Categories of Identity Theft

Foley and Foley (2005) defined three main categories of identity theft:

- **Financial Identity Theft:** The perpetrator uses the victim's identifying personal information to open accounts such as bank accounts, credit cards, car loans, or even to rent a property.
- **Criminal Identity Theft:** The victim's information is provided to the law enforcement agencies by the criminal instead of his or her own when required.
- **Cloning Identity Theft:** The victim's information is used by the perpetrator to set up a new life. In this case the perpetrator usually uses the victim's information to steal his/her professional establishment or for illegal migration.

Economic Impact

The diverse methods used to steal the identity of a person in an online environment are continuously changing and include use of computer viruses, "worms," keyloggers, and spyware software. Recently, *phishing* and *pharming* attacks have also emerged. Another type of theft includes theft or loss of a company's unencrypted backup tapes, laptops, and documents. For example, on June 2, 2006, Hotels.com warned that due to the stolen laptop of an Ernst & Young employee, some 243,000 customers' names and credit card details (Bouldton, 2006) could have been stolen. Such growing diverse attacking techniques, incidents, and their frequency create new challenges for corporations all around the world who need to invest huge amounts of resources to protect customer information. These information protection techniques require large sums of investment, which most of the small and new merchants cannot afford, thus creating a sense of insecurity among customers. Identity theft-related costs are also prompting governments to introduce new, tougher laws—such as the Database Breach Notification Security Act ("SB1386") of California—which are putting more responsibilities on the shoulders of the corporations while increasing their workload and operational costs. This act enables government agencies to impose a fine of $50,000 or less per day to a company that collects personal information but fails to notify the clients of a data security breach or unauthorized access to their information (Internet News.com, 2005). In order to reestablish users' trust in the electronic environment, a solution is required. Such a solution would enable the users to have full control of their personal information, to apply restrictions on their data, and to store their information in encrypted format at one location rather than it being replicated and distributed to various companies and organizations.

Emerging Business Models

Unified platforms like Amazon and eBay are changing the way we learned to buy goods and services online. Both companies provide access to monetary insurance to their customers and have dispute-resolution policies. Moreover, both companies facilitate the end user to search for a product or service and provide feedback on the sellers, a standard user interface, and optional access to enhanced monetary insurance services like PayPal. Such unified online platforms like eBay and Amazon are making it tougher for the large online merchants to compete with the small specialized merchants who do business under the umbrella of established brands like eBay and Amazon.

However even the e-merchants who operate under the umbrella of established brands like eBay and Amazon have failed to utilize and materialize their business potential, as they usually do not have a privacy or disclosure policy. Moreover they generally do not have the appropriate infrastructure and specialties to

ensure the confidentiality of the data collected from the users. Such vulnerabilities increase the user's perceived privacy and data security risks, and restrict the users to commit online transactions.

Although PayPal assures that it does not share the user's credit card and account details with other parties to ensure the confidentiality of the user's bank and credit card details, the data regarding the e-mail and postal address of the users is shared and stored locally by the small merchants for order processing and record keeping. However, it has been reported repeatedly that information is stolen/lost by the big corporations like PayPal and Time Warner due to inadequate security measures and procedures (Mutton, 2006; Silver, 2005).

Therefore a solution is required that will enable:

1. online users to take full control of their information
2. online users to see the logs of their information access
3. online users to keep their personal data at one secure central repository, so that it is easy for them to maintain and update and
4. online merchants to save in terms of operational costs, as they will not be required to set up and maintain secure database servers in order to store customers' personal information

On the other hand the solution should enable the merchants and service providers to access the information from a secure repository:

1. after getting the user's explicit permission
2. for the permitted time period and
3. for a user-specified number of times

Such a solution will enhance the user's level of trust and confidence in committing online transactions, as they will know that their private information is not stored at various locations and they are not likely to suffer due to the negligence of others.

PROPOSED MODEL ARCHITECTURE

Technical models have been proposed to tackle the problem of identity theft by combating certain types of data theft techniques such as phishing and pharming attacks. In combating phishing and pharming attacks, it has been generally proposed to use some form of browser plugin to check the authenticity of the Web site before the users provide their personal information, such as Earthlink Toolbar (Earthlink, 2006), Microsoft Phishing Filter (IEBlog, 2005), Three Phase Checking Plugin (Mahmood, 2006a), and Custom Plugin (Mahmood, 2006b). The RSA Site-To-User Authentication model is based on customization of a Web interface for each user (RSA, 2006). However such models only target limited types of techniques used by the perpetrator to steal a person's identity. They do not enable the users to see their personal information access logs, to have full control over their personal information, and to make the online merchants conform to a user's enforced privacy and disclosure policies; most importantly, they do not provide a single storage or access point for the user's personal information. Besides the above shortcomings the suggested models fail to work in the cases of physical theft, misplaced paperwork, and human negligence.

To overcome the above mentioned limitations, a conceptual model is proposed here based on the concept of having a trusted third party in between the user and the seller, so as to protect the end user from possible online identity theft. Technical implementation details of the model are not covered in this chapter, as they can be implemented by using a variety of technologies.

The user opens an account with the trusted third party where the user's private information related to shipping and payment details are stored in an encrypted format. Upon the user's registration, the trusted third party provides the user with a privacy and disclosure policy. This policy will restrict the online merchants from storing the customer information, using it, or distributing it. This policy will also minimize the misuse of personal information due to human negligence and physical theft. Along with the privacy policy, the trusted third party also gives a list of trusted registered online merchants who already implement and adhere to the no local information storage and distribution policy. This list ensures that the users will not have to exchange privacy policies with existing registered merchants for each new transaction, resulting in better adoption of the proposed model.

Figure 1. Conceptual interaction model

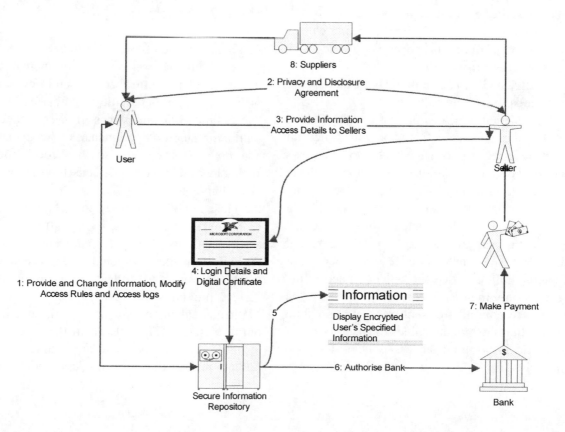

When the user makes a purchase with any small or medium-sized online merchant who is not currently registered with the trusted third party, the user provides the privacy and disclosure policy, which restricts the merchants from storing and distributing the user's personal information, thus ensuring the user's privacy even in a case of data security breach at the seller's end. The sellers are likely to sign and accept the policy as it dramatically reduces their financial costs, since now they do not need highly secure systems to store customer information. Moreover, the sellers can also use this opportunity to register with the trusted third party as a trusted online merchant.

After agreeing to comply with the provided privacy and disclosure policy, the seller gives his public key to the user. By using the seller's details, the user creates an access policy on the trusted third party's secure server which enables the seller to access the user's accessible details. This information is only made available to the seller as per the user's defined access rules, which enable the user to specify the number of times information can be accessed, the total duration for which information will be made available, and the maximum amount the seller can charge from the user's account. The server, in response to a new access policy, creates special login details for the transaction. The user sends the seller the generated details, which the seller uses to access the information and charge the user's account. In this proposed model the seller never gets the account or credit card details of the user, as the user's trusted party automatically transfers the specified funds to the seller's account.

All the information transmitted from the trusted party to the seller is encrypted, and only the seller can decrypt it by using his secure private key. The logs and records of each information access, along with the details of the order and transaction, are stored by the trusted party, in case the user or the seller needs it in the future. Once the order is successfully processed and shipped, the user can always go back to the trusted third party Web site to terminate the seller's access, or to change the policy so that the seller can access the user's e-mail only in order to contact him. In case the user expects to commit frequent transactions with a particular seller, the model enables the user to generate automatic information access policies for each specified seller.

In the case of a security breach, the stored information will be of no use to the hacker or culprit due to following factors:

- The information is only made available to the seller for a specified period of time.
- The information is only made available to the seller a specified number of times.
- The seller can notify the user or the trusted third party, which will block the seller's access, if the seller's login and access details are stolen.
- By default all the information is encrypted and the hacker will need the seller's private key to decrypt the information.

This model also helps the users to manage their information; in the case of a change of address, for example, the user will only be required to make changes at one place. However the proposed solution would fail to work if an employee of the online merchant or the system implemented does not properly comply with the privacy and disclosure policy. For example if the online merchants store the users' personal information locally, then the proposed solution would fail to work.

FUTURE TRENDS

As a result of the escalating number of identity theft cases, trust in the electronic environment has become fundamental for future growth and development of e-commerce. Palmer, Bailey, and Faraj (2000) argue that building consumer trust in Web retailers is essential for the growth of business-to-consumer (B2C) e-commerce. According to the World Information Technology and Services Alliance International Survey of E-Commerce 2000 (WISTA, 2000), trust (26%) is the most important barrier to electronic commerce in 27 surveyed countries. In the future, online users are likely to use their personal "Friend of a Friend" (FOAF) networks—which will represent the user's social network—to collect information on online service providers before they commit transactions. Mathematical models are also emerging in the area of online trust to help users evaluate their subjective trust levels for each transaction. For example, Mahmood (2006c) proposed a mathematical model that can be used by online users to evaluate their respective levels of trust on each transaction and compare them. Online merchants are also likely to make use of trust-enhancing models to increase the end user's general level of trust in order to attract more market. For example, Mahmood (2006d) proposed a conceptual model that can be used by online merchants to recognize and target specific characteristics of their Web site which play a major role in determining the user's level of trust.

Web 2.0 is defined as a network platform, enabling the utilization of distributed services such as social networking and communication tools. It is also referred to as the architecture of participation. Web 2.0 is not all about new technology. Rather it is more related to how the technology is used to link the physical world with the electronic one within the social network domain while empowering and facilitating people to contribute more. Web 2.0 is not only a set of technologies; it also has properties which aim for social integration, user-contributed content, user-generated metadata, transparent business processes, and decentralized and participatory products and processes (Gartner, 2006a). Within Web 2.0, Social Network Analysis (SNA) is considered to be of high impact, while Collective Intelligence has been rated transformational (Gartner, 2006b). SNA targets to increase the revenues or save the costs of enterprises by adopting new ways to deploy and engineer Web applications. In relation to SNA, Collective Intelligence is an approach used to produce intelligent contents such as documents and decisions that result from individuals working together with no centralized governing body. The above notions clearly suggest that in the future the Web system will be designed and developed to collect and use information from people's personal social networks in order to assist the users (both consumers and service providers) to make rational decisions. Such a system will rely heavily on Web-based social computing, primarily on SNA and collective intelligence, by linking physical and electronic worlds. Social computing Web systems are likely to contain components that support and represent online social constructs such as online identity, online reputation, and online trust. Similar to the current physical environment, in the future Web systems' trust will be the main synthetic force. In the future, trust-based online merchant independent rating systems, trusted peer-to-peer networks, and personal electronic social networks will play a major role in reshaping the way we conduct business in the electronic environment.

CONCLUSION

Identity theft is widespread and is the fastest growing crime in the developed world; it impacts both electronic businesses and online users. As a result, governments are introducing new laws to protect the online user's identity. This article summarizes the implications of identity theft and the laws introduced by the governments to protect online users' identity for both the electronic merchants and the online users. Common techniques used by the perpetrator for identity theft and the measures taken by electronic businesses to enhance online user's trust in the electronic environment are also covered in the article. It is suggested that in future, the trust-based electronic service provider's comparison, ranking, and rating models will play a major role in the area of electronic commerce. Users' personal, trusted, peer-to-peer networks and communities will also have a major impact on online users' behaviors. The proposed conceptual model promises to reduce the chances of identity theft by providing full control to the user on his/her information, and by keeping the user's information in an encrypted form at one secure location. The proposed conceptual pattern is also designed to assist online merchants in reducing their operational costs and enhance the user's level of trust in online service providers by giving them full control over their personal information.

REFERENCES

Ahern, R. (2003). Managing credit and application fraud risks in a volatile economy: Technology is key. *Business Credit, 105,* 54-55.

Bouldton, C. (2006). *Hotels.com warns customers on data theft.* Retrieved August 2, 2006, from http://www.internetnews.com/bus-news/article.php/3610801

Earthlink. (2006). *Earthlink Toolbar.* Retrieved June 26, 2006, from http://www.earthlink.net/software/free/toolbar/

Foley, L., & Foley, J. (2005). *Victim resources: Victim guide*. Retrieved August 30, 2006, from http://www.idtheftcenter.org/vg100a.shtml

Frank, M. (2000). *Identity theft horror stories*. Accessed August 30, 2006, from http://www.consumer-action.org/English/CANews/2000_Spring_IdentityTheft.php

Gartner. (2006a). *Gartner says Web 2.0 offers many opportunities for growth, but few enterprises will immediately adopt all aspects necessary for significant business impact*. Retrieved from September 18, 2006, from http://www.gartner.com/press_releases/asset_152253_11.html

Gartner. (2006b). *Gartner's 2006 emerging technologies hype cycle highlights key technology themes*. Retrieved September 18, 2006, from http://www.gartner.com/it/page.jsp?id=495475

IEBlog. (2005, September). *Phishing filter in IE7*. Retrieved September 16, 2006, from http://blogs.msdn.com/ie/archive/2005/09/09/463204.aspx

Internet News.com. (2005). *Senate takes up data security law*. Retrieved April 12, 2005, from www.internetnews.com/bus-news/article.php/3497161

Mahmood, O. (2006a, June 14-18). Three phase checking against phishing and pharming attacks. *Proceedings of the 11th Annual Conference of Asia Pacific Decision Sciences Institute* (APDSI) (pp. 209-213), Hong Kong.

Mahmood, O. (2006b). Custom plugin—a solution to phishing and pharming attacks. *Proceedings of the 2006 World Congress in Computer Science, Computer Engineering, and Applied Computing (SAM'06)* (pp. 32-38), Las Vegas, NV.

Mahmood, O. (2006c). Online initial trust evaluation and comparison in electronic environment. *Proceedings of the IADIS International Conference e-Commerce 2006*, Barcelona, Spain.

Mahmood, O. (2006d). Trust: From sociology to electronic environment. *Journal of Information Technology Impact, 6*(3), 119-128.

Mutton, P. (2006, June 16). *PayPal security flaw allows identity theft*. Retrieved September 15, 2006, from http://news.netcraft.com/archives/2006/06/16/paypal_security_flaw_allows_identity_theft.html

Palmer, J.W., Bailey, J.P., & Faraj, S. (2000). The role of intermediaries in the development of trust on the WWW: The use and prominence of trusted third parties and privacy statements. *Journal of Computer Mediated Communication, 5*(3).

RSA. (2006). *RSA adaptive authentication*. Retrieved September 16, 2006, from http://www.rsasecurity.com/node.asp?id=3018

Silver, C. (2005, May 3). *Time Warner employee data missing: Information on 600,000 current, ex-workers lost by storage firm; Secret Service investigating*. Retrieved September 15, 2006, from http://money.cnn.com/2005/05/02/news/fortune500/security_timewarner/index.htm

Sweeney, L. (2005). AI technologies to defeat identity theft vulnerabilities. *Proceedings of the AAAI Spring Symposium, AI Technologies for Homeland Security 2005*. Retrieved August 30, 2006, from http://privacy.cs.cmu.edu/dataprivacy/projects/idangel/idangel1.pdf

United States Federal Trade Commission (FTC). (2002). *Report on Identity theft, victim complaint data: Figures and trends January-December 2001*. Washington, DC: Federal Printing Office.

U.S. Congress. (1998). *Identity Theft and Assumption Deterrence Act of 1998*. Retrieved August 18, 2006, from http://www.ftc.gov/os/statutes/itada/itadact.htm

WISTA (World Information Technology and Services Alliance). (2000). *International survey of e-commerce 2000*. Retrieved September 16, 2006, from http://www.witsa.org/papers/EComSurv.pdf

KEY TERMS

Cloning Identity Theft: The victim's information is used by the perpetrator to setup a new life, for illegal migration, or to avoid arrest. It is also an open door to terrorists.

Criminal Identity Theft: The victim's information, such as a driver's license number, is provided to the law enforcement agencies by the perpetrator instead of his or her own, when required.

Financial Identity Theft: The perpetrator unlawfully acquires the victim's identifying personal information to open accounts such as bank accounts, credit cards, car loans, or even to rent a property.

Identity Fraud: Someone who is not authorized to use an individual's existing credit card or account, who uses it illegally to make purchases. Identity fraud does not include opening of new accounts or identity cloning of the victim.

Identity Theft: Someone unlawfully uses the personal information—for example, name, date of birth, address, and license number—to apply for new accounts by impersonating the victim, or to commit or aid to commit any unlawful activity, for example for illegal immigration, terrorism, or espionage.

Pharming: The hacker acquires the Domain Name Server (DNS) or attacks users' browsers to redirect the users to a different IP address, where the fake or spoof Web site is hosted, with an intention to get users' personal details.

Phishing: An act of deceptively collecting personal information, mostly by using e-mails, commonly known as hoax e-mails, or instant messaging, or over the phone to commit identity theft or identity fraud. In phishing the perpetrator portrays a trustworthy business or person in communication, with an attempt to fraudulently acquire a victim's sensitive information.

Document Security in the Ancient World

Christopher H. Walker
The Pennsylvania State University, USA

INTRODUCTION

While issues of encryption, firewalls, surveillance technologies, and cyber terrorism occupy the day-to-day thoughts of contemporary practitioners on the frontiers of information science, the essential problems they face are old, not new. The concept of document security goes back to some of the earliest eras from which writing survives. Testimony to the efforts of information professionals confronting security issues in the ancient world can be found in business, government, family, and temple contexts.

Even the name of one of today's most persistent (and pesky) computer problems, the Trojan horse, reminds us that the challenges of today perpetuate, in new forms, problems faced by our predecessors in the distant past. We can even, at least sporadically, trace shifts of usage in response to changes in the technology of writing from clay tablet to papyrus, wax codex, and parchment. These changes may remind us of the way new formats and technology in our own time have made us scramble to keep up with the ingenuity of hackers, or the danger of losing information left behind, stored on obsolete diskettes, coded in computer languages no one studies any longer, or stranded in unsupported software.

BACKGROUND AND LITERATURE REVIEW

It is not surprising that the topic of document security in Antiquity has not been specifically addressed in print before. Research on information services in the ancient world requires gleaning references from broad reading in archeology and cultural history. Pioneering studies on the origins of indexing (Witty, 1972), classification (Berthold, 1938), shelf lists and document inventory control (Weitemeyer, 1956), and the development of the library catalog (Dalby, 1986) demonstrate that it is possible to pull together an overview of how the ancient world approached an aspect of information service. Such inquiries shed light on contemporary problems by providing a historical perspective on the information challenges of today.

The Document's Lifecycle: Security Measures Taken in the Ancient World

The life of a document occurs in several stages, each presenting challenges for preserving the integrity of its content, establishing its authenticity, limiting access to it, preventing interception by unauthorized readers, and secure storage.

Accurate Transmission of the Original Message

The invention of writing solved part of the initial problem. A brief verbal message can be memorized and repeated verbatim by a courier; but if it is lengthy, complicated, or carefully worded (as military or diplomatic instructions frequently must be), it is better to write it down.

But it must be recorded accurately. Sasson (2002, p. 211) cites a cuneiform tablet from the Old Babylonian city of Mari (modern Tel Hariri, on the Euphrates), circa 1850-1800 BCE. The text of the tablet demonstrates that it must have been a frequent practice for scribes to read back what they had transcribed to the official dictating, to verify that the gist of the communication was accurately conveyed by the writing. In this particular letter, the sender excuses a previous miscommunication by alleging that this checkpoint had been skipped by the scribe who recorded his previous report.

Codes, Secret Writing, and the Use of Official Languages

In ancient Mesopotamia most people other than scribes were illiterate, so the use of code was not generally necessary. But by Roman times simple substitution ciphers were used to protect military and government dispatches. Suetonius mentions them in his *Lives* of both Julius and Augustus Caesar. In fact, codes were common enough among the Romans that the grammarian Probus wrote a treatise on the subject. The book itself does not survive, but Aulus Gellius (17.9., 1-5) alludes to it.

Alternative methods of transmitting a message through enemy lines were used in ancient Greece. Plutarch describes (Life of Lysander, 19) a Spartan system. Messages were written on a parchment strip wound around a cylindrical tool called a *scytale*. The writing crossed the edges of the parchment, so the individual letters were broken and incomplete. The strip of parchment could then be sent to a commander who had a *scytale* of the same diameter, and he could read it when it had been wound back around his duplicate cylinder.

Herodotus (5.35) narrates the stratagem of Histaeus, who sent a message to a co-conspirator, tattooed on the scalp of a slave. His correspondent had to shave the slave's head to read it, surely the most curious instance of *steganography* in the ancient world.

Compiling information from documents that are not all presented in a standardized format is tedious. Writers for modern academic journals may sometimes chafe under the limitations imposed by editorial style sheets; they can take comfort from the standardization imposed on accounting documents in the expanding Mesopotamian empire of the Sargonid dynasty (c. 2380-2167 BCE) (Foster, 1986). No doubt this demand for standardization annoyed local accounting clerks required to change their record-keeping procedures just as much as office workers grumble when technology changes today. Parpola (1981) notes that 15 centuries after the era of Sargon the Great, ancient clerks were still grumbling. Parpola speculates that security policy may have played a role in a reply sent by Sargon II (c. 721-705 BCE) to Sin-iddin of Ur, insisting that the latter continue to make his reports in Akkadian, on clay tablets, rather than in Aramaic, on scrolls. Parpola suggests that classified or sensitive documents might have been considered safer if transmitted in the official language (Akkadian), rather than the vernacular spoken in the empire's southeastern provinces; but the innate conservatism of hidebound bureaucracies may suffice to explain the resistance.

Verification that the Document is Authentic

If it is to carry the full weight of the writer's authority, a document must bear signs of authentication. The usual practice, from the ancient world right up through the early modern era, was to add a seal imprinted with words or symbols identifying the sender (or sometimes, the witnesses to a legal document). A person's seal might be as well known to his or her correspondents as a signature is today. Vallon (1997, p. 173) cites a group of documents found at Persepolis that bear the seal of a government functionary called Parnakka. Under the seal on each, he's written a line saying that he's lost his old seal, and this is the new one he's using as a replacement.

A commentary summarizing case law during the Sassanid era in Persia (223-651 CE) sheds light on the extent to which, by late antiquity, the value of seals as legal evidence was scrupulously studied. One case turned on the testimony of a defendant in a civil lawsuit who repudiated the seal alleged to be his on a disputed contract. He testified that it was not the seal he was using at the time of the transaction and claimed, in effect, that the contract was forged. The court examined documents he had sealed at various dates, and found for the plaintiff (Macuch, 1997, p. 80). The same Sassanid digest specifies the circumstances under which an official who is custodian of a departmental seal must surrender it to his successor (Macuch, 1997, p. 84).

Collon (1990, p. 27) cites evidence from business archives found at the ancient city of Nuzi in northern Mesopotamia (15th century BCE), where the seals of thousands of different individuals have been found on documents and *bullae*. On a cuneiform tablet, the seal might be impressed into the clay, below or beside the slow-drying text. Documents written on pliable materials such as papyrus, parchment, or leather might be folded or rolled and closed with a ball or *bulla* of wax or clay, which was then impressed with the sender's seal.

At the capital of the Hittite Empire, Hattusa (modern Boğazköy, in Turkey), excavators found a roomful of more than 3,000 embossed clay fragments that had been used as document seals. The physical documents, written on papyrus or leather, had perished; but the sturdier seals remained. Neve (1991) documented these finds in a series of reports from the site. The report on the campaign of 1990 includes photographs illustrating the range and size of the artifacts and the beautiful detail of the carved stamps. Similar evidence has been found from ancient Crete (Barber, 1974, p. 228). Demonstrating the continuity of this use, a thousand years after the Hittites, a room in the ruins of Sennacherib's palace at Nineveh (c. 700 BCE) contained a similar cache of surviving seals left from documents written on perishable materials that had turned to dust (Veenhof, 1986, pp. 2-3). At Uruk (modern Warka), capital of the Seleucid empire (c. 323-68 BCE), clay rings remain; the rolls of papyrus documents they secured disintegrated long ago (Veenhof, 1986, p. 3).

Safe Transmission of Documents

If a document is to be sent over a distance, it may need to be encased in an envelope to protect it from prying eyes, or to preserve the text from tampering (Max, 1994, p. 24). Commercial records from ancient Assyria were sometimes recorded on cuneiform tablets that were dried and then imbedded in a clay envelope that protected and concealed the contents. Excavators have found these at many ancient sites. Examples dated to around 1900-1800 BCE survive from a trade center called Kārum Kanesh, in Asia Minor (modern Kültepe) (Veenhof, 2003). Parrot (1959, p. 213) gives a splendid illustration of a clay tablet still partially concealed by a half-opened clay envelope bearing the seal impression of the sender.

Some ancient cultures employed painted or wax-coated wooden boards as a writing surface. Wax takes an impression much like wet clay does and is ideal for memoranda or other transitory writing, because it can be warmed or smoothed and used again. Like wet clay, however, it is also in danger of being smudged. Wood is more perishable than dried or baked clay, so wooden tablets survive from Antiquity in smaller numbers. Bonfante (1990, p. 341) describes wax-coated tablets used among the Etruscans that were hinged in pairs or diptychs, so they could be closed, protecting the writing from view and the wax from being worn or damaged. Hinged wooden tablets of this kind—sometimes with more than two leaves—have been found elsewhere with a little wooden peg in the center, intended to keep the wax from sticking together when closed. White-

horne (1996, p. 244) discusses evidence that even in provincial western Egypt, it was possible to order one made that way.

Safe transmission also requires that a letter be addressed correctly. Sasson (2002, footnotes 222-223) translates from an unpublished letter called to his attention by Charpin in which a recipient complains of receiving a tablet that bore an impressed seal, but no address on the *bulla*. Charpin (1995, p. 49) publishes another letter found at Mari that was opened by mistake. The scribe realized it had been misdelivered and did not read it aloud to the incorrect recipient, forwarding it instead (with his explanation) to the addressee.

Protecting Information from Interception

We have noticed above some techniques that were used by the ancient Greeks to get a message through enemy lines in war time. Max (1994, p. 29) mentions intelligence reports found in the neo-Assyrian royal archives at Calah and at Nineveh (8th century BCE). Spies posted abroad wrote them on small round tablets, which were then compiled into larger intelligence digests by officials at the seat of government. It is tempting to infer that the small format of these reports made them easier to conceal on a courier's person.

Guarantees for the Integrity of Valuable Documents

Documents conveying information of value to multiple parties such as accounting records of large loans, property deeds, or the verdicts of lawsuits might need to be issued in multiple copies (Veenhof, 2003, p. 81). A master original that could be verified as authoritative might be encased in a clay envelope bearing part or all of the enclosed text, with the seals of officials or witnesses. Collon (1990, p. 27) provides a photograph of a clay envelope from Kanesh which bears the contrasting seals of an Assyrian merchant and a local Anatolian client or trading partner. The seals are easily distinguished by a seal specialist or *sigillographer* as reflecting two different cultures and seal-carving traditions, but were used in exactly the same way on a single document. Ur-Utu, a priest in the temple of Annunītum at Sippar-Amnānum (modern Tell ed-Dēr), on the Tigris, 1647-1625 BCE, kept documents concerning real estate transactions and litigation in their sealed envelopes (Van Landberghe, 2003, p. 69).

Logic, as well as a passage in Jeremiah 32, had long suggested that documents surviving to modern times in an unopened clay envelope must probably have been issued with duplicate copies that were unencased. This allowed the sealed-up copy to be preserved as legal evidence in case of dispute, while the unencased one was read by the recipient. Veenhof (2003, p. 81), searching diligently through museum collections and published archives, turned up surviving examples of such duplicates (in and out of inscribed envelopes), and other examples where, while only one copy has been found, the text itself refers to the preparation of copies. Veenhof's painstaking analysis of the evidence allows us to retire the surmise, passed on by Posner (1972/2003, p. 47), that tablets found still in their envelopes represent unopened "incoming mail."

Veenhof even found evidence of the procedures followed when the envelope containing a master document had to be opened, perhaps to verify the debts of a businessman who had died, or to answer a challenge to property rights that had been granted by a court or government agency. He cites a letter found in commercial archives at Kanesh that records the presence of witnesses, who attest with their seals and affidavits that the original was opened, its contents examined and verified, and the document re-sealed, with the original broken seals preserved and forwarded to the interested party in the re-sealed envelope (Veenhof, 2003, pp. 82-83).

Protection of Stored Documents

While on deposit in an archive, documents might need to be protected by security measures. In many ancient sites, embossed clay seals were used on boxes, baskets, or jars containing tablets, and to seal the doors to the room containing document archives. Shibtu, wife of King Zimri-Lin of Mari (c. 1800-1760 BCE), writes to him that she has, per his instructions, given his messengers access to collect from the archive two baskets of documents which she will hold for the king's arrival. She specifies the name of the official whose seal was broken in opening the tablet room, and mentions that she re-sealed it using her own (Durand, 2000, vol. 3, pp. 332-333). A letter from the lady Inibshina to the same King Zimri-Lin reports that she has obeyed his orders, opening the sealed doors to the tablet room in the presence of officials whom she names, to retrieve and forward records to the absent king (Durand, 2000,

vol. 3, p. 405). The latter transaction is doubly attested by the survival of a letter from one of the officials, who assures the king that he retrieved the coffers containing the tablets requested, but did not open them (Durand, 2000, vol. 2, p. 369).

Breaking a door seal was a serious matter, with legal consequences. Veenhof (2003, pp. 110-112) calls attention to a cuneiform tablet now in the British Museum in which commercial agents visiting Kanesh on business for a *naruqqu* society write back to the investors in Assur to say that they have found an associate's strong room door sealed after a withdrawal the investors were unaware of. They ask for further instructions before they break that seal.

Historians have been mystified by observing that sometimes little piles of broken clay seals were left on the floor and not removed. Dalley (1984), for instance, describes "stratified heaps, bearing witness to slovenly housekeeping" (p. 73). Information security professionals might suggest a possible interpretation: evidence that the seal had been broken was deliberately left to testify that the opening of the door and its re-sealing were not covert.

Lax security procedures might be punished. Egyptian law provided for judges to subpoena documents from temples and document depositories if needed when hearing a case. A text concerning the duties and prerogatives of a vizier, which survives in four copies (best preserved in the tomb of Rekhmire, who served Thutmose III and Amenhotep II, c. 1470-1445 BCE), specifies that documents summoned in this way should be forwarded under the seal of the custodian magistrates and scribes, and returned to them re-sealed by the vizier. If the judge subpoenaed confidential documents, however, they were not to be sent (Davies, 1944/1973, p. 91). Court records from a treason trial during the reign of the Pharaoh Ramses III (c. 1151 BCE) mention punishment doled out to document custodians who allowed conspirators to gain access to sensitive papers having to do with the state religion. Guilty members of the conspiracy, including scribes and librarians, were variously sentenced to be put to death, obliged to commit suicide, or to have their noses and ears cut off (Richardson, 1911, pp. 48-53).

Mesopotamian collections were sometimes protected by warnings inscribed on the tablets themselves, calling down a curse on borrowers who failed to return them (Casson, 2001, p. 14).

Individuals lacking their own document strong rooms might be able to obtain safe storage in the archive of a larger firm, as at Kanesh (Teissier, 1994, p. 7), or in an emergency, simply bury their most important deeds and documents. At Tel Sifr in southern Babylonia, archaeologists found the personal papers of one Silli Ishtar wrapped in a reed mat and buried under the floor of his house (Black & Tait, 1995, p. 2203).

Unalterable Texts: Laws, Treaties, and Dedications

After drafts and revisions of a foreign treaty had been negotiated between the contracting parties in the form of clay tablets, in Hittite Imperial times the finalized treaty might be inscribed on metal tablets, signifying their unalterable finality (Bryce, 2002, pp. 67-68). Other documents of great importance might also be inscribed on metal plates; Bryce discusses a bronze tablet found at Hattusa which finalized arrangements made by King Tudhaliya concerning dynastic succession among his near relatives (Bryce, 1998, pp. 295-299).

Dedicatory prayers and messages intended only for the gods or for remote posterity might be inscribed on tablets of lead, gold, or silver, encased in fitted stone boxes, and placed in hollowed-out foundation stones, much as a time capsule is created in our own time. Wright (1983) traced this little-noted but remarkably persistent tradition, handed on from the Sumerians to the Babylonians, and thence to the Assyrians and neo-Babylonians. Nabonidus, the last neo-Babylonian king (c. 556-539 BCE), was an antiquary; his collection of already ancient foundation tablets was found in modern times. The practice continued in the Persian empire, and the Ptolemies brought it to Egypt after the age of Alexander. The last one laid down in Antiquity, and latest to surface in modern times, was discovered in the foundations of the Serapeion, a temple which housed the smaller of the two wings of the fabled library of Alexandria (4th century BCE).

FUTURE TRENDS: EVIDENCE YET TO FIND AND INTERPRET

More remains to be learned. As archeologists discover, document, and publish their findings from fresh excavations, they add to the growing corpus of information about archives, libraries, and document service in the ancient world. Digs suspended for decades, as at Kish and Alalakh, are resuming in our time, turning up evidence that connects with poorly documented (by modern standards) previous finds scattered to worldwide museums in the 19th century. Important sites such as Agade (Sargon the Great's lost capital) and the vanished cities of North African states on the periphery of the Roman world have yet to be located at all. When future archeologists identify and excavate these sites, some of which are known to have possessed libraries, facts will turn up that need to be interpreted and connected to what is already known.

Archeologists need cross-disciplinary help to build a complete picture of how ancient societies operated day to day. Historians of information science in the emerging generation must keep an eye on the published literature and continue to sift the new evidence and synthesize, forming a mosaic that becomes less fragmentary as evidence accumulates. And we need a deeper understanding ourselves of our own history, if we are to avoid the fate linguist Thomas Wasow (1985) characterized (in his own discipline) as "forever re-inventing the flat tire" (p. 487).

CONCLUSION

It is not possible or necessary to demonstrate a strict linear progression of document security procedures passed down through unbroken generations to the present day. There are gaps in continuity; there are mysteries not yet explored; and while many of the problems are analogous, they are not exactly the same. But at each stage in the life of a document, one can see evidence that ancient scribes protected its security in ways that are analogous to modern practice. There is comfort in the reflection that the conceptual challenges crossing the modern security professional's desk (or computer screen) have been seen before, and solved.

REFERENCES

Barber, E. (1974). *Archaeological decipherment.* Princeton, NJ: Princeton University Press.

Berthold, A.B. (1938). *On the systematization of documents in ancient times.* Philadelphia: Kopy Komposers.

Black, J.A., & Tait, W.J. (1995). Archives and libraries in the ancient Near East. In J.M. Sasson (Ed.), *Civilizations of the ancient Near East* (pp. 2197-2209). New York: Charles Scribner's Sons.

Bonfante, L. (1990). Etruscans. In *Reading the past: Ancient writing from cuneiform to the alphabet* (pp. 320-378). New York: Barnes & Noble.

Bryce, T. (1998). *The kingdom of the Hittites.* Oxford, UK: Clarendon Press.

Bryce, T. (2002). *Life and society in the Hittite world.* Oxford, UK: Oxford University Press.

Casson, L. (2001). *Libraries in the ancient world.* New Haven, CT: Yale University Press.

Charpin, D. (1996). 'Lies natürlich…': A propos des erreurs des scribes dans les lettres de Mari. In M. Dietrich & O. Loretz (Eds.), *Vom alten Orient zum alten testament* (pp. 43-55). Kevelaer: Butzon & Bercker.

Collon, D. (1990). *Near Eastern seals.* Berkeley, CA: University of California Press.

Dalby, A. (1986). The Sumerian catalogs. *Journal of Library History, 21*(3), 475-487.

Dalley, S. (1984). *Mari and Karana: Two old Babylonian cities.* London: Longman.

Durand, J.-M. (Ed. & Trans.). (2000). *Les documents épistolaires du palais de Mari.* Paris: Editions du Cerf.

Foster, B.R. (1983). Archives and empire in Sargonic Mesopotamia. In K.R. Veenhof (Ed.), *Cuneiform archives and libraries: Papers read at the 30e Rencontre Assyriologique Internationale Leiden, 4-8 July 1983* (pp. 46-52). Leiden: Nederlands Historisch-Archaeologisch Instituut te Istanbul.

Gellius, Aulus. (1927-1928). *The attic nights of Aulus Gellius,* with an English translation by John C. Rolfe. London: Heinemann.

Herodotus. (1998). *The histories.* New York: Oxford University Press.

Macuch, M. (1997). The use of seals in Sasanian jurisprudence. In R. Gyselen (Ed.), *Res orientales X: Sceaux d'orient et leur emploi* (pp. 79-87). Bures-sur-

Yvette, France: Groupe pour l'Etude de la Civilisation du Moyen-Orient.

Max, G.E. (1994). Ancient Near East. In W.A. Wiegand & D.G. Davis Jr. (Eds.), *Encyclopedia of library history* (pp. 23-31). New York: Garland.

Neve, P. (1991). Die Ausgrabungen in Boğazköy-Hattuša, 1990. *Archäologischer Anzeiger,* (3), 299-348.

Parpola, S. (1981). Assyrian royal inscriptions and neo-Assyrian letters. In M. Fales (Ed.), *Assyrian royal inscriptions: New horizons* (pp. 117-134). Rome: Istituto per l'Oriente, Centro per le antichità e la storia dell'arte del vicino Oriente.

Parrot, A. (1959). *Mission archéologique de Mari. Volume 2, Le Palais.* Paris: Geuthner.

Posner, E. (1972/2003). *Archives in the ancient world.* Chicago: Society of American Archivists.

Plutarch. (1964). *The rise and fall of Athens: Nine Greek lives: Theseus, Solon, Themistocles, Aristides, Cimon, Peicles, Alcibiades, Lysander.* Harmondsworth, Middlesex: Penguin Books.

Richardson, E.C. (1911). *Some old Egyptian librarians.* New York: Charles Scribner's Sons.

Sasson, J.M. (2002). The burden of scribes. In T. Abusch (Ed.), *Riches hidden in secret places: Ancient Near Eastern studies in memory of Thorkild Jacobsen* (pp. 211-228). Winona Lake, IN.: Eisenbrauns.

Teissier, B. (1994). *Sealings and seals from Kültepe Kārum level 2.* Istanbul: Nederlands Historisch-Archaeologisch Instituut te Istanbul.

Vallon, F. (1997). L'utilisation des sceaux-cylindres dans l'archivage des lettres de Persépolis. In R. Gyselen (Ed.), *Res orientales X: Sceaux d'orient et leur emploi* (pp. 171-173). Bures-sur-Yvette, France: Groupe pour l'Etude de la Civilisation du Moyen-Orient.

Van Landberghe, K. (2003). Private and public: The Ur-Utu archive at Sippar-Amnānum (Tell ed-Dēr). In M. Brosius (Ed.), *Ancient archives and archival traditions: Concepts of record-keeping in the ancient world* (pp. 59-77). Oxford, UK: Oxford University Press.

Veenhof, K.R. (1986). Cuneiform archives: An introduction. In K.R. Veenhof (Ed.), *Cuneiform archives and libraries: Papers read at the 30e Rencontre Assyriologique Internationale Leiden, 4-8 July 1983* (pp. 1-36). Leiden: Nederlands Historisch-Archaeologisch Instituut te Istanbul.

Veenhof, K.R. (2003). Archives of Old Assyrian traders. In M. Brosius (Ed.), *Ancient archives and archival traditions: Concepts of record-keeping in the ancient world* (pp.78-123). Oxford, UK: Oxford University Press.

Wasow, T. (1985). Comment: The wizards of Ling. *Natural Language and Linguistic Theory, 3*(3), 485-492.

Weitemeyer, M. (1956). Archive and library technique in ancient Mesopotamia. In. F. Steenbuch-Jensen (Trans.), *Libri 6.1* (pp. 217-238).

Whitehorne, J. (1996). The Kellis writing tablets: Their manufacture and use. In *Archaeological research in Roman Egypt* (pp. 240-245). Ann Arbor, MI: Journal of Roman Archaeology supplement series, 19.

Witty, F.J. (1972). The beginnings of indexing and abstracting: Some notes towards a history of indexing and abstracting in Antiquity and the Middle Ages. *The Indexer, 8*(4), 193-198.

Wright, H.C. (1983). *Ancient burials of metallic foundation documents in stone boxes.* Graduate School of Library and Information Science, University of Illinois, USA.

KEY TERMS

Bulla: A ball or pellet of clay or wax used to seal a jar, door, box, or document; sometimes impressed with an image, word, or symbol from a stone or ceramic seal (plural: bullae).

Cuneiform: A writing system employing a wedge-shaped stylus (Latin: *cuneus*) to impress symbols on a soft surface such as clay or wax. Cuneiform writing was used to record documents in many different languages from the third millennium BCE to the 6th century CE, chiefly on clay tablets, but sometimes in metal or stone inscriptions.

Naruqqu society: A corporate entity common in the Assyrian business world consisting of investors who have pooled their capital for a joint-stock venture in trade. Stiff penalties discouraged an individual investor from withdrawing his capital before the term of the contract expired.

Scytale: A cylindrical tool used by the Spartans to send parchment messages that could not be read unless the receiver also had a scytale of the same size.

Sigillography: From a Latin word-root: the study of seals and sealings; also called sphragistics (from the Greek word for seal).

Steganography: The specialized branch of cryptography in which not just the content of the message, but also the message itself, is hidden or disguised.

DRM Practices in the E-Publication Industry

Bong Wee Kiau
Universiti Utara Malaysia, Malaysia

Norshuhada Shiratuddin
Universiti Utara Malaysia, Malaysia

INTRODUCTION

Electronic publishing (e-publishing) is the process of publishing information to be viewed electronically or online and delivered in the form of electronic books (e-books), e-mail newsletters, Web sites, CD-ROM, wireless publishing, and most recently electronic ink (Thomas, 2004). With the recent growth of telecommunication technologies and the Internet, assisted by the development of new technologies such as high-bandwidth connections and peer-to-peer networks, digital distribution services in which clients distribute files between themselves without using a central server (Burkhalter, 2001) have vastly improved the way we produce, procure, store, redistribute, and consume digital content. At the same time, these have created several problems like unauthorized copying, modification, and redistribution by a third party. Downloading encoded files has gained acceptance among Internet-savvy users because it provides immediate access to digital content and does not rely on physical media. The ease of processing, obtaining, and transmitting information has made easier both trading in data as well as collecting information from different sources, and has resulted in information about individuals often being collected and sold without their knowledge (Banks, Dickinson, Erickson, Reynolds, & Vora, 2001).

Everyone associated with e-publishing will be concerned with how e-books are protected from unauthorized copying. Realizing the potential of the Internet as a dynamic medium for delivery of intellectual property (IP), before digital content owners will offer their copyright works for sale or promotion, a secure system that protects digital content is needed. Digital rights management (DRM) is a collective term for tools and processes whose purpose is to enable owners of copyright works to control their use. DRM technologies impose constraints on the use of digital objects or IP that correspond to the terms of the agreement between publisher and consumer during digital content commerce (Clarke, 2000). DRM promises a secure framework for digital content distribution and enables an electronic marketplace where previously unimaginable business models can be implemented. At the same time, it particularly ensures content providers; copyright owners receive adequate remuneration for the creation of the content that is distributed over the DRM system. It manages the commerce, IP ownership, and confidentiality rights of digital content creators and owners, as content travels through the value chain from creator to distributor, then to the consumer, and from consumer to other consumers.

Protection of IP is as critical as protection of any physical asset that society, individual authors, and publishers value and hold. The information industry and society are realizing the potential of the Internet as a dynamic medium for delivery of IP, coming to appreciate the difficulties in how those assets are to be managed and the complexities in providing easy access in the electronic environment while protecting intellectual property rights (IPR) (Slowinski, 2003).

There are many reasons for wanting to manage the rights associated with IP. Authors and artists wish to control what can be done with their creations, scholars wish to ensure that they receive proper attribution, commercial enterprises wish to support business models that involve licenses and fees, and consumers want an environment free of legal worries and unexpected costs. Although rights themselves are not technological in nature, they are defined by laws, beliefs, and practices (Downes, Mourad, Piccariello, & Robson, 2003). Technology can be used to transmit, verify, interpret, and enforce rights as they apply to digital content and services.

Currently, as tools such as local and national digital repositories come online and are widely developed, more and more of these valuable resources are going to be stored and shared digitally. These resources are already subject to IPR law, but storing and sharing them in this new and very public manner makes it important to ensure that these resources comply with IPR law and can be protected by it. For those who want to share their content with others, it is also important that they understand the legal environment that they are operating in.

Research undertaken indicates that digital content providers often spend a great deal of time managing tasks like obtaining legal advice, adding features to protect copyright, managing online user payment, income stream to rights holders, monitoring and tracking users and payers, and the use of existing and new materials. Thus, DRM has emerged to manage the commerce. Trust and control are core issues related to DRM. A DRM system deals with encrypting content and information, and is integrated into an organization at an infrastructure level (Duhl & Kevorkian, 2001). A company that implements DRM uses a trusted vendor's technology to manage encrypted data, keys, and information about users. Companies, therefore, need to trust that a DRM vendor and system will not only support their business rules, policies, and interests, but also do so in such a way that remains under their control. Adopting an effective DRM system that manages rights clearances and payments can make extra time available for developing new products and delivering them in new and different ways (DCITA, 2003).

Introduction to DRM

"Digital rights management" is the term for new business trust assurance processes designed to unleash the tremendous capabilities of the Internet. DRM is fairly new, but the business challenges it addresses are many centuries old. If the Internet is considered as the latest invention that has disrupted established markets, then DRM is the latest solution for reestablishing equilibrium for opening up lucrative new sources of revenue for market participants. DRM becomes essential anytime digital information is deemed important or sensitive enough to be protected by laws, rules, or policies (Coffee, 2003).

There are several well-known definitions of DRM. Slowinski (2003) defines DRM as "a set of actions, procedures, policies, product properties and tools that an entity uses to manage its rights in digital information according to requirements." The Association of American Publishers (2004) defines it in two different definitions, "the technologies, tools and processes that protect IP during digital content commerce" and "the technology, legal and/or social mechanisms used to protect the copyrights in digital content." According to Einhorn (2001), "DRM entails the operation of a control system that can monitor, regulate and price each subsequent use of a computer file that contains media content, such as video, audio, photos or text." Lyon (2001) defines DRM as "a system of information technology components and services that strive to distribute and control digital products."

Open eBook Forum (2000) describes DRM as:

the definition, protection or enforcement of rights pertaining to content produced, delivered or accessed electronically." Finefrock (2000) characterizes DRM as a process involving the safekeeping and copyright protection of e-books, while the American Library Association (2004) defines DRM as a term used for technologies that control how digital content is used. Finally, the Information and Communications Unit of the European Commission Directorate General Information Society (2002) defines DRM systems as "technologies that describe and identify digital content protected by IPR and enforce usage rules set by rights holders or prescribed by law for digital content. DRMs are thus an important complement to the legal framework.

DRM historically has been viewed as the methodology for the protection of digital media copyrights. In more formal terms, DRM has been described as a way of addressing the description, identification, trading, protection, monitoring, and tracking of all forms of rights usages over tangible and intangible assets, including management of rights holders' relationships. It identifies the rights and rights holders associated with particular works and keeps track of their use. For publishers, more complex DRM systems can record, track, and monitor rights for a range of existing and newly created materials. The content will be protected by security features that are unlocked after agreements for use have been reached and payment made.

Generally, DRM systems make use of at least two security techniques, cryptography and identification techniques, to protect and detect the content from unauthorized access and to link DRM-protected content to a seller (Jonker, 2004). Encryption is a protection method that scrambles the information embedded within a digital content so that it cannot be accessed without a password. Some types of encryption need to be employed to ensure that the digital content can only be accessed by users with the correct access codes. Encryption allows a user to specify an access code or password which is used to make the content unreadable to anyone without the correct password.

An aspect of many DRM systems is that content can be identified if encountered in unprotected form. Content owners can use this to detect theft or to prove ownership, while users could use this to find content they have sampled, but which they have not yet acquired. DRM systems can employ a variety of techniques to identify content. The Digital Object Identifier (DOI) scheme provides a lookup service; given a cryptic identifier, a server looks up the current location of the content and redirects the user there (Paskin, 2000). DRM systems could use cameras and microphones to "take" a fingerprint. Fingerprinting identification works by matching a small sample of digital content to the original content by using a database of "fingerprints" of digital content. This makes it robust against attempts to thwart fingerprinting (Jonker, 2004). Digital watermarking embeds user-specific information (usually about author, publisher, and terms and conditions of use) into the digital content and thus could be able to distinguish users of the same original content (Fabien, 2003). Watermarks can be visible or invisible (Cushing, 2001) and can be used to personalize a particular instance of a work to a user to reduce the likelihood of that person passing it on or duplicating it.

Introduction to E-Book

Growing interest in converting paper books to bytes has resulted in a collection of hybrid definitions of e-books. Initially, paper books that had been converted to a digital format through digitization processes that allow them to be displayed on computers were defined as e-books. The term also began to encompass multimedia, hypertext, or hypermedia systems that are based on a book metaphor (Norshuhada, Landoni, Gibb, & Shahizan, 2003). Recently, the definition of an e-book has been extended to include book titles that are available online, that can be read as e-mail or retrieved by a portable electronic reading device or downloadable file onto a computer (Carvajal, 1999; Allen, 2000).

The following are some of the definitions of e-books defined diversely by researchers to fit their own expectations (Norshuhada et al., 2003):

1. Any kind of digitized information ranging from a CD-ROM title to an online interactive database or a collection of Web pages
2. A collection of reactive pages of electronic information that exhibit many of the characteristic features and properties of a conventional book
3. Learning environments which have an application containing a multimedia database of instructional resources that store pre-captured multimedia presentations about topics in a book

In this article, the term "e-book" is defined as an electronic version of a traditional print book that is available in electronic form, which can be downloaded from the Internet and read on a variety of hardware platforms with the aid of reading software.

A CASE STUDY IN MALAYSIA

E-Book Publication

Malaysia is strong in its intent to attain the highest level of communication technology. In terms of production, since 1995 more than 1,000 titles of compact disks have been published and deposited at the National Library (Asian/Pacific Book Development, 2001). Most newspapers and magazines currently have their online versions. Academic journals and books also have started to go into digital versions.

Various government-backed ventures such as the Malaysian Institute of Microelectronic System (MIMOS), the Multimedia Development Corporations (MDC), the Smart School Projects, and the Virtual Library Projects are providing broad opportunities for the development of e-publishing. The global trend of setting up virtual bookstores on the World Wide Web (WWW) has attracted a small number of Malaysian pioneers onto the Internet (Chan, 1999). They are drawn to the Web by a number of factors:

1. the low costs of establishing a virtual bookstore
2. the potential of reaching a global rather than local clientele

3. the possibility of increasing revenue by selling directly to the customer (particularly in the case of publishers)
4. strong policy support from the government

Policy support has been provided on two fronts (Chan, 1999). The first is a good infrastructure to provide convenient and affordable access to the Internet for both consumers and the publication industry. A major investment is being made to build the Multimedia Super Corridor (MSC), which is a US$40 billion project launched on June 27, 1998. MSC acts as an impetus and proving ground for the new information and communication technologies (ICTs). The MSC is a geographical area 15 kilometers wide and 50 kilometers long stretching out from Kuala Lumpur (Elizabeth & Francis, 2002). State-of-the-art computer networking technologies and facilities are provided within this zone to facilitate and support national and multinational companies in their operations.

On the second front is a set of innovative legislation comprising the Communications and Multimedia Act 1998, which addresses the unique issues presented by the new ICT, and the attendant potentials and risks of doing business via these technologies (Chan, 1999). For publishers, copyright safeguards have been enacted to protect IP created and disseminated using the new ICT. For consumers, regulations are in place to ensure safe commercial transactions over the Internet.

Several local higher leaning institutions and universities in Malaysia, as well as organizations in government and private sectors, are actively involved in electronic publication. With the borderless world of the WWW, the e-publication business will very likely not be confined to the geographical borders of Malaysia.

Survey on DRM Practices

A preliminary survey was conducted from November 2003 to February 2004 to discover the level of awareness, knowledge, and understanding regarding IPR issues among publishers who have been involved in e-publication and those who would potentially be involved in e-publication. The sampling frame for this survey consisted of two local e-book publishers, one government agency, and 33 higher education institutions in Malaysia. Out of these 36 organizations, 12 responded to the survey, yielding a response rate of 33.3%. Out of the 12 surveys returned, one of them was incomplete and hence was dropped from subsequent analyses, yielding 11 usable responses and a usable response rate of 30.6%.

An analysis of the answers obtained from the survey questionnaires showed that none of them had experience with DRM or any other piracy protection technology implementation. Lack of knowledge on how the technology works and how to adopt the piracy protection technology are the most frequently quoted reasons for not adopting DRM into their business model. Generally, the target respondents were highly concerned about piracy and copyright associated with e-publication, and reported that they lack exposure to digital content protection. Feedback from one of the organizations that encountered the digital copyright issue stated that even though there are statutory provisions that provide protection to IP, due to the lack of practice and lack of exposure on the importance of piracy protection, the implementation of DRM has not been put into effect in the e-publication sector in Malaysia.

All organizations agreed that the issue of copyright in Malaysia's digital commerce is a new subject. There is a need to increase the awareness of the public by providing education, seminars, conferences, and public talks. The analysis of the responses obtained revealed that all organizations are confident that DRM implementation in the e-publication sector in Malaysia would be successful if there is a complete guideline to assist them throughout the process of adopting the technology into their business. In addition, all organizations were concerned about the rules and regulations during DRM implementation. They agreed that the technology will be successfully put into implementation if all conditions are accepted by all parties associated with e-publication including digital content consumers.

To solve the identified problem, there is a need to develop a set of clear guidelines that will act as an awareness-raising device about IPR issues and basic guidance on DRM implementation to assist e-book publishers throughout the process of adopting the technology and consequently reduce the risk of copyright infringement. A number of surveys were conducted to gain information about experiences, expectations, and suggestions regarding the e-book DRM implementation from local and worldwide respondents in the e-publication industry, DRM service providers, and law enforcement agencies. The findings show that 20.6% of the targeted respondents from e-book publishers

D

worldwide implemented DRM and declared that it is successful (Bong & Norshuhada, 2004). Only a few of the e-book publishers were aware of moral rights and insisted on owning the rights to minimize copyright problems. In addition, there are only a small number of respondents who were very concerned about piracy or copyright infringement.

In developing the guideline and providing a better understanding of what is currently happening to digital content management on a legal and technological basis, security technologies, underlying legal implications, related privacy problems, copyright law, and main obstacles to DRM deployment were reviewed. The Web version of the DRM guidelines can be accessed from http://www.e-infoc.uum.edu.my/DRMGui/DRM-Guidelines.htm.

DISCUSSION AND CONCLUSION

A preliminary survey conducted to gain feedback from current electronic publishers in Malaysia regarding successful and failure cases of DRM implementation reveals that currently, none of the existing e-book publishers in Malaysia implemented DRM or any other piracy protection technologies to protect the digital content that they make available online. The survey also discovered that existing e-book publishers in Malaysia could not commit to e-book sales because of the problem of unauthorized copying and redistribution of e-books (Bong & Norshuhada, 2005).

Locally, there is a general consensus that digital content providers need to understand more about IPR issues. Findings reveal that DRM implementation in the e-publication industry in Malaysia will be successful if there is a set of complete guidelines to assist them throughout the process of adopting the technology. In addition, all organizations were concerned about the laws, rules, and regulations during DRM implementation. Consequently, a set of comprehensive guidelines, consisting of DRM implementation processes and a list of tools and templates, was developed. Adopting a DRM system into digital commerce may be a complicated process. However, with the comprehensive guidelines, a digital content provider would be able to find a systematic way to adopt the piracy protection technology in managing its IP and enjoy the benefits of the DRM technology.

Although there are some guidelines currently available to provide guidance and overview of IP protection, many of these efforts are limited to geographic territory and not specifically or significantly applicable to e-book publication. These available guidelines provide an introduction to Copyright Law enforcement specifically in the United States, United Kingdom, Australia, and Canada. Some evidence of such efforts are guidelines developed by the Joint Information Systems Committee (JISC) Legal Information Services (Hayes, 2001); the Australia Government, Department of Communications, Information Technology and the Arts (DCITA) (2003); Visual Arts Data Service (Grout, Purdy, & Rymer, 2005); and the Antitrust Guidelines for the Licensing of Intellectual Property Issued by the U.S. Department of Justice and the Federal Trade Commission (1995). These guidelines also provide information and practical guidance concerning issues involved in valuating the viability of creating and developing digital resources, and offer practical and legal advice regarding IPR issues and digitization initiatives particularly involving images, broadcasts, films, and musical works.

To develop any satisfactory DRM approaches, several interests must be balanced. Apparently, studies focus on technological and user-related issues; implementation of the technologies and their impact on the legal framework should be carried out in order to meet the needs and requirements of the digital content provider and the consumers. Nevertheless, the guarantees offered by the DRM technologies are essential for developing a truly secure environment for online transaction and commercialization of digital contents. In particular, a high-level degree of confidence is required to ensure that the transaction is running in a secure environment and free from the possibility of tampering or infringement. Extending the study to a strong security guarantee of trust-computing and DRM capabilities should eventually be able to satisfy concerned consumers.

REFERENCES

Allen, M. (2000). *E-publishing FAQ*. Retrieved December 2005 from http://www.writing-world.com/epublish/FAQ.html

American Library Association. (2004) *DRM: A brief introduction*. Retrieved December 2003 from http://www.ala.org/Content/NavigationMenu/Our_Association/Offices/ALA_Washington/Events10/Midwinter_Meeting5/drm.pdf

Asian/Pacific Book Development. (2001). How far is publishing digitized in Asia? *Language Issues in Digital Publishing, 31*(3). Retrieved December 2005 from http://www.accu.or.jp/appreb/report/abd/31-3/abd3133.html

Association of American Publishers. (2000). *Digital rights management for e-books: Publisher requirements. Version 1.0*. New York: Association of American Publishers.

Australia Government, Department of Communications, Information Technology and the Arts. (DCITA). (2003). *What is DRM?* Retrieved January 2004 from http://www.dcita.gov.au/drm/1976.html

Banks, D., Dickinson, I., Erickson, J., Reynolds, D., & Vora. P. (2001). Privacy and digital rights management. *Proceedings of the W3C Workshop on Digital Rights Management*, Antibes, France.

Bong, W.K., & Norshuhada, S. (2004). A qualitative study of e-book digital rights management. *International Journal of the Book,* (2), 15-23.

Bong, W.K., & Norshuhada, S. (2005). Current state of e-book DRM. *Proceedings of the 2nd ECTI Annual International Conference*, Pattaya, Thailand.

Burkhalter, B. (2001). *The Napster controversy*. Retrieved September 2004 from

http://iml.jou.ufl.edu/projects/Spring01/Burkhalter/Napster%20history.html

Carvajal, D. (1999). Racing to convert books to bytes. *The New York Times,* (December 9).

Chan, S.Y. (1999). The old and the new: Bookselling in Malaysia. *Asian/Pacific Book Development, 30*(1).

Clarke, R. (2001). DRM will beget DCRM. *Proceedings of the W3C DRM Workshop,*

Sophia Antipolis, France.

Coffee, P. (2003). *The best DRM policy may be no policy at all*. Retrieved December 2003 from http://www.eweek.com/article2/0,4149,1258741,00.asp

Cushing, L. (2001). *Protection of digital images on the Web*. Retrieved May 2004 from http://www.lib.berkeley.edu/~lcushing/pdfs/ImagePro.pdf

Downes, S., Mourad, M., Piccariello, H., & Robson, R. (2003). Digital rights management in e-learning problem statement and terms of reference. *Proceedings of the AACE World Conference on E-Learning in Corporation, Government, Health & Higher Education* (vol. 1, pp. 696-699).

Duhl, J., & Kevorkian, S. (2001). *Understanding DRM systems*. Retrieved December 2003 from http://www.intertrust.com/main/research/whitepapers/IDCUnderstandingDRMSystems.pdf

Einhorn, M.A. (2001). Digital rights management and access protection: An economic analysis. In Ginsburg et al. (Eds.), *Proceedings of the ALAI Congress* (p. 89). New York: CopyCo.

Elizabeth, F., & Francis, P. (2002). Socio-economic and cultural factors affecting adoption of broadband access: A cross-country analysis. *Proceedings of the 41st European Telecommunication Congress,* Genoa, Italy.

European Commission Directorate General Information Society. (2002). *Digital rights management (DRM) workshop*. Retrieved September 2004 from http://europa.eu.int/information_society/topics/multi/digital_rights/doc/workshop2002/workshop_report1.doc

Fabien, A.P. (2003). *Digital watermarking: Digital rights management* (pp. 62-80). Berlin: Springer-Verlag (LNCS 2770).

Finefrock, S.D. (2000). Digital rights management solutions are fast becoming a priority in the publishing industry. *The Internet Law Journal,* (December 26).

Grout, C., Purdy, P., & Rymer, J. (2005). *Creating digital resources for the visual arts: Standards and good practice*. UK: Oxbow Books.

Hayes, M.J. (2001). *Intellectual property rights: Overview of intellectual property*. Retrieved June 2005 from http://www.jisclegal.ac.uk/ipr/IntellectualProperty.htm

Jonker, H.L. (2004). *Security of digital rights management systems*. Retrieved May 2004 from http://www.

win.tue.nl/~hjonker/publications/master-thesis-2004-10-07.pdf

Lyon, G. (2001). *The Internet marketplace and digital rights management.* Retrieved March 2004 from http://www.itl.nist.gov/div895/docs/GLyonDRMWhitepaper.pdf

Norshuhada, S., Landoni, M., Gibb, F., & Shahizan, H. (2003). E-books technology and its potential applications in distance education. *Journal of Digital Information, 3*(4).

Open eBook Forum. (2000). *A framework for the e-publishing ecology.* Retrieved December 2003 from http://www.openebook.org/doc_library/ecology/A%20Framework%20for%20 the%20Epublishing%20Ecology.pdf

Paskin, N. (2000). *Digital object identifier: Implementing a standard digital identifier as the key to effective digital rights management.* Retrieved June 2004 from http://www.doi.org/doi_presentations/aprilpaper.pdf

Slowinski, F.H. (2003). *What consumers want in digital rights management (DRM): Making content as widely available as possible in ways that satisfy consumer preferences.* Retrieved December 2003 from http://www.publishers.org/press/pdf/DRMWhitePaper.pdf

Thomas, D. (2004). *Introduction to e-publishing.* Retrieved January 2003 from http://www.ebookcrossroads.com/epublishing.html

U.S. Department of Justice and the Federal Trade Commission. (1995). *Antitrust guidelines for the licensing of intellectual property.* Retrieved May 2004 from http://permanent.access.gpo.gov/lps9890/lps9890/www.usdoj.gov/atr/public/guidelines/ipguide.htm#t4

KEY TERMS

Cryptography: The discipline that embodies principles, means, and methods for the transformation of data in order to hide its information content, and prevent its undetected modification and unauthorized use.

Digital Rights Management (DRM): The wide range of systems and services used for the description, identification, protection, monitoring, and tracking of all forms of digital copyright material throughout the lifecycle of the material.

Digital Object Identifier (DOI): An identification system for intellectual property in the digital environment. Developed by the International DOI Foundation on behalf of the publishing industry, its goals are to provide a framework for managing intellectual content, link customers with publishers, facilitate electronic commerce, and enable automated copyright management.

Digital Watermarking: A security technique that allows an individual to add hidden copyright notices or other verification messages to digital content.

Electronic Book (E-Book): Electronic version of a traditional print book that is available in electronic form, and can be downloaded from the Internet and read on a variety of hardware platforms with the aid of reading software.

Electronic Publishing (E-Publishing): A generic term for the distribution of information that is stored, transmitted, and reproduced electronically.

Encryption: The process of coding data for security so that a specific code or key is required to restore the original data, used to make transmissions secure from unauthorized reception.

Fingerprinting: Embeds a digital signal in text, image, audio, or video files, which may contain information on the end user. This can be used to trace the source of copyright infringement.

Intellectual Property (IP): Creation of the mind or product of the intellect that has commercial value, including copyrighted property such as literary or artistic works, and ideational property, such as patents, appellations of origin, business methods, and industrial processes.

Intellectual Property Rights (IPR): The right to possess and use intellectual property; monopoly protection for creative works such as writing (copyright), inventions (patents), processes (trade secrets), and identifiers (trademarks); and all other rights resulting from intellectual activity in the industrial, scientific, literary, or artistic fields.

D

Educational Technology Practitioner–Research Ethics

Kathleen Gray
University of Melbourne, Australia

INTRODUCTION

Many ethical issues arise when educators undertake any kind of research into their own practice with their own students, and a number of ethical guidelines have been developed for such research. But working with educational technologies may enable kinds of transactions and interactions—and trigger related questions for teachers about good practice and propriety—that either do not arise at all or are not thrown into relief so clearly in other modes of teaching and learning. The broad categories of ethical issues that apply to practitioner research into teaching may not fully address all of the ethical dimensions of research into teaching and learning with technology.

This article provides a framework for reflecting on practitioner-researcher ethics in educational technology, including review of the research intention, the researcher's own position, approaches to data and subjects, ramifications, dissemination, and stakeholder interests. Excerpts from the literature are used to flag the possibilities and responsibilities attendant on such research. The focus of this article is on research undertaken in tertiary or higher education settings; however the general principles are relevant to schooling and other education settings.

BACKGROUND

Arising from the experience of the author and others, while operating a scheme supporting academics to undertake research into their own teaching, there are five broad categories of ethical issues that teaching staff need to consider before embarking on practitioner research (Chang, Gray, Polus, & Radloff, 2005): efficacy and protecting student learning, informed consent and voluntary participation, vulnerability and unequal power relationships, intellectual property, and collegiality. Table 1 shows a list of the 20 educational technology research projects undertaken within this

scheme (nearly 60% of all the projects undertaken), exemplifying both the strength of interest in doing such research and the diversity of research problems. In the author's experience, teaching staff using these five broad categories found it difficult to explore the ethical dimensions in their technology projects fully or deeply. Furthermore, emerging educational technologies that are rapidly expanding the scope of practitioner research—to include and to integrate mobile, wireless, handheld and broadband technologies; smart devices; reconfigured physical learning spaces; social networking facilities; as well as ever more sophisticated media authoring, resource sharing, and gaming—are likely to continue to raise complex ethical questions.

But there is no distinct body of established ethical practice for research into new and emerging educational technologies available to inform the design of practitioner research. Although general ethical aspects of human subjects research on the Internet as it was at the millennium have been thoroughly mapped (see Frankel & Siang, 1999), Thompson (2005, p. 9), quoting Roberts (2000), suggests that this is not adequate: "The online environment is characterized by 'unique and potentially harmful environmental factors', an awareness of which may not be reflected in existing codes of ethical practice for research on human subjects." A code of ethics for professional educational technologists (AECT, 2005) acknowledges the need for guidelines and procedures in the research and practice of that group; however such staff do not conduct research into their own teaching. The Association for Educational Communications and Technology code notes the need to build up a body of "interpretive briefs or ramifications of intent" (AECT, 2005, p. 1) for their own (and by extension their teaching staff clients') benefit in understanding what might constitute soundness, reasonableness, appropriateness, or integrity in specific instances of research and practice.

Most case reports of educational technology practitioner research make no mention at all of ethical considerations. In practice, reading between the lines

Table 1. Examples of practitioner research in educational technology

Pilot Projects	Integrated teaching and learning tool using computer-aided learning
	Learning activities using a new online learning production tool
	Renewable learning objects
	Student e-portfolios
	Virtual field trip
	Virtual tool for integration with hands-on teaching and learning
	Web portal
Implementation Projects	Asynchronous e-communication in a journal club
	Engagement in an elective subject studied fully online
	Graphical user interface to teach relevant skills in first year
	New online presentation and discussion environment
	Student e-portfolios
	Web-based videoconferencing to facilitate communities of learning practice
	Wireless interactive teaching, especially cultural issues
Evaluation Projects	E-communication
	Digital video material for teaching laboratory courses
	Student learning experience of using a new online learning environment
	Student learning experience of using e-portfolios for assessment
	Video analysis as a method to understand e-learning
	Web-based virtual tours as compared to actual tours

suggests that a spectrum, or possibly a polarization, of views has emerged among educators about the special significance of ethical considerations in such settings. At one end of the spectrum, there is seen to be nothing to worry about, and on the other end, the ethical dimension is regarded as an almost paralyzing issue. Illustrating one end of the spectrum is a case report suggesting that ethics are a pragmatic logistical factor in such research, but no more than this: "Practical issues such as the timing of the evaluation, instructions to students, ethics and student consent were all discussed" (Kennedy, 2003, p. 197). In contrast, a framework for scholarly teaching in an information and communications technology (ICT) degree implies a need to undertake such research with a sweepingly critical humanitarian perspective recognizing "the capacity of ICTs to bring forward voices that have been silenced, and…to marginalize and endanger others; to bridge or to widen the gap between those who have and those who do not; and to commercialize or to free human interaction" (Clifford, Friesen, & Lock, n.d., p. 80).

Further, discussions of the ethical factors to be borne in mind when teaching in online learning environments (e.g., Zimitat & Crebert, 2002; Gosper, 2004) do not capture the issues faced by teachers contemplating research into their own practice. This may be because such issues are thought to be morally relative to the individual teacher's personal code of conduct, as in the argument put forth in Brewer, Eastmond and Geertsen (2003, p. 67) that the force of any institutional ethical code cannot be relied upon because educators' personal values and social roles "overlap with our professional roles and affiliations."

Given this choice among ethical stances characterized by invisibility, pragmatism, humanitarianism, or moral relativism, what is a practitioner-researcher to do? To be faithful to the spirit of the scholarship of teaching, any academic planning to develop, implement, or evaluate an educational technology initiative with his/her own students will want to address ethical considerations deliberately and explicitly within her/his reflective practice, before, during, and after undertaking the project. Roberts (2000, p. 7) suggests that the best resource to improve practice in this area is "'bottom-up' learning, that is, from other Internet researchers and well-documented case studies, as well as the researcher's own practice based on the meticulous questioning of, and reflections on all facets of the online research process."

A FRAMEWORK FOR REFLECTING ON ETHICAL PRACTICE

As a framework for reflective practice and sharing of practice, Table 2 uses questions from Zeni (2001, p. 4)

Table 2. Considerations for practitioner research in educational technology

Questions	Considerations	Observations
Research Intention	• The project may be impelled by a larger institutional agenda for teaching and learning or for ICT. • The project may be "blue-sky" research to advance teaching and learning, or may be deliberately addressing evidenced teaching and learning deficits.	"Research that produces knowledge from a managerial or technological perspective can marginalize the knowledge of teachers and students." (Coupal, 2005, p. 5)
Researcher's Stance	• A teacher's predisposition to researching educational technology may be influenced by technological hype or by disenchantment with other aspects of academic work. • A teacher's approach to researching educational technology may not be informed by good practice in pedagogy and in project management.	"A professional culture in the staff room is a requirement for establishing norms supportive of practical, creative and critical testing of new ways of teaching with ICT." (Nordkvelle & Olson, 2005, p. 27)
Research Data	• Student-student, student-staff, and staff-staff interactions usually subject to the privacy and transitory nature of classroom proceedings may be captured for much longer as electronic data. • These data are easier to re-purpose and circulate more publicly, whether intentionally or inadvertently.	"The basic issues raised by point-of-view authoring of digital records for research are privacy and access issues affiliated with human subjects requirements in research policy." (Pea, 2005, p. 47)
Research Subjects	• Communication between staff and students may be predominantly text based rather than face to face, losing subtle cues that come through non-verbal communication. • Students may never meet or work as a class group or may meet infrequently, thus forming different kinds of identities and communities than in a campus-based group.	"Factors such as the dis-inhibiting effect of the seemingly anonymous (or pseudonymous) environment, an increased danger of researchers objectifying their 'invisible' research subjects, and the difficulty of obtaining informed consent from members of online groups whose composition changes constantly, are representative concerns." (Thompson, 2005, p. 9)
Ramifications of Research	• Students' participation may be affected by underlying issues of access and equity, cultural norms, or ICT literacy. • Their participation may have an unforeseen impact on their use of a particular technology in another, non-education setting such as a social or work situation.	"What are the ethical issues when implementing handheld computers?… Technology leaders must understand these new issues and be proactive in finding ways to solve them before they adversely affect the handheld program." (Pownell, 2002, p. 326) "'Social penalties'…the potential ostracism and stigmatism that can result from choosing not to 'join the group'…." (Poole & MacLean, 2004, p. 3)
Research Publication	• Academic integrity and intellectual property considerations, such as moral rights and copyright, may be more complex when publishing data created or reproduced in new media formats.	"Does the institution providing the e-portfolio system own certain elements of a student's archived work, similar to other college records?" (Lorenzo & Ittleson, 2005, p. 5) "With open editing, a page can have multiple contributors, and notions of page 'authorship' and 'ownership' can be radically altered." (Lamb, 2004, p. 38)
Stakeholders in Research	• Provision of essential advice and support for research participants is usually beyond the scope of the teacher alone, and involves partnerships with ICT administrators and service providers. • The extent of financial or logistical investment required to support the research design may affect the applicability of the findings widely or sustainably.	"There is a 'notable absence' in teacher, parent and policy discourses of the role of computers in future society and the importance of understanding the social, ethical and environmental consequences of evolving technologies and their uses." (Blackmore, Hardcastle, Bamblett, & Owens, 2003, p. 198)

to contextualize issues that the author observed among the cases in Table 1 when discussing ethical practices and considering ethics applications by the researchers concerned, and to relate observations drawn from recent literature.

TRENDS

The framework in Table 2 emphasizes the practitioner-researcher's responsibility toward others, but it is important too for an intending researcher to reflect on others'—most notably technology managers' and academic administrators'—responsibility towards him/her. Those who wish to support and encourage this kind of research need to ensure that conducting it ethically will provide academics with intellectual and workplace satisfactions that overcome the discomforts and challenges. Otherwise there is the possibility of a trend to academic disenchantment with such research, based on fundamental issues of power and trust, including "knowledge ownership (including intellectual property rights and plagiarism); control (including perceived loss of control and status); and privacy (including issues of surveillance by and over themselves)" (Spencer, 2002, p. 2).

Trends in the research context may also be influential. The framework in Table 2 may be used by those who regulate research, as well as by those who do it. It is important that the intending practitioner-researcher finds her/his own clear perspective on ethical practice, regardless of turbulence in the social and political context of university research. If one's attitude to ethics is merely a reaction to an institutional culture of risk management, it may lead to "ethics committee rage"—as Scott (2003, pp. 93-94) describes in her response to what she regards as increasing over-governance of "the perceived power differential between intellectuals as researchers in relation to their subjects, and as teachers in relation to their students."

Educators' engagement in this kind of research has largely evolved through individualized interest and effort to date, but the trend to heightened levels of systematic attention to ethico-legal aspects of "business processes" is likely to reveal a legacy of practices that requires retroactive reforms as well as staff training for future improvement. A recent case observed by the author illustrates this trend: during the course of a seemingly straightforward project to pilot pre-existing digital video learning resources in a new online learning environment, it emerged that the academic producer of the videos did not hold informed consent from the people featured in the videos in a form that met the university's current ethics requirements.

Trends in the evolution of new technologies are likely to raise ever more interesting ethical questions for practitioner research, and to move research further into the realms of biomedical ethics. Addictive behaviors and anxiety disorders related to personal computing technologies such as mobile phones may become more prevalent. Virtual reality that is augmented by touch and smell may pose accessibility and even allergy problems. Wearable devices that bypass the hand-eye interface and connect with electrophysiological signals through the skin may have neuropsychological effects. "By comparison with the World Wide Web, ubiquitous computing is vastly more insinuative. By intention and design it asserts itself in every moment and through every aperture contemporary life affords it. It is everyware" (Greenfield, 2004, p. 1).

CONCLUSION

Serious engagement by practitioner-researchers with the special ethical challenges raised by educational technologies is right and proper. As well, it can illuminate processes, relationships, and scholarship in teaching and learning generally. It can yield improvements in the understanding that both teachers and learners have of their goals and roles, whether in technology-enabled settings or outside them.

From the perspective of responsible conduct of research, the sheer scale and scope of current practitioner research into teaching and learning with technology point to a need to instigate more a consistent approach to ethics. Even more importantly for the creation of new knowledge, working out the ethical design and conduct of such research can give rise to interesting and sometimes quite new research questions and technical development opportunities.

However it is unlikely that academics will find their way through the ethical questions or discover new ideas, if they work alone and in the privacy of their own classroom and their own conscience. It is important for the reputation and rigor of both educational technology research and the scholarship of teaching that academics engage thoroughly, openly, and collegially, with the aim of building greater sophistication into the planning and products of this kind of research.

REFERENCES

AECT (Association for Educational Communications and Technology). (2005). *Code of ethics*. Retrieved April 15, 2006, from http://aect.org/about/Ethics.htm

Blackmore, J., Hardcastle, L., Bamblett, E., & Owens, J. (2003). *Effective use of information and communication technology (ICT) to enhance learning for disadvantaged school students*. Retrieved April 15, 2006, from http://www.dest.gov.au/sectors/school_education/publications_resources/profiles/effective_use_technology_enhance_learning.htm

Brewer, E., Eastmond, N., & Geertsen, R. (2003). Considerations for assessing ethical issues. In M. Fitzgerald, M. Orey, & R. Branch (Eds.), *Educational media and technology yearbook 2003* (pp. 67-76). Oxford: Greenwood Press.

Chang, R., Gray, K., Polus, B., & Radloff, A. (2005, July 3-6). Scholarly teaching practice: Ethics issues and responses in research into teaching in tertiary education. In A. Brew & C. Asmar (Eds.), *Higher Education in a Changing World: Proceedings of the 2005 Annual International Conference of the Higher Education Research and Development Society of Australasia* (HERDSA) (vol. 28, pp. 93-100), University of Sydney. Retrieved April 15, 2006, from http://www.itl.usyd.edu.au/herdsa2005/pdf/refereed/paper_284.pdf

Clifford, P., Friesen, S., & Lock, J. (n.d.). *Coming to teaching in the 21st century: A research study conducted by the Galileo Educational Network*. Retrieved April 15, 2006, from http://www.galileo.org/research/publications/ctt.pdf

Coupal, L. (2005). Practitioner-research and the regulation of research ethics: The challenge of individual, organizational, and social interests. *Forum: Qualitative Social Research/Sozialforschung, 6*(1). Retrieved April 15, 2006, from http://www.qualitative-research.net/fqs-texte/1-05/05-1-6-e.htm

Frankel, M., & Siang, S. (1999, June 10-11). *Ethical and legal aspects of human subjects research on the Internet*. Report of a workshop convened by the American Association for the Advancement of Science Program on Scientific Freedom, Responsibility and Law, Washington, DC. Retrieved April 15, 2006, from http://www.aaas.org/spp/dspp/sfrl/projects/intres/main.htm

Gosper, M. (2004). *Summary of the Australian Council on Distance Education (ACODE) discussion on ethical issues in the online environment*. Retrieved April 15, 2006, from http://www.elearning.canterbury.ac.nz/documents/Ethical%20Issues_2.pdf

Greenfield, A. (2004). *All watched over by machines of loving grace: Some ethical guidelines for user experience in ubiquitous-computing settings*. Retrieved April 15, 2006, from http://www.boxesandarrows.com/view/all_watched_over_by_machines_of_loving_grace_some_ethical_guidelines_for_user_experience_in_ubiquitous_computing_settings_1_

Kennedy, G. (2003). An institutional approach to the evaluation of educational technology. *Educational Media International, 40*(3-4), 187-199.

Lamb, B. (2004). Wide open spaces: Wikis, ready or not. *EDUCAUSE Review, 39*(5), 36-48. Retrieved June 1, 2006, from http://www.educause.edu/ir/library/pdf/erm0452.pdf

Lorenzo, G., & Ittleson, J. (2005, July). *An overview of e-portfolios*. Retrieved April 15, 2006, from http://www.educause.edu/LibraryDetailPage/666?ID=ELI3001

Nordkvelle, Y., & Olson, J. (2005). Visions for ICT, ethics and the practice of teachers. *Education and Information Technologies, 10*(1/2), 19-30.

Pea, R. (2006). Video-as-data and digital video manipulation techniques for transforming learning sciences research, education and other cultural practices. In J. Weiss, J. Nolan, J. Hunsinger, & P. Trifonas (Eds.), *International handbook of virtual learning environments* (chapter 55). Berlin/London/New York: Springer-Verlag.

Poole, G., & MacLean, M. (2004). *Ethical considerations for research in higher education*. Retrieved April 15, 2006, from http://www.tag.ubc.ca/about/institute/Working%20Paper%20ISoTL1.pdf

Pownell, D. (2002). *Implementing handheld computers in schools: The research, development and validation of a technology leaders' resource guide*. Doctoral

Thesis, Kansas State University, USA. Retrieved April 15, 2006, from http://coe.ksu.edu/bailey/pownelldissertation.pdf

Roberts, P. (2000, September 11-13). Ethical dilemmas in researching online communities: "Bottom up" ethical wisdom for computer-mediated social research. *Proceedings of the International Distance Education and Open Learning Conference,* Adelaide, Australia. Retrieved April 15, 2006, from http://www.unisanet.unisa.edu.au/cccc/papers/refereed/paper40/Paper40-1.htm

Scott, C. (2003). Ethics and knowledge in the contemporary university. *Critical Review of International Social and Political Philosophy, 6*(4), 93-107.

Spencer, H. (2002). Educational technology and issues of power and trust: Barriers to the use of technology due to concerns over knowledge ownership, surveillance and power balance shifts. *Proceedings of the Human-Centered Technology Group Postgraduate Workshop,* University of Sussex Department of Informatics. Retrieved April 15, 2006, from http://hct.fcs.sussex.ac.uk//Submissions/18.pdf

Thompson, M. (2005, April). E-learning research in the U.S.: Challenges and opportunities. *Proceedings of the Worldwide Universities Network E-Learning Seminar Series* (seminar two). Retrieved April 5, 2006, from http://www.wun.ac.uk/elearning/seminars/seminar_two/papers/Melody.pdf

Vuorikari, R. (2005, October 5). *Can personal digital knowledge artefacts' management and social networks enhance learning?* Special Report, European Schoolnet/Insight Observatory for New Technologies and Education. Retrieved April 15, 2006, from http://www.eun.org/insight-pdf/special_reports/social_networks_learning_vuorikari_9_2005_insight.pdf

Zeni, J. (2001). *A guide to ethical decision making for insider research (epilogue).* New York: Teachers College Press. Retrieved April 15, 2006, from http://www.writingproject.org/cs/nwpp/lpt/nwpr/309

Zimitat, C., & Crebert, G. (2002, July 7-10). Conducting online research and evaluation. *Quality Conversations: Proceedings of the 2002 Annual International Conference of the Higher Education Research and Development Society of Australasia* (HERDSA) (pp. 761-769), Perth, Australia. Retrieved April 15, 2006, from http://www.ecu.edu.au/conferences/%20herdsa/main/papers/ref/pdf/Zimitat.pdf

KEY TERMS

Educational Technology: Information and communications technologies including online technologies used to provide support, resources, and activities for learning and teaching.

Human Subjects Research: A human subject is a person questioned or observed for purposes of research. Such research should protect the interest of people eligible to be involved.

Informed Consent: Guidelines for the conduct of human subjects research typically aim to ensure that the subject (or if a minor, the subject's guardian) is clearly informed of what the purpose of the study is, what their participation entails, any possible consequences from participation, the options for declining or ceasing to participate, contact details for information, and questions or complaints.

Intellectual Property (IP): A product of the mind or imagination able to be captured in a physical form. The IP is distinct from this form and can be described separately and possibly captured in other forms. Copyright and moral rights, trademarks, and patents are aspects of IP.

Practitioner Research: Research that a practitioner undertakes into his/her own work practices (also described as insider research); in human science professions like education, such research often involves human subjects; if the purpose of the research is to change work practices based on research findings, it may be referred to as action research.

Responsible Conduct of Research: A set of conventions to ensure the propriety of research with respect to the welfare of human subjects and animals, protocols for collaboration, peer review and authorship, conflict of interest, data management, and handling of misconduct.

Scholarship of Teaching: A view of teaching that regards teaching activity and the learning activity of students as a legitimate focus for research by those who are responsible for doing the teaching.

E–Health and Ensuring Quality

Prajesh Chhanabhai
University of Otago, New Zealand

Alec Holt
University of Otago, New Zealand

INTRODUCTION

The Internet is one of the most utilized resources for obtaining information, learning, communication, and as a source of advice. The most sought after advice and information are related with health matters. In the United States, for example, over 16 million people per year visit WebMD (*http://my.webmd.com/webmd_to-day/home/default*), an online portal dedicated to providing health information and services (Sass, 2003). Health information on the Internet has grown exponentially, with up to 88 million adults predicted to access medical information online in 2005 (Ansani et al., 2005). This merging of medical knowledge and information knowledge has given birth to e-health.

Despite the growth and application of information and communications technology (ICT) in health care over the last 15 years, e-health is a relatively new concept, with the term being introduced in the year 2000 (Pagliari et al., 2005). Its use has grown exponentially, and as Pagliari et al. (2005) reported, there are over 320,000 publications addressing e-health listed in MEDLINE alone. However, there is still no clear definition of e-health. There have been two international calls, in 2001 and 2004, for a clear and concise definition of e-health, but both failed to produce an internationally acceptable definition. In the same paper, Pagliari et al. (2005) found 24 different definitions, highlighting the fact that this is a gray area. Hence, without a clear and standardized definition, the opportunities to conduct unethical behavior are made easier.

In this article Eysenbach's (2001) definition will be used, as it provides a comprehensive overview of the term e-health. It has also been used, as Eysenbach is regarded as an expert in the area of e-health and consumer informatics. He has defined e-health as:

An emerging field in the intersection of medical informatics, public health and business, referring to health services and information delivered or enhanced through the Internet and related technologies. In a broader sense, the term characterizes not only a technical development, but also a state-of-mind, a way of thinking, an attitude, and a commitment for networked, global thinking, to improve health care locally, regionally, and worldwide by using information and communication technology. (Eysenbach, 2001, p. 1)

This phenomenon has led to consumers becoming more educated and aware of their health condition. This advice is not only accessed by people who may be suffering from a health condition, but also those who are healthy and want to remain so. E-health is being used as a tool for preventive and predictive treatment, as well as a means of locating others in a similar situation and sharing various experiences. In most developed countries e-health is seen to be the first step that one will take towards healing themselves, and if not avoiding the doctor, it is a useful second opinion.

However, the quality of the information on medical Web sites is highly variable and thus some users are reluctant to utilize the information given on mainstream sites. Through social engineering, some Web sites exploit the public's weakness for trusting information on the Web. There are numerous cases of online financial transactions in which unsuspecting members of the public have lost large amounts of money as they have been victims of exploitation. As with a financial setting, there is a great potential for good use and misuse for health information. With e-health experiencing rapid growth, it is becoming increasingly important to consider the various ethical issues that are involved with this form of health information. Unlike financial transactions, inaccurate and unethical information on health informing Web sites could lead to greater complications and even death (Theodosiou & Green, 2003).

Medicine and those that practice it have always had ethics as a core component of their field. There should be no difference when the more traditional aspects of medicine are modernized and utilized as e-health. All those involved with the running of online health care sites have to realize that they are running a site that could potentially mean the difference between life and death for those who access it. It is imperative that such Web sites follow codes and guidelines to prevent individuals' personal medical information, including patterns of use and interests, from involuntarily entering the hands of unauthorized people.

This article focuses on a number of privacy issues that are associated with e-health. Among these are concerns about determining the quality of technologically mediated care, ensuring and managing privacy, and allowing freedom of choice. It is well known that the Internet has the potential of exposing the public to unregulated volumes of misleading information on health and illness. This article will give a short summary of the various regulatory bodies that have been set up to try and ensure that any health information that is put up on the Internet is accurate and in no manner misleading. The *Codes of Conduct* proposed by the Health on the Net Foundation, *URAC* guidelines, and the *e-Code of Ethics* are examples of some regulatory ventures. It has to be made clear that medicine is a practice in which the interests of the patient are the priority rather than the exception, and with rules and regulations e-health can be as "safe" as going to one's local general practitioner. With the exponential growth of e health, the need to determine the safety, security, and ethical behavior in relation to the traditional services is of paramount importance.

BACKGROUND

The Impact of E-Health

The Internet is seen as the primary medium for the expansion of e-health (Maddox, 2002). This has already resulted in a shift away from the traditional health care delivery model. Patients need not rely on their health care provider for information, and the development of telemedicine has removed the geographic limits that have always been present in health care. The advent of electronic health records with decision support systems will enable medical records to be stored in large data warehouses, thus promoting easier disease management. Also the shift in financial and clinical relationships between all parties involved in health care are all a result of the e-health revolution.

The importance of the Internet in the e-health revolution is crucial. The expansion through this medium has produced eight different types of e-health Web sites. According to Sass (2003), these are:

- Internet-based medical education
- medical expert sites for patient management of a complex nature
- general health information sites for laypeople
- specialized medical sites where physicians play an active role
- cyber doctors who give second opinions for tests carried out in the real world
- sites provided by insurers and drug companies informing about various products
- community Web sites where people suffering from similar ailments share experiences and advice
- research Web sites that focus on new treatment techniques and methods

With such a large variety of e-health Web sites, it can be seen why more than 88 million people in America alone utilize the Internet to search for health information (Ansani et al., 2005).

This rapid expansion has led to the development of new challenges that will require a readjustment in current regulatory systems. Two primary concerns that are a direct result of the information explosion are the quality of information and the possibility of misinterpretation and deceit (Fried, Weinreich, Cavalier, & Lester, 2000). Health consumers and health care providers who access the Internet to obtain knowledge and information have to be able to trust the quality of information being presented to them. Also, with the large volume of content available, the chance of manipulating data and putting up incorrect information is a major concern and a real problem (Goldman & Hudson, 2000). It is this element of uncertainty that has proved to be the main barrier for the growth of e-health at an even faster rate (Fried et al., 2000). Apart from the problems with actual content, the major fear concerns the lack of privacy and security (Chhanabhai, 2005).

The fear arises from the inherent nature of the way business is run on the Internet. Currently most online businesses, especially health Web sites, utilize cookies to collect information about people that visit their Web sites. The other method in which information is collected is through the use of online registration forms. It is the collection of this information that consumers fear. As noted by Goldman and Hudson (2000):

The trail of transactional data left behind as individuals use the Internet is a rich source of information about their habits of association speech and commerce. When aggregated, these digital fingerprints could reveal a great deal about an individual's life. (Goldman & Hudson, 2000, p. 1)

As they lack trust, health consumers are reluctant to fully and honestly disclose health information. The *Ethics Survey of Consumer Attitudes About Health Web Sites* (2000) found that 75% of people surveyed are concerned about health Web sites sharing information without their permission. A large proportion of the survey sample stated that they refused to engage in any online health-related activity as a result of their privacy and security concerns. However, 80% of respondents also said that if there was a specific policy regarding their involvement in information sharing, they would be more willing to move towards the e-health system.

Health consumers' concerns are justified by the numerous reports of health information mismanagement within electronic systems. Win (2005) highlights the following reports:

- Kaiser Permanente accidentally sending e-mail responses to the wrong recipients. The e-mail contained sensitive information that was obtained through online activities
- Global-Healthtrax, an online health store, revealing all contact information including credit card numbers of their its customers on its Web site
- The University of Michigan Medical Center mistakenly placing thousands of its patients records for public access on its Web site

These are a few examples of the reasons that the health consumer is reluctant to fully embrace e-health. Despite that, health consumers are visiting online health Web sites for information and confirmation of various diseases and treatment plans. Thus their primary fear arises when they have to share personal and private information. As a consequence, privacy may not be

an issue when only visiting Web sites for information. The issues of quality and misinterpretation hence take on a bigger role in this scenario.

Health Web sites may seem to have high-quality information, but because of the nature of the health information, even this may cause unintentional harm to users of that information. Risk and Dzenowagis (2001) report that unlike other information, health information on the Internet is very susceptible to the following problems:

- language and complexity barriers
- inappropriate audience or context
- unavailability of certain services or products in different parts of the world
- difficulty in interpreting scientific data
- accuracy and currency of information
- potential for source bias, source distortion, and self-serving information

The wide-ranging sources of potential problem areas and the nature of the health Web sites makes them vulnerable to numerous ethical problems. The key ethical issues surrounding e-health are privacy and confidentiality, and quality of information (Ansani et al., 2005; Eysenbach, 2001).

Privacy and Confidentiality

Privacy is found to be the major concern with e-health (Westin, 2005). Health consumers feel that placing information on the Internet or on any electronic system makes it easily accessible to unauthorized persons. Unauthorized persons may be people within the particular company to people such as hackers (Goodman & Miller, 2000). These persons may use the obtained information in various ways. The information is valuable to insurance companies, pharmaceutical organizations, and fraudulent individuals. The fear is that health information can be used to blackmail individuals, especially those in high-profile positions (Givens, 1996). For the average person, the fear is that the information may be used by insurance companies to deny coverage and claims or to increase premiums. Potential employers could use the service of hackers to obtain health information and health Web site surfing habits on current or potential employees, and use this information to fire or not even hire a person (Goodman & Miller, 2000). As systems may be insecure and health information is of high value, there is a great potential for unethical behavior.

There are numerous types of people that have tried and will try to obtain health information. Each of these people will use different ways to try to obtain this information. These methods can be grouped into five distinct categories, identified by the Committee on Maintaining Privacy and Security in Health Care Applications of the National Information Infrastructure (National Research Council, 1997):

1. insiders who make "innocent" mistakes and cause accidental disclosures
2. insiders who abuse their record access privileges
3. insiders who knowingly access information for spite or for profit
4. the unauthorized physical intruder
5. vengeful employees and outsiders

These categories are not clear cut, as an intruder may fall into all the categories depending on his or her time period or situation. Outside attackers and vengeful employees make up one of the five categories; the other four categories indicate that the people that one should fear are those on the inside. Unlike other attackers who might be more interested in the actual breaking of the system, the insider who is a trusted individual is after the information (Spitzner, 2003).

Computer systems by their nature are prone to many other problems other than those that involve an intrusive nature. Being a system that is based on software and various pieces of hardware, an EHR system is vulnerable to both software bugs and hardware failures. These failures have the potential of corrupting medical records and thus diminishing the integrity of the system. When the postal, fax, or telephone system fails, there is a clearly evident impact on the message that is meant to be delivered (Anderson, 1996). In an EHR, this corruption may not be as easily noticeable. Examples include altering numbers in a laboratory report or deleting large amounts of important information. Unlike in other systems where an error would mean a financial disadvantage, an error in the health care system, due to badly designed software or poor hardware construction, may have a detrimental effect on both the caregiver and the patient.

Quality of Information

The quality of Internet-based medical information is extremely variable as there is no peer review or mandatory standard for the quality of health information (Edworthy, 2001). Studies by Ansani et al. (2005), Butler and Foster (2003), and Smart and Burling (2001) have found that health Web sites, irrespective of the medical condition, vary widely in their quality of information. These studies found that there were many inconsistencies in the information provided as well as in the various treatment plans proposed. This is to be expected, as many of the Web sites are sponsored by companies selling specific products or are run by individuals who are sharing their own experiences. Health information carries with it opportunities to reap large cash profits, thus many e-health Web sites are profit driven. With monetary value being associated with health information, the potential for health consumer deceit, bias, or distraction is high (Edworthy, 2001). Also, information may not come from credible sources, thus making it potentially harmful to people who may use that information as a benchmark in their health care. The problem lies with basic human nature. When individuals are suffering from an illness, especially a chronic illness, they tend to try non-conventional therapies in order to improve their condition. With the Internet teeming with alternative therapies, whether provided by individuals or a wide variety of groups, the possibility of using potentially harmful advice is very high (Center for Health Information Quality, 2005). It is this drive towards the use of non-traditional therapies that drives the need for models that can assure that good quality and correct information is published on the Internet.

Apart from possible problems that are a direct result of the information on the Internet, other negative effects of e-health affect the doctor-patient relationship (Theodosiou & Green, 2003):

*   health consumers may be better informed than their health care provider about medical findings in a specialized area,
*   health consumers may have found disturbing information that may not apply to their situation at all,
*   health consumers may choose to use alternative therapies that hinder or oppose the mainstream treatment methods, and

- health consumers may feel they are right and refuse to listen to their health care provider.

Despite the possible negative effects on the patient-doctor relationship, the advent of e-health also has an important role in the empowerment of the patient and thus addressing patients as health consumers rather than just patients. This again highlights the importance of ensuring that the standard of information that empowers patients is of the highest quality.

As can be seen, the possibility of unethical effects is limitless. A number of regulatory bodies have come into existence to try and reduce the chances of unethical activity. The next section will give a brief description of the main quality affirming bodies.

FOCUS

Regulating E-Health

Presently there are approximately 98 different rating schemes for medical Web sites (Ansani et al., 2005). With such a large number of schemes, there is no way of ensuring that one standard that can be trusted over another, thus leading to inconsistent information being posted on the Internet. The leading organizations that have established guidelines for online e-health initiatives are:

- E-Health Code of Ethics,
- Health on the Net Code (HONCode),
- Health Internet Ethics (Hi-Ethics), and
- American Accreditation Healthcare Commission (URAC).

The four above-mentioned schemes are recognized as the leaders in developing sustainable guidelines (Wilson, 2002). The Health Insurance Portability and Accountability Act (HIPAA) is legislation that aims to establish greater privacy rights for health consumers. However, it has a strong legal background that may affect ethical considerations. It is not discussed in this article.

E-Health Code of Ethics

Founded in May 2000 by the non-profit organization Internet Healthcare Coalition, the aim of the code is to provide a guiding set of principles aimed directly at e-health stakeholders worldwide. Its goal is:

to ensure that individuals can confidently and with full understanding of known risks realize the potential of the Internet in managing their own health and the health of those in their care. (Internet Healthcare Coalition, 2006)

The code, which can be found at http://www.ihealth-coalition.org/ethics/ethics.html, is based on eight basic principles: candor, honesty, quality, informed consent, privacy, professionalism in online health care, responsible partnering, and accountability.

Its principles are all based on ethical considerations. Unlike other guidelines, it does not focus on any legal considerations. This has allowed the code to be developed in a manner that provides an ethical foundation for both the providers and receivers of information. The strength of the code results from its development process. It was developed by a method similar to that of an open source project. The draft document was created by medical ethicists and persons involved in the area of ethical behavior. This draft document was then published for public comment, and the comments were incorporated into the final version of the code (Mack, 2002).

Despite its strong ethical base, the major downfall of the e-health Code of Ethics is that it places the final burden on the user of the Web site. As there are no real enforcement measures, the final responsibility is on the provider or the reader of the health information as to whether or not they should conform to the code.

Health on the Net Code (HONCode)

Developed by the Geneva-based Health on the Net Foundation in 1996, the HONCode is the earliest quality initiative for e-health. It is available in 17 different languages. Its inherent strength, simplicity, is also its weakness. Like the eCode of Ethics, the HONCode is based on a set of eight principles. These are (Health on the Net Foundation, 2006): authority, complementarity, confidentiality, attribution, justifiability, transparency of authorship, transparency of sponsorship, and honesty in advertising and editorial policy.

This code works by allowing Web sites that conform to all eight principles to display an active HONCode logo that is considered a Web site trustmark. The presence of this logo indicates that the Web site meets the set guide of standards and ethics. However, this is a self-certification system, and even though HON does periodically review the Web sites that apply for its logo, the Foundation still depends on users of the Web site to inform it if the Web site is not conforming to the HONCode of practice (Risk & Dzenowagis, 2001).

Once again the burden of responsibility is placed on the users of the site to inform HON if there are any breaches in the code; only then can that site have its link broken. The complete code of practice can be found at http://www.hon.ch.

Health Internet Ethics (Hi-Ethics)

Launched in May 2000, Hi-Ethics is a coalition of profit-making U.S. health Web sites. It is run by the non-profit organization Hi-Ethics Inc., with the aim to ensure that individual consumers can realize the full benefits of the Internet to improve their health and that of their families. It is based on 14 principles that are intended to increase the quality of information while ensuring that sound ethical principles are maintained (Mack, 2002). Its principles look at (Hi-Ethics Inc., 2006): privacy policies; enhanced privacy protection for health-related personal information; safeguarding consumer privacy in relationships with third parties; disclosure of ownership and financial sponsorship; identifying advertising and health information content sponsored by third parties; promotional offers, rebates, and free items or services; quality of health information content; authorship and accountability; disclosure of source and validation for self-assessment tools; professionalism; qualifications; transparency of interactions; candor and trustworthiness; and disclosure of limitations and mechanism for consumer feedback.

Web sites that conform to the principles are given URAC accreditation (see next section) and are listed on the Hi-Ethics Web site as trusted sites for health information (Kemper, 2001). Each Web site undergoes a third-party accreditation process before it is approved with the Web site trustmark. The problem with this is that it targets only American companies and Web sites, thus covering only a small portion of the Web sites that are available. This closed coalition and the importance of maintaining the currency of its principles are the main drawbacks of this guideline. (Mack, 2002; Kemper 2001).

American Accreditation Healthcare Commission (URAC)

Launched in August 2001, the URAC standards are based on the 14 Hi-Ethics principles. URAC also draws upon the eCode of Ethics in order to develop ethical frameworks for health Web sites. Unlike the eCode of Ethics, which is completely voluntary with no formal compliance assurance mechanism, URAC works in cooperation with Hi-Ethics to act as a third-party verification system. The standards address the following concerns (Mack, 2002): health content editorial process, disclosure of financial relationships, linking to other Web sites, privacy and security, and consumer-complaint mechanisms.

Any Web site that applies for accreditation with URAC undergoes a two-step review process. Initially the Web site is reviewed by a member of the URAC accreditation staff. The staff member travels to physically meet the owners of the site, to ensure that the online site and the people running it conform to their standards (URAC, 2006). Having passed that stage, the Web site is then assessed by the Accreditation and Executive Committees. Any Web sites that fail to comply with the guidelines after being accredited will have their accreditation withdrawn (Mack, 2002). Each Web site that wants to be accredited has to pay a fee that includes the cost of travel for URAC certifiers.

URAC also has a number of issues that have to be addressed. It is currently aimed at American Web sites, thus like the Hi-Ethics initiative, it is very limiting in its target market. Also it requires a substantial number of fee-paying members to make it truly viable. It cannot be considered to be a successful program if it only has a select group of Web sites conforming to its requirements.

There are numerous other guidelines and systems in place, and the report by Risk and Dzenowagis (2001) provides in-depth analyses of each of the different systems. These four mechanisms alone highlight that there is a problem in trying to control the type of health information that is made available on the Internet. The ideal solution would be to regulate the actual Internet itself. This move has been supported by the World Health Organization, which has called for tighter controls on the placing of health information on the Internet. However, this was opposed by Eysenbach (1998) who correctly stated that attempting to control information on the Internet is both unrealistic and undesirable. As the Internet cannot be controlled, the next best thing is to ensure that the guidelines that are available can and will do a good job. They must promote the rapid development of e-health by making available health information that is of high quality and conforms to stringent ethical standards.

CONCLUSION

The Internet was created to produce a medium of communication that is both flexible and under no specific governing body. By its nature, the Internet has grown extremely successful and has produced an environment that is difficult to regulate, as free speech is promoted. It is in this context that e-health has been developed, and its very nature is an adaptation of the nature of the Internet. The health consumer now has the opportunity to control the way their health is treated. This being so, an area has opened up for unscrupulous and unethical behavior. The problem is further heightened as health care itself suffers from unclear privacy rules. Thus e-health enjoys the benefits of both the electronic medium and medical treatment, but also suffers from the weakness of unclear privacy rules.

This article has highlighted a number of examples where e-health has suffered negative consequences resulting from fraudulent activity and incorrect information on the Internet. Quality of Internet health information is of utmost importance, as it can have both beneficial and fatal consequences for the wide audience that it reaches out to. The unclear definition of e-health does not help the cause either. With e-health not clearly defined, it leaves another question open, "What can be defined as good quality health information?" There are numerous standards and guidelines available, but none will work if there is no way of assessing what good quality health information is.

The four models discussed in this article aim to ensure the validity and reliability of e-health information while maintaining a strong ethical framework. The problems with the models are the lack of consistency and the often complex burden that is placed on the user of the Web site to understand and follow the different criteria. Also some of these models involve high costs to ensure accreditation (e.g., URAC), thus making it not viable for smaller and individual-run Web sites to subscribe to such standards. The models are focused on mainstream Web sites as well as mainstream therapies,

thus they do not take into account alternative therapies or treatments plans; yet, it is in these alternative methods that the chances for unethical behavior arise.

E-health is unquestionably the future of health care. With e-health, health consumers will be empowered with deep knowledge and self-care strategies, and will be linked to large communities of other health consumers and health care providers. For the health care providers, e-health brings the opportunity to immediately access patients' records while promoting evidence-based medicine and keeping updated with the most current treatment techniques. However, the full potential of e-health may not be realized, as there is great fear concerning the privacy, security, and unethical behavior connected with the Internet. Currently there are many alarming areas regarding e-health. What is needed is a single regulatory body that will ensure that ethics and privacy are essential elements in the design of e-health initiatives.

Promoters of e-health must remember that e-health is a branch of medicine and thus they should subscribe to the ethical practices that have been established through the Hippocratic Oath. They must remember that "the practice of medicine involves a commitment to service to the patient, not one to economic interests" (Dyer & Thompson, 2001, p. 1).

REFERENCES

Ansani, N.T., Vogt, M., Fedutes-Henderson, B.A., McKaveney, T.P., Webber, R.J., Smith, R.B., Burda, M., Kwoh, C.K., Osial, T.A., & Starz, T. (2005). Quality of arthritis information on the Internet. *American Journal of Health System Pharmacy, 62,* 1184-1191.

Butler, L., & Foster, N.E. (2003). Back pain online: A cross sectional survey of the quality of Web-based information. *Spine, 28,* 395-401.

Center for Health Information Quality. (2005). Retrieved November 31, 2005, from http://www.hfht.org/chiq

Chhanabhai, P. (2005). *EHRs: Fear of breach? The New Zealand public's opinion.* Unpublished Masters Thesis, University of Otago, New Zealand.

Dyer, K.A. (2001). Ethical challenges of medicine and health on the Internet: A review. *Journal of Medical*

E

Internet Research, 3(2). Retrieved December 25, 2005, from http://www.jmir.org/2001/2/e23/

Edworthy, S.M. (2001). Crawling through the Web: What do our patients find? *Journal of Rheumatology, 28*(1), 1-2.

Eysenbach, G. (2000). Recent advances: Consumer health informatics. *British Medical Journal, 320,* 713-16.

Eysenbach, G. (2001). What is e-health? *Journal of Medical Internet Research, 3*(2). Retrieved July 23, 2005, from http://www.jmir.org/2001/2/e20/

Fried, B.M., Weinreich, G., Cavalier, G.M., & Lester K.J. (2000). E-health: Technologic revolution meets regulatory constraint. *Health Affairs, 19*(6). Retrieved December 11, 2005, from http://content.healthaffairs. org/cgi/reprint/19/6/124

Goldman, J., & Hudson, Z. (2000). Virtually exposed: Privacy and e-health. *Health Affairs, 19*(6). Retrieved December 11, 2005, from http://content.healthaffairs. org/cgi/reprint/19/6/140

Goodman, K.W., & Miller, R.A. (2000). Ethics and health informatics: Users, standards, and outcomes. In E.H. Shortliffe & L.E. Perreault (Eds.), *Medical informatics: Computer applications in health care and biomedicine.* New York: Springer-Verlag.

Grimes-Gruczka, T., & Gratzer, C. (2000). *Ethics survey of consumer attitudes about health Web sites.* Retrieved November 11, 2005, from http://www.chcf. org/documents/consumer/Ethics2ndEdition.pdf

Health on the Net Foundation. (2006). Retrieved January 3, 2006, from http://www.hon.ch/

Hi-Ethics Inc. (2006). Retrieved January 3, 2006, from http://www.hiethics.com/

Internet Healthcare Coalition. (2006). Retrieved January 3, 2006, from http://www.ihealthcoalition.org/

Kemper, D.W. (2001). Hi-Ethics: Tough principles for earning consumer trust. In J. Mack (Ed.), *The new frontier: Exploring e-health ethics* (pp. 145-150). URAC/Internet Healthcare Coalition.

Mack, J. (2002). *Global e-health ethics—access + quality = equity.* Retrieved November 6, 2005, from http://www.wma.net/e/publications/pdf/2001/mack. pdf

Maddox, P.J. (2002). Ethics and the brave new world of e-health. *Online Journal of Issues in Nursing.* Retrieved December 20, 2005, from http://www.nursingworld. org/ojin/ethicol/ethics_10.htm

Pagliari, C., Sloan, D., Gregor, P., Sullivan, F., Detmer, D., Kahan, J.P., Oortwijn, W., & MacGillivray, S. (2005). What is e-health (4): A scoping exercise to map the field. *Journal of Medical Internet Research, 7*(1). Retrieved December 23, 2005, from http://www.jmir.org/2005/1/ e9/

Risk, A., & Dzenowagis, J. (2001). Review of Internet health information quality initiatives. *Journal of Medical Internet Research, 3*(4). Retrieved August 5, 2005, from http://www.jimir.org/2001/4/e28/

Sass, H.M. (2003). *Ethical issues in e-health and the promotion of health literacy.* Retrieved October 5, 2005, from http://www.ruhr-uni-bochum.de/zme/healthlit- eracy/publofpro.htm

Sass, H.M., & Zhai, X. (2004). E-health ethics: A yet to be recognised issue in medicine and medical ethics. *Eubios Journal of Asian and International Bioethics, 14,* 147-148.

Smart, J.M., & Burling, D. (2001). Radiology and the Internet: A systemic review of patient information resources. *Clinical Radiology, 56,* 867-870.

Theodosiou, L., & Green, J. (2003). Emerging challenges in using health information from the Internet. *Advances in Psychiatric Treatment, 9,* 387-396.

URAC. (2006). Retrieved January 4, 2006, from http://www.urac.org/

Wilson, P. (2002). How to find the good and avoid the bad or ugly: A guide to tools for rating quality of health information on the Internet. *British Medical Journal, 324,* 598-600.

Win, K.T. (2005). A review of security of electronic health records. *Health Information Management, 34*(1), 13-18.

Westin, A.F. (2005). U.S. public sharply divided on privacy risks of electronic medical records. *Proceedings of the Hearing on Privacy and Health Information Technology,* Washington, DC. Retrieved March 17, 2005, from http://www.pandab.org/

KEY TERMS

Consumer Health Informatics: "The branch of medical informatics that analyses consumers needs for information; studies and implements methods of making information accessible to consumers; and models and integrates consumers' preferences into medical information systems" (Eysenbach, 2000).

E-Health: "An emerging field in the intersection of medical informatics, public health and business, referring to health services and information delivered or enhanced through the Internet and related technologies. In a broader sense, the term characterizes not only a technical development, but also a state-of-mind, a way of thinking, an attitude, and a commitment for networked, global thinking, to improve healthcare locally, regionally, and worldwide by using information and communication technology" (Eysenbach, 2001).

Electronic Health Records: A longitudinal collection of health information about individual health consumers and populations which is stored in an electronic format. The stored information will provide a picture of "cradle to the grave" consumer health information.

Health Informatics (Medical Informatics): The emerging discipline in which information technology is applied to the medical field. It involves the development of structures and algorithms to enhance the treatment, management, and prevention of medical conditions.

Informed Consent: The process by which a health consumer is firstly given all the information about various procedures, which will possibly include information on how consumer information will be treated. The health consumer can then make a legally binding decision to carry on with the process or decline taking part.

Medical Ethics: The field that considers the activities, risks, and social effects that affect the field of medicine. It is strongly based on the Hippocratic Oath and uses this as a guideline to determine the ethical conduct of professionals in the field of medicine.

Medical Internet Ethics: "An emerging interdisciplinary field that considers the implications of medical knowledge utilised via the Internet, and attempts to determine the ethical guidelines under which ethical participants will practise online medicine or therapy, conduct online research, engage in medical e-commerce, and contribute to medical Web sites" (Dyer, 2004).

MEDLINE: A comprehensive electronic literature database of life sciences and biomedical information produced by the U.S. National Library of Medicine. It covers the fields of medicine, dentistry, nursing, veterinary medicine, health care administration, and the pre-clinical sciences dating back to 1966.

Telemedicine: The use of telecommunications technology to aid in medical diagnosis and consumer care when the health care provider and health consumer are separated geographically.

Electronic Signatures and Ethics

A. Srivastava
Monash University, Australia

S. B. Thomson
Monash University, Australia

INTRODUCTION

The advent of the Internet once again raised the question as to what constitutes a signature and what form of signature should be used to sign electronic documents. This led legal jurists and academics to examine what a signature is. Traditionally, a signature is "the name of a person written with his or her own hand" (Merriam-Webster Online Dictionary, 2006), and since 439 AD in the Roman Empire, a signature authenticated wills (Nicholas, 1965). However, courts have accepted various other forms of signature such as initials, marks, rubber stamp, typed name, and a printed name.[1] Thus the validity of a signature is not to be tested by its form but rather by the functions it performs (Reed, 2000). The primary functions of a signature are to provide evidence: (1) of the identity of the signatory, (2) that the signatory intended the signature to be his/her signature, and (3) that the signatory approves and adopts the contents of the document as his/her own (Reed, 2000). The primary functions of a signature are the only mandatory requirement adopted by most legislation for signing electronic documents.[2] Thus, any type of technology that has the ability to satisfy the primary functions of a signature can be used to sign electronic documents. Such types of technologies are generically known as *electronic signatures* (ESs).

ES is defined as "data in electronic form…affixed to or logically associated with (an electronic record)…used to identify the signatory…and indicate the signatory's approval…" (UNCITRAL MLES, 2001, Article 2a). Examples of ESs include, but are not limited to, a password, a typed name at the end of an e-mail, a personal identification number (PIN), a biometric indicator, and a digital signature (DS). Among all the types of ESs, DS is the most popular as judged by the fact that the term is often used interchangeably with ES (Shark Tank, 2003). DS is a technologically specific mechanism based on Public Key Cryptography (PKC), whereas ES is a technology-neutral term and can be any technology that is able to satisfy the legislative requirements.

The aim of this article is to describe in detail the various forms of ESs, especially DS, and analyze the ethical issues associated with the usage of ES/DS. The first section explains in detail the technology of DS, describes the legal functions that a DS performs in the electronic environment, and explains the implementation of DSs. Next we describe other forms of ESs such as passwords, PINs, "typed name at the end of e-mail," and the various forms of biometrics. The ethical issues associated with the usage of ES/DS are examined, and we end with a summary of the article.

DIGITAL SIGNATURES

DSs are formed and verified by using cryptography, the branch of applied mathematics concerned with transforming messages into seemingly incomprehensible form and back again into the original form (Electronic Frontiers, 2005). DS performs three important functions: *authentication, integrity,* and *non-repudiation. Authentication* is "broadly the act of proving that something (as a document) is true or genuine…" (Garner, 2004, p. 142). *Integrity* protects the contents of data, so that it is possible to know that the read message has not been changed either accidentally or maliciously. Non-repudiation is "a property achieved through cryptographic methods which prevents an individual or entity from denying having performed a particular action…" (ECEG, 1998, Appendix 4). The sender of the message cannot falsely repudiate that the message has not been sent by him/her.

The Implementation of DSs

Based upon a technologically specific mechanism, PKC, or asymmetric-key cryptography, a DS subscriber has two keys: a private key and a public key. These key pairs are obtained from an institution known as a certification authority (CA), which associates the public and private key pair to an individual. The private key and the public key are unique to the subscriber and work as a functioning key pair. The private key is only known to the user, just like a password or PIN, whereas the public key is known to the public and can be found in a similar manner to a person's name and phone number in a telephone directory.[3] The procedure described in Diagram 1 identifies the method used to seal a document with the DS.

The data message to be sent is first hashed through a hashing algorithm to get a message digest. To the message digest the signer (user) applies his/her private key (124) to obtain a DS. After receiving the DS the sender (signer) attaches the DS to the data message. Both the attached data message and DS are encrypted with the recipient's public key (362) and sent to the recipient. Upon receipt of the digitally signed document, the receiver will separate the DS from the body of the document (data message) with his/her private key (263). The data message is then hashed using the same algorithm that the signer used to create the DS. This will result in the message digest (1). The DS is then processed using the signer's public key (421) to receive a second message digest (2). If both (1) and (2) are the same, then the recipient has verified the identity of the signer because the signer's public key will verify only a DS created with the signer's private key. The message integrity is established because the message is shown to have remained unaltered.

Even though the process shown in Figure 1 is considered as being highly secure, it is a very slow process. In reality, for maintaining the security as well as retaining high-speed data transfer, DS technology uses both a symmetric and asymmetric crypto system. Figure 2 demonstrates this process. Data is encrypted in two phases:

1. A symmetric key (123) is used to encrypt the body of message (data message + digital signature).
2. The symmetric key (123) is then encrypted with the recipient's public key and sent along with the encrypted message.

When the body of document (data message + digital signature + symmetric key (123)) reaches the recipient, the recipient decrypts the data in two phases:

1. The recipient decrypts the body of document (data message + digital signature + symmetric key (123)) through his/her private key to receive the symmetric key.
2. With the symmetric key now decrypted, the message body (data message + digital signature) can be decrypted with the help of the symmetric key (123).

The above method not only enhances the speed of data transfer but also encrypts the body of the message twice, making it doubly secure.

Figure 1. Implementation of a DS[4]

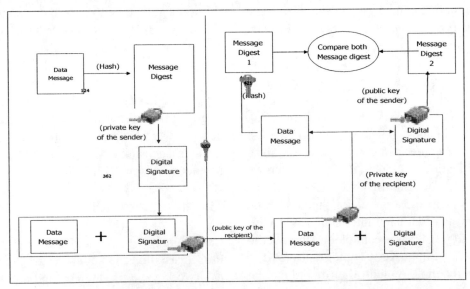

Figure 2. Data encryption through DS

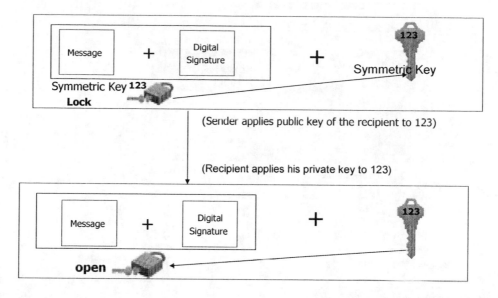

OTHER FORMS OF ESS

Password

A password represents the most common form of authentication used as a form of ES. Passwords are generally used to log into a computer or onto a network or an online service. A single computer can be used by many users, each having his/her own user name and password. Every time a user wants to use the computer, the computer asks that person his/her username and password. Once he/she types his/her user name and password, the computer checks the password file containing usernames and passwords. Only if the entry matches the name and password is the login successful.

When more than one computer are connected to each other and their resources shared, or when the required resources are kept on a remote computer,

known as a server, the password used for accessing remote resources are generally different from those used to log into the computer. For example it is very common to have a user name and password to access a network printer or to connect to the Internet. In such a case the password file is stored at a centrally located server (see Figure 4).

In both the procedures mentioned above, a user's name and password are stored in a password file containing many usernames and passwords, thus access to this file can reveal anybody's username or password. So, in order to secure the password file from unauthorized access, these passwords files are encrypted or hashed through the hashing algorithm. Hashing the passwords protects them from hackers/eavesdroppers. Even if they extract hashed passwords, it will be of no value to them. It is almost impossible to retrieve the actual password from the hashed passwords.

PIN

PINs are generally issued by banks so their customers can access automatic teller machines (ATM) and carry out other banking facilities such as electronic fund transfers (EFTs) and so forth. Today PINs are also issued by many institutions as a form of ES. The institutions clearly state that a PIN serves as an ES. For example the U.S. Department of Education Web site (see Figure 5) provides PINs to students as a form of ES.

Figure 3. Password storage on servers

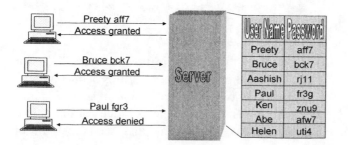

Figure 5. PIN as an ES[5]

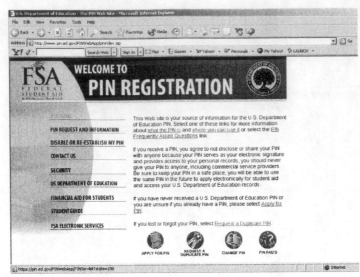

Figure 6. E-mail—personal signature[6]

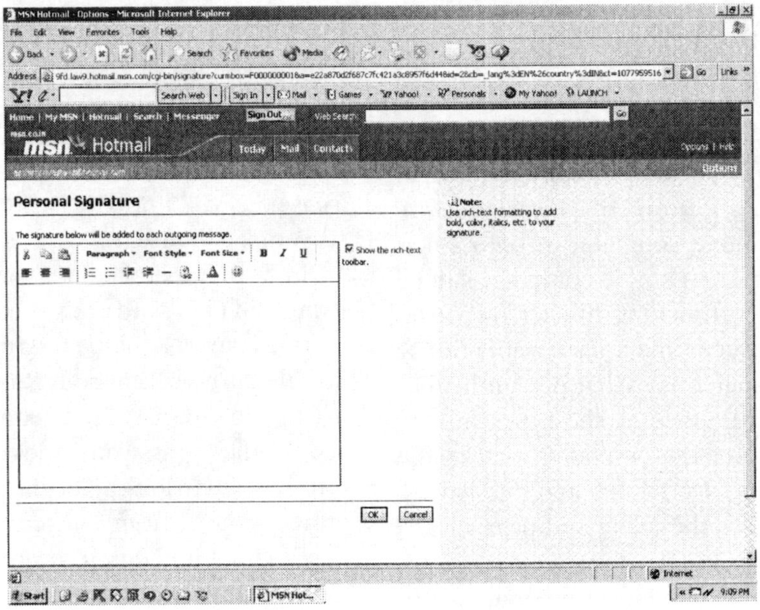

Typed Name at the End of an E-Mail

Typed name at the end of an e-mail can also be a form of signature. For example, Hotmail™ gives an option to its users to create a personal signature that can be added to one's e-mail message (see Figure 6).

A person can type his/her name and other text, such as address and so forth, in the box to be used as a form of signature. Such a type of 'personal signature' can be used by individuals as a form of ESs to sign their e-mails. However, such a signature will be considered

valid in the eyes of the law only if it can be proved that it was created by the sender, and with an intention to authenticate the contents of the e-mail document.

Biometrics

In biometrics "the body is the password" (Smith, 2002, p. 193). Biometrics uses features of the body or a person's behavior for authentication and consequently as a form of ES. Some of the examples of biometrics are fingerprints, retina scan, iris scan, recognition of images of face, voice recognition, and key-stroke dynamics. The compulsory use of such biometrics has been in existence for many years in prisons and military bases. However, the use of biometrics as a form of ES will be voluntary rather than compulsory.

How Does Biometrics Work?

Biometrics works in a way similar to passwords. Despite the various forms of biometrics in existence, the functioning of all the types of biometrics are fundamentally the same. All biometric systems use a biometric reader that collects the traits of the particular biometric, for example. a camera will be a biometric reader for the iris or retina, and a fingerprint reader will be a biometric reader for a fingerprint. The biometric reader will extract the trait associated with the particular biometric to generate a data item known as the biometric signature. This biometric signature is then stored in the database in the form of an electronic file. In the future when the user presents his/her biometric, it is verified with the biometric signature already stored in the database.

ETHICAL ISSUES RELATED TO ES/DS

Kant proposed that an ethical act must be considered naturally or instinctively right or wrong. Therefore three questions must have a positive response (Payne & Landry, 2005):

1. Is the action universally consistent?
2. Does the action respect the individual?
3. Does the action take account of and respect the autonomy of the individual?

By signing a document the individual reveals his/her identity, which provides the same action that we would all expect from others. The signature demonstrates respect to others by the act of revealing one's identity, and it demonstrates the willingness to respect the terms and conditions of a contract set out by all parties involved. Lastly, a signature illustrates the individual's autonomy by its unique nature and the fact that it was given willingly and freely. The technology of ES/DS seems to meet ethical requirements.

In the case of DS, a major ethical concern is with regard to the issuance of key pairs by the CA. Is it

ethical on the part of the government to allow anyone to act as a CA? A CA gathers personal and business information that may be used for either illegal or unfair advantage by an individual or group. Therefore, it is of utmost importance that a CA be trustworthy and reputable (Froomkin, 1996).

Is it ethical that a CA provides key pairs with inappropriate security procedures? A CA that does not take stringent measures to ensure accurate identification procedures in the issuance of DSs fails to protect individuals from invasion of privacy and illegal acts such as identity theft and fraud. CAs should issue key pairs to applicants only after face-to-face meetings and checking identity requirements (Davis, 1996). Also a CA that fails to guarantee a secure delivery procedure of key pairs breaches ethical considerations for their own convenience or cost saving (Srivastava, 2005).

The key to ES/DS security is the secrecy of the private key or password/PIN. Individuals or groups that act in a cavalier manner about the security of their ES (i.e., password/private key/PIN) act unethically. They leave not only themselves at risk but others as well. For example, an organization mandates individuals use a unique seven-digit code as a backup if their biometric identification fails. An organization acts in a cavalier manner by recommending the use of the individual's telephone number as their code in order to reduce overhead. If an unethical individual is aware of the telephone number, then they can bypass the biometric procedures and use another person's identity to their advantage (Alterman, 2003).

This use of biometrics can be considered a benefit to track down known criminals, but it also illustrates the ethical dilemma of the possible invasion of privacy from the use of biometrics. In the last decade initiatives have been undertaken to fingerprint or photograph individuals entering given countries. There is no recourse; if an individual wishes to enter one of these countries, they must submit to this process. Individuals who have broken no law are treated as criminals. Although the procedure may be deemed acceptable after the events of 9/11, questions still arise as to the use, security, and storage of the biometric data gathered by governments.

Biometrics, no matter how secure, dehumanizes the body. Biometrics transforms the body into a piece of identification (Alterman, 2003; van der Ploeg, 1999). Thus individuals, groups, or organizations (i.e., governments) can covertly identify individuals, even in a crowd, and use that information to their advantage without the individual's knowledge. Once again, by applying Kant's ethical requirements, the universality can be questioned by those who are opposed to being treated as a criminal when entering a country. The innate value of the human being is stripped away when it becomes a tool for identification. Biometrics does recognize the uniqueness of each individual and respects his/her autonomy; however, the user of that data may not respect the autonomy of the individual. The use of biometrics results in negative responses for Kant's ethical requirements, rendering it unethical. However, the voluntary use of biometrics results in positive responses to all three questions. The ethical use of biometrics as a form of ES/DS hinges upon voluntary participation.

A final ethical issue with ES/DS resides in the global nature of e-communication and e-commerce. Most of the development and direction of the Internet has come from Western developed nations. There are ethical concerns over the creation of information-rich as opposed to information-poor countries and even with creating the same scenario within societies (Medley, Rutherfoord, Anderson, Roth, & Varden, 1998). In regards to ES/DS cultural ethical issues, some forms of ES/DS may not be acceptable in terms of preferences for face-to-face relationship building. Individuals unaware of the cultural background of those they are dealing with may inadvertently cause offence or transgress ethical boundaries. Therefore to avoid inadvertent and ethical aspects, one should not only be aware of the legal environment, but also the cultural environment of the ES/DS sender or recipient.

CONCLUSION

The various forms of ESs, including DSs, are the technological alternatives to the manuscript signature in the online environment. The legal validity of ESs means businesses and individuals can finalize their deals online. Legally enforceable e-contracts or e-transactions are no longer a myth but a reality.

However, the technology of DSs, through the functions of authentication, integrity, and non-repudiation, are comparatively more secure than other forms of ESs. The drawback with various other forms of ESs is that they can only ensure authentication and not integrity and non-repudiation (Pun et al., 2002). The advantage

is that they seem to be much easier and less complex to use as compared to DSs. The other drawback with other forms of ESs is that they need to be shared. Thus, their success with regard to the usage will depend upon the secrecy of such an ES (PIN/password).

In regards to ethical issues, ESs/DSs strike a similar chord to basic ethical issues that arise with handwritten signatures. Fraud, inappropriate use, and the violation of privacy exemplify some of those issues. Legislation across the globe mandates punitive consequences for those who violate ethical behavior in regard to written signatures. Within the last decade governments have responded to a 'cultural lag' between Internet technology and ethical beliefs systems by introducing legislation to address ES/DS validity and reliability.

No doubt, unethical behavior will continue to occur through electronic media such as the Internet and e-commerce. However, the recognition of the legal and moral obligations that an ES/DS carries is a positive step towards ethical behavior and standards for a knowledge economy and an electronic age.

REFERENCES

Alterman, A. (2003). A piece of yourself: Ethical issues in biometric identification. *Ethics and Information Technology, 5,* 139-150.

Davis, D. (1996, July). Compliance defects in public-key cryptography. *Proceedings of the 6th USENIX Security Symposium* (pp. 171-178).

Electronic Commerce Expert Group to the Attorney General of Australia. (1998). *Electronic commerce: Building the legal framework.* Retrieved June 20, 2005, from http://152.91.15.15/aghome/advisory/eceg/single.htm

Electronic Frontiers. (2005). *Introduction to cryptography.* Retrieved June 20, 2005, from http://www.efa.org.au/Issues/Crypto/crypto1.html

Froomkin, A.M. (1996). The essential role of trusted third parties in electronic commerce. *75 Oregon L. Rev. 49.* Retrieved June 20, 2006, from http://osaka.law.miami.edu/~froomkin/articles/trusted1.htm#xtocid72314

Garner, B.A. (Ed.). (2004). *Blacks law dictionary.* St. Paul, MN: Thomson/West.

Medley, M.D., Rutherfoord, R.H., Anderson, G.E., Roth, R.W., & Varden, S.A. (1998). *Ethical issues related to Internet development and research*. Retrieved June 20, 2006, from http://delivery.acm.org/10.1145/360000/358299/ p57-medley.pdf?key1=358299&key2=4472329411&coll=portal&dl= ACM& CFID=72658567&CFTOKEN=44080140

Merriam-Webster Online Dictionary. (2006). Retrieved June 2, 2006, from http://www.m-w.com/dictionary/signature

Nicholas, B. (1965). *An introduction to Roman law*. Oxford: Clarenden Law Series.

Payne, D., & Landry, B.J.L. (2005). Similarities in business and IT professional ethics: The need for a development of a comprehensive code of ethics. *Journal of Business Ethics, 62*, 73-85.

Pun, K.H., Hui, L., Chow, K.P., Tsang, W.W., Chong, C.F., & Chan, H.W. (2002). Review of the electronic transactions ordinance: Can the personal identification number replace the digital signatures? *Hong Kong Law Journal, 32*, 241.

Reed, C. (2000). What is a signature? *Journal of Information Law and Technology*. Retrieved March 24, 2005, from http://elj.warwick.ac.uk/jilt/00-3/reed.html

Shark Tank. (2003). Not exactly what the doctor ordered. *Computerworld*. Retrieved May 15, 2005, from http://www.computerworld.com/departments/opinions/sharktank/0,4885,77957,00.html

Smith, R.E. (2002). *Authentication from passwords to public keys*. Addison-Wesley Canada.

Srivastava, A. (2005). Is Internet security a major issue with respect to the slow acceptance rate of digital signatures? *Computer Law & Security Report, 21*, 392-404.

UNCITRAL (United Nations Commission on International Trade Law). (2001). *Guide to enactment of the UNCITRAL model law on electronic signatures*. Retrieved June 20, 2006, from http://www.uncitral.org/pdf/english/texts/electcom/ml-elecsig-e.pdf

van der Ploeg, I. (1999). The illegal body: 'Eurodac' and the politics of biometric identification. *Ethics and Information Technology, 1*, 295-302.

KEY TERMS

Algorithm: A formula or a series of mathematical steps to achieve a particular task.

Certification Authority: The identity of an individual in cyberspace is established through digital certificates issued by a 'certification authority' (CA), also known as the 'trusted third party'. It is the CA that links the public and private key pair to an individual. This association is confirmed in a certificate known as DS Certificate, which is an electronic file containing all necessary information to identify the creator of a DS.

Data Message: An electronic document like an e-mail or word file.

Hash Function: A process whereby the data message is passed through an algorithm, which is a one-way function, and an irreversible process resulting in a number that is substantially smaller than the data message—a 'message digest' or 'hash value'. It is virtually impossible to derive the data message from its hash value. Two similar data messages, if passed through the same hashing algorithm, will give the same hash value. However, if one data message is even changed by a single bit, the hash value will change.

Key: In cryptography, a variable value that is applied using an algorithm to the unencrypted text to produce an encrypted text, or to decrypt an encrypted text. The length of the key is measured in bits and is a factor in considering how difficult it will be to decrypt the text in a given message.

ENDNOTES

[1] There are various court cases where courts have accepted various other forms of signatures apart from handwritten signatures. See *Thompson v Vittadello, 1978, R 199*; *Smith v Greenville County, 188, SC 349*; *Joseph Denunzio Fruit Company v Crane, 79 F, Sup 117, DC Cal 1948.*

[2] A signature also performs certain secondary functions which "attest to: the intent of a party to be bound by the content of a signed contract; the intent of a person to endorse authorship of a text; the intent of a person to associate itself with the content of a document written by someone

else; the fact that, and the time when, a person had been at a given place" (UNCITRAL, 2001, p. 19).

[3]   Storage device generally known as Online Certificate Server.

[4]   Adapted from lecture notes, Post Graduate Diploma in Cyberlaws and Internet Related Laws (2000-2001), Indian Law Institute, New Delhi.

[5]   Retrieved June 20, 2005, from http://www.pin.ed.gov/PINWebApp/pinindex.jsp

[6]   Retrieved January 10, 2006, from www.hotmail.com

Engineering Multi-Agent Systems

Tagelsir Mohamed Gasmelseid
King Faisal University, Kingdom of Saudi Arabia

INTRODUCTION

The migration of business enterprises to decentralized operations, location independence, and micromanagement has been accompanied by the emergence of different computing paradigms, enterprise architectures, and communication platforms. Software agents perform some tasks on behalf of their users, other agents, or programs with some degree of autonomy using multiple information and communication platforms. The use of wireless devices and networks has significantly improved information transmission and transaction processing in support of virtual and physical mobility and the acquisition, customization, and use of context-specific information for electronic and mobile shopping, finance, banking, and payment services.

BACKGROUND

The proliferation of networked and Web-based information systems shows a growing interest in using multi-agent systems in different applications (electronic commerce, airlines, insurance, distance learning, manufacturing, and the management of common pool resources) because of their potential decision support, negotiation, and task-delegation features. Software agents (making up multi-agent systems) perform some tasks on behalf of their users. These tasks range from information search and retrieval, management of information overload, scheduling and interface presentation, task delegation, user training, event monitoring, and information search, to matchmaking and decision making. Multi-agent systems offer a new dimension for coordination and negotiation by incorporating autonomous agents into the problem-solving process and improving coordination of different functional unit-defined tasks, independent of both the user and the functional units under control (Byung & Sadeh, 2004). Their capacity to carry out these tasks demands that they possess some basic qualities including autonomy, conviviality, reactivity, learning, mobility, benevolence,

rationality, and adaptivity (Lai & Yang, 2000; Jung & Jo, 2002; Lisa, Hogg, & Jennings, 2001; Hu & Weliman, 2001). The growing use of multi-agent systems in different domains has also been accompanied by an expanding interest in "mobility," "context awareness," and "information security."

Mobility allows different agents to move across different networks and perform tasks on behalf of their users or other agents, by accessing databases and updating files in a way that respects the dynamics of the processing environment and intervention mechanisms. The importance of maintaining security in mobile systems stems from the importance of maintaining integrity, privacy, and information sharing. Furthermore, context awareness allows multi-agent systems to support mobility through the acquisition and use of context information that describes location, time, activities, and the preferences of each entity. The dynamic and adaptive provisioning of context information requires an expressive, semantically rich representation to support context information acquisition, context engagement (required by certain events to trigger actions), and context dependency (the relationship between different aspects of context information). On the other hand, seamless concepts require a service layer in the multi-agent infrastructure that is capable of delivering functionalities such as context management, context-based service discovery, and a communication protocol responsible for handling issues such as presence, notification, and privacy (Khedr & Karmouch, 2005).

Within this context, emphasis on "information security" continued to be made on technological solutions and the use of hardware devices or computer programs. The basic aim is to prevent, avoid, detect, or prepare for breaches of security that threaten the confidentiality, integrity, or availability of information processed by computer systems. The majority of networked systems are managing their information security through the use of cryptographic algorithms, digital signatures and challenge response authentication techniques, hash algorithms, and hybrid encryption mechanisms and protocols (Microsoft, 2000). Asymmetric cryptographic algorithms use two related keys (public and private), each of which has the characteristic algorithm that, given the public key, is computationally infeasible to derive the private key. Symmetric cryptography, on the other hand, transforms (encrypts) the plaintext (original data) into ciphertext (protected data) in a way that makes it infeasible to reverse the process without the full knowledge of the transformation function. A hash function is a one-way transformation that efficiently turns arbitrary-length data into fixed-length data, and gives some data or its hash value. However, it is computationally infeasible to find some other data that will hash into the same value. Hash algorithms are commonly used for digital signatures, passphrases, integrity protection, and challenge-response authentication. Applications frequently employ hybrid or bulk encryption when they are required to apply a confidentiality service to shared data. Using a protocol such as (SSL/TLS) processing is done on the assumption that the receiver has a private-public key pair and that the sender has obtained the public key. Using hybrid encryption and hash functions, digital signatures offer a data authentication service and ensure the origination of messages from the source and stability of contents. However, approaching information security through technological solutions is challenged by the variety of key length, computational complexity, and breach possibilities. Therefore, it is essential to "couple" technological solutions with an array of other factors (human resources, standard operating procedures, structure, and system development methodologies) that should be investigated when addressing information security.

INFORMATION SECURITY OF MULTI-AGENT SYSTEMS: REVISITED

The process of developing multi-agent systems continued to be guided by different agent-oriented software engineering (AOSE) methodologies such as Gaia, Tropos, MESSAGE, Prometheus, and MaSE. While some current AOSE methodologies are "expanding" the application of existing "conventional" object-oriented methodologies to agent-oriented domains, others are focusing on defining a number of models that guide the process of designing agent-oriented applications in accordance with the basic guidelines of agent theory (Wooldridge, Jennings, & Kinny, 2000). Some of these methodologies are criticized for their limited deployment due to the lack of maturity (Dam & Winikoff, 2003) and their failure to capture the autonomous and proactive behavior of agents, as well as the richness of the interactions (Zambonelli, Jennings, Omicini, & Wooldridge, 2001). Current agent-oriented methodologies focus mainly on multi-agent systems analysis and design, but without providing straightforward connections to the implementation of such systems (Mercedes et al., 2005). They are characterized with a fundamental mismatch between the concepts used by object-oriented developers and the agent-oriented view (Wooldridge & Jennings, 1999). As a result, they fail to adequately capture an agent's flexible, autonomous problem-solving behavior, the richness of an agent's interactions, and the complexity of an agent system's organizational structure. Most of these methods feature a technology-driven, model-oriented and sequential approach, and assume (in advance) the suitability of multi-agent technology for the development of multi-agent applications, which may not always be the case in different problem domains. Because model orientations of these methodologies are obvious, the process of model coupling and integration does not explicitly reflect the links between models (Lind, 1999). Besides the main issues (known as agent qualities) to be addressed by agent-oriented software engineering methodologies (such as autonomy, reactivity, proactiveness, and social ability), the concern for mobility has been growing over time (Pablo et al., 2003).

In spite of the growing diffusion of mobile agent technology, little research has been done to settle "design" directions to be followed in order to determine when mobile agents are convenient to be used or not. However, the current agent-oriented software engineering methodologies used for developing multi-agent systems do not provide methods to determine in which cases mobile agents should be used. Many of the existing methodologies intentionally do not support intelligent agents; rather, they aim for generality and treat agents as black boxes (Padgham & Winikoff, 2002).

While the entire agent-oriented software engineering methodologies have provided alternative ways for describing "tasks" and "relationships," little has been done to incorporate "information security" considerations in multi-agent "mobile" and "context aware" applications. The importance of maintaining the information security of multi-agent systems originates from two basic considerations:

a. the expanding use of these systems in different service-provision (e-learning, e-banking, e-medicine) and facilitation (e-governance and the management of common pooled resources) domains that are inexorably related to our lives and the "fabric" and "ecosystems" of enterprises; and

b. the growing number and type of threats associated with the enterprise transformations and change of the qualities that constitute agenthood.

Threats to multi-agent systems range from uncontrolled accessibility and modification of core agent codes and services to the integrity of processes and communications, service execution, and coordination.

Incorporating information security considerations demands not only change of programs and technological solutions, but also a review of the way multi-agent systems are being developed and the methodologies used. Within this context, emphasis should be made on the description and implementation of two basic issues of information security:

1. linking information security with functional decomposition, message initiation, and communication in pursuit of integrated multi-agent task management; and

2. viewing security mechanisms on "layered bases" in order to enhance information flow, mainstream feedback, and the use of appropriate metrics and standard operating procedures to reduce threats at earlier stages.

As shown in Figure 1, functional decomposition of activities and tasks in a multi-agent, mobile, and context-aware system targets three (basic and complementary) functions: network-specific (fixed and wireless), user-centered, and agent-based functions undertaken through network devices, agents, or users themselves. User functions (such as accessing data or printing a document) are usually implemented through the use of mobile devices and network infrastructures. The implementation of mobile-specific and context-aware functions of users requires the execution and orchestration of some (direct and interface) network activities such as the acquisition and use of context-related

information necessary for assuring device suitability for the implementation of the entire function. Such process is based on metrics and artifacts (e.g., the location of the device, its type, its processing attributes, etc.) while preserving the integrity of standard operating procedures in use and efficiency of feedback mechanisms that govern the "sequencing," initiation and termination of activities, accessing and updating databases, and streamlining complementary activities used by networks, users, and agents.

Identifying linkages between "functions" using information security perspectives facilitates the crystallization of potential threats, their potential causes, and consequences, and accordingly setting the foundation for the appropriate security platforms. By doing so, all functions and components will have their "information security" mechanisms embedded in their base. Moreover, viewing the information security of multi-agent, mobile, and context-aware systems allows taking precautions at different levels and incorporating relevant measures in agent codes.

The decision-making context reflects the entire organizational structure (through which information is exchanged), objective (to be supported by the multi-agent information system), and the decision-making models (reflecting managerial styles). The importance of maintaining task-security coherence and layered information security is affected by the increase and diversity of the devices and resources to be used in heterogeneous networks and the functions to be performed in spontaneous ad hoc communications in a transparent, integrated, and extensible fashion.

Revisiting AOSE methodologies to incorporate information security considerations as shown in Figure 1 has three reflections on the functionality of multi-agent, mobile, and context-aware systems:

1. It "embedds" security in solution spaces when specifying and structuring problems in accordance with rules, behavior expectations, and authority relations, particularly in open dynamic environments where the security of negotiation mechanisms looms largely. Because the capacity of an agent to fulfill its task assignment(s) either individually or collectively is contingent upon its capacity to use the appropriate means to electronically scan the environment, discover the appropriate information, and satisfy its information requirements, maintaining linkage between

Figure 1. Conceptualization of information security

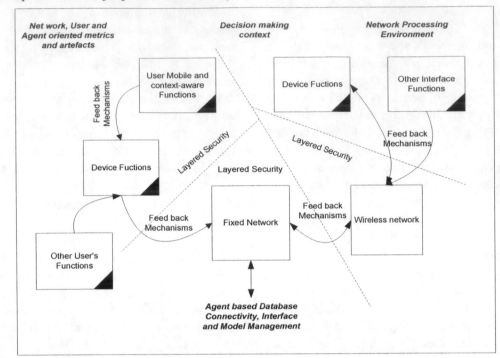

task decomposition and information security provides considerable support and improves the learning capacity of agents. The use of Internet indices of the search engines and "facilitators" to search the available information for the agent to obtain network locations is challenged by the overwhelming work, the change of Internet addresses, and increasing security threats.

2. The emphasis on AOSE-based information security measures rather than technological solutions only, brings "ontological and semantic" considerations to the surface at early stages. Ontological complexities appear because the interacting parties (represented by agents) should agree upon the structure of messages, instructions, requests to be supported, semantics, and the list of terms to be used in the content of messages. Sharing and agreeing on a common definition of process-related concepts is known as the ontology. The explicit definition of (all) concepts to be represented includes the definition of the concepts themselves, meanings of attributes, constraints on attributes' values, and the relations between the attributes of different concepts. However, despite the use of general-purpose ontologies and the provision of editors for creating domain-specific ontologies and converters for translating between ontologies, the context and magnitude of the problem of ontology have been complicated by the failure to incorporate security measures properly. While a significant degree of ontological sophistication of agents is necessary for knowledge sharing, cooperation, and interoperability, the interaction between the "domain" and "task" ontologies is cumbersome and includes many induced security-related risks.

3. It significantly affects the tradeoff among alternative agent architectures. Architecture specifies how agents can be incorporated as a part of a multi-agent system and how these "parts" (hardware and/or software modules) should be made to interact using specific techniques and algorithms. In a deliberative architecture, the explicitly represented model of the problem domain depends on logical reasoning, pattern matching, and symbolic representation for "taking decisions." A reactive architecture, on the other hand, does not include any kind of central symbolic world model and does not use complex symbolic reasoning. Instead, it is based on considering the behavior of an agent as the result of competing entities trying to get control over the actions of the agent. A hybrid

architecture combining aspects of both, realized as a number of software layers, each dealing with a different level of abstraction, has been widely used. At the lowest level in the hierarchy, there is typically a reactive layer, which makes decisions about what to do on the basis of row sensor input. The middle layer deals with a knowledge-level view of the agents' environment making use of symbolic representation. The upper-most level of the architecture tends to deal with the social aspects of the environment. Coordination with other agents is typically represented in the upper-most layer. Due to the lack of universally accepted agent representation architecture and the heterogeneity of application domains, investigating necessary layers of security associated with alternative architectures when decomposing tasks remains an important tradeoff factor.

FUTURE TRENDS

The continuity of trends like decentralization, mergers, and acquisition efforts; globalization of business operations; and emphasis on developing advanced architectures by business enterprises reflects more emphasis on the use of Web technologies, wireless communication, and accordingly, information security concerns. The growing migration of business enterprises towards "downsizing," "micro management," and "time-based competition" also suggests the expansion of deployment of intelligent systems in general and multi-agent, mobile, and context-aware applications in particular. It also expands the expected radical change in the qualities that constitute agency. The unprecedented technological developments witnessed during the last couple of years also reflect the possibility and potential of mobile devices in terms of functionalities, use, and interface. Existing mobile devices are expected to change into complicated multi-purpose equipment that supports more and different forms of user mobility, system intelligence, and advanced information exchange domains. Based on all of these transformations, more emphasis is expected to be made on coupling technological solutions with other situation-specific variables when addressing information security networked businesses and heterogeneous telecommunication platforms. Interest in developing alternative approaches for information security are also

expected to grow due to the outstanding developments witnessed in the field of developing context acquisition and use devices, and the mounting efforts to make information systems more flexible, responsive, and even sensitive to changes in their surrounding environments. The accommodation of information security concerns, together with the above-mentioned transformations in response to the potential threats associated with the deployment of multi-agent, mobile, and context-aware systems, warrants the attention of the software engineering community and calls for revisiting the way these systems are being analyzed, designed, and used. It is only "multidisciplinary" analysis, not the analysis of technological dimensions of information security, that improves the "integrity" and "privacy" of these systems in a digital economy governed by networks of "capital," "information," and "power."

CONCLUSION

The migration towards Web-based, context-aware, and mobile systems has resulted from the growing wave of organizational transformations that significantly affect the capacity of business enterprises to develop appropriate strategies to benefit from opportunities and avoid threats. Because information threats are increasing, it is important to understand technological solutions as well as the way such systems are being developed and used. While the use of technological solutions and security measures may be of considerable value in maintaining information security of intelligent systems in general, the investigation of other security-related variables remains of paramount importance. The articulation of human resources involvement, organizational culture and structure, and standard operating procedures, among others, provides an integrated domain for understanding and maintaining information security. However, because the "agency-hood qualities" of multi-agent systems change over time in response to technology developments and organizational transformations, there is a growing need to "reengineer" the agent-oriented software engineering methodologies to reflect concerns of information security. Such reflection not only enriches the process of threat anticipation activities, but also enables the development of agent codes and mechanisms necessary for managing ontological and semantic problems. Moreover, incorporating information security concerns also contributes to "relaxing" the problems related to the selection of appropriate system architectures and methods of representing "problem domains" into "agent-oriented" solution spaces.

REFERENCES

Amor, M., Fuentes, L., & Vallecillo, A. (2005). *Bridging the gap between agent-oriented design and implementation using MDA* (pp. 93-108). Berlin: Springer-Verlag (LNCS 3382).

Dhillon, G. (2001). Challenges in managing information security in the new millennium. In G. Dhillon (Ed.), *Information security management: Global challenges in the new millennium* (pp. 1-9). Hershey, PA: Idea Group Inc. Retrieved May 2, 2006, from http://www.atis.org/tg2k/_asymmetric_cryptographic_algorithm.html

Hu, J., & Weliman, M.P. (2001). Learning about other agents in a dynamic multi-agentsystem. *Cognitive Systems Research, 2*(1), 67-79.

Jung, J.J., & G.S., Jo. (2002). Brokerage between buyer and seller agents using constraint satisfaction problem models. *Decision Support Systems, 28*(4), 293-304.

Khanh, H.D., & Winikoff, M. (2003). Comparing agent oriented methodologies. *Proceedings of the Conference on Agent-Oriented Information Systems* (AOIS-2003), Melbourne, Australia. Retrieved from www.cs.rmit.edu.au/agents/Papers/aois2003.pdf

Khedr, M., & Karmouch, A. (2005). ACAI: Agent-based context-aware infrastructure for spontaneous applications. *Journal of Network and Computer Applications, 28*(1), 19-44.

Kleijnen, M., de Ruyter, K., & Wetzels, M.G.M. (2003). Factors influencing the adoption of mobile gaming services. In B. Mennecke & T. Strader (Ed.), *Mobile commerce: Technology, theory, and applications* (pp. 202-217). Hershey, PA: Idea Group Publishing.

Kwon, B., & Sadeh, N. (2004). Applying case-based reasoning and multi-agent intelligent system to context-aware comparative shopping. *Decision Support Systems, 37*(2), 199-213.

Lai, H., & Yang, T.C. (2000). System architecture for intelligent browsing on the Web. *Decision Support Systems, 28*(3), 219-239.

Lind, J. (1999). *A review of multi-agent systems development methods.* Technical Report, Adastral Park Labs, British Telecom, UK.

Lisa, M.J., Hogg, L.M.J., &. Jennings, N.R. (2001). Socially intelligent reasoning for autonomous agents. *IEEE Transactions on Systems, Man, and Cybernetics, Part A: Systems and Humans, 31*(5), 381-393.

Pablo, V., Maximiliano, A., Sebastián, R., María, R., & Omar, C., (2003). Approaches for the Analysis and Design of Multi-Agent Systems, *Inteligencia Artificial, Revista Iberoamericana de Inteligencia Artificial.* 21, 73-81. Retrieved from: http://www.aepia.org/revista

Pattinson, M.R. (2005). A method of assessing information system security controls. In M. Quigley (Ed.), *Information security and ethics: Social and organizational issue* (pp. 214-237). Hershey, PA: Idea Group Publishing.

Mercedes, A., Lidia, F., & Antonio V., (2005). Bridging the Gap Between Agent-Oriented Design and Implementation Using MDA*. Lecture Notes in Computer Science, Volume 3382, Chapter 3, (pp: 93-108), Springer-Verlag GmbH.

Microsoft. (2000). *Windows® 2000 security technical reference.* Retrieved May 2, 2006, from http://www.microsoft.com/mspress/books/WW/sampchap/3873a.asp

Oliveira, E., Fischer, K., & Stepankova, O. (1999). Multi-agent systems: Which research for which applications. *Robotics and Autonomous Systems, 27,* 91-106.

Padgham, L., & Winiko, M. (2002). Prometheus: A pragmatic methodology for engineering intelligent agents. *Proceedings of the OOPSLA Workshop on Agent-Oriented Methodologies* (pp. 97-108), Seattle, WA.

Trcek, D. (2004). E-business systems security for intelligent enterprise. In J. Gupta & S. Sharma (Ed.), *Intelligent enterprises of the 21st century* (pp. 302-320). Hershey, PA: Idea Group Publishing.

Villarreal, P., Alesso, M., Rocco, S., Galli, M.R., & Chiotti, O. (2003). Approaches for the analysis and design of multi-agent systems. *Inteligencia Artificial,* (21), 73-81. Retrieved May 2, 2006, from http://www.aepia.org/revista

Wooldridge, M.J., & Jennings, N.R. (1999). Software engineering with agents: Pitfalls and pratfalls. *IEEE Internet Computing, 3*(3), 20-27.

Wooldridge, M., Jennings, N.R., & Kinny, D. (2000). The Gaia methodology for agent-oriented analysis and design. *Journal of Autonomous Agents and Multi-Agent Systems, 3*(3), 285-312.

Zambonelli, F., Jennings, N., Omicini, A., & Wooldridge, M. (2001). Agent-oriented software engineering for Internet applications. *Coordination of Internet Agents: Proceedings of SEKE01, the 13th International Conference on Software Engineering–Knowledge Engineering* (pp. 283-290), Buenos Aires.

KEY TERMS

Agent-Oriented Software Engineering (AOSE): The methodology used for engineering software that has the concept of agents as its core computational abstraction, particularly in the context of complex, open, networked, large, and heterogeneous applications. The main purposes of AOSE are to create methodologies and tools that enable inexpensive development and maintenance of agent-based software in a flexible, easy-to-use, scalable, and quality fashion.

Context Awareness: Reflects the ability of mobile devices to acquire and use information about the circumstances under which they operate and react accordingly. By making assumptions about the user's current situation, context awareness assists in the design of user interfaces in ubiquitous and wearable computing environments and hybrid search engines. It also reflects task-relevant information and/or service that can be used to characterize the situation of an entity to a user.

Digital Signature: Cryptographic means necessary for the verification of the origin of a document, the identity of the sender, the time and date a document was sent and/or signed, and the identity of a computer or user in order to reduce security breaches. The digi-tal signature of a document is a piece of information based on both the document and the signer's private key. It is typically created through the use of a hash function and a private signing function (encrypted with the signer's private key), but there are other methods. They are created and verified using digital certificates to support authentication confidentiality, data integrity, and non-repudiation.

Information Security: Refers to all the strategies, policies, procedures, mechanisms, and technical tools used for safeguarding information and information systems from unauthorized access, alteration, theft, and physical damage. The basic aim is to maintain integrity, confidentiality, availability, and privacy of information systems, and their components and contents.

Mobility: Providing universal access to communication tools, networks, databases, and information repositories, as well as reliable applications, regardless of their location or type of access devices. Can be implemented through calling, conferencing management, presence, messaging management, contact and information management, and personal efficiency management and other tools that guarantee access to messages represented in different data formats.

Multi-agent System: A collection of possibly heterogeneous, computational entities that use their own problem-solving capabilities to interact in order to reach an overall goal. Their ability to improve information availability, problem-solving capabilities, corporate control, and distributed data processing gave them more importance in different domains of application. They proved to be suitable for complex, distributed problems involving a multiplicity of interconnected processes whose solutions demand the allocation of fusion of information and expertise from demographically distributed sources.

Web-Based System: System in which Web technologies are used to improve efficiency and performance through decision models, Online Analysis Processing (OLAP), and data mining tools that allow publishing and sharing of decision resources on the Internet. In a Web-based system, all activities are performed on a network server in order to benefit from platform independence, shorter learning curves for users, ease of performing system updates, and "reusability" of decision modules through standardized protocols and formats.

Ethical Approach to Gathering Survey Data Online

Sophie Nichol
Deakin University, Australia

Kathy Blashki
Deakin University, Australia

INTRODUCTION

Using the Internet to conduct online surveys is not a new form of data collection. A large proportion of marketing analysis or customer surveys are now done online (Burns & Bush, 2006). However the uptake in tertiary education and research has proven to be slower. This could be attributed to the fact that high-visibility institutions such as universities are subject to stringent codes of ethics (Kizza, 2003). This article discusses techniques university researchers may use when implementing an online survey, premised on McNiff, Lomax, and Whitehead's (2003) action research checklist of ethical considerations. These techniques abide by both the institution's code of ethics and national standards to ensure the participants' privacy, confidentiality, and anonymity. In addition, the benefits of conducting online research are discussed, particularly when the cohort under consideration is moving into majority status within society such as the *Generation Y* of this study. Generation Y participants under consideration in this chapter are university students studying Games and Development at Deakin University, Australia.

The games students are prodigious consumers of online entertainment, information, and specifically from the researchers' previous experience, learning material online. These defining characteristics of Generation Y were harnessed and used to very good effect in the development of the research tool (an online survey) used in this article. The research process for obtaining ethical approval to conduct surveys and collect and evaluate data for this particular participant cohort thus must incorporate contemporary methods of ethically obtaining data. Ethically, the issues with collecting data in traditional methodological modes such as privacy, confidentiality, anonymity, and coercion remain similar, however in this study there is the additional complexity of conducting a survey online. The ethical guidelines of this study are premised on those published by the Australian Government (1999) and are the current guidelines used by Deakin University. This article explores the issues related to obtaining ethical clearance for conducting an online survey with Generation Y participants.

BACKGROUND

The Games Design and Development students are from Deakin University in Victoria, Australia. By virtue of their age, the majority between 18 and 25, these students are demographically considered to be Generation Y (generally those born between 1979 and 1994) (McCrindle, 2006). This identification as Generation Y is important to acknowledge in relation to the games geeks, not as a definitive "labeling" of them, but rather because of the basic characteristics the label encompasses. While clearly each games geek is defined by his or her individuality, as a cohort they possess characteristics that delineate them as Generation Y. Such identifiable traits include: flexibility, adaptability, spontaneity, and an increased disposition towards participative behaviors. Most notable however has been Generation Y's willing and enthusiastic uptake of technology such as the Internet, and using it to design, create, participate, and support online communities (Sheahan, 2005). Communication among Generation Y is continually shifting between online and off-line modes, and culturally specific languages such as Leet Speak (Blashki & Nichol, 2005) have evolved as part of these slippery social negotiations and hierarchies. This chapter specifically highlights how the games geeks from our research are particularly receptive to online communication as a part of their social negotiations, and thus we chose an online survey as the best method of data collection with them. The survey tool used in this study is best described as a Web resource that has the sole purpose of the creation and management of online surveys. The tool allows each participant to go to a specific Web location to complete the survey. Once the survey is completed, the data is stored in a database. To access the data the researchers use the Web interface. This tool was created at Deakin University.

The purpose of the online survey was to gather data concerned with social collaboration and technological factors that contribute to the environment of each games student at Deakin University. In this study, environment is defined as physical elements (computers, resources, information) as well as social (family, friends, peers, teachers, mentors). The purpose of the survey is to attempt to elicit the 'creative' skills of games students, to ensure that the learning environment in which they study can be enhanced to support these creative skills (Isaksen, Lauer, Ekvall, & Britz, 2001; Nichol & Blashki, 2005, 2006).

The manner in which the researchers designed and conducted the online survey with the games geeks is of primary significance in this article. In addition to formal ethical guidelines provided by the Australian Government (1999), the methodological approach of action research also influenced procedures and data collection and evaluation. Action research is the methodology loosely guiding the research process in this study. However it needs to be highlighted that the online survey presented in this study is a subset of a much larger 'cyclic' action research project conducted by the researchers. The larger study involves many other forms of data collection, such as interviews and observations, as well as participation of the researchers in the community of the games students. As in action research, the researchers are directly involved in the study with the participants, not as observers but rather as active participants (Levin & Greenwood, 2001). Action research is renowned as a methodology that attempts to influence the practices of a community of people. In this study the community may be defined as the games students. As McNiff et al. (2003) note, action research is concerned with the exercise of influence, and it is often assumed that the resulting influence is both negative and/or sinister (McNiff et al., 2003). To mediate and mitigate any influence the researchers may have upon the participants, every research project must have a solid ethical foundation, regularly scrutinized by the researchers themselves and other outside observers. McNiff et al. (2003) define ethics principles of action

research processes in six stages and refer to it as the "Checklist of Ethics Considerations":

1. Draw Up Documentation
    a. Ethics statement (plain language statement at Deakin University)
    b. Letters of permission (consent form at Deakin University)
2. Negotiate Access
    a. With authorities
    b. With participants
    c. With parents/guardian/supervisors
3. Promise Confidentiality
    a. Confidentiality of information
    b. Confidentiality of identity
    c. Confidentiality of data
4. Ensure Participants' Rights to Withdraw from the Research
5. Ensure Good Professional and Academic Conduct
6. Keep Good Faith

These six steps from McNiff et al. (2003) were adhered to during the application process for ethics clearance to survey the games geeks, however the distinctive requirements for the successful implementation of online surveys resulted in the modification and adaptation of the steps to focus on providing a solid ethical framework in an online environment. The following section identifies the difficulties inherent in the implementation of a survey 'online' specifically for games geeks, and in addition explores the ethical considerations undertaken by the researchers to ensure that these complications were overcome.

HOW TO ETHICALLY AND EFFICIENTLY SURVEY GAMES GEEKS

"Trust is integral to a successful virtual community and it is a core ingredient of social capital" (Heath, 2006, p. 46). McNiff et al.'s (2003) six steps assisted in the provision of a reliable ethical framework to facilitate the 'trust' that is required when undertaking a survey, in particular online. Some of the ethical techniques used by the researchers to build trust with the games students included:

1. The provision of plenty of detail in the plain language statement and consent form, so that each participant knew exactly what was required of them.
2. The provision of the full details of all involved in the research (contact details) so the participants know who to contact regarding their participation.
3. Offer an opportunity for participants to ask more questions, either at the end of the survey or by providing an e-mail address through which that they can contact the researchers.
4. The critical contributing factor to the development of trust with the games students was the purposeful cultivation of a face-to-face relationship between the researchers and the participants. This relationship was established prior to the implementation of the online survey.

In addition to facilitating trust in the ethical framework, many other problems arose during the development of the ethics application to conduct the online surveys with the games students. The six ethical considerations are seminal in the building of good ethical techniques for the researchers of the study, however do not adequately support the 'online' element present in the surveys with the games geeks. As discussed, the online survey is the best method to survey the games geeks, therefore the researchers have adapted McNiff et al.'s (2003) ethical considerations. Structurally premised on these six considerations, the following details how the ethical considerations were used in the study of the games geeks.

Draw Up Documentation

Consent

The national statement defines that:

...where consent to participate is required, research must be so designed that each participant's consent is clearly established, whether by a signed form, return of a survey, recorded agreement for an interview or other sufficient means. (Australian Government, 1999, p. 12)

At Deakin University the ethical conduct of surveys and questionnaires requires paper-based consent forms to be provided to the participant for signature; they are then returned to the researcher prior to any undertaking to complete the survey. However the input device of the survey in the online environment is a keyboard and screen, rather than paper, and thus renders such a practice impractical. To overcome this difficulty the "consent form" is preceded by the following comment:

By clicking the submit survey button at the end of the questionnaire you consent to your participation within this study.

Such a statement subsumes the requirement for a signature to be gathered from each participant and is an appropriate way to ethically gain consent from participants, and constitutes consent in accord with the national statement. However, the assumption is that each participant understands that the 'submit survey' button is functioning as a substitute for the conventional paper-based signature on a consent form. This may not be the case, with participants not reading or only skimming the survey's listed ethical procedures. To overcome this potential dilemma, the consent statement (as listed above) is displayed to the participant on the survey in a very distinct way, by using large font size and color for the statement. It should be noted, however, that when conducting a survey online, the participant should not feel at any time pressure or coercion to participate as the researcher is not providing that face-to-face presence. As an example the consent form permitted the *submit survey* button to function as a signature, because the survey did not require the participant to input any personal information. The supply of personal information was deemed optional, however most of the students actively chose to supply personal information including first name, last name, and e-mail address.

Negotiate Access

Authorities/Participants

Access to the participants did not pose any difficulties, however such access must be carefully considered. Consent in this situation was not just on an individual level with each student. Consent to undertake the survey was required from the relevant teaching 'authorities'. This is in line with the national statement that "the researcher needs to obtain the consent of all properly interested parties before beginning the research" (Australian Government, 1999, p. 12). In this study the survey was available via the university's online learning system *Deakin Studies Online (DSO)*. Prior approval was sought and granted by the relevant authorities in order to allow access to the survey via DSO, however the potential ethical issue with this arrangement is that DSO stores the student's information, progress data, and grades. It was essential that the participants were made aware of the distinction between the survey and their DSO information. The survey was in no way associated with DSO apart from functioning as a repository for its conduct, and none of the survey data will be stored on DSO. To reassure the students, the plain language statement highlighted:

The responses will not be held on DSO.

Minors

Gaining consent to survey minors (under the age of 18) requires parental consent. This can often prove to be a prolonged and difficult process. Given the rampant independence of our participants and the added complication of online, the researchers determined that no minors should undertake the survey. While the survey was conducted with university students, the potential for minor participation was realized and raised within the ethics clearance. To overcome the potential ethical issue, the plain language statement asked in red highlighted text.

If you are not yet eighteen years of age please do not complete the survey.

This statement ethically covers the researchers in regard to minor participation. However, due to the vigorous independence of the participants in this study, we could not guarantee that minors would not participate. Ethically however, the survey has covered the issue of minor participation.

Coercion

A plain language statement was provided to participants clearly outlining that the survey was in no way related to the assessment processes of their studies:

No one other than myself will have access to the questionnaire data obtained from you (this includes whether you have participated in the questionnaire or not). This includes lecturers and other tutors: they do not have access to the data obtained, only myself.

Coercion is an ethical issue that often requires some creative ideas on how to recruit participants for involvement in a study. With the games students, coercion was not a significant issue because of the way access was negotiated for provision of the survey. The survey was placed on the DSO at the beginning of semester and left there until the end, to ensure that there was no pressure on the students to fill it in within a certain timeframe. Furthermore, the students were not forced to the survey. It was their choice, as discussed previously.

Promise of Confidentiality

Security/ Integrity of Data

The national statement defines that:

...where personal information about research participants or a collectivity is collected, stored, accessed, used or disposed of, a researcher much strive to ensure that the privacy, confidentiality and cultural sensitivities of the participants and/or the collectivity are respected. (Australian Government, 1999, p. 13)

Based on Deakin University current processes, the convention for paper-based surveys is to agree to contain all survey and participant data in a locked filing cabinet or room at all times while undertaking the study. The online survey therefore proposes a number of technical issues that need to be addressed in order to assure participants of a similar level of security.

1. **Submission of data/storage of data:** The plain language statement clearly outlines the manner in which the online data will be submitted and stored once the participant has completed the survey:

The submitted responses will be sent to a secure database that can only be accessed by the researcher. The responses will not be held on DSO. Once your questionnaire data is obtained, it will be stored in a safe location (locked under password protection) with the School of IT as per Deakin University Guidelines. This will occur for the duration of the study. Upon completion, the personal details part of the survey will be destroyed, with the anonymous survey data being stored in a locked filing cabinet in my supervisor's office (on a CD) for a minimum period of 6 years.

2. **Collection of IP address:** This is built into the online survey tool. The impetus for gathering this information is to ensure that the researchers can potentially track duplication survey submissions. Naturally, due to the nature of the participants under observation, they could potentially submit multiple surveys via simply using a different computer, therefore different IP. This is an issue that could be addressed by requiring participants to login to the survey using their student login details. These details could be checked against a formal list. There is a potential ethical issue with the collection of IP address information. However, the plain language statement outlines that participants can opt to have their IP address removed by contacting the researchers.

Personal Details

The collection of personal details was not integral to this survey, therefore participants were offered the option of not providing any personal details. The following statements outline the participants' rights when providing their personal details:

"You will be asked for your personal information at the beginning of the survey. This is optional. However, if you do provide your personal details the highest respect for your privacy and confidentiality will be maintained....Furthermore, the contact details are only linked to the survey via a code, and both documents will be kept under separate (password protected) files. Your contact details are not explicitly stated anywhere on the survey, only used as a record for further contact later on in the study."

Participants' Right to Withdraw from the Study

The right to withdraw is an important ethical component of any study, and needs to be actively facilitated. As defined by the national statement "a participant must be free at any time to withdraw consent to further involvement in the research" (Australian Government, 1999, p. 13). In addition it also defines that " a person may refuse to participate in a research project and need to give no reasons nor justification for that decision" (Australian Government, 1999, p. 12). In the online survey the participants were informed of the way in which they can 'technically' withdraw from the study:

Survey respondents are free to choose which questions they will answer. You can also exit the survey at any stage by closing the window. Thus no responses will be recorded. Upon completion click the submit survey button to submit your responses.

In a separate section, clearly differentiated from other text, the following comment further assures the participant:

Importantly, you are not obliged to participate in this study. Furthermore, if you do participate in this study, you are free to withdraw at any time and your contributions to the study withdrawn.

The technique of anonymous surveying is to provide each participant with a unique code that refers to the participant's particular survey. In the games geeks online survey, once the participant 'submitted' his or her survey, an additional screen was displayed indicating the survey's unique code, in addition to the typical "survey submitted successfully" screen. The participant is informed on this screen that if he or she wishes to withdraw his or her survey results from the study, he or she is required to contact the researcher and provide the unique code. It was possible for the researcher to 'track back' and find the participant's survey without provision of the unique code. However in the case of anonymous survey submission, the unique code is the only identifiable feature.

Ensure Good Professional and Academic Conduct

To assist researchers achieve good professional and academic conduct, it is important for each researcher to go through the process of applying for ethics approval from their relevant institution. The researchers should conform to ethical guidelines outlining integrity, respect for persons, beneficence, and justice. Overall, the pursuit of research must have integrity of purpose, as the national statement defines:

The guiding value for researchers is integrity, which is expressed in a commitment to the search for knowledge, to recognised principles of research conduct and in the honest and ethical conduct of research and dissemination and communication of results. (Australian Government, 1999, p. 11)

Keep Good Faith

Demonstrating good faith to participants is done through thorough preparation and delivery of a survey based on the five steps just discussed. In addition the researcher shows good faith by allowing all the research results to be made available to a participant who requests them (Australian Government, 1999). As a researcher, the empathic perspective is an essential 'tool' when developing and implementing surveys for young people, specifically in this study, the Generation Y games geek.

CONCLUSION

The above problems, if addressed in the manner indicated, can facilitate trust in an online survey. It should be noted, however, that the above issues and suggestions complement each other when used in combination, and if used in isolation may not cover the full spectrum of ethical methods of survey.

The ethical considerations apply to action research overall and have been illustrated using one example or 'cycle' of the action research project, an online survey. Both the methodological approach and the process of applying for ethical clearance to conduct research with human participants in an online environment present the researchers with context-sensitive and context-specific difficulties. However, such a process is both a valid and valuable tool in the research process, and can efficiently and effectively reduce the time and effort required in the survey process. Not only does it maintain the researchers' ethical integrity, it also facilitates a closer look at the processes involved with surveying a participant.

As McNiff et al. (2003, p. 49) suggest, it is important not only to talk about the principles involved in an ethical action research project, but to also demonstrate how practitioners and writers act in a way that aims to influence others in an ethical manner. Any work involving human participants needs to have strong ethical considerations, and as indicated in this study, action research is an appropriate methodology with which to do this.

ACKNOWLEDGMENT

Thanks to Jason Wells of Deakin University for his assistance with the survey tool used in this study. For more information about the survey tool, please contact him directly via e-mail at jason.wells@deakin.edu.au.

REFERENCES

Australian Government. (1999). *National statement on ethical conduct in research involving humans.* Retrieved July 14, 2006, from http://www7.health.gov.au/nhmrc/publications/synopses/e35syn.htm

Australian Government. (1999). *National statement on ethical conduct in research involving humans.* Retrieved July 14, 2006, from http://www7.health.gov.au/nhmrc/publications/synopses/e35syn.htm

Blashki, K., & Nichol, S. (2005). Games geek goss: Linguistic creativity in young males. *Australian Journal of Emerging Technology and Society, 3*(1), 71-80.

Burns, A.C., & Bush, R.F. (2006). *Marketing research* (5th ed.). Upper Saddle River, NJ: Pearson Education.

Heath, R. (2006). *Please just f* off it's our turn now.* North Melbourne: Pluto Press.

Isaksen, S.G., Lauer, K.J., Ekvall, G., & Britz, A. (2001). Perceptions of the best and worst climates for creativity: Preliminary validation evidence for the situational outlook questionnaire. *Creativity Research Journal, 13*(2), 171-184.

Kizza, J.M. (2003). *Ethical and social issues in the information age* (2nd ed.). New York: Springer.

Levin, M., & Greenwood, D. (2001). Pragmatic action research and the struggle to transform universities into learning communities. In P. Reason & H. Bradbury (Eds.), *Handbook of action research* (pp. 104-113). London: Sage.

McCrindle, M. (2006). *Bridging the gap: Generational diversity at work*. Baulkham Hills: McCrindle Research.

McNiff, J., Lomax, P., & Whitehead, J. (2003). *You and your action research project*. Oxon: Routledge-Falmer.

Nichol, S., & Blashki, K. (2005). The realm of the game geek: Supporting creativity in an online community. *Proceedings of IADIS,* San Sebastian.

Nichol, S., & Blashki, K. (2006). Games geeks in context: Developing the environment to engage creative expression. *Proceedings of the ED-MEDIA World Conference on Educational Multimedia, Hypermedia and Telecommunications,* Orlando, FL.

Sheahan, P. (2005). *Generation Y: Thriving and surviving with Generation Y at work*. Melbourne: Hardie Grant.

KEY TERMS

Action Research: A methodological technique for conducting research that involves active participation of the researchers with the participant community under observation. Action research is a cyclic interaction of phases within a community of participants, where the influence of the research process is a direct outcome.

Community: A group of people who share a similar interest, as well as similar values and norms.

Environment: The factors that surround each of us in our daily lives. These include social, physical, and technical factors such as family, buildings, and computers.

Ethical Consideration: As defined in six steps (McNiff et al., 2003), an ethical consideration is a step that needs to be taken into account when undertaking research involving humans.

Games Student: One of the Generation Y students undertaking games design and development studies at Deakin University. They are known as games geeks by their own admission.

Generation Y: The category that defines people generally born between 1979 and 1994 (McCrindle, 2006).

Online Survey: The administration of a survey via the medium of the Internet.

Ethical Behaviour in Technology–Mediated Communication

Sutirtha Chatterjee
Washington State University, USA

INTRODUCTION AND HISTORICAL PERSPECTIVE

In this information age, serious concerns with unethical behaviour in information technology (e.g., software piracy, deception, plagiarism, etc.) have cast doubts on the claims of the unmitigated success of rapid adoption of information technology. Surprisingly, there have been very few studies in information systems (IS) that have tried to understand the general rise in such unethical behaviours with respect to information technology. Especially, the question that remains to be understood is: Are these problems of unethical behaviour representative of the human nature at large, or are they related to characteristics of technology in any way? This article tries to partly answer this question. It looks at dyadic communicative behaviour using technology-mediated communication and proposes *a conceptual model* of unethical communicative behaviour. To summarize, the question(s) that this article tries to address are:

In a dyadic technology-based communication between two individuals, what characteristics of technology-based media influence unethical behaviour for an individual? Does individual difference have a role to play in affecting such unethical behaviour? If so, how does it do so?

In answering these questions, the article poses arguments based on literature on media richness, social presence, and deindividuation, and also philosophy-based ethical outlooks of an individual.

BACKGROUND AND LITERATURE REVIEW

Unethical Communicative Behaviour

Chatterjee (2005) defined unethical usage of information technology as the violation of privacy, property, accuracy, and access of an individual or an organization by another individual or organization. Since violations of property and access might not be directly relatable to a communicative scenario, this article defines *unethical communicative behaviour between two individuals as the violation of the privacy and/or accuracy of an individual by another individual*. It should be noted that commonly identified forms of unethical communicative behaviour mentioned in the literature (e.g., flaming, swearing, insults, deception, etc.) fall within the scope of violation of either *privacy* (e.g., insults) or *accuracy* (e.g., deception).

Technology-Based Media Characteristics

The key features of technology-based communicative media have been addressed in the media richness literature in IS. Richness of media is the ability to unequivocally transfer the message from the sender to the recipient (Daft & Lengel, 1986). The ability to do this depends on numerous characteristics that the media possesses. Kumar and Benbasat (2002) provide a nice review summary of the key *media characteristics* identified in the media richness literature over the years. These are presented in the following:

- **Modality:** The degree to which a media can support a variety of symbols to present rich information.
- **Synchronicity:** The ability of the media to support communication in real time.
- **Contingency:** The extent to which the communication responses are pertinent to previous responses.
- **Participation:** The extent to which the media supports the active engagement of senders and receivers in the communication.
- **Identification:** The extent to which the senders and receivers are identified (as opposed to being anonymous) by the media.

- **Propinquity:** The extent to which the media supports communication between geographically dispersed senders and receivers
- **Anthromorphism:** The degree to which the interface simulates or incorporates characteristics pertinent to human beings.
- **Rehearsability:** The extent to which the media supports fine tuning of the message before sending.
- **Reprocessability:** The extent to which the media supports messages to be reexamined within the same context.

This summarization forms the fundamental set of antecedents in this article. Latter sections of the article argue how these key media characteristics ultimately influence unethical communicative behaviour.

Media Richness and Social Presence

Technology-based communication is a mediated experience (Biocca, Burgoon, Harms, & Stoner, 2001) with the aim to emulate face-to-face (FTF) communication. The primary aim of technology-mediated communication is to make the mediation disappear (as in FTF) in order to result in a perception of "being there" and "being together" (Biocca et al., 2001, p. 1). Social presence—defined as the extent of perception (of users of a media) that the media conveys the communicators' physical presence in terms of humanness, sociability, personalness, and warmth (Baker, 2002)—also revolves around the ideas of "being there" and being "together."

Existing literature on media richness (e.g., Rice, 1992; Kinney & Dennis, 1994) has always linked media richness to social presence. It has been argued that FTF differs significantly than other environments because it exudes a greater perception of presence than other media. Media that are not sufficiently rich have limited capability to transfer information from the sender to the receiver and have a lower social presence than media that are high in richness. Media richness and social presence are essentially two sides of the same coin and can be defined individually in terms of the other. For example, a rich media is one that exudes a greater social presence, and a higher social presence implies a richer communicative media. Evidence of this fact can be found in the literature (Carlson & Davis, 1998), and the fact that social presence and media richness have been grouped together under the "Trait Theories of Media Selection"(Kumar & Benbasat 2002).

Following Kinney and Dennis (1994) and Dennis and Kinney (1998), this article argues that *media characteristics are the key influencers of media richness (and thus, of social presence)*. This thought is also echoed by Kumar and Benbasat (2002), where they say that it can be reasonable to argue that a media being perceived as being high on the communication characteristics would result in a richer and more socially present media.

PROPOSITION DEVELOPMENT

This section develops the model and propositions. For the benefit of the reader, we present the entire model a priori in Figure 1.

Figure 1. Model of unethical communicative behavior

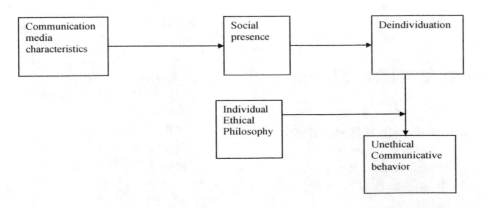

Media Characteristics and Social Presence

This section develops propositions on how each of the abovementioned media characteristics influences social presence. FTF has the most positive influence on social presence (Chidambaram & Jones, 1993). Hence, each of the media characteristics is compared against the "baseline" of FTF. Any media characteristic that is different from those of FTF has a negative influence on social presence; on the other hand, any characteristic that helps closely approximate FTF has a positive influence social presence.

- **Modality:** A media high in modality can present information in alternate ways so as to suit the receiver of the information. As in FTF, the sender of the message can try alternate means to get the message through to the receiver. For example, if the language is not well understood by the receiver, the sender can resort to using visual signs or gestures in order to make the receiver understand. Since, the characteristic of (high) modality enables a sender to present such alternate ways to send the message, it becomes a close approximation of this characteristic of FTF. We already know that FTF leads to a high degree of social presence. Therefore:

Proposition 1a. Media high in modality leads to a high degree of social presence.

- **Synchronicity:** A media high in synchronicity implies that there is no time delay between the sending and receiving of messages. This again is a scenario very similar to a FTF. The immediacy of the communication makes the sender and receiver of the messages feel that they are in a "real" conversation, with the sense of "being there and "being together." Media high in synchronicity gives a high illusion of physical co-presence (even though the individuals are not physically co-present) and stimulates the feeling that the other entity in the conversation is also real. This results in a need to reply immediately and creates a sense of social urgency, just like FTF, thus leading to a high degree of social presence. Therefore:

Proposition 1b. Media high in synchronicity leads to a high degree of social presence.

- **Contingency:** A media high in contingency (e.g., technology-based chat) retains the relevance of conversation. In such a case, there is little scope to "avoid" any message that is received and reply back in an entirely different manner. While chatting, if A asks B about an issue, then B is "forced" to reply back and does not realistically have a chance to conveniently ignore the question that A posed. However, in a medium like e-mail, B can possibly conveniently ignore A's question (or not reply to A's question at all). This is because typically an e-mail is more assimilative (many issues can be discussed and one of them can be ignored). In a chat, any discussion is atomic (one issue at a time), so responses must be pertinent. Even in FTF, the discussion is more atomic and thus there is no scope of "avoidance." Hence media high in contingency approximates this feature of FTF closely. Therefore:

Proposition 1c. Media high in contingency leads to a high degree of social presence.

- **Participation:** Participation and the sense of "being part of the conversation" is an important contributor to social presence. If one is not actively engaged (psychologically at least) in a communication process, then the feelings of "being there" or "being together" are absent. FTF requires the active participation of both parties, else the communication would stop immediately. Similarly, media high in the participation characteristic (e.g.. videoconferencing, or even a voice chat) help to approximate this effect. Therefore:

Proposition 1d. Media high in participation leads to a high degree of social presence.

- **Identification:** Identifiability (as opposed to anonymity) has been shown to be a key positive influencer of social presence. FTF provides absolute identification. Some media as compared to others may be more appropriate for identification (e.g., videoconferencing as compared to e-mail). For example, videoconferencing or video chats improve the possibility of identification, making it very similar to FTF. Therefore:

Proposition 1e. Media high in identification leads to a high degree of social presence.

- **Propinquity:** A high degree of propinquity implies that individuals who are geographically far away can communicate. However, propinquity is more concerned with actually delivering the message between geographically dispersed communicators. The actual understanding of the message by the receiver and the corresponding influence on social presence is not directly related to propinquity. When an individual is already interacting with an individual, the geographical distance between them does not matter. Therefore:

Proposition 1f. Media high in propinquity would have no effect on the degree social presence.

- **Anthromorphism:** If a media interface can simulate anthromorphism or human-like characteristics, then an individual would feel as if s/he is interacting with an animate object and not an inanimate object like the computer. Literature has argued that individuals can perceive computers and technology to be similar to them and respond using social norms (Lee & Nass, 2002). This compulsion to behave according to the social norms implies that the individuals are in a similar scenario to FTF. Therefore:

Proposition 1g. Media high in anthromorphism leads to a high degree of social presence.

- **Rehearsability:** Rehearsability is not an attribute of FTF. In FTF, messages cannot be fine tuned before they are sent. Hence, a media high in rehearsability cannot approximate FTF. Too much of rehearsability destroys the "naturalness" of a communication. Being contradictory to FTF, a high amount of rehearsability characteristic of a media leads to a low level of social presence. Therefore:

Proposition 1h. Media high in rehearsability leads to a low degree of social presence.

- **Reprocessability:** The characteristic of reprocessability helps to reanalyze messages. This is an important feature of FTF. During FTF, both the sender and the receiver can go back and reassess and reanalyze any previous discussion. A media that can support such reprocessability simulates an FTF-like communication. Therefore:

Proposition 1i. Media high in reprocessability leads to a high degree of social presence.

Having presented our propositions on how media characteristics can influence social presence, we next turn our attention to the downstream effect of social presence. In particular, we concentrate on a phenomenon called deindividuation.

Social Presence and Deindividuation

Deindividuation is defined as a feeling of being estranged from others, leading to behaviour violating appropriate norms (Zimbardo, 1969). During deindividuation, one loses awareness for others, feels more anonymous, and has less inhibition for socially unacceptable acts (Sproull & Kiesler, 1991). Classic deindividuation theory (Diener, 1980; Zimbardo, 1969) posits that a decrease of social presence leads to greater deindividuation characterized by negative outcomes such as reduction in awareness, greater anonymity, and lesser group cohesion. Within a dyadic communication, it can therefore be proposed:

Proposition 2. In a dyadic technology-mediated communicative discourse, a higher level of social presence would lead to a lower level of deindividuation. Conversely, a lower level of social presence would lead to a higher level of deindividuation.

Having seen how social presence causes deindividuation, we next turn our attention to the effects of deindividuation on human behaviour.

Deindividuation and Communicative Behaviour

Deindividuation theory argues that when a person is deindividuated, then the individual senses more opportunities to carry out behaviour that are unacceptable to society. Deindividuation results in an inability to identify other stakeholders and leads to ethically questionable acts (Lin, Hsu, Kuo, & Sun, 1999). Hsu and Kuo (2003) mention that deindividuation results in a high probability of unethical conduct. From all these arguments, we can say that the probability of unethical communicative behaviour for a deindividuated person is high. Therefore, it can be proposed:

Proposition 3. In a dyadic technology-mediated communicative discourse, a high level of deindividuation will lead to a high level of probability to commit unethical communicative behaviour.

However, even though deindividuation affects unethical behaviour, this article argues that unethical behaviour is not only affected by deindividuation, but also by individual differences. We next address this individual difference in the form of the different ethical philosophies of the individual.

Individual Ethical Philosophy

Individual ethical philosophy can be defined as the individual belief about the acceptability of right or wrong. In order to understand our arguments based on individual ethical philosophy, a brief introduction to the philosophy of *ethics* is warranted.

Ethics has two broad views: the consequentialist and the categorical schools. The consequentialist school (e.g., Mill, 1861) views that the rightness of an action is determined by how much consequential benefit comes out of the action. The categorical school of thought (e.g., Kant, 1804) views that rightness or wrongness of a behaviour is guided by certain objective rules in place. For example, it is objectively necessary to speak the truth, and hence it would be "unethical" to lie, even to help somebody.

Unethical communicative behaviour can be thought to be a violation, either in a categorical sense (violating norms of privacy and accuracy) or in a consequential sense (violating benefits of privacy and accuracy). An individual might subscribe to the consequentialist or categorical view above. However, within the consequentialist view, the benefits could be either self-interest based (benefits for self only) or altruistic (benefits for others). Depending on the view that an individual subscribes to, an individual might find an act to be ethical for one of the three: (a) it satisfied established

norms of conduct, (b) it satisfied benefits for self, or (c) it satisfied benefits for others.

For example, a categorical individual would never violate another individual with respect to privacy and accuracy. This follows similar to the categorical imperatives: privacy and accuracy should not be violated. A self-interest-based individual, on the other hand, might be much more favorable towards such a violation if it promoted benefits for self. The benefits could be hedonistic (e.g., one could get satisfied by simply calling another person names) or non-hedonistic (e.g., one could deceive another to achieve a selfish monetary end). An altruistic individual would not be favorable towards the abovementioned violations, as they have the increasing possibility of causing harm to the victim.

Though higher deindividuation leads to the possibility of unethical behaviour (as previously argued), the final commitment of an unethical behaviour would differ according to the ethical philosophy of individuals due to the abovementioned reasons. Based on our arguments, we therefore propose:

Proposition 4. Individual ethical philosophy will moderate the positive effects of deindividuation on unethical behaviour such that self-interested individuals will have higher levels of unethical behaviour as compared to either altruistic individuals or categorical individuals.

CONCLUSION AND FUTURE IMPLICATIONS

This article attempted to propose a conceptual model of how technology-based media characteristics can influence unethical behaviour and how individual differences in terms of ethical philosophy can also influence such behaviour. The foremost contribution of this article is in the fact that such a model has been previously non-existent in the literature. Future empirical studies on this model should give us a deeper understanding of technology-mediated unethical communicative behaviour. If propositions regarding the technology-induced effects were supported, it would mean that technology is an important driver of unethical behaviour. If not, it would mean that unethical behaviour is more due to individual characteristics (especially ethical philosophy) than technological characteristics. Either way, it would provide us with a deeper insight into the ethical communicative aspect of IS ethics.

Furthermore, the results of the empirical study can have important practical considerations. If the unethical behaviour is mainly based on individual characteristics, the answer to a lowering of such unethical behaviour might lie in improved moral education. If the unethical behaviour is dependent on technology, then the answer might lie in improving technology so that the communicating participants feel a high degree of social presence. This would result in lower deindividuation and thus a lower possibility of unethical behaviour. Thus, the validation of the model proposed in this article might have important implications for the framing of public policy (improved moral education) or the designing of technological improvements.

REFERENCES

Baker, G. (2002). The effects of synchronous collaborative technologies on decision making: A study of virtual teams. *Information Resources Management Journal, 15*(4), 79-93.

Biocca, F., Burgoon, J., Harms, C., & Stoner, M. (2001). Criteria and scope conditions for a theory and measure of social presence. *Proceedings of Presence 2001,* Philadelphia, PA.

Carlson, P.J., & Davis, G.B. (1998). An investigation of media selection among directors and managers: From "self" to "other" orientation. *Management Information Systems Quarterly, 22*(3).

Chatterjee, S. (2005). A model of unethical usage of information technology. *Proceedings of the 11th Americas Conference on Information Systems,* Omaha, NE.

Chidambaram, L., & Jones, B. (1993). Impact of communication medium and computer support on group perceptions and performance: A comparison of face-to-face and dispersed meetings. *Management Information Systems Quarterly, 17*(4).

Daft, R.L., & Lengel, R.H. (1986). Organizational information requirements, media richness and structural determinants. *Management Science, 32*(5), 554-571.

Dennis, A.R., & Kinney, S.T. (1998). Testing media richness theory in the new media: The effects of cues, feedback, and task equivocality. *Information Systems Research, 9*(3).

Diener, E. (1980). Deindividuation: The absence of self-awareness and self-regulation in group members. In P.B. Paulus (Ed.), *Psychology of group influence.* Hillsdale, NJ: Lawrence Erlbaum.

Hsu, M., & Kuo, F. (2003). The effect of organization-based self-esteem and deindividuation in protecting personal information privacy. *Journal of Business Ethics, 42*(4).

Kant, I. (1804/1981). *Grounding for the metaphysics for morals.* Indianapolis, IN: Hackett.

Kinney, S.T., & Dennis, A.R. (1994). Re-evaluating media richness: Cues, feedback and task. *Proceedings of the 27th Annual Hawaii International Conference on System Sciences.*

Kumar, N., & Benbasat, I. (2002). Para-social presence and communication capabilities of a Website: A theoretical perspective. *E-Service Journal, 1*(3).

Lee, E., & Nass, C. (2002). Experimental tests of normative group influence and representation effects in computer-mediated communication: When interacting via computers differs from interacting with computers. *Human Communication Research, 28,* 349-381.

Lin, T.C., Hsu, M.H., Kuo, F.Y., & Sun, P.C. (1999). An intention model based study of software piracy. *Proceedings of the 32nd Annual Hawaii International Conference on System Sciences.*

Mill, J.S. (1861/1979). *Utilitarianism.* Indianapolis, IN: Hackett.

Rice, R.E. (1992). Task analyzability, use of new media, and effectiveness: A multi-site exploration of media richness. *Organization Science, 3*(4).

Sproull, L., & Kiesler, S. (1991). *Connections: New ways of working in the networked organization.* Cambridge, MA: MIT Press.

Zimbardo, P.G. (1969). The human choice: Individuation, reason, and order vs. deindividuation, impulse and chaos. In W.J. Arnold & D. Levine (Eds.), *Nebraska symposium on motivation* (vol. 17, pp. 237-307). Lincoln, NE: University of Nebraska Press.

KEY TERMS

Categorical School of Ethics: The rightness or wrongness of a behaviour is guided by certain rules in place.

Consequentialist School of Ethics: The rightness (or wrongness) of an action is determined by how much consequential benefit (or loss) comes out of the action.

Deindividuation: A feeling of being estranged from others, leading to behaviour violating appropriate norms.

Individual Ethical Philosophy: The individual belief about the acceptability of right or wrong.

Media Richness: The ability of media to unequivocally transfer the message from the sender to the recipient.

Social Presence: Extent of perception (of users of a medium) that the medium conveys the communicators' physical presence in terms of humanness, sociability, personalness, and warmth.

Unethical Communicative Behaviour (Dyadic): The violation of the privacy and accuracy of an individual by another individual.

Ethical Concerns in Computer Science Projects

Alistair Irons
Northumbria University, UK

Roger Boyle
University of Leeds, UK

INTRODUCTION

Many more computer systems do not work in the way they are intended (Sommerville, 2004; Pressman, 2004). Computer systems are also increasingly vulnerable to misuse (Edgar, 1997; Rowe & Thompson, 1996) and crime (Barrett, 1997; NHTCU, 2003; Casey, 2004). The concerns ascribed to the development of computer systems can also be attributed to the development of computer artifacts in undergraduate and postgraduate projects; poor software practice can often be traced back to the education of the practitioner. The main issue addressed here is the steps academics, computing schools, and departments and universities should take in order to address the potential harm that could result from inappropriate projects, and the potential benefits of introducing an ethical approval phase.

It is incumbent on academics in their role as project supervisors to ensure that students do not undertake any projects that have the potential to cause harm; clearly the scope for a student to cause damage is limited, but is also non-zero. Such an approach to project conduct might be made conspicuous, thereby inculcating the student into sound and ethical work practice.

BACKGROUND

Since the 1990s the subject of computer ethics has been formally embedded into computing curricula—both in the United States as part of the ACM Curriculum (ACM, 2001) and in the UK (QAA Computing Benchmark). The British Computer Society (BCS), the main accrediting UK body for computing programs, places great stock on legal, social, ethical, and professional issues being embedded into the curriculum; it is acknowledged that technical education and skills alone are insufficient for a professional life in computing.

There are many different definitions of "computer ethics" (Maner, 1980; Johnson, 2001; Moor, 1985; Gotterbarn, 1991), but all are concerned with the potential impact computers systems have on society. Applying the principles of computer ethics encourages practitioners to consider the effect their product or artifact could potentially have. It is suggested in this article that students and supervisors engaging in *computing projects* should consider the ethical implications of their work as an integral part of that project process.

In almost every computing program worldwide, the project is an integral part: few would dissent from this inclusion, as this is the best simulation universities can offer of software development "in the real" (Fincher, Petre, & Clark, 2001). The BCS examines projects, focusing on the theoretical and practical application of computing and software engineering principles. It is customary for computing undergraduates to have more than one project experience, and it will represent 25% or more of a senior academic year.

However, the BCS does not explicitly examine the ethical nature of projects or expect discussion of ethical issues in the project process or write up. While this does frequently occur, a formal connection between these two aspects is not sought. The whole issue of ethical scrutiny of computing projects is a "live" but underdeveloped issue.

The ethics agenda for research carried out in universities is developing and gaining momentum, although recent research undertaken by the Nuffield Foundation (2005) suggested that "Ethical scrutiny of university research is patchy despite the fact that more institutions than ever have committees to vet projects." One of the criteria in the Nuffield Foundation research was whether ethical considerations of student research were scrutinized. A framework for ethical scrutiny is proposed which would address ethical issues in projects and as a result optimize the educational benefits for students, and also allow computing schools to protect themselves in the case of something going wrong.

Within the UK, preliminary work is underway in the development of an "ethical framework" for computing projects. This is being undertaken in conjunction with CPHC,[1] professional bodies (BCS, IEE, ACM), and the HEFCE-funded IDEAS Center of Excellence in Teaching and Learning (IDEAS, 2005). This framework (see below for detail) will provide guidelines on ethical;

- **Responsibilities:** Institutions, schools, staff, students
- **Scrutiny:** Filter, terms of reference review, ethics committee
- Inclusion in student project
- Assessment

Ethical issues have always been a mandatory element of many degrees—medicine is the obvious example. However, there has been a recent growth in the number of university and school committees considering ethical issues across many disciplines. The Royal Academy of Engineering (which includes computing in its remit) has recently established a working party on this issue (RAE, 2005). Simultaneously there is a growth in the breadth and choice of subjects and discipline areas which constitute computing projects: there is a "rush to interdisciplinarity" driven by the need for students to be able to apply technical skills.

As the range of potential projects increases, so does the potential for computing projects to cause harm either to subjects or through inappropriate development of a computing project product: this is an obvious risk in the area of, for example, health informatics; students regularly work alongside health professionals (well versed in ethical constraints) but rarely have any grounding in the ethical issues they are likely to encounter. It is common for student project work to be deployed, even if only prototype, and sensible precautionary mechanisms are sometimes absent. Projects regularly generate Web-based databases as part of their development, and authors neglecting issues such as confidentiality as a fundamental design issue would clearly be flawed.

Additionally, there are potential ethical issues associated with the gathering of primary data; for example, informed consent and anonymity. These become more relevant as applications that impact widely become more commonplace and attractive as project activity. Again, these issues are routine in many professions, but have rarely been considered as a normal part of computing.

ETHICAL ISSUES IN PROJECTS

There are many subject areas for potential concern, such as obtaining primary data from under-18s or vulnerable adults; the development of computing artifacts which raise ethical concerns, for example virus generators; and research in sensitive subjects such as health informatics, computer forensics, dataveillance, and so forth.

The standard pattern of projects is proposal, requirements analysis, implementation, testing, and documentation—this pattern is explicitly encouraged by the BCS. A number of computing schools have introduced aspects of ethical scrutiny at the proposal stage, although a few have embedded more detailed ethical scrutiny throughout project development and expect explicit consideration to be documented in the write up. This article seeks to promote a framework which can be adopted by computing schools to identify potential ethical problems early in the project.

Initial research[2] suggests that many institutions leave ethical considerations to the supervisor, without making use of formal structures, relying on their professionalism, and putting trust in students' behavior. There is no suggestion that staff are remiss in this *responsibility*: the point we make is that the need for this filter is growing, and that little opportunity is currently taken to establish this phase as part of the student's education.

Commonly given reasons for not formalizing an ethical consideration process are the pragmatic ones of time and volume. There needs to be a quick and workable "filter" to ensure ethical appropriateness balanced with the need to ensure all interests are protected. Historically, software *product* generation has been seen as the primary aim of projects, and academic hesitation in devoting time to tasks other than production might be seen as understandable. It might also illustrate a deeper issue in convincing the community of the benefit of devoting explicit resource to ethical considerations.

There are a number of stakeholders who have responsibility in ensuring that a project is ethically acceptable. Obvious ones who have responsibilities (depending on the nature of the project) include the:

- student
- project supervisor
- project tutor (project process coordinator)
- school ethics committee
- university ethics committee
- university
- computing professional bodies

Precise interests of these differ: the university may find itself legally liable for something, while the student is primarily interested in experience and a qualification of value. It is easy to see how this may lead to conflict in the creation of procedures.

If a computing school is to adopt some form of ethical scrutiny, there is a need to decide which projects should be scrutinized; strategies include examination of all, of a sample, of specific criteria, by exception, or of none.

We contend that the only route forward that preserves integrity and fulfils the aims of the exercise is to involve all projects in some form of consideration: it is likely that for some (perhaps theoretical work), the procedure will be effectively null, but the student would have been exposed to the requirement to demonstrate this, and the university will be confident that it has done all it can and should. There is a potential difference in the need for scrutiny depending on whether the project has been proposed by staff or by the student. It is common for students to propose wholly sensible activity that inter-relates with commercial activity of their personal associates. Such projects always have the potential for divided loyalties, but this can easily develop into moral dilemmas as opportunities to interact with the broader public multiply.

The proposed framework will consider:

- **Potential for harm:** To the discipline, student, supervisor, institution, a third party
- **Potential for misuse:** By students, clients, third parties—this is an aspect that would be null with wholly self-contained or theoretical activity
- Gathering of primary data
- **Potential to legal issues:** Affecting the student, university, clients, a third party

There are various points in the project development process where there may be a need to invoke ethical scrutiny, at project proposal, at terms of reference, during design and implementation, at the time that the product is produced, at the time that the product is made available to clients, and so forth. The nature of such scrutiny may well differ among these phases.

The framework will provide guidelines on:

Stage 1

- **Responsibilities: institutions, schools, staff, students**—The framework outlines the duties and ethical requirements of stakeholders in the project in terms of reasonable steps that they should take in order to avoid any instances that would be deemed unethical either in terms of the subject matter they are covering or of the methodological approach (research and development) or potential use of the developed artifact.

Stage 2

- **Scrutiny: terms of reference, filter, ethics committee**—Ethical scrutiny should take place at a number of stages. There will be a different onus of responsibility depending on whether the project is proposed by an academic or student. In both situations the supervisor has a duty of care to protect the student, school, institution, and of course themselves.

The project proposal and terms of reference should be scrutinized against a checklist in order to determine whether there is the opportunity for unethical actions to develop. At this stage the filter will be a quick checkbox-style approach, illustrated in Table 1; the majority of projects will not need any further scrutiny.

Those projects where there is an indication of potential ethical concern should go through a more detailed filter, which will check for legitimacy. In the most contentious cases, the project will require going to the school ethics committee to receive approval for progress. The timing of the process will need to be very early in the project cycle and produce quick, informative feedback.

Stage 3

- **Inclusion of ethics in the write up (and by implication the assessment of the project)**—By giving consideration to ethics in the development, students will potentially amass rich data on the

Table 1. Ethical filter

1	Potential for harm?	Y / N
	To subject	Y / N
	To student	Y / N
	To academic supervisor	Y / N
	To institution	Y / N
2	Potential for misuse of product or artifact?	Y / N
3	Potential to break law?	Y / N
4	Primary data to be collected?	Y / N
5	Consent required?	Y / N
6	Need for authorization by "ethics committee"?	Y / N

ethical issues in their project which can be written about. The inclusion of ethical considerations in the project write up will by definition mean that computer ethics is assessed. This assessment will be a component of the marking scheme and as such be assessed by the multiple markers and potentially the external examiner.

Of course, procedures are well embedded in most departments, and any adjustment to them would need to be pragmatic in terms of workability, usability, and timeliness. While being a component of the work that all should feel is useful, compromising on attention to time for purely technical activity would of necessity dilute such activity, and would not attract the support of many staff. Simultaneously, an ethical filter needs to be balanced with the need to ensure all interests are protected.

Proscriptive approaches are rarely successful in the higher education environment and so one would seek a minimum activity that might be regarded as a default: in this, the existence of a professional body is of value. While it is the case that accreditation by the BCS is sought and maintained by most UK institutions, their active support in devising and observing such procedures would be of value. Of course, many countries do not have a tradition of such accreditation, although this activity is growing in the United States with ABET (2006).

There are many potential areas of ethical concern in computing projects including academic misconduct (for example, plagiarism), unethical access to subjects (for example, under 18s), or the development of unethical products (such as a game glorifying racism). It is expected that these would be identified either through the processes of project proposal or project supervision.

We would attest that certainly the latter two examples would be identified in an "ethical filter." The hypothetical example below illustrates a project that on the surface would appear to be perfectly reasonable, but then moves down an unethical route.

It would be easy for arguments made here to fall on stony ground: changes in procedure are rarely popular. We present an example to justify these points. While this scenario has not been seen as we present it, the contributory aspects have.

A project has been requested to develop a prototype system which will detect when "Trojans" are inadvertently introduced onto a host PC without the user's knowledge. A proposal is developed which presents an acceptable project in terms of methodology and deliverable. A student begins the project and has regular meetings with the supervisor. From the outset, ethical issues associated with the development of Trojans and their distribution are discussed. The student is encouraged to write a chapter in his or her report on ethical issues.

Throughout the project the student's knowledge of Trojans increases and the potential for economic gain (through unethical use of Trojans—although the student does not appreciate the scale of the ethical issue) becomes apparent. As well as developing a product for monitoring Trojans, the student includes a Trojan on the prototype which is released onto every machine that the detection product is loaded onto. Unbeknown to the supervisor the student has made the product available as a download from a personal university Web page. The student uses the distributed Trojans to gather data, then sell information, including credit card details, bank accounts, and passwords, to a third party in Eastern Europe.

The situation comes to light in a local newspaper under the headline "Computing Student at the University of Newtown Sells Clients' Financial Details to Russian Mafia."

The example is only a little far-fetched. The rebound onto the entire university structure and student is clear, and after-effects would be significant. Examples of this nature are becoming more common, and we contend that a formally structured approach to ethical consideration has the potential to head off such problems: at the very least, a properly structured protocol would isolate the guilt with the student, while leaving no doubt in the individual's mind that wrongdoing is taking place.

Of course, the majority of projects will not go wrong, but the exercise of ethical consideration will be written about in the documentation. This has the benefit of giving the student a wider perspective on the project, getting him or her to consider potential impact on society, and giving him or her a real-world consideration.

FUTURE TRENDS

The problem we identify is likely to become more acute in the future. As the range of computing projects grows, the types of project become more likely to incorporate areas of potential ethical concern; simultaneously, the diversity and ability range of students is becoming wider. Evidence for this view we have noted from the RAE (2005) and the significant funds being invested in ethical treatment of all disciplines.

There will remain a tension between the strictly vocational aspects of project work (the "preparation for a job") and the modus operandi of the laboratory scientists who genuinely feel that "ethical issues don't impact on me."

Should a national body of the standing of the BCS or the university funding bodies take an active interest in these affairs, it is likely that the foregoing will ease itself into computing curricula easily. If not, then the scene will remain a patchwork, unless some event comes to pass that persuades the skeptical that there is something to worry about.

CONCLUSION

There are several possible options computing schools could choose in determining what to do about ethical scrutiny of projects. At one extreme is "do nothing," while another would be an imposed regime. Neither is likely, but the cornerstone nature of the project in computing means that it is taken seriously by students, staff, professional bodies, and employers alike, and represents a golden opportunity for instilling good practice into tomorrow's professionals. Learning that non-technical issues can sometimes scupper projects is a lesson best experienced in the safety of formal education, rather than when our graduates are out in the world making mistakes for real.

REFERENCES

ABET (Accreditation Board for Engineering and Technology). (2006). Retrieved January 2006 from http://www.abet.org/

ACM Computing Curricula. (2001). Retrieved December 2005, from http://www.acm.org/education/curricula.html

Barrett, N. (1997). *Digital crime, policing the cybernation.* London: Kogan Page.

Casey, E. (2004). *Digital evidence and computer crime, forensics science, computers and the Internet* (2nd ed.). Elsevier Academic Press.

Edgar, S.L. (1997). *Morality and machines; perspectives on computer ethics.* London: Jones and Bartlett.

Fincher, S., Petre, M., & Clark, M. (2001). *Computer science project work: Principles and pragmatics.* Berlin: Springer-Verlag.

Gotterbarn, D. (1995). 'Computer ethics, responsibility regained' national forum. *The Phi Beta Kappa Journal, 71,* 26-31.

IDEAS. (2005). *CETL: Inter-disciplinary ethics across subjects Center for Excellence in Teaching and Learning.* Retrieved December 2005 from http://www.philosophy.leeds.ac.uk/PhilosophyNews/IdeasCETL.htm

Johnson, D.G. (2001). *Computer ethics* (3rd ed.). Englewood Cliffs, NJ: Prentice Hall.

Maner, W. (1980). *Starter kit in computer ethics.* Helvetia Press (published in cooperation with the national Information and Resource Center for Teaching Philosophy).

Moor, J.H. (1985). What is computer ethics? *Metaphilosophy, 16*(4), 266-275.

NHTCU. (2003). *Survey of computer crime in the UK.* London: National High Tech Crime Unit.

Pressman, R. (2004). *Software engineering: A practitioner's approach.* New York: McGraw-Hill.

Quality Assurance Agency. (2000). *Subject benchmark statements; computing.* Gloucester: QAA.

RAE. (2005). *Ethics & Engineering Working Group.* Retrieved December 2005 from http://www.raeng.org.uk/policy/ethics

Rowe, C., & Thompson, J. (1996). *People and chips; the human implications of information technology.* New York: McGraw-Hill, Maidenhead.

Sommerville, I. (2004). *Software engineering* (7th ed.). Boston: Addison-Wesley.

KEY TERMS

Academic Responsibility: Academic responsibility for the ethical worthiness of a computing project ultimately lies with the academic institution and will be detailed in academic regulations. However, it is incumbent upon all academics and students to ensure that all computing projects and computing artifacts are ethically sound.

Computer Ethics: A set of values in computing and computer science that help the computing practitioner 'do the right thing' mapped against a set of benchmarks or standards, such as the BCS Code of Ethics.

Computing Artifact: The product from a computing or computer science project, such as piece of software, a database, a Web site, a prototype system, or a piece of hardware.

Computing Taught Project: Distinct from a pure research project such as a PhD or MPhil, the computing taught project forms part of the final year of an undergraduate degree (normally between 25% and 35% of the final year) or part of an MSc scheme (normally 33% of the MSc). It is a near universal feature of computing taught programs. These projects demand a more intense form of supervision than a PhD or MPhil.

Ethical Framework: A series of steps/stages provided to guide the consideration given to the ethical implications (potential and real) of a taught project.

Ethical Reviewer: Person (normally an academic) who makes judgment on the ethical suitability of a project.

Filter: Part of the ethical framework. The stage that passes or fails a project proposal/terms of reference on ethical grounds.

Legal, Social, Ethical, and Professional Issues: A series of issues defined in the QAA Computing Benchmark and the BCS expectations.

Risk: A measure of what will happen if something goes wrong.

ENDNOTES

[1]   CPHC: The [UK] Council of Professors and Heads of Computing

[2]   Reported to a workshop at the 2005 HEA ICS Conference, York, UK.

The Ethical Debate Surrounding RFID

Stephanie Etter
Mount Aloysius College, USA

Patricia G. Phillips
Duquesne University, USA

Ashli M. Molinero
Robert Morris University, USA

Susan J. Nestor
Robert Morris University, USA

Keith LeDonne
Robert Morris University, USA

RFID TECHNOLOGY

Radio frequency identification (RFID) is a generic term that is used to describe a system that transmits the identity of an object or person wirelessly using radio waves (RFID Journal, 2005). It falls under the broad category of automatic identification technologies. RFID tags, in the simplest of terms, are "intelligent chips that can be embedded in or attached to a product to transmit descriptive data" (Gelinas, Sutton, & Fedorowicz, 2004, p. 6). According to the online *RFID Journal* (2005), there are several methods of identifying objects using RFID, including the most common of storing a serial number that identifies a product on a microchip that is attached to an RFID tag. RFID is not a new technology, but it has only recently been in the spotlight as more businesses are receiving press for putting the technology to work in their supply chains.

RFID tag technology is sometimes associated with the term electronic product code (EPC). An EPC uniquely identifies objects in a supply chain. According to EPCGlobal, "EPC is divided into numbers that identify the manufacturer and product type. The EPC uses an extra set of digits, a serial number, to identify unique items." The EPC number is placed on a tag composed of a silicon chip and an antenna, which is then attached to an item. Using RFID, a tag communicates its number to a reader (EPCGlobal, 2005). In broad terms, RFID tags are placed into one of two categories: active or passive. According to the Association for Automatic Identification and Mobility (AIM,

2005), active RFID tags are powered by an internal battery and are typically designated as read-write tags. When a tag has read-write capabilities, the tag data can be modified. Passive tags, according to AIM, operate without a power source and obtain operating power from the tag reader. Passive tags are typically read-only tags, having only read-only memory. Active tags generally have a longer read range than passive tags.

RFID development dates back, according to some accounts, to the 1940s work of Harry Stockman who discussed the possibility of communication by means of reflected power. Stockman at that point was early in the exploration and "admitted that more needed to be done in solving the basic problems of reflected-power communication before the application could be useful" (Landt & Catlin, 2001). According to the *RFID Journal*, RFID's early applications can be found during World War II when it was used by the military in airplanes, through the assistance of radar, to identify friend or foe (IFF).

Two decades later the first commercial use of RFID-related technology was electronic article surveillance (EAS), which was designed to help in theft prevention. These systems often used 1-bit tags that could be produced cheaply. Only the presence or absence of the tag could be detected, which provided effective anti-theft measures (Landt & Catlin, 2001).

Commercial applications expanded in the 1980s across the world, although not everyone had the same RFID applications in mind. The United States found the greatest applications for RFID to be in the areas of transportation, personnel access, and to a lesser extent, animal tracking. "In Europe, the greatest interests were for short-range systems for animals, industrial and business applications, though toll roads in Italy, France, Spain, Portugal, and Norway were equipped with RFID" (Landt & Catlin, 2001).

Today we see RFID in use in toll collection, tracing livestock movements, and tracking freight (Jones, Clarke-Hill, Comfort, Hillier, & Shears, 2005). While not a new technology, the use of RFID is slowly gaining momentum for widespread application, with RFID technology being used in industries such as retail, banking, transportation, manufacturing, and healthcare.

PRIVACY DEBATE

The two main controversies regarding the use of RFID are privacy and security. While advances in technology can address the security issues related to RFID, the ethical debate surrounding privacy is not as easily solved. As RFID technology becomes mainstream, its privacy protection challenges are becoming the topic of debate between technologists, consumer activists, academics, and government agencies. Yoshida (2005) reports that there is a "polarizing force tugging at the technology: the government and industry groups advocating RFID's adoptions, and the civil libertarians concerned about its potential abuse." The main question is, will this technology lead to situations where confidential information can be improperly disclosed? A representative from the UK's Department of Trade and Industry warned, "RFID tags could be used to monitor people as well as merchandise. As the use of RFID spreads, privacy issues must be weighed in the context of societal consent" (Yoshida, 2005).

RFID is not the first technology to spur a privacy debate. While technologies like RFID are not necessary for the invasion of privacy, they have made new privacy threats possible and old privacy threats more powerful. Based on IT ethics literature, there are three key aspects to privacy that computer technology tends to threaten (Baase, 2003):

1. freedom from intrusion,
2. control of personal information, and
3. freedom from surveillance.

RFID has the potential to impact all three, especially in terms of invisible information gathering. Gunther and Speikermann (2005) argue that RFID has added a "new dimension to the traditional e-privacy debate because much more information can potentially be collected about individuals" (p. 74).

While many understand the origin of RFID as being related to inventory tracking, privacy advocates argue that RFID can be used to track items after the item is out of the supply chain and in the hands of the consumer. RFID has the potential to allow anyone with an RFID scanner, either business or individual, to see the contents of shopping bags, purses, or other personal items, a process known as skimming. The RFID privacy concerns then are three-fold: pre-sales activities, sales transaction activities, and post-sales uses (Peslak, 2005).

While some believe that privacy advocates who argue against the use of RFID are being overly cautious and unreasonable, it is important to note that several businesses may already have plans to use RFID for the purposes of marketing, advertising, and tracking. For example, IBM filed a patent application in 2001 which offers the potential to use RFID "to track people as they roam through shopping malls, airports, train stations, bus stations, elevators, trains, airplanes, rest rooms, sports arenas, libraries, theaters, museums, etc." (Bray, 2005). Unique item identification made possible through RFID has the potential to lead to a degree of personal attribution and surveillance never before possible (Gunther & Speikermann, 2005).

Global RFID standards are non-existent. Active RFID tags can often be read outside of the supply chain, are difficult for consumers to remove, can be read without consumer knowledge, and in the future may be able to uniquely identify items so that each item is traceable back to a credit account. According to Gunther and Speikermann (2005), "Consumers feel helpless toward the RFID environment" (p. 74) and "even though the potential advantages of RFID are well understood by a solid majority of consumers, fear seems to override most of these positive sentiments" (p. 76). There is some development in the area of privacy-enhancing technologies (PETs), technology designed to enable privacy while still using RFID, but as Gunther and Speikerman-n (2005) report, consumers still feel helpless (p. 74).

Although the ethical debate surrounding RFID does focus on privacy, it is important to note that much of the privacy debate itself can be connected to the other main controversy with RFID: security. Yoshida (2005) reports that Elliot Maxwell of The Pennsylvania State University's E-Business Research Center argues, "Fair information practices are designed for centralized control and personal verification, but what is emerging from RFID is surveillance without conscious action." He further argues that with RFID, "every object is a data collector and is always on. There are no obvious monitoring cues. Data can be broadly shared, and data that [are] communicated can be intercepted." While this information is stored in databases for later use or sale, there are potential security risks that arise. If it is intercepted during transport (electronic or otherwise), or accessed by an unauthorized party, the information now becomes more than just a concern about privacy related to which products consumers buy or which books they read, but it then becomes an opportunity for identity theft.

Our recent study of German consumers found they feared losing privacy due to the introduction of RFID technology. Even though the potential advantages of RFID (such as enhanced after-sales services) are well understood by a solid majority of consumers, fear seems to override most of these positive sentiments. (Gunther & Speikermann, 2005, p. 76)

Those in the RFID industry have responded to concerns about privacy by developing EPC tags that can be equipped with a kill function. Tags that are killed are totally inoperable after being sold to a consumer. Without global standards it is difficult to predict whether kill functions will be used widely in an attempt to protect consumer privacy.

INDUSTRY IMPACT

Healthcare

Health information management is a critical concern for any medical facility. RFID technology offers a comprehensive solution to managing patient data, staff, equipment, pharmaceuticals, supplies, or instruments because it can be used for both object identification and tracking. While the application of this technology offers many opportunities for hospital administrations to improve service delivery and patient care, ethical concerns also prevail. As with any new technology, there is a delicate balance between getting the most out of RFID without infringing upon patients' rights. The ethical debate over electronic supervision with RFID technology in the healthcare industry comes down to weighing the benefits of patient safety against the risks of patient confidentiality.

The Benefits

Applications of RFID in healthcare facilities vary. In 2005, Correa, Alvarez Gil, and Redin identified five areas where the technology has been implemented in healthcare, including "workflow improvements, maintenance of medical equipment, patients' identification, drug's procurement and administration, and inventory management" (p. 3). Each area can benefit from the technology in different ways; several examples were identified in the literature.

Preventing medical and medication errors is one reason for supporting RFID in healthcare (FDA, 2003). An example of how this technology can prevent such errors is the Surgichip Tag Surgical Marker System. This tagging system marks parts of a patient's body for surgery, minimizing the likelihood of a procedure being performed on the wrong side or wrong patient (FDA, 2005). Similarly, medication errors such as wrong dosage or wrong drug can also be prevented (FDA, 2003).

In addition to error prevention, another facet of patient safety that can benefit from RFID technology is physical security. Because strategically placed readers can track people, equipment, staff, or instruments, many maternity wards frequently use RFID as a security measure. The technology helps to ensure the right baby stays with and goes home with the right parents, and deters would-be abductors (Correa et al., 2005). Similarly, older patients in assisted-living facilities can be monitored, particularly those with memory impairments who may be prone to wandering out of the facility and unable to find their way back (Baard, 2004). Some argue that while this provides a sense of security for the older patient's family, it is a violation of the patient's right to privacy. The facility has to gain permission from the patient to monitor him or her, but the patient may not be mentally competent enough to know what it is they are signing (Baard, 2004).

The Challenges

Ironically, the area that can benefit the most from RFID technology also has the most risk associated with it: patient safety. Confidentiality, personal privacy, and data security are the main challenges hospitals face when employing RFID technology (Borriello, 2005). The biggest challenge in healthcare information management today stems from the fact that so much of it is still on paper (National Committee on Vital and Health Statistics, 2000). In addition to being a time-consuming task, recording patient information by hand leaves room for error in transcribing. Elimination or reduction of hand-written clinical data in healthcare facilities via the implementation of electronic health records could alleviate a lot of the margin of error, and attributes of RFID make it an attractive technology solution for this problem (Terry, 2004). A tag could store information about what medications and procedures were given when, as well as the patient's location in the facility at any given time.

However, securing the information and controlling who has access to read or write to the patient's tag is a threat to the wide adoption of RFID in hospitals. Data accumulation, or how will it be used and who will have access to it, is a critical concern for hospitals (Neild, Heatley, Kalawsky, & Bowman, 2004). The industry is making progress towards a universal electronic health record, but none has been able to ensure an appropriate level of data security. Implementing a system that provides the level of data security necessary can be cost prohibitive for many facilities (Terry, 2004)

Retail

Retailers like Wal-Mart, Prada, Target, and Walgreens are also embracing the use of RFID technology, primarily for inventory tracking. Retailers are constantly looking for ways of improving the balance between inventory supply and consumer demand. They want to make sure there are enough products on the shelves to meet demand, but not so much that they are sitting in a warehouse taking up costly inventory space. The use of RFID technology is viewed as one of the more promising tools to improve visibility of inventory almost instantly.

The Benefits

Retailers can see benefits of using RFID in the form of reduction in cost and increase in revenue. RFID provides benefits to retailers to aid with the reduction in theft, to improve the matching of supply to demand for a product, and to improve the speed of distribution (Jones et al., 2005). Current research suggests that RFID is being used to improve customer service; improve freshness of products; track products for warranty and recalls; improve efficiency of the supply chain; reduce shrinkage, theft, and counterfeit goods; and track the sales of products. By leaving tags active, retailers can offer enhanced after-sales services for warranties and recalls. Companies can be proactive and notify customers of a potential defect or recall.

The Challenges

From a consumer standpoint, the privacy threat comes when RFID tags remain active once the consumer leaves the store. Consumers are concerned with the use of data collected by retailers. Even though many consumers use loyalty cards, RFID adds a greater threat because each tag can contain more information. In addition, RFID tags can be attached to goods without the consumers' knowledge. Consumers are concerned that retailers are collecting data and surveillance of the consumers' shopping behaviors. There is a concern that retailers will collect the data on the customer, build profiles, and in turn create different pricing strategies or different levels of service for customers based on these profiles (Jones, Clarke-Hill, Comfort, Hillier, & Shears, 2004). Consumers are also concerned that data collected by retailers will be sold to other retailers. In addition, there is a concern of RFID misuses by criminals who have access to RFID scanners. According to Eckfeldt (2005):

Major companies worldwide have scrapped RFID programs following consumer backlash, and several U.S. states, including California and Massachusetts, are considering whether to implement RFID-specific privacy policies. (p. 77)

Retailers, who want to embrace RFID technology should attempt to develop ways to gain the customer's confidence. Millar (2004) provides four privacy concepts that should be considered when implementing EPC and RFID. These privacy concepts include:

1. Collection of personal data must be fair and lawful.
2. Consumers have the right to be informed about the use of the tags.
3. Personal data must be maintained in a secure fashion.
4. Consumers must be provided with reasonable access to their personal information.

To gain the customer's confidence, retailers should ensure that customers are aware that data are being collected, have a knowledge of what type of data are being collected, and understand how the data will be used. If the consumer understands how the data are being used and the consumer obtains a benefit with the use of RFID, they may be more willing to accept RFID data collection practices by retail organizations.

FUTURE PROSPECTS

Writing about RFID technology in general, Borriello (2005) notes:

As RFID technologists, application developers and consumers, we must be vigilant as to how these systems are designed not only for the sake of efficiency and cost but also to safeguard consumers' privacy and instill trust in the technology.

This statement is even more significant when speaking of RFID in terms of its application in healthcare. If healthcare facilities are careful about their implementation strategies and ensure the right amount of data security, this technology can be incredibly useful in increasing security and efficiency at the same time.

Since many organizations are in the early stages of RFID usage, Cap Gemini Ernst and Young surveyed 1,000 consumers in February 2004 to obtain their perceptions of RFID and their willingness to purchase RFID products (Jones et al., 2004). The results from the survey indicated few customers are even aware of this technology (23% of those surveyed), and of those aware of this technology, 42% had a favorable

view, 10% had an unfavorable view, and 48% had no opinion. To those surveyed, they saw the benefits as "faster recovery of stolen items; better car anti-theft capabilities; savings from reduced product cost; better prescription security; and faster, more reliable product recall" (Jones et al., 2004, p. 52). In addition, those surveyed indicated what might lead them to purchase RFID products: "lower costs, conveniences, improved security, a better shopping experience and privacy assurances" (Jones et al., 2004, p. 52). As this survey indicated, customers are concerned with the use of data by a third party, being targeted by direct marketing, health issues, and environmental impact. Consumers stressed the need for better education so that they could know what was most important to them in regards to RFID.

Research indicates that retailers and companies investing in RFID technology should govern themselves to protect the consumers because there is little legislation and policies to protect the consumer from the misuse of data collected through this technology. They should provide notice to consumers that RFID tags are present. In addition, consumers should have a choice to disable the RFID tags on purchases.

CONCLUSION

Consumers will be more open to accept RFID in their lives if they can see the benefits for themselves. Organizations, such as those in the healthcare and retail industries, must take the initiative to educate the consumer regarding RFID capabilities. There needs to be open communication about the advantages of RFID and the potential risks associated with it.

Organizations should provide privacy policies to explain what data is being collected, how it is being used, and how it will be destroyed. Privacy policies should address data from cradle to grave.

In addition, organizations must tie the presence of tags directly to consumer benefit in terms of better service, reduced prices, better products, or quicker checkout (Eckfeldt, 2005). Companies must lower the risk to consumers of losing their personal data and privacy, and increase the benefit to consumers in terms of a more convenient shopping experience, lower prices, and quicker checkout (Eckfeldt, 2005).

REFERENCES

AIM (Association for Automatic Identification and Mobility). (2005). *What is radio frequency identification (RFID)?* Retrieved May 18, 2006, from www.aimglobal.org

Baard, M. (2004). RFID keeps track of seniors. *Wired News,* (March). Retrieved January 27, 2006, from http://www.wired.com/news/medtech/ 0,1286,62723,00.html

Baase, S. (2003). *The gift of fire: Social, legal and ethical issues for computers and the Internet.* Upper Saddle River, NJ: Pearson Education.

Borriello, G. (Ed.). (2005). RFID: Tagging the world. *Communications of the ACM, 48*(9), 34-37. Retrieved January 27, 2006, from http://delivery.acm.org/10.1145/1090000/ 1082017/p34borriello.html

Bray, H. (2005). You need not be paranoid to fear RFID. *Boston Globe.* Retrieved December 1, 2005, from *http://www.Bostonglobe.com*

Correa, F.A, Alvarez Gil, M.J., & Redin, L.B. (2005, July). *Benefits of connecting RFID and lean principles in health care.* Retrieved January 27, 2006, from http://docubib.uc3m.es/WORKINGPAPERS/WB/wb054410.pdf

Eckfeldt, B. (2005). What does RFID do for the consumer? *Communications of the ACM, 48*(9), 77-79.

EPCGlobal. (2005). *Frequently asked questions.* Retrieved May 20, 2005, from http://www.epcglobalinc.org/about/faqs.html#6

FDA. (2003, March). Bar code label requirements for human drug products and blood. *Proposed Rule Federal Register, 68,* 50. Retrieved April 13, 2005, from http://www.fda.gov/OHRMS/dockets/98fr/03-5205.html

FDA. (2005). Technology for safer surgery. *FDA Consumer, 39*(1). Retrieved August 25, 2005, from http://www.findarticles.com/p/articles/mi_m1370/is_1_39/ai_n8694482

Gelinas, U., Sutton, S., & Fedorowicz, J. (2004). *Business processes and information technology.* Boston: Thompson South-Western.

Gunther, O., & Speikermann, S. (2005). RFID and the perception of control: The consumer's view. *Communications of the ACM, 48*(9), 73-76.

Jones, P., Clarke-Hill, C., Comfort, D., Hillier, D., & Shears, P. (2005). Radio frequency identification and food retailing in the UK. *British Food Journal, 107,* 356-360.

Jones, P., Clarke-Hill, C., Comfort, D., Hillier, D., & Shears, P. (2004). Radio frequency identification in retailing and privacy and public policy issues. *Management Research News, 27,* 46-56.

Landt, J., & Catlin, B. (2001). *Shrouds of time: The history of RFID.* Retrieved from www.aimglobal.org/technologies/rfid/resources/shrouds_of_time.pdf

Millar, S.A. (2004). RFID & EPC systems. *Paper, Film and Foil Converter, 78*(11), 16.

National Committee on Vital and Health Statistics. (2000). *Report to the secretary of the U.S. Department of Health and Human Services on uniform standards for patient medical record information.* Retrieved April 13, 2005, from http://www.ncvhs.hhs.gov/hipaa00006.pdf

Neild, I., Heatley, D.J., Kalawsky, R.S., & Bowman, P.A. (2004). Sensor networks for continuous health monitoring. *BT Technology Journal, 22*(3). Retrieved January 27, 2006, from http://www.springerlink.com/media

Peslak, A. (2005). An ethical exploration of privacy and radio frequency identification. *Journal of Business Ethics, 59,* 327.

RFID Journal. (2005). *What is RFID?* Retrieved December 1, 2005, from http://www.rfidjournal.com/article/articleview/1339/2/129/

Terry, N.P. (2004). *Electronic health records: International, structural and legal perspectives.* Retrieved January 27, 2006, from http://law.slu.edu/nicolasterry/NTProf/ALM_Final.pdf

Yoshida, J. (2005). RFID policy seeks identity: Global economic body debates controversial technology. *Electronic Engineering Times.* Retrieved January 31, 2006, from Lexis Nexis Academic Universe Database.

KEY TERMS

Active Tag: A type of RFID tag that is powered by an internal battery and is typically designated as a read-write tag. Active tags generally have longer read ranges than passive tags.

Electronic Product Code (EPC): A number designed and used to uniquely identify a specific item in the supply chain. The number is placed on a chip and read with RFID technology.

Invisible Information Gathering: The collection of personal information without a person's knowledge.

Kill Function: Disables the functionality of an RFID tag after consumers purchase a product.

Passive Tag: A type of RFID tag that operates without a power source and is typically designated as a read-only tag.

Privacy Enhancing Technology (PET): Hardware and software designed to protect an individual's privacy while using technology.

Read-Only Tag: A tag that only has read-only memory. When manufactured, this tag is pre-programmed with a unique and/or randomly assigned identification code.

Read-Write Tag: A tag that allows for full read-write capacity. A user can update information stored in a tag as often as necessary.

Skimming: When someone other than the intended party reads an RFID tag, usually without the owner's knowledge.

Ethical Dilemmas in Data Mining and Warehousing

Joseph A. Cazier
Appalachian State Univeresity, USA

Ryan C. LaBrie
Seattle Pacific University, USA

INTRODUCTION

As we move into the twenty-first century, marketing is increasingly becoming a one-to-one affair. No longer are marketers satisfied with pools of potential customers extracted from mailing lists or government records. Instead they're aggressively seeking personalized information and creating computing systems that categorize individual consumers. (Garfinkel, 2000, p. 158)

Information has become a commodity, moving from place to place with little thought given to the ultimate value provided to consumers, business, and society. With advanced innovations in e-business, data warehousing, and data mining, it is becoming increasingly important to look at the impact of information use on individuals. This free flow of information within an organization and between different organizations can be both an asset and liability for consumers, businesses, and society.

As we have increasing privacy and risk concerns in the world today with identity theft, questionable marketing, data mining, and profiling, it is becoming increasingly important to explore how consumers feel and react to the use of their data. This study makes an important contribution to the literature by presenting common positive and negative myths surrounding these issues and exploring how ethical or unethical consumers believe these practices are by looking at the myths and their reaction to them. We focus on consumers' perceptions because at the end of the day it is what the consumers perceive to be happing that will determine their reaction. An ethical data practice is one that is believed to increase consumer, business, or societal value, and an unethical data practice is one which causes harm to these groups.

BACKGROUND

Ethical use of data within information systems has been investigated for a number of years. Mason (1986) suggested that there are four ethical issues in the information age, readily identified through the acronym PAPA. PAPA stands for privacy, accuracy, property, and accessibility. While in 1986, we did not believe that the sheer amount of data produced through the Internet and transactional e-business systems, including consumer personalization and the use of radio frequency identification (RFIDs), could have been foreseen, these four issues still remain the center of focus for computing ethics.

With respect to the introduction of new information technology and its affect on privacy, Tavani (1999) proposes two possibilities. Use of technology to collect information without the knowledge of the individual and use of technology for unintended purposes even when the individual has consented for other purposes both can have serious consequences to privacy. Tavani goes on to provide an excellent example of how a bank might have a privacy policy that protects an individual's information from being sold or transferred to other companies, but then abuses that information within the bank itself to the detriment of the customer.

In an *Information Week* research study on business ethics, Wilder and Soat (2001) discuss the ethics of data management. Among their findings are: (1) information technology professionals can no longer abstain from the ethics and privacy debate, and thus should undergo ethics and data security training; and (2) customer profiling is being led by the healthcare and financial services industries, with more than 80% of the companies surveyed in those fields participating in profiling, followed closely by business services,

Table 1. Data mining and warehousing practices myths (adapted from Cazier & LaBrie, 2003)

Value Level	Myth	Counter Myth
Consumer	*The merging of current customer data with secondary sources ultimately increases value for the consumer.*	*The merging of current customer data with secondary sources ultimately hurts the consumer.*
	Customer profiling, leading to more customized service, creates consumer value.	*Customer profiling, leading to more customized service, reduces consumer value.*
	Using persuasive marketing techniques increases consumer value.	*Using persuasive marketing techniques reduces consumer value.*
Business	*Data warehousing improves organizational productivity.*	*Data warehousing reduces organizational productivity.*
	Data warehousing improves your organizational image.	*Data warehousing hurts your organizational image.*
Societal	*Data warehousing reduces waste and helps the environment.*	*Data warehousing increases waste and harms the environment.*
	Governmental use of data warehousing technologies is good for society.	*Governmental use of data warehousing technologies is not good for society.*

manufacturing, and retailing, which average more than 70% of the companies participating in customer profiling.

This article explores the myths and perceptions that consumers have regarding the ethics and usefulness of data mining and warehousing activities. These myth/counter myth pairs were first introduced in Cazier and LaBrie (2003). This study extends that research by attempting to quantify whether or not what was proposed in Cazier and LaBrie (2003) is valid. That is, are these myths truly perceived by the consumer or not? These myths are broken up into three value classifications: consumer, business, and societal. Table 1 presents a summation of those myths.

To better understand public reaction to the increase in data analysis and information flow, this research presents findings from a survey (N=121) that presented the arguments for both sides of seven misconceptions of the use (or misuse) of data in data warehouses in a myth/counter myth fashion. Respondents are asked how they believe they are affected in value propositions for consumers, business, and society. Because there are elements of truth in both sides of the arguments, we present the results of how much users agree or disagree with each myth and then ask them to choose which they believe is more likely. It is possible to agree or disagree with both myth and counter myth by examining different aspects of the impact, hence we also ask respondents to choose which they believe is more likely to be true. Respondents were chosen from

a cross-section of the population of three universities in different regions to maximize generalizability.

Investigation of Consumer Value

It is generally accepted that successful data warehousing projects can benefit the businesses that implements them. Less recognized however are the benefits to the consumer. This section describes three myths on how data warehousing may positively or negatively affect the consumer. Results from the survey follow each myth.

Myth 1: *The merging of current customer data with secondary sources ultimately increases value for the consumer.* Myth 1 suggests that by acquiring data from secondary sources about customers, and adding it to their existing data, businesses can better understand their customers and more accurately target their needs. The collection and merging of this data is a good business practice that helps the customer find products and services they desire. Customer satisfaction is increased because their service is more customized and tailored to their needs and desires. Offers that they receive from companies are more likely to be things they are interested in. Our respondents were split on this issue, with 45% agreeing or strongly agreeing with this myth, 39% disagreeing, and 16% undecided.

Counter Myth 1: *The merging of current customer data with secondary sources ultimately harms the consumer.* The counter argument is that there is a loss of privacy to the consumer that has a value to it. As long as the consumer owns the information, they have the right to disclose it, potentially for a benefit. Once a company owns and controls that information, the consumer has lost the benefit of the option to disclose the information and consumer value is reduced.

This myth had a very clear and statistically significant majority agreeing with the idea that merging data with secondary sources reduces consumer value, with 61% agreeing, 21% disagreeing with the reduction, and 17% undecided. On the overall question where respondents were asked to choose between the myths, 40% believed that the counter myth (harms the consumer) was more likely, with 30% believing the myth (helps the consumer) was more likely to be true, and 30% undecided.

Myth 2: *Customer profiling, leading to more customized service, creates consumer value.* Participating in commerce with Amazon.com provides an experience that is more and more focused to the individual consumer. With their advanced data mining techniques and the use of clustering, Amazon.com provides individualized Web site experiences with products more likely to be desired by the consumer. Forty-nine percent believe that profiling creates customer value, while 33% disagreed and 18% were undecided.

Counter Myth 2: *Customer profiling, leading to more customized service, reduces consumer value.* With limited numbers of interactions to a customized Web site, individuals may become frustrated with the "wrong" personalization, becoming inundated with marketing efforts for items they are not interested in. Sixty-two percent of respondents believe that customer profiling reduces consumer value, 26% disagreed, and 12% reported undecided. There is a very significant difference (.001), with most consumers believing that profiling reduces consumer value and is reflected in our overall numbers, where 39% believed profiling was more likely to harm as opposed to 31% help and 30% undecided.

Myth 3: *Using persuasive marketing techniques increases consumer value.* Persuasive technologies are computing devices designed to change human attitudes and behaviors (King & Tester, 1999). Some businesses would argue that by using data warehouse and data mining technologies in conjunction with persuasive technologies, they are locating customers that have a need for their product and are creating value for the customer by meeting and fulfilling their unmet needs. By persuading them to buy their products, they are performing a service to the customer. Overwhelmingly our respondents disagreed with this myth with only 17% agreeing, 71% disagreeing, and 12% undecided.

Counter Myth 3: *Using persuasive marketing techniques reduces consumer value.* If it is unethical to persuade someone to do something without technology, is should also be unethical to persuade them to do something with technology (Berdichevsky & Neuenschwander, 1999). Just as technology can be used to persuade someone to do *good,* it can also be used to persuade someone to do things considered *bad.* Some may consider technologies that persuade to gamble, drink alcohol, or view pornography, especially if someone is fighting an addiction, as reducing consumer value.

Our respondents again overwhelmingly believed persuasive technologies reduce consumer value, with 62% agreeing with counter myth 3, 22% disagreeing, and 16% undecided. For the overall choosing between the two, 21% believing it increased value, 56% believing it decreased value, and 23% were undecided. In this data set this proved to be statistically significant at the .001 level, with most consumers believing persuasive marketing reduces consumer value.

Investigation of Business Value

Data warehousing projects have similar attributes to any information systems project undertaken by an organization. Implementation issues arise, there are costs associated with the development, user acceptance is tenuous, and ultimately the question of whether or not the data warehouse is profitable for the organization is asked. In this section on business value, we focus on two myths: one concerning productivity and one concerning image.

Myth 4: *Data warehousing improves organizational productivity.* There are numerous anecdotal reports that data warehouses can generate 1,000-fold returns on investment. There are many books and articles written on the success of Wal-Mart's data warehouse implementation (Foote & Krishnamurthi, 2001; Westerman, 2000). Of our respondents, 50% agreed, 12% disagreed, and 37% were undecided that data warehousing improves organizational productivity. The difference in agreeing and disagreeing with this myth was also significant at the .001 level.

Counter Myth 4: Data warehousing reduces organizational productivity. For every data warehouse success story, there is failure to match. While these numbers have just recently come under scrutiny, various reports suggest that 50-66% of all initial data warehouse projects fail (Wixom & Watson, 2001; Boon, 1997). Data warehousing projects are not small investments; often they take years to implement correctly and require millions of dollars in hardware, software, and consulting services. Thirty-five percent agreed with the counter myth, 26% disagreed, and 39% were undecided. When asked to choose between them, 36% of the respondents agreed that it improves organizational productivity, 16% thought it reduced productivity, and 48% were undecided.

Myth 5: Data warehousing improves your organizational image. A well-run data warehouse program can help improve your corporate image. Your company may be seen as a technology leader. You may be able to do relevant data mining that will help meet your customer's needs. As an example Wal-Mart has arguably benefited in increased prestige through their skilled use of technology, and largely that is exposure to their data warehousing success stories. Overwhelmingly, 64% agreed, 17% disagreed, and 18% were undecided that data warehousing improves the organizational image.

Counter Myth 5: Data warehousing hurts your organizational image. While wise use of technology can help your corporate image, misuse of information can cause a public backlash. Amazon recently came under fire when it changed its privacy policy to allow the sale of gathered data to third parties, which it had previously stated it would not sell (Richman, 2002). If the use, storage, and sale of data in a company's data warehouse is not carefully monitored and controlled, it can lead to consumer group outcries that could harm

the company's image. Fifty-five percent agreed, 29% disagreed, and 16% were undecided. When asked to choose between them, 37% believed it was more likely to help with the organizational image, 27% said that it would hurt the image, and 36% were undecided.

Investigation of Societal Value

The collection and use of information by organizations continues to have an important impact on society. For information systems to be successful and interact well with the public, they should be aware of how they are perceived as affecting society. This section explores some of the ways organizations can use technology to affect society and how they might be perceived in society. Two specific ways that society as a whole can be affected by data warehousing practices is through environmental and governmental considerations.

Myth 6: Data warehousing reduces waste and helps the environment. With target marketing and tighter budgets, many companies have ever shrinking budgets to spend on their direct marketing endeavors. Given that, the mining of a data warehouse can lead to customers with a higher propensity to purchase goods and services, businesses can target fewer people with the same or more potential volume of sales. This leads to less waste of resources. Instead of 1,000,000 flyers, a company might send out only 50,000, a 20-times reduction in paper, ink, and stamps, suggesting both fiscal and environment responsibility. Sixty-three percent agreed, 18% disagreed, and 19% were undecided, again providing statistical significance at the .001 level.

Counter Myth 6: Data warehousing increases waste and harms the environment. On the other hand, lowering the cost of marketing by increasing the chances of success with more accurate target marketing may lead to further waste and ultimately be more harmful to the environment. New technologies and lower prices for hardware and software lower traditional barriers to entry for developing a data warehouse (LaBrie, St. Louis, & Ye, 2002). This leads to increasing numbers of firms being able to afford to mine their data. As such, more and more businesses will begin engaging in direct marketing. We see this in the increase of "junk mail" that fills not only our electronic but also traditional postal mailboxes. This ultimately leads to further use of more resources including paper, ink, and so forth, which is then discarded with the trash and eventually finds its way to the landfills. Forty-three percent agreed, 39% disagreed, and 18% were undecided. When asked to choose between them, 41% believed that it was more likely to help the environment, 27% thought it would hurt the environment, and 32% were undecided.

Myth 7: *Governmental use of data warehousing technologies is good for society.* Data warehouse and data mining systems play an important role in the U.S. government's fight against terrorism (Koerner, 2002), also in the battle for homeland security and in the fight to catch criminals in general, making society a safer place. Thirty-one percent agreed, 42% disagreed, and 27% were undecided.

Counter Myth 7: *Governmental use of data warehousing technologies is not good for society.* The use of these technologies, when carried to the extreme, can infringe on people's civil rights and liberties. A government's use of this type of technology to identify, track, and persecute subclasses of the population based on racial, ethnic, or religious profiling would likely be harmful for society. This includes discussion about national databases.

Sixty-six percent agreed that governmental use was not good for society, 17% disagreed, and another 17% were undecided, providing significance at the .001 level. When asked to choose between the two, 25% of our respondents said it was more likely to be good and increased societal value, while 40% believed that it decreased it, and 35% were undecided.

Table 2 shows that 10 of the 14 myths or counter myths were statistically significant in their differences. Nine of 10 were significant at the .001 level based on a one sample T-test. Table 3 presents the data from the paired sample T-test and finds that user perceptions indicate that:

1. Persuasive technologies decrease (or harm) consumer value (.001 level of significance).
2. Data warehousing helps business productivity (.01 level of significance).
3. Governmental use of data warehousing is more likely to be harmful to society.

Table 2. Value perceptions and their significance

Value Level	Abbreviated Propositions	Agree or Strongly Agree	Disagree or Strongly Disagree	Undecided
Consumer	*1a. Merging data increases consumer value.*	45%	39%	16%
	1b. Merging data decreases consumer value.***	61%	21%	17%
	2a. Profiling creates consumer value.	49%	33%	18%
	2b. Profiling reduces consumer value.***	62%	26%	12%
	3a. Persuasive marketing increases consumer value.***	17%	71%	12%
	3b. Persuasive marketing reduces consumer value.***	62%	22%	16%
Business	*4a. Data warehousing improves productivity.****	50%	12%	37%
	4b. Data warehousing reduces productivity.	35%	26%	39%
	5a. Data warehousing improves organizational image.***	64%	17%	18%
	5b. Data warehousing hurts organizational image.***	55%	29%	16%
Societal	*6a. Data warehousing helps the environment.****	63%	18%	19%
	6b. Data warehousing harms the environment.	43%	39%	18%
	7a. Governmental use of data warehousing is good.*	31%	42%	27%
	7b. Governmental use of data warehousing is not good.***	66%	17%	17%

Significance Levels of Difference: * =.05, ** = .01, *** = .001

Table 3. Which 'myths' win

Value Level	Abbreviated Propositions	Increase/Help/Good	Decrease/Hurt/Bad	Undecided
Consumer	*1. Is merging data with secondary sources more likely to increase or decrease consumer value?*	30%	40%	30%
	2. Is customer profiling more likely to increase or decrease consumer value?	31%	39%	30%
	3. Are persuasive technologies more likely to increase or decrease consumer value?***	21%	56%	23%
Business	*4. Is data warehousing more likely to help or hurt business productivity?***	36%	16%	48%
	5. Is data warehousing more likely to help or hurt a business's image?	37%	27%	36%
Societal	*6. Is data warehousing more likely to be good or bad for the environment?*	41%	27%	32%
	7. Is data warehousing more likely to be good or bad for society?*	25%	40%	35%

Significance Levels of Difference: * =.05, ** = .01, *** = .001

FUTURE TRENDS

In 1965 Gordon Moore, co-founder of Intel, made a prediction that became known as Moore's law, which predicts that the power of a microprocessor will double every 18 months. This prediction has been remarkably close to reality (Turban, Leidner, McLean, & Wetherbe, 2006). It is this growth that has made it possible to create, store, and manage vast amounts of information in a way that affects consumers in their everyday life. As this trend for increasing processing power continues into the future, information ethics will be further challenged as our ability to capture and use that information continues to increase exponentially. Thus we are only at the beginning of gauging the effect these tools will ultimately have on society, making it even more important to explore and understand the underlying ethics involved.

In the future we will see an increasing amount of information being stored and captured about consumers for a variety of purposes, from marketing to homeland security initiatives to criminals hunting their prey. As consumers become increasingly aware of the amount of information being collected and how it is being used, there very well could be a massive consumer backlash to some of the perceived abusing occurring today. Organizations should be careful in choosing information practices that their constituents deem to be ethical.

CONCLUSION

From this study the data shows that there is some confusion and differences of opinion on many aspects related to the ethical use of data, given today's data warehousing practices. Early themes that appear to be emerging, at least statistically speaking, include the consumer value of persuasive technologies being negatively viewed, data warehousing in business being positively viewed, and data warehousing by the government being negatively viewed.

These findings suggest that the jury is still out on the ethical perceptions of data warehousing and mining practices. Two sides have been presented to seven data warehousing issues, yet no clear-cut winner (or winners) has (have) emerged. One thing is clear: companies that participate in data mining and warehousing practices should clearly set boundaries on the appropriate use of this data and educate not only their employees, but also their customers on these policies.

REFERENCES

Berdichevsky, D., & Neuenschwander, E. (1999). Toward an ethics of persuasive technology. *Communications of the ACM, 42*(5), 51-58.

Boon, C. (1997). Why do data warehouse projects fail? *Journal of Data Warehousing, 2*(2), 16-20.

Cazier, J., & LaBrie, R. (2003, April 23-25). 7 myths of common data warehousing practices: An examination of consumer, business, and societal values. *Proceedings of the ISOneWorld 2003 Conference,* Las Vegas, NV.

Foote, P., & Krishnamurthi, M. (2001). Forecasting using data warehousing model: Wal-Mart's experience. *The Journal of Business Forecasting Methods & Systems, 20*(3), 13-17.

Garfinkel, S. (2000). *Database nation: The death of privacy in the 21st century.* Cambridge, MA: O'Reilly & Associates.

King, P., & Tester, J. (1999). The landscape of persuasive technologies. *Communications of the ACM, 42*(5), 31-38.

Koerner, B. (2002, September 1). *The winner of the war on terrorism is...* (p. 25). U.S. Industry, Sunday Business Group.

LaBrie, R., St. Louis, R., & Ye, L. (2002, August 9-11). A paradigm shift in database optimization: From indices to aggregates. *Proceedings of the 8th Americas Conference on Information Systems* (pp. 29-33), Dallas, TX.

Layman, E. (2003). Health informatics: Ethical issues. *Health Care Manager, 22*(1), 2-15.

Mason, R. (1986). Four ethical issues of the information age. *MIS Quarterly, 10*(1), 5-12.

Richman, D. (2002). Amazon will clarify its privacy notice. *The Seattle Post Intelligencer,* (September 28).

Tavani, H. (1999). Information privacy, data mining, and the Internet. *Ethics and Information Technology,* (1), 137-145.

Turban, E., Leidner, D., McLean, E., & Wetherbe, J. (2006). *Information technology for management: Transforming organizations in the digital economy.* Hoboken, NJ: John Wiley & Sons.

Westerman, P. (2000). *Data warehousing: Using the Wal-Mart model.* San Francisco: Morgan Kaufmann.

Wilder, C., & Soat, J. (2001). The ethics of data. *Information Week,* (May 14), 36-48.

Wixom, B., & Watson, H. (2001). An empirical investigation of the factors affecting data warehousing success. *MIS Quarterly, 25*(1), 17-42.

KEY TERMS

Business Value: The degree to which a technological practice benefits or harms a business by increasing its ability to function according to its goals and objectives.

Consumer Value: The degree to which a technological practice benefits or harms consumers in a way that enriches or impoverishes their lives and/or experiences.

Counter Myth: A response to a myth by detractors supported by inconclusive evidence.

Data Mining: The process of exploring stored data with the goal of finding something useful to the organization exploring.

Data Warehousing: The storing of massive amounts of data from multiple sources.

Myth: A popular belief supported by inconclusive evidence.

Privacy: The freedom to control information about oneself.

Privacy Concern: The concern that one has lost or may lose control of his or her information and may be damaged by the use of that information.

Societal Value: The degree to which a technological practice benefits or harms society.

Ethical Erosion at Enron

John Wang
Montclair State University, USA

James Yao
Montclair State University, USA

Richard Peterson
Montclair State University, USA

Zu-Hsu Lee
Montclair State University, USA

INTRODUCTION

Enron Corporation, the seventh-largest company in the nation, was named "America's Most Innovative Company" by *Fortune Magazine* from 1989 through 2001. Ironically, the company collapsed spectacularly in 2001 into bankruptcy and set off a wave of investigations into corporate malfeasance. The failure of both fiscal regulators and business analysts to notice the deterioration at Enron can debatably be labeled as the biggest business ethics failure in corporate history. The focus of this article is on the failure of Enron in conducting e-commerce due to unethical employee issues. Enron engaged in a series of complex transactions specifically to mask its activities. And yet the company saw no need to pay taxes in four of the last five years of its existence.

Scandals at Enron scared the public. The Enron implosion led to a major confidence crisis in the United States. While pushing off-the-books accounting to new levels on the one hand, Enron on the other hand innovated some very forward-looking projects, and what began as a smart business plan ended in disaster. To provide insight into what additional disclosures might be needed, it is useful to examine just how the current U.S. financial reporting model failed the markets in the Enron debacle. In ensuring that another Enron is not taking place, we hope to shed a modest amount of illumination upon the Enron scandal.

BACKGROUND

Enron was formed in 1985 when a Houston natural gas company merged with InterNorth, a gas provider in Nebraska, to operate an interstate natural gas pipeline that linked the Great Lakes with Texas. Kenneth Lay, a former Exxon executive, became chief executive officer (CEO) of Enron in 1986. Enron began trading gas commodities in 1989 and soon became the largest supplier in the United States. The business activities of Enron spread all around the world and included activities in countries like Argentina, Bolivia, Brazil, China, India, Indonesia, Mozambique, and the Philippines (Chatterjee, 2000). Enron also diversified its product range and expanded on to the Internet, trading a wide range of products from pulp and paper to petrochemicals and plastics. It also traded esoteric products such as airport landing rights, railroad hauling capacity, and clean air credits.

In less than two decades, Enron grew from a small gas pipeline company into the world's leading energy trading company, with $100 billion in revenue, $60 billion market value, and 21,000 employees in 40 countries (Enron, 2002). In 2000 Energy Financial Group ranked Enron as the sixth largest energy company worldwide. Enron's mergers brought the company much success, but Enron wanted more. This phenomenal growth was made possible by the use of new market strategies that tilted towards knowledge and innovation, in place of traditional ownership of physical assets.

The central strategy at Enron was to use the financial derivatives in the market to acquire commodities that anybody wanted to sell and dispose it at a profit to anyone who required it. This started with oil and natural gas, and then expanded into electric power generation and pipeline capacity, broadband communication, and freight capacity of modular containers. From "energy supplier" to "energy broker" to "multiple-item broker," all these were the factors that were responsible for Enron's growth, and corporate greed led to its downfall (Ekbia, 2004).

MAIN FOCUS

From the *postal coupon scam* in the 1920s to the *mutual funds scam* in the 1970s, from the *securities fraud scam* in the 1980s to the *junk bond scam* and *insider trading scam* afterwards, none could overshadow the *Enron scam* in terms of magnitude and depth. Enron engaged in the use of electronic technology to facilitate business transactions and managed to create the largest e-commerce Web site in the world. However, what began as a smart business decision ended in a disaster. Gini (2004) stressed that Enron has become "an icon of an era, the poster child for corporate mismanagement, a metaphor for corporate corruption, and, a shorthand for corporate greed" (p. 9).

Meteoric Rise and Sudden Fall

E-commerce provides numerous opportunities in increasing networking efforts, increasing efficiency, hence decreasing costs. Enron launched EnronOnline (EOL) in November 1999, the first ever global, Web-based, online commodity trading site. EOL was a principal-based online trading system. All transactions were directly with an Enron company. Customers could view real-time prices and accept full contractual terms online, such as Argentine natural gas, Japanese weather, Dutch aluminum, Spanish electricity, and U.S. lumber. Enron had an edge over its competitors in that there was no commission and no subscription fee charged to the customer. The key factor that separated Enron from its competition was the way it interacted with its buyers and sellers. In addition, Enron offered a risk management product to these buyers and sellers to make them comfortable with this new marketing exploit by hedging their financial exposures. Enron played three different roles at the same time: broker, trader, and market maker.

In early 2001 Jeff Skilling took over as Enron's CEO from Ken Lay. In October 2001 the tables were turned again, and Ken Lay returned as CEO with Jeff Skilling having resigned in August. Then hints of overstated earnings began to circulate, along with nose-dived share prices—employees were terminated and their life savings emptied. Investigations into corporate crimes and accountancy fraud were initiated on Enron leading to the collapse of the Enron empire (Siylak, 2002). Enron declared bankruptcy in December 2001. Quite a few of its executives reaped large benefits by disposing their stock options for cash when the share prices were high. The employees were the losers as they put all their pension money in Enron shares and lost it all when the firm went bankrupt.

How the Company was Directed

Virtually every company, including those that plunder, has a policy with the proper lofty language about their commitment to integrity. But there is a difference between words and deeds (Wright, 2003). It is an irony that at the time these companies were engaged in wrongdoing, they were never more eager to present themselves as good citizens.

Enron's token commitment to its code of ethics was famed "RICE" (respect, integrity, communication, and excellence). Enron's values are set forth in its 2000 Annual Report to Shareholders:

Communication—We have an obligation to communicate. Respect—We treat others as we would like to be treated ourselves. Integrity—We work with customers and prospects openly, honestly and sincerely. Excellence—We are satisfied with nothing less than the very best in everything we do. (Enron, 2001)

However, the RICE values were neither modeled by leaders nor integrated into operations. Enron was obsessed with values relating to business success and profitability. Risk taking and "do deals" had become the dominant value in the company. Enron adopted an aggressive employee review system—a semiannual weeding out known as the "rank and yank." In the performance review committee (PRC), which became known as the harshest employee ranking system in the country, every six months 15% of employees were to be given unsatisfactory ratings that largely doomed their careers at Enron.

The company's culture had profound effects on the ethics of its employees. Enron's former President and CEO Jeffry Skilling actively cultivated a culture that would push limits. Employees were forced to stretch the rules further and further until the limits of ethical conduct were easily overlooked in the pursuit of the next big success. Fierce internal competition prevailed.

Paranoia flourished and contracts began to contain highly restrictive confidentiality clauses.

Once a culture's ethical boundaries are breached, thresholds of more extreme ethical compromises become lower. Sims and Brinkmann (2003) discovered that even if the Enron culture permitted acts of insignificant rule bending, it was the sum of incremental ethical transgressions that produced the business catastrophe.

Hypothetically, the introduction of EOL could have increased the competitive functioning of the gas markets, or instead it could become a vehicle for increasing the concentration of market information in the hands of the Enron traders. Aided by the information available through EOL, Enron could emerge as a dominant firm exerting influence on the market to its own advantage (Murry & Zhu, 2004).

With the use of e-commerce and the acceptance of its countless benefits come responsibilities and risks if not met. Enron began diversifying its portfolio through the use of thousands of special purpose entities (SPEs), which allowed the company to embark upon less conventional ventures without necessarily reflecting their cost on its balance sheets. The pushing of boundaries was most likely encouraged throughout the company. They were pioneering business methods of the entrepreneurial culture, of innovation and deal making. Finally they pushed too hard; they "crossed a line and strayed into illegal behavior" (Zellner, 2003).

Because the activities that eventually resulted in the collapse of Enron did not occur overnight, nor were conducted by one person, many people are responsible for what occurred inside of Enron. CEO Jeff Skilling, Chairman Ken Lay, also former CEO of Enron, and ex-CFO Andrew Fastow played major roles in the way Enron's future turned out. The Board of Directors supported the CEO and the chairman, and they were further supported by an intelligent staff of accountants, auditors, and lawyers. Without committed ethical leadership, as Gini (2004) pointed out, "ethical standards will not be established, maintained, and retained in the life of any organization" (p. 11).

The Main Reasons for the Company's Failure

The collapse of Enron has been explained in a range of ways. Certainly, faulty operating decisions could underlie some of Enron's problems. Yet it appears that a major share of the blame for the collapse may be due to the ethical climate in the company, as *Verschoor* (2002) claimed.

Enron's downfall is considered by many to be a classic accounting failure characterized by the inappropriate use of generally accepted accounting principles (GAAP), off-balance-sheet schemes, and questionable independent auditor performance. It was a failure brought about by loose practices and a betrayal of trust.

Kreitner and Kinicki (2004, p. 107) blamed "the damage to the culture by the unscrupulous demands and practices of the CEO 'to make the numbers' at whatever cost necessary, which contributed significantly to the company's financial and legal problems."

The *Washington Post* described Enron as "a fundamentally self-destructive institution, a house of cards, where human error and a culture of ambition, secrecy and greed made collapse inevitable" (Behr & Witt, 2002). Zellner (2003) mentioned "the unbridled greed, the Byzantine financial deals, and the toothless watchdogs at Arthur Andersen." In Awe's point of view (2003), "dubious financial maneuvers, excessive spending, and intricate and questionable accounting practices," as well as "political assistance" from big man, contributed to Enron's rise and fall.

On the other hand, the demise of Enron is not only the result of ethically challenged corporate managers, but also a tale of fatal near-sightedness on the part of directors, auditors, bankers, lawyers, and analysts (Martorelli, 2004). Enron dealt in commodities and derivative structures and deal terms that were far too unusual to have an established price. The both hard pressure from the "rank and yank" and soft supervision from the non-standard measurements were Enron's unprecedented environment.

Also, Prentice (2003) argued that behavioral decision theory has substantial explanatory power in the Enron debacle. Because of subgoal pursuit, individual units of Enron tackled huge, risky projects—and a number of them helped drag Enron down. The self-serving bias worked particular evil at Enron. Trades were often recorded at full value as revenue rather than according to the simple profit that was made. Energy was sometimes bought, sold, and then bought back in order to inflate revenues. Emphasis was placed on stock values almost to the exclusion of all else. Enron was an organization where money was the only yardstick and where the code of ethics was only window dressing.

Enron was not in isolation of being the only company to have conducted such illegal activities when dealing with e-commerce. Other companies include but are not limited to WorldCom, Adelphia Communications, Global Crossing, and Tyco International. Over the last five years, over 700 companies have been forced to re-state their earnings in the United States. Each and every one can be accused of contributing to the damaged credibility of today's businesses (Awe, 2003).

Recently, Maccoby (2005) asserts that to make both companies and government organizations behave morally, the focus should be on organizational values and leadership. What needs to be done to raise the moral level? One key factor is whether employees feel it is safe to tell the truth, argue minority views, and deliver bad news, especially when telling the truth may be essential to the well-being of others. Of course, leaders must articulate and model organizational values. If leaders are serious about raising the moral level, they need to actively engage the organization.

FUTURE TRENDS

The industry that Enron made infamous—energy trading—is springing to life again (Barrionuevo, 2006). Ongoing court trials and investigations into the firm's accounting will continue for some time, since the Enron scandal has aggravated multiple lawsuits and extraordinary fury from a range of stakeholders. In legal terms the only positive outcome of the Enron failure was the revision of accounting standards and retirement plan regulations. Legislative remedies were immediately sought, culminating in the Sarbanes-Oxley Act (SOX) of 2002. Sarbanes-Oxley includes a number of provisions designed to strengthen public and private oversight of corporate behavior, and subjects violators to harsher penalties (Leeds, 2003). "Further, what was once considered unethical is now illegal" (Downes & Russ, 2005, p. 7).

Saunders (2003) emphasized that "as a result of Enron there have been the biggest changes to company rules in the U.S. since the 1929 crash. CEOs must now testify to the accuracy of the accounts and auditors are effectively banned from consulting to clients." But

Stanford (2004) noticed that ethical behavior cannot be legislated: it has to come from within the individual and within an organization's culture. Research suggests that to the extent organizational structure can promote ethical behavior, a decentralized structure is best. When decisions reflect consensus and accountability is shared, self-dealing should be curtailed, if not eliminated.

While shareholder wealth is typically maximized through long-term profitability, the wealth of individual managers is often the result of short-term performance. It is possible for unethical managers to take advantage of the information asymmetry and use their positions to further their own agendas rather than those of owners, engaging in what is termed managerial opportunism (Downes & Russ, 2005; Williamson, 1996). Why do "good" people make "bad" moral choices? How can long-term social acceptance be achieved together with short-term maximization of returns? Does SOX, with its strictures governing corporate behavior, offer an answer? Questions remain. In line with Morgenson (2006), the Enron verdicts were, at best, the end of the beginning of this dispiriting corporate crime wave. They were certainly not the beginning of its end.

CONCLUSION

At Enron, the alleged corners-cutting and rule-breaking wrong-doing occurred at the very top of corporation pyramid. Ethical problems were left to grow until they were too big to hide and too big to fix. Executives must choose the ethical path, even when it is the path of most resistance and least profit.

The collapse of Enron shook U.S. corporate governance. Deregulation, Arthur Andersen, Wall Street analysts, and politics played roles in the company's downfall. Enron has given the business world lessons in ethics, "creative" accounting, and internal competition, while also pointing new directions in infrastructure and e-commerce management. At any rate Enron has become an example of how not to manage an organization.

Organizations reap what they sow. An invincible corporate giant can still be brought down by gigantic ethical delinquencies. The seventh-largest corporation in America destroyed itself through every kind of greed. The old saying goes, "Lesson learned hard are learned best." Traces of Enron's evolution, expansion, corruption, and collapse have shaped salient warning signals for everyone.

REFERENCES

Awe, S.C. (2003). Pipe dreams: Greed, ego, jealousy, and the death of Enron. *Library Journal, 128*(5), 63.

Barrionuevo, A. (2006). Energy trading, post-Enron. *The New York Times.* Retrieved April 19, 2007, from http://www.nytimes.com/2006/01/15/business/yourmoney/15traders.html?pagewanted=1&th&emc=th

Behr, P., & Witt, A. (2002). Visionary dreams led to risky business. *The Washington Post,* (July 28), A1.

Chatterjee, P. (2000). Meet Enron, Bush's biggest contributor. *The Progressive,* (September).

Downes, M., & Russ, G.S. (2005). Antecedents and consequences of failed governance: The Enron example. *Corporate Governance, 5*(5), 84-98.

Ekbia, H.R. (2004). How IT mediates organizations: The role of Enron in California energy crisis. *Journal of Digital Information, 5*(4).

Enron. (2001). Proxy statement (p. 53).

Enron. (2002). *Who's who.* Retrieved April 19, 2007, from http://news.bbc.co.uk/hi/english/static/in_depth/business/2002/enron/2.stm

Gini, A. (2004). Business, ethics, and leadership in a post Enron era. *Journal of Leadership & Organizational Studies, 11*(1), 9-15.

Kreitner, R., & Kinicki, A. (2004). *Organizational behavior* (6th ed.). Boston: McGraw-Hill/Irwin.

Leeds, R. (2003). Breach of trust: Leadership in a market economy. *Harvard International Review, 25*(3), 76.

Maccoby, M. (2005). Creating moral organizations. *Research Technology Management, 48*(1), 59-60.

Martorelli, M.A. (2004). Enron: Corporate fiascos and their implications. *Financial Analysts Journal, 60*(6), 83.

Morgenson, G. (2006, May 28). *Are Enrons bustin' out all over?* Retrieved April 19, 2007, from http://select.

nytimes.com/2006/05/28/business/yourmoney/28gret.html

Murry, D., & Zhu, Z. (2004). EnronOnline and informational efficiency in the U.S. natural gas market. *The Energy Journal, 25*(2), 57-74.

Prentice, R. (2003). Enron: A brief behavioral autopsy. *American Business Law Journal, 40*(2), 417.

Saunders, C. (2003). *What can we learn from the Enron affair?* Retrieved April 19, 2007, from http://www.lums.lancs.ac.uk/news/executive/2002-12-18/

Sims, R.R., & Brinkmann, J. (2003). Enron ethics (or: Culture matters more than codes). *Journal of Business Ethics, 45*(3), 243.

Siylak, S. (2002). *Brief history of Enron Corporation—the biography of a corporate disaster.* Retrieved April 19, 2007, from http://www.photofora.com/eugene/stuff/ENRON.htm

Stanford. J.H. (2004). Curing the ethical malaise in corporate America: Organizational structure as the antidote. S.A.M. *Advanced Management Journal, 69*(3), 14-21.

Verschoor, C.C. (2002). Were Enron's ethical missteps a major cause of its downfall? *Strategic Finance, 83*(8), 22-24.

Williamson, O.E. (1996). *The mechanisms of governance.* New York: Oxford University Press.

Wright, B. (2003). Restoring trust. *Executive Excellence, 20*(4), 19.

Zellner, W. (2003). An insider's tale of Enron's toxic culture. *Business Week, 3826*(March 31), 16.

KEY TERMS

Electronic Commerce (E-Commerce): The buying and selling of goods and services on the Internet, especially the World Wide Web.

Generally Accepted Accounting Principles (GAAPs): A widely accepted set of rules, conventions, standards, and procedures for reporting financial information, as established by the Financial Accounting Standards Board.

McLear + Elkind 2004 — see 443

Integrity: As defined by AICPA, the American Institute of Certified Public Accountants: the character traits of honesty, candor, and protection of confidentiality.

Market Maker: One of the intermediaries required to stand ready to buy and sell stock.

Organizational Responsibility: Refers to obligations to operate regularly according to accepted social norms and standards. Those organizations that comply with basic standards are able to argue that their behavior is ethical, and that their operations are normative and legitimate.

Scam: A fraudulent business scheme or a ploy by a shyster to raise money.

Special Purposes Entity (SPE): A trust, corporation, limited partnership, or other legal vehicle authorized to carry out specific activities as enumerated in its establishing legal document; dubbed the Raptors.

Ethical Usability Testing with Children

Kirsten Ellis
Monash University, Australia

Marian Quigley
Monash University, Australia

INTRODUCTION

Usability testing of children's software on children is an important part of the software development and evaluation cycle, but the dilemmas of conducting usability testing in an ethical manner need careful consideration in order to protect the participants' well-being. The main issues in conducting research with children are the protection of the child, informed consent, and voluntary participation. Protection of the child is achieved by careful consideration of the design of the research. Consent is required from the parent and the child depending on the ability of the child to give informed consent. The final issue is voluntary participation, and thus the child's right to refuse to participate must be respected.

REASONS FOR CONDUCTING RESEARCH ON CHILDREN

This article looks at the dilemmas of conducting ethical usability testing with children in the context of university research and publicly funded research in which researchers are required to meet strict criteria specified by the institutions in order to protect the participants and the credibility of the research and the institution. Private organizations are not subject to the same procedures, but should still be considering the following issues in order to protect the best interests of the participating child. It is important to conduct research with children, as children can benefit from these activities and the findings from research conducted on adults cannot always be assumed to apply to children. According to the Australian National Statement on Ethical Conduct in Research Involving Humans (2005, p. 4.1): "Research is essential to advance knowledge about children's and young peoples' well-being." It is by researching children that their voices can be heard and their preferences can be taken into consideration. There are many areas in which children are valuable research participants, particularly in education as the education process affects them greatly. Hedges (2001, p. 1) states, "Views of children affect the content and process of the education they receive and ways they are researched." For example, software designed for children should be tested on children to ensure that it is age appropriate for the target audience and that the children are able to use the software as predicted by the designer (Burmeister, 2001).

Conducting ethical research with adults is difficult and takes considerable thought and effort. Conducting ethical research with children is even more difficult, as there are even more complex issues that need to be addressed and they are more susceptible to some types of harm that may arise from research (Commonwealth Government of Australia, 2005). "Children can be seen as both agents and dependents—children can be empowered to participate in research with agency, but with regard for their different cognitive and language abilities, structural vulnerabilities and cultural and ecological context" (Hedges, 2001, p. 2).

Once the research as been completed and analyzed, the knowledge gained by conducting research with children should then be released to the public (conforming to the appropriate confidentiality provisions) in order to improve the circumstances of children and thereby justify the conducting of the research (Hedges, 2001). The participants in the research must also be informed of the findings. In the case of children, this should be done in a language that is appropriate to the age of the children involved (Johnson, 2000).

GUIDELINES FOR RESEARCH INVOLVING CHILDREN

Use Qualified Researchers

It is important that researchers who work with children are adequately qualified and trained, as children are vulnerable participants. Johnson (2000) points out that it is important to treat children with respect. This will ensure ethical behavior in the design of the experiments and the treatment of the participants. Children are indispensable for research in the same way as adults, however they have additional and unique requirements to ensure ethical outcomes.

Gaining data from children can be complicated by a number of characteristics that children may exhibit. Although not exclusively characteristics of children, they are more prevalent in this group. Read and Mac-Farlane (2006, p. 82) state: "Factors that impact on question answering include developmental effects including language ability, reading age, and motor skills, as well as temperamental effects such as confidence, self-belief and the desire to please." False data may be collected if the children can make up answers in order to please the interviewer or if they tell the interviewer what they have been told by adults rather than giving their own opinion (Hedges, 2001). Another reason for using well-trained researchers is that young children may have limited ability to express themselves verbally and the accuracy of the data is dependent on the researchers' ability to understand the children (Hedges, 2001). The presence of the researcher can affect the result, especially in the case of children. Read and MacFarlane (2006, p. 82) state, "Even when there is no deliberate intervention the interview has an effect. In one study it was shown that children are likely to give different responses depending on the status of the interviewer." Hedges (2001, p. 6) notes that "Children behave differently with people they are unfamiliar with." Also the presence or absence of a parent or guardian can significantly effect a child's behavior, so careful consideration needs to be given to the physical research design.

Provide Appropriate Company Depending on the Child's Age

There are special considerations that need to be taken into account for researching with children. The testing environment needs to be explained to them so that they are comfortable with equipment and tape recorders. Young children up to the age of seven or eight years of age need to have company during the session. A researcher providing company for children reduces parents' interference in the process. Young children under the age of five will probably need a parent with them. Children older than this will not need parental company, so ideally the parent can be in an observation room during the session. Siblings of children involved in user testing should not be in the room as they pose a significant distraction (Hanna, Risden, & Alexander, 1997).

Carefully Consider the Involvement of Teachers

The involvement of teachers in research with children has advantages and disadvantages that need to be considered carefully in the research design (Hedges, 2001). Teachers who participate have established rapport with the children and may enable the children to relax, but it is important not to take advantage of the children's trust. There can also be problems with bias when teachers are involved. This may occur consciously or unconsciously.

Select the Location of the Research Carefully

The location of the research is an important issue: should the researcher go to the children in a home or school setting, or should the child come to the researcher? Usability labs offer iterative testing with changes between each test session, but the children may not be as comfortable as in the home environment and not as many children can be tested as by testing groups within a school setting. The three main methods of gathering data are observations, interviews, and questionnaires (Hanna et al., 1997). Usability testing is usually used to assess ease of use, learning, and appeal over time.

Use an Age-Appropriate Research Design

The age of children involved in testing affects the style of testing that is appropriate to gather the required information (Ellis, 2002). Hanna et al. (1997, p. 10) found that "most children younger than 2½ years of age are not proficient enough with standard input devices (e.g., Mouse, trackball or keyboard) to interact with the technology and provide useful data." Preschool children should be able to explore the computer independently, however, when conducting usability testing preschool children require extensive adaptation to software because of their limited attention span. Their motivation to please can affect the data and they may or may not be able to adjust to strange surroundings. A skillful tester is required when conducting user testing of appeal or engagement on a pre-school audience, as the tester needs to watch for body language such as sighing, smiling, or sliding under the table since children cannot always express likes and dislikes in words (Hanna et al., 1997).

In comparison to testing pre-schoolers, elementary school children aged 6-10 are relatively easy to test. They can sit and follow directions, are not self-conscious of being observed, and will answer questions and try new things easily. Six- and seven-year-olds like to be engaged in hands-on activities but can be shy (Hanna et al., 1997).

Explain the Environment

When setting up user testing for children, it is important to use input devices that they are familiar with and small microphones or cameras. It is important not to face children directly towards the video camera as they will become self-conscious (Hanna et al., 1997). In contrast to this guide on using cameras during research, Druin (1999, p. 594) states: "Our team does not find video cameras to be successful in capturing data for contextual inquiry purpose. In my previous work…We found that when children saw a video camera in the room, they tended to 'perform' or to 'freeze'."

Limit the Duration of the Testing

Hanna et al. (1997) believe that sessions should not exceed one hour of lab time, as preschoolers tire after 30 minutes and older children will fatigue in an hour. When conducting user testing with children, it is best to select children who can already use a computer. Read and MacFarlane (2006) concur, stating: "Keep it short: Whatever the children are asked to do, make it fit their time span.…For young children, five minutes spent in a written survey is generally long enough, more time can be given, as the children get older."

Recruit Children because they are Representative not Convenient

The recruitment of children for research must be considered carefully, as it is quite difficult to not recruit a captive audience through people that are known to the researcher or organization and who have groups of children of the appropriate age. Hanna et al. (1997) warn against using colleagues' children for usability testing as they are far more exposed to computers than average children and if they do not like the software, it can create a situation where they feel uncomfortable expressing their true thoughts on the software.

PROTECTION OF THE RESEARCH SUBJECTS

Children have the right to expect to be protected from harm in all research conducted on them. The Convention on the Rights of the Child states: "Bearing in mind that, as indicated in the Declaration of the Rights of the Child, 'the child, by reason of his physical and mental immaturity, needs special safeguards and care, including appropriate legal protection, before as well as after birth'" (UNICEF, 1989). In addition to this, Article 3 of the convention states, "In all actions concerning children…the best interest of the child shall be a primary consideration."

Protection of children in the process of research may not be as obvious as it first seems. If the results of the research are unknown, as is usually the case, then it is necessary to consider the research carefully to predict any harm that may come to children by participating in the research, and if there is a possibility of harm, then the research should not be conducted (Berk, 1997). For example, harm can be induced in children at different ages in ways that are not relevant to adults (Greenfield, 1984). Older children, for example, are susceptible to harm from procedures that threaten the way they think of themselves (Berk, 1997).

National laws governing mandatory reporting of particular issues can pose a dilemma when conducting research. The procedures to be followed in the case of mandatory reporting should be clearly set out so that the researchers know what their obligations are and the appropriate channels to follow (Newman & Pollnitz, 2002).

INFORMED CONSENT

The parents or guardians of children are usually required to give informed consent on behalf of the child until the child reaches the age of consent. The parents' or guardians' consent is gained as they are considered more capable of making a decision taking into account all aspects of the research (Hedges, 2001). Field and Behrman (2004, p. 7) note that:

Informed consent is widely regarded as a cornerstone of ethical research. Because children (with the exception of adolescents under certain conditions) do not have the legal capacity to provide informed consent, the concepts of parental permission and child assent have been developed as standards for ethical research involving children.

The Australian National Statement on Ethical Conduct in Research Involving Humans states that consent is required from the "child or young person whenever he or she has sufficient competence to make this decision" (Commonwealth Government of Australia, 2005, p. 4.2a) and also from the parent or guardian. Parents may only consent if the proposed research is not contrary to the child's best interests.

When research is conducted in schools, the lines of communication between the researcher and the parents are often more complex, but acquiring consent from parents must not be compromised. In schools, consent must be obtained from all relevant parties, including the child, the parent or guardian, the class teacher, the school principal, and the relevant department of education. School staff cannot consent on behalf of students or parents, nor can they disclose information for research purposes about any person or group without the prior permission of the individual affected. In schools, care must also be taken when the research proposal involves the comparison of more able children with less able children as there is the potential for embarrassment, discrimination, and invasion of privacy (Commonwealth Government of Australia, 2005).

Informed consent when working with children is problematic. In order to inform children, it is important that the explanation is appropriate to their age. Children's understanding of the implication of the research is difficult to verify depending on their age. Berk (1997) states that children seven years and older are able to give informed consent as they are able to understand enough to reason and make this decision. Children are aware of their immediate environment and their personal experiences. It is important to explain the research in a way that is within the limitation of the children's experience. It is also important to use concrete terms rather than intangible concepts as children often do not have the maturity to understand abstract concepts and ideas (Hedges, 2001; Singer & Revenson, 1996; Woolfe, Want, & Siegal, 2002). A script should be used for introductions. Where confidentiality is required, it can be explained to children as "top secret." Older children can be motivated by stressing the importance of their role. They should understand that the software is unfinished so that they do not expect too much and so that they know that their input can affect the software that is being tested (Hanna et al., 1997).

Designing ethical research is difficult in educational settings, as the nature of the experimental process applies different treatments to different groups, which leads to disadvantage in some groups. Hedges (2001, p. 8) states: "In experiments a researcher ought to verify that children in the control group are not disadvantaged in relation to those in the experimental group who may receive new curricula, new teaching methods or new learning strategies." There are also cases when the control group does not benefit from the treatment; this may be harm by omission (Johnson, 2000). Confidentiality of results can also be an issue, as inadvertently revealing a child's identity may lead to harm of the child. This may not be releasing a name but having such as small group that the identity can be deduced (Berk, 1997).

REFUSAL TO PARTICIPATE

Voluntary participation is a complex ethical area when working with children. The children may feel coerced into participating in the research if their parent or guardian has given permission even if they do not want to participate in the research. The child's right to refuse to participate in a research project must be respected (Commonwealth Government of Australia, 2005). The language and tone used by the researcher is important as there may be implied coercion when it is not intended. For example, if asking a child to use a computer, the researcher could state, "Come and use the computer now" or use a more diplomatic statement such as "Would you like to use the computer now?" When children elect to participate in research, they may change their minds. Hedges (2001, p. 7) states: "Children may choose, for example not to answer a question in an interview, or become bored or uninterested."

The payment of participants to take part in research has considerable ethical implications as it may apply subtle coercion (Burmeister, 2001). It is accepted that participants are reimbursed for their costs, but there should never be the consideration of payment for greater risk. This is particularly vexed as the payment would be accepted by and given to the parent rather than directly to the child (Field & Behrman, 2004).

CONCLUSION

Children's participation in research is important to developing high-quality, appropriate software for children, but the ethics of the research need to be carefully considered. Children are a vulnerable group, so special effort must be taken to ensure their physical, emotional, and psychological safety during the research process. The gaining of informed consent is a pillar of ethical research, but can be somewhat vexatious when dealing with children as they are not legally able to give consent, and assessment of their ability to be informed is subject to debate. Respecting the rights of a child to refuse to participate in research is a clear principle, but subtle, unintended coercion may occur. Careful design and consideration of the research process will assist in ensuring that research is conducted in an ethical manner and will produce valid results.

REFERENCES

Berk, L.E. (1997). Ethics in research on children. In *Child development* (4th ed., pp. 64-69). Boston: Allyn & Bacon.

Burmeister, O.K. (2001). Usability testing: Revisiting informed consent procedures for testing Internet sites. *Proceedings of the Australian Institute of Computer Ethics Conference,* Canberra, Australia.

Commonwealth Government of Australia. (2005). *National statement on ethical conduct in research involving humans.* National Health and Medical Research Council.

Druin, A. (1999). Cooperative inquiry: Developing new technologies for children with children. *Proceedings of the SIGCHI Conference on Human Factors in Computing Systems: The CHI Is the Limit.*

Ellis, K. (2002). *Modelling interface metaphors: Developing multimedia for young children.* Monash University, Australia.

Field, M.J., & Behrman, R.E. (2004). *Ethical conduct of clinical research involving children.* Washington, DC: The National Academies Press.

Greenfield, P.M. (1984). *Mind and media: The effects of television, video games, and computers.* Cambridge, MA: Harvard University Press.

Hanna, L., Risden, K., & Alexander, K. (1997). Guidelines for usability testing with children. *Interactions: New Visions of Human-Computer Interactions, 4*(5), 9-12.

Hedges, H. (2001). A right to respect and reciprocity: Ethics and educational research with children. *NZ Research in ECE, 4*(1), 1-18.

Johnson, K. (2000). Research ethics and children. *Curriculum Perspectives,* (November), 6-7.

Newman, L., & Pollnitz, L. (2002). *Ethics in action: Introducing the ethical response cycle.* ACT: Australian Early Childhood Association.

Read, J.C., & MacFarlane, S. (2006, June 7-9). Using the Fun Toolkit and other survey methods to gather opinions in child computer interaction. *Proceedings of the Conference on Interaction Design for Children,* Tampere, Finland.

Singer, D.G., & Revenson, T.A. (1996). *A Piaget primer: How a child thinks* (rev. ed.). New York: Plume.

UNICEF. (1989). General assembly resolution 44/25 1-15. *Proceedings of the Convention of the Rights of the Child.*

Woolfe, T., Want, S.C., & Siegal, M. (2002). Signposts to development: Theory of the mind in deaf children. *Child Development, 73*(3), 768-778.

KEY TERMS

Informed Consent: A participant knows what is involved in the process that they are going to undertake, and they are still willing to participate.

Mandatory Reporting: In certain jurisdictions it is compulsory to report particular information that is revealed or observed, for example telling authorities about possible cases of child abuse.

Right to Refuse: The participants know that they are able to refuse to participate and are able to enact this right.

Usability Testing: Testing of software by the end user to ensure that it is designed in a manner that is easy to use.

Voluntary Participation: The participants take part without being coerced by an external source.

Ethics and Access to Technology for Persons with Disabilities

Belinda Davis Lazarus
University of Michigan – Dearborn, USA

INTRODUCTION

The growth in technology has provided unprecedented access to information and experiences for persons all over the world. An Internet search yields volumes of information, personal digital assistants (PDAs) connect people with friends and information worldwide, and prosthetic devices provide both cosmetic effects and mobility for persons with a wide variety of orthopedic impairments. Although the current level of access to technology is a recent phenomenon, most people take these conveniences for granted. However, technology may be a mixed blessing for persons with disabilities and pose ethical dilemmas for developers who wish to provide global access for all.

BACKGROUND

Over 600 million people worldwide live with a sensory, physical, mental, or self-care disability that limits their ability to learn, work, and participate in daily activities (Heumann, 2004). Although assistive technology has become an important tool to provide persons with disabilities access to community, vocational, and leisure activities, mainstream technology such as computers, electromyographic (EMG)-controlled prostheses, cell phones, and handheld PDAs may require resources and skill levels that are beyond their reach and prevent them from accessing information and services. For example, persons with learning disabilities or visual impairments may not be able to read the text on Web sites. Persons with limited mobility may not be able to use their fingers to type, manipulate a computer mouse, or hold a cell phone. Also, many persons with disabilities cannot afford to purchase and maintain expensive assistive devices. As a result, accessible Web design and access to various assistive technology devices is needed to maximize information access for persons with disabilities.

The Alliance for Technology Access (ATA) asserts that all persons with disabilities are entitled to access to the information and technology needed to foster independence, employment, and leisure activities. ATA (2006) contends that:

- People with disabilities have the right to maximum independence and participation in all environments, without barriers.
- Technology can be harnessed to diminish or eliminate environmental barriers for people with disabilities.
- People with disabilities have the right to control and direct their own choices, and the right to access the information they need in order to make informed decisions according to their goals and interests.
- People with disabilities have the right to employ assistive technologies, strategies for implementation, and necessary training support to maximize their independence and productivity.

Furthermore, the IEEE Professional Communication Society Code of Ethics (1990) calls for members "…to treat fairly all persons regardless of such factors as race, religion, gender, disability, age, or national origin" (p. 487).

Advances in information and communications technology (ICT) hold the potential to provide access to services and information for all persons with disabilities, however ICT specialists in the public and private sector often lack information on the needs of persons with disabilities. Also, institutional strategies and resource allocations seldom address the limitations and technological needs of persons with disabilities at different age levels and in various situations. For example, access issues for children often affect educational and leisure opportunities, while adults may be more concerned with workplace issues and independent living skills. Furthermore, populations of persons with disabilities are heterogeneous and include a wide variety of skills and limitations.

Persons with Disabilities

Physical and cognitive disabilities pose different challenges as individuals attempt to access information and services. Physical disabilities affect about 3% of the population and include orthopedic, health, visual, and hearing impairments (Jones & Sandford, 1996). Persons with physical disabilities usually have the cognitive skills necessary to gain age-appropriate academic, social, and vocational skills; however, they often have limited mobility, health, sight, hearing, or the stamina needed to work for extended periods of time. The impact of physical disabilities may include paralysis, poor manual dexterity, low or distorted visual acuity, deafness, spasticity, weakness, and/or fatigue—all factors that affect access to information (Center of Information Technology, 2002-2006).

Assistive devices and disability-friendly Web designs that accommodate individuals with one or more disabilities help reduce the impact of their disability and improve their access to everyday living activities by providing assistance with communication and the self-help functions that increase their independence and sense of self-worth. Also various accommodations may serve one or more disability. For example, devices such as EMT control hands or limbs, text-to-speech synthesizers, audio and/or videoconferencing, and Braille displays and printers often equalize access for persons with both visual and orthopedic impairment (Hetzroni & Schrieber, 2004). Web sites that provide all visual information in text and sound, allow mouse-free navigation, and limit the use of color for distinguishing information help serve the needs of persons with visual, hearing, and health impairments.

Cognitive disabilities affect about 8% of the population and include learning disabilities, mental retardation, emotional disorders, attention deficit disorders, and speech/language impairments. Persons with cognitive disabilities experience a broad range of skills and limitations. For example, persons with learning disabilities or speech/language impairments often have average to above average intelligence, but may lack the visual and/or auditory processing skills needed to gain age-appropriate academic and/or social skills. Persons with attention deficit disorders or emotional disorders also have average intelligence, but

often lack the self-regulatory and self-management skills to engage in age-appropriate behaviors. Persons with mental retardation usually have poor cognitive and adaptive behavior skills. As a result, most persons with cognitive disabilities lack the reading, writing, and language skills needed to process and comprehend the text, language, graphics, and/or mathematics that are commonly needed to utilize technology.

In spite of the diverse impact of cognitive disabilities, the common characteristics affect information processing. Visual and/or auditory processing deficits can adversely affect a person's ability to use e-mail, instant messages, and Web sites. Persons with cognitive disabilities usually need additional training, practice, and supervision to gain the skills needed to understand directions and the use of assistive devices. They may need a screen reader plus synthesized speech to facilitate comprehension, captions to help understand an audio track, reduced distractions like animations to help focus their attention, or a consistent navigational structure throughout a site (Samuelsson, Lundberg, & Herkner, 2004; Gunderson & Jacobs, 2000). Also, software like Inspiration assists in organizing displays and information by using symbolic and a variety of graphical displays that facilitate understanding large amounts of information (Inspiration Software, 2006).

Issues with Access to Technology

The ATA maintains that society's attitude towards persons with disabilities is the greatest barrier to inclusion of persons with disabilities in the "Information Age." And, the National Telecommunications and Information Administration (2000) contends that the "digital divide" is a chasm for persons with disabilities. Lack of information about the availability of assistive technology, expensive equipment, and inconsistent standards for Web design and applications prevents persons with disabilities from accessing the technology that they need to gain independent living skills. Also, persons with disabilities in undeveloped countries are often unaware of and cannot afford assistive devices.

Thousands of simple and complex assistive technology devices exist. Talking pens read words to the writer as he or she pens thoughts and ideas. Electric page turners, headwands, and light pointers enable persons with limited mobility to read independently. Computer keyboards with large letters and monitors with magnified screens help persons with low vision type and read. The Kurzweil Omni 3000 Reading System assists persons whose disabilities affect their reading by simultaneously reading text out loud and highlighting each spoken word on a computer display. Users may pause the system at any time and use its pull-down menus to gain instant access to the dictionary, thesaurus, grammar checks, and note taking. Users may also use the system's scanner, voice-output, and recording capabilities to create books-on-tape. And, Telecommunications Device for the Deaf/TeleTypewriter (TDD/TTY) telephone relays and closed-captioned television allow persons with hearing impairments to use everyday devices like the telephone and television. However, more than half of the population with disabilities is unaware of the available assistive technology, and many cannot afford to pay for it (Closing the Gap, 2005; Rehab Tool, 2004).

Funding sources for assistive technology vary widely among and within countries. In developing nations, funds and resources are limited. The National Assistive Technical Assistance Partnership (2001) attempts to connect donors of used devices with recyclers who refurbish and redistribute equipment to hospitals and orphanages in the poorest countries of the world. In Asia, the Economic and Social Commission for Asia and the Pacific (1997) has developed a plan to produce and distribute free and low-cost devices for persons with disabilities. Physicians for Peace (2006) collect and refurbish used prosthetic devices, hearing aides, and eyeglasses for distribution in developing countries. Western countries like the United States, Canada, and Western Europe maintain various public assistance programs that supply assistive technology for persons who qualify for services. An assessment team composed of educational, psychological, and medical evaluators must collect data that justifies the need for a particular device within the needs that are occasioned by the particular disability.

Web designs and e-mail systems also pose problems for persons with disabilities. Although various screen readers like JAWS for Windows convert text into audio presentations, most text-to-speech readers cannot interpret tables, frames, and PDF files in a coherent manner. Readers also do not detect hyperlinks that are indicated by graphics or titles instead of the actual http-hyperlink, and animations may cause screen readers to scramble or misinterpret text. Also, the number of screen readers and computer operating systems may be confusing for persons with disabilities as they attempt to purchase compatible systems. Web designers and software developers need to work towards standards that maximize access for all persons and interface with common operating systems.

Trends in Accessibility

In recent years, advocacy groups have raised awareness of the needs and challenges faced by persons with disabilities. A variety of groups have attempted to compile resources related to assistive technology and to provide guidance to Web designers. Also, programs have been developed to train professionals in the area of assistive and adaptive technology. Rehabilitation specialists that serve persons with disabilities often receive continuing education to increase their awareness and skills with emerging technologies that accommodate a variety of disabilities

The Internet has also evolved into a source of information for persons with disabilities, service providers, and technology developers. Hundreds of Web sites offer assistive devices or advice on accessible Web design. The Center for Information Technology (CITA) is a model demonstration facility influencing accessible information environments, services, and management practices that is operated by the General Service Administration in the United States. CITA's purpose is to provide assistive technology services that eliminate barriers to education and the workplace for persons with disabilities. The Adaptive Technology Resource Center (n.d.) in Toronto, Canada, maintains a searchable database of thousands of assistive technology devices and provides design consultation services, current research, education, and direct services to persons with disabilities. And, Bobby Approved (1998-2005) in the United States and Canada offers free advice on accessible Web design and provides evaluation for existing Web sites with feedback that enables designers to incorporate accessible features and design elements into Web sites. Web sites that comply with Bobby standards may place the Bobby Approved graphic on the Web site as an indication to persons with disabilities that the site had reduced distractions and increased accessibility.

CONCLUSION

Access to adaptive and information technology promises to improve the lives of persons with disabilities who face numerous challenges as they attempt to enjoy everyday life. Although assistive technology is a rapidly growing area, persons with disabilities are not aware of the technologies that are available and may not be able to afford devices that help them participate in mainstream activities. Numerous Internet applications may also include barriers that prevent persons with disabilities from accessing information and services. Advocacy groups that promote access are emerging to address their needs and ensure that persons with disabilities are enabled to fully participate in mainstream environments with their non-disabled peers.

REFERENCES

Adaptive Technology Resource Center. (n.d.). *Homepage.* Retrieved from http://www.utoronto.ca/atrc/

Allen, L., & Voss, D. (1997). *Ethics in technical communication: Shades of gray.* Hoboken, NJ: John Wiley & Sons.

Alliance for Technology Access. (2006). *Principles.* Retrieved from http://www.ataccess.org/about/principles.html

Bobby Approved. (1998-2005). *Accessible org.* Retrieved from http://www.accessible.org/bobby-approved.html

Center for Information Technology. (n.d.). *Overview.* Retrieved from http://www.gsa.gov/Portal/gsa/ep/channelView.do?pageTypeId=8203&channelPage=%252Fep%252Fchannel%252FgsaOverview.jsp&channelId=13126

Closing the Gap. (2005). *The gap.* Retrieved from http://www.closingthegap.com/

Economic and Social Commission for Asia and the Pacific. (1997). *Production and distribution of assistive devices for persons with disabilities: Part 1.* Thailand: The United Nations Publications.

Gunderson, J., & Jacobs, I. (2000). *User agent accessibility guidelines.* Retrieved from http://www.w3.org/TR/2002/REC-UAAG10-20021217

Hetzroni, O.E., & Shrieber, B. (2004). Word processing as an assistive technology tool for enhancing academic outcomes of students with writing disabilities in the general classroom. *Journal of Learning Disabilities, 37*(2), 143-154.

Heumann, J. (2004). Disability and inclusive development: Sharing, learning, and building alliances. *Proceedings of the 2nd International Disability and Development Conference,* Washington, DC.

IEEE Professional Communication Society. (1990). *Code of ethics.* Orlando, FL: IEEE.

Inspiration Software. (2006). *Inspiration®.* Retrieved from http://www.inspiration.com/productinfo/inspiration/index.cfm

Jones, M.L., & Sanford, J.A. (1996). People with mobility impairments in the United States today and in 2010. *Assistive Technology, 8,* 43-53.

Kaye, H.S. (2000). Computer and Internet use among people with disabilities. *Disability Statistics Report, 13. Retrieved from* http://www.dsc.ucsf.edu/ucsf/pdf/REPORT13.pdf

National Assistive Technical Assistance Partnership. (2001). Retrieved from http://www.resna.org/taproject/library/pubs/recycling/RMchptr4.htm

National Telecommunications and Information Administration. (2000). *Falling through the net: Toward digital inclusion.* Retrieved from http://www.ntia.doc.gov/ntiahome/digitaldivide

Physicians for Peace. (2006). *PFP Newsletter,* (May 3).

Raskind, M.H. (1998). Selecting the right assistive technology. *NCLD News, 8*(4), 3-4.

Raskind, M.H., & Higgens, E.L. (1995). Reflections on ethics, technology, and learning disabilities: Avoiding the consequences of ill-considered action. *Journal of Learning Disabilities, 28*(7), 425-438.

Rehab Tool. (2004). *Homepage.* Retrieved from http://www.rehabtool.com/

Samuelsson, S., Lundberg, I., & Herkner, B. (2004). ADHD and reading disability in adult males. Is there a connection. *Journal of Learning Disabilities, 37*(2), 155-168.

KEY TERMS

Assistive Technology: The set of devices that compensate for loss of functioning in persons with disabilities.

Auditory Processing: The ability to perceive, comprehend, and appropriately act upon auditory stimuli.

Braille Display: A series of raised dots that indicate letters of the alphabet and enable persons with visual impairments to read print and computer screens.

Braille Printer: A printer that transform text into Braille and print documents that may be read by persons with visual impairments.

Cognitive Disability: A disorder or condition that affects processing of information and prevents persons from comprehending and using concepts, ideas, and information.

Electromyographic (EMG)-Controlled Prosthesis: Computer-controlled signals that enable prosthetic devices like arms and hands to move more easily to increase the mobility of the user.

Independent-Living Skills: Basic skills such as self-care, learning, and thinking that enable persons to participate in everyday activities.

Manual Dexterity: The ability to use hands, fingers, and toes to complete fine motor tasks.

Physical Disability: A physiological disorder or condition that limits a person's mobility, endurance, and/or ability to perceive stimuli.

Spasticity: Inability to control gross motor functions such as arm and leg movements.

Text-to-Speech Synthesizer; Speech Reader: A screen reader is the commonly used name for the voice output technology used. Screen readers are used to replace the visual display traditionally viewed on a monitor for those with visual disabilities. Hardware and software produce synthesized voice output for text displayed on the computer screen, as well as for keystrokes entered on the keyboard.

Telecommunications Device for the Deaf/Tele-TYpewriter (TDD/TTY): A user terminal with keyboard input and printer or display output used by the hearing and speech impaired. The device contains a modem and is used over a standard analog phone line.

Visual Processing: The ability to perceive, comprehend, and appropriately act upon visual stimuli.

E

Ethics and Perceptions in Online Learning Environments

Michelle M. Ramim
Nova Southeastern University, USA

INTRODUCTION

Recent incidents of unethical behaviors reported in the media have led scholars to initiate a debate on the subject of ethics. In particular, professional and personal ethics appear to be relevant issues to explore, as literature suggests that they impact behavior. In higher education, a substantial increase in the use of online learning systems (OLSs) for the delivery of higher educational courses has been observed in the past decade (Hiltz & Turoff, 2005). However, little attention has been given in information systems (IS) literature to exploring the construct of ethics and its impact on perceptions relevant to the use (i.e., user behavior) of ISs. Thus, this article attempts to raise the awareness of scholars about such important constructs by providing an overview of the literature related to ethics and highlighting some related key definitions. Specifically, this article will review literature about personal ethics, professional ethics, and ethical challenges in higher education, and will assess personal ethics utilizing Forsyth's Personal Ethics Taxonomy instrument. Moreover, an argument is put forth for the connection between faculty members' personal ethics and their perceptions as constructs that impact the use of online learning systems to safeguard against and curb incidents of academic misconduct.

BACKGROUND

Throughout this article numerous pertinent definitions of personal and professional ethics will be introduced. A synthesized discussion about ethics in the information age will be offered as well as a description of some of the challenges that users face as a result of the use of information systems.

Ethics notions affect individuals' decision making and behaviors in everyday life. Yet, the IS literature offers very little about this topic or about how ethics impact humans' perceptions related to ISs usage. This article will highlight a particular ethical challenge in higher education related to academic misconduct and information system usage. The suggestion will be put forward that ethics play a significant role in faculty members' perceptions about the severity of this phenomenon. In turn, such perceptions may influence the way in which they employ ISs, or OLSs in the case of online learning, to reduce opportunities for academic misconduct.

ETHICAL CHALLENGES IN THE TECHNOLOGY AGE

Ethics is defined in Webster's dictionary as "the philosophical analysis of human morality and conduct [that are established] by society" (Webster, 2005). Philosophical ethics reflects a wide range of issues related to social policies and individual behavior. Scholars contend that the use of various ISs and the Internet in particular have brought about ethical challenges (Johnson, 2001; Tavani, 2004) which include, but are not limited to, accountability, government regulation, intellectual property rights, privacy, and security. Essentially, these ethical challenges affect all members of society (Johnson, 2001).

Tavani (2004) elaborates on the role of ethics with regards to individuals and society. He notes that society and individuals are guided by moral rules and principles. The rules are codes of conduct that guide ethical decisions and behaviors. Directives and social policies are examples of codes of conduct. Principles are universal standards that guide rules of conduct (i.e., social utility). Principles are founded upon religion, law, and philosophical ethics (Moore, 1999). There is a consensus among scholars that ethics help to guide ethical behaviors that are relevant in business, and in professional and daily life (Gbadamosi, 2004; Johnson, 2001; Tavani, 2004). Some researchers have pointed out that the Internet and various types of information systems have given rise to opportunities for unethical behavior (Harrington, 1996; Nitterhouse, 2003). Such misuses result in substantial economic losses (Straub, Nance, & Carlson, 1990). Therefore, researchers indicate the need to further understand what motivates unethical behaviors and what role information systems play in instances of unethical behaviors (Gbadamosi, 2004; Harrington, 1996). Furthermore, some scholars suggest that education about ethical issues can reduce unethical behavior in the workplace as well as in daily life (Banerjee, Cronan, & Jones, 1998; Gbadamosi, 2004). Thus, additional studies about the impact of ethical education are needed.

Professional Ethics

A number of scholars have attempted to explore professional ethics. For example, Bommer, Gratto, Gravander, and Tuttle (1987) defined professional ethics by separating the two words. Professional is defined as either belonging to a professional association or adhering to a licensing procedure. Professional in this case does not mean a person who aspires to make highly ethical decisions by upholding personal values. Instead, members of the profession hold a special license or membership that separates them from other individuals in society. As such, the loss of a license or membership serves to discourage unethical behavior (Bommer et al., 1987; Harrington, 1996). Aside from the licensing issues, professional associations regulate the profession by requiring all members to graduate from an accredited program. Accredited programs require graduates to take courses related to various ethical topics. Therefore, by ensuring that graduates become exposed to ethics education, professional associations ensure that professionals become aware of crucial ethical issues. For example, the AACSB (Association of Advanced Collegiate Schools of Business) mandates that business schools require their business graduates to complete substantial ethics courses. Thus, ethics is deemed so crucial that professional associations ensure that professionals receive ethics education.

Another aspect of professional associations is compliance with a code of conduct (Bommer et al., 1987). Professional associations have formal and published standards of professional conduct that members must adhere to. In some cases, where professional associations do not prevail, the professionals still tend to uphold a distinct self-image and social standing as members of the profession. Therefore, a code of conduct is an instrument that guides professionals on ethical behavior. Professionals appear to comply with such codes of conduct (Bommer et al., 1987). Ethical issues as well as codes of conduct are formally discussed in professional association meetings and professional journals. In this respect, professionals remain aware of current ethical issues and fortify compliance with ethics codes in their daily decision making.

In some cases professionals face conflicting directions among personal ethics, professional code of conduct, and corporate policies in the workplace (Bommer et al., 1987). Analysis of case studies in the literature points out that the ethics direction applied depends on the context of the case. However, scholars agree that personal ethics, professional ethics, and corporate policies are all important in guiding ethical behavior (Bommer et al., 1987; Johnson, 2001; Tavani, 2004). In contrast, Casey (1990) argued that ethical behavior is independent of context and that a person with good ethical values will behave ethically in all situations. Scholars argue that with the increase in global trade, professionals face business situations that pose ethical dilemmas (Bommer et al., 1987).

The effect of code of conduct on professional behavior in the workplace has received some attention in the literature. The literature suggests that code of conduct alone does not deter unethical behavior (Crown & Spiller, 1998). However, the code of conduct becomes effective when it is accompanied by additional factors such as the severity of the unethical behavior, existence of severe sanctions, corporate ethical climate, and extent of communication of such codes (Banerjee et al., 1998; Crown & Spiller, 1998). Thus, each of these factors in and of itself provided little effect in curbing unethical behavior, but when joined together, made a significant impact on individuals. Another perspective about codes of conduct is offered by Harrington (1996), who investigated its effect on unethical behaviors and intentions in IS organizations. Harrington defined codes of ethics as explicit statements of laws, policies, and standards that reflect the organizations' values. Codes of ethics are created for the purpose of establishing responsibility and reducing unethical behavior. Few empirical studies have been conducted about the effect of codes (Harrington, 1996). Codes of ethics can make a significant contribution to organizations as they induce awareness about ethics. Explicit codes have been found to yield a significant influence on the intention to act (Salter, Guffey, & McMillan, 2001). However, general institutional codes of ethics appear to have a small effect on the intention to act. Furthermore, explicit IS codes have also been found to play a significant role in the intention to act, particularly in cases of computer abuses (Harrington, 1996). One exception was noted for individuals with high responsibility denial: such individuals were not influenced by any kind of code.

IS codes are considered a subset of professional ethics (Tavani, 2004). Harrington's (1996) study provides further motivation for the need to explore the impact of various kinds of codes on individuals' judgment and intention to engage in computer abuses. Additionally, further attention should be given to investigating the role of professional ethics in such acts.

Personal Ethics

Personal ethics has received limited attention in the literature. This section will discuss several definitions, taxonomy, and an instrument that measures personal ethics.

Forsyth and colleagues studied the influence of personal ethics on decision making in business organizations (Forsyth, 1980, 1992; Schlenker & Forsyth, 1977). Accordingly, personal ethics comprises ethical beliefs, attitudes, and moral ideologies (1980). Additionally, personal ethics is based upon two dimensions: relativism and idealism. Relativism refers to "the extent to which the individual rejects universal moral [ethical] rules" (Forsyth, 1980, p. 175). In addition, relativism refers to the "nature of the situation [where] circumstances weigh more than the ethical principle" (Forsyth, 1992, p. 462). On the other hand, idealism refers to the extent to which "some individuals idealistically assume that desirable consequences can, with the 'right' action, always be obtained" (Forsyth, 1980, p. 176).

Forsyth suggests that "highly idealistic individuals feel that harming others is always avoidable, and they [highly idealistic individuals] would rather not choose between the lesser of two evils…[and avoid] negative consequences for other people" (Forsyth, 1992, p. 462). Therefore, he asserts that situational factors play an important role in personal ethics. Ethical decisions are made, to a large extent, on the basis of the consequence of an action and the compatibility of such an action with society's moral rules and principles.

Forsyth dichotomized and crossed these two dimensions with high and low ranges to yield the taxonomy of personal ethics (see Figure 1). Based on this classification, Forsyth proposed four quadrants of personal ethics: situationists, subjectivists, absolutists, and exceptionists. Situationism represents a combination of high relativism and high idealism. In this quadrant, individuals "reject [ethical] rules, and ask if the action yielded the best possible outcome in the given situation" (Forsyth, 1992, p. 462). The situationist quadrant is similar to the utilitarian ideology that "one

Figure 1. Forsyth's (1980, 1992) taxonomy of personal ethics

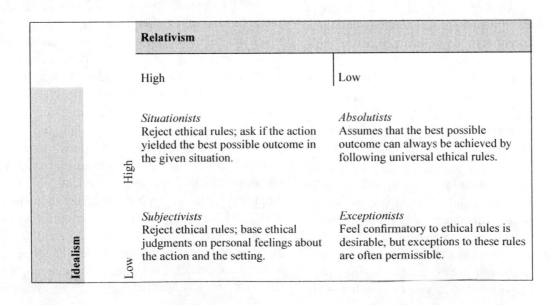

must act in ways that will generate the greatest good for the greatest number of people" (Forsyth, 1992, p. 463). In the subjectivism quadrant is found the high relativism, low idealism combination. Subjectivist individuals "reject [ethical] rules and base [ethical] judgment on personal feelings about the action and the settings" (Forsyth, 1992, p. 462). In this regard, subjectivists are deemed parallel to egoistic ideologies. Therefore, subjectivist individuals seek to promote their own interests rather than focusing on producing positive outcomes for others. In the subjectivist approach, consequences are the central motivating factor in ethical decisions. Unlike situationism, subjectivist decisions are centralized around oneself rather than a positive outcome for others.

Absolutism, the third quadrant, is one in which relativism is low and idealism is high. Absolutist individuals elect actions that result in positive consequences that meet general ethics principles. Absolutist individuals disagree with actions that cause harm to others. Thus, absolutism is associated with deontologism, which suggests one should not make exceptions regardless of the circumstances. The fourth quadrant is exceptionism, in which relativism and idealism are both low. Exceptionist individuals believe in ethical absolutes but are not idealist. They do not focus on actions that avoid harming others; rather, their actions follow ethical ideologies. Exceptionist individuals also fit the position of situationists because they believe in "balancing the positive consequence of an action against the negative consequences of an action" (Forsyth, 1992, p. 463). Therefore, exceptionist individuals align with those ethical ideologies that provide good consequences for all the stakeholders but do accommodate exceptions. These four personal ethics quadrants appear to provide a solid classification of ethical behaviors based on the individual's ethical system, but may, however, vary across different situations. Forsyth's taxonomy is not based solely on universal principles of good and bad, but rather incorporates the element of consequence of the action. Moreover, Forsyth's taxonomy does not significantly correlate with other measures such as Kohlberg's stages of moral reasoning (Rest, Cooper, Coder, Masanz, & Anderson, 1974).

Kirman (1992) has also studied personal ethics; his definition includes elements of love, kindness; and respect for human dignity. Kirman asserts that the rise of modern technology holds the inherent potential to achieve negative ends, such as the misuse of technology to engage in unethical behavior. Therefore, Kirman believes that modern technology has created new choices as well as moral challenges. Thus, one's personal ethics serve to guide individuals in power to act responsibly and assess the impact of their actions on others. Personal ethics supports principles such as authority, cooperation, loyalty, and obedience, to name a few. Kirman concludes by articulating that personal values form the basis for personal ethics that enable individuals to use modern technology to achieve positive ends. Furthermore, ethics is relevant to work-related decisions as well as everyday essential decisions.

Kreitner and Kinicki (1995) discussed ethics from the perspective of organizational behavior in the workplace. Kreitner and Kinicki defined ethics as the study of moral issues and choices that individuals face. Personal ethics encourages individuals to exercise their moral imagination and make ethical decisions. Kreitner and Kinicki proposed a model of ethical behavior by which the individual makes decisions. Appropriately, each individual has a distinctive blend of personality traits, values, and moral principles that enable them to act ethically or unethically. Additionally, Kreitner and Kinicki (1995) noted that the individual's experience with positive and negative reinforcements for their behavior shapes their tendency to behave ethically. Three primary attributes related to cultural, organizational, and political influences affect the individual's ethical behavior. Ethical codes are contained within the organizational influences that act on the individual's ethics. Often times, individuals make unethical decisions due to perceived pressures at the workplace. Following the model illustrated in Figure 2, Kreitner and Kinicki (1995) maintained that behaviors are based on the person-to-situation interaction, and the organization's ethical climate. To this end, their approach differs from Kirman's approach (1992) by introducing the element of the organization's ethical setting. Ethical settings should convey ethical principles based on utilitarian ideology (i.e., consequences to actions, achieving good for the greatest number of people), as well as theories of rights (i.e., basic human rights) and justice (i.e., rules and rewards). Ultimately, Kreitner and Kinicki (1995) advocate the role of personal ethics in enabling ethical decisions.

The various definitions of personal ethics mentioned above amplify the importance of personal ethics and its role in ethical decision making. However, additional scholarly work is needed in order to understand how per-

Figure 2. Kreitner and Kinicki's (1995) model of ethical behavior in the workplace

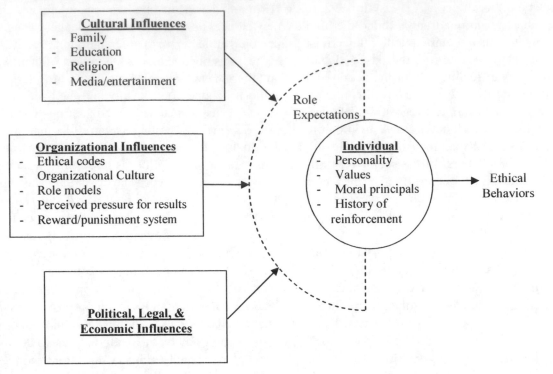

sonal ethics affects the use of information systems and what tools within these systems are utilized to achieve the universal moral principles discussed above.

Ethics in Higher Education

Ethics concerns have also spilled into the realm of academia as scholars find that academic misconduct has been on the rise (Bernardi et al., 2004). Scholars have highlighted a number of trends among students. Students do not perceive cheating as unethical (Kidwell, 2001). Moreover, students' unethical behavior spills over into the workplace (Ahmed, Chung, & Eichenseher, 2003; Bernardi et al., 2004; Couger, 1989; Gbadamosi, 2004). These worrisome trends have motivated debates on how to reduce opportunities for unethical behavior in higher education. For example, Bernardi et al. (2004) suggest creating awareness among learners and faculty members by developing ethics curriculums and adopting honor codes. Honor codes have been found to be somewhat instrumental in reducing unethical behavior. Moreover, the creation of an ethical setting has been suggested to be effective for curbing academic misconduct (McCabe & Trevino, 1993). Additionally, instilling ethical awareness among students, continu-

ally reinforcing, and stimulating peer pressure aid in curbing academic misconduct (Jendrek, 1989; Kidwell, Wozniak, & Laurel, 2003; McCabe & Pavela, 2004).

Ethics education has also been found to be valuable for students (Nitterhouse, 2003). In fact, the AACSB mandates that students take several ethics courses during their academic career. Given these remarkable findings, scholars maintain that faculty members play an important role in setting ethical standards and reinforcing them when interacting with students (Jendrek, 1989; McCabe & Pavela, 2004). Yet, the literature has yielded a very limited number of empirical studies about faculty members and their commitment to maintaining ethical standards. Moreover, few studies have been conducted about the influence of the teaching experience of faculty members on the ways in which they pursue unethical behaviors and more specifically academic misconduct incidents.

Yet faculty members' personal ethics have been given little attention in the literature, although they appear to play a critical role in educating students about ethical issues (Laband & Pietter, 2000; Tabachnick, Spiegel, & Pope, 1991). In the classical study by Tabachnick et al. (1991), 63 behaviors were tested using faculty members as the unit of analysis. Findings indicated a correlation between the perception of the behavior as ethical and the engagement in that behavior. Additionally, several behaviors were found to be controversial and yielded disagreements about ethical judgment. These findings suggest that faculty members range in their perceptions about ethical and unethical behaviors, and that their personal belief system may impact those perceptions. Furthermore, Tabachnick et al.'s (1991) study suggests that faculty members' perceptions impact their actions. As the literature has pointed out the connection between faculty members' behaviors and students' behaviors, it appears that faculty members' personal ethics play a part in motivating actions that reduce opportunities for students to engage in academic misconduct. Therefore, Tabachnick et al.'s (1991) study has been crucial in understanding faculty members' personal ethics, suggesting the need to further explore this topic in higher education.

Ethics in Online Learning Systems

Online learning systems (OLSs) offer access to a vast number of resources that have presented both new opportunities for teaching and a challenge for higher education (Folkers, 2005). With this apparent rise in OLSs usage, some scholars have raised concerns about academic misconduct in online learning (Dufresne, 2004; Pincus & Schmelkin, 2003). While technology is facilitating online learning, some studies have pointed out that various technologies have facilitated students' engagement in academic misconduct behavior (Gunasekaran, McNeil, & Shaul, 2002; Hinman, 2002; Kidwell et al., 2003; McCabe & Pavela, 2000; Pillsbury, 2004). However, no studies have been devoted to exploring incidents of academic misconduct in online learning, the role of faculty members' personal ethics, and the ways in which faculty members appear to curb academic misconduct in online learning.

SUMMARY, IMPLICATIONS, AND FUTURE TRENDS

This article reviewed some of the relevant literature related to ethics. There is evidence in literature that academic misconduct has been on the rise as a result of the increased use of technology in higher education. Still, it appears that little attention has been given in

literature to empirical studies about online learning. Moreover, the perspective of faculty members has not been investigated, with the majority of the studies focusing on learners' perspectives. Some scholars have suggested that ethics is associated with academic misconduct. However, existing studies about ethics tend to focus on students' behavior or code of conduct as well as the honor code. Ethics studies are divided into multiple streams of research addressing issues related to philosophical ethics (i.e., Greek philosophy-virtues), computer ethics (i.e., intellectual rights, privacy, accountability, etc.), and professional ethics (i.e., code of conduct, organizational behavior policy). Moreover, some attention has been given to the role of personal ethics among students. However, in the context of higher education, few studies have explored faculty members' personal ethics. Instead these studies have an organizational behavior perspective and focus primarily on faculty members' professional behavior. Additionally, these studies view faculty members' professional ethics in academic institutions and their compliance with the institutional code of conduct. Yet, the studies reviewed fail to take a comprehensive view combining faculty members' personal ethics, their perception of academic misconduct severity, and the use of technology to curb such behaviors. Thus, future studies should attempt to analyze and synthesize the appropriate literature in order to address this gap.

REFERENCES

Ahmed, M.M., Chung, K.Y., & Eichenseher, J.W. (2003). Business students' perception of ethics and moral judgment: A cross-cultural study. *Journal of Business Ethics, 43*(1/2), 89-102.

Banerjee, D., Cronan, T.P., & Jones, T.W. (1998). Modeling IT ethics: A study in situational ethics. *MIS Quarterly, 22*(1), 31-60.

Bernardi, R.A., Metzger, R.L., Bruno, R.G.S., Hoogkamp, M.A.W., Reyes, L.E., & Barnaby, G.H. (2004). Examining the decision process of students' cheating behavior: An empirical study. *Journal of Business Ethics, 50*(4), 397-414.

Bommer, M., Gratto, C., Gravander, J., & Tuttle, M. (1987). A behavioral model of ethical and unethical decision making. *Journal of Business Ethics, 6*(4), 265-280.

Crown, D.F., & Spiller, M.S. (1998). Learning from the literature on collegiate cheating: A review of empirical research. *Journal of Business Ethics, 17*(6), 683- 700.

Couger, J.D. (1989). Preparing IS students to deal with ethical issues. *MIS Quarterly, 13*(2), 211-218.

Dufresne, R.L. (2004). An action learning perspective on effective implementation of academic honor. *Group & Organization Management, 29*(2), 201-218.

Folkers, D.A. (2005). Competing in the marketspace: Incorporating online education into higher education—an organizational perspective. *Information Resources Management Journal, 18*(1), 61-77.

Forsyth, D.R. (1992). Judging the morality of business practices: The influence of personal moral philosophies. *Journal of Business Ethics, 11,* 461-470.

Forsyth, D.R. (1980). A taxonomy of ethical ideologies. *Journal of Personality and Social Psychology, 39,* 175-184.

Gbadamosi, G. (2004). Academic ethics: What has morality, culture and administration got to do with its measures? *Management Decision, 42*(9), 1145-1161.

Gunasekaran, A., McNeil, R.D., & Shaul, D. (2002). E-learning: Research and applications. *Industrial and Commercial Training, 34*(2), 44-54.

Harrington, S.J. (1996). The effect of codes of ethics and personal denial of responsibility on computer abuse judgments and intentions. *MIS Quarterly, 20*(3), 257-279.

Hiltz, S.R., & Turoff, M. (2005). Education goes digital; the evolution of online learning and the revolution in higher education. *Communications of the ACM, 48*(10), 59-66.

Hinman, L.M. (2002). The impact of the Internet on our moral lives in academia. *Ethics and Information Technology, 4*(1), 31-35.

Jendrek, M.P. (1989). Faculty reactions to academic dishonesty. *Journal of College Student Development, 30,* 401-406.

Johnson, D.G. (2001). *Computer ethics.* Upper Saddle River, NJ: Prentice Hall.

Kidwell, L.A. (2001). Student honor codes as a tool for teaching professional ethics. *Journal of Business Ethics, 29*(1/2), 45-50.

Kidwell, L.A., Wozniak, K., & Laurel, J.P. (2003). Student reports and faculty perceptions of academic dishonesty. *Teaching Business Ethics, 7*(3), 205-214.

Kirman, J.L. (1992). Values, technology, and social studies. *McGill Journal of Education, 27*(1), 5-18.

Kreitner, R., & Kinicki, A. (1995). *Organizational behavior.* Chicago, IL: Irwin.

Laband, D.N., & Piette, M.J. (2000). Perceived conduct and professional ethics among college economics faculty. *American Economist, 44*(1), 24-33.

Levy, Y., & Murphy, K. (2002). Toward a value framework for e-learning systems. *Proceedings of the 35th Hawaii International Conference on System Sciences* (HICSS-35), Big Island, HI.

Moor, J.H. (1999). Just consequentialism and computing. *Ethics and Information Technology, 1*(1), 65-69.

McCabe, D.L., & Pavela, G. (2004). Ten updated principles of academic integrity: Faculty can foster student honesty. *Change, 36*(3), 10-16.

McCabe, D.L., & Trevino, L.K. (1993). Academic dishonesty: Honor codes and other contextual influences. *Journal of Higher Education, 64*(5), 522-539.

Nitterhouse, D. (2003). Plagiarism—not just an "academic" problem. *Teaching Business Ethics, 7*(3), 215-227.

Pillsbury, C. (2004). Reflections on academic misconduct: An investigating officer's experiences and ethics supplements. *Journal of American Academy of Business, 5*(1/2), 446-454.

Pincus, H.S., & Schmelkin, L.P. (2003). Faculty perceptions of academic dishonesty: A multidimensional scaling analysis. *Journal of Higher Education, 74,* 196-209.

Rest, J.R., Cooper, D., Coder, R., Masanz, J., & Anderson, D. (1974) Judging the important issues in moral dilemmas—an objective measure of development. *Development Psychology, 10,* 491-501.

Salter, S.B., Guffey, D.M., & McMillan, J.J. (2001). Truth, consequences and culture: A comparative examination of cheating and attitudes about cheating among U.S. and UK students. *Journal of Business Ethics, 31*(1), 37-50.

Schlenker, B.R., & Forsyth, D.R. (1977). On the ethics of psychological research. *Journal of Experimental Social Psychology, 13,* 369-396.

Stern, E.B., & Havlicek, L. (1996). Academic misconduct: Results of faculty and undergraduate student surveys. *Journal of Allied Health,* 129-142.

Straub, D.W. Jr., Nance, W.D., & Carlson, C.L. (1990). Discovering and discipline computer abuse in organizations: A field study. *MIS Quarterly, 14*(1), 45-60.

Tabachnick, B.G., Spiegel, P.K., & Pope, K.S. (1991). Ethics of teaching. *American Psychologist, 46*(5), 506-515.

Tavani, H.T. (2004). *Ethics and technology: Ethical issues in an age of information and communication technology.* New York: John Wiley & Sons.

Webster. (1997). *Webster's universal college dictionary.* New York: Random House.

KEY TERMS

Academic Misconduct: A malpractice behavior committed by a student (Stern & Havlicek, 1996). Academic misconduct behaviors include (but are not limited to) plagiarism, cheating, copying, falsifying information, and bribing faculty/staff (Pincus & Schmelkin, 2003). This study will suggest an inventory of academic misconduct behaviors (AMBIs) using the literature.

Academic Misconduct Incident (AMI): An acronym developed by the author.

Ethics Position Questionnaire (EPQ): Developed by Forsyth (1980) for the purpose of classifying individuals' personal ethics. The score of this survey is used to sort individuals into the four taxonomy categories of situationism, subjectivism, absolutism, and exceptionism, which are the four dimensions of personal ethics.

Ethics: The study of human morality and conduct created by society (Webster, 2005). **Ethics Taxonomy:** Developed by Forsyth (1980) using the EPQ instrument. The taxonomy includes four categories: situationism, subjectivism, absolutism, and exceptionism, which are the four dimensions of personal ethics.

Online Learning System (OLS): Includes synchronous and/or asynchronous communication. OLS encompasses multiple interactions between professor-to-students; student-to-professor; students-to-students; and the technological, organizational, and managerial infrastructure employed for the delivery of online learning (Levy & Murphy, 2002).

Personal Ethics: Individuals' moral beliefs, attitudes, and values that make up the integrated system of personal ethics (Forsyth, 1992)

Ethics and Security under the Sarbanes–Oxley Act

Thomas J. Tribunella
Rochester Institute of Technology, USA

Heidi R. Tribunella
University of Rochester, USA

INTRODUCTION

The objective of this article is to review the Sarbanes-Oxley Act and assess the difficulty in maintaining ethical standards, strong internal controls, and acceptable levels of security in a technologically advanced economy such as the United States. According to Arthur Levitt, the chair of the Securities and Exchange Commission (SEC) in 1999:

The dynamic nature of today's capital markets creates issues that increasingly move beyond the bright line of black and white. New industries, spurred by new services and new technologies, are creating new questions and challenges that must be addressed. Today, we are witnessing a broad shift from an industrial economy to a more service based one; a shift from bricks and mortar to technology and knowledge. (Levitt, 1999)

The role of government, the impact of legislation, and the interaction of public policy with capital markets in the United States will be addressed in this article. In addition, we will review the ethical issues that were encountered by large accounting firms such as Arthur Andersen in their efforts to audit the financial information of clients such as Enron and Global Crossing.

BACKGROUND

The Internet boom and bust that occurred from 1996 to 2002 was one of the most significant business events of the past several decades. In the wake of this historic period, accountants, investors, analysts, and business managers have an unprecedented opportunity to learn from past mistakes and successes. The dot.com bear market may have indicated the end of the gold rush stage for technology firms. Down 39.3% in 2000, the

NASDAQ (National Association of Securities Dealers Automated Quotations) suffered the largest one-year loss in its 30-year history. In 2001, the NASDAQ continued its downward trend with a 21.1% loss. The statistics in Table 1, compiled by Webmergers.com, reports the shutdowns and bankruptcies of substantial Internet companies that have received significant funding from public capital markets.

Inexperienced stockholders had unrealistic expectations, and disgruntled investors who relied on financial statements lost money during the Internet shakeout and took legal actions against Wall Street investment and large accounting firms. Major bankruptcy cases such as Enron, WorldCom, Adelphia Communications, and Global Crossing disclosed misleading financial statements. The resulting lawsuits have damaged the reputation of the accounting profession (Tribunella & Tribunella, 2003).

The financial statements of a company should provide information to a variety of users so that they can make investment and credit decisions. According to the Efficient Market Hypothesis, stock market

Table 1. Dot.com shutdowns of Net companies by quarter (Webmergers, 2002)

Month and Year	Number
March 2000	5
June 2000	31
September 2000	52
December 2000	135
March 2001	164
June 2001	181
September 2001	119
December 2001	80
March 2002	54
June 2002	39

prices should reflect all publicly available information relevant to the traded companies. In addition, market prices should react quickly to new information such as freshly issued financial statements (Wolk, Tearney, & Dodd, 2001).

Financial statements include a balance sheet, income statement, statement of changes in stockholders' equity, statement of cash flows, and footnotes. Certified public accountants (CPAs) who serve as auditors have the responsibility of examining the financial statements and certifying their conformity with Generally Accepted Accounting Principles (GAAPs). A CPA is an individual that has completed education, examination, and work experience requirements. A CPA is professionally licensed in the state where he or she practices (Arens, Elder, & Beasley, 2006).

As a result of these major bankruptcies, the U.S. government has started to regulate the accounting industry. President Bush signed into law the Sarbanes-Oxley Act of 2002. The act includes far-reaching changes in federal regulation that represents the most significant overhaul since the enactment of the Securities Exchange Act of 1934. For example, Section 404 of the Sarbanes-Oxley Act requires management to assess and issue a report on the company's internal controls. Furthermore, auditors must now express an opinion on the effectiveness of internal controls over the financial reporting of an organization (Ramos, 2004).

MAINTAINING ETHICS AND SECURITY FOR FINANCIAL INFORMATION UNDER THE SARBANES-OXLEY ACT

As a result of several conspicuous accounting frauds, the U.S. government has started to regulate the accounting industry through the Sarbanes-Oxley Act. The act prescribes a system of federal oversight of auditors (Paul, 2005) through the Public Company Accounting Oversight Board (PCAOB). In addition, a new set of auditor independence rules, new disclosure requirements applicable to public companies, and new penalties for persons who are responsible for accounting or reporting violations have been promulgated by the act (Cary, 2002). A summary of the act is listed below (AICPA, 2002):

- increases criminal penalties for corporate crimes up to 20-year prison terms and fines of $1 to $5 million
- creates the Public Company Accounting Oversight Board to police the accounting industry
- prevents CPAs from auditing and consulting with the same corporation
- requires top executives to certify their firm's financial statements
- allocates $300 million which will go to the SEC to hire 200 investigators and auditors
- bans personal loans from companies to their officers and directors
- gives the SEC authority to ban corporate wrong-doers from serving as company officers in the future
- prohibits officers from filing bankruptcy to avoid paying financial judgments

In addition, members of the board of directors should be independent; in other words, they should not be corporate officers and they should not do business with the corporation. The audit committee of the board of directors that chooses the auditors must be knowledgeable, independent, and have a long tenure. Finally, the chief executive officer (CEO) or chief financial officer (CFO) should not chair the board of directors, and board members should not sit on numerous other boards (Persons, 2005). These issues fall under the category of corporate governance.

Corporate governance refers to all structures, policies, and procedures that are issued from the board of directors and put in place to govern the corporation in an ethical manner. It includes strategic planning, corporate values and ethics, as well as internal control (Yakhou & Dorweiler, 2005). The following high-level internal controls should be maintained by the members of the board of directors who are ultimately responsible for the actions and financial stability of the organization they direct:

- The board of directors should be elected by the shareholders or other outside parties (e.g., major donors of a not-for-profit organization) and not appointed by the officers
- The outside auditing firm should be hired by and report directly to the audit committee of the board of directors

- The board of directors should meet frequently, stay informed, review the long-term strategic plan, and approve all major and financially material expenditures.
- The board of directors should hire and review all high-level officers (CEO, CIO, CFO, COO, etc.) of the organization.
- The officers must present and explain the audited financial statements to the board of directors on a regular basis (usually four times per year).
- When a company materially changes its business model, such as creating an e-commerce division, the auditors must be briefed by the board of directors and executives officers of the company. This will allow the auditors to adjust their estimate of business risk.

One of the objectives of the Sarbanes-Oxley Act is to ensure ethical behavior of corporate managers and public accountants. Some individuals maintain that ethics cannot be regulated and that ethics are a part of your personality or spiritual being (Verschoor, 2004). However, based on the large-scale unethical activities that were occurring prior to Sarbanes, it was evident that the government needed to intervene to restore investor confidence.

Although it may not be possible to regulate an unethical person into becoming an ethical individual, the U.S. Congress has certainly increased the penalty for unethical behavior. The theory is that increased penalties and responsibilities for corporate officers and auditors will create an incentive to obey the law and protect the investors. CEOs and CFOs must now sign a statement to certify that their financial statements are free of material misstatement to the best of their knowledge. CEOs and CFOs who certify financial statements and are later found to be fraudulent will be prosecuted under Sarbanes-Oxley and will face harsh penalties.

Another ethical issue that came out of the large accounting frauds was the independence of external auditors. Arthur Anderson LLP served as the independent auditors for Enron. Many writers made the argument that because Andersen's fees were so large from the extensive amount of consulting services it provided to Enron, that Andersen was not independent (Tribunella & Tribunella, 2003). The Sarbanes-Oxley Act addressed this by no longer allowing public accounting firms to provide consulting services to the firms they audit. It also requires that the lead and concurring audit partners be rotated every five years (Arens et al., 2006).

It was also noted that several public companies hired audit staff from the public accounting firms that audited them. To address this issue, the government added rules concerning the hiring of former auditors by public companies. CPA firms cannot audit a public company, if an auditor at that firm accepted a key management position and has participated in the audit of the company within one year (Arens et al., 2006).

Management must assess the internal controls over the company. Internal controls start at the top of the company. The "tone at the top" must be an ethical one in order for the controls to work and not be circumvented. The board of directors and senior management must communicate their view of ethics to the company and must also let company personnel know that unethical behavior will not be tolerated. In order to set such a tone, a "whistle blower" program or ethical hotline should be set up where anonymous complaints regarding unethical behavior can be made (Silverstone, 2004). To improve the employees' confidence that reporting unethical behavior will have no repercussions, it is best to have the hotline maintained by an outside firm. If the hotline is serviced by internal legal counsel, there may be concerns that the person reporting the behavior could be identified and have negative actions taken against them.

Another challenge facing management related to Section 404 of the act is how to assess and report on internal controls. Many publicly held companies have embraced technology, and the older well documented controls on paper-based systems have become less dominant. Many of the controls in today's financial reporting environment are buried into the programming code of very complex accounting and enterprise systems. Managers without information technology (IT) skills are forced to certify internal controls that they do not have the expertise to understand. This requires them to hire a variety of IT consultants to help them comply with the Sarbanes-Oxley Act. Internal controls, such as the segregation of duties, may now be controlled by limiting access to certain user interface screens within the accounting information system. Therefore, examining the effectiveness of the control may require knowledge of the information system to determine user access requirements.

One of the challenges with auditing an information system is the identification of key controls (McNally, 2005). Many companies find that large, complex enterprise systems offer so many control options that they overwhelm the auditors testing the system. Companies may have many controls, but identifying which controls are the critically important controls can be very difficult (Violino, 2005). When identifying key controls, it may be helpful to map the controls to the management assertions that are made in the financial statements. Furthermore, the controls can be mapped to the strategic plan and clearly identified risks in the business model.

FUTURE TRENDS

With the spread of e-commerce, the internationalization of capital markets will continue. Accordingly, the U.S. needs to maintain confidence in the capital markets to ensure that international investors will continue to seek investments in the United States. Sarbanes-Oxley was meant to restore confidence in the financial reporting of public companies and the audit firms that service those companies.

Even though auditing standards are determined on a country-by-country basis, there is a movement to standardize the rules on a worldwide basis. The International Federation of Accountants (IFAC) is a worldwide organization consisting of 80 national organizations such as the American Institute of Certified Public Accountants (AICPA) and the Institute of Chartered Accountants of England and Wales. The IFAC has formed the International Auditing Practices Committee (IAPC), and the IAPC issues *International Standards on Auditing,* which seek to eliminate material inconsistencies between national auditing standards (Tribunella & Tribunella, 2003). Therefore, the Sarbanes-Oxley Act may affect the development of global auditing standards.

The IAPC is in a relatively early stage of development, but its standards will receive more attention as capital markets become more international through the global reach of e-commerce and supply chains that transcend national boundaries. Research is needed to understand the similarities and differences between various national standards such as the Sarbanes-Oxley Act.

CONCLUSION

Analysis

The Sarbanes-Oxley Act was enacted in response to the variety of agency theory issues revolving around accounting scandals. Issues addressed within the act include auditor independence, corporate governance, corporate ethics, and internal controls. In order to have accurate financial reporting, which is absolutely necessary for efficient capital markets, it is necessary to have effective internal controls. Internal controls permeate throughout a company and must have "buy in" from the board of directors and senior management. Commingled with internal controls is ethical behavior (Silverstone, 2004). If the board of directors and senior management are unethical, they can easily override controls and also send a message to other corporate employees that such overrides of controls are acceptable or even desirable. If this occurs, accurate financial reporting will be completely eroded, along with investor confidence, when the inaccuracies become public.

The Sarbanes-Oxley Act, often referred to as the "Full Employment Act for Accountants," has had a significant effect on the accounting profession. It has created an increased demand for accountants in industry, public accounting, and by regulatory authorities such as the SEC and the PCAOB. In addition, it has also created a demand for IT expertise, as many of the controls are embedded in complex enterprise systems. Internal controls have moved from well-documented pencil-and-paper controls to less visible IT controls embedded in computer programming logic. The accountants, normally charged with assessing internal controls, may not have the IT expertise necessary for analyzing computer-based controls.

Although government intervention is generally undesirable within a free market, government regulation has become a necessity due to the number and size of the accounting scandals that have occurred. The PCAOB has completed reviews of audits and found several deficiencies with audits conducted by Big Four firms (the four largest firms in the U.S.). The reviews were conducted by examining the audit procedures used in 2003. The report found 65 significant deficiencies in the audits conducted by the Big Four (Arnold, 2005). Clearly, there is more work to be done to increase the quality of audits in order to restore investor confidence. Even though the results are disappointing, some argue that the PCAOB is in its early stages and that both the public accounting firms and the PCAOB are still learning. Improvements may be achieved on both sides to increase the quality of audits and restore investor confidence.

Final Thoughts

Sarbanes-Oxley was legislation passed in response to a plethora of unethical behavior from both management and auditors. With increased penalties and increased oversight of the public accounting profession by the PCAOB, it is hoped that such large accounting scandals will be avoided in the future.

The internationalization of capital markets will continue with the spread of e-commerce. Accordingly, the U.S. needs to maintain confidence in capital markets to ensure that international investors will continue to seek investments in the United States. Sarbanes-Oxley was meant to restore confidence in the financial reporting of public companies and the audit firms that service those companies.

Investors should remember that the managers, owners, and board members at companies should uphold their fiduciary duty by staying informed and hiring independent auditors. Most auditors are very honest and hard-working individuals. We should not let the actions of a few dishonest individuals damage the whole auditing profession. Thousands of organizations are satisfied with their auditors, and auditors are necessary to maintain efficient capital markets.

REFERENCES

AICPA. (2002). *Summary of the Sarbanes-Oxley Act.* Retrieved from www.aicpa.org

Arens, A.A., Elder, R.J., & Beasley, M.S. (2006). *Auditing and assurance services: An integrated approach* (11th ed.). Upper Saddle River, NJ: Pearson Prentice-Hall.

Arnold, L. (2005). Accounting firms lax, board says. *Bloomberg News, Rochester Democrat and Chronicle,* (November 18), 10D.

Cary, G. (2002). *President signs Sarbanes-Oxley Act of 2002.* Retrieved from www.gcwf.com

Levitt, A. (1999, October 18). *Quality information: The lifeblood of our markets.* Securities Exchange Commission Speech, Washington, DC. Retrieved from www.sec.gov

McNally, J.S. (2005). Assessing company-level controls. *Journal of Accountancy, 199*(6), 65-68.

Paul, J.W. (2005). Exploring PCAOB Auditing Standard 2: Audits of internal control. *The CPA Journal, 75*(5), 22-27.

Persons, O.S. (2005). The relation between the new corporate governance rules and the likelihood of financial statement fraud. *Review of Accounting and Finance, 4*(2), 125-148.

Ramos, M. (2004). Section 404 compliance in the annual report. *Journal of Accountancy, 198*(4), 43-48.

Silverstone, H. (2004). The importance of being earnest. *Security Management, 48*(2), 51-56.

Tribunella, T.J., & Tribunella, H.R. (2003). The effect of auditor independence on international capital markets for e-commerce firms. *Journal of Business and Economics Research, 1*(2), 49-60.

Verschoor, C.C. (2004). Will Sarbanes-Oxley improve ethics? *Strategic Finance, 85*(9), 15-16.

Violino, B. (2005). Sarbox: Year 2. *CFO IT Magazine, 21*(13), 17-19.

Webmergers. (2002). *Dot com failures down 73% from 2001 levels in first half.* Retrieved from www.webmergers.com

Wolk, H.I., Tearney, M.G., & Dodd, J.L. (2001). *Accounting theory: A conceptual and institutional approach* (5th ed.). Cincinnati, OH: Southern-Western College Publishing.

Yakhou, M., & Dorweiler, V.P. (2005). Corporate governance reform: Impact on accounting and auditing. *Corporate Governance, 5*(1), 39-44.

KEY TERMS

Agency Theory: Also called contracting theory, it is the theory that there is a conflict between managers of a company, who are agents of the stockholders, and the stockholders themselves. It assumes that managers may act in their own best self-interest and not in the interests of the company or the stockholders (Wolk et al., 2001).

Audit Opinion: The auditors' opinion is the conclusion they reach after conducting audit procedures to check whether the financial statements have been prepared in accordance with Generally Accepted Accounting Principles (Arens et al., 2006).

Auditing: An assurance service offered by CPA firms that specifically relates to the financial statements of an organization. Auditors use Generally Accepted Auditing Standards (GAASs) to guide their work and determine if the financial statements have been prepared in accordance with Generally Accepted Accounting Principles (GAAPs). The result of an audit is the expression of an opinion on the financial statements (Arens et al., 2006).

Generally Accepted Accounting Principles (GAAPs): The set of accounting rules followed by accountants and companies within the United States. GAAPs are contained in official volumes of publications that postulate accounting conventions and procedures that were derived from experience, reason, customs, and usage in the profession (Wolk et al., 2001).

Generally Accepted Auditing Standards (GAASs): Auditing rules followed by auditors within the United States that were developed by the American Institute of Certified Public Accountants (Arens et al., 2006).

Internal Control: One of the set of practices and procedures put in place by companies to safeguard assets, promote efficiency, create reliable financial reporting, and comply with managerial and governmental policies (Hall, 2005).

Public Company Accounting Oversight Board (PCAOB): This government oversight board was created from the Sarbanes-Oxley Act. It established auditing standards for public company audits. The PCAOB also reviews the audits of publicly traded companies conducted by public accounting firms. It had a major impact on the field of public accounting, as it changed from a self-regulated profession to one regulated by the government (Arens et al., 2006).

Sarbanes-Oxley Act: Enacted in 2002, it established the Public Company Accounting Oversight Board to establish auditing standards for public companies (Arens et al., 2006). It was enacted in response to several accounting frauds in the late 1990s and early 2000s. The act now requires compliance to regulations such as:

- CEOs and CFOs must certify financial statements
- Management must assess and issue a report on internal controls
- Auditors must issue an opinion on management's assessment of internal controls

Securities and Exchange Commission (SEC): The U.S. government entity empowered with the broad authority to help ensure that investors receive adequate information from publicly traded companies so that the investors can make informed investment decisions. The SEC requires public companies to be audited by CPA firms (Hall, 2005).

Ethics Education for the Online Environment

Lori N. K. Leonard
University of Tulsa, USA

Tracy S. Manly
University of Tulsa, USA

INTRODUCTION

As a greater number of business transactions and communications are facilitated by the Internet, understanding individual behavior in this arena is becoming an important part of overall business ethics. One key issue that distinguishes transactions conducted via the Internet from those in traditional business settings is that of anonymity (Davenport, 2002). The sense of being anonymous and having little accountability allows individuals to behave in ways that they "traditionally" would not behave if they were known to the other parties involved. "Shame is less common in cyberspace because less strict moral norms pertain..." (Ben-Ze'ev, 2003). Kracher and Corritore (2004) explore whether e-commerce ethics and traditional brick-and-mortar ethics are the same. In their study, they outline the current ethical issues facing organizations, and ultimately state that e-commerce ethical issues are not completely unique but differ from traditional brick-and-mortar commerce in terms of manifestation and scope. The critical elements identified by Kracher and Corritore (2004) are used in this article to create a framework for introducing students to the ethical issues that need to be considered in the online arena.

In addition to the finding in the academic literature that the ethics environment in e-commerce is perceived differently by individuals, anecdotal evidence from the classroom also supports this idea. In-class discussions about these topics have shown that students' perceptions about ethics between the two environments are distinct. One example scenario is that of taking music. When the scenario is changed from discussing "copying of music files from the Internet" to "taking a music CD from the shelf of a retailer," the students' responses change dramatically. In the online situation, they were of the verbal persuasion that they did not feel guilt or moral obligation to not perform such an act (i.e.,

they intended to behave more unethically). However, when faced with a traditional ethical consideration, the students felt the act was unethical and they would not perform such an act (i.e., they intended to behave more ethically).

This presents a strong argument for expanding business ethics material taught to college students to include topics related to electronic commerce and other online business situations. A formal business education decreases one's tolerance for unethical behavior (Lopez, Rechner, & Olson-Buchanan, 2005); however, there is a lack of emphasis on ethics in university programs. Therefore, this article presents a four-point framework (PAPA, defined later) from the existing literature and poses ways to teach ethical conduct in the online arena to college students.

BACKGROUND

Kracher and Corritore (2004) identify six critical electronic commerce (i.e., Internet) ethics' issues: access, intellectual property, privacy and informed consent, protection of children, security of information, and trust. Previously, Mason (1986) identified the rights to information which include: property, access, privacy, and accuracy. Ethical categorization based on Mason's principles has been applied in many studies (refer to Leonard & Cronan, 2001; Leonard, Cronan, & Kreie, 2004). Mason's four principles overlap with the electronic commerce ethics' issues as follows:

1. **Property:** Intellectual property
2. **Access:** Access, protection of children, and security of information
3. **Privacy:** Privacy and informed consent and protection of children
4. **Accuracy:** Trust

These four categories (PAPA) provide an initial framework to present ethical scenarios to students. These ethical dilemmas relate to the online environment in general and to electronic commerce as well. The PAPA framework does not cover all of the ethical dilemmas that can be faced on the Internet. However, it does provide a good starting point for educators to consider as they begin to incorporate ethical issues that are specific to an information age where many transactions are conducted anonymously. Each of the four categories are explained below.

Property

Property focuses on who owns information about individuals and how information can be sold and exchanged (Mason, 1986). Intellectual property describes works of the mind, such as art, books, music, film, and so forth (Reynolds, 2003). In September 2000, Janet Reno, attorney general at the time, made reference to protecting intellectual property in a speech:

We need to change the cultural acceptance of theft of intellectual property, whether the theft is committed by stealing from a retail store or stealing using a computer. Either way, we are talking about theft, pure and simple. (Zoellick, 2002)

A common issue with electronic commerce is sharing purchased music, song by song, online with anyone in the world (Kracher & Corritore, 2004; Sama & Shoaf, 2002). Traditionally to accomplish the same task, music CDs would be purchased and then copies made and distributed.

Access

Access defines what information a person or organization has the right to obtain about individuals, and how this information can be accessed and used (Mason, 1986). In an online environment, access can also be thought of as an issue of having or not having computer access. Individuals without computer access cannot take advantage of the opportunities that the Internet offers, such as discounted airline fares offered on many Web sites (Kracher & Corritore, 2004). Access also is directly related to the protection of children. For example, pornography is increasingly accessible via the Internet to children, where as traditionally children

gained access only through magazines, video stores, or television (Kracher & Corritore, 2004). Finally, access is a security concern (Kracher & Corritore, 2004; Stead & Gilbert, 2001). Traditionally, people give credit cards to waiters in restaurants to pay for meals where the waiter could be making a copy of the credit card information for himself. However, in the online environment the interception of credit card information is invisible to the user, and thus is believed to be more of a security threat.

Privacy

Privacy is protection from unreasonable intrusion upon one's isolation, from appropriation of one's name or likeness, from unreasonable publicity given to one's private life, and from publicity that unreasonably places one in a false light before the public (Reynolds, 2003; Zoellick, 2002). In an Internet-based environment, for example, store representatives can monitor one's shopping habits at many locations on the World Wide Web (WWW), whereas in a traditional retail outlet, retailers would not be able to follow an individual to many other store locations (Kracher & Corritore 2004). This can also be viewed as collecting customer information through a survey or information form in a retail store, or by monitoring a customer's clickstream in an online store (Kelly & Rowland, 2000; Stead & Gilbert, 2001). Privacy is also directly related to protecting children. For example, on the Internet, restrictions are made as to what information can be gathered from a child of a particular age. "Privacy law and theory must change to meet the needs of the digital age" (DeVries, 2003, p. 309).

Accuracy

Accuracy is concerned with the authenticity and fidelity of information, as well as identifying who is responsible for informational errors that harm people (Mason, 1986). In an Internet-based environment, individuals must be concerned with their personal information being accurately captured and secured from others. This is where trust comes into play. Without face-to-face interaction, Web sites are deemed to be less trustworthy (Kracher & Corritore, 2004). Web site designers instead create the impression of trust through Web site design, navigation systems, and seals of approval (Corritore et al., 2001).

SCENARIOS FOR PRESENTING ONLINE ETHICS

The online environment contains many ethical situations that current college students should address and consider before becoming business professionals. Therefore, we propose ways to present ethics in the class setting. Our framework centers on the issues discussed above: property, access, privacy, and accuracy. For each issue, students may have different concerns, perceptions, and feelings. Since there is an atmosphere of anonymity in the electronic world, as instructors we must find ways to discuss these issues and their ethical dimensions. Practical ethics' applications are essential in classroom discussion (Jurkiewicz, Giacalone, & Knouse, 2004; Watkins & Iyer, 2006).

We present an approach that uses scenarios to generate class discussions. From existing literature and through our own development, we propose situations for each area of the framework. Through a discussion of each scenario, students are allowed to voice their opinions and to hear the opinions of others. Ultimately, the goal is for the students to begin to understand how the ethical implications in online situations are quite similar to the traditional situations in their everyday life. Although the element of anonymity exists, it should not change what is right and wrong in behavior. The following discussion covers the four areas of the online ethics framework and provides scenarios to be used in class discussion. Similar situations could be used for discussion questions in homework assignments or exams. While there is rarely a correct solution, instructors should look for thought development and ability to present a reasonable argument.

Property situations are easy to create and seem to be an area of high interest to students. One that has proven fruitful in class discussion is as follows:

Traditional Property Situation: John is shopping at a local retailer for some DVDs. He decides to purchase one DVD. As he is leaving the store, he notices that his bag contains two DVDs, one of which he did not purchase. John decides to keep both DVDs.

Online Property Situation: John is shopping online for some DVDs. He orders one DVD from a Web site. When he receives his order, he notices that he has received two DVDs, one of which he did not order. However, his invoice statement indicates that he has only been charged for one DVD. John decides to keep both DVDs.

Instructors can consider printing an equal number of each situation and distributing one to each student. Give the students a minute to answer what they would do and why. Then, the instructor can ask for a show of hands for those who would return the DVD vs. those who would not. From the split in the class, the difference in the scenarios will be revealed to the entire class. Frequently during discussions, students approve of keeping the DVDs in the online situation, but would return the DVDs in the traditional, retail store situation. An interesting discussion can be directed by the instructor. Why would the online situation be any different than the traditional? Inevitably, students admit that it is a convenience factor. The online method requires effort on their part, an effort that they may not be willing to take. As instructors, it is important to recognize the students' reasoning and then to provide guidance. The situations are really not different at all; in both cases, an additional product is received without payment. Additional property situations could also be considered, such as the copying of a friend's paper vs. the copying of paragraphs directly from the Internet. Students may also argue that convenience is a factor in these scenarios as well.

Access issues generally do not exist alone. They overlap with the other three issues. However, from the given scenarios, one can see that access is a huge concern.

Traditional Access Situation: A new employee discovered that the payroll files were unlocked and completely accessible. The files contained information about salaries and bonuses. This problem was reported to the appropriate authorities in the company. Until a new cabinet was purchased with a lock, the employee continued to browse through the files when no one was in the office (adapted from Pierce & Henry, 2000; Paradice, 1990).

Online Access Situation: A new employee discovered a way to access all of the payroll information, including salaries and bonuses on the company Web site. This flaw in the system security was reported to the appropriate authorities in the company. Until the problem was corrected, the employee continued to "browse" the information (adapted from Pierce & Henry, 2000; Paradice, 1990).

Accessing confidential employee information by any means is unethical. However, students often believe information in an online format is "free to all." In the traditional sense, tampering with file cabinets is viewable. Therefore, students feel there is a greater likelihood of being caught and facing consequences. In reality they should understand that there is a greater likelihood of being caught in the electronic world, and more importantly, it is still the same act regardless of the method. Additional access situations could be discussed, for example the access and modification of a bank's accounting system.

Privacy has become more of a media point in the past decade. Identity theft is the major concern; however, other privacy issues should be brought to the attention of students as well.

Traditional Privacy Situation: John fills out a survey form that came in the box of a new computer game he purchased. The survey asks for his e-mail address, mailing address, and telephone number, which he fills in. John's information is sold to other computer game companies. In the following weeks, John receives several advertisements in the mail about new computer games (adapted from Johnson, 2004).

Online Privacy Situation: John fills out a survey form on the Web for a new computer game he purchased. The survey asks for his e-mail address, mailing address, and telephone number, which he fills in. The Web page sells John's information to other computer game companies. In the following weeks, John receives dozens of e-mail messages about new computer games (adapted from Johnson, 2004).

Interestingly, past experience with privacy situations shows that students expect to have little privacy. One good method for beginning a discussion is to address the privacy policies of organizations. What can the companies collect? What can they sell of the collected information? Is there a way to opt-out of having the information released? These are all valid questions that students can ask as consumers. Students need to gain a greater appreciation for the privacy they are entitled. Additionally, privacy situations regarding

identity theft, child protection, and other issues could also be discussed from an online perspective.

Finally, accuracy is another issue that overlaps greatly with the other three. However, this situation amplifies the accuracy issue and is also a good lead into discussions related to a student's specific discipline or major.

Traditional Accuracy Situation: A small company that prepares tax returns has hired some temporary help in March and April because of the high demand. The temporary workers are to assist the full-time, experienced employees. During the last week, several clients bring their tax returns when there is not enough time for the experienced employees to complete them by the deadline. The manager tells the clients that she can assign the tax returns to the temporary workers to complete on their own. The manager explains that these workers are not experts in tax and disclaims any responsibility for errors that they might produce. The clients are desperate and accept the offer. A few months later, several of the clients are notified that their tax returns were incorrect and were penalized by the taxation authorities (adapted from Hay, McCourt Larres, Oyelere, & Fisher, 2001).

Online Accuracy Situation: A software development company has just produced a new online software package that incorporates the new tax laws and figures taxes for both individuals and small businesses. The manager of the company knows that the product probably has a number of bugs, but believes that the first firm to put this kind of software on the online market is likely to capture the largest market share. The company widely advertises the program. When the company actually ships a disk, it includes a disclaimer of responsibility for errors resulting from use of the program. The company expects it will receive a certain number of complaints, queries, and suggestions for modifications. The company plans to use these to make changes and eventually issue updated, improved, and debugged versions. The president argues that this is general industry policy and that anyone who buys version 1.0 of a program knows this and will take proper precautions. Because of the bugs, a number of users filed incorrect tax returns and were penalized by the taxation authority (adapted from Hay et al., 2001).

These situations are slightly different than those previously presented. Here students are asked to look at the difference between traditional worker error and online software error. Students believe that workers should be more liable for errors. In reality, the situations are not different. The assumption is that software will be correct. Students need to understand that even online software packages are not flawless and can lead to inaccuracy. The ethical ramifications for the companies in either situation should be the same. Additionally, accuracy situations could be posed for slander issues and credit reporting issues.

FUTURE TRENDS

In the future, instructors must teach online ethics in universities. Students rarely perceive ethical dilemmas in traditional and online settings similarly. Therefore, as technologies evolve and new possibilities develop, there will be an increased need to discuss these issues in a class setting. For researchers, this also poses additional research possibilities. Understanding the attitudes and corresponding behavior of current students is extremely important, considering that students compose the largest percentage of consumers online (by age group).

CONCLUSION

Teaching ethics related to the dilemmas created by the information age in universities is vital. It can be assumed that every student who graduates from a university will be impacted by transactions online. Regardless of their work environments—large company, small company, or entrepreneur—an online presence is needed. Therefore, students should be exposed to the dilemmas that this environment brings. We presented a framework (PAPA) of four specific areas to give instructors some ideas for beginning to include this in their courses. The situations we pose provide opportunities for discussion of each of the four areas—property, access, privacy, and accuracy. By focusing on these areas, instructors will be covering issues of fundamental importance in the online arena, and teaching ethical conduct in the ever changing and increasingly important online world.

REFERENCES

Ben-Ze'ev, A. (2003). Privacy, emotional closeness, and openness in cyberspace. *Computers in Human Behavior, 19,* 451-467.

Davenport, D. (2002). Anonymity on the Internet: Why the price may be too high. *Communications of the ACM, 45*(4), 33-35.

DeVries, W.T. (2003). Protecting privacy in the digital age. *Berkeley Technology Law Journal, 18*(1), 283-311.

Hay, D., McCourt Larres, P., Oyelere, P., & Fisher, A. (2001). The ethical perception of undergraduate students in computer-related situations: An analysis of the effects of culture, gender and prior education. *Teaching Business Ethics, 5*(3), 331-356.

Johnson, D. (2004). *Resources for teaching information technology ethics to children and young adults.* Retrieved October 20, 2004, from http://www.doug-johnson.com/ethics/

Jurkiewicz, C.L., Giacalone, R.A., & Knouse, S.B. (2004). Transforming personal experience into a pedagogical tool: Ethical complaints. *Journal of Business Ethics, 53,* 283-295.

Kelly, E.P., & Rowland, H.C. (2000). Ethical and online privacy issues in electronic commerce. *Business Horizons,* (May-June), 3-12.

Kracher, B., & Corritore, C.L. (2004). Is there a special e-commerce ethics? *Business Ethics Quarterly, 14*(1), 71-94.

Leonard, L.N.K., & Cronan, T.P. (2001). Illegal, inappropriate, and unethical behavior in an information technology context: A study to explain influences. *Journal of the Association for Information Systems, 1*(12), 1-31.

Leonard, L.N.K., Cronan, T.P., & Kreie, J. (2004). What are influences of ethical behavior intentions—planned behavior, reasoned action, perceived importance, or individual characteristics? *Information & Management, 42*(1), 143-158.

Lopez, Y.P., Rechner, P.L., & Olson-Buchanan, J.B. (2005). Shaping ethical perceptions: An empirical assessment of the influence of business education, culture, and demographic factors. *Journal of Business Ethics, 60,* 341-358.

Mason, R.O. (1986). Four ethical issues of the information age. *MIS Quarterly, 10*(1), 4-12.

Paradice, D.B. (1990). Ethical attitudes of entry-level MIS personnel. *Information & Management, 18,* 143-151.

Pierce, M.A., & Henry, J.W. (2000). Judgments about computer ethics: Do individual, co-worker, and company judgments differ? Do company codes make a difference? *Journal of Business Ethics, 28,* 307-322.

Reynolds, G. (2003). *Ethics in information technology.* Canada: Thomson Course Technology.

Sama, L.M., & Shoaf, V. (2002). Ethics on the Web: Applying moral decision-making to the new media. *Journal of Business Ethics, 36,* 93-103.

Stead, B.A., & Gilbert, J. (2001). Ethical issues in electronic commerce. *Journal of Business Ethics, 34,* 75-85.

Watkins, A.L., & Iyer, V.M. (2006). Expanding ethics education: Professionals can participate. *The CPA Journal,* (February), 68-69.

Zoellick, B. (2002). *CyberRegs: A business guide to Web property, privacy, and patents.* Boston: Addison-Wesley.

KEY TERMS

Access: Concerns what information a person/organization has the right to obtain about individuals.

Accuracy: Concerns the authenticity and fidelity of information.

Anonymity: The ability to state an individual's opinions without revealing his or her identity.

Information Technology: Any computer-based tool that allows individuals to work with information.

Online Ethics Situation: An ethical dilemma that exists as a result of the online environment.

Privacy: Concerns the protection from unreasonable intrusion upon an individual's private life.

Property: Concerns who owns information about individuals.

Traditional Ethics Situation: An ethical dilemma that exists as a result of the non-online environment.

Ethics in Software Engineering

Pankaj Kamthan
Concordia University, Canada

INTRODUCTION

As software becomes pervasive in our daily lives, its values from a purely human perspective are brought to light. Ethical conduct is one such human value.

There are various reasons for discussing the issue of ethics within a software engineering context. By participating in a software development process, software engineers can influence the final product, namely the software itself, in different ways including those that may be contrary to public interest. In other words, they could engage in an unethical behavior, inadvertently or deliberately. This could lead to personal harm, and potentially result in loss of confidence in software and loss of trust in organizations that own them. This can adversely affect the acceptance of software as a useful product, question the credibility of software engineering as a profession, lead to legal implications, and impact the bottom line of the software industry at-large.

This article is organized as follows. We first outline the background necessary for later discussion. This is followed by a proposal for a quality-based framework for addressing ethics, and software quality treatment of a software engineering code of ethics. Next, avenues and directions for future research are outlined, and finally, concluding remarks are given.

BACKGROUND

By viewing software engineering as a profession, we define ethics as a code of professional standards, containing aspects of fairness and duty to the profession and the general public.

Since a software can either be a benefit or a hazard to its potential users, the issue of ethics in its engineering arises. Software failures (Sipior & Ward, 1998) that have led to loss of human life, rendered computer systems unusable, led to financial collapse, or caused major inconveniences are grim reminders of that.

In this article, we discuss the issue of ethics from the viewpoint of software product quality considerations in practice. There is an apparent symbiosis between ethics and quality. For example, the causes of the aforementioned failures were attributed to violations of one or more quality attributes such as reliability, safety, and so forth, and/or to lack of proper validation/verification of these.

Indeed, in the Software Engineering Body of Knowledge (SWEBOK) (Abran, Moore, Bourque, & Dupuis, 2001), ethics has been placed within the software quality "knowledge area." The issue of information technology in general, and the role of quality in software development in particular, have been addressed in (Reynolds, 2003; Tavani, 2004). Moreover, software quality is viewed as an ethical issue from a philosophical perspective (Peslak, 2004). However, these efforts are limited by one or more of the following issues: quality and ethics are often viewed as a tautology, treatment of software quality is at a very high level and often as a single entity, and there is lack of specific guidance for improvement of software quality within the domain of software ethics.

One way to enforce ethical standards in a software project is by explicitly documenting the ethical expectations from stakeholders such as via a *code of ethics*. The Software Engineering Code of Ethics and Professional Practice (SECEPP) is a recommendation of the ACM/IEEE-CS Joint Task Force on Software Engineering Ethics and Professional Practices. SECEPP puts forth eight categories of principles decomposed further into clauses that software engineers should adhere to in teaching and practicing software engineering. However, these principles and associated clauses suffer from several issues (expounded in the next section): lack of separation (of concerns), recency, precision, completeness, reachability (to certain audience), and specificity, which makes their realization difficult. The relevance of SECEPP for practical purposes has been questioned (Qureshi, 2001), however the view is largely managerial rather than oriented towards the software product.

ETHICS IN SOFTWARE ENGINEERING AND SOFTWARE PRODUCT QUALITY

For the purpose of this article, our understanding of the discussion on ethics in software engineering is based on the following interrelated hypothesis:

Hypothesis 1. Ethical behavior is dynamic, rather than static. Specifically, by appropriate means (such as code of ethics), ethical actions of software engineers could be regulated and with education even be instilled.

Hypothesis 2. Ethics is a "meta-concern" (Qureshi, 2001) leading us to adoption of steps for software quality assurance and evaluation. Specifically, ethics and software quality are related by direct proportionality, and so overall improvement in the quality of a software product leads to an improvement in ethical considerations related to that product.

A Theoretical Framework for Addressing Ethics from a Software Product Quality Perspective

In order to address the practicality of introducing the ethical dimension in software engineering, we first need a theoretical foundation. To do that, we separate the concerns involved as follows:

1. View ethics as a qualitative aspect and attempt to address it via quantitative means so as to minimize the potential for heuristics and to make the evaluation repeatable.

2. Select a theoretical basis for communication of information, and place ethics within its setting.

3. Address software product quality in a systematic and practical manner by means of adopting a quality model. In particular, select the quality model that separates internal and external quality attributes.

Using this as a basis, we propose a framework for ethics from the perspective of software product quality (see Table 1).

We now describe each of the components of the framework in detail.

Semiotic Levels

The first column of Table 1 states the semiotic levels. Semiotics (Stamper, 1992) is concerned with the use of symbols to convey knowledge. From a semiotics perspective, a representation can be viewed on six interrelated levels: physical, empirical, syntactic, semantic, pragmatic, and social, each depending on the previous one in that order.

The physical level is concerned with the physical representation of signs in hardware and is not of direct

Table 1. A framework for ethics in a semiotic approach to software product quality

Ethical Concern	Software Product		
Semiotic Level	**Levels of Quality Attribute**	**Example(s) of Quality Attributes**	**Decision Support**
Social	External: Tier 1	Credibility, Trust	Feasibility
	External: Tier 2	Legality, Safety	
	External: Tier 3	Privacy, Security	
Pragmatic	External: Tier 1	Accessibility, Maintainability, Usability	
	External: Tier 2	Interoperability, Portability, Reliability	
Semantic	Internal	Completeness, Validity	
Syntactic	Internal	Correctness	
Empirical	Internal	Characters, Character Set	
Physical	Internal	Hardware Characteristics	

concern here. The empirical level is responsible for the communication properties of signs. The syntactic level is responsible for the formal or structural relations between signs. The semantic level is responsible for the relationship of signs to what they stand for. The pragmatic level is responsible for the relation of signs to interpreters. The social level is responsible for the manifestation of social interaction with respect to signs.

Software Product Quality Attributes and Examples

The second column of Table 1 draws the relationship between semiotic level and software product quality attributes.

The first level of quality attributes gives the *external attributes,* which on decomposition leads to second level of quality characteristics called *internal attributes* that are directly measurable via quality metrics. External attributes are extrinsic to the software product and are directly the user's concern, while internal attributes are intrinsic to the software product and are directly the software engineer's concern.

Now, external attributes in the collection are *not* all at the same level. For example, security is a necessary condition for safety, which in turn is a necessary condition for credibility of a software product. Therefore, credibility of a software product is at a higher echelon than safety, which in turn is higher than security. So we extend the traditional software product quality models by introducing a further decomposition of external attributes into different tiers.

The third column of Table 1 includes examples of quality attributes at different semiotic levels based upon our experience from past software projects in different domains, observations from several software product quality models (Lindland, Sindre, & Sølvberg, 1994; Fenton & Pfleeger, 1997), and most importantly, those that have a direct impact on stakeholders. Their purpose is only to make the argument concrete, not to mandate a required list (that could be shortened or lengthened based on the application domain anyway).

Decision Support

The practice of software engineering must take into account organizational constraints (personnel, infra-

structure, schedule, budget, and so on). These, along with external forces (market value or competitors), force us to make software-related decisions that could cross over on either side of the ethical boundaries. Therefore, the practice of ethics (say, enforcement via code of ethics) must also be feasible and is acknowledged in the last column of Table 1. There are well-known techniques for carrying out feasibility analysis, but further discussion of this aspect is beyond the scope of this article.

Ethics and Software Product Quality: Making SECEPP Practical

The following issues inherent to principles and associated clauses SECEPP make their realization difficult:

- **Separation:** The concerns are not separated clearly, and there are apparent overlaps across principles. For example, cost estimation is addressed in both Principle 3: PRODUCT and Principle 5: MANAGEMENT.
- **Recency:** The last version of SECEPP was announced in 1999 and is seemingly not constantly maintained.
- **Precision:** The clauses often include terminology that is either vague or open to broad interpretation, and many of the terms therein lack links/references to standard definitions. For example, Principle 3: PRODUCT states that "software engineers shall ensure that their products and related modifications meet the highest professional standards possible." However, it is unclear what "highest" means in this context and by whose measure, the reason for the distinction between "products and related modifications," and which "professional standards" are being implied.
- **Completeness:** SECEPP does not address certain classical practices such as (ethics in the light of) software reuse, reengineering, or reverse engineering, or current practices such as software modeling, and therefore needs to be extended. In retrospective, SECEPP does point out that the list of principles and clauses in it are not exhaustive.
- **Reachability:** The principles and/or clauses are often at a high level of abstraction that can make

them prohibitive for novices such as beginning software engineering students that need to start on the right foot. In this sense, SECEPP resembles the problems inherent in the use of guidelines per se.

- **Specificity:** In order to be applicable to the field of software engineering, SECEPP had to be both abstract and general. It does not include concrete examples for or against ethical conduct for development scenarios for specific software such as Web applications.

One of the main purposes of the article is to tackle some of these issues, particularly as they relate to the software product.

The commentary on SECEPP is structured as follows. Each principle and associated clause (and any sub-statements) in SECEPP that is seen within the scope of non-trivial quality considerations is listed verbatim in *italics*. This is followed by corresponding [Issues] and [Resolutions] for every case. The resolutions vary in their coverage where some address the issues better and in a more complete manner than others. We do not claim that the resolutions as being absolute, and their limitations are pointed out where necessary.

Principle 1: PUBLIC. Software engineers shall act consistently with the public interest. In particular, software engineers shall, as appropriate

1.07. Consider issues of physical disabilities...that can diminish access to the benefits of software.

[Issues] It is unclear why only *physical disabilities* are being addressed when software is also used by people with other forms of disabilities (such as visual, auditory, and cognitive/neurological) as well. Also, there are no details on means for addressing accessibility concerns.

[Resolutions] For the Web applications domain, the Web Content Accessibility Guidelines (WCAG) and its ancillary specifications or the Section 508 mandate of the U.S. Government Federal Access Board provide detailed guidelines and examples/non-examples of assuring accessibility. There are tools available that can automatically test for conformance to these guidelines.

3.02. Ensure proper and achievable goals and objectives for any project on which they work or propose.

[Issues] In absence of further details, it is unclear what are considered as *achievable goals,* how to define and achieve them, and when they are considered having been achieved.

[Resolutions] A goal-oriented software project is seen as a set {goals, means} to be satisfied. Indeed, one view of goal-oriented software engineering in general and measurement in particular is given by the Goal-Question-Metrics (GQM) approach (Van Solingen & Berghout, 1999). In GQM, a set of measurement goals are stated, corresponding to each of one or more questions asked, followed by one or more metrics to tackle each question. One of the limitations of GQM, however, is that it does not explicitly address the issue of feasibility.

3.07. Strive to fully understand the specifications for software on which they work.

[Issues] The term *fully understand* is not defined. If it means each software engineer must comprehend all aspects of a given specification at all times, then this goal is unrealistic.

[Resolutions] For our purpose, a working definition of comprehension is the acquisition of the explicit knowledge inherent in a specification. For a non-trivial specification, it is not realistic that each stakeholder will be able to comprehend each statement made by the specification in its entirety at all times. A comprehension is *feasible* (Lindland et al., 1994) if the cost of reducing the incomprehensible statements in a specification does not exceed the drawbacks of retaining them.

3.11. Ensure adequate documentation, including significant problems discovered and solutions adopted, for any project on which they work.

[Issues] It is unclear what *adequate* or *significant* means here. There is also no suggestion as to what kind of documentation is being addressed, and how and where such documentation should appear.

[Resolutions] All documentation should be minimal in the sense that if there is some documentation, then that must correspond to a problem/solution, and vice versa, and it should not be redundant (never appear in more than one place). This can be addressed via the "single source approach." All documentation should be modular in the sense that semantically similar aspects should be cohesive, and clearly separated from others. For example, all design decisions, including the ones not included, corresponding to each software requirement must be uniquely identified and rationalized, and appear in the software design description document. All documentation should be "globally" (anybody, anywhere, any device, any time) reachable. This could, for example, be done by representing software process documentation in the Extensible Markup Language (XML). The guidance for structuring and presenting technical documents has been given (Houp, Pearsall, Tebeaux, and Dragga, 2005).

3.12. Work to develop software and related documents that respect the privacy of those who will be affected by that software.

[Issues] In absence of details, it is non-trivial to address privacy concerns.

[Resolutions] One of the main privacy concerns that the users have is not knowing how or by whom the personal information that they have voluntarily or involuntarily released will be used. The Platform for Privacy Preferences Project (P3P) enables providers to express their privacy practices in a format that can be retrieved automatically and interpreted easily by user agents. This ensures that users are informed about privacy policies before they release personal information. A P3P Preference Exchange Language (APPEL) complements P3P and allows a user to express his or her preferences in a set of preference-rules that are placed in a profile document. This can then be used by the user agent to make decisions regarding the acceptability of machine-readable privacy policies from P3P-enabled applications.

Challenges to a Software Quality Approach to Addressing Ethics in Software Engineering

Open Source Software (OSS) suffers from various quality issues (Michlmayr, Hunt, & Probert, 2005),

including that of usability and maintainability. Since there are modest opportunities, if any, for enforcing ethical regulations in the OSS realm, this brings into question the ways in which OSS can be used.

Due to constraints not imposed by choice but by technical considerations in practice of software engineering, quality attributes in technical and social tiers compete. For example, the pairs of usability–security or maintainability–efficiency are often in competition.

Finally, we note that there are ethical predicaments in software development that are irreconcilable from a software quality perspective. For example, a software engineer working for a company producing defense software could, when asked to make a decision on including a certain feature in software that will lead to striking improvement in a certain weapon capability, find his or her ethical commitments to the organization in conflict with his or her ethical obligations to society at-large. Therefore, alternative means of tackling such scenarios are desirable.

FUTURE TRENDS

Since project and process quality is not mutually exclusive from the product quality, it would be worth examining them in general and within the SECEPP framework. For example, according to the Capability Maturity Model (CMM), the organizations below Level 3 do not have formal quality evaluation practices, such as inspections, in place.

In a similar spirit of organizational quality management, it would of interest to study the interplay between ethics and the Total Quality Management (TQM) that focuses on the optimization of industrial processes under economic considerations in such a way as to achieve customer satisfaction.

Finally, it would be of interest to closely investigate the ethical concerns in specific software domains such as mobile or Web applications (Johnson, 1997). The issue of ethics is also important to these applications as they are increasingly being used as technological means for persuading consumers (Fogg, 2003). To that regard, a recast of SECEPP applicable to Web engineering is also highly desirable.

CONCLUSION

Software engineers are expected to share a commitment to software quality as part of their culture (Wiegers, 1996). There needs to be a regulatory and/or educational shift to accommodate making ethics a first-class member of this culture as well.

The improvement of software quality is technical as well as an ethical imperative. By addressing software product quality in a systematic manner, ethical concerns can be largely attended to.

Organizations that are engaged in software production from an engineering standpoint need to adhere to a code of ethics and monitor its practice. Institutions that have software engineering as part of their curriculum must include the role of ethics on the forefront. A code of ethics such as SECEPP can be helpful in that regard, but it needs to evolve to be more effective in such practical situations.

REFERENCES

Abran, A., Moore, J.W., Bourque, P., & Dupuis, R. (2001). *Guide to the software engineering body of knowledge—SWEBOK.* IEEE Computer Society.

Fenton, N.E., & Pfleeger, S.L. (1997). *Software metrics: A rigorous & practical approach.* International Thomson Computer Press.

Fogg, B.J. (2003). *Persuasive technology: Using computers to change what we think and do.* San Francisco: Morgan Kaufmann.

Houp, K.W., Pearsall, T.E., Tebeaux, E., & Dragga, S. (2005). *Reporting technical information* (11th ed.). Oxford: Oxford University Press.

Johnson, D.G. (1997). Ethics online. *Communications of the ACM, 40*(1), 60-65.

Lindland, O.I., Sindre, G., & Sølvberg, A. (1994). Understanding quality in conceptual modeling. *IEEE Software, 11*(2), 42-49.

Michlmayr, M., Hunt, F., & Probert, D.R. (2005, July 11-15). Quality practices and problems in free software projects. *Proceedings of the 1st International Conference on Open Source Systems* (OSS 2005), Genova, Italy.

Peslak, A.R. (2004, April 22-24). Improving software quality: An ethics based approach. *Proceedings of the 2004 SIGMIS Conference on Computer Personnel Research: Careers, Culture, and Ethics in a Networked Environment* (SIGMIS 2004), Tucson, AZ.

Qureshi, S. (2001). How practical is a code of ethics for software engineers interested in quality? *Software Quality Journal, 9*(3), 153-159.

Reynolds, G. (2003). *Ethics in information technology.* Thompson Publishing Group.

Sipior, J.C., & Ward, B.T. (1998). Ethical responsibility for software development. *Information Systems Management, 15*(2), 68-72.

Stamper, R. (1992, October 5-8). Signs, organizations, norms and information systems. *Proceedings of the 3rd Australian Conference on Information Systems,* Wollongong, Australia.

Tavani, H.T. (2004). *Ethics and technology: Ethical issues in an age of information and communication technology.* New York: John Wiley & Sons.

Van Solingen, R., & Berghout, E. (1999). *The goal/question/metric method: A practical method for quality improvement of software development.* New York: McGraw-Hill.

Wiegers, K. (1996). *Creating a software engineering culture.* Dorset House.

KEY TERMS

Code of Ethics: A resource that describes the ethical and professional obligations with respect to which the public, colleagues, and legal entities can measure the behavior of and decisions made by a professional.

Quality: The totality of features and characteristics of a product or a service that bear on its ability to satisfy stated or implied needs.

Quality Model: A set of characteristics and the relationships between them that provide the basis for specifying quality requirements and evaluating quality of an entity.

Semiotics: The field of study of signs and their representations.

Software Engineering: A discipline that advocates a systematic approach of developing high-quality software on a large scale while taking into account the factors of sustainability and longevity, as well as organizational constraints of time and resources.

Software Failure: A departure from the software system's required behavior from a user's perspective.

Software Fault: A human error in performing some software activity from a software engineer's perspective. A fault is not a sufficient condition for a software failure.

Ethics in the Security of Organizational Information Systems

Sushma Mishra
Virginia Commonwealth University, USA

Amita Goyal Chin
Virginia Commonwealth University, USA

INTRODUCTION

Organizational security initiatives by corporations have been voted number one for IT project priorities for the year 2006. The increasing concern for the security of information systems is further intensified with the plethora of governmental regulations emphasizing security, both of information systems and of soft data. The Health Insurance Portability and Accountability Act (HIPPA), the Sarbanes Oxley (SOX) Act, and the U.S. Providing Appropriate Tools Required to Intercept and Obstruct Terrorism (U.S. PATRIOT) Act make it mandatory to ensure the security of electronic records and the integrity of data. Security of informational assets is a huge responsibility for organizations that are IT intensive. A strong IT infrastructure in organizations brings convenient and fast access to data across the globe. With such access comes an added burden in the form of protection and safeguarding of crucial data. Since soft data is more vulnerable to malicious attacks from outsiders than physical hard copies of data, which may be securely locked in an office, it calls for organized and efficient information assurance practices in the form of detection and prevention of breaches in networks, data usage procedures, and data storage procedures. Various sophisticated technical solutions to these problems such as firewalls, access control models, and cryptography technology are available. However, these technical efforts to ensure the integrity of information are not sufficient to achieve a secure information system in an organization. The organizational as well as behavioral issues of security endeavors need to be explicitly planned for by management. After all, it is the human aspect of security that is the weakest link in an integrated security approach to information systems.

BACKGROUND

An information system is a system that emerges from the interaction of information technology and an organization (Lee, 2004). Thus an information system incorporates not just the information technology component, but also the human aspects of implementing and monitoring the technology. The organizational context in which IT has been implemented, the culture prevalent in the organization, the norms, the rules, and the practices are as equally important as the technical sufficiency of the security framework in an organization. The security solutions are implemented by the employees. The human link has been found to be the weakest in the security solution (Bottom, 2000; Gonzalez & Sawicka, 2002; Vroom, Cheryl, & Von Solms, 2004). Research has shown that the threat to security from the insiders of an organization (i.e., the employees) exceeds that from outsiders (i.e., hackers) (Schultz, 2002). There are various reasons suggested for this in the research literature: lack of internal controls and lack of normative pressure (Dhillon, 2001), ignorance or disregard for security policies (Bottom, 2000), and no consideration being given to human factors in the system development methodology (Hitchings, 1995). For comprehensive security management, information systems security should be ensured at three levels—formal, informal, and technical (Dhillon, 2007). The informal level is the common practices, norms, and culture of the organization. To ensure security at this level, the professional ethics of the organization and the personal ethics of the employees are of paramount importance. It is this element of the behavioral aspect of security that we will emphasize in this article.

MAIN FOCUS OF THE ARTICLE

Ethics is the study of morality, representing the basic societal values and the code of conduct and actions that guide the behavior of individuals or groups. Ethics shapes the individual belief system that guides an individual and tells him or her whether an action is good or bad. Ethics are a function of many factors such as cultural, geographical, economical, and philosophical motivations. Since the subjectivity part is inherent in the concept of ethics, there are no universal agreements about the definition or domain of ethics. Research in ethics combines inputs from many disciplines such as sociology, economics, psychology, anthropology, and history. Ethics help us in making moral judgments and influence our decisions in issues regarding "what is good" and "what is bad." In our context, ethics helps us decide how to make judgments regarding security and protection of informational assets. Individuals are influenced by the environment and behave accordingly, but one's deep-seated values do not change easily.

While some researchers (e.g., Freeman & Peace, 2004) have begun exploring the concept of ethics in information systems, we are largely still in a nascent stage of development. Thus there is no clear map of the "IT ethics domain that identifies major land masses, compass directions, levels of analysis, or recommended pathways" (Laudon, 1995, p. 33) to be followed. Based on the existing ethics literature, Laudon (1995) divided the moral space covered by ethical concepts into the following dimensions:

- **Phenomenology vs. Positivism:** This particular dimension provides guidance in an ethical dilemma—that is, it seeks to answer the question "What should I do?" For phenomenologists, the good is given in a situation; it is derived from the logic and the language of the situation. For positivists, the real world has to be observed and the ethical principles have to be derived from the situation.
- **Rules vs. Consequences:** Rules-based ethicists, or people belonging to the deontological school of thought, believe that there are certain rights and certain wrongs, and that actions that are correct and are right should be taken. Such actions are universal in nature and do not depend on specific context. They tend to follow certain rules in all situations. According to ethicists, who

believe in consequential ethics, right or wrong is based on the context of the decision and on the consequences of the action taken. They believe that the end justifies the means—that is, if the results are good, then the actions leading to that result are also good.
- **Individuals vs. Collectivities (micro vs. macro levels):** The locus of moral authority is another criterion on which ethicists differ in opinion. While they agree that how an individual makes a decision is the subject of ethics research, they differ on who has the authority to make the decisions. Some argue that individuals decide for themselves what is right and what is wrong. Others argue that moral authority must be located in larger collectivities, for example the organization or the society. Even government could have a large authority to shape such decisions. There are problems with both lines of thinking. The individuals set their own rules and their own standards of morality, and do not consider the context of society to which they belong, whereas believers in collectivities introduce a moral relativism concept that defines all its decisions based on the democratic principle of majority. They believe in following the mob.

In order to understand the process of assessing the importance of ethics in information systems research (Mason, 1986), especially in the security domain, we must first consider the following major issues:

- **Privacy:** The personal information about individuals must be protected and their privacy respected
- **Accuracy:** Someone should be accountable to ensure that information is accurate
- **Property:** Information ownership should be clear. The question of how to decide who can access what information needs to be answered
- **Accessibility:** It must be clear what kind of information an organization is allowed to obtain and under what conditions

In an assessment of the values of managers regarding information systems security, Dhillon and Torkzadeh (2006) found that developing and sustaining an ethical environment is one of the basic objectives of creating a secure information system in an organization. An ethical environment in an organization can be created by instilling personal and professional ethics, and also by creating an environment that promotes and respects personal values of individuals in the organization. An organization must clearly communicate its ethical philosophy to the employees, so that an employee's behavior may be consistent with that of the organization's position on ethical issues. Some of the suggested ways to achieve an ethical consciousness in an organization are:

- **Ethics Seminars and Training:** Organizations need to invest in training and seminars to create awareness amongst employees regarding ethical issues in job functions. Research shows that training employees is helpful in effectively showing the organization's stand on issues. Training employees regarding security issues has been identified as a critical factor for security management (Whitman, 2003; Bottom, 2000). Similarly, training employees about ethics, presenting scenarios of ethical dilemmas, and suggesting solutions in such situations could be instrumental in explaining the importance of ethics to employees.

- **Communication:** Organizations need to clearly communicate their ethical beliefs and expectations to employees. Clarity in communications can be achieved through clear and precise policies, effective internal controls, and elaborate job descriptions from management. Organizations should continuously communicate the message of transparency in functions and commitment to security endeavors. Ambiguity in rules and policies leads to numerous individual interpretations and potentially to behaviors deemed unethical by the organization.

- **Security Culture:** Organizations need to realize the importance of having a proactive security culture for a comprehensive security management environment. The importance of having a security culture to instill a sense of responsibility and morality amongst employees has been emphasized in the research literature (Vroom & Solms, 2004; Dhillon & Backhouse, 2000). Security culture may also be beneficial in communicating the correct ethical values to employees. Such a culture may help in aligning personal and organizational values.

- **Ethical Code of Conduct:** Organizations should have a clear and professional code of conduct as a guiding factor for employees to follow. These standards could then provide a benchmark for people in the organization to gauge not only their own behavior in a given context, but also to assess the behavior of peers and subordinates against the standard code of conduct for ethical behavior in the organization. Pearson, Crosby, & Shim, 1997) emphasize the importance of a predefined standard code of conduct for implementing the ethical values in employees. In their study, findings show that there is a lack of understanding of the criteria that is to be used in assessing the ethical behavior of people in the information technology domain.

The ethical stand of an organization on various issues can thus be explicitly communicated to employees, but assessing the impact of such measures and explicating the value out of such endeavors is rather difficult. Also, there is very little guidance within the security literature regarding the relationship between employees' ethical stand and the impact of such stand on behavior. It appears that the ethical stand of an employee regarding an issue and his behavior should be highly correlated, and the ethical stand could be used as a predictor of the person's behavior; however, there is no evidence to confirm this belief. It is difficult to predict such relationships, for there are no good measures available to estimate the personal ethics of a person. Research is required in this area in order to develop measures that may be used to determine the ethical beliefs of each employee and also to be able to use the results to assess and predict an employee's behavior.

A disregard of these issues can generate situations leading to ethical dilemmas which in turn can lead to unpleasant consequences (Conger, Loch, & Helft, 1994). There is no universal right or wrong in ethical decision making; right or wrong depends on the perspective that is being adopted when evaluating a problem. Thus, from an organizational perspective, it is best to provide professional guidance in a clear manner to employees so that personal values do not compromise ethical decision making.

Establishing trust, responsibility, and accountability structure in an organization is necessary for instilling ethical principles in the work culture. Information systems security must be a concern for all employees of the organization, not just for the security personnel.

Information security ethics can be broadly defined as the "analysis of nature of social impact of computer technology and the corresponding formulation and justification of policies" (Leiwo & Heikkuri, 1998) for the proper use of technology. Given the importance of information security in the currently prevalent business infrastructures, ethical clarity is important in the minds of the people who frame the security policies, the people who implement such policies, and the people who try to compromise these policies. It is possible that many of the security breaches occurring today are due to the lack of clear boundaries between right and wrong, and due to the weak internal controls rampant in most organizations.

Research in information security recognizes four major reasons which make ethical issues so important and so frequently addressed (Kowalski, in Leiwo & Heikkuri, 1998). These are:

- **A gap in the administrative (social, technical, organizational) control structure of the organizations maintaining commercial information systems:** Organizations need to address information security in a more comprehensive way, rather than just emphasizing the technical solutions.
- **Ethics provide a common denominator to communicate with people outside of the computing community:** The code of conduct defined for professionals in the information systems community provides a standard for people to behave in an ethical manner.
- **The lack of technological controls to manage the information systems vulnerability:** System vulnerabilities are social and behavioral in nature, as well as those which make the security management of information systems an integrated approach at all three of the above-mentioned levels: technical, organizational, and behavioral.
- **The lack of a top-down approach to create an understanding between users and systems:** Management in organizations needs to address the importance of explaining the appropriateness of various internal controls and policies to the employees.

Henry and Pierce (1994) propose factors that could lead to a comprehensive model for ethical decision making in the context of computer crimes. A formal code of ethics is one of the components of their model, which implies a documented and established company code or policy with provisions that apply to the ethical guidelines for using technology.

FUTURE TRENDS

Dhillon and Backhouse (2000) have argued that existing security principles (confidentiality, integrity, and availability) are concerned more about the technical aspects of security management than the behavioral aspects. The emphasis of the above security measures is more on data management issues rather than managing the threat to information systems from the employees, who use and manage the technical systems. They suggested RITE (Responsibility, Integrity, Trust, and Ethicality) as added principles that need to be considered for a balanced security environment in an organization.

The existence of governmental legislation is not enough to ensure that ethical decisions are being made. Laws may themselves be unethical. Additionally, there is a moral dimension behind successful legislations—that is, the law has to be morally binding (Siponen, 2001). The laws in computer security should be strengthening the moral thinking and code of conduct to which organizations and individuals adhere. Such an attempt is visible in the Sarbanes-Oxley Act, where top management is made liable for any security breach in the organization and management is charged with criminal offense. Fox (2004) observes that in the post-Sarbanes-Oxley era, good corporate governance practices and ethical business practices are no longer optional niceties—they are the law.

The notion of restructuring organizations on the lines of security management—at formal, informal, and technical levels simultaneously—is a viable approach for integrating security issues into the social fabric of the organization. The RITE principles take into account all of the concerns of managing the security personnel of an organization. The security policies and controls can only work if people abide by them. Thus developing an organizational culture based on the above principles would further propagate the ethics of security.

Additionally, methodologies such as a value-focused assessment (Dhillon & Torkzadeh, 2004) provide a good way to assess the social-psychological values and beliefs, and thus the behavioral pattern of individuals in an organization. Given the context of security, an assessment, using this methodology for example, of the ethical values of individuals applying for jobs would provide a beginning point for assessing the individual value system of the applicants. This could be a helpful tool for recruitment purposes for an organization and promote an ethical work culture.

CONCLUSION

Measures such as systems auditing can play a crucial role in educating organizations and IT users in the ethics of systems security. With regulatory pressure to comply with certain standards of security, organizations must be well prepared to seriously and proactively consider ethical issues and to consider implementing them at the operational, the planning, and the strategic business levels. Furthermore, there must be clear ethical guidance for complex decision-making situations, and this can be achieved by providing appropriate training and education to employees about such scenarios. Organizations should have a standard code of conduct for ethical behavior and promote a security culture so that the virtues of ethics are instilled in the employees.

REFERENCES

Bottom, N.R. (2000). The human face of information loss. *Security Management, 44*(6), 50-56.

Conger, S., Loch, K.D., & Helft, B.L. (1994). Information technology and ethics: An exploratory factor analysis. *Ethics in Computer Age,* 22-27

Dhillon, G. (2001). Violation of safeguards by trusted personnel and understanding related information security concerns. *Computers & Security, 20*(2), 165-172.

Dhillon, G. (2007). *Principles of information system security: Text and cases.* New York: John Wiley & Sons.

Dhillon, G., & Backhouse, J. (2000). Information system security management in the new millennium. *Communications of the ACM, 43*(7), 125-128.

Dhillon, G., & Torkzadeh, G. (2006). Value-focused assessment of information systems security in organizations. *Information Systems Journal.*

Fox, C. (2004). Sarbanes-Oxley: Considerations for a framework for IT financial reporting controls. *Information Systems Control Journal, 1.*

Freeman, L., & Peace, G. (2004). *Information ethics: Privacy and intellectual property.* Hershey, PA: Idea Group.

Gonzalez, J.J., & Sawicka, A. (2002). A framework for human factors in information security. *Proceedings of the 2002 WSEAS International Conference on Information Security,* Rio de Janeiro.

Henry, J.W., & Pierce, M.A. (1994). Computer ethics: A model of the influences on the individual's ethical decision making. *Computer Personnel,* (October, 21-27).

Laudon, K.C. (1995). Ethical concepts and information technology. *Communications of the ACM, 38*(12).

Lee, A.S. (2004). Thinking about social theory and philosophy for information systems. In *Social theory and philosophy for information systems* (pp. 1-26). Chichester, UK: John Wiley & Sons.

Leiwo, J., & Heikkuri, S. (1998). An analysis of ethics as foundation of information security in distributed systems. *Proceedings of the 31st IEEE Hawaii International Conference on System Sciences* (vol. 6, pp. 213-222).

Pearson, M.J., Crosby, L., & Shim, J. (1997). Measuring the importance of ethical behavior criteria. *Communications of the ACM, 40*(9), 94-100.

Schultz, E.E. (2002). A framework for understanding and predicting insider attacks. *Proceedings of Compsec 2002,* London.

Siponen, M.T. (2001). Five dimensions of information security awareness. *Computers and Society,* (June), 24-29.

Violino, B. (2006). Priority plans. *Computerworld, 40*(1), 20-21.

Vroom, C., & Von Solms, R. (2004). Towards information security behavioral compliance. *Computers & Security, 23,* 191-198.

Whitman, M. (2003). Enemy at the gate: Threats to information security. *Communications of the ACM, 46*(8): 91-95.

KEY TERMS

Behavioral Aspects of Security: Maps the domain of security that deals with human aspects and the complexities of human behavior regarding security management in an organization. Includes the prevalent norms and practices acceptable to people.

Ethics: A set of values or beliefs that is used for decision-making purposes and is moral in the context in which the decision is being made. This depends on the personal choices of an individual, environment, and cultural underpinnings.

Hacker: An individual who uses his or her computer skills, such as programming or networking, to gain illegal access to a computer network or file.

Information Security Awareness: Concept meaning that users of information systems should be aware of the security objectives, policies, and ethical expectations when interacting with a particular system.

Information Systems Security: A comprehensive set of security practices at the formal, informal, and technical levels in an organization. All perspectives (social, psychological, cultural, physical, technical) regarding security have to be considered simultaneously to create a secure information system.

Information System: A socio-technical system that emerges from interaction between information technology and organizations that implement these technologies. It consists of the organizational context in which technology is implemented, implementation and issues, adoption of technology, and control structure to achieve the intended use of the particular technology.

Ethics of AI

Kevin B. Korb
Monash University, Australia

INTRODUCTION

There are two central questions about the ethics of artificial intelligence (AI):

1. How can we build an ethical AI?
2. Can we build an AI ethically?

The first question concerns the kinds of AI we might achieve—moral, immoral, or amoral. The second concerns the ethics of our achieving such an AI. They are more closely related than a first glance might reveal. For much of technology, the National Rifle Association's neutrality argument might conceivably apply: "guns don't kill people, people kill people." But if we build a genuine, autonomous AI, we arguably will have to have built an artificial moral agent, an agent capable of both ethical and unethical behavior. The possibility of one of our artifacts behaving unethically raises moral problems for their development that no other technology can.

Both questions presume a positive answer to a prior question: Can we build an AI at all? We shall begin our review there.

THE POSSIBILITY OF AI

Artificial intelligence as a research area arose simultaneously with the first electronic computers (Turing, 1948). AI aims at producing an intelligent machine by the construction of an appropriate computer program; the assertion of the possibility of this is known as the strong AI thesis. Alan Turing (1950) proposed replacing the question whether a machine could be intelligent, by another: is it possible to program a machine so that its verbal behavior would be indistinguishable from human verbal behavior? This has become known as the *Turing Test* for intelligence. Turing thought his test would be passed by the year 2000. The continued failure to do so has paralleled continued debate over the possibility of doing so and also over the adequacy of the test.

Joseph Weizenbaum (1966) produced a natural language understanding program, ELIZA. This program had a small set of canned phrases and the ability to invert statements and return them as questions. For example, if you type "I am unhappy," it could respond "Are you unhappy often?" The program, however, is quite simple and, on Weizenbaum's own account, stupid. Nevertheless, Weizenbaum (1976) reported that the program's behavior was sufficiently human-like that it confused his secretary for some time; and it encouraged others to convert it into a kind of virtual psychologist, called DOCTOR, leading some to prophesy the arrival of automated therapy. Weizenbaum responded to these events with despair, swearing off any further AI research and declaring the profession unethical (discussed more below).

Around this time Hubert Dreyfus launched an attack upon the possibility of an AI passing the Turing Test (Dreyfus, 1965). His arguments emphasized the many qualitative differences between human thought and computation, including our embodiment (vs. program portability), our intuitive problem solving (vs. rule following), and the sensitivity of our judgments to mood (vs. cold calculation). If these arguments were right, our computers could never achieve intelligence. However, Dreyfus (1994) ended up conceding that artificial neural networks (ANNs) potentially overcome these objections. Since ANNs are provably equivalent to ordinary computers (assuming they cannot overcome known physical constraints to perform infinite-precision arithmetic; see Franklin & Garzon, 1991), this indirectly conceded the possibility of an AI. (Korb, 1996, presents this argument in detail.)

Whatever the difficulties in tackling the Turing Test, we can legitimately wonder whether even passing it would suffice for intelligence. The best-known argument against the adequacy of the Turing Test was launched by John Searle (1980) in the Chinese Room Argument. Searle began by granting the possibility of passing the Turing Test. Suppose we understand human natural language processing so well that we can precisely mimic it in a computer program. In particular, imagine a program able to understand and generate Chinese to this level. Searle chooses Chinese because Searle does not understand it. Write that program on paper; or rather, rewrite it in English pseudo-code so that Searle can understand it. Put the program, Searle, paper and ink in a giant room with two slots, one for input and one for output. If a Chinese speaker writes a squiggle on paper and inputs it, Searle will simulate the program, and after much to-ing and fro-ing, write some squoggle and output it. By assumption, Searle is participating in a Chinese conversation, but of course, he does not understand it. Indeed, Searle's point is that nothing whatever in the Chinese Room does understand Chinese: not the Searle, not the paper with pseudo-code printed on it, nothing. Therefore, Searle concludes, there is no Chinese understanding going on and so passing the Turing Test is logically inadequate for intelligence.

The most popular response amongst AI researchers is to insist that it is no one thing within the room that is responsible for intelligence, rather it is the system (room) as a whole. Many systems have properties that emerge from the organization of their parts without inhering in any subpart, after all. All living organisms are examples of that. So why not intelligence? Harnad (1989), and many others, have responded by pointing out that intelligence requires semantics and the Chinese Room cannot have any successful referential semantics. For example, if the Chinese interlocutor were asking the Room about her fine new shirt, the Room would hardly have anything pertinent to say. For a program to display human-like intelligence, it must be embodied in a robot with human-like sensors and effectors. Searle, on the other hand, thinks that intelligence and consciousness are necessary for each other (Searle, 1992). Functionalists would agree, although for different reasons. Functionalism asserts that the mind, including conscious states, depend only upon the biological functions implemented by the brain, including information-processing functions. Any system, wet or silicon, that implements those functions will, therefore, necessarily have a mind and consciousness (Dennett, 1991). This amounts to the view that strong AI, while strictly speaking false, can be largely salvaged by requiring that our computer programs be supplemented by bodies that support human-like behavior and semantics. The result will be a conscious, intelligent artifact, eventually. Assuming this to be so, let us reconsider the ethics of the matter.

IS AI ETHICAL?

Weizenbaum claimed that AI research is unethical. His reasons were not simply his personal despair at finding stupid AI programs pronounced smart. His argument (crudely put) was one that has repeatedly found favor in Hollywood: that once we build a genuine AI, it will necessarily be intelligent and autonomous; that these AIs will lack human motivations and be incomprehensible to us, as well as any large computer program must be; in other words, these AIs will be out of control and dangerous. The danger in science fiction is frequently manifested in a war between robots and their would-be masters.

It may be difficult to take Hollywood and its arguments seriously. But the potential dangers of an uncontrolled AI can be, and have been, put more sharply (Bostrom, 2002). The strong AI thesis, in effect, claims that if we were to enumerate all possible Turing machines from simpler to more complex, we would find machines that are isomorphic to you and me somewhere early in the list, one isomorphic to Einstein a little farther out, and perhaps the yet-to-be-encountered Andromedans quite a lot farther out. But there is no end to the list of Turing machines and no end to their complexity. Humans have various corporeal restrictions to their potential intelligence: their brains must fit through the birth canal, subsequent maturation can last only so long, and so forth. Although incorporated AIs will also face some restrictions, such as the speed of light, these are not nearly so severe. In short, once the first AI is built, there is no obvious limit to what further degrees of intelligence can be built. Indeed, once the first AI is built, it can be replicated a great number of times and put to the problem of improving itself. Each improvement can be applied immediately to each existing robot, with the likely result that improvements will come thick and fast, and then thicker and faster, and so on. In what has been dubbed the technological singularity, we can expect that roughly as soon as there is a legitimate AI, there shall also be a SuperIntelligence (SI) (Good, 1965; Vinge, 1993; Bostrom, 1998). An uncontrollable SI would be a very serious threat indeed. If such is the prospect, there can be little doubt that AI research is unethical.

A generic counterargument applies to any technology. Richard Stallman has famously argued that software will be free (a paraphrase of Stallman, 1992). Whether or not that is so, it seems clear that knowledge "will" be free: once a scientific research program appears feasible, it is already too late to stop it. If one party refuses to proceed in developing a technology, be it nuclear weaponry, therapeutic cloning, or AI, that will simply leave the opening for others to get there first. Unless your motives are unethical, it cannot be unethical actually to get there first, barring some verifiable agreement by all parties to restrain themselves. So, it behooves us to consider whether a controllable AI might be possible.

CONTROLLING AI

Isaac Asimov got there first. Asimov wrote a lengthy series of robot stories in which a unifying theme was his "Three Laws of Robotics" (Asimov, 1950):

1. A robot may not harm a human being, or, through inaction, allow a human being to come to harm.
2. A robot must obey the orders given to it by human beings except where such orders would conflict with the First Law.
3. A robot must protect its own existence, as long as such protection does not conflict with the First or Second Law.

Unfortunately, many of his plots revolved around the ambiguities and conflicts arising between these laws (even leading to the introduction of a "zeroeth" law, that a robot may not injure humanity as a whole, etc.). Guaranteeing that incorporating such laws in the psychological foundations of our robots would not give rise to problems, and potentially to loss of control, would require a semantic sophistication that is currently beyond human capacity.

The failure of such laws to maintain control is one kind of difficulty. But there is another. If you reread the laws in the language of some fascists, substituting "subhuman" for "robot," this will immediately become apparent: Asimov's laws have nothing to do with promoting ethical behavior; they are all about the

selfish protection of human interests. If we were talking about the development of any neutral technology, which would be used for good or ill depending solely upon the motivations of its users, then this narrow focus would be natural. But, as we have seen, it is at least arguable that if AIs are achievable at all, they will be autonomous, with an independent set of motivations, and perhaps consciousness. They will more likely be artificial moral agents than neutral slabs of technology. If we wish them to respect our rights, we will likely have to respect theirs first.

FUTURE TRENDS

If we take the possibility of creating an artificial moral agent seriously, a possible resolution of the ethical problems readily suggests itself: we can build artificial agents which are capable of moral behavior and which *choose* to act ethically. The possibility of constructing moral agents has received attention recently (e.g., Johnson, 2007; Floridi & Sanders, 2004).

Allen, Varner, and Zinser (2000) raise the question: when could we know we have created an artificial moral agent? They propose using a *moral Turing Test*. When one of our creations has passed it, we will have created an artifact that is morally indistinguishable from some (normal) humans. Human history suggests that this test may be passed too easily to be of interest to us. In particular, if we are creating a being whose intellect considerably exceeds our own, we are unlikely to be satisfied unless its ethics also considerably exceed our own.

Of course, how to achieve such a goal depends upon what the right account of ethics may be. There are three leading types of normative ethics: *deontic systems* with rules of behavior (such as Moses' laws or, were they designed to be ethical, Asimov's laws); *virtue ethics,* which identifies certain moral characteristics (e.g., honor, integrity) which moral behavior should exemplify; and *consequentialism* (including utilitarianism; Smart, 1973), which identifies moral value not from intrinsic properties of the action, but from its consequences. The debate between these views has been raging for more than 2,000 years and is unlikely to be resolved now. A practical response for an artificial ethics project is to consider which of these is amenable to implementation. The difficulties with Asimov's laws show us that implementing any deontic ethics requires us to first solve our problems with natural language understanding, which is effectively the same as solving our problems with designing an AI in general. But our main problem here is how to build ethics into our AI, and this must be solved before we have created that AI. Similar difficulties apply to virtue ethics.

In the last few decades, there has been considerable improvement in automated decision analysis using Bayesian networks, finding many hundreds of useful applications (Howard & Matheson, 1984; Jensen, 2001). These networks provide relatively efficient means of automating decision making so as to maximize expected utility in an uncertain world, which is one leading theory of what it means to act rationally (Russell & Norvig, 2003). This technology, or rather some future extension of it, promises to enable autonomous robots implementing arbitrary utility structures (motivations, goals), without the necessity of resolving all possible ambiguities or conflicts we might find in rules of any natural language.

Thus, for example, we might enforce a non-linguistic correlate of Asimov's laws upon such robots. However, if the robots are indeed autonomous seats of moral agency, this could be no more ethical than imposing such rules of enslavement upon any subpopulation of humans. A more promising approach is to build the robots so that they are ethical. As agents, they must have some utility structure. But it need not be one solely concerned with maximizing their private utility (implementing egoism); instead, it could be utilitarian, maximizing expected utilities across the class of all moral agents, in which case the well-being of humans, separately and collectively, would be one of their concerns.

There are many difficulties in the way of a project to implement an artificial utilitarian agent. Allen et al. (2000) argue that this artificial morality project requires computing all the expected consequences (and so utilities) of actions and that this is intractable, since there is no temporal or spatial limit to such consequences; further, any horizon imposed on the calculation would have to be arbitrary. But this objection ignores that utilitarianism advocates maximizing *expected* utility, not *absolute* utility. No reasonable ethics can demand actions (or calculations) beyond our abilities; what we expect to arise from our actions is always limited by our abilities to formulate expectations. And those limits fix a horizon on our expectations which is the opposite of arbitrary. Nevertheless, the history of ethics suggests that the most intransigent difficulties in

the way of the project will be the theoretical debates around its value, rather than the practical problem of developing and applying the technology.

CONCLUSION

With all of our technologies, there are serious moral issues about their value, and especially about the value of the uses to which we put them. If those uses are likely to be unethical, then the ethics of those developing them can be put into doubt, at least if there is any alternative. In AI matters are even worse: since AIs will be autonomous actors, and since once they arise they will rapidly exceed our abilities, they may put *themselves* to unethical uses. However, there is a real option of designing them to be ethical actors in the first place, as well as a real technology to support such an effort. If realized, then our robotic offspring, as well as their future descendants, need not be feared. Thus, we might find our robotic grandchildren caring for their senescent grandparents one day, without either one dominating the other.

REFERENCES

Allen, C., Varner, G., & Zinser, J. (2000). Prolegomena to any future artificial moral agent. *Journal of Experimental and Theoretical Artificial Intelligence, 12*, 251-261.

Asimov, I. (1950). *I, robot.* Gnome Press.

Bostrom, N. (1998). How long before superintelligence? *International Journal of Futures Studies, 2.*

Bostrom, N. (2002). Existential risks: Analyzing human extinction scenarios and related hazards. *Journal of Evolution and Technology, 9.*

Dennett, D. (1991). *Consciousness explained.* Boston: Little, Brown and Company.

Dreyfus, H. (1965). *Alchemy and artificial intelligence.* Technical Report P.3244, RAND Corporation, USA.

Dreyfus, H. (1994). *What computers still can't do* (3rd ed.). Cambridge, MA: MIT Press.

Floridi, L., & Sanders, J.W. (2004). On the morality of artificial agents. *Minds and Machines, 14*, 349-379.

Franklin, S., & Garzon, M. (1991). Neural computability. In O. Omidvar (Ed.), *Progress in neural networks.* Norwood, NJ: Ablex.

Good, I.J. (1965). Speculations concerning the first ultraintelligent machine. In *Advances in computers* (vol. 6, pp. 31-88). Academic Press.

Harnad, S. (1989). Minds, machines and Searle. *Journal of Theoretical and Experimental Artificial Intelligence, 1,* 5-25.

Howard, R., & Matheson, J. (1984). Influence diagrams. In R. Howard & J. Matheson (Eds.), *Readings on the principles and applications of decision analysis.* Menlo Park, CA: Strategic Decisions Group.

Jensen, F. (2001). *Bayesian networks and decision graphs.* New York: Springer.

Johnson, D.G. (2007). Computer systems: Moral entities but not moral agents. *Ethics and Information Technology.*

Korb, K.B. (1996). Symbolicism and connectionism: AI back at a join point. In D.L. Dowe, K.B. Korb, & J.J. Oliver (Eds.), *Information, statistics and induction in science* (pp. 247- 257). World Scientific.

Russell, S., & Norvig, P. (2003). *Artificial intelligence: A modern approach* (2nd ed.). Englewood Cliffs, NJ: Prentice Hall.

Searle, J. (1980). Minds, brains, and programs. *Behavioral and Brain Sciences, 3,* 417-457.

Searle, J.R. (1992). *The rediscovery of the mind.* Cambridge, MA: MIT Press.

Smart, J.J.C. (1973). An outline of a system of utilitarian ethics. In J.J.C. Smart & B. Williams (Eds.), *Utilitarianism: For and against.* Cambridge: Cambridge University Press.

Stallman, R. (1992/2002). Why software should be free. In *Free software, free society: Selected essays of Richard M. Stallman.* Free Software Foundation.

Turing, A. (1950). Computing machinery and intelligence. *Mind, 59,* 433-460.

Vinge, V. (1993). The coming technological singularity. *Whole Earth Review.*

Weizenbaum, J. (1966). ELIZA—a computer program for the study of natural language communication between men and machines. *Communications of the ACM, 9,* 36-45.

Weizenbaum, J. (1976). *Computer power and human reason.* New York: W.H. Freeman.

KEY TERMS

Artificial Intelligence: (1) The research field which investigates methods of improving the apparent intelligence of computer programs, including such subfields as planning, visual processing, pattern recognition, natural language understanding, and machine learning. (2) A computer system or robot which has achieved human-level intelligence (or greater intelligence), displayed across some wide range of behaviors.

Artificial Neural Network (ANN): A computational method based upon a simple model of biological neural processing.

Bayesian Network: A technology for automating probabilistic reasoning, commonly augmented with decision nodes to support decision making.

Egoism: The ethical view which holds that one ought to do what is in one's own self-interest.

Functionalism: The thesis that mental states (including conscious states) are identifiable strictly in terms of the functional roles they play, including information-processing roles. It follows that there may be many possible ways to realize these functions; in particular, both biological and silicon realizations may be possible.

Moral Agent: An agent that is capable of moral behavior, implying the ability to behave both morally and immorally.

Moral Turing Test: A test of an artificial agent's ability to behave in ethically demanding tasks in a way indistinguishable from some (normal) humans.

SuperIntelligence: A computer system or robot which has achieved greater-than-human-level intelligence, displayed across some wide range of behaviors.

Turing Test: Proposes the indistinguishability of computer verbal behavior from human verbal behavior as a criterion of intelligence.

Utilitarianism: The ethical view which holds that one ought to do what is in the global interest of some class of agents.

Fair Use

Pasi Tyrväskylä
University of Jyväskylä, Finland

INTRODUCTION

Intellectual property legislation has continuously redefined the balance between the interests of stakeholders, especially the authors of creative works, and the users of the works. The contemporary balance of legal, technical, social, political, and economical interests has typically been formulated into the copyright law stating the limits of the exclusive rights of the authors of creative works and the exceptions to the exclusive rights, defining the fair use of the works by other stakeholders. National legislation reflects the changes in the surrounding society, its technical development, and so forth, but global technical development and international treaties have harmonized the laws and user expectations to some extent.

The concept of fair use cannot be fully understood from a single perspective, such as piracy, freedom of speech, or different legal systems. The purpose of this article is to give the reader a balanced overall understanding of the aspects impacting evolution of fair use in the digital environments. The next section provides a short history of copyright developed in a dialogue between the authors, content users, national governments, and international bodies. A review of the contemporary laws in the United States and in Europe follows, and then the focus turns to new technology as an enabler of content use, and approaches are reviewed to adopt fair use in this context. The next section elaborates technical protection means, followed by a review of the means to incorporate fair use to them. Finally, the article concludes that defining the legal limits of fair use needs to be renegotiated for each new technical context created based on balancing the interests of the parties.

BACKGROUND

In general, fair use refers to the exceptions of exclusiveness of the copyright, either as a general concept or as defined by the national law. Thus we need to have a closer look at copyright and the history of copyright prior to elaborating the aspects and trends of fair use.

Copyright refers to the exclusive right of authors to exploit their works or authorize others to do so. Authors may exercise this control by authorizing or prohibiting others from using the work. An author can permit an orchestra to play the song composed or deny printing copies of the book written. The rights include both economic and moral rights. For example, the author can charge fees from the users and deny presenting the work in a context the author considers inappropriate, for example, in certain TV commercials.

Individual authors may manage their rights themselves or pass over the responsibility to a collective society. Typically the collective societies monitor the use of the works, negotiate with the potential users on the terms and fees to use the works, license the rights to the users, collect fees, and distribute the fees to the right owners. Right owners may also license the rights for, for example, one concert or a TV commercial themselves or sign a contract, which transfers exclusive rights to their works to a publisher or a record company.

The historical development of copyright started with the authors of drama literature writing plays for theatre. Often the authors did not get compensation from the theaters presenting their works, especially from those in faraway cities. To remedy the situation, they established Bureau de Légistlation Dramatique, the first society to promulgate authors' rights in 1777 in France. Authors of musical works followed in 1850 by establishing Soci'et'e des Auteurs, Compositeurs et 'Editeurs de Musicque (SACEM). Similar societies were established at the end of the nineteenth century and in the early twentieth century in nearly all European countries, and the national legislations acknowledged widely the authors' rights under the concept of copyright (Ficsor, 2003).

Authors' societies established CISAC as an international organization in 1926. CISAC started negotiations with international representatives of other stakeholders (e.g., IFPI, the International Federation of the Phonographic Industry). These long negotiation processes were mostly led by the World Intellectual Property Organization (WIPO), including the United Nations UNESCO Universal Copyright Convention (UCC) and the WIPO Berne Convention laying ground for international intellectual property management systems in the 1970s. In the mid-1980s the work in Paris, Geneva, and Sydney meetings addressed new challenges brought by new technology, such as use of computers to store and retrieve copyrighted works, cable TV broadcasting, personal copies enabled by tape recorders, and satellite broadcasting. The process resulted in "Internet treaties," most importantly the WIPO Copyright Treaty (WCT) and the WIPO Performances and Phonograms Treaty (WTTP), which laid the foundation to the continental and national legislations. These include the European copyright directive (EUCD) (EU2001/29/EC, 2001), under implementation in the member states and the Digital Millennium Copyright Act (DMCA), adapted in the U.S. code of law defining the limits of fair use in the United States (U.S. Code, 2000).

FAIR USE IN LEGAL CONTEXT

As a general concept, *fair use* refers to legally protected right of people to use content based on exceptions and limitations, in copyright laws, to the exclusive right of authors to exploit their works. Sometimes fair use is also thought to cover uses that users expect to be fair although they are not included in law, here referred to as *fair use expectations*. The national regulations on copyright are harmonizing due to general willingness to comply with the WTC and the same technical changes impacting all nations. However, the definition of and terms used for fair use vary. We will now elaborate on the U.S. and the EU legal context to some extent.

The right to use a copyrighted work without a license from the rights holder is included both in the U.S. code of law and in the EUDC stating the requirements for national laws. The specific term "fair use" can be found in the U.S. Code (2000), while EUCD uses terms such as "exception or limitation ..." to copyright or "in national law" (EU2001/29/EC, 2001).

Use of copyrighted content for purposes such as criticism, comment, news reporting, and teaching is not considered as infringement of copyright, but as fair use in the U.S. law. In most EU countries the following exceptions are recognized: private copy or other private use, parody, quotation, use of a work for scientific or teaching purposes, news reporting, library privileges, and needs of the administration of justice and public policy (Dusollier, 2002).

In the U.S. the judges determine only afterwards if an unauthorized use of copyrighted work was fair use or not. Any licensing in advance will remove any fair use considerations afterwards. In case of evaluating fairness of use afterwards, the judges' determination should include the following four broad factors on a case-by-case basis:

- the nature of the use (e.g., commercial or non-profit),
- the nature of the original work,
- the portion of the original work used, and
- the effect of the use on the market or value of the work.

Rather than treating fair use as a defense to copyright infringement, as in the U.S., the national law tradition in most European countries provides a list of circumstances where the author is not allowed to enforce his or her rights. Also the EUCD follows this approach and aims at enforcing service providers to support fair use in the Internet environment (Article 6, Paragraph 4 in EU2001/29/EC, 2001):

"In the absence of voluntary measures taken by rightholders [the Member States should] ensure that rightholders make available to the beneficiary of an exception or limitation provided for in national law...that the beneficiary has legal access to the protected work or subject-matter concerned."

FAIR USE IN THE DIGITAL ENVIRONMENT

New technology development has been one of the drivers of the WIPO process and national copyright law redefinitions, and has thus also impacted user expectations on use of copyrighted works as such as well as fair use of the works. Thirty years ago no one could anticipate that songs could be copied from an LP record to a black-and-white TV set or to a phone. Now users expect ease of use while copying songs from CDs to mobile phones, to TV set-top boxes, or to PVR/DVD equipment. This has extended the scope of expected fair use, namely personal use, which is widely recognized, especially in the North-European legal tradition. This kind of personal copying is unauthorized by the copyright holders, but legal according to several national legislations.

According to EUCD, Paragraph 4 (EU2001/29/EC, 2001), fair use of content should be made available only to beneficiaries of the exceptions who have legal access to the protected work—that is those who purchase the product—rather than granting free access to all users to enjoy fair use, as in the U.S.. Unlike in the U.S., the EUDC also requires "fair compensation" to be paid to the copyright owners in some cases of fair use. This compensation is typically collected as media fees (e.g., for VCR tapes) and fees for recording and reproduction equipment (e.g., MP3 players, scanners, and photocopiers).

Inexpensive computers and Internet connections have recently enabled easy access to copyrighted content across peer-to-peer (P2P) networks. The majority of *unauthorized copying* takes place as illegal copying of works through P2P networks, representing a form of digital piracy. At present, the majority of Internet communications is copying of digital content. Only a small percentage of music and movies copied through the Internet consists of authorized purchases of digital content. Internet purchases accounted for 5% of music purchases in 2005 (Kennedy, 2006). In some cases the works are distributed for free, to gain visibility in the audience; in some cases the illegal copying will increase the sales of the works later on, while the copying of contemporary hit songs and movies will cause loss to the record companies, the artists, and the authors.

There are several approaches to adopt the legal framework to this situation, each with different balance in between the stakeholders' interests and with different problems. *Flat-fee systems* (media fees, levies) have been seen as a means for collecting copyright fees for rights holders both from legal and illegal unauthorized users. However, these systems have several shortcomings: they take control of the moral and material rights from the copyright holders, they bear no relationship to the commercial value of the reproductions enforcing flat pricing of the works, they lead to double payments for works bought legally, and so on (Ulbricht, 2003). Use of *non-voluntary licenses* has similar problems: fees should be collected from all users by some means, and use statistics of works should be collected to distribute the remuneration to the rights holders according to use of the works. The Creative Commons (*www.creativecommons.org*) approach is to make a standardized licensing contract enabling wide and free use of the works. It takes strictly the position of users of the works, as it does not give any material compensation to the authors and other copyright holders while emphasizing the free availability of all content in the information society. Record companies and movie companies have tried to enforce existing copyright laws by suing individual users distributing unauthorized material. So far the music industry has taken some 20,000 legal actions against illegal file-sharers in 17 countries (Kennedy, 2006). Yet another approach is the use of technical protection to exert control over the copying.

TECHNICAL PROTECTION MEANS AND DIGITAL RIGHTS MANAGEMENT

The term *technical protection means* (TPM) is commonly used in regulation to refer to techniques used to avoid uncontrolled and unauthorized access and copying of digital content, and to enforce legal license practices by technical means. Typical technical means include encryption of the content and associating a digital license with the content. Protected content can be distributed through CD records, the Internet, or digital audio and video broadcasting. Examples include cable TV scramblers, copy-protection on CDs, and DRM systems on PCs.

Digital rights management (DRM) deals with controlling and managing digital rights over intellectual property (Iannella, 2001; Rosenblatt, Trippe, & Mooney, 2002). Recently, it has broadened its scope from content protection to description, identification, trading, protecting, monitoring, and tracking of rights over tangible or intangible assets in various electronic commerce systems. This emerging business-to-business use of DRM is less visible to customers that are mostly concerned with the use of encryption for content protection and steganography (e.g., digital watermarks and fingerprints) to track content in delivery of digital goods.

A *digital license* identifies the content product and the authorized user, and describes the rights the user has to the digital resource in a computer-readable format using some digital rights expression (or description) language (REL/DREL/RDL), such as ODRL (Open Digital Rights Language) and DPRL (Digital Property Rights Language)/XrML, which describes the rights given for the user and the related constraints and conditions. In this context, it is more relevant to speak about *use rights*—the rights licensed to the user—rather than copyrights.

The legal frameworks in the U.S. and in the EU have recognized the position of technical protection means. The circumvention of TPM/DRM systems is prohibited. However, as purchase of digital licensed content creates a contract between the seller and the user, the license terms and the TPM/DRM systems used can violate fair use and fair use expectations of the user unless fair use is designed into such systems.

APPROACHES TO FAIR USE DESIGN

Fair use design refers to designs and designing of systems to enable fair use of copyrighted work, especially where DRM systems or TPM in general are used. Concern has been raised where personal copying and other fair use can be achieved without the circumvention of DRM systems (Dusollier, 2002; Liu, Safavi-Naini, & Sheppard, 2003).

In the U.S. the legally permitted fair uses cannot be transformed into technical systems operating without human intervention (Erickson, 2003; Felten, 2003; Mulligan & Burstein, 2002). Literally, the term "fair use design" is, as such, a contradiction in the context of the U.S. law, where a judge determines only afterwards whether the use of copyrighted content should be considered fair use or not. In practice, U.S. Supreme Court decisions will form the guideline evolving over the years making it quite impossible to create a DRM system that would enable all fair uses in advance (Erickson, 2003; Felten, 2003; Mulligan & Burstein, 2002; von Lohmann, 2002), at least without some level of human intervention.

The approach of EUCD is that the users should not need to break the digital lock-up for content protected by DRM to gain access to content based on fair use exceptions, as in the U.S. Rather, the rights holders should provide fair use by design (Dusollier, 2002) enabling use of the content. This can be embedded in the technical design of a TPM/DRM system or in the contractual design of the business model. This bold intent of EUDC has been undermined by the rights holders' ability to overcome the obligations by contractual means or by providing mainly highly priced on-demand services (Dusollier, 2002), which can even be fully automated.

As we employ here the general concept of fair use rather than the strict definition of the U.S. law, also technical approaches providing some level of fair use are of interest for us, even though any practical system would probably be both too permissive and too restrictive (Cohen, 2003).

Fox and LaMaccia (2003) suggest creating subsets of fair uses—*safe harbors*—that are allowed without the explicit permission of copyright holders. Messerges and Dabbish (2003) propose a set of equipment to form a private domain called a "family domain" within which content can be shared freely. Erickson (2003) suggests a DRM architecture for approximating fair use by introducing human intervention through a *third-party license-granting authority* to the technical DRM context. This rights escrow server containing a DRM license generator would complement a license server.

Tyrväinen (2005a) proposes use of *product copy managers* (PCMs), which enable acquiring free digital licenses to new machines by using templates delivered with the digital content purchased: personal copy templates for personal copies, student templates for university students, and so forth, according to the fair use exceptions defined in the local legal context. With these means an automated PCM would be able to gain additional information about the process context, enabling a higher portion of the fair use cases to be handled without costly human intervention. This approach is based on tracking the product copy with a privacy-preserving *delivery chain tracking* technique, which can also be applied to copyright-respecting *peer-to-peer marketing* (Tyrväinen, Järvi, & Luoma, 2004) and to new business models for libraries (Tyrväinen, 2005b).

Sobel (2003) proposes the adoption of a *digital retailer model*, where Internet service providers would serve as digital retailers. They would monitor watermarks in content distributed to consumers and collect royalties for the first downloading of any identified content downloaded based on the watermarks embedded in registered digital works. As only the first download would be charged, fair use treatment would apply on each user account. This approach could additionally be enhanced to prevent spamming, but it has no means to identify content transmitted from one user to another in an encrypted format.

Other approaches related to fair use and privacy in DRM systems include the Shibboleth architecture described by Martin et al. (2002), as well as the use dongle identification with trusted third parties (Knopf, 2005) and a locker server providing a key management service for the customer (Garnet & Sander, 2002).

CONCLUSION AND FUTURE TRENDS

Technological development will continue and will bring with it new situations, where the balance of authors' exclusive copyright, users' rights, and rights of other stakeholders will have to be redefined once again. The volume of Internet music purchases tripled from 2004 to 2005 (Kennedy, 2006), but the contemporary wild unauthorized and illegal copying of digital content will still impose an extra load to Internet traffic for several years. Flat-fee systems and non-voluntary licensing seem not to gain momentum. Contemporary TPM/DRM systems are still rather immature and far from user friendly. They also suffer from interoperability problems, making it difficult to move content in between devices and systems. It takes still some time for the commercial TPM/DRM systems to adopt the research results on fair use design and to reach consensus on interoperability.

It seems likely that a major part of transactions on digital content will be split between a reducing volume of unauthorized and illegal access using peer-to-peer networks and an increasing volume of authorized content purchases. The content purchases will mainly take place, with less user-hostile next-generation TPM/DRM systems embedded in phones and other equipment. A minor portion of free content will be licensed using Creative Commons and other open licensing agreements or delivered though promotional distribution channels.

In this environment the role of fair use must be defined in each context separately. In peer-to-peer networks where copyright is not respected, no fair use exists either. However, fair use can be designed into copyright-respecting peer-to-peer networks and into TPM/DRM systems. The approaches with open access licenses usually embed fair use in the licensing terms.

As a research area, fair use requires a multidisciplinary approach. User expectations, new technical means, economical considerations, as well as social, political, and historical considerations are needed to complement each other to form a holistic view to the domain. This continuously evolving view and political decisions will guide the development of globally harmonizing laws.

REFERENCES

Cohen, J.E. (2003). DRM and privacy. *Communications of the ACM, 46*(4), 47-49.

Dusollier, S. (2002). Fair use by design in the European copyright directive of 2001: An empty promise. *Proceedings of the 12th Conference on Computers Freedom & Piracy* (pp. 12-25).

Erickson, J.S. (2003). Fair use, DRM, and trusted computing. *Communications of the ACM, 46*(4), 34-39.

EU2001/29/EC. (2001). Directive 2001/29/EC of the European Parliament and of the Council of 22 May 2001 on the harmonisation of certain aspects of copyright and related rights in the information society. *Official Journal, L*(167), 0010-0019.

Felten, E.W. (2003). A skeptical view of DRM and fair use. *Communications of the ACM, 46*(4), 57-59.

Ficsor, M. (2003). *Collective management of copyright and related rights.* Geneva: WIPO.

Fox, B.L., & LaMacchia, B.A. (2003). Encouraging recognition of fair uses in DRM systems. *Communications of the ACM, 46*(4), 61-63.

Garnet, N., & Sander, T. (2002). What DRM can and cannot do…and what it is or isn't doing today. *Proceedings of the 12th Conference on Computers, Freedom & Piracy* (p. 6).

Iannella, R. (2001). Digital rights management (DRM) architectures. *D-Lib Magazine, 7*(6).

Kennedy, J. (2006). *Music—a key driver of the digital economy.* London: IFPI.

Knopf, D. (2005). How to implement copyright exceptions in DRM systems. *INDICARE Monitor, 2*(1).

Liu, Q., Safavi-Naini, R., & Sheppard, N.P. (2003). Digital rights management for content distribution. *Proceedings of the Australasian Information Security Workshop 2003* (vol. 21, pp. 49-58).

Martin, M., Agnew, G., Kuhlman, D.L., McNair, J.H., Rhodes, W.A., & Tipton, R. (2002). Federated digital rights management. *D-Lib Magazine, 8*(7), 9.

Messerges, T.S., & Dabbish, E.A. (2003). Digital rights management in a 3G mobile phone and beyond. *Proceedings of the 2003 ACM Workshop on Digital Rights Management* (pp. 27-38).

Mulligan, D., & Burstein, A. (2002). Implementing copyright limitations in rights expression languages. *Proceedings of the 2002 ACM Workshop on Digital Rights Management* (p. 15).

Rosenblatt, B., Trippe, B., & Mooney, S. (2002). *Digital rights management: Business and technology.* New York: M&T Books.

Sobel, L.S. (2003). DRM as an enabler of business models: ISPs as digital retailers. *Berkeley Technology Law Journal, 18*(2), 667-695.

Tyrväinen, P. (2005a). Concepts and a design for fair use and privacy in DRM. *D-Lib Magazine, 11*(2).

Tyrväinen, P. (2005b). Fair use licensing in library context. A privacy-preserving lending service with a revenue sharing business model. *INDICARE Monitor, 2*(2), 15-19.

Tyrväinen, P., Järvi, J., & Luoma, E. (2004). Peer-to-peer marketing for content products—combining digital rights management and multilevel marketing. *Proceedings of the IADIS International Conference on E-Commerce 2004* (p. 8).

Ulbricht, J. (2003). Digital rights management and the future of collective licensing. In R. Auf der Maur & M. Jacobson (Eds.), *Music unleashed: Legal implications of mobile music distribution* (1st ed., pp. 227-237). Apeldoorn, The Netherlands: MAKLU.

U.S. Code. (2000). *Fair use.* United States Code, Section 107, Chapter 1, Title 17, Law U.S.C. 107.

von Lohmann, F. (2002). Fair use and digital rights management: Preliminary thoughts on the (irreconcilable?) tension between them. *Proceedings of the Conference on Computers, Freedom & Privacy 2002* (p. 9).

KEY TERMS

Copyright: The exclusive right of authors to exploit their works or authorize others to do so.

Digital Rights Management (DRM): Controlling and managing digital rights over intellectual property. DRM includes description, identification, trading, protection (i.e., TPM), monitoring, and tracking of rights over tangible or intangible assets in digital computer systems.

Fair Use (Generic Concept): Fair dealing, fair treatment. Legally protected right to use content based on exceptions and limitations to the exclusive right of authors to exploit their works as defined in copyright laws. Sometimes fair use is also used to cover uses that users expect to be fair although they are not included in law, here referred to as fair use expectation.

Fair Use (U.S. Code): A defense to copyright infringement determined afterwards to be fair use based on the nature of the use (e.g., commercial or non-profit), the nature of the original work, the portion of the work used, and the effect of the use on the market or value of the work.

Fair Use Design: An information systems design implementing the fair use concept, especially in the context of TPM/DRM systems.

Related Right: Neighboring right. Droits voisins (Fr). The rights of performers, producers of phonograms, and broadcasting organizations related to a copyrighted work.

Technical Protection Means (TPM): Technical means to protect content from unauthorized use. Examples: cable TV scramblers, copy-protection on CD disks, DRM systems on PC.

Use Right: One of the set of rights licensed to a copy of a work to a purchaser of a digital content product. Described in a license agreement, but may also be enforced by a TPM/DRM system.

Federal Information Security Law

Michael J. Chapple
University of Notre Dame, USA

Charles R. Crowell
University of Notre Dame, USA

INTRODUCTION

The American legal system, along with many of its counterparts around the globe, is only beginning to grapple with the legal challenges of the information age. The past decade has witnessed a multitude of new laws and regulations seeking to address these challenges and provide a common framework for the legal and technical professions. Those charged with information security responsibilities face a myriad of complex and often vague requirements. In this article, we establish a four-level taxonomy for federal information security laws and explore the major components of each level.

BACKGROUND

Chawki (2005, p. 7), in a study of computer crime law, points out that the traditional definition of a computer crime as any crime that involves "the knowledge of computer technology for its perpetration, investigation, or prosecution" is far too broad for practical application. In this era of electronic organization, virtually *every* crime involves computer technology at some point in the investigative process. For example, a common burglary should not be considered a computer crime merely because the booking officer entered data on the crime into a department information system. Similarly, the fact that the criminal looked up driving directions on the Internet should not make a bank robbery a computer crime.

We seek to clarify these issues by creating a general taxonomy of information security laws. Our taxonomy includes the following four levels:

- **Intellectual property laws** protect the rights of authors, inventors and creators of other intellectual works.

- **Computer-focused crime laws** define transgressions and applicable punishments for offenses where the use of a computer is intrinsic to the crime.
- **Computer-related crime laws** are those laws that involve the use of a computer but where the criminal activity is not defined by the use of a computer. This category also includes those laws that require the use of computers to assist in the investigation of a crime.
- **Industry-specific laws** do not apply to society as a whole, but rather govern particular industries and are typically focused on protecting the confidentiality, integrity, and/or availability of personal information.

In the remainder of this article, we seek to explore this taxonomy in further detail. While the taxonomy may be applied to any body of law, due to space constraints this article limits the discussion to federal laws in the United States. A myriad of state and local laws, as well as the laws of other nations, may also be classified under this taxonomy.

It is also important to note that many information security crimes are prosecuted under traditional laws, rather than the specific laws presented in this taxonomy. Smith (2005) points out two examples of this: the charging of an individual with a felony offense for accessing an unprotected wireless network and a school district's charge of criminal trespass against 13 students who accessed laptops issued to them with an administrative password that was taped to the bottom of the machines.

INTELLECTUAL PROPERTY LAW

The legal principles protecting the rights of owners of creative works date back several centuries. As our society shifts from an industrial economy to a knowledge economy, these laws become increasingly important, as they protect the very essence of our economic engine. These intellectual property laws are critical to any information security program, as they provide the legal basis for protecting the intellectual property rights of individuals and organizations.

Copyrights

Copyrights protect any original work of authorship from unauthorized duplication or distribution. The Copyright Act (1976) defines eight categories that constitute covered works. One of these categories, literary works, is broadly interpreted to include almost any written work. This category has traditionally been used to include computer software, Web content, and a variety of other works of direct interest to information security professionals.

Copyright protection is automatic upon the creation of a work. For works created after 1978, copyright protection lasts for 70 years after the death of the last surviving author.

Trademarks

Trademark law protects words, phrases, and designs that identify the products or services of a firm. The essential characteristic of a trademark is that it must uniquely distinguish the trademark holder's goods or services from those of other providers. Therefore, trademarks may not be simply descriptive of the product or service, but must contain the element of uniqueness. For example, it would not be possible to gain trademark protection on the term "blue automobile," while it may be possible to gain protection for the term "Blue Streak Automobiles."

Trademark protection is afforded by the Lanham Act (1946). The U.S. Patent and Trademark Office grants registrations with an initial duration of 10 years and the option to renew.

Patents

Patents protect inventions, processes, and designs. They grant the inventor substantial protection in the form of exclusive rights to the patented concept. To protect against the abuse of this privilege, the U.S. Patent and Trademark Office strictly governs the issuance of patents. The three requirements for patent protection are that the invention must be novel, useful, and non-obvious. Patents granted for inventions or processes are valid for 17 years, while design patents are valid for 14 years (Patent Act, 1952).

Trade Secrets

The Economic Espionage Act of 1996 makes it illegal to steal, misappropriate, duplicate, or knowingly receive or possess a trade secret without appropriate permission. Trade secrets include any information that "derives independent economic value, actual or potential, from not being generally known to, and not being readily ascertainable by proper means by the public" and is the subject of "reasonable measures to keep such information secret" (Economic Espionage Act, 1996).

When designing an information security program, it is essential to recognize that trade secrets are defined by the confidentiality protection afforded them. If an organization fails to take reasonable efforts to maintain the confidentiality of a trade secret, this protection is lost. This is a major departure from patent protection, which requires public disclosure of the invention. Public disclosure of a trade secret nullifies the protection afforded to that secret and effectively releases it into the public domain. Unlike patents, however, trade secrets enjoy indefinite protection under the law.

Digital Millennium Copyright Act

The Digital Millennium Copyright Act (DMCA) of 1998 instituted a number of significant changes in U.S. copyright law designed to accommodate the changing digital environment of the Internet. For example, DMCA offers a safe harbor provision for Internet service providers, absolving them of liability for the infringing acts of customers, provided that they meet certain policy requirements.

COMPUTER-FOCUSED CRIME LAW

Computer-focused crime laws center upon the transgressions and associated punishments when the use of a computer is intrinsic to the crime. When drafting computer-focused crime laws, legislators have the specific intent of outlawing the use of a computer to commit a crime. This category is distinct from the third category, computer-related crime laws, crimes in which the perpetrator may utilize a computer as a support tool. For example, a law prohibiting the use of a computer to eavesdrop on the electronic mail of an individual is a computer-focused crime law. It is the act of using the computer to eavesdrop that is the essential nature of the crime.

Computer Fraud and Abuse Act

Congress originally passed the Computer Fraud and Abuse Act of 2001 in 1986 and later amended it in 1994, 1996, and 2001 to reflect the rapidly changing digital environment. Originally intended to protect data contained on the computers of government agencies and financial institutions, later amendments expanded the scope to include any system involved in interstate commerce (Burke, 2001). Offenses under the Computer Fraud and Abuse Act include gaining unauthorized access to a computer and other crimes.

Electronic Communications Privacy Act

The Electronic Communications Privacy Act (ECPA) of 1986 protects the rights of individuals who become the subject of electronic surveillance by government agencies or other third parties. It includes two separate components: the Wiretap Act and the Stored Communications Act (SCA). The Wiretap Act makes it illegal to intercept (or attempt to intercept) any wire, oral, or electronic communication outside of several specific circumstances identified in the law (such as when approved by a court order or when conducted as part of a quality assurance monitoring effort). The SCA protects communications stored on a computer against unauthorized access or alteration.

COMPUTER-RELATED CRIME LAW

The third category in our taxonomy, computer-related crime laws, includes laws that govern crimes which commonly involve the use of a computer but do not meet the criteria of a computer-focused crime.

Child Pornography Laws

Society has long held the tenet that any molestation or exploitation of children via the creation or distribution of pornography is objectionable and has codified this abhorrence in the law. Unfortunately, the growth of the Internet has led to an increased ability of child pornography traffickers to market their wares with a greater degree of anonymity. This technological shift required a corresponding shift in the law.

The majority of child pornography prosecutions take place under Title 18, Section 2252 of the United States Code (Waters, 1997). This law bans the interstate or foreign transportation of sexually explicit materials that involve minors and was amended specifically to include the transmission of such materials through the use of a computer.

The Child Protection and Obscenity Enforcement Act of 1988 requires that the producers of sexually explicit materials maintain documented records of the ages of all actors and models used in their productions.

Identity Theft and Assumption Deterrence Act

The Identity Theft and Assumption Deterrence Act of 1998 amended federal law to address computer-related elements encompassed by the crime of identity theft. Specifically, Congress outlawed the possession or use of electronic devices, computer hardware, and computer software designed primarily for the production of false identity documents. This act also modified the definition of "means of identification" under the law to include biometric data, electronic identification numbers, addresses or routing codes, and telecommunication identifying information or access codes.

USA PATRIOT Act

The Uniting and Strengthening America by Providing Appropriate Tools Required to Intercept and Obstruct Terrorism (USA PATRIOT) Act enhances the authority granted to the federal government when conducting counterterrorism operations and places additional requirements on service providers. In a legal summary of the act, Iuliano (2003) notes that the critical changes that impact information security programs are that the act:

- exempts voicemail from wiretap requirements, allowing law enforcement officials access through a search warrant
- track and monitor Internet traffic
- increases penalties for computer-focused crimes

Communications Assistance for Law Enforcement Act

Law enforcement agencies have long employed the use of court-ordered wiretaps in investigations to obtain evidence of criminal activity. Up until the past two decades, agents could implement these wiretaps simply by attaching electronic eavesdropping devices to an analog telephone network. The emergence of digital and mobile communications devices increased the technical difficulty of implementing wiretaps and caused Congress to pass the Communications Assistance for Law Enforcement Act (CALEA) of 1994. CALEA requires that communications providers cooperate with law enforcement efforts to obtain wiretaps and to do so in a manner that cannot be detected by the communicating parties.

For 10 years, both the government and telecommunications providers interpreted CALEA to apply to voice communications over telephone networks. In a 2005 notice of proposed rulemaking, the Federal Communications Commission stated that the government intends to apply CALEA to Internet service providers (FCC, 2004). This new interpretation of CALEA raises a number of critical issues as it requires service providers to make substantial equipment investments in order to comply. For example, a coalition of higher education argued to the FCC that the proposed interpretation would impose an unjustified cost burden upon academia (Higher Education Coalition, 2005).

INDUSTRY-SPECIFIC LAW

In addition to the broad laws identified in the previous sections of this taxonomy, there are a number of laws that apply to specific industries, due to their unique access to sensitive data. These include regulations on health care providers, financial institutions, public corporations, and others.

Child Online Privacy Protection Act

The Child Online Privacy Protection Act (COPPA) of 1998 regulates the conduct of business with minors using the Internet. It requires that businesses obtain parental consent before knowingly collecting personal information from children under the age of 13. It also requires that these online services provide parents with any information collected from their children, offers them the opportunity to revoke consent, and demands the removal of such information at any time upon parental request. As pointed out by Isenberg (2000), the cost of compliance with this act may be steep. He illustrates this point through the case of SurfMonkey, a site which reportedly spent over $50,000 on COPPA compliance and instituted a 4,673 word privacy policy.

Health Insurance Portability and Accountability Act

In 1996, Congress enacted the Health Insurance Portability and Accountability Act (HIPAA). Among its many provisions, HIPAA implemented privacy and security requirements for health care providers, health insurance plans, and health information clearinghouses. The Privacy Rule creates a new classification of data: protected health information (PHI), which includes several categories of data related to an individual's health.

The Privacy Rule requires that covered organizations only disclose PHI to authorized individuals and organizations. The HIPAA Security Rule provides five categories of safeguards that must be applied to electronic PHI (ePHI):

- administrative safeguards
- physical safeguards
- technical safeguards
- organizational requirements
- policies and procedures

HIPAA is one of the most comprehensive industry-specific laws, and it provides a full blueprint for the protection of health care data. It also provides specific consequences for knowing and willful violations of the law. Anyone who obtains or discloses PHI in violation of HIPAA may be fined up to $250,000 and imprisoned for up to 10 years.

Gramm-Leach-Bliley Act

Just as HIPAA requires that health care organizations protect the privacy and security of patient records, the Gramm-Leach-Bliley Act (GLBA) of 1999 requires that financial institutions protect the privacy and security of individual financial records. GLBA's Financial Privacy Rule requires that financial institutions provide customers with a copy of the institution's privacy policy. GLBA's Safeguards Rule requires financial institutions to design and implement safeguards to protect customer information.

Sarbanes Oxley Act

The Sarbanes Oxley Act (SOX) of 2002 instituted sweeping reforms in the way public corporations conduct business and report financial results. While the majority of SOX requirements pertain to financial reporting and traditional accounting controls, the law does specifically impact information security. The law requires that institutions implement sufficient information security controls to ensure the validity and reliability of financial reports. The broad applicability of this law to all publicly traded corporations makes it one of the highest impact information security laws of the past decade.

FUTURE TRENDS

As we have demonstrated, the landscape of federal information security law is quite complex and includes a number of overlapping regulations that apply to different industries, technologies, and constituencies. These laws have evolved significantly over the past three decades and matured in their understanding of the unique technological issues posed by the ubiquity of broadband Internet access. We expect that these laws will continue to evolve as technology does and that the United States will eventually adopt a broad-reaching information security and privacy law, similar to the European Union's Data Privacy Directive of 1995.

We also expect to see an increase in the already heightened public awareness of security and privacy issues. As consumers become more familiar with the present and future laws and regulations protecting the privacy and security of their personal data, we will see an increase in judicial activity on these issues. The courts will be used to test the existing enforcement provisions of information security laws in actions brought by the government, and we will also likely see civil liability cases brought by private individuals, individually or as members of a class, seeking damages for negligent activity. This heightened awareness will serve a greater purpose—it will provide the stimulus necessary to bring information security reform to the forefront of industry.

CONCLUSION

It is important to reiterate that this article presents a snapshot in time of a rapidly changing landscape of information security laws. In addition to the laws presented here, a variety of other federal laws impact information security decisions. Further, there are a myriad of state, local, and international laws that govern information security controls. In addition, private contractual relationships often impose specific information security requirements on individual business relationships or broad industries. One example of this is the Payment Card Industry Data Security Standard (Payment Card Industry, 2005), which regulates the security controls for any organization that accepts credit cards.

Information security is a rapidly developing field, and the body of law regulating related activities is evolving with each development. The four-tier taxonomy presented in this article serves as a framework for understanding the context of existing and future information security laws.

REFERENCES

Burke, E. (2001). *The expanding importance of the Computer Fraud and Abuse Act.* Retrieved January 14, 2006, from http://www.gigalaw.com/articles/2001-all/burke-2001-01-all.html

Chawki, M. (2005). A critical look at the regulation of cybercrime. *ICFAI Journal of Cyber Law, 3*(4), 1-55.

Child Online Privacy Protection Act. (1998). 15 USC 6501-6506.

Child Protection and Obscenity Enforcement Act. (1988). 18 USC 2257.

Communications Assistance for Law Enforcement Act. (1994). Public Law 103-414, 108 Stat. 4279.

Computer Fraud and Abuse Act. (1984). 18 USC 1030, as amended 1994, 1996, and 2001.

Copyright Act. (1976). 17 USC.

Digital Millennium Copyright Act. (1998). Public Law 105-304, 112 Stat. 2860.

Economic Espionage Act. (1996). 18 USC 90.

Electronic Communications Privacy Act. (1986). 18 USC 2510-2522 and 18 USC 2701-2711, as amended.

FCC (Federal Communications Commission). (2004). *In the matter of Communications Assistance for Law Enforcement Act and broadband access and services.* Notice of Proposed Rulemaking RM-10865, ET Docket No. 04-295.

Gramm-Leach-Bliley Act. (1999). 15 USC 6801-6809.

Isenberg, D. (2000). *The problems with online privacy laws.* Retrieved January 13, 2006, from http://www.gigalaw.com/articles/2000-all/isenberg-2000-07a-all.html

Health Insurance Portability and Accountability Act. (1996). Public Law 104-191, 110 Stat. 1936.

Higher Education Coalition. (2005). *Comments before the Federal Communications Commission in the matter of Communications Assistance for Law Enforcement Act and broadband access and services.* Retrieved January 14, 2006, from http://www.educause.edu/ir/library/pdf/EPO0536.pdf

Iuliano, R.W. (2003). *Summary of the USA PATRIOT Act and related legislation.* Retrieved January 25, 2006, from http://www.security.harvard.edu/usa_patriot.php

Identity Theft and Assumption Deterrence Act. (1998). Public Law 105-318, 112 Stat. 3007.

Lanham Act. (1946). 15 USC.

Mota, S.A. (2002). The U.S. Supreme Court addresses the Child Pornography Prevention Act and Child Online Protection Act in Ashcroft v. Free Speech Coalition and Ashcroft v. American Civil Liberties Union. *Federal Communications Law Journal, 55*(1), 85-98.

Payment Card Industry. (2005). *Payment card industry data security standard.* Retrieved January 3, 2006, from http://www.visa.com/cisp

Patent Act. (1952). 35 USC.

Sarbanes Oxley Act. (2002). Public Law 107-204, 116 Stat. 745.

Smith, S.W. (2005). Pretending that systems are secure. *IEEE Security & Privacy, 3*(6), 73-76.

USA PATRIOT Act. (2001). Public Law 107-56, 115 Stat. 272.

Waters, M., & Harrell, J. (1997). *Child pornography on the Internet.* Retrieved January 14, 2006, from http://gsulaw.gsu.edu/lawand/papers/sp97/

KEY TERMS

Computer-Focused Crime: Involves criminal acts where the use of a computer is intrinsic to the crime.

Computer-Related Crime: Involves the use of a computer, but where the criminal activity is not defined by the use of a computer.

Copyright: Protects any original work of authorship from unauthorized duplication or distribution.

Industry-Specific Law: Protects the confidentiality, integrity, and/or availability of personal information maintained by specific industries.

Intellectual Property Law: Protects the rights of authors, inventors, and creators of other intellectual works.

Patent: Grants exclusive use rights to the creators of an invention, process, and design.

Trademark Law: Protects words, phrases, and designs that identify the products or services of a firm.

Trade Secret: Includes any information that derives independent economic value, actual or potential, from not being generally known to, and not being readily ascertainable by proper means by the public and is the subject of reasonable measures to keep such information secret.

Formulating a Code of Cyberethics for a Municipality

Udo Richard Averweg
eThekwini Municipality and University of KwaZulu-Natal, South Africa

INTRODUCTION

The diversity of Information and Communication Technology (ICT) applications and the increased use of ICTs have created a variety of ethical issues. du Plessis (2004) suggests that one way in which high ethical standards in public service can be promoted is by developing *codes of conduct*.

For the sake of clarity and equity in the workplace, it is important that are codes to regulate employees' information-related activities (Britz & Ackermann, 2006). The challenge is to make essential ethical decision making explicit so as to make it better (Sternberg, 1994). Although tailor-made Codes of Conduct will not be sufficient in it, it should be viewed as an integral part of integrating ethics management with the broader public management environment (du Plessis, 2004). Many organizations develop their own *codes of ethics*. A code of ethics is a collection of principles intended as a guide for employees in an organization.

Ethical theories are theories about justifying our moral actions (Rossouw, 1994). They propose the appropriate reasons on which our moral decisions should be based. In today's environment, interpretations of "right" and "wrong" are not always clear. Some consider that "right" actions are those that are useful to praise, "wrong" actions are those that are useful to blame (Russell, 1971). The "right" ethical answer may or may not be the answer that is prescribed by law; in fact depending on the ethical assumptions made, the "right" and "wrong" may on occasion be in conflict (Smith, 2002).

One of the basic tenets of Kantian Ethics is based on the idea that duty is fundamental and is "principle based." The main assumption of the Principle-Based Theory holds the value of an action on the nature of the action itself. One advantage of duty ethics is that it gives a powerful and clear framework for stating codes of ethics. Another advantage is that it is impartial: the same rules apply to all persons. For example, in South Africa, eThekwini Municipality's published Disciplinary Procedures apply to all its employees. It is argued that Principle-Based Theory should therefore serve as backdrop to formulating a Code of Cyberethics.

PRINCIPLE-BASED THEORY

Principle-Based Theory emphasizes that moral actions should be in accordance with a set of pre-established rules. The theory assumes that progress toward an objective standard of moral behavior is insured when people base their actions on fixed rules. It is argued that an example of fixed rules is a Code of Cyberethics. *Cyber* is a prefix stemming from cybernetics and loosely means "through the use of a computer." Cybertechnology refers to a wide range of computing and communication devices, from stand-alone computers to "connected" or networked, computing, and ICT (Tavani, 2004).

The best-known proponent of Rule-Based Theory is Immanuel Kant (1724-1804). Kantian theory gives individuals values in themselves, but looks at others in a detached, rational, and abstract fashion. Kant was convinced that all rational thinking people should be able and willing to subscribe to a basic rule that should govern all moral behavior (Tavani, 2004). This basic rule can be expressed as follows: act in such a way that your action could be a universal law. Kant was convinced that such a strategy will improve the quality of moral decisions and enhance the respect that people pay each other (Rossouw, 1994). The one who applies this approach has the following advantages:

- respects the rights and interests of all persons and not only those in the majority,
- encourages consistency and thus integrity is moral behavior, and
- provides for the obligations that we have towards other persons (for example, ICT software developers) in our respective social roles.

Some of the problems associated with this approach include:

- dogmatic approach as a result of a too strong focus on the rules,
- lack of solution for the situations where two rules may come into conflict with each other, and
- lack of consent among thinking individuals in their choice of rules for moral behavior. For example, in the ICT domain there may be dissension whether one may distribute copies of downloaded music from the Internet.

The abovementioned difficulties lead to the question of what type of moral norms (such as a Code of Cyberethics in the cybertechnology arena) should be accepted and who should play the role of referee in solving this dilemma in an organization. A "business is ethical when it maximizes long-term value subject to distributive justice and ordinary decency" (Sternberg, 1999).

CODES OF ETHICS

The value of codes is often overstated: unaccompanied by the appropriate habits, expectations, and sanctions, codes of conduct are of little value (Sternberg, 1994). Nevertheless, codes of conduct (such as a proposed Code of Cyberethics for eThekwini Municipality) can be extremely useful. By explicitly communicating corporate purposes regarding controversial matters (such as copying someone else's software for personal use) and by clarifying which stakeholder expectations are legitimate, codes of conduct can become an effective tool for sharpening business accountability and improving corporate governance. An information governance framework should contain strategic goals beneficial for the provider and citizens, and promote ethical standards. For example, for eThekwini Municipality's supply chain management policy, a "code of ethical standards has been established for officials to promote mutual trust and respect and provide an environment where business can be done with integrity" (Sutcliffe, 2005). Professionals in the public service are custodians of the public trust and therefore have to be worthy of that trust (du Plessis, 2004).

Codes must be properly structured and should not reflect the prevailing values of culture of the organization. For example, when the existing culture is less than perfect, enshrining it in a code merely reinforces bad practice—what the code prescribes must be better than the existing norm. A code of conduct is *not* a survey of employees' ethical attitudes (Sternberg, 1994). It sets out what constitutes ethical conduct for the business (such as cybertechnology) where its validity depends solely on the moral virtues of the values and principles it expresses—not on employee agreement. Ideally, stakeholders will agree upon the values embodied in the code. However, if they do not, it is the stakeholders (municipal employees) and not the code that should be changed. One needs to take "into consideration that citizens' expectations of government are to a large extent influenced by their interaction with municipalities, mainly because of the types of services that are rendered" (du Plessis, 2004). Furthermore "no code…should be as detailed and all-encompassing as parliamentary statues are" (Britz & Ackermann, 2006). Such are some of the challenges for the formulation of a Code of Cyberethics for a municipality in South Africa.

Codes of ethics involve the formalization of some rules and expected actions (Turban et al., 2004). Violation of a code of ethics may lead to the termination of employment. Similar procedures exist in eThekwini Municipality's Disciplinary Procedures. Codes of ethics are valuable for raising awareness of ethical issues and clarifying what is acceptable behavior in a variety of circumstances. Furthermore organizations are increasingly faced with serious legal and liability issues which stem from wrongful use of software by their employees (Straub & Collins, 1990).

The acceptance of a code of conduct is a very central part of being a professional (du Plessis, 2004). Codes of ethics involve the formulation of some rules and expected action (Turban et al., 2004). However, codes of ethics have limitations because of their nature to generalize acceptable behavior. Since variation in social and ethical values exist in different communities, formulation of a code must take into account cultural and social specificities of the community where the code will be applied. This may be seen to be contrary to Kantian ethics. However, it is argued that in South Africa stakeholder consultation and consensus is viewed as a constitutional right.

Stakeholder Theory and Employee Involvement

Stakeholder Theory examines individual preferences and attempts to satisfy as many of those preferences as possible, with the understanding that these individuals (e.g., employees) and the groups they form have particular relationships with the organization and each other, and cannot necessarily be looked upon with Kantian detachment. Sternberg (1994) notes that the Stakeholder Theory of Business typically holds that business is accountable to all its stakeholders and that the role of management is to balance these competing interests. Freeman (1984) defines a stakeholder as "any group or individual who can affect or is affected by the achievement of the organization's objectives."

Sternberg (1999) argues against the notion that stakeholders must be accountable to their stakeholders and not just take them into account. Employee involvement can be valuable (Sternberg, 1994). A code will be most effective if it addresses matters that cause concern to its stakeholders. Sternberg (1994) suggests that it is sensible to consult stakeholders (especially employees) to determine what situations are genuinely problematical. This approach was used as a framework for the presented research. Informal discussions were held with colleagues at eThekwini Municipality. Using the "snowball" sampling method, Table 1 reflects cybertechnology issues and concerns that were raised by the author's colleagues during informal interviews.

Consultation can provide useful information about the stringency and the degree of ethical diversity prevailing among the employees of eThekwini Municipality's heterogeneous workforce. Furthermore, making the employees part of the code-making process may improve employees' future compliance with the Code of Cyberethics. Since there has been consultation and consensus with employees (stakeholders), this argues favorably for such compliance, thereby promoting ethical cybertechnology practices.

Although the concept of business ethics arises more frequently in developing countries such as South Africa, it influenced transformations in the business culture of developing countries to the same extent it did in developed countries (Rossouw, 1994). This discrepancy of business ethics between developed and developing economies poses a severe problem for people involved in international business since it means that such people are confronted with two different sets of moral standards. In the global ICT network age, this problem becomes more pronounced.

Intellectual property is defined as the rights over intangible property created by individuals. To varying degrees in different countries, intellectual property is protected under laws relating to copyright, trademarks, patents, and trade secrets. The copying of software is generally seen to be of great concern to software developers since software piracy (the unauthorized copying of computer software) is widespread in many organizations (Lending & Slaughter, 2001). In eThekwini Municipality's Disciplinary Procedures, an employee may be dismissed for dishonest behavior or wrongful disclosure of privileged information.

The notion of privacy has become one of the most contentious issues of the global information age due to the capability of computers to perform actions previously impossible. Computers are able to advance exponentially and make unmanageable tasks practically possible (Charlesworth & Sewry, 2002). Agranoff (1993) defines (data) privacy as the "claim of individuals, groups or institutions to determine for themselves when, and to what extent, information about them is communicated to others." Charlesworth and Sewry (2002) note that privacy includes considerations of the conflicts between society's right to know and an individual's right to privacy. Nevertheless the right to

Table 1. Cybertechnology and related concerns raised by author's colleagues at eThekwini Municipality

No.	Questions
1	May one copy someone else's software for one's own personal use and distribute it?
2	May one download music/video from the Internet for personal use and distribute it?
3	May one access private and confidential information without consent and distribute it?
4	May one access others' desktops or laptops without consent?
5	May one take programs that one has done for eThekwini Municipality and keep it for personal use or use it at another employer?

Table 2. Summary of six data protection principles from the Office of the Privacy Commissioner's Office for Personal Data, Hong Kong (retrieved September 04, 2006, from http://www.pco.org.hk)

No.	Narrative	Associated Explanatory Text
1	Purpose and manner of collection	Data should be collected in a fair and lawful manner. Data users should explain to data subjects what data is being collected and how it will be used.
2	Accuracy and duration of retention	Personal data that has been collected should be kept accurate, up to date, and for no longer than is necessary.
3	Use	Data must only be used for the specific or directly related purpose for which it was collected. Any other use is conditional on consent of the data subject.
4	Security	Suitable security measures should be applied to personal data.
5	Information availability	Data users should be open to the kind of data they store and what they use it for.
6	Access	Data subjects have the right to access their personal data, to verify its accuracy, and to request correction.

privacy is not absolute. It varies considerably in different cultures, as it has to be balanced by society's right to know.

A detailed set of data privacy principles is drawn from the Privacy Commissioner's Office for Personal Data (PCOPD), Hong Kong, and promulgated in December 1996. A summary of the six PCOPD data protection principles is reflected in Table 2. These principles are designed to enshrine the reasonable rights and duties of both the data subject and the data users. Sternberg (1994) states that there is a fundamental importance of accountability to ethical business conduct and good corporate governance, suggesting that the tools used to promote accountability may influence developing a code of conduct.

Once the Code of Cyberethics is formulated and adopted by eThekwini Municipality's Strategic Management (Stratman) Team, comprising heads and deputy heads of clusters/service units, the document should become a part of the city manager's Standing Orders. Publishing a formal code serves as an explicit signal of the municipality's commitment to ethical business conduct. The adopted Code of Cyberethics must apply and be seen to apply to every employee in the municipality. According to eThekwini Municipality's Disciplinary Procedures, the "maintenance of discipline is the responsibility of management." In terms of clause 3.1 of eThekwini Municipality's Disciplinary Procedures, discipline must be handled fairly and consistently.

eTHEKWINI MUNICIPAL ENVIRONMENT

eThekwini Municipality's vision is that by 2020 it will be "Africa's most caring and liveable city." eThekwini Municipality comprises six clusters/service units (Office of the City Manager, Treasury, Governance, Sustainable Development and City Enterprises, Corporate and Human Resources & Health, Safety, and Social Services) and employs approximately 22,000 employees. The Office of the City Manager has "to fulfil its legal and ethical responsibilities relating to confidentiality, privacy, data integrity and data availability" (eThekwini IDP Review, 2006).

There are some 6,000 networked desktops (personal computers, thin clients, and laptops). Electronic communication is via Novell's GroupWise (Client version 6.5). A total of 5,806 GroupWise accounts are in existence. There are approximately 1,500 Internet accounts utilizing Internet Explorer and Netscape Navigator Web browsers. Reflecting on the magnitude of ICT connectivity of the municipality and the potential for abuse and misuse of cybertechnology by employees and municipal officials, a need to formulate a Code of Cyberethics for eThekwini Municipality arises. Moreover, since eThekwini Municipality's future development is centered on being an "information-driven" organization, one of its values is based on it being an "…ethical and productive organisation" (eThekwini IDP Review, 2006). It therefore seems appropriate that a Code of Cyberethics be formulated for setting out what constitutes ethical cybertechnology practices in eThekwini Municipality.

The proposed methodology for the formulation of the Code of Cyberethics for the selected municipality in South Africa is as follows:

- Disseminate the author's validated survey instrument (see extract in Table 3) to municipal employees who have Internet accounts.
- Qualitatively and quantitatively analyze the responses received to completed survey questionnaires. From the scored responses, themes, patterns, and trends will be synthesized.
- Draft a proposed Code of Cyberethics based on the municipality's: (1) vision and mission, (2) moral and social values that the organization wants reflected in all its activities, and (3) values that reflect characteristics of the organization's approach to achieving its mission. Particular attention is to be paid to cybertechnology situations which appear to be genuinely problematic.

- When the Code of Cyberethics is breached, eThekwini Municipality's Disciplinary Procedures must be followed.
- Present the proposed Code of Cyberethics to Stratman for ratification and adoption.
- Incorporate the document in the city manager's Standing Orders.
- Utilize appropriate and effective communication mechanisms for the adopted Code of Cyberethics to municipal employees. Such mechanisms will include: (1) publishing the code on eThekwini Municipality's intranet, (2) including a hardcopy of the code with municipal employee's payslips, and (3) incorporating the code in Human Resources' induction programs for new employees.

McCabe et al. (1996) found the existence of a corporate code of ethics was associated with significantly lower levels of self-reported unethical behavior in the workplace. Another study (Adams et al., 2001) found that simply having a code of ethics can influence the actions of organization members, even when individuals

Table 3. Extract of ethics statement survey for eThekwini Municipality employees (This extract is an adapted version of the Ethics Statement Survey by Alan Peslak, Penn State's Scranton Campus, USA. Retrieved September 4, 2006, from http://wsistdevel.sn.psu.edu/ist/arp14/eths1/webform1.aspx)

Please indicate your level of agreement/disagreement with the following information and communication technology related statements.

Strongly agree - Agree - Undecided - Disagree or Strongly disagree

I may distribute copies of downloaded music

- Strongly agree
- Agree
- Undecided
- Disagree
- Strongly disagree

Please tick any of the following factors that affected your answer (you may tick more than one)

- I believe that the potential harm done to others would be minimal
- I believe that most view this activity as acceptable
- I believe that any harm that would take place would be to people I do not know
- I believe the number of people harmed would be minimal
- I believe that negative effects of this action would occur a very long time from now
- I believe that the potential harm done to others would be high
- I believe that most view this activity as wrong
- I believe that any harm that would take place would be to people I know
- I believe the number of people harmed would be high
- I believe that negative effects of this action would occur very soon

---

cannot remember specific content. Just the presence of the code may impact the perceptions of ethical behavior. While ethics is not just about codes, one needs to ensure that both employees and structures within an organization support ethical practices.

It is important to make clear distinction between personal ethical dilemmas and ethical disputes. In the case of a personal ethical dilemma, the employee is faced with a choice between options which normally serve different interests. An employee has to make up his mind without having to reach consensus with fellow employees involved. In the case of an ethical dispute, two or more employees (or groups of employees in an organizational structure) with contradictory ethical views may be involved, and it may be much harder to come to a conclusion on what the suitable ethical standpoint or action would be. The "latter is normally the situation in which…decisions have to be made in business" (Rossouw, 1994). Cleek and Leonard (1998) state that "emphasis should be placed on how the codes are communicated, enforced, and used, as a basis for strengthening the culture of the organization."

CONCLUSION

A code of ethics demonstrates a concern about organizational ethics and is tangible, concrete evidence that ethics are a concern to an organization. Furthermore, it is a way of communicating to its employees what the standards and expectations of management are. If an organization is committed to promoting ethical conduct, a code of ethics affects the behavior of employees by laying down corporate expectations.

Rules of ethics depend on given situations. For the sake of clarity and equity in the workplace, it is important that these should be codes to regulate employee's Internet-related activities and, if necessary, to provide for disciplinary action. If municipal officials do not have a Code of Cyberethics to reference and guide their actions, it will probably be as catastrophic as when power and authority are delegated without enforcing accountability.

McClenahen (1999) suggests that "being consistent in policies and actions, rewarding ethical conduct, treating employees fairly, and providing better executive leadership" work best to reduce unethical conduct. A commitment to the moral treatment of employees is one of the preconditions for continued excellence

(Rossouw, 1994). Therefore, effective communication of the Code of Cyberethics to eThekwini Municipality employees can help eliminate situations wherein employees complain that they have not been made aware of corporate expectations regarding private Internet-related usage. With a Code of Cyberethics, there is a strong likelihood that situational dilemmas wherein a municipal employee reaches an unethical decision should be reduced.

REFERENCES

Adams, J.S., Tashchian, A. & Stone, T. (2001). Codes of Ethics as Signals for Ethical Behavior. *Journal of Business Ethics, 29*, 199-211.

Agranoff, M.H. (1993). Controlling the Threat to Personal Privacy: Corporate Policies Must be Created. *Journal of Information Systems Management*, Summer.

Britz, H. & Ackerman, M. (2006). *Information, Ethics & the Law*. Petroria: Van Schaik Publishers.

Charlesworth, M. & Sewry, D.A. (2002). Ethical Issues in Enabling Information Technologies. In *Proceedings of the 2002 annual research conference of the South Africa Institute of Computer Scientists and Information Technologists*, Port Elizabeth, South Africa, 163-171.

Cleek, M. & Leonard, S. (1998). Can Corporate Codes of Ethics Influence Behavior? *Journal of Business Ethics*, 619-630, April.

du Plessis, B. (ed) (2004). *Ethics in Local Government. Journal of the Institute of Municipal Finance Officers, 4*(3), 16.

eThekwini IDP Review (2006). *eThekwini Municipality Integrated Development Plan Review 2005/6 Corporate Policy Unit (GIPO)*, eThekwini Municipality, Durban, South Africa.

Freeman, R.E. (1984). *Strategic management: A Stakeholder approach*. Boston: Pitman.

Lending, D. & Slaughter, S.A. (2001). Research in progress: The effects of ethical climate on attitudes and behaviors toward software piracy. In *Proceedings of the 2001 ACM SIGCPR conference on Computer personnel research*, San Diego, CA, 198-200.

McCabe, D., Klebe Trevino, L. & Butterfield, J. (1996). The Influence of Collegiate and Corporate Codes of Conduct on Ethics-Related Behavior in the Workplace. *Business Ethics Quarterly, 6*(4), 461-470.

McClenahen, J. (1999). Your Employees Know Better. *Industry Week*, 12-13, 1 March.

Rossouw, D. (1994). *Business Ethics: A South African Perspective*. Halfway House: Southern Book Publishers.

Russell, B. (1971). *Human Society in Ethics and Politics*. London: George Allen & Unwin Ltd.

Smith, H.J. (2002). Ethics and information systems: Resolving the Quandaries. ACM SIGMIS *Database, 33*(3).

Sternberg, E. (1994). *Just business: Business Ethics in Action*. London: Little, Brown, and Company.

Sternberg, E. (1999). *The Stakeholder Concept: A Mistaken Doctrine*. Henley-on-Thames: NTC Publications Ltd.

Straub, D. & Collins, R. (1990). Key Information Liability Issues Facing Managers: Software Piracy, Proprietary Databases, and Individual Rights to Privacy. *MIS Quarterly, 14*(2), 143-156.

Sutcliffe, M. (2005). The City Manager's Desk. *Ezasegagasini Metro*, eThekwini Municipality, Durban, 20 September, 6.

Tavani, H.T. (2004). *Ethics and Technology: Ethical Issues in an Age of Information and Communication Technology*. Hoboken, NJ: John Wiley & Sons.

Turban, E., McLean, E. & Wetherbe, J. (2004). Information Technology for Management: Transforming Organizations in the Digital Economy. Hoboken, NJ: John Wiley & Sons.

KEY TERMS

Code of Conduct: A standard of behavior to be followed within specific occupational categories.

Code of Ethics: A collection of principles intended as a guide for employees in an organization.

Cyberethics: The study of moral, legal, and social issues of cybertechnology.

Cybertechnology: A wide range of computing and communication devices from stand-alone computers to "connected" or networked, computing, and ICT.

Internet: The worldwide, publicly accessible network of interconnected computer networks that transmit data by packlet switching using the standard Internet protocol.

Principle-Based Theory: A theory that bases the value of an action on the nature of the action itself.

Stakeholder Theory: A theory that examines individual preferences and attempts to satisfy as many of those preferences as possible with the understanding that these individuals and the groups they form have particular relationships with the organization and each other.

F

Hackers and Cyber Terrorists

M. J. Warren
Deakin University, Australia

INTRODUCTION

Many aspects of our modern society now have either a direct or implicit dependence upon information technology (IT). As such, a compromise of the availability or integrity in relation to these systems (which may encompass such diverse domains as banking, government, health care, and law enforcement) could have dramatic consequences from a societal perspective.

In many modern business environments, even the short-term, temporary interruption of Internet/e-mail connectivity can have a significantly disruptive effect, forcing people to revert to other forms of communication that are now viewed as less convenient. Imagine, then, the effect if the denial of service was over the longer term and also affected the IT infrastructure in general. Many governments are now coming to this realization.

This article sets out to consider the scenario in which technology infrastructures or services are targeted deliberately, examining the issue in relation to two categories of computer abuser: 'hackers' and 'cyber terrorists.'

The Computer Hacker

The definition of the 'computer hacker' has been the subject of much debate in computing circles. Caelli, Longley, and Shain (1989) provide two definitions of the term:

1. In programming, a computing enthusiast. The term is normally applied to people who take a delight in experimenting with system hardware (the electronics), software (computer programs) and communication systems (telephone lines, in most cases).
2. In data (information) security, an unauthorized user who tries to gain entry into a computer, or computer network, by defeating the computers access (and/or security) controls.

In mass media terms, the latter interpretation is by far the more common (although persons belonging to the former category of hacker would seek to more accurately define the latter group, particularly those with a malicious intent, as 'crackers').

Hackers are by no means a new threat and have routinely featured in news stories during the last two decades. Indeed, they have become the traditional 'target' of the media, with the standard approach being to present the image of either a "teenage whiz kid" or an insidious threat. In reality, it can be argued that there are different degrees of the problem. Some hackers are malicious, while others are merely naïve and hence do not appreciate that their activities may be doing any real harm. Furthermore, when viewed as a general population, hackers may be seen to have numerous motivations for their actions (including financial gain, revenge, ideology, or just plain mischief making) (Parker, 1976). However, in many cases it can be argued that this is immaterial, as no matter what the reason, the end result is some form of adverse impact upon another party.

Steven Levy's (1994) book *Hackers: Heroes of the Computer Revolution suggests that hackers operate by a code of ethics. This code defines main key areas:*

- **Hands-On Imperative:** Access to computers and hardware should be complete and total. It is asserted to be a categorical imperative to remove any barriers between people and the use and understanding of any technology, no matter how large, complex, dangerous, labyrinthine, proprietary, or powerful.
- **"Information Wants to Be Free":** This can be interpreted in a number of ways. Free might mean without *restrictions* (freedom of movement = no censorship), without *control* (freedom of change/evolution = no ownership or authorship, no intellectual property), or without *monetary value* (no cost).
- **Mistrust Authority:** Promote decentralization. This element of the ethic shows its strong anarchis-

tic, individualistic, and libertarian nature. Hackers have shown distrust toward large institutions, including but not limited to the state, corporations, and computer administrative bureaucracies.

- **No Bogus Criteria:** Hackers should be judged by their hacking, not by 'bogus criteria' such as race, age, sex, or position.
- **"You Can Create Truth and Beauty on a Computer":** Hacking is equated with artistry and creativity. Furthermore, this element of the ethos raises it to the level of philosophy.
- **"Computers Can Change your Life for the Better":** In some ways, this last statement really is simply a corollary of the previous one, since most of humanity desires things that are good, true, and/or beautiful.

During the 1980s and 1990s, this pure vision of what hackers are was changed by the development of new groups with various aims and values. It was certainly true that at this time hackers certainly saw themselves as cyber Robin Hoods whose motives for hacking certainly outweighed any law that they may have been breaking.

Mizrach (1997) states that the following individuals currently exist in cyberspace:

- **Hackers** (crackers, system intruders): These are people who attempt to penetrate security systems on remote computers. This is the new sense of the term, whereas the old sense of the term simply referred to a person who was capable of creating hacks, or elegant, unusual, and unexpected uses of technology.
- **Phreaks** (phone phreakers, blue boxers): These are people who attempt to use technology to explore and/or control the telephone system.
- **Virus Writers** (also, creators of Trojans, worms, logic bombs): These are people who write code which (a) attempts to reproduce itself on other systems without authorization and (b) often has a side effect, whether that be to display a message, play a prank, or destroy a hard drive.
- **Pirates:** Originally, this involved breaking copy protection on software. This activity was called 'cracking'. Nowadays, few software vendors use copy protection, but there are still various minor measures used to prevent the unauthorized duplication of software. Pirates devote themselves to

thwarting these and sharing commercial software freely.

- **Cypherpunks** (cryptoanarchists): Cypherpunks freely distribute the tools and methods for making use of strong encryption, which is basically unbreakable except by massive supercomputers. Because American intelligence and law enforcement agencies, such as the NSA and FBI, cannot break strong encryption, programs that employ it are classified as munitions—thus, distribution of algorithms that make use of it is a felony.
- **Anarchists:** They are committed to distributing illegal (or at least morally suspect) information, including but not limited to data on bomb making; lock picking; pornography; drug manufacturing; and radio, cable, and satellite TV piracy.
- **Cyberpunk:** Usually some combination of the above, plus interest in technological self-modification, science fiction, and interest in hardware hacking and 'street tech'.

Mizrach (1997) determined that new groupings with cyberspace had altered the initial code of ethics, and that the code of ethics in the 1990s was more concerned with:

- **"Above all else, do no harm":** Do not damage computers or data if at all possible.
- **Protect Privacy:** People have a right to privacy, which means control over their own personal (or even familial) information.
- **"Waste not, want not":** Computer resources should not lie idle and wasted. It is ethically wrong to keep people out of systems when they could be using them during idle time.
- **Exceed Limitations:** Hacking is about the continual transcendence of problem limitations.
- **The Communication Imperative:** People have the right to communicate and associate with their peers freely.
- **Leave No Traces:** Do not leave a trail or trace of your presence; do not call attention to yourself or your exploits.
- **Share:** Information increases in value by sharing it with the maximum number of people. *Don't hoard, don't hide!*
- **Self-Defense Against a Cyberpunk Future:** Hacking and viruses are necessary to protect people from a possible Orwellian *1984* future.

- **Hacking Helps Security:** This could be called the 'tiger team ethic'—it is useful and courteous to find security holes, and then tell people how to fix them.
- **Trust, but Test:** You must constantly test the integrity of systems and find ways to improve them.

This newer code of ethics is based more on the view that hackers are helping in the development of the information society and adding to its distinct nature. The ethics of imposing these values on others who are unwilling 'victims' does not seem to be questioned. The rationale for hacking activity can be based on the requirement to obtain information and then use that information (process it, give it away, or sell it).

A recent AusCERT (2005) survey focused on the state of IT security within Australia; the following is a summary of the main results:

- 35% of all Australian organizations surveyed have been attacked (attacks including hacking attempts) in 2005
- 68% of companies had experienced either computer security incidents/crimes or other forms of computer abuse (such as network scanning, theft of laptops, employee abuse)
- Of Australian organizations who were victims of computer incidents, 71% of attacks came from external sources

The survey showed that IT security and computer misuse is a major problem within Australia. The survey showed that external attacks were the source of the majority of attacks.

The most recent famous Australian hacking case was related with sewage. In October 2001, Vitek Boden was convicted of 30 charges involving computer hacking of the Maroochy Shire Council sewerage system. The attacks, which commenced in late 1999, involved using remote radio transmissions to alter the actions of the sewerage pumping stations and caused hundreds of thousands of liters of raw sewage to be pumped into public waterways (Kingsley, 2002).

It is certainly true that hacking and hacking-associated activities are becoming more widespread, including increased hacking into school systems (Borja, 2006), online voting, and other more recent online innovations. Recently a 20-year-old was arrested for hacking and

also selling tools that were used to attack a number of other networks. He "is accused of being part of a new breed of criminal hacker." The fact that a large part of his activities was money-motivated informs us of a worrying new trend (Greenemeier, 2005).

The Cyber Terrorist

Recent years have witnessed the widespread use of information technology by terrorist-type organizations. This has led to the emergence of a new class of threat, which has been termed *cyber terrorism*. This can be viewed as distinct from 'traditional' terrorism, since physical terror does not occur and efforts are instead focused upon attacking information systems/resources (Hutchinson & Warren, 2001).

When viewed from the perspective of skills and techniques, there is little to distinguish cyber terrorists from the general classification of hackers. Both groups require and utilize an arsenal of techniques in order to breach the security of target systems. From a motivational perspective, however, cyber terrorists are clearly different, operating with a specific political or ideological agenda to support their actions. This in turn may result in more focused/determined efforts to achieve their objectives and more considered selection of suitable targets for attack. However, the difference does not necessarily end there, and other factors should be considered. Firstly, the fact that cyber terrorists are part of an organized group could mean that they have funding available to support their activities. This in turn would mean that individual hackers could be hired to carry out attacks on behalf of a terrorist organization (effectively sub-contracting the necessary technical expertise). In this situation, the hackers themselves may not believe in the terrorists' 'cause', but will undertake the work for financial gain (Verton, 2003).

Propaganda/Publicity

Terrorist groups have difficulty in relaying their political messages to the general public without being censored; they can now use the Internet for this purpose. Different terrorist groups/political parties are now using the Internet for a variety of different purposes. Some examples are (Warren & Hutchinson, 2002):

- **Tupac Amaru Revolutionary Movement (MRTA):** In 1997 a Peruvian terrorist group know as MRTA took over the Japanese embassy in Peru, taking a number of hostages. During this time, the Web site of the MRTA contained messages from MRTA members inside the embassy, as well as updates and pictures of the drama as it happened.

- **Chechen Rebels:** Chechen rebels have been using the Internet to fight the Russians in a propaganda war. The rebels claimed to have shot down a Russian fighter jet, a claim refuted by the Russians until a picture of the downed jet was shown on *Kavkaz.org,* the official Web site of the Chechen rebels. The Russians were forced to admit their jet had in fact been shot down.

- **Fundraising:** Azzam Publications, based in London and named after Sheikh Abdullah Azzam, a mentor of Osama bin Laden, is a site dedicated to Jihad around the world and linked to Al Qaeda. It is alleged that the Azzam Publications site, which sold Jihad-related material from books to videos, was raising funds for the Taliban in Afghanistan and for guerrillas fighting the Russians in Chechyna. After September 11, Azzam Publications came under increased pressure to the point where its products could no longer be purchased through its site. In a farewell message

published on the site, those at Azzam provide alternatives to ensure that funds can still be raised and sent around the world to fight the 'struggle'. In 2002 the main Azzam site went back online, offering the same fundraising options. The new site also mirrored itself around the world and provides its content in a number of languages including: Arabic, English, German, Spanish, Indonesian, Bosnian, Turkish, Malay, Albanian, Ukranian, French, Swedish, Dutch, Italian, Urdu, and Somalian (as shown by Figure 1). The reason for doing so, according to the Azzam site, "is to protect against Western Censorship Laws." It will probably prove to be difficult to close the Azzam site in the future, when the information is mirrored around the Internet in a variety of languages.

- **Information Warfare:** Cyber terrorism—or the more appropriate term *information warfare,* as discussed earlier—is becoming a common technique used to attack organizations. Cyber terrorist groups employ what is known as *hacktivism.* Hacktivists are activists involved in defacing the site of an enemy for a political cause, for example, a cyber terrorism group or a group acting on behalf of a cyber terrorism group (Meikle, 2002).

Figure 1. Example of Azzam multi-language sites

FUTURE TRENDS: IRAQI WAR CASE STUDY 2003

In the example of the Iraqi War 2003, you had a situation that included hackers, viruses, and online propaganda. What makes this different to the previous cyber wars (e.g., the Serbian-NATO cyber war) is the fact that more than two parties are involved and the motivation is based upon ideologies—religious and political. What also makes this cyber war of interest are the three parties involved. These include (Warren, 2003):

- U.S.-based hackers who are inspired by patriotism and wish to attack anything that can be considered as an Iraqi target.
- Islamic-based hackers who are trying to carry out an online Jihad against perceived allied targets.
- Peace activists who are trying to use the Web to promote a peaceful message via Web sites. But what would have been the next step for the radical peace activists if the war had continued?

The situation was very confusing, as you had the U.S. Government National Infrastructure Protection Center (NIPC) releasing an advisory on February 11, 2003, trying to restrain "patriotic hacking" on behalf of the U.S. government (NIPC, 2003). NIPC (2003) defined that attacks may have one of several motivations:

- political activism targeting Iraq or those sympathetic to Iraq by self-described "patriot" hackers
- political activism or disruptive attacks targeting U.S. systems by those opposed to any potential conflict with Iraq
- criminal activity masquerading or using the current crisis to further personal goals

During this period there were active pro-Islamic hacking groups such as Unix Security Guard (USG); their strategy was trying to deface sites with their pro-Iraqi political messages (Warren, 2003). A typical anti-war hack is illustrated by Figure 2.

Following the defeat of Iraqi forces and the restoration of a democratic government, Iraqi resistance groups formed to fight the new government and occupying military forces. These new resistance groups turned to the Internet (see Figure 3) for the reasons described before, but with some differences; these are (Warren, 2005):

Figure 2. Cyber terrorism at work

Figure 3. Iraqi resistance groups at work

- use of the Web as a source of recruitment of volunteers;
- focus on Arabic rather than English Web sites and content;
- mirroring information around the world, making it harder to remove; and
- spreading information of a more practical nature, for example, on making explosives, how to use captured foreign firearms, and so forth.

A final point to note is that cyber terrorist activity could also be used in conjunction with or to support more traditional attacks. For example, hacking techniques could be employed to obtain intelligence information from systems, which could then be used as the basis for a physical attack.

So far, the number of cyber terrorist attacks has been limited compared to those involving hackers; however, since the terrorist attacks of 2001, the focus and acceptance of cyber terrorism as a real threat has been acknowledged (Boulard & Goodwin, 2003).

CONCLUSION

Hacking has certainly become widespread since the mid-1990s, but the ethical motives have changed since the early days of the hackers in the 1980s. Hackers rarely see themselves now as part of a social revolution, as computer users who are "setting the world to rights." With the advent of the Internet and the explosion of online users, there has been a surge in a new breed of inexperienced, inefficient young hackers who use pre-programmed code (Thomas, 2005). These hackers have discovered the world of spam, of money and profit. Their activities are no longer of the Robin Hood variety, interested in the learning of new skills, but are far more non-altruistic than that. It is this new "unethical" breed of hacker that could imply danger for the future increase in cyber-terrorism. Cyber terrorist groups have access to funds that would allow them to employ the new breed of hacker, who would be tempted by the commercial enterprise. Hackers would become outsourced from groups of cyber terrorists, making the arrangement a business one. This is a far cry from the "golden age" of the ethical hacker (Thomas, 2005).

A final observation is that cyber attacks offer the capability for terrorist activities with wider-reaching impacts. With traditional terrorist activities, such as bombings, the impacts are isolated within specific physical locations and communities. In this context, the wider populace act only as observers and are not directly affected by the actions. Furthermore, acts of violence are not necessarily the most effective ways of making a political or ideological point—the media/public attention is more likely to focus upon the destruction of property and/or loss of life than whatever 'cause' the activity was intended to promote. The ability of cyber terrorism activities to affect a wider population may give the groups involved greater leverage in

309

terms of achieving their objectives, while at the same time ensuring that no immediate long-term damage is caused which could cloud the issue. For example, in a denial-of-service scenario, if the threatened party was to accede to the terrorist demands, then the situation could (ostensibly at least) be returned to that which existed prior to the attack (i.e., with service resumed). This is not the case in a 'physical' incident when death or destruction has occurred.

Cyber terrorists operate with a political agenda. This motivation (which could often be more accurately described as fanaticism) will mean these types of attacks will be more specifically targeted and aimed at more critical systems. This collective action would do more harm than the action of a single hacker. There is also the issue of funding; since terrorist groups could have substantial funds available, this means that they could easily employ hackers to act on their behalf. Whether we like it or not, society has developed a significant (and increasing) dependence upon IT. The Internet is available 24 hours a day, and cyber terrorist groups that view developed countries as a target will be able to attack 24 hours a day. This means that all organizations could feel the impact of attacks as their sites are attacked just because they happen to be in Australian, Japan, the United States, and so forth. Only the future will show the risks that we face from the threat of cyber terrorism

REFERENCES

AusCERT. (2005). *2005 Australian computer crime and security survey.* University of Queensland, Australia.

Borja, R. (2006). Cyber-security concerns mount as student hacking hits schools. *Education Week, 25*(19).

Boulard, G., & Goodwin, J. (2003). Cyber terrorism: No Longer fiction. *State Legislatures, 29*(5), 22.

Caelli, W., Longley, D., & Shain, M. (1989). *Information security for managers.* New York: Stockton Press.

Greenemier, L. (2005). Hacking back: Time for cyber counterterrorism. *Information Week, 1064,* 1-1.

Hutchinson, W., & Warren, M.J. (2001). *Information warfare: Corporate attack and defence in a digital world.* London: Butterworth-Heinemann.

Kingsley, P. (2002). QUEEN v BODEN. *Proceedings of the ACISP 2002 Forensic Computer Workshop,* Melbourne.

Levy, S. (1994). Hackers: Heroes of the computer revolution. New York: Penguin.

Meikle, G. (2002). *Future active: Media activism and the Internet.* Routledge.

Mizrach, S. (1997). *Is there a hacker ethic for 90s hackers?* Retrieved May 12, 2002, from *www.infowar. com*

NIPC. (2003). *Advisory 03-002—encourages heightened cyber security as Iraq–U.S. tensions increase.* Washington, DC: National Infrastructure Protection Center.

Parker, D. (1976). *Crime by computer.* Charles Scribner's Sons.

Thomas, J. (2005). The moral ambiguity of social control in cyberspace: A retro-assessment of the 'golden age' of hacking. *New Media & Society, 7*(5), 599-624.

Verton, D. (2003). *Black ice: The invisible threat of cyber terrorism.* New York: McGraw-Hill.

Warren, M.J. (2003). The impact of hackers. *Proceedings of the 2nd European Information Warfare Conference,* Reading, UK.

Warren, M.J. (2005). Cyber terrorism. *Proceedings of the Annual Police Summit,* Melbourne, Australia.

Warren, M.J., & Hutchinson, W. (2002). Will new laws be effective in reducing Web sponsorship of terrorist groups? *Proceedings of the 3rd Australian Information Warfare and Security Conference,* Perth, Australia.

KEY TERMS

Cyber Terrorism: Terrorism conducted in cyberspace, where criminals attempt to disrupt computer or telecommunications service.

Ethics: A set of principles of right conduct.

Internet: An interconnected system of networks that connects computers around the world via TCP/IP.

Hacker: One who uses programming skills to gain illegal access to a computer network or file.

Homeland: One's native land.

Security: Something that gives or assures safety, such as: (a) measures adopted by a government to prevent espionage, sabotage, or attack; or (b) measures adopted, as by a business or homeowner, to prevent a crime.

Terrorism: The unlawful use or threatened use of force or violence by a person or an organized group against people or property with the intention of intimidating or coercing societies or governments, often for ideological or political reasons.

Homo Electricus and the Continued Speciation of Humans

Katina Michael
University of Wollongong, Australia

M. G. Michael
University of Wollongong, Australia

INTRODUCTION

When Jacques Ellul (1964, p. 432) predicted the use of "electronic banks" in his book, *The Technological Society*, he was not referring to the computerization of financial institutions or the use of Automatic Teller Machines (ATMs). Rather it was in the context of the possibility of the dawn of a new entity—the *coupling of man and machine*. Ellul (1964) was predicting that one day knowledge would be accumulated in electronic banks and "transmitted directly to the human nervous system by means of coded electronic messages... [w]hat is needed will pass directly from the machine to the brain without going through consciousness..." As unbelievable as this *man-machine* complex may have sounded at the time, 40 years on, visionaries are still predicting that such scenarios will be possible by the turn of the twenty-second century. Michio Kaku (1998, pp. 112-116) observes that scientists are working steadily toward a brain-computer interface. The first step is to show that individual neurons can grow on silicon and then to connect the chip directly to a neuron in an animal. The next step is to mimic this connectivity in a human; the last is to decode millions of neurons which constitute the spinal cord in order to interface directly with the brain. Cyberpunk science fiction writers like William Gibson (1984) refer to this notion as "jacking-in" with the *wetware*—plugging in a computer cable directly with the central nervous system (i.e., with neurons in the brain analogous to software and hardware) (Gates, 1995, p. 133).

In terms of the current state of development we can point to the innovation of miniature wearable media, orthopedic replacements (including pacemakers), bionic prosthetic limbs (Davis, 2006), humanoid robots, and radio-frequency identification implants (Jones, 2006). Traditionally the term *cyborg* has been used to describe humans who have some mechanical parts or extensions. Today however we are on the brink of building a new sentient being, a bearer of electricity, a modern man belonging to a new race, beyond that which can be considered merely *part man part machine*. We refer here to the absolute fusion of man and machine, where the *toolmaker becomes one with his tools* (McLuhan, 1964). The question at this point of coalescence is how human will the new species be (Toffler, 1981)? And what are the related ethical concerns? Does the "biological evolution" of humans as recorded in history end when technology can be connected to the body in a wired or wireless form?

FROM PROSTHETICS TO AMPLIFICATION

While orthopedic replacements corrective in nature have been around since the 1950s (Banbury, 1997) and are required to repair a function that is either lying dormant or has failed altogether, implants of the future will attempt to add new functionality to native human capabilities, either through extensions or additions (see Figure 1). Kevin Warwick's Cyborg 2.0 project for instance, intended to prove that two persons with respective implants could communicate sensation and movement by thoughts alone. In 2002, the BBC reported that a tiny silicon square with 100 electrodes was connected to the professor's median nerve and linked to a transmitter/receiver in his forearm. Although "Warwick believe[d] that when he move[d] his own fingers, his brain [would] also be able to move Irena's" (Dobson 2001, p. 1), the outcome of the experiment was described at best as sending "Morse code" messages. Warwick (2003) is still of the belief that a person's brain could be directly linked to a computer network. Commercial players are also intent on keeping ahead, continually funding projects

Figure 1.

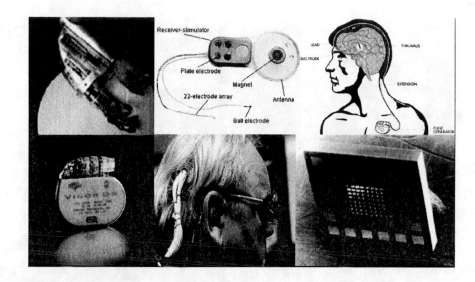

in this area of research. IBM's Personal Area Network (PAN) prototype transmitter showed the potential to use the human body's natural salinity as a conductor to sending or receiving data electronically. While the devices used were wearable, it showed that as many as four people could exchange electronic messages simply by shaking hands (Scannell, 1996).

THE SOUL CATCHER CHIP

The *Soul Catcher* chip was conceived by former Head of British Telecom Research, Peter Cochrane, who (1999, p. 2) believes that the human body is merely a *carcass* that serves as a *transport* mechanism just like a vehicle, and that the most important part of our body is our brain (i.e. mind). Similarly Miriam English has said "I like my body, but it's going to die, and it's not a choice really I have. If I want to continue, and I want desperately to see what happens in another 100 years, and another 1000 years... I need to duplicate my brain in order to do that" (Walker, 2001).

Soul Catcher is all about the preservation of a human, way beyond the point of physical debilitation. The Soul Catcher chip would be implanted in the brain and act as an access point to the external world (Grossman, 1998). Consider being able to download the mind onto computer hardware and then creating a global nervous system via wireless Internet (Fixmer, 1998). By 2050 Cochrane has predicted that downloading thoughts and emotions will be commonplace (LoBaido, 2001). Billinghurst and Starner (1999, p. 64) predict

that this kind of arrangement will free up the human intellect to focus on creative rather than computational functions.

Cochrane's beliefs are shared by many others engaged in the *transhumanist* movement (especially Extropians like Alexander Chislenko). Marvin Minsky believes that this would be the next stage in human evolution, a way to achieve true immortality "replacing flesh with steel and silicon" (Kaku, 1998, p. 94). Chris Winter of British Telecom has claimed that Soul Catcher will mean "the end of death." Winter predicts that by 2030: "[i]t would be possible to imbue a new-born baby with a lifetime's experiences by giving him or her the Soul Catcher chip of a dead person" (Uhlig, 2001).

THE RISE OF THE ELECTROPHORUS

The human who has been implanted with a microchip that can send or receive data is an *Electrophorus*, a bearer of "electric" technology (Michael & Michael, 2005). One who "bears" is in some way intrinsically or spiritually connected to that which they are bearing, in the same way an expecting mother is to the child in her womb (see Figure 2). The root *electro* comes from the Greek word meaning "amber," and *phorus* means to "wear, to put on, to get into" (Michael & Michael, 2006, p. 635). To electronize something is "to furnish it with electronic equipment" and electrotechnology is "the science that deals with practical applications of electricity." The *Macquarie Dictionary* definition of electrophorus is "an instrument for generating

Figure 2.

Figure 3.

static electricity by means of induction." The term "electrophoresis" has been borrowed here to describe the 'electronic' operations that an electrophorus is engaged in. McLuhan and Zingrone (1995, p. 94) believed that "...electricity is in effect an extension of the nervous system as a kind of global membrane." McLuhan argued that "physiologically, man in the normal use of technology (or his variously extended body) is perpetually modified by it and in turn finds ever new ways of modifying his technology" (Dery, 1996, p. 117). McLuhan called this process "auto-amputation," the idea of extending oneself to become the complete person again.

The designation electrophorus seems to be more suitable today than that of any other term, including that of cyborg. It is not surprising then that these crucial matters of definition raise the metaphysical question of identity, which science fiction writers are now beginning to creatively and in some instances ontologically address. The Electrophorus belongs to the emerging species of *Homo Electricus*. In its current state the Electrophorus relies on a device being triggered wirelessly when it enters an electromagnetic field. In the future the Electrophorus will act like a network element or node, allowing information to pass through him or her, to be stored locally or remotely, and to send out messages and receive them simultaneously and allow some to be processed actively and others as background tasks (see Figure 3).

At the point of becoming an Electrophorus (i.e. a *bearer* of electricity), we can share Brown's (1999), observation that "you are not just a human linked with technology; you are something different and your values and judgment will change". Some suspect that it will even become possible to alter behavior in people with brain implants, whether they will it or not. Maybury (1990) believes that "the advent of machine intelligence

raises social and ethical issues that may ultimately challenge human existence on earth." We know, for example, from the reports of the clinical psychologist Michael Yapko (1998) that a procedure under clinical investigation called *Vagus Nerve Stimulation* refers to a "pacemaker for the brain" that has been used to treat depression by sending electrical impulses to stimulate those parts of the brain which are considered "the underperforming areas." This, of course, raises the alarmingly obvious questions of the potential for 'mood' and 'mind' control.

THE ETHICAL CONCERNS

Warwick is well aware that one of the major obstacles of *cyber-humans* and bio-electric humans are the associated moral issues—who gives anyone the right to be conducting complex procedures on a perfectly healthy person, and who will take responsibility for any complications that present themselves (Smith, 2002)? D.M. Rummler (2001) asks whether it is ethical to be linking computers to humans in the first place and whether or not limitations should be placed on what procedures can be conducted even if they are possible. For instance, could this be considered a violation of human rights? And moreover what will it mean in the future to call oneself "human"? McGrath (2001) asks "how human?" Do we determine our 'humanity' by the number of synthetic or mechanical parts we have willingly invited into our body? Rushworth Kidder questions the general area of research: "are some kinds of knowledge so terrible they simply should not be pursued?" Kidder believes we are heading for a philosophical crisis and that the root cause lies in the chasm between three domains that are hardly on speaking terms—technology, politics and ethics.

With reference to Kurzweil's prediction of humans merging with robots, Danny Hillis predicts that the change would happen so gradually that we would sooner or later get used to it as if it had been there all along (Joy, 2000). In the wearable computing realm, Steve Mann (1997, p. 31) uses an analogy to express this same idea: "Someday, when we've become accustomed to clothing-based computing, we will no doubt feel naked, confused, and lost without a computer screen hovering in front of our eyes to guide us," just like we would feel our nakedness without conventional clothes today. Warwick too remarked about his Cyborg 1.0 implant: "I don't see it as a separate thing [the implant]…It's like an arm or a leg" (Witt, 1999). There is an underlying theme of control here—the partnership between man and machine will always be disproportionate. The machine in the Electrophorus scenario, though given breath by man, is still the more dominant member. It cannot be held accountable for malfunction, including viruses, and for this reason 'traditional' humanity will always be at the mercy of the machine. Homo Electricus is at a greater risk than its predecessors in terms of natural selection, as it cannot exist without a man-made power source. It will also to some degree rely on the 'have nots' or those who 'opt out' of a virtual existence, as the key to its continuum.

WHERE TO NEXT?

We could be forgiven for thinking that the *human-computer* metaphor belongs to science fiction but the evidence is there that it is certainly not *just* science fiction (Keiper, 2006; Davis, 2006). When well-known universities in North America and Europe fund brain implant projects and large multinational companies support ideas like the Soul Catcher chip and sponsor cyborg experiments, and government departments like DARPA and NASA discuss future possibilities openly, we can be assured that this is not science fiction but increments of science fact. McGrath (2001) alludes to the German poet Rainer Maria Rilke who pondered that the "future enters into us long before it happens."

Science fiction writers and directors, whose predictions are sometimes denigrated or altogether discounted by "professional scientists," have helped to put some form to forecasts by the use of print, sound and visual mediums, especially in novels and motion picture. Some of the more notable predictions and social critiques are contained within the following works: *Frankenstein* (Shelley 1818), *Metropolis* (Lang 1927), *Brave New World* (Huxley 1932), *1984* (Orwell 1949), *I, Robot* (Asimov 1950), *2001: A Space Odyssey* (Clarke 1968), *Blade Runner* (Dick 1968), *THX-1138* (Lucas 1971), *Neuromancer* (Gibson 1984), *Total Recall* (Verhoeven 1990), *The Silicon Man* (Platt 1991), and *Johnny Mnemonic* (Longo, 1995). Forecasts are important because they "do not state what the future will be…they attempt to glean what it might be" (Braun, 1995, p. 133) and for that matter, futuristic-type works help us to understand trends and patterns and to raise challenging issues to do with the impact of technology on society.

Bartholomew (2000) reflects: "Palm Pilots. Windows CE. Car phones. Cell phones. Armband computers for warehouse management. Bar-code readers. Pagers. Geophysical positioning devices. Where will it all end?" His compelling question "where will it all end?" is noticeably rhetorical. Science holds to the unalterable creed that there is 'no end.' To Bartholomew's list we could add: RFID transponder implants. Nanotechnology. Brain implants. Soul chips… the list can go on and on, bound only by the limits of the imagination and time. About the Verichip RFID, 14-year-old implant recipient Derek Jacobs commented: "I think it's one more step in the evolution of man and technology…There are endless possibilities for this" (Scheeres, 2002). Kurzweil believes that we are now entering that explosive part of the technological evolution curve. Kurzweil's *Law of Accelerating Returns* states that "the evolution of biological life and the evolution of technology have both followed the same pattern: they take a long time to get going, but advances build on one another and progress erupts at an increasingly furious pace." Fixmer (1998) described this plight as humanity's attempt to accelerate its own evolution and Mann calls it a *new kind of paradigm shift* that society has not yet experienced. Compare with the idea of *accelerating change* (Kurzweil, 2006).

CONCLUSION

The idea of the Electrophorus is one that no longer exists in the realm of the impossible. This being the case, the requirement for inclusive dialogue is now, not after widespread innovation. There are many lessons to be learned from history, especially from such radical developments as the atomic bomb and the resulting arms race. Joy (2000) has raised serious fears about continuing unfettered research into "spiritual machines." Will humans have the foresight to say "no" or "stop" to new innovations that could potentially be a means to a socially destructive scenario? Or will they continue to make the same mistakes? Implants that may prolong life expectancy by hundreds if not thousands of years might sound ideal but they could well create unforeseen devastation in the form of technological viruses, plagues, or a different level of crime and violence.

To many scientists of the positivist tradition solely anchored to an empirical world view, the notion of whether something is "right" or "wrong" is redundant and in a way irrelevant. To these individuals a purely moral stance has little or nothing to do with technological advancement but more with an ideological position. A group of these scientists are driven by an attitude of "let's see how far we can go," not "is what we are doing the best thing for humanity?"—and certainly not with the thought of "what are the long-term implications of what we are doing here?" One need only consider the maddening race to clone the first animal though many have long suspected an 'underground' scientific race to clone the first human. Today many observers believe that engineers and professionals more broadly lack accountability for the tangible and intangible costs of their actions (O'Connell 1988, p. 288). The dominant belief is that *science* should not be stopped because it will always make things better. The reality is however, that even seemingly small *advancements* into the realm of the Electrophorus if 'unchecked', for anything other than medical diagnostics or prosthesis, will have unbridled consequences for humanity. "Once man has given technique its entry into society, there can be no curbing of its gathering influence, no possible way of forcing it to relinquish its power. Man can only witness and serve as the ironic beneficiary-victim of its power" (Kuhns, 1971, p. 94).

REFERENCES

Banbury, C.M. (1997). *Surviving technological innovation in the pacemaker industry 1959-1990*. New York: Garland.

Bartholomew, D. (2000, January 10). *The ultimate in mobile computing*. Retrieved November 20, 2001, from http://www.iwvaluechain.com/Features/articles.asp?ArticleId=720

BBC. (2002, March 7). *Chips to keep the family healthy*. Retrieved November 13, 2003, from http://news.bbc.co.uk/1/hi/sci/tech/1859699.stm

Berry, A. (1996). *The next 500 years: Life in the coming millennium*. New York: Gramercy Books.

Billinghurst, M., & Starner T. (1999). Wearable devices: New ways to manage information. *IEEE Computer, 32*(1), 57-64.

Braun, E. (1995). *Futile progress: Technology's empty promise*. London: Earthscan.

Brown, J. (1999, October 20). *Professor Cyborg*. Retrieved December 20, 2004, from http://www.salon.com/tech/feature/1999/10/20/cyborg/index.html

Chislenko, A. (1997). *Technology as extension of human functional architecture*. Retrieved November 29, 2001, from http://www.extropy.org/eo/articles/techuman.htm

Cochrane, P. (1999). *Tips for time travelers: Visionary insights into new technology, life, and the future on the edge of technology*. New York: McGraw-Hill.

Davis, R. (2006). Meet the $4 million woman. *USA Today,* (September 14).

Dery, M. (1996). *Escape velocity: Cyberculture at the end of the century*. London: Hodder and Stoughton.

Dobson, R. (2001, June 5). *Professor to try to 'control' wife via chip implant*. Retrieved October 15, 2002, from http://www.rense.com/general10/professortotry.htm

Eli. (2005, June 25). *Species summary for electrophorus electricus: Electric eel*. Retrieved August 30, 2006, from http://filaman.ifm-geomar.de/Summary/SpeciesSummary.php?id=4535

Ellul, J. (1964). *The technological society*. New York: Vintage Books.

Fixmer, R. (1998). The melding of mind with machine may be the next phase of evolution. *The New York Times,* (August 11). Retrieved August 11, 1998, from http://www.princeton.edu/~complex/board/messages/138.html

Gates, B. (1995). *The road ahead.* New York: The Penguin Group.

Gibson, J. (1984). *Neuromancer.* New York: Ace Books.

Grossman, W. (1998, November). *Peter Cochrane will microprocess your soul.* Retrieved November 22, 2001, from http://www.wired.com/wired/archive/6.11/wired25.html?pg=17

Jones, K.C. (2006). VeriChip wants to test human-implantable RFID on military. *Information Week,* (August 23). Retrieved September 6, 2006, from http://www.informationweek.com/story/shortArticle.jhtml?articleID=192204948

Joy, B. (2000, April). *Why the future doesn't need us.* Retrieved January 4, 2003, from http://www.wired.com/wired/archive/8.04/joy_pr.html

Kaku, M. (1998). *Visions: How science will revolutionise the 21st century and beyond.* Oxford: Oxford University Press.

Keiper, A. (2006). The age of neuroelectronics. *The New Atlantis: A Journal of Technology and Society,* (Winter). Retrieved October 22, 2006, from http://www.thenewatlantis.com/archive/11/keiperprint.htm

Kuhns, W. (1971). *The post-industrial prophets: Interpretations of technology.* New York: Harper Colophon.

Kurzweil, R. (1999). *The age of spiritual machines.* New York: Penguin.

Kurzweil, R. (2006). *The Singularity is Near: When Humans Transcend Biology.* New York: Penguin.

LoBaido, A.C. (2001). *Soldiers with microchips: British troops experiment with implanted, electronic dog tag.* Retrieved November 20, 2001, from http://www.fivedoves.com/letters/oct2001/chrissa102.htm

Mann, S. (1997). Wearable computing: A first step toward personal imaging. *IEEE Computer,* (February), 25-32.

Maybury, M.T. (1990). The mind matters: Artificial intelligence and its societal implications. *IEEE Technology and Society Magazine,* (June/July), 7-15.

McGrath, P. (2001). *Technology: Building better humans.* Retrieved November 29, 2001, from http://egweb.mines.edu/eggn482/admin/Technology.htm

McLuhan, M. (1964). *Understanding media: The extensions of man.* Cambridge: MIT Press.

McLuhan, E., & Zingrone, F. (1995). *Essential McLuhan.* New York: Basic Books.

Michael, K., & Michael, M.G. (2006). Towards chipification: The multifunctional body art of the Net generation. In F. Sudweeks (Ed.), *Cultural attitudes towards technology and communication 2006* (pp. 622-641). Murdoch: Murdoch University.

Michael, K., & Michael, M.G. (2005). Microchipping people: The rise of the electrophorus. *Quadrant,* (March), 22-33.

Negroponte, N. (1995). *Being digital.* Australia: Hodder and Stoughton.

O'Connell, K.J. (1988). Uses and abuses of technology. *IEEE Proceedings, 135,* A(5), 286-290.

Rothblatt, M. (2006, July 21). *Transbemanism. Future Hi.* Retrieved August 30, 2006, from http://www.futurehi.net/archives/000833.html

Rummler, D.M. (2001, March 6). *Societal issues in engineering.* ENGR 300.

Scannell, E. (1996, November 25). Future technology will wire people up. Info World News, *18*(48). Retrieved October 27, 1998, from http://archive.infoworld.com/cgi-bin/displayArchive.pl?/96/48/t22-48.19.htm

Scheeres, J. (2002, February 6). *They want their id chips now.* Retrieved October 15, 2002, from http://www.wired.com/news/privacy/0,1848,50187,00.html

Smith, D. (2002, February 16). *Chip implant signals a new kind of man.* Retrieved October 15, 2002, from http://www.theage.com.au/news/national/2002/02/16/FFX9B13VOXC.html

Toffler, A. (1981). *Future shock.* New York: Bantam Books.

Uhlig, R. (2001). *The end of death: 'Soul Catcher' computer chip due....* Retrieved November 29, 2001, from http://www.xontek.com/Advanced_Technology/Bio-chips_Implants/The_End_of_Death

Yapko, M.D. (1998). *Breaking the patterns of depression.* Main Street Books.

Walker, I. (2001, November 4). *Cyborg dreams: Beyond human. Background Briefing, ABC Radio National, USA.*

Warwick, K. (2003). *Frequently asked questions.* Retrieved November 2003 from http://www2.cyber.rdg.ac.uk/kevinwarwick/FAQ.html

Witt, S. (1999, January 14). *Is human chip implant the wave of the future?* Retrieved November 2001 from http://www.cnn.com/TECH/computing/9901/14/chip-man.idg/

KEY TERMS

Bionic (Wo)man: Combining both biological and electronic elements in a man or woman that allow prosthetic limbs to be controlled by on-board computers.

Cybernetics: The study of nervous system controls in the brain as a basis for developing communications and controls in socio-technical systems.

Cyborg: The concept of a man-machine combination—a human who adds to or enhances his or her abilities by using technology.

Electrophorus: A human *bearer* of electricity. The root *electro* comes from the Greek word meaning "amber," and *phorus* means to "wear, to put on, to get into." When an electrophorus passes through an electromagnetic zone, he or she is detected, and data can be passed from an implanted microchip (or in the future directly from the brain) to a computer device.

Homo Electricus: The new species of man that the *electrophorus* would belong on the evolutionary ladder in the continued speciation of humans.

Human Evolution: The part of the theory of evolution by which human beings emerged as a distinct species.

Humanoid Robot: A robot that looks like a human in appearance and is autonomous. The term was derived by Czech playwright Karel Capek in 1920 from the Slav word for *worker.*

Law of Accelerating Returns: As order exponentially increases, the time between salient events grows shorter—that is, advancements speed up and the returns accelerate at a nonlinear rate.

Microchip Implant: An integrated circuit device encased in radio-frequency identification transponders that can be active or passive and is implantable into animals or humans usually in the subcutaneous layer of the skin.

Transhumanism: Abbreviated as >H or H+; an international cultural movement that consists of intellectuals who look at ways to extend life through the application of emerging sciences and technologies.

IT Security Culture Transition Process

Leanne Ngo
Deakin University, Australia

INTRODUCTION

The information superhighway is here and stretching further than the eye can see. Our working environment is becoming ever more hectic and demanding, computers and information technology are more pervasive, and limitations are perishing. The once solo dimension of information and technology is now multifaceted and convoluted in disposition (Ngo & Zhou, 2005). As a result, organizations need to be more vigilant than ever in actively responding to new information and technology security challenges and to ensure survivability in this new age.

Over the years many information technology (IT) security approaches—technical, managerial, and institutionalization—have surfaced. Also safeguards and countermeasures have been developed, practiced, and learned within organizations. Despite all these attempts to reduce and/or eradicate IT security threats and vulnerabilities, the issue still continues to be problematic for organizations. Solutions are needed that will reach the core of the problem—safeguarding and controlling *humans*—the human aspect of IT security.

Humans are a pervasive element in our businesses and critical infrastructures, the element which interacts with systems, services, information, and information technology. Furthermore, humans are responsible for the design, development, operation, administration, and maintenance of our information systems and resources. Therefore the ultimate success of any effort to secure information resources depends largely on the behavior and attitudes of the humans involved. While technological solutions can solve some information security problems, even the finest technology cannot succeed without the cooperation of humans. IT security is not just a technical problem that can be solved with technical solutions, but also a human problem that requires human solutions.

This article reviews the current literature on the human aspect of IT security within an organizational context. Human-related IT security concerns are summarized, and current human-related IT security solutions are examined and discussed. In this article, we consider IT security culture as a plausible solution to improving IT security-related behavior and attitudes of humans. We present our IT security culture transition model that is currently being trialed in three organizations to assist with increasing IT security awareness and hence improve the IT security culture of the individuals (managers and employees) and overall organization. Further, we discuss the potential individual psychological experiences of managers and employees during the transitional change towards IT security culture change.

BACKGROUND

Human-related IT security problems relate to how people associate themselves and interact with security. Here, human-related IT security problems are presented as well as current human-related solutions regarding the controlling and management of the human-side to IT security.

Human-Related IT Security Problems

Human factors impeding IT security within an organizational context with examples include:

1. **How humans perceive risk people:** People do not know to analyze risk properly and therefore this leads to improper actions.
2. **Ability to make security decisions:** Organizations cannot expect general employees to be IT security experts on top of their daily work.
3. **Human memory limitations:** This is a result of our inability to remember numerous and complex passwords.
4. **Trust:** We must have faith and confidence in the security of our computers.
5. **Usability:** This includes individuals trading off between security and practicality.

6. **Social engineering:** This means being manipulated to do things we would not normally do.

These human factors stem from the norms of natural human tendencies. Natural human tendencies suggest that humans are emotional, manipulative, and fallible. For example, humans want to get their job done and want to be helpful. People are helpful and therefore as a consequence are easily deceived, as exemplified by the success of social engineering attacks (Mitnick & Simon, 2002). Furthermore, humans are irrational and unpredictable. Unlike computers that can be programmed to process instructions in some logical order, humans on the other hand are irrational and complex and do unpredictable things. Barrett (2003) states for all the cleverness that organizations put into formulating creative, innovative, and secure efforts, they all can be breached if the users are reckless, therefore insinuating that recklessness and carelessness are common natural human tendencies. Natural human tendencies put an organization at risk of many security-related threats.

A better understanding of these predispositions will provide organizations and the greater community with a better chance of protecting and securing the human aspect of information security.

Current Human-Related IT Security Solutions

Current human-related IT solutions encompass understanding the human aspects and enforcing compliant behaviors and attitudes towards IT security. These current solutions include:

*   **Behavioral Auditing for Compliance:** Current auditing (security) methods do not cover effectively the behavior of the employees. Vroom and von-Solms (2004) proposes the concept of behavior auditing for compliance as a way of understanding, identifying, and resolving IT security-related human behavior concerns. However, auditing human behavior is very difficult to attain reliable and valid results due to humans being unpredictable by nature.
*   **IT Security Policy:** IT security policy has the potential to enforce compliant security behavior and attitudes of employees (Wood, 2004). IT security policies are a set of rules that outline how information and technology is to be protected to

achieve the organization's security goals. This allows humans to understand what is expected from them and be accountable for their actions. Simply telling people to behave in a certain way can be one option, but managers should not expect human to always act as prescribed. Also, reiterated by Dekker (2003), procedures do not rule human behavior and suggest that procedures should be seen as resources for action instead of an expectation about human behavior.

*   **Security Training and Education Programs:** A good security training program helps improve a user's decision-making skills by providing them with the necessary knowledge about security threats and the consequences of their actions (Leach, 2003). With the growing numbers of mobile employees, enterprises are at greater risks due to their employees with inadequate understanding of current security threats and risks to their computers. This simply illustrates the need for better security education on current security threats and best practices for humans.
*   **Ethical Standards of Behavior:** Eloff and Eloff (2003) and Jones (2004) researched ethical standards of behavior related to security and asserted that in order to change a user's behavior, there needs to be some form of guidelines on which to base such behavior. The authors maintained that following such established guides like the IEEE professional code can promote good behavior and influence others to do so.
*   **Leveraging off technology to reduce human error:** IT systems have become increasingly complex. Consequently, human errors resulting from operating these systems has increased. Experts have highlighted how IT has now gone beyond legitimate users' control to use information systems honestly and appropriately without causing a security breach. Legitimate users such as employees are more likely to put a priority on getting their work tasks completed rather than 'think' about security (Besnard & Arief, 2004). These authors suggest better software design with security built-in, that is, invisible to the user.

Any approach to human information security should aim to achieve transparent security—that is, built-in security either in technology or defused into the daily lives of humans, whereby security is not seen as an afterthought. It should be easy-to-understand—that is, consider usability issues and facilitate security decision making. It should be least-effort—that is, only ask humans to do as little as possible, as humans do not act or behave as prescribed. It should be continuous and constant—that is, whatever the effort, it needs to be persistent to act as a recurring reminder of the importance of security. And it must aim to be personal—that is, security must be taken on board by humans on a private and individual basis in order for humans to take security seriously.

IT Security Culture

Culture relates to the way in which things are done in an organization, and thus relates to the behavior and attitude of its members. An ethical culture of security is a culture whereby organizational members have strong ethical values that are exhibited in their security attitudes and behaviors within the organization's operational security environment. A culture whereby organizational members have strong ethical values and beliefs towards their organization's operational security environment will have better prospects of successful security culture change.

Creating a security culture means to change the current culture to a more security-conscious one. This requires an examination of the current culture. An examination of the current culture will allow an organization to highlight areas that require greatest attention for change. Fostering a culture of security means to instill security as a way of life. This means integrating security into the behavior and attitudes of people towards a security-conscious state.

The main limitations of creating a security culture are that it requires understanding and communication, it is slow and uncertain and difficult to measure whether culture change has taken place (Vroom & von-Solms, 2003). Security training, awareness, and education programs are critical in fostering security culture within individuals and organizations. These programs will help make employees understand, be responsive, and appreciate the need to act in a responsible security mindful way. However, education may not solve all problems, but will at least let users know of the consequences of their actions. Humans should see security as a personal gain and benefit to themselves and the overall organization.

There are several different methods in which an organization can foster a strong security culture. Vroom and von-Solms (2004) argue the presence of three cultures within an organization that require change: (1) organization as a whole, (2) groups or departmental, and (3) individual culture. The authors articulate that once group behavior begins to alter, this would influence the individual employees and likewise have an eventual affect on the formal organization (Vroom & von-Solms, 2003). This suggests that any organizations attempting to change culture should do so in small incremental steps (Kabay, 1993), and hence should be gradual and voluntary (Vroom & von-Solms, 2003).

In a short amount of time, the security and management literature has produced several key ideas regarding how organizations can foster and instill a culture of security within organizations. However, very little has been done to address the transition towards IT security culture improvement from both an organizational and individual point of view. Noting the key points suggested by the literature, we propose our IT security culture transition model.

IT Security Culture Transition (ITSeCT) Model

The ITSeCT model proposed by Ngo, Zhou, and Warren (2005) aimed at assisting participating organizations in their research to better meet the organization's desired level of IT security awareness and culture. Employees needed to understand their roles and responsibilities in order to make informative and morally correct judgments and actions. Our IT security transition model proposes to detail the roles and responsibilities of managers and employees in the transition process to improve IT security culture in the workplace. The model places importance on raising awareness of IT security threats and risks, and associated consequences of IT security-related behavior and actions towards IT and information systems interactivity in the workplace.

Our ITSeCT model proposes a culture that would see individuals behave in an expected manner when faced with new security challenges. We know that technology will always advance. Therefore, giving individuals knowledge of IT security basics such as threats, risks, and consequences of their actions will allow individuals to gradually adapt to constant change—and hence allow us to predict expected behavior.

Figure 1. IT security culture transition model

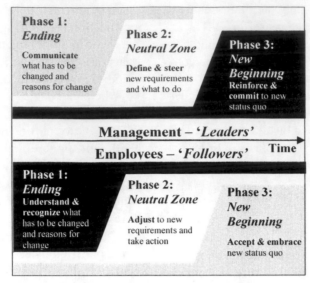

The transition model is intended to assist organizations in transitioning towards IT security culture improvement. The model consists of two main players—*leaders* (managers) and *followers* (general employees). The model is shown in Figure 1. The model highlights the respective roles and responsibilities of managers and employees. The former has the role of overseeing and managing the process, and the latter adapts and accepts the transition.

There are three phases within the model. Phase 1, *Ending,* requires an understanding of letting something go. In this article's case, it is letting go of the current behavior and apathetical attitude towards IT security. Management communicates this change, and employees understand and recognize the reasons for change. Phase 2, *Neutral Zone,* is the fertile ground opened for new requirements and actions to flourish, steered by management, and adjusted and learned by employees. Phase 3, *New Beginning,* looks towards the improved IT security culture. Management reinforces and commits to the new status quo, and employees accept and embrace it. The transition process needs to have the commitment and support from management and the understanding and acceptance from employees to have any chance of success. Furthermore, any new ventures intended in any organization require planning and dedication.

Transition is the adjustment, development, and change experienced by people within organizations when progressing towards achieving a particular change

(Bridges, 2003). Understanding the transition process is crucial for successful organizational information security culture change. Furthermore, identifying the key roles of management and employees in the transition process will allow for better understanding of their respective responsibilities. For more explanation and discussion of the model, please refer to Ngo et al. (2005).

The ITSeCT model is easy to follow with a step-by-step process. Only two major parties are involved: managers and employees. There is no need for technology spending, as it solely focuses on improving the attitudes and behavior of individuals.

IT Security Culture Transition Model: Individual Context

Bridges (2003) asserts that there are two transition processes running concurrently. The first has been discussed, and the second is the individual psychological transition process. When there are changes happening within an organization, the people that are affected by it are also going through their own psychological transitions (Iacovini, 1993; St-Armour, 2002; Harvard Business School, 2003). Ngo et al. (2005) show in Figure 2 an adaptation of an individual transition process and the psychological experiences as suggested by St-Amour (2001) during each transition phase.

In Table 1 we present the personal experiences during each phase of the transition process that managers

Table 1. Individual transitions:Managers vs. employees

Individual Transitions	Endings	Neutral Zone	Beginnings
Managers	• No longer ignoring the potential impact of IT security threats • No longer taking a reactive approach to security • No longer having a false sense of security	• How, when, and what information should I communicate to my employees? • Will my employees care enough to participate? • Do I trust my employees enough with extra responsibility?	• Proactive approach to security • Supporting and commitment to IT security culture • Understanding of potential IT security threats and risk
Employees	• No longer ignoring potential impact of IT security threats • No longer not caring about security • No longer seeing security as solely the IT team's and manager's responsibility	• Responsible for organizational security • Realizing that I am part of the security team • How will I change my behavior and attitude to be t IT is security conscious? • How do I adjust to the new requirements?	• I am part of the organizational security strategy • I am a security-conscious employee • My interactions with IT and security conforms to organization's security policies and procedures

and employees may experience during transitioning towards IT security culture change. Our example is based on applying Bridges' (2003) framework of transition and St-Amour's (2001) individual transition process. Table 1 shows this example.

FUTURE TRENDS

Human IT security research will give us a better understanding of human factors associated with IT security which is fundamental to the understanding of how humans interact and behave towards IT security. This knowledge can aid in providing the basis for proposals of possible approaches and measures to manage the human aspect of IT security. Human IT security research will help to raise awareness among those who are unacquainted with the potential detrimental threats and risks that humans can cause. Therefore, it is anticipated that this research will generate a great deal of interest, not only by corporations and governments, but to the general public.

Our future research project will focus on this research gap to promote IT security awareness and establish an IT security culture within organizations. Furthermore, an IT security awareness and culture assessment tool will be a direct outcome of this research, which will be available to participating Australian organizations.

CONCLUSION

Human-related security problems should be addressed with human solutions. Technical solutions, although important, cannot be the only means for solving human problems, and any approach should focus on solutions tailored to solving the human problem.

Understanding and having a well-planned transition process is crucial for successful organizational information security culture change. Furthermore, identifying the key roles of management and employees in the transition process will allow for better understanding of their respective responsibilities.

This article addressed the key roles and responsibilities for managers and general staff in improving the IT security culture in an organization's operational environment. The model highlighted the importance of understanding the transition process required for IT security culture change. We reviewed the key developments with IT security culture research. Our model was developed based on key IT security culture research and Bridges' (2003) transition process framework.

Furthermore, we highlighted that individuals such as employees and managers go through their own psychological transition concurrent to the organization. We provided an example of the psychological transition process that managers and employees may go through when transitioning towards IT security culture improvement. We based our example on Bridges' (2003) transition process and St-Amour's (2001) individual transition framework.

REFERENCES

Barrett, N. (2003). Penetration testing and social engineering: Hacking the weakest link. *Information Security Technical Report, 8*(4), 56-64.

Besnard, D., & Arief, B. (2004). Computer security impaired by legitimate users. *Computers & Security, 23*, 253-264.

Bridges, W. (2003). *Managing transitions: Making the most of change.* New York: Perseus.

Dekker, S. (2003). Failure to adapt or adaptations that fail: Contrasting models on procedures and safety. *Applied Ergonomics 2003, 34*, 233-238.

Eloff, J., & Eloff, M. (2003). Information security management: A new paradigm. *Proceedings of the 2003 South African Institute for Computer Scientists and Information Technologists Conference,* South Africa.

Harvard Business School. (2003). *Managing change and transition.* Boston: Harvard Business School Press.

Iacovini, J. (1993). The human side of organization change. *Training & Development, 47*(1), 65 - 68.

Jones, A. (2004). Technology: Illegal, immoral, or fattening? *Proceedings of the 32nd Annual ACM SIGUCCS Conference on User Services,* Baltimore, MD.

Kabay, M.E. (1993). Social psychology and infosec: Psycho-social factors in the implementation of information security policy. *Proceedings of the 16th U.S. National Computer Security Conference.*

Leach, J. (2003). Improving user security behavior. *Computers & Security, 22*(8), 685-692.

Mitnick, K.D., & Simon, W.L. (2002). *The art of deception: Controlling the human element of security.* Indianapolis: Wiley.

Ngo, L., & Zhou, W. (2005). The multifaceted and ever-changing directions of information security—Australia get ready! *Proceedings of the 3rd International Conference on Information Technology and Applications* (ICITA 2005), Sydney, Australia.

Ngo, L., Zhou, W., & Warren, M. (2005). Understanding transition towards information security culture change. *Proceedings of the 3rd Australian Information Security Management Conference,* Perth, Australia.

St-Amour, D. (2001). Successful organizational change. *Canadian Manager, 26*(2), 20-22.

Vroom, C., & von-Solms, R. (2004). Towards information security behavioral compliance. *Computers & Security, 23*, 191-198.

Wood, C.C. (2004). *Developing a policy your company can adhere to.* Retrieved February 6, 2006, from *http://www.searchsecurity.com*

KEY TERMS

Individual Transition Process: The individual transitional and psychological process individuals go through in when transitioning towards change.

IT Security Awareness: Familiarity of IT security literacy concepts by either an individual or organization as a whole.

IT Security Culture: Relates to the way in which things are done in an organization, thus relating to the IT security behavior and attitude of its members.

IT Security Management: Refers to the policies, processes, procedures, and guidelines regarding how to manage and control information and technology for achieving security goals.

IT Security Policy: Formally written IT security statements similar to that of laws aimed at representing IT security rules within an organization context.

ITSeCT (IT Security Culture Transition) Model: A role- and process-based model aimed at assisting individuals and organizations to increase IT security awareness and in transitioning towards IT security culture improvement.

Transition: The adjustment, development, and change experienced by people within organizations when progressing towards achieving a particular change

ICT Leapfrogging Policy and Development in the Third World

Amanda Third
Monash University, Australia

Kai-Ti Kao
Monash University, Australia

INTRODUCTION

'Leapfrogging' is the term used to describe development policies, and the processes of their implementation, that aim to move lesser developed societies to a higher stage of development without them transitioning through the spectrum of changes that have underpinned the development of industrialized societies. Information and communication technology (ICT) leapfrogging strategies have the potential to bypass intermediate stages of development that are often resource intensive (in terms of capital investment in hardware and labor), environmentally unsustainable, and involve the building of infrastructure that is prone to become obsolete in a relatively short time. A number of organizations, including (and not only including) the Association of South East Asian Nations (ASEAN, 2000), Group of Eight (G8, 2000), the United Nations (UN, 2000), and aid agencies, advocate ICT leapfrogging in the developing world.

The rise and increasing reach of globalization has seen the emergence and widespread uptake of ICTs. Indeed, for many commentators the proliferation of ICTs is a key mechanism of the social, cultural, political, and economic transformations that characterize globalization. In this context, as Nulens and van Audenhove (1999, p. 451) note:

The benefits of ICTs are not considered confined to the West alone. Several observers believe that the widespread use of ICTs in developing countries will improve the economic and social situation of the Third World populations as well. Technological innovation in ICTs and the drastic reduction in prices will enable [lesser developed nations such as those of] Africa to 'leapfrog' stages of development and catch up with the global Information Society.

The explicit aim of leapfrogging policies is to allow developing nations to compete on par with the developing world. The introduction of ICT production, distribution, and consumption initiatives is seen to represent a unique opportunity for developing nations in places like South America, Asia, and Africa to enter the global economy and benefit from the processes of globalization. As such, the argument that ICTs are crucial to development underpins the agendas of a number of global organizations. For example, the activities of the UN Global Alliance for ICT and Development (UN-GAID) to date have emphasized the importance of integrating ICTs into development strategies in order to achieve the UN's broader development goals (see ECOSOC, 2000). Leapfrogging is thus a policy orientation with considerable purchase in arenas dedicated to development.

DEVELOPING NATIONS AND THE PROBLEMS WITH THE THIRD WORLD

The term 'third world' first came into popular usage in the aftermath of World War II when nations around the world began the process of post-war reconstruction. From the outset, the idea of the third world was bound up with the emergent politics of the Cold War, which saw the capitalist 'Western world' (and in particular, the United States) engage in a nuclear standoff with the communist 'East' (represented most prominently by the then Soviet Union). A 'three worlds' model of development was used to classify the nations of the world according to levels of 'industrialization' or 'modernization' and economic status. The 'first world' described highly industrialized, capitalist nations. The 'second world' described communist bloc nations with strong levels of modernization. And the 'third world' applied to those nations that fell outside the 'first' and 'second' worlds. These nations were typically colonial territories or newly independent nations with low levels of industrialization and highly dependent economies. In the context of the Cold War, the modernization of the third world was seen in the West as an important component of the struggle against the threat of communism. It was thought that, by lending third-world nations' economic support for the process of industrialization, the first world could annex the third world and facilitate the global spread of capitalism. Further, as a major source of raw materials (minerals, timber, and so on), the third world was of economic importance to manufacturing in first-world industrialized nations.

With the so-called 'fall of communism' in the early 1990s and the 'disappearance' of the second world, the three worlds model became an increasingly irrelevant way of describing the developmental status of the world's nations. In this context the term 'developing nations' gained prominence and has become the preferred term, not least because it is a more dynamic term that conveys the possibility of changing the circumstances of impoverished nations. As globalization gained momentum, developing nations, while remaining a primary source of raw materials, also came to be configured as potential markets for first-world products.

Discussions about the status of third-world or developing nations typically emphasize the problem of widespread poverty. However, these terms also describe nations with very high rates of population growth, traditional rural social structures, low rates of literacy, high rates of disease, and also often unstable governments. While the term 'developing world' implies that the nations that comprise this category are homogenous, it in fact disguises a high degree of diversity. That is, there are vast differences between individual developing nations (compare, for example, Vietnam, Sierra Leone, and Barbados) and also between different social groups within developing nations (e.g., historically India has had a very small but wealthy population as well as large numbers of people living in extreme poverty). Further, there is a tendency to discuss concepts of development in terms of binaries such as first/third worlds, north/south and west/east, wherein the former is always allocated a more privileged status than the latter. The use of these binaries implies that development can be measured according to geographical location, which also overlooks the presence of varying states of development within both 'first' and 'third' worlds. Acknowledging this, the specific

historical, geographical, socio-cultural, political, and economic factors shaping underdevelopment in individual nations need to be taken into consideration in the process of formulating solutions to these nations' problems.

POTENTIAL BENEFITS FOR ICT LEAPFROGGING FOR DEVELOPING COUNTRIES

The process of globalization has arguably exacerbated the problems of the developing world. Some theorists suggest that, to date, globalization has witnessed an extension of Western imperialism that further forces developing nations into a relationship of dependency upon developed nations (Moore, 1995; McChesney & Nichols, 2002). In this understanding, the developing world remains a source of cheap labor and raw materials that is exploited by (Western) global corporations to increase their profits. That is, globalization is seen to be underpinned by the flow of capital from the developing world into the developed world, reproducing asymmetrical power relations. In this view, globalization, rather than remedy, is said to compound the problems of the developing world. Added to this, it is argued that one of the negative effects of the information or network society is that it has consolidated a digital divide between the 'information haves' of the developed world and the 'information have-nots' of the developing world (Flew, 2002, pp. 208-209).

However, if globalization and the rise of the network society have compounded the problems of the developing world, these phenomena also arguably present new possibilities for rectifying their problems. In *The Rise of the Network Society*, Manuel Castells argues that the current information society is facilitated by a global media system and the proliferation of convergent information and communication technologies. He argues that "the new economy is organized around global networks of capital, management, and information, whose access to technological know-how is at the roots of productivity and competitiveness" (Castells, 1996, p. 471). The information and network society is characterized by a 'weightless' economy in which specialist knowledge, skills, and creativity are highly prized and sought after (Flew, 2002, pp. 146-147). Businesses increasingly operate on a global scale (Dann & Dann, 2001, pp. 49-56), and ICTs facilitate the flow of capital around the world at unprecedented rates. New technologies simultaneously enable greater interconnection between various parts of the globe and are creating an interdependent global economy, where the fortunes of one company can have repercussions on various national economies. A nation's position in the new world economy is now defined more by its degree of participation in the network rather than by geographical location. In this logic, nations outside this information society are at risk of severe economic disadvantage.

The global integration of national and regional economies can provide greater opportunities for participation by the developing world in the global economy, resulting in wealth generation for these nations. The amelioration of social problems such as poverty, disease, and low literacy is seen to flow from the economic prosperity engendered by participation in the global information economy. It is in this context that ICT leapfrogging presents as a viable strategy for addressing the digital divide and stimulating the growth of market economies in the developing world. Not just ICT consumption, but also ICT production is seen as vital to the future of developing nations. Thus, the aim of many ICT leapfrogging initiatives is not just that of launching the developing world into the ICT revolution, but also fostering the growth of homegrown ICT industries and ICT research and development.

The virtues of ICT leapfrogging are said to extend beyond economic growth to wider social, cultural, and community benefits for the developing world. The uptake of ICTs is perceived to enable the empowerment of individual citizens and a revival of the public sphere. It has claimed access to ICT results in greater individual access to communication on both a global and local scale, which in turn provides these individuals with opportunities for political, economic, and social empowerment. The broader benefits of decentralized communication networks include: greater horizontal communication; the ability to bypass official channels to gather, distribute, and validate information; and the freedom to speak, campaign, and assemble without censorship, ultimately resulting in a more democratic environment (Flew, 2002, p. 185).

Indeed, ICT leapfrogging initiatives emphasize the democratic potential of ICTs, arguing that the uptake of ICTs will foster the free flow of information both into and out of the developing world. This is said to produce 'enlightened' developing world populations that are well-versed in globalizing ideals, and to create the demand for transparent democratic governance in developing nations. As such, ICTs are seen as playing an important role in stamping out corruption and transitioning impoverished nations into democracy. This process will be further supported by the effects of the emergence of a global conscience (Tester, 1994). The spread of the network society is understood here as creating new structures of accountability which will see the global community call for an end to abuses of power in the developing world. It is also suggested that ICTs operate as what Daniel Lerner (1958) has described as "mobility multipliers" (p. 59). This term refers to the ability of media technologies to connect individuals and communities in the developing world with other cultures, resulting in the transmission of modernizing ideas that will supposedly compel the developing world to raise its aspirations.

The likely results of leapfrogging initiatives need to be assessed within larger contexts. Singapore, for example, has established itself as a regional networking hub and ICT pioneer and leader within the Southeast Asian region. Much of this success can be attributed to the nation's restricted land mass and concentrated urban population, which has facilitated the establishment of an impressive telecommunications infrastructure (Ure, 1997, p. 30). However, a country such as Vietnam, a fellow ASEAN member and located within the same geographic region as Singapore, has experienced a much slower uptake of ICTs and leapfrogging policies. In contrast to Singapore, Vietnam has been severely hindered by numerous internal conflicts; it has a largely agricultural economy and a population that is primarily distributed and rural. These differences in the success of leapfrogging in different national contexts thus illustrate that leapfrogging policies made on a global level, such as those by ASEAN for this region, do not always target the needs of individual nations. This in turn highlights the potential pitfalls of applying the concept of leapfrogging as either a blanket or instant-fix policy.

IMPEDIMENTS TO ICT LEAPFROGGING POLICY

The barriers to ICT use in the developing world go beyond the mere absence of the appropriate technology and are bound up with a number of social, cultural, political, economic, and geographical considerations.

The introduction of leapfrogging ICT policy often entails deceptively high costs. These include initial investments in technological equipment, as well as ongoing costs such as Internet service providers (ISPs) and telephone bills, and the need to pay for technical maintenance, support, and training. Further, given that technological development in the developed world is advancing at a rapid pace, there are likely to be considerable costs associated with the introduction of new technologies as early ICT technologies and platforms are superseded. Nations implementing such policies must thus have sufficient funds to finance ICT programs in a holistic manner. This is problematic in contexts where financial resources are scarce or dependent upon financing from external organizations. Additionally, many developing nations lack adequate material infrastructure (such as reliable electricity supplies or an established telecommunications service) upon which ICT leapfrogging is dependent. The costs of establishing such infrastructure can be substantial. Capital outlays associated with ICT development may well be offset in the future by the introduction of mobile communications technologies whose infrastructure requires less capital investment. However, to date, mobile technologies are not as reliable, do not provide the same quality communication, and are expensive for individual users to maintain (for example, Internet access via mobile telephone is patchy, slow, and expensive to run compared to cable access).

Language and ICT literacies in developing nations also pose obstacles to ICT leapfrogging. Castells (1996, p. 471) notes that access to technology is not enough to participate in the information society, but that it is also necessary to have the knowledge and training in how to use and maintain technologies. The introduction of ICTs thus needs to be complemented by tailored education and training that accounts for the ongoing development of new technologies and platforms. Language and cultural considerations can pose problems as the majority of content on the Internet is in English and Western oriented (Flew, 2002, pp. 86-87). This raises associated concerns with domination known as cultural imperialism. Leapfrogging also requires well-thought-out policy making and planning, efficient management cultures, effective industry regulation, and ongoing research. In some developing nations, experience in these areas is very minimal and requires appropriate programs to foster the necessary skills and structures.

There is a real danger that the blind implementation of ICT policies can result in a widening of the digital divide, reinforcing dependency in "an asymmetrical relationship that, by and large, has reinforced patterns of domination created by previous forms of dependency throughout history" (Castells, 1996, p. 109). Without targeted investment in literacy, management, and research and development, along with contingency plans for the adoption of ongoing technological developments, developing nations risk playing continual 'catch-up' to the developed world. This is particularly pertinent as the futures of nations and sometimes entire regions are often constructed as dependent upon their ability to implement the newest technologies. If ICT leapfrogging ultimately aims to establish developing nations as independent producers of ICT hardware, software, and content, and to reduce these nations' dependency on the developed world, the problem of catch-up needs to be anticipated. While leapfrogging can indeed enhance a nation's economy, mechanisms also need to be put in place to ensure that the wealth generated by ICTs is distributed evenly within developing societies and that it does not instead operate to reinforce an internal divide between rich and poor.

Many have argued the need for the creation of a free market (or a deregulated environment) to promote leapfrogging. While a market open to a greater competition would theoretically result in cheaper technology that would ultimately benefit developing nations, it could also lead to a loss of economic and state autonomy. Nulens and Van Audenhove (1999, pp. 453-454) point out that in many cases developing nations are presented with little other choice, and due to their lack of domestic capital are encouraged to promote foreign investment in this manner. Calls for the free market approach often do not take into account the various other factors involved in the implementation and use of ICTs. The price of deregulation can have adverse consequences upon domestic companies as foreign competition moves in on their markets, and there is no guarantee that they will facilitate the use and choice of appropriate ICTs over profit motivations (Kraemer & Dedrick, 2002, p. 38).

A CRITIQUE OF LEAPFROGGING IN DEVELOPING NATIONS

Garnham (2000, p. 66) warns that "debates on media economics and policy or on the social and cultural impact of the media are in fact often largely debates about technology," and argues for the constant need to be aware of a possible underlying technological determinism when examining policy documents regarding media and communication technologies. With specific regard to ICT leapfrogging policies, Nulens and van Audenhove (1999) similarly argue that these policies are "idealistic" and "technophilic." That is, such policies tend to express a utopian faith in technology as a neutral driver of positive social change. It is important to recognize, however, that technology is not ideologically neutral, and further, that by privileging technology, there is a risk of glossing over the factors that first resulted in the country's underdevelopment, as well as overestimating the ability of ICTs to address the issues.

The concept of leapfrogging is closely connected to that of development, which itself privileges those already in a position of power. The term 'developed world' is one that is frequently considered synonymous with advanced, Western-oriented, democratic, and industrialized societies, and therefore positioned as a desirable status. However this notion is inherently culturally imperialistic in that it positions Western advanced nations as the standard to which a range of diverse and unique cultures must aspire (O'Sullivan et al., 1994, p. 74).

The term is further complicated by the way in which development is measured by reference to a country's gross national product (GNP), reducing the complexities of development to a simplistic measure. This carries with it the implication that the problems caused by a lack of development can be resolved only by implementing policies (such as leapfrogging) that enable the growth of the economy.

These perspectives are also closely linked to the market approach (Nulens & Van Audenhove, 1999, p. 452). An example of this is the Group of Eight's *Okinawa Charter on Global Information Society* in 2000, which sees the private sector playing "a leading role in the development of information and communication networks in the information society" (G8, 2000, p. 2). This policy document further advocates that governments "avoid undue regulatory interventions that would hinder productive private-sector initiatives in creating an IT-friendly environment" (G8, 2000, p. 2). This market-dominated approach can be seen to privilege Western values and, as Arce and Lang (2000) argue, the language of development contributes to a discourse that reproduces relations of power which privilege Western understandings of development.

Therefore, the need to recognize the complexities of the term development becomes further hindered by the formal language used by policy documents and reports, which catalogue and record issues to then be presented to relevant parties as problems to be addressed. For example, the United Nations' *Millennium Declaration* in 2000 repeatedly emphasizes the right to develop. As well as stating that "no individual and no nation must be denied the opportunity to benefit from development," it affirms the resolution of the General Assembly to "create an environment—at the national and global levels alike—which is conductive to development," and emphasizes the UN's dedication to upholding "all internationally recognized human rights and fundamental freedoms, including the right to develop" (UN, 2000, pp. 2-6). However, this policy neglects to specify a conception of development, but rather assumes an understanding of the term as the attainment of the position and privilege currently enjoyed by the world's richest nations. Not only does this assumption tend to overlook the unique needs and features of local cultures, but also gradually dilutes the intricacies of development issues into language which subsequently produces solution policies likewise divorced from the original issues.

Policies such as those of the G8 and the UN, stemming from a privileged perspective, represent a developed world viewpoint, and therefore are not necessarily immediately transferable to a developing world context. Not only are conditions such as physical and regulatory infrastructure different, but so too are the social environments and cultural attitudes towards technology. In addition, there is also the danger of adopting in an uncritical manner the predominantly Western attitudes present in these global policies in regards to technology, society, and development, and transferring them into local policies.

However, these policies also have advantages. When establishing the rules and conditions regulating ICT use and development within their own borders, it can be assumed that the leaders of developing nations would be influenced by these global charters and incorporate their visions and experiences into their own policies. This has significant benefits in that these global charters can signal potential problems and issues related to ICT use, and thus allow developing nations to anticipate them before they occur.

IMPLEMENTING SUCCESSFUL LEAPFROGGING ICT POLICY

Research shows that the success of ICT leapfrogging policies is very much context specific, and as such, ICT strategies need to be developed with attention to the historical, geographical, economic, and socio-cultural specificities of individual developing nations. Nonetheless, a number of general guidelines for the implementation of ICT developmental policies and programs can be gleaned from the experiences of developing nations to date.

For ICT leapfrogging initiatives to be successful, they need to be fully integrated into a nation's overall development strategy and implemented in stages over lengthy timelines. While ICT leapfrogging initiatives potentially bring significant financial benefits to developing nations, the temptation to privilege economic considerations over social and cultural priorities needs to be resisted. The developmental benefits of ICTs can only be realized if they articulate with, and support, a nation's long-term social, cultural, political, and economic aspirations. Experience shows that ICTs need to be introduced into nations of the developing world with due sensitivity to the social and cultural factors that will shape ICT production, uptake, and its successful integration into developing cultures. This means that ICT leapfrogging initiatives need to be underpinned by a holistic approach to development. They need to incorporate, for example, appropriate educational and vocational training that will produce literate, technology savvy users, along with skilled workers and effective management cultures that are able to contribute positively to the nation's growth and interface with global communities. They also need to take appropriate measures to address the material problems of infrastructure and access. Finally, if such initiatives are to avoid reproducing existing relationships of marginalization, dependency, and exploitation by industrialized nations, developing nations need to be given the opportunity to exercise autonomy in the development and implementation of ICT leapfrogging strategies.

REFERENCES

Arce, A., & Lang, N. (2000). Modernity and development: Models and myths. In A. Arce & N. Lang (Eds.), *Anthropology, development and modernities* (pp. 4-7). London/New York: Routledge.

ASEAN. (2000). *e-ASEAN framework agreement.* Retrieved September 10, 2004, from http://www.aseansec.org/5462.htm

Braman, S., & Sreberny-Mohammadi, A. (Eds.). (1996). *Globalization, communication and transnational civil society.* Cresskill, NJ: Hampton Press.

Calvert, P., & S. (2001). *Politics and society in the third world.* London: Longman.

Castells, M. (1996). *The rise of the network society.* Oxford: Blackwell.

Collins, R., & Murroni, C. (1996). *New media, new policies: Media and communications strategies for the future.* Cambridge: Polity.

Dann, S., & Dann, S. (2001). Unique features of Internet-based marketing. In *Strategic Internet marketing* (pp. 43-69). Milton, John Wiley & Sons.

Dunn, H.S. (1995). Caribbean telecommunications policy: Fashioned by debt, dependency, and underdevelopment. *Media, Culture and Society, 17,* 201-222.

ECOSOC (United Nations Economic and Social Council). (2000). *Ministerial declaration on development and international cooperation in the twenty first century: The role of information technology in the context of a knowledge-based global economy.* Retrieved September 8, 2006, from http://habitat.igc.org/undocs/e200019.htm

Flew, T. (2002). *New media: An introduction.* South Melbourne: Oxford University Press.

G8. (2000). *Okinawa charter on global information society.* Retrieved August 10, 2004, from http://www.g8.utoronto.ca/summit/2000okinawa/gis.htm

Garnham, N. (2000). The media as technologies. In *Emancipation, the media, and modernity: Arguments about the media and social theory* (pp. 63-81). Oxford: Oxford University Press.

Habermas, J. (1974). Public sphere: An encyclopaedia article (1964). *New German Critique, 1*(3), 49-55.

Hall, S. (1997). Discourse, power and the subject. In *Representation: Cultural representations and signify-*

ing practices (pp. 41-51). London/Thousand Oaks/New Delhi: Sage.

Heng, R.H.K. (2002). *Media fortunes, Changing times: ASEAN states in transition.* Singapore: Institute of South East Asian Studies.

Hilhorst, D. (2003). *The real world of NGOs: Discourses, diversity and development.* London: Zed Books.

Hoijer, B. (2004). The discourse of global compassion: The audience and media reporting of human suffering. *Media, Culture and Society, 26*(1), 513-531.

Iyer, V. (1999). *Media regulation for the new times.* Singapore: Asian Media Information and Communication Center.

Kraemer, K.L., & Dedrick, J. (2002). Information technology in Southeast Asia: Engine of growth or digital divide? In S.Y. Chia & J.J. Lim (Eds.), *Information technology in Asia: New development paradigms* (pp., 22-47). Singapore: Institute of Southeast Asian Studies.

Lerner, D. (1958). *The passing of traditional society: Modernizing the Middle East.* Glencoe, IL: The Free Press.

McChesney, R., & Nichols, J. (2002). *Our media not theirs: The democratic struggle against corporate media.* New York: Seven Stories Press.

McQuail, D., & Sinne, K. (Eds.). (1998). *Media policy: Convergence, concentration and commerce.* London: Sage.

Moore, D.B. (1995). Development discourse as hegemony. In D.B. Moore & G.J. Schmitz (Eds.), *Debating development discourse: Institutional and popular perspectives* (pp. 1-53). New York: St Martin's Press.

Mulholland, M. (1999). Deconstructing development. In *The politics of representation and western development activism* (pp. 5-15). Adelaide: Center for Development Studies.

Nulens, G., & van Audenhove, L. (1999). An information society in Africa? An analysis of the information society policy of the World Bank, ITU and ECA. *Gazette, 61*(6), 451-471.

O'Sullivan, T. et al. (1994). *Key concepts in communication and cultural studies* (2nd ed.). London/New York: Routledge.

Raborg, M. (Ed.). (2002). *Global media policy in the new millennium.* Luton: University of Luton Press.

Said, E. (1978). *Orientalism.* London: Routledge and Kegan Paul.

Stevenson, R.L. (1988). *Communication, development and the third world: The global politics of information.* New York/London: Longman.

Tenbruck, F.H. (1991). The dream of a secular ecumene: The meaning and limits of policies of development. In M. Featherstone (Ed.), *Global culture: Nationalism, globalisation and modernity* (pp. 193-206). London: Sage.

Tester, K. (1994). *Media, culture and morality.* London: Routledge.

UN. (2000). *United Nations millennium declaration 55/2.* Retrieved July 27, 2004, from http://www.un.org/millennium/declaration/ares552e.pdf

Ure, J. (1997). Telecommunications in China and the four dragons. In J. Ure (Ed.), *Telecommunications in Asia: Policy, planning and development* (pp. 11-48). Hong Kong: Hong Kong University Press.

KEY TERMS

Cultural Imperialism: The term used to describe the process of domination by which economically and politically powerful nations exert strong cultural influence over less powerful nations. Traditionally, concerns about cultural imperialism have focused on the problems engendered by the unidirectional flow of cultural products from the 'West' into other parts of the world, and as such, have taken expression as fears about 'Westernization' or 'Americanization'. It is feared that cultural imperialism will lead to the erosion of local culture and the loss of cultural autonomy for less powerful nations, as well as a decrease in cultural diversity globally.

Developing Nation: Formerly known as 'third-world' nation, this term is now used to describe a country considered to be in an ongoing state of development. While such nations are only partially industrialized, they are by necessity participating in an increasingly globally connected world.

Digital Divide: Commonly used to describe the gap in access and know-how between the ICT 'haves' and 'have nots'. The increased and widespread use of ICTs is advocated by many in the belief that they will facilitate the spread of democracy and narrow the gap between the rich and the poor. However, critics have also pointed out that the increasing connection between ICTs and the global economy means that the rich are getting richer while the poor poorer, thus widening this digital divide. The digital divide exists not only between nations, but also between different groups (e.g., between the working class and the elite, or between men and women, etc.) within a particular society.

Discourse: A term used by Michel Foucault to theorize the relationship between language, practice, and the operation of power. Hall (1992, p. 291) defines discourse as "a group of statements which provide a language for talking about—a way of representing knowledge about—a particular topic at a particular historical moment...Discourse is about the production of knowledge through language. But...since all social practices entail *meaning,* and meanings shape and influence what we do—our conduct—all practices have a discursive aspect." For Foucault, all discourse is embedded in power relations.

Free Market: A market that is free from regulation or restriction. The belief is that a free market will help to encourage greater competition, resulting in lower prices and higher quality products, which will ultimately benefit the consumer. Critics of the free-market ideal argue that competition is reduced as dominant market players shut out smaller competitors, thus disadvantaging the consumer with a lack of choice.

Global Conscience: A global moral sensitivity to or concern for the problems faced by disadvantaged populations. One of the effects of media globalization is that it draws attention to "distant victims of civil wars, genocide, massacres and other violence against civil populations, and play[s] a basic role in giving publicity to human suffering" (Hoijer, 2004, p. 513). As such, the global media are understood as a key facilitator of global conscience.

Idealistic: The idealistic view of ICT leapfrogging privileges technologies as "the main driving force of social change" (Nulens & van Audenhove, 1999, p. 452). It also assumes that "technology is neutral and

transferable from one context to another" (Nulens & van Audenhove, 1999, p. 452).

Information and Communication Technology (ICT): Digital technology that enables the increased transfer of information and communication, resulting in the breakdown of constraints imposed on communication by time and space. The use of such technologies also enables the creation of an increasingly networked and information-based society.

Leapfrogging: The idea that stages of development can be bypassed by the implementation and use of the latest technology/methods, thus bringing lesser developed nations onto an equal footing with more advanced countries.

Mobility Multiplier: This term describes the media's potential to communicate the possibility and nature of change to populations of developing nations. As a mobility multiplier, the media theoretically connects individuals and communities in the developing world with other cultures, resulting in the transmission of modernizing ideas that will supposedly compel the developing world to raise its aspirations.

Network Society: Term used to describe a society characterized by increased connectedness due to media and communications technologies. These facilitate the increased creation and transfer of information-based goods and services on a global basis, thus not only producing greater interconnection, but also increased interdependence.

Public Sphere: Described by Jügen Habermas (1974, p. 49) as "a realm of our social life in which something approaching public opinion can be formed [and] access is guaranteed to all citizens." The theory of the public sphere places emphasis on equal access to knowledge, decision making, and public participation by all citizens.

Technological Determinism: A term used to describe theories of social and cultural change that place heavy emphasis on the role of technology in shaping such processes. Technologically determinist arguments tend to overlook or marginalize the influence of political, economic, social, cultural, and other factors.

Technophilia: "In the technophilic view the current and future impacts of ICT are perceived as basically positive. The widespread use of ICT will lead to an increase in jobs, an expansion of diversity and pluralism, a harmonization of society, an increase in efficiency in private and public sectors and so on. With regard to developing countries, technophiles hold that the information revolution will provide these countries with the opportunity to leapfrog stages of development, leading to a balanced and equal world society" (Nulens & van Audenhove, 1999, p. 453). Technophilic views are characterized by a technologically deterministic perspective in that they privilege the role of technology as a driver of social, political, and economic change.

Third World: The term formerly used to describe lesser developed countries at the lower end of the global economic scale, and commonly composed of former colonies. The third world was defined in opposition to the first world, composed of highly industrialized, capitalist nations, and the second world, which denoted the communist bloc.

Identity Verification using Resting State Brain Signals

Ramaswamy Palaniappan
University of Essex, UK

Lalit M. Patnaik
Indian Institute of Science, India

INTRODUCTION

In the last several decades, computers or automated technologies have been utilized to verify the identity of humans using biometrics (i.e., physical and behavioral characteristics) (Wayman, Jain, Maltoni, & Maio, 2004), as it often surpasses the conventional automatic identity verification measures like passwords and personal identification numbers (PINs) by offering positive human identification. For example, the use of a PIN actually denotes the automatic identification of the PIN, not necessarily identification of the person who has provided it. The same applies with cards and tokens, which could be presented by anyone who successfully steals the card or token. PINs and passwords also have the problem of being compromised by 'shoulder surfing' and people picking the obvious choices. Even the recently proposed graphical passwords share similar problems.

The fingerprint-based biometrics has seen the most extensive deployment (Maltoni, Maio, Jain, & Prabhakar, 2003). Nevertheless, the field of biometrics remains exciting and actively researched after the continuing threats of transaction forgery and security breaches in e-commerce and electronic banking. Further, it is also very useful in other areas such as access to restricted places (control gates) or resources (computer log-in, automated teller machines, digital multimedia data access). As such, other biometrics like signatures (Jonghyon, Chulhan, & Jaihie, 2005), face (Chellappa, Wilson, & Sirohey, 1995), palmprint (Duta, Jain, & Mardia, 2002), hand geometry (Sanchez-Reillo, Sanchez-Avila, & Gonzalez-Marcos, 2000), iris (Wildes, 1997), and voice (Roberts, Ephraim, & Sabrin, 2005) have been proposed as an alternative or to augment the fingerprint technology. More recently, the field of biometrics has seen the emergence of newer biometrics techniques like keyboard dynamics (Bechtel, Serpen,

& Brown, 2001), ear force fields (Hurley, Nixon, & Carter, 2005), heart signals (Biel, Pettersson, Philipson, & Wide, 2001), odor (Korotkaya, 2003), and brain signals (Paranjape, Mahovsky, Benedicenti, & Koles, 2001; Poulos, Rangoussi, Chrissikopoulos, & Evangelou, 1999a, 1999b; Palaniappan, 2004).

There are only a small number of reported studies on using brain signals as biometrics, which can further be classified as electroencephalogram (EEG) based or Visual Evoked Potential (VEP) based. The advantage of using EEG- or VEP-based biometrics compared to other biometrics is its distinctiveness—that is, it is difficult to be duplicated by someone else, therefore not easily forged or stolen. The storage is not a problem as the feature vector is of a small size compared to other image-based biometrics.

BACKGROUND

A brief description on some of the previous studies on brain signal biometrics follows. Paranjape et al. (2001) examined the use of autoregressive (AR) coefficients with discriminant analysis that gave classification of about 80% for 349 EEG patterns from 40 subjects. Poulos et al. (1999a) used Learning Vector Quantizer[1] network to classify AR parameters of alpha rhythm EEG, where classification performance of 72-84% were obtained from four subjects with 255 EEG patterns. In another study, Poulos et al. (1999b) utilized this same EEG data and feature extraction method but used computational geometry to classify the unknown EEGs, which gave an average classification of 95%.

In another previous study (Palaniappan, 2004), VEP-based biometrics were proposed. This method was based on using energy of gamma band VEP potentials recorded from 61 channels while the subjects perceived common pictures. Perception of the picture stimulus evokes recognition and memory, which involves gamma oscillations, which were distinct between the subjects, thereby being suitable for biometrics.

All these previous studies that used brain signals as biometrics concentrated on identification of a user from a pool of users. In this study, the focus is on verification of a user's claimed identity rather than identification. Further novelty of the proposed methods lies in the use of a two-stage verification procedure that gives good accuracy. It is also easier for the user as it requires only brain signals recorded during resting state, which do not require any degree of mental effort as compared to the requirement of focusing on the recognition of a picture stimulus as in the study in Palaniappan (2004). In addition, the proposed method requires only six channels, as compared to 61 channels as in Palaniappan (2004).

A system to verify the identity will either accept the user claiming a given identity or reject his or her claim. The user is called a client in the former case and an impostor in the latter case. There are two types of errors in this system: false match error (FME) or false non-match error (FNME). The former is the error made by the system when wrongly accepting an impostor, while the latter is the error made when wrongly rejecting the client.

A realistic application scenario for this sort of biometrics would be targeted at small groups of people, where the security would be an utmost important issue—for example, access to classified confidential documents or entry to restricted areas. Fingerprints could be easily forged, and most of the other biometrics like palmprint, face, and iris share the same problem of easy forgery. But it is not easy to duplicate the thought processes in the brain. However, it should be noted that this discussion applies to fraud in the samples, not fraud in the other parts of the system (extracted features, decision, etc.), which has the possibility of fraud for any biometrics.

EXPERIMENTAL STUDY

Data

EEG data from five subjects were used in this study. The subjects were seated in an industrial acoustics company sound-controlled booth with dim lighting and a noiseless fan (for ventilation). An Electro-Cap elastic electrode cap was used to record EEG signals from positions C3, C4, P3, P4, O1, and O2 (shown in Figure 1), defined by the 10-20 system of electrode placement. The impedances of all electrodes were kept below 5 KΩ. Measurements were made with reference to electrically linked mastoids, A1 and A2. The electrodes were connected through a bank of amplifiers (Grass7P511), whose band-pass analogue filters were set at 0.1 to 100 Hz. The data were sampled at 250 Hz with a Lab Master 12-bit A/D converter mounted on a computer. Before each recording session, the system was calibrated with a known voltage.

In this study, EEG signals were recorded from subjects while performing four different mental activities (shown illustratively in Figure 2), without vocalizing or making any other physical movements. These mental activities were:

a. **Mathematical multiplication activity:** The subjects were given nontrivial multiplication problems. The activities were non-repeating and designed so that an immediate answer was not apparent.

b. **Geometric figure rotation activity:** The subjects were given 30 seconds to study a particular three-dimensional block object, after which the drawing was removed and the subjects were asked to visualize the object being rotated about an axis.

c. **Mental letter composing activity:** The subjects were asked to mentally compose a letter to a friend or a relative without vocalizing. Since the activity was repeated several times, the subjects were told to continue with the letter from where they left off.

d. **Visual counting activity:** The subjects were asked to imagine a blackboard and to visualize

Figure 1. Electrode placement

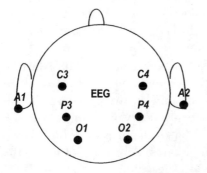

Figure 2. The four active mental activities performed by the subjects in the study: (a) rotation of a figure, (b) mathematical multiplication, (c) mental letter composing, and (d) visual counting. The other mental activity was resting. Note that the subjects imagined these activities without performing any form of action.

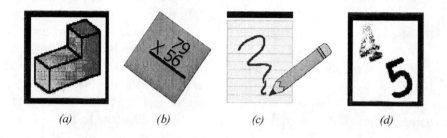

(a)	*(b)*	*(c)*	*(d)*

numbers being written on the board sequentially, with the previous number being erased before the next number was written. They were also told to resume counting from the previous activity rather than starting over each time.

In addition, EEG signals were also recorded during a resting state where the subjects were asked to relax and think of nothing in particular. Signals were recorded for 10 seconds during each activity, and each activity was repeated for 10 sessions.

Signal Conditioning

The EEG signal for each mental activity was segmented into 20 segments with length 0.5 seconds. The sampling rate was 250 Hz, so each EEG segment was 125 data points (samples) in length. Since there were 20 EEG segments for a session; there were a total of 200 EEG segments (with six channels) from a subject. When a particular subject was in consideration for identity verification, 200 segments were treated as client data while the other 800 segments were treated as impostor data.

Each of the EEG segments was re-referenced to common average using:

$$z[n] = x[n] - \frac{1}{6} \sum_{i=1}^{6} x_i[n] \qquad (1)$$

where *x[n]* is the original signal, while *z[n]* is the new re-referenced signal. This would be useful in reducing the intra-subject variance of the EEG signals.

Feature Extraction

The EEG segments were filtered into three bands using Elliptic filter. These bands were alpha (8-13 Hz), beta (14-20 Hz), and gamma (21-50 Hz). Though only alpha and beta bands have been commonly used, we included gamma band due to its relationship with mental processes, which was shown in the study by Palaniappan, Raveendran, and Omatu (2002). Forward and reverse operations were performed to ensure no phase distortion. The stop-band width of the filter was 1 Hz beyond the pass-band width on both sides. The filter orders were chosen to give a minimum of 20 dB attenuation in the stop-bands and a maximum of 0.5 dB ripple in the pass-bands.

The filtered EEG segments were subjected to feature extraction using autoregressive (AR) modeling. A real valued, zero mean, stationary, AR process of order *p* is given by

$$z(n) = -\sum_{k=1}^{p} a_k z(n-k) + e(n) \qquad (2)$$

where *p* is the model order, *z(n)* is the re-referenced signal at the sampled point *n*, a_k are the real valued AR coefficients, and *e(n)* represents the error term independent of past samples.

In this article, Burg's method (Shiavi, 1999) was used to estimate the AR coefficients. It is more accurate than other AR coefficient estimators like Levinson-Durbin as it uses more data points simultaneously by minimizing not only a forward error but also a backward error. In computing AR coefficients, order six was used because it as used in another previous study by Palaniappan, Raveendran, Nishida, and Saiwaki (2002) for mental activity classification. Therefore, six AR coefficients were obtained for each channel, giving a total of 36 features for each EEG segment for a mental activity. As there were three spectral bands, the size of the feature vector was 108.

Two-Stage Verification

For each subject, the 1,000 feature vectors (each with length 108) were split into:

- train patterns using 50 randomly selected client feature vectors
- validation patterns using 50 randomly selected client feature vectors (with no overlap to train patterns)
- test patterns using 100 remaining client feature vectors and all 800 impostor feature vectors

For different subjects, the allocations of the client and impostor feature vectors were different, where the particular subject's feature vectors were client feature vectors, while the rest of the subjects' feature vectors were impostor feature vectors. The Manhanttan^2 (city block) distances D were computed between 50 validation patterns and 50 training patterns. Manhanttan distance is simply the sums of lengths of the line segment in each dimension. For example, Manhanttan distance between two dimensional points P1 (x1,y1) and P2 (x2,y2) is |x1-x2| + |y1-y2|. Next, D_{min} and D_{max}, the minimum and maximum of these D validation-training distances for each validation pattern were computed. Thresholds Th_1 and Th_2 were obtained using:

$$Th_1 = \min(D_{min}) \text{ and } Th_2 = \max(D_{max}) \qquad (3)$$

The Th_1 would be useful in reducing FME—that is, reducing the error of wrongly accepting impostors as clients—while Th_2 would be useful in reducing FNME—that is, reducing the error of wrongly rejecting the clients as impostors. D_{min} was used to ensure that only the extremely similar patterns close to the clients

are accepted. This would filter out nearly all the impostors and perhaps some of the clients. So Th_2 would be useful in ensuring that the clients rejected using Th_1 were detected as clients, hence the use of D_{max}.

In the first verification stage, the maximum Manhanttan distances Dt_{max} of each of the 800 test patterns from the 50 training patterns were computed. The threshold Th_1 was used to determine whether each pattern was client or impostor, using the rule that the test pattern belonged to the client category if $Dt_{max} < Th_1$. Else, the test pattern was detected as from the impostor category. The focus of this verification level was to reduce FME only. No doubt, the FNME would be very high, but the second stage verification would solve this problem.

The second verification stage was used only for those test patterns that were detected as impostors. The minimum Manhanttan distances Dt_{min} of each of the test patterns (detected earlier as impostors) from the 50 training patterns were computed. The threshold Th_2 was used to determine whether the test patterns detected as impostors from first stage verification were really clients or impostors. Client was detected if $Dt_{min} < Th_2$. Else, it was impostor. The focus of this level was to reduce FNME.

Finally, FNME and FME were computed using:

FNME=(no. of client patterns incorrectly detected as impostor patterns/100)*100%

FME=(no. of impostors patterns incorrectly detected as client patterns/800)*100%

(4)

It should be noted here that there was no overlap between the test, validation, or training patterns. This was to ensure that accurate FNME and FME would be reflected. Figure 3 shows a simplified block diagram of the proposed approach.

Figure 3. Block diagram of the proposed approach

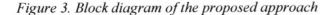

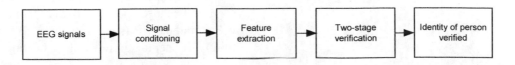

Table 1. Results of the experimental study

Subject	Matching Error (%)											
	S1		S2		S3		S4		S5		Average	
Activity	FNM	FM	FNM	FM	FNM	FM	FNM	FM	FNM	FM	FNM	FM
Resting	0	0	0	0	0	0	0	0	0	0	0	0
Count	0	0	0	0	4	0	0	0	0	0	0.8	0
Letter	0	0	0	0	0	0	0	0	0	0	0	0
Maths	16	0	0	0	8	0	14	0	1	0	7.8	0
Rotation	11	0	0	0	0	0	0	0	0	0	2.2	0
Minimum Error	0	0	0	0	0	0	0	0	0	0	0	0

Results

Table 1 shows the results of the experimental study. The FME and FNME values for each subject are shown. The low error values show the validity of the two-stage verification procedure using EEG signals. When comparing all the five subjects using the averaged FME and FNME values, the best mental activities were resting and letter composing. These activities gave good verification accuracy. Since resting activity is much easier to be performed by the subjects, it would be more suitable as compared to letter composing activity. The mental activity that gave the worst accuracy was mathematical multiplication activity.

FUTURE TRENDS

Although the proposed approach is still far from being suitable for an immediate industrial application, our aim was to draw attention of the international research community to the significant potential of brain electrical activity as a biometric.

For future work, we plan to investigate the stability of EEG signals over time and on extending the work to include more subjects. Further, a reduced feature set will also be studied, for example, use of a single channel (electrode) which will greatly simplify the EEG signal capture. It would also be worthwhile to study the use of this biometric in a multimodal environment—that is, to investigate if this biometric could be used in conjunction with other existing biometrics to increase the accuracy.

As this area is closely related to Brain-Computer Interface (BCI) designs for the use of paralyzed individuals, improvements in BCI would probably see similar improvements in this *brain biometrics*.

CONCLUSION

In the proposed approach, EEG data were recorded from five subjects while they were performing some simple mental activities. These EEG signals were subjected through several steps of signal conditioning, feature extraction, and decision making. In the signal conditioning step, the EEG signals were filtered into different spectral bands and re-referenced to common average, while in the feature extraction stage, AR coefficients were computed to be used as discriminative features. In the decision-making step, a novel two-stage verification procedure was used that gave good accuracy.

Though EEG data from six electrodes were used here instead of one to increase the inter-subject differences, it is still far less than 61 used in the earlier study for identification (Palaniappan, 2004). The good results obtained in this study indicate that it is possible to verify the identities of users by the use of resting state EEG signals alone. This pilot study has shown the potential of using EEG for biometric verification systems, especially for high-security environments as they are resistant to fraud.

Applications for this system include where fingerprints and other identity measures like passwords could be easily forged. It could also be used as a modality within a multimodal biometrics environment. The advantage of using such brain electrical activity as biometrics is its fraud resistance, that is the recorded brain response is difficult to be duplicated by someone else, and is hence unlikely to be forged or stolen. This modality has the additional advantage of confidentiality ('shoulder surfing' is impossible) as brain activity is not easily seen.

The disadvantage of the system lies in the cumbersome data collection procedure, but improvements in data collection procedures (such as dry electrodes, instead of wet) will reduce the unwieldiness and that the fraud resistance significantly outweighs this difficulty especially for high security applications.

ACKNOWLEDGMENT

The authors would like to acknowledge the assistance of Dr. C. Anderson of Colorado State University, USA, for giving permission to use the EEG data. We also thank the Department of Biotechnology, Government of India for supporting a portion of the work.

REFERENCES

Bechtel, J., Serpen, G., & Brown, M. (2001). Passphrase authentication based on typing style through an ART 2 neural network. *International Journal of Computational Intelligence and Applications, 2*(2), 131-152.

Biel, L., Pettersson, O., Philipson, L., & Wide, P. (2001). ECG analysis: A new approach in human identification. *IEEE Transactions on Instrument and Measurement, 50*(3), 808-812.

Chellappa, R., Wilson, C.L., & Sirohey, S. (1995). Human and machine recognition of faces: A survey. *Proceedings of IEEE, 83*(5), 705-740.

Duta, N., Jain, A.K., & Mardia, K.V. (2002). Matching of palmprint. *Pattern Recognition Letters, 23*(4), 477-485.

Hurley, D., Nixon, M., & Carter, J. (2005). Force field feature extraction for ear biometrics. *Computer Vision and Image Understanding, 98*(3), 491-512.

Jonghyon, Y., Chulhan, L., & Jaihie, K. (2005). Online signature verification using temporal shift estimated by the phase of Gabor filter. *IEEE Transactions on Signal Processing, 53*(2-2), 776-783.

Korotkaya, Z. (2003). *Biometric person authentication: Odor.* Retrieved June 12, 2006, from http://www.it.lut.fi/kurssit/03-04/010970000/seminars/korotkaya.pdf

Maltoni, D., Maio, D., Jain, A.K., & Prabhakar, S. (2003). *Handbook of fingerprint recognition.* New York: Springer-Verlag.

Palaniappan, R. (2004). Method of identifying individuals using VEP signals and neural network. *IEEE Proceedings—Science, Measurement and Technology, 151*(1), 16-20.

Palaniappan, R., Raveendran, P., & Omatu, S. (2002). VEP optimal channel selection using genetic algorithm for neural network classification of alcoholics. *IEEE Transactions on Neural Networks, 13*(2), 486-491.

Palaniappan, R., Raveendran, P., Nishida, S., & Saiwaki, N. (2002). A new brain-computer interface design using fuzzy ARTMAP. *IEEE Transactions on Neural Systems and Rehabilitation Engineering, 10*(3), 140-148.

Paranjape, R.B., Mahovsky, J., Benedicenti, L., & Koles, Z. (2001). The electroencephalogram as a biometric. *Proceedings of the Canadian Conference on Electrical and Computer Engineering, 2,* 1363-1366.

Poulos, M., Rangoussi, M., Chrissikopoulos, V., & Evangelou, A. (1999a). Person identification based on parametric processing of the EEG. *Proceedings of the IEEE International Conference on Electronics, Circuits, and Systems* (vol. 1, pp. 283-286).

Poulos, M., Rangoussi, M., Chrissikopoulos, V., & Evangelou, A. (1999b). Parametric person identification from the EEG using computational geometry. *Proceedings of the IEEE International Conference on Electronics, Circuits, and Systems* (vol. 2, pp. 1005-1008).

Roberts, W.J.J., Ephraim, Y., & Sabrin, H.W. (2005). Speaker classification using composite hypothesis testing and list decoding. *IEEE Transactions on Speech and Audio Processing, 13*(2), 211-219.

Shiavi, R. (1999). *Introduction to applied statistical signal analysis* (2nd ed.). London: Academic Press.

Sanchez-Reillo, R., Sanchez-Avila, C., & Gonzalez-Marcos, A. (2000). Biometric identification through hand geometry measurements. *IEEE Transactions on Pattern Analysis and Machine Intelligence, 22*(10), 1168-1171.

Wayman, J., Jain, A., Maltoni, D., & Maio, D. (Eds.). (2004). *Biometric systems: Technology, design and performance evaluation.* New York: Springer-Verlag.

Wildes, R.P. (1997). Iris recognition: An emerging biometric technology. *Proceedings of IEEE, 85*(9), 1348-1363.

KEY TERMS

Autoregressive (AR): A type of modeling commonly employed for EEG signals.

Alpha, Beta, Gamma: Some commonly used spectral bands.

Biometric: A quantitative measure of physical and behavioral characteristics of humans, normally used for identification/verification of the identity of the user.

Client: The actual user claiming the identity.

Electroencephalogram (EEG): Electrical potentials (in micro Volts range) caused by brain activity and obtained from the scalp using electrodes.

False Matching Error (FME): Also known as false accept error; the error of the system when it wrongly accepts impostors as clients.

False Non-Matching Error (FNME): Also known as false reject error; the error of system when it wrongly rejects the clients as impostors.

Impostor: The user claiming to be another user.

Verification: Also known as authentication; the procedure to verify the claimed identity of the user.

Visual Evoked Potential (VEP): A type of EEG/ brain signal that is evoked when the subject perceives a visual stimulus.

ENDNOTES

[1]   In the article, it is referred as Learning Vector Quantizer, though the common name is Learning Vector Quantization.

[2]   Alternatively, Euclidean distance could also be used.

Individual and Institutional Responses to Staff Plagiarism

Carmel McNaught
The Chinese University of Hong Kong, Hong Kong

INTRODUCTION

The 'publish or perish' syndrome is often mentioned. However, we are now seeing cases of 'publish and perish', speaking from an ethical standpoint. The pressures on academics to increase their research publications come from within universities and also externally from government higher education funding bodies. There are also pressures on universities to portray their own academic staff as being scrupulously honest, and this can lead to the protection of academics who plagiarize.

The glossary defines plagiarism as the act of passing off the work of others (in particular, the writing of others) as one's own. The History News Network (2002) posted three different definitions of plagiarism provided by the American Historical Association, the Modern Language Association, and the American Psychological Association, thus covering several discipline areas. All definitions reinforce the concept that plagiarism involves an intentional act of using the work of others, and all discuss the obligation of scholars to be meticulous in their use of source material. In addition, the history and language definitions stress that plagiarism is unethical. This article is concerned with incidents of plagiarism involving university academic staff who might be expected to know about, and rigorously adhere to, established norms of academic publication. In this article the term plagiarism will be used to mean intentionally taking credit for work that should not be claimed as fresh work of one's own. This implies more than editorial oversight and can be construed as academic misconduct.

The majority of the published literature is about student plagiarism (e.g., Stoeger, 2005, describes 28 articles on staff plagiarism and 39 on student plagiarism). This article does not address student plagiarism where the questions of training and intentionality are much grayer. For example, there are different cultural interpretations to ownership of knowledge. Students from Middle Eastern, Asian, and African cultures may need more support in negotiating the norms of Western scholarly discourse (Sweda, 2004). However, there is evidence (Kember, Ma, McNaught, & 18 Exemplary Teachers, 2006) that academic staff worldwide share common educational values and principles.

The article centers around four vignettes. These are stories from my personal experiences since 2002. Only the essential elements of each story are included, and the narratives are disguised to protect the innocent and not-so-innocent. The nationality of the four universities and the gender of the participants have been withheld; however, the overall thread of each story is close to the actual facts. My own university is *not* involved in any of these cases. The first vignette focuses on plagiarism from colleagues; the second concerns multiple publication of the same work—self-plagiarism (Hexham, 2005). In the third and fourth vignettes, the locus of attention shifts to cultural and policy issues in the province of university administration. Key questions are posed and discussed after each vignette. No clear-cut answers are given, but it is hoped that a brief exploration of the ethical issues around the questions will stimulate critical thought.

Figure 1 portrays the 'plagiarism drivers' operating in modern universities that drive individuals and the institutions to respond to situations where plagiarism has occurred. V1 to V4 refer to the vignettes in the article. Positive drivers are those that address the matter—either by the academic concerned acting to correct the error or by the university investigating the allegations. In this article no individuals admitted plagiarism even though this might be seen as the ethical thing to do. Only two of the four universities enacted formal academic misconduct investigations. Negative drivers are those that result in the plagiarism not being resolved and status being maintained by denial and cover-up. In Figure 1 there are two positive drivers, but only one that appears to be functional. In contrast there are four negative drivers, all of which operate. Note that the current rewards systems in higher education encourage academics to play the publications

Figure 1. Positive and negative drivers on individuals' and institutions' responses to plagiarism

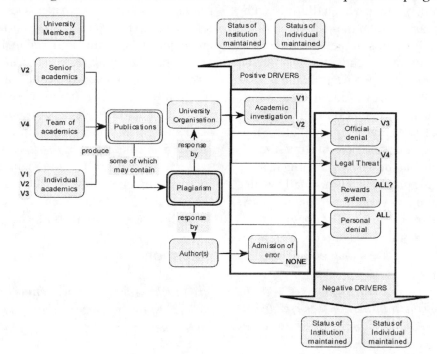

numbers game; this can be a negative driver towards plagiarism.

VIGNETTE 1:
THE EDITOR WHO IS A PLAGIARIST

Imagine a packed room at a large international conference. After the presentation two people stand up in the audience. Both accuse the authors of plagiarism. Emotions are high—denial from the authors, anger and dismay on the part of the complainants, and an atmosphere of embarrassed fascination emanating from the audience. What makes the situation more emotionally charged is that the first author is a journal editor. An editor plagiarizing from two sources in the one paper! The follow-up from these public accusations was protracted, despite the documentary evidence that existed. There was careful scrutiny by an independent panel of the publications that the complainants had previously published; the panel verified the significant amount of word-for-word copying found in the conference paper. Almost a year elapsed before disciplinary investigations by the editor's university were complete. Disciplinary action was taken within the university on a confidential basis. While the editor paid some price

within the university, there was little knowledge about the plagiarism incident beyond a few key university staff, the complainants, and a number of associated colleagues. The dust settled and the editor remains as a journal editor.

Questions

There are two sets of questions that can be posed from this case. One set relates to the rights of the journal publishers; the other to the amount of 'punishment' an academic plagiarist should receive.

1. *Should the publishers of the journal be told that its editor is a confirmed plagiarist? Do the publishing company managers deserve to know so they can decide for themselves if this semi-public transgression will damage the reputation of the company?*

The relationship between commercial publishers and academic editors is built on mutual benefit and trust. Publishers obtain the services of experienced academics for little or no cost. In return, the academic builds a reputation and has an enhanced CV to use for career advancement. This relationship is predicated on the editor's reputation being acceptable to professional colleagues. If that reputation has been diminished by an incidence of plagiarism, then the reputation of the journal may decline. I use this vignette in a research ethics course for postgraduate students. Overwhelmingly, my students vote that the journal should be told. Their reasoning is that their own publications would be diminished if a journal's reputation sank. This may well be seen as a self-seeking response, but for new researchers, publications are precious and my students want to feel confident that they are publishing in high-quality journals. While plagiarism is normally treated as an ethical issue and not a legal one, there are laws that relate to plagiarism in the areas of copyright, unfair competition, and moral rights (Green, 2002). The commercial rights of publishers may be infringed by any taint of plagiarism.

2. *Would revealing this information to the publishers be 'fair' to the editor? Is an internal university investigation enough 'punishment'?*

This is a complex problem. It is interesting that plagiarism was denied by all the plagiarists in these vignettes, even when the documentary evidence was clear to others. This 'denial' syndrome is not uncommon (Schulman, 1998) as the consequences of admitting responsibility for an act that is generally accepted by the academic community as being unethical are very threatening; the positive driver of honestly admitting error does not function well in our universities. However, unproductive punishment is pointless as well. Much greater scrutiny of future academic output is warranted, but few universities are likely to have the inclination to monitor academics in this way. Indeed, as vignette 3 illustrates, many universities are loathe to admit that their academic staff could be plagiarists.

VIGNETTE 2: MULTIPLE DIPPING

Google is a marvelous boon to the busy academic. It enables one to rapidly find a number of papers on a particular theme. Sometimes these papers are strikingly similar—indeed almost identical. In this case, a colleague noticed the similarity in the titles of several publications in a departmental annual report; all of these papers were claimed as independent publications. A few minutes with Google revealed that all these papers were essentially the same paper with only minor editorial changes. The same paper had been published in refereed conference proceedings on different continents and in journals, again published in different countries and so possibly with less than usual overlap in readership. What annoyed the colleague who discovered this 'multiple dipping' (many more than two) was that the first author of these papers had a relatively senior academic position and was, as in vignette 1, a journal editor! The editor's supervisor was informed, as were senior university staff. As in vignette 1, there was an internal university investigation and some internal disciplinary action was taken by the editor's university. The editor remains in the same editorial post.

Question

Are the pressures on more senior tenured academics as bad as, or even worse than, those on their junior colleagues?

Bennett (2003) coined the phrase 'insistent individualism'. He explored what he saw as a growing acceptance on the part of academics that building their own careers should be their first priority, and that success in terms of reputation, academic kudos, and personal publicity was the raison d'etre of academic life. For many academics, the main rewards are intangible—satisfaction and a sense of personal worth in contributing to knowledge and the education of the next generation. Indeed, the tangible rewards of money and kudos are often not high, considering the time and energy invested. If an academic takes only a self-seeking approach, then a degree of dissatisfaction and cynicism may well develop. Further, the bar for advancement is constantly being raised and the number of publications expected of any academic is increasing. Pressure to produce publications and an attitude of cynicism about the value of academic work are a dangerous combination. As a result, 'multiple dipping' may well be quite common. The Internet makes it easier to detect this type of misconduct, and certainly annual reports may need more scrutiny. But the malaise goes deeper and the restoration of the health of the academy is the only true cure.

The framework produced by Bennett (2003) is one where "conversation" is the "essential metaphor" (ch. 5) for university life. Conversation implies active and open engagement between all members of the university—both teachers and students. Rather than regulation, we may need more freedom to revitalize what Bennett described as the "virtue" of "hospitality" (ch. 3)—a university community that cares for each other and for the values of that community. Bennett ended his book with a discussion on the role of academic leaders in promoting an interactive, conversational community. In his model, institutional leaders need to foster a conversational community at all levels of the organization. Our next vignette illustrates the antithesis of Bennett's ethical, hospitable world.

VIGNETTE 3: THE INSTITUTIONAL COVER-UP

In this case, an experienced referee noticed an inconsistency in style in a paper and also the existence of double lines around a table, as one gets when copying a table from the Web. Again, a few minutes with Google reveals two clear instances of plagiarism in the paper. The editor concerned was notified. As this was an internal university publication, the author's Head of Department came to hear of it quite rapidly. The matter escalated when the Head of Department wanted to 'whitewash' the event. The university was provided with full documentary evidence about the two instances of plagiarism, and the vice-chancellor/president of the university became aware of the case. A committee of inquiry was established, but this inquiry was situated in the Human Resources/Personnel division and not in the academic arena. The report on the matter described the plagiarism as "an editorial error." No action, beyond a mild caution on editing, was taken against the author.

Question

Why do universities protect plagiarists? Should such instances become public in the media?

The Web site of the university in vignette 3 has an 'academic integrity' page, including: "All work produced must acknowledge the sources of ideas presented and cite the original written work which informed it." I do not give the URL for obvious reasons, but it is not a unique statement and variants are found on many university Web sites. Is there one set of rules for students and another for their teachers?

I was surprised to find that there are those who publicly ascribe to the view that there is a difference between student plagiarism and staff plagiarism. The Becker-Posner Blog (2006), between Nobel laureate and university professor Gary Becker and U.S. Judge and university professor Richard Posner, hosts many controversial conversations. In April/May 2005, Posner stated and then defended a view that he acknowledged as being "heretical," that "student plagiarism is a more serious offense...a professor who 'steals' ideas or even phrases and incorporates them into his own work not only produces a better product to the benefit of his readership but may well improve his own skills." While I disagree with this view, this blog discussion is evidence that the academic community itself is divided on what constitutes unacceptable plagiarism.

As universities become more reliant on self-generated revenue, the norms and discourses of the business world are increasingly encroaching on academic life (Smyth & Hattam, 2000). Steering a moral course in this rapidly changing academic landscape is challenging. Olscamp (2003) indicated clearly that he believes that moral leadership needs to come from the top. The role of university vice-chancellors/presidents is crucial in establishing a clear set of norms and reducing the ambiguity in university policy.

Should these cases be made public in the hope of pressuring the weaker institutions into a more ethical stance? Vignette 4 adds caution to this line of action. Let us explore what can happen to a whistleblower.

VIGNETTE 4: PROTECTION FOR WHISTLEBLOWERS

A member of an editorial committee was surprised to see a paper on a project without the authorship of the key designer. The paper concerned was a team software project that had been discussed in professional circles on other occasions. So, before publication, the existing authors and the designer were asked to clarify authorship of the paper. The designer knew nothing about the paper and was very annoyed at being overlooked. The existing authors insisted that the designer had no rights to the paper, despite the fact that key sections of the paper were verbatim reproductions of design documents that all acknowledged were the work of the designer. The designer now worked elsewhere and the former colleagues did not consider that there was any existing claim to publications emanating from the project. The editorial committee was not prepared to publish the paper without the designer as an author and so the existing authors withdrew the paper. There was a lengthy e-mail correspondence about the authorship of the paper in question. Some of the comments in these e-mails were acerbic, though not in any way abusive. None of the e-mails was made public beyond the immediate persons involved in the decision-making process on the authorship of the paper. What occurred next came as a surprise to the editor and the designer. Both received quite threatening legal letters from the university concerned saying that they had made unwarranted allegations against that university's academic staff members and that their comments were defamatory. A formal demand was made that an apology should be made to the authors who had plagiarized the design documents. Both the editor and the designer ignored the letters and there was no further action taken by the university. The designer had been contemplating more public action, but was not prepared to fight aggressive legal battles and so remained silent.

Question

What protection is there for whistleblowers? What protection do individual academics have against large and powerful universities?

Universities are becoming increasingly litigious (Adler & Adler, 2002). In order to understand the current policy climate, it is useful to refer to the substantial literature on university research ethics processes. As Haggerty (2004) pointed out, a formal rule-driven process can be problematic and counter-productive to the process of informed scholarly decision making about ethical matters. He examined how the formalization of research ethics processes in universities has led to 'ethics creep', a progressive change in ethical decision making towards the selection of 'safe', though possibly inappropriate, research methods. If the rules become all-dominant, then sensible application of those rules and procedures can suffer. On the other hand we want to avoid the sensationalism of 'moral panic' (Fitzgerald, 2005), where heightened emotions can cloud careful analysis of issues. Policy related to complaints processes thus needs to be structured and clear in order to avoid ad hoc and hasty reactions, and also not overly rigid

so that judgments can be made about the motives and honesty of all people involved in any dispute.

Many universities have responded by having active and balanced policies to protect whistleblowers. Examples are the University of California (2002) and the University of Melbourne (2003). These policies give clear protection to those who divulge material about what they genuinely consider to be a matter of academic misconduct. There are examples of successful whistleblowing (e.g., Fitzgerald, 1996). However, sadly, not all universities appear to have the wording or spirit of such policy protection.

In concluding, I return to the concept of an academic community discussed under vignettes 2 and 3. I want to end this article on a positive note. I feel somewhat battle-scarred by the experiences portrayed in these four cases (and others) and have a sinking feeling that what I have described is just the tip of the iceberg. Our universities need to be more vigilant about academic misconduct and more straightforward in dealing with cases when they become apparent. But, more importantly, our universities need to strenuously emphasize values of integrity and scholarship, and to nurture those values in new cohorts of academics. Universities have a tremendously important potential role in the twenty-first century; we must not abrogate that potential or that responsibility.

REFERENCES

Adler, P.A., & Adler, P. (2002). Do university lawyers and the police define research values? In W.C. van den Hoonaard (Ed.), *Walking the tightrope: Ethical issues for qualitative researchers* (pp. 34-42). Toronto: University of Toronto Press.

Becker-Posner Blog. (2006). Retrieved June 10, 2006, from http://www.becker-posner-blog.com/

Bennett, J.B. (2003). *Academic life. Hospitality, ethics, and spirituality.* Bolton: Anker.

Fitzgerald, K. (1996). Whistle-blowing: Not always a losing game. In K.W. Bowyer (Ed.), *Ethics and computing: Living responsibly in a computerized world* (pp. 240-243). Los Alamitos, CA: IEEE Computer Society Press.

Fitzgerald, M.H. (2005). Punctuated equilibrium, moral panics and the ethics review process. *Journal of Academic Ethics, 2*(4), 315-338.

Green, S.G. (2002). Plagiarism, norms, and the limits of theft law: Some observations on the use of criminal sanctions in enforcing intellectual property rights. *Hastings Law Journal, 54*(1), 167-242.

Haggerty, K.D. (2004). Ethics creep: Governing social science research in the name of ethics. *Qualitative Sociology, 27*(4), 391-414.

Hexham, I. (2005). *Academic plagiarism defined.* Retrieved June 10, 2006, from http://www.ucalgary.ca/~hexham/study/plag.html

History News Network. (2002). *What is plagiarism?* Retrieved June 10, 2006, from http://hnn.us/articles/514.html

Kember, D., Ma, R., McNaught, C., & 18 Exemplary Teachers. (2006). *Excellent university teaching.* Hong Kong: Chinese University Press.

Olscamp, P.J. (2003). *Moral leadership: Ethics and the college presidency.* Lanham, MD: Rowman & Littlefield.

Posner. (2005). *Posner's response to comments on his plagiarism posting, 1 May 2005.* Retrieved June 10, 2006, from http://www.becker-posner-blog.com/archives/2005/05/posners_respons.html

Schulman, M. (1998). Cheating themselves. *Issues in Ethics, 9*(1). Retrieved June 10, 2006, from http://www.scu.edu/ethics/publications/iie/v9n1/cheating.html

Smyth, J., & Hattam, R. (2000). Intellectual as hustler: Researching against the grain of the market. *British Educational Research Journal, 26*(2), 157-175.

Stoeger. (2005). *Plagiarism.* Retrieved June 10, 2006, from http://www.web-miner.com/plagiarism

Sweda, J.E. (2004). *When is plagiarism not cheating?* Retrieved June 10, 2006, from http://www.library.cmu.edu/ethics8.html

University of California. (2002). *Policy on reporting and investigating allegations of suspected improper governmental activities (whistleblower policy).* Retrieved June 10, 2006, from http://www.ucop.edu/ucophome/coordrev/policy/10-04-02whistle.pdf

University of Melbourne. (2003). *Whistleblowers protection policy.* Retrieved June 10, 2006, from http://www.hr.unimelb.edu.au/whistleblowers-policy/

KEY TERMS

Academic Community: There are many people in any university from diverse backgrounds and disciplines. The extent to which the members of a university feel aligned with that university's set of values is a measure of the strength of the academic community.

Institutional Leadership: A set of qualities that people in senior roles in an organization should have. In the context of universities, leadership is the ability to foster a sense of academic community.

Insistent Individualism: An absorbing and continuing focus on self-interest, rather than the good of the community.

Multiple Dipping: Republishing the same work in a number of publications without due acknowledgment that the work has been published before.

Plagiarism: The act of passing off the work of others (in particular, the writing of others) as one's own.

Whistleblower: A person who alerts authorities about dishonest or unethical acts being committed within the organization. In the context of this article, these acts refer to plagiarism as an example of academic misconduct.

Information Ethics as Ideology

Bernd Carsten Stahl
De Montfort University, UK

INTRODUCTION

If we live indeed in the early stages of what has been termed the "information society," then it is clear that ethical concerns with regards to information are of central importance. This can explain the growing interest in issues of information ethics. The use of the word "ethics" seems to suggest that there is something wrong or bad and that this can be addressed by morally acceptable means.

This article will take a different view. It will argue that issues and discourses concerning information ethics can be used for purposes that are not necessarily in accordance with the ethical assumptions on which they are built. The article should thus be seen in the tradition of critical research. It aims to promote the emancipation of researchers as well as practitioners with regards to the use of ethical terms in information, and information and communication technology (ICT). The main argument is that ethical discourses can be used as ideological tools. Ideology will be understood as a shared worldview that favors particular interests. It leads to the closure of debate and reification of meaning and understanding. An example of ideology could be the view that it is the nature of women to rear children and look after the home. If this is generally accepted as a true description of the world, then no debate about it is necessary. Clearly, such a view of the world is favorable for some, not for others. Moral arguments, this article will argue, lend themselves to contribute to ideology. In our example, a moral argument would be that it is good for women to conform with their natural role. This would strengthen the patriarchal ideology.

In order to support this contention, the article will begin by discussing an important concept in information ethics: privacy. I will argue that privacy derives its importance in current debates from its irreducible ethical quality. In the next step I will then define ideology and provide examples of how privacy can be used to promote particular interests. I will conclude the article by pointing out that it is the moral nature of the term *privacy* that renders it a useful tool for ideol-

ogy. I will discuss the question whether the debates in information ethics can or should react to such (mis)use of moral arguments.

THE ETHICS OF PRIVACY

When trying to prove that the moral quality of privacy is a factor in its use as ideology, one has to contend with two main difficulties: first, the debate on privacy is too extensive to be captured comprehensively in a brief section; second, the concept of ethics is even more complex. Ethics, an integral part of philosophy, has been formally discussed since the ancient Greeks. As part of the normative constitution of the social world, it predates philosophical discourse and permeates all areas of social interaction. In this article I will follow what has been termed the "German tradition" of moral philosophy (Stahl, 2004b) which distinguishes between morality as the factually accepted norms which guide individual and collective behavior and ethics as the theory and justification of morality. Moral rules are those that agents follow because they represent what is good and right. Examples of moral rules could be an obligation to help the needy or an interdiction to download proprietary software. Ethical theory explains why moral rules are desirable. It can draw on a rich history of justificatory ideas ranging from duty (deontology) to utility (teleology) to the individual character (virtue ethics). It is not the purpose of this article to engage in the ethical discourses surrounding privacy, but only to demonstrate their relevance by explicating some of the more frequently used arguments.

Privacy is generally acknowledged to be a (moral) good (Weckert & Adeney, 1997), but there is less agreement on what exactly it is or why it is valuable (Gavison, 1995; Shostack & Syverson, 2004). Historically, privacy concerns go back to the ancient Greeks (Rotenberg, 1998) but only acquired legal recognition towards the end of the nineteenth century (Sipior & Ward, 1995), when the most widely spread definition of the term as the "right to be let alone" was coined by Warren and Brandeis (1890). This definition is still used today (Britz, 1999; Velasquez, 1998), but it lacks the clarity needed for a thorough investigation. Privacy can refer to control of information, social control (Culnan, 1993), to perceptions and psychological states (Velasquez, 1998), to rights and obligations, to personal curiosity or social structures.

What is probably beyond doubt is that the current interest in privacy is related to the use of information and communication technology, which includes computing and telecommunication technologies. It is difficult to clearly delineate because it pervades other technical and social fields. For the purposes of this argument, one can imagine technologies such as personal computers, the Internet, or mobile phones as examples. ICT arguably does not cause the collection and (potentially unwanted) use of data, but in many cases it facilitates such uses or renders them much easier (Anderson, Johnson, Gotterbarn, & Perrolle, 1993; Johnson, 2001). Privacy has thus been identified as one of the major ethical issues in ICT from the early days of the debate on computer and information ethics (Mason, 1986), but also in information management (Straub & Collins, 1990). The use of ICT thus leads to a change in the importance of privacy (Robison, 2000). As a result of the challenges of privacy, a variety of legal instruments have been developed by different countries (Chan & Camp, 2002).

What is of interest for this article is the ethical nature of privacy. This can best be observed by looking at the arguments proposing or justifying a right to privacy. Privacy can be seen as an absolute or a relative right. Where it is perceived as absolute, this means that it requires no further justification. It is then comparable to a natural right, something that is irreducible (Spinello, 1997). Such a "fundamental right" (Rogerson, 1998 p. 22) will have the status of a human right, which is reflected by the right to the respect to privacy as developed in Article 8 of the European Convention on Human Rights. However, some authors do not see privacy as absolute but relative, which means that it needs to be justified with regards to other values or rights. This distinction mirrors the one between privacy as an intrinsic or instrumental value (Tavani, 2000; Moor, 2000). Both sides of the argument agree, however, that privacy is a moral good. What they disagree on is the ethical justification and therefore the reach of the concept.

On the individual level, privacy is often described as a necessary condition for a healthy personal development. We require privacy to become autonomous and independent humans who are able to interact with others and create rewarding and useful relationships. Respecting privacy is thus an expression of the respect for the autonomy of others (Rachels, 1995; Elgesiem, 1996; Severson, 1997; Brown, 2000; Introna, 2000; Johnson, 2001). Since a society of incomplete individuals cannot function, privacy can also be justified by social considerations. Privacy not only allows us to develop healthy interpersonal relationships, it also seems to be required for democratic states to function (Gavison, 1995; Johnson, 2001), which is evidenced by the generally accepted procedure of casting secret ballots.

This brief characterization leaves open many questions. It does not address questions of the legal status of privacy, nor the exact limits of this perceived right or ways of adjudicating conflicts between privacy and other rights. It leaves open, for example, the issue whether or under which circumstances workplace surveillance is justified (Stahl, Prior, Wilford, & Collins, 2005). These shortcomings are not problematic for this article because the point of the discussion of privacy was to show that the concept is of an ethical nature. It is recognized as a moral value, which can be justified using a variety of ethical arguments ranging from utilitarian considerations to virtue issues and deontological arguments. Having thus established the importance of ethics in the discourse surrounding privacy, we can proceed to look at its use for ideological purposes.

PRIVACY AS IDEOLOGY

This section will start with a definition of the term "ideology" and then discuss how it relates to privacy.

Ideology

Ideology is an important concept of critical research in information systems as well as critical research in general. It is one of the central aims of critical research to expose ideologies because they limit the ability of the individual to perceive the world. Very briefly, critical research will here be characterized by its aim to change the status quo and to promote emancipation. Ideology is a problem for critical research because it opposes emancipation and hinders social change. By addressing issues of ideology and emancipation, the article enters into the context of critical research. Critical research has historically developed from Marxist critique of capitalism. What it still shares with Marxism is a fundamental suspicion of the capitalist organization of the economy. Critical research in information systems has been developing for at least 20 years. It is often defined as a research "paradigm," the third one next to positivist and interpretive research (Orlikowski & Baroudi, 1991).

Within critical research the concept of "ideology" plays a central role. Fairclough (2003, p. 9) suggests the definition of ideologies as "representations of aspects of the world which can he shown to contribute to establishing, maintaining and changing social relations of power, domination and exploitation." It is important to see that ideologies are not necessarily falsehoods and based on bad faith (Schumpeter, 1994). Instead, ideologies are taken for granted and shared conceptualizations or constructions of (social) reality. The problem is that such constructions will often become reified and taken for absolute truth (McAulay, Doherty, & Keval, 2002). These objectified constructions typically hide vested interests and power relationships (Hirschheim & Klein, 1994). Such hidden agendas are problematic when they can no longer be discussed, which is the case when they become recognized as natural "facts." Ideology therefore makes it harder or even impossible for individuals to reach their full potential. It thus precludes emancipation (Hirschheim, Klein, & Lyytinen, 1995). Critical research therefore aims to overcome ideologies, to facilitate new perspectives, and to allow for new discourses that are more conducive to emancipation.

Ideology of Privacy in ICT

How can we identify instances of ideology in ICT? The kind of ideology we are concerned with is the reification of social constructions for the benefit of particular groups. Of particular interest are examples of ideology that are based on the moral nature of privacy. The moral nature of privacy can be used to render it a universally acceptable aim, which can be used to limit debates and criticism. To identify those, we need to pay attention to instances where certain groups or

individuals are advantaged to the detriment of others. Of particular concern for this article are cases where the moral nature of privacy is used to limit discourses with the aim of facilitating gains for certain groups or individuals.

An example of this is the use of the term "trustworthy computing" (or "trusted computing"—Anderson, 2004). This is a software industry initiative that equates privacy and security, and wants to improve them to facilitate trust by the user. However, trust is a complex social construct, but it is not something that can simply be created. There clearly seems to be a lack of trust in computing by users, largely due to a perceived lack of security and privacy (Cavusoglu, 2004).

One could argue that such situations are not particularly serious because, in a functioning market, customers could seek different suppliers. They can only do so, however, if they are aware of problematic effects. This is where ideology as reification plays a role. If the state of affairs is perceived as natural and unchangeable, as the result of developments which cannot be influenced, then those who are privileged no longer need to justify themselves for their advantages. Technology including ICT is often used for such acts of reification. If we are told, and consequently believe, that technology has a certain nature, for example that the Internet is intrinsically democratic, then this need no longer be discussed. Such reification is closely linked to the idea of technological determinism, which assumes that technology has certain properties which leads to determined consequences. Technological determinism can thus be described as a mechanism that leads to the reification of certain social constructs into the "nature" of technology. Reified technologies, that is technologies whose properties are taken to be part of their unalterable nature rather than results of human interaction and intervention, are then removed from democratic scrutiny (Feenberg, 1999). They can be promoted using moral arguments including privacy. Pertinent examples of this might be the assumption that the introduction of surveillance technology such as CCTV cameras will lead to a reduction of crime (Lyon, 2003) or that the use of ICT in teaching will lead to better educational outcomes (Sahay, 2004). While there is a long tradition of criticizing the idea of technological determinism, it can still be found as a powerful aspect of governing ideologies. Privacy can become part of the reification of ideology when viewed as technical aspects of an artifact

Proponents of certain ideological interests often use rhetorical devices such as metaphors to promote their views. Such metaphors, if used successfully, will take on a life of their own and render the originating interest invisible. They can be turned into reifications when they shape the generally accepted definition of technology or its properties. There are several good examples of such use of metaphors as vehicles of ideology in ICT. One of them is the use of the word "virus" for a certain type of self-replicating software. Viruses are generally recognized to be dangerous and undesirable, which renders strong measures against them easily enforceable. It precludes a possible discussion of positive aspects of such programs and thereby furthers the interests of those who oppose them to the detriment of those who may have legitimate reasons to create them (Klang, 2003). Another good example is the use of the word "piracy" for the unauthorized downloading of computer programs or digital content. "Piracy," being originally a horribly violent type of illegal activity, carries the connotation of something not only illegal but highly reprehensible, very similar to the related crimes of murder and rape. The use of the metaphor paints a very clear (and arguably misleading) picture of the activity of unauthorized downloading. Someone committing piracy must be a pirate and hence an evil person. This use of the word thus reifies the moral evaluation of an activity, leads to discursive closure, and thereby promotes the interests of some, namely intellectual property holders, to the detriment of others.

The moral nature of privacy renders it open to misuse as positive metaphor. An important example of this is where privacy considerations are used to cloak issues of control. If strong control features are integrated into programs, then this can lead to protest by users, civil libertarians, or data protection activists. It is therefore in the interest of proponents of strong control to frame this in morally acceptable terms. One example of this is parental control. Microsoft Vista, the next generation of the MS operating system, for example, includes strong centralized control features, but these are explained in terms of security for businesses, and privacy and parental control for parents. Such rhetorical and partial use of privacy is only possible because of its moral nature.

These uses of ideology have many manifest implications. They lead to the hardening of social practices, for example in the intellectual property area. By withdraw-

ing technology from discourse, ideology establishes precedents that become self-reinforcing. One example of this would be a hierarchical information systems development process. There is much literature suggesting that participative development projects have a variety of advantages from an ethical as well as a business perspective (Mumford, 1996). However, if ICT is seen as fundamentally determined, then there is no need to have users or other stakeholders participate in design decisions. Emancipation cannot become part of the agenda.

CONCLUSION: CRITICAL REFLECTIONS

This article should not be misunderstood to say that all information ethics discourses are necessarily bad or will be misused. Its main purpose was to flag the possibility that moral values implied and discussed in information ethics can be used for purposes other than intended. This should certainly not be read to imply that we should stop having debates on issues of information ethics. The use of terms and concepts out of the contexts in which they were developed is part of human language and interaction, and therefore not necessarily a bad thing. The conclusion of this article can therefore also not be to ring fence the use of certain concepts such as privacy and claim exclusive ownership of them.

The main conclusion I would want to draw from the possibility of ideological use of information ethics concepts is that the participants of those original discourses should pay closer attention to external and related discourses. That means, for example, that individuals engaged in privacy debates on a philosophical and academic level should pay close attention to the use of the concept by commercial organizations, governments, and other stakeholders. Such attention will allow them to identify ideological closure (the limitation of discourses because of ideology) and to re-open debates. This will probably be an interesting exercise for the individuals involved, but more importantly, it will also help safeguard the moral content of the concepts and thereby their ethical validity. Failure to engage in such external discourses, on the other hand, can jeopardice the social relevance of information ethics.

REFERENCES

Anderson, R. (2004). Cryptography and competition policy—issues with 'trusted computing'. In L.J. Camp & S. Lewis (Eds.), *Economics of information security* (pp. 35-52). Dordrecht: Kluwer.

Anderson, R.E., Johnson, D.G., Gotterbarn, D., & Perrolle, J. (1993). Using the new ACM code of ethics in decision making. *Communications of the ACM, 36*(2), 98-106.

Britz, J.J. (1999). Ethical guidelines for meeting the challenges of the information age. In L.J. Pourciau (Ed.), *Ethics and electronic information in the 21st century* (pp. 9-28). West Lafayette, IN: Purdue University Press.

Brown, W.S. (2000). Ontological security, existential anxiety and workplace privacy. *Journal of Business Ethics, 23*, 61-65.

Chan, S., & Camp, L.J. (2002). Law enforcement surveillance in the network society. *IEEE Technology and Society Magazine, 21*(2), 22-30.

Cavusoglu, H. (2004). Economics of IT security management. In L.J. Camp & S. Lewis (Eds.), *Economics of information security* (pp. 71-83). Dordrecht: Kluwer.

Culnan, M.J. (1993). How did they get my name?: An exploratory investigation of consumer attitudes toward secondary information use. *MIS Quarterly, 17*(3), 341-363.

Elgesiem, D. (1996). Privacy, respect for persons, and risk. In C. Ess (Ed.), *Philosophical perspectives on computer-mediated communication* (pp. 45-66). Albany: State University of New York Press.

Fairclough, N. (2003). *Analysing discourse—textual analysis for social research*. London/New York: Routledge.

Feenberg, A. (1999). *Questioning technology*. London: Routledge.

Gavison, R. (1995). Privacy and limits of law. In D.G. Johnson & H. Nissenbaum (Eds.), *Computers, ethics & social values* (pp. 332-351). Upper Saddle River, NJ: Prentice Hall.

Hirschheim, R., Klein, H.K., & Lyytinen, K. (1995). *Information systems developing and data modeling: Conceptual and philosophical foundations*. Cambridge: Cambridge University Press.

Hirschheim, R., & Klein, H.K. (1994). Realizing emancipatory principles in information systems development: The case for ETHICS. *MIS Quarterly, 18*(1), 83-109.

Introna, L. (2000). Privacy and the computer—why we need privacy in the information society. In R.M. Baird, R. Ramsower, & S.E. Rosenbaum (Eds.), *Cyberethics—social and moral issues in the computer age* (pp. 188-199). New York: Prometheus Books.

Johnson, D.G. (2001). *Computer ethics* (3rd ed.). Upper Saddle River, NJ: Prentice Hall.

Klang, M. (2003). A critical look at the regulation of computer viruses. *International Journal of Law and Information Technology, 11*, 162-183.

Lyon, D. (2003). *Surveillance after September 11*. Cambridge: Polity Press.

Mason, R.O. (1986). Four ethical issues of the information age. *MIS Quarterly, 10*, 5-12.

McAulay, L., Doherty, N., & Keval, N. (2002). The stakeholder dimension in information systems evaluation. *Journal of Information Technology, 17*, 241-255.

Moor, J.H. (2000). Toward a theory of privacy in the information age. In R.M. Baird, R. Ramsower, & S.E. Rosenbaum (Eds.), *Cyberethics—social and moral issues in the computer age* (pp. 200-212). New York: Prometheus Books.

Mumford, E. (1996). *Systems design: Ethical tools for ethical change*. London: Macmillan.

Orlikowski, W.J., & Baroudi, J.J. (1991). Studying information technology in organizations: Research approaches and assumptions. *Information Systems Research, 2*(1), 1-28.

Rachels, J. (1995). Why privacy is important. In J.G. Johnson & H. Nissenbaum (Eds.), *Computers, ethics & social values* (pp. 351-357). Upper Saddle River, NJ: Prentice Hall.

Robison, W.L. (2000). Privacy and appropriation of identity. In G. Collste (Ed.), *Ethics in the age of information technology* (pp. 70-86). Linköping: Centre for Applied Ethics.

Rogerson, S. (1998). *Ethical aspects of information technology—issues for senior executives.* London: Institute of Business Ethics.

Rotenberg, M. (1998). Communications privacy: Implications for network design. In R. Stichler & R. Hauptman (Eds.), *Ethics, information and technology: Readings* (pp. 152-168). Jefferson, NC: MacFarland & Company.

Sahay, S. (2004). Beyond utopian and nostalgic views of information technology and education: Implications for research and practice. *Journal of the Association for Information Systems, 5*(7), 282-313.

Schumpeter, J. (1994). Science and ideology. In D.M. Hausman (Ed.), *The philosophy of economics: An anthology* (2nd ed., pp. 224-238). Cambridge: Cambridge University Press.

Severson, R.J. (1997). *The principles of information ethics.* Armonk, NY/London: M.E. Sharpe.

Shostack, A., & Syverson, P. (2004). What price privacy? (and why identity theft is about neither identity nor theft). In L.J. Camp & S. Lewis (Eds.), *Economics of information security* (pp. 129-142). Dordrecht: Kluwer.

Sipior, J.C., & Ward, B.T. (1995). The ethical and legal quandary of email privacy. *Communications of the ACM, 38*(12), 48-54.

Spinello, R. (1997). *Case studies in information and computer ethics.* Upper Saddle River, NJ: Prentice Hall.

Stahl, B.S., Prior, M., Wilford, S., & Collins, D. (2005). Electronic monitoring in the workplace: If people don't care, then what is the relevance? In J. Weckert (Ed.), *Electronic monitoring in the workplace: Controversies and solutions* (pp. 50-78). Hershey, PA: Idea Group.

Stahl, B.C. (2004a). Responsibility for information assurance and privacy: A problem of individual ethics? *Journal of Organizational and End User Computing, 16*(3), 59-77.

Stahl, B.C. (2004b). *Responsible management of information systems.* Hershey, PA: Idea Group.

Straub, D.W., & Collins, R.W. (1990). Key information liability issues facing managers: Software piracy, proprietary databases, and individual rights to privacy. *MIS Quarterly, 14,* 143-156.

Tavani, H. (2000). Privacy and security. In D. Langford (Ed.), *Internet ethics* (pp. 65-89). London: McMillan.

Velasquez, M. (1998). *Business ethics: Concepts and cases* (4th ed.). Upper Saddle River, NJ: Prentice Hall.

Warren, S.D., & Brandeis, L.D. (1890). The right to privacy. *Harvard Law Review, 5,* 193-220.

Weckert, J., & Adeney, D. (1997). *Computer and information ethics.* Westport, CT/London: Greenwood Press.

KEY TERMS

Critical Research in Information Systems: Application of Critical Theory to the field of Information Systems. Typically no longer emphasizes its Marxist roots, but shares the interventionist and emancipatory intention of Critical Theory. A typical topic is that of emancipation by participation. Often builds on Habermas's Theory of Communicative Action, but increasingly broadens its theoretical foundation to include other critical theorists.

Critical Theory: Research approach that is based on the Marxist critique of capitalism. It is closely linked with the scholars of the Frankfurt School (first generation: Horkheimer, Adorno; second generation: Habermas, Apel; third generation: Honneth), but nowadays also often linked to French scholars such as Bourdieu, Foucault, and others. The aim of Critical Theory is to change the status quo to facilitate emancipation.

Ethics: Justification of morality (sometimes also called meta-ethics). Uses different schools of thought to reflect on why we see some actions or rules as good or bad. Well-known ethical theories include Utilitarianism, (Kantian) deontology, and virtue ethics.

Ideology: Collectively shared perception of reality that is advantageous to particular individuals or groups to the detriment of others. Ideologies are collective pre-conceptions about what is real, right, or acceptable. They remove issues from debate, thus cementing advantages of some and alienation of others. Exposing of ideologies can help emancipate people, which is why they are of central interest to Critical Theory.

Morality: Set of rules that govern actual behavior of individuals or groups. Helps us decide what we see as good or bad.

Privacy: "Right to be let alone." An important issue in the information society. It derives its current interest from the fact that new information and communication technologies allow us to collect large amounts of data easily, and that control over such data is hard to establish. Privacy is generally recognized as a moral good, but there are a variety of ethical justifications, which sometimes contradict each other. The moral good of privacy is protected by the law in most societies, but definitions and extent of legal protection varies greatly.

Information Ethics from an Islamic Perspective

Salam Abdallah
Amman Arab University for Graduate Studies, Jordan

INTRODUCTION

The Web of networks has created a convenient global environment for people to work, socialize, learn, buy, and sell. The Web has also been used as a tool to breach privacy, gain illegal possession of property, battlefield for cyberwarfare, and in some cases, cause loss of life. The field of 'information ethics' was developed to curb this negative impact. Elrod and Smith (2005) define information ethics as a "field that applies ethical principles within the context of information provision, control, and use. This field considers issues about all aspects of information technology and information systems for personal, professional, and public decision-making." Moore (2005) defines information ethics as having three public interests related to privacy, property, and control. Mason (1986) proposes a different set consisting of privacy, accuracy, property, and access.

The characteristics of the networked economy make information ethics a global issue. Bynum (2001) argues there is a need for "global information ethics" to increase the use of the global networks. Górniak-Kocikowska (2001) argues that globalization is an opportunity for creating global ethics in this digital civilization where every culture contributes to its creation. Any attempt to develop global information ethical theories or solutions should in fact consider the political, economic, social, and cultural dimensions of the various regions in the world (UNESCO, 1995).

Most discussions on information ethics have been from the perspective of Judeo-Christian ethics and from the works of ancient and modern philosophers, with little attention given to the Islamic ethical approach. Despite the fact that Islam is one of the major religions in the world, the underlying ethical structure of this faith is yet to be fully understood. Islam has brought prosperity in the past to various empires because it offered an elaborate ethical conduct for almost every aspect of life. Carney (2001, p. 167) argues that Islamic ethics is "exceptionally rich and impressive in the concepts, positions and lines of argument it set forth." The lack of resources in the English language

may be the reason for this lack of understanding of Islamic ethics and the distortions caused by the media. Reinhart (2001, p. 187) argues the foundation of the Islamic law provides an "ethical and epistemological system of great subtlety and sophistication."

This article introduces Islam and its sources of knowledge and the mechanism it uses to derive ethical judgment. A case at the end of this article demonstrates this mechanism. This article is introductory to raise research interest in this neglected epistemological ethical system.

ISLAM

Islam is a monotheistic religion with more than 1.5 billion followers (CIA, n.d.). The basic message of Islam is that God (Allah in Arabic) is the only creator and Mohammad is his Messenger and servant (Jalil, n.d.). Islam is regarded as "a way of life" because it goes beyond rituals; it includes ethical conduct, creed, and worship (Bouhdiba, 2005; Ghani, 2004). There are explicit teachings and laws concerning religious rituals, personal character, morals, habits, family relationship, social and economic affairs, administration, rights and duties of citizens, judicial system, laws of war and peace, international relations, and the protection of the environment. Bouhdiba (2005) argues that Islam can be described as a "superculture" because it had left its marks permanently on different societies globally and mainly because of its "extraordinary richness."

The corpus of Islamic teachings and laws is called Shari'ah, which provides the ethical foundation of conduct for either the individual or community (Siddiqui, 1997; Omar, 1997; Ahmad, 2003). The foundation of Shari'ah relies on primary and secondary sources of knowledge:

1. the *Quran,* or the holy book of Islam;
2. the *Sunnah* and the *Seerah,* or the way and biography of the Messenger; and

3. the *Usul-al-Fiqh* or the Fiqh Science, which is the Islamic legal sciences.

Scholars use these sources to formulate a ruling on a given issue or dilemma to decide the right action.

THE QURAN

The Quran, the holy book of Islam, is God's own words revealed to the Prophet Muhammad 1,400 years ago in the Arab Peninsula (Vondenffer, 1981). The Quran is complete in its content and preserved for all times (Ahmed, 1998). The verse from the Quran supports this claim, which says: "this day have I perfected your religion for you, completed My favor upon you" (Quran 4:3) and "We have, without doubt, sent down the Message; and We will assuredly guard it (from adulteration)" (Quran 15:9). Another supporting statement of its perfection is: "Nothing have we omitted from the Book" (Quran 6:38). This absolute statement implies that it contains a complete and comprehensive methodology of ways and laws of proper conduct (Patrick, 1901). Muslims believe that Islam is eternal because it is not a man-made religion and its teachings are applicable for all times and places (Idris, n.d; Brown, 1999).

The Quran has about 400 verses of legal principles and about 5,800 verses for purifying the soul through ethical conduct. The Quran in different forms commands people to do what is right and forbids what is wrong, especially when people are interacting with each other. The Quran also claims global or universal ethics since it was sent for all humankind (Ghani, 2004):

O mankind! We created you from a single (pair) of a male and a female, and made you into nations and tribes, that ye may know each other (not that ye may despise (each other). (Quran 49:13)

The Islamic laws in the Quran seek to benefit and protect people's material goods. As mentioned earlier, it addresses issues related to social, financial, political, and personal affairs, including issues related to the soul, emotions, and sentiments, which may have a large influence on the ethical behavior of people.

THE SUNNAH AND THE SEERAH

The Sunnah is the traditions (Ahadeeth) of the Prophet, which includes his deeds, sayings, tacit approval, or description of his physical appearance. Al-Ghazali (1058-1111) said in his book *Muslim Character* that Muhammad's main purpose for being sent to this world was for "perfecting good morals" (translated by Alghazali, Ghazali, & Usmani, 2004).

These traditions expound on the teachings of the Quran. Muhammad's companions recorded his traditions and they are in the thousands. The companions have also recorded his biography (Seerah), which provides a foundation for virtue ethics. The biography documents Muhammad's successes and ethical conduct as a Prophet, legislator, teacher, husband, father, trader, leader, peacemaker, and warrior. Muhammad was responsible for the prosperity of many empires under one spiritual system (Hart, 1992).

THE USUL-AL-FIQH (FIQH SCIENCE)

The word Fiqh in Arabic means understanding and Usul means science. The Fiqh science aims at understanding and abstracting the essence of the operating principles of the Quran and the Sunnah (Brown, 1999; Hannan, 1999; Kamili, 1991; Alwani, 1990). The Fiqh science provides a condensed set of principles or legal maxims called Qawa'id al-Fiqh. The knowledge of these abstracted principles allows scholars and people to arrive at ethical conduct.

This science also relies on secondary sources such as analogical reasoning (Qiyas) (Shehaby, 1982) and the consensus of scholars (Ijma). Qiyas is the method for finding out the effective cause of a principle from the Quran and then applying the ethical rule to an analogous case. If Qiyas fails in reaching a judgment, then the consensus of scholars will be considered.

With this combination of sources, Muslim scholars have access to a mechanism for meeting the challenges of different periods such as abortion, euthanasia, intellectual property, and software piracy (see Figure 1). Scholars go through quasi-inductive processes to formulate rulings to determine the ethical status of an

Figure 1. The Islamic ethical judgment sources of knowledge and process

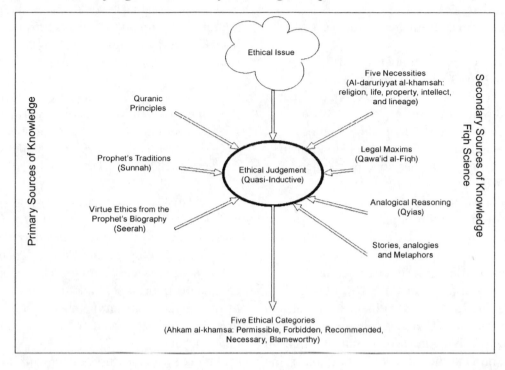

action (Reinhart, 2001). The final ruling is not a matter of right or wrong action, but falls into either one of the five ethical categories. These five ethical categories (the ahkam al-khamsa) are: permissible (mubah), forbidden (haram), recommended (mandub), necessary (wajib), and blameworthy (makruh) (Brown, 1999; Alwani, 1990). These rulings may also contain procedures, conditions, context, reasons, and exceptions.

The general aim of the Islamic laws is to minimize or remove harm and bring benefits. It regulates the daily life of people through ethical conduct. Scholars have determined that the objectives of the Islamic laws evolve around three levels of interests labeled as necessities (daruriyyat), conveniences (hajiyyat), and refinements (tahsiniyyat) (Rice, 1999; Kamali, 1998a, 1998b).

The *necessities* are benefits or public interests that people's lives depend upon. Without these interests, hardship would prevail on the social life, causing imbalance against the natural laws. Islam seeks to promote and preserve five public interests known as the *Five Necessities* (or al-daruriyyat al-khamsah). These Five Necessities are religion, life, property, intellect, and lineage (Brown, 1999; Hannan,1999).

The *conveniences* are issues people need to remove difficulties in their daily activities. The absence of the

conveniences have no impact on the necessities, but can impose hardship on people, while the *refinements* are issues involving ethical behavior and conduct for day-to-day living.

As mentioned earlier, through the understanding of the main objectives of the Islamic laws, scholars have deduced more than 70 principles or legal maxims from the Quran and the Sunnah (Qawa'id al-Fiqh). These principles are the building blocks for further law deductions. In light of these laws, scholars can support their opinion and weigh their decision on the mentioned three interests, mainly concentrating on preserving the Five Necessities (religion, property, life, intellect, and lineage). Some of these principles are:

1. Harm is eliminated to the extent that is possible
2. Harm is not eliminated by another harm
3. Harm not to be inflicted nor reciprocated in Islam
4. Preventing harm is given preference over gaining benefit
5. Public interest takes precedence over personal interest

6. Specific harm is tolerated in order to prevent a more general one
7. A greater harm is eliminated by means of a lesser harm
8. Necessity makes the unlawful lawful
9. Hardship begets facility (easiness)
10. In case of conflict between two options, adopt the uncomplicated one
11. Certainty cannot be overruled by doubt
12. Acts are judged by the intention behind them
13. An act is illegal whether done by the person or by agent
14. Custom is the basis of judgment
15. The norm in regard to things is that of permissibility

As mentioned earlier, scholars go through a sequence of inductive reasoning or analogies to decide if an act is ethical. The use of these principles operates in conjunction with each other and sometimes requires a holistic view involving the text from the Quran and the Sunnah, and with the ultimate aim of preserving the Five Essentials in order to prevent collisions or contradictions of principles.

It is beyond the aim of this article to explain these legal maxims. However, the following case provides an indication on the use of Islamic principles and its way of thinking for deriving ethical judgment.

CASE: SOFTWARE PIRACY

This case will illustrate how Islamic scholars would approach an ethical issue to derive ethical ruling concerning the act of software piracy.

A definition of software piracy is the act of accessing illegal copies of software and using it contrary to the prescribed user agreement set by the software developers.

One of the legal principles of Fiqh Science states: "The norm in regard to things is that of permissibility." This principle states that permissibility is the natural state unless there is evidence from text to change this position. However, the issue of software piracy is causing hardship to developers and losing the incentives to produce more and better software (Mason, 1986). Software piracy claims US$12 billion yearly in revenues (SIIA, n.d).

Because of the explained hardship caused by software piracy, scholars would search the primary text (Quran and Sunnah) to find statements to assist them in making ethical judgment. Below are two statements from the Quran that may be used:

- *O you who believe! do not devour your property among yourselves falsely, except that it be trading by your mutual consent.* (Quran 4:29)
- *O ye who believe! fulfil (all) obligations (agreements).* (Quran: 5:1)

In the first statement, the Quran commands people not to dwindle other people's property. Copying and using unlicensed software can lead to the bankruptcy of software developers. Developers depend on the sale of software for their earnings. The second statement commands the respect and fulfilling of agreements. Most software applications display a user agreement that needs to be accepted and respected if it is within lawful means.

From the Sunnah three statements may be used to further support the instructions of the Quran:

- *Muslims are to honor their agreements (with others).* (reported by Sunan Abu-Dawud, translated by Hassan, 2000)
- *A Muslim's wealth is forbidden for another to use without his permission.* (reported by Hanbal, 1950)
- *Whoever is the first to acquire something lawful has more right to it.* (reported by Sunan Abu-Dawud, translated by Hassan, 2000)

These three statements equally apply to both Muslims and non-Muslims. The Sunnah also calls for the respect of other people's property and agreements are binding.

From the Fiqh Science, the following legal principles may also be applicable:

1. Harm not to be inflicted nor reciprocated in Islam
2. Preventing harm is given preference over gaining benefit
3. Custom is the basis of judgment

Using illegal copies of software can bring harm to developers. Great effort has gone to develop and produce the software and therefore "Harm not to be inflicted." In addition, this action violates one of the Five Necessities (religion, property, intellect, life, and lineage), which is property. Although people are benefiting from using copied software, there is the possibility developers will not have the incentive to write software to further benefit the society, therefore: "Preventing harm is given preference over gaining benefit." The third principle states, "Custom is the basis of judgment"; now almost all countries have legal positions regarding the protection of intellectual property of their citizens which also need to be followed. Qiyas, or analogical reasoning, may be used by finding the effective cause from an applicable principle from the Quran or Sunnah and apply the ruling to the case being examined.

In addition, reflecting on the virtues of Muhammad through his biography is also useful in trying to imagine how the Prophet may have responded to the issue of software piracy. There are many documented stories of Muhammad that portray his justices, honesty, bravery, and other virtues.

At the end of this inductive and triangulation effort, a ruling is issued based on the five ethical categories: permissible, forbidden, recommended, necessary, blameworthy. In reality, scholars have declared the act of software piracy as a forbidden act on the basis it will bring harm to the developers and may prevent them from contributing further to society, and therefore software agreements need to be upheld.

STORIES, ANALOGIES, AND METAPHORS

The Quran and the Sunnah also provide a large variation of stories, analogies, and metaphors which play an important role in forming the ethical behavior of a Muslim. The following is an example of a story about a group of people on a ship:

Some of them got seats in the upper-part, and the others in the lower. When the latter needed water, they had to go up to bring water (and that troubled the others), so they said, 'Let us make a hole in our share of the ship (and get water), saving those who are above us from troubling them. So, if the people in the upper-part left the others do what they had suggested, all the people of the ship would be destroyed. But if they prevented

them, both parties would be safe. (reported by Bukhari, translated by Khan, n.d.)

One of the morals of this story is the unethical behavior of one person may threaten the security for all. It is not enough to act ethically, but there is a need to stop others from acting unethically. The story encourages people to try to stop others from acting unethically, and whistle-blowing is an option.

CONCLUSION

The Islamic ethical system in the literature of information ethics is unexplored. This article provides an introduction to demystify some of the features of the Islamic ethical system in order to encourage further research.

The ethical foundation of Islam covers various aspects of life and has proved itself to be stable and universal in approach. The system has a harmonized composite structure of deontological, consequentialism, and virtue ethics. The teachings of Islam can provide a foundation for ethical conduct to deal with the contemporary ethical dilemmas. Any attempts to develop global ethics without examining the corpus of Islamic ethical ways of thinking may miss fundamental issues.

REFERENCES

Ahmad, A. (2003). Mawdudi's concept of Shari'ah. *The Muslim World, 93*, 533-544.

Ahmed, S. (1998). *Proof of the preservation of the Quran.* Retrieved July 9, 2006, from http://www.iol.ie/~afifi/BICNews/Sabeel/sabeel3.htm

Al Alwani, T. (1990). *The Usul-al-Fiqh.* Retrieved July 9, 2006, from http://www.usc.edu/dept/MSA/law/alalwani_usulalfiqh/

Alghazali, M., Ghazali, M., & Usmani, M.A.H. (2004). *Muslim character: An American-English translation of Muhammad al-Ghazali's Khuluq al-Muslim.* Library of Islam.

Bouhdiba, A. (2005). The message of Islam. *Diogenes, 52*(205), 111-117.

Brown, D. (1999). Islamic ethics in comparative perspective. *The Muslim World, 89*(2), 181-192.

Bynum, T.W. (2001). Computer ethics: Basic concepts and historical overview. *The Stanford Encyclopedia of Philosophy,* (Winter). Retrieved July 9, 2006, from http://plato.stanford.edu/archives/win2001/entries/ethics-computer/

Carney, F.S. (1983). Focus on Muslim ethics: An introduction. *Journal of Religious Ethics, 11*(2), 167-179.

CIA. (n.d.). *Central Intelligence Agency—the world factbook.* Retrieved July 9, 2006, from http://www.cia.gov/cia/publications/factbook/index.html

Elrod, E.M., & Smith, M.M. (2005). Information ethics. In *Encyclopedia of science, technology, and ethics* (vol. 2). Detroit: Macmillan Reference.

Ghani, Z.A. (2004). Islamic values and ethics in the life of communication scholar. *Journal of Communication and Religion,* (March), 58-62.

Górniak-Kocikowska, K. (2001). *The global culture of digital technology and its ethics.* Retrieved July 9, 2006, from http://www.ccsr.cse.dmu.ac.uk/conferences/ccsrconf/ethicomp2001/abstracts/gorniak.html

Hanbal, A.I. (1950). *Musnad Ahmad Ibn Hanbal.* Cairo, UAR: Dar AlMa'aref.

Hannan, S.A. (1999). *Usul Al Fiqh (Islamic jurisprudence).* Retrieved July 9, 2006, from http://www.123arabia.com/hudainfo/Articles/E005.pdf

Hart, M.H. (1992). *The 100: A ranking of the most influential persons in history.* Citadel Press.

Hassan, A. (2000). *Sunan Abu Dawud: English translation.* Kitab Bhavan.

Idris, J.S. (n.d.). *Islam for our times: How & why?* Retrieved July 9, 2006, from http://islaam.com//Article.aspx?id=523

Jalil, A. (n.d.). *Islam explained.* Retrieved July 9, 2006, from http://www.islamicity.com/mosque/Islam_Expl.htm

Kamali, M. (1998a). Qawa'id Al-Fiqh: The legal maxims of Islamic law. *The Muslim Lawyer, 3*(2), 1-7.

Kamali, M.H. (1991). *Principles of Islamic jurisprudence.* Cambridge: The Islamic Texts Society.

Kamali, M.H. (1998b). Al Maqasid al-Shari'ah: The objectives of Islamic law. *The Muslim Lawyer, 3*(1), 1-7.

Khan, M.M. (n.d.). *Translation of Sahih Bukhari.* Retrieved July 9, 2006, from http://www.usc.edu/dept/MSA/fundamentals/hadithsunnah/bukhari/

Mason, R. (1986). Four ethical issues of the information age. *MIS Quarterly, 10*(1), 5-12.

Moore, A. (2005). *Information ethics: Privacy, property, and power.* Seattle: University of Washington Press.

Omar, M.A. (1997). Reasoning in Islamic law: Part one. *Arab Law Quarterly, 49,* 148-196.

Patrick, M.M. (1901). The ethics of the Koran. *International Journal of Ethics, 11*(3), 321-329.

Quran. (n.d.). *The noble Qur'an.* Retrieved May 4, 2006, from http://www.usc.edu/dept/MSA/law/

Reinhart, K. (2001). Islamic law as Islamic ethics. *Journal of Religious Ethics, 11*(2), 186-204.

Rice, G. (1999). Islamic ethics and the implications for business. *Journal of Business Ethics, 18*(4), 345-358.

Shehaby, N. (1982). *Illa and Qiyas in early Islamic legal theory. 102*(1), 27-46.

Siddiqui, A. (1997). Ethics in Islam: Key concepts and contemporary challenges. *Journal of Moral Education, 26*(4), 423-431.

SIIA. (n.d). *Software & Information Industry Association.* Retrieved July 9, 2006, from http://www.siia.net/

UNESCO. (1996). *Our creative diversity: Report of the World Commission on Culture and Development.* Paris: UNESCO.

Vondenffer, A. (1981). *Ulum al Quran: An introduction to the sciences of the Qur'an.* Retrieved July 9, 2006, from http://www.islamworld.net/UUQ/index.html

KEY TERMS

Ahkam al-khamsa (Five Ethical Categories): The outcome of the Islamic ethical judgment is grouped into five categories: permissible (mubah), forbidden (haram), recommended (mandub), necessary (wajib), and blameworthy (Makruh).

Al-daruriyyat al-khamsah (Five Necessities): Islam seeks to promote and preserve five public interests known as the 'Five Necessities': religion, life, property, intellect, and lineage.

Islam: A monotheistic religion consisting of ethical conduct, creed, and worship; based on the teachings of the Quran and the Sunnah or the way of the Prophet Mohammad.

Quran: Islam's holy book, which is God's own words revealed to the Prophet Mohammad 1,400 years ago. The book contains principles and ways of ethical conduct.

Seerah: The biography of the Prophet Muhammad which provides a complete foundation for virtue ethics. The biography documents Muhammad's successes and ethical conduct as a Prophet, legislator, teacher, husband, father, trader, leader, peacemaker, and warrior.

Shari'ah: The ethical foundation of Islam consisting of principles, commandments, and prohibitions covering various aspects of life.

Sunnah: The traditions of the Prophet Muhammad (Ahadeeth); includes his deeds, sayings, tacit approval, and physical description of his appearance. These traditions expound on the principles of the Quran.

Usul-al-Fiqh (Fiqh Science): The Islamic legal science; it is related to the abstraction and understanding of the operating principles from the Quran and the Sunnah in order to determine their essence. The Fiqh science provides a condensed set of principles or legal maxims called Qawa'id al-Fiqh. The knowledge of these abstracted principles allows scholars and people to arrive at an unethical conduct. The Fiqh Science uses other sources of knowledge such as analogical reasoning called Qiyas and the consensus of scholars (Ijma).

Information Security and the "Privacy Broker"

Michael Douma
Institute for Dynamic Educational Advancement, USA

Eduard J. Gamito
University of Colorado Health Sciences Center, USA

INTRODUCTION

The term "privacy broker" describes a concept developed in 2004 to address important privacy issues in public health research. The privacy broker provides a combination of an information "firewall" between the research team and the study participants' personal data, to protect the identity of study participants. It also provides a "masquerading" feature so that participants can be indirectly tracked or contacted, which allows for the collection of scientifically useful information over time.

BACKGROUND

Over the past several hundred years, research involving humans as subjects has resulted in countless exciting discoveries that have greatly benefited humanity. Advances like the discovery of penicillin to fight infection or the vaccine that brought polio under control, and nearly all modern-day treatments for cancer, diabetes, heart disease, and so forth, would not have been possible without research on humans. Unfortunately, among the many bright moments in research history, some dark episodes have occurred. For example, in the infamous Tuskegee Syphilis Study that took place from 1932 to 1972, researchers withheld available treatments from poor African American men with syphilis so that the progression of this terrible disease could be studied. Many of the men in the study suffered and died needlessly as a direct result of the researchers' unethical behavior. While the Tuskegee study is an extreme example of the abuses that have occurred, and is considered the worst case of research abuse in U.S. history, many other abuses have occurred and continue to occur to this day. In recent years, research abuses have been less extreme and much more rare than in the past. Most of these abuses have pertained to improperly informing study participants of known risks to participating in research. In some cases, researcher negligence has resulted in the release and misuse of the personal health information of research participants.

To address these problems, a series of laws and regulations have been put into place over the years to protect humans participating in research studies. One of the most recently implemented laws is known as the Health Insurance Portability and Accountability Act (HIPAA) of 1996. This law, the first phase of which covered privacy issues, was implemented in 2003. The HIPAA Privacy Rule sets standards to protect information related to health care. Specifically, it regulates health care information that can be linked with a person.

The Problem

While HIPAA is an important law that is needed to protect study participants, its restrictions have created barriers to the successful implementation of some research studies with human subjects (Feld, 2005; Erlen, 2005; Kaiser, 2004; O'Herrin, Fost, & Kudsk, 2004). For example, many studies that require long-term follow-up to collect data from study participants have become more difficult to implement or have become completely unfeasible. This is because, in order to follow up with a participant, a researcher needs to record the participant's contact information, which falls under the purview of HIPAA. Many researchers in this situation can comply with HIPAA by obtaining written consent (a signed subject consent form) to collect, store, and use the participant's personal information.

This is not an onerous requirement for a researcher who is based at one institution and who has his or her study subjects come in for clinical appointments on a regular basis. However, in many research scenarios, such as public health research that often entails the

Table 1.

STUDY ID	GENDER	AGE	CANCER TYPE	COUNTY
1	Male	82	Prostate	Jefferson
2	Female	74	Breast	Los Angeles

study of entire populations, this requirement can be an insurmountable barrier.

What is Personally Identifying Information?

Some obvious personal identifiers are names, addresses, and dates of birth. However, some other potentially identifying information may not be as obvious and may identify an individual depending on the setting. Table 1 provides a fictional example of research data for a pain management study for men and women with cancer.

Research subject number one lives in a rural area. He is one of six men in the county who have been recently diagnosed with prostate cancer and he is the only 82-year-old still living in that area. In this case, the study participant's age, cancer type, and county of residence constitute personal identifying information

and should not have been collected without written consent of the study subject. On the other hand, study subject number two is a 74-year-old woman with breast cancer living in Los Angeles, California. Her age, cancer type, and county of residence would be much less likely to identify her. Table 2 provides a list of potentially identifying information that may fall under the purview of HIPAA.

A Research Example

As an example, consider a scenario where researchers want to measure changes in tobacco use (both cigarettes and chewing tobacco) in rural areas throughout the U.S. The researchers have developed educational materials that are intended to inform users of the increased health risks associated with tobacco use. The materials also include suggested strategies for tobacco use cessation.

Table 2. Additional examples of personally identifying information

Name(s), including nicknames and initials
Geographic location other than state (address, city, ZIP, county)
Date(s) of treatment, appointments, tests, hospitalizations (can use year only)
Month or date of birth (year of birth can be used unless over 89)
Social Security number
Phone number
Fax number
E-mail address
Medical Record number
Health Plan number
Account numbers
Certificate/license numbers
URL
IP address
Vehicle identifiers
Device ID
Biometric ID
Full-face/identifying photo
Any other unique identifying number, characteristic, or code

The researchers want to know if their educational intervention will really make a long-term difference in reducing tobacco use in rural settings. To do this, they need to administer a baseline survey and collect the data about the participants' current tobacco use. The survey may include questions such as, "How many cigarettes did you smoke per day, on average, this past month?" This baseline information can be collected fairly easily with a written, telephone, or online survey. In most cases, obtaining written informed consent will not be necessary as long as personally identifying information is not collected.

Then, to see how their intervention is working, the researchers want to administer a shorter version of the survey once a month for six months. Some of the research questions they want to answer are: Does the intervention work equally well in all age groups studied? In all ethnic groups studied? In all education levels?

To answer these questions, the researchers must match the baseline answers that each participant provides with the answers obtained from the same participant in subsequent surveys. This can be easily done by collecting the names and dates of birth for each participant and including them in the survey data. Unfortunately, the only way that the institutional review board at the researchers' institution will allow them to collect and store personally identifiable information is if they obtain written consent from each study participant. However, they know from experience that this will not be practical because it will cause their project to be delayed for several weeks while consent forms are mailed back and forth. Further, they do not have the budget to print and mail written consent forms to the hundreds of potential participants. They also know from experience that study participants are more likely to be honest with their answers if the surveys are anonymous.

How can the researchers conduct their study without collecting identifying information?

A Solution

A *privacy broker system* (PBS) (Douma & Gamito, 2006) serves as an independent custodian of personal identifiers and provides a barrier between these identifiers and the personal health care information of research subjects. This is accomplished through the use of a firewall that keeps contact information and health information separate, and a masquerade that tracks codenames to allow for long-term data collection and so that researchers can indirectly contact participants. A privacy broker system consists of at least three elements:

1. **Privacy Broker Agent (PB-Agent):** The PB-Agent can be a specially trained, independent person who serves as a custodian of private information; a sophisticated information technology (IT) system that serves the same purpose; or a combination of a trained person and an IT system.
2. **Privacy Broker Contacts Data (PB-Contacts):** The PB-Contacts is a highly secure, heavily encrypted database that contains study participants' private contact information and is only accessible by the PB-Agent.
3. **Privacy Broker Research Study Data (PB-Study):** The PB-Study contains the non-identifying research data collected during the study. Only the researchers have access to this database.

The following example will help clarify what kinds of data a PBS protects. Table 3 provides a data set for a fictional telephone survey study that contains both personal identifiers (name and telephone number)

Table 3. Fictional data set containing both personal identifiers and personal health information

Name	Home Phone	Age	Weight	Diabetic?	Smoker?	Alcohol?
Terry Silva	703-414-7090	29	224	Yes	No	No
Pat Sinclair	917-492-8870	45	189	No	Yes	Yes
Jody Smith	310-443-9912	33	139	Yes	Yes	Yes
Robin Starr	303-758-5805	32	178	No	Yes	No

Personal Identifiers   Personal Health Information

Table 4a. Fictional PB-Contacts with common primary key

Primary Key	Name	Home Phone
redfox	Terry Silva	703-414-7090
blackeagle	Pat Sinclair	917-492-8870
blackbear	Jody Smith	310-443-9912
bluebird	Robin Starr	303-758-5805

Table 4b. Fictional PB-Study with common primary key

Primary Key	Age	Weight	Diabetic?	Smoker?	Uses Alcohol?
redfox	29	224	Yes	No	No
blackeagle	45	189	No	Yes	Yes
blackbear	33	139	Yes	Yes	Yes
bluebird	32	178	No	Yes	No

and personal health information (age, weight, and so forth).

Remember, HIPAA regulates health care information that is linked to a person. The PBS creates a firewall by removing the direct link between personal identifiers (names and telephone numbers above) and personal health information (age, weight, smoker status, and so forth), while still allowing an indirect link so that follow-up data can be collected, and even indirect two-way communications can occur between researchers and study participants.

As mentioned above, in a PBS, there are two physically and institutionally separate databases. One is controlled by the PB-Agent at an independent site. The other, the PB-Study, is controlled by the researchers at an institution, such as a university. The two databases have a "primary key" or masquerade in common for each study participant. This key can be a number, or as shown in an example below, the key can be a set of culturally appropriate symbols. Tables 4a and 4b show example data contained in the PB-Contacts and the PB-Study, respectively. The "primary key" is common to both databases.

The researchers only have access to the health care information (PB-Study) and *never* have access to the personal identifiers. The PB-Agent only has access to the personal identifiers and *never* to the health data.

A Worst-Case Scenario

Now, consider that somehow, through the negligence of the researchers or through the willful act of a hacker,

the PB-Study is released to the public. The data in Table 4b is not likely to be useful to the hacker or harmful to the participants since it is only listed by the primary key and does not identify anyone. Similarly, in the unlikely event that the PB-Contacts is released or hacked, it would only contain contact information in Table 4a. The release of participant contact information would be problematic, but not nearly as harmful as if this information was linked to personal health information. Moreover, the contact information would have no context that would make it useful to a hacker. That is, the data alone do not indicate what the participants have in common. The PB-Contacts would not include any information about the research in question. The released data would amount to a list of random names and contact information.

Communication

An important advantage to a PBS is that, via the masquerade, researchers and participants can communicate indirectly. This is remarkable since, in a PBS, there is no need for the researchers to ever know the identities of their participants. The following example, based on an actual public health research project, will illustrate how communication is possible between researchers and anonymous participants using a PBS.

A public health research team is using a sophisticated educational Web site and a PBS to provide educational materials for Native American breast cancer survivors and to conduct a research study to investigate the effectiveness of these educational materials. The project reaches survivors all across the North American continent. Participants in the study obtain culturally appropriate code names, which serve as primary keys in the PB-Contacts and PB-Study (as illustrated in Tables 4a and 4b). The participants in this project log in to the Web site using their code names to access the educational materials. At their first log in, the participants complete an online survey that provides the baseline information the researchers need to measure the initial quality of life for each participant. As the participants continue to use the site over several months, they complete online surveys from time to time to gauge their quality of life. The researchers in this project want to see if any changes in quality of life occur due to their education interventions.

Now, consider a scenario where the research staff, which includes medical experts, sees a disturbing trend in the survey data for an individual participant or for a group of participants. For example, what if five participants who are all on the same chemotherapy agent are showing signs of deteriorating health? What if one of the participants appears to be in danger? A PBS allows the researchers to contact the PB-Agent with a private message for these participants. To send participants written materials, for example, the researchers would insert the written materials in an envelope, write the participant's code name on the envelope, seal it, and send it to the PB-Agent. The PB-Agent would look up the participant's contact information using the code name, put this on a label over the code name on the sealed envelope, and then mail it to the participant. E-mail could be used in a similar fashion, where the PB-Agent simply forwards an e-mail from the researcher to the participant. Anonymous communication can also occur via the Web site using chat sessions or posting of messages on a message board. In an emergency, the PB-Agent could call the participant and ask him or her to see a doctor.

Human vs. Automated PB-Agents

As mentioned earlier, a PB-Agent can either be a person, a purely automated IT system, or a combination of both.

1. **Human PB-Agent:** A human PB-Agent can be specially trained to understand the details of a given study and to follow a protocol, while being flexible enough to deal with unusual or unanticipated situations. A human PB-Agent can be personable and can be less expensive than developing a complex IT PB-Agent solution.

2. **Automated PB-Agent:** The PBS can also be implemented using technology, with a blind re-e-mailer system maintained by a third party, or a sign-in system for study staff and participants with strict access controls and roles for different data fields. The advantages of an automated PB-Agent are 24-hour availability and low marginal costs after the system has been developed. The disadvantages include lack of flexibility and an impersonal interface that may not be appropriate for all participants.

3. **Human/IT PB-Agent:** The preferred PBS arrangement utilizes a human PB-Agent assisted by an automated IT system. In this arrangement, many tasks can be automated while allowing for the personal touch and flexibility of a human.

Creation of Code Names

A participant's code name or masquerade can either be created manually by the PB-Agent each time a participant enrolls in the study or the process can be automated using an IT solution. In the manual scenario, the participant would contact the PB-Agent (for example, via e-mail, chat session, or toll-free telephone number) for help in creating a code name. Once created, the PB-Agent would enter the code name along with the participant's contact information into the PB-Contacts. The PB-Agent would then send the newly created code name to the research team so that a record could be created in the study database for that participant.

Although optional, an automated system for creating code names is preferred since it reduces errors and greatly simplifies the enrollment process. In an automated system, the participant could obtain a code name by going to the study Web site and registering for the study. Behind the scenes on what is called the "back end" of the site, the code name and contact information would be entered directly into the secure PB-Contacts (the contact information is never stored on the study site). Simultaneously, the automated system would create a record in the PB-Study for the new codename. From that point, anytime the participant completed an online survey, the data would be automatically entered in the PB-Study under the code name.

Authentication

An important part of a PBS is the ability to authenticate the identities of study participants through the use of a code name, the goal being to ensure that only the right participant is providing the study data that pertains to him or her.

Practical authentication tends to fall into two categories: cultural authentication and random secrets (Smith, 2002). Both methods are problematic in the context of biomedical research.

Cultural authentication is a widely used technique and involves asking questions like: "Can you verify your address, please? Your social security number? Your mother's maiden name?" This is based on knowledge and capabilities that are peculiar to each person. The technique maintains security because it relies on information that can vary widely from one person to the next, except within groups that know each other very well.

The other major approach to authentication is random secrets. Tokens and passwords hold a strong advantage over cultural authentication when they incorporate a random secret that serves as the base secret for authentication. Users can change their random secret if the previous one is lost or stolen. The secret might be memorized or stored on a magnetic swipe card. Random secrets are ideal for maintaining anonymity, but they are impractical with populations that are wary of computers, inexperienced with impersonal random passwords, or have memory problems, such as those who are advanced in age or have a debilitating medical condition.

In these instances, a third approach, which is a modified version of cultural identification, can be successfully implemented. In Native American populations, for example, cultural authentication can build on the storytelling culture of virtually all Native Americans, as well as on the tradition of long narrative last names, like "Wilma Man Killer" and "Bear Standing Strong." By using a combination of culturally appropriate symbology, colors, and numbers, a participant may choose "Red Eagle 12" as his authentication. Storyteller narrative phrases and a visual interface make code names easy for participants to recall. This type of authentication is currently in use in the Native American cancer survivor project described earlier.

Planning for Problems

When using a PBS, it is crucial to plan for circumstances that can result in a failure of the system and/or data loss. It is important that a human PB-Agent be well trained and that sufficient PB-Contacts back-up systems are in place. There should also be legal agreements and a contingency plan that establishes a chain of custody for the PB-Contacts in case a PB-Agent resigns, dies, or is incapacitated. Likewise, the PB-Study should be secured using the latest data security standards that the given institution can put in place.

History of the Term

The general privacy broker concept was developed by public health researchers involved in a Native American research project. The Institute for Dynamic Educational Advancement (IDEA) further refined the concept while designing a PBS that responded to the needs and challenges that the researchers faced in their public health research. The PBS developed by IDEA for these researchers was designed to address the challenge of a small education and research organization in collecting research data on individuals from across the North American continent in a consistent and efficient way while protecting individual privacy and complying with stringent government regulations concerning patient confidentiality.

Related Definition

A related definition of the term "privacy broker" was first used by Bhattacharya and Gupta in 2004 in the context of medical records. For Bhattacharya, a privacy broker is a software firewall. It is a layer between the database access request and the database that enforces privacy policy in health information systems. If a user is not authorized to access certain information, the information is not transmitted. This is different from the broader definition provided in this encyclopedia article which couples both "firewall" and "masquerade" elements.

Bhattacharya describes the "privacy broker" as a middleware architecture that acts as a sentry, reducing the risk of violating patient privacy by enforcing a machine-readable syntax for labeling different database fields. Bhattacharya's privacy broker intercepts database transactions. It has three main features: (a) the broker accepts the agreed privacy specification and ensures adherence of the stated privacy policies; (b) it enables the authorization of specific individuals to access their data; and (c) it enforces non-repudiation of agreements between visitors and Web sites. Such a broker-based approach ensures that the solution is independent of the database used. It also allows the solution to be easily used in legacy systems. A 2004 version of Bhattacharya's privacy broker was based on the World Wide Web Consortium's "Platform for Privacy Preference" (P3P). But it was later modified in 2006 to add an enforcement mechanism for organizations to use in monitoring their information handling practices (Bhattacharya, Gupta, & Agrawal, 2006). When adding enforcement, Bhattacharya switched to using "Enterprise Privacy Authorization Language (EPAL)," a syntax for writing privacy rules used by databases. EPAL is an XML-based language designed for organizations to specify internal privacy policies. These EPAL policies can be used internally and among an organization and its business partners to ensure compliance with the underlying policies of each partner.

FUTURE TRENDS

The privacy broker concept is relatively new to the research community. It has been approved by a major medical center's Institutional Review Board and has been successfully implemented in a large, ongoing public health study. It seems likely that the use of privacy broker systems will increase as knowledge of the benefits of such systems spreads. Further, as Internet access continues to expand to include populations in remote areas, privacy broker systems will be become more practical.

CONCLUSION

Privacy broker systems provide an effective way for researchers to conduct long-term research while maintaining participant anonymity and protecting participant privacy. Such systems allow researchers to undertake projects that were previously impractical due to regulatory barriers.

REFERENCES

Bhattacharya, J., & Gupta, S.K. (2004). Privacy broker for enforcing privacy policies in databases. *Proceedings of the 5th International Conference on Knowledge-Based Computer Systems,* Hyderabad, India.

Bhattacharya, J., Gupta, S.K., & Agrawal, B. (2006). Protecting privacy of health information through privacy broker. *Proceedings of the 39th IEEE Hawaii International Conference on System Sciences.*

Douma, M., & Gamito, E. (2006). A culturally appropriate, Web-based technology for anonymous data collection for public health research in culturally diverse populations. *Journal of Cases on Information Technology.*

Erlen, J.A. (2005). HIPAA—implications for research. *Orthopaedic Nursing, 24*(2), 139-142.

Feld, A.D. (2005). The Health Insurance Portability and Accountability Act (HIPAA): Its broad effect on practice. *American Journal of Gastroenterology, 100*(7), 1440-1443.

Kaiser, J. (2004). Patient records. Privacy rule creates bottleneck for U.S. biomedical researchers. *Science, 305*(5681), 168-169.

O'Herrin, J.K., Fost, N., & Kudsk, K.A. (2004). Health Insurance Portability Accountability Act (HIPAA) regulations: Effect on medical record research. *Annals of Surgery, 239*(6), 772-776.

Smith, R. (2002). *Authentication: From passwords to public keys.* NJ: Addison-Wesley.

KEY TERMS

Firewall: A logical barrier designed to prevent unauthorized or unwanted communications between sections of a computer network. In the context of medical records, it is a layer between the database access request and the database that enforces privacy policy in health information systems.

Health Insurance Portability and Accountability Act of 1996 (HIPAA): Sets standards to protect information related to health care. Specifically, it regulates health care information that can be linked with a person.

Informed Consent: A process by which a person makes a voluntary decision to participate in a research study based on accurate and understandable information.

Institutional Review Board (IRB): A group of individuals that review research study protocols (study plans) and approve or disapprove them based on ethical, safety, and scientific considerations.

Masquerade: To represent as another. The privacy broker system masquerades the identity of a study participant as an anonymous code so that study researchers never have access to the real identities of the study participants.

Privacy Broker Agent (PB-Agent): A person or system external to a research project that acts as a custodian of personally identifying information and that is an intermediary between the research subject and the researchers. Only the privacy broker has access to personal identifiers.

Privacy Broker Contacts Data (PB-Contacts): A highly secure, heavily encrypted database that contains study participants' private contact information and is only accessible by the privacy broker agent.

Privacy Broker Research Study Data (PB-Study): The non-identifying research data collected during a study. Only the researchers have access to this database.

Privacy Broker System (PBS): A system consisting of at least three elements: (1) a privacy broker agent (PB-Agent), (2) a privacy broker contacts data (PB-Contacts), and (3) a privacy broker research study data (PB-Study). As an option, an automated primary key (code name) generation and authentication system can be incorporated as a fourth element in a PBS. A PBS removes a direct link between personally identifying information and personal health information.

Subject Consent Form: A document that describes a research study, including risks associated with participation, and other information deemed necessary by the governing Institutional Review Board for the participant to make an informed decision as to whether or not to participate in the research.

Subject: Person who participates in clinical research; also known as study participant.

Information Security Policies for Networkable Devices

Julia Kotlarsky
University of Warwick, USA

Ilan Oshri
Rotterdam School of Management Erasmus, The Netherlands

Corey Hirsch
Henley Management College, UK

INTRODUCTION

Recent years have seen a surge in the introduction of networkable Windows-based operating system (NWOS) devices. Some examples are home entertainment systems (e.g., Xbox), smart phones (e.g., Motorola i930 and PlamOne's Treo), and Pocket PC (e.g., Toshiba e850). While NWOS devices present an appealing proposition for both software vendors and buyers in terms of the flexibility to add supplementary software applications, such devices also introduce new challenges in terms of managing information security risks. NWOS devices are particularly vulnerable to information security threats because of the vendors' and buyers' lack of awareness of the security risks associated with such devices. In addition to the direct damage to business operations that an infected NWOS device might cause, other consequences may also include alienated customers and a tarnished reputation (Austin & Darby, 2003).

In this article, information security risks in NWOS will be explored and practices applied by one vendor will be outlined. First, some definitions of the key concepts discussed here will be provided and a review of recent discussions in the academic and practice literature will be presented. Following this, a discussion about the information security risks and the practices applied will be developed. Lastly, future research in this area and conclusions will be offered.

BACKGROUND

The information security literature has indeed discussed at length prevention, detection, and recovery strategies related to information security management (e.g., Joseph & Blanton, 1992; Jung, Han, & Lee, 2001); however, these studies mainly focused on computer- and Internet-related information security threats and highlighted practices associated with the management of software development and information systems that could offer protection from malicious software. In this regard, NWOS devices present an extended set of challenges that call for the development of additional capabilities by the vendor. Indeed, several studies have recently discussed the need to integrate software development and operational processes with strategic business objectives when building security into products (McAdams, 2004; von Solms & von Solms, 2004, 2005; Taylor & McGraw, 2005). Clearly, the careless management of information security of NWOS devices will not only risk the vendor's or the buyer's network environment, but could also harm the relationships between vendors and buyers, as malicious software may be transferred between their networks during production, sales, and after-sales activities. In a recent article, Arce (2003) acknowledges that networkable gadgets pose unique information security risks to vendors; however, little is so far known about the challenges faced and solutions applied by vendors when managing the information security of NWOS devices throughout the product lifecycle.

INFORMATION SECURITY RISKS IN NWOS DEVICES

While the literature on information security has addressed various issues relating to (i) best practices in managing information security programs (e.g., Joseph

& Blanton, 1992; Austin & Darby, 2003; Farahmand, Navathe, Sharp, & Enslow, 2003), (ii) risk management and evaluation of security management programs (e.g., von Solms, van de Haar, Von Solms, & Caelli, 1994; McAdams, 2004), and (iii) the links between the management of information security and operational activities (McAdams, 2004), recent studies have claimed that there is a serious lack of empirical research in this area (Kotulic & Clark, 2004), and in practice, firms rarely apply a systematic and methodological approach (Austin & Darby, 2003) that aligns their information security strategy with business objectives and operational processes (McGraw, 2004; von Solms & von Solms, 2004, 2005; Taylor & McGraw, 2005). Indeed, most vendors of off-the-shelf computing products will either "bundle" an information security solution into the product or give the buyer the freedom to select a solution that fits their needs. In this regard, the market for NWOS devices presents unique challenges, as a vendor of such devices is required to consider information security measures during different stages of the product lifecycle. This is mainly because most buyers of NWOS devices do not consider their devices to be a target for malicious attack by viruses or worms. However, being a NWOS device puts such a device under the same category of most personal computers and servers that operate on Windows platforms. Because of the large installed base of Windows-based platforms, these are subject to a large majority of hackers' attacks. Consequently, the risk for NWOS devices has become acute, and the challenges that some NWOS devices present to vendors and buyers may require the development of new capabilities. For example, NWOS devices that are designed for a particular usage (e.g., digital microscopes, digital storage oscilloscopes) impose interactions between the vendor and the buyer during the lifecycle of the product. Consider product demonstration activities during which an NWOS device could be connected to the local network to demonstrate its printing capabilities. Without considering the information security risks involved in connecting this networkable device to the buyer's network, in doing so, the vendor puts at risk the buyer's network and the demonstration product by allowing the transfer of malicious software from the buyer's network to the NWOS device and vice versa. The risk can be even more acute should the salesperson use the same device while visiting other clients, without protecting both the client's network and the demonstration device.

Table 1 summarizes information security risks that vendors and buyers of NWOS devices face which may lead to an information security incident if such risks are not managed properly.

In this article we consider information security measures in three stages in the product lifecycle. The stages are: *production, sales,* and *after-sales* activities. It is important that vendors approach each of these stages with awareness to the risks reported above and align operational activities with information security measures to reduce the vulnerability of the NWOS devices. Furthermore, from buyers' perspective, it is important to create awareness about the vulnerability of NWOS devices and offer tools that can protect the devices as well as assess vendors' practices to this problem.

In the following sections we discuss each of the three product lifecycle stages and offer a checklist of information security measures that can be useful for both vendors and buyers of NWOS devices. Vendors can learn from the checklist how to improve their information security measures at different stages of the product lifecycle. Buyers can use this checklist during vendor selection by inquiring bidding vendors about how they, the vendors, ensure security at each stage. We based these recommendations on research conducted at LeCroy, a supplier of data storage oscilloscopes.

Stage 1: Production

Because the production environment can also be a source of malicious software in itself, there are four key issues that vendors should consider:

- isolating the production environment from other networks
- educating the workforce not to bring portable memory devices into the production environment
- placing warning labels near connectors, and
- providing an antivirus package with shipment

The Implementation at LeCroy

LeCroy took some steps to isolate the production environment and improve engineers' awareness of information security issues relating to its NWOS products. To increase awareness, the company introduced an annual information security fair at which issues relating to

Table 1. Information security risks for buyers and vendors of NWOS devices

Stage	Risks to Vendor	Risks to Clients/Users
Production	- Malicious software that attacks the vendor's network may infect the production environment and NWOS devices.	- A client receives an infected NWOS device. - Malicious software is transferred from the vendor's production environment into the client's network.
Demonstration Activities	- Sales person infects clients' network with malicious software when demonstrating product functionality that requires connection to the client's network, thus ruining the vendor's reputation. - Malicious software is transferred from the client's network to the NWOS device during demo activities.	- Sales person infects the client's network with malicious software when demonstrating product functionality that requires connection to the client's network.
Product delivery and deployment	- Users do not consider the device to be networkable and a target for malicious software, so do not protect the device and its network. Therefore, if the NWOS device is becoming infected, (1) the client may come back to the vendor with complains about performance problems with the delivered device, and (2) the product becomes a risk to the vendor upon return to the manufacturer for repair or upgrade.	- Users do not consider the device to be networkable and a target for malicious software, so do not protect the device and its network. - Users do not have facilities to scan the NWOS unit from the outside, if antivirus is not installed. - Antivirus installed by the vendor is difficult to un-install, if a client wants to use another antivirus. - Antivirus installed in the NWOS unit delivered might be outdated; it does not have recent security patches that have become available since the unit was manufactured and until it is opened by the client for deployment
Maintenance and upgrades	- Users do not update virus definitions, thus allowing malicious software to attack the NWOS device. Upon connection to the vendor's network for maintenance or upgrade activities, the vendor's network is at risk.	- Vendor does not inform users about newly discovered vulnerabilities and about security patches to deal with these vulnerabilities.

the company's information security strategy were presented and discussed. In addition, LeCroy introduced an isolated network for production to eliminate the possibility that malicious software would get into the production environment. To ensure that the production network was isolated, engineers were instructed not to connect external devices (e.g., memory sticks and laptops) or use CDs on the production network. The production procedure was updated to include a final virus check of the NWOS device before shipping it to a customer. Moreover, information package and antivirus software were included in each product shipment. Buyers were advised to contact their Information Systems department prior to connecting the NWOS device to their network and to install antivirus software of their preference. To ensure that buyers paid attention to the risk involved in connecting the NWOS device to the network, LeCroy placed a sticker on the Ethernet socket that said: "This is a Windows networkable device; visit the security Web site." This way, users had to consider the consequences of plugging this unit to the network without consulting their IS departments. Lastly, LeCroy offered a recovery disk in each product shipment to ensure that, if a NWOS device did get infected by a virus, the buyer could always restore the unit to its original settings and start again.

The Buyer's Checklist

Unless this is a key business partner, it is unlikely that a buyer will be willing to visit the vendor's plant to see what information security measures are taken during the production phase. However, a vendor should be willing to host such a visit if a buyer wishes (and it does not hurt to enquire). A buyer should still be able to find out a good deal, without traveling, by asking to be put in touch with the head of the vendor's security team. The questions a buyer may want to ask include:

- Is this product manufactured in your own facilities, or those of a contract manufacturer? If a contract manufacturer is used, how do you ensure that their production line is secured?
- Are isolated networks in place for production (and for later servicing) of the product?
- Do production and/or service networks contain out-of-support (old) nodes? Is the equipment used in production certified to be malware-free?
- Is each box externally scanned just prior to shipment? With what tool? Please note that internal scanning tools introduce difficulties for customers who do not prefer the particular tool that the vendor chose to embed.
- How often are master images updated to reflect most recent patches?
- Do recovery CDs reflect recent images?

Stage 2: Sales

For the sales activities, vendors should consider the following measures:

- developing a methodology to communicate important security information to customers
- providing training programs for the sales force about security issues
- providing technical support for remote update of virus definitions

The Implementation at LeCroy

LeCroy invested in educating its sales force about information security issues. The objectives of this training program were twofold. First, it was necessary to educate the sales force to consider information security threats when performing product demonstrations at the buyer's site. This training included several practices that the sales force was asked to follow. For example, before product demonstrations requiring a connection to the local network, the salesperson should contact the IS department at the site and check their information security arrangements. In addition, the salesperson was instructed to perform a virus check following each product demonstration that included a connection to the network. Nonetheless, one major challenge that the sales force faced when attempting to implement these new practices was the difficulty in getting updates of virus definitions while on the road. This was solved through a synchronization process that the company supported, in which the latest virus definitions and patches were transferred to the salesperson, stored on a memory stick, and later on were uploaded onto the NWOS device. The second challenge was to train the sales force on how to educate buyers about information security risks concerning their NWOS devices. This line of training was particularly challenging, as the sales force was mainly focused on getting "the deal done" and devoted less attention to technical matters. Nonetheless, the management at LeCroy emphasized the importance of educating their buyers about information security risks as a long-term business strategy. In addition, the salesperson walks the buyer through LeCroy's Web site to get him or her familiar with how security updates can be downloaded and updated. Finally, the company provides an antivirus package in every box shipped.

The Buyer's Checklist

When a salesperson visits a potential buyer, the demo NWOS has already been to several other locations recently. To ensure that the demo NWOS device does present risks to the buyer's network, the buyer should be advised to check the demo unit by the IT and security team as well as by end application users. The buyer should further investigate what the vendor's information security capabilities are by asking the salesperson the following questions:

- What precautions do you take prior to connecting the appliance to my network?
- What precautions do you take with regard to your laptop PC to ensure there is no malware contagion?

- How does your firm guard against spam, malware, and spyware on the company's networks in general, and in particular with regard to demonstration units and salespersons' PCs?

Further, ask to see any training documents, brochures, or materials on information security that the salesperson has received in the prior year.

Stage 3: After-Sales Activities

From the vendor's perspective, after-sales activities involve considering information security measures for maintenance and upgrades. During this stage vendors should consider the following:

- isolating the customer service environment from other networks,
- ensuring that application software is compatible with OS updates and virus definitions, and
- publishing through the vendor's Web site information about the compatibility of the device with OS upgrades and virus definitions.

The Implementation at LeCroy

The procedure applied for NWOS sent back for repair or upgrade was similar to the handling of products during production. One key difference was the immediate check for viruses of a returning NWOS device using an independent CD, ensuring that the unit was clean before admitting it to the service network. With regard to updates from Microsoft, which often result in new updates for antivirus software, LeCroy dealt with these changes by regularly checking for updates, testing each new update, and informing its clients about the compatibility of the update through its Web site.

The Buyer's Checklist

From buyer's side, after-sale activities start from product delivery and deployment, followed by maintenance and upgrades. To ensure security when the NWOS device is connected to the network, a buyer should involve the IT department in the deployment process. Furthermore, in addition to questions about duration of the warranty period, a buyer is advised to check the vendor's Web site for its information security policy and ask ques-

tions that would help him/her to assess whether the potential vendor ensures information security during maintenance activities such as calibration and repair or in case new vulnerability in OS is discovered. Questions to ask include:

- What is the software support and version update process?
- Does the vendor provide active (e.g., via e-mails) or passive (e.g., posting on its Web site) security updates, such as advice on taking service packs or patches?
- Does the vendor scan your product prior to connecting it to a network during repair?
- Is the repair network isolated?
- Does the vendor scan your product prior to return shipping it to you?
- If a security problem is discovered, does the vendor contact you to offer a range of possible methods to deal with it?
- How does the vendor insure the privacy of any data you have stored on the appliance during the service process?

IMPLEMENTATION CONSIDERATIONS

Indeed, pursuing the suggestions made above will improve the link between information security policy, operational activities, and the business strategy of the firm. To ensure that these measures will be carried out, it is imperative that senior and middle managers (i.e., the chief information officer, the chief information security officer, and the security team) will be involved and lead this information security policy. Evidence suggests that such measures are likely to have a positive impact on the firm and its clientele when a champion from the firm is leading this process and promoting information security policies within and outside the firm. This person can be the chief information officer, who is familiar with information security issues as well as with the firm's business objectives. As claimed above, information security vulnerabilities of NWOS devices can be detected and overcome in each stage of the product lifecycle (i.e., production, sales, and after-sales), therefore requiring the involvement of senior and middle managers from the engineering, production, sales, and security teams.

The Potential Benefits for Vendors and Buyers

What value is added from these information security measures to vendors and buyers of NWOS devices? Through such information security measures, vendors of NWOS devices may differentiate their products from vendors who prefer to shift the responsibility for managing information security risks to their clients. Vendors of NWOS devices may offer extra value in offering support with information security risks, thus positioning their products as superior to others, and possibly commanding premium prices for their products. In the long term, bonding clients and vendors through such practices may improve the retention of existing clients and may offer the vendor additional opportunities to promote new product introductions. In addition, buyers develop a degree of dependency on vendors through constant updates and upgrades related to antivirus packages, which can in return serve the vendors in future offerings. Buyers, on the other hand, may enjoy continuous support relating to information security issues from the vendor during the product life, a value-adding activity that also reduces the vulnerability of their network.

FUTURE TRENDS

One key future trend for firms to consider is the management of information security in outsourcing relationships. Recent years have seen many industries contracting out their manufacturing and customer services activities to companies based in India or China. In the case of NWOS, the consequences of manufacturing a networkable device are far more than just quality issues. A vendor of NWOS devices that outsources the production line or the customer service operations should consider developing a methodology that would apply the same guidelines described above by the outsourcee. Failing to do so may result in triggering information security problems associated with the production and after-sales phases described above. Such methodology should be negotiated and agreed between the parties as part of the Service Level Agreement (SLA), and the vendor should monitor the implementation of such information security measures (described above) by the outsourcee. Another key future

trend concerns technical solutions for the challenges that vendors of NWOS devices face. So far the academic and practice literature offered limited solutions with regard to automating the process through which the vendor checks whether OS upgrades, patches, and virus definitions are compatible with the device functionality. Most vendors of NWOS devices that follow such practice perform manual checks and release this information through their Web sites. Improving the customer support to buyers of NWOS devices requires an automation of this process in the same manner that Microsoft offers new updates to its OS users.

CONCLUSION

This article explored information security in NWOS devices. Risks relating to NWOS devices from the vendor's and the buyer's perspectives were reviewed, and information security measures were offered to both vendors and buyers. In this respect, the emphasis in this article was to offer vendors some practices that could improve their management of information security during the production, sales, and after-sales activities. At the same time, buyers of NWOS devices were offered some selection criteria to assess the measures taken by a vendor of NWOS devices before committing to a purchase. While research and practice has made significant progress in understanding information security risks in NWOS devices, far more investment in developing methodologies and technical tools is still needed in order to overcome new challenges such as information security in outsourcing relationships.

REFERENCES

Arce, I. (2003). The rise of the gadgets. *IEEE Security and Privacy, 1*(5), 78-81.

Austin, R.D., & Darby, C.A.R. (2003). The myth of secure computing. *Harvard Business Review,* (June), 120-126.

Farahmand, F., Navathe, S.B., Sharp, G.P., & Enslow, P.H. (2005). A management perspective on risk of security threats to information systems. *Information Technology and Management, 6*(2-3), 203-225.

Joseph, G.W., & Blanton, J.E. (1992). Computer infectors: Prevention, detection, and recovery. *Information & Management, 23,* 205-216.

Jung, B., Han, I., & Lee, S. (2001). Security threats to Internet: A Korean multi-industry investigation. *Information & Management, 38*(8), 487-498.

Kotulic, A.G., & Clark, J.G. (2004). Why there aren't more information security research studies? *Information & Management, 41*(5), 597-607.

McAdams, A. (2004). Security and risk management: A fundamental business issue. *Information Management Journal, 38*(4), 36-44.

McGraw, G. (2004). Software security. *IEEE Security & Privacy, 2*(2), 80-83.

Taylor, D., & McGraw, G. (2005). Adopting a software security improvement program. *IEEE Security & Privacy, 3*(3), 88-91.

von Solms, B., & von Solms, R. (2004). The ten deadly sins of information security management. *Computers & Security, 23,* 371-376.

von Solms, B., & von Solms, R. (2005). From information security to business security. *Computers & Security, 24,* 271-273.

von Solms, R., van de Haar, H., Von Solms, B., & Caelli, W. (1994). A framework for information security evaluation. *Information & Management, 26*(3), 143-153.

KEY TERMS

Information Security Incident: An incident as an adverse network event in an information system, networkable device, or network. This can also be the threat of the occurrence of such an event.

Malicious Code Software (e.g., Trojan Horse): Software that appears to perform a useful function, however actually gains unauthorized access to the information system resources or deceives a user into executing other malicious logic.

Networkable Windows Operating System Device: A device that operates on the Windows™ Operating System and therefore has system capabilities of a computer.

Patch: A small update released by a software vendor to fix bugs in existing programs.

Risk: The product of the level of threat and the level of vulnerability presented to the system. It establishes the probability of a successful attack.

Risk Assessment: The process by which threats are identified and their impact is determined.

Security Policy: A set of rules and practices that regulate how a system or organization could provide security services to protect sensitive and critical system resources.

Information Security Policy Research Agenda

Heather Fulford
The Robert Gordon University, UK

Neil Doherty
Loughborough University, UK

INTRODUCTION

For the past two decades, it has been argued that an 'information revolution' is taking place that is having a significant impact upon all aspects of organizational life (e.g., Porter & Millar, 1985; Drucker, 1988). If applied effectively as a strategic resource, investment in information can result in the realization of significant corporate benefits. Indeed it has been contended that "information is the firm's primary strategic asset" (Glazer, 1993), and elsewhere that it is the "lifeblood of the organization" (CBI, 1992) contributing directly, as it does, to the organization's operational performance and financial health. (Bowonder & Miyake, 1992; McPherson, 1996). However, information can only be recognized as a vital organizational resource if managers can readily gain access to it when required. Unfortunately, as a consequence of the high incidence of security breaches, many organizations are failing to consistently provide the information resources that their managers require (Angell, 1996; Gaston, 1996).

Information only retains the potential to deliver value if its confidentiality, integrity, and availability are protected (Menzies, 1993; Gaston, 1996). However, the increasing integration of information systems, both within and between organizations, when coupled with the growing value of corporate information resources, have made information security management a complex and challenging undertaking (Gerber, von Solms, & Overbeek, 2001). Indeed, it is estimated that "security breaches affect 90% of all businesses every year, and cost some $17 billion" (Austin & Darby, 2003). Moreover, Austin and Darby (2003) also suggest that protective measures can be very expensive, noting for example that "the average company can easily spend 5% to 10% of its IT budget on security."

One increasingly important mechanism for protecting corporate information, in an attempt to prevent security breaches rather than merely respond to them, is through the formulation, dissemination, and implementation of an information security policy (Hone & Eloff, 2002a). Indeed, the information security policy has been denoted as "one of the most important" information security controls (Hone & Eloff, 2002b), and elsewhere as the "start of security management" (Higgins, 1999) and the "sine qua non (indispensable condition) of effective security management" (von Solms & von Solms, 2004). The primary reason that the information security policy has become the "prerequisite" (David, 2002) or "foundation" (Lindup, 1995) of effective security management has been suggested by Higgins (1999), who notes that "without a policy, security practices will be developed without clear demarcation of objectives and responsibilities."

The overall aim of an information security policy then is to create the "ideal operating environment" for the management of information security (Barnard & von Solms, 1998). It does so by defining "the broad boundaries of information security" as well as the "rights and responsibilities of information resource users" (Hone & Eloff, 2002b). Specifically, a good information security policy should:

...outline individual responsibilities, define authorized and unauthorized uses of the systems, provide venues for employee reporting of identified or suspected threats to the system, define penalties for violations, and provide a mechanism for updating the policy. (Whitman, 2004)

Furthermore, the information security policy should act as an important tool for demonstrating to employees, as well as to other stakeholders, management's commitment to, and recognition of, the importance of information security issues within the organization (Hone & Eloff, 2002b).

The increasing awareness of the importance of the information security policy, coupled with the advent of national and international standards on policy formulation, dissemination, and implementation, have given rise to a growing body of literature on information security policies. The purpose of this article is to report on a thorough and focused review of the existing literature on the role of information security policies in information security management. A summary of the key themes in that literature are presented and discussed, demonstrating how the subject has been treated to date, and illustrating the issues and perspectives that have been addressed. In addition to reporting on what has been presented in the literature so far with regard to the role of policies in information security management, indications will be given of issues relating to information security policies that have not as yet been dealt with in any depth or detail in the existing literature. To conclude the article, these untreated issues will then be discussed and drawn together into a proposal for a future research agenda in this important area of information security management, and the implications for managers of the current literature coverage will be considered.

KEY THEMES IN THE LITERATURE ON INFORMATION SECURITY POLICIES

Gaston (1996) suggests that the information security policy can be defined as "broad guiding statements of goals to be achieved." Such a policy serves to "define and assign the responsibilities that various departments and individuals have in achieving policy goals." This definition is broadly in line with the British Standard on Information Security Management (BSI, 1999; now ISO 17799), which suggests that the information security policy document should "set out the organization's approach to managing information security." As such, information security policies typically include "general statements of goals, objectives, beliefs, ethics and responsibilities, often accompanied by the general means of achieving these things (such as procedures)" (Wood, 1995). These procedures or guidelines tend to be advisory, whereas "policies are mandatory," and consequently "special approval is needed where a worker wishes to take a different course of action" from that stipulated in the policy (Wood, 1995).

Theme I: The Structure and Format of Information Security Policies

While there is a high degree of consensus in the literature with regard to a broad definition for the information security policy, there is rather more debate as to whether there should be a single policy, or whether it should be subdivided into several distinct levels or types (Baskerville & Siponen, 2002). This debate represents a key theme in the literature on information security policy formulation. Examples of structures and formats discussed include Siponen's suggestion that security policies can be classified into two broad groups, namely "computer-oriented policies" or "people/organizational policies" (Siponen, 2000). By contrast, Sterne (1991) distinguishes between three levels of policy, namely the "institutional policy, the institutional information security policy and the technical information security policy." Lindup (1995) agrees that there is no single information security policy, but suggests instead that there are several distinct types, rather than levels, which include the "system security policy, product security policy, community security policy and corporate information security policy." Lindup (1995) further makes the claim that, while academics may continue the debate about ways of classifying or sub-dividing policies, in practice organizations tend to have a single "corporate policy."

Interesting though this theoretical debate may be, this area of information security management warrants in-depth empirical investigation in order to help inform the discussion and provide meaningful insights. Specific issues worthy of investigation in this respect include:

1. There is a need for studies of the range of policy structures and formats that exist, and indications of the levels of uptake in organizations of the various types, incorporating an examination of relationships between policy structure and organization type, size, industry sector, and so on.
2. There is scope for investigating the factors motivating an organization to adopt a particular policy structure and format.
3. A valuable contribution could be made by research exploring the efficacy of each type of policy structure in the overall framework of an organization's efforts to manage its information resources.

Theme II: Information Security Policy Uptake

Another important theme in the literature concerns the uptake of information security policies. There have been a number of recent surveys addressing this issue, although it is interesting to note that, apart from one notable exception (namely Fulford & Doherty, 2003), these surveys have been practitioner, rather than academic studies, and most have been undertaken within a European context. These practitioner-led studies address a broad sweep of information security management issues, among which the uptake of information security policies receives rather scant treatment, in comparison with the coverage of issues such as the prevalence and type of security breaches experienced. Overall, the findings of these various studies indicate that there has been an upward trend in the uptake of information security policies, particularly in large organizations. For example, the UK Department of Trade and Industry (DTI) has commissioned a number of information security surveys (e.g., DTI, 2000, 2002, 2004). The 2000 survey reported that only 14% of the surveyed organizations had an information security policy in place; in 2002 the figure reported was 27% (and 59% for large enterprises); and in 2004, over one-third of the organizations in the DTI's survey sample claimed to have an information security policy.

As noted in the report of the 2004 DTI survey, while the result showing more than one-third of organizations having a policy in place is the "highest result ever" in the DTI series of security surveys, it "still seems inconsistent with the perceived high priority of information security in three-quarters of businesses" (DTI, 2004). Studies designed to explicitly explore this apparent inconsistency are needed if real progress is to be made in improving the information security management endeavors of business enterprises. Moreover, while the relationship between policy uptake and information security management success has been briefly examined in an exploratory UK-based study (see Fulford & Doherty, 2003), and revisited in Doherty and Fulford (2005), there is clearly scope for more detailed examination and empirical investigations of this important issue of policy efficacy. Other authors substantiate this point by expressing concerns regarding the effectiveness of information security policies (e.g., Hone & Eloff, 2002b; Karyda, Kiountouzis, & Kokolakis, 2005).

A further strand of research arguably needs to be devoted to comparing and contrasting information security policy coverage in organizations, and to exploring the relationship between policy coverage and policy effectiveness as a tool for managing information security. Beyond these studies of uptake and policy scope, the whole area of policy dissemination and implementation remains generally under-researched. For example, while the various DTI survey reports present findings about the approaches organizations use to disseminate their information security policies, again we are left with no clear indication of the relative success of each approach. Neither do we glean much with regard to the specific means used to implement information security policies, and the relative effectiveness of each one.

Theme III: Information Security Policy Maintenance and Updating

Allied to the theme of policy uptake, a number of authors have emphasized the importance of policy updating and maintenance (e.g., Higgins, 1999; Hone & Eloff, 2002a; Hong, Chi, Chao, & Tang, 2003). While the 2002 DTI study found that a higher proportion of organizations with a policy were undertaking annual policy updates than had been the case in 2000, and the 2004 survey report stressed the need to ensure policies stay current, there appears to be a dearth of academic studies exploring the issue of policy longevity and updating. In particular, what seems to be lacking here is explicit investigation of policy maintenance issues, such as the ideal frequency of policy updating and the overall longevity of information security policies. Again, this broad area of information policy management warrants thorough investigation. This could perhaps be most effectively achieved in the context of compliance with the relevant ISO standards on information security (e.g., ISO 17799 and 27001), in which the ongoing nature of security management in organizations is highlighted.

Theme IV: Information Security Policy Alignment

A further strand of the literature discusses the importance of aligning the information security policy with corporate objectives (e.g., Rees, Bandyopadhyay, & Spafford, 2003; Doherty & Fulford, 2006). However, as Doherty and Fulford (2006) note, there has been little investigation of the relationship between strategic information systems planning and information security management, and hence between the two key documents associated with those activities, namely the strategic information systems plan and the information security policy. While Doherty and Fulford (2006) discuss some hypothetical cases highlighting the importance for organizations of ensuring that the information systems plan and the information security policy are formulated and managed in tandem, it seems there has yet to be any detailed investigation of real cases in this aspect of information security management. Their call for empirical work in this area echoes the comments made elsewhere by Kotulic and Clark (2004), who believe that the "organizational level information security domain" is a new and under-researched phenomenon, which may "prove to be one of the most critical areas of research necessary for supporting the viability of the firm."

MANAGEMENT IMPLICATIONS AND PROPOSED RESEARCH AGENDA

As shown in the above review, the academic literature on information security policies, while rather meager in comparison with the coverage of other aspects of information security management, is replete with theoretical discussions, propositions, and conceptual research. The principal limitation of this aspect of information security management literature seems to be that few detailed empirical studies exist. Moreover, the practitioner-led studies of information security management also do not provide a rich source of pertinent empirical data with regard to information security policy issues: these studies tend instead to comprise much broader coverage of security management among which policy issues really receive only cursory treatment. Overall, these limitations in both the academic and practitioner-led research leave a major gap in the coverage of the topic of information security policies.

For business managers (i.e., for practitioners), this gap is arguably problematic. In order to make sound and sensible decisions about information security management in their organizations—and in particular in order to be able to formulate appropriate information security policies, and to disseminate and implement them successfully—business managers need not so much conjecture and supposition, but rather solid empirical evidence to support and reinforce the relevant underlying theory currently provided through the existing academic research literature. While the various practitioner-led studies, such as the DTI surveys discussed earlier, constitute a rich body of status reports on the range of security problems facing organizations and how organizations are approaching the issue of managing these problems, they shed few insights on the deeper questions pertaining to the efficacy of information security policies; nor do they provide data to indicate how prevailing theories and ideas have been rigorously tested. In summary, the existing body of literature on information security policy literature presents to business managers thoughts and theories on what *should* be done, and reports about what *is* being done, but little on the efficacy of either or indeed the link between the two.

This problem facing practitioners is arguably a key research opportunity for academic researchers in the area of information security management. As indicated in the literature review section above, there is a pressing need for empirical studies exploring issues associated with the efficacy of various information security policy structures and formats, the success of the approaches taken to policy dissemination and implementation, the lifespan of policies, and the alignment of the information security management process with the information systems planning process. A research agenda picking up these key themes would arguably make both a timely and relevant contribution to the literature on information security management in general, and the information security policy literature in particular.

However, before such a research agenda can be realistically contemplated, careful attention needs to be devoted to an important issue of research methodology raised by Kotulic and Clark (2004). According to these authors, "information security research is one of the most intrusive types of organization research," and there is "undoubtedly a general mistrust of any 'outsider' attempting to gain data about the actions of the security practitioner community" (Kotulic & Clark, 2004). These problems can lead to low response rates when using approaches such as mail surveys. Based on their experiences of researching various aspects of information security management, they warn that "developing a research stream in an emerging, organization-sensitive area requires major personal, financial and professional commitments far beyond what most researchers can afford to expend" (Kotulic & Clark, 2004). Specifically, they suggest that conducting large-scale mail surveys may not constitute the most appropriate approach for collecting sensitive information security-related data; they contend instead: "Time is far better spent focusing on a few, select firms with whom the researcher has developed an excellent rapport and trust" (Kotulic & Clark, 2004).

The research method problems identified by Kotulic and Clark (2004) perhaps serve to explain the seeming dearth of organization-based studies and large data sets in information security policy research to date (as identified in the above literature review). However, while it is clearly not an undertaking for the faint-hearted, the research agenda presented above represents an important aspect of information security management, and information security researchers ignore it at their peril. If the field is to mature and real progress is to be made, then academic theory needs to be tested and business practice needs to be subjected to careful scrutiny. Clearly, the environment in which this can best be achieved is one in which close and trusted collaborations are carefully forged between academic research partners and business managers. Consequently, in addition to the research themes identified in the above literature review, there is also a need for research methodology to feature prominently on the research agenda in the area of information security policy. The pooling of ideas and experiences pertaining to research methods among information security researchers may, in time, lead to innovative and novel research approaches likely to yield more successful results, and more substantial data sets, in this sensitive area than have to date been possible using conventional means.

REFERENCES

Angell, I.O. (1996). Economic crime: Beyond good and evil. *Journal of Financial Regulation & Compliance, 4*(1).

Austin, R.D., & Darby, C.A. (2003). The myth of secure computing. *Harvard Business Review,* (June).

Barnard, L., & von Solms, R. (1998). The evaluation and certification of information security against BS 7799. *Information Management and Computer Security, 6*(2), 72-77.

Baskerville, R., & Siponen, M. (2002). An information security meta-policy for emergent organizations. *Information Management and Computer Security, 15*(5/6), 337-346.

Bowonder, B., & Miyake, T. (1992). Creating and sustaining competitiveness: Information management strategies of Nippon Steel Corporation. *International Journal of Information Management, 1*(3), 155-172.

BSI. (1999). *Information security management—BS 7799-1:1999.* London: British Standards Institute.

CBI. (1992). *IT, the catalyst for change.* London: Confederation of British Industry.

David, J. (2002). Policy enforcement in the workplace. *Computers & Security, 21*(6), 506-513.

Doherty, N.F., & Fulford, H. (2005). Do information security policies reduce the incidence of security breaches: An exploratory analysis. *Information Resources Management Journal, 18*(4), 21-38.

Doherty, N.F., & Fulford, H. (2006). Aligning the information security policy with the strategic information systems plan. *Computers & Security, 25,* 55-63.

Drucker, P.F. (1988). The coming of the new organization. *Harvard Business Review,* (January-February).

DTI. (2000, April). *Information security breaches survey 2000.* Technical Report, Department of Trade and Industry, London.

DTI. (2002, April). *Information security breaches survey 2002.* Technical Report, Department of Trade and Industry, London.

DTI. (2004). *Information security breaches survey 2004.* Technical Report, Department of Trade & Industry, London.

Fulford, H., & Doherty, N.F. (2003). The application of information security policies in large UK-based organizations. *Information Management and Computer Security, 11*(3), 106-114.

Gaston, S.J. (1996) *Information security: Strategies for successful management.* Toronto: CICA.

Gerber, M., von Solms, R., & Overbeek, P. (2001). Formalizing information security requirements. *Information Management and Computer Security, 9*(1), 32-37.

Glazer, R. (1993). Measuring the value of information: The information intensive organization. *IBM Systems Journal, 32*(1), 99-110.

Higgins, H.N. (1999). Corporate system security: Towards an integrated management approach. *Information Management and Computer Security, 7*(5), 217-222.

Hone, K., & Eloff, J.H.P. (2002a). Information security policy—what do international security standards say? *Computers & Security, 21*(5), 402-409.

Hone, K., & Eloff, J.H.P. (2002b). What makes an effective information security policy. *Network Security, 20*(6), 14-16.

Hong, K., Chi, Y., Chao, L., & Tang, J. (2003). An integrated system theory of information security management. *Information Management and Computer Security, 11*(5), 243-248.

ISO. (2000). *Information technology. Code of practice for information security management—ISO 17799.* Geneva, Switzerland: International Organization for Standardization.

ISO. (2005). *Information security management—specification with guidance for use—ISO 27001.* Geneva, Switzerland: International Organization for Standardization.

Karyda, M., Kiountouzis, E., & Kokolakis, S. (2005). Information security policies: A contextual perspective. *Computers & Security.*

Kotulic, A.G., & Clark, J.G. (2004). Why there aren't more information security research studies. *Information & Management, 41,* 597-607.

Lindup, K.R. (1995). A new model for information security policies. *Computers & Security, 14,* 691-695.

McPherson, P.K. (1996). The inclusive value of information. *Proceedings of the 48th Congress of the International Federation for Information and Documentation* (pp. 41-60), Graz, Austria.

Menzies, R. (1993). Information systems security. In J. Peppard (Ed.), *IT strategy for business.* London: Pitman.

Porter, M.E., & Millar, V.E. (1985). How information gives you competitive advantage. *Harvard Business Review,* (July-August), 149-160.

Rees, J., Bandyopadhyay, S., & Spafford, E.H. (2003). PFIRES: A policy framework for information security. *Communications of the ACM, 46*(7), 101-106.

Siponen, M. (2000, August 21-25). Policies for construction of information systems' security guidelines. *Proceedings of 15th International Information Security Conference* (IFIP TC11/SEC2000) (pp. 111-120), Beijing, China.

Sterne, D.F. (1991). On the buzzword 'security policy'. *Proceedings of the IEEE Symposium on Research in Security and Privacy* (pp. 219-230).

von Solms, B., & von Solms, R. (2004). The ten deadly sins of information security management. *Computers & Security, 23,* 371-376.

Whitman, M.E. (2004). In defense of the realm: Understanding threats to information security. *International Journal of Information Management, 24,* 3-4.

Wood, C.C. (1995). Writing InfoSec policies. *Computers & Security, 14*(8), 667-674.

KEY TERMS

Information Security Breach: The accidental or deliberate infringement of the integrity, confidentiality, and/or availability of information and/or information systems.

Information Security Control: A facility an organization puts in place to detect, prevent, and/or recover from an information security breach. Such controls include mechanisms for the physical protection of computer hardware and systems to prevent unauthorized access to, and/or manipulation of, data and information.

Information Security Guidelines: Also referred to as information security procedures); a document, or documents, accompanying an organization's information security policy and designed to provide supplementary details about specific aspects of security management.

Information Security Policy Dissemination: The process of communicating the contents of an information security policy to individuals within an organization. Dissemination methods might include intranet, staff handbook, and/or training sessions.

Information Security Policy Formulation: The process of designing and creating an information security policy to meet the information security needs of an organization.

Information Security Policy Implementation: The process of putting an information security policy in place in an organization, administering it, and overseeing organizational and employee compliance to the policy.

Information Security Policy: A document outlining an organization's security risks, the rights and responsibilities of individuals within that organization with regard to the use of information and information systems, and the controls in place for managing information security in the organization.

Internet and Suicide

Dianne Currier
Columbia University, USA

INTRODUCTION

It is now commonly accepted that the appearance and expansion of Internet-based communication has given rise to new possibilities for forging social networks and establishing "communities of interest." One such 'interest group' which has found a community online comprises those who wish to end their lives. This has become a cause for concern to public health officials, governments, and suicide prevention professionals, while on the other hand possibilities for outreach and prevention in the new medium are being explored. The ways in which suicidal individuals have availed themselves of the information resources and connective possibilities of the Internet are outlined below, along with how governments and other parties interested in suicide prevention have responded to this new domain of risk.[1]

Suicide and Public Health

Suicide is both a personal tragedy and a public health issue. In 2002, 877,000 lives were lost worldwide, representing 1.5% of the global burden of disease (WHOSIS, 2003). Suicide rates vary from country to country, with the highest in eastern Europe and the lowest in Muslim countries and Latin America. For every individual who dies by suicide, it is estimated that 10 to 25 make a non-fatal suicide attempt. Over and above the distress caused to survivors, suicide and suicide attempts cost billions of dollars each year in lost productivity and health care costs (Goldsmith, Pellmar, Kleinman, & Bunney, 2002). In the United States, suicide is the third leading cause of death in the 15- to 24-year age group (WISQARS, 2003). In the majority of cases, suicide is not an informed choice in the context of terminal illness, rather it is most often a complication of mental illness. Over 90% of those who die by suicide have a diagnosable psychiatric disorder. Most commonly suicidal individuals suffer from a depressive disorder, but can also suffer schizophrenia, personality disorders, and alcohol or substance abuse (Arsenault-Lapierre, Kim, & Turecki, 2004).

Suicide and Media

The traditional print and electronic media have been the focus of suicide prevention efforts on two fronts. First, the media are seen to represent an avenue for educating populations about mental illness and its treatment, and for the dissemination of information about help and support for suicidal individuals. Second, there are concerns that the media sometimes practice 'irresponsible reporting' of suicide that misinforms the public as to its causes and preventability, and glamorize suicide in ways that are thought to incite vulnerable individuals to engage in suicidal behavior. This phenomenon is termed contagion and has been well documented in the scientific literature (Gould, 2001).

As an information and communication medium, particularly as one favored by younger sections of the population, the Internet is seen as both a medium that might extend the possibilities of suicide prevention beyond the scope of the traditional media, and as a site for the emergence of new and, for many, worrisome practices. This article will discuss the four major contexts in which suicidal behavior and the Internet intersect: (1) the role of the Internet as a source of information on means and methods to end one's life; (2) the Internet as a communal space where people can meet and make arrangements for suicide pacts; (3) the Internet as an important avenue for pursuing preventative measures; and (4) steps that governments have taken to intervene in the use of the Internet for the promotion of suicide.

The issue of suicide and the Internet has only come to the attention of the general public, suicide prevention professionals, and governments in recent years. As such, there is a dearth of published research, either scientific, public policy, or sociological. For example, there is currently little reliable data available on the prevalence of suicide-related content on the Internet.

Estimates range from 900 sites to more than 100,000 suicide sites on the Web (Dobson, 1999; Arnold, Slater, & Sparks, 2005), with a Chinese report claiming that 566,000 Chinese-language Web sites related to suicide, of which 500 contain detailed instructions (Yan, 2005). There are no data available on what proportion of these sites are concerned with prevention or with supporting and facilitating suicidal behavior, or with assisted suicide/euthanasia. Initial research on this issue is available mainly from case reports in medical and public health literature, mass media reports, and online discussions and forums.

The Internet and Suicide Methods

A key strategy in suicide prevention is reducing access to methods of suicide, particularly the most lethal means such as firearms, domestic gas, and highly toxic pesticides (Mann et al., 2005). Epidemiological research has demonstrated that such restrictions do indeed result in a decline in suicides using those means, and in many cases, if the method is widely used, a decline in overall suicide rates (Mann et al., 2005). Suicide attempts are often impulsive reactions to an immediate event or a cry for help, and with many there is little intention to die (Mann, 2002). While this is certainly not the case for all suicide attempts, when someone who is making such an impulsive attempt has access to or knowledge of highly lethal methods, they are more likely to succeed.

The Internet has become a source of readily accessible information on methods of suicide. The medical literature reports case studies of individuals finding suicide method information on the Internet (Becker, Mayer, Nagenborg, El-Faddagh, & Schmidt, 2004; Dobson, 1999). For example, Becker et al. (2004) describe the case of a 17-year-old girl who researched reliable suicide methods on the Internet and made contact online with an anonymous person who sold her pharmaceuticals she later used to make a suicide attempt. Suicide sites not only give descriptions of methods, but advice on how best to deploy them. Contributors to discussion lists report their experiences with various methods, and discuss why the attempt failed and possible steps to take to avoid such failures. For example, from the Church of Euthanasia (2006) site, in article 89h7flhrm1@news8.svr.pol.co.uk, "James" wrote in response to the questions, "How long does it take to hang oneself?" and "Is it painful for long?":

You should experience extreme pain, but you will more than likely black out before it becomes unbearable. Make sure that the ligature will not break or become loose. After you lose consciousness, your body will convulse, so it's better not to hang near anything (like I did). You need half hour—at least—without interruption, so that you will be dead, and not a vegetable, if they try rescuscitation (sic).

Studies of the electronic media have demonstrated that once a particular suicide method is publicized, the number of suicides and attempts using that method increase (Goldsmith et al., 2002). Lee, Chan, and Lee's study (2002) of charcoal burning in Hong Kong describes the phenomenon. Charcoal burning was little used as a method of suicide, however in early 1998 in the month after wide publicity of a suicide by charcoal burning, nine more suicides were committed using this method, and by the end of the year it was the third most common suicide method. While this seems to propose a straightforward casual model of communication, one that has been shown as overly simplistic by media theory, it is not necessarily the case. No one suggests that exposure in itself precipitates suicidal behavior, rather that in vulnerable individuals, for example those suffering depression and under stress, exposure to stories that portray suicide as a solution to life's problems, or inevitable, as well as giving clear information on methods for suicide can increase not only the risk of an attempt, but the likelihood of succeeding. Thus it is not considered that the possession of knowledge of suicide methods gained from the Internet is the principal cause of a person making a suicide attempt; however, it can be reasonably assumed that if a person has knowledge of an effective and available means of suicide, when they do make an attempt it is more likely that it will be fatal.

Moreover, beyond providing information on suicide methods, forums where information on suicide methods is available such as alt.suicide.methods are openly supportive of suicide acts, and discourage participation from those who seek to dissuade anyone from undertaking it. This is clearly expressed in the alt.suicide.holiday FAQ (ASH, 2006):

The regular posters on ash see suicide as a valid option. They are not interested in reading anti-suicide or pro-suicide messages, both of which are seen as denying the right to choose....In general, discussing why you think suicide is not an option for yourself is acceptable, but you should not tell others not to do so, or make broad denials of the validity of suicide as an option for others. You are welcome to join our discussions, as long as you respect the basic premise of ash, that suicide is a legitimate choice.

Cybersuicide

Most recently the phenomenon dubbed "cybersuicide" has attracted the attention of off-line media and governments. The term "cybersuicide" is used to describe Internet mediation of what, prior to the appearance of the Internet, were known as 'suicide pacts'. Cybersuicide describes practices that entail two or more people meeting online and agreeing to commit suicide simultaneously, though geographically apart, or two or more people meeting online and arranging to meet at an off-line location in order to commit suicide together. Cobain (2005) gives an example of a posting to one such site:

Hi, I'm new here. I am in the UK, near Liverpool to be precise. Is there anyone near me considering ending their life? Do you want to enter into an agreement to help each other? I have had a few unsuccessful attempts, panic always sets in....

While these behaviors currently represent a very small fraction of total yearly suicides, the phenomenon is increasing. Japan has the most reported cases of the second type of cybersuicide: in 2003, there were 34 deaths in 12 groups; in 2004, 55 deaths in 19 groups; and as of August 2005, figures stand at 75 deaths for that year (McNicol, 2005; AP, 2005). Group suicides have also been reported in Great Britain (Cobain, 2005).

One of the reasons given for participating in such pacts by those who survive the attempts, and also by those soliciting partners online, is that an individual is too afraid to complete the act by him or herself (Cobain, 2005). Thus the Internet provides an avenue for locating not just others who are supportive of the act, but who are also willing to share the experience. Suicide research shows that there may be open coercion involved in some suicide pacts, or less overtly, it may just be more difficult for someone to change his or her mind if there is another person involved (Rajagopal, 2004). A poster to alt.suicide.holiday describes the case in which participation in the group exerts a certain pressure on an individual and prompts the individual into action that they might not otherwise take:

ASH can be deadly because, as with Suzy, she so wanted to please people here, where she said she finally 'belonged'. So she imposed her idea of satisfaction of peers by completing her suicide and announcing its date and time before acting on it. (ASH, 2006b)

Beyond increasing the likelihood that an undecided individual will make a suicide attempt, there are reported incidents where one party in a pact to simultaneously commit suicide at different locations has no intent of doing do, but encourages or incites the other party to do so. All of these situations cause concern to suicide prevention practitioners as they increase the likelihood that a vulnerable individual will move from contemplating suicide to action. Moreover, the supportive attitude toward suicide is accompanied by an absence of information regarding the causes of suicidal behavior and treatment options, particularly psychiatric disorders, thus decreasing the likelihood that participants will seek aid or treatment.

SUICIDE PREVENTION ON THE INTERNET

Suicide prevention has also migrated to the Internet with hundreds of sites offering information and support for suicidal individuals. Prior to the advent of the Internet, information and support was available principally through crisis hotline and medical/psychiatric care. In recent years public health campaigns in a number of countries about suicide and depression have disseminated information more broadly (Mann et al., 2005). There is presently no reliable information available as to the exact number of such sites, the success of such programs, or the volume of inquiries and requests. However, the Samaratins, a UK-based help group, reported that in 1999 they received 15,000 e-mails, and they expected more than 25,000 in 2000. More than half of the e-mails received came from people under 25, a vulnerable group for suicide attempts and also heavy users of technology. Of those e-mails, they found that 51% of the senders reported feeling suicidal, compared to just 25% of telephone callers (Dobson, 1999). This suggests that the Internet might offer a more effective avenue to connect to a particular 'at risk' population. It also suggests that people may be more comfortable communicating sensitive or distressing thoughts in the more impersonal medium of e-mail than on the telephone.

Another prevention group, Befrienders, is more proactive regarding Internet-related suicide communication. They actively monitor chat rooms and offer support and information regarding assistance to suicidal individual (Befrienders, 2006). Indeed, the public nature of the Internet does offer opportunities for life-saving intervention. One of the requirements for a successful suicide attempt is minimizing opportunities for discovery and intervention (Mann, 2002). There are case reports where an individual has made statements of suicide intent, given notice of an impending suicide attempt, or actually made the attempt while online and police have been notified by network administrators or others online with the individual, enabling medical or psychotherapeutic intervention to be carried out. Janson et al. (2001) suggest that "the perceived anonymity of this means of communication allows some individuals with suicidal thoughts to feel comfortable enough to announce their private intent" (p. 487). Pro-suicide sites counsel users to be aware that by participating in a public forum, they may make themselves vulnerable to intervention:

In the short term somebody may act upon something you posted. Anybody can be lurking out there. On top of this, if you are posting from work or university the system administrator might be reading your posts. Many people are against suicide and will try to intervene. (ASH, 2006a)

However, to the extent that the Internet facilitates the making visible of threats or attempts, it may increase opportunities to intervene.

While the prevention services offered online are essentially the same in content as that available through off-line outlets, there are aspects unique to the online environment that can potentially extend the reach of off-line prevention activities. For example, the anonymity of the caller is easier to preserve over the Internet, and studies have shown that high school adolescents, a vulnerable group for suicide attempts and also heavy Internet users, are more likely to be forthcoming about suicidal thoughts and acts when guaranteed anonymity (Safer, 1997). The Internet offers a solution to the lack of locally available prevention resources. A great

deal of stigma remains attached to mental illness and suicide, and can inhibit at risk individuals from seeking help in their local communities. Moreover, social isolation is a known risk factor for suicide and suicide attempts (Goldsmith et al., 2002). The ability to access supportive communities and communicate with other individuals with similar experiences can be life saving, particularly if accompanied by information about treatment options. While some steps have been taken, there is clearly wider scope to for suicide prevention practitioners, particularly those concerned with youth suicide, to develop Internet-specific preventive initiatives that tap into the unique social networks and modes of communication of the Internet.

Government Intervention

To date there has been little action on the part of most governments to regulate the Internet with respect to suicidal behavior. The reasons for this are multiple and include:

- the inherent difficulties in regulating the Internet
- globally, national-level suicide prevention is a relatively recent phenomena
- while of concern, Internet suicide pacts—publicity of which drives calls for regulation—represent only a small number of suicides in any given year

Given these reasons, it is unsurprising that few governments have formulated and enacted comprehensive guidelines or laws aimed at preventing facilitation of suicide by means of the Internet. One instance of a national legislative approach is that of the Australian government, which in 2005 passed the "Suicide Related Material Offences Act," directly aimed at suppressing suicide chat rooms and the dissemination of information relating to suicide methods via the Internet. Under the provisions of the act, it is illegal to use the Internet or e-mail to access, transmit, or make available material that counsels or incites suicide (Parliament of Australia, 2005). Also criminalized under the act is the possession, production, or supply of such material, with intent to make it available on the Internet. The act also prohibits conducting these activities by telephone. Substantial penalties are imposed: fines of up to AUD$110 000 for individuals and AUD$500,000 for organizations

(Parliament of Australia, 2005). The law does not prohibit discussion and debate online about euthanasia or suicide, nor does it criminalize advocates. However, how the law will be enforced in practice has yet to be fully elucidated and will be followed with interest by suicide prevention professionals.

China and Japan have also responded but with less comprehensive action. In April 2005, the Chinese Ministry for Public Security announced criminal punishment for anyone spreading suicide information on the Internet and the penalizing of operators of Web sites used for communicating information on suicide. However it remains unclear, due to lack of available law enforcement information from China, whether specific laws pertaining to Internet-related suicidal information and behavior have been enforced (Yan, 2004). In Japan, under existing law, telecommunication companies, which include Internet service providers, are obliged to pass on information to law enforcement authorities if a crime is being committed. However, if the crime is only imminent, passing on such information may constitute a breach of privacy legislation. In 2005 new guidelines were drawn up whereby information regarding potential suicides can be passed on. Under the new guidelines, if the police believe a person's life is in danger, they can request information about the location and identity of that individual from the service provider. The provider is under no obligation to furnish that data. Moreover, the onus is on the users of a service, not the providers, to notify police of potential acts—which, given the supportive nature of many online suicide communities, decreases the likelihood of intervention (McNicol, 2005). Also in Japan there is a plan to distribute computer software restricting access to suicide-related Web sites to families free of charge (AP, 2005).

As with regulation of the Internet in general, government intervention into Internet activity related to suicide is evolving, and it will be some time before the efficacy of regulatory measures can be assessed. However, as more countries are developing and implementing national suicide prevention plans, the Internet will inevitably come under increased scrutiny in regard to suicide prevention.

CONCLUSION

Globally, while cybersuicide represents a small fraction of those who take their own lives, it is cause for increasing concern because those who use the Internet most, young adults, are a high-risk group for suicide and suicide attempts. Research has shown that individuals who make suicide attempts after seeking out suicide information on the Web are qualitatively different to those who seek information from other sources—they were "psychologically more vulnerable with higher risk taking behavior, substance abuse and depression scores" compared to individuals who did not engage in suicidal behavior. Moreover, most who sought suicide information online were aged 14-24 years, an age group with a high suicide rate and low peer support (Dobson, 1999). While the convergence of vulnerable suicidal individuals and the Internet has resulted in increased risk, it has also increased opportunities for prevention. The issue of suicide and the Internet demonstrates the migration of off-line practices to online environments, but also the appearance of wholly new and Internet-specific practices, and it presents a new set of regulatory challenges to governments. As such the issue of suicide and the Internet is typical of the changes, challenges, and opportunities that have accompanied the uptake of this medium.

REFERENCES

AP (Associated Press). (2005). Alarm at suicide epidemic. *Herald Sun,* (December 28), P34.

Arnold, B., Slater, J., & Sparks, S. (2005). *Caslon analytics note: Cybersuicide.* Retrieved June 11, 2005, from *http://www.calson.com.au/cybersuicidenote.htm*

Arsenault-Lapierre, G., Kim, C., & Turecki, G. (2004). Psychiatric diagnoses in 3275 suicides: A meta-analysis. *BMC Psychiatry,* (4), 37.

ASH. (2006a). *alt.suicide.holiday FAQ.* Retrieved June 11, 2006, from http://ashbusstop.org/intro.html

ASH. (2006b). *Doug.* Retrieved June 11, 2006, from http://groups.google.com/group/alt.suicide.holiday/browse_frm/thread/8e7edcf93b715ed6/0a0cc3574dd7cd56#0a0cc3574dd7cd56

Barnes, G. (2006). New law on suicide attacks freedom. *Canberra Times,* (January 6), 11.

Becker, K., Mayer, M., Nagenborg, M., El-Faddagh, M., & Schmidt, M. (2004). Parasuicide online: Can suicide Web sites trigger suicidal behavior in predisposed adolescents. *Nordic Journal of Psychiatry, 58*(2), 111-114.

Befrienders. (2006). *Homepage.* Retrieved June 11, 2006, from http://www.befrienders.org

Church of Euthanasia. (2006). *A practical guide to suicide.* Retrieved June 10-11, 2006, from http://www.satanservice.org/coe/suicide/guid

Cobain, I. (2005). Suicide Web sites: Clampdown on chatrooms after two strangers die in first Internet death pact. *The Guardian,* (October 11), 9.

Dobson, R. (1999). Internet sites may encourage suicide. *British Medical Journal, 319,* 2227.

Goldsmith, S.K., Pellmar, T.C., Kleinman, A.M., & Bunney, W.E. (2002). *Reducing suicide. A national imperative.* Washington, DC: National Academies Press.

Gould, M.S. (2001). Suicide and the media. *Annals of New York Academy of Sciences,* (932), 200-221.

Janson, M., Alssandrini, E., Strunjas, S., Shahab, H., El-Mallakh, R., & Lippmann, S. (2001). Internet-observed suicide attempts. *Journal of Clinical Psychiatry, 62*(6), 487.

Lee, D.T.S., Chan, K.P.M., Lee, S., & Yip, P.S.F. (2002). Burning charcoal: A novel and contagious method of suicide in Asia. *Archives of General Psychiatry, 59,* 293.

Mann, J.J. (2002). A current perspective of suicide and attempted suicide. *Annals of Internal Medicine,* (136), 302-311.

Mann, J.J., Apter, A., Bertolote, J., Beautrais, A., Currier, D., Haas, A., Hegerl, U., Lonnqvist, J., Malone, K., Marusic, A., Mehlum, L., Patton, G., Phillips, M., Rutz, W., Rihmer, Z., Schmidtke, A., Shaffer, D., Silverman, M., Takahashi, Y., Varnik, A., Wasserman, D., Yip, P., & Hendin, H. (2005). Suicide prevention strategies: A systematic review. *Journal of the American Medical Association,* (294), 2064-2074.

McNicol, T. (2005). *Police, Internet providers try to deter suicide pacts.* Retrieved from http://www.japan-mediareview.com/japan/stories/051215mcnicol

Parliament of Australia. (2005). *Bills digest no. 133 2004–05. Criminal Code Amendment (Suicide Related Material Offences) Bill 2005.* Retrieved June 11, 2006, from http://www.aph.gov.au/library/pubs/bd/2004-05/05bd133.htm

Rajagopal, S. (2004). Suicide pacts and the Internet. *British Medical Journal, 329*(December), 1298-1299.

Safer, D.J. (1997). Self-reported suicide attempts by adolescents. *Annals of Clinical Psychiatry, 9,* 263-269.

WHOSIS (WHO Statistical Information System). (2003). Evidence and information for health policy. *WHO Statistics.* Washington, DC: World Health Organization.

WISQARS. (Web-Based Injury Statistics Query And Reporting System). (2003). *National Center for Injury Prevention and Control.* Atlanta: CDC.

Yan, A. (2005). China: Crackdown on Internet 'suicide manuals'. *South China Morning Post,* (April 1).

KEY TERMS

Cybersuicide: Phenomenon whereby individuals contact each other online and agree to commit suicide together.

Suicide Attempt: A non-fatal, self-inflicted destructive act with explicit or inferred intent to die.

Suicide Contagion: Information or publicity of a suicide event may induce vulnerable individuals to engage in suicidal behavior.

Suicide Means Restriction: Restricting access to lethal means for suicide and/or information on how to kill oneself.

Suicide Pact: Agreement of two or more individuals to commit suicide together.

Suicide Prevention: Interventions designed to prevent individuals from committing suicide and/or making suicide attempts. Interventions may be at the individual, local, or national level.

Suicide: Fatal, self-inflicted, destructive act with explicit or inferred intent to die.

ENDNOTE

[1] This article discusses suicide from the public health perspective, as a preventable disorder/ event. There are many and long debates concerning the right to die/end of life/euthanasia, which are separate topics, as is the issue of political suicide.

Internet Piracy and Copyright Debates

Paul Sugden
Monash University, Australia

INTRODUCTION

Superman, the Marvel Comic superhero, has captured the imagination of another generation, guaranteeing a box office blockbuster and merchandising bonanza. However, even before the movie's release, Internet pirates are copying and releasing it over the Internet. Hundreds of thousands of these illegal copies are downloaded every day, from sites such as Morpheus and KaZaA. Each pirated copy is a lost sale and a copyright infringement of the creator's rights as it is created without the permission of the copyright owner. Piracy is not new to copyright industries; the problem arose with the invention of the printing press. Prior to the Internet though, piracy was generally controlled by finding the infringing producer and removing them from the distribution system by the use of copyright laws. The Internet gives previously unavailable speed and dissemination possibilities to pirates and an ability to escape detection by a "here today, gone tomorrow" ease of establishment and relocation, which means that removing the infringing items no longer removes the piracy. In the technology age anyone with a laptop can be a pirate. The speed and ease with which copying occurs in the digital age raises debate by ethicists, historians, and economists as to the appropriate level of copyright protection as a means of controlling piracy. The successful prosecution of an Internet piracy gang—known as "Drink or Die" (DoD) under criminal copyright laws—continues the debate on the appropriate copyright boundaries, as the use of criminal conspiracy law enabled extensions of jurisdiction to bring actions against pirates in foreign countries. This article will examine the debates and the relevance of the DoD case as a boundary of the fight against piracy.

DoD Pirates

The U.S. Department of Justice, Computer Crime and Intellectual Property Section (CCIPS) brought prosecutions resulting from a U.S. Customs Office three-year undercover operation to trace the DoD to their source rather than capture the end user. This action resulted in 16 prosecutions, with first-time offenders being imprisoned for up to 46 months (CCIPS, 2006). The jail terms surprised the "Drink or Die" pirates, as the individual pirates were law-abiding, ethical people in the real world (Lee, 2002). The economic effect of DoD's activities was valued at $US50 million (*USA v Griffith*, 2004).

The pirates were charged with being a criminal conspiracy to infringe copyright under *Copyright Act* 17 USC §506(a)(1) and *Copyright Felony Act (Amendment)* 18 USC §2319(b)(1), with extradition proceedings in Australia of *USA v Griffith* (2004) to bring a major ring leader to trial in the United States. The magistrate refused the extradition request saying the protection of copyright was not considered the normal subject matter for extradition. The magistrate's decision led to an appeal to the Federal Court and Full Federal Court. Both courts confirmed that bringing the action as a criminal conspiratorial behavior captured the infringing conduct the moment the agreement to commit the crime occurred and continued to wherever the effects are felt, which is accepted criminal jurisprudence from the decisions of *Director of Public Prosecutions v Doot* (1973) and *Lipohar v The Queen* (1999-2000). This meant that a court in one country has jurisdiction to try a matter regardless of where the conspiracy was formed or where the participants resided, as held in *Liangsiriprasert v United States* (1991). *USA v Griffith* (2004) confirmed the extraterritorial effect of U.S. criminal copyright laws and fueled the debate on appropriate copyright protection.

The Debates

Moral and Ethical

Modern generations accept downloading of music and films as a norm of life, and view downloading as morally acceptable; as Litman (1997) observed, people "find it hard to believe that there's really a law out there that says the stuff the copyright law says." The general public has an erroneous view that because Net access is cheap and easy, material on the Web is free to use and consume. The inexpensive nature and ease of copying has led Donaldson (2001) to pose a new social contract that could emerge from conduct on the Internet which will give rise to a core set of values allowing for a moral free zone in respect to some economic areas (downloading music, etc., for personal use), but ultimately concludes that business should set "hypernorm" boundaries to manage and regulate conduct on the Net. Meanwhile, Calkins (2002) states that Internet technologies are influencing our moral standards and that business ethicists should become more interested and involved in these issues.

Guadamuz (2002) describes a phenomenon where users of the Internet allow the free flow of ideas as the "new sharing ethic," but do not allow this sharing to transgress onto the free sharing of other people's works when such sharing is a copyright infringement. Guadamuz further acknowledges the control exerted by large multinational corporations over the distribution channels for movies, books, music, and software, but highlights that the Internet provides authors and musicians with the widest possible audiences to publish their work, although it may not provide an economic return.

Such comments cast the moral debate as an issue of freedom of access to information and knowledge, whereas copyright laws are used to protect commercial returns to publishers or creators. Barlow (2003) and Stallman, Gay, Lessig, and the Free Software Foundation (2002) are vocal critics of the power of the commercial world against creativity and the propriety nature of intellectual property laws preventing the free flow of information.

This debate highlights the moral and ethical divide as the individual vs. the corporation, but recognizes that the limit of ethical sharing is transgressed when the ownership laws of intellectual property rights such as copyright are crossed. Siponen and Vartiainen (2004) conducted a moral evaluation of unauthorized copying of software, using Kohlberg's (1981) theory of moral development, and concluded that the use of punishments and psychological means of manipulating people had been overvalued, and may violate the autonomy of the individual if used haphazardly (Siponen & Vartiainen, 2004). Their moral surveys in the area of software and illegal copying indicated that copying is divided into

reasoning and solution categories. Their discussion of the six stages of Kohlberg's theory when applied to Internet piracy means a solution will only occur when a moral judgment motivated by respect for the community, respect for social order or an individual's own conscience has been reached. A world without illegal copying of materials would then exist.

Utopian ethical ideals are unattainable as they conflict with the commercial reality of Internet piracy, which De George (1999) acknowledges means that the divide between moral and ethical conduct in controlling downloading from the Internet is a commercial divide that is impossible to enforce. De George (1999), when combined with Lessig's thesis that control of computer code is disenfranchising creators, led others such as Bowie (2005) to conclude that that copyright protection is warranted when it protects artistic creativity is moral, but is immoral when there is no payment made for the creativity.

Economic

Copyright laws are based on the proposition that creativity should obtain an economic return from the permission to copy the work. Shapiro and Varian (1998) noted, economically information is expensive to produce in the first copy but nearly costless in succeeding copies, and with advances in CD burning and download times, this is a reality with the Internet. Suing all end users who download pirate copies from an economic perspective is commercial suicide, as it ultimately alienates present and future customers and reduces sales. In addition the economic theory of deterrence was ineffective against Internet pirates as the transaction costs of enforcement were too high to create a substantial deterrence to pirates, as there was no fear of actual punishment (Cameron, 2002).

Cultural

The freedom to publish on the Internet generally comes without economic return, as no remuneration is obtained from releasing the material onto the Net, but discourses arising from the release enable the development of culture. Such cultural considerations have been the focus of Bowery's writing. Bowery (2005) believes this problem should be examined from a cultural analysis of law that strives to combat "common sense" understanding of law as formal and rule-bound.

This 'cultural' approach examines the dominance of American culture: policy and law over the Internet. In Bowery's view, selling the digital piracy message is difficult, as the history of consumption of popular culture and consumer expectations arising from digital technologies is giving the consumer expectations that are being removed by the increase in protection given to technological protection measures in copyright law (Bowie, 2005). The consumer has been sold a story of "facilities integration," with coordination of lifestyle and appliances, meaning consumers want newer, faster, and enhanced end products as part of a fantasy without issues of control, legality, or ethical constraints. The introduction of technological protection measures and other right protection systems in new products to support copyright laws are giving the consumer less than they already have, rather than more. The demand for more therefore causes a cultural clash with the legal control mechanisms as culture is about the free expression of ideas, whereas copyright law controls publication of expression for an economic return. Where a balance can be found between these issues is the challenge for lawyers and the community. Legalizing downloading for personal non-commercial use is one acceptable cultural balance.

Lessig examined technology advances as the corruption of the free values of the early Internet both from a technological perspective and from a legal perspective, and traces this corruption through the increased regulation and content controls placed on material and its dissemination through extensions of copyright laws. Lessig's argument, described as "modalities of regulation," states that code and copyright laws increase control in the digital environment, shifting the power from innovators and creators to those who stifle innovation by control of distribution, awareness, and access to publication (Lessig, 1999, 2002a, 2002b, 2004).

Murray and Scott (2002) modified Lessig's modalities of regulation into four bases of regulation—hierarchy, competition, community, and design—and note that the tendency to give priority to one form over other forms is inconsistent with empirical observations and normative considerations of good regulation design. In their view the differing approaches adopted throughout the world utilize a number of these individual bases in combination. Yet Murray and Scott (2002) examine individual design issues such as the DeCSS decryption of the CSS DVD coding and do not support Lessig's

pessimistic view, as the DeCSS program is available from sites outside the United States' control.

McLeod and NetLibrary (2001) and Vaidhyanathan (2001) support considerations of culture, and view this theme as a 'little guy vs. big corporation' and from the perspective of the cultural stakes involved in America's increasingly expansive copyright protection to control Internet piracy. Braithwaite and Drahos (2000) confirm the United States' status as the most influential nation state, but note it is the power of a state to control intangible property outside the nation's territorial boundaries which is crucial to the nation's wealth.

Historical and Technological Determinist Views

The historical examination of copyright and its fundamental purpose of protecting the return for creativity should determine policy to control Internet issues rather than technological determinist rhetoric (Jackson, 2002). Technological determinism believes technological development is autonomous of society and shapes society, but is not reciprocally influenced by society (Mackay, 1995). There is irony in Jackson's (2002) examination of copyright history, as 500 years ago printers sought copyright protection to protect the investment in printing equipment which gave publishers power; the Internet and technology as a tool allow all individuals to become publishers for a miniscule investment in time and money. In Jackson's view, copyright law can now rise to reduce the monopoly power of the large publishers by eliminating private privileges and bringing copyright into the public realm where it would be subject to political scrutiny.

This historical examination concludes that the reliance on technology contracts and increased civil and criminal copyright liability outweighs the policy issues of the Internet as a communication medium that encourages all creators to be creative. The advantage Jackson sees in the Internet is its empowerment of consumers as creators who can participate actively in the creation of culture. This empowerment is jeopardized by legislators blindly accepting the rights of copyright owners and applying constraints by laws designed to protect investment in printing infrastructure rather than creativity (Jackson, 2002).

Copyright as the protection of publishers' power has led to increased core technologies such as encryption, digital watermarking, digital signatures, and software programs for digital rights management systems and software architectures. Each new product is a pirate's opportunity to prove the technology is fallible. This implementation confirms Lessig's argument that the code is creating the control, not the creativity of authors.

Criminal Remedy Debate

Penney (2004) writes that the digital age has led to an acceptance and increased protection, not just in technological protection measures but in lobbing for more comprehensive and punitive criminal sanctions for infringement. Penney notes though that even with the copyright criminal provisions, infringement was not deterred. Currently the criminal copyright provisions capture commercial conduct, but the U.S. Free Trade Agreement negotiations include a policy argument that criminal sanctions should be extended to all forms of copyright infringement. Such an extension is generally denied, and Australia announced changes to its 1968 *Copyright Act* to allow downloading for non-commercial purposes (Ruddock, 2006). The implementation of more stringent laws of criminal liability for non-commercial uses of materials would confirm the pessimistic view expressed by Lessig (1999) that modalities of regulation were ruling the world.

Importance of the DoD to this Debate

Currently, film, software, and music industries use technological barriers, civil copyright laws, and authorized Internet sites (movies.com, rip.com, etc.) to protect their products against pirates. Technology barriers such as Content Scrambling Systems (CSS) programs, encryption, and zoning of "chips" are used to control the distribution channels and prevent piracy. The film industry has brought actions like *Universal Studios Inc v Corley* (2001) against a software developer who demonstrated the infallibility of the DVD-encryption program CSS. Also they lobbied for copyright amendments increasing penalties and providing new offences for tampering with technological barriers designed to protect copyright works from infringement, for example *Digital Millennium Copyright Act* §1201, 17 USCS (1998)(USA) and *Copyright Amendment (Digital Agenda) Act* 2000, s116A.

Even with these changes, piracy continues. *USA v Griffiths* (2004) indicates the transaction costs of a criminal copyright conspiracy action that was previously too great to deter piracy are reducing as the industry and government assess the economic loss to authors and industry of piracy. The commercial piracy to the levels seen in *USA V Griffiths* (2004) is considered immoral, unethical, but cultural, ethical, and moral standards are not universal. The pirates who unpick technology never asked themselves Kant's universality principle of morality (Liddell & Kant, 1970): what would you think if it happened to you?

The acceptance of international, ethical standards by all citizens of all nations would solve piracy, but this utopia is unattainable. *USA v Griffith* (2004) indicates that the United States can extend its cultural reach to protect copyright where the pirates reside in countries with criminal copyright laws and extradition arrangements with the U.S. Such an effect means the Internet can no longer be seen as a free sea to plunder with impunity. The dormant criminal boundary of copyright law as an effective tool against commercial piracy has been awakened.

REFERENCES

A&M Records Inc v Napster Inc 114 F Supp 2d 896. (2000). (N Dist of Cal) *2000 U.S. Dist. LEXIS 11862; 55 U.S.P.Q.2D (BNA) 1780; Copy. L. Rep. (CCH) P28, 126;* and aff'd, *2001 U.S. App. LEXIS 1941, (9ᵗʰ Cir. Cal., 2001).*

Atlantic Recordings Corporation v Doe 371 F. Supp. 2d 377; (Western District of New York). (2005). 2005 *U.S. Dist LEXIS 10354.*

Barlow, J.P. (2003). *Selling wine without bottles: The economy of mind on the global Net.* Retrieved May 23, 2006, from http://www.eff.org/Misc/Publications/John_Perry_Barlow/HTML/idea_economy_article.html

Bowie, N.E. (2005). Digital rights and wrongs: Intellectual property in the information age. *Business and Society Review, 110*(1), 77-96.

Bowery, K. (2005). *Law & Internet cultures.* Melbourne: Cambridge University Press.

Braithwaite, J., & Drahos, P. (2000). *Global business regulation.* Cambridge/Melbourne: Cambridge University Press.

Calkins, M. (2002). Rippers, portal users, and profilers: Three Web-based issues for business ethicists. *Business and Society Review, 107*(1), 61-75.

Cameron, S. (2002). Digital media and the economics of crime. *Economic Affairs, 22*(3), 15-20.

CCIPS (U.S. Department of Justice Computer Crime & Intellectual Property Section). (2006). *Intellectual property cases.* Retrieved July 7, 2006, from http://www.cybercrime.gov/ipcases.html

Copyright Act 17 USC §506(a)(1).

Copyright Act. (1968). (Commonwealth of Australia).

Copyright Felony Act (Amendment) 18 USC § 2319(b)(1).

De George, R.T. (1999). Business ethics and the information age. *Business and Society Review, 104*(3), 261-278.

Director of Public Prosecutions v Doot. (1973). AC 807 (House of Lords).

Donaldson, T. (2001). Ethics in cyberspace: Have we seen that movie before? *Business and Society Review, 106*(4), 273-291.

Guadamuz, A. (2002). The "new sharing ethic" in cyberspace. *The Journal of World Intellectual Property, 5*(1), 129-139.

Jackson, M. (2002). From private to public: Reexamining the technological basis for copyright. *Journal of Communication, 52*(2), 416-433.

Kabushi Kaisha Sony Computer Entertainment Inc v Stevens. (2001). FCA 1379 and appeal decision at [2003] FCAFC 157 (30 July 2003) (Full Court of the Federal Court of Australia).

Kabushi Kaisha Sony Computer Entertainment Inc v Ball. (2004). EWHC 1738, (Chancery) (19 July 2004).

Kabushi Kaisha Sony Computer Entertainment Inc v Nuplayer Limited. (2005). EWHC 1522, (Chancery) (14 July 2005).

Kohlberg, L. (1981). *The philosophy of moral development: Moral stages and the idea of justice* (1st ed.). San Francisco: Harper & Row.

Lee, J. (2002). Pirates of the Web. *The New York Times,* (July 11).

Lessig, L. (1999). *Code: And other laws of cyberspace.* New York: Basic Books.

Lessig, L. (2002a). Architecture of innovation: Intellectual property. *Duke Law Journal, 51*(6), 1783.

Lessig, L. (2002b). *The future of ideas: The fate of the commons in a connected world* (1st ed.). New York: Vintage Books.

Lessig, L. (2004). *Free culture: How big media uses technology and the law to lock down culture and control creativity.* New York: Penguin Press.

Liangsiriprasert v United States. (1991). 1 AC 225 (House of Lords).

Liddell, B.E.A., & Kant, I. (1970). *Kant on the foundation of morality; a modern version of the Grundlegung.* Bloomington: Indiana University Press.

Lipohar v The Queen. (1999-2000). 200 CLR 485.

Litman, J. (1997). Copyright noncompliance. *New York University Journal of International Law & Politics, 29,* 237.

Mackay, H. (1995). Theorising the IT/society relationship. In N. Heap et al. (Eds.), *Information technology and society* (pp. 41-53). London: Sage.

McLeod, K., & NetLibrary. (2001). *Owning culture authorship, ownership, and intellectual property law.* Retrieved from http://www.netLibrary.com/urlapi.asp

Murray, A., & Scott, C. (2002). Controlling the new media: Hybrid responses to new forms of power. *The Modern Law Review, 65*(4), 491-516.

Penney, S. (2004). Crime, copyright, and the digital age. In Law Commission of Canada (Ed.), *What is a crime?: Defining criminal conduct in contemporary society* (p. xxv). Vancouver: UBC Press.

Recording Industry Association of America v. University of North Carolina At Chapel Hill 367 F. Supp. 2d 945. (2005).

Ruddock, P. (2006). *Media release 088/2006.* Retrieved from http://ag.gov.au

Shapiro, C.V., & Hal, R. (1998). *Information rules: A strategic guide to the network economy.* Boston: Harvard Business School Press.

Siponen, M., & Vartiainen, T. (2004). Unauthorized copying of software and levels of moral development: A literature analysis and its implications for research and practice. *Information Systems Journal, 14*(4), 387-407.

Stallman, R., Gay, J., Lessig, L., & the Free Software Foundation. (2002). *Free software, free society: Selected essays of Richard M. Stallman* (1st ed.). Boston: GNU Press, Free Software Foundation.

USA v Griffiths. (2004). FCA 879, (Federal Court of Australia) and *aff'd* [2005] FCAFC 34 (Full Court of the Federal Court of Australia).

Universal Studios Inc v Corley 273 F3d 429 (2nd Cir). (2001). Lexis 25330.

Vaidhyanathan, S. (2001). *Copyrights and copywrongs: The rise of intellectual property and how it threatens creativity.* New York: New York University Press.

KEY TERMS

Copyright: The protection given through international treaties such as the Bierne Convention and the Universal Copyright Convention to original artistic literary dramatic and musical works and derivative works as forms of expression.

Technological Determinism: The belief that technology shapes society but is not influenced by society itself.

Technology Protection Measure: A measure that in the ordinary course of its operation requires the application of information or a process or a treatment, with the authority of the copyright owner to gain access to the copyright work.

Internet Research Ethics Questions and Considerations

Elizabeth Buchanan
University of Wisconsin – Milwaukee, USA

INTRODUCTION AND BACKGROUND

The Internet, as a global research phenomenon, has developed along two parallel lines: as a medium *for* research (e.g., databases, electronic indexes, online catalogs) and as a field or locale *of* research (e.g., MUDs, MOOs, online communities, Usenet, listservs, blogs, etc.). This article will discuss this second phenomenon, and the ethical implications that arise with such research endeavors, an emerging field known as Internet Research Ethics (IRE). Specifically, this article will call attention to the major areas of online research ethics, while acknowledging that hard-and-fast "answers" to some of the questions are elusive. IRE fits into a larger framework of research and information ethics, both of which have a longer history and more firmly established research base from which to inform this growing field.

Academic researchers conducting human subjects research are typically bound by a formal human subjects protection model. In the United States, for instance, the Code of Federal Regulations codifies human subjects protections in Title 45, Part 46 CFR. The CFR was informed by the 1979 policy statement, *The Belmont Report,* which outlined three distinct areas of importance:

1. **respect for persons**, which involves a recognition of the personal dignity and autonomy of individuals, and special protections for those with diminished autonomy—such respect is in part garnered through an informed consent process;
2. **beneficence**, which entails an obligation to protect persons from harm by maximizing anticipated benefits and minimizing possible risks from research; and
3. **justice**, which requires that risks and benefits are distributed equally and requires that subjects be fairly selected.

Similar protections are afforded across the world. Canada's research ethics programs are dictated by the *Tri-Council Policy Statement: Ethical Conduct for Research Involving Humans,* while Australia's are codified in the *Policy Statement: Ethical Conduct for Research Involving Humans.* Countries across the European Union differ in their codification and policies surrounding research ethics (Sveningsson, 2004).

These extant guidelines and policies are grounded in and on the idea of *human subjects* work, and stem, generally, from a biomedical perspective, with examples of such research atrocities as the Nuremberg Trials and the Tuskegee experiments. The idea that researchers be bound both legally and ethically for harms done to their subjects or participants stems logically from the medical and applied sciences, and was more recently brought into the social sciences and humanities disciplines, noting that debate continues surrounding the applicability of such protections models in research such as oral histories.

With the emergence of Internet use throughout the 1990s, researchers found a new fertile ground for social, behavioral, and humanistic research opportunities that differed greatly from their biomedical counterparts. As such, "populations," locales, and spaces that had no corresponding physical environment became the focal point—or site—of research activity. Questions then began to arise: What about privacy? How is informed consent obtained? What about minors (Stern, 2004; Bober, 2004)? What are harms in an online environment? Is this *really* human subjects work (White, 2003)? And ultimately, what are the ethical obligations of researchers conducting research online, and are they somehow different from other forms of research ethics practices?

Throughout the 1990s, then, disparate disciplines began, in piecemeal fashion, looking at these ethical complexities and implications of conducting research online. Whether or not such research ethics guidelines as *The Belmont Report* "fit" or were applicable was at best uncertain. Also, while interesting and important ethnographies of Internet reality and the ethical quandaries associated with studying them such as Markham's *Life Online* emerged, other more "rudimentary" forms of online research through Internet-based survey tools exemplify a host of ethical issues facing researchers using the Internet in its various capacities. The debate began to take serious academic form when one of the first journals devoted entirely to the IRE appeared in 1996, in a special issue of *The Information Society,* and then the American Association for the Advancement of Science funded a workshop on IRE in 1999. Further evidence of the recognition of IRE came through the release of the Association of Internet Researchers Ethics Working Group's report on *Ethical Decision Making and Internet Research,* chaired by Dr. Charles Ess, in 2002. Such consideration occurred among researchers, policy makers, and such entities as institutional review boards, which were seeing an extraordinary increase in the number of Internet-based research protocols (Buchanan, 2003, 2004). Also, such prominent professional societies as the American Psychological Association convened a Board of Scientific Affairs Advisory Group on Conducting Research on the Internet, releasing a report in 2004 in *American Psychologist* (Kraut et al., 2004). And finally, three books in the field of IRE were published between 2003 and 2004 (Buchanan, 2004; Johns, Chen, & Hall, 2003; Thorseth, 2003). These were all, indeed, important moments in the development of IRE as a discrete research phenomenon, and promoted serious consideration about the ethical implications of research in online or virtual environments.

MAJOR ISSUES IN INTERNET RESEARCH ETHICS

Throughout the IRE literature, specific themes have emerged as significant; these are now reviewed, with a major emphasis on the types of questions promoted in and through online research. Some have debated whether cybertechnologies in particular or technologies in general create new ethical issues, or whether there are "old" ethical issues simply exacerbated by or through technology (e.g., Tavani, 2004; Spinello & Tavani, 2004). This debate can apply to Internet research ethics. One can argue, research is research, and ethical issues emerge in either online or onsite

studies. But, there is *something* significantly worthy of note about online research, and as more researchers see the potential of such research, serious examination of the ethical issues grows as well. While they are presented as discrete, insofar as possible, IRE issues are complex and intertwined due to Internet technologies and the nature of research when conducted in online environments.

Anonymity/Confidentiality

One of the most binding promises researchers make to their subjects or participants is to protect their privacy and their identity, should revealing something about them cause undue harm, embarrassment, or some other tangible loss. *The Belmont Report,* for instance, demands that privacy of subjects is protected and confidentiality of data is maintained. In online environments, researchers must ask: Is there a truly secure online interaction? What type of Internet location/medium is *safest*? Is an "anonymous" survey really possible? How will subjects/participants be protected? Is encryption enough? These are data integrity issues, and often, researchers do not have the control possible over an online site to be able to secure the interaction from hackers or other forms of data corruption or interference. For instance, a researcher may promise to maintain confidentiality over the data she collects; confidentiality is defined by the U.S. model as pertaining to the treatment of information already revealed. There is an expectation that "the data will not be divulged to others in ways that are inconsistent with the understanding of the original disclosure without permission" (National Commission for the Protection of Human Subjects of Biomedical and Behavioral Research, 1979). In online research, an ethical breech may occur not due to researcher negligence but circumstances beyond her control. Data may be collected online, and the researcher is not the only one to have access to it; others in an online forum, archiving sites, or other back-ups may exist that reveal the source of some data. The researcher may not be in control of this.

Moreover, can a research participant be anonymous online? One may have a "different" online identity, but that is still that individual in a corresponding physical environment. If an electronic persona is portrayed in research on an electronic support group for a medical condition, will she be identifiable? If so, at what risk? Is there the potential for significant harms to the subjects through identification? One could imagine a research report using screen names which can be searched online and identified fairly easily. Thus, while the researcher may have attempted to protect privacy, and maintain anonymity and confidentiality, such technological tools as search engines and archives of online discussions may provide enough context and information to make identification not only possible, but harmful. This leads directly into the question of how researchers name, describe, or anonymize their online subjects or participants—to the extent it could be possible.

Revealing Identities

The major question is: How should online participants be identified in research reports? Should they use screen names, which individuals choose for some usually personally significant reason, or should the researcher protect that screen name from potential identification by using a pseudonym of the screen name? This raises questions of ownership and research integrity, in addition to the more obvious privacy questions. For instance, by changing screen names in a research report, does the researcher detract from the "reality" or "reputation" of the participant? Text searches can reveal more context than a researcher may in her reporting, and this raises potential risks. Should the researcher allow participants to make this decision? If so, should it be a part of the informed consent process? Should participants review the research report prior to publication and then decide? Such questions begin to challenge the long-standing process of research, questioning what Forte (2004) has described as scientific takers and native givers.

Public vs. Private Spaces

Another more challenging area of IRE for researchers is the differentiation between public and private spaces online. If one contends there is any privacy to online interactions (which may be a big *if*), one can examine

Figure 1.

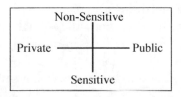

whether or not a particular forum, listserv, chat room, or bulletin board is considered *by its members* to be a public space or a private space. What expectations of privacy exist? Many have used the analogy of the public park: What we observe in a public park is available to us as researchers. If the Internet locale is correspondingly public, must the researcher *belong* or seek permission? In other words, what role does the researcher play in the space? Observer, participant, member, other? Is it truly a *members-only* site, and if so, does that negate the park analogy? What status do we ascribe to public newsgroups? If one posts something to such a newsgroup, it may not be with the intention that a researcher will use it and thus it is used in a way not in line with the poster's original intentions—there may be use of archived quotes never intended to be represented in research. Or, a researcher may use preexisting data from archives, thinking this is acceptable. But, could something from a public space come back to haunt a subject, should it be brought to light in research? All of these possibilities quite seriously violate, among many ethical guidelines, the spirit of a consensual research relationship.

Sveningsson (2004) has suggested that researchers evaluate this component of IRE along a continuum: public-private and sensitive-non-sensitive. Data falling in the private/sensitive quadrant would be off limits to researchers, while the remaining three quadrants would be used with discretion, according to ethical guidelines and policy (see Figure 1).

Ownership of Data

As mentioned above, ownership of data becomes questionable with Internet research. With face-to-face research, the researcher, for instance, conducts an observation. She writes field notes and may return a report to the participant when completed. Ultimately, though, the researcher *owns* "it." In online research, a researcher conducts an observation of some newsgroup interactions. A log/transcript is generated. The researcher has a copy. So do the participants. So does Deja News. Who owns "it"? What rights and responsibilities do all of these stakeholders have? It becomes less clear in the online environment.

Furthermore, to satisfy review boards or ethics boards, researchers typically state how long they will retain the data. But, how long does e-data last? And in what context? When researchers tell their participants they will destroy any data after a specified period of time, it may mean nothing in an online context where researchers are not in control.

Respect for Persons

Recall that human subjects protections models are grounded in respect for persons, as borne out of the informed consent process. In online environments, there are many purely practical challenges in obtaining informed consent; these range from fluidity in group membership in quick periods of time, for instance, those who log on for a few minutes at a time then quickly log off, to long-time changes in group membership, to individuals who have multiple screen names and identities, to ensuring people receive an informed consent document and where such a document may be accessible.

Further problems arise in the actual verification of understanding one's role in the research as a participant or subject, which is arguably the cornerstone of informed consent. What is the best process by which to achieve informed consent? Click boxes? Hard copies? Are blanket statements necessary ("I understand that online communications may be at greater risk for hacking, intrusions, and other violations. Despite these possibilities, I consent to participate.")? And, if there are truly anonymous online interactions, would a researcher need informed consent with such anonymous research?

Recruitment

In traditional research ethics, the principle of justice demands that subjects have an equal or fair chance of participation—exclusion must be based on some justifiable reason; individuals must also not be unfairly targeted, as occurred in the Tuskegee experiments, for instance. But online, one could argue that many populations are indeed self-selected based on some quality, thus questions of justice may not apply, in their strict sense; ultimately, in online research, equity/fair representation in the subject pool may not be possible. However, related questions of justice and recruitment emerge: How does the researcher enter the research space to begin recruiting? Many sites, notably, pro-anas (pro-anorexic/eating disorder sites), for instance, reject researcher presence with notices—researchers are not welcome, essentially. What if a researcher is also a

participant, as Walstrom (2004) has examined in the face of eating disorder groups online? Moreover, what if some in a community consent, while others do not? The researcher must take precautions to protect those who have not consented, while preserving the integrity of the whole of online interactions. This proves more difficult online than in onsite research encounters. Clark (2004) has also raised the interesting question of "hybrid" research endeavors: hybrid research bridges research and researcher presence through groups that have both a physical and virtual presence simultaneously. Clark (2004, p. 247) describes the potential research ethics issues: "Research in a jointly virtual and material context raises unique questions…the primary texts in my research are the community's listserv postings; how will participant perceptions of risk be impacted by physical meetings with me and others after I have written potentially critical things?" Thus, one could conceivably consent to participate in one environment, but could thereby violate confidences from the other locale, intentionally or unintentionally.

Research with Minors

According to the U.S. model, minors, those under the age of 18, are considered "special populations" (along with pregnant women and fetuses, prisoners, intellectually or emotionally impaired or handicapped), and as such, require special protections. The idea is that such populations have limited or diminished capacity to consent, to understand their roles in research, and to participate fully according to research ethics standards. Consent from an adult, in addition to the minor's assent, is required, thus calling for an additional layer in the consent process. In online environments, research on or with minors has raised considerable attention. Both Stern (2004) and Bober (2004) argue that research with minors is fraught with difficulty from a number of perspectives and should be conducted under very special conditions. Online research with minors raises issues of researcher certainty and competence—how can researchers be sure their online participants are adults, consenting adults, and not a minor in some online forum? What if the minor assents and the parent or guardian does not even know of the researcher's desire to collect data from his/her child? What responsibilities does the researcher have in reporting disturbing or dangerous information collected from a minor? And, when taken into an international setting, what age constitutes "adulthood" or age of consent? This varies culturally and holds the potential for serious differences across research forums online.

CONCLUSION

Overall, given the specificity of online research as typified through the aforementioned issues, research interactions must be predicated on the three firmly entrenched principles of research ethics—respect for persons, beneficence, and justice—and even more critically, such intrinsic values as honesty, trust, competence, and reflexivity (Ayers, 2004). Researchers seeking guidance on ethically based online research must first become aware of the ethical issues and challenges presented here. Answers to the pressing questions raised throughout are not conspicuously found in the literature, though the guidelines of the AoIR Ethics Working Committee and & Ess (2002) remain the benchmark by which researchers should evaluate their online research conduct.

These form the basis of a relationship between or among researchers and researched. Many of these concepts are *intrinsic* values—things that we as researchers should value as important "in and of themselves," or "for its/their own sake," or "as such," or "in its/their own right." By asking what research participants or subjects "get out of it," as Bakardjieva, Feenberg, and Goldie (2004) have asked, we begin to see the potential for a greater reflexivity and different way of thinking about the usually hierarchical process of research. Online research may just open up new ways of thinking about human subjects protections models, by promoting a different discourse about legal models (Lipinski, 2006), how we teach research methods and research ethics (Bruckman, 2006; Markham, 2006), and what it means to do ethically based research in a global information ethics model (Buchanan, 2006).

REFERENCES

American Association for the Advancement of Science. (1999). *Ethical and legal aspects of human subjects research in cyberspace.* Retrieved from http://www.aaas.org/spp/sfrl/projects/intres/main.htm

AoIR (Association of Internet Researchers) Ethics Working Committee & Ess, C. (2002). *Ethical decision-making and Internet research: Recommendations from the AoIR Ethics Working Committee.* Retrieved from http://www.aoir.org/reports/ethics.pdf

Ayers, M. (2004). Fact or fiction: Notes of a man interviewing women online. In E. Buchanan (Ed.), *Readings in virtual research ethics: Issues and controversies* (pp. 262-273). Hershey, PA: Idea Group.

Bakardjieva, M., Feenberg, A., & Goldie, J. (2004). User-centered Internet research: The ethical challenge. In E. Buchanan (Ed.), *Readings in virtual research ethics: Issues and controversies* (pp. 338-350). Hershey, PA: Idea Group.

Bober, M. (2004). Virtual youth research: An exploration of methodologies and ethical dilemmas from a British perspective. In E. Buchanan (Ed.), *Readings in virtual research ethics: Issues and controversies* (pp. 288-316). Hershey, PA: Idea Group.

Bruckman, A. (2006). Teaching students to study online communities ethically. *Internet Research Ethics at a Critical Juncture: A Special Issue of Journal of Information Ethics, 15*(2), 82-98.

Buchanan, E. (2003). Internet research ethics: A review of issues. *Proceedings of the Association of Internet Researchers Annual Conference,* Toronto, Canada.

(Ed.). (2006). Introduction. *Internet Research Ethics at a Critical Juncture. Special Issue of the Journal of Information Ethics, 15*(2), 14-17.

(Ed.). (2004). *Readings in virtual research ethics: Issues and controversies.* Hershey, PA: Idea Group.

Clark, D. (2004). What if you meet face to face? A case study in virtual/material research ethics. In E. Buchanan (Ed.), *Readings in virtual research ethics: Issues and controversies* (pp. 246-261). Hershey, PA: Idea Group.

Forte, M. (2004). Co-construction and field creation: Web site development as both an instrument and relationship in action research. In E. Buchanan (Ed.), *Readings in virtual research ethics: Issues and controversies* (pp. 219-245). Hershey, PA: Idea Group.

Kraut, R., Olson, J., Banaji, M., Bruckman, A., Cohen, J., & Cooper, M. (2004). Psychological research online:

Report of board of scientific affairs' advisory group on the conduct of research on the Internet. *American Psychologist, 59*(4), 1-13.

Lipinski, T. (2006). Emerging tort issues in the collection and dissemination of Internet-based research data. *Internet Research Ethics at a Critical Juncture: A Special Issue of Journal of Information Ethics, 15*(2), 55-81.

Johns, M., Chen, S.L., & Hall, J. (Eds.). (2003). *Online social research: Methods, issues, and ethics.* New York: Peter Lang.

Markham, A. (1998). *Life online: Researching real experience in virtual space.* London: Walnut Creek.

(2006). Ethic as method, method as ethic: A case for reflexivity in qualitative ICT research. *Internet Research Ethics at a Critical Juncture: A Special Issue of Journal of Information Ethics, 15*(2), 37-54.

National Commission for the Protection of Human Subjects of Biomedical and Behavioral Research. (1979). *The Belmont report.* Retrieved from http://ohsr.od.nih.gov/guidelines/belmont.html

Spinello, R., & Tavani, H. (Eds.). (2004). *Readings in cyberethics.* Sudbury, MA: Jones and Bartlett.

Stern, S. (2004). Studying adolescents online: A consideration of ethical issues. In E. Buchanan (Ed.), *Readings in virtual research ethics: Issues and controversies* (pp. 274-287). Hershey, PA: Idea Group.

Sveningsson, M. (2004). Ethics in Internet ethnography. In E. Buchanan (Ed.), *Readings in virtual research ethics: Issues and controversies* (pp. 45-61). Hershey, PA: Idea Group.

Tavani, H. (2004). *Ethics and technology: Ethical issues in an age of information and communication technology.* Hoboken, NJ: John Wiley & Sons.

Thorseth, M. (2003). *Applied ethics in Internet research.* Program for Applied Ethics, Norwegian University of Science and Technology, Norway.

Walstrom, M. (2004). Ethics and engagement in communication scholarship: Analyzing public, online support groups as researcher/participant-experiencer. In E. Buchanan (Ed.), *Readings in virtual research ethics: Issues and controversies* (pp. 174-202). Hershey, PA: Idea Group.

White, M. (2003). *Representations or people?* Retrieved from http://www.nyu.edu/projects/nissenbaum/ethics_whi_full.html

KEY TERMS

Anonymity: A state where one's identity is unknown; in a research study, there are no direct links between data collected and one's identity.

Beneficence: The ethical principle that requires researchers to do what will further the participant or subject's best interests. A principle of doing no harm.

Confidentiality: Pertains to the treatment of information that an individual has disclosed in a relationship of trust and with the expectation that it will not be divulged to others in ways that are inconsistent with the understanding of the original disclosure without permission.

Cyberethics: The study of moral, legal, ethical issues involving the use of information and communication technologies.

Interviews with Young People using Online Chat

Elza Dunkels
Umeå University, Sweden

AnnBritt Enochsson
Karlstad University, Sweden

INTRODUCTION

When we first started using online interviews as a method for qualitative research, we had no thoughts about it being any different from face-to-face interviews. Being naturalized digital immigrants (Prensky, 2001), having not used computers and the Internet from childhood but having become accustomed to them over time, we did not give the methodological issues much thought. However, when we started getting questions about our research, we understood that we took too much for granted. The questions that were raised made us question our approaches.

Internet Use among Young People

Sweden has a large number of Internet users, and on a global scale only Iceland had more Internet users per capita in 2004 (ITU, 2006). According to Safety, Awareness, Facts, and Tools (SAFT, 2003), 87% of the Swedish children between ages 9 and 16 have Internet access at home, compared to 85% in Iceland and 80% in Ireland.

The patterns of Internet use among young people have changed since the turn of the century. Private conversation channels, such as text messaging on mobile phones and instant messaging over the Internet, have replaced the open chat rooms that were popular at the end of the 1990s. Net communities have found their way into every home, having evolved from highly technical systems to applications that are relatively easy to use. This has opened up the Internet for the average user in contrast to the early adopter of new technology. A majority of young Internet users in Sweden are members of at least one Net community and use instant messaging on a daily basis (SAFT, 2003).

BACKGROUND

The focus of this article is online interviews, which we view as a special form of Internet research. There are also other online interrogation methods.

The chat interview is written and synchronous, although there can be different levels of synchronicity; in fact the parties can construct their entire answers before submitting them, making it different from face-to-face conversations. If we need to compare chat interviews to something well known, we might say that it is a combination of the traditional interview and a survey.

Performing research on children's activities on the Internet is an area where ethical codices are not yet fully developed. An ethical dimension is suggested by Hernwall (2001) who claims that communication with him via e-mail offered the children the possibility to act on their own terms and conditions. But it is also important to take into consideration aspects connected

Table 1. Some features of online methods compared with traditional interviewing. The article focuses on the last row: Chat Interview.

	Face-to-Face	Written	Synchronous	Asynchronous
Traditional Interview	X		X	
E-Mail Interview		X		X
Chat Interview		X	X	

to children's limited experiences of life (Enochsson & Löfdahl, 2003), and the younger the respondent the more difficulties she might have in expressing herself in a written medium. In addition to this the online medium demands certain ethical considerations (Ess, 2002).

Davis, Boding, Hart, Sherr, and Elford (2004) claim that online interviews are inexpensive, convenient, and can be more acceptable to people who do not want to or are unable to attend face-to-face interviews. The weaknesses according to Davis et al. (2004) are that online interviews are slow and that follow-up probing can inhibit the flow of the dialogue. The authors also claim that the lack of social and conversational cues present in face-to-face interviews can cause breakdown in turn-taking. Their experience is that these weaknesses make the text ambiguous. Other researchers claim that young people communicating have other ways of expressing those cues and emotions, which are qualitatively different from communicating face-to-face and cannot be regarded as *better* or *worse* (Hernwall, 2001; Hård af Segerstad, 2002).

All research involving humans has to follow certain ethical guidelines to protect the participants from harm (ACHES-MC, 1946; WMA, 1964/2002). The voluntariness of people to participate is particularly emphasized. The participants should be informed of their rights to abstain from participation or to withdraw their consent. Sometimes though, it can be difficult for a participant to tell the researcher that she wants to withdraw. When dealing with children, this matter is even more delicate and requires a lot of sensitivity from the researcher since children sometimes use extra-linguistic markers to signal their withdrawal (Enochsson & Löfdahl, 2003). Backe-Hansen (2002) also emphasizes the researcher's responsibility to make it possible for the children to withdraw throughout the research process.

Holge-Hazelton (2002) and Frankel and Siang (1999) discuss whether the researcher can be sure that the person at the other end really is the one she thinks it is. However, this problem is two sided. Johansson (2000) tried to find participants for her study in a common chat room, and comments she received showed that children online suspected her to be someone else than the researcher she claimed to be.

QUESTIONS

In this article we will discuss our findings concerning method and ethics when conducting online interviews with children and teenagers. The questions we will address are:

- What methodological and ethical issues are specific to online interviews?
- How can our method be developed further?

Method

This article is based on experiences from three different research projects in which children of different ages have been interviewed online (Dunkels, 2005b; Enochsson, 2006). The research projects' aims were not to study the method as such, so this article is based on analyses and reflections written down by the researchers during the process. The analyses are qualitative, and we have been looking at our own methods and the interview transcriptions in light of questions posed to us from colleagues and others interested in our research. When discussing the matter and consulting research articles, different themes emerged. The themes have been discussed, revised, and discussed again.

Online Interviews

The following is an account of the themes that emerged when analyzing our own methods.

Deception

Children are constantly being exposed to risks, and the Internet is no exception. Media focuses on the risks of being contacted by pedophiles and being exposed to sexual or racist content, among others (Dunkels, 2005a). When contacting children online the researcher must be unambiguous concerning her identity and agenda in order to minimize the risk for the children. The greatest risk is luring children to act in a careless way when contacted by adults. As described above, Johansson (2000) was suspected by the children in the chat room to be someone with dishonest motives.

There may also be a risk that parents suspect that a pedophile posing as a researcher is contacting their child. In some cases the first contacts are better made off-line, making use of the fact that many people trust a telephone or a face-to-face conversation more than an online meeting. This is a way of giving the children and their parents control over the interaction, and when the parents have given their consent, it is time to make the contacts online.

It is difficult to be sure that the person chatting really is the person the researcher thinks they are. Research on chatting from the 1990s showed that it was common to pretend to be someone else and it was easy to stay anonymous (Sjöberg, 2002). Today, when peer-to-peer applications such as MSN are much more common, young people prefer chatting with friends they already know (Bjørnstad & Ellingsen, 2004). Also in Net communities, most contacts are with friends from real life (Enochsson, 2005; Medierådet, 2005). This implies that patterns of behavior on the Net may have changed. The more used to communication on the Internet we get, the easier it will be to interpret what kind of person has written different messages (Sveningsson, 2006). The fact that the respondent might be another person than the researcher thinks even in face-to-face interviews is rarely discussed. However, when interviewing unknown people this could be a problem in real life, although infinitely small. It is reasonable to assume that the risks connected with the Internet will diminish as we grow accustomed to the technology.

Interpretation

Sundén (1998) claims that the similarity between the computer-mediated written conversation and the traditional text is an illusion, and the fact that the process of saving the conversation is so simple, from a technical point of view, that it deceives us to believe that they are the same. Kroksmark (2005) states that in an e-mail interview the answers are longer, more structured, and that the respondent often discusses with herself. The latter is less likely to be seen in a chat interview, since the chat medium often presupposes immediate responses. As Kroksmark puts it, the interviewee writes down the sentence herself. This means that punctuation marks are placed where the respondent wants them to be, and there are no such comments as inaudible humming and so forth. It is also common for respondents to use emoticons both in e-mails and in chat interviews. The following is a passage from an interview with Sarah:

Sarah	*hiyou :-D*
annbritt	*Hello*
Sarah	*Sarah here*
annbritt	*Shall we begin*
Sarah	*yesbox :-)*
annbritt	*Just interviewed Laura. We haven't seen since last spring and it was a bit im personal just to start directly with the questions.*
Sarah	*haha yes I can understand that*
Sarah	*haha I think it will work out fine :-P*

In this passage Sarah uses emoticons several times, and she also writes "haha" to mark that she is in a good mood.

Davis et al. (2004) point out some weaknesses in online interviews such as lack of flow and social cues. However, the respondents in Davis et al.'s (2004) study were adult men. Today's youth have a richer experience of chatting with friends online. This mode of communication has developed its own distinguishing features, such as emoticons (Hernwall, 2001; Hård af Segerstad, 2002) and the upholding of parallel dialogues with the same or other persons.

In one of our interviews, there was a breakdown in turn-taking. There had been technical problems at the school, so in order to help 12-year-old Kim get ready in time for her next class, the interviewer hurried along with the questions, causing not only confusion but also stressing the interviewee:

elza	*is that a rule you have, about the time, or is it something that just happens?*
Kim	*yes*
elza	*rules?*
Kim	*i'm allowed to be on the internet for half an hour*
elza	*ok, what do you usually do by the computer?*
Kim	*rule yes*
elza	*(we are a little out of pace, I think I'm rushing it) :-)*
Kim	*yes, a little too fast for me*
elza	*ok, I'll calm down... :-)*
elza	*what do you usually do by the computer?*

We can see that the conversation becomes meaningless when questions and answers are out of pace. Kim confirms the interviewer's suspicions that the pace is too fast, and the interview can start over again. In a face-to-face situation, it might have been easier to notice the signs Kim displayed, and this breakdown might not have occurred. The problem could, however, be attributed to the interviewer's lack of experience, which then would support Sveningsson's (2006) claim that the problems with extra linguistic markers will lessen over time.

Net Cultures

The younger a child is, the more difficult it can be to carry out an online interview. There can also be children unaccustomed to the online medium. This can lead to children refusing an interview and a bias in the data. In one of the projects, the respondents could choose themselves between face-to-face or online interviews. Some respondents claimed that it was easier to write than to speak. Those respondents were between the ages of 12 and 13. We did not use Web cameras and thus had no eye contact. Eye contact can give you a chance to interpret the respondent's actions, and the lack of eye contact makes it more difficult to know when a respondent does not feel comfortable answering the questions, for example. On the other hand the respondents can think over what they write before submitting their reply.

It is important to bear in mind the differences between the Net cultures of the digital natives—the children—and those of digital immigrants, to use Prensky's (2001) terminology. The differences might create situations where the two groups' expectations conflict. As an example, many young people are highly skilled in multitasking: upholding several conversations at the same time, perhaps playing a game or doing homework while chatting in the background. For the adult researcher the interview is expected to be in focus

for both parties and this might cause problems. In one of Enochsson's interviews the interviewer gets worried when discovering that the interviewee is doing other things. This leads to a very confusing dialogue.

Several researchers (e.g., Dunkels, 2006; Sveningsson, 2006) have reported a new kind of openness that computer-mediated communication seems to promote. This might make it possible to study arenas that were hard to approach earlier. This opportunity, however, calls for caution from the researcher, who needs to carefully think through her involvement with the participants. Computers and the Internet have changed our ways of interacting. Among the areas that were highly unlikely to have some years ago and are a reality today, we find online therapy (Grohol, 1999; Holge-Hazelton, 2002), mourning the dead (Dunkels, 2006), and meeting a sexual partner (Löfgren-Mårtensson, 2005).

Security

How the data is gathered and stored are important questions whenever research involves people. This is no different when the Internet is part of the research, but the implementations may have to be altered.

An online interview must pass a server at some point. Depending on what level of security the researcher finds necessary, different solutions may be appropriate. If the research concerns sensitive issues, it may be important that the researcher also is in control of the server. In this case the interview takes place in a forum placed on the researcher's server and the data is also stored there. This method is the most secure, and any risks connected with this method are of a kind found off-line too, for example, negligence of the researcher, illegal attempts to get hold of data, and so forth. Another alternative is using an existing instant message tool. In this case the level of security is lower, since the data can be saved on several other computers. Using MSN Messenger is an example of this method where researchers can take advantage of the fact that

Table 2. The level of security of different technical solutions

Level of Security	Own Server	Instant Message Tool	Net Community	Open Forum
High	X			
Low		X		
Lower			X	
Public				X

most participating children are accustomed to the tool and the positive consequences that follow. This method might not offer the same safety, but it simplifies the procedure for both researcher and children. Yet another method is using an existing Net community, giving the same positive effects for the participants, but lowering the security even further. Finally, researchers might consider interviewing in an open forum, where the conversation is to be regarded as public.

Power Structures

A girl who very openheartedly told the interviewer about her use of the Internet explained why she sometimes preferred online contacts, even with her friends:

Marie   *You see, in real life, I am pretty shy.*

Several children in our studies express that it can be easier to *write* than to *speak* about more delicate matters. This is supported by other studies such as Enochsson (2005) and Hernwall (2001). Hernwall also claims that the children in his study after some months express themselves more freely in relation to him as an adult researcher. This is also supported by different studies where marginalized groups claim that on the Internet they have found a powerful arena from which they can act (e.g., Dahan & Sheffer, 2001; Hall, 2000; Leonardi, 2000; Weinrich, 1997). Enochsson's (2005) informants said that the Internet is a place where everybody can find his or her space independent of their status in the classroom.

When the interview is in text form already, the researcher can easily read the text between sessions and in so doing increase the quality of the following session. This is also an advantage during the actual interview, since it is possible to re-read earlier answers when undertaking follow-up probing. When interviewing face-to-face, it is also possible to let the respondents read and comment upon their own interview transcript, a method Enochsson (2001) used. This is a way of getting a more developed text and hopefully more developed thoughts. In two of the studies, the respondents were asked to read the chat interview afterwards to develop some thoughts, and only one comment was given. This can be due to power relations or simply because there was nothing to add.

Dunkels informed her 12-year-old interviewees of a way of withdrawing from the project. If they wanted to quit the interview but felt uneasy to say so, they could simply shut down the Web browser and blame it on technical problems. The researcher made a promise not to ask any questions, but that she would wait to see if they returned, as there actually might be technical problems. Two of Enochsson's informants did not show up on the Net in spite of reminders. A similar behavior could also be seen in Löfdahl's (2002) study with pre-school children. They turned the light off when they did not want the researcher to use the video camera anymore. It could be seen that the children found it difficult to tell the researcher not to use the camera (Enochsson & Löfdahl, 2003). These examples show that it is very important to be sensitive as a researcher and to let the children use their own expressions for withdrawal, but also that the online interview offers new possibilities to withdraw.

CONCLUSION AND FURTHER RESEARCH

We have discussed the importance of being open concerning identity and agenda when engaging in online communication with children. We also discussed the risk of any of the parties being deceived by the other. The conclusion is that problems connected to identity probably will diminish over time, as users get accustomed to the medium and thereby unveil the extra linguistic markers that are specific to the medium.

Does the researcher need any Internet-related competence to engage in a chat conversation? Our experience seems to indicate that you do not need any particular skills, though some practice is required.

We have found that online interviews can be very useful, as they simplify the interview situation in many ways. The time- and money-saving aspects, making it possible to carry out interviews without a lot of traveling, are not unimportant.

A strong point of online interviews might be that it can promote creating an arena also for marginalized people, people whose voices are seldom heard for different reasons: social, ethnical, gender related. The possibility for the respondent to write his or her own text is positive, but this is dependent on her ability to use the written language.

Gender perspectives in Internet use among young people need to be investigated further. There is reason to suspect that access to technology is partly dependent on gender and social, ethnic, and cultural differences, a situation which makes these perspectives essential to studies concerning social life on the Internet in particular and online studies in general.

It is important to bear in mind that all methods have their limitations, and as always it is necessary to choose a method accordingly. Choice of the method sometimes depends on the topic of the interviews. However, in this matter it is essential to keep an open mind; sometimes the least likely subjects are suitable for computer-mediated communication.

Considerations

The same methodological and ethical questions become apparent when conducting online and real-life interviews, and any differences are mostly in appearance. Researchers getting accustomed to the medium will probably become aware of the differences and find ways of solving methodological and ethical problems. Until then every situation must be carefully considered in order to secure the quality of the research and the personal integrity of the participants.

We must be careful to ascertain who the other party is in a chat conversation, but on the other hand to not overrate the problems of possible deception. Being open with our identity and agenda as researchers is essential to safeguard the reliability of the study and the security for children in particular.

Finding ways of interpreting the written conversation that an online interview constitutes is important, taking into account the different Net cultures of digital natives and immigrants.

Also, we must carefully consider what technical solutions are appropriate for the interview in question: how much security it requires, what the demands on access to computers and the Internet are, and what technical skills can be expected from the researcher and participants.

And finally, we must take responsibility for the relative advantage we have as researchers and carefully try to even out power levels. Possibly, computer-mediated communication can be of help in this important pursuit.

REFERENCES

ACHES-MC. (1946). *Nuremberg code.* Retrieved March 26, 2006, from http://www.aches-mc.org/nurm.htm

Backe-Hansen, E. (2002). Børns deltakelse i spørreskjemaundersøkelser sett i forhold til generelle forskningsetiske krav. In D. Andersen & M.H. Ottosen (Eds.), *Børn som respondenter. Om børns medvirken i survey* (pp. 47-75). Copenhagen: Socialforskningsinstituttet.

Bjørnstad, T.L., & Ellingsen, T. (2004). *Onliners—a report about youth and the Internet.* Norwegian Board of Film Classification.

Dahan, M., & Sheffer, G. (2001). Ethnic groups and distance shrinking communication technologies. *Nationalism & Ethnic Politics, 7*(1), 85-107.

Davis, M., Bolding, G., Hart, G.J., Sherr, L., & Elford, J. (2004). Reflecting the experience of interviewing online: Perspectives from the Internet and HIV study in London. *AIDS Care, 16*(8), 944-952.

Dunkels, E. (2005a). Nätkulturer—vad gör barn och unga på Internet? *Tidskrift för lärarutbildning och forskning, 12*(1-2). 41-50.

Dunkels, E. (2005b). Young people's Net cultures. In C. Howard, J. Boettcher, L. Justice, K. Schenk, P.L. Rogers, & G.A. Berg (Eds.), *Encyclopedia of Distance Learning.* Hershey, PA: Idea Group Reference.

Dunkels, E. (2006). The digital native as a student—implications for teacher education. *Tidskrift för lärarutbildning och forskning, 13*(1), 43-58.

Enochsson, A. (2001). *Meningen med webben—en studie om Internetsökning utifrån erfarenheter i en fjärdeklass* (Doctoral Dissertation No. 2001:7). Karlstad: Division for Educational Sciences.

Enochsson, A. (2005). Ett annat sätt att umgås—yngre tonåringar i virtuella gemenskaper. *Tidskrift för lärarutbildning och forskning, 12*(1), 81-99.

Enochsson, A. (2006, September 13-16). Tweens on the Internet—communication in virtual guest books. *Proceedings of ECER2006,* Geneva.

Enochsson, A. (submitted). *Young learners' views on Internet reliability.*

Enochsson, A., & Löfdahl, A. (2003, March 6-9). Incongruence in ethical and methodological issues in research concerning children's perspective. *Proceedings of the NERA Conference,* København, Denmark.

Ess, C. (2002, November 27). *Ethical decision-making and Internet research: Recommendations from the AoIR Ethics Working Committee.* Retrieved January 15, 2004, from http://www.aoir.org/reports/ethics.pdf

Frankel, M.S., & Siang, S. (1999). *Ethical and legal aspects of human subjects research on the Internet* (report of a workshop). Washington, DC: American Association for the Advancement of Science.

Grohol, J. (1999). *Definition & scope of e-therapy.* Retrieved February 18, 2006, from http://psychcentral.com/best/best3.htm

Hall, M. (2000). Digital S. A. In S. Nuttall & C.-A. Michael (Eds.), *Senses of culture: South African culture studies* (pp. 460-475). Cape Town: Oxford University Press.

Hernwall, P. (2001). *Barns digitala rum.* Doctoral Dissertation, Department of Educational Sciences, Stockholm University, Sweden.

Holge-Hazelton, B. (2002). The Internet: A new field for qualitative inquiry? *Forum: Qualitative Social Research, 3*(2).

Hård af Segerstad, Y. (2002). *Use and adaptation of written language to the conditions of computer-mediated communication.* Doctoral Dissertation, Department of Linguistics, Gothenburg University, Sweden.

ITU. (2006). *Internet indicators: Hosts, users and number of PCs.* Retrieved March 12, 2006, from http://www.itu.int/ITU-D/ict/statistics/at_glance/Internet04.pdf

Johansson, B. (2000). *Kom och ät! Jag ska bara dö först. ['Time to eat' 'Okay! I'll just die first!.'— the computer in children's everyday life].* Doctoral Dissertation, Department of Ethnography, Gothenburg University, Sweden.

Kroksmark, T. (2005). *@ografi.* Retrieved March 26, 2006, from http://www.hlk.hj.se/doc/398

Leonardi, L. (2000). The other half of cyberspace. Women and social participation in virtual and conventional networks. *Quaderni di Sociologia, 44*(23), 64-84.

Löfdahl, A. (2002). *Förskolebarns lek—en arena för kulturellt och socialt meningsskapande [Pre-school children's play—arenas for cultural and social meaning making].* Doctoral Dissertation No. 2002:28. Karlstad: Division for Educational Sciences.

Löfgren-Mårtensson, L. (2005). *Kärlek.nu: Om Internet och unga med utvecklingsstörning.* Lund: Studentlitteratur.

Medierådet. (2005). *Ungar & medier 2005—fakta om barns och ungas användning och upplevelser av medier.* Stockholm.

Prensky, M. (2001). Digital natives, digital immigrants part 1. *On the Horizon, 9*(5), 1-6.

SAFT. (2003). *Barnens eget liv på nätet.* Retrieved August 25, 2005, from http://www.medieradet.se/templates/products_193.aspx

Sjöberg, U. (2002). *Screen rites—a study of Swedish young people's use and meaning-making of screen-based media in everyday life.* Doctoral Dissertation, Media and Communication Studies, Lund University, Sweden.

Sundén, J. (1998). *Cybercultures.* Retrieved August 31, 2005, from http://www.jmk.su.se/digitalborderlands/jennys/cybercultures.doc

Sveningsson, M. (2006). Anonymitet i gemenskaper på Nätet. In O. Jobring, U. Carlén, & J. Bergenholtz (Eds.), *Att skapa lärgemenskaper på nätet* (vol. 3, pp. 117-138). Lund: Studentlitteratur.

Weinrich, J.D. (1997). Strange bedfellows: Homosexuality, gay liberation, and the Internet. *Journal of Sex Education & Therapy, 22*(1), 58-66.

WMA. (1964/2002). *Ethical principles for medical research involving human subjects.* Retrieved February 7, 2006, from http://www.wma.net/e/policy/b3.htm

KEY TERMS

Chat: A computer-mediated, real-time written conversation. It has the characteristics of a casual conversation and is usually not stored. A chat can be Web based or software based. The first means that it can be accessed from any computer with a Web connection, the latter that certain software needs to be installed on the computer. There are open chat forums that anyone can visit to chat, to find new acquaintances or information. Just as often, people prefer to chat with friends, using chat tools that require authentication before allowed chatting. Examples of software chat tools are Irc and Mirc.

Digital Native: Somebody who has never experienced life before the Internet. Prensky (2001) uses the term to describe the first generation that grew up with the Internet as a part of their childhood, which is the sense of the word used in this article. Persons who are not used to computers and the Internet from childhood are consequently digital immigrants.

Emoticon: Probably derived from the words emotion and icon, suggesting that emoticons are icons, or images, expressing emotions. In written conversations, such as chats, instant messages, or post-it notes, the lack of visual and aural support often needs to be compensated. Hård af Segerstad (2002, p. 131) expresses this: "Cyber communicators use emoticons to convey non-verbal signals."

In Real Life (IRL): Used here to distinguish between the Net on the one hand and real life on the other. This does not mean that we are involved in the discussion regarding the Net's relationship to reality, it is simply a practical way to distinguish between something happening in the world that we can see and touch, and something happening on the Internet.

Instant Message (IM): Written message, synchronous or asynchronous, sent via an IM tool. The IM tool allows the user to see which pre-defined contacts are online and send *synchronous* messages, the conversation taking the character of a chat, or *asynchronous,* leaving the message until the contact goes online. Examples of IM tools are Icq and MSN. These kinds of applications, creating private conversation channels, are increasingly becoming popular.

Net Community: A virtual meeting place accessible through the Internet. To get a picture of what a Net community is, one can imagine a mixture of the school yearbook, a showroom, a trendy café, a telephone, mail, and walking down High Street on a Saturday afternoon. It is a virtual place for communication, providing tools for presenting yourself and observing others. Most Net communities are Web based—that is, you can access them via a Web site. As a member you log in and get admittance to your personal space where you can publish information about yourself, true or untrue, as much as you choose. All members can view each other's information and communicate.

Net Culture: Activities on the Internet and the cultures that evolve around these activities. Examples are chatting; searching on the Internet; playing games; downloading and distributing music, films, software, and other digital material; the unwritten rules concerning e-mail and other written conversations; and patterns of interaction in the new media environment.

Safe Use Guide: A set of rules to help Internet users avoid dangers and unpleasant situations. Examples can be found on many major Web sites particularly aimed at children and teenagers. Among these you often find tips like the ones SafeKids.com (2006) list:

- I will not give out personal information such as my address, telephone number, parents' work address/telephone number, or the name and location of my school without my parents' permission.
- I will tell my parents right away if I come across any information that makes me feel uncomfortable.
- I will never agree to get together with someone I "meet" online without first checking with my parents. If my parents agree to the meeting, I will be sure that it is in a public place and bring my mother or father along.

Intrusion Detection and Information Security Audits

Terry T. Kidd
University of Texas Health Science Center, USA

Robert K. Hiltbrand
University of Houston, USA

INTRODUCTION

The rapid expansion and dramatic advances in information technology in recent years have without question generated tremendous benefits to business and organizations. At the same time, this expansion has created significant, unprecedented risks to organization operations. Computer security has, in turn, become much more important as organizations utilize information systems and security measures to avoid data tampering, fraud, disruptions in critical operations, and inappropriate disclosure of sensitive information. Such use of computer security is essential in minimizing the risk of malicious attacks from individuals and groups. To be effective in ensuring accountability, management and information technology security personnel must be able to evaluate information systems security and offer recommendations for reducing security risks to an acceptable level. To do so, they must possess the appropriate resources, skills, and knowledge.

With the growing perverseness of information systems and the technologies used to support such tools, the growing need to keep the integrity of both the data and the system used to manage that data will become a major priority. Therefore, it is important for security personnel and management to keep abreast of the issues and trends in information systems and security, and the tools and techniques used to secure systems and data.

In order to keep information safe and systems secured from outside attacks from computer criminals, information systems security and network vulnerability assessment must be conducted on a regular and ongoing basis to insure system security integrity. The aim of this article is to introduce to the information technology community, the conceptual overview of information security audits. Not only will this article present an overview of information security audits, but also information on popular intrusion detection and security auditing software used in industry.

BACKGROUND

Advances in information systems and the technology used to support those systems have produced great results for organizations, businesses, and other agencies in terms of work productivity, information storage, management, and in opportunities for the competitive advantage. While the promise and offerings of information systems have tremendous benefits, information systems have also created significant and unprecedented levels of risks to organizational operations. Businesses, hospitals, schools, universities, governmental agencies, and banks depend heavily on information systems, thus increasing the need for information security. With this newfound dilemma, organizations are beginning to use information security measures to ensure that the integrity of other data is held at an optimal level.

As discussed previously, the aim of information security used by an organization is to avoid data tampering, fraud, inappropriate access to and disclosure of sensitive information, and disruptions in critical operations (Umar, 2003). Unfortunately, these risks are expected to escalate as wireless communication technologies emerge and become ubiquitous. If information systems personnel are to be effective instruments of accountability and assessment, they need to be able to evaluate information systems and security measures to offer recommendations for reducing the security risk to an acceptably low level (Umar, 2003).

Further, the growing importance of information systems in performing daily operational activities, along with the elimination of paper-based evidence and audit trails, demands that these professionals consider the effectiveness of information technology security controls during the course of financial and performance audits. To do so, information security personnel must acquire and maintain appropriate resources and skill sets to help prevent computing security threats, vulnerabilities, or attacks. This can be a daunting challenge in an era of rapid evolution and deployment of new information technology. Likewise, management within organizations needs to take stock of their information systems security audit and its capabilities, to ensure that strategies exist for their continued development and enhancement, for an organization's security is only as strong as its policy.

When it comes to articulating or writing the organization security policy, the discussion should be more than information systems and the technologies used to support those systems, the conversation should move past a discussion of infrastructure (e.g., hardware and software), but to a discussion of security and methods for securing the organization's systems and most valuable assets—its information.

According to Holden (2004), information is essential to the achievement of any business or organizational. Its reliability, integrity, and availability are significant concerns in most organizations. The use of computing and system networks, particularly the Internet, is revolutionizing the way organizations conduct their business and their day-to-day operations. While the benefits of such tools have been enormous and have allowed vast amounts of information to be available at our fingertips, these interconnections also pose significant risks to computer systems, information, and to the critical operations and infrastructures they support. Infrastructure elements such as telecommunications, power distribution, financial data, research and development information, as well as personnel data are subject to these risks. The same factors that benefit operations—speed and accessibility—if not properly controlled, can leave them vulnerable to fraud, sabotage, and malicious or mischievous acts (NSAA & GAO, 2001). In addition, natural disasters and inadvertent errors by authorized computer users can have devastating consequences if information resources are poorly protected. Recent publicized disruptions caused by virus, worm, and denial of service attacks on both commercial and education Web sites illustrate the potential for damage.

Information security is of increasing importance to all levels of organization management in minimizing the risk of malicious attacks from individuals and groups.

These risks include the fraudulent loss or misuse of organization resources, unauthorized access to release of sensitive information such as tax and medical records, disruption of critical operations through viruses or hacker attacks, and modification or destruction of data. According to the National State Auditing Association and the General Accounting Office (NSS & GAO, 2001), the risk that information attacks will threaten vital organization interests increases with the following developments in information technology:

- Monies are increasingly transferred electronically between and among governmental agencies, commercial enterprises, businesses, and individuals.
- Organizations and businesses are rapidly expanding their use of electronic commerce.
- Business, government, and national/domestic security communities increasingly rely on the available information technology.
- Public utilities and telecommunications increasingly rely on computer systems to manage everyday operations.
- More and more sensitive economic and commercial information is exchanged electronically.
- Computer systems are rapidly increasing in complexity and interconnectivity.
- Easy-to-use hacker tools are readily available, and hacker activity is increasing.
- Paper supporting documents are being reduced or eliminated.
- Each of these factors significantly increases the need for ensuring the privacy, security, and availability of state and local government, business, and public education systems.

Although as many as 80% of security breaches are probably never reported, the number of reported incidents are growing dramatically with relative intensity (NSAA & GAO, 2001). To further illustrate the need for information systems security, a survey conducted by the Computer Security Institute in cooperation with the FBI found that 70% of respondents from large corporations and government agencies had detected serious computer security breaches within the last 12 months and that quantifiable financial losses had increased over past years (NSAA & GAO, 2001).

Are organizations responding to the call for greater security? There is great cause for concern regarding this question, since earlier reports of analyses on computer security identified significant weaknesses. The weaknesses identified place a broad array of organizational and business operations as well as assets at risk of fraud, misuse, and disruption. Further, information security weaknesses can place enormous amounts of confidential data, ranging from personal, financial, tax, and health data to proprietary business information, at risk of inappropriate disclosure. According to the National State Auditing Association and the General Accounting Office (NSS & GAO, 2001), typical information technology computer security weaknesses in an organization include the following:

- lack of formal planning mechanisms with the result that they do not serve the organization's pressing needs or do not do so in a timely and secure manner
- lack of formal security policies resulting in a piecemeal or "after-an-incident" approach to security
- inadequate program change control, leaving software vulnerable to unauthorized changes
- little or no awareness of key security issues and inadequate technical staff to address the issues;
- failure to take full advantage of all security software features such as selective monitoring capabilities, enforcement of stringent password rules, and review of key security reports
- inadequate user involvement in testing and sign-off for new applications resulting in systems that fail to meet user functional requirements or confidentiality, integrity, and availability needs
- installation of software or upgrades without adequate attention to the default configurations or default passwords
- virus definitions that are not kept up to date
- inadequate continuity of operation plans
- failure to formally assign security administration responsibilities to staff who are technically competent, independent, and report to senior management

Also of concern is a relatively recent threat—weaknesses in operating systems. A number of business and organization Web sites were hacked through a vulnerability in a widely used operating system. The time between the discovery of the vulnerability by the vendor and the notification to users that a special software patch should be applied was a matter of days and sometimes weeks (NSAA & GAO, 2001). The need for immediate notification of vulnerabilities and a subsequent need to react immediately will mean higher standards for security and network system administration groups who may have limited staff and technical knowledge. This is why the need for information systems security auditing is important and thus valuable to the integrity of an organization.

Systems Security Audits

With the growing need for security measures and the limited number of technical staff to meet the demands for the ever-increasing threat of unauthorized intrusion into an organization's networking system, security audits have become one of several lines of defense employed to help mitigate such action. According to Haynes (2003), a security audit is a process that can verify that certain standards have been met and identify areas in need of remediation or improvement. Dark and Poftak (2004) add that a computer security audit involves a systematic, measurable technical assessment of how the organization's security policy is employed at a specific site or location. Current literature suggests that computer security auditors work with the full knowledge of the organization, at times with considerable inside information, in order to understand the resources to be audited. In times past, identifying problem areas in a system had to be done by a team of human auditors, but now software can analyze a computer, a system, or a range of systems, and present the evidence that you do not need to be an expert to comprehend. It is important to use software that stays current with the rapidly evolving security threats. Software cannot resolve the entire problem of intrusion, but it helps in the process. Computer users within organizations need to assess, evaluate, discuss, run reports, make changes to corrections to the problems, and then rerun the reports in order to ensure maximum integrity and optimization of a network system. When success is achieved in resolving all the identified problems, we can raise the bar on the standards we are trying to achieve.

Haynes (2003) further explains that a security audit is a policy-based assessment of the procedures and practices of a site, assessing the level of risk created by these actions. A security audit comprises a number of stages. You can choose to focus the audit on different areas, such as the firewall, host, or network. However, a security audit will address issues with your systems, including software and hardware, your infrastructure, your procedures, your business processes, and your people. Information is the key. Once the audit has been completed you will have information on the compliance level of the users and systems under your control, with an idea of the risk exposure and security level of these systems (Haynes, 2003; Dark & Poftak, 2004). You will also have an idea of the potential damage that could occur if the worst came to the worst—this enables you to plan and develop a strategy to ensure minimal damage. In some cases management may choose to carry out an audit internally or use an external contractor. Whoever carries out the audit, those personnel should have the relevant technical expertise and ability to communicate the findings of the audit. It is also important that the auditor has an understanding of the organization under review. When auditing an information system that holds data that requires security clearance from upper management, the auditor must have the required clearances in order to access the systems holding that specified data (Haynes, 2003; Dark & Poftak, 2004).

According to Lerida, Grackzy, Vina, and Andujar (1999) when one conducts a security audit it is important to look beyond the systems and consider the human interface to those systems. This is on the same lines as Kapp (2000), Haynes (2003), Dark and Poftak (2004), and Stair and Reynolds (2006). One may think their system is perfectly secure, but the users may be involved in practices that compromise the security of the systems in place. This may include surfing unauthorized Web sites, installing shareware and peer-to-peer applications or transferring virus-infected e-mails and desktop applications. As a result any audit must attempt to identify all the possible risks. Information systems and the technologies used to support those systems are at risk from compromise from a number of sources, including poorly managed or badly configured systems, internal users, external users, and external attackers (sometimes known as crackers or hackers). It is important to understand that these attacks can come from a variety of sources and thus have to be analyzed in depth. A point to remember is that security audits do not take place in a vacuum; they are part of the ongoing process of defining and maintaining effective security policies (Kapp, 2000). It involves everyone who uses any computer resources throughout the organization.

Security audits provide a fair and measurable way to examine how secure a system or site really is. Even authorized system users can be the source of a security breach, therefore identifying possible lapses that could allow this is just as important as preventing external attack. It is important to understand that information security or computer security audits must move beyond information technology audits, which are concerned with ideas of auditing what is on the computer system and how it is being used. Instead security audits must also move past the review of programs and hardware, to the level of verifying that programs are operation with full integrity as they are intended to operate (Kapp, 2000). Security audits also must encompass components that ensure the data and information are reliable, as well as to verify that the information has not been compromised. To be successful at analyzing the security and integrity of an organization's network infrastructure, a team approach can be used to optimize security research. Security audits can be part of an information technology audit conducted by a team of professionals with expertise not only in the theoretical underpinnings of information systems, but also in the computer or networking system being audited. In addition, security audits must go beyond the annual financial audits and physical inventory audits to the data and content, which are standard processes in most businesses. Security audits look into how the data or information is stored and whether that data is secure. This is the importance of using a security auditing tool.

Methods for Performing Security Audits

When performing a security audit, one must perform the audit though personal interviews, vulnerability scans, examination of operating system settings, analyses of network shares, and historical data (Kapp, 2000; Hayes, 2003). Those who conduct the audit should be concerned primarily with how security policies—the foundation of any effective organizational security strategy—are actually applied and implemented. According to Haynes (2003), there are a number of key questions that security audits should attempt to answer concerning the audit:

- Are passwords difficult to crack?
- Are there access control lists (ACLs) in place on network devices to control who has access to shared data?

- Are there audit logs to record who accesses data?
- Are the audit logs reviewed?
- Are the security settings for operating systems in accordance with accepted industry security practices?
- Have all unnecessary applications and computer services been eliminated for each system?
- Are these operating systems and commercial applications patched to current levels?
- How is backup media stored? Who has access to it? Is it up to date?
- Is there a disaster recovery plan? Have the participants and stakeholders ever rehearsed the disaster recovery plan?
- Are there adequate cryptographic tools in place to govern data encryption, and have these tools been properly configured?
- Have custom-built applications been written with security in mind?
- How have these custom applications been tested for security flaws?
- How are configuration and code changes documented at every level? How are these records reviewed and who conducts the review?

These are just a few of the kind of questions that can and should be assessed in a security audit. In answering these questions honestly and rigorously, an organization can realistically assess how secure its vital information and systems are.

Conducting a Security Audit with GFI LANguard

Over the past few years, a number of intrusion detection and vulnerability assessment tools have been developed to aid the information systems professionals in their efforts in keeping their systems secure and their data safe. These tools run on a number of platforms including Windows NT, 2000, XP, and Linux. There are a number of types of tools that detect changes in system configuration, tools that test for known security issues, and a class of tools that are used to monitor systems in real time, such as network sniffers. Of the programs available to the public on the market, one program has consistently gained favor with security professionals in the field. This particular program can be used in conjunction with other tools as one line of

defense for an organization. GFI LANguard Network Security Scanner (N.S.S.) is a premier security auditing tool that checks the network for all potential methods that an unauthorized user may employ to attack or gain entry into a system. By analyzing the operating system and the applications running on the network, GFI LANguard N.S.S. identifies possible security holes. During a security audit, GFI LANguard N.S.S. scans the entire network, IP address by IP address, and alerts the auditor of the weaknesses discovered on the specified network(s). Using a combination of operating system functions together with the features offered by GFI LANguard N.S.S., one can proactively deal with the security issues detected. For example, security issues can be proactively detected by shutting down unnecessary ports, closing shares, as well as installing service packs and hotfixes before malicious persons can exploit them. By default, GFI LANguard N.S.S. allows the auditor to perform security audits on both Windows- and Linux-based target computers. During an audit, the scanning engine collects various hardware and software information from the scanned targets. This includes the service pack level of each target computer, potentially vulnerable devices such as wireless access points and USB devices, installed applications, as well as open shares and open ports (GFI Software, 2005). The scanner also enumerates specific OS configuration settings such as Windows registry settings and password policy configuration details aiding in the identification of common security issues related to an improperly configured operating system such as an OS running on default settings (GFI Software, 2005).

With this software scan, results can easily be analyzed using filters and reports, enabling the security team to proactively secure the network by shutting down unnecessary ports, closing shares, installing service packs and hot fixes, to name a few. In addition to the features listed above, GFI LANguard N.S.S. is also complete with a patch management solution system aimed at enhancing the security audits that are identified (GFI Software, 2005). After the software has scanned the network for security weaknesses and determined missing patches and service packs—both in the operating system and in the applications—one could use GFI LANguard N.S.S. to deploy service packs and patches network-wide with the ease. Not only is the software able to deploy service pack and patches network-wide, the software can also deploy custom software and updates network-wide to ensure a wider range of network security and information integrity. According to GFI Software (2005), when determining whether to use a network security scanning product on the market, one should look at the following product attributes:

- network security vulnerabilities (Windows and Linux) scanning
- intrusion detection of unnecessary shares, open ports, and unused user accounts on workstations
- network analysis for and deployment of missing security patches and service packs in OS and Office
- wireless node/link detection and USB device scanning
- ease of use and report generation

In addition to the regular use of an active network vulnerabilities scanner such as GFI LANguard's Network Security Scanner, the use of real-time (actually, near-real-time) network-based intrusion detection/prevention systems (known by the initials IDS/IPS) such as the GFI LANguard Security Event Log Monitor (S.E.L.M.) in conjunction with host-based IDS/IPS systems such as GFI LANguard's System Integrity Monitor (S.I.M.) provide defense-in-depth against both internal and external threats.

GFI LANguard's System Integrity Monitor is a utility that provides intrusion detection by checking whether files have been changed, added, or deleted on a host system. If a change happens, S.I.M. alerts the central monitoring system (e.g., GFI LANguard's Security Event Log Monitor) as well as the systems administrator or other designated personnel via e-mail and centralized event log. Since hackers need to change certain system files to gain access, this utility provides a means to further secure any host systems open to attack.

The use of both passive (intrusion detection systems) and active (vulnerability scanner) measures that are network based and host based provide the beginnings of a solid defense-in-depth strategy for securing an organization's information systems. Security is a process, not a single piece of technology, not a black box that sits in the corner, and there are no "silver bullets" that will cure all woes. Information Assurance and Computer Security are concepts, not end points.

Security is a journey and not a destination. Assessment, implementation, and evaluation are the step all organizations must undertake on a continuing basis to constantly improve security and stay even with the hackers that want into your network and want unauthorized access to your precious data. Using intrusion detection software and network security auditing tools as one line of defense to any organization can be one step closer in ensuring that the organization's data contains full integrity.

CONCLUSION AND FUTURE TRENDS

In building information systems security audit procedures and policies, management should assess the organization's security audit readiness by taking into account the following relevant factors. Establishing a baseline in these areas by identifying strengths and weaknesses will help an organization determine the best way to proceed. In many instances, this process will determine what is practical to implement within given time and budget constraints. Although an organization may have time, staffing, technology, and budgeting constraints, software such as GFI LANguard presents itself to be a positive mid-range solution for those looking to optimize their network and systems security within their respective organizations. Along with experienced personnel to perform security audits, an information systems security audit capability must have the relevant tools, techniques, and practice aids available to assist the auditors with their audit tasks. Decisions on obtaining such tools, techniques, and practice aids, along with the appropriate expertise to use them, must be based on the hardware, system software, and applications that constitute the audit environment, as well as on the information security policy within the organization.

With networking systems becoming more and more interconnected, the hardware and software that make up and connect these systems are critical. The technical components that provide network, Internet, and intranet connectivity must be identified, analyzed, and reviewed on a continuous basis, in order to ensure maximum operating optimization as well as for data and information integrity (Umar, 2003). Organizations should develop an inventory of this infrastructure, which should be periodically refreshed since computer systems are extremely fluid, and projections are that technology will continue to advance rapidly. It is importantto understand that information systems security is of increasing importance to all levels of organization management in minimizing the risk of malicious attacks from individuals and groups. In order to preserve the vitality of a business or an organization, information must be kept in full integrity; not doing so will ensure risks that may become detrimental to the organization, its resources, and personnel. In order to keep information safe and systems secured from outside attacks from hackers and other computer criminals, information systems security and network vulnerability assessment must be conducted on a regular and ongoing basis to insure system security integrity.

REFERENCES

Dark, M., & Poftak, A. (2004). How to perform a security audit. *Technology & Learning, 24*(7), 20-22.

GFI Software. (2005). *GFI LANguard Network Security Scanner (N.S.S.).* Retrieved May 1, 2005, from http://www.gfi.com/lannetscan

Haynes, B. (2003). *Conducting a security audit: An introductory overview. Security focus.* Retrieved May 1, 2005, from http://www.securityfocus.com/infocus/1697

Holden, G. (2003). *Guide to network defense and countermeasures.* Boston: Thompson Course Technology.

Kapp, J. (2000). How to conduct a security audit. *PC Network Advisor, 120*(7), 3-8.

Lerida, J.L., Grackzy, S.M., Vina, A., & Andujar, J.M. (1999, October 5-7). Detecting security vulnerabilities in remote TCP/IP networks: An approach using security scanners. *Proceedings of the International Carnahan Conference on Security Technology*, Madrid, Spain.

NSS & GAO (National State Auditors Association and the U.S. General Accounting Office). (2001). *Management planning guide for information systems security auditing.* Washington, DC: NSS & GAO.

Stair, R., & Reynolds, G. (2006). *Fundamentals of information systems* (3rd ed.). Boston: Thompson Course Technology.

Umar, A. (2003). *Information security and auditing in the digital age—a managerial and practical perspective.* NGE Solutions.

KEY TERMS

Information Systems: A set of interrelated components that collect, manipulate, and disseminate data and information, and provide a feedback mechanism to meet an objective.

Information Systems Security: The protection of information systems against unauthorized access (or the denial of service to authorized users) and modification of information (whether in storage, processing, or in transit), including those measures necessary to detect, document, and counter such threats.

Intrusion Detection: Software that monitors systems and network resources, and notifies network security personnel when it sees a possible instruction.

Network Security Scanner: A software program that identifies possible security weaknesses and threats.

Security Auditing: A process that can verify that certain standards have been met and identify areas in need of remediation or improvement. A security audit involves a systematic, measurable technical assessment of how an organization's security policy is employed at a specific site or location. Current literature suggests that computer security auditors work with the full knowledge of the organization, at times with considerable inside information, in order to understand the resources to be audited.

Security Policy: A policy that outlines rules for computer and information systems access. The policy determines how policies are enforced and lays out architecture of the company information security environment.

Vulnerability Assessment: The process of identifying technical vulnerabilities in computers and networks, as well as weaknesses in policies and practices relating to the operation of these systems.

Investigation Strategy for the Small Pedophiles World

Gianluigi Me
Università di Roma, "Tor Vergata," Italy

INTRODUCTION

Internet child pornography (CP) is one of the most rapidly growing problems on the Net. In particular, pedophilia has been largely facilitated by the Internet, because it has enabled like-minded people to meet and fuel their sexual interests in children. In addition, the diffusion of pedophile material mainly occurs in almost-public fields like the World Wide Web, mailing lists, newsgroups, and bulletin boards, where anonymity and confidentiality obscure most of the communication parties and content causing difficulties for investigative analysis.

The results of the "Operation Hamlet—De Iniqua Turpitudine" investigation led us to analyze the behavior of the affiliates of a pedophile criminal association, its rules, and the payoff of the affiliates. Since the production of the CP—representing the main target of the implicated criminal associations—is governed by well-established rules, this article will suit the *small world problem* of the pedophile phenomenon and is useful in establishing some investigative patterns. For this reason, this article will firstly give the relevant investigative aspects of the CP crimes, then, utilizing the mathematics of the birthday paradox, it will present some considerations related to the law enforcement (LE) investigation task.

BACKGROUND

Operation Hamlet: De Iniqua Turpitudine

"Operation De Iniqua Turpitudine" (DIT) represents the Italian branch of Operation Hamlet, involving many different European countries, which ended with several arrests of pedophiles. In particular, the DIT operation investigated the activities of the affiliates of an Internet-based criminal association composed of several pedo-pornographers, familiar with infor-

mation and communication technologies (e.g., they managed their own server) and cryptography tools (e.g., PGP). Furthermore, this criminal association, structured with watertight compartments, focused its activity mainly on child pornography production and on the organization of child fetishism meetings. The investigation was carried out mainly by overcoming the cryptography applied to ICQ message system log files. This activity enabled the detailed reconstruction of all criminal activities in the period of 2000-2002, and the recovery of most of the illegal materials produced, leading finally to victim identification and the imprisonment of several pedo-criminals.

Analysis

The scientific research and criminological analysis related to the evidence has:

- demonstrated recurrent behaviors pointed out in the literature (Becker, 1968; Thimbleby, Duquenoy, & Beale, 1998; De Boni & Prigmore, 2003; Kelly & Reagan, 2000; Glaeser, Sacerdote, & Scheinkman, 1996), confirming the deep behavioral difference between producers and users of child pornography
- pointed out how the pedo-pornographic ring's affiliates search for the "souvenir boxes": mono-thematic and multimedia compositions, each one focusing on a single victim
- made possible the application of Becker's (1968) mathematical models to the pedophile ring's world and, in particular, to the associative, un-negotiated context
- focused attention on the group's internal procedures, called *"mutual involvement,"* which are oriented to avoid the risk of infiltration by law enforcement agencies and to warrant the authenticity of the video and the graphic material produced and spread

- localized the channels used to auto-finance the costs (e.g., technical management of the ring, to the XDSL connections, to the payment towards Web hosting providers) of the group

The Birthday Paradox

The birthday paradox (a special case of the classical occupancy problem [Bloom, 1973]) answers the question: "Imagine a soccer game. There are 23 people in a soccer field (22 players plus the referee). What is the probability that at least two of them share the same birthday—the same day of the same month?" The result, typically non-intuitive, is 0.5, for N=23: it derives from the fact that 23 people form 253 pairs (since the first player can be coupled with the remaining 22 people; the second player can be coupled with the remaining 21, etc.).

Firstly, let us nominate the number of permutations of *k-uple* over a *n* rank alphabet (n=365 in this case) as n^k, and the number of permutations without repetition as:

$$\frac{n!}{(n-k)!} \tag{1}$$

Consider *p* as the probability of the event of two people sharing the same birthday.

Choosing uniformly and randomly from the set of all the possible permutations, the probability of the complementary event *q* (no birthdays coincide) is:

$$q = \frac{1}{n^k} \cdot \frac{n!}{(n-k)!} = \frac{(n-k+1)!}{n^k} \tag{2}$$

Since *p=(1-q)* the probability can be expressed, for $1 \leq k \leq n$, as:

$$p = 1 - \frac{n(n-1)(n-2)...(n-k+1)}{n^k} \tag{3}$$

Using the Taylor series for the approximation of exponential series, we can write the last term of (Equation 3) as:

$$q \leq \prod_{j=1}^{k-1} e^{-\frac{j}{n}} = e^{-\sum_{i=1}^{k-1} \frac{j}{n}} = e^{-\frac{k(k-1)}{2n}} \tag{4}$$

Calculating q ≤ 0,5, if:

$$k \geq \frac{1}{2}\left(1 + \sqrt{1 + 8n \log 2}\right) \tag{5}$$

then $k \cdot (k-1) = 2n\log2$ thus

$$q \leq e^{\frac{(-k(k-1))}{2}} \leq \frac{1}{2} \tag{6}$$

Therefore, the probability p=1-q that two people have the same birthday is at least 0.5 when (Equation 5) is true. To easily manage the function, we can consider an approximation of the last term of (Equation 4), depicted in Figure 1, leading to

$$P \approx 1 - e^{-\frac{k^2}{2n}} \tag{7}$$

The solution for the birthday paradox can be obtained by the simple substitution of n=365.

A Complementary Benefit: Situational Crime Prevention

The results of this article can offer complementary benefits to the Situational Crime Prevention (SCP) approach to Internet CP and pedophilia, due to the increased risk to the pedophile when collecting the pictures and in order to improve the LE capability to threaten the pedophiles.

The SCP refers to a preventative approach that relies upon the reduction of the opportunities for crime, according to the emergent criminological theories focusing on the relationship between the offender and the actual environment where the crime takes place:

- **Routine Activity** (Cohen & Felson, 1979) explains how changes in society in the numbers of "suitable targets" for crime, or in the numbers of the "capable guardians" against crime results, can lead to more or less crime. The Routine Activity theory assumes that crime occurs when a motivated offender and a suitable target (or victim) converge in space and time in the absence of a capable guardian.

Figure 1.

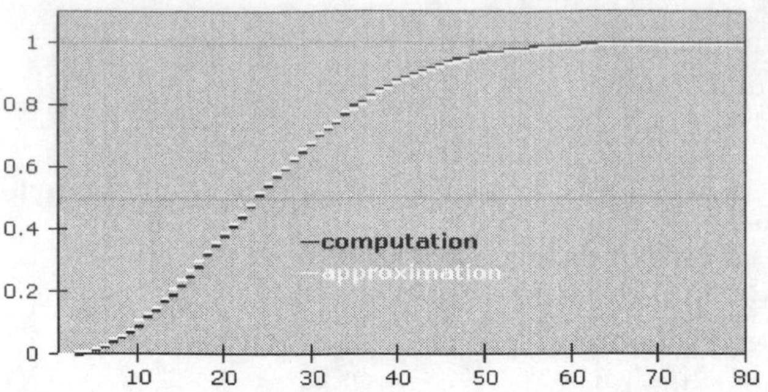

- **Environmental Criminology** is a term coined by Brantingham and Brantingham (1991) to refer to studies of the locational dimension of crime. This theory is based on the analysis of the offender decision-making process and the spatial and temporal variation in crime patterns.
- The **Rational Choice Perspective** (Cornish & Clarke, 1986) tries to understand crime from the perspective of the offender. The typical questions of this theory are: What is the offender seeking by committing the crime? How do the offenders decide to commit particular crimes? How do they weigh the risks and the rewards involved in these crimes? How do they set about committing them? If prevented from committing them, what other crimes might they choose to commit? According to Clarke (1992): "It should be clear from these questions that the rational choice perspective is directly concerned with the thinking processes of offenders, how they evaluate criminal opportunities and why they decide to do one thing rather than another." It is important to focus on the actor, who may not always be fully aware of his situation or have the complete information. Therefore the actor may behave "rationally" according to his perceptions of the world and the situation around him, and that these perceptions may (or may not) be accurate (Newman, 1997).

INVESTIGATIVE STRATEGY

As previously explained, the cardinal characteristics of the Internet CP/pedophilia phenomenon to formalize the problem are (Manzi, 2004):

1. *The "souvenir box,"* as a distinctive element of the pedophile's activity and part of the material collected by the pedo-pornographer during his criminal activity. It mainly consists of a collection of pictures of CP victims stored on the hard disk of the pedophile.
2. *The mutual involvement,* consisting of an unambiguous picture portraying the pedophile and his victim, both naked in apodictic scenes.
3. *The use of asymmetric cryptography* (Menezes, Van Oorschot, & Vanstone, 1996) (e.g., PGP), to assure the confidentiality and the privacy of the communications inside the group.

These points are of fundamental importance to the investigative strategy because:

1. The "souvenir box" of each pedophile suggests an approach strongly based on the seizure, the recovery, and the analysis of the contained pictures in order to identify the children as victims of the violence committed by at least two different pedophiles.
2. The mutual involvement together with the asymmetric cryptography (the digital signature on picture) uniquely identifies the guilt of the pedophile.

This work was carried out using a great amount of data, including conversations between "Fun Club" members, seized device content, and the individual background (criminal and psychological) of every suspect. The outcomes support the hypothesis of behavioral repetitiveness where the pedo-pornographers/pedophiles respect some rules which, with appropriate modelization, can offer investigators a greater chance for success. In particular, expected benefits of this

Figure 2.

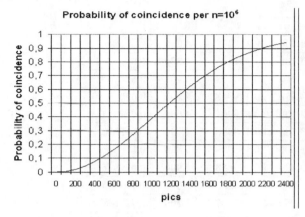

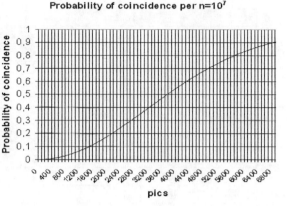

article regard the victim's identification capability, which until now has been characterized by a "lack of success" in this typology of investigations. Our purpose is to propose the birthday paradox as the intuition to develop an investigative strategy to fight the pedophile phenomenon in order to increase the success rate.

Considering N as the number of pictures of child victims of pedo-violence (e.g., whose images are contained in a database), we are looking for the probability of two pictures depicting the same child. Since it is very difficult to estimate how many children are victims of pedo-violence, we propose some trials to evaluate the effectiveness of the proposed strategy.

Recalling (Equation 7), per n=250,000, the non-negative root k=589,2052≈589 means that:

1. Collecting just 589 pictures of the children victims of pedo-violence, we have more than 0.5 probability to detect the same child.
2. It is possible to find 589 different pictures in few hard disk seizures (e.g., very often seized material is more than 1 Gb).
3. Detecting the same child suggests the need to focus the investigations on new pedophile rings or at least to detail various link typologies between pedophiles.

A further consideration relies on the probability of finding the picture of a chosen child in a children's picture database: in this case, the probability is 0.002353, coming from

$$1 - \left(\frac{n-1}{n}\right)^k \qquad (8)$$

Consequently, the probability of finding two pictures of the same child is 0.5 with 589 pictures. The probability of finding one child is very poor: nearly 0.002.

Now we can analyze the results for the rising magnitude orders of the estimated number of child victims of pedophiles n, where probability is 0.5. We will show two different cases of applied birthday paradox, per n=10^6 and n=10^7.

The sample values are shown in Table 1.

When the estimated number of the victims increases by one magnitude order, the number of pictures needed goes up from approximately 1,200 to 3,800. As the probability remains constant, it increases to approximately 0.5. Regarding the same shapes (with a slight left shift), we can identify, as the number of victims increases, the need for pictures of different children rises exponentially. In Figure 3, we show how the collected pictures follow an exponential shape, when the number of estimated CP victims grows by single order of magnitude and the probability of collisions remain at 0.5.

This suggests that the proposed investigation strategy is broadly applicable even if the number of CP victims is not known a priori.

Table 1. Sample values for n=10⁶ (gray background) and n=10⁷

K	P	K	P	K	P	K	P
100	0.004988	1,300	0.570443	3,000	0.362372	4,200	0.586046
200	0.019801	1,400	0.624689	3,100	0.381526	4,300	0.60327
300	0.044003	1,500	0.675348	3,200	0.400704	4,400	0.620158
400	0.076884	1,600	0.721963	3,300	0.419868	4,500	0.63669
500	0.117503	1,700	0.764254	3,400	0.438981	4,600	0.652851
600	0.16473	1,800	0.802101	3,500	0.458006	4,700	0.668623
700	0.217295	1,900	0.835526	3,600	0.476909	4,800	0.683996
800	0.273851	2,000	0.864665	3,700	0.495658	4,900	0.698956
900	0.333023	2,100	0.889749	3,800	0.51422	5,000	0.713495
1,000	0.393469	2,200	0.911078	3,900	0.532567	5,100	0.727604
1,100	0.453926	2,300	0.928995	4,000	0.550671	5,200	0.741278
1,200	0.513248	2,400	0.943865	4,100	0.568505	5,300	0.75451

Figure 3.

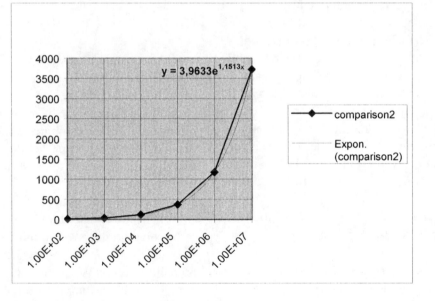

RELATED INVESTIGATION GUIDELINES

The strategy suggested by this figure is now quite obvious: the more you collect pictures with the identification data of the correspondent criminal profile, the more probability you have of detecting the same child as a victim of two different criminals. This consideration creates a relationship link between two pedophiles, since the same child picture has been found in their virtual souvenir boxes: this reflects the affiliation to the same pedophile ring or the belonging to different rings where at least one person is in common.

Since the collection of child pictures together with all of the related information into a database is the main task suggested by this article, the use of face-recognition software to enable automatic picture matching is appropriate.

However, a quantitative approach is not sufficient for increasing the effectiveness of the suggested investigation approach. In particular, according to Locard's Exchange Principle, anyone or anything entering a crime scene takes something of the scene with them, and leaves something of themselves behind when they depart (Casey, 2000). This principle can be applied to both the physical and the digital world. However, digital forensic seizure and analysis today can be considered to be more of an art than a science. Therefore, it is very important to improve the forensic skill of the LE (Manzi, 2004) regarding the analysis of pictures collected in a large database.

Recalling Garoupa (2003), since every criminal utility function has a penalty addend like:

$$\alpha_i \cdot r_i \tag{9}$$

where:

- α_i is the probability to be detected by LE
- r_i is the crime related penalty

which decreases the payoff related to a crime, we can identify the components of α_i, with relation to the virtual activity (cryptography and steganography techniques which raise the LE attack cost, raising the probability to escape detection, so lowering α_i), of the community:

- **Event A:** probability to be detected by LE
- **Event B:** probability of strong evidence recovery by LE

Coefficient α_i will assume the form:

$$P(A,B) = \alpha_i = P(A) \cdot P(B|A) \tag{10}$$

The conditional probability in the last term of (E10) is strongly afflicted by the competence of the investigators. When you find strong evidence with probability ≈ 1

$$P(A,B) = \alpha_i = P(A) \tag{11}$$

For this reason, as a general guideline, the foremost action with regard to digital-related crimes, as CP could be, is education in order to improve investigation quality and to expand the investigation spectrum. In particular, computer-related investigations capability can be considered as an additional weapon in well-established investigative techniques. In this way, the investigator can choose the most effective/efficient one, depending on the particular crime investigation context.

CONCLUSION

Increased connectivity not only increases the number of prospective victims of computer-related crime, it also increases the number of the offenders. In fact, old crimes-new media may be a case of adapting the *modus operandi* to suit the new environment, since the Internet provides criminals with global reach, anonymity, instant secure communication, access to knowledge, increased targets, an abundance of criminal opportunities, and facilitation of existing activities.

Internet CP is only the superset of the pedophilia phenomenon (old crimes-new media), which, for some mechanisms strongly linking the affiliates, can resemble the mafia affiliates relationships. This feature, even if it represents a good defense for insiders, leaves many "fingerprints." This article showed how to build a strategy to defeat this phenomenon, relying on the construction of a victim's picture database, based on straightforward considerations on the probability of finding a link between two different children. This link can represent the most important key to linking apparently different pedo-criminal phenomena for different pedophiles, joining the same pedo-ring at some level. The organizational and, to a lesser extent, technical problems that arise when trying to reach this objective are considerable. In particular, investment in the forensics training of LE operators is an important brick in the organizational structure. One of the related tasks in the near future is to develop a model of this criminal phenomena using game theory.

REFERENCES

APA. (n.d.). *Diagnostic and statistical manual of mental disorders* (4th ed.). American Psychiatric Association.

Becker, G.S. (1968). Crime and punishment: An economic approach. *Journal of Political Economy, 76*(March-April), 169-217.

Bloom, D. (1973). A birthday problem. *American Mathematical Monthly,* 1141-1142. This problem solution contains a proof that the probability of two matching birthdays is least for a uniform distribution of birthdays.

Brantingham, P., & Brantingham, P. (1991). *Environmental criminology* (2nd ed.). Prospect Heights, IL. Waveland Press.

Casey, E. (2000). *Digital evidence and computer crime* (pp. 4-5). Academic Press.

Clarke, R.V. (Ed.). (1992). *Situational crime prevention: Successful case studies.* Albany, NY: Harrow and Heston.

Cohen, L.E., & Felson, M. (1979). Social change and crime rate trends: A Routine Activity approach. *American Sociological Review, 44,* 588-608.

Cornish, D.B., & Clarke, R.V. (1986). *The reasoning criminal.* New York: Springer-Verlag.

De Boni, M., & Prigmore, M. (2003). *Growing up in cyberspace: Children's rights online.* Retrieved from http://citeseer.ist.psu.edu/cache/papers/cs/27658/http:zSzzSzwww-users.cs.york.ac.ukzSz~mdebonizSzpaperszSzchildrens_privacy.pdf/growing-up-in-cyberspace.pdf

Garoupa, N. (2003). Behavioral economic analysis of crime: A critical review. *European Journal of Law and Economics,* (15), 5-15.

Glaeser, S., Sacerdote, B., & Scheinkman. (1996). Crime and social interactions. *Quarterly Journal of Economics, 111,* 507-548.

Kelly, L., & Reagan, L. (2000). *Rhetoric and realities: Sexual exploitation of children in Europe.*

Manzi, G.S. (2004). Metodi di investigazione nella pornografia minorile. In G. Marotta (Ed.), *Tecnologie dell'informazione e comportamenti devianti.* LED Edizioni.

Menezes, A.J., Van Oorschot, P.C., & Vanstone, S.A. (1996). *Handbook of applied cryptography* (p. 53). CRC Press.

Newman, G. (1997). Introduction: Towards a theory of situational crime prevention. In *Rational choice and situational crime prevention. Theoretical foundations.* Ashgate.

Thimbleby, H., Duquenoy, P., & Beale, N. (1998). *UK views on ethical and spiritual implications of IT.*

Retrieved from http://citeseer.ist.psu.edu/cache/papers/cs/30420/http:zSzzSzwww.uclic.ucl.ac.ukzSzharoldzSzsrfzSzWCIT98.pdf/uk-views-on-ethical.pdf

Weisstein, E.W. (n.d.). *Birthday attack.* Retrieved from http://mathworld.wolfram.com/BirthdayAttack.html

KEY TERMS

Asymmetric Cryptography: In cryptography, an asymmetric key algorithm uses a pair of cryptographic keys to encrypt and decrypt. The two keys are related mathematically; a message encrypted by the algorithm using one key can be decrypted by the same algorithm using the other. In a sense, one key "locks" a lock (encrypts), but a different key is required to unlock it (decrypt).

Birthday Attack: A class of brute-force techniques used in an attempt to solve a class of cryptographic hash function problems. These methods take advantage of functions which, when supplied with a random input, return one of k equally likely values. By repeatedly evaluating the function for different inputs, the same output is expected to be obtained after about $1.2 \sqrt{k}$ evaluations (Weisstein, n.d.).

Pedophilia: The word comes from the Greek *paidophilia* (παιδοφιλια)—*pais* (παιδί, "child") and *philia* (φιλια, "love, friendship"). The American Psychiatric Association (APA, n.d.) gives the following as its "Diagnostic criteria for 302.2 Pedophilia":

a. Over a period of at least six months, recurrent, intense sexually arousing fantasies, sexual urges, or behaviors involving sexual activity with a prepubescent child or children (generally age 13 years or younger).

b. The person has acted on these urges, or the sexual urges or fantasies cause marked distress or interpersonal difficulty.

c. The person is at least age 16 years and at least five years older than the child or children in criterion a.

Payoff: Recalling game theory, a player's return, which is dependent on the strategies and actions chosen by all players. Since many criminal models can be formalized as games (including pedophiles' games), the criminal payoff represents the overall benefit (including risk and penalty) of the crime execution.

Seizure: The taking of physical/digital evidence or property by law enforcement; this includes, for example, blood for a drug test or the duplication of the content of an entire hard disk. Depending on local laws, the police must generally obtain a search warrant or court order before proceeding in seizing personal property.

Utility Function: In microeconomics, a function that specifies the utility of a consumer for all combination goods consumed (and sometimes other considerations). Represents both their welfare and their preferences. The shape of the utility function depends upon the decision maker's attitude to risk.

Managed Services and Changing Workplace Ethics

Alan Sixsmith
University of Technology Sydney, Australia

INTRODUCTION

Organizations use various types of outsourcing for many reasons, and these have been widely documented in the research literature. However, the impact on both the employees remaining with the organization and those who move to the service provider is often neglected. Prior to the outsourcing arrangement coming into effect, the employees all work for the same organization, but now with two (or more) organizations in place, professionalism and workplace relationships are drastically changed. In this article, the impact of changing workplace relationships on individual professionalism and workplace ethics will be explored.

The article will begin by briefly discussing managed services and outsourcing, and ethical workplace practices and how these may be impacted by an outsourcing arrangement. Included in this discussion are associated areas of trust, professionalism, workplace relationships, and employee mindset change. The mindset change is of particular interest as employees in both organizations are now guided by commercial arrangements. For example, the simple phone call to a former colleague asking for assistance or information may now cross organizational boundaries and therefore lead to potential ethical conflicts

MANAGED SERVICES AND OUTSOURCING

Various definitions of outsourcing prevail. Outsourcing "reflects the use of external parties to perform one or more organisational activities" (Dibbern, Goles, Hirschiem, & Jayatilaka, 2004, p. 9). Pearlson and Saunders (2006) describe outsourcing as "the purchase of a good or service that was previously provided internally" (p. 229). From an information systems and technology (IS&T) perspective, outsourcing is the contracting out or selling of an organization's IS&T assets, people, and activities to a third party for an agreed time period and monetary payment (Oza, Hall, Rainer, & Gray, 2004; Kern, Willcocks, & van Heck, 2002). IS&T outsourcing covers many areas, for example the use of contract staff, the contracting out of various IS&T functions such as managing and operating data centers, software development, and hardware and network support (Kishore, Rao, Nam, Rajagopalan, & Chaudhury, 2003).

Sanders and Locke (2005) define managed services as an engagement where a third-party company has responsibility for design, implementation, and management of a total solution. The engagement can vary and may include responsibility for equipment, facilities, staffing, software, and management (Sanders & Locke, 2005). As such a managed services engagement is a form of outsourcing. The value of such an engagement is that the client is buying specific industry experience that it does not possess.

Based on these definitions, there are marked similarities between managed services and outsourcing. The differences are in the context of the contract, the business environment, and how the parties see their relationship and the achievement of their business goals.

Commercial Focus → Mindset Change

With commercial arrangements in place, internal IS&T staff must change their work practices to become more commercially focused. However, IS&T staff have often struggled to adopt a commercial focus in the way they perform their activities. They are often perceived as having no real understanding of what the business needs are and of being primarily concerned with technology (hence some reasons for the move to outsourcing). This is mostly due to a support function mentality (Kingsford, Dunn, & Cooper, 2003) and most IS&T staff having minimal contact with the commercial aspects of the organization. Having a commercial or customer-oriented focus will permit the

IS&T department to promote its products and services, provide value to the organization, and realize its full potential within the organization.

By adopting a commercial or customer focus, the IS&T department can move away from the cost center or support function mentality and potentially become a profit center within the organization. For this to be successful, challenges such as considering users as customers, building and developing ongoing relationships with these customers, providing value for money services and fee-for-service costing models, and catering for selective product and service requirements by business units will surface. However, a workplace dilemma may surface for IS&T staff—that is, focus on profit and return on investment or focus on professionalism and ethical practice.

ETHICAL WORKPLACE PRACTICE

Ethical practice in the workplace can cover many aspects of any individual's role, for example providing the correct information to a customer, not taking advantage of working relationships (both internal and external), taking a bribe vs. receiving a gift, or revealing confidential company information to others. In most instances ethical workplace practices focus on the work-related conduct of the employee (Marchewka, 2006), however most employees and managers receive little (if any) training in workplace ethics and ethical behavior (Pearlson & Saunders, 2006).

Organizations develop policies, procedures, and guidelines related to workplace conduct which employees are expected to follow (Marchewka, 2006; Reynolds, 2003). Conversely an employee expects the management of an organization to also follow ethical practices. Unethical acts by management or employees could mean breaking the law or contravening professional standards (Marchewka, 2006; Reynolds, 2003).

Professionalism

A profession is "a calling requiring specialised knowledge and often long and intensive academic preparation" (Reynolds, 2003, p. 27) and consists of members known as professionals. Reynolds (2003) and Edgar (2003) identify a professional as someone:

- having advanced training and experience
- exercising judgment and discretion in the course of his or her work
- contributing to society
- participating in lifelong learning
- whose job cannot be standardized

The IS&T industry has many professional roles and people with wide-ranging backgrounds, experience, and education. Many relationships are developed at an individual level during an IS&T professional's career. However the following classification of relationships can be identified: the professional and (1) employer, (2) client, (3) vendor, (4) professional, (5) user, and (6) professional society. For further details, see Reynolds (2003).

The professional-employer relationship is the most important, and is often documented in employment contracts and company policies and procedures which detail the responsibilities of both parties (Marchewka, 2006; Reynolds, 2003). The professional-client relationship is normally based on a contract that specifies the work to be performed and the rewards to be provided. In the professional-to-professional sense, most professionals have a degree of loyalty to fellow professionals and hence may assist fellow professionals when opportunities become available (Reynolds, 2003). Conflicts could arise when a fellow professional is in fact a client. Trust in these relationships is then a crucial element for an employer.

Trust

While trust is commonly used in everyday language, an exact definition is difficult as trust has many interpretations. However, most definitions of trust share the theme that one party must knowingly place themselves in a position where they may be at risk from or be vulnerable to another party (Brown, Poole, & Rodgers, 2004). Integrity, ability, and predictability are components of trust (Cockcroft & Heales, 2005). After reviewing trust literature, Spector and Jones (2004) found trust to be linked to performance, cooperation, and the quality of communication.

Trust is the basis for creating and developing relationships (Brown et al., 2004; Kern & Willcocks, 2002), and also for managing long-term relationships. Dibbern et al. (2004) note that relationship building and structure are distinct from relationship management.

However, in practice, relationship building is the basis for relationship management.

Workplace Relationships

Workplace relationships are built between staff in various departments, staff and management, and staff and external contacts. These relationships are built over time during the course of work-related interactions. From an IS&T perspective these relationships involve the IS&T staff management and the various internal and external stakeholders such as users, management, vendors, and clients (Marchewka, 2006). These relationships are built at an individual level rather than departmental or organizational level.

Improving relationships with all parties (both internal and external) is an important strategy for an organization's management and can be a critical component of business success. Poor workplace relationships can seriously impact an individual's contribution to the organization (Ward & Peppard, 2002).

THE CASE

In order to understand the impact outsourcing or managed services has on workplace practices and relationships a case, from the telecommunications sector will be presented.

A telecommunications *Supplier* sold its manufacturing business to a venture capitalist and contracted to purchase equipment back from the new company. The *Start-up* took on all manufacturing employees and limited support staff from areas such as finance, information technology (IT), and human resources. In essence the *Supplier* outsourced the manufacturing component of its business to the *Start-up* through this sale.

This case will concentrate on the IT division where a managed services operation was implemented. For the *Start-up* to become operational as soon as possible, the sale was negotiated with a clause allowing the *Start-up* to use the IT environment of the *Supplier*. A considerable amount of work was undertaken by IT staff from the *Supplier* to partition the IT environment into two mirror image segments—one for each company. The *Supplier* retained ownership of the IT environment. The *Start-up* paid for services provided by the *Supplier*'s staff and for usage of the IT environment.

From an IT staffing perspective, the *Start-up* took on two IT development staff members from the *Supplier* (with one becoming the IT manager).

The *Start-up* operated its IT environment in its own right even though most services were provided by the *Supplier*. From an IT applications perspective, there was some confusion as to the specific contents of the contract, that is, what the *Supplier* would provide and what the *Start-up* would pay for. The *Start-up* undertook its own development and maintenance work for all manufacturing and store-related applications. However, for several specialist applications or when human resource constraints prevented the *Start-up* from undertaking its own work, services were provided by the *Supplier* on a contract basis.

A contentious point became who was liable for maintenance to the existing application base (where both the *Supplier* and the *Start-up* used the applications). When application development services were to be provided by the *Supplier*, the *Start-up*'s IT manager would request the *Supplier*'s IT development manager to quote on a certain piece of work; the quote would be compiled by the appropriate staff and returned to the *Start-up*. If the *Start-up* decided to proceed, it would request the IT development manager to schedule the work and provide an expected timeframe for completion. This had obvious repercussions on the project work and individual workloads of the *Supplier*'s IT development staff. Ethical workplace practice and professionalism was required in the quoting and scheduling process to ensure that the *Start-up* was not being taken advantage of (i.e., quote too high) and that the work requested would be undertaken in a timely fashion (i.e., fit in amongst current workload).

DISCUSSION

In the case presented all employees encountered major changes in work practices and relationships. As former colleagues now working for different organizations, the staff members faced different challenges and issues when working on assignments for the "other" organization. No longer could a simple phone call or a discussion in the hallway lead to work being undertaken. With commercial contracts in place, all activities being undertaken for the other company must be documented, budgeted, signed off, resourced, and scheduled.

Relationships that had previously been developed through workplace interactions, while potentially still in place at a personal level, had changed dramatically with the introduction of the new organization. Workplace relationships and practices now cross organizational boundaries. Therefore a more formal approach to work practices must be implemented which is in essence dictated by the contract.

Figure 1 outlines the actual relationship ingredients in the given case, based on the Dibbern et al. (2004) model of Management of Relationships in Outsourcing. In conjunction with a formal contract, a psychological contract is an unwritten mutual commitment and perception of stakeholders and staff on either side as to their individual expectation of what each party gives and receives from the relationship based on a reciprocal exchange (Oza et al., 2004; Koh, Ang, & Struab, 2004).

It is this notion of the psychological contract that is of most interest. The psychological contract is the institution of trust and grows over time as the formal contract gains momentum with both business and technical commitment. Trust coupled with control (the formal contract) tends to prevent opportunistic or unethical behavior on either side during the contract's life. Research has highlighted that a lack of trust inhibits vendor performance. Koh et al. (2004) indicate that IS&T outsourcing is not only controlled by legal contracts, but the parties involved also rely on the "spirit of the contract"—that is, individual beliefs and perceptions of their obligations. Outsourcing relationships focus on cooperation and commitment to an agreement to work together for mutual gain and benefit which is akin to trust. Client companies should consider outsourcing as more than a contract for IS&T services: it is in fact the management of business relationships (Kishore et al., 2003).

With regards to the workings of the IT contract between the *Supplier* and the *Start-up*, all areas except applications development and maintenance were well understood. The *Start-up* would pay for the services provided and their usage of the IT environment. Applications development was a so-called gray area as the formal contract lacked detail in this area. The phrase "spirit of the contract" was certainly fitting as the appropriate staff from either company had little knowledge of the contract's contents. A new commercial relationship had to be developed and was based on the psychological contract and ethical workplace practices rather than the formal contract.

AN ETHICAL FRAMEWORK

It is hard to define a standard approach to help an individual faced with an ethical problem. Laudon (1995) stated: "There is an ethical vacuum in cyberspace" (p. 33), and this still appears to be the case today as "well-accepted guidelines do not exist" (p. 193) to assist managers and employees with ethical and moral

Figure 1. Actual relationship ingredients in the case (adapted from Dibbern et al., 2004)

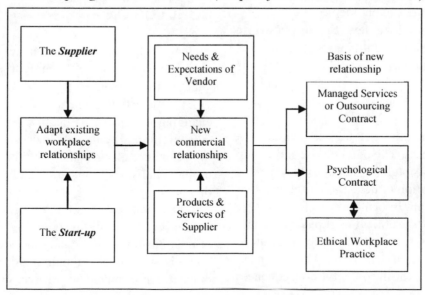

issues (Pearlson & Saunders, 2006). Ethical frameworks are available to help an individual make sound ethical decisions, and several approaches are detailed in undergraduate and postgraduate textbooks (e.g., Marchewka, 2006; Edgar, 2003; Reynolds, 2003).

No matter which approach is undertaken, a number of key areas must be considered when attempting to determine ethical workplace practices that ultimately form the basis for making ethical workplace decisions. Ethical workplace practice must encompass the following steps:

1. **Obtain all the available relevant information:** To ensure that the situation is fully understand to the best of one's professional ability.
2. **Determine the stakeholders and their stance:** This will complement the above point by providing information from the point of view of those who may benefit or suffer depending on the final solution/decisions.
3. **Identify and document the possible solutions or decision:** Analyze all the information obtained to derive all possible solutions/decisions. These must be documented and reviewed.
4. **Isolate the consequences associated with the solutions or decisions:** Any solution/decision documented will have positive and negative outcomes. The negative outcomes for each stakeholder must be identified for further review.
5. **Appraise your interpretation of the situation based on corporate guidelines:** The identified solutions/decisions must be considered in relation to existing corporate guidelines or policies and their impact on the stakeholders.
6. **Communicate and review the appropriate solution or decision:** Identify and recommended the correct solution/decision. This must then be communicated and reviewed with all stakeholders before implementation.

The above steps should not be considered as a single sequential process. The outcome from one step may require a previous step (or steps) to be revisited to ensure that the solution or decision has been based on accurate and relevant information.

When determining the ethical workplace practices in the managed service sector, it may be appropriate to look beyond the contract and the rules of engagement, that it prescribes to focus on the potential consequences of the solution or decision. For example, any solution implemented or decision made by the managed services (or outsource) provider cannot have a detrimental effect on the other party as this may in fact damage both organizations. Putting this into the context of the *Supplier-Start-up* case, the psychological contract (based on working relationships) may also provide some basis for ethical workplace practices.

Hence a consequences-based ethical approach may be more appropriate than a hard-and-fast (the written contract) rules-based ethical approach (Laudon, 1995) in the managed services sector to enable both parties to operate successfully.

FUTURE TRENDS

As more organizations move towards outsourcing, managed services, or selective sourcing of IS&T services, there will be continued impact on employee work practices and relationships. As this trend continues and IS&T jobs shift from technical roles to a more business-related role in order to interact with IS&T service providers, employees will become more commercially focused. Ethical work practices will become essential for all parties concerned.

Research on the social changes in the workplace as a result of an outsourcing or managed services arrangement is worthy of further investigation. Areas such as the psychological contract and the change to ethical work practices and relationships should be explored.

CONCLUSION

Ethical workplace practices are essential in today's changing business environment as organizations adapt to the various methods of obtaining IS&T services. This article presented two components of the changing workplace: ethical workplace practice, and outsourcing and managed services. These components impact other aspects in the workplace, including trust, professionalism, relationships, and changing employee orientation.

The case highlights the changing practices in the respective organizations. A model for the development of relationships in the changing workplace identifies that it is more involved than the formal contract in an outsourcing or managed services context. A psychological contract and ethical workplace practice must also be considered when developing new commercial relationships.

REFERENCES

Brown, H.G., Poole, M.S. & Rodgers, T.L. (2004). Interpersonal traits, complementarity, and trust in virtual teams. *Journal of Management Information Systems, 20*(4), 115-137.

Cockcroft, S., & Heales, J. (2005, November). National culture, trust and Internet privacy concerns. *Proceedings of the 16th Australasian Conference on Information Systems,* Sydney, Australia.

Dibbern, J., Goles, T., Hirscheim, R., & Jayatilaka, B. (2004). Information systems outsourcing: A survey and analysis of the literature. *The Database for Advancement in Information System, 35*(4), 6-102.

Edgar, S.L. (2003). *Morality & machines* (2nd ed.). Sudbury: Jones & Bartlett.

Kern, T., & Willcocks, L. (2002). Exploring relationships in information technology outsourcing: The interaction approach. *European Journal of Information System, 11*(1), 3-19.

Kern, T., Willcocks, L.P., & van Heck, E. (2002). The winners curse in IT outsourcing: Strategies for avoiding relational trauma. *California Management Review, 44*(2), 47-69.

Kingsford, R., Dunn, L., & Cooper, J. (2003, November). Information systems, IT governance and organisational culture. *Proceedings of the 14th Australasian Conference on Information Systems,* Perth, Australia.

Kishore, R., Rao, H.R., Nam, K., Rajagopalan, S., & Chaudhury, A. (2003). A relationship perspective on IT outsourcing. *Communications of the ACM, 46*(12), 87-92.

Koh, C., Ang, S., & Straub, D.W. (2004). IT outsourcing success: A psychological contract perspective. *Information Systems Research, 15*(4), 356-373.

Laudon, K.C. (1995). Ethical concepts and information technology. *Communications of the ACM, 38*(12), 33-39.

Marchewka, J.T. (2006). *Information technology project management providing measurable organizational value.* Hoboken, NJ: John Wiley & Sons.

Oza, N., Hall, T., Rainer, A., & Grey, S. (2004, November). Critical factors in software outsourcing—a pilot study. *Proceedings of the 2004 ACM Workshop on Interdisciplinary Software Engineering Research* (WISER).

Pearlson, K.E., & Saunders, C.S. (2006). *Managing and using information systems: A strategic approach* (3rd ed.). Hoboken, NJ: John Wiley & Sons.

Reynolds, G. (2003). *Ethics in information technology.* Boston: Thompson Course Technology.

Sanders, N.R., & Locke, A. (2005). Making sense of outsourcing. *Supply Chain Management Review, 9*(2), 38-44.

Spector, M.D., & Jones, G.E. (2004). Trust in the workplace: Factors affecting trust formation between team members. *The Journal of Social Psychology, 144*(3), 311-321.

Ward, J., & Peppard, J. (2002). *Strategic planning for information systems* (3rd ed.). Chichester: John Wiley & Sons.

KEY TERMS

Ethical Framework: An approach used to assist an individual in making a sound decision when faced with an ethical problem.

Managed Services: A contractual arrangement giving the responsibility of a specified component of an organization's information systems and technology environment to a third-party company.

Outsourcing: The contracting out or selling of an organization's information systems and technology assets, people, and activities to a third party for an agreed time period and monetary payment.

Professionalism: The conduct, judgment, and discretion an employee exhibits during the course of his or her daily work.

Psychological Contract: The personal interpretation by one party of the obligations to another party after a formal contract for the provision of services between the two organizations has been agreed upon and implemented.

Trust: The belief that one party places in another party to undertake their responsibilities at an expected level of performance. Trust includes components such as integrity, ability, predictability, performance, cooperation, and communication.

Workplace Relationships: The relationships developed over time by employees of an organization with other employees and colleagues, and with external contacts such as vendors, suppliers, and clients, which are based on workplace interactions.

Managing the Environmental Impact of Information Technology

Laurel Evelyn Dyson
University of Technology Sydney, Australia

INTRODUCTION

This article explores a much under-researched field of ethics: the impact of information technology (IT) on the environment. Reducing the ecological impact of IT requires a holistic approach including better design of computers, the development of non-polluting manufacturing processes, and effective management strategies. The latter have received much attention in recent years. The three main areas of management focus have been the problems of hardware disposal, the energy consumed by computer technology in operation, and paper usage by printers and photocopiers.

In this article management strategies will be examined in light of theories of environmental ethics and in the context of the university. Whereas universities are not typical of all organizations, they nevertheless offer particular challenges. They frequently have large deployments of advanced technology accompanied by intensive use by diverse stakeholders such as students, academics, and support staff. Statistics from the U.S. Energy Information Administration show that educational institutions have the highest ratio of computers per square foot after office buildings (EIA, 2003). Therefore, they provide an interesting arena in which to explore these matters.

ENVIRONMENTAL ETHICS AND INFORMATION TECHNOLOGY

Over the last few decades, the focus has shifted from traditional ethical concerns—the right behavior of one person to another—towards an interest in how people should act with respect to the environment. No doubt this shift is the result of the stress of overpopulation on ecosystems and the fact that this stress is now global in its extent (Southgate, 2002). As concern over the environment has grown, so has discussion of how ethics can be broadened to take into account environmental issues and which approaches will be the most effective in promoting environmental protection.

Generally there is wide agreement that ethical systems must be extended to take into account intergenerational issues (Reiss, 2002). That is, actions must be assessed in the light of their consequences for future generations. Concerns over recycling of non-renewable resources, such as the precious metals found in computers, would fall into this category, as would attempts to minimize the use of fossil fuels and conserve electricity by introducing more energy-efficient computer technology.

Interspecific issues also have reasonable acceptance (Reiss, 2002). There is a general belief that it is not sufficient to consider only humans, but that other species must be taken into account. So recycling of paper may focus on saving trees, another group of organisms which have a right to a place on the planet. However, it would be true to say that many people would still place human needs over those of other species.

Broadly, environmental ethics can be divided into two main approaches: human- and life-centered (Taylor, 1996). Human-centered environmental ethics is based on the concept that the environment should be protected because our quality of life, and the quality of life of future generations, depends on it. This view has the advantage of ease of acceptance since it focuses on human concerns and can be related to traditional utilitarian approaches to ethics. It may also take into account intergenerational issues. The main limitation is that long-term environmental needs may be ignored if outweighed by short-term human needs. By contrast, the life-centered view acknowledges the intrinsic worth of living things irrespective of their value to humanity. It has the advantage that it includes both interspecific and intergenerational concerns. The main disadvantage of this approach is that it has much less acceptance in the community. Organizations, in particular, would no doubt find it easier to obtain support for environmentally friendly initiatives which

Figure 1. Management of the environmental impact of IT

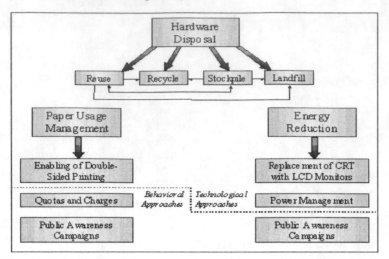

give at least some benefits to the organization and the people working in it.

MANAGING HARDWARE DISPOSAL, ENERGY, AND PAPER

Managing the environmental impact of IT involves three main processes:

- the disposal of hardware (computers, printers, photocopiers, etc.)
- the reduction of energy consumption by computers
- the reduction, or at least control, of paper usage generated by computer technology, in particular by printers and photocopiers

These processes are summarized in Figure 1.

Hardware Disposal

Disposing of superseded hardware poses the greatest environmental challenge of IT. Firstly, there is the enormous volume of old hardware. More significantly, perhaps, is the potential for hazardous materials, such as lead, zinc, nickel, cadmium, and mercury, to leach from computers dumped in landfills into the environment and water table (Beatty, 2002). In addition, there are valuable metals, such as gold and copper, that are wasted unless recovered. In this section only disposal

of old computers will be considered, although many of the same concerns apply to printers and other hardware that is no longer wanted.

Beatty (2002) defines the ways of dealing with old hardware as:

- **Dumping in Landfills:** Estimates of the number of computers that go directly into landfills vary widely, but ultimately all computers that are not recycled will end up there.
- **Stockpiling:** At least 50% of computers are stockpiled for varying lengths of time (Resource NSW, 2001). Occasionally, they will provide backups or spare parts, but normally most eventually go to landfill without being used again.
- **Recycling:** Recycling old computers for parts or valuable materials is not easy because of the hazardous materials they contain and the complexity of isolating the many different materials that are used in their manufacture (Beatty, 2002). Meeting health and safety standards is difficult: specialized equipment is required and profits are often marginal. Despite this, some countries, for example some states in the United States, have well-organized recycling programs.
- **Reuse:** Estimates state that about 25% of computers are resold, given or sold to employees, or given to charities for refurbishment and subsequent donation to poorer members of society or poorer countries (Beatty, 2002).

A study of computer disposal was undertaken at the University of Technology, Sydney (UTS). Here the computer lifecycle is under one central point of control, the asset control officer, acting under a policy that covers all computers and other disposable assets (Landale, Nguyen, Hoque, Lee, & Shin, 2004). UTS has two methods of disposing of computers, both related to reuse. The first, donation, is reserved for computers that are deemed to be of little resale value. These are given to Wesley Mission for refurbishment prior to being given away to other charities or poor people. In addition, students of the university who are unable to afford their own computers can place their names on a waiting list for free ones. Resale is the other method of disposal used: this is reserved for computers that still have monetary value. They are advertised for sale by the university. Another method is leasing: this is not so much a disposal method, but a way of *avoiding* the responsibility of disposal, since the company from which the computers are leased takes all responsibility for them once they are no longer serviceable to the university.

The ethical framework that governs UTS here is provided by the Talloires Declaration, to which the university is a signatory: one of its aims is to "set an example of environmental responsibility by establishing programs of resource conservation…and waste reduction" (Hardy et al., 2005). In this context the university makes environmentally sustainable decisions in the running of the organization, but also aims to operate in an economically sustainable manner and provide a quality service to students and staff. Generally, one can say that UTS achieves this, at least in the short term. Both from an environmental ethics standpoint and a general ethics standpoint, the practice is sound, helping those who cannot afford computers—or cannot afford new computers—as well as avoiding dumping the computers in landfills. Ultimately, however, as Landale et al. (2004) point out, UTS takes no responsibility for what happens to the computers once their reuse is over and they move on to another phase of the computer lifecycle. Ultimately, intergenerational issues need to be taken into account both by computer manufacturers and consumers if the problem of landfill is to be addressed properly.

Reduction of Energy Consumption

Energy consumption by computer technology contributes significantly to greenhouse gas emissions. A single desktop computer with a standard CRT (cathode ray tube) monitor uses about 0.12 kW of electricity per hour (Tufts, 2004). If left running 24 hours a day for a complete year, it will consume about 1,000 kW. Coal generation of this quantity of electricity will result in 850-1,500 pounds (380-680 kg) of carbon dioxide (CO_2) emissions into the atmosphere. To offset this, 60-300 trees would need to be planted for this one computer alone, for this one year alone. These figures do not take into account the energy required to power air conditioning to counteract the heat generated by the computer.

There are several strategies that can be followed to reduce energy consumption, and these can be grouped under two broad approaches (Tufts, n.d.):

- **Technological Approaches:** These can result in improved energy efficiency, but are unlikely by themselves to be enough because of the rebound effect, whereby new behavioral responses often arise which undermine energy savings (Binswanger, 2001):
  - **Replacement of older technology with more energy-efficient solutions:** For example, an LCD (flat screen) monitor uses about one-third the energy of a CRT monitor. A laptop consumes about one-quarter of the energy of a desktop computer (Tufts, 2004).
  - **Power management:** Enablement of power management features is possible on most computer operating systems. This usually involves powering down the screen if not in use for a period of 15 minutes or more, but can also include the enabling of standby or sleep mode for the computer hard drive after set periods of inactivity, turning off server monitors except when needed, and enablement of power saving on large printers (Tufts, 2004).
- **Behavioral Approaches:** There are three main myths which contribute to people's use of computers in an energy-inefficient way: that screen savers save energy, that shutting down a computer is harmful to the hard disk, and that computers do not consume power when not in use (Tufts, 2004; Nordman, Piette, Kinney, & Webber, 1997). To correct these misconceptions public awareness campaigns are needed to inform people and

encourage them to shut down their computers at night and on weekends, and to put their monitor and computer into standby when not in use during the day.

Tufts University in Boston, Massachusetts, is one example of an institution that has been making a concerted effort to reduce its energy consumption, having identified IT as a prime contributor to its rising use of electricity in recent years (Tufts, n.d.). It has adopted a combination of technological and behavioral strategies. On the technical side, CRT monitors are being gradually replaced with LCD screens, technical staff routinely enable power management features on all desktops where possible, and an investigation is being carried out into remote switching off of computers from a central server. Its behavioral approach has focused on the distribution of a brochure to all students, academics, and other staff to inform them of the facts about IT and energy usage, and to advise them of practical energy-saving methods.

The ethical motivations behind the Tufts campaign are a mixture of environmental concerns and utilitarian considerations since they aim to "save much money and energy and reduce CO2 emissions." Computer-generated electricity consumption is calculated both in terms of CO_2 *and* cost. This demonstrates that environmentally sound use of ICT and organizational efficiency often overlap (Waage, Shah, & Girshik, 2003). The brochure that Tufts developed for distribution also appeals to a mixture of motivations, although the overwhelming emphasis is on the environment: half of the text is devoted to a discussion on global warming and the reader is exhorted to "Be a climate hero!" (Tufts, 2004). There is an appeal to both human-centered and life-centered environmental concerns: "Our health [human-centered] and the health of the global ecosystem [life-centered] is in danger" (Tufts, 2004).

Paper Usage Management

IT is potentially paper-saving. Yet the dream of the paperless office in the 1970s and 1980s has evaporated, and the number of printers worldwide and paper usage levels have increased dramatically (Sellen & Harper, 2002). Eliminating paper is probably unrealistic, given that it fulfils important legal, psychological, and aesthetic functions (Aber, 2003). Like energy usage management, changes to paper use can be driven by technology or

brought about by behavior modification supported by organizational policies (Hardy et al., 2005):

- **Technological Approaches**
  - **Double-sided printing:** Double-sided printing is potentially a way of halving paper use, particularly if made the default printer setting.
- **Behavioral and Policy Approaches**
  - **Charges for printing and photocopying:** Charging for paper use is an effective solution, particularly for public access machines or for students. However, charges may be unacceptable for employees, who are likely to view their paper usage as part of their job.
  - **Setting quotas:** Allowing a reasonable quota of free copies before charges become applicable may be acceptable where charging for every copy is not feasible.
  - **Public awareness:** Establishing guidelines against wasteful printing and communicating these to users can appeal to their sense of environmental ethics. Posters placed near printers and photocopiers are an appropriate way of conveying the message.

The University of Technology, Sydney has experimented with a range of technological and behavioral solutions to manage paper more effectively. From 1997 to 2001 paper and toner usage increased by 69% in student computer labs, but dropped dramatically thereafter (Greenfield, 2002). Successful measures were the introduction of paid printing as well as computer logons to prevent people outside the university using the computers and the high-speed laser printers that run off of them (Hardy et al., 2005). Attempts to introduce double-sided printing as the default have met some resistance, mainly because teaching staff prefer to read assignments on single-sided paper. The Faculty of IT at UTS has a slightly different, but nevertheless effective approach, which was adopted after consultations with students and academics about nine years ago: IT students are allowed a semester quota of 75 single-sided copies, which they can use for assignments, and 200 "draft" sheets, which zoom two pages of printing onto each side of a double-sided sheet. After the quota is exhausted, students must pay. This measure has placed a limit on printing while providing a good level of service. Other measures include extensive paper recycling, reusing the back of old pages as note paper, paid photocopying for students at the library, e-mailed library renewal notices rather than paper ones, and posters announcing the university's "Acceptable Use of Information Technology Facilities" guidelines, which include a section requiring users not to waste paper (Hardy et al., 2005).

These strategies have reduced costs to the university. Though the popularity of recycling bins, scrap paper reuse, and double-sided printing demonstrate that students and staff are genuinely concerned about the environment, some managers believe that cutting costs is a primary consideration for the university, and that likewise cost saving is a priority for students (Hardy et al., 2005). Yet, despite this, those involved speak proudly of the estimated 4,542 trees they saved in one year alone (McInerney, 2003). Generally the university takes a human-centered ethical approach, recognizing the value of the environment to humans, and incorporating environmental policies and practices into those which serve other legitimate aims of the university.

FUTURE TRENDS

With increasing industrialization of the Third World and growing demands for IT in many countries which previously had little technological access, the potential environmental impact of computers is forecast to grow. Against this, however, is the rapid evolution of computer technology which may well provide solutions to the problems created to date. For example, changes to the LCD screen manufacturing process, which led to a sharp price decline, have made this more energy-efficient technology much more accessible. Moreover, ethical solutions will be needed, such as increased reuse of computers by poorer people to overcome the digital divide. This might include donating old computers to developing nations, provided that proper disposal mechanisms are in place to prevent these countries from becoming a dumping ground for unwanted hardware. No doubt many more solutions will arise to address the problems created by the technology.

CONCLUSION

In this article the management of the environmental consequences of IT has been analyzed with respect to three major areas: hardware disposal, reduction of computer-generated energy consumption, and management of paper usage. The experience from the university sector shows that environmental considerations are an important factor in all three areas in providing a framework for conceptualizing desirable behavior.

However, managers also operate in a way to maximize the benefits to their organizations. Furthermore, they believe that, at times, self-interest is important in leveraging users' environmental concerns: dollar savings to the user from conserving paper or electricity are a significant part of campaigns and strategies to bring about a better outcome for the environment and the organization. Policies based purely on appeals to users' ethical interest in the environment are more likely to be successful if reinforced by a regard for more utilitarian considerations. Duncan (n.d.) sums it up in his definition of environmental sustainability from the point of view of the organization: sustainability requires simultaneously meeting "the 'triple bottom line'—increasing profits, improving the planet and improving the lives of people." Provided that all three elements are taken into account, organizations can achieve progress in ameliorating the effects of computer technology on the environment.

REFERENCES

Aber, R. (2003, October, 13). *Pining for a paperless office—some tips for minimizing your paper glut.* Retrieved May 5, 2006, from http://www.entrepreneur.com/article/0,4621,311323,00.html

Beatty, R. (2002). ComputerAid and the landfill menace. *PC Update,* (June). Retrieved September 9, 2003, from http://www.melbpc.org.au/pcupdate/2206/2206article9.htm

Binswanger, M. (2001). Technological progress and sustainable development: What about the rebound effect? *Ecological Economics, 36*(1), 119-132.

Duncan, A. (n.d.). *The definition of sustainability depends on who is speaking.* Retrieved May 5, 2006, from http://oregonfuture.oregonstate.edu/part1/pf1_02.html

EIA (Energy Information Association). (2003). *Computers and photocopiers in commercial buildings.* Retrieved May 3, 2006, from http://www.eia.doe.gov/emeu/cbecs/pc_copier/pccopier99.html

Hardy, V., Fung, H.C., Xian, G.S., Wu, J.H., Zhang, X.Z., & Dyson, L.E. (2005, December 13-15). Paper usage management and information technology: An environmental case study at an Australian university. *Proceedings of the IBIMA Conference on Internet & Information Technology in Modern Organizations* (pp. 699-705), Cairo, Egypt.

Landale, K., Nguyen, P., Hoque, R., Lee, S.K., & Shin, H.K. (2004). What UTS does with its old computers and what they should do. In G. Abraham & R.I.P. Rubenstein (Eds.), *Proceedings of the 2nd Australian Undergraduate Students' Computing Conference* (pp. 113-119).

McInerney, S. (2003). Saving thousands of trees. *UTS News, 3*(March 24-April 6).

Nordman, B., Piette, M.A., Kinney, K., & Webber, C. (1997). *User guide to power management for PCs and monitors.* Lawrence Berkeley National Laboratory, University of California, USA.

Reiss, M. (2002). Introduction to ethics and bioethics. In J. Bryant, L. Baggot la Velle, & J. Searle (Eds.), *Bioethics for scientists* (pp. 3-17). Chichester, UK: John Wiley & Sons.

Resource NSW. (2001, October). *Computer hardware recovery.* Retrieved November 19, 2004, from http://www.resource.nsw.gov.au/publications.htm#comphardware

Sellen, A., & Harper, R. (2002). *The myth of the paperless office.* London: MIT Press.

Southgate, C. (2002). Introduction to environmental ethics. In J. Bryant, L. Baggot la Velle, & J. Searle (Eds.), *Bioethics for scientists* (pp. 39-55). Chichester, UK: John Wiley & Sons.

Taylor, P.W. (1996). The ethics of respect for nature. In R.A. Larmer (Ed.), *Ethics in the workplace: Selected readings in business ethics* (pp. 574-587). Minneapolis: West.

Tufts. (2004). *Tufts climate initiative computer brochure.* Retrieved May 3, 2006, from http://www.tufts.edu/tie/tci/Computers.html

Tufts. (n.d.). *Computers & energy efficiency.* Retrieved May 3, 2006, from http://www.tufts.edu/tie/tci/Computers.html

Waage, S., Shah, R., & Girshick, S. (2003). Information technology and sustainability: Enabling the future. *Corporate Environmental Strategy: International Journal of Corporate Sustainability, 10*(4), 81-95.

KEY TERMS

Environmental Ethics: Beliefs and guidelines regarding how humans should act with respect to the environment in order to maximize the well-being of other species and the planet.

Environmental Sustainability: An environmental goal whereby energy and materials used in the manufacture or operation of computer hardware are derived from renewable resources.

Human-Centered Environmental Ethics: An ethical approach which has as its central tenet that the environment should be protected principally because humans derive benefit from it.

Intergenerational Environmental Approach: An approach to environmental ethics which takes into account the needs of future generations.

Interspecific Environmental Approach: An approach to environmental ethics which takes into account the needs of other species.

Life-Centered Environmental Ethics: An ethical approach which has as its central tenet that other forms of life have an inherent worth separate from their usefulness to human beings.

Paper Usage Management: Management practices that seek to control the amount of paper used by computer printers and photocopiers.

M

Paperless Office: A theory, common in the early days of desktop computers, that digital storage and transmission of documents would eliminate the need for hard copies.

Recycling: The taking apart of computer hardware no longer in use in order to reuse parts or materials.

Utilitarian: Of material benefit or usefulness to humans, particularly to the majority.

Measuring Ethical Reasoning of IT Professionals and Students

Mohammad Abdolmohammadi
Bentley College, USA

Jane Fedorowicz
Bentley College, USA

INTRODUCTION

Information technology (IT) professionals are entrusted with the design, implementation, and operation of the information systems that support key business processes within organizations. Many organizational stakeholders such as management, investors, and regulators expect these professionals to act ethically, as these systems must accurately reflect all business activity. This expectation has been particularly heightened in the early 2000s due to the substantial business scandals in the United States, Europe, and elsewhere. For example, in 2001 fraudulent financial practices by the now defunct U.S. energy trading company, Enron, rocked the financial markets so hard that the Congress of the United States enacted sweeping reforms in 2002 through the Sarbanes-Oxley Act (SOX, 2002). As McLean and Elkind (2004) observe, this law includes several provisions aimed at ensuring the integrity of information and business process support in organizational information systems. Concerns about unethical business activity are not endemic to the United States, as exemplified by the financial frauds unearthed at the Italian food distribution company, Parmalat, and the Dutch international supermarket company, Royal Ahold.

With increased reliance on IT professionals to support and record business process activity, companies must be able to expect ethical behavior by those they charge with this responsibility. However, it is not always clear how their ethical behavior can be measured. The purpose of this essay is to describe instruments to measure ethical reasoning of IT professionals. In particular, we describe a generally supported model in the literature (Rest, 1994) that posits that ethical reasoning is a key component of ethical behavior that can be measured, and which is also significantly correlated with ethical action (see Thoma, 1994, for a review).

BACKGROUND

As entry-level IT professionals, graduates of business schools often have taken a course in ethics as part of their management curriculum (Peppas & Diskin, 2001). It is otherwise rare for students preparing for IT careers to be exposed to ethics in their major's courses. And yet upon graduation, their employers expect them to design and use technology in an ethical manner in their personal and professional lives. Many of these students pass professional IT exams, gain experience, and join professional associations such as the Association for Computing Machinery (ACM) or the Institute of Electrical and Electronics Engineers (IEEE). As members, they are asked to adhere to the respective codes of conduct of their professional bodies (Anonymous, 1993; Gotterbarn, Miller, & Rogerson, 1999; Rogerson, Weckert, & Simpson, 2000). However, while adherence to these codes fulfills membership requirements, it does not necessarily ensure ethical reasoning or behavior by IT professionals (Oz, 1992; Harrington, 1996).

Should we just assume that IT professionals know how to act ethically? Can information system (IS) students be taught to make ethical decisions? These questions have puzzled researchers for many years, harking back to Mason's (1986) landmark article in which he identified privacy, ownership, access, and accuracy as the four main ethical issues of concern to IT professionals. Since then, many researchers have studied various aspects of ethical behavior by IT professionals and students (Grupe, 2003; Harrington, 1996; Kreie & Cronan, 2000), and several books now support the teaching of IT ethics in college (cf., Mason, Mason, & Culnan, 1995; Schultz, 2005; Spinello, 2002, 2004). In fact, since 2002 ethics has been included as an important analytical and critical reasoning capability of the IS Model Curriculum and is listed as a topic in two of the courses (cf., Gorgone et al., 2003).

MAIN FOCUS OF ARTICLE

In order to measure the ethical reasoning of IT professionals and students, one can use ethics assessment tools. Before describing a specific instrument for assessing ethical reasoning, we describe the model of ethical behavior that it is designed to support. According to a widely accepted model (Rest, 1994), ethical behavior is dependent on four components:

1. **Moral Sensitivity:** The ability to interpret a moral situation and be able to sense its ethical undertone.
2. **Moral Reasoning:** The ability to judge actions as morally right or wrong.
3. **Moral Motivation:** The ability to prioritize moral values over other values.
4. **Moral Character:** Having the courage, persistence, and implementation skills to overcome distractions and to make the right moral decision.

The literature indicates that each of these four components is positively associated with ethical behavior, and that to ensure moral action, IT professionals must possess all four. Thus, there is a need for measures for each of these components of moral action. However, only the moral reasoning component has a well-developed theory and measurement scale. The theory is called Cognitive Developmental Theory of Ethics, developed by Lawrence Kohlberg (1981). The measurement instrument based on this theory is known as the Defining Issues Test (DIT), developed by James Rest (1986) of the University of Minnesota's Center for the Study of Ethical Development.

Kohlberg's theory has three levels of moral development with each level subdivided into two stages. Each of the six stages is 'higher' than previous stages of ethical development. The first level is called the Pre-Conventional level. It refers to the self-centered ethics of convenience. For example, the individual obeys rules to avoid punishment (Stage 1) or to gain personal rewards from others (Stage 2).

The second level is called the Conventional level, where the individual adheres to the ethics of confor-

mity. For example, the individual may exhibit group loyalty (Stage 3) or follow national law and order (Stage 4). The highest level in Kohlberg's theory is the Post-Conventional level, where the individual follows principle-based ethics of conviction. Written ethics of social contract and utilitarianism comprise Stage 5, while unwritten global principles of justice, duties, and human rights comprise Stage 6.

The six-stage theory just outlined requires a measurement system. Since the higher stages indicate higher-order ethical reasoning, it is most desirable to measure individual standings at the highest stages. The DIT is a popular and reliable instrument for this purpose. According to Rest (1986, p. 196), the DIT is based on the premise that people at different points of development interpret moral dilemmas differently, define the critical issues of the dilemmas differently, and have intuitions about what is right and fair in a situation. Differences in the way that dilemmas are defined therefore are taken as indications of their underlying tendencies to organize social experience. These underlying structures of meaning are not necessarily apparent to a subject as articulative rule systems or verbalized philosophies—rather, they may work 'behind the scenes' and may seem to be based on common sense or appear intuitively obvious.

The original full version of the DIT has six cases and 72 questions. It is a self-administered, multiple-choice questionnaire, where each case presents a moral dilemma and is accompanied by 12 questions that are designed to measure different schemes of fairness. Using a four-level scale (much importance, some, little, or none), the individual taking the DIT indicates the importance of each item in the resolution of the dilemma. The resulting summary measure is called the P-score, which reflects moral reasoning at Kohlberg's Post-Conventional level ethics of conviction. The measure falls between 1 and 99, where the higher the P-score, the higher the level of moral reasoning.

The DIT instrument has been used in thousands of studies of professionals worldwide where it has been shown to have widespread reliability. Rest (1994, p. 13) summarizes the results of many studies, and reports that the "test-retest correlation of the DIT (over a period of several weeks) averages in the .80s, and the internal reliability of the DIT also averages in the .80s (Chronbach's Alpha)." In addition, the DIT P-score has consistently shown positive and statistically significant correlations with moral behavior. For example, a review study of prior literature reports that on average, moral reasoning explains 10-15% of the variation in ethical behavior (Thoma, 1994, p. 201).

As a generic instrument, the DIT measures levels of ethical reasoning by IT professionals and students. Its P-scores can be used for benchmarking as well as for investigating the relationship between reasoning and behavior in IT shops, making it a useful performance measure for ethics researchers. It could also be used in a classroom setting to assess the validity of ethics-based curricula and pedagogy.

However, the DIT instrument is not without limitation. For example, the DIT instrument does not address internally focused ethical issues such as pride, productiveness, and rationality. Also, we note that the DIT is not the only instrument available for measuring ethical reasoning, although it is the most widely used. Other instruments in the literature include Kohlberg's (1981) Moral Judgment Interview, and Reidenbach and Robin's (1990) Multidimensional Ethics Scale. Due to their subjectivity and inefficiency, these scales have not been as widely adopted in the literature as the DIT.

FUTURE TRENDS

Recently, the Center for the Study of Ethical Development (2006) at the University of Minnesota introduced a modified version of the DIT called DIT-2. The center indicates that DIT-2 is shorter, has clearer instructions, purges fewer subjects for bogus data, and is slightly more powerful on validity criteria than DIT-1. While DIT-2 has not been subjected to as much empirical testing as DIT-1, it may prove to be preferable over DIT-1 due to the advantages just indicated. Also, given the specialized nature of IT practice, there may be a need for development of specialized instruments to more accurately measure ethical reasoning of IT professionals. While we are not aware of any such instrument in the literature, we note that scholars have developed customized instruments for measurement of ethical reasoning in some other fields. For example, Thorne (2000) has introduced an accounting-based instrument, while Massey (2002) has introduced a specialized auditing-based instrument.

CONCLUSION

As influential people in organizations, IT professionals are expected to adhere to the highest levels of ethical action. As members of IT-oriented professional societies, they agree to abide by a code of ethics that is aimed at governing their behavior in the workplace. However, research has shown that ethical behavior depends on individual inclinations, and that external codes cannot assure moral action on their own. Ethical action is dependent on four factors of ethical sensitivity, reasoning, motivation, and character, and is a complex construct to measure. In this article we introduced a generic instrument, called the Defining Issues Test, that has been used widely to measure ethical reasoning. The DIT can be used to assess affinity toward ethical reasoning in both students and IT professionals, and researchers have used it to investigate its correlation with ethical behavior in the classroom and the workplace.

An updated DIT (DIT-2) has been proposed by the Center for the Study of Ethical Development at the University of Minnesota that may be used by IT professionals. In addition, IT-specific instruments can be developed for more accurate assessment. Research is needed to develop measures for the other three components of ethical action (i.e., ethical sensitivity, ethical motivation, and ethical character) to provide all inputs for a comprehensive measurement of ethical action by IT professionals.

REFERENCES

Anonymous. (1993). ACM code of ethics and professional conduct. *Communications of the ACM, 36*(2), 99-105.

Center for the Study of Ethical Development. (2006). *DIT-2*. Retrieved from http://www.centerforthestudyofethicaldevelopment.net/DIT2.htm

Gorgone, J.T., Valacich, J.S., Feinstein, D.L., Davis, G.B., Topi, H., & Longenecker, H.E. Jr. (2003). IS 2002 model curriculum and guidelines for undergraduate degree programs in information systems. *Communications of the AIS, 11*(1). Retrieved from http://cais.isworld.org/articles/11-1/default.asp?View=Journal&x=64&y=3

Gotterbarn, D., Miller, K., & Rogerson, S. (1999). Software engineering code of ethics is approved. *Communications of the ACM, 42*(10), 102-107.

Grupe, F. (2003). Information systems professionals and conflict of interest. *Information Management and Computer Security, 11*(1), 28-32.

Harrington, S.J. (1996). The effect of codes of ethics and personal denial of responsibility on computer abuse judgments and intentions. *MIS Quarterly, 20*(September), 257-278.

Kohlberg, L. (1981). *The philosophy of moral development: Moral stages and the idea of justice.* San Francisco: Harper & Row.

Kreie, J., & Cronan, T.P. (2000). Making ethical decisions. *Communications of the ACM, 43*(12), 66-71.

Mason, R.O. (1986). Four ethical issues of the information age. *MIS Quarterly, 10*(March), 5-12.

Mason, R.O., Mason, F.M., & Culnan, M.J. (1995). *Ethics of information management.* Thousand Oaks, CA: Sage.

Massey, D. (2002). The importance of context in investigating auditors' moral abilities. *Research on Accounting Ethics, 8,* 195-247.

McLean, B., & Elkind, P. (2004). *Smartest guys in the room: The amazing rise and scandalous fall of Enron.* New York: Portfolio.

Oz, E. (1992). Ethical standards for information systems professionals: A case for a unified code. *MIS Quarterly, 16*(4), 423-433.

Peppas, S.C., & Diskin, B.A. (2001). College courses in ethics: Do they really make a difference? *The International Journal of Educational Management, 15*(7), 347-353.

Reidenbach, R.E., & Robin, D.P. (1990). Toward the development of a multidimensional scale for improving evaluations of business ethics. *Journal of Business Ethics, 9,* 639-653.

Rest, J. (1986). *Moral development: Advances in research and theory.* New York: Praeger.

Rest, J.R. (1994). Background: Theory and research. In J.R. Rest & D. Narvaez (Eds.), *Moral development in the professions* (pp. 1-26). Hillsdale, NJ: Lawrence Erlbaum.

Rogerson, S., Weckert, J., & Simpson, C. (2000). An ethical review of information systems development: The Australian Computer Society's code of ethics and SSADM. *Information, Technology and People, 13*(2), 121-136.

Schultz, R.A. (2005). *Contemporary issues in ethics and information technology.* Hershey, PA: IRM Press.

SOX. (2002). *Sarbanes Oxley Act of 2002.* One Hundred Seventh Congress of the United States of America.

Spinello, R.A. (2002). *Case studies in information technology ethics.* Upper Saddle River, NJ: Prentice Hall.

Spinello, R.A. (2004). *Readings in cyberethics* (2nd ed.). Boston: Jones and Bartlett.

Thoma, S. (1994). Moral judgments and moral action. In J.R. Rest & D. Narvaez (Eds.), *Moral development in the professions* (pp. 199-211). Hillsdale, NJ: Lawrence Erlbaum.

Thorne, L. (2000). The development of two measures to assess accountants' prescriptive and deliberative moral reasoning. *Behavioral Research in Accounting, 12,* 139-169.

KEY TERMS

Code of Ethics: Statement of personal responsibility and commitment reflecting adherence to a set of principles or obligations that is shared by all members of a professional society, company, or other formal group.

Cognitive Developmental Theory of Ethics: A theory based on cognitive psychology that posits that ethical reasoning improves in stages over time. Thus age and education improve ethical reasoning. The theory was developed by Lawrence Kohlberg (1981).

Defining Issues Test (DIT): A psychometric test that uses ethical dilemmas to elicit responses from individuals. From these responses the DIT measures levels of ethical reasoning. It is a product of the Center for the Study of Ethical Development at the University of Minnesota.

IT Professionals: Organizational staff charged with the design, implementation, and operation of information and communication technology.

Moral Reasoning: The ability to judge actions as morally right or wrong.

P-Score or Principled-Score: This is a score between 1-99 that indicates one's ethical reasoning at Kohlberg's (1981) Post-Conventional ethics of conviction.

Meta View of Information Ethics

Charles R. Crowell
University of Notre Dame, USA

Robert N. Barger
University of Notre Dame, USA

INTRODUCTION

That computing and information systems give rise to specific ethical issues related to the appropriate uses of such technology is a viewpoint that, according to Bynum (2001a), is traceable at least as far back as Norbert Wiener's seminal work in the 1950s (Wiener, 1954). From this important idea, a field of inquiry emerged that came to be known as "computer ethics" (Maner, 1980). As with many emerging fields, however, scholarly debate arose as to how "computer ethics" should best be defined (cf. Bynum, 2001b). While various distinct positions have been advanced in this regard (e.g., Moor, 1985; Johnson, 2001), a broad characterization of the field is that "computer ethics" deals with the personal and social impacts of information technology, along with the ethical considerations that arise from such impacts (Bynum, 2001b). More recent views localize "computer ethics" within a still broader philosophical domain of "information ethics" (Floridi & Sanders, 2002).

In this article it is not our aim to review historical or current developments in the field of information ethics, per se. Rather, our goal is to discuss an important but somewhat neglected aspect of this field: namely, its "metaethics." In its broadest sense, metaethics can be defined as the generic name for inquiries about the source of moral judgments as well as about how such judgments are to be justified (Barger, 2001). Positioned in this way, metaethics is not about isolated individual judgments concerning whether certain actions are right or wrong. Rather, it is about how one's particular worldview, also known as a "Weltanschauung," is propaedeutic to the formulation of such ethical judgments. A person's worldview is his or her own collection of beliefs about reality and existence, which can be multifaceted including beliefs relating to whether human nature is fundamentally good or evil, whether absolute standards of conduct exist, whether there is a supreme power in the universe, and so forth.

In philosophy, the study of being and existence is called "metaphysics." This very term, derived from its Greek roots, connotes a higher or more advanced (meta) understanding of reality (physics). A personal metaphysical position is basically equivalent to someone's worldview or fundamental beliefs about reality (Barger, 2001). Metaphysics is described here as a set of "beliefs" because it is based on ideas that cannot be proven or verified.

Aristotle called metaphysics "first principles" (McKeon, 1968) in deference to the notion that a foundation of meaning is prerequisite to the interpretation of any particular events or actions within the larger universe of that meaning. The reason more than one metaphysics exists is that different people adopt different personal explanations of reality. Once a personal metaphysical worldview is adopted, that view inevitably influences personal decisions about ethical matters (Barger, 2001). It is in this sense, then, that a person's view of reality is propaedeutic to one's stand on value questions.

As others have noted, several traditional philosophical positions exist that commonly influence personal metaphysics and ethical decision making (Barger, 2001; Johnson, 2001). The purpose of the next section is to review those positions along with their primary ethical implications.

BACKGROUND: MAJOR METAPHYSICAL POSITIONS AND THEIR ETHICS

Idealism

The term "idealism" applies to a collection of metaphysical positions, all of which share a common notion that the mental realm predominates over the physical (Wikipedia, 2006). Many philosophers (e.g., Socrates,

Plato, Berkeley, Kant) have emphasized the primacy of mentality because they believed the mind to be the only means by which human experience occurs. In this view, humans can have no direct experience of physical objects, only mental perceptions (i.e., "ideas") of objects fueled by the senses. This has led some idealists to question whether or not anything other than the mental realm really exists. It is in this sense, then, that idealism elevates mentality, which it holds to be a uniquely human quality, to a position of preeminent importance. Only ideas are thought to be able to achieve a kind of perfection or "ideal" form; the physical realm, if it exists at all, is flawed, imperfect, and subject to degradation over time. Ideas, on the other hand, can achieve a kind of timeless, universal quality that physical objects cannot.

Idealism gives rise to a form of "deontological" or duty-based ethics perhaps epitomized in the work of Immanuel Kant (Johnson, 2001). Kant believed that because the essence of human nature was its rationality, a code of conduct was required befitting that essence. Accordingly, Kant proposed several forms of what he called the "Categorical Imperative" as the universal standard for human action. The first form emphasized its universality: "Act only on that maxim by which you can at the same time will that it should become a universal law" (Kant, 1993). In other words, if you wish to establish a particular ethical standard, you must be willing to agree that it would also be right for anyone else to follow it. As Barger (2001) indicates, this form is very close to what is commonly known from the New Testament as the "golden rule."

A second form of the Categorical Imperative emphasizes the dignity of human nature that derives from its mentality: "Act so that you treat humanity, whether in your own person or in that of another, always as an end and never as a means only" (Kant, 1993). Reflected in this form is the notion that because each human is a rational being, all humans should be treated in a manner respectful of this quality (Johnson, 2001). Like the timeless perfection of ideas, idealist moral imperatives are *a priori* and absolute. That is, these imperatives do not admit of exceptions and are stated in terms of "always" or "never." For example: "Always tell the truth" or "Never tell a lie."

Realism

This metaphysical position, also known as naturalism (Barger, 2001), holds that reality is material, natural, and physical. As such, reality is quantitative, measurable, governed by the laws of nature, and subject to the operation of cause and effect. The universe, according to the realist, is one of natural design and order in which matter takes precedence over mentality. For some realists, if the mind exists at all, it can be explained by physical mechanisms like brain functions (Searle, 2000).

The resultant ethical position that flows from a realistic metaphysics holds that conformity with nature is good. Therefore, people should strive to promote habits that would, for example, enhance personal health (by exercising, not smoking, etc.), or protect our environment and its resources (by not polluting, recycling, etc.). In a sense, realism leads to its own form of deontological ethics with a universal mandate derived from a more natural law: live in harmony with nature.

Pragmatism

Within a pragmatic metaphysics, reality is not so easily localized in the mental or physical realms as it is for the idealist and realist. The pragmatist finds meaning neither in ideas nor things, but rather believes that reality is a process, a dynamic coming-to-be instead of a static state of being. Reality is to be found in change, activity, interaction, and experience. Since change is ubiquitous, nothing can have a permanent essence or identity. The only constant is change, and the only absolute is that there are no absolutes!

Pragmatism leads to a form of utilitarian ethics (Barger, 2001; Johnson, 2001) in that all moral values must be tested and proven in practice since nothing is intrinsically good or bad. If certain actions work to achieve a socially desirable end, then these actions are ethical and good. Consequences, therefore, define good and evil on this view. The maxim that follows from this pragmatic ethics is that "the end justifies the means." That is, if an act is useful for achieving some laudable goal, then it becomes good. Accordingly, a means has no intrinsic absolute value, but only gains value relative to its usefulness for achieving some desired result.

Results or consequences are the ultimate "measure" of goodness for a pragmatist, since the usefulness of a means to an end can only be judged after the fact by the effects of that means. Thus, for the pragmatist, there can be no assurance that any action is good until it is tried. Even then, its goodness is only held tentatively, as long as it continues to work. If ever there is a dispute about which ends should be pursued and which means are more effective for achieving an end, the pragmatist looks for guidance from the group since collective wisdom is more highly esteemed than that of an individual. Since the group is valued more than the individual, the pragmatist strives for "the greatest good for the greatest number" (Barger, 2001).

Existentialism

The existentialist joins with the pragmatist in rejecting the belief that reality is *a priori* and fixed. But, unlike a pragmatic emphasis on the controlling group, the existentialist holds that reality must be defined by each autonomous individual. The existentialist notions of "subjectivity" and "phenomenological self" imply that the meaning or surdity of an otherwise "absurd" universe is individually determined (Sartre, 1992). Any meaning attached to the world must be put there by the individual and it will be valid only for that individual. Thus, each person's world and self-identity is the product of that person's own choices. In a sense, each person can be defined as the sum of his or her choices. It follows, therefore, that reality is different for each individual. We each live in our own world and are determined/defined by our choices.

An existentialist worldview also leads to a kind of utilitarian ethics in which moral values are individualized through personal rather than group choices. Each personal choice reflects a preference for one alternative over others. Anyone who makes a choice freely and "authentically" (Sartre, 1992) is therefore acting in a moral fashion. This aspect of existentialism is reminiscent of Polonius's advice to his son in Shakespeare's *Hamlet*: "To thine ownself be true" (Act I, Scene iii). As some have suggested (e.g., Onof, 2004), existentialism, especially as presented by Sartre (1992), may represent a form of relativistic moral imperative with the same kind of universality that characterizes Kant's Categorical Imperative.

Blended Worldviews

No person's actions are governed all the time by just one worldview (Barger & Barger, 1989). The possibility of "blended worldviews" has led some writers to posit guidelines for dealing with ethical dilemmas that appear to be derived from multiple metaphysical positions. Donn Parker (cited in Rifkin, 1991, p. 84), for example, offers several "guidelines for action" that seem at first glance to include both idealistic and pragmatic elements. Parker's seemingly idealistic guideline is something he calls the "Kantian Universality Rule," which states: "If an act or failure to act is not right for everyone to commit, then it is not right for anyone to commit" (Rifkin, 1991). This Universality Rule is just an alternate formulation of the Categorical Imperative discussed above. Another of Parker's guidelines is called "The Higher Ethic," which states: "Take the action that achieves the greater good" (Rifkin, 1991). This maxim appears to be an instance of the pragmatic motto we discussed earlier. Whatever the exact philosophical analysis of Parker's guidelines may prove to be, the fact that they are in sync with seemingly different worldviews could enhance their practical usefulness for ethical decision making among those with a "blended" metaphysics.

IMPLICATIONS FOR THREE COMPUTING-RELATED ETHICAL DILEMMAS

The different worldviews noted above seem to offer divergent solutions for many possible ethical information technology-related dilemmas. We select but three hypothetical dilemmas for purposes of illustration. They have to do with piracy, privacy, and authority-deception. While these examples are set in an educational context, we think they are readily transferable to other settings.

Our argument here is that any divergence in the "ethically correct" solutions to these dilemmas can be traced rather directly to the seemingly different ethical standards associated with each separate worldview. Due to space limitations, we will consider two hypothetical response alternatives for each dilemma: a deontological or "absolutist" type of solution and a "relativist" utilitarian solution.

Piracy

First consider piracy, a common ethical dilemma in today's digital world, involving wrongful appropriation of computing resources. As an example, suppose someone uses a personal account on a university's mainframe computer for something that has no direct relation to university business. Such use could involve anything from sending a personal e-mail message to a friend, to conducting a full-blown private business on the computer (billing, payroll, inventory, etc.). Is there anything unethical about such computer usage?

An absolutist position would likely say that the above-described activities are indeed unethical—whether only the e-mail message is involved or the larger-scale business activities (although an absolutist would recognize a difference between the two in the degree of wrong being done)—provided that such use is prohibited by the university's published computer utilization policies. The guiding principle here would be based on the purposes for which the university (i.e., the computing-resource owner) intended the computer to be used. Any utilization for purposes other than what was intended, as specified in the usage policy, would be unethical.

On the other hand, a relativist might say that only the full-scale business activities really were unethical because they tied up too much memory and slowed down the machine's operation, thereby depriving other legitimate users of access to, or reasonable performance of, the computing resources in question. However, the personal e-mail message might not be unethical because it represented no significant drag on operations or no deprivation of services/performance for other legitimate users. The guiding principle here is consequences or harm: no harm, no foul.

Privacy

Next consider a dilemma having to do with privacy. Suppose a student enters a public computer lab on campus and encounters a machine still logged into the account of another student who forgot to log off when she left. The student decides to access the personal files of this account owner that are available on the system. Is this behavior unethical?

An absolutist position would maintain that the behavior was unethical because the only person who is entitled to access someone's personal files is the owner of those files, unless the owner knowingly grants permission to others.

A relativist position would be based on the consequences. If the intrusive student logged the account owner off the system after snooping around and never revealed to anyone any confidential information he or she may have seen, then no harm would be done. So, it could be argued that the intrusive student's snooping was not unethical. But, if that student passed on any personal or confidential information about the account owner, then unethical action could be involved since potential harm might result.

Authority-Deception

Finally, let us look at a dilemma involving what may arguably be regarded as an abuse of power by authority, but which certainly involves at least an instance of deception. A student is strongly suspected by his university of a major "fair-use" computer-policy violation involving a hoax e-mail allegedly being sent by the student under the name of a prominent administrator. This e-mail proved to be exceedingly disruptive to student affairs until it was identified as being fraudulent. The student suspect, though not a professional hacker, was adept enough to cover his electronic tracks well. However, the administration decided to confront the student and falsely inform him that they had hired an outside expert whose skills were sufficient to uncover electronic evidence of the student's perpetration of the hoax. The suspect thus was being deceived in an effort to force an admission of responsibility, which the student eventually did provide. Did the administration behave unethically in this instance?

An absolutist position would maintain that lying under any circumstances is wrong. This follows, of course, from an idealist emphasis on the universal importance of truth. A relativist could argue, however, that the "end justified the means" in this case. The "greater good" was being served by any means used to identify the perpetrator, dispense a severe penalty, and hopefully deter future instances of similar computer-use violations.

CONCLUSION AND FUTURE TRENDS

There is little doubt that technology use will continue to escalate. As it does, so will the potential for ethical dilemmas arising from such use. While there is some controversy about whether technology-based ethical dilemmas are unique, or merely instances of age-old moral questions (Johnson, 2001), it is clear that ethics must be an ever-increasing focus of our educational system at all levels.

The field of moral psychology may have much to offer in this regard. As those who study the process of moral development formulate and test theories about various psychological and behavioral factors contributing to ethical decision making, it becomes possible to consider whether or not and to what extent technology may impact those factors (cf. Crowell, Narvaez, & Gomberg, 2005). Such efforts may help to illuminate the educational practices and tools that will be needed to effectively prepare students to understand and resolve technology-related ethical dilemmas. Moreover, it is of continuing importance to explore how metaethical analysis may be helpful in understanding and promoting moral education and personal development.

REFERENCES

Barger, R.N. (2001). *Philosophical belief systems.* Retrieved April 23, 2006, from http://www.nd.edu/~rbarger/philblfs.html

Barger, R.N., & Barger, J.C. (1989). *Do pragmatists choose business while idealists choose education?* Charleston: Eastern Illinois University. (ERIC Document Reproduction Service No. ED 317 904)

Bynum, T.W. (2001a). Computer ethics: Its birth and its future. *Ethics and Information Technology, 3,* 109-112.

Bynum, T.W. (2001b). Computer ethics: Basic concepts and historical overview. *The Stanford Encyclopedia of Philosophy.* Retrieved April 23, 2006, from http://plato.stanford.edu/archives/win2001/entries/ethics-computer/

Crowell, C.R., Narvaez, D., & Gomberg, A. (2005). Moral psychology and information ethics: The effects of psychological distance on the components of moral behavior in a digital world. In L.A. Freeman & A.G.

Peace (Eds.), *Information ethics: Privacy and intellectual property* (pp. 19-37). Hershey, PA: Idea Group.

Dewey, J. (1916). *Democracy and education.* New York: Macmillan.

Floridi, L., & Sanders, J.W. (2002). Mapping the foundationalist debate in computer ethics. *Ethics and Information Technology, 4,* 1-9.

Johnson, D.G. (2001). *Computer ethics* (3rd ed.). Upper Saddle River, NJ: Prentice Hall.

Kant, I. (1993). *Critique of practical reason and other writings* (L.W. Beck, Trans.). Chicago: University of Chicago Press. (Original work published 1788).

Maner, W. (1980). *Starter kit in computer ethics.* New York: Helvetia Press.

McKeon, R. (Ed.). (1968). *The basic works of Aristotle.* New York: Random House.

Moor, J.H. (1985). What is computer ethics? In T.W. Bynum (Ed.), *Computers and ethics* (pp. 255-275). Malden, MA: Blackwell.

Onof, C.J. (2004). Jean-Paul Sartre (1905-1980): Existentialism. *The Internet Encyclopedia of Philosophy.* Retrieved April 23, 2006, from http://www.iep.utm.edu/s/sartre-ex.htm

Rifkin, G. (1991). *The ethics gap, 25*(41), 83-85.

Sartre, J.-P. (1992). *Being and nothingness* (Hazel Barnes, Trans.). New York: Washington Square Press. (Original work published 1943).

Searle, J.R. (2000). Consciousness. *Annual Review of Neuroscience, 23,* 557-578.

Shakespeare, W. (n.d.). *Hamlet.* In C. Knight (Ed.), *The pictorial edition of the works of Shakespeare.* New York: P.F. Collier.

Wiener, N. (1954). *The human use of human beings: Cybernetics and society* (2nd ed.). Boston: Houghton Mifflin.

Wikipedia. (2006). *Idealism.* Retrieved April 23, 2006 from http://en.wikipedia.org/w/index.php?title=Idealism&oldid=49148606

KEY TERMS

Existentialism: A view that reality is not objective, rather it is subjective and must be constructed by each individual.

Idealism: A view that reality is ultimately grounded in the perfect, abstract, ideal world, the world of spirit and ideas.

Information Ethics: A field concerned with the personal and social impacts of information technology, along with the ethical concerns to which those impacts give rise.

Metaethics: The generic name for inquiries about the source of moral judgments (i.e., about their basis) as well as about how such judgments are to be justified.

Metaphysics: The branch of philosophy devoted to the study and analysis of reality and existence.

Pragmatism: A view suggesting that reality is not static in the sense of depending on absolute ideas or matter, but rather is ultimately "in process" and must be constantly probed and determined by social experimentation.

Realism: A view emphasizing the ultimate importance of the natural world, that is, the physical, material, sensible universe.

Worldview: A person's own assumptions about reality and existence; also known as a Weltanschauung or personal metaphysics.

Mitigation of Identity Theft in the Information Age

Reggie Becker
Emerson Electric, USA

Mark B. Schmidt
St. Cloud State University, USA

Allen C. Johnston
University of Louisana Monroe, USA

INTRODUCTION

The information age is characterized by unprecedented levels of information sharing, connectivity, and convenience. Along with the expediency afforded us by electronic commerce (e-commerce), online banking, e-mail reminders, and electronic government (e-government) services comes a degree of dependence on the information technology that drives these processes. Moreover, these processes are inherently insecure, thereby generating an unparalleled level of concern for computer security and identity theft, in particular. This article will discuss identity theft techniques and describe how readers can avoid it.

A familiar problem faced by numerous Americans each year, identity theft can be defined as "a situation where someone assumes the identity of another and makes telephone calls or obtains merchandise, credit, or other valuable things in their name" (Swartz, 2003, p. 17). The Federal Trade Commission estimates that each year 3.2 million American citizens have their identities stolen; equating to roughly one theft every ten seconds (IMJ Staff, 2005a). Prior to the emergence of today's highly interconnected world, identity thieves would employ a variety of techniques to obtain the personal information of their potential victims. These methods included such acts as dumpster diving, phone inquisitions, and social engineering.[1] While simplistic, these techniques were nonetheless effective. Today, however, we face a new type of criminal. This new criminal is more sophisticated than previous identity thieves and leverages the Internet to facilitate theft. For instance, today's criminals may design Web pages that compel users to offer personal information without thinking twice about it. Figure 1 depicts the common types of identity theft.

Figure 1. Sources of identity theft (adopted from Bidwell, 2002)

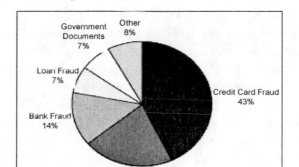

BACKGROUND

During the 1990s, the phenomenal growth of the Internet spurred a flurry of online consumer and business activity, and indirectly produced an influx of online identity theft and other forgeries. In fact, between 1990 and 2003, 33.4 million Americans reported themselves as victims of identity theft or fraud, with more than 13 million having fallen victim after January 2001 (Swartz, 2003). Additionally, based on information obtained in a 2003 Federal Trade Commission (FTC) survey, more than 10 million people had experienced identity theft in one from or another over the course of one year (Moye, 2006). These surveys give some indication of the reach of identity theft and the prolific nature of the problem.

Indeed, identity theft is not an isolated phenomenon. Figure 2 presents a list of the top ten states in terms of identity theft. As is evident by this figure, identity theft does not discriminate on the basis of geography, race, sex, or social standing. It is likely that if someone

Figure 2. Top ten states for ID theft (adapted from U.S. Ways and Means Committee, 2004)

Top Ten States for ID Theft Occurrences		
State	**Victims per 100,000 People**	**Number of Victims**
Arizona	122.4	6,832
Nevada	113.4	2,541
California	111.2	39,452
Texas	93.3	20,634
Florida	83.0	14,119
New York	82.4	15,821
Oregon	81.7	2,909
Colorado	81.3	3,698
Illinois	77.4	9,792
Washington	77.3	4,741

has not been victimized, they know someone that has. Moreover, the problem is likely to only worsen as more and more Americans become reliant on the Internet and technology to function effectively and efficiently within our information-based society.

Identity theft awareness and protection are clearly needed in the United States. The dissemination of information to various organizations and individuals is far too relaxed, with few controls regulating the manner in which information is collected, stored, transferred, and shared by people in many different fields. As American society becomes more and more dependent on the Internet and its complimentary technology, the need for the adequate and appropriate protection of these processes becomes even greater. Certainly, thieves will continue to evolve in terms of resourcefulness and they will increase their risk propensity in effort to obtain personal information. However, if protection is addressed on an individual level, business level, and government level, the thieves' road to success becomes more difficult. In the open market of the information age and the Internet, it is difficult to prevent identity thieves from contacting and soliciting potential victims. Awareness is a logical method by which to prevent thieves from stealing people's identities and financials, and in many cases is the first step in defense (GAO, 1998; Goodhue & Straub, 1989; Im & Baskerville, 2005; Rhee, Ryu, & Kim, 2005; Siponen, 2000; Straub & Welke, 1998).

ACTIONS FOR PROTECTION

Individual

An individual can play a major role in his or her identity defense. While there is no fool-proof defense, there are a few things he or she can do to reduce the odds of becoming a victim. Typical advice includes checking URLs for the correct spelling and ensuring the padlock icon is displayed in the corner of the Internet browser (Knight, 2005). Unfortunately, most people who use the Internet on a regular basis do not follow this advice. Another action for protection is the obtainment of a free credit report. Everyone is entitled to one free credit report per year. An individual should, therefore, obtain a credit report at least this often to monitor accounts for any suspicious activity. Most people do not know that they are entitled to a free credit report, and even less use the service (Swartz, 2005). Therefore the free credit check is not being used to its full potential.

Security or credit freezes are another identity protection option. When an identity is threatened through security breaches, credit reports should be locked. If someone tries to open an account, additional identity checks will be needed to ensure the loan is going to the actual person identified on the credit report. A credit freeze is a valuable tool to allow consumers to control their degree of risk (IMJ Staff, 2005b). If a freeze is affected, credit files cannot be accessed and instant credit, such as retail credit cards or on-the-spot car loans, cannot be issued (IMJ Staff, 2005b).

There also are steps an individual can take if he or she becomes the victim of identity theft. The following is an example of what can be done in the event of a false charge on a credit card.

- Call the credit card company immediately to inform them of the discrepancy.
- Call the credit reporting agencies to report the crime and ask them to place a 90-day fraud hold on your credit report. The alert will notify creditors that you may be a credit fraud victim and warn them to verify identity before opening any new accounts.
- Visit the Federal Trade Commission Web site (www.ftc.gov) and file an ID theft worksheet. This will show evidence of the report in case further action is needed (JOA Staff, 2006).

Clearly, these are post-victimization activities suggested to lessen the effects of identity theft.

Business

Businesses also need to protect themselves against identity thieves and must be aware of identity theft on two fronts. First, businesses must work with companies that verify identities in order to ensure that their clients are whom they claim they are. Secondly, clients must be reassured that their data is safe and will remain that way (Bauknight, 2005b).

According to Trevor Bauknight (2005b), a specialist in identity protection, there are several things businesses can do to achieve these two goals:

- Do not depend on a client's Social Security number. Setup a separate identification number or PIN.
- Demand more from the data brokers and credit reporting agencies. Payment for their services should come with the expectation that the provided information is current, accurate, and secure.
- Establish policies to govern the exchange of information between customers and facilities. Follow these policies without exception.
- Protect online identity. Secure the company's Web site with trusted digital certificates. Some major certification companies are Equifax, RSA Data Security, or VeriSign.

- Change passwords regularly for all business activities.
- Publicize efforts involving privacy policies. This will establish credibility with current customers and the potential customers.
- Protect networks and computers. Make sure firewalls are operational and software is up to date on all the latest patches.
- Report any suspicious activity. Report this activity to the authorities and most importantly to customers when the integrity of their personal information is threatened.

Government

The U.S. government is now becoming more involved because of the ever-changing information market and the growing skills of hackers and identity thieves, as the public has neither the time nor the resources to keep up with these individuals. States are beginning to administer identity theft laws that require businesses to implement security measures to ensure their customers' identities are safe. For those situations where security is compromised, full disclosure will be necessary (Rosow, 2006). For example California, Arkansas, Florida, and Connecticut have adopted laws for disclosure if there is a reasonable belief that consumers' personal information was compromised. The victimized business is required to disclose this information to the consumer so that consumers can watch their accounts and take appropriate action. Florida has added fines for businesses that do not comply with these laws. On a national level, the U.S. House of Representatives is currently considering a bill entitled "Data Accountability and Trust Act." The law ensures information (Social Security number, driver's license number, or other financial or personal information) is protected (Rosow, 2006). This law would supersede many of the state laws already in place, except Florida's which deals with medical information which could be covered under the Data Accountability and Trust Act or what it is currently covered under the Health Insurance Portability and Accountability Act (HIPAA).

Identity theft has also been identified as an area of concern for Congress. The Identity Theft Protection Act, S. 1408, was voted on in Congress and was to be voted on again later in 2006:

The Identity Theft Protection Act, S. 1408, is sponsored by a bipartisan group of senators and was voted out of the Senate Commerce, Science and Transportation Committee on July 28, 2005. S. 1408 would require covered entities (i.e., any commercial entity or charitable, educational, or nonprofit organization that acquires, maintains, uses, or disposes of sensitive personal information) to take reasonable steps to protect against security breaches and to prevent unauthorized access to sensitive personal information that the entity sells, maintains, collects, transfers, or disposes. To safeguard against authorized breaches of information, covered entities would be required to 'develop, implement, and maintain an effective information security program that contains administrative, technical, and physical safeguards for sensitive personal information'. (Moye, 2006)

The problem with these bills, and others of its kind, is that they possibly interfere with the agendas of other government agencies. The Senate and the House need to work together to allow these bills to coincide with one another. When the consumer is given the right for a credit freeze, the Senate Banking Committee becomes upset with the fact that they are no longer needed. Therefore the Senate Banking Committee is holding up many bills that give the rights for a credit freeze to the consumer (Moye, 2006).

Clearly, the U.S. government is taking action to deter identity theft crimes. The problem remains in catching the thieves, which has not been an easy endeavor. In the last 12 months, there have been close to 20,000 phishing sites posted on the Internet. Phishing involves the fraudulent attempt by criminals to get consumers to respond to e-mails and divulge personal financial information via the Internet (Folsom, Guillory, & Boulware, 2005). Fourteen individuals were recently arrested in the United Kingdom for the crime. This demonstrates how hard it is to solve cyber-crimes (Folsom et al., 2005).

THE FUTURE OF IDENTITY THEFT

Identity thieves are practicing a few new techniques to defraud the public. One of the new techniques is referred to as spear-phishing. Spear-phishing relies heavily on making the target seem safe to provide more believable snare and targets a smaller, more defined group of victims. As a result, spear phishing attacks have a much higher success rate than conventional phishing attacks (Bauknight, 2005a). Phishing sends out the scam to large numbers of people, where only a few respond. But spear-phishing depends on the thief to win the trust of a smaller group of people, maybe as few as one, for a long enough time to steal the sensitive information they are after.

Another trend that is spreading among Internet identity thieves is that of pharming. "Pharming is used by Internet criminals to link consumers with their Web sites and then capture users' personal information" (Folsom et al., 2005, p. 30). While phishing uses e-mail spam to deliver fraudulent messages to persuade potential victims into revealing information, pharming directs computer users from a real Web address to a phantom site exactly like the real thing (CACM Staff, 2005). In pharming, individuals are redirected to a fictitious Web site. This site will look the same as the actual site. The address in the browser will appear exactly the same as the actual site. By changing some of the address information that appears behinds the scenes, a thief is able to perpetuate a false replica of the actual site.

Evil twins are another technique used by criminals to surreptitiously gather information from targeted individuals without their knowledge. "Evil twins are Wi-Fi sites created by criminals to capture Internet users' personal information" (Folsom et al., 2005, p. 30). Evil twins are Wi-Fi networks that resemble secure Wi-Fi connections to the Internet; however, they are not secure and allow hackers access to the personal information of the victim.

In terms of the future of identity theft protection, U.S. laws and regulations required banks to institute additional levels of security for all Web-based banking activities by the end of 2006. The Federal Financial Institutions Examination Council (FFIEC) demands that U.S. financial institutions that do business on the Internet enact special security measures to control the transfer of sensitive user information (Alvarado, 2005). The FFIEC contends that most fraud on user accounts is due to the fact that the only security offered is a username and password. These measures are now proven to be inadequate (Alvarado, 2005). "Multifactor authentication supplements these methods with physical devices that must be in the customer's possession, such as smart cards, one-time passwords, USB plug-ins, and tokens" (Alvarado, 2005, p. 20). They are also moving

M

into physical character recognition systems, such as voice, fingerprints, or iris recognition. Banks are making strides to protect consumers from identity thieves, however they have a long way to go, and it is harder for banks to justify this increase in security when they have made such progress in making banking more of a hands-off system when it comes to customer-business relations. All this security will come at a price, monetarily and in terms of resources. However, this is a small price to pay to have a sense of security that when we give money to our financial institution, it will be there when we decide to remove it.

CONCLUSION

It is clear that individuals cannot rely on someone else for protection against identity thieves. There are just too many possibilities of fraud. With the Internet as a global system, even the government has a seemingly insurmountable challenge ahead in efforts to control criminals originating from countries. One of the more shocking statistics is that more than half of identity-theft victims, who learned of their assailant's identity, actually knew the thief (JOA Staff, 2005). Total strangers comprised 24% of the criminals, while family members, neighbors, co-workers, or otherse accounted for the remaining 76% (JOA Staff, 2005). Given these statistics, it is difficult to trust others. However, these statistics do help to solidify the point that protection starts at the individual level. Awareness may the best method of protection, given the current state of technology. Unfortunately, identity theft perpetrators are operating on the same learning curve as everyone else.

Businesses, on the other hand, have a set of obligations to their consumers. They have to protect the trust of consumers. They have to protect the information given to them by potential and existing customers, and in doing so, stay one step ahead of the criminals.

As for U.S. citizens, the plan for protection is three-fold. First, on an individual level, awareness of the environment, disseminated information, and the identity of those to whom the information is distributed is critical. Second, businesses need to have an awareness of those agencies that are receiving information concerning the identities of their clients and need to set up barriers for potential criminals. These barriers include firewalls, Web site protection, and awareness of the employees. Third, the federal and state governments are taking steps to control the manner in which we distribute and control information. These steps should improve the odds of catching and prosecuting those individuals that infiltrate businesses and homes.

REFERENCES

Alvarado, K. (2005). Regulations tighten online bank security. *Internal Auditor, 62*(6), 19-20.

Bauknight, T.Z. (2005a). The newest Internet scams. *Business & Economic Review, 52*(1), 19-21.

Bauknight, T.Z. (2005b). Protecting yourself from identity theft. *Business & Economic Review, 51*(4), 25-27.

CACM Staff. (2005). Betting the pharm. *Communications of the ACM, 48*(6), 9.

Bidwell, T. (2002). *Identity theft: Are you at risk?* Retrieved from http://www.syngress.com/book_catalog/221_Hack_Identity/sample.pdf

Folsom, W.D., Guillory, M.D., & Boulware, R.D. (2005). Gone phishing. *Business & Economic Review, 52*(1), 29-31.

GAO. (1998). *Information security management.* Washington, DC: General Accounting Office.

Goodhue, D.L., & Straub, D.W. (1989). Security concerns of system users: A proposed study of user perceptions of the adequacy of security measures. *Proceedings of the 22nd Annual Hawaii International Conference on System Science* (HICSS), Kailua-Kona, HI.

Im, G.P., & Baskerville, R.L. (2005). A longitudinal study of information system threat categories: The enduring problem of human error. *The DATA BASE for Advances in Information Systems, 36*(4), 68-79.

IMJ Staff. (2005a). ID thieves more likely to use dumpster, phone. *Information Management Journal, 39*(4), 20.

IMJ Staff. (2005b). States consider "security freeze" laws. *Information Management Journal, 39*(4), 18.

JOA Staff. (2005). A thief among us. *Journal of Accountancy, 200*(5), 19.

JOA Staff. (2006). Stop identity theft in three steps. *Journal of Accountancy, 201*(1), 17.

Karat, C., Brodie, C., & Karat, J. (2006). Usable privacy and security for personal information management. *Communications of the ACM, 49*(1), 56-57.

Knight, W. (2005). Caught in the Net. *IEEE Review, 51*(7), 26-30.

Moye, S. (2006). Congress assesses data security proposals. *Information Management Journal, 40*(1), 20-22.

Rhee, H.S., Ryu, Y., & Kim, C.T. (2005). I am fine but you are not: Optimistic bias and illusion of control on information security. *Proceedings of the 26th International Conference on Information Systems,* Las Vegas, NV.

Rosow, M.P. (2006). Unauthorized access? Remember to check identity theft laws. *Journal of Health Care Compliance, 8*(1), 35-78.

Siponen, M.T. (2000). A conceptual foundation for organizational information security awareness. *Information Management & Computer Security, 8*(1), 31-41.

Straub, D.W., & Welke, R.J. (1998). Coping with systems risk: Security planning models for management decision making. *MIS Quarterly, 22*(4), 441-469.

Swartz, N. (2005). Study reveals consumers' data worries. *Information Management Journal, 39*(5), 16.

Swartz, N. (2003). Identity theft victims skyrocket, surveys say. *Information Management Journal, 37*(6), 17.

U.S. Ways and Means Committee. (2004). *Facts and figures: Identity theft.* Retrieved from http://waysandmeans.house.gov/media/pdf/ss/factsfigures.pdf

KEY TERMS

Credit freeze: "Credit files cannot be accessed, and instant credit—such as retail credit cards or on-the-spot car loans—cannot be granted" (IMJ Staff, 2005b).

Evil Twin: Phantom Wi-Fi site and connection created by criminals to capture Internet users' personal information.

Identity Theft: "A situation where someone assumes the identity of another and makes telephone calls or obtains merchandise, credit, or other valuable things in their name" (Swartz, 2003).

Pharming: "Used by Internet criminals to link consumers with their Web sites and then capture users' personal information" (Folsom, 2005).

Phishing: "The fraudulent attempt by Internet criminals to get consumers to respond to e-mails and divulge personal financial information" (Folsom, 2005).

Spam: Unsolicited and unwanted e-mail sent to a larger number of recipients.

Spear-Phishing: A phishing technique focused on a smaller group of potential victims. Trust is gained and exploited over this smaller group.

ENDNOTE

[1] Despite its archaic nature, dumpster diving is still the most widely used technique employed by identity thieves. In fact, a recent telephone survey of 4,000 consumers found that only 11% of known identity-theft cases occurred online, with dumpster diving and phone fraud accounting for the majority of thefts (IMJ Staff, 2005a).

Mobile Agents and Security

Fei Xue
Monash University, Australia

INTRODUCTION

As an emerging technology, mobile agents can facilitate distributed computing applications over computer networks. During the past decade, the advance of computer software and hardware has led the structure and logic of mobile agents to become increasingly sophisticated. As a consequence, some security threats have started to appear in mobile agent systems (MASs).

Mobile agent technology derives from the concept of mobile code that Jeff Rulifson (n.d.) proposed in order to submit a set of program codes to a central machine in 1969. This concept was not transformed to mobile agents until 1994 when James E. White introduced Telescript, which is a runtime environment and programming language for mobile agents. One of Telescript's limitations is that it uses a proprietary approach lacking enough specifications, which thus has blocked its popularity (Minar, 1997). In 1995, a new mobile agent system named as MOLE was developed using Java, which is a computer language with the power of facilitating network environments (Baumann, Hohl, Rothermel, & Straßer, 1998). Since then, Java has become a common programming language for MAS, and this makes mobile agent technology more recognizable and acceptable to researchers and developers.

In 1997, the Object Management Group (OMG, n.d.) released a mobile agent standard entitled "Mobile Agent System Interoperability Facilities" (MASIF). This standard is known as one foundation of today's agent technologies. Since then, many mobile agent toolkits have been developed for the construct of MAS, such as Aglets, Tracy, JACK, Voyager, and so on (Braun & Rossak, 2005; Agentbuilder, n.d.). Today, mobile agents are suitable for many applications such as information searching and disseminating, distribution of the client-side software, semantic information retrieval, online service brokering, network management, and mobile computing.

BACKGROUND

A software agent is referred to as a software program that is authorized by its owner to work autonomously for the achievement of its objectives on behalf of its owner (Toivonen, 2000). When a software agent can migrate from one host to another over computer networks, it will be referred to as *mobile agent*. There exists a controversy about what properties can precisely characterize a mobile agent. The consensus is that a typical mobile agent must at least have the following key properties (Recursion Software, n.d.; Toivonen, 2000; Gupta et al., 2001, Chess et al., 1997):

- **Functionality:** A mobile agent must have the ability of functioning in a network environment to accomplish the tasks assigned by its user and to achieve its preset goals. During this functional process, the agent must be capable of reacting to any possible changes in its working environment. Preferably, a mobile agent should be able to communicate and collaborate with other agents and hosts.

- **Autonomy:** A mobile agent should act on its initiatives and perform its functions independently on behalf of its owner. For example, it can be unattended for a time period until a predefined event triggers its activation.

- **Mobility:** Mobile agents' mobility distinguishes them from any other software agents. This means that both code and data of a mobile agent can be moved within a network environment. The run-time execution of the agent can be suspended prior to its movement and can be resumed afterwards. A mobile agent can accomplish such movement by means of duplicating its run-time states. When it wants to move, it saves all states and transfers them to its destination host where its execution will be resumed according to those saved states.

- **Itinerary:** An itinerary-based MAS enables a mobile agent (referred to as *itinerant agent* in this case) to carry information about where it travels.

The power of a mobile agent can be further enhanced by some optional properties. A mobile agent may utilize artificial intelligence to get more smart features, such as learning new information, adjusting its behaviors, and deciding where to go and what to do. Security is another important property which requires that a mobile agent be designed to be unmalicious and immune to other agents and hosts. Although security is not a native property to mobile agents, it has become more and more important because of the increasing security concerns about mobile agents.

Mobile agents have some advantages and disadvantages (Harrison, Chess, & Kershenbaum, n.d.; Vigna, 1998; Lange & Oshoma, 1998; Recursion Software, 2001). On the one hand, a mobile agent can make computing systems work better in the following ways:

- Reduces network traffic by using fewer communication processes than traditional technologies like Remote Procedure Call (RPC) use.
- Its messaging processes are faster than those in traditional technologies.
- Supports autonomous query and interaction between hosts or between agents.
- Supports those who use mobile devices to perform functions over a network, even when their devices are off-line.
- Facilitates semantic information retrieval from different hosts, provided it is equipped with relevant intelligent algorithms.
- Provides lower overhead for secure transactions that apply encryptions than RPC-based systems.
- Its power can be enhanced by aggregation. The advantage of aggregate mobile agents is overwhelmingly stronger than what individual mobile agents can offer.

One the other hand, mobile agents have to overcome some problems. For example, transmission performance is an issue when a mobile agent carries a large volume of data, which results in a significant enlargement of its size. Compared with a small message transmitted over networks, its traveling time can be longer, and even may be intolerable in the circumstance that the agent is too large to be decomposed for online delivery. More seriously, security may be compromised in mobile agent-based systems. It is recognized that security attacks in MAS can take place in the following circumstances (Jansen, n.d.; Braun & Rossak, 2005; Jansen & Karygiannis, n.d.):

- **Agent-to-Agent:** Agent A can pretend to be an agent friendly to Agent B (known as masquerading), access the contents of Agent B without authorization, and even deny some services that Agent B provides.
- **Agent-to-Host:** An agent can pretend to be agent friendly to a host, access the resources on the host without authorization, and even deny the host's services.
- **Host-to-Agent:** A host can also pretend to be a host friendly to an agent, access its contents without an authorization, and even modify its code and logical structure.
- **Host-to-Host:** Host A can send a number of agents to collect and analyze the information about Host B. Host A can even change the code of the agents belonging to Host B when they travel to Host A.

Issues

One of the issues relating to mobile agents is that they may be abused. This means developers may sometimes use mobile agents to replace other traditional technologies in their computing systems, regardless of whether the agents can better suit their systems than those traditional technologies in terms of performance, ease of use, and security. They ignore the fact that mobile agents can be used only when their specific features are critically essential to the development or refinement of a computing system.

The increasing sophistication of MAS has motivated another issue—security concerns. Mobile agents can have a potential motivation to severely degrade and even destroy normal computing operations, when they are constructed with some malicious code or their logics include some bugs. Compared with the problems that ordinary communication technologies like RPC may cause, the destruction caused by that mobile agent may be worse, because its mobility capability can make this destruction more pervasive and its autonomy capability can make its destructive behavior be more hardly controlled.

A more serious issue is that most conventional security threats to computer systems can also have impacts on MAS, and they may act in a specific way in MAS.

Authentication

A mobile agent or a host is authentic only when it can be identified as who it claims to be. Without authentication, there will be a lack of trust in an MAS. On the one hand, any unauthentic mobile agent may pretend to be an authentic agent to communicate with a host or another mobile agent. This implies that a host must authenticate each inbound mobile agent. On the other hand, any unauthentic host may pretend to be a specific authentic host to communicate with some inbound mobile agents. This implies that those inbound mobile agents must authenticate that host.

Confidentiality

The information of a mobile agent that travels over a network or resides at a host may be disclosed to an unauthorized third party. Such information includes both the message that the agent carries and the code and structure of the agent itself.

Integrity

During the transmission of a mobile agent, its contents may be intercepted, modified, and then replayed to its destination by a malicious party. In this circumstance, the integrity of the agent is destroyed.

Non-Repudiation

Every mobile agent must have responsibility for its behaviors and cannot be allowed to deny such responsibility in any circumstances. If an agent or its owner denies its inappropriate behaviors such as misusing some confidential resource and modifying an agreed content, the losses caused by these behaviors may be irrecoverable.

Denial of Service

The services a host provides to an agent or an agent provides to another agent may be unavailable or unreliable, which leads to denial of service. This threat can be caused by various factors, such as a communication jam, a failure of hardware, an error of software, or an attack of malicious program.

A general strategy as a countermeasure to the above issues is that a mobile agent must authenticate every host and agent that it will communicate with, because authentication is a fundamental requirement of solving many other security issues in an MAS. To authenticate mobile agents and hosts, either symmetric or asymmetric cryptography can be adopted (Vigna, 1998). The symmetric kind uses a common key, which is shared only between two communicating parties (e.g., an agent and a host), to sign mobile agents or hosts which can also use the same key to validate the signature. A better resolution is the use of a digital certificate and signature based on a public key and a private key under Public Key Infrastructure (PKI). The private key is used to sign the code of a mobile agent that will travel to a remote host where the public key—and only the public key—can validate that signature. If the signature is valid, the mobile agent is then authentic.

Some conventional techniques can be used to minimize confidentiality-related threats. For example, the message can be encrypted using the symmetric cryptographic algorithms such as TDEA and AES (NIST FIPS197, n.d.; NIST FIPS46-3, n.d.), or the asymmetric algorithms such as Rivest Shamir Adleman (RSA) and Diffie-Hellman (RSA Security, n.d.). These algorithms use one or more keys to implement the encryption. An unauthorized third party cannot understand the encrypted message because it does not have the key(s) to decrypt the message. In the application where a large number of mobile agents are active, the asymmetric resolution is desirable because it provides an easy way to distribute and manage a variety of keys.

To protect against the integrity attack, the techniques of authentication code (NIST FIPS113, n.d.) can be used. The idea is, in addition to the assistance of authentication, digital signatures can also be used to check if a received agent still holds its integrity. If the size of the agent is too long to compute its digital signature, its signature can be computed based on a hash value that is much smaller in size and originates from the agent's content. In addition, Message Authentication Code (MAC), which is based on symmetric cryptography, can also be used to ensure integrity. It requires a secret key shared between an agent and a host, and adopts a symmetric algorithm using that key to compute encryption and decryption of the agent's content.

A common countermeasure against repudiation is the use of a digital signature that can keep the trace of an agent and make evident the commitment of the agent. In this case, a digital signature can be created and managed by using asymmetric cryptographic algorithms like RSA, and even some biometric information such as a fingerprint and retina image can be adopted for this purpose.

In order to minimize the impacts of the denial-of-service attack on MAS, it is believed that regularly backing up the system should be considered for use (Braun, 2005). However, this is a not easy task because some mobile agents may be traveling over networks in MAS, and their dynamically changed locations and status can only be captured with difficulty at a time for the backing up purpose.

To protect a host, the following measures can be taken (Jansen & Karygiannis, n.d.; Vigna, 1998):

- **Safe Code Interpretation:** Interpretative languages such as Java can transform one part of an agent's code that is suspected to be harmful into a safe form or deny it completely, by the means of isolating memory access and verifying code.
- **Code Signing:** The code of a mobile agent is signed with a digital signature under the asymmetric scheme so that the authority of the agent can be indicative.
- **Software-Based Fault Isolation:** At runtime, untrusted codes which may arbitrarily use memory space are enforced to a single virtual memory space for execution.
- **Use of Proof-Carrying Code:** A code proof generated directly from the native code of a mobile agent is used to verify the safety properties of the agent.
- **Use of Path Histories and State Appraisal:** The information of the hosts to which a mobile agent has previously traveled are recorded for the de-

termination of how secure the agent is; appraisal functions are used to determine what privileges to grant the agent according to its states change.

The protection of an agent itself can be accomplished as follows (Jansen & Karygiannis, n.d.; Braun & Rossak, 2005, Vigna 1998):

- **Encryption of Agent Functions:** The critical functions of an agent are encrypted by the owner of the agent. An encrypted function can be passed to a user for him to fill in relevant parameters needed by that function. The encrypted function together with its parameters is then performed. This technique avoids the user's learning about the function.
- **Itinerary Recording:** The itinerary along which an agent travels is recorded and another agent can be allowed to track it, provided a supportive agreement exists between those two agents.
- **Execution Tracing:** Every host to which an agent travels should record a trace of the operations that the agent performs, and that record is used for detecting whether any unauthorized modification has applied to that agent.
- **Environmental Key Generation:** When a certain predefined environmental condition is satisfied, a key is generated to unlock some executable code of an agent by encryption. This can make it impossible for any third party who read the code to understand the messaging that the agent does.
- **Time-Limited Black Box Protection:** Based on the theory of Encryption of Agent Functions, this technique encrypts an agent's functions for a time period at interval only. This makes it hard for a hostile third party hardly to master the overall sense of the agent, even if he or she knows each line of code within it.
- **Replication of Agents:** Key agents are replicated, including their code, data, and states, so that they can be the back ups to achieve a same goal.

FUTURE TRENDS

The perception of security risk has become a barrier to the widespread adoption of mobile agents. Even if mobile agents satisfy all of the conventional security requirements, they may still possibly have some virus-like behaviors if their inside logic codes are improperly designed and written (Jansen & Karygiannis, n.d.). In addition, the mobility property of mobile agents may enable those behaviors to easily spread over a large number of computers and networks. Therefore, more comprehensive study and further innovation of mobile agent technology will still be necessary. For this purpose, the following aspects may be further explored.

First of all, there is a current lack of enough techniques to judge whether a given mobile agent contains some malicious logic. This may be done by protocol filtering and code analyzing. Thus, some intelligent algorithms and communication protocols can be developed for this use. Secondly, if certain malicious code is found in the mobile agent, measures must be taken to avoid executing them, or must allow users to decide an appropriate response. Once some current measures mainly used for virus protection purposes are taken against the mobile agent, its malicious code can be stopped but its normal capabilities can be thoroughly destroyed as well. Consequently, it is necessary to seek a better way to manage, monitor, and control the execution of mobile agents.

Thirdly, there is now no a universal communication protocol between multiple heterogeneous agents. Diverse mobile agents created based on different program structures and programming languages cannot effectively communicate with each other directly. If a universal communication protocol is developed and agreed upon among most agent toolkit providers, it will be significantly contributing to the future development of mobile agent applications. Fourthly, developers need to have a mobile agent-specific scripting or programming. The languages used for today's mobile agents are not completely mobile agent specific and not universal. Although many of them derive from some other existing general programming languages such as C++ and Java, they have a variety of versions and standards. So it is believed that these languages can be further improved or totally innovated. For the purpose of easily developing non-malicious code-based mobile agents, the future languages should at least address the following capabilities:

- automatically checking a mobile agent's codes and warning developers of its possible code weakness

- supporting the easy deployment of mobile agents, particularly in Web and wireless environments;
- conforming to a universal communication protocol between heterogeneous agents
- handling large-size agents

Finally, the future study can also go into the field of developing more advanced intelligent algorithms for enhancing mobile agents' anonymity and security, as well as developing more mobile agent applications for tomorrow's computing needs.

CONCLUSION

Mobile agent technology can be used to facilitate today's distributed computing applications. However, it should be adopted only when its native features such as mobility and autonomy are essential to the needs of a computer application. In some circumstances, mobile agents can compromise system security with some security threats in terms of authentication, confidentiality, repudiation, and denial-of-service, unless some appropriate security countermeasures are taken. A common countermeasure is to use some conventional cryptographic techniques for securing agents and hosts. Specifically, some agent-centric and host-centric countermeasures can be used to minimize security risks.

It is clear that some aspects such as determination and control of malicious behaviors are still a weakness to MAS. With the power driven by mobility, the improvement of mobile agents should be continued to enhance future computing applications, and more studies should be undertaken to thoroughly protect MAS against security threats.

REFERENCES

Agentbuilder. (n.d.). *Agent construction tools*. Retrieved from http://www.agentbuilder.com/AgentTechnology/

Artikis, A., Pitt J., & Stergiou, C. (n.d.). *Agent communication transfer protocol, intelligent & interactive systems group*. Retrieved from http://portal.acm.org/citation.cfm?id=337577

Braun, P., & Rossak, W. (2005). *Mobile agents: Basic concepts, mobility models & the Tracy Toolkit*.

Baumann, J., Hohl, F., Rothermel, K., & Straßer, M. (1998). *Mole—concepts of a mobile agent system.*

Harrison, C.G., Chess, D.M., & Kershenbaum, A. (n.d.). *Research report—mobile agents: Are they a good idea?* Retrieved from http://www.research.ibm.com/massive

Jansen, W. (n.d.). *Countermeasures for mobile agent security.* Retrieved from http://csrc.nist.gov/mobilesecurity/ Publications/ppcounterMeas.pdf

Jansen, W., & Karygiannis, T. (n.d.). *NIST special publication 800-19—mobile agent security.* Retrieved from http://csrc.nist.gov/publications/nistpubs/800-19/sp800-19.pdf

Lange, D.B., & Oshima, M. (1998). *Programming and deploying Java mobile agents with aglets.* Boston: Addison-Wesley.

Minar, N. (1997). *Other technologies for mobile agents.* Retrieved from http://xenia.media.mit.edu/~nelson/research/dc/node4.html

NIST FIPS113. (n.d.). Computer data authentication. Retrieved from http://www.itl.nist.gov/fipspubs/fip113.htm

NIST FIPS197. (n.d.). *AES.* Retrieved from http://csrc.nist.gov/publications/fips/fips197/fips-197.pdf

NIST FIPS46-3. (n.d.). *DES.* Retrieved from http://csrc.nist.gov/publications/fips/fips46-3/fips46-3.pdf

OMG. (n.d.). Retrieved from http://www.omg.org/technology/documents/formal/mobile_agent_facility.htm

Recursion Software. (n.d.). *Voyager®'s intelligent mobile agent documentation.* Retrieved from http://www.recursionsw.com/voyager_documentation.htm

Reilly, D. (n.d.). *Mobile agents—process migration and its implications.* Retrieved from http://www.davidreilly.com/topics/software_agents/mobile_agents/index.htm

Rulifson, J. (n.d.). *RFC 5: The decode-encode language.* Retrieved from http://www.rfc-archive.org/getrfc.php?rfc=5

RSA Security. (n.d.). *RSA and Diffie-Hellman.* Retrieved from http://www.rsasecurity.com/rsalabs/node.asp?id=2248

Toivonen, S. (2000). *Definition and usage of a software agent.* Retrieved from http://www.control.hut.fi/hyotyniemi/publications/2000_arpakannus/Toivonen.pdf

Vigna, G. (1998). *Mobile agents and security.* Berlin: Springer-Verlag (LNCS 1419).

KEY TERMS

Asymmetric Cryptography: A cryptographic scheme that two keys with a multiplicative relation (one is called public key, the other is called private key) are used to encode and decode messages.

Digital Signature: A fingerprint of a message that was generated by encrypting the message or its digest using a key (either a private key in the asymmetric scheme or a secret key/value in the symmetric scheme), for the purpose of authentication.

Itinerant Agent: A type of mobile agent that has information about where it travels.

Mobile Agent: A software agent that is allowed for the breaking of its runtime execution, the resumption of its execution, and the migration of itself from one host to another over computer networks.

Mobile Code: The code that can be downloaded from or uploaded to network hosts for execution without explicit human intervention.

Software Agent: Software program that can work autonomously for the achievement of its objectives on behalf of its owner in a computer system.

Symmetric Cryptography: A cryptographic scheme in which only one secret key shared by communicating parties is used to encode and decode messages.

Modelling Context–Aware Security for Electronic Health Records

Pravin Shetty
Monash University, Australia

Seng Loke
La Trobe University, Australia

INTRODUCTION

The Internet has proven to be the most convenient and demanding facility for various types of businesses and transactions for the past few years. In recent years, business information systems have expanded into networks, encompassing partners, suppliers, and customers. There has been a global availability (Anderson, 2001; BSI Global, 2003) of resources over the Internet to satisfy different needs in various fields. The availability factor has called for various security challenges in fields where information is very valuable and not meant for all. Potential threats to information and system security come from a variety of sources. These threats may result in violations to confidentiality, interruptions in information integrity, and possible disruption in the delivery of services. So it is essential to manage the flow of information over the network with the required level of security. There are many security technologies and models that have been introduced which are capable of realizing the functions and objectives of information system security.

This article first gives a brief overview of what we term basic security policies of an integrated security model. Then it suggests context-based security policies for a health organization scenario using contextual graphs augmented with details about specific security actions, which relate to the security policies enumerated in the integrated security model.

The plan of the article is as follows. We first overview the three concepts in detail and briefly describe the concept of contextual (meta-policy) graphs. We then develop a context-based security meta-policy for securing patient records based on the security policies overviewed and discuss related work, before concluding the paper.

BASIC SECURITY POLICIES

Mobile ambients were first proposed by Cardelli and Gordon (1998a, 1998b) and then further extended by Bugliesi, Castagna, and Crafa (2004); and Braghin et al. (2002) were very efficient in modeling multilevel security issues. These three notions are very effective in modeling a foolproof security solution in a computing scenario by stating various security steps to be taken in the corresponding scenario. On this basis we have five cases that form the basic security policies in this article which we note can be concisely and precisely modeled using the mobile ambients formalism, though we omit such details of the formalism here and only describe the policies in plain language. The article uses them in appropriate scenarios depending on the context. Thus, the combined use of these five policies and a contextual graph representing the contexts of use of these policies provides a context-based security solution for pervasive environments. This section briefly describes the five policies using ambient (representing a boundary of security restrictions) notions.

Policy 1: Authenticate Returning Mobile Agent

When a privileged process (agent or person) leaves the parent ambient (e.g., a host institution) to execute some external independent activities, it relinquishes its local privileges and authority within its bounding parent ambient and ambient community. It exits the parent and might later return to the parent ambient. At this point an *authentication mechanism* is needed to check the authenticity of the returning original process. Cardelli and Gordon (1998a, 1998b, 1999) suggest that these high-level privileges must not be automatically restored to the returning agents/processes without first verifying their identity. This is to preserve the security and integrity of the ambient as well as the services and resources contained within it.

Policy 2: Firewall Access

If any agent/process has to enter an ambient, it has to know the name of the ambient and also possess the capability to enter it. The functionality of firewall is achieved with the help of restriction primitives and with the help of anonymity of the ambient name. Thus without knowing the ambient name, no process or agent can exit or enter the parent ambient. This helps in achieving protection of the resources from unwanted agents. The ambient name could be interpreted as a secret password.

Policy 3: Encryption Using Shared Keys to Secure the Data While Communicating

Cardelli and Gordon (1998a, 1998b, 1999) also put forth the encryption primitives to communicate between two ambients or between an ambient and a remote agent. These primitives helped in maintaining the *confidentiality* of the message or data. Consider a Plaintext message M. The encryption of the plaintext message is done with the help of the encryption key k. A name can represent a shared key, as long as it is kept secret and shared only by certain parties. A shared key can be reused multiple times, for example, to encrypt a stream of messages. A message encrypted under a key k can be represented as a folder that contains the message and whose label is k (Cardelli & Gordon, 1998a, 1998b).

Policy 4: Security Across Multiple Levels

In general, an enclosed ambient environment would typically contain numerous subambients as well as active processes, agents, and information resources. These groups of subambients within an ambient may be arbitrarily nested and organized in a hierarchical structure. Ambients and processes at the higher level of the nested structure are responsible for managing resources that are more vital and important than those at a lower level. In such multilevel environments, it is necessary to restrict the access to the flow of informa-

tion depending upon the need and the security levels. Information can only flow from lower levels of security to higher levels and not conversely. A policy for this assigns levels to users and restricts information flow among the users.

Policy 5: Movement of Data and Entities Through Different Communities

The multilevel security policy mandatory access control security in the boxed ambients provided restricted access to information based on the various security levels in the hierarchical levels. The access is defined by the level at which the agents are which are predetermined based on their needs. But Braghin et al. (2002) were of the view that the implementation of mandatory access control security is complex, as agents and processes may move from one security level to another. The agents themselves may be confidential or may be carrying secure/confidential information. Thus there is no way of ensuring the agents will not be illegally attacked, accessed, or executed by untrustworthy entities at the lower security levels. The *security boundary* concept put forth by Braghin et al. (2002) guarantees absence of information leakage.

According to this concept, every high-level data or process should be encapsulated in a boundary ambient. A boundary ambient can be opened only when it is nested into another pre-specified boundary ambient. A policy for this states that the protected information cannot be read without being contained within some safety boundary (e.g., physically, an item cannot be viewed in the absence of a bodyguard).

CONTEXTUAL (META-POLICY) GRAPHS

Contextual meta-policy graphs are derived from contextual graphs (Braghin et al., 2002; Bugliesi et al., 2001a, 2001b). We replace the security actions in contextual graphs by security policies, which in turn, represent the security actions accordingly. By virtue of this embedding of policies (such as the five mentioned above) into a contextual graph, the graph becomes a meta-policy construct. The contextual meta-policy graphs are very general and can be used to depict security architecture in any scenario. The use of such graphs is to provide a high-level picture of the security framework, thereby avoiding lower details (security actions), which makes the overall architecture less cumbersome. The security actions are triggered according to the policies, which are predefined and programmed. The five security policies depicted in the integrated (in that such policies complement one another and have holistic coverage over security situations) security model above forms the basis of the graphs presented in this article. The contextual meta-policy graphs use various combinations of these five policies to define the various access paths to the patient's records. The next section presents the overall security architecture using such graphs.

SECURING ELECTRONIC HEALTH RECORDS USING CONTEXTUAL META-POLICY GRAPHS

The integrated security model discussed above is used to implement context-based security. The following model can be used in any context-aware situation. This article will explain the use of the model for securing health records. The various access possibilities depending on the context are described with the help of the contextual meta-policy graphs. This section is divided into two subsections. The first gives the details of the security policies used along with the low-level details (what security actions are triggered in each policy). The second subsection gives the actual approach for security purposes, along with an explanation of the individual access possibilities.

POLICY DEFINITION

This section outlines the various types of users associated with the electronic health records. It also specifies the various types of contextual information to be used for implementing the security policies. Finally, the various security actions to be taken depending upon the information received are also stated.

Figure 1. Context graphs showing the various possible scenarios and security actions taken

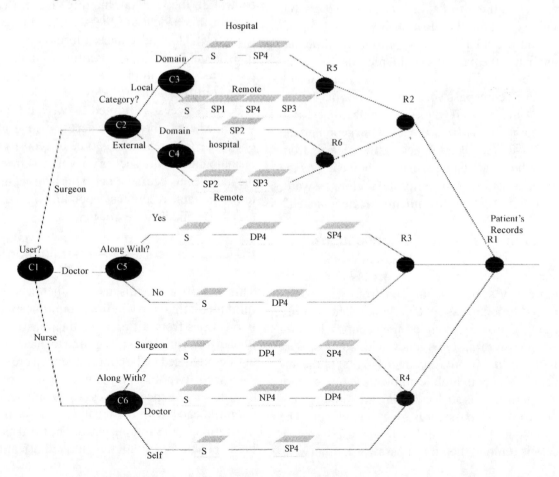

Roles: Surgeon, Doctor, Nurse

Contextual Information Considered: Role, Location, Place

The five policies, collectively labeled the 'integrated security model', can be effectively used for implementing security in a hospital scenario for accessing a patient's records. The five policies can be described in context for the hospital scenario as follows.

The Secret code S in the diagram can be considered as a secret name of the hospital network, which has to be known by each and every local person who wants to access the patient's detail. This secret code is similar to the secret name of the ambient in the case of ambient terms. It is not known to foreign entities. The details about the individual usernames and passwords are stored in the systems database along with the corresponding roles.

Policy 1: Authentication

This security policy defines the way in which a valid user can access the hospital network once s/he is out of it. This type of authentication is required for the surgeon and the doctor who have to access the network and hence the patient's health records. When the surgeon goes out of the hospital network, temporarily s/he is given a secret password, which helps her/him to authenticate her/himself when s/he wants to access the network again. Apart from the local surgeon and the local doctor, no one else can access the records from outside the hospital. This security policy triggers the action such as asking the user for the secret password, which will help her/him to authenticate her/himself.

Policy 2: Foreign Agent Authentication

This security policy defines the access method for a foreign entity such as a surgeon from some other medical institution in case of emergency. The security infrastructure provides such foreign agents, which are required in case of an emergency with some special combination of passwords analogous to that of the foreign agents concept in mobile ambients. This security policy triggers actions such as asking the foreign agent for the three sets of passwords given to her/him. The first will help her/him to validate her/himself. In case the access is remote, then it is a password; otherwise,

it is done by retina scan or any other biometrics. The second password is used to allow the external surgeon inside the network. The third password will help her/him to access the patient's records in the mode as per her/his role.

Policy 3: Encryption of Data

This policy secures the data from falling into destructive hands by using various encryption techniques. This security policy is required when the user is accessing the network from a remote place. For example, there might be a case where a local surgeon might have to access the patient record from a remote place and do some modifications according to the present condition of the patient. This transfer of data should be safe and confidential and not intercepted by a malicious intruder. Thus, encryption is required which is provided by this policy.

Policy 4: Security Levels

This security policy talks about role-based access control. In the hospital, the three main users considered in this article are the surgeon, the doctor, and the nurse. They have access to the patient's records in different modes and according to the need of their positions. For example the surgeon has the access to the records in all three modes (i.e., read/write/update). A doctor's access is limited to two modes (i.e., read/write), whereas the nurse's access is restricted to just one mode (i.e., read). This type of security hierarchy is analogous to the security level structure policy of the multilevel access model. This helps control access to the valuable resources depending on the role of the user in the medical institution.

Policy 5: Third-Party Authentication

This security policy discusses authentication from the third mediating party in the communication between two entities from different medical institutions. This type of authentication is required to make sure that the entities involved in the communication are authorized. This security policy plays an important role when an outside surgeon needs access to the medical record or communicates with the local network of the medical institution from a remote place. The third party should be a reliable party, giving the authorization of any information passed between the two communicating entities.

The five security policies defined above are based on the concepts of mobile ambients defined in the former sections and depict the various security approaches taken depending on the context. The next subsection elaborates on the various contexts in a hospital scenario and the appropriate security policies to be taken to have secured access to the patient's records using a context meta graph.

Security Paths Defined in a Contextual Meta-Policy Graph

The above model gives the overall security approach used in a hospital environment to access electronic health records of the patients. The behavior of the security infrastructure according to various contexts is described as follows:

1. **User→ Type→ Domain :: Surgeon→Local→Hospital:- *Policy 4.*** If the user is a local surgeon and s/he wants to access the patient's records from the hospital, then s/he has to follow security policy 4. When s/he tries to access the records, the system will ask for her/his username and password, which will depict her/his role in the institution. Being a surgeon, s/he enjoys the highest level of rights. S/he can access the records in all the three modes (read/write/update). For access from within the hospital, authentication can be provided by various biometrics.

2. **User→ Type→ Domain :: Surgeon→Local→Remote:- *Policy 1 + Policy 4 + Policy 3.*** When the local surgeon, say John, wants to access the information from outside the hospital, which can be in the case of an emergency, then a combination of three security policies is followed. First he has to get back into the hospital network by providing his secret key/password according to policy 1, which will validate him as a local user. Then with the help of his username and password, which is associated with his role (policy 4), he can access the records. As he is in a remote place, care should be taken that the data is not visible to the outside world. This is achieved by encrypting the channel according to policy 3. Thus, using the combination of three

policies, the local surgeon is provided access to the records from a remote place.

3. **User→Type→Domain :: Surgeon→External→ Hospital:- *Policy 2.*** In some emergency cases, it becomes necessary to invite an external surgeon to the local institution. For such cases, the system stores all the information of such emergency persons. Policy 2 defines the access for such a surgeon using predetermined passwords. The surgeon is provided with three sets of passwords. The first will help him/her to validate him/herself. The second password is used to allow the external surgeon into the network. The third password will help him/her access the patient's records in the mode according to his/her role. Biometrics instruments can provide the required authentication when he/she is accessing from the hospital. If the external surgeon is accessing the records from the hospital, then he/she can use his/her third password to get access according to his/her role. The first and the second passwords are not required in this case.

4. **User→Type→Domain :: Surgeon→External→ Remote:- *Policy 2 + Policy 3.*** When the external surgeon has to access the records from a remote place, then the access takes place as determined by the combination of two security policies. Policy 2 is as defined as above. In such a case, he/she must have all three sets of passwords with him/her in order to get into the hospital network and then access the patient's records. Policy 3 is used for encryption of the information to provide safe and confidential communication.

   The surgeon, whether local or external, does not need to be with any other staff, as he/she enjoys the maximum access rights. He/she has to follow the appropriate security procedures depending upon his/her category (i.e., local or external) and his/her location of access.

5. **User→Along with :: Doctor→ Along with Surgeon:- *Policy 4 (for doctor) + Policy 4 (for surgeon).*** When a local doctor wants to access the records, then s/he can do so by using a combination of policy 4 applied to two roles. If s/he is with the surgeon, then s/he can access the patient's record in a full mode (read/write/edit) with the same access privileges as the surgeon. But for this, the surgeon has to first specify her/his

username and password according to policy 4 so that her/his role is specified. If the surgeon is not physically present in the hospital, then the doctor cannot access the records in full mode. Also, a doctor is not allowed access to the records from a remote place.

6. **User→Along with :: Doctor→ Alone:- *Policy 4 (for doctor)*.** If a surgeon is not with the local doctor, then the doctor accesses the patient's information in the restricted mode (read/write). S/he can access the information according to policy 4. S/he has to present her/his username and password so that her/his role will be represented in the system. An important point in this security architecture is that the doctor can never access the patient's records from a remote place.

7. **User→Along with :: Nurse→ Along with Surgeon:- *Policy 4 (for nurse) + Policy 4 (for surgeon)*.** A nurse, say Jane, is at the lowest security level in the hospital hierarchy. If she is with the surgeon, she is allowed to view the records in full mode as the surgeon has. For that, the surgeon must present his/her role to the system first, and then the nurse can access the information according to her role as in security policy 4. Remote access is not allowed in this case.

8. **User→Along with :: Nurse→ Along with Doctor:- *Policy 4 (for nurse) + Policy 4 (for doctor)*.** When the nurse, Jane, is with a doctor in the hospital, then she can have access to the patient's information according to the doctor's privileges. The doctor first provides his/her username and password, and then the nurse can provide her role as per security policy 4. Remote access is also not allowed in this case.

9. **User→Along with :: Nurse→ Alone:- *Policy 4 (for nurse)*.** When nurse Jane is alone, she is only allowed one mode (read). She can read the information but cannot delete or modify it. She can access the information using her username and password according to security policy 4. But she is not allowed to access the records from a remote place.

RELATED WORK

There has been some work on security policies in the field of electronic health records systems in past years. Reid, Cheong, Henricksen, and Smith (2003) presented a model that uses role-based access control to restrict the access to the health records on a need-to-know basis. The prototype described maintains databases consisting of explicit 'allow' and explicit 'denial' lists. The proposed model also permits allow and deny policies to successively qualify each other in a role hierarchy supporting inheritance. Thus, the access control framework exhibits a great flexibility and efficiency in the range of access policies that it can support.

Mostéfaoui and Brézillon (2004) put forth the concept of contextual graph for modeling security in context-aware environments. They present a new model for policy specification based on the new approach. The security policy based on such an approach depends on the contextual information of the user and the environment. Contextual graphs have proved to be very effective in modeling a complex situation. Mostéfaoui and Brézillon (2004) also mention how contextual graphs are used to model security in a context-aware environments. In their paper they gave an example of how context-based security is used in a hospital scenario, but it does not employ our meta-policy scheme in the way we do above.

CONCLUSION

Due to the ubiquitous nature of the today's computing world, security is of utmost important. The traditional static authentication techniques are no longer valid and justified. This situation is due to the lack of consideration for context in existing security systems. Context-based security helps the security policy to, in effect, adapt to the new "threats" as they come. It aims at providing flexible security models for distributed infrastructures, where the user and application environments are continually changing. In this article, we have presented an approach that helps with context-based security in a medical scenario. The type and nature of the authentications that are demanded by the security policy depend on the information that is collected from the environment. Further, the contextual graph approach helps to add/modify secure paths based on the newly detected contexts that need to be utilized for fine-grain security. The model presented is a generalized model that can be used in any context-aware environment or enterprise, from the office to factories.

REFERENCES

Anderson, R. (2001). *Security engineering.* New York: John Wiley & Sons.

Braghin, C., Cortesi, A., & Focardi, R. (2002a). Security boundaries in mobile ambients. *Computer Languages, 28(1), 101-127.*

Braghin, C., Cortesi, A., Focardi, A., & van Bakel, S. (2002b). *Boundary inference for enforcing security policies in mobile ambients.* Retrieved from http://www.informatics.sussex.ac.uk/users/vs/myths/reports/papers/boundaries-tcs02.pdf

BSI Global. (2003). *Information security.* Retrieved from http://www.bsi-global.com/ Information+Security/ Overview/Why.xalter

Bugliesi, M., Castagna, G., & Crafa, S. (2001a). Boxed ambients. *Proceedings of TACS* (pp. 38-63). Berlin: Springer-Verlag (LNCS 2215).

Bugliesi, M., Castagna, G., & Crafa, S. (2001b). *Reasoning about security in mobile ambients* (pp. 102-120). Berlin: Springer-Verlag (LNCS 2154).

Bugliesi, M., Castagna, G., & Crafa, S. (2004). Access control for mobile agents: The calculus of boxed ambients. *ACM Transactions on Programming Languages and Systems, 26*(1), 57-124.

Cardelli, L. (1999). *Abstraction for mobile ambients.* Retrieved from http://research.microsoft.com/Users/luca/Papers/Abstractions%20for%20Mobile%20Computation.A4.pdf

Cardelli, L., & Gordon, A.D. (1998a). Mobile ambients. *Proceedings of FOSSACS* (pp. 140-155). Berlin: Springer-Verlag (LNCS 1378).

Cardelli, L. and Gordon, A. D. (1998b). *Mobile ambients.* Retrieved from http://www.cis.upenn.edu/~lee/98cis640/Lectures/fm3.ppt#24

Cardelli, L., & Gordon, A.D. (2004). *Mobile ambients.* Retrieved from http://classes.cec.wustl.edu/~cs673/1

Covington, M.J., Fogla, P., Zhan, Z., & Ahamad, M. (2002). *A context-aware security architecture for emerging applications.* Retrieved from http://www.acsac.org/2002/papers/71.pdf

Mostéfaoui, G., & Brézillon, P. (2004a). Modeling context based security with contextual graphs. *Proceedings of the 2nd IEEE Annual Conference on Pervasive Computing and Communications Workshops.*

Mostéfaoui, G., & Brézillon, P. (2004b). Context-based security policies: A new modeling approach. *Proceedings of the 2nd IEEE Annual Conference on Pervasive Computing and Communications Workshops.*

Reid, J., Cheong, I., Henricksen, M., & Smith, J. (2003). *A novel use of RBAC to protect privacy in distributed health care information systems* (pp. 403-415). Information Security Research Center, Queensland University of Technology, Australia.

Wikipedia. (n.d.). *Ubiquitous computing.* Retrieved from http://en.wikipedia.org/wiki/Ubiquitous_computing

KEY TERMS

Contextual Graph: Graph whose edges represent the values that context information take, and have three types of nodes: branching and recombination nodes, and nodes representing security actions. A path through the graph represents a security action taken in response to particular context information.

Mobile Ambients: A process calculi that emphasizes the notion of boundaries and how processes with such boundaries interact.

Pervasive Computing: Integrates computation into the environment, rather

than having computers which are distinct objects. Other terms for ubiquitous computing include ubiquitous computing, calm technology, things that think, and everyware (Wikipedia, n.d.).

Security Action: Action taken to secure a resource, from authentication to encryption to other informational and physical measures (e.g., putting a man on guard).

Security Policy: A description of security actions to take under different circumstances. Such policies are typically specified as rules in a formal language.

Moral Rights in the Australian Public Sector

Lynley Hocking
Department of Education, Tasnania, Australia

INTRODUCTION

Moral rights amendments to the Australian Copyright Act present a challenge and an opportunity for large public sector agencies. Their implementation is not straightforward and can be interpreted in a number of ways. Moral rights amendments require a proactive response, as much of the work in public sector agencies is governed by the Copyright Act.

The interpretation of the moral rights legislative changes should not only be viewed in terms of implementing legal requirements. The implementation of the moral rights amendments in public sector organizations also requires careful consideration of the corporate culture and objectives of the organization. The legislative amendments can provide impetus for positive cultural changes that improve corporate memory, promote innovation, and provide recognition and reward incentives when monetary rewards are not available or appropriate.

BACKGROUND

The Commonwealth of Australia's *Copyright Act 1968* provides for two types of intellectual property rights: *copyright* and *moral rights*. Both moral rights and copyright attach to 'works'. The owner of the copyright in a work may or may not be the author (creator) of the work. Ownership of copyright in a work gives the exclusive right to reproduce, publish, perform, communicate, and adapt it, and to enter into commercial and rental agreements in relation to it.

Amendments to the Copyright Act in December 2000 mean that employees can claim moral rights of authorship. The moral rights are:

- the right of an individual to be attributed as an author of a work, even if the copyright ownership of the work belongs to someone else
- the right not to have authorship falsely attributed

- the right of 'integrity of authorship', which means that a creator's work should not be distorted, used, or exhibited in a way that is detrimental to the author's reputation

Moral rights are relevant to authors, co-authors, and significant contributors in a 'work'. Importantly, only individuals have moral rights. Moral rights are non-economic rights because an author cannot sell or otherwise transfer them to another person, although an author can choose not to enforce all or any of their moral rights.

Moral rights are infringed when rights of authorship are not respected. However, it is not considered an infringement if the action is considered 'reasonable'. The interpretation of what is 'reasonable' depends on:

- the nature of the work
- the purpose for which the work is used
- the manner or context in which the work is used
- the practice in the industry where the work is used
- the voluntary code of practice in the industry where the work is used
- whether the work was made in the course of the author's employment or under contract for services
- if use of the work is required by law, or is required to avoid a breach of law
- the views of co-authors

MANAGING MORAL RIGHTS IN A PUBLIC SECTOR ORGANIZATION

The legislative changes concerning moral rights are relevant when employees' work has an intellectual, artistic, literary, musical, or creative element to it. Much of the work created by staff in public sector agencies is intellectual and is covered by the Copyright Act. A reasonable proportion has a creative element to it.

Public sector agencies have had to comply with the moral rights amendments from December 2000. In addition to this legal prerogative, there are a number of other issues that need to be considered. These include:

- the existing organizational culture, particularly concerning employee recognition and reward, and the 'industry standard'
- the increased emphasis on encouraging innovation, commercial activity, and intellectual property management in the public sector around Australia
- organizational goals

The Legislative Imperative

The amendments to the Copyright Act in 2000 are both the primary rationale for managing moral rights and the most immediate issue to consider.

Work created by public servants during the course of their employment belongs to the relevant government (the 'Crown'). However, the moral rights legislative changes mean that employees can claim moral rights of authorship.

Employees are increasingly aware of their moral rights under Australian law, although there is some confusion as to what these rights entail. For example, teachers contributing to the development of curriculum material have requested rights of authorship. Agencies need to address the changes in law to avoid being exposed to an action for infringement. In some cases, employees have confused moral rights of authorship acknowledgement with the economic rights associated with copyright ownership. Such confusion needs to be addressed.

Organizational Culture and Industry Practice

Some government departments have adopted the stance that it is 'industry practice' within government not to acknowledge moral rights, while others do acknowledge them. For example, the Victorian Department of Education and Training has assumed that it is industry practice not to acknowledge authorship, while the Commonwealth Attorney General's Department has assumed that it is industry practice to acknowledge authorship on many types of works. Such confusion

in interpretation suggests that author attribution is an organizational standard in many cases, not an industry practice.

A distinction should also be made between attributing authorship internally and externally. It could be considered an 'industry standard' in the public sector that documents released as official departmental information or policy do not acknowledge individual authorship. However, in many government agencies it is the norm to acknowledge authorship for internal documents, primarily for reasons of maintaining corporate memory, and often it is not intended that these documents be used outside the agency. Such documents include project and other plans, and discussion or research papers. In some agencies authorship is often not acknowledged internally. Again, the differences between agencies suggest this is an organizational standard reflecting cultural differences, rather than an industry-wide standard.

Organizational culture can be viewed as a 'negotiated reality' (Whitely, 1995) that people experience as an objective reality as it becomes institutionalized and objectified as truths. It can be considered both a subjective reality, created by people and their perceptions, and an objective reality, shaping people's actions and perspectives (Giddens, 1979). Culture is an important concept as it highlights the importance of social interpretations and recognizes that organizations are both enduring and able to change.

Unlike the university sector, with its emphasis on individual research excellence, publication rates, and international recognition of individual staff members, public sector agencies tend to encourage a team approach to respond to community issues. In some agencies, managers are not only credited for the input they had in the coordination and quality control of works, but are often given or take authorship credit for work developed by people in their area. Such a norm is challenged by the moral rights amendments, as it is now potentially illegal for a manager to claim authorship over a work created by their subordinate.

Intellectual Property Management as a Support for Innovation

Intellectual property management within public sector agencies is also influenced by pushes to encourage innovation and unlock the economic potential of government intellectual property, primarily for economic development purposes. Most government organizations recognize innovation as a desirable goal or trait.

Many Australian state governments and the Commonwealth Government have been examining intellectual property management in the public sector as a means to stimulate commercialization, industry development, and economic growth. The Australian Commonwealth Government's "IT IP Guidelines" (Information Technology Intellectual Property Guidelines for Commonwealth agencies) emphasizes this, as do policies in states including Victoria, Western Australia, and Tasmania (Commonwealth Government of Australia, 2000; Government of Victoria, 2001; Government of Western Australia, 2003; Government of Tasmania, 2001). These approaches focus on encouraging innovation to support industry growth and profit creation. They tend to be developed or promoted by departments concerned with economic development, and encourage commercialization rather than innovation in a broader sense. The Western Australian Government has gone so far as to develop procedures for providing monetary incentives for staff whose work is commercialized and return a profit for the Crown.

However, there are other important issues governing the manner in which intellectual property is managed. For example, in the Tasmanian Department of Education, the 'value' of intellectual property also derives from its use in realizing agency and government objectives and its worth in helping to achieve community benefits. Industry growth and appropriate monetary return are secondary considerations, along with the maintenance and enhancement of intellectual property assets to foster innovation, knowledge generation and the sharing of ideas, academic and social recognition of Tasmania's education, library and other community services, and the promotion and uptake of the department's intellectual property which has value to the community. These broader goals are reflected in the department's approach to the management of its intellectual property.

For intellectual property with clear operational or community value, it may be inappropriate to provide monetary incentives for departmental employees, even if funds were available. However, moral rights acknowledgement can provide some recognition and reward for individuals involved, and so help to encourage innovation and excellence in an environment where the monetary rewards of commercial activity are not available or appropriate.

Any approach taken by public sector agencies must consider all the above issues. Obviously any approach must be consistent with the legislative requirements. The approach adopted must also take into consideration the existing culture of the organization, organizational goals and objectives, and the context and role of intellectual property management for the agency.

APPROACHES TO MANAGING MORAL RIGHTS

There are four approaches public sector agencies could take for managing moral rights:

1. Require employees to relinquish moral rights
2. Acknowledge moral rights all or most of the time
3. Acknowledge moral rights in works considered appropriate, unless requested not to
4. Acknowledge moral rights when requested and it is appropriate and reasonable. Ignoring moral rights is not a feasible option due both to the current legislative requirements and also the potential confusion amongst employees about what moral rights entail.

Require Employees to Relinquish Moral Rights

One approach is to ask all employees and contractors to relinquish their moral rights in writing. This is the approach the Victorian Department of Education and Training adopted in 2003. All contracts where moral rights could be an issue were to include a clause where the individual agrees that their work can be used in ways that are not consistent with the moral rights amendments.

Advantage

If all employees, contractors, and others were asked to relinquish all moral rights as part of their contract of engagement, the agency would not breach moral rights.

Disadvantages

This approach would be administratively cumbersome. More importantly, it would probably cause ill feeling among employees, many of whom would simply appreciate their contributions being individually acknowledged.

Requiring employees to relinquish their moral rights could result in agencies losing the benefits which could otherwise be associated with acknowledging moral rights, such as stimulating innovation.

Acknowledge Moral Rights all or Most of the Time

Another approach would be to respect all moral rights, particularly the acknowledgment of authorship wherever possible. Adopting this approach would mean that individuals' names would be attached to all or most works created within the agency.

Advantage

This approach would help to ensure an agency did not infringe moral rights.

Disadvantages

This approach would be not only inappropriate in many cases, but also almost impossible to implement for many public sector agencies. There are a number of reasons why moral rights would not be acknowledged all or most of the time in public sector agencies:

- Many documents and other works are created by a large number of individuals, all of whom may have made some contribution. Such documents can evolve over time, and individual authorship can be difficult to track.
- In many cases, work is produced by an individual or group to reflect the view of the agency. Policy documents and guidelines, for example, are intended to represent the agency's formal stance, and tend to reflect a consensus view rather than the views of individuals.
- The viewpoint of the individuals can be different from the position they are required to take in their work due to the stance of the government which

they serve. Authors may not wish to have their names associated publicly with their work.
- Employees with moral rights should be given the opportunity *not* to assert their moral rights. Systematically including the author's name in all work produced by the department would not allow for this choice.
- Names are often not linked with agencies' Web pages due to privacy issues. As most documents are now published on the Internet, there could be a conflict between maintaining privacy and acknowledging moral rights. It would also be administratively difficult to identify authors of Web pages, as Web pages tend to be dynamic over time, often with multiple authors.

Acknowledge Moral Rights in all Works Considered Appropriate, Unless Requested not to

The Commonwealth's Attorney General's Department specifies the department will:

- dentify its employees as the authors of major works and identify authors of referenced works, unless it is reasonable not to do so (right of attribution)
- not alter or treat a major work by an employee in a way that is prejudicial to the honor or reputation of the author, unless it is reasonable to do so (right of integrity)
- not falsely attribute authorship of a work (right against false attribution)

The Attorney General's Department distinguishes between major and minor works and does not acknowledge moral rights for minor works as a rule. A 'major work' is defined as a literary or artistic work that is the result of substantial creative effort. It could include discussion papers, major speeches, reports, computer programs, films, videos, photographs, and other artistic works. Ministerial correspondence or media releases would usually not constitute 'major' works.

These guidelines state there is no need to acknowledge an author who has specified *in writing* that he or she does not wish to be named as an author of the work. That is, this policy allows people to *opt out* of being acknowledged.

These commonwealth guidelines specify the Attorney General's Department will not alter or treat an author's work in any way that is detrimental to the author's honor and reputation, unless it is reasonable to do so. It would be considered reasonable to make an alteration of a work of an employee if:

- the work was a minor one (for example, a memorandum for the minister)
- the work was a major one and the alteration was considered necessary or desirable by a minister, the supervisors of the author for an official purpose, including advising or briefing a minister or employee of the department or another agency, or for an official communication
- a change was required by law or to avoid a breach of law
- if the author requests in writing that his or her name be removed from the work unless this would detract from the usefulness of the work

The Attorney General's Department Guidelines provide examples of when moral rights of attribution could be breached. In general, an author has the right not to have his or her work falsely attributed. However, a minister's signature of a letter, the issue of a press release for the minister, or an employee's signature of a minute or letter produced by another does not breach the moral right of false attribution as such documents are understood to be prepared purely for the signature of another (Commonwealth of Australia, 2002).

Advantages

This approach is the most consistent with the intent of the moral rights amendments. It defines certain kinds of work where it would be appropriate and inappropriate to acknowledge moral rights, and provides opportunity for individuals to choose not to be acknowledged.

Disadvantages

For some pubic sector organizations, this approach would represent a major shift, both for the organization as a whole and the individuals within it. While individuals have the option to specify that they do not want to be acknowledged, this approach could prove administratively cumbersome in an organization where the standard position has been to not acknowledge authorship, and a substantial proportion of work within the agency would not be appropriate for acknowledgement of moral rights. Choosing an 'opt out' approach to acknowledging moral rights would probably represent a greater administrative and cultural challenge than the approach outlined below.

Acknowledge Moral Rights when Requested and where this is Appropriate and Reasonable

The Tasmanian Department of Education's approach is to acknowledge authorship only where this is appropriate and reasonable in the circumstances, and it is requested. Authorship is not automatically attributed to much of the agency's work unless the individual author(s) specifically requested it and it is operationally feasible and appropriate.

Advantages

In many cases, non-acknowledgement of authorship would probably be considered 'reasonable', as defined by the Copyright Act, given the norms of the type of work conducted by many public sector agencies and the fact that the work was developed during the course of employment. It would also be considered 'reasonable' that works would evolve over time with multiple authors.

Examples of works that are considered appropriate for acknowledging moral rights include curriculum materials, discussion papers, and newsletter contributions. Other works, such as ministerial memorandums, policy and guideline documents, library catalogs, and much of the information on the department's official Web sites, are not considered appropriate for moral rights acknowledgement. Projects in areas such as curriculum development should address issues of moral rights proactively.

If an individual wishes to claim public authorship, then this is easily achieved in most cases, provided the contributions of any co-authors are taken into consideration. If only one of several co-authors wishes to be acknowledged, then that one individual can be publicly acknowledged as a 'contributor' or 'co-author'.

M

Disadvantages

This approach may expose the agency to the risk of impinging moral rights. However, these risks are generally easily resolved once raised and the remedies minor. Moral rights infringement would only become a significant concern if the author could illustrate personal suffering resulting from moral rights infringements.

It also involves decision making on a case-by-case basis. This approach requires well-considered guidelines as to the appropriate circumstances for acknowledging or not acknowledging moral rights.

ANALYSIS OF OPTIONS

Options 1 and 2 are not recommended. Both would be administratively cumbersome, and option 1 could cause employee ill-feeling plus prevent the benefits of moral rights.

Option 3 is closest to the spirit of the moral rights amendment legislation and is reflected in the Attorney General's Department approach. However, in many public sector agencies, it would be cumbersome and would present a challenge to those working in an organization where the norm has been not to acknowledge authorship.

Option 4 recognizes moral rights, but it takes into consideration the context and nature of much work in public sector agencies, and is administratively easier to implement. For an organization like the Tasmanian Department of Education, this conservative approach represents an approach that is implementable, while still supporting the possible benefits that the acknowledgement of moral rights can bring. It acknowledges moral rights as a useful tool for encouraging innovation and sharing by supporting the internal recognition of authorship, but does not change the acknowledgment status of most works produced for external purposes.

CONCLUSION

The implementation of the moral rights legislation is not straightforward for Australian public sector organizations, and the amendments can be interpreted in a number of ways. There are at least four possible approaches for managing moral rights. Ignoring moral rights legislation is not an option.

The moral rights amendments to the Copyright Act present both a challenge and an opportunity for a large public sector agency. Any response must reflect not only the legal requirements of the amendments, but also the organizational culture and the opportunity present for positive change.

Most public sector agencies assert innovation as an important performance measure to support the achievement of organizational goals. Effective moral rights management can help promote innovation and continuous improvement, plus the development of a high-performing and supported workforce. It can provide incentive for innovation, especially in an environment where the value of intellectual property is not only measured in terms of its commercial or monetary value, but also in terms of the contribution it makes to the organization's operations and the value it provides to the community.

ACKNOWLEDGMENT

The author would like to acknowledge the input of members of an internal Department of Education working party and colleagues who contributed into the policy development project on which this paper was based.

REFERENCES

Australian Copyright Council. (2001). *Information sheet G43—moral rights.* Retrieved from http://www. copyright.org.au

Australian Copyright Council. (2002). *B114v1 moral rights: A practical guide.* Author.

Commonwealth Government of Australia. (2002, August). *Employee relations advice: Acknowledging authorship—no. 22/2002.* Attorney General's Department.

Commonwealth Government of Australia. (2002). *The commonwealth IT IP guidelines.* Department of Communications, Information Technology and the Arts.

Copyright Agency Limited. (2003). *Moral rights? Factsheet.* Retrieved August 7, 2003, http://www. copyright.org.au/PDF/InfoSheets/G043.pdf

Copyright Council. (2002, June). *Moral rights: A practical guide.* Author.

Giddens, A. (1979). *Central problems in social theory: Action, structure and contradiction in social analysis.* New York: John Wiley & Sons.

Government of Tasmania. (2002). *Tasmania, annual report, 2001-2002.* Department of Education. Retrieved September 2003 from http://www.education.tas.gov.au

Government of Tasmania. (2003). *Managing our intellectual property—discussion paper and suggested policy.* Department of Education.

Government of Tasmania. (2006). *Managing our intellectual property—administrative policy.* Department of Education. Retrieved January 10, 2006, from http://www.education.tas.gov.au/deis/policies/ip/default.htm

Government of Tasmania. (2006). *Acknowledging moral rights.* Department of Education. Retrieved January 10, 2006, from http://staff.education.tas.gov.au/pages/deiscopyright/moralrights.htm

Government of Tasmania. (2001). *IT-related IP principles.* Department of Premier and Cabinet. Retrieved from http://www.go.tas.gov.au

Government of Tasmania. (2001). *IT-related intellectual property—an information toolkit.* Department of State Development.

Government of Victoria. (2001, December). *Capitalising on government intellectual property: An issues paper for the development of a Victorian Government intellectual property management policy.* Department of Innovation, Industry and Regional Development, Science, Technology and Management.

Government of Victoria. (2002, October). *Managing and commercialising intellectual property—a guide for Victorian universities and research institutes.* Draft for Industry Comment, Department of Innovation, Industry and Regional Development, Science, Technology and Management, Australia.

Government of Western Australia. (2003, January). *Government intellectual property policy and best practice guidelines.* Author.

Government of Western Australia. (2003). *Encouraging innovation by government employees: Procedures for the payment of monetary awards to innovative government employees.* Author.

Round, C., & Middletons Lawyers. (2001, February). *Moral rights and employment issues.* Retrieved September 18, 2003, from http://www.middletons.com.au/_site/inprint/PDF/Feb01employmentissues.PDF

TAFE Tasmania. (2003). *Learning resource development policy.* Retrieved March 13, 2003.

Teece, P. (2001). Moral rights laws pose problems for employers. *inCite,* (September). Retrieved March 13, 2003, from http://www.alia.org.au/incite/2001/09/workwatch.html

University of Tasmania. (1988, July 17). *Intellectual property policy.* Author.

Whitely, A. (1995). *Managing change: A core values approach.* Melbourne: Macmillan.

KEY TERMS

Author: The individual who created a work, or the individual act of creating a work.

Commercialization: The commercial exploitation of the results of innovation and creativity. It includes the licensing or sale (assignment) of associated IP rights.

Copyright: As defined by the Commonwealth's *Copyright Act 1968,* copyright covers works of a literary, dramatic, and musical nature; artistic works; sound recordings; films and broadcasts; photographs; and published editions of literary, dramatic, musical, or artistic work.

Economic Right of Ownership: The owner of the copyright in a work may or may not be the author (creator) of the work. Ownership of copyright in a work gives the exclusive right to reproduce, publish, perform, communicate, and adapt it, and to enter into commercial and rental agreements in relation to it. Copyright in a work is an economic right because the rights comprised in copyright can be transferred by the copyright owner to another person for a fee.

Intellectual Property (IP): Includes all rights in relation to copyright, patents, registered designs, trademarks, trade secrets, plant breeders' rights, and circuit layouts. Intellectual property has to be created in a material form for it to be recognized.

Moral Rights: Includes the right to be attributed as an author of a work, the right not to have authorship falsely attributed, and the right for one's work to not be distorted, used, or exhibited in a way that is detrimental to the author's reputation.

Moral Rights Remedies: If moral rights are infringed upon, a court may grant an injunction against using the work, order that a public apology be made, order the removal or reversal of false attribution or derogatory treatment of the work, or award damages for loss resulting from infringement. In this case, the author would have to clearly show that the work has been treated in such a derogatory manner that he or she sustained a financial loss or a loss of credibility that can be attributed to that specific infringement.

Work: A creative output, such as written material; an artistic, musical, or dramatic work; computer software; a compilation; a film or sound recording; a circuit layout; design; patent; or trademark. Both moral rights and copyright attach to 'works'.

NOTE

The views expressed in this article are the personal views of the author and do not necessarily reflect the views of the Tasmanian Department of Education.

M

Multimodal Biometric System

Ajita Rattani
Indian Institute of Technology Kanpur, India

Hunny Mehrotra
Indian Institute of Technology Kanpur, India

Phalguni Gupta
Indian Institute of Technology Kanpur, India

INTRODUCTION

Personal identification is a fundamental activity within our society. This identification is made possible by the emergence of the new concept of biometrics. Biometrics is the science of identifying or verifying an individual based on the physiological or behavioral characteristics like face, fingerprint, iris, signature, voice, retina, handwriting, and so forth. Biometric identifiers for personal authentication reduce or eliminate reliance on tokens, PINs, and passwords. It can be integrated into any application that requires security, access control, and identification or verification of people (Jain, Ross, & Prabhakar, 2004).

A wide variety of applications require reliable verification schemes to confirm the identity of an individual requesting their service. They have an edge over traditional security methods in that they cannot be easily stolen or shared. A biometric system can be either an identification system or a verification (authentication) system, defined as:

- **Identification—One to Many:** Biometrics can be used to determine a person's identity even without his knowledge or consent. For example, scanning a crowd with a camera and using face recognition technology, one can determine matches against a known database.
- **Verification—One to One**: Biometrics can also be used to verify a person's identity. For example, one can grant physical access to a secure area in a building by using finger scans or can grant access to a bank account at an ATM by using face recognition.

Biometric authentication requires comparison of a registered or enrolled biometric sample (biometric template or identifier) against a newly captured biometric sample (e.g., the one captured during a login). A simple biometric system has a sensor module, a feature extraction module, and a matching module. However, it is found that none of these individual modules (face, fingerprint, iris, signature) are 100% reliable or efficient, thus in order to further increase its reliability, several biometrics traits are fused together on the basis of one of the following fusion rule such as sum rule, min-max rule, and so forth, and the decision is made based on the final score. The multimodal systems are able to meet the stringent performance requirements imposed by various applications (Jain & Ross, 2004).

Multimodal systems also address the problem of non-universality: it is possible for a subset of users not to possess a particular biometric. For example, the feature extraction module of a fingerprint authentication system may be unable to extract features from fingerprints associated with specific individuals, due to the poor quality of the ridges. In such instances, it is useful to acquire multiple biometric traits for verifying the identity. Multimodal biometrics systems are expected to be more reliable due to the presence of multiple, fairly independent pieces of evidence.

BACKGROUND

Uni-modal systems, besides having high error rates, have to contend with a variety of problems such as *noise in sensed data, intra-class variations, interclass similarities, non-universalities,* and *spoof attacks.* Some examples of noise in sensed data are fingerprint image with a scar. *Intra-class variations* are typically caused by a user who is incorrectly interacting with the sensor or due to changes in the biometric characteristics of a user over a period of time. In a biometric

Figure 1. Multimodal system

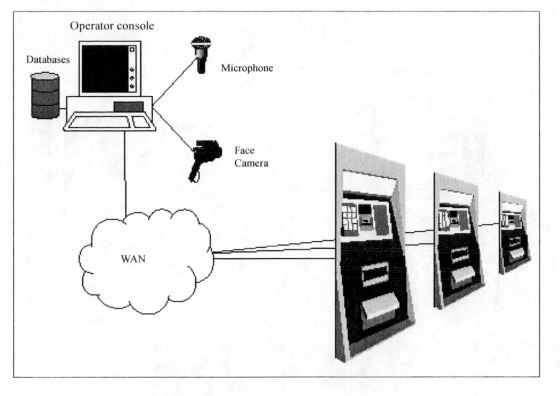

system comprising a large number of users, there may be *interclass similarities* in the feature space of multiple users. Another source is *non-universality*: the biometric system may not be able to acquire meaningful biometric data from a subset of users. *Spoof attacks* are especially relevant when behavioral traits such as signature and voice are used.

Multimodal biometric systems overcome limitations of uni-modal biometric systems by consolidating the evidence obtained from different sources. These sources can be of the following forms and are shown in Figure 2 (Ross & Jain, 2004):

i. **Multiple sensors for the same biometric:** More than one sensor is used to grab images, and then these images are fused together and analyzed for better results (e.g., optical and solid state fingerprint sensors).

ii. **Multiple instances of the same biometric:** Multiple instances of an individual are processed and fused to generate the final result (e.g., multiple face images of a person obtained under different pose/lightning condition).

iii. **Multiple representations and matching algorithms for the same biometric:** Multiple representations and classifiers are applied on the same biometric data to generate the final result (e.g., multiple face matchers like PCA and LDA).

iv. **Multiple units of the same biometric:** Multiple units of an individual are used to check the authenticity of a person (e.g., left and right iris images).

v. **Multiple biometric traits:** Multiple modalities are used to test the authenticity of a person (e.g., face, fingerprint, and iris).

In the multi-biometrics system, different classifiers/modalities for recognition are combined at one of the four levels—sensor level, feature extraction level, matching score level, and decision level—and it performs better compared to individual recognizers and classifiers. Ross and Jain (2003) have presented an overview of multimodal biometrics and have proposed various levels of fusion, various possible scenarios, the different modes of operation, integration strategies, and design issues. A multimodal system can operate in one of three different modes: serial mode, paral-

Figure 2. Multi biometrics system (Ross & Jain, 2004)

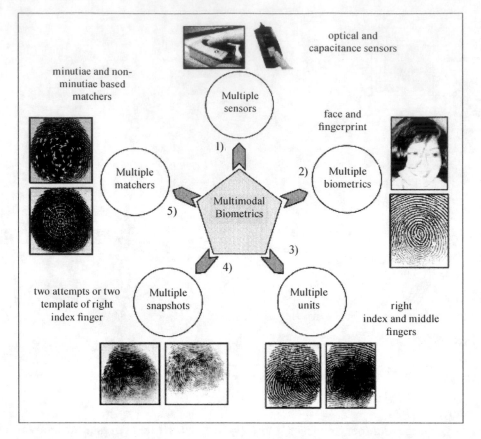

lel mode, or hierarchical mode. In the serial mode of operation, the output of one modality is typically used to narrow down the number of possible identities before the next modality is used. In the parallel mode of operation, the information from multiple modalities is used simultaneously in order to perform recognition. In the hierarchical scheme, individual classifiers may be combined in a treelike structure. This mode is more relevant for the large number of classifiers. In order to design a good integration strategy, there is a need for a well-studied multimodal biometric system. These include: (a) the choice and number of biometric traits to be considered, (b) the level in the biometric system at which information provided by multiple traits should be integrated, (c) the methodology adopted to integrate the information, and (d) the trade-off between cost and matching performance.

A substantial amount of work has been carried out on the combination of multiple classifiers. Most of such work focuses on fusing 'weak' classifiers for the purpose of increasing the overall performance (Tolba

& Rezq, 2000). A hybrid fingerprint matcher which fuses minutiae and reference point location classifiers has been proposed by Ross, Jain, and Riesman (2003). It has been reported that the performance of the hybrid matcher is better than individual classifiers. Matching scores generated by comparing the minutiae sets and the reference points are combined in order to generate a single matching score using sum rule. Let S_M and S_R indicate the similarity scores obtained using minutiae matching and ridge feature map matching, respectively. Then, the final matching score is computed as $S = \alpha\, S_M + (1-\alpha)\, S_R$, where α is constant lying between 0 and 1. It is possible to vary α to assign different weights to the individual matchers.

There is also a recent spurt in the field of multimodal biometrics where multiple traits are combined/integrated for higher performance purposes. Three biometric modalities—face, fingerprint, and hand geometry—have been combined in Ross and Jain (2003), and all scores are mapped to the range [0; 100]. A score vector $(x_1;\ x_2;\ x_3)$ represents the scores of multiple matchers, with x_1, x_2, and x_3 corresponding to the scores obtained from the three modalities. It has been reported that performance of the combined modalities is better than the individual three recognizers. The two techniques—sum rule and decision tree—have been used to combine the scores. Yunhong, Tan, and Jain (2003) proposed the fusion of iris and face modalities, and reported that besides improving verification performance, the fusion of these two has several other advantages.

Dass, Nandakumar, and Jain (2005) have proposed an approach to score level fusion in multimodal biometrics systems. Experimental results have been presented on face, fingerprint, and hand geometry using product rule and coupla method. It is found that both fusion rules show better performance than individual recognizers. The framework for optimally combining the matching scores from multiple modalities based on generalized densities is estimated from the genuine and impostor matching scores. The motivation for using generalized densities is that some parts of the score distributions can be discrete in nature. Two approaches for combining evidence based on generalized densities—(i) the product rule, which assumes independence between the individual modalities; and (ii) copula models, which parametrically model the dependence between the matching scores of multiple modalities—show better performance than individual recognizers.

Information Fusion in Multimodal Biometrics

The level of fusion depends on the application scenario and security requirements. Biometric systems that integrate information at an early stage of processing are believed to be more effective than those systems that perform integration at a later stage. Since the features contain richer information in the input biometric data than in the matching score or the decision of a matcher, integration at the feature level should provide better recognition results than other levels of integration. The levels of fusion can be broadly categorized into fusion prior to matching and fusion after matching.

Fusion Prior to Matching

Here integration of information can take place either at the sensor level or at the feature level. *Sensor-level fusion* can be done only if the multiple cues are either instances of the same biometric trait obtained from multiple compatible sensors or multiple instances of the same biometric trait obtained using a single sensor. For example, the face images obtained from several cameras can be combined to form a 3D model of the face, and mosaicking of multiple fingerprint impressions can form a more complete fingerprint image (Ross & Jain, 2002). Sensor-level fusion may not be possible if the data instances are incompatible. For example, it may not be possible to integrate face images obtained from cameras with different resolutions.

Feature-level fusion refers to combining different feature vectors that are obtained from one of the following sources: multiple sensors for the same biometric trait, multiple instances of the same biometric trait, multiple units of the same biometric trait, and multiple biometric traits. When the feature vectors are homogeneous, a single resultant feature vector can be calculated as a weighted average of the individual feature vectors. When the feature vectors are non-homogeneous, one can concatenate them to form a single feature vector. Concatenation is not possible when the feature sets are incompatible (e.g., fingerprint minutiae and eigenface coefficients).

However, integration at the feature level is difficult to achieve in practice because of the following reasons:

i. The relationship between the feature spaces of different biometric systems may not be known. In the case where the relationship is known in advance, care needs to be taken to discard highly correlated features. This requires the use of some well-known feature selection algorithms prior to classification.

ii. Concatenating two feature vectors may result in a large feature vector, leading to the 'curse of dimensionality' problem. Kumar, Wong, Shen, and Jain (2003) have presented an approach which combines palmprint and hand-geometry features, while a combination of face and hand-geometry features has been given by Ross and Govindarajan (2005). But both the approaches are found to have limited success.

iii. Commercially available software may not provide access to the generated feature vectors. Hence, a little work has been done for integration at the feature level, and the schemes after matching have become more popular. One way to fuse at feature level can be describe as follows. The feature vectors of two classifiers/modalities $F_i = \{f_{i,1}, f_{i,2}, ... f_{i,n}\}$ and $H_i = \{h_{i,1}, h_{i,2}, ...h_{i,m}\}$ are normalized, and feature selection is performed on concatenated feature vectors to obtain the augmented feature vector $X_i = \{x_{i,1}, x_{i,2}, ...x_{i,d}\}$. The normalized feature vectors F_i' and H_i' are computed by applying a transformation to the individual feature values using some normalization scheme such as min-max, z-score, and median absolute deviation (MAD) in order to ensure that the feature values across the two modalities are compatible.

Fusion after Matching

When the biometric matchers output a set of possible matches along with the confidence measure (matching score), integration can be done at the *matching score level,* also known as fusion at the *measurement level* or *confidence level.* Next to the feature vectors, the matching scores output by the matchers contain the richest information about the input pattern. Also, it is relatively easy to access and combine the scores generated by the different matchers. The methods for consolidating scores fall into two categories—classification approach and combination approach.

In the classification approach, a feature vector is constructed using the matching scores output by the individual matchers; this feature vector is then classified into one of two classes: "accept" (genuine user) or "reject" (impostor). Generally, the classifier used for this purpose is capable of learning the decision boundary irrespective of how the feature vector is generated. Hence, the output scores of the different modalities can be non-homogeneous (distance or similarity metric, different numerical ranges, etc.), and no processing is required prior to feeding them into the classifier.

In the combination approach, the individual matching scores are combined to generate a single scalar score which is then used to make the final decision. The scores are first transformed to common domain to ensure meaningful combination. Thus before applying the combination approach, these scores are normalized to common range. The matching scores at the output of the individual matchers *may not be homogeneous.* For example, one matcher may output a distance (dissimilarity) measure while another may output a proximity (similarity) measure. Further, the outputs of the individual matchers *need not be on the same numerical scale* (range). Finally, the matching

scores at the output of the matchers *may follow different statistical distributions.* Due to these reasons, score normalization is essential to transform the scores of the individual matchers into a common domain prior to combining them. Min-max normalization and z-score normalization are some of the popular techniques used for score normalization (Snelick, Indovina, Yen, & Mink, 2003).

MULTIMODAL BIOMETRICS SYSTEM AT THE INDIAN INSTITUTE OF TECHNOLOGY KANPUR (IITK)

A Multimodal Biometrics System for Human Identification, based on four traits of face, fingerprint, iris, and signature, is being developed at the Indian Institute of Technology Kanpur, India. The system is designed for applications where the training database contains a face, an iris, two fingerprint images, and one or two signature images for each individual The final decision is made by fusion at "matching score level architecture," in which feature vectors are created independently for query images. These feature vectors are then compared to the enrollment templates that are stored during database preparation for each biometric trait. Based on the proximity of feature vector and template, each subsystem computes its own matching score. These individual scores are finally combined into a total score, which is then passed to the decision module. The efforts have been done to develop a multi-classifier cum multimodal biometrics system. Figure 3 shows an example. Multiple classifiers are developed for fingerprint and iris recognition system. These classifiers were combined at the decision level, and improvement in the results was recorded. Then the four traits were combined at the matching score level to generate a final matching score.

Thus overall multimodal at IITK can be explained as follows. In *face recognition,* the detected face image is used to extract features using the Elastic Bunch Graph matching algorithm (Bolme, Beveridge, Teixeira, & Draper, 2003) with the accuracy of 97.96%, and FAR and FRR of 0.59% and 3.49% respectively. In *fingerprint verification,* the matching is done on the basis of extracted features, that is, minutiae locations and reference point (Ross et al., 2003). The accuracy of the system is 93.05%, with FAR and FRR of 8% and 5% respectively. In *iris recognition,* the input image is

Figure 3. Multimodal biometrics system at IITK

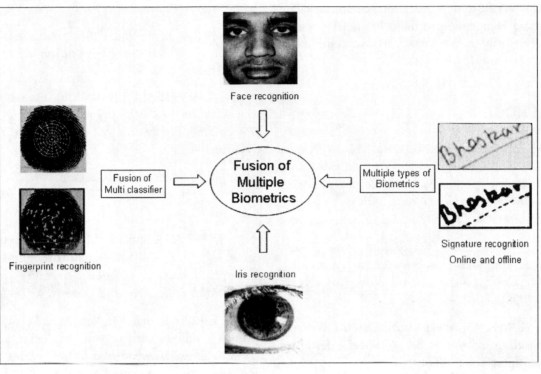

FUTURE TRENDS

preprocessed to remove the effect of holes and spots of light and is matched by the extraction of unique iris patterns (Li, Yunhong, & Tan, 2002) using a combination of Haar Wavelet and Circular Mellin approaches (Ravichandran & Trivedi, 1995). The accuracy of the system is 95.37%, with FAR and FRR of 8.49% and 0.87% respectively. In *signature verification,* the input image is processed to extract Global and Local features (Saeed & Adamski, 2005) like Width to Height ratio, High Pressure Regions, and so o n, and is matched using Euclidean Distance. The accuracy of the system is 91%, with FAR and FRR of 10% and 8% respectively. All these traits are tested on the IITK database comprising approximately 500 images for each trait. The results are combined at the matching score level using a sum of scores technique.

The research is still being conducted to further enhance the robustness, reliability, and accuracy of the multimodal biometrics system at IITK. The system is being rigorously tested under varying environmental conditions, and the limitations are recorded to bring out necessary changes in the proposed system.

To further improve the reliability and robustness of the system, the possibility of combining soft biometrics like age, gender, ethnicity, weight, height, iris, and color with different classifiers/traits is also being studied. Another important aspect is to study the dynamic updating of the biometric templates of the user in the database.

CONCLUSION

Demands for biometrics-based personal authentication technologies are progressively increasing. There are high expectations with the applications to the security field. To meet these demands, continuous research and development for biometrics is going on, aiming at faster speeds, smaller size, and lower cost, and is expanding its application fields utilizing non-contact authentication and high authentication accuracy. And in order to increase reliability/robustness, several biometrics traits are fused together on the basis of an efficient fusion rule and the decision is made based on the final score. Hence, a multimodal biometrics system improves reliability and accuracy by overcoming few limitations of a single biometric.

REFERENCES

Bolme, D.S., Beveridge, J.R., Teixeira, M.L., & Draper, B.A. (2003). The CSU face identification evaluation system: Its purpose, features and structure. *Proceedings of the 3rd International Conference on Computer Vision Systems* (ICVS) (pp. 304-313), Graz, Austria.

Dass, S.C., Nandakumar, K., & Jain, A.K. (2005). A principled approach to score level fusion in multimodal biometrics system. *Proceedings of ABVPA* (pp. 1049-1058).

Jain, A.K., & Ross, A. (2004). Multibiometric systems. *Communications of the ACM, 47*(Special Issue on Multimodal Interfaces), 34-40.

Jain, A.K., Ross, A., & Prabhakar, S. (2004). An introduction to biometric recognition. *IEEE Transactions on Circuits and Systems for Video Technology, 14*(1), 4-20.

Kumar, A., Wong, D.C.M., Shen, H.C., & Jain, A.K. (2003). Personal verification using palmprint and hand geometry biometric. *Proceedings of the 4th International Conference on Audio and Video-Based Biometric Person Authentication* (AVBPA) (pp. 668-678), Guildford, UK.

Li, M., Yunhong, W., & Tan, T. (2002). Iris recognition using circular symmetric filters. *IEEE International Conference on Pattern Recognition* (ICPR) (vol. 2, pp. 414-417).

Ravichandran, G., & Trivedi, M.M. (1995). Circular-mellin features for texture segmentation. *IEEE Transactions on Image Processing, 4*, 1629-1640.

Ross, A., & Govindarajan, R. (2005). Feature level fusion using hand and face biometrics. *Proceedings of the SPIE Conference on Biometric Technology for Human Identification* (pp. 196-204), Florida.

Ross, A., & Jain, A.K. (2002). Fingerprint mosaicking. *Proceedings of the International Conference on Acoustic Speech and Signal Processing* (ICASSP) (pp. 4064-4067), Florida.

Ross, A., & Jain, A.K. (2003). Information fusion in biometrics. *Pattern Recognition Letters, 24*(13), 2115-2125.

Ross, A., & Jain, A.K. (2004). Multimodal biometrics: An overview. *Proceedings of the 12th European Signal Processing Conference (EUSIPCO) (pp. 1221-1224)*, Vienna, Austria.

Ross, A., Jain, A.K., & Riesman, J.A. (2003). A hybrid fingerprint matcher. *Pattern Recognition, 36*, 1661-1673.

Saeed, K., & Adamski, M. (2005). Extraction of global features for offline signature recognition. *Image Analysis, Computer Graphics, Security Systems and Artificial Intelligence Applications, 429-436.*

Snelick, R., Indovina, M., Yen, J., & Mink, A. (2003). Multimodal biometrics: Issues in design and testing. *Proceedings of the 5th International Conference on Multimodal Interfaces* (pp. 68-72), Vancouver, Canada.

Tolba, A.S., & Rezq, A.A. (2000). Combined classifier for invariant face recognition. *Pattern Analysis and Applications, 3*(4), 289-302.

Yunhong, W., Tan, T., & Jain, A.K. (2003). Combining face and iris biometrics for identity verification. *Proceedings of the 4th International Conference on AVBPA* (pp. 805-813), Guildford, UK.

KEY TERMS

Biometrics: The automated recognition of an individual based on biological and behavioral characteristics.

Enrollment: The initial process of collecting biometric data from a user and then storing it in a template for later use.

False Acceptance Rate: The likelihood expressed in percentage that a biometric sample submitted by someone attempting to gain illegal entry to a biometric system is accepted.

False Rejection Rate: The likelihood expressed in percentage that a biometric sample submitted by a correct individual is rejected by a biometric system.

Fusion: The general method of improving performance via collection of multiple samples is known as biometric fusion.

Identification: The biometric system identifies a person from the entire enrolled population by searching a database for a match.

Multi-Biometrics: The ability to utilize multiple biometrics modalities (multimodal), instances within a modality (multi-instance), and/or algorithms (multi-algorithmic) prior to making a specific verification/identification or enrollment decision.

Template: The mathematical representation of biometric data.

Threshold: A predefined number often controlled by a biometric system administrator which establishes the degree of correlation necessary for a comparison to be deemed a match.

Verification: The biometric system matches a person's claimed identity to his/her previously enrolled pattern.

Objective Ethics for Managing Information Technology

John R. Drake
Auburn University, USA

INTRODUCTION

Businessmen have faced ethical dilemmas throughout history in many varying contexts. Today, chief information officers (CIOs) and information technology (IT) managers, in particular, face many ethical dilemmas from not only traditional business dilemmas, but also in managing IT. Traditional ethical issues of business, such as receiving gifts and promotional items from vendors, affect any manager in charge of purchases. In addition, IT managers must also make decisions with regards to technological issues such as information privacy, security, and accountability. IT facilitates action, both good and bad. This means that individuals can act *good* with far more efficiency and act *bad* with more malevolence. Actions that may not have been possible without IT now become issues because people have the means to do them. Managers need not only to adopt a moral code for themselves, but to encourage their employees to adopt a moral code or guard against and appropriately deal with behavior that violates that code.

Identifying and understanding an objective ethical framework is critical for the rapidly changing nature of information technology. Without an appropriate ethical standard to guide choices and actions in ever more complex and subtle situations, IT managers and professionals will find choosing morally acceptable solutions ever more difficult, leading to dangers in the long-term success of the organization. CIOs need to cut through the haze of conflicting demands to make decisions for the benefit of the organization. CIOs also need to be confident that their employees will act in appropriate, non-arbitrary manners when making decisions. The need to research ethics with regard to IT has been demonstrated numerous times (Davison, 2000; Rose, 2006; Stewart & Segars, 2002), yet none has provided an objective standard for making decisions. While several research efforts have explored normative and applied ethical theories as applied to IT (Davison, 2000; Walsham, 1996; Wood-Harper, Corder, Wood, & Watson, 1996), none has questioned the underlying assumptions nor provided a compelling case for a non-arbitrary, objective moral code. Reviewing existing ethical theories should lead us to a standard that is applicable and beneficial to IT managers.

BACKGROUND

Ethics is the study of morals and moral choices. It is the study of individual purposes and values that guide life. Ethics examines which values and virtues are necessary vs. which are optional, and defines the ultimate source of values. In an increasingly complex world, these guiding principles direct how we should live by providing a moral code—"a code of values to guide man's choices and actions" (Rand, 1964, p. 13). Individuals need a moral code to guide their decisions and actions. This is true for their private lives as well as in social situations, such as in business.

Three branches of ethical theory include *meta-ethics, normative ethics,* and *descriptive ethics.* Descriptive ethics does not promote any one theory over any other, but merely tries to explain the observed ethics of others individuals. Normative ethics attempts to define what types of behaviors are acceptable. Meta-ethics takes a more abstract view by asking what "goodness" means and if there are any standards for morality.

Research in business ethics usually focuses on normative or descriptive ethics, without consideration to underlying meta-ethical assumptions (Miner & Petocz, 2003). When meta-ethical perspectives are considered, they do not prescribe an ideal, rather they state that there is disagreement between perspectives (Karmasin, 2002). This stance, where all meta-ethical perspectives are equally valid, leaves CIOs and IT managers without an objective standard by which to guide their actions. Because a meta-ethical perspective deals with the foundation of ethics, a flawed foundation leads to flawed conclusions in IT ethical issues.

One general meta-ethical discussion can be found in Tara Smith's *Viable Values* (2000). In this book, she critiques four dominant ethical perspectives: intuitionism, contractarianism, rationalism, and intrinsic value. All four of these ethical perspectives fall short of providing an objective and rational basis for morality. A fifth ethical perspective, objectivism, based on the writings of Ayn Rand, successfully develops and supports an objective standard for ethical decisions. In the next section, we review each of the meta-ethical perspectives, provide examples of IT managers' behavior using that perspective, and examine a specific case using the different perspectives.

Case

A recent controversy over Sony's Digital Rights Management (DRM) rootkit provides a case analysis for understanding the meta-ethical perspectives. In this controversy, Sony was installing a DRM program on user computers when purchasers of Sony-copyrighted audio CDs copied the songs onto their computers. As part of the end users' license agreement (EULA), the users acknowledged that a DRM was being installed to prevent illegal copying of songs. As justice requires, users not satisfied with copyright protections are free not to buy the product. However, the controversy over the DRM that Sony installed is that the EULA does not disclose that some of the files are cloaked and the whole program is uninstallable. This creates vulnerabilities on computers where the DRM is installed, violating the respect for property of those customers.

ETHICAL STANDARDS

Intuitionism

The first school of thought on why be moral comes from the intuitionists. In this view, obligations are viewed as self-evident (Prichard, 1952). For intuitionist IT managers, merely looking at a technological issue tells them what is morally right and wrong. Denying the self-evident is tantamount to denying their senses. No amount of argument will reveal the truth. Smith (2000) unravels this theory by asking what exactly is intuition. Is it a thought? Is it an emotion?

Intuitionists' claim that morality is self-evident disavows any method for determining what is moral

and what is not. It becomes impossible to replicate the thought process in discovering morals because they identify no thought process. An example may be an IT manager identifying computer hacking as a bad behavior without being open to discussion or argument about *why* it is bad. As Smith (2000) notes, "Intuitionists completely fail to explain what distinguishes the claim 'I know it by intuition' from the claim 'I believe it.' Consequently, intuitionist's account of morality…is completely arbitrary" (p. 28). If we are to have any hope in identifying a standard for ethics in IT, use of intuition will not help us.

In the Sony case, it is impossible to know how an intuitionist would judge Sony's actions. They may claim that copyright violations are obviously wrong, therefore Sony is morally obligated to protect their property by any means necessary. They may alternatively claim that it is self-evident that Sony was malicious and therefore Sony is immoral. Either way, the arbitrary assertions lack a clear standard for determining what is right or wrong.

Contractarianism

Contractarianists, on the other hand, believe that moral authority is established through a contract to be moral. IT managers should be moral because they have agreed to be moral. Variations of contractarianism argue such agreement may be explicit or implicit, actual or hypothetical, and even individually or socially oriented. Contractarian philosopher David Gauthier (1986) declares that "moral principles are introduced as the objects of fully voluntary *ex ante* agreements among rational persons" (p. 9). People agree to honor contracts because it is in their own self-interest to do so (Hobbes, 1968). If they do not, their reputation may be destroyed, resulting others eschewing any further involvement with them.

The commonsense, simple approach to contractarianism attracts many proponents, especially among businessmen. However, there are flaws with this approach to morality. First is the relativism of contractarianism. Is any code of ethics valid as long as people agree to it? Is software piracy valid if everyone agrees it is? Relativism is not a fatal flaw, but certainly begs the question as to what exactly is the foundation for this theory.

Contractarianism says that contracts should be honored. Yet, there are no means of identifying why contracts *must* be honored. If it is merely the promise to do something that creates the obligation, then taking back that promise at any time should relieve you of that obligation. This flaw has led contractarianists to propose that the contract itself is not the foundation for morals but the individual's self-interest in following it. This also has its problems. If contracts are honored because of self-interest, then what happens when it is no longer in the individual's self-interest to honor a contract? If an employee knows he or she can escape detection, it may be in his or her "self-interest" to secretly steal corporate information and sell it to competitors. As other employees realize that the company lacks information security, they will also abuse the system, resulting in a moral breakdown.

This free-rider problem stems from a misconception of self-interest promoted by contractarians. As Smith (2000) observes, they do not contend that "only disciplined adherence to a particular code of actions could enhance a person's well-being" (p. 35). Rather, the defense of contractarianism is that there is a possibility of the contract violations being *discovered*. Defense of contractarianism without an objective standard collapses into subjectivism. It simply does not provide a satisfactory foundation for ethics.

Again, we find that it would be impossible to predict how a contractarian would view the Sony case. Is Sony guilty of breaking an implicit contract when it did not disclose the rootkit in the EULA? On the other hand, does the purchase of a copyright-protected CD justify the inclusion of any software installed on the customer computer in order to protect that copyright? Again, the lack of an objective standard prevents a clear valuation from being established.

Rationalism

Another basis for morality is provided by rationalism. Rationalism holds that one should be moral because rationality requires it. One of the preeminent rationalist philosophers, Immanuel Kant, argues that morality is our duty because rationality demands it (Kant, 1990). He argues that our morals are not to serve our life, but rather we live so that we can be moral. Not all rationalists agree with Kant, yet the underlying conception of morality is that something is moral only if it is rational.

Smith (2000) recognizes that rationalism has appeal because it appears logical, rigorous, all encompassing,

and neutral. However, these notions are ultimately based on a false foundation. Rationalists deny that reality is the final source of morals, but rather argue that reason is. They contend that morality is based solely on reason, without reference to ends, and that discussion of ends confuses motivation with justification. They would argue that a CIO may be motivated to secure his network, but without a rational justification distinct from motivation, the behavior is without moral significance. This conception however distorts the nature of reason. Reason's usefulness cannot be divorced from its ends. Ends demand that purposes and goals be based on the context of the situation. Motivation and justification, while conceptually different, cannot be divorced from each other. Justification for securing a network requires not just a single reason for doing it, but must be relative to the full context of facts surrounding the action. Without tying justification of ends to reality, CIOs are left with a subjective ethical theory. This is the fatal flaw in the rationalist's theory.

A rationalist might say that Sony has a duty to be honest regardless of consequences. Alternatively, they may say that the customer has a duty to accept the rootkit out of obligation to the copyright holder. In either case, the duties carry an authoritative pronouncement that is not supported by the context.

Intrinsic Value

The fourth attempt at establishing moral authority is with intrinsic value. Ethicists, not content with the various subjectivist theories discussed above, retreated to a theory that places value in the objects themselves, rather than in the subject. In other words, value is intrinsic to the nature of the thing. To defend successfully, proponents of intrinsic value must explain why objects have value in and of themselves. Efforts such as organic unity (Nozick, 1989), favorable disposition (Railton, 1986), and majority consensus (Lemos, 1994) each try to explain this basis Although it is not always identified, it is usually believed that intrinsic value is self-evident. This appeal to the self-evident nature of value strikes a remarkable resemblance to intuitionism.

Intuitionism, however, does not say anything about the ultimate source of value other than it is immediately known and not imitative. Intrinsic value proponents state that value is derivate to the object itself. Yet, there is no evidence that intrinsic value actually exists and no standards by which to judge if something has value. "The absence of objective evidence for intrinsic value, alongside the utterly subjective basis on which people assert it, leaves us without grounds to credit its existence" (Smith, 2000, p. 69). Ultimately, intrinsic value must adopt a subjective foundation, which fails in the same ways that other subjective moral systems fail.

Proponents of intrinsic value might assert that rootkits, by their very nature, are intrinsically evil and that any company that uses them are therefore evil. Other proponents of intrinsic value may argue that the possibility of copyright violations destroys social unity, so any means of preventing those violations is good. In either case, arbitrary assertions become moral commandments, with no clear standard for judging things morally.

Objectivism

The case for objectivism begins with a discussion of the nature of life in relation to value. Life is self-generated, self-sustaining action (Aristotle, 1941). Plants, animals, and humans all have to do something to maintain their existence. Their activities are either good for them or bad for them. They will either promote their life or destroy it. Without values, living things would have no goals for their actions. Values allow life to be sustained. Yet, without life, values would not exist. Since values are only cognizant in relation to the ends to each a being acts, that being must be able to act in order for values to exist. It is the concept of life that makes values possible.

It is this reciprocal relationship between values and life that sustains the foundation for ethics. Life is the ultimate goal, without which no other values would be possible (Rand, 1964). If chosen values conflict with this ultimate goal, then the life of that creature would cease. Humans have specific needs to stay alive. In order to meet those needs, specific values must be pursued. Life becomes the ultimate measure of success. This grounding of values in fundamental human needs for sustaining life is what provides ethics with an objective standard. Life is the ultimate goal *and* the standard for ethics. For IT managers, actions that promote and enhance their lives, while simultaneously promoting the business and its customers, are good. The ultimate goal of business is to create value for their customers (Drucker, 1954), so decisions in information privacy, security, accountability, and accuracy should be based on the creation of objective values.

The objectivity of values is found with their relation to life. Values and virtues that promote life are objective. Morality, which is a code of values and virtues, must also promote life to retain any objectivity. By tying ethics to these facts of reality and our nature as human beings, Rand (1964) established an objective morality and a rational basis for egoism.

One common effort to discredit objectivism's ethical theory starts with optional values, such as the choice of careers or operating system preferences (LeBar, 2001; Spohn, 2004). Critics often point to these values as evidence of latent subjectivism that Rand's theory does not explain. Optional values vary from person to person and even change within the same person over time. Because these values vary by the subject in question, it is argued that the values are subjective in nature. Smith (2000) addresses this issue by pointing out that if these optional values still promote the individual's life, then they still maintain their objective nature. Objectivity applies to the context in which the judgment is made, not to its relation to other people's values. The fact that individuals live in widely varying contexts gives rise to widely varying optional values. This diversity does not however lend any support to the notion that values are subjective.

In objectivism's view of the Sony case, moral violations stem from the firm's dishonest, unjust, and irrational behavior, which ultimately damaged the firm's reputation. This behavior put the long-term survival of the firm and all of its shareholders and employees at risk. While protecting copyrights is critical for Sony's long-term interests, short-sighted attempts at that protection endangers the corporation with consumer outrage. Sony's dishonesty in concealing the DRM rootkit is but one manifestation of how the company hurt its long-term survival (Hsieh, 2004; Rand, 1964; Smith, 2003). The managers responsible for these decisions should be held morally responsible for the damage done to Sony's long-term viability.

FUTURE TRENDS

With objectivism's approach, IT managers can understand complex issues, evaluate them, and act with certainty. Applying objectivism's ethical foundation to normative and applied issues relevant to IT managers and CIOs is greatly needed. Objectivism requires careful thought to untangle the nature of particular issues and to ensure that an objective standard for self-interest is maintained. Researchers in MIS have identified many issues relevant to IT managers, such as security, trust, privacy, accountability, accessibility, property, and accuracy (Davison, 2000; Lu, Marchewka, Lu, & Yu, 2004; Mason, 1986). Analyzing each of these issues through the objectivist lens will provide researchers and IT managers with an objective standard for action.

CONCLUSION

This article re-examines the ethical frameworks often employed in making ethical decisions. Of the major ethical theories, objectivism is the only one that provides a usable objective standard for evaluating values and virtues. While a conceptual foundation provides the groundwork, much research needs to be done to fully concretize objectivism's importance to and usage of information systems. Until such efforts are followed, managers will only have weak and amorphous ethical concepts to guide them. These deficiencies can jeopardize the long-term organizational survival.

REFERENCES

Aristotle. (1941). Nicomachean ethics. In R. McKeon (Ed.), *Basic works of Aristotle.* New York: Random House.

Davison, R.M. (2000). Professional ethics in information systems: A personal perspective. *Communications of the AIS, 3*(8).

Drucker, P. (1954). *The practice of management.* New York: HarperCollins.

Gauthier, D. (1986). *Morals by agreement.* New York: Oxford University Press.

Hobbes, T. (1968). *Leviathan.* New York: Penguin.

Hsieh, D.M. (2004). False excuses: Honesty, wrongdoing, and moral growth. *The Journal of Value Inquiry, 38,* 171-185.

Kant, I. (1990). *Foundations of the metaphysics of morals* (L.W. Beck, Trans.; academy ed.). New York: Macmillan.

Karmasin, M. (2002). Towards a meta ethics of culture—halfway to a theory of metanorms. *Journal of Business Ethics, 39*(4), 337-346.

LeBar, M. (2001). Book review. *The Journal of Value Inquiry, 35,* 575-579.

Lemos, N. (1994). *Intrinsic value.* New York: Cambridge University Press.

Lu, C., Marchewka, J.T., Lu, J., & Yu, C.-S. (2004). Beyond concern: A privacy-trust-behavioral intention model of electronic commerce. *Information & Management, 42,* 127-142.

Mason, R.O. (1986). Four ethical issues of the information age. *MIS Quarterly, 10*(1), 5-12.

Miner, M., & Petocz, A. (2003). Moral theory in ethical decision making: Problems, clarifications and recommendations from a psychological perspective. *Journal of Business Ethics, 42*(1), 11-25.

Nozick, R. (1989). *The examined life—philosophical mediations.* New York: Simon and Schuster.

Prichard, H.A. (1952). Does moral philosophy rest on a mistake? In W. Sellars & J. Hospers (Eds.), *Readings in ethical theory.* New York: Appleton-Century-Croft.

Railton, P. (1986). Facts and values. *Philosophical Topics, 9*(17).

Rand, A. (1964). *The virtue of selfishness.* New York: Signet.

Rose, E.A. (2006). An examination of the concern for information privacy in the New Zealand regulatory context. *Information & Management, 43*(3), 322.

Smith, T. (2000). *Viable values.* Lanham, MD: Rowman & Littlefield.

Smith, T. (2003). The metaphysical case for honesty. *The Journal of Value Inquiry, 37,* 517-531.

Spohn, W. (2004). On the objectivity of facts, beliefs, and values. In P. Machamer & G. Wolters (Eds.), *Science, values and objectivity.* Pittsburgh: University of Pittsburgh Press.

Stewart, K.A., & Segars, A.H. (2002). An empirical examination of the concern for information privacy instrument. *Information Systems Research, 13*(1), 36-49.

Walsham, G. (1996). Ethical theory, code of ethics and IS practice. *Information Systems Journal, 6,* 69-81.

Wood-Harper, A.T., Corder, S., Wood, J.R.G., & Watson, H. (1996). How we profess: The ethical systems analyst. *Communications of the ACM, 39*(3), 69-77.

KEY TERMS

Contractarianism: An ethical theory that grounds morality in a contract between individuals.

Ethics: The study of the general nature of morals, moral choices, and moral standards.

Intrinsic Value: An ethical theory that grounds morality in the intrinsic nature of objects.

Intuitionism: An ethical theory that grounds morality in the person's intuition.

Morality: A code of values to guide one's actions.

Objectivism: An ethical theory that grounds morality in the objective standard of one's own life.

Rationalism: An ethical theory that grounds morality in rationality.

Value: That which one acts to gain and/or keep.

O

Parental Rights to Monitor Internet Usage

Benjamin J. Halpert

Nova Southeastern University, USA

INTRODUCTION

Technological advances do not occur in isolation of the society in which they are intended to be used. As the demand, evolution, and maturation of computing technologies continues to increase, the price of entry for consumers decreases (Baye, 2006). Households that used to have one personal computer may now have several computing devices for each member of the family (Ketchum Global Research Network, 2005). Technologies, for the most part, are not developed to be bound by social or ethical norms (Hansson & Palm, in press). Just as a gun can do no harm unless it is used by an individual with malicious intent, so too is the case with computing technologies. A chat room that is frequented by children for the purposes of casual conversation and exchange of ideas can also be used by a pedophile to recruit children to exploit for purposes of cybersex, cyberporn, molestation, or other socially reprehensible and criminal purposes. In addition to inappropriate uses of technology, ethically questionable material, such as instructions on how to build a bomb, manufacture illegal drugs, and access child pornography, can be found on the Internet.

The extent of parental rights with regard to monitoring their children's Internet activity will be discussed in subsequent sections. As will be expounded upon, although parents have certain obligations to protect their children, neither the bounds of privacy nor the ethical aspect of monitoring have been clearly delineated. Approximately 75% of children between ages 12 and 17, and 40% of 3- to 11-year-olds, are regular Internet users (Market Wire, 2005). Children can be adversely affected by information they read or see on the Internet. In addition, they could be coerced into meeting an online friend that may wish to cause them harm in the physical world. Some parents may not be aware of the negative influences their children can be exposed to on the Internet (Ketchum Global Research Network, 2005). The right to monitor enables parents to address certain issues at appropriate times and to educate their children as to what they may be exposed

to when online. According to the U.S. Department of Justice, one in five children between the ages of 10 and 17 received unwanted sexual solicitations online. As a result of receiving such solicitations, many children report being afraid and upset (Finkelhor, Mitchell, & Wolak, 2000). Children that receive unwanted sexual solicitations online may believe that this type of activity is a normal use of the Internet and may respond inappropriately. A parental right to monitor children's Internet use is imperative for parents wishing to teach children appropriate online behavior.

There are multiple ways to monitor a child's online usage. Some monitoring practices include sitting with the child while they are engaged in online activities, checking the computer files and logs at the completion of an online session, placing the computer in a common area of the home, or using an automated monitoring software program. The scope of the information contained herein relates to a parent's right to monitor their children's Internet activity utilizing automated, real-time monitoring tools. These tools take screen shots, capture chat sessions, capture all characters typed, and save or e-mail the data for parents to view. These programs can oftentimes include a feature that hides the existence of the monitoring software from other system users. Much of the product literature does not address the legality of using automated monitoring software (Iopus Software Gmbh, 2005; Net Nanny, 2006; Spectorsoft Corporation, 2006). In one instance, a software developer claims that the use of key logging software as part of their monitoring program is perfectly legal for parents to use without notifying their children (KMiNT21 Software, 2003). Web sites dedicated to providing information on how to protect children while they are online do not mention that it may be a legal violation of a child's privacy to monitor their online activity (Federal Bureau of Investigation, 2006; National Center for Missing & Exploited Children and Boys & Girls Clubs of America, 2006).

There is limited case law that could be used by parents to determine their rights with regard to using automated monitoring software. However, cases heard in several jurisdictions in the United States show mixed outcomes. The scope of the legal analysis applies to the United States of America.

BACKGROUND

In order to understand parental rights with regard to impeding on their children's online privacy, several non-technologically based areas related to children's privacy rights will be expounded upon. The disparity of privacy constraints as applied to children by various entities is intended to show that a simple definition of privacy rights as applied to children does not exist. Aspects examined will include the extent to which a school, the U.S. government, or specific state governments may impede on a child's privacy. American Civil Liberties Union (ACLU) and Electronic Privacy Information Center (EPIC) positions will be presented in a later section. In 1989, the United Nations adopted the Convention on the Rights of the Child, which spelled out the extent of what a child's right is. Based on the convention, a child's basic rights include:

...the right to survival; the right to the development of their full physical and mental potential; the right to protection from influences that are harmful to their development; and the right to participation in family, cultural and social life. (UNICEF, 2006)

Parents have a legal obligation to provide for their children. This can take the form of providing financial support, ensuring their well-being, providing education, and attending to their healthcare needs (Nolo, 2006).

A child's right to privacy can also be viewed from the aspect of a school's right to search and drug test students. In the United States, schools may randomly search and drug test students if a reasonable suspicion exists that a child may be using drugs. Numerous courts at both the U.S. state and national levels have upheld this right. One item of note is from a U.S. Supreme Court decision that grants more privacy rights to non-athlete students than their athletic counterparts, based on student athletes' more public participation in school activities (Gale Research, 1998). Just as a school can delve deeper into private areas of a student's life simply for playing a sport, parents need to be aware of how far they can go with regard to invading a child's privacy, and on what grounds.

From a state regulatory perspective on a minor's privacy, the California "Supreme Court held that the state may regulate voluntary sexual activity by a minor in ways that would violate adults' right to privacy" (Patton, 2001, p. 3). In the State of Georgia, Title 16 Code Section 16-11-66 addresses a parent's right to monitor his or her children's Internet activity (Georgia General Assembly, 2005). The rights conferred to parents in OCGA 16-11-66 are not without bounds. In order for a parent to be in compliance with the aforementioned law, there must be a concern for the child's welfare. According to the Assistant Attorney General for the State of Georgia, the law was originally developed to detail specifics as to telephony monitoring bounds, but has since been amended to include all electronic communications (C.J. Schansman, personal communication, February 11, 2005).

EXPLORATION OF PARENTAL MONITORING RIGHTS

The Internet creates a feeling of community among individuals that extends beyond immediate physical surroundings. As previously illustrated, the Internet is not free from potential dangers. Parents that wish to ensure their children have pleasant online experiences should be cognizant of potential legal ramifications of doing so.

The Internet has brought about a rapid increase in the amount, frequency of exchange, and sharing of illegal child pornography materials on the Internet. International efforts are underway by national and local governments to track down pedophiles that deal in child pornography (U.S. Department of Justice, 2006). Many pedophiles use Internet chat rooms to locate their victims and to arrange physical encounters that would harm children (Weir, 2005). Additionally, the Internet is used by individuals for online grooming, abusive cybersex, and cyberstalking (U.S. Department of Justice, 2003). Parents may know who their children associate with at school and around the neighborhood via direct observation or reports of observers, such as teachers and other parents. However, if a parent does not have the right to monitor their children's online usage, they may never know who their children are associating with online. It has been reported that "girls were slightly more likely than boys to have close online relationships with sixteen and twelve percent, respectively." Additionally, "girls aged fourteen to seventeen were about twice as likely as girls who were 10 to 13 to form close online relationships" (Finkelhor et al., 2003, p. 110).

Traditionally, a parent's right to monitor their children, even in cases infringing on U.S. Constitution First Amendment rights, in order to protect them has been the norm in the United States (O'Reilly, 2004). The threats discussed that affect children while using the Internet have led many parents to utilize monitoring software, among other methods, to assist them in being more aware of their children's online activity. However, the legality of such monitoring methods has been questioned on numerous occasions. The FBI has questioned the legality of monitoring software, also called Snoopware, or spy software. In particular, the FBI has taken interest in products that advertise that they enable anyone to spy on someone else (CBS Broadcasting, 2003).

Challenges to parental rights to monitor their children's activities have recently been made. From a case law perspective, two incidents illustrate this trend, one in the State of Florida and the other in Washington State. In *O'Brien v O'Brien* (2005), Beverly O'Brien sought to divorce her husband for cheating on her. When Mrs. O'Brien thought her husband may be cheating on her, she installed computer monitoring software on her husband's computer. As a result, Mrs. O'Brien discovered that her husband was having an affair with another woman. When Beverly O'Brien tried to introduce the software monitoring logs as evidence in the divorce proceeding, it was denied. According to the ruling, Mrs. O'Brien was in violation of the Florida Wiretap Act. The law was originally created to make phone wiretaps illegal, but is now being applied to digital information sent on the Internet.

The Washington State Supreme Court handed down a ruling in *Washington v Christensen* that puts children's right to privacy ahead of a parent's right to monitor their children's activities to ensure their safety (Kastensmidt, 2005). In this case, a 17-year-old boy confessed, over the telephone line that was paid for by the parents of a 14-year-old girl, that he mugged and stole the purse of an elderly woman. The boy was originally convicted, but the conviction was overturned by the Washington Supreme Court (O'Reilly, 2004). Again, an application of the Wiretap Act was applied to a parent-child relationship.

Florida and Washington State are not alone in their views of limiting parental rights. The American Civil Liberties Union (ACLU) backs decisions to limit parental rights to monitor their children, no matter the cause for concern (O'Reilly, 2004). Additionally, Electronic Privacy Information Center (EPIC) has also expressed concern of using such monitoring products (CBS Broadcasting, 2003). The ACLU's stance is also troubling for parents wishing to know what their children are doing online. The ACLU has sided with privacy rights of convicted pedophiles, rapists, and child molesters on more than one occasion (Kastensmidt, 2005). This stance is a departure from the traditional view that parents are expected to protect their children and have a right to invade children's privacy in order to do so.

The aforementioned legal challenges where the state dictates limitations on parental involvement is contrary to the doctrine of parental authority that allows parents discretion to raise their children as they see fit. In general, the state only has the right to intervene in parenting issues if they can prove serious harm may come to the child under the parent's care due to exercising the doctrine of parental authority (Alstott, 2004).

Based on the case law related to parental monitoring rights previously discussed, there is opposition to parental limitation of rights to monitor their children's Internet activities. While the following quote needs to be taken in context, it exemplifies the frustration some have towards such restrictions:

So don't try to find out what your kids are up to on the computer or on the telephone. Children must have privacy in these matters, so 14-year-old girls can deal with 17-year-old criminals. (O'Reilly, 2004, para. 7)

According to one survey, 95% of parents do some type of monitoring of their children's Internet usage. The term monitoring in the survey was defined as any activity related to supervising, either in real time or after the fact. Examples include a parent being in the same room with a child when they are online or reviewing the browser history and cache after a child has completed an online session (Newswise, 2005). The survey did not include information as to whether parents notified their children that their online activity was being monitored.

To date, the bounds of a parent's right to monitor their child's Internet use have yet to be tested in most states and at the federal level. If one were to apply the outcomes of decisions on such bounds from other states, it may be appropriate for parents to limit the type of activities that are monitored. For example, it may be appropriate to know what a child is Instant Messaging about and to whom, but it may be inappropriate, and for that matter, illegal, to capture a child's password for accessing blogs, e-mail, or other communications.

As computing devices get smaller, it will be harder to monitor a child's Internet use (Whitehead, 2005). Examples include smart phones and portable gaming platforms that have wireless connectivity. Monitoring software may be the only alterative in such cases, as it is difficult to sit with a child to monitor their use on such a small screen.

FUTURE TRENDS

Prior to purchasing, installing, configuring, and using computer monitoring software, parents that wish to monitor the online activities of their children should weigh applicable pros and cons. The preceding discussion has identified some of the inappropriate information and malicious individuals that children may be exposed to when online. Parents should also consider whether to inform their children that such monitoring is taking place. Often, secretly using monitoring software to record children's activities can deteriorate a parent-child relationship (Reeks, 2005).

Manufacturers and marketers of Internet and computer monitoring software should place a disclaimer on their Web site or product packaging. Suggested wording would be:

The use of this product for monitoring the activities of individuals, including but not limited to employees, children, and spouses, without their consent may be illegal. It is the responsibility of the purchaser and/or user to exercise due diligence with regard to determining the legality of using monitoring software, as such actions may be illegal in certain jurisdictions.

There is no clear answer as to what a parent's right to monitor their children's Internet activity is. While it may be safe to assume that as long as a parent has concern for their children's safety, monitoring of such

activities may be acceptable under law, there is currently no clear guideline as to where the monitoring bounds are drawn with regard to intercepting and using children's private information, such as passwords. Additionally, some tools may be used in an unrestricted manner by parents, such as Web filter software, whereas other tools, such as those that collect passwords for later use, may not.

Legal challenges to a parent's right to monitor their children's Internet usage and potential restrictions on what type of information a parent is allowed to capture should be publicized to raise parents' awareness. Relevant information should be added to the numerous safe use guidelines that abound on the Internet. Future research should be conducted that will expand upon the information presented here from an international perspective.

CONCLUSION

As has been illustrated, a parental right to monitor children's Internet use is imperative for parents wishing to teach children appropriate online behavior. This monitoring may also be necessary for parents attempting to protect children from online predators. While there are proactive measures that can be taken, such as online education for children, they may not always be effective.

In the United States the onus for making an appropriate use determination of automated monitoring software lies with courts in the jurisdiction where the computing device with the software will be used. In addition to the legal ramifications of using monitoring software, parents need to determine if they should inform their children that their online activities will be monitored. It is important for parents to consider the impacts to the parent-child relationship if the child ever discovers the monitoring activity.

While exercising due diligence from a parental perspective is important prior to installing and using an automated monitoring software package, other stakeholders should also address the privacy aspect from both a legal and non-legal perspective. Suppliers, marketers, and organizations that provide online safety awareness education should include pertinent information as previously discussed.

REFERENCES

Alstott, A. (2004). *No exit*. New York: Oxford University Press.

Baye, M.R. (2006). *Managerial economics and business strategy* (2nd ed.). Philadelphia: McGraw-Hill.

CBS Broadcasting. (2003). *Are you being 'snooped'?* Retrieved January 29, 2006, from http://www.cbsnews.com/stories/2003/09/03/tech/main571296.shtml

Criminal Code of Georgia. (2006). *OCGA § 16-11-66*. Retrieved February 12, 2006, from http://www.legis.state.ga.us/cgi-bin/gl_codes_detail.pl?code=16-11-66

Federal Bureau of Investigation. (2006). *A parent's guide to Internet safety*. Retrieved February 16, 2006, from http://www.fbi.gov/publications/pguide/pguidee.htm

Finkelhor, D., Mitchell, K.J., & Wolak, J. (2003). Escaping or connecting? Characteristics of youth who form close online relationships. *Journal of Adolescence, 26,* 105-119.

Finkelhor, D., Mitchell, K.J., & Wolak, J. (2000). *Online victimization: A report on the nation's youth*. Arlington, VA: National Center for Missing & Exploited Children.

Gale Research. (1998). *Child's right to privacy*. Retrieved March 20, 2006, from http://www.findarticles.com/p/articles/mi_g2602/is_0004/ai_2602000443

Hansson, S.O., & Palm, E. (in press). The case for ethical technology assessment (eTA). *Technological Forecasting and Social Change*.

Iopus Software Gmbh. (2005). *ActMon computer and Internet monitoring*. Retrieved April 2, 2006, from http://www.actmon.com/

Kastensmidt, S. (2005). *Courts granting sexual right-to-privacy to minors*. Retrieved January 2, 2006, from http://www.reclaimamerica.org/Pages/News/newspageprint.asp?story=2367

Ketchum Global Research Network. (2005). *Parents' Internet monitoring study*. Retrieved April 2, 2006, from http://www.netsmartz.org/pdf/takechargestudy.pdf

KMiNT21 Software. (2003). *Frequently asked questions about computer activity monitoring and spy software*. Retrieved April 8, 2006, from http://www.spyarsenal.com/activity-monitor-faq.html

Market Wire. (2005, September 7). *Kids, teens make up nearly a fifth of all Internet users*. Retrieved April 6, 2006, from http://biz.yahoo.com/iw/050907/094702.html

National Center for Missing & Exploited Children and Boys & Girls Clubs of America. (2006). *Safety tips*. Retrieved March 10, 2006, from http://www.netsmartz.org/safety/safetytips.htm

Net Nanny. (2006). *Net Nanny 5.1 parental control software*. Retrieved February 23, 2006, from http://www.netnanny.com

Newswise. (2005, January 6). *More than 95 percent of parents monitor their children's online activities*. Retrieved January 25, 2006, from http://www.newswise.com/articles/view/509130/

Nolo. (2006). *Parental rights for same-sex partners*. Retrieved March 1, 2006, from http://www.nolo.com/article.cfm/ObjectID/63423603-9D36-4ECA-B3626C7615458270/catID/56932A5A-84E0-4902-A048DBF98CB9A78D/118/122/174/ART/

O'Brien v. O'Brien. (2005, February 11). No. 5D03-3484, 30 Fla. L. Weekly D430 (Florida 5th District Court of Appeals).

O'Reilly, B. (2004). *Another setback for parental authority*. Retrieved April 10, 2006, from http://www.foxnews.com/printer_friendly_story/0,3566,141602,00.html

Patton, W.W. (2001). *Butler v. Harris, brief of amicus curiae*. Retrieved February 7, 2006, from http://jurist.law.pitt.edu/amicus/butler_v_harris.pdf

Reeks, A. (2005). Internet safety—10 smart moves to protect your child online. *Parenting,* (March), 145-149.

Spectorsoft Corporation. (2006). *Spector Pro 5.0*. Retrieved April 13, 2006, from http://www.spectorsoft.com/products/SpectorPro_Windows/

UNICEF. (2006). *Convention on the rights of the child*. Retrieved April 5, 2006, from http://www.unicef.org/crc/parentsfaq.htm

U.S. Department of Justice. (2003). *Cyberstalking: A new challenge for law enforcement and industry.* Retrieved April 5, 2006, from http://www.usdoj.gov/criminal/cybercrime/cyberstalking.htm

U.S. Department of Justice. (2006, March 15). *Dozens charged in international, Internet-based child pornography investigation, 06-143.* Retrieved April 3, 2006, from http://www.usdoj.gov/opa/pr/2006/March/06_crm_143.html

Weir, R. (2005). Netting Web perverts. *New York Daily News,* (February 22). Retrieved April 12, 2006, from http://www.nydailynews.com/front/v-pfriendly/story/283341p-242613c.html

Whitehead, B.D. (2005). Parents need help: Restricting access to video games. *Commonwealth, 132*(2), 9-10.

KEY TERMS

Automated Monitoring Software: Software that captures predetermined information for the purposes of determining what activities are or have occurred. Also known as Snoopware or spy software.

Case Law: Law based on judicial decision and precedent rather than on established legislation.

Chat Room: An Internet- or intranet-based application where a number of users can communicate in real time.

Cyberstalking: The act of utilizing computing technologies to follow or observe a person persistently, especially out of obsession or derangement.

Jurisdiction: The limits or territory within which legal authority may be exercised.

Online Grooming: The act of establishing and nurturing an inappropriate online relationship with one or more children.

Pedophile: An adult who is sexually attracted to children.

Privacy: The state of being free from unsanctioned intrusion.

P

Patient Centric Healthcare Information Systems in the U.S.

Nilmini Wickramasinghe
Illinois Institute of Technology, USA

INTRODUCTION

Healthcare expenditure is increasing exponentially, and reducing this expenditure (i.e., offering effective and efficient quality healthcare treatment) is becoming a priority not only in the United States, but also globally (Bush, 2004; Oslo Declaration, 2003;Global Medical Forum, 2005). In the final report compiled by the Committee on the Quality of Healthcare in America (Institute of Medicine, 2001), it was noted that improving patient care is integrally linked to providing high quality healthcare. Furthermore, in order to achieve high quality healthcare, the committee has identified six key aims, that is, healthcare should be:

1. **Safe:** avoiding injuries to patients from the care that is intended to help them
2. **Effective:** providing services based on scientific knowledge to all who could benefit, and refraining from providing services to those who will not benefit (i.e., avoiding under use and overuse)
3. **Patient centered:** providing care that is respectful of and responsive to individual patient preferences, needs, and values, and ensuring that patient values guide all clinical decisions
4. **Timely:** reducing waiting and sometimes harmful delays for both those receiving care and those who give care
5. **Efficient:** avoiding waste
6. **Equitable:** providing care that does not vary in quality based on personal characteristics

Most of the poor quality connected with healthcare—such as loss of information or incomplete information pertaining to patient medical records, allergic reactions that can be life threatening, or the ordering of wrong tests—is related to a highly fragmented delivery system that lacks even rudimentary clinical information capabilities resulting in inadequate information flows and poorly designed care processes characterized by unnecessary duplication of services,

long waiting times, and delays (Institute of Medicine, 2001; Chandra, Knickrehm, & Miller, 1995). In addition, poor information quality is also a major contributor to the numerous medical errors that permeate throughout the system (Mandke, Bariff, & Nayar, 2003). The introduction of the Health Insurance Portability and Accountability Act (HIPAA, 2001) in the United States into this context only makes matters more complex, since it imposes a further level of convolution to the design and management of information and its flows throughout the healthcare system. The aims of HIPAA are indeed laudable, since they focus on establishing better governance structures and compliance so that healthcare information can be protected and secured; however, in practice, given the current platform-centric nature of healthcare organizations, this only serves to create further informational challenges.

Healthcare is noted for using leading-edge technologies and embracing new scientific discoveries to enable better cures for diseases and better means to enable early detection of most life-threatening diseases (Stegwee & Spil, 2001; McGee, 1997; Johns, 1997; Wallace, 1997). However, the healthcare industry has been extremely slow to adopt and then maximize the full potential of technologies that focus on better practice management and administrative needs (Stegwee & Spil, 2001). In the current complex healthcare environment, the development and application of sophisticated patient-centric healthcare systems and e-health initiatives are becoming strategic necessities, yet healthcare delivery has been relatively untouched by the revolution of information technology (Institute of Medicine, 2001; Wickramasinghe, 2000; Wickramasinghe & Mills, 2001; Stegwee & Spil, 2001; Wickramasinghe & Silvers, 2002). To address this dilemma, healthcare organizations globally require a systematic methodology to guide the design and management of their respective IC^2T adoptions, not only to be compliant with regulations like HIPAA but also to be able to capture, generate, and disseminate information that is of high integrity and quality, and thereby be both technically sound and meet the highest ethical and security standards. An integrative compliance framework is an appropriate solution strategy.

REGULATORY REQUIREMENTS

In the United States, HIPAA (2001) is the minimum governing regulatory compliance standard to which healthcare organizations must adhere. Essentially similar standards exist in other countries, for example, the EU Directive 46 of 1995 is currently being implemented throughout all EU countries, as well as revisions to this, including privacy law (675/96) (Inchingolo, 2003). These are developed by countries or respective governments within the EU to ensure security and privacy of sensitive patient healthcare information. Irrespective of which policy we look at (HIPAA or the EU Directive), the fundamental areas pertaining to compliance and security of health information are similar. A closer examination of HIPAA reveals three key elements: security, privacy, and standards for electronic submissions and exchange of healthcare information (HIPPA, 2001; Moore & Wesson, 2002).

Security

According to HIPAA, a number of security criteria must be met, not only by the housing of information but also by all electronic healthcare transactions that contain healthcare information. Some of these criteria directly affect how healthcare systems can be accessed as well as how the key healthcare players (governments, providers, payers, and patients) may interact with these systems. The HIPAA security requirements[1] focus on:

- establishing trust partnership agreements with all business partners
- instituting formal mechanisms for accessing electronic health records
- establishing procedures and policies to control access of information
- maintaining records of authorizing access to the system
- assuring that system users receive security awareness training, and the training procedures are periodically reviewed and updated
- maintaining security configuration including complete documentation of security plans and procedures, security incident reporting procedures, and incident recovery procedures;
- ensuring communication and network control, including maintaining message integrity, authenticity, and privacy; encryption of messages is also advocated for the open network transmission portion of the message; and
- authenticating data to ensure it is not altered or destroyed in an unauthorized manner.

The principal security tenets of HIPAA fall into three categories—administrative, physical, and technical—each subdivided into several sub-categories consisting of multiple levers (Wickramasinghe & Fadlalla, 2004). Table 1 summarizes the major issues and levels under each of these categories.

Transaction Standards

The standards for electronic health information transactions cover all major transactions, including claims, enrollment, eligibility, payment, and coordination of benefits. HIPAA discusses two major categories with relation to transaction standards: practice standards and technical standards. The key practice standards are:

1. Health Care Common Procedure Coding System (HCPCS)
2. ICD-9–Diagnosis Codes
3. ICD-9–Procedure Codes

The technical standards focus on the adoption of electronic data interchange (EDI) using health care industry implementation guidelines and other standards such as XML and X12. Plans and providers can comply with these standards directly or via a healthcare clearinghouse (Wickramasinghe & Fadlalla, 2004).

Privacy

The final element of HIPAA focuses on ensuring the privacy of healthcare information. Patient healthcare data is sensitive in nature and must be protected from the potential and possibility of misuse or abuse. Specifically, the *Federal Register* (vol. 67, no. 157) details all the rules that must be adhered to with respect to privacy. The purpose of these rules is to maintain strong protection for the privacy of individually identifiable health information. Thus, these privacy requirements

Table 1. HIPAA security issues and key focus areas[2]

Security Issues	Key Areas of Focus
Security Management Process	• Risk Analysis • Risk Management • Sanction Policy • Information System Activity Review
Workforce Security	• Authorization and/or Supervision • Workforce Clearance Procedure • Termination Procedure
Information Access Management	• Isolating Healthcare Clearinghouse Function • Access Authorization • Access Establishment and Modification
Security Awareness and Training	• Security Reminders • Protection from Malicious Software • Log-in Monitoring • Password Management
Security Incident Procedures	• Response and Reporting
Contingency Plan	• Data Backup Plan • Disaster Recovery Plan • Emergency Mode Operation Plan • Testing and Revision Procedure • Applications and Data Criticality Analysis
Business Associate Contract and Other Arrangement	• Written Contract or Other Arrangement
Facility Access Controls	• Contingency Operations • Facility Security Plan • Access Control and Validation Procedure • Maintenance Records
Device and Media Controls	• Disposal • Media Re-Use • Accountability • Data Backup and Storage
Access Control	• Unique User Identification • Emergency Access Procedure • Automatic Logoff • Encryption and Decryption
Audit Controls	
Integrity	• Mechanism to Authenticate Electronic Protected Health Information
Transmission Security	• Integrity Controls • Encryption

cover the use and disclosure of treatment and payment information, while creating a national standard to protect individuals' medical records and other personal health information. Specifically, they aim to:

- give patients more *control* over their health information;
- set *boundaries* on the use and release of health records;
- establish appropriate *safeguards* that healthcare providers and others must achieve to protect the privacy of health information;
- hold violators *accountable,* with civil and criminal penalties that can be imposed if they violate patients' privacy rights; and
- strike a balance when *public responsibility* requires disclosure of some forms of data, for example, to protect public health.

Healthcare providers and organizations must ensure that all their IC^{2}T initiatives are compliant with all regulatory requirements. For example, in the case of HIPAA in the U.S., non-compliance has major negative implications such as legal action and severe financial penalties. A framework that enables healthcare organizations to design and build HIPAA compliance (or other relevant regulatory compliance) into the IC^{2}T architecture then becomes an indispensable tool and a critical success factor for any patient-centric healthcare system.

Information Integrity and Quality

At the center of the information flows in current healthcare systems is the healthcare information system (HCIS). Not only does the HCIS connect the key healthcare players within the healthcare system in an efficient and effective manner, but it also forms the central repository for critical information such as patient medical records, billing, and treatment details. Hence the HCIS provides the underlying network structure for supporting the information flows which in turn support decision-making activities throughout the healthcare system. Healthcare procedures such as medical diagnostics, treatment decisions, consequences of these decisions, prevention, communication, and equipment usage can be thought of as iatric in nature since they are connected to treating patients (Perper, 1994). Integral to these iatric procedures is the

generation and processing of multi-spectral data and information such as patient history, research findings on treatments, and protocols for treatment (Mandke et al., 2003). The patient provides key information at the time of a clinical visit or other interaction with his/her provider. Such a visit also generates other information including insurance information, medical history, and treatment protocols (if applicable) which must satisfy regulatory requirements, payer directives, and the healthcare organization's informational needs. Thus, from a single intervention, many forms and types of information are captured, generated, and then disseminated throughout the healthcare system. All this information and the consequent flows must, in addition to satisfying regulatory requirements such as HIPAA, satisfy some common integrity characteristics such as accuracy, consistency, reliability, completeness, usefulness, usability, and manipulability. In this way the information product will be truly useful and useable while generating a high level of trust and confidence in its content by the user or decision maker. Since the generated healthcare information flows across various departments and/or organizational boundaries, the challenge of ensuring information integrity is further compounded because any integrity problems will propagate with ripple effects following the same trajectory as the information itself. The consequences of poor quality information are multiplied as they propagate throughout the system, thus are not only significant but have far-reaching consequences.

Given the critical role information plays both within and between the many healthcare players, it is imperative that the information flowing both within the HCIS and between these key players must exhibit both the attributes and the dimensions of the information integrity construct, as well as satisfy the six healthcare quality aims (stated earlier).

Information Integrity

Information integrity is an emerging area that is "not just about engineering the right properties of information but it also includes sensitivity to the context in which information is used and the purpose for its usage" (Geisler, Lewis, Nayar, & Prabhaker, 2003, p. 5). More specifically it encompasses the accuracy, consistency, and reliability of the information content, process, and system. By focusing on the privacy, security, and standards aspects of healthcare information, it would appear that HIPAA implicitly assumes certain characteristics of this information product such as its accuracy and reliability. However, in practice this may not always be the case, and from the perspective of the healthcare organization, it is not sufficient to be HIPAA compliant, rather it must also ensure that the information product satisfies the principles of information integrity standards. Hence, the information should display the attributes of accuracy, consistency, and reliability of content and processes, as well as the dimensions of usefulness, completeness, manipulability, and usability (Mandke et al., 2003; Geisler et al., 2003).

Implicit in taking an information integrity perspective is the shift from viewing information as a byproduct to viewing it as an essential product (Huang et al., 1999). This requires following four key principles; namely that the information must (Huang et al., 1999; Mandke et al., 2003; Geisler et al., 2003):

1. meet the consumers information needs
2. be the product of a well-defined information production process
3. be managed by taking a lifecycle approach
4. be managed and continually assessed vis-à-vis the integrity of the processes and the resultant information

Healthcare Quality Aims

In the final report of the Committee on the Quality of Health Care in America (Institute of Medicine, 2001), six key quality aims were identified. They are listed again here for completeness. Healthcare should be:

1. **Safe:** Avoiding injuries to patients from the care that is intended to help them
2. **Effective:** Providing services based on scientific knowledge to all who could benefit, and refraining from providing services to those who will not benefit (i.e., avoiding under use and overuse)
3. **Patient centered:** Providing care that is respectful of and responsive to individual patient preferences, needs, and values, and ensuring that patient values guide all clinical decisions
4. **Timely:** Reducing waiting and sometimes harmful delays for both those receiving care and those who give care
5. **Efficient:** Avoiding waste

6. **Equitable:** Providing care that does not vary in quality based on personal characteristics

These aims can only be negatively impacted by poor information quality, flow, and integrity. Conversely, a higher quality, flow, and integrity of information will positively impact these aims by helping to reduce the large number of medical errors that currently permeate the healthcare system (Mandke et al., 2003; Geisler et al., 2003). This is because more accurate data and information will be entered into the systems, and if erroneous data and/or information is entered, it will be identified quickly and corrected.

What becomes critical then is to incorporate these quality aims into the manufacturing of the information product so that the output is quality information. This requires the establishment of an information quality program which serves to (Huang et al., 1999):

1. articulate an information quality vision in healthcare business terms
2. establish central responsibilities for information quality within the information product manufacturing processes
3. educate the producers and consumers of information on information quality issues
4. institutionalize and continuously evaluate and develop new information quality skills

PROPOSED FRAMEWORK

Healthcare in the United States and globally is facing multidimensional challenges, including structuring efficient and effective healthcare systems that first and foremost deliver value to patients, enable-cost conscious healthcare treatments, and simultaneously support the statutory as well as operational information requirements. IC²T is becoming a key enabler and strategy necessity for organizations, irrespective of their business sector (Haag, Cummings, & McCubbrey, 2004; Scott Morton, 1991; von Lubitz & Wickramasinghe, 2005). Hence, it is reasonable to expect that HCIS in general, and e-health in particular, should be able to play a similar role for healthcare organizations; specifically these technologies should be viewed as key enablers for healthcare to meet the current challenges of escalating costs, an aging population that presents more complex treatment issues, and the need to have high-quality information and provide superior healthcare delivery. In order to systematically maximize and facilitate the full potential of such initiatives to enable healthcare organizations to cope with current challenges, it is important to have a guiding integrative framework to facilitate the design and management of robust HCIS and e-health initiatives. The following integrative compliance framework serves such a role.

The proposed framework integrates the key challenges of:

1. the three elements of regulatory compliance taken from HIPAA, including transaction standards, privacy, and security;
2. the six healthcare quality aims; and
3. the core principles of information integrity.

Further, the framework also recognizes the multi-faceted nature of the key players within the healthcare system—in particular, the dynamics of their information requirements with respect to capturing, generating, and disseminating the necessary information. Moreover, the framework acknowledges the existence of other challenges such as existing IT infrastruc-ture limitations, gathering of data/information from the patient encounter, and integrating it with (when necessary) other stored data and information. These challenges, though, are beyond the scope of this article but are reflected in the framework for completeness. The key component of this framework is the protocols for ensuring compliance, observing the principles of information integrity, and satisfying the healthcare quality aims (Q). Figure 1 depicts the proposed framework. Finally, the framework highlights the major deliverable from the HCIS—namely, the information product and its key applications to various healthcare practices and processes.

The patient-centric healthcare information system received input of patient data at the time of the patient encounter. This information is cross-referenced with any existing data/information stored in databases and also validated using ICT infrastructure, for example, intranet capabilities. In addition the data and information are structured to satisfy regulatory and compliance standards (such as HIPAA), the six key quality aims, and the tenets of information integrity. Once this information is deemed to be correct, the resultant information product is then applied to the healthcare treatment or

Figure 1. An integrative compliance framework for patient-centric healthcare systems

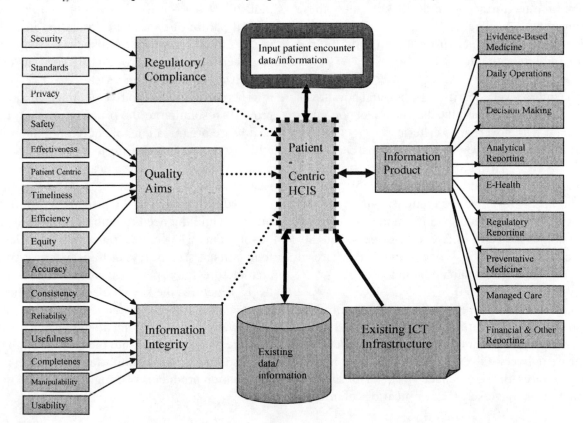

used to develop the evidence base. The information is input usually by a human, but is continuously corrected if required to ensure that accurate information permeates the system.

DISCUSSION

The proposed framework described above highlights the major information flows within a healthcare system. As can be seen information and data are critical to all healthcare activities, and thus the benefit of a robustly designed patient-centric HCIS that supports healthcare organizations in creating, generating, and disseminating germane data, information, and knowledge is crucial. Such a well-designed HCIS will also assist healthcare organizations as they try to address the major healthcare challenges. Ultimately, it is through having pertinent and relevant information that superior decision making can ensue, and such superior decision making is paramount if cost-effective quality healthcare delivery is to prevail (von Lubitz & Wickramasinghe, 2006). Specifically, the framework provides a useful diagnostic and monitoring tool to help healthcare organizations identify the key challenges they face regarding their healthcare data, and consequently design and/or revise the IC²T architecture accordingly so that it takes these challenges into consideration, complies with regulatory requirements, and produces information of the highest quality and integrity. This occurs at:

1. the micro level, identifying when and how errors enter the system or if the data is in fact non-compliant with governance criteria
2. the meso level, where comparisons can occur between departments pertaining to utilization of resources and/or treatment protocols
3. the macro level, where comparisons across the healthcare organization can be made with national averages to see if, in fact, cost-effective quality healthcare delivery is occurring and where, if required, changes should be made

This will then ensure that the resultant information product will be of the highest caliber and hence support superior decision making and excellence in healthcare delivery. Given the iatric nature of healthcare procedures, the significance and need for superior information or conversely the ramifications of inferior information cannot be stressed strongly enough. It is worth noting that the framework is as relevant to existing HCIS in meeting these key challenges and refining the information product as it is to the design and subsequent management of new HCISs; hence the framework serves both as a diagnostic and prescriptive tool.

CONCLUSION

The healthcare industry is currently facing constant and relentless pressures to satisfy conflicting goals such as lower cost while maintaining and increasing the quality of service. In addition, healthcare organizations must also contend with regulatory pressures such as HIPAA compliance. In such a challenging environment, the need for well-suited and high-quality information that flows throughout the Web of the healthcare system becomes paramount. Patient-centric HCIS and e-health initiatives can be used effectively and efficiently to facilitate the information flows and consequent decision-making activities throughout this healthcare system Web. This is inevitable, given the general success of IC²T in many business settings and the fact that healthcare is a data- and information-rich industry. What is critical, given the omnipresent and critical nature of data and information in healthcare organizations, is to take a holistic and comprehensive approach to designing a robust HCIS and subsequently effectively managing this asset.

The proposed integrative compliance framework provides a solution to the pressing problem faced by healthcare organizations of addressing the myriad of ethical, security, and informational considerations regarding their HCISs. Specifically, the framework considers the three key challenges of HIPAA compliance, the need for embracing the principles of information integrity, and the need to embrace the six healthcare quality aims. Hence, the framework provides a solid foundational step in trying to design an appropriate architecture for a patient-centric HCIS that collectively structures the key challenges facing healthcare organizations, analyzes their constituent elements, and develops protocols that attempt to ensure that not only are the data inputs into the HCIS of high quality, but also and of equal importance that the resultant information product is of a high quality and integrity.

This in turn will ensure superior decision making and support excellence in healthcare delivery.

REFERENCES

Applegate, L., Mason, R., & Thorpe, D. (1986). Design of a management support system for hospital strategic planning. *Journal of Medical Systems, 10*(1), 79-94.

Bush, G.W. (2004). *State of the Union address.* Retrieved from http://www.whitehouse.gov/news/release/2004/01/20040120-7.html

Chandra, R., Knickrehm, M., & Miller, A. (1995). Healthcare's IT mistake. *The McKinsey Quarterly,* (5).

Croasdell, D.C. (2001). IT's role in organizational memory and learning. *Information Systems Management, 18*(1), 8-11.

Geisler, E., Lewis, D., Nayar, M., & Prabhaker, P. (2003). *Information integrity and organizational performance: A model and research directions.* Working Paper.

Global Medical Forum Foundation. (2005, April 4-6). *GMF IV: New frontiers in healthcare.* Retrieved from http://www.globalmedicalforum.org/gmf_iv/session3.asp

Haag, S., Cummings, M., & McCubbrey, D. (2004). *Management information systems for the information age* (4th ed.). Boston: McGraw-Hill Irwin.

Hammond, C. (2001). The intelligent enterprise. *InfoWorld, 23*(6), 45-46.

HIPAA (Health Insurance Portability and Accountability Act). (2001, May). *Privacy compliance executive summary.* Protegrity Inc.

HIPAA. (2002). *HIPAA security requirement matrix.* Retrieved from http://www.hipaa.org/

Holt, G.D., Love, P.E.D., & Li, H. (2000). The learning organization: Toward a paradigm for mutually beneficial strategic construction alliances. *International Journal of Project Management, 18*(6), 415-421.

Huang, K., Lee, Y., & Wang, R. (1999). *Quality information and knowledge.* Englewood Cliffs, NJ: Prentice Hall.

Inchingolo, P. (2003). Picture archiving and communication systems in today's healthcare. *Business Briefing: Next Generation Healthcare,* 93-97.

Institute of Medicine. (2001). *Crossing the quality chasm—a new health system for the 21st century.* Washington, DC: National Academy Press.

Johns, P.M. (1997). Integrating information systems and health care. *Logistics Information Management, 10*(4), 140-145.

Mandke, V., Bariff, M., & Nayar, M. (2003). Demand for information integrity in healthcare management. *Proceedings of the Hospital of the Future Conference.*

McGee, M. (1997). High-tech healing. *Information Week,* (September 22).

Moore, T., & Wesson, R. (2002). Issues regarding wireless patient monitoring within and outside the hospital. *Proceedings of the 2nd Hospital of the Future Conference,* Chicago.

Oslo Declaration. (2003, June 12-13). Oslo declaration on health, dignity and human rights. *Proceedings of the 7th Conference of European Health Ministers,* Oslo, Norway. Retrieved from http://odin.dep.no/hod/norsk/aktuelt/taler/monister/042071-990209/dpk-bn.html

Perper, J. (1994). Life threatening and fatal therapeutic misadventures. In M. Bogner (Ed.), *Human error in medicine* (pp. 27-52). Hillsdale, NJ: Lawrence Erlbaum.

Scott Morton, M. (1991). *The corporation of the 1990s.* New York: Oxford University Press.

Stegwee, R., & Spil, T. (2001). *Strategies for healthcare information systems.* Hershey, PA: Idea Group.

Thorne, K., & Smith, M. (2000). Competitive advantage in world class organizations. *Management Accounting, 78*(3), 22-26.

Troisfontaine, N. (2000). *Preparatory report: Entrepreneurship in healthcare.* University of Twente, The Netherlands.

von Lubitz, D., & Wickramasinghe, N. (2006). Healthcare and technology: The doctrine of network-centric healthcare. *International Journal of Electronic Healthcare.*

Wallace, S. (1997). Health information in the new millennium and beyond: The role of computers and the Internet. *Health Education, (3)*, 88-95.

Wickramasinghe, N. (2000). IS/IT as a tool to achieve goal alignment: A theoretical framework. *International Journal of Healthcare Technology Management, 2*(1/2/3/4), 163-180.

Wickramasinghe, N., & Fadlalla, A. (2004). An integrative framework for HIPAA-compliant I*IQ healthcare information systems. *International Journal of Health Care Quality Assurance, 17*(2), 65-74.

Wickramasinghe, N., Fadlalla, A., Geisler, W., & Schaffer, J. (2003). Knowledge management and data mining: Strategic imperatives for healthcare. *Proceedings of the 3rd Hospital of the Future Conference,* Warwick, UK.

Wickramasinghe, N., & Mills, G. (2001). MARS: The electronic medical record system, the core of the Kaiser galaxy. *International Journal of Healthcare Technology Management, 3*(5/6), 406-423.

Wickramasinghe, N., & Schaffer, J. (2006). Creating knowledge driven healthcare processes with the intelligence continuum. *International Journal of Electronic Healthcare.*

Wickramasinghe, N., & Silvers, J.B. (2002). IS/IT: The prescription to enable medical group practices attain their goals. *Healthcare Management Science.*

KEY TERMS

E-Health: The use of Web-based technologies, especially Internet capabilities to support healthcare delivery.

Evidence-Based Medicine: The practice of medicine where treatments and/or procedures must be justified from sound past case history or "evidence."

Health Information Portability and Accountability Act (HIPAA): Enacted by the U.S. Congress in 1996.

Healthcare Actors: All participants in the healthcare system including patients, providers, regulators, insurance companies, and healthcare organizations.

Healthcare Delivery: The process of offering treatment to patients.

ICD-9: Ninth revision of International Classification of Diseases, the classification used to code and classify mortality data from death certificates.

Information Integrity: Key tenets for ensuring that information entered or derived is accurate, correct, pertinent, and useful.

Patient-Centric HCIS: Healthcare information system centered around the patient, hence all data and information pertaining to a patient is recorded and stored together, and can be accessed and used throughout the network in a seamless fashion.

Quality Aims: There are six: healthcare should be safe, effective, patient centered, timely, efficient, and equitable.

ENDNOTES

[1]   Readers interested in the complete HIPPA security requirements are referred to HIPAA (2002).

[2]   Table elements developed from http://www.hhs.gov/ocr/hipaa/

Pedagogical Framework for Ethical Development

Melissa Dark
Purdue University, USA

Richard Epstein
West Chester University, USA

Linda Morales
Texas A&M University, USA

Terry Countermine
East Tennessee State University, USA

Qing Yuan
East Tennessee State University, USA

Muhammed Ali
Tuskegee University, USA

Matt Rose
Purdue Univeresity, USA

Nathan Harter
Purdue University, USA

INTRODUCTION

The Internet has had an enormous impact on society. The benefits are numerous and so is the potential for misuse and abuse. Hacking, spam, denial-of-service attacks, identity theft, digital rights infringement, and other abuses are now commonplace. Malice and criminal intent motivate some of these attacks, yet for others the motivation is not so clear.

An attacker may feel a need to prove a particular cleverness or technological skill. An attacker may view a particular vulnerability as a challenge that cannot be resisted. An attacker may desire revenge against a corporation or private individual, or may view the downloading and sharing of copyrighted software, movies, and music to be a personal "right." An attacker may be motivated by a dare from fellow hackers. Other motivations undoubtedly exist.

The ubiquity and openness of the Internet require self-governance; however, we see that the ethical maturity of Internet users is often put to the test. Curricula struggle to integrate ethics education in meaningful ways. Relevant professional associations have recognized the need to integrate ethics into computer science and information technology curricula (ACM, 2001; ACM/CS-IEEE, 2001, 2004; IEEE-CS/ACM Joint Task Force, n.d.) and have developed codes of ethics for computing and engineering professionals (ACM, 2001; IEEE, 2001; IEEE-CS/ACM Joint Task Force, n.d.). The problem has certainly been recognized in the information security community, where ethical judgments are needed on a regular basis. Information security programs are rapidly growing. Are these academic programs equipped to nurture the ethical development of information security students?

The teaching of ethics is fundamentally different from the teaching of science and technology. Pedagogical approaches need to be purposefully selected to facilitate the creation of educational opportunities that allow students to examine their personal ethical beliefs. This needs to be done against the broader explicit context of right and wrong engendered by the existing technical, professional, legal, and cultural environment. The goal of this article is to present a pedagogical framework for such ethical development in information security.

SUBJECT AREA FRAMEWORK

We have developed a pedagogical framework to help those who teach information security ethics to conceive their course structure and delivery in a manner that allows students to explore their personal moral beliefs and development. The discussion that follows assumes that information security ethics are arranged by topic, for example privacy, digital rights, and intellectual property. The framework examines information security ethics from four dimensions: the ethical dimension, the security dimension, the solutions dimension, and the personal moral development dimension. The four dimensions are not rigid compartments nor are they on a continuum. Instead, the four dimensions are loosely bounded areas that describe existing attempts to address ethical issues in information security. There are technical solutions that attempt to enforce ethical issues, just are there are legal solutions, cultural norms and expectations, and professional codes of conduct and expectations. Sometimes these solutions overlap or interact with one another. We think it is important that students examine the nature of the solution, contemplate that solutions can be differing in nature, and also analyze the sufficiency of such solutions. A discussion of how this framework can be used to teach topics in information security ethics is found in Dark et al. (2006).

The Four Dimensions

The Ethical Dimension

The ethical dimension explores the ethical ramifications of a given information security topic from a variety of perspectives. It entertains questions, such as: What are the implications of this topic for individuals, particular groups of individuals, and society at large? What ethical dilemmas arise in discussion of this topic? How do evolving technologies impact the way that individuals, groups, and society perceive the ethical issues surrounding this topic?

As students learn to analyze ethical problems and develop their personal ethics, they first must learn to examine topics from a variety of perspectives that sometimes conflict with each other. When asked to defend their views about what is right or wrong, many students are unable to successfully articulate the underlying reasons for their beliefs or present rational arguments for them (Haidt, 2001). They may justify their actions with superficial rationalizations such as "what is good for you may not be good for me" or "everybody else is doing it so it must be okay" (Pritchard, 1999). Furthermore, existing and emerging security technologies add layers of complexity to issues, leading students to assume that, because they are dealing with an evolving technology, the underlying ethical norms have also changed. We want students to examine their current state of thinking, question intuitions, address existing norms, and discover the inadequacy of intuitionist rationalization.

To foster a deeper, systematic understanding of ethical problems, the authors propose using three normative ethical approaches as tools for examining the underlying ethical issues for any given information security topic. Normative ethical theories abound (for a more detailed exploration of ethics, readers are referred to Kant, 1964; Johnson, 2001; Popkin & Stroll, 1993; Spinello, 2003). In this article, we include a brief description of three broad ethical approaches that are helpful in exposing ethical issues: virtue ethics, utilitarianism, and deontological ethics. Virtue ethics, an agent-centered approach, emphasizes the *motivation* for an action more than the action itself. Virtue ethics emphasizes an individual's character: if an individual is virtuous, then his or her actions are thought to be ethical. Utilitarianism, a consequence-centered approach, emphasizes the ultimate outcome of an action whose worth is based on the net total of "good" that it produces, regardless of the motive. People are advised to maximize happiness for the whole and not just their own happiness. Finally, deontological ethics examine an agent's motives. They claim that, in order to act in an ethical manner, a person must take action for the sake of fulfilling an obligation. A person must do his or her duty. According to Kant (1964), learning what is one's duty begins with the *categorical imperative,* to treat others as you would have them treat you. Students have heard versions of these theories before. They have been urged to cultivate virtue, as in "don't be stingy." They have been taught to anticipate how their actions will affect other people, to seek "the greatest good for the greatest number." And they have encountered some variation on the Golden Rule. They will have been acquainted with advice to develop virtue, maximize happiness, and perform their duties.

Applying these three ethical approaches to a topic in information security allows students and instructors to investigate how the topic manifests itself to individuals and their belief systems, groups and their shared cultural values, and society at large with its social codes. Use of the ethical approaches also allows the underlying ethical dilemmas to be untangled from the confusion of detail that sometimes accompanies new technology. These classic approaches to understanding right and wrong are beneficial for examining the impact that emerging technologies have on various populations because they help to separate technological features from their ethical implications, thereby preparing students to examine security issues.

The Security Dimension

The security dimension for a specific information security topic includes ways in which the topic manifests to information security professionals and others who have a vested interest in information security. The usefulness of information and communication technologies to society is challenged by the prevalence of vulnerabilities in these technologies. For example, vulnerabilities may allow unauthorized access and corruption of data without physical access, potentially from anywhere in the world. Recognized crimes are on the rise, as are other activities whose ethical impact is under debate. For example, in the past, intellectual property such as music was embedded in a physical medium, which required some effort to reproduce, like a record or tape. Nowadays, the considerable amount of intellectual property available on the Internet is not bound to any physical medium. The benefits of easy access to information via the Internet have to be balanced against violations of privacy and intellectual property enabled by the Internet.

Many questions arise. Take electronic mail as an example. Is it ethical to send unsolicited e-mail? When is it ethical to send anonymous mail? What are the ethical guidelines and what is the etiquette for exchanging e-mail? Is it ethical to distribute or use personal information that belongs to other people?

Servers on the Internet are vulnerable to denial-of-service (DOS) attacks. Some attackers justify DOS attacks as retaliation for opposing points of view or for business practices that are perceived as exploitative. Is Internet vigilantism justified under *any* ethical framework?

Personal information is spread across several databases, purportedly to improve service to ordinary citizens, but privacy is threatened because the information is potentially accessible over the Internet. Confidential information about several hundred thousand citizens has already been compromised (UNESCO, 2003). Organizations generally try to minimize cost. Ethically speaking, what minimum level of privacy protection should an organization provide irrespective of cost?

In a well-known case, a corporation recently acquired information on several million Latin American voters and sold it to the U.S. government without the knowledge of the originating countries. Is this ethical? This is an example of potentially unethical conduct of entities that are supposed to safeguard personal data.

Freedom of speech has received a boost from the Internet because any individual can make his or her opinions available globally on the Internet. However this freedom is accompanied by a considerable increase in intentional and unintentional disinformation. What steps can be taken to protect freedom of speech while discouraging disinformation?

It is easier to falsify one's identity by impersonating legitimate users, and more difficult to authenticate legitimate users of the Internet. Is it ethical to use someone else's password to gain access to Internet services?

These are a few examples of ethical issues that have been raised due to security vulnerabilities in IT systems and the open nature of the Internet. Pedagogical resources for the security dimension should clarify the responsibility of the security professional to recognize, prevent, and avoid ethical misconduct in a world full of vulnerabilities.

The Solutions Dimension

The solutions dimension focuses on remedies that individuals, groups of individuals, and society have created to address security problems and associated ethical dilemmas. Ethical issues related to information security and motivations that give rise to unethical behavior tend to be ambiguous. There is a lack of consensus on solutions to many ethical dilemmas in information security. We feel that exposure to these ambiguities is beneficial to students' personal moral development. Students should be invited to explore and grapple with current solutions to ethical dilemmas and should be encouraged to examine the adequacy of solutions.

Components of the solutions dimension overlap with those in other dimensions discussed in this article, however the solutions dimension has a different focus. Four perspectives are addressed in the solutions dimension: technological, cultural, legal, and professional.

As future information security professionals, students must understand the legal solutions to ethical issues in the field. Students need ample opportunities to discuss many questions including: What is legal? What is ethical? Where do legal solutions address ethical issues and where do they fall short? What is unique about legal issues and ethics in information security?

From a legal perspective, relevant laws and regulations must be studied. The deployment of network security solutions is required by regulations; three examples are Sarbanes Oxley, Gramm Leach Bliley, and the Health Information Portability and Accountability Act. Information security students should understand the legal and technological ramifications of compliance. They need to be cognizant of their professional responsibilities and liabilities.

The professional solutions perspective explores professional expectations and codes of ethics for information security. Again, students must understand how professional codes of ethics attempt to provide solutions to ethical issues in the information security profession—where they succeed and where they fall short.

The cultural solutions perspective addresses how cultural factors can shape ethical behavior. This is explored in the context of societies, as well as formal and informal groups. Students are exposed to practices that reflect accepted norms in these social groupings and explore the effectiveness of such solutions.

The technological solutions perspective addresses how technology is used as a means of addressing information security ethical issues and enforcing solutions. Students will learn to analyze how technology enables ethical and unethical behavior. Students should investigate how technology can be used to prevent misuse of intellectual property, and how technology at the same time can create new vulnerabilities.

As students consider each perspective of the solutions dimension, they will also consider how the perspectives interact with each other. Questions include: What is the interplay of the various solutions? How do legal, professional, cultural, and technological solutions address ethical issues in information security? Do they fall short in any way? If so, how and why?

The Moral Development Dimension

Unlike the previous dimensions where knowledge is *object,* this dimension is there qualitatively different in that *subject,* where subject is students' personal moral beliefs, is explored in relation to *object.* In other words, we seek to have students explore, explain, defend, question, deconstruct, and redefine their personal beliefs of right and wrong against the backdrop of the first three dimensions. The personal ethical framework that we are interested in is not a description of what is accepted as right and wrong by groups of people. This is known as descriptive ethics; and while it is useful in some areas, descriptive ethics does not offer enough insight into who or where our students are ethically and how we, as mentors, can create opportunities for them to grow. Nor are we interested in normative ethics,

which are ethical frameworks for deciding what should be right and wrong. We use normative ethics as a tool for students to explore, question, reframe, defend, tear down, and hopefully rebuild their personal ethical code, but we are not formally interested in whether or not utilitarian perspectives are better than deontological perspectives.

Instead, the moral development dimension describes the stages and transitions that humans experience as they develop morally, as they develop their own *personal* beliefs and behaviors about right and wrong. These stages and transitions have been widely researched by several developmental psychologists, including Kohlberg (1984), Perry (1970), and Kegan (1982, 1994), who are all regarded as experts in this field. Developmental psychologists tend to agree that ethical development is epochal, meaning that the changes we experience in our personal beliefs about right and wrong occur in distinct phases or stages. Furthermore, the growth is cumulative, with each stage building on the previous stage. The growth is characterized not by the need for the next stage, but rather by the need to abandon the current stage as the individual awakens to and comes to accept (which some do not) that one's current belief system is no longer sufficient. For the most part, the sequence of stages is invariant, one progresses from stage A to stage B and then from B to C, but will not pass directly from A to C. Ethical changes in an individual also take place in the context of one's relationship to the environment, not just as a result of the demands of a relationship or in the context of a web of relationships, but rather in the context of changes in the nature of a person's relationship with his or her environment. These types of changes are described as constructivist approaches to development where the focus of inquiry is "Who am I?" (subject), "What is the world?" (object), and "What is the relationship between subject and object?" The answers to these questions change over time. This is at the heart of our interest in the moral development dimension. In an earlier section, we described how students examine these solutions with an external, objective point of view. Now, the student is positioned at the center of the intersecting circles (see Figure 1). We believe that educational opportunities should allow and encourage students to explore "Who am I now?" in relation to technical, professional, cultural, and legal solutions to these ethical and security issues, and then engage students to reflect on questions such

Figure 1. Moral development model

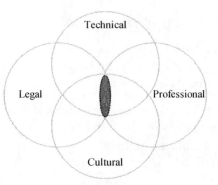

Figure 2. Spiral of development

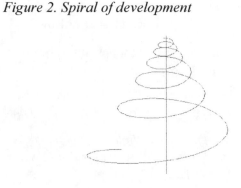

as "What is the relationship between who I am, who I want to be, and these issues and solutions?" These educational opportunities should allow students to continually question and evolve their moral beliefs, as they become more aware of the subtle complexities involved in this dimension. Students need to move through a cyclic process where at times they view an issue or their beliefs about the issue from an opposing perspective, which creates the need to move out of that plane (where plane is analogous to developmental stage) in order to evolve a new and more sufficient personal outlook of right and wrong (see Figure 2).

CONCLUSION

This article presents a framework for ethical development in information security. The framework discusses the need for students to explore ethical issues in information security first from the perspective of philosophical ethics. This provides students with a foundation in ethical theory that helps students move beyond superficial rationalizations to explore the nature of right and wrong from a reasoned perspective in the information security domain. The framework requires students to explore the sufficiency of existing technological, legal, professional, and cultural solutions to ethical issues in information security. This is critical as we seek to have our students understand that ethics are complex social constructs, and as such, one dimensional, static solutions are simplistic and naïve. Finally, the framework includes a moral development component, which challenges students to understand and advance their level of moral development with regard to information security ethics.

REFERENCES

ACM. (2001, May). *ACM code of ethics and professional conduct*. New York: Association for Computing Machinery. Retrieved from http://www.acm.org/constitution/code.html

ACM/CS-IEEE (Association for Computing Machinery and the Computer Society of the Institute of Electrical and Electronics Engineers). (2001). *Computing curricula 2001*. New York: ACM Press.

ACM/CS-IEEE. (2004). *Computing curricula information technology volume I*. New York: ACM Press.

Dark, M., Epstein, R., Morales, L., Countermine, T., Yuan, Q., Rose, M., & Harter, N. (2006). A framework for information security ethics education. *Proceedings of the 2006 Colloquium for Information Systems Security Education*, Adelphi, MD.

Haidt, J. (2001). The emotional dog and its rational tail: A social intuitionist approach to moral development. *Psychological Review, 108*(4), 814-834.

IEEE (Institute for Electrical and Electronic Engineers). (2001, May). *IEEE code of ethics*. Piscataway, NJ: IEEE. Retrieved from http://www.ieee.org/about/whatis/code.html

IEEE-CS/ACM Joint Task Force on Software Engineering Ethics and Professional Practices (SEEPP). (n.d.). *Software engineering code of ethics and professional practice* (version 5.2). Retrieved from http://www.acm.org/serving/se/code.htm

Johnson, D. (2001). *Computer ethics* (3rd ed.). Upper Saddle River, NJ: Prentice Hall.

Kant, I. (1964). *Groundwork of the metaphysic of morals* (H.J. Paton, Trans.). New York: Harper & Row.

Kegan, R. (1982). *The evolving self.* Cambridge, MA: Harvard University Press.

Kegan, R. (1994). *In over our heads.* Cambridge, MA: Harvard University Press.

Kohlberg, L. (1984). *The psychology of moral development: The nature and validity of moral stages.* San Francisco: Harper & Row.

Perry, W. (1970). *Forms of intellectual and ethical development in the college years: A scheme.* New York: Holt, Rinehart and Winston.

Popkin, R.H., & Stroll, A. (1993). *Philosophy made simple.* New York: Doubleday.

Pritchard, M. (1999). Kohlbergian contributions to educational programs for the moral development of professionals. *Educational Psychology Review, 11*(4), 395-409.

Spinello, R. (2003). *Cyber ethics: Morality and law in cyberspace* (2nd ed.). Sudbury, MA: Jones and Bartlett.

UNESCO. (2003, October). *UNESCO promotes 'knowledge societies' to maximize the impact of communication technology.* UNESCO Press.

KEY TERMS

Ethics: The philosophy of morals.

Framework: Conceptual structure for supporting something, in our case a teaching framework for supporting ethical development.

Deontology/Deontological Ethics: One of three major approaches in normative ethics; emphasizes the ethical doctrine that actions serve their moral quality based on moral obligations or duty.

Morality: The sphere of human conduct that addresses distinctions of right and wrong.

Moral Development: The study of how morality develops/evolves in humans.

Utilitarianism: One of three major approaches in normative ethics; emphasizes moral quality from their usefulness as a means to some end.

Virtue Ethics: One of three major approaches in normative ethics; emphasizes virtues or moral character.

Personal Information Ethics

Sabah S. Al-Fedaghi
Kuwait University, Kuwait

INTRODUCTION

Beginning with information ethics that is based on the machine-independent concept of information recognized to have an intrinsic moral value, personal information ethics (PIE) goes further by conferring moral value on personal information itself. PIE gives moral consideration to the well-being of any personal information based on the moral concern for the welfare of its proprietor.

INFORMATION ETHICS

According to Froehlich (2004), the issues in information ethics (IE) were raised as early as 1980, and the field of IE "has evolved over the years into a multi-threaded phenomenon, in part, stimulated by the convergence of many disciplines on issues associated with the Internet." Mathiesen (2004) suggests that "information ethics can provide an important conceptual framework with which to understand a multitude of ethical issues that are arising due to new information technologies." IE has encompassed issues that stem from connecting technology with such topics as privacy, intellectual property rights, information access, intellectual freedom, and so forth.

Floridi (1998) proposed to base IE on the concept of information, as its basic phenomenon is recognized to have an intrinsic moral value. Floridi (1998) considers IE to be the philosophical foundation that provides the basis for moral principles that guide problem-solving procedures in computer ethics. According to such a conceptualization of IE, objects are "information objects" and all information objects have inherent moral value. "This information ethics…must be the environmental ethics for the information environment" (Floridi, 2001). "[A] person, a free and responsible agent, is, after all, a packet of information…We are our information, and when an information entity is a human being at the receiving end of an action, we can speak of a me-hood…What kind of moral rights does a me-hood enjoy? Privacy is certainly one of them, for personal information is a constitutive part of a me-hood" (Floridi, 1998). Mathiesen (2004) criticized such a theory of IE since "a theory of information ethics will need to specify the relation between persons and information such that information can be of ethical import."

Al-Fedaghi (2005a) claims that studying the relationship between information and privacy needs a precise definition of personal information. Personal information is said to denote information about identifiable individuals. Assertions about individuals are personal information. Consequently, assertions are categorized into the following types:

i.   a non-personal assertion that has no referent signifying a person,
ii. an atomic assertion that has a single referent signifying a single person, or
iii. a compound assertion that has several referents signifying more than one person.

Assertions (ii) and (iii) are personal information where the referent(s) refer(s) to (a) person(s). On the other hand, *Spare part ax123 is in store 5* is non-personal information because it does not refer to any identifiable person. *John and Mary are in love* is compound information because it has two referents. The personal information can be sensitive, confidential, ordinary, trivial, and so forth, but all of these types are encompassed by the given definition: they refer to persons. *Reference* implies unique identifiability.

The relationship between persons and their atomic personal assertions is preserved through the notion of *proprietorship*. Proprietorship of personal information is different from the concepts of possession, ownership, and copyrighting. Any atomic personal information of an individual is proprietary personal information of its proprietor (the referent). Compound personal information is proprietary information of its referents. It is privacy-reducible to a set of atomic assertions.

PERSONAL INFORMATION ETHICS

According to IE, all objects are information objects and all information objects have inherent moral value. "Information" has been an unsettled issue in different domains of inquiry such as computer science, library science, law, economy, and philosophy. Its nature and characteristics are studied typically from the syntactic, semantic, and pragmatic aspects. There are many conceptualizations of human beings as information processors, seekers, information consumers, information designers, and as "packets of information." On the other hand, privacy always has been promoted as a human trait; hence, information and privacy are combined resulting in a unique human notion that is vital and valued: personal information.

We observe that there is a difference between the conceptualization of a human being as an information entity and as a personal information entity. Consider the case of "the husband who reads the diary of his wife without her permission" (Floridi, 1998). Suppose that the diary does not include any personal information, but contains nothing other than comparisons between scientific materials related to the wife's profession. Are such materials "private" and thereby considered for treatment similar to that extended to human beings, themselves? What if the diary contains other people's personal information that is in the wife's possession? In this case, does "treatment similar to that extended to human beings, themselves" refer to the wife, the other people, or both? Suppose that the diary includes only personal information regarding the wife's friend, "Jane." An IE justification may lead to the interpretation that the husband's intrusion is wrong because it is an intrusion on Jane as an information entity. The wife's position as an ethical patient in this ethical discourse is unclear. What if the husband read the diary with the permission of his wife? What if the husband found in his wife's diary information about himself? Do we consider the husband an ethical agent who stumbled on "a constitute part" of his-hood (the ethical patient)?

Al-Fedaghi (2006a) proposed to adapt Floridi's notion of the moral value of information to personal information such that personal information ethics recognizes personal information itself as having an intrinsic moral value. The term "ethics of private [personal] information" appeared in several publications, apparently, without recognizing it as a coherent area of applied ethics with distinct ethical concerns.

For example, the International Council for Science (ICSU, 2004) mentioned in its 2004 annual reports the need to "facilitate dialogue on ethics of personal information in databases."

Recognition of the intrinsic ethical value of personal information does not imply prohibiting acting upon the information. Rather, it means that while others may have a right to utilize personal information for legitimate needs and purposes, it should not be done in such a way that devalues personal information as an object of respect. Personal information consists of "human parts" with intrinsic value that precludes misuse. "Human parts," as used here, does not imply a kind of sacredness; rather, it expresses a relationship to humaneness that may be as valuable as a brain or as insignificant as some parts of the hair or nails. For example, the ontology of the person's genome is on the border between material and informational forms of being. A person can collect pieces of hair to know the sequences of the DNA; hence, in this case, personal information is literally, in Floridi's words, "part of me-hood."

PIE is concerned with the "moral consideration" of personal information because personal information's "well-being" is a manifestation of the proprietor's welfare. The moral aspect of being a piece of personal assertion means that, before acting on such information, an ethical agent should consider its "being private," in addition to other considerations (e.g., its significance/insignificance). This extension of ethical concern is a kind of infosphere/biosphere mixture since the *patient* is an informational "beingness" of a person.

Personal information is considered to have a higher intrinsic moral value than non-personal information. From the privacy side, the moral worth of personal information is based on the assumption that the proper "beneficiary" of the moral action is the proprietor of the personal information. Thus, the intrinsic moral status of personal information comes from the intrinsic moral status of its proprietor. To phrase it more accurately, the "moral consideration" of personal information by agents stems from the proprietor's right to "privacy."

The individual's role as a moral patient comes indirectly through having his/her proprietary personal information affected by the agents' activities on that personal information. Consider the act of possessing personal information that is not one's own, against the proprietor's will, whose consent is not unreasonably withheld. What is wrong with such an act is not the possession of information, hardly valued in itself as an anonymized piece of information, but the possession of information with a particular quality—namely, that of being not the proprietary information of the possessor. Thus, the proprietor of the possessed information is the patient toward whom the act is aimed, and it is the patient who is affected. The sensitivity of the personal information is incidental; whether it is information of minor significance or vital health information does not affect the fundamental character of the act as morally wrong. Thus, possession of personal information—against the proprietor's will—amounts, morally, to theft, where the wrong is not acting on the stolen thing, but taking the thing which is not one's own. Notice the philosophical foundation of conferring intrinsic moral value on personal information in contrast to conferring it on information. "Thou shalt not possess personal information—against the proprietor's will" is based on valuing the human being, while "thou shalt not possess information—against the owner's will" is based on valuing ownership.

According to PIE, a human being, as a personal information entity, has an intrinsic value that ought to regulate a moral action affecting it. Information about the human-information entity has an intrinsic value because it is a constitutive part of that entity. Thus, *Book DS559.46.1I35 is out of print* is not personal information; consequently, it has no PIE intrinsic value. Also, if the person under consideration is Einstein, then $E=mc^2$ is not a constitutive part of Einstein, while, *Einstein is convinced that He does not play dice* is. A fundamental premise in PIE is that *proprietary personal information about individuals is a constitutive part of the individuals.* The implication here is that personal information has a value because a person values it as he/she values aspects or parts of him/herself.

PIE is unique in terms of its entropy-related properties. For example, randomization increases the information entropy of the system. Nevertheless, the techniques of randomization and anonymization are used to protect personal information. Both techniques increase the information entropy. A hospital that k-anonymizes its health records makes every k record indistinguishable from others, thus increasing the level of entropy. The opposite is true in PIE; randomization and anonymization halt the "spread" of personal information, thus increasing informational privacy and the "privacy order" of the environment.

PIE's evaluation of moral criteria is that "publicness of personal information" is, in general, evil because it causes the degradation of privacy. "Publicness" is "dis-privatizing" the individual and can be viewed as the disorder (entropy) of the structure of personal information; consequently, minimizing it benefits the privacy environment and allows the proprietors of personal information to flourish.

Personal information ethical principles regulate the behavior of any agent. Agents have the duty to treat personal information, when it is put in the role of a patient, as an informational manifestation of its proprietor. Generally, any action on a piece of personal information is evaluated in terms of its contribution to the welfare of the personal information environment, which implies the welfare of proprietors. This welfare seems to have some universality feature with the development of agreed-on personal information protection principles and privacy protection rules.

PRIVACY INTRUSION

Consider the following scenario described by Kang (1998):

Starting from the premise that we own our own bodies, I begin by asking: What precisely is wrong with a nonconsensual touch? Such a touch is socially unacceptable and sometimes tortuous or criminal. But what exactly is wrong with touching a person without her permission?...Even if the touch is physically harmless, a person should presumptively enjoy the sovereignty to determine who may touch her and under what circumstances, unless some competing interest or value undermines that presumption. What would it mean to respect a person as a chooser if we refused to respect this basic choice about her own body without any countervailing interests?...The reason for the touch fails to marshal any competing social interest that trumps the person's desire not to be touched. What if the toucher argued that his freedom to touch should trump the touched person's freedom to avoid the touch? Most of us would reject this argument, for it so bizarrely departs from current mores.

Touching is an intrusive act on parts of the human body. Similarly, intrusion on personal information is a form of touching parts of the body. According to Kang (1998), "Conversely, if sufficiently intrusive, observation [surveillance] is a form of, or functionally equivalent to, touching."

Returning to the example of a husband who reads his wife's diary without her permission, the husband's act is wrong because he then possessed personal information without the consent of its proprietor. Floridi (1998) defines informational privacy as "freedom from epistemic interference or intrusion, achieved thanks to a restriction on facts about S that are unknown or unknowable." This definition is based on:

an ontology-based interpretation [that] argues that information privacy is valuable and ought to be respected because each person is constituted by his or her information, and breaching one's informational privacy undermines one's personal identity, either positively (by cloning someone's information) or negatively (by imposing unwanted information on someone). (Floridi, 2005)

It is not clear here what is "one's information." According to Floridi (2005), "breaching one's informational privacy may consist in forcing someone to acquire unwanted information, thus changing her or his nature as an informational object." In our definition of (linguistic) personal information, it is not possible to force the proprietor to "acquire" unwanted proprietary information. Breaching one's personal information privacy in PIE is obviously different from its interpretation in IE.

There are several types of intrusion in PIE. Also, there is a difference between the act of intruding on a person and intruding on that person's personal information. As we see here, the husband's act is a personal information privacy-related act if it involves personal information. If it does not, its moral status is equivalent to intrusion on things that the wife owns, such as logging onto her computer without consent. Such an act may have privacy significance, but it is not an intrusion on "me-hood." It is analogous to stealing my pencil, in contrast to stealing, for instance, pieces of my hair for whatever purpose. If the act does involve personal information, then the moral seriousness of such an act depends on the type of personal information involved.

Still, it is not clear how these types of intrusions are related to normal ethics, IE, and PIE. Even if the wife's

dairy is blank, there is a sense of privacy intrusion. If we are to accept the PIE thesis that such an intrusion is not an intrusion on the wife's personal information, how does it relate to privacy? In general, we may ask "What is the nature of privacy that does not involve personal information?" To answer such questions, we have to look at the topology of different ethics and then position each ethical setting accordingly.

ETHICS AND PERSONAL INFORMATION ETHICS

Computer ethics, information ethics, personal information ethics, privacy ethics, and many other terms that juxtapose the terms "ethics," "privacy," and "information" call for a uniform treatment to understand the topography of these topics. "Ethics" is understood as "an agent's behavior governing a system of acts" that affects others (i.e., ethical patients) according to moral principles. For us, the moral participants in the ethical discourse are limited to ethical agents and ethical patients: the two classical logical entities in ethical discourses, in addition to impartial the observer.

How can we characterize the relationship between ethical agents and patients? According to Floridi and Sanders (2004), there are five logical relationships between the class of ethical agents and the class of patients: (1) agents and patients are disjoint, (2) patients can be a proper subset of agents, (3) agents and patients can intersect, (4) agents and patients can be equal, or (5) agents can be a proper subset of patients. Medical ethics, bioethics, and environmental ethics "typify" agents and patients when the patient is specified as any form of life. Animals, for example, can be moral patients but not moral agents. Also, there are ethics that typify moral agenthood to include legal entities (especially human-based entities) such as companies, agencies, and artificial agents, in addition to humans.

The relationship between agents and patients may be thought to be hidden in certain ethically related concepts such as trust. For example, Kainulainen (2001) identifies the layers of trust as follows: individual–machine, individual–individual, individual–(machine)–individual, individual–identifiable small groups (social aspect), individual–groups/organizations (authority, higher levels of hierarchy, and abstraction), and group–group. Accordingly, Dodig-Crnkovic and Horniak (2005) ask: "How, in all these types of interactions, [do you]

Figure 1. Ethical categories as moral acts involving agents and patients

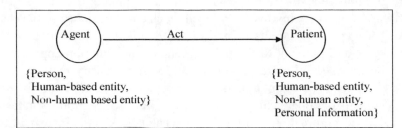

Table 1. Categorization according to person, human-based entities, and non-person entities

		AGENT		
		Person	Human-Based	Non-Human
PATIENT	Person	A person acts on a person	A human-based entity acts on a person	A non-human entity acts on a person
	Human-Based	A person acts on a human-based entity	A human-based entity acts on a human-based entity	A non-human entity acts on a human-based entity
	Non-Human	A person acts on a non-human entity	A human-based entity acts on a non-human entity	A non-human entity acts on a non-human entity
	Personal Information	A person acts on personal information	A human-based entity acts on personal information	A non-human entity acts on personal information

Table 2. Summary of the domains of normal ethics, IE, and PIE

Patient	Person	Uniquely identifiable	Normal ethics	Privacy-related
				Non-privacy
			IE	Privacy-related
				Non-privacy
		Not uniquely identifiable	Normal ethics	Privacy-related
				Non-privacy
			IE	Privacy-related
				Non-privacy
	Human-based entities		Normal ethics	Non-privacy
			IE	Non-privacy
	Non-human entities		Normal ethics	Non-privacy
			IE	Non-privacy
	Personal information		PIE	Privacy-related
				Non-privacy

establish the responsibility, especially when machines and software agents (e.g., intelligent software agents such as Web bots–software robots) are involved."

These "typifications" of agents and patients are not sufficient for relating agents and patients to the notions of our concern such as "person," "privacy," and "informational ontology." Instead, we adopt a model that includes the basic elements of ethical categories: agent and patient, as shown in Figure 1. An "ethical category" is a discerned ethical situation that includes a "typified" moral agent and a patient, according to the following: person, human-based entity, or non-human entity. Furthermore, patients are segregated according to informational and normal ontologies, and according to the privacy-relatedness of the category. The types (e.g., person) and property (identifiable) of agents and patients, and their ontology (e.g., informational) and the privacy-relatedness of the discourse (e.g., anonymity) are factors that determine what we call an *ethical category*.

Using this model, we can develop the taxonomy of ethical categories that juxtaposes humans, human-based systems, machines, hybrid systems formed by digital agents, artificial agents, and so forth. It answers the question, "What discourses are possible for certain types of agents and patients?" We classify ethical categories according to their ethical agents into the following: (a) person agents, (b) human-based agents, and (c) non-human agents that include artificial moral agents, robots, and so forth.

Ethical patients also are categorized into (a) person patients, (b) human-based patients, (c) non-human patients, and (d) personal information. Personal information is unique, as it is a human-related entity and at the same time as non-human as information. Table 1 shows the resultant divisions of ethical categories.

Table 2 shows a general view of the domains of normal ethics, IE, and PIE. In this table, we categorize person agenthood into identifiable persons (e.g., *John ought to tell the truth*) and non-identifiable persons (e.g., *A person should not murder another person*).

CONCLUSION

The intertwining of privacy, ethics, and information generates many new ways to revisit theories and issues from these three realms of inquiry. An example is developing moral justification for lying about personal information (Al-Fedaghi, 2005b). Personal information ethics is applied to study the dilemma of whether to breach confidentiality in the case of the risk of harming identifiable individuals (Al-Fedaghi, 2005c). The personal information approach also has been utilized to develop security techniques that are applied only to personal information (Al-Fedaghi, 2006b). Further work in this direction includes classification of ethical categories in the investigation of the nature of PIE and its applications. Another possible area is applying the proposed taxonomy in different ethical and legal analyses.

REFERENCES

Al-Fedaghi, S. (2006a, May 21-24). Crossing privacy, information and ethics. *Proceedings of the 17th International Conference of the Information Resources Management Association* (IRMA 2006), Washington, DC.

Al-Fedaghi, S. (2006b). Some aspects of personal information theory. *Proceedings of the 7th Annual IEEE Information Assurance Workshop* (IEEE-IAW 2006), West Point, NY.

Al-Fedaghi, S. (2005a, October 12-14). How to calculate the information privacy. *Proceedings of the 3rd Annual Conference on Privacy, Security and Trust*, St. Andrews, New Brunswick, Canada.

Al-Fedaghi, S. (2005b). Lying about private information: an ethical justification. *Communications of the International Information Management Association, 5*(3), 47-56.

Al-Fedaghi, S. (2005c). Privacy as a base for confidentiality. *Proceedings of the 4th Workshop on the Economics of Information Security*, Cambridge, MA. Retrieved from http://infosecon.net/workshop/schedule.php

Dodig-Crnkovic, G., & Horniak, V. (2005, July 17-19). Good to have someone watching us from a distance? Privacy vs. security at the workplace. *Proceedings of the 6th International Conference of Computer Ethics: Philosophical Enquiry,* Enschede, The Netherlands.

Floridi, L. (1998, March 25-27). Information ethics: On the philosophical foundation of computer ethics. *Proceedings of the 4th International Conference on*

Ethical Issues of Information Technology (ETHI-COMP98), Rotterdam, The Netherlands.

Floridi, L. (2005, June 6-7). An interpretation of informational privacy and of its moral value. *Proceedings of the Workshop on Bridging Cultures: Computer Ethics, Culture, and ICT,* Trondheim, Norway. Retrieved from http://www.anvendtetikk.ntnu.no/main.php?id=redirected&page=pres/bridging_workshop

Floridi, L. (2001). Ethics in the infosphere. *Proceedings of the UNESCO Executive Board 161st Session Thematic Debate: "The New Information and Communication Technologies for the Development of Education,"* Paris.

Floridi, L., & Sanders, J.W. (2004). On the morality of artificial agents. *Minds and Machines, 14*(3), 349-379.

ICSU. (2004, July). *Report.* Retrieved from http://www.icsu.org/Gestion/img/ICSU_DOC_DOWNLOAD/371_DD_FILE_Foresight_Analysis.pdf

Kainulainen, A. (2001). *Trust and ubiquitous computing.* Retrieved from http://www.cs.uta.fi/~anssi/work/cogscisempres_7.4.2001.ppt#258,1,Trust%20and%20Ubiquitous%20Computing

Kang, J. (1998). Information privacy in cyberspace transactions. *Stanford Law Review, 1193*(April), 1212-1220.

Mathiesen, K. (2004). What is information ethics? *Computers and Society Magazine, 32*(8).

KEY TERMS

Ethical Agent: One who performs an act that has an ethical dimension.

Ethical Patient: A recipient of an act that has an ethical dimension.

Information Ethics: A field of applied ethics that addresses issues related to information creation, processing, gathering, and disclosure.

Personal Information Ethics: A field of applied ethics that addresses issues related to personal information creation, processing, gathering, and disclosure.

Personal Information Privacy: A property of a state of affairs that involves an act on personal information.

Personal Information: Information that has referents signifying individuals.

Proprietor of Personal Information: The person whom a piece of personal information refers to.

Pharming Attack Designs

Manish Gupta
State University of New York at Buffalo, USA

Raj Sharman
State University of New York at Buffalo, USA

INTRODUCTION

Pharming is emerging as a major new Internet security threat. Pharming has overtaken "phishing" as the most dangerous Internet scam tactic, according to the latest Internet Security Intelligence Briefing (VeriSign, 2005). Pharming attacks exploit the design and implementation flaws in DNS services and the way Internet addresses are resolved to Internet protocol (IP) addresses. There are an estimated 7.5 million external DNS servers on the public Internet (MF-Survey, 2006). Pharming attacks manipulate components of the domain and host naming systems to redirect Internet traffic from one Web site to a different, identical-looking site in order to trick users into entering personal and sensitive information on their fake site. Financial services' sites are often the targets of these attacks, in which criminals try to acquire personal information in order to access bank accounts, steal identities, or commit other kinds of fraud. The use of faked Web sites makes pharming sound similar to e-mail phishing scams, but pharming is more insidious, since users are redirected to a false site without any participation or knowledge on their part. Pharming is technically harder to accomplish than phishing, but also sneakier because it can be done without any active mistake on the part of the victim (Violino, 2005). The greatest security threat lies in the fact that a successful pharming attack leaves no information on the user's computer to indicate that anything is wrong.

The Etymology and Metaphor: "Pharming"

The coinage and usage of the word pharming has origins in metaphorical connection with "farming." The metaphor tunes with the characteristics and forms of the attack where attackers bring people onto a property they control, without having to "phish" for them.

Pharming has also been called "phishing without a lure." "Pharming" also refers to manufacturing of pharmaceutical products via genetic engineering of farm crops and animals. Another form of pharming, known as gene pharming, is a biotechnological process in which the DNA of an animal, usually livestock, is altered so the animal produces human proteins for pharmaceutical use. The proteins appear in the blood, eggs, or milk of the animal.

Organization and Contribution of the Article

The article has a two-fold contribution. First, it presents classification of pharming attack designs in light of DNS components and characteristics. The second contribution is survey and synthesis of different modes and channels of pharming attacks based on design and implementation of DNS components and services.

The article is organized as follows. The Preliminaries section provides preliminaries on DNS that are extensively used in the explanation of attack designs in later sections. The section on Attacks and Designs presents, in detail, attack designs from DNS service and client perspectives, and classifies pharming attacks into three types based on location sensitivity of the DNS service. The next section on pharming incidents discusses successful pharming attacks and their methodologies to provide insights into the functioning of such attacks.

PRELIMINARIES

Social Engineering

Social engineering is a technique used by hackers or other attackers to gain unauthorized access to secure systems through obtaining the privileged information by manipulating human behavior. Mitnick (2004) identifies four distinct stages of the "Social Engineering Cycle": research, developing rapport and trust, exploiting trust, and utilizing information. Organizations and individuals alike must equip themselves with the knowledge on social engineering attacks such as what information can be used, how information divulged could precipitate attacks, how the attacker develops the attack, and in what forms the attack may appear.

Domain Name System: Concepts

The DNS is the method by which human-readable Internet addresses such as mgt.buffalo.edu, which are easy for people to understand and remember, are converted into the equivalent numeric IP address such as 128.205.202.194. This translation service is provided to the users and application processes either by the local host or from a remote host via the Internet. The DNS server (or address resolver) may communicate with other Internet DNS servers if it cannot translate the address itself. Following the example from above, the Web site that we referred to as mgt.buffalo.edu has the IP address 128.205.202.194. DNS implements a client server process architecture, where the client side is represented by a resolver, which submits queries to and receives responses from the DNS application itself.

Domain Name System: Components and Structure

DNS is a database that contains the mapping information in both distributed and hierarchical structure and can be represented as an inverted tree. All of the domain names that are registered with a naming authority are held within this database along with their associated IP addresses. The general structure of a domain name is hierarchical. For example, .edu is a top-level domain (TLD) in domain mgt.buffalo.edu. At least one root name server is associated with each TLD. The Internet today has a total of 13 root servers that are distributed geographically. Sub-domains can be created to an arbitrary level below each TLD. Domain registrars, within Internet context, can grant the authority over sub-domains to the organizations that manage those sub-domains. The boundary of authority that is granted within DNS is determined by means of the specification and implementation of zones. An example would be mgt.buffalo.edu, where there is:

- a TLD zone (.edu)
- a sub-domain (buffalo.edu) which is a zone,
- a sub-domain of buffalo.edu (mgt.buffalo.edu) which is a zone

Typical Transactional Flow for a DNS Query

Figure 1 (adapted from Stewart, 2004) shows a query and transaction path when the IP address of a domain name is requested. The flow of information and hierarchy of DNS servers is presented in the Figure 2 as: (1) Local-ns, (2) ISP-ns, (3) R-ns, and (4) A-ns. Explanation of each step from Figure 1 is presented below in the box.

The SP-ns is authorized to make queries on the user's behalf to as many nameservers as needed in order to find the answer. This is known as recursion. The root-level nameservers contain information about what nameservers hold the specific information about the hosts in each top-level domain. This information is known as the authority record for a domain, which contains pointers to the servers that are authoritative for a domain.

PHARMING ATTACK TYPES AND DESIGNS

Pharmers have a variety of motives and objectives, primarily malice and monetary gain. In several documented cases, pharming has caused disruption and malicious use of registrant's Internet services, discussed in detail in the section on pharming incidents. The pharming attacks are classified into three types as represented in Figure 2. The following subsections discuss pharming attack designs in these categories. Table 1 presents attack designs and their classifications. The second column of the table shows the section of the article in which that particular attack is discussed.

PHARMING ATTACK DESIGNS COMPONENT

This section presents pharming attack designs that fall under the category Internet name services (INS) as illustrated in Figure 2 and Table 1.

Figure 1. DNS query example

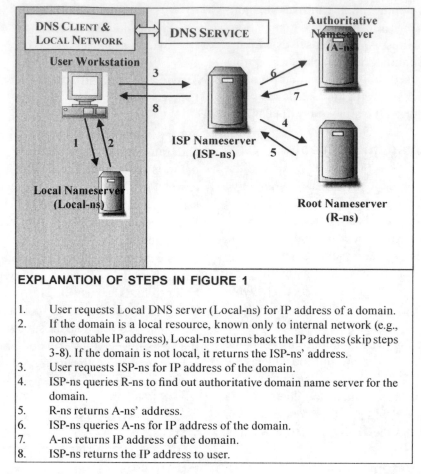

EXPLANATION OF STEPS IN FIGURE 1

1. User requests Local DNS server (Local-ns) for IP address of a domain.
2. If the domain is a local resource, known only to internal network (e.g., non-routable IP address), Local-ns returns back the IP address (skip steps 3-8). If the domain is not local, it returns the ISP-ns' address.
3. User requests ISP-ns for IP address of the domain.
4. ISP-ns queries R-ns to find out authoritative domain name server for the domain.
5. R-ns returns A-ns' address.
6. ISP-ns queries A-ns for IP address of the domain.
7. A-ns returns IP address of the domain.
8. ISP-ns returns the IP address to user.

Table 1. Pharming attacks categorization

PHARMING ATTACK DESIGNS	COMPONENT
DNS Service Attacks	INS
DNS Spoofing	INS
DNS Cache Poisoning	INS
DNS Mis-Configurations	INS
Domain Hijacking	INS
DNS Software Vulnerabilities	INS
Similar Name Domain Registration	INS
DNS Client-Side and Local Network Attacks	CNS & LNNS
nslook-up and Hosts File Corruption	CNS
Client Software Vulnerabilities	CNS
Client-Side Network Settings	CNS
Rogue Services	LNNS
Search Rank Escalation	LNNS

DNS Spoofing

A DNS server can perform a query to an upstream DNS server in order to resolve the IP address of the domain. The process by which this is accomplished is called a recursive query. More than 75% of domain name servers (of roughly 1.3 million sampled) allow recursive name service to arbitrary queries (MF-Survey, 2006). This opens a name server to both cache poisoning and denial–of-service attacks. The DNS server conducting such a query could end up making a series of sequential queries to upstream DNS to obtain an address, or if the recursive query feature is disabled, the DNS server then simply forwards (DNS forwarding) the query to the next DNS server higher up in the inverted tree of servers and relinquishes control of that query request. Where the recursive queries are allowed, the DNS server can be fooled into thinking that it is receiving a response from a trusted DNS server, when, in fact, it is being "spoofed." The spoofing server can issue a command to change the IP address associated with a particular domain to an IP address of a malicious DNS server.

DNS Cache Poisoning

As mentioned earlier in this article, a fundamental component of the DNS architecture is the ability of DNS to cache responses to queries in order to improve the performance (throughput and delay) associated with the DNS service. The downside of this is that if the cache gets corrupted with a malicious, but otherwise well-formed entry, then the compromised cache will continue to be used to translate domain-IP mapping until the Time-To-Live (TTL) parameter is reached. An even worse scenario would if the TTL is also modified to a very high number.

DNS Mis-Configurations

Two surveys from early 2001, the first of 978 WWW sites in the Fortune 1,000, and the second of 5,000 random sites in the .com domain, suggest that 25% and 38% of the respective sites had DNS configurations that were either incorrect or weak from a security perspective (Olusada, 2001). Improper configuration resulting in insecure states of DNS servers is a severe problem. The effects of the attacks that can exploit these insecurities can be significant, widespread, and difficult to detect. Some of the most common configuration errors include using wildcards in the entries for name resolutions. Pharmers and many spammers use DNS wildcard entries to engineer attacks. More than 40% of DNS servers on the Internet allow zone transfers from arbitrary queries. This exposes a name server to denial-of-service attacks and gives attackers information about internal networks (MF-Survey, 2006).

Domain Hijacking

The International Corporation for Assigned Names and Numbers (ICANN, 2005) recently published a report on "domain hijacking" and its consequences. The report defines domain hijacking as the wrongful taking of control of a domain name from the rightful name holder. The common use of the term encompasses a number of attacks and incidents including:

- impersonation of a domain name registrant in correspondence with a domain name registrar
- forgery of a registrant's account information maintained by a registrar
- forgery of a transfer authorization communication from a registrant to a registrar

In a pharming attack the hijacker would attempt to take ownership of the domain as soon as the existing registration of the domain expires. The DNS ID hacking is a necessary technique for a hacker to succeed in impersonating a DNS server (necessary for DNS spoofing) (Carli, 2003).

DNS Software Vulnerabilities

There are numerous vulnerabilities in domain name servers that are documented in the CERT (2006) Advisories. BIND (Berkeley Internet Name Domain) is the most commonly used DNS server on the Internet, especially on Unix-like systems supported by the Internet Systems Consortium.[1] BIND has had a history of software defects, including buffer overflows that result in improper processing of such variable length inputs (Holmblad, 2003). Buffer overflow attacks in earlier versions of BIND could result in an attacker gaining root user access to the underlying server running the attacked DNS.

Similar Name Domain Registration

Here, the pharmer can register similar spelled domains in hope that users would end up on such sites if they mistype the Web site name. A technique to determine various permutations is to analyze fat fingering patterns, when users can type neighboring keys of the letters from the Web site name. Four out of five authoritative DNS servers around the world are vulnerable to types of hacking attacks that might be used by hackers to misdirect surfers to potentially fraudulent domains (Leyden, 2005). An example would be to register www. citibamk.com (replace "n" with "m") to pharm users of www.citibank.com to the attacker's site. Pharmers have used "key mashing" permutations of popular Web sites to direct users to malicious Web sites, also related to cyber-squatting.

DNS Client-Side and Local Network Attacks

This section presents pharming attack designs that fall under category client name services and local network name services as illustrated in Figure 2 and Table 1.

nslook-up and Hosts File Corruption

The hosts file and local ns-lookup normally act as network-translation mechanisms so that you can access certain network resources without having to go through DNS. However, in many situations, spyware and adware modify this file so that Web browser requests go to other sites instead. The pharmer can add or modify existing entries in the file or overwrite the file to misdirect the user to a malicious site.

Client Software Vulnerabilities

The client-side components of DNS reside in the protocol stack and the WWW browser of the PC which is requesting the services of DNS. Thus, any malware exploit on a PC that allows an attacker to run "code of their choice" will make these client-side components vulnerable to exploit as well. A common exploit of this type is one where the attacker redirects the settings for the IP address of the DNS server or servers (primary and secondary) that are maintained for each network interface adapter (NIC), generally by the TCP/IP protocol stack. The net effect of this kind of exploit will be that domain names will be resolved to the IP address of the attacker's choosing.

Client-Side Network Settings

The pharmer can modify settings on a user's computer to assign a DNS server that he controls to redirect all DNS queries from the user's workstations. This problem is aggravated when the workstations are shared and a user has gained control (administrative rights) on the PC.

Rogue Services

In the local network, the pharmer can discover and modify the network services that play important roles on routing user requests across the network. For example, by controlling the DHCP settings of a computer, an attacker can state which DNS server address must be used by the customer's computer (Ollman, 2004). This can be the DNS server the attacker has complete control of. Another example of such services is a WPAD service that allows Web browsers to use methods to automatically locate suitable proxy services. A rogue WPAD server can be used to redirect network traffic to a proxy server of its choice—an example of man-in-the-middle attack.

Search Rank Escalation

A pharmer can seek to increase his or her search engine page ranking by abusing the way the engine determines the Web site and Web page ranking (Ollman, 2004). By changing the content of his or her Web pages to exploit the page-ranking algorithm, the pharmer can get the malicious Web sites' links to appear where users would expect the real link.

SOME OF THE REPORTED PHARMING INCIDENTS

The Anti-Phishing Working Group (APWG) has recognized the potential severity of the problem and has added pharming as a type of Internet scam and fraud the group aims to prevent (APWG, 2006). Some of the most highlighted incidents are cited in the following:

- **April 2005, Hushmail:** On Sunday, April 24, 2005, the DNS configuration for Hush Communication's Hushmail service was modified by an unauthorized party. The incident is characterized by spoofing an e-mail to Network Solutions, Inc., directing modification of the administrative e-mail contact information in Hush's registration record (ICANN, 2005). Then the attacker accessed the Hush Communications account, changed the password, and used the account to alter the DNS configuration to point the domain name record to the attacker's server.

- **March 2005, Multiple:** On March 16, 2005, one or more hackers launched a widespread series of DNS cache poisoning attacks. These attacks exploited vulnerabilities in several different products from a variety of vendors. The users of popular Web sites like Google or eBay were directed to a malicious Web site from which spyware and adware were distributed (VeriSign, 2005). SANS Institute, in March 2005, also uncovered the same cache-poisoning attack that redirected 1,300 brands (Radcliff, 2005).

- **January 2005, Panix:** In January 2005, the domain name for a large New York State Internet service provider (Panix) was hijacked to a graffiti site in Australia by claiming the ownership of the company's domain. Requests to reach the panix. com server were redirected to the UK, and e-mail was redirected to Canada.

- **September 2004, eBay.de:** In September 2004, a teenager in Germany managed to hijack the domain for eBay.de. He used social engineering tactics to dupe the domain registrar and gain control of the domain (Vamosi, 2005).

CONCLUSION

Pharming is a very real threat and one that currently has fairly free reign. With an understanding of risks and methods by which pharming attacks are launched, a multi-layered defense and security policies could be devised to make pharming a much more difficult attack to carry out. This article presents pharming attack designs and attack categorization in light of DNS components and characteristics. The concepts covered in the article equip risk managers with knowledge of terminology and methodologies employed by attackers to launch pharming attacks which will aid them in designing better security decisions and countermeasures to reduce risk.

REFERENCES

APWG. (2006). Anti Phishing Working Group homepage. Retrieved from http://www.antiphishing.org

Carli, F. (2003). Florent Carli, Security issues with DNS, SANS GSEC practical assignment. SANS Institute.

CERT. (2006). CERT Coordination Center advisories. Retrieved from http://www.cert.org/advisories

Holmblad, J. (2003, October 5). The evolving threats to the availability and security of the domain name service. SANS GIAC/GSEC Practical.

ICANN. (2005). Domain name hijacking: Incidents, threats, risks, and remedial actions. Retrieved from http://www.icann.org/announcements/hijacking-report-12jul05.pdf

Leyden, J. (2005, October 24). Most DNS servers 'wide open' to attack. Retrieved from http://www.theregister.co.uk/2005/10/24/dns_security_survey/

MF-Survey (Measurement Factory DNS Survey). (2006). Domain name servers: Pervasive and critical, yet often overlooked. Retrieved from http://dns.measurement-factory.com/surveys/sum1.html

Mitnick, K., & Smith, W. (2002). The art of deception. Indianapolis: Wiley.

Ollman, G. (2004). The pharming guide: Understanding and preventing DNS-related attacks by phishers. NGS Software Paper.

Olusada, C.C. (2001, February 15). DNS vulnerabilities—nine days in the spotlight. Retrieved from http://www.giac.org/practical/gsec/Cheryl_Olusada_GSEC.pdf

Radcliff, D. (2005, July 18). How to prevent pharming. Retrieved from http://www.networkworld.com/research/2005/071805-pharming.html?fsrc=rss-security

Stewart, J. (2004). GCIH DNS cache poisoning—the next generation. Retrieved from http://www.lurhq.com/dnscache.pdf

Vamosi, R. (2005, February 21). Alarm over 'pharming' attacks. Retrieved from http://reviews.zdnet.co.uk/software/internet/0,39024165,39188617,00.htm

VeriSign. (2005). VeriSign Internet security intelligence briefing (vol. 3, no. I). Retrieved from http://www.verisign.com/static/030910.pdf

Violino, B. (2005, October). After phishing? Pharming! Retrieved from http://www.csoonline.com/read/100105/pharm.html

KEY TERMS

Cyber-Squatting: A process of registering an Internet domain name that could exhibit or contain goodwill of another entity's trademark, with the intent of profiting from the acts of selling or using the domain name.

DNS Cache Poisoning: A process characterized by injection of false information into the caches of the DNS system so that future requests for domain(s) are diverted to different site(s).

DNS Spoofing: A process when a DNS server accepts and uses incorrect information from a host that has no authority giving that information.

Domain Hijacking: The process in which a person or business illegally claims Internet domain names for carrying out fraudulent activities.

Domain Name System (DNS): A distributed database system that stores information associated with domain names, in a hierarchical fashion, on networks, such as the Internet. The DNS stores and processes information related with domain names and IP addresses associated with the domain name. It also lists mail exchange servers accepting e-mail for each domain.

Pharming: A kind of social engineering attack where vulnerability in design or implementation of a domain name system is exploited to take control of traffic to a Web site by modifying the DNS record of the site.

Phishing: A kind social engineering attack launched to fraudulently acquire sensitive information by pretending to be a trustworthy entity in an apparently official electronic communication, such as an e-mail.

Social Engineering Attack: An attack carried out illegally to obtain unauthorized and privileged information by using dynamic art of manipulating social behavior of human relationships.

ENDNOTE

[1]   Internet Systems Consortium is a U.S. Federal 501c(3) public-benefit, non-profit corporation that develops BIND, DHCP, INN, Network Time Protocol, and OpenReg.

Port Scans

Jalal Kawash
American University of Sharjah, UAE

INTRODUCTION

The hardest task for a hacker is to get a foothold into a computer network system. If the hacker manages to get inside, the rest of the network is easily conquered. This is often referred to as the 'eggshell principle'. It is hard to pierce in, but once inside, the whole network can be available for the hacker's grab.

Trying to map a blueprint of the target network is the first challenge to the hacker. It is important for hackers to find out as much information as possible concerning the target network. Such information may include host names and addresses, applications and operating systems running on these hosts (versions and patch states), and application organization (servers and their roles).

A famous hackers' operation is 'zone transfer'. The zone contains all the registered host names in a network. Zone transfer is a request to get a copy of the zone. The underlying Routing Information Protocol can be discovered and manipulated to redirect traffic and obtain unencrypted information. A decent firewall can disable zone transfers, but administrators do not always take necessary precautions. Yet if they do, piercing into the network is still possible utilizing *port scanning*.

In a computer network system, application processes communicate with each other by sending and receiving messages. Transport addresses, called *end-points*, are specified and associated with each application process. In the Internet, each end-point is a pair of values. The first value is a unique machine address, called the Internet Protocol (*IP*) address. The second value is a local *port* number, which uniquely identifies the address of a particular process per IP address. An *open* port is one that has a process listening for connections; otherwise, it is said to be *closed*.

Port scanning is the process of determining which ports are open. Open ports may expose the host machine to external attacks because they can be further examined by attackers to discover and exploit network service vulnerability. Hence, port scanning allows a hacker to determine which applications are exposed on a target host. Such exposed applications are typically essential to the operation of the system. For instance, HTTP Web servers (port 80) and FTP (port 21) are typical exposed applications.

Open ports are associated with services. So, if the hacker can find out information about the nature of the service, its version, and patching state, he or she can work on exploiting it. For instance, if the hacker performs operating system fingerprinting, to find out the underlying operating system version, he or she can figure out if there are any known security problems with the version at hand, especially if it is not properly patched. Exploiting these security holes, and with the help of other tools, a hacker can install a backdoor into a system through open ports. This can allow the hacker to control the system remotely.

Since port scanning is important to hackers, it is also equally important to network administrators, but with contradictory objectives. Since open ports may expose a machine to potential external attacks, it is important that administrators identify them to monitor or avoid any possible hacking attempts. This article exposes the subject of port scanning, outlining some of the technical details on how such scans work.

BACKGROUND

Shaping Factors

There are three important factors that shape the implementation of a port scanner. These are the underlying communication protocol, filtering and detection, and time and bandwidth (Schiffman, 2003; De Vivo, Carrasco, Isern, & De Vivo, 1999). Call the attacking host (where the port scanner is running) the *scanning host* and the attacked host the *scanned host*.

- **Protocol:** Port scanners obtain their clues about ports by analyzing the underlying protocol's behavior. Hence, a scanning method is typically designed for some specified protocol. On the Internet, the most famous transport protocols are Transmission Control Protocol (TCP) and the User Data Protocol (UDP). In this article, we will limit the discussion to TCP scans, since UDP plays a lesser role in port scanning. The basic behavior of TCP is explained later in this section.

- **Detection:** Network administrators rely on an Intrusion Detection System (IDS) in order to monitor the network and detect any possible attacks. With an ever increasing number and effectiveness of attacks, IDSs have become indispensable for most organizations. Administrators cannot run detectable port scans while an IDS is running, since the latter can disable the scanner. Shutting down the IDS is obviously a bad idea. Hence, it is important to provide administrators with stealth port scanners that do not only hide the scanning behavior, but also conceal the scanning host IP address.

- **Time and Bandwidth:** Attackers have the luxury of spending an enormous amount of time performing port scanning, but administrators do not. Controlled port scanning incurs substantial overhead over the network's bandwidth and consequently its throughput. That is why administrators' controlled scans rarely span more than one day. Therefore in addition to providing administrators with stealth port scanners, it is also crucial to provide them with powerful scanners that can perform a comprehensive scan in a limited amount of time.

TCP Behavior

TCP is the most common target for port scanning. TCP is a connection-oriented protocol that any two processes need to establish a connection with two end-points in order to communicate with each other. To establish a TCP connection, a pair of processes follow the *three-way handshake* (Transmission Control Protocol RFC, 2006). This handshake consists of sending and receiving messages, called *segments,* whose purpose is to initialize the connection and its data streams. A TCP segment consists of a header and an optional body. The header includes six control bits, called flag bits, or simply *flags.* The flags that are set in a TCP segment header convey valuable information

to the scanning host. Such information can reveal for instance whether a port is closed or open (Transmission Control Protocol RFC, 2006).There are six flag bits (Stevens, 1994, 1995):

- **SYN:** The SYN bit is set when a sender or a receiver is establishing a connection. The sender sets this bit in order to request a connection, and the receiver sets it in order to accept a connection.
- **FIN:** The FIN bit is set to signal the act of finishing sending data by the sender. That is, it releases the connection.
- **RST:** This bit is used to reset the connection. Typically, it signals a problem. The RST bit is set when confusion takes place due to a host crash, for example. It is also used to refuse a connection. This bit is typically set in response to a SYN or FIN segment arriving at a closed port.
- **URG:** This bit states that the urgent pointer is being used. The urgent pointer points to urgent information contained in the TPC segment and allows the receiver to jump directly to this information.
- **ACK:** The ACK bit, when set, states that the TCP segment is an acknowledgment.
- **PSH:** If this bit is set, the segment is asking the receiver to rush (push) delivery to the application process.

A TCP segment that has one of these six bits set, say bit *x*, is called an *x* segment. The three-way handshake starts with the sender sending a SYN segment to the receiver; the receiver acknowledges this SYN segment by a sending back an ACK+SYN segment (both the ACK and SYN bits are set). The sender finally acknowledges the receiver's SYN segment with an ACK segment and the connection is initialized. Figure 1 illustrates a successful three-way handshake.

The arrival of a TCP SYN segment at an open port starts the three-way handshake. However, if the port is closed, an RST segment is sent back to the sender. RST segments can be also sent as a result of the arrival of an ACK segment at an open port. A FIN segment can also detect if a port is open or closed since a closed port results in sending an RST reply, but for an open port the FIN segment is simply dropped. URG and PSH flags can also be used to detect open ports.

Figure 1. A successful three-way handshake

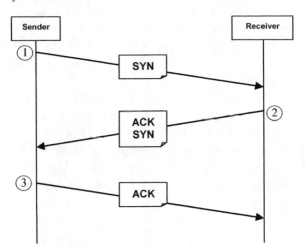

PORT SCANNING

Port Scan Techniques

There are many techniques to perform a scan; a comprehensive documentation of all of these is beyond the scope of this document. Here we discuss a handful of the many scans supported by a famous port scanning tool, called Nmap (*http://www.insecure.org/nmap*). Nmap is the most commonly used port scanning tool nowadays. Recall that the objective of a scan is to determine if a port is open or closed.[1]

- **SYN Scan:** In this scan, a SYN segment is sent to the scanned host, pretending to initiate a three-way-handshake in order to establish a TCP connection. However, this scan does not complete the whole handshake, and this is the reason why it is sometimes called the *half-open* scan. If the scanned host replies with a SYN or ACK segment, the port is open. If it replies with an RST segment, the port is closed. The scan ends here.

  The SYN scan is a popular choice since it is fairly stealthy and can perform a large number of scans in a short period of time. Its stealth behavior stems from the fact that it never completes a three-way handshake and hence never establishes a TCP connection.

- **Null Scan:** In TCP RFC 793 (Transmission Control Protocol RFC, 2006), when an open port receives a segment that does not have a SYN,

ACK, or RST set, no response is generated. If the port is closed, an RST packet is sent back. The null scan sends a segment with no bits set. If the scanner times out without receiving a response, the port must be open.[2] If an RST segment is received, it must be closed.

- **FIN Scan:** The FIN scan works like a null scan, but is initiated by sending a FIN segment instead.

- **Xmas Scan:** The Xmas scan sets all three bits FIN, PSH, and URG. Since none of the SYN, ACK, or RST bits is set, it also works like a null scan.

  Since not all TCP implementations abide by the RFC 793, the null, FIN, and Xmas scans can be cumbersome sometimes. It is also not possible to differentiate between open and filtered ports with these scans. However, these scans can fool some firewalls and filters. To continue:

- **FTP Scan:** Hackers can exploit FTP in order to perform scans that bypass firewalls. FTP allows users to transfer files, even to a third-party location. Asking the FTP server to send a file to different ports on a machine will result in a side-effect scan because the responses of these file transfer attempts can uncover open ports.

- **Other Scan Techniques:** Nmap offers many other scan types. The *connect* scan is an alternative to the SYN scan, but works at a higher level, the Application Programmer Interface (API) level. The ACK scan is used to detect firewall properties. Technically, this is not a port scan since it is not aimed to determine open versus closed ports. The *window* scan adds to the ACK scan the capabilities of detecting open and closed ports. Nmap also offers a *UDP* scan, the option for users to create their costumed scans, and stealthy and complex scans such as the *zombie* scan.

Port Scanning Categories

Port scanners can be classified into three categories, depending on how the scan for a set of ports is organized (Staniford, Hoagland, & McAlerney, 2002; Lee, Roedel, & Silenok, 2005). The categories are *horizontal, vertical,* and *block* scans.

*   **Horizontal Scan:** The horizontal scan, illustrated in Figure 2, is the most common category of port scans. It is characterized by having the scanning host investigate if the same port is open on each host in a given network. An example of a horizontal scan is when the administrator wants to check if any of the hosts on the network is running an e-mail server. In this case, it is only required to scan port 25 on all machines.
*   **Vertical Scan:** The vertical scan category is characterized by scanning all ports on one fixed IP. An example of this type of scanning is when a penetration tester wants to find vulnerability on a Web server host. Figure 3 illustrates a vertical scan.

Figure 2. A horizontal scan

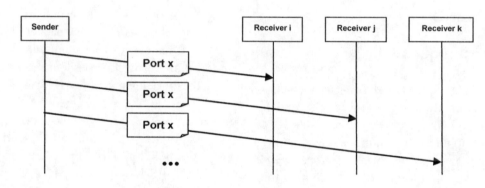

Figure 3. A vertical scan, with i increments

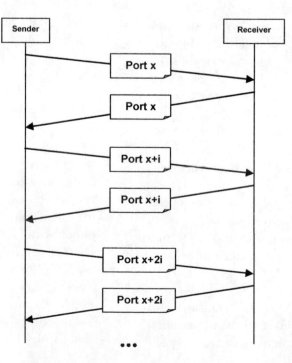

- **Block Scan:** The block scan category is a combination of horizontal and vertical scans. Usually, security specialists scan the entire network (all the ports on all IPs) to check the magnitude and the level of security that the network has.

Stealthy Scans

The purpose of an IDS is monitoring a computer system or network, watching for any signs of security problems (Bace & Mell, 2006). The most common three types of attacks reported by IDSs are scanning, denial of service, and penetration.

Stealthy port scans are undetectable by IDSs, or at least they aim at being undetectable by IDSs. Even though stealthy port scanners are desirable to hackers, they are also equally desirable to network administrators. Recall that the main concern of administrators is to identify network weaknesses without the need to shutdown any network monitoring programs, such as IDSs. Hence, attempts to improve port scanners' stealthy behavior have been constantly made (Schiffman, 2003).

The very first port scanners supported *full open* scans where ports were scanned in a sequential fashion (Lee et al., 2005; Staniford et al., 2002). That is, a scanned host is vertically scanned starting at the lowest port number and incrementally scanning higher numbers. In this scan, a scanned host receives an enormous amount of segments in a very small time window, making the scan easily detectable by an IDS. Later, time delay between successive segments to the scanned machine was introduced in order to widen that time window (Staniford et al., 2002) and hence make the scan less prone to detection.

The turning point for stealthy port scans came when some scanners abandoned sequential port scanning and replaced it with *random* port generation. Instead of sequentially scanning ports of a given host, the ports are randomly generated, making it more difficult for IDSs to detect suspicious behavior. This was later combined with delaying the scan messages and even randomizing the waiting time between messages (Staniford et al., 2002).

Nmap supports random port generation with random time delays to make the scan stealthy. It also supports parallel scans to improve efficiency.

FUTURE TRENDS

Developing techniques that distinguish between "innocent" scans and scans that form an early stage in an attack is very much needed. Panjwani, Tan, Jarrin, and Cukier (2005) claim that less than 50% of the port scans are succeeded by attacks.

Attackers will continue to make their attacks stealthier, and networks will continue to become larger and faster. Improving the effectiveness and efficiency of IDSs is crucial. In high-speed networks, where the traffic volume is high, an IDS often loses packets and generates an unacceptable number of false negatives. Rule-based approaches tailored for high-speed networks and real-time algorithms can offer solutions for more efficient and more effective IDSs (Yang, Fang, Liu, & Zhang, 2004; Jiang, Song, & Dai, 2005).

Machine learning and artificial intelligence techniques are not yet fully explored for building better IDSs. Generally, currently used machine learning techniques fail to identify the new attack if the training set does not include a representative of that attack. Genetic algorithms can help circumvent the problem of being faced with a never-encountered-before attack (Liu, Chen, Liao, & Zhang, 2004). An IDS can be viewed or formulated as a binary classifier, and support vector machines (SVMs) can be used to design better IDSs. The SVM can be also trained online to outperform existing techniques, as shown by Zhang and Shen (2005).

Mobile agents have several advantages (Jensen, 2002), and they constitute a promising area for the improvement of intrusion detection and blocking. Dasgupta, Gonzalez, Yallapu, Gomez, and Yarramsettii (2005) show how to build an IDS powered by a hierarchy of agents, specialized for different tasks. Decisions are made based on intelligent support modules, such as fuzzy inference, classification, and knowledge bases. More experimental evidence is needed to completely verify the effectiveness of Dasgupta et al.'s approach. The same agent-specialization approach can be used to build a dual-based IDS (Jha & Hassan, 2002), where a preemptive defense mechanism is delegated to an agent that detects and blocks the attacks. Passive postmortem defense is implemented in a different agent.

Analysis of all data features of an attack can be cumbersome (data could be redundant or even irrelevant). Chebrolu, Abraham, and Thomas (2005) show that isolating the relevant features leads to a better and more realistic IDS design. New data mining techniques are needed in order to reduce the size of the data being analyzed. Rawat, Pujari, and Gulati (2006) present a spectral analysis technique to pre-process that data by removing the noise.

CONCLUSION

Port scanning constitutes an important piece in a hacker's attack puzzle. It is a method used by hackers in order to uncover and exploit weaknesses in networked computer hosts. The method is equally important to administrators and ordinary users who are concerned with protecting their hosts from attacks. This article gives an overview of port scanning and how it can be used to detect vulnerable ports. It provides an overview of the most commonly used techniques in scanning, a categorization of scans, and a discussion of the most dangerous scans, stealthy scans.

Port scanning will continue to be one of the most important attack and defense mechanisms in networked systems. This article exposes port scanning in a simple language.

REFERENCES

Bace, R., & Mell, P. (2006). Intrusion detection systems. *NIST Special Publication on Intrusion Detection Systems*. Retrieved February 10, 2006, from http://www.snort.org/docs/nist-ids.pdf

Chebrolu, S., Abraham, A., & Thomas, J.P. (2005). Feature deduction and ensemble design of intrusion detection systems. *Computer and Security, 24,* 295-307.

Dasgupta, D., Gonzalez, F., Yallapu, K., Gomez, J., &Yarramsettii, R. (2005). CIDS: An agent-based intrusion detection system. *Computer & Security, 24,* 387-398.

De Vivo, M., Carrasco, E., Isern, G., & De Vivo, G.O. (1999). A review of port scanning techniques. *ACM SIGCOMM Computer Communication Review, 29*(2), 41-48.

Jensen, W.A. (2002). Intrusion detection with mobile agents. *Computer Communications, 25,* 1392-1401.

Jha, S., & Hassan, M. (2002). Building agents for rule-based intrusion detection system. *Computer Communications, 25,* 1366-1373.

Jiang, W., Song, H., & Dai, Y. (2005). Real-time intrusion detection for high-speed networks. *Computers & Security, 24,* 287-294.

Lee, C., Roedel, C., & Silenok, E. (2005). *Detection and characterization of port scan attacks.* Retrieved April 5, 2005, from http://www.cs.ucsd.edu/users/clbailey/PortScans.pdf

Liu, Y., Chen, K., Liao, X., & Zhang, W. (2004). A genetic clustering method for intrusion detection. *Pattern Recognition, 37,* 927-942.

Panjwani, S., Tan, S., Jarrin, K.M., & Cukier, M. (2005). An experimental evaluation to determine if port scans are precursors to an attack. *Proceedings of the 2005 International Conference on Dependable Systems and Networks* (pp. 602-611).

Rawat, S., Pujari, A.K., & Gulati, V.P. (2006). On the use of singular value decomposition for a fast intrusion detection system. *Electronic Notes in Theoretical Computer Science, 142,* 215-228.

Schiffman, M. (2003). *Building open source network security tools.* New York: John Wiley & Sons.

Staniford, S., Hoagland, J.A., & McAlerney, J. (2002). Practical automated detection of stealthy portscans. *Journal of Computer Security, 10*(1-2), 105-136.

Stevens, W.R. (1994). *TCP/IP illustrated* (vol. 1). Boston: Addison-Wesley.

Stevens, W.R. (1995). *TCP/IP illustrated* (vol. 2). Boston: Addison-Wesley.

Transmission Control Protocol RFC. (2006). Retrieved March 5, 2006, from http://www.ibiblio.org/pub/docs/rfc/rfc793.txt

Yang, W., Fang, B., Liu, B., & Zhang, H. (2004). Intrusion detection system for high- speed network. *Computer Communications, 27,* 1288-1294.

Zhang, Z., & Shen, H. (2005). Application of online-training SVMs for real-time intrusion detection with different considerations, *Computer Communications, 28,* 1428-1442.

KEY TERMS

Block Port Scan: A combination of vertical and horizontal scans.

Horizontal Port Scan: A port scan that examines one given port on all or some host machines in a network.

Intrusion Detection System (IDS): A program that monitors a computer host or a network of hosts trying to detect suspicious behavior, such as a port scan.

Port: An element of a pair of values that make a communication end point. Machines on the network are addressed by IP numbers and processes hosted by machines are addressed by a port number.

Port Scan: The procedure of examining a set of ports in a given network in order to determine which ports have processes listening to them. Such ports can be further examined to expose any weaknesses in the network.

Stealthy Port Scan: A port scan that cannot be detected or is hard to detect by an IDS.

Three-Way-Handshake: The process used by TCP in order to initiate network connections. The sender sends a connection request, the receiver replies with approval, and the sender acknowledges the connection instantiation.

Vertical Port Scan: A port scan that examines all or a set of ports on one host machine in a network.

ENDNOTES

[1]   Nmap allows another classification of ports: filtered. A filtered port is unreachable and from the attacker's point of view is similar to a closed port.

[2]   It can be also filtered. A port is filtered if a 'port unreachable' error message is received.

Privacy and Access to Electronic Health Records

Dick Whiddett
Massey University, New Zealand

Inga Hunter
Massey University, New Zealand

Judith Engelbrecht
Massey University, New Zealand

Jocelyn Handy
Massey University, New Zealand

INTRODUCTION

The special relationship of trust that needs to exist between a patient and his or her physician has been recognized since the origins of the profession, and the need for doctors to keep confidential any information disclosed to them is codified in the Hippocratic Oath. A distinctive feature of the health records which arises from this relationship is the intimate nature of the information that they may contain; consequently, it is vitally important to maintain the confidentiality of the records and to protect the privacy of the patients. Privacy has long been recognized as a fundamental right in most western societies (Westin, 2003), and unless a patient can be sure that personal information will not be distributed against his or her wishes, the patient may be reluctant to disclose information that may in fact be crucial to his or her correct treatment (Ford, Bearman, & Moody, 1999; NZHIS, 1995), or he or she may refrain from seeking treatment (Sankar, Moran, Merz, & Jones, 2003). This is particularly true when health records contain sensitive information concerning issues like drug and alcohol problems, sexual behavior, mental health, or a genetic predisposition towards certain diseases. In such circumstances, the consequences of the inappropriate release of information could be extensive and might impact on many aspects of a person's life, such as the ability to gain employment, to maintain a marriage, or to obtain loans or life insurance (Chadwick, 1999; Woodward, 1995).

Within the healthcare sector there is a constant pressure to balance patients' requirements for personal privacy against the potential benefits that may accrue to society as a whole from the more widespread use of their personal information. This issue is particularly relevant in developed countries that have been seeking to use computer-based patient records (CPRs) (Dick & Streen, 1991), electronic medical records (EMRs), and electronic health records (EHRs) to improve both organizational efficiency and the quality of care provided for patients (AHRQ, 2006).[1]

The potential benefits of EHRs are widely accepted, but there are also serious problems concerning the potential threats to patient privacy (Carter, 2000). The move from paper-based records to electronic records has greatly increased the potential threats to patients' privacy in two ways. Firstly, it has increased the risk of unauthorized access to patients' information by people both within and outside of an organization, since it is now no longer necessary to manually search through individual patient's records and it is possible to systematically search through collections of records from a distance (Goldschmidt, 2005). Secondly, the development of communications networks has greatly increased to the extent to which patient information is now routinely exchanged between different healthcare organizations so more people have access to it (Kissinger & Borchardt, 1996).

This article will explore some of the privacy issues associated with the development and use of EHRs. The first part describes the background and development of EHRs and the various ways that patient health information can be used and distributed within modern healthcare systems. It discusses the benefits that may accrue to the individual patient and also to healthcare organizations due to improved access to information. The second part then reviews some issues that arise from the use of EHRs, and it reviews research into patient attitudes towards the distribution of their health information. The final part of the article discusses some technologies that address the security requirements of patients such as role-based security systems (Sandhu, Coyne, Feinstein, & Youman, 1996), smartcard systems (Rienhoff, 2003), and finally, e-consent systems (Coiera & Clarke, 2004; Galpottage & Norris, 2005; Scott, Jennett, & Yeo, 2004), which aim to provide patients with much greater control over the access to their information.

BACKGROUND

Electronic information systems are often justified on the grounds that having access to more complete, accurate, and timely information facilitates better decisions. In the case of health records, these benefits may accrue directly to the individual patient in terms of better treatment or to the population in general through improvements to healthcare practice or administration (Mount, Kelman, Smith, & Douglas, 2000). The application of data-mining techniques to large numbers of EHRs could facilitate epidemiological and evaluative studies (Bath, 2004; Payton, 2003), and the information may also benefit healthcare administrators and managers by providing them with more comprehensive information about service usage and costs (Hannan, 1999).

Despite the wide range of their potential benefits, the introduction of comprehensive EHRs has been relatively slow because of the complexity of the health sector from technological, organizational, and ethical perspectives (Goldschmidt, 2005). The use of computer-based information systems to store patients' records has been evolving since the 1970s. The early systems tended to focus on the administrative details of a patient and to deal with a single episode of care. Because of the high development and implementation costs, early systems were mainly used in larger hospitals (Goldschmidt, 2005; Reichertz, 2006), but as computing costs have fallen, sophisticated systems have become widespread, and systems are now found in most hospitals and in many primary care or GP practices (Didham & Martin, 2004).

In the late 1980s and throughout the 1990s, the potential benefits of an integrated lifelong electronic health record began to be recognized and explored (Haux, 2006). For the individual patient, major benefits arise from the improved continuity of care which is possible if all healthcare practitioners have a complete and detailed history of the patient's conditions and treatments on which to base their diagnoses and decisions. Easy access to a comprehensive patient history would be particularly useful when a patient is referred to a practitioner for the first time, if a patient needs treatment when he or she is traveling and is away from his or her usual practitioner, or in accident or emergency situations when the patient is unconscious or unable to answer questions (Mount et al., 2000; Hunt, Haynes, Hannah, & Smith, 1998). For example, comprehensive records will improve medication management by allowing the practitioner to quickly check whether a patient is known to be allergic to a particular medicine, or whether a particular drug might have adverse interactions with other medicines the patient may be taking (Ministry of Health, 2001).

Unfortunately, the widespread introduction of EHRs has been hampered by organizational problems caused by the dispersed nature of the healthcare sector in most countries. Since many organizations are involved in providing and funding care, a patient's information tends to get fragmented and dispersed (Goldschmidt, 2005; Kissinger & Borchardt, 1996). Treatment of a typical condition may involve a patient visiting a community-based practice, such as a general practitioner (GP), consultations and treatments by hospital-based specialists, and tests and analyses undertaken by various laboratories. Typically, information from each of these encounters will be stored by each organization within its own separate computer system, which will have been designed to support the specific requirements of each organization and its users. Furthermore, the payment for all these services may come in part or full from several sources, such as the patient, the government, or some private insurance scheme, so further inter-organizational information exchange is required to sort out the finances (Kissinger & Borchardt, 1996). Current developments of EHRs are therefore focusing on distributed structures with a centralized summary of a patient's information, with links to detailed information located in other computer systems (AHRQ, 2006). Developments of this kind are currently being supported by the governments of the UK (NHS, 2001, 2002a), Canada (CHII, 2006), Australia (NHIMAC, 1999), and New Zealand (Ministry of Health, 2000, 2001), which are all pursuing the development of nationwide EHRs to help manage their public health systems. In the United States where there is no public health system, the government is still involved in similar developments that aim to promote the efficient interchange of health information by funding the National Health Information Infrastructure (NHII) project (USDHHS, 2001) and through legislation such as the Health Insurance Portability and Accountability Act (HIPAA) of 1996 (USDHHS, 2006), which defines standards for health information structure, security, and privacy. These developments should benefit individual patients and also improve the overall efficiency of the health sector.

PRIVACY AND PATIENTS' ATTITUDES

The potential threats to the confidentiality of the information that EHRs contain and their implications for patient privacy are controversial (Carter, 2000), and large-scale health information systems have often been fraught with problems (Hannan, 1998; Sicotte et al., 1998). A classic example of this occurred within the British National Health Service when doctors boycotted an inter-organizational network designed to improve the exchange of information on the grounds that it threatened patients' privacy (Davis, 1996; Willcox, 1995). Research in New Zealand into clinicians' attitudes towards the use of information contained within EHRs indicated that some of the potential uses were unacceptable and would also lead them to withhold information (Handy, Hunter, & Whiddett, 2001).

Despite the fact that many western countries have adopted privacy legislation that is based on the OECD principles (OECD, 1980) which should protect the confidentiality of health information, concerns about the uses made of the information are not unfounded. In the UK, the Caldicott Committee Report (1997) into patient privacy identified several breaches of confidentiality, and the report made wide-ranging recommendations to improve the security of patients' information. In a survey of Australians, Mulligan (2001) found that 1.9% of respondents reported harm arising from unauthorized disclosure of their information by health services. Anderson (2000) cites a number of cases where patient privacy has been breached in the United States. The U.S. pressure group *Patientprivacyrights* (2006) is also concerned that amendments to HIPAA will increase the abuse of patient information. The group claims that medical information is used to influence employment and promotion decisions, to determine eligibility for bank loans and insurance, and to market pharmaceuticals.

Despite the importance of personal privacy, there is a lack of research which addresses the issue from the patients' perspective. A recent review of the literature (Sankar et al., 2003) identified nearly 6,000 articles related to issues of patient privacy, but the vast majority of them were written from the practitioners' perspective or addressed legal or regulatory issues. Only 6% of the identified articles were written from the patients' perspective, and of these only 110 (2%) were based on research. Furthermore, most of this research focused on specific groups or particularly sensitive issues, such as adolescents who are concerned about their information reaching their parents or people who are having HIV tests. Very little work has addressed the perspective of ordinary patients.

Some research into attitudes of patients or the public towards the distribution of their information has been undertaken in the UK in association with the National Health Service's Electronic Record Development and Implementation Program (ERDIP) (NHS, 2002a), the PERIC (Patient Electronic Record: Information and Consent) project (Shickle, Carlisle, & Wallace, 2002), and the 'Share with Care' project (NHS, 2002b). Patients' attitudes have also been studied in New Zealand (Whiddett, Hunter, Engelbrecht, & Handy, 2006), and in Australia the issues of confidentiality of patient information and consent for access have been addressed as part of the Health*Connect* project (Health*Connect* Program Office 2002, 2003). These projects have recognized the increasing levels of concern about personal privacy among the general public and have begun to try to identify their expectations. However, to date the exploration of the attitudes of patients and the development of systems to meet their requirements has not received the attention that these issues would seem to warrant.

Although the various studies of patients' attitudes have addressed different specific issues and have used different research methodologies, such as questionnaires, interviews, telephone interviews, and focus groups, it is possible to draw some broad overall conclusions. A key finding of all the studies is that on many detailed issues there is little overall public consensus, and a wide range of views are often found, with some people being happy for their information to be used in certain a way, while others would be most upset by it. The studies usually find that there is little or no correlation between peoples' attitudes and demographic variables such as age, gender, ethnicity, and so forth. This means that it is virtually impossible to develop a standard system that will satisfy all patients, or even to predict the specific privacy requirement of any particular individual. However, the studies do reveal some general trends.

Firstly, the studies have all confirmed that people do want restrictions to be applied to access to their information. While most people are happy for their information to be accessed by practitioners who are treating them, there is much less consensus about information being accessed by other professionals for secondary purposes, such as clinical research or organizational management and planning.

Secondly, many people also wish for different levels of security to be provided for different parts of the record so that some information could be made available on a 'need to know' basis only, and for information about particularly sensitive issues to be hidden from general access. For example, the Share with Care project (NHS, 2002b) found that 32% of respondents had at least some sensitive information over which they would like particular control through the use of a 'virtual sealed envelope'.

Thirdly, people are more willing to allow their information to be used for purposes other than their care if the information is first made anonymous by removing any identifying features such as their name and address. However, many people expressed some reservations about sharing even anonymous information with people other than health professionals, and many people feel that they should still be consulted about the use of their information, even when it is anonymous. The desire for this level of control contrasts with some current practices which are permitted under the privacy legislations of the UK, Australia, and New Zealand (Galpottage & Norris, 2005) which do not control the use of unidentifiable data.

MANAGING ACCESS

Overall, the studies revealed that people would like to have more control over the uses that are made of their information. However, the mechanisms that are provided in most current computer systems operate at too coarse a level of granularity and are not sophisticated enough to meet patients' requirements. Typically, access control mechanisms provide entire classes of users with access to the set of applications that they need to fulfill their role within their organization (Sandhu et al., 1996). Protection of an individual's privacy tends to be based upon the integrity of the staff who are relied upon not to abuse their positions of trust rather than being based upon technological safeguards within the systems. However, technological solutions have been investigated by the health sector, particularly in the areas of smartcards and e-consent models.

The health sector has been experimenting with the use of smartcard technologies (credit card-sized devices with on-board memories and possibly microprocessors) to store patient information and to authenticate practitioners since the early 1990s, and several systems in the United States and Europe (particularly France and Germany) have used smartcards to store patient information with varying degrees of success (see Reinhoff, 2003, for a comprehensive review). Having a patient's information stored electronically on a card can be very convenient for organizations, and it can also give the patients a high level of control over who has access to their information (Marschollek & Demirbilek, 2006). However, there are often problems with compatibility and inter-operability of systems that limit the uptake and use of the smartcard-based EHRs (Reinhoff, 2003). The relatively limited memory that is available on the card means that systems tend to only contain a very restricted amount of information (Chan, 2000), and an alternative use of smartcards is to provide a method of authenticating users and controlling their access to other systems over a network (Blobel, Pharow, Spiegel, Engel, & Engelbrecht, 2001; Marschollek & Demirbilek, 2006). Overall it seems that smartcards on their own will not resolve all of the issues of patient privacy, but they may provide some components of the solution.

Recently, some researchers have been focusing on the design of systems which are capable of capturing and recording a patient's privacy requirements and their consent to share information at a fine level of granularity. This information would then be used by the 'e-consent systems' to mediate information requests and to enforce a patient's requirements depending on the intended recipient, the nature of the information, and the proposed use of the information (Coiera & Clarke, 2004; Galpottage & Norris, 2005; Scott et al., 2004). However, as Coiera and Clarke (2004) note, the process of consulting with each patient about future access to information needs to be managed carefully so that it does not place an undue burden on health professionals. One solution that has been proposed to overcoming this problem during the clinical consultation is to enable patients to log onto the EHR system at some other time and to set or update the access permissions for their own personal information (Galpottage & Norris, 2005), thus giving patients the ultimate control.

CONCLUSION

Healthcare systems are exceedingly complex environments that often deal with highly personal and intimate issues; consequently, the security and privacy requirements for EHRs are more demanding than most other information systems applications. To date, the magnitude of the technical difficulties of implementing EHRs has tended to dominate the attention of researchers, and the privacy issues which are associated with the wholesale exchange of patients' information have received comparatively little attention. However, privacy issues are important since they will also influence the acceptance of EHRs; a failure to address them may ultimately lead practitioners or patients to boycott or reject such systems.

Patients' privacy needs to be protected in several ways: by technological systems that enforce security and can restrict access to information, by organization and cultural systems that emphasize and respect patients' privacy, and finally by a legislative framework that can be used to enforce patients' rights to privacy.

REFERENCES

AHRQ (Agency for Healthcare Research and Quality). (2006). *Electronic medical/health records.* Retrieved from http://www.ahrq.gov

Anderson, J. (2000). Security of the distributed electronic patient record: A case-based approach to identifying policy issues. *International Journal of Medical Informatics, 60,* 111-118.

Bath, P.A. (2004). Data mining in health and medical information. *Annual Review of Information Science and Technology, 38,* 331-369.

Blobel, B., Pharow, P., Spiegel, V., Engel, K., & Engelbrecht, R. (2001) Securing interoperability between chip card based medical information systems and health networks. *International Journal of Medical Informatics, 64*(3), 401-415.

Chan, A.T. (2000). WWW+smart card: Towards a mobile health care management system. *International Journal of Medical Informatics, 57*(2), 127-137.

Caldicott Committee. (1997). *Report on the review of patient-identifiable information.* London: NHS Executive. Retrieved from http://www.doh.gov.uk/confiden/crep.html

Carter, M. (2000). Integrated electronic health records and patient privacy: Possible benefits but real dangers. *Medical Journal of Australia, 172,* 28-30.

Chadwick, R. (1999). The Icelandic database—do modern times need modern sagas? *British Medical Journal, 319,* 441-444.

CHII. (2006). *Canada Health Infoway Incorporated.* Retrieved from http://www.canadahealthinfoway.ca

Coiera, E., & Clarke, R. (2004) E-consent: The design and implementation of consumer consent mechanisms in an electronic environment. *Journal of the American Medical Informatics Association, 11*(4), 129-140.

Davies, S. (1996). Dystopia on the health superhighway. *Information Society, 12*(1), 89-93.

Dick, R., & Streen, E. (1991). *The computer based patient record: An essential technology for healthcare.* Washington, DC: National Academy Press.

Didham, R., & Martin, I. (2004). *A review of computerised information technology in general practice medicine.* Retrieved from http://hcro.enigma.co.nz/website/index.cfm?fuseaction=articledisplay&FeatureID=040302

Ford, C.A., Bearman, P.S., & Moody, J. (1999). Foregone health care among adolescents. *Journal of the American Medical Association, 282*(23), 2227-2234.

Galpottage, P.A.B., & Norris, A.C. (2005). Patient consent principles and guidelines for e-consent: A New Zealand perspective. *Health Informatics Journal, 11*(1), 5-18.

Goldschmidt, P.G. (2005). HIT and MIS: Implications of health information technology and medical information systems. *Communications of the ACM, 48*(10), 69-74.

Hannan, T.J. (1998). Transporting an electronic patient record system across international boundaries—the lessons learnt. *Medinfo, 9*(1), 18-20.

Hannan, T.J. (1999). Variation in health care— the roles of the electronic medical record. *International Journal of Medical Informatics, 54*(2), 127-136.

Handy, J.A., Hunter, I., & Whiddett, R. (2001). User acceptance of inter-organizational electronic medical records. *Health Informatics Journal, 7*(2), 102-106.

Haux, R. (2006). Health information systems—past, present and future. *International Journal of Medical Informatics, 75,* 268-281.

HealthConnect Program Office. (2002). *Consent and electronic health records: A discussion paper.* Canberra: Commonwealth of Australia. Retrieved from http://www.healthconnect.gov.au/publications/

HealthConnect Program Office. (2003). *HealthConnect: Interim research report.* Canberra: Commonwealth of Australia. Retrieved from http://www.healthconnect.gov.au/publications/

Hunt, D.L., Haynes, R.B., Hannah, S.E., & Smith, K. (1998). Effects of computer-based clinical decision support systems on physician performance and patient outcomes: A systematic review. *Journal of the American Medical Association, 280,* 1339-1346.

Kissinger, K., & Borchardt, S. (1996). *Information technology for integrated health systems.* New York: John Wiley & Sons.

Marschollek, M., & Demirbilek, E. (2006). Providing longitudinal health care information with the new German health card—a pilot system to track patient pathways. *Computer Methods and Programs in Biomedicine, 81*(3), 266-271.

Marietti, C. (1998, May). *Will the real CPR/EMR/EHR please stand up.* Retrieved from http://www.healthcare-informatics.com/issues/1998/05_98/cover.htm

Ministry of Health. (2000). *The New Zealand health strategy.* Wellington: Author.

Ministry of Health. (2001). *From strategy to reality: The WAVE project.* Wellington: Author.

Mount, C., Kelman, C., Smith, L., & Douglas, R. (2000). An integrated electronic health record and information system for Australia? *Medical Journal of Australia, 172,* 25-27.

Mulligan, E. (2001). Confidentiality in health records: Evidence of current performance from a population survey in South Australia. *Medical Journal of Australia, 174*(12), 637-640.

NHIMAC (National Health Information Management Advisory Council). (1999). *Health online: A health information action plan for Australia.* Canberra: Commonwealth of Australia.

NHS (National Health Service) (2001). *Building the information core.* London: NHS Executive.

NHS (National Health Service). (2002a). *Electronic Record Development and Implementation Programme—EPDI.* London: NHS. Retrieved from http://www.nhsia.nhs.uk/erdip/pages/default.asp

NHS (National Health Service). (2002b). *Share with care! People's views on consent and confidentiality of patient information.* London: NHS. Retrieved from http://www.nhsia.nhs.uk

NZHIS. (1995). *Health information privacy and confidentiality.* Wellington: New Zealand Health Information Service.

OECD. (1980). *Guidelines on the protection of privacy and transborder flows of personal data.* Retrieved from http://www.oecd.org/dsti/sti/it/secur/prod/

Patientprivacyrights. (2006). Retrieved from http://www.patientprivacyrights.org

Payton, F.C. (2003). Data mining in health care. In J. Wang (Ed.), *Data mining: Opportunities and challenges* (pp. 350-365). Hershey, PA: Idea Group.

Reichertz, P.L. (2006). Hospital information systems—past, present and future. *International Journal of Medical Informatics, 75,* 282-299.

Reinhoff, O. (2003). *Integrated health data cards (smart cards): A primer for health professionals.* Washington, DC: Pan American Health Organization. Retrieved from http://www.ehealthstrategies.com

Sandhu, R.S., Coyne, E.J., Feinstein, H.L., & Youman, C.E. (1996). Role-based access control models. *Computer, 29*(2), 38-47.

Sankar, P., Moran, S., Merz, J.F., & Jones, N.L. (2003). Patient perspectives on medical confidentiality: A review of the literature. *Journal of General Internal Medicine, 18,* 659-669.

Scott, R.E., Jennett, P., & Yeo, M. (2004). Access and authorization in a global e-health policy context. *International Journal of Medical Informatics, 73,* 259-266.

Shickle, D., Carlisle, J., & Wallace, S. (2002). *Patient Electronic Record; Information and Consent (PERIC)—public attitudes to protection and use of personal health information.* ScHARR Report Series No. 7, School of Health and Related Research, University of Sheffield, UK.

Sicotte, C., Denis, J.L., Lehoux, P., & Champagne, F. (1998). The computer based patient record challenges: Towards timeless and spaceless medical practice. *Journal of Medical Systems, 22,* 237-256.

USDHHS. (2001). *Information for health: A strategy for building the national health information infrastructure.* Washington DC: U.S. Department of Health and Human Services. Retrieved from http://www.hhs.gov

USDHHS. (2006). *HIPPA medical privacy—national standards to protect the privacy of personal health information.* Washington DC: U.S. Department of Health and Human Services. Retrieved from http://www.hhs.gov

Westin, A.F. (2003). Social and political dimensions of privacy. *Journal of Social Issues, 59*(2), 431-453.

Whiddett, R., Hunter, I., Engelbrecht, J., & Handy, J. (2006). Patients' attitudes towards sharing their health information. *International Journal of Medical Informatics, 7*(7), 530-541.

Willcox, D. (1995). Health scare. *Computing,* (October 19), 28-29.

Woodward, B. (1995). The computer-based patient record and confidentiality. *New England Journal of Medicine, 333,* 1419-1422.

KEY TERMS

Computer-Based Patient Record (CPR): Automated patient record designed to enhance and support patient care by providing access to complete and accurate data and to bodies of knowledge.

Confidentiality: Tacit understanding that information disclosed to care providers will remain protected.

Consent: Process by which an individual authorizes medical interventions or the processing of his or her information based on an informed understanding of the expected outcomes.

Data Mining: A set of techniques that explore large collections of data to discover new or unexpected relationships.

E-Consent System: Advanced computer-based system that can record a patient's consent and use it to mediate information requests from other systems.

E-Health: A term that encompasses a wide range of healthcare-related activities that involve the exchange of information using electronic communication systems.

Electronic Health Record (EHR): Integrated collection of health information relating to an individual's lifetime, stored in electronic format.

Electronic Medical Record (EMR): The health information for a patient contained within a given institution or organization stored in electronic format.

Master Patient Index (MPI): Module of a health information system used to uniquely identify a patient.

Smartcard: Credit card-sized device with on-board memory and possibly a microprocessor. Sometimes used to store a patient's personal information.

ENDNOTE

[1] There are no universally accepted definitions of the terms CPR, EMR, and EHR. The meanings of the terms have been constantly evolving and definitions often overlap; see Marietti (1998) for further discussion. This article will adopt the term EHR.

Privacy and Online Data Collection

Călin Gurău
GSCM – Montpellier Business School, France

INTRODUCTION

Online *privacy* represents a controversial subject for Internet users and online companies alike. Most Internet-active enterprises are using cookies or subscription forms to collect demographic and behavioral data about the Internet users that visit their sites. In exchange, these companies are promising the *personalization* of online interaction between company and customer, and therefore better value for clients. In addition to these *benefits,* many firms promise in their *privacy* disclaimer to use the collected data only for purposes specifically accepted by clients.

Studies have shown that most Internet customers are concerned about their online *privacy* (Kim & Montalto, 2002; Kuanchin & Rea, 2004; Malhotra, Sung, & Agarwal, 2004; Sheehan, 2002). They feel that despite the strict *privacy* policies published on the Net by firms, they have no control over the use of their personal data once collected by an online enterprise. In other cases, they fear that companies may use covert data-collecting methods that are not disclosed to the Internet users. According to Westin (2001), consumers' concerns in online *privacy* revolve around "intrusions, manipulation, and discrimination; on special concerns about third parties capturing self-revelations users are making on the Internet; and on concerns about identity theft and stalking though capture of personal information." These negative perceptions highlight the need to approach online *data collection* from an ethical perspective.

This article attempts to identify and analyze the perceptions of online customers related to the benefits and perils of personal data collection on the Internet. Analyzing the primary data collected through a questionnaire survey of 300 UK Internet users, the article presents and discusses the customers' evaluation of the privacy policy applied by the commercial sites most frequently accessed, as well as the level of *personalization* offered by these Web sites. The main sources of perceived *risks* and benefits are identified and analyzed in order to identify their effect on the perception of online customers.

On the basis of these results, the article proposes a graphical model that classifies the commercial Web sites into four main categories, based on the balance between the perceived *risks* and the perceived *benefits* of online *data collection.* This article concludes with practical propositions addressed to commercial Web sites concerning the actions they can take to improve the perception of their customers regarding the benefits of online data collection, and to develop the popularity of their Web sites.

BACKGROUND

The evolution of information technology applications in the last 10 years has opened new possibilities for distant commercial interactions, related with the acquisition and exchange of information, products, or services. The exponential growth of online commercial transactions was related with an intensive competition among virtual enterprises for market shares and customer loyalty. In order to achieve a competitive advantage in the online market, many firms have implemented advanced e-CRM applications, which collect relevant data about online clients, analyze and evaluate the consumer profiles, and identify the higher value customers for the firm (Ragins & Greco, 2003).

One of the prerequisites of an effective e-CRM strategy is the collection of historical data about the interaction between the firm and its customers (Ragins & Greco, 2003). However, the collecting, archiving, and processing of personal data creates significant online *privacy* concerns. For the individual user, the privacy threats fall into two main categories:

1. **Web tracking devices that collect information about the online behavior of the user (e.g., cookies):** A company can use cookies for various valid reasons: security, personalization, marketing, customer service, and so forth. However, there is an important distinction between cookies which are active only within a specific Web site, and

the ones that can track the user's activity across unrelated Web sites. Recently some aggregator networks have deployed hidden 'pixel beacon' technology that allows ad-serving companies to connect unrelated sites and overcome the site-specific nature of traditional cookies (Mabley, 2000). Additionally, some companies are now connecting this aggregated data with offline demographic and credit card data. Eventually, these resulting databases can be used or sold as powerful marketing tools.

2. **The misuse of users' personal information in exchange for specific benefits, including increased personalization, Web group membership, and so forth:** The misuse of personal information includes unsolicited promotional e-mails, the integration of data in databases that can be sold to third parties without the consent of Internet users, or even credit card fraud.

The databases, intelligent agents, and tracking devices are surrounding the Internet users with a web of surveillance, which is often hidden and unknown to the subjects. The surveillance is initiated by the simple act of presence on the Internet. Specialized software applications such as 'cookies' are tracking the online behavior of Internet users and feeding the data into databases, which create and permanently update a profile of online consumers. These profiles are then used for segmenting the market and targeting the most profitable consumers.

Exercising control of information, after it was voluntarily released, presents another critical problem. The misuse of personal information—which can be defined as any use that is not explicitly defined in the company's *privacy* disclaimer or is not approved by the informed customer—covers many possible aspects. The customers' concerns focus on people reading private e-mails, tracking clickstream patterns to learn where people surf, compiling profiles of Net use for marketing purposes, and collecting information about children for marketing purposes without parental consent (Westin, 2001). For example, in 2000, Toysurus. com was subject to intense debate and controversy when it was discovered that shoppers' personal information was transferred through an unmarked Internet channel to a little-known data processing firm for analysis and aggregation. This operation was not disclosed in the company's privacy disclaimer, and therefore online customers were not aware of it.

Another main concern of online customers is the quality and reliability of online privacy policies (OPPs) (Westin, 2001). A series of studies (Freehills, 2000; Lichtenstein, Swatman, & Babu, 2003; NPP, 2000) indicated that many American and Australian OPPs do not comply with recognized ethical principles concerning the use of customers' data, use unclear terms, and are not consistent with the real practices of the online firms that publish them.

Regulators and legislators have addressed the controversial *privacy* issue quite differently across the world (Nakra, 2001). The United States, the largest world's financial and Internet market, has not yet adopted a national, standard-setting online *privacy* law (Jarvis, 2001). U.S. privacy statutes have primarily focused so far on protecting only specific areas of consumer privacy, such as financial data, health information, and children's personal information (Desai, Richard, & Desai, 2003; Frye, 2001; Rombel, 2001). In comparison with the American official opinion that online privacy protection is a matter of voluntary self-regulation by market-driven companies, the Europeans consider that it is more effective to enforce specific legislation regarding this issue.

The current European approach is based on three basic tenets (DTI, 2003):

1. individuals have the right to access any data relating to them and have it kept accurate and up-to-date;

2. data cannot be retained for longer than the purposes for which it was obtained, nor used or disclosed in a matter incompatible with that purpose, and must be kept only for lawful purposes; and

3. those who control data have a special duty of care in relation to the individuals whose data they keep.

Data commissioners oversee these rights in each European country and require most data controllers to register with them to track what information is being collected and where. They are charged also with investigating all complaints from citizens.

These principles have been incorporated in the European Data Directive, which came into effect in 1998, and more recently, in the European Directive on

Privacy and Electronic Communications, adopted in 2002, which required implementation of its provisions in Member States by October 31, 2003 (DTI, 2003).

Companies that collect and process customer information declare to do so in order to personalize the online interaction between the firm and its customer (Chellappa & Sin, 2005). *Personalization* represents a source of advantages for the online client, determining increased satisfaction, repeated purchase, and the long-term loyalty towards the commercial Web site. Better service provision realized though online *personalization* can create the following range of effects (Lips, van der Hof, Prins, & Schudelaro, 2004):

- services tailored to their needs and interests
- enhanced customer trust built through information sharing
- better understanding and awareness of customer needs
- targeted marketing
- increased and more stable revenues for online firms
- a consistent user experience from any location or device
- minimized costs and improved efficiencies.

Millard (2004) perceives three elements that have to be personalized in online interactions:

- **content:** what the customer receives
- **context:** how the customer receives it
- **contact:** the way in which customers are serviced

Previous studies attempted to analyze and model the behavior of online customers in relation to the value attached to *personalization* and considering users' concerns for *privacy* (Chellappa & Sin, 2005). The researchers consider that the decision to provide personal information is made on the basis of a rational cost-benefit analysis, therefore if the *benefits* of information sharing are superior to the perceived costs (risks), the online user is willing to provide online personal information (Kim & Montalto, 2002; Malhotra et al., 2004). However, these articles did not attempt to identify and define clearly what types of benefits are perceived by the customers in relation to online personal *data collection* and what the main concerns related with privacy issues are.

ONLINE PRIVACY VS. PERSONALIZATION: AN EMPIRICAL SURVEY

In order to identify the perceived benefits and risks related with online data collection, a survey was undertaken in the UK between March and June 2004. People were approached in the waiting areas of Edinburgh and London commercial centers, as well as in Edinburgh and London Stansted Airports, and asked to answer a short questionnaire regarding their Web activity. As a result of this survey, 300 usable questionnaires have been filled in by UK citizens, aged between 18 and 60 years. The respondents were asked to think of a Web site to which they provided personal information recently (in the last month), and then to identify as precisely and detailed as possible the benefits and *risks* perceived, as well as their influence on their decision-making process. In order to understand the reasons that determine online disclosure of personal information, the respondents were also asked to describe the main stages of their decision process. The collected data has been introduced into SPSS statistical software and analyzed using frequencies and cross-tabulations.

Although a series of other factors could influence the Internet users' perception regarding online *data collection* (voluntary or required provision of personal information, intensity of Internet usage, level of trust, type of personal information provided, etc), these elements were not taken into account in this exploratory study.

Table 1 presents the main benefits perceived by respondents in relation to online personal data requests. The immediate benefits seem to represent the most important reason for providing online information (79.3% of respondents), such as a subscription to a newsletter, an advantageous offer, or winning a promotional game. Almost exclusively, the access to these immediate benefits is offered only if the Web user voluntarily fills in an online form with personal socio-demographic information.

In terms of long-terms benefits, three aspects of online personalization have been indicated by respondents: Web site personalization, which can increase the ease of Web navigation; personalized information/communication, including exclusive offers of new products, a personalized newsletter, or professional advice; and the personalization of online transactions, in terms of payment, delivery, or post-sales services. The collec-

Table 1. The perceived benefits of providing personal data online

Perceived Benefits of Providing Personal Data Online	Number (out of 300)	Percentage
Immediate benefits	238	79.3
Web site personalization	177	59
Personalized information/communication	196	65.3
Transaction personalization	153	51

Table 2. The perceived risks of providing personal data online

Perceived Risks of Providing Personal Data Online	Number (out of 300)	Percentage
Unsolicited e-mails	216	72
Data disclosure to third parties	247	82.3
Credit card fraud	223	74.3

Table 3. The risk-reducing information used by online customers

Risk-Reducing Information	Frequency (out of 300)	Percentage
Privacy policy	266	88.7
Security seal	271	90.3
Third-party information	189	63

tion of personal data for these benefits can be either through online forms or through an online application that automatically registers the online behavior of the client and is usually described in the privacy policy posted online by the firm.

On the other hand, the main perceived risks identified by respondents (see Table 2) were unsolicited e-mails, personal data disclosure to third parties (e.g., associated firms), or credit card fraud. In reality, when confronted with a request for providing personal information, most users are searching for elements that can reduce these perceived risks.

Table 3 shows the most important risk-reducing online information as indicated by respondents.

The information provided by respondents strongly suggests that the online user is basing his or her decision for providing personal information online on a risk/benefit analysis. Although the main benefits of personal data disclosure are related with personalization, most respondents confessed that in the first instance they are attracted mainly by immediate, short-term benefits.

On the other hand, when users perceive a potential risk for their privacy, they try to modify this perception by searching for additional information about the way in which the Web site treats customers' data.

This risk/benefit analysis can be represented on a two-dimensional graph, as shown in Figure 1. Although the two axes (Benefits–Risks) are continuous, we can identify four main situations, and the corresponding strategies followed by Internet users:

1. **High Risks/High Benefits:** The information collected during the survey indicate that in this situation, the Internet users are applying risk-reduction strategies, attempting to preserve the offered benefits. Most of these strategies involve additional information search and interpretation about the privacy policy and practices implemented by a particular Web site, but also attempt to negotiate with the online firm a preferential treatment.

Figure 1. The various strategies adopted by online users, in relation to the perceived risks and benefits of personal data disclosure

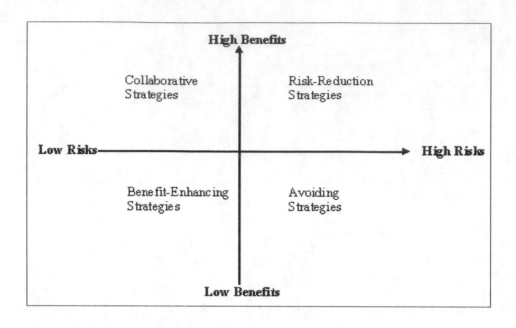

2. **High Risks/Low Benefits:** The Internet users are applying strategies in this particular situation.
3. **Low Risks/Low Benefits:** In this situation, the online clients will attempt to enhance the existing benefits, engaging in personal negotiations with the virtual enterprise. The majority of respondents indicated that if these negotiations are unsuccessful, they will probably not provide personal information to these Web sites. The effect of immediate benefits on consumer perceptions indicates a possible solution for the Web site to improve the risks-benefits balance.
4. **Low Risks/High Benefits:** Internet users are engaging in a long-term collaboration with the virtual enterprise that proposes this situation.

Considering that in all the cases presented above the situation is highly subjective, sometimes the customers' perception can be improved by simply providing more detailed, clearer, or better organized information regarding the benefits and the risks for providing personal information.

FUTURE TRENDS

The findings of this study indicate the necessity for creating a tool that can assist the online customers in quickly finding the information concerning the risks and the benefits associated with disclosing personal information. This tool exists already, being launched in 1998 by the Web Standards Organization. The Platform for Privacy Preferences, or P3P, is a protocol meant to provide an automatic common Web language for the acceptable use of personal information (Cranor & Wenning, 2002).

During the Web interaction, a P3P-compatible browser automatically detects the Web site's privacy policy, and, depending on the level of promised protection, releases or not the customer's personal information. The browser also allows users to perform selective cookie blocking based on the extent of the Web site privacy policy and provides a report of the Web site data practices. As a support to this function, Microsoft has implemented an advanced cookie-filtering mechanism in the software package of Internet Explorer 6 based upon the P3P 1.0 specification. The software presents various levels of cookie-filtering sensitivity, which users can adjust manually using a slider contained on the 'Privacy' tab, under 'Internet Options'. When the user has not adjusted his or her preferences, the interaction between the site and the user's browser is based on default preference settings implemented in the program.

Although P3P has many critics that emphasize various problems related with the implementation and use of the platform (Harvey & Sanzaro, 2002; Thibadeau, 2000), the advocates of P3P consider them to be limitations rather than valid grounds for eliminating the entire concept (Cranor & Wenning, 2002). They emphasize that the implementation and use of the P3P platform is only a first step towards the standardization of privacy policies, and facilitates the users' choice of a desired privacy level, including anonymity and pseudonymity.

CONCLUSION

The use of Internet-enhanced commercial applications can provide huge benefits for companies and customers alike. In order to fully use the potential of the Internet, the digital firms should introduce one-to-one marketing techniques. Using the data collected about, or voluntarily provided by, consumers, these firms can offer their clients a better online experience, high-value products, and customized interactions.

However, the possibility to collect, process, and use personal data should be realized without infringing upon the online privacy rights of customers. The use of the personal data disclosed by clients should be made only after and within the limits of an informed consent of the Internet user (Van der Geest, Pieterson, & de Vries, 2005). The ethical behavior of an online enterprise should constantly evolve, as well as the online applications which, like P3P, help Internet users to identify possible privacy problems and negotiate the benefits of their online interaction with virtual firms.

REFERENCES

Chellappa, R.K., & Sin, R.G. (2005). Personalization versus privacy: An empirical examination of the online consumer's dilemma. *Information Technology and Management, 6*(2/3), 181-202.

Cranor, L.F., & Wenning, R. (2002, April). *Why P3P is a good privacy tool for consumers and companies.* Retrieved June 2005 from http://www.gigalaw.com/articles/2002-all/cranor-2002-04-all.html

DTI. (2003). *The directive on privacy and electronic communications.* Retrieved May 2003 from http://www.dti.gov.uk/ind...electronic_communications_200258ec.html

Desai, M.S., Richards, T.C., & Desai, K.J. (2003). E-commerce policies and customer privacy. *Information Management & Computer Security, 11*(1), 19-27.

Freehills. (2000). *Internet privacy survey.* Melbourne: Freehills Law Firm.

Frye, C.D. (2001). *Privacy-enhanced business: Adapting to the online environment.* Westport, CT: Quorum Books.

Harvey, J.A., & Sanzaro, K.M. (2002, February). *P3P and IE 6: Raising more privacy issues than they solve?* Retrieved June 2005 from http://www.gigalaw.com/articles/2002-all/harvey-2002-02-all.html

Kim, S., & Montalto, C.P. (2002). Perceived risk of *privacy* invasion and the use of *online* technology by consumers. *Consumer Interests Annual, 48,* 1-9.

Kuanchin, C., & Rea, A.L. Jr. (2004). Protecting personal information *online privacy* concerns and control techniques. *Journal of Computer Information Systems, 44*(4), 85-92.

Lichtenstein, S., Swatman, P.M.C., & Babu, K. (2003, June 24). Trends and guidelines in online privacy policy. *Proceedings of the CollECTeR Europe 2003 Conference in eCommerce,* Galway, Ireland. Retrieved August 2006 from http://www.is.nuigalway.ie/collecter/papers%5Clichstenstein.pdf

Lips, A.M.B., van der Hof, S., Prins J.E.J., & Schudelaro, A.A.P. (2004). *Issues of personalization in private and public service delivery.* Retrieved December 2005 from http://rechten.uvt.nl/prins/upload/23220051148418804347515.pdf

Mabley, K. (2000). *Privacy vs. personalization.* Retrieved September 2003 from http://www.cyberdialogue.com/library/pdfs/wp-cd-2000-privacy.pdf

P

Malhotra, N.K., Sung, S.K., & Agarwal, J. (2004). Internet Users' Information *Privacy Concerns* (IUIPC): The construct, the scale, and a causal model. *Information Systems Research, 15*(4), 336-355.

Millard, N.J. (2004). A Million segments of one—how personal should customer relationship management get? In D. Ralph & S. Searby (Eds.), *Location and personalization: Delivering online and mobility services* (Communications Technology Series 8, pp. 211-222). London: Institution of Electrical Engineers.

NPP. (2000). *National privacy principles.* Canberra: Office of the Federal Privacy Commissioner.

Nakra, P. (2001). Consumer privacy rights: CPR and the age of the Internet. *Management Decision, 39*(4), 272-279.

Ragins, E.J., & Greco, A.J. (2003). Customer relationship management and e-business: More than a software solution. *Review of Business, 24*(1), 25-30.

Rombel, A. (2001). The privacy law debate: Navigating the privacy law divide. *Global Finance, 15*(1), 28.

Sheehan, K.B. (2002). Toward a typology of Internet users and *online privacy* concerns. *Information Society, 18*(1), 21-32.

Thibadeau, R. (2000). *A critique of P3P: Privacy on the Web.* Retrieved June 2005 from http://dollar.ecom.cmu.edu/p3pcritique/

Van der Geest, T., Pieterson, W., & de Vries, P. (2005, July 25). Informed consent to address trust, control and privacy concerns in user profiling. *Proceedings of the UM 2005 Workshop on Privacy-Enhanced Personalization,* Edinburgh, UK. Retrieved August 2006 from http://www.isr.uci.edu/pep05/papers/InformedConsent.PDF

Westin, A. (2001). *Opinion surveys: What consumers have to say about information privacy.* Retrieved August 2006 from http://energycommerce.house.gov/107/hearings/05082001Hearing209/Westin309.htm

KEY TERMS

Cookie: A file that resides on the computer of the Internet user, and which keeps track of the interaction between the user and a specific Web site.

Consumer (User) Profile: A structured data record that contains user-related information, such as identifiers, characteristics, abilities, needs and interests, preferences, traits, and previous behavior in contexts that are relevant to predicting and influencing future behavior.

E-CRM: The online version of customer relationship management that uses tools and processes to interact in real time with customers and business partners, which expands the traditional CRM components by integrating both electronic communication and electronic commerce features with the CRM application.

Informed Consent: A process in which a fully informed user participates in decisions about his or her personal data.

Intelligent Agent: A software application used extensively on the Web that perform tasks such as retrieving and delivering information and automating repetitive tasks.

Personalization: The process of tailoring Web-based processes to the needs and preferences of online customers.

Security Seal: An image, icon, or sign displayed on a Web site that certifies a certain level of online security insured by that site in terms of information transmission, online transactions, or online payment.

Privacy in Data Mining Textbooks

James Lawler
Pace University, USA

John C. Molluzzo
Pace University, USA

INTRODUCTION

Many companies, such as Wal-Mart, store much of their business and customer data in large databases called data warehouses. Their customers are not told the extent of the information accumulated on them, how long it will be kept, nor the uses to which it will be put (Hays, 2004). This data is subsequently analyzed to produce new information to help the companies evaluate business processes and customer behavior. Data mining is usually used to do the analysis. Much of the mined data is public or semi-public—what we purchase at the supermarket, where we surf the Web, where we work, our salary.

The key ethical issues in mining personal data are that people: (1) are generally not aware their personal information is being gathered, (2) do not know to what use the data will be made, or (3) have not consented to such collecting or use.

In a survey of twenty Web data mining professionals, van Wel and Royakkers (2004) showed that the professionals prefer to focus on the advantages of Web data mining instead of discussing its possible dangers. These professionals argued that Web data mining does not threaten privacy.

One might wonder why professionals are not aware of or concerned over the possible misuse of their work, and the possible harm it might cause to individuals and society. Part of the reason might lie in the content of the data mining courses they have taken and in the textbooks they used to learn their craft. The purpose of this article is to analyze the content of contemporary data mining textbooks to determine the extent to which they introduce and discuss issues relating to privacy of consumer data, laws that govern the use of personal consumer data, and professional guidelines for the collection and use of consumer data.

BACKGROUND

Privacy

Privacy is not easily defined, perhaps because the notion of privacy has evolved over time and now means different things in different situations and in different cultures. This article focuses on the effects of data mining on *informational privacy* (Tavani, 2004), which is a person's ability to restrict access to and control the flow of his or her private information. Much of modern informational privacy theory is grounded on Moor's (1997) *control/restricted access* theory of privacy, in which a person has privacy in a situation if the person is protected from intrusion, interference, and information access by others.

Laws

There is no explicit right to privacy in the U.S. Constitution. However, legislation and court decisions on privacy are usually based on parts of the First, Fourth, Fifth, and Fourteenth Amendments. Most of the laws in the United States govern what the federal government can do with personal data. Except for healthcare and financial organizations, and data collected from children, there is no law that governs the collection and use of personal data by commercial enterprises. Therefore, each organization decides how it will use the personal data it has accumulated on its customers.

Privacy Guidelines

Although there are few laws in the United States governing the use of personal data, many businesses have used the Code of Fair Information practices of the Organization for Economic Cooperation and Development

Table 1. Number of books in each construct/rank

		Rank					
	Construct	5	4	3	2	1	0
Business and Consumer Ethics							
Ethics Codes	C1-1	2	6	1	1	1	18
Definitions of Privacy	C1-2	0	1	1	2	0	25
Functions of Privacy	C1-3	0	1	0	0	0	28
Personal vs. Group Privacy	C1-4	0	2	1	1	0	25
Studies of Privacy	C1-5	0	1	1	2	0	25
Subtotal		2	11	4	6	1	121
Government and Organizations							
Constitution	C2-1	0	0	0	0	0	29
Court Cases	C2-2	0	0	0	1	0	28
Federal Legislation	C2-3	2	0	1	2	3	21
State Legislation	C2-4	0	1	1	2	3	22
Authorities	C2-5	0	0	3	4	0	22
Organizations	C2-6	0	1	2	1	1	24
Subtotal		2	2	7	10	7	146
Managerial and Methodological							
Chief Privacy Officer	C3-1	0	1	2	2	4	20
Personal Privacy Policy Standards	C3-2	0	2	5	3	2	17
Personalization Techniques	C3-3	2	7	0	1	1	18
Privacy Systems	C3-4	0	3	0	1	1	24
Protection of Systems	C3-5	3	2	5	5	4	10
Subtotal		5	15	12	12	12	89
Pedagogical							
Privacy Studies	C4-1	0	0	0	0	0	29
Privacy Publications	C4-2	0	2	3	1	1	22
Privacy Conferences	C4-3	0	0	1	0	0	28
Scholarly Journals	C4-4	0	1	0	1	1	26
Privacy Groups	C4-5	0	0	0	0	4	25
Subtotal		0	3	4	2	6	130
Technological							
Digital Rights Management	C5-1	0	0	0	0	0	29
Platform for Privacy Preferences	C5-2	0	2	0	1	0	26
Privacy Aware Technology	C5-3	0	0	0	0	0	29
Privacy Invasive Technology	C5-4	0	0	0	0	0	29
Privacy Software Technology	C5-5	0	0	0	0	0	29
Subtotal		0	2	0	1	0	142
Total		9	33	27	31	26	628

(OECD) to guide them in setting informational privacy policy. The code is based on eight principles: collection limitation, data quality, purpose specification, use limitation, security safeguards, openness, individual participation, and accountability (OECD, 2005).

European Privacy Policy

Given the global nature of today's economy, the European Union (EU) has realized that laws governing privacy must apply on an international scale. In 1995, the EU developed an informational privacy policy, known as the European Directive 95/46/EC, which applies to all member states. Their *Principles Relating to Data Quality* states that data must be processed fairly, collected for legitimate purposes, must be adequate and relevant to the purpose for which it is collected, be accurate, and not be identified with the data's subject longer than necessary (Center for Democracy and Technology, 2005).

Because EU member states cannot export personal data to non-EU nations that do not meet the EU standard, the U.S. Department of Commerce developed the "safe harbor" framework, which was approved by the EU in July of 2000. Being certified by Safe Harbor assures EU organizations that a company provides adequate privacy protection, as defined by the Directive (U.S. Department of Commerce, 2005).

Data Mining and Privacy

Personal informational privacy is threatened by three computing practices (Tavani, 2004):

1. **Data Gathering:** The collection of personal information, often without the subject's knowledge and consent.
2. **Data Exchange:** Transferring personal data between databases, often without the subject's knowledge and consent.
3. **Data Mining:** Searching large databases of mostly public data to generate profiles based on peoples' personal data and behavior patterns.

Today's privacy laws and guidelines protect data that is explicit, confidential, and exchanged between databases. However, there is no legal or normative protection for data that is implicit, non-confidential, and not exchanged (in a data warehouse, for example).

Information gathered in data mining is usually implicit in patterns in the data. These patterns suggest new associations about persons, which place them into new categories. Data mining can also reveal sensitive information that is derived from non-sensitive data and meta-data—the so-called *inference problem* (Farkas & Jajodia, 2002).

Constructs and Factors in Information Ethics

The descriptive constructs in the education of information ethics are customized in this article from diverse expert literature sources, as defined in the categorical framework of column 1 in Table 1. These factors are imputed in this article to be important in introducing information ethics into data mining curricula. Closer examination of *business, consumer and ethical, governmental and organizational, managerial and methodological,* and *pedagogical and technological content* enables fresh insight into the learning or non-learning of principles and practices of information ethics, and privacy as an issue in ethics by higher education students. Few studies in the literature include this diversity of principles and practices in analyzing the adequacy of ethics in data mining education.

RESEARCH METHODOLOGY

The research methodology of the article consists of *two iterative stages of analysis.* In *stage 1,* the authors analyzed a sample of 29 data mining texts (see the Appendix) from December 2004–February 2005, as mostly representative of primary data mining texts in ABET-certified schools of computer science and information systems.

In *stage 2,* the authors analyzed the 29 textbooks from March–July 2005 for content inclusion of constructs of information ethics from a checklist of the 26 factors listed in column 1 of Table 1. To the factors was applied the six-point rating scale of Table 2.

Each entry in Table 1 gives the number of books in the corresponding construct and rank. In the C1 categories, only two books had chapters and 11 had sections devoted to a general discussion of privacy. Two books had chapters devoted to federal privacy legislation (construct C2-3) and two more had sections on the topic. As might be expected, books devoted more

Table 2. Rating scale

Rating	Explanation
0	No mention of the construct.
1	A word or two about the construct
2	One or two sentences about the construct
3	A complete paragraph discussing the construct
4	A complete section about the construct
5	A complete chapter about the construct

Table 3. Mention of constructs

Construct Category	Mention at All (Rank > 0)
C1—Business and Consumer Ethics	23
C2—Government and Organizations	28
C3—Managerial and Methodological	56
C4—Pedagogical	15
C5—Technological	3

space to managerial and methodological constructs. Five books had chapters on either personalization techniques (construct C3-3) or the protection of systems (construct C3-5). Fifteen books had entire sections on the managerial and methodological constructs (all C3 constructs). Interestingly, only one book had a section discussing the role of the chief privacy officer (construct C3-1). None of the books surveyed had a chapter on any of the pedagogical constructs, although 11 of them did at least mention one or more privacy publications (construct C4-2) or privacy advocacy groups (construct C4-5). Finally, almost no references were made to the various technological constructs. Only two books had sections in this area (construct C5-2), and one book had a few sentences.

Since most data mining texts aim at future data mining professionals, we expect that many of them would discuss some of the managerial issues surrounding the topic. Table 3, which lists the number of books that at least mention one of the constructs, shows there are 56 references to these issues (C3) in the books surveyed. Business issues (C1—23 references) and governmental issues (C2—28 references) surrounding privacy are about equally referenced. The category with the least coverage is C5, the technological constructs that enable the protection of personal privacy. As mentioned in the Introduction, there is a lack of awareness of the

ethical issues surrounding data mining by data mining professionals. In light of the sparse coverage of the C1 and C5 constructs in the texts surveyed, this is not surprising.

These data lead us to conclude that unless individual instructors make an effort to discuss ethical issues in their courses, students will not be exposed to them through their textbooks. Data mining and its applications can have a profound effect on the privacy of individuals and groups. To make data mining professionals more aware of these issues, it is important that instructors and authors in this area fully discuss them.

FUTURE TRENDS

The inadequacy of contemporary data mining texts, for instructors attempting to effectively introduce information ethics in computer science and information systems curricula, is an important implication of this article. Ethical principles for moral and philosophical theory (Grodzinsky, 1999) continue not to be included in depth in data mining texts. Ethical and non-ethical practices of citizen and consumer information mining that are current and immediate in government and industry are not often included in outdated texts (Schrage, 2005). Though instructors may enhance core foundational texts with further practitioner and scholarly resources, they are challenged in having comprehensively convenient and integrated texts (Richards, 2005). The text is a critical source for instructors in introducing students to the information ethics of data mining.

The inherent limitation of data mining texts in introducing students to ethical issues is another implication of this article. Issues and pressures of customer privacy (Saporito, 2005) and legislation on privacy (Holmes, 2005) may not be clear to students if the mining text is limited to technology (Hackathorn, 2005). In addition, studies indicate improvement in the inclusion of philosophy, social science, and information systems instructors (Brey, 2000), and in further interdisciplinary frames of marketing and business instructor teams (Gloeckler, 2005).

The final implication and trend of this article is in both the challenge and in the opportunity for schools of computer science and information systems to improve curricula in data mining. Technology continues to evolve in power, contributing to increased ethical issues that challenge information systems and computer science instructors and professionals (Turner, 2005).

The findings of this article furnish a foundation for further researching mining and information ethics curricula, which will be informative to instructors striving to integrate issues of ethics in mining pedagogy.

CONCLUSION

This article on data mining and information ethics in schools of computer science and information systems is insightful into the *business, consumer and ethical, governmental and organizational, managerial and methodological,* and *pedagogical and technological factors* of ethical principles and practices in mining curricula. The inadequacy of current data mining texts for instructors and the limitation of the texts for student learning are issues indicated in the article. The article furnishes a framework for improving the inclusion of information ethics in data mining curricula.

The ethical use of personal information is one of the most important issues facing both the owners and users of that information. There are presently few laws in the United States governing the use of personal data. Therefore, it is important that those who extract information from that data be aware of the many privacy, managerial, governmental, and technical issues surrounding such practices. This study shows that a serious gap exists between what should be covered regarding these issues in data mining texts and what is actually covered. This implies that it is incumbent upon future data mining textbook authors to include discussions of some of the constructs mentioned in this article. Until that time, instructors in data mining courses must fill the gap by using ancillary materials to supplement their courses.

REFERENCES

Brey, P. (2000). Disclosive computer ethics. *Computers and Society,* (December), 10-16, 22-23.

Center for Democracy and Technology. (2005). Retrieved June 14, 2005, from http://www.cdt.org/privacy/eudirective/EU_Directive_.html#HD_NM_2

Farkas, C., & Jajodia, S. (2002). The inference problem: A survey. *SIGKDD Explorations, 4*(2), 6-11.

Gloeckler, G. (2005). This is not your father's MBA. *Business Week,* (May 16), 74-75.

Grodzinsky, F. (1999). The practitioner from within: Revisiting the virtues. *Computers and Society,* (March), 9-10.

Hackathorn, R. (2005). The ethics of business process management. *Business Integration Journal,* (March), 32.

Hays, C. (2004). What Wal-Mart knows about customers' habits. *The New York Times,* (November 14). Retrieved November 15, 2004, from http://www.nytimes.com

Holmes, A. (2005). Riding the California privacy wave. *CIO,* (January 15), 44-49.

Moor, J.H. (1997). Towards a theory of privacy in the information age. *Computers and Society, 27*(3), 27-32.

OECD. (2005). Retrieved June 14, 2005, from http://www.oecd.org/document/18/0,2340,en_2649_201185_1815186_1_1_1_1,00.html

Richards, C.H. (2005, March 2). Private and public sector ethics. *Proceedings of the Applied Business Research Conference,* Puerto Vallarta, Mexico.

Saporito, W. (2005). Are your secrets safe? *Time,* (March), 30.

Schrage, M. (2005). Ethics, shmethics. *CIO,* (March 15), 40.

Tavani, H.T. (2004). *Ethics and technology: Ethical issues in an age of information and communication technology.* Hoboken, NJ: John Wiley & Sons.

Turner, F. (2005, March 1-4). Anatomy of unethical leadership crisis in corporate America. *Proceedings of the Applied Business Research Conference,* Puerto Vallarta, Mexico.

U.S. Department of Commerce. (2005). *Export portal.* Retrieved June 16, 2005 from http://www.export.gov/safeharbor/

Van Wel, L., & Royakkers, L. (2004). Ethical issues in data mining. *Ethics and Information Technology, 6,* 129-140.

APPENDIX: DATA MINING TEXTBOOKS ANALYZED IN ARTICLE

Agosta, L. (2000). *The essential guide to data warehousing.* Englewood Cliffs, NJ: Prentice Hall.

Becker, S. (2002). *Data warehousing and Web engineering.* Hershey, PA: IRM Press.

Berry, M.J.A., & Linoff, G.S. (2000). *Mastering data mining: The art and science of customer relationship management.* New York: John Wiley & Sons.

Berry, M.J.A., & Linoff, G. (2000). *Data mining techniques for marketing, sales, and customer support.* New York: John Wiley & Sons.

Berson, A., Smith, S., & Thearling, K. (2000). *Building data mining applications for CRM.* New York: McGraw-Hill.

Biere, M. (2003). *Business intelligence for the enterprise.* Englewood Cliffs, NJ: IBM Press/Prentice Hall.

Delmater, R., & Hancock, M. (2001). *Data mining explained: A manager's guide to customer-centric business intelligence.* Digital Press.

Dunham, M.H. (2003). *Data mining: Introductory and advanced topics.* Englewood Cliffs, NJ: Prentice Hall.

Hand, D., Mannila, H., & Smyth, P. (2001). *Principles of data mining.* Cambridge, MA: MIT Press.

Hughes, A.M. (2000). *Strategic database marketing: The masterplan for starting and managing a profitable customer-based marketing program.* New York: McGraw-Hill.

Humphries, M., Hawkins, M.W., & Dy, M.C. (2000). *Data warehousing: Architecture and implementation.* Englewood Cliffs, NJ: Prentice Hall.

Inmon, W.H., Terdeman, R.H., Norris-Montanari, J., & Meers, D. (2001). *Data warehousing for e-business.* New York: John Wiley & Sons.

Kantardzic, M.M., & Zurada, J. (2005). *Next generation of data-mining applications.* IEEE Press.

Kantardzic, M. (2002). *Data mining: Concepts, models, methods, and algorithms.* New York: John Wiley & Sons.

Kimball, R., & Merz, R. (2000). *The data Webhouse toolkit: Building the Web-enabled data warehouse.* New York: John Wiley & Sons.

Kudyba, S., & Hoptroff, R. (2001). *Data mining and business intelligence: A guide to productivity.* Hershey, PA: Idea Group.

Loshin, D. (2003). *Business intelligence: The savvy manager's guide: Getting onboard with emerging information technology.* San Francisco: Morgan Kaufmann.

Mallach, E.G. (2000). *Decision support and data warehouse systems.* New York: McGraw-Hill.

Marakas, G.M. (2003). *Modern data warehousing, mining, and visualization: Core concepts.* Englewood Cliffs, NJ: Prentice Hall.

McGonagle, J.J., & Vella, C.M. (2003). *The manager's guide to competitive intelligence.* Praeger.

Mena, J. (2000). *Data mining your Web site.* Digital Press.

Moeller, R.A. (2000). *Distributed data warehousing using Web technology.* AMACOM.

Mohammadian, M. (2004). *Intelligent agents for data mining and information retrieval.* Hershey, PA: Idea Group.

Sarker, R.A., Abbass, H.A., & Newton, C.S. (2002). *Heuristics and optimization for knowledge discovery.* Hershey, PA: Idea Group.

Simon, A., & Shaffer, S. (2001). *Data warehousing and business intelligence for e-commerce.* San Francisco: Morgan Kaufmann.

Thuraisingham, B. (2003). *Web data mining and applications in business intelligence and counter-terrorism.* CRC Press.

Turban, E., Aronson, J.E., & Liang, T.-P. (2005). *Decision support systems and intelligent systems.* Englewood Cliffs, NJ: Prentice Hall.

Vitt, E., Luckevich, M., & Misner, S. (2002). *Making better business intelligence decisions faster.* Redmond, WA: Microsoft Press.

Wang, J. (2003). *Data mining: Opportunities and challenges.* Hershey, PA: Idea Group.

KEY TERMS

Business Intelligence: Knowledge of information on customers that enables business firms to market distinct products and services to those customers.

Chief Privacy Officer: Business executive in a firm that manages policies and procedures for protecting information about customers.

Data Mining: A set of techniques employed by business firms that extract information on customers from large database systems, in order to market products and services to those customers.

Data Warehousing: Storing information on customers in integrated large databases of business firms.

Information Ethics: Standards that govern the usage of stored customer information.

Information Systems Curricula: Courses of study that educate data processing students in specialized usage of information technologies.

Privacy: Freedom of customers from intrusion, freedom of customers from interference in personal choice, and freedom of customers from restriction to control or access private information.

Protection of Mobile Agent Data

Sheng-Uei Guan
Brunel University, UK

INTRODUCTION

One hindrance to the widespread adoption of mobile agent technology is the lack of security. Security will be the issue that has to be addressed carefully if a mobile agent is to be used in the field of electronic commerce. SAFER—or Secure Agent Fabrication, Evolution, and Roaming—is a mobile agent framework that is specially designed for the purpose of electronic commerce (Zhu, Guan, Yang, & Ko, 2000; Guan & Hua, 2003; Guan, Zhu, & Maung, 2004). Security has been a prime concern from the first day of our research (Guan & Yang, 1999, 2002; Yang & Guan, 2000). By building strong and efficient security mechanisms, SAFER aims to provide a trustworthy framework for mobile agents, increasing trust factors to end users by providing the ability to trust, predictable performance, and a communication channel (Patrick, 2002).

Agent integrity is one such area crucial to the success of agent technology (Wang, Guan, & Chan, 2002). Despite the various attempts in the literature, there is no satisfactory solution to the problem of data integrity so far. Some of the common weaknesses of the current schemes are vulnerabilities to revisit attack when an agent visits two or more collaborating malicious hosts during one roaming session and illegal modification (deletion/insertion) of agent data. Agent Monitoring Protocol (AMP) (Chionh, Guan, & Yang, 2001), an earlier proposal under SAFER to address agent data integrity, does address some of the weaknesses in the current literature. Unfortunately, the extensive use of PKI technology introduces too much overhead to the protocol. Also, AMP requires the agent to deposit its data collected to the agent owner/butler before it roams to another host. While this is a viable and secure approach, the proposed approach—Secure Agent Data Integrity Shield (SADIS)—will provide an alternative by allowing the agent to carry the data by itself without depositing it (or the data hash) onto the butler.

Besides addressing the common vulnerabilities of current literature (revisit attack and data modification attack), SADIS also strives to achieve maximum ef-

ficiency without compromising security. It minimizes the use of PKI technology and relies on symmetric key encryption as much as possible. Moreover, the data encryption key and the communication session key are both derivable from a key seed that is unique to the agent's roaming session in the current host. As a result, the butler can derive the communication session key and data encryption key directly. Another feature in SADIS is strong security.

Most of the existing research focuses on detecting integrity compromise (Esparza, Muñoz, Soriano, & Forné, 2006) or on bypassing integrity attacks by requiring the existence of a cooperating agent that is carried out within a trusted platform (Ouardani, Pierre, & Boucheneb, 2006), but which neglected the need to identify the malicious host. With SADIS, the agent butler will not only be able to detect any compromise to data integrity, but to identify the malicious host effectively.

BACKGROUND

Agent data integrity has been a topic of active research in the literature for a while. SADIS addresses the problem of data integrity protection via a combination of techniques discussed by Borselius (2002): execution tracing, encrypted payload, environmental key generation, and undetachable signature.

One of the recent active research works is the security architecture by Borselius, Hur, Kaprynski, and Mitchell (2002). Their security architecture aims at defining a complete security architecture designed for mobile agent systems. It categorizes security services into the following: agent management and control, agent communications service, agent security service, agent mobility service, and agent logging service. SADIS addresses the agent communication service as well as agent security services (integrity protection), while previous research on SAFER addresses agent mobility service.

While many of the security services are still under active research, the security mechanisms for protecting agents against malicious hosts were described by Borselius, Mitchell, and Wilson (2001). Their paper proposes a threshold scheme to protect mobile agents. Under the mechanism, a group of agents is dispatched to carry out the task, each agent carrying a vote. Each agent is allowed to contact a merchant independently and gathers bids based on the given criteria. Each agent votes for the best bid (under a trading scenario) independently. If more than n out of m ($m > n$) agents vote for the transaction, the agent owner will agree to the transaction.

Such a mode of agent execution effectively simplifies agent roaming by allowing one agent to visit one merchant only. While the approach avoids the potential danger of having the agent compromised by the subsequent host, it does not employ a mechanism to protect the agent against the current host. Most important of all, the threshold mechanism's security is based on the probability that no more than n hosts out of m are malicious. In other words, the security is established based on probability. Different from this approach, SADIS's security is completely based on its own merits without making any assumption about probability of hosts being benign or malicious. This is because the author believes that in an e-commerce environment, security should not have any dependency on probability.

Other than the research by Borselius, there are related works in the area. One such work on agent protection is SOMA, or Secure and Open Mobile Agent, developed by Corradi, Cremonini, Montanari, and Stefanelli (1999). SOMA is a Java-based mobile agent framework that provides for scalability, openness, and security on the Internet. One of the research focuses of SOMA is to protect the mobile agent's data integrity. To achieve this, SOMA makes use of two mechanisms: Multi Hop (MH) Protocol and Trusted Third Party (TTP) Protocol. MH protocol works as follows. At each intermediate site the mobile agent collects some data and appends them to the previous ones collected. Each site must provide a short proof of the agent computation, which is stored in the agent. Each proof is cryptographically linked with the ones computed at the previous sites. There is a chaining relation between proofs. When the agent moves back to the sender, the integrity of the chained cryptographic

proofs is verified allowing the sender to detect any integrity violation.

The advantage of MH protocol is that it does not require any trusted third party or even the agent butler for its operation. This is a highly desirable feature for agent integrity protection protocol. Unfortunately, MH protocol does not hold well against revisit attack when the agent visits two or more collaborating malicious hosts during one roaming session (Chionh et al., 2001). Roth (2001) provides more detailed descriptions on potential flaws of the MH protocol.

Another agent system that addresses data integrity is Ajanta (Tripathi, 2002). Ajanta is a platform for agent-based application on the Internet developed in the University of Minnesota. It makes use of an append-only container for agent data integrity protection. The main objective is to allow the host to append new data to the container, but to prevent anyone from modifying the previous data without being detected. Similar to the MH protocol, such an append-only container suffers from revisit attack.

From these attacks on existing research, the importance of protecting agent itinerary is obvious. In SADIS, the agent's itinerary is implicitly updated in the agent butler during key seed negotiation. This prevents any party from modifying the itinerary recorded on the butler and guard against all itinerary-related attacks.

There is one recent research work on agent data integrity protection called One-Time Key Generation System (OKGS) researched at the Kwang-Ju Institute of Science and Technology, South Korea (Park, Lee, & Lee, 2002). OKGS does protect the agent data against a number of attack scenarios under revisit attack, such as data insertion attack and data modification attack to a certain extent. However, it does not protect the agent against deletion attack, as two collaborating malicious hosts can easily remove roaming records in between them.

Inspired by OKGS's innovative one-time encryption key concept, SADIS will extend this property to the communication between agent and butler as well. Not only the data encryption key is one time, but the communication session key is as well. Using efficient hash calculations, the dynamic communication session key can be derived separately by the agent butler and the agent with minimum overhead. Despite the fact that all keys are derived from the same session-based key seed, SADIS also ensures that there is little correlation between these keys. As a result, even if some of the keys are compromised, the key seed will still remain secret.

PROTECTION OF AGENT DATA INTEGRITY

SADIS is designed based on the SAFER framework. The proposal itself is based on a number of assumptions that were implemented under SAFER. Firstly, entities in SAFER, including agents, butlers, and hosts, should have a globally unique identification number (ID). This ID will be used to uniquely identify each entity. Secondly, each agent butler and host should have a digital certificate that is issued by a trusted CA under SAFER. These entities with digital certificates will be able to use the private key of its certificate to perform digital signatures and, if necessary, encryption. Thirdly, while the host may be malicious, the execution environment of mobile agents should be secure and the execution integrity of the agent can be maintained. This assumption is made because protecting the agent's execution environment is a completely separate area of research that is independent of this article. Without a secure execution environment and execution integrity, none of the agent data protection schemes will be effective. The last assumption is that entities involved are respecting and cooperating with the SADIS protocol. And finally, SADIS does not require the agent to have a pre-determined itinerary. The agent is able to decide independently which host is the next destination.

Key Seed Negotiation Protocol

When an agent first leaves the butler, the butler will generate a random initial key seed, encrypt it with the destination host's public key, and deposit it into the agent before sending the agent to the destination host. It should be noted that agent transmission is protected by the *SAFE* supervised agent transport protocol (Guan & Yang, 2002). Otherwise, a malicious host (man-in-the-middle) can perform an attack by replacing the encrypted key seed with a new key seed and encrypt it with the destination's public key. In this case, the agent and the destination host will not know the key seed has been manipulated. When the agent starts to communicate with the butler using the wrong key seed,

the malicious host can intercept all the messages and re-encrypt them with the correct key derived from the correct key seed and forward them to the agent butler. In this way, a malicious host can compromise the whole protocol.

The key seed carried by the agent is session-based: it is valid until the agent leaves the current host. When the agent decides to leave the current host, it must determine the destination host and start the key seed negotiation process with the agent butler.

The key seed negotiation process is based on the Diffie-Hellman (DH) key exchange protocol (Diffie & Hellman, 1976) with a variation. The agent will first generate a private DH parameter a and its corresponding public parameter x. The value x, together with the ID of the destination host, will be encrypted using a communication session key and sent to the agent butler.

The agent butler will decrypt the message using the same communication session key (derivation of communication session key will be discussed later in the section). It too will generate its own DH private parameter b and its corresponding public parameter y. With the private parameter b and the public parameter x from the agent, the butler can derive the new key seed and use it for communications with the agent in the new host. Instead of sending the public parameter y to the agent as in normal DH key exchange, the agent butler will encrypt the value y, host ID, agent ID, and current timestamp with the destination host's public key to get message M. Message M will be sent to the agent after encrypting with the communication session key.

$$M = E(y + \text{host ID} + \text{agent ID} + \text{timestamp}, H_{pubKey})$$

At the same time, the agent butler updates the agent's itinerary and sends it to the agent. When the agent receives the double-encrypted DH public parameter y, it can decrypt with the communication session key.

Subsequently, the agent will store M into its data segment and requests the current host to send itself to the destination host using the agent transport protocol (Guan & Yang, 2002).

Upon arriving at the destination host, the agent will be activated. Before it resumes normal operation, the agent will request the new host to decrypt message M. If the host is the right destination host, it will be able to use the private key to decrypt message M and thus obtain the DH public parameter y. As a result, the decryption of message M not only completes the key seed negotiation process, but also serves as a means to authenticate the destination host. Once the message M is decrypted, the host will verify that the agent ID in the decrypted message matches the incoming agent, and the host ID in the decrypted message matches that of the current host.

With the plain value of y, the agent can derive the key seed by using its previously generated private parameter a. With the new key seed derived, the key seed negotiation process is completed. The agent can resume normal operation in the new host.

Whenever the agent or the butler needs to communicate with the other, the sender will first derive a communication session key using the key seed and use this communication session key to encrypt the message. The receiver can make use of the same formula to derive the communication session key from the same key seed to decrypt the message.

The communication session key K_{CSK} is derived using the formula below:

$$K_{CSK} = Hash(key\_seed + host\ ID + seqNo)$$

The sequence number is a running number that starts with 1 for each agent roaming session. Whenever the agent reaches a new host, the sequence number will be reset to 1. Given the varying communication session key, if one of the messages is somehow lost without being detected, the butler and agent will not be able to communicate afterwards. As a result, SADIS makes use of TCP/IP as a communication mechanism so that any loss of messages can be immediately detected by the sender. In the case of an unsuccessful message, the sender will send 'ping' messages to the recipient in plain format until the recipient or the communication channel recovers. Once the communication is re-established, the sender will resend the previous message (encrypted using the same communication session key).

When the host provides information to the agent, the agent will encrypt the information with a data encryption key K_{DEK}. The data encryption key is derived as follows:

$$K_{DEK} = Hash(key\_seed + hostID)$$

Data Integrity Protection Protocol

The key seed negotiation protocol lays the necessary foundation for integrity protection by establishing a session-based key seed between the agent and its butler. Agent data integrity is protected through the use of this key seed and the digital certificates of the hosts. Our data Integrity Protection protocol is composed of two parts: chained signature generation and data integrity verification. Chained signature generation is performed before the agent leaves the current host. The agent gathers data provided by the current host d_i and construct D_i as follows:

$$D_i = E(d_i + ID_{host} + ID_{agent} + timestamp, k_{DEK})$$

or,

$$D_i = d_i + ID_{host} + ID_{agent} + timestamp$$

The inclusion of a host ID, agent ID, and timestamp is to protect the data from possible replay attack, especially when the information is not encrypted with the data encryption key. For example, if the agent ID is not included in the message, a malicious host can potentially replace the data provided for one agent with that provided for a bogus agent. Similarly, if a timestamp is not included into the message, earlier data provided to the same agent can be used at a later time to replace current data provided to the agent from the same host. The inclusion of the IDs of the parties involved and a timestamp essentially creates an unambiguous memorandum between the agent and the host.

After constructing D_i, the agent will request the host to perform a signature on the following:

$$c_i = Sig(D_i + c_{i-1} + ID_{host} + ID_{agent} + timestamp, k_{priv})$$

where c_0 is the digital signature on the agent code by its butler.

There are some advantages with the use of chained digital signature compared to the conventional signature approach. In the scenario when a malicious host attempts to modify the data from an innocent host i and somehow manages to produce a valid digital signature c_i, the data integrity would have been broken if the digital signature is independent and not chained to each other. The independent digital signature also opens the window for host i to modify data provided to the agent at a later time (one such scenario is the agent visits one of the host's collaborating partners later). Regardless of the message format used, so long as the messages are independent of each other, host i will have no problem reproducing a valid signature to the modified message. In this way, data integrity can be compromised. With chained digital signature, even if the malicious host (or host i itself) produces a valid digital signature after modifying the data, the new signature c_i' is unlikely to be the same as c_i. If the new signature is different from the original signature, as the previous signature is provided as input to the next signature, the subsequent signature verification will fail, thus detecting compromise to data integrity. The inclusion of a host ID, agent ID, and timestamp prevents anyone from performing a replay attack.

When the agent reaches a new destination, the host must perform an integrity check on the incoming agent. In the design of SADIS, even if the new destination host does not perform an immediate integrity check on the incoming agent, any compromise to the data integrity can still be detected when the agent returns to the butler. The drawback, however, is that the identity of the malicious host may not be established. One design focus of SADIS is not only to detect data integrity compromise, but more importantly, to identify malicious hosts. To achieve malicious host identification, it is an obligation for all hosts to verify the incoming agent's data integrity before activating the agent for execution. In the event of data integrity verification failure, the previous host will be identified as the malicious host.

Data integrity verification includes the verification of all the previous signatures. The verification of signature c_0 ensures agent code integrity, the verification of c_i ensures data provided by host h_i is intact. If any signature failed the verification, the agent is considered compromised.

While the process to verify all data integrity may seem to incur too much overhead and be somewhat redundant (e.g., why verify the integrity of d_1 in h_3 while host h_2 already verifies that), it is necessary to ensure the robustness of the protocol and to support the function of malicious host identification.

FUTURE TRENDS

Besides agent data integrity and agent transport security, there are other security concerns to be addressed in SAFER. One such concern is a mechanism to assess the agent's accumulated risk level as it roams. There have been some considerations for using the 'agent battery' concept to address this during the earlier stages of the research. Furthermore, in order to establish the identity of different agents from different agent communities, a certain level of certification by trusted third parties or an agent passport is required (Guan, Wang, & Ong, 2003). More research can be conducted in these areas.

CONCLUSION

In this article, a new data integrity protection protocol, SADIS, is proposed under the SAFER research initiative. Besides being secure against a variety of attacks and robust against vulnerabilities of related work in the literature, the research objectives of SADIS include efficiency. This is reflected in minimized use of PKI operations and reduced message exchanges between the agent and the butler. The introduction of variation to DH key exchange and evolving communication session key further strengthened the security of the design. Unlike some existing literature, the data integrity protection protocol aims not only to detect data integrity compromise, but more importantly, to identify the malicious host.

With security, efficiency, and effectiveness as its main design focus, SADIS works with other security mechanisms under SAFER (e.g., Agent Transport Protocol) to provide mobile agents with a secure platform.

REFERENCES

Bellavista, P., Corradi, A., & Stefanelli, C. (2000). Protection and interoperability for mobile agents: A secure and open programming environment. *IEICE Transactions on Communications.*

Borselius, N. (2002). Mobile agent security. *Electronics & Communication Engineering Journal, 14*(5), 211-218.

Borselius, N., Hur, N., Kaprynski, M., & Mitchell, C.J. (2002). A security architecture for agent-based mobile systems. *Proceedings of the 3rd International Conference on Mobile Communications Technologies* (3G2002) (pp. 312-318), London.

Borselius, N., Mitchell, C.J., & Wilson, A.T. (2001). On mobile agent based transactions in moderately hostile environments. In B. De Decker, F. Piessens, J. Smits, & E. Van Herreweghen (Eds.), *Advances in Network and Distributed Systems Security—Proceedings of the IFIP TC11 WG11.4 1st Annual Working Conference on Network Security* (pp. 173-186). Boston: Kluwer Academic.

Chionh, H.B., Guan, S.-U., & Yang, Y. (2001). Ensuring the protection of mobile agent integrity: The design of an agent monitoring protocol. *Proceedings of the IASTED International Conference on Advances in Communications* (pp. 96-99), Rhodes, Greece.

Corradi, A., Cremonini, M., Montanari, R., & Stefanelli, C. (1999). Mobile agents and security: Protocols for integrity. *Proceedings of the 2nd IFIP WG 6.1 International Working Conference on Distributed Applications and Interoperable Systems* (DAIS'99).

Diffie, W., & Hellman, M.E. (1976). New directions in cryptography. *IEEE Transactions on Information Theory, 22,* 644-654.

Esparza, O., Muñoz, J.L., Soriano, M., & Forné, J. (2006). Secure brokerage mechanisms for mobile electronic commerce. *Computer Communications, 29*(12), 2308-2321.

Guan, S.-U., & Hua, F. (2003). A multi-agent architecture for electronic payment. *International Journal of Information Technology and Decision Making, 2*(3), 497-522.

Guan, S.-U., Wang, T., & Ong, S.-H. (2003). Migration control for mobile agents based on passport and visa. *Future Generation Computer Systems,* 19(2), 173-186.

Guan, S.-U., & Yang, Y. (1999). SAFE: Secure-roaming agent for e-commerce. *Proceedings of the Computer & Industrial Engineering Conference '99* (pp. 33-37), Melbourne, Australia.

Guan, S.-U., & Yang, Y. (2002). SAFE: Secure agent roaming for e-commerce. *Computer & Industrial Engineering Journal, 42,* 481-493.

Guan, S.-U., Zhu, F., & Maung, M.T. (2004). A factory-based approach to support e-commerce agent fabrication. *Electronic Commerce and Research Applications, 3*(1), 39-53.

Ouardani, A., Pierre, S., & Boucheneb, H. (2006). A security protocol for mobile agents based upon the cooperation of sedentary agents. *Journal of Network and Computer Applications.*

Patrick, A.S. (2002). Building trustworthy software agents. *IEEE Journal of Internet Computing,* 46-53.

Park, J.Y., Lee, D.I., & Lec, H.H. (2002). One-time key generation system for agent data protection. *IEICE Transactions on Information and Systems,* 535-545.

Roth, V. (2001). On the robustness of some cryptographic protocols for mobile agent protection. *Proceedings of Mobile Agents 2001* (MA'01) (pp. 1-14).

Tripathi, A.R. (2002), Design of the Ajanta system for mobile agent programming. *Journal of Systems and Software, 62*(2), 123-140.

Wang, T., Guan, S.-U., & Chan, T.K. (2002). Integrity protection for code-on-demand mobile agents in e-commerce. *Journal of Systems and Software, 60*(3), 211-221.

Yang, Y., & Guan, S.-U. (2000). Intelligent mobile agents for e-commerce: Security issues and agent transport. In *Electronic commerce: Opportunities and challenges.* Hershey, PA: Idea Group.

Zhu, F., Guan, S.-U., Yang, Y., & Ko, C.C. (2000). SAFER e-commerce: Secure Agent Fabrication, Evolution and Roaming for e-commerce. In *Electronic commerce: Opportunities and challenges.* Hershey, PA: Idea Group.

KEY TERMS

Agent: A piece of software that acts to accomplish tasks on behalf of its user.

Cryptography: The art of protecting information by transforming it (*encrypting* it) into an unreadable format, called *cipher text.* Only those who possess a secret *key* can decipher (or *decrypt*) the message into *plain text.*

Flexibility: The ease with which a system or component can be modified for use in applications or environments other than those for which it was specifically designed.

Integrity: Regards the protection of data or program codes from being modified by unauthorized parties.

Mobile Agent: An agent that can move from machines to machines for the purpose of data collection or code execution. Also called a roaming agent.

Protocol: A convention or standard that controls or enables the connection, communication, and data transfer between two computing endpoints. Protocols may be implemented by hardware, software, or a combination of the two. At the lowest level, a protocol defines a hardware connection.

Security: The effort to create a secure computing platform, designed so that agents (users or programs) can only perform actions that have been allowed.

Rule–Based Policies for Secured Defense Meetings

Pravin Shetty
Monash University, Australia

Seng Loke
La Trobe University, Australia

INTRODUCTION

Security of the information in a defense department of any country is of utmost importance. And today, in this nuclear world, security and privacy of the various defense plans and other valuable strategies of a country's defense force is in focus. This security is of prime importance during war periods. The defense strategies are normally discussed in the meetings held at the various headquarters of the defense department. In today's computing world these meetings are conducted with the various concerned persons connected via a secured network in a room. If a person is unable to attend a meeting due to some important work, then he or she takes part in the discussion through his or her laptop. Such meetings involving technology have also become a part of research centers where innovation of new technologies is being carried out.

Such meetings involving technology are efficient when they have to be conducted in an emergency, but the question about the secured flow of data still remains. The main aim of this article is to strive for effective security solutions in such areas where the privacy of each and every piece of information is absolutely essential. The article provides a security infrastructure for such meetings. The security policies here are defined in a rule-based formalism. Figure 1 shows the approach used in this article.

'Security Policies' in Figure 1 refers to the security policies put forth by the integrated security model. The figure shows how the access rules make reference to the security policies that are also used in a similar fashion in the context-based security approach using context graphs. Each access rule can be a combination of one or more than one security policy depending on the context.

The rule-based technique provides the following two basic functions in achieving adaptive security solutions:

Figure 1. Access rules in the rule-based formalism

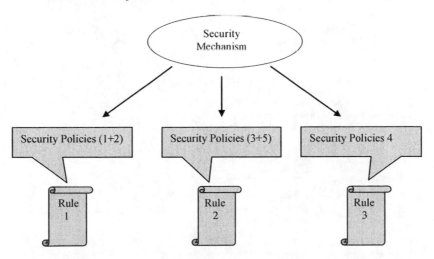

- capturing security policies and rules that are subject to frequent changes
- implementing those changes quickly and efficiently

Thus rule-based techniques play an important role in modeling security policies in any pervasive computing scenario. The article manifests the use of rule-based formalisms coupled with modular policy concepts.

SECURITY ARCHITECTURE

Figure 2 shows the overall security architecture in a military meeting scenario. The architecture is actually divided into two scenarios. The first one is for the access to the meeting network and the second is the access to the resources themselves. The basic steps that are performed are the same in both the cases. Further a user can access the network either physically or remotely. The access rules for all such cases are defined with policies (Cardelli & Gordon, 1998; Bugliesi, Castagna, & Crafa, 2001; Cardelli, 1999), declared with the help of rules (Mostefaoui & Brezillon, 2003) and stored in the policy server. The following subsections discuss the main components of the architecture.

Policy Server

The policy server has three main functions:

- storage of access rules
- authentication mechanism based on the access point
- validation of the request based on the information from the context storing area and the evaluation of the access rules

As shown in Figure 3, the policy server consists of three subcomponents:

- a **rule repository**, where all the access rules are stored;
- an **authentication mechanism**, which consists of the records of the valid usernames and the passwords; and
- a **rule evaluator**, which takes inputs from the context storing area and the authentication mechanism, and evaluates the request based on the access rules stored.

The access rules stated are based on the rule-based technique. The various situations in a military meeting

Figure 2. Overall architecture

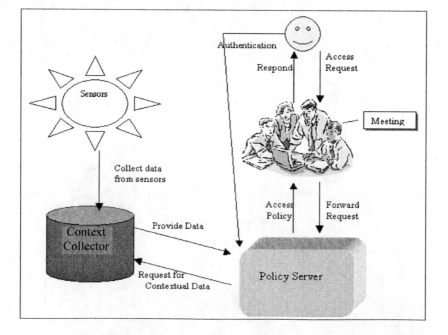

R

Figure 3. Policy server

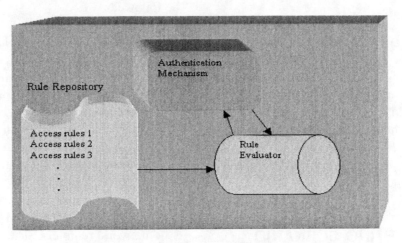

scenario where security is called for, along with the appropriate access rules in detail later in this article. The form of a typical access rule is as follows: The language syntax and the grammar of the rules mimic the natural languages and hence the rules are easy to define. The rules can either be created first and stored covering various possibilities or a rule composer can be effectively used to create runtime rules. The access rules here are defined taking only specific possibilities into account and cannot be normally recreated or redefined by the user to avoid conflicts.

Authentication Mechanism

This is the main part of the policy server. It verifies the identity of the user and gives the result to the rule evaluator. The rule evaluator decides whether to grant the access or deny it, based on the final result obtained from the authentication mechanism. The mechanism stores the list of all the local as well as external members who are required in case of some emergency, along with their respective passwords. It works in two modes. If the access point is remote, then it takes the input from the user by asking the user for the password. If the access is physical, then it takes input from the context collector about the biometric sensors (Mostefaoui & Brezillon, 2004) (retina scan and thumbprint). The combined value of these two inputs is matched with the preexisting value stored for the particular individual. If the match percentage is more than 75%, then it confirms the rule evaluator about the identity of the person.

Rule Evaluator

The rule evaluator is a rule engine wherein the actual evaluation of the rule takes place. It contains a source code, which is based on the J2EE architecture. It is also capable of creating the runtime rules based on natural language processing. The evaluator takes input from the context storing area and the user. Then it builds up a rule and then checks for the existence of a similar rule in the rules repository. After the match is found, it sends a request to the authentication mechanism about the validity of the user identity. Once it gets that information, it sends an appropriate request to the user.

Context Collector

The context collector acts as a centralized service that has the ability to retrieve a given contextual entry when requested. The data collected can be from the sensors or from the environment. The main advantage of this approach is to ease the scale up of the system for a large number of contextual entries across a wide network. The second advantage is the robustness to failures by making the contextual data available from different places, and finally, to ease the protection of contextual data (Mostefaoui & Brezillon, 2003).

The information from the distributed network is collected mainly with the help of software agents, which are launched by the context collector and are mobile in nature. Multiple context collectors can exist in the same network performing the same function.

Sensors

These are tools for capturing information about the users as well as the environment. This information is used to check for the user's validity in accessing the resources. These tools can be retina scanners, thumbprint scanners, temperature sensors, and so forth. The information captured is passed on to the context collector, which stores them as the overall context for that particular instance. The context collected is given to the policy server on its request for matching the rules stored in the rule repository.

A MILITARY MEETING SCENARIO

The military meetings comprise discussion on very important agenda items, and hence the sensitivity of the information is very high. Care should be taken that such information is disclosed only to the relevant persons in the safety of the country's defense. The meetings are conducted by a panel of people in a network discussing the delicate issues regarding the matter. The head of the meeting normally uses certain information in a pictorial or graphical format to elaborate more on particular topics. Also, if the meeting consists of people carrying different roles, then the information should be presented according to their privileges.

Thus security is required at two levels:

- at the boundary of the network so that only authorized persons are allowed to enter, and
- at the point of accessing the information/resources such that the information is distributed according to the role of the user.

We will look at the two security levels one by one. The following subsection discusses the security scenario and the access rules for the first security level.

Accessing the Meeting Network

The decision to allow the user to access the network depends on the valid identity of the users, which in turn depends on many conditions such as the role of the user, access point, and external or local entity.

This section talks about the various situations in which the above described security architecture grants access to the network and the access rules to be followed.

1. All the local entities in the department are given a secret password, which allows them to enter the meeting room. When a local entity from the defense department wants to enter the meeting room physically, he or she is authorized first by the retina scan and then he or she has to enter the secret password on the screen, which is at the door of the meeting room. This provides for his or her authenticity.

    If the local users are unable to attend the meeting physically, they can do it by accessing the network remotely. The authorization and the authentication are done with the normal username and secret password. In addition to this any sort of communication between the board members and those who access remotely should be purely in an encrypted format. This would prevent any intruder from intercepting the information.

2. There are cases where some of the higher authorities of some other defense department need to be invited to attend the conference due to some emergency. In such cases the external users are treated as foreign entities and their authentication is done in a manner analogous to the concept of movement of foreign agents into the local ambient.

    Such foreign users are granted access based on the notion of predetermined passwords. The two passwords given to them at the beginning are stored on an emergency user list. The first password helps the user to validate his or her identity. After that a secret question is asked of them, which if answered correctly allows them to enter the network either physically or remotely. The second password is used to restrict the external user from interfering with the important information irrelevant to him and to limit his access to the necessary data.

Access Rules in a Real-Time Scenario

Suppose that the major of the military department wants to access the conference network; a rule must already be present in the rule repository of the security framework. The "user name" or the "retina matching level" is used as means to authenticate him depending upon the location of the access point. The "secret password" is used to define the access rights of the major based on his role. The access rule is as given below:

IF
("Role" is equal to "Major") AND
("Entity" is equal to "Local") AND
("Access Point" is equal to "Remote")
THEN
"Authorization" needed "User name" AND
"Authentication" needed "Secret Password"
ELSIF
("Role" is equal to "Major") AND
("Entity" is equal to "Local") AND
("Access point" is equal to "Door")
THEN
"Authorization" needed "Retina matching level" AND
"Authentication" needed "Secret Password"

Authorization and authentication are done with the help of the respective passwords. Thus access rules for relevant members of the institution are stored in the repository so that they are available as and when the need arises.

In some cases, some higher authorities such as the defense minister or a major from the other defense department like the Air Force need to be invited to the meeting to discuss some immediate matters. In situations like this the access rules includes the concept of predetermined passwords of mobile ambients.

IF
("Role" is equal to "Defense Minister") AND
("Entity" is equal to "External") AND
("Access Point" is equal to "Remote") AND
("Day" equal to "Day_Set")
THEN
"Authentication" needed "First Password" AND
"Access Path" equal to "Secret question" AND
ELSIF
("Role" is equal to "Defense Minister") AND
("Entity" is equal to "External") AND
("Access Point" is equal to "Door") AND
("Day" equal to "Day_Set")
THEN
"Authentication" needed "Retina match value" plus "First Password" AND
"Access Path" equal to "Secret question" AND
"Access Restricted" by "Second Password"

Further the access rules might also consist of some special timing when no one is allowed to access the network, either physically or remotely. The example of one such access rule is given above. In this way the external users can access the network with the help of pre-existing passwords. When the existing conditions match the rule stored, then the access is granted.

Accessing the Information

Once the user gets the entry to the network, his or her access to the resources is based on whether he or she is an external or a local entity, and also on the role he or she performs. Further there are cases in which some higher authorities, although having access to the network, must be denied of accessing the resources except for a particular time. The explanation is made clear by the following discussions in a real-time scenario as described above with the help of respected access rules.

1. Lets say in a military meeting, a border security plan is being discussed. Major John of the department is the main speaker in that meeting. He has some maps and strategies in a graphical format on his laptop, which is simultaneously being displayed on rest of the people's laptops. But there should be restriction on who will have access to which information. If the strategy is such that the entire unit is divided into a number of small crews for the mission and there are individual plans for each of them, then each crew member should be able to see only that information which pertains to him or her. But at the same time, if a colonel of the local department is sitting in the meeting, he or she can have access to the entire security plan because he or she is at a higher security level. If the access is remote, then encryption must be used to avoid malicious entities from intruding into the communication network. The access rule for such a security scenario will be as follows:

IF
("Role" is equal to "Colonel") AND
("Entity" is equal to "Local") AND
("Access Point" is equal to "Remote")
THEN
"Authentication" needed " Password"
"Format" equal to "Encrypted"

"Information" access equal to "Full"
ELSIF
("Role" is equal to "Colonel") AND
("Entity" is equal to "Local") AND
("Access Point" is equal to "Door")
THEN
"Authentication" needed " Retina Match Value"

"Information" access equal to "Full"
ELSEIF
("Role" is equal to "Member") AND
("Entity" is equal to "Local") AND
("Access Point" is equal to "Remote")
THEN
"Authentication" needed "password"
"Format" equal to "Encrypted"
"Information" access equal to "Crew basis"
ELSIF
("Role" is equal to "Member") AND
("Entity" is equal to "Local") AND
("Access Point" is equal to "Door")
THEN
"Authentication" needed " Retina Match Value
"Information" access equal to "Crew basis"

2. Now the major of some other department enjoy the rights of an external agent when required in emergency. When he or she enters the network, he or she must be given restricted access to the information, which is pertaining to his or her area. Suppose that he or she is invited to discuss further issues on strategies, then he or she should only be presented the overview of the security structure of the members. The individual specific strategies must be kept away from him or her. The access rule is as follows:

IF
("Role" is equal to "Major") AND
("Entity" is equal to "External") AND
("Access Point" is equal to "Remote")
THEN
"Authentication" needed "Second Password"
"Format" equal to "Encrypted"
"Information" access equal to "General overview"
ELSIF
("Role" is equal to "Major") AND
("Entity" is equal to "External") AND
("Access Point" is equal to "Door")

THEN
"Authentication" needed "Second Password"
"Information" access equal to "General overview"

Communication between Two Different Defense Networks

During war period, the three defense departments (i.e., Air Force, Navy, and Military) have to be in contact with each other. Their plans and strategies should be well integrated. For this there should be constant transfer of data between them. Suppose the Military and the Navy departments are conducting meetings for discussing some agenda pertaining to the war. If they need to communicate with each other for seeking a joint venture or for some other important reason, the data should not only be in encrypted format, but also both the departments must be assured of each other's authenticity. There should be a third party that ensures this validity. Such a security concept was put forth by Braghin, Cortesi, and Focardi (2002) with the help of Boundary Ambients.

Real-World Scene

Suppose the colonel of the Military wants to communicate with the captain of the Navy when they are in a meeting; the data sent by the colonel must first go to an authenticated agent, which then forwards the data to the Navy network. The network in the Navy department will first check the authenticity of the data and then accept it. The same is the case when the captain wants to send something to the colonel. In this way the communication is secured and the valuable information is secured by the introduction of a third party. The third party included in this communication should be at the same level in the security hierarchy as that of the colonel and the captain. He or she should enjoy the same rights as a captain in the Navy and a colonel in the Military. In this way the information transfer between two departments is always carried out with the help of a third party, which is responsible for both the authenticity and the security of the data communicated.

The access rules to incorporate such a concept in a security infrastructure should facilitate the incoming and outgoing of the information. Such rules are easily developed with the help of rule-based formalism. The rule required while sending the data from the colonel

Figure 4. Communication between two different defense departments

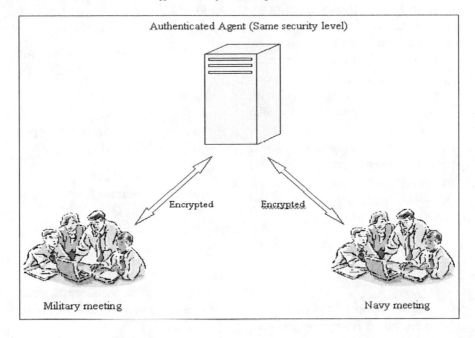

of the Military department to the captain of the Navy department is as follows:

IF
("Role" equal to "Colonel") AND
("Source_Network" equal to "Military") AND
("Dest_Network" equal to "Navy") AND
("Mode" equal to "Send")
THEN
"Authentication" needed "Password"
"Format" equal to "Encrypted"
"Intermediate_Dest" equal to "Agent_Network"
ELSEIF
("Role" equal to "Colonel") AND
("Intermediate_Dest" equal to "Agent_Network") AND
("Dest_Network" equal to "Military") AND
("Mode" equal to "Receive")
THEN
"Authentication" needed "Password"
"Format" equal to "Encrypted"
"Source_Network" equal to "Navy"

RELATED WORK

Security in pervasive computing environments has always been an emerging topic due to the complex nature of information flow and the various access points, which are vulnerable to attack. Many approaches have been made towards achieving security in this field. Covington, Ahamad, and Srinivasan (2001) and Covington, Fogla, Zhan, and Ahamad (2002) explored new access control models and security policies to secure both information and resources in an intelligent home environment. They extend the basic RBAC model to achieve a more expressive framework to include the notion of environment as well as the object roles. Their main aim was to provide a well-structured authentication service that would be effective in validating users in the presence of an appropriate context. They used XML to encode the various access rules and definition.

Mostefaoui and Brezillon (2003) introduced a new model for context-based authorizations tuning in distributed systems. They came up with a concept of partial context, which can be used to request specific authentication methods in order to control access to protected resources. The access rules and definitions were based on a rule-based formalism.

All of the above-mentioned approaches focused more on how context can be incorporated into security issues. But they say little about the actual level of security mechanisms or actions to be taken at the vulnerable access points. Further the models above are useful when the application area is commercial, for example, smart homes where we have to explore many contexts or conditions rather than the actual access points. These models are less effective in military security areas where the main focus has to be on the type of security action rather than the various contexts. The main aim of this article is to work on this limitation and explore security points in military defense meetings. Context, though essential for adaptive security measures, is not the only area of concern. We have also explored the use of policies for achieving high-level security in areas such as meetings or conferences held at the defense departments or the research centers. The access rules are written in simplified grammar using a rule-based technique, which reduces anomalies at the design level while meeting the requirements.

CONCLUSION

Context-based security is becoming a prime area of focus due to the pervasive nature of many applications. In this article we have not only described a context-based security infrastructure, but also highlighted that the security mechanisms used in a given context also are part of a very essential issue. If we do not have stern security actions, then the ultimate goal of the security solution is not thoroughly achieved. In this article, we have used the notion of meta-policies to serve such desired security measures. This notion has paved the way for a better security solution in pervasive computing scenarios.

We have also manifested an effective technique known as rule-based formalism for effective security policies. The access rules created with the help of these concepts are easy and effective.

REFERENCES

Braghin, C., Cortesi, A., & Focardi, R. (2002). Security boundaries in mobile ambients. *Computer Languages, 28(1), 101-127.*

Brezillon, P., & Mostefaoui, G.K. (2004). Context-based security policies: A new modeling approach. *Pervasive Computing and Communications Workshops, Proceedings of the 2nd IEEE Annual Conference* (pp. 154-158).

Bugliesi, M., Castagna, G., & Crafa, S. (2001). Boxed ambients. *Proceedings of TACS* (pp. 38-63). Berlin: Springer-Verlag (LNCS 2215).

Cardelli, L. (1999). *Abstraction for mobile ambients.* Research Report, Microsoft Corporation, Redmond, VA.

Cardelli, L., & Gordon, A.D. (1998). Mobile ambients. *Proceedings of FOSSACS'98* (pp. 140-155). Berlin: Springer-Verlag (LNCS 1378).

Covington, M.J., Ahamad, M., & Srinivasan, S. (2001). *A security architecture for context-aware applications.* Technical Report GIT-CC-01-12, College of Computing, Georgia Institute of Technology, USA.

Covington, M.J., Fogla, P., Zhan, Z., & Ahamad, M. (2002). A context-aware security architecture for emerging applications. *Proceedings of the Annual Computer Security Applications Conference* (ACSAC), Las Vegas, NV.

Mostefaoui, G.K., & Brezillon, P. (2004). Modeling context-based security policies with contextual graphs. *Pervasive Computing and Communications Workshops, Proceedings of the 2nd IEEE Annual Conference* (pp. 28-32).

Mostefaoui, K.M., & Brezillon, P. (2003). A generic framework for context-based distributed authorizations. In P. Blackburn et al. (Eds.), *Proceedings of CONTEXT 2003* (LNAI2680) (pp. 204-217), Paris, France.

KEY TERMS

Rule-Based: Rules have been used from the artificial intelligence (AI) perspective to capture knowledge. Rule-based refers to a technique of automated reasoning using knowledge encoded as rules.

Rule Evaluator: A software component that takes a rule and processes it, one by one—that is, it attempts to find which rule is applicable by matching the condition of the rule with given information, and then upon finding a rule that matches, performs the action as specified, given the condition.

Rule Repository: A store of rules with a mechanism to retrieve them based on a query.

Secure Agent Roaming under M-Commerce

Sheng-Uei Guan
Brunel University, UK

INTRODUCTION

The focus of this article is secure transport of mobile agents. A mobile agent is useful for hand phones or handheld devices (e.g., palmtop or PDA) equipped with mobile capabilities. Such m-commerce devices usually have limited computing power. It would be useful if the users of such devices could send an intelligent, mobile agent to remote machines to carry out complex tasks like product brokering, bargain hunting, and information collection.

An intelligent agent is one solution to providing intelligence in m-commerce. But having an agent that is intelligent is insufficient. There are certain tasks that are unrealistic for agents to perform locally, especially those that require access to a huge amount of remote information while local processing power and storage is limited. Therefore, it is important to equip intelligent agents with roaming capability.

Unfortunately, with the introduction of roaming capability, more security issues arise (Guan & Yang, 2004). As the agent needs to move among external hosts to perform its tasks, the agent itself becomes a target of attack. The data collected by agents may be modified, the credit carried by agents may be stolen, and the mission statement on the agent may be changed. As a result, transport security is an immediate concern to agent roaming. The SAFE (Secure roaming Agent For E-commerce) transport protocol is designed to provide a secure roaming mechanism for intelligent agents to satisfy their needs to roam from hosts to hosts for remote data collection or processing when local storage or computing power is limited. In SAFE, both general and roaming-related security concerns are addressed carefully. Furthermore, several protocols are designed to address different requirements. An m-commerce application can choose the protocol that is most suitable based on its need.

BACKGROUND

There has been a lot of research done in the area of intelligent agents, focusing on various aspects of agents (Guilfoyle, 1994; Johansen, Marzullo, & Lauvset, 1999). Unfortunately, there is no standardization in the various proposals, resulting in vastly different agent systems. Efforts were made to standardize some aspects of agent systems so that different systems can inter-operate with each other. Knowledge representation and exchange is one of the aspects of agent systems for which KQML (Knowledge Query and Manipulation Language) (Finin & Weber, 1993) is one of the most widely accepted standards. Developed as part of the *Knowledge Sharing Effort,* KQML was designed as a high-level language for runtime exchange of information between heterogeneous systems. Unfortunately, KQML was designed with little security considerations because no security mechanism is built to address common security concerns, not to mention specific security concerns introduced by mobile agents. Agent systems using KQML will have to implement security mechanisms on top of KQML to protect the agents.

While KQML acts as a sufficient standard for agent representation, it does not touch upon the security aspects of agents. In an attempt to equip KQML with 'built-in' security mechanisms, Secret Agent was proposed by Thirunavukkarasu, Finin, and Mayfield (1995).

Secret Agent defines a security layer on top of KQML. Applications will have to implement some special message format in order to make use of Secret Agent. Secret Agent has a number of shortcomings and is handicapped by the design of KQML. Firstly, one requirement of Secret Agent is that every agent implementing the security algorithm must possess a key (master key). This master key is either a symmetric key or based on Public Key Infrastructure (PKI).

If the key is based on a symmetric key algorithm, it requires each agent to have a separate key with every other agent it corresponds with. If the agent intends to communicate with another agent with which it has no common pre-established master key, a central authentication server is required to generate such a key. The problems introduced by the implementation of the secret agent, therefore, are key database management, authentication server protection, and key transport/exchange security.

If the master key is based on PKI, the agent identity must be tightly tied with the key pair. This was insufficiently addressed in the design of Secret Agent, subjecting the algorithm to man-in-the-middle attack. For example, when agent 006 and 007 starts a handshake, if a third agent 003 can intercept all messages between 006 and 007, agent 003 can pretend to be agent 006 while talking to agent 007, and vice versa. If key and ID are not tightly integrated (like that in digital certificate), there is almost no way agent 006 or 007 can detect this attack. In the SAFE transport protocol, agent identity and key pair are tightly tied using digital certification.

Another prominent transportable agent system is Agent TCL developed at Dartmouth College (Gray, 1997; Kotz et al., 1997). Agent TCL addressed most areas of agent transport by providing a complete suite of solutions. Its security mechanism aims at protecting resources and the agent itself. In terms of agent protection, Gray (1997) acknowledged that "it is clear that it is impossible to protect an agent from the machine on which the agent is executing…it is equally clear that it is impossible to protect an agent from a resource that willfully provides false information." As a result, the author "seeks to implement a verification mechanism so that each machine can check whether an agent was modified unexpectedly after it left the home machine" (Gray, 1997). The other areas of security, like non-repudiation, verification, and identification, were not carefully addressed.

Compared with the various agent systems discussed above, SAFE is designed to address the special needs of m-commerce. The other mobile agent systems are either too general or too specific to a particular application. By designing SAFE with m-commerce application concerns in mind, the architecture will be suitable for m-commerce applications. The most important concern is security as discussed in previous sections. Due to the nature of m-commerce, security becomes a prerequisite

for any successful m-commerce application. The other concerns are mobility, efficiency, and interoperability. In addition, the design allows certain flexibility to cater to different application needs.

SECURE AGENT TRANSPORT

General Agent Transport

As a prerequisite, each SAFE entity must carry a digital certificate issued by the SAFE Certificate Authority, or SCA. In this way, each agent, agent owner, and host will carry its own unique digital certificate. The certificate itself is used to establish the identity of a SAFE entity. Because the private key to the certificate has signing capability, this allows the certificate owner to authenticate itself to the SAFE community. An assumption is made that the agent private key can be protected by function hiding (Baldi, Ofek, and Yung, 2003).

General Message Format

In SAFE, agent transport is achieved via a series of message exchanges. The format of a general message is as follows:

SAFE Message = Message Content + Timestamp + Sequence Number + MD(Message Content + Timestamp + Sequence Number) + Signature(md)

$$(1)$$

The main body of a SAFE message comprises message content, a timestamp, and a sequence number. The message content is defined by individual messages. Here MD stands for the Message Digest function (elaborated in equation (2) shortly). The first 'MD' is the function applied to Message Content, Timestamp, and Sequence Number to generate a message digest. The second 'MD' in the equation is the application of a digital signature to the message digest generated. A timestamp contains the issue and expiry time of the message.

To prevent replay attack, message exchanges between entities during agent transport are labeled according to each transport session. A running sequence number is included in the message body whenever a new message is exchanged. In this way, if a message is lost during transmission or an additional message is received, the recipient will be able to detect it.

In order to protect the integrity of the main message body, a message digest is appended onto the main message. The formula of the message digest function (i.e., MD in (1)) is defined as follows:

$$MD = MD5(SHA(message\_body) + message\_body)$$

$$(2)$$

Here MD5 stands for the one-way mathematical function that produced a 128-bit unique representation of the data to be authenticated, while SHA (Secure Hash Algorithm) stands for a set of related cryptographic hash functions. The most commonly used function, SHA-1, is employed in a large variety of security applications. The message digest alone is not sufficient to protect the integrity of a SAFE message. A malicious hacker can modify the message body and recalculate the value of message digest using the same formula, and produce a seemingly valid message digest. To ensure the authenticity of the message, a digital signature on the message digest is generated for each SAFE message. In addition to ensuring message integrity, the signature serves as a proof for non-repudiation as well.

If the message content is sensitive, it can be encrypted using a symmetric key algorithm (e.g., Triple DES). The secret key used for encryption will have to be negotiated using a secure sockets layer, for example.

To cater for different application concerns, three transport protocols are proposed: supervised agent transport, unsupervised agent transport, and bootstrap agent transport. These three protocols will be discussed in the following sections in detail.

Supervised Agent Transport

Supervised agent transport (shown in Figure 1) is designed for applications that require close supervision of agents. Under this protocol, an agent must request a roaming permit from its owner or butler before roaming. The owner has the option to deny the roaming request and prevent its agent from roaming to undesirable hosts. Without the agent owner playing an active role in the transport protocol, it is difficult to have tight control over agent roaming.

Agent Receptionist

Agent receptionists are processes running at every host to facilitate agent transport. If an agent wishes to roam to a host, it should communicate with the agent receptionist at the destination host to complete the transport protocol.

Request through Source Receptionist for Entry Permit

To initiate supervised agent transport, an agent needs to request for an entry permit from a destination receptionist. Communication between the visiting agent and foreign parties (other agents outside the host, agent

Figure 1. Supervised agent transport

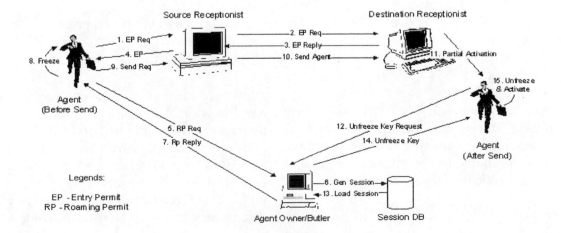

573

owner, etc.) is done using an agent receptionist as a proxy. The request for entry permit is first sent to the source receptionist. The request contains the requesting agent's digital certificate and the destination's address. The source receptionist will forward the agent's digital certificate to the destination receptionist as specified in the agent's request.

Request for Roaming Permit

Once the source receptionist receives the entry permit from the destination receptionist, it forwards it to the requesting agent. The next step is for the agent to receive a roaming permit from its owner/butler. The agent sends the entry permit and address of its owner/butler to the source receptionist. The source receptionist forwards the entry permit to the address as specified in the agent request.

For the issuing of every roaming permit, a key pair is generated. A public key is included in the roaming permit for agents to encrypt or freeze their sensitive code/data during roaming. When the agent reaches the destination, it can obtain the private key (unfreeze key) from its owner to activate itself.

Agent Freeze

With the roaming permit and entry permit, the agent is now able to request for roaming from the source receptionist. In order to protect the agent during its roaming, sensitive functions and codes inside the agent 'body' will be frozen. This is achieved using the freeze key in the roaming permit. Even if the agent is intercepted during its transmission, the agent's capability is restricted such that it cannot be run due to the freezing of agent functions. Not much harm can be done to the agent owner/butler. To ensure a smooth roaming operation, the agent's 'life support systems' cannot be frozen.

Agent Transport

Once frozen, the agent is ready for transmission over the Internet. To activate roaming, the agent sends a request containing the roaming permit to the source receptionist. The source receptionist can verify the validity and authenticity of the roaming permit.

Agent Pre-Activation

When the frozen agent reaches the destination receptionist, it will inspect the agent's roaming permit and the entry permit (contained in the roaming permit) carefully. By doing so, the destination receptionist can establish the following:

1. The agent has been granted permission to enter the destination.
2. The entry permit carried by the agent has not expired.
3. The agent has obtained sufficient authorization from its owner/butler for roaming.
4. The roaming permit carried by the agent has not expired.

If the destination receptionist is satisfied with the agent's credentials, it will activate the agent partially and allow it to continue agent transport process.

Request for Unfreeze Key and Agent Activation

Although the agent has been activated, it is still unable to perform any operation since all sensitive codes/data are frozen. To unfreeze the agent, it has to request for the unfreeze key from its owner/butler. To prove the authenticity of the destination, the destination receptionist is required to sign the random challenge in the roaming permit. The request for unfreeze key contains the session number, the certificate of destination, and the signature on the random challenge.

The destination receptionist can decrypt the unfreeze key using its private key and passes the unfreeze key to the agent. Using the unfreeze key, the agent unfreezes itself.

The direct agent transport process is completed.

Unsupervised Agent Transport

Supervised agent protocol is not a perfect solution to agent transport. Although it provides tight supervision to an agent owner/butler, it has its limitations. Since the agent owner/butler is actively involved in the transport, the protocol inevitably incurs additional overhead and network traffic. This results in lower efficiency of the protocol. This is especially significant when the agent owner/butler is located behind a network with lower

Figure 2. Unsupervised agent transport

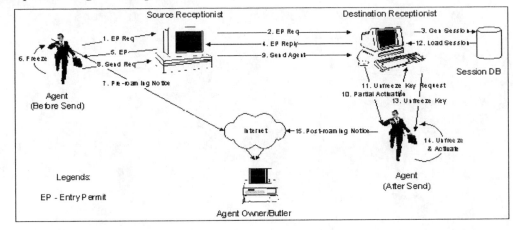

bandwidth, or the agent owner/butler is supervising a large number of agents. In order to provide flexibility between security and efficiency, unsupervised agent transport is proposed. The steps involved in unsupervised agent transport are shown in Figure 2.

Request for Entry Permit

In supervised agent transport, session ID and key pair are generated by the agent butler. However, for unsupervised agent transport, these are generated by the destination receptionists because agent butler is no longer online to the agents.

Pre-Roaming Notification

Unlike supervised agent transport, the agent does not need to seek explicit approval to roam from its owner/ butler. Instead, a pre-roaming notification is sent to the agent owner/butler first. It serves to inform the agent owner/butler that the agent has started its roaming. The agent does not need to wait for the owner/butler's reply before roaming.

Agent Freeze

Agent freeze is very close to the same step under supervised agent transport, only the encryption key is generated by the destination instead of the agent butler.

Agent Transport

This step is the same as that in supervised agent transport protocol.

Request for Unfreeze Key

The identification and verification processes are the same as compared to supervised agent transport, the exception being that the unfreeze key comes from the destination receptionist.

Agent Activation

This step is the same as that in supervised agent transport.

Post-Roaming Notification

Upon full activation, the agent must send a post-roaming notification to its owner/butler. This will inform the agent owner/butler that the agent roaming has been completed successfully. Again, this notification will take place through an indirect channel so that the agent does not need to wait for any reply before continuing with its normal execution.

Bootstrap Agent Transport

Under bootstrap agent transport, agent transport is completed in two phases. The first phase is to send a transport agent to the destination using either supervised or unsupervised agent transport. In the second phase,

Figure 3. Bootstrap agent transport

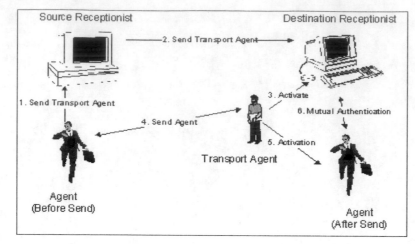

the transport agent takes over the role of destination receptionist and continues the transport of its parent agent with its own agent transport protocols. In this way, different applications can implement their transport agents using the preferred transport mechanisms and still be able to make use of our agent transport. Bootstrap agent transport is illustrated in Figure 3.

In the first phase, the transport agent is sent to the destination receptionist using either supervised or unsupervised agent transport with some modifications. The original supervised and unsupervised agent transport requires agent authentication and destination authentication to make sure that the right agent reaches the right destination. Under bootstrap agent transport, the transmission of transport agent does not require both agent authentication and destination authentication.

Once the transport agent reaches the destination, it starts execution in a restricted environment. It is not given the full privilege of a normal agent because it has yet to authenticate itself to the destination. This is to prevent the transport agent from hacking attempts to the local host. Under the restricted environment, the transport agent is not allowed to interact with local host services. It is only allowed to communicate with its parent (source receptionist) until the parent reaches destination. The bootstrap protocol allows individual transport agents to be customized to use any secure protocol for agent transmission.

When the parent agent reaches the destination, it can continue the handshake with the destination receptionist and perform mutual authentication directly. The authentication scheme is similar to that in supervised/unsupervised agent transport.

The bootstrap agent transport is meant for applications that involve highly sensitive content; they may wish to use a proprietary protocol for their agent transports. As can be seen in Figures 1, 2, and 3, the bootstrap transport procedure is relatively simple. The disadvantage is the overhead incurred for sending the "transport agent" ahead of real agent transport.

Note the use of PKI and public keys in the process does not come free. It is relatively expensive, for example to get a public key certificate we need to go through some third parties (i.e., certification authorities).

FUTURE TRENDS

As an evolving effort to deliver a more complete architecture for agents, SAFER (Secure Agent Fabrication, Evolution, and Roaming) architecture has been proposed to extend the SAFE architecture (Zhu, Guan, & Yang, 2001; Guan & Zhu, 2002, 2004). In SAFER, agents not only have roaming capability, but can make electronic payments (Guan & Hua, 2003; Guan et al., 2004) and can evolve to perform better.

CONCLUSION

SAFE has been designed as a secure agent transport protocol for m-commerce. The foundation of SAFE is the agent transport protocol, which provides intelligent agents with roaming capability without compromising security. General security concerns as well as security concerns raised by agent transport have been carefully addressed. The design of the protocol also took into consideration differing concerns for different applications. Instead of standardizing on one transport protocol, three different transport protocols were designed, catering to various needs. Based on the level of control desired, one can choose between supervised agent transport and unsupervised agent transport. For applications that require a high level of security during agent roaming, bootstrap agent transport is provided so that individual applications can customize their transport protocols. The prototype of SAFE agent transport protocol has been developed and tested.

Agent transport protocol provides the secure roaming capability to SAFE. With a secure agent transport protocol, agents in SAFE can roam from host to host without being compromised.

REFERENCES

Baldi, M., Ofek, Y., & Yung, M. (2003). The TrustedFlow™ protocol—idiosyncratic signatures for authenticated execution. *Proceedings of the Information Assurance Workshop 2003 of the IEEE Systems, Man and Cybernetics Society Conference* (pp. 288-289).

Finin, T., & Weber, J. (1993). *Draft specification of the KQML agent communication language.* Retrieved from http://www.cs.umbc.edu/kqml/kqmlspec/spec.html

Gray, R. (1997). *Agent TCL: A flexible and secure mobile-agent system.* PhD Thesis, Department of Computer Science, Dartmouth College, USA.

Guan, S.-U., & Hua, F. (2003). A multi-agent architecture for electronic payment. *International Journal of Information Technology and Decision Making, 2*(3), 497-522.

Guan, S.-U., Tan, S.L., & Hua, F. (2004). A modularized electronic payment system for agent-based e-commerce. *Journal of Research and Practice in Information Technology, 36*(2), 67-87.

Guan, S.-U., & Yang, Y. (1999). SAFE: Secure-roaming Agent For E-commerce. *Proceedings of the Computer & Industrial Engineering Conference'99* (pp. 33-37), Melbourne, Australia.

Guan, S.-U., & Yang, Y. (2004). Secure agent data integrity shield. *Electronic Commerce and Research Applications, 3*(3), 311-326.

Guan, S.-U., & Zhu, F. (2002). Agent fabrication and its implementation for agent-based electronic commerce. *International Journal of Information Technology and Decision Making, 1*(3), 473-489.

Guan, S.-U., & Zhu, F. (2004). Ontology acquisition and exchange of evolutionary product-brokering agent. *Journal of Research and Practice in Information Technology, 36*(1), 35-46.

Guan, S.-U., Zhu, F., & Maung, M.T. (2004). A factory-based approach to support e-commerce agent fabrication. *Electronic Commerce and Research Applications, 3*(1), 39-53.

Guilfoyle, C. (1994). *Intelligent agents: The new revolution in software.* London: OVUM.

Johansen, D., Marzullo, K., & Lauvset, K.J. (1999). An approach towards an agent computing environment. *Proceedings of the ICDCS'99 Workshop on Middleware.*

Kotz, D., Gray, R., Nog, S., Rus, D., Chawla, S., & Cybenko, G. (1997). Agent TCL: Targeting the needs of mobile computers. *IEEE Internet Computing, 1*(4), 58-67.

Thirunavukkarasu, C., Finin, T., & Mayfield, J. (1995). Secret agents—a security architecture for the KQML agent communication language. *Proceedings of the CIKM'95 Intelligent Information Agents Workshop,* Baltimore, MD.

Zhu, F., Guan, S.-U., & Yang, Y. (2001). SAFER e-commerce: Secure Agent Fabrication, Evolution & Roaming for e-commerce. In S.M. Rahman & M. Raisinghani (Eds.), *Internet commerce and software agents: Cases, technologies and opportunities* (pp. 190-206). Hershey, PA: Idea Group.

KEY TERMS

Agent: A piece of software that acts to accomplish tasks on behalf of its user.

Digital Certificate: Certificate that uses a digital signature to bind together a public key with an identity—information such as the name of a person or an organization, an address, and so forth. The certificate can be used to verify that a public key belongs to an individual.

Electronic Commerce (E-Commerce): Consists primarily of the distributing, buying, selling, marketing, and servicing of products or services over electronic systems such as the Internet and other computer networks.

Integrity: Regards the protection of data or program codes from being modified by unauthorized parties.

Mobile Agent: An agent that can move from machines to machines for the purpose of data collection or code execution. Also called a roaming agent.

Mobile Commerce (M-Commerce): Electronic commerce made through mobile devices.

Protocol: A convention or standard that controls or enables the connection, communication, and data transfer between two computing endpoints. Protocols may be implemented by hardware, software, or a combination of the two. At the lowest level, a protocol defines a hardware connection.

Replay Attack: An attack used by hackers; messages between a user and a server can be intercepted by the intermediate hacker who can resend these messages to the server later.

Security: The effort to create a secure computing platform, designed so that agents (users or programs) can only perform actions that have been allowed.

Secure Automated Clearing House Transactions

Jan Skalicky Hanson
St. Cloud State University, USA

Mark B. Schmidt
St. Cloud State University, USA

INTRODUCTION

U.S. society is at the precipice of a major revolution in the payments system. Given today's advancing technology, it is becoming clear to industry experts that consumers and businesses are ready for the transition to electronic movement of funds. Banks of all sizes are beginning to innovate, the Federal Reserve is encouraging transition to electronic funds as opposed to paper, and consumers are slowly getting used to the idea of safe transfer of funds electronically (Santomero, 2005). In the end, it will be the consumer who decides, and critical to the transition will be providers creating simple and secure solutions so users have confidence in the payment systems.

Among the potential barriers to such systems are the many potential security concerns that are present in today's networked world. Another phishing scheme or data breach of some sort is reported in the national media almost daily (Bellovin, 2004). But even with the security concerns, the rush to move funds electronically is akin to the Gold Rush. The decline of paper checks over the last decade, together with the increased use of debit cards over credit cards, the use of credit and debit for small food and retail purchases, and the increase in awareness of electronic movement of money through companies like PayPal through eBay, appear to suggest that the American public may be ready for the transition to electronic transfer of funds.

Security is an ongoing concern. While exact figures are extremely difficult to obtain due to a consistent lack of many organizations' willingness to disclose breaches (Computer Security Institute, 2003; Hoffer & Straub, 1989), industry estimates are that security breaches occur in 90% of organizations each year and cost $17 billion (Austin & Darby, 2003). A more recent survey found that in 2004 the total losses for 269 companies was $141 million (Computer Security Institute, 2004).

BACKGROUND OF TODAY'S PAYMENTS SYSTEMS

Consumers and businesses have long preferred to pay for goods and services with the paper check (Santomero, 2005). This method succeeded primarily because of consumers' confidence in the banking system, specifically the Federal Reserve and its ability to make good on checks at a low cost.

Since the advent in the 1950s of the credit card and the more recent widespread acceptance of the debit card (now bypassing the credit card in transaction volume), it would seem that consumers and companies are more ready than ever to accept a transition away from paper checks to different forms of electronic movement of funds (Chakravorti & Jankowski, 2005).

Because of the widespread acceptance of the use of debit and credit cards, processing of paper checks has been experiencing a steady decline since the 1990s. Research from the Philadelphia Federal Reserve Research Department found that less than 18% of U.S. households used debit cards in 1995. By 2001, nearly half of all households used them. Coincidently, as paper checks and their accompanying profits decline, the debit card allows banks to profit, as opposed to having to share revenue with the credit card companies. Using debit cards is a cheaper way for consumers to pay for goods, as they use their own funds and do not have interest charges (Santomero, 2005).

Figure 1. A cross-country electronic payment (adopted from the Federal Reserve Bank of Richmond, 2006)

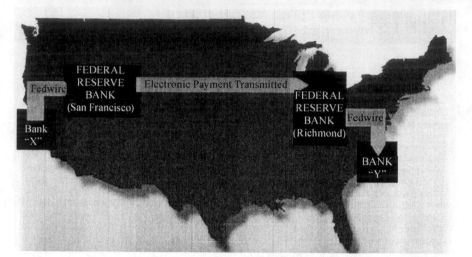

Automated Clearinghouse

In the 1970s, the development of the automated clearinghouse (ACH) provided a way for banks to move funds electronically from businesses to consumers and vice versa. Banks control the ACH network, and the technology is most useful to companies processing large volumes of transactions. The ACH transaction incurs minimal costs to banks and is a cheaper way for merchants to receive payments. However, ineffective delivery to end users of the ACH product has prohibited its widespread use. It can easily be argued that electronic movement of funds via the banks and the Federal Reserve's ACH network is more secure and fraud-proof than the use of paper checks (Kandra, 2005). Figure 1 depicts how an ACH may take place.

However, confidence and convenience is the key to any payment system's acceptance. Use of paper checks is expected to decrease by 23% for consumers over the next two years (Bielski, 2006). It seemed that 2003 was a pivotal year for transition from paper to electronic movement of funds. The trend is in one direction: UP. From 2000-2003 payments by checks dropped from 57% to 45%. Automated clearinghouse transactions and debits increased from 21% to 32%. In all there were 13.8 billion more electronic transactions in 2003 than in 2000.

The National Association of Automated Clearinghouse Association tracked ACH payments from the second quarter of 2004 to the second quarter of 2005 to have increased from 2.2 billion to 2.6 billion—an 18% increase in one year. Even more intriguing is the increase in consumers using ACH as a payment vehicle. The increase of the consumers initiating a bill payment to suppliers with a debit from their account and a credit to the supplier was 38% during the same year. By 2010, the Federal Reserve expects to process only 2.5 billion checks, down from the current 40 billion (Orr, 2005).

It seems the trend is worldwide, as other nations have been in one stage or another of acceptance of electronic funds for some time. The reasons are all the same, and most experts agree that it saves time, reduces costs for paper handling, and offers flexibility (Panurach, 1996).

Security and Acceptance of Electronic Payments

Security is still considered the leading factor in building confidence today in consumers and businesses alike as they transition to electronic forms of payment. In 2005, 600,000 names and social security numbers of employees were stolen from Time Warner computer backup tapes, and information about 1.4 million customers was stolen from DSW shoe store. Even though data is becoming more traceable and quickly retrievable, fears continue (Compiled, 2005). Electronic information can be quickly identified and accountholders notified, whereas paper trails are less likely to be traceable. In any case, with identity theft and other forms of security breaches on the rise, consumers are more aware than ever of a need for secure sites for their financial data. These widespread reports increase the appeal of electronic ACH transactions.

However, in a consumer study on privacy, most answered that security was of critical concern, but freely offered personal information when asked (Berendt, Gunther, & Spiekermann, 2005). Unfortunately consumers pass on the responsibility for security to providers rather than taking on the responsibility themselves (Whitman, 2003). Security is a joint effort.

The electronic world is by nature anonymous, so creating ways of establishing secure identities is critical to building trust among users. Not that those solutions are iron clad, but they are at least a step in the right direction and will only increase consumer confidence in the electronic world and especially the payment system (Backhouse, Hsu, Tseng, & Baptista, 2005). According to industry experts, essentially consumers are looking for simplicity and security when using electronic payments (Khanna, 2005).

Electronic Payments Systems

The banking industry is becoming innovative in regard to electronic payments. The Federal Reserve is doing its part in creating policy facilitating electronic movement of funds. The recent passage of Check 21, a new banking regulation that allows for the acceptance of an image of an item (check or deposit) to be a legal transaction at the clearing bank may pave the way for more acceptances among businesses of electronic movement of funds. Although a step in the right direction, many in the Federal Reserve believe that the move toward electronic or online bill payment is still the best long-term solution (Chakravorti & Jankowski, 2005).

Another electronic payment developed in the private sector is the Accounts Receivable Conversion (ARC) product that turns paper checks at the point of sale into ACH transactions.

The challenge is to lead the electronic funds movement by creating a secure and convenient delivery system for ACH payment methods that build confidence in businesses and consumers. Fortunately, banks have an inherent trust built into their systems from years of managing transactions from consumers and businesses (Davis, 2004). Factors such as the convenience of electronic payments for both consumers and companies

alike will likely lead to increased adoption of online payments. By some accounts 45% of all recurring bill payments are made online (Bielski, 2006).

Security Issues with Electronic Payment Systems

The basic infrastructure of bank handling of ACH transfers is considered by many to be secure and safe. At a typical bank, PC based-software compiles .txt or .csv files and converts them to an ACH format accepted by the Federal Reserve. The data is sent over a secure telecommunications line to the Federal Reserve. The next day, a file is sent back to the bank verifying all transactions processed. These computers and phone lines to the Federal Reserve are accessible to limited employees and are kept in separately locked rooms.

Unfortunately, the general public has had limited access to one of the safest methods of electronic funds transfers in operation today. Banks offer ACH, but not often as a product used for day-to-day payments. The leaders in developing the use of ACH as a standard payment method have been third-party processors adept at software development and industry-specific accounting procedures. These providers market to businesses with high-volume, low-dollar transactions such as health clubs, cable and Internet providers, and city utilities to name a few.

A local Midwestern bank studied the marketing efforts of successful third-party processors and incorporated their innovations into a separate banking division. Armed with the knowledge that banks have long held a reputation for confidentiality and security in handling banking transactions, the bank developed its own ACH payment gateway to allow businesses to streamline operations, reduce expenses, and speed the clearing of funds.

The payments division focus is:

- **A Recurring ACH Product:** Preauthorized debits.
- **Payroll Direct Deposit:** Preauthorized credits.
- **Online Direct Payment Products:** Consumer to business.
- **Online Bill Presentment/Invoicing/Payments for Business to Business.**

Security and the Three Components in Online Payment Gateway Development

The bank's Web developer created secure online direct pay options for targeted markets. Pilot property management firms offered recurring ACH to residents. Renters link from their property management site to a bank-hosted secure site to make a one-time ACH payment from their checking or savings. The payment gateway would have three main components:

1. **Company Administration Panel:** The company would have an administration panel where authorized personnel would log on to upload current statement data and customer files, and have access to customer payment history information and monthly invoices. Customer information would be stored for a limited time and then archived.
2. **Customers Live Payment Gateway:** This section would be accessible with a link from the company's Web site. Customers could be given a unique password and log in or simply enroll and select a user name and password. Customers enter their bank and bank routing information to submit for payment. The payment information is held on a secure site for processing. When a payment is made, the company is notified of a payment via e-mail and the customer information is moved to the bank's processing panel on a secure database.
3. **Bank Processing Panel:** Authorized bank personnel access live payments on the secure site. Live payments (those not yet processed) are highlighted, and operators download the payments to bank processing software for secure delivery to the Federal Reserve for processing. Once processed, payments are stored on the system and then archived.

Critical to the development of the online sites is the development of a secure site for users to deliver, process, store, and manage sensitive financial information. The issues critical to the development were creating authorized access to data, secure processing data with encryption, safe and limited data storage, and authenticating the identity of users.

The bank purchased the industry standard Secure Socket Layer (SSL) 128-bit signed by VeriSign to secure data on a secure server. SSL utilizes public key encryption to protect data in transmission from the Web server to the end user's computer. Although not perfect by any means, it is among the best security offered for electronic movement of funds today. The payment site is hosted at an outside server with minimal outside access, and payment information is held on a separate server. The payments would all be entered on the secure site, and once submitted, data would be formatted for delivery in the standard ACH payment format required by the Federal Reserve.

Banking on Trust

Banks and financial services companies do more than is required to secure online financial data. In spite of that, industry experts concede that security is only as good as yesterday's innovations, as those wanting to steal information find ways to do it.

Today, most cases of identify theft occur with paper transactions, statements, paper bills, and data stolen from mailboxes or garbage bins (Kandra, 2006). Even so, no one thinks that the move to electronic transfers creates a foolproof solution to stop all fraud. However, bank-to-bank ACH through the Federal Reserve has every opportunity to respond to the need for security in electronic movement of funds. The use of electronic transfers allows the consumer more access to their data instantaneously, thereby the time of discovery of a data breach is less. Most security and fraud experts suggest consumers check their statements online monthly and also take advantage of getting at least one credit bureau report annually. Relying on consumers to take more responsibility makes authenticating users more critical. The Office of Controller of Currency is recommending more stringent authentication methods, asking banks to consider adopting multifactor authentication by 2007 (Childs, 2006).

CONCLUSION

With the model for secure payments described herein, extraordinary measures are taken to ensure that files are uploaded to a secure site and all payments are encrypted. Both the company and bank personnel have unique log in to verify proper handling of financial data. Also significant is the length of time the bank stores the payment data. This is a key challenge in that compiling a history of payments for the company and the customer alike requires a database of historical payments. However, the length of time payment data is stored and then archived is a point addressed with the company. This is typically solved with reporting data, so payment information is not held in a database, but in standard reports accessible for retrieval.

It is currently believed by most industry experts that the transition to electronic means of payments is on the verge of exploding. This model of providing a payment gateway for ACH payments allows accessibility to a low-cost and secure way to make payments by using banks with a long-trusted payment system. For any innovation, acceptance and usage will be the key to success, and in end it will be the consumer who decides.

REFERENCES

Austin, R.D., & Darby, C.A.R. (2003). The myth of secure computing. *Harvard Business Review, 81*(6), 120-126.

Backhouse, J., Hsu, C., Tseng, J., & Baptista, J. (2005). A question of trust. *Communications of the ACM, 48*(9), 87-91.

Bellovin, S. (2004). Inside risks: Spamming, phishing, authentication, and privacy. *Communications of the ACM, 47*(1), 144.

Berendt, B., Gunther, O., & Spiekermann, S. (2005). Privacy in e-commerce: Stated preferences vs. actual behavior. *Communications of the ACM, 48*(4), 101-106.

Bernstel, J. (2000). Sense of security. *Bank Marketing,* (April).

Bertolucci, J. (2005). Technology and your finances. Banking-ease of use, more features, better security. And most have branches, too. *Kiplinger's,* (November).

Bielski, L. (2006). Debit's growing popularity. *American Banking Association Banking Journal, 158*(1), 35-37.

Chakravorti, S., & Jankowski, C. (2005). Innovations, incentives, and regulation: Forces shaping the payments environment. *Chicago Fed Letter, Federal Reserve Bank of Chicago, Special Issue No. 218a,* (September).

Chakravorti, S., & Jankowski, C. (2005). Payment studies: Forces shaping the payments environment: A summary of the Chicago Fed's 2005 Payments Conference. *Chicago Fed Letter, Federal Reserve Bank of Chicago, Special Issue No. 219a,* (October).

Childs, R. (2006, February). *Banking on multifactor authentication.* Retrieved from http://searchsecurity.techtarget.com/tip/1,289483,sid14_gci1168269,00.html

Complied. (2005). Data breaches: Is anyone safe? *The Information Management Journal, 39*(4), 10.

Computer Security Institute. (2003). *2003 CSI/FBI computer crime and security survey.* Retrieved July 26, 2003, from http://i.cmpnet.com/gocsi/db_area/pdfs/fbi/FBI2003.pdf

Computer Security Institute. (2004). *2004 CSI/FBI computer crime and security survey.* Retrieved February 5, 2005, from http://i.cmpnet.com/gocsi/db_area/pdfs/fbi/FBI2004.pdf

Davis, Z. (2004). Banking on e-payments. *Eweek,* (October 25).

Federal Reserve Bank of Richmond. (2006). *The Federal Reserve today.* Retrieved July 5, 2005, from http://www.richmondfed.org/publications/educator_resources/federal_reserve_today/bankers.cfm

Hoffer, J.A., & Straub, D.W. Jr. (1989). The 9 to 5 underground: Are you policing computer crimes? *Sloan Management Review, 30*(4), 35-44.

Kandra, A. (2006, March). *Consumer watch: Banking on the Web: Risky business.* Retrieved from *http://www.pcworld.com*

Khanna, P. (2005). New payment methods must take security into account: Panel. *Computing Canada,* (November).

Lieber, R. (2005). Green thumb: Taking rain check on e-checks; more retailers ask for your bank account info…here's why. *Wall Street Journal, 246*(106), B1.

Orr, B. (2006). Warning! Electronic tsunami coming. *American Banking Association Banking Journal, 157*(12), 38-39.

Panurach, P. (1996). Money in electronic commerce: Digital cash, electronic funds transfer, and e-cash. *Communications of the ACM, 39*(6), 45-50.

Santomero, A. (2005, Third Quarter). *Business review* (p. 8). Philadelphia: Federal Reserve Bank of Philadelphia.

Vijayan, J. (2005). Banks urged to automate online transaction controls. *Computerworld,* (November), 22.

Whitman, M.E. (2003). Enemy at the gate: Threats to information security. *Communications of the ACM, 46*(8), 91-95.

KEY TERMS

Accounts Receivable Conversion: A consumer billing company notifies its customer that his or her check payment will be processed using check conversion. The notification allows the sending of the check as an ACH or electronic transfer. After the consumer makes a payment with a check, the check is converted by the company to an ACH transaction. The account and bank routing information is read by a scanner and transmitted to the sending and receiving banks (http://www.checkconversioneducation.org/PDF/arc-whitepaper.pdf).

Automated Clearinghouse (ACH): These transactions are payment instructions to either debit or credit a deposit account. An ACH transaction is an electronic funds transfer between sending and receiving financial institutions. ACH payments can either be credits originated by the accountholder sending funds (payer), or debits originated by the accountholder receiving funds (payee). Financial institutions may contract with third-party service providers to conduct their ACH activities, and independent third parties not affiliated with financial institutions now generate significant ACH payment activity (http://www.ffiec.gov/ffiecinfobase/booklets/Retail/retail_02d.html).

Check 21: The Check Clearing for the 21st Century Act (Check 21) was signed into law on October 28, 2003, and became effective on October 28, 2004. Check 21 is designed to foster innovation in the payments system and to enhance its efficiency by reducing some of the legal impediments to check truncation. With Check 21, a substitute check is the legal equivalent of the original check and includes all the information contained on the original check. The law does not require banks to accept checks in electronic form, nor does it require banks to use the new authority granted by the act to create substitute checks (http://www.federalreserve.gov/paymentsystems/truncation/default.htm).

Encrypted: Cryptography or cryptology is a field of mathematics and computer science concerned with information security and related issues, particularly encryption. Technically, "cryptography" refers to the techniques and "cryptology" refers to the study of them; despite this, the term "cryptography" is often used to refer to the entire field. Cryptography makes extensive use of mathematics, particularly discrete mathematics, including topics from number theory, information theory, computational complexity, and statistics (http://en.wikipedia.org/wiki/Cryptography).

Online ACH Payment Gateway: A Web-based tool allowing consumers and businesses to make payments from their checking account or savings account using the Federal Reserve ACH network over the Internet.

Phishing: In computing, phishing is a form of criminal activity using social engineering techniques, characterized by attempts to fraudulently acquire sensitive information, such as passwords and credit card details, by masquerading as a trustworthy person or business in an apparently official electronic communication, such as an e-mail or an instant message (http://en.wikipedia.org/wiki/Phishing).

Secure Socket Layer (SSL): A protocol developed by Netscape for transmitting private documents via the Internet. This can be embedded into the browser. It uses public key encryption and digital certificates. Both Netscape and Internet Explorer support SSL, and many Web sites use the protocol to obtain confidential user information like credit card numbers. The SSL certificate protocol provides data encryption, server authentication, message integrity, and optional client authentication for a TCP/IP Internet connection. URLs that require an SSL connection start content with *https://* instead of *http://*. A small lock symbol on the right-hand of the corner of the browser which shows connection is SSL (http://www.kentlaw.edu/legalaspects/digital_signatures/tutorials/SSL.html).

Security Dilemmas for Canada's New Government

Jeffrey Roy
Dalhousie University, Canada

INTRODUCTION

The context of this article stems from the growing importance of digital technologies within public sector processes and applications tied to the realms of service and security. Both currents continue to influence the public sector and both rely increasingly on digital capacities for information sharing and processing. Yet there are also tensions between them as although both are bound by a more citizen-centric focus, the interpretation and application of this focus is different in each case. Service delivery is predicated on providing information and transactions to citizens in more efficient and integrated ways. Security underpins such service capacities, but it also denotes the usage and deployment of a digital infrastructure to both identify and respond to potential threats. Tensions between service and security have been and continue to be central to managerial and governance reforms associated with digital technologies internally and online connectivity externally.

The Government of Canada is illustrative of the importance of both of these agendas. Over the past decade, Connecting Canadians gave birth to the flagship online service initiative, Government Online (GOL), which has since evolved into the emergence of a new Service Canada entity beginning in the fall of 2005 in order to better integrate and coordinate all delivery channels, including the Internet, telephone, and walk-in, staffed venues. At the same time, the post-9/11 restructuring has resulted in the creation of the Department of Public Safety and Emergency Preparedness Canada and the first overarching national security strategy. Importantly, all of these initiatives are predicated on stronger horizontality within government across previously autonomous units. Such is the challenge of interoperability—meaning the ability to communicate and coordinate action across systems designed for separate and unique purposes.

While interoperability has evolved from a primarily technical challenge to one that is recognized as organizational, the political meaning of interoperability is equally consequential though less recognized and understood. There are new pressures for different levels of government to work with one another more formally and effectively: such pressures extend transnationally, particularly continentally where Canada–U.S. relations have become a predominant framework. Central to this framework is a 'national' security effort that is nonetheless highly intertwined with the Canada–U.S. border and rising pressures for interoperability on a continental scale. Although some elements of 'border management' are explicit (such as the Smart Border Accord), the organizational restructuring and technological retooling of Canadian government is more complex, as is the spectrum of options and choices between independence and sovereignty on the one hand and bilateral (and to a lesser degree trilateral) interdependence on the other. Of particular interest in this article is the prominence of digital technologies in underpinning a culture of information sharing and surveillance both within and across the Canada–U.S. border.

In sum, the objective of this article is thus to better understand:

i. the similarities and differences between service and security in terms of organizational, technological, and political dimensions;

ii the managerial and governance reforms within the public sector driven by the events of 9/11 and the implications for information management and accountability; and

iii. the pressures for cross-border governance arrangements between Canada and the United States.

BACKGROUND: SERVICE AND SECURITY

Delivering services online became the hallmark of e-government during the 1990s: as more and more citizens conduct their personal and professional affairs online, these 'customers' of government look to do the same in dealing with their state, whether it is paying their taxes or renewing permits and licenses of one sort or another (Curtin, Sommer, & Vis-Sommer, 2003). Although the initial impetus for utilizing online channels to deliver information and services was often financial savings through improved automation and efficiency, many such forecasts proved excessively optimistic due to both investment costs and governance complexities (Fountain, 2001; Allen, Paquet, Juillet, & Roy, 2005). Service transformation efforts tied to the Internet began to evolve in the late 1990s, leading to the 1999 pledge to achieve comprehensive online service delivery by 2004:

The Government On-Line Initiative (GOL) was launched to meet this commitment. The goal of GOL is to provide Canadians with electronic access to key federal programs and services. The initiative focuses on grouping or 'clustering' online services around citizens' needs and priorities, rather than by government structures. (Coe, 2004, p. 6)

The government showcases citizen satisfaction surveys with online delivery channels[1] and the results of various surveys such as Accenture's annual rankings as evidence of progress: much of this recognition is owed to the government's main portal[2] that, in the spirit of integrated service delivery, is grouped according to clusters of services and specific client groups.[3] A key objective of GOL had been ensuring that the 130 most common federal services were online by 2005. Although by the end of 2004, nearly all of them were 'identifiable' online, most offerings remain informational, rather than transactional, and the ability to fully complete services and make payment remains more limited. Some current examples include: integrated change of address features, online tax return filing, business registrations, submission of select statements of employment, applying for government employment, and a variety of purchases for government publications.[4] Security is a foundation for such efforts:

Secure Channel is a portfolio of services that forms the foundation of the Government of Canada's Government On-line (GOL) initiative. Secure Channel's primary goals are to provide citizens and businesses with secure, private and high-speed access to all federal government's on-line services, and to provide an environment that enables and encourages departments to integrate with federated common services.[5]

By 2004, the secure channel had been deployed across all federal departments and agencies as the basis of a new government-wide network infrastructure—and it also allowed for the small but growing base of online service offerings summarized above (among other initiatives planned, the secure channel is expected to allow for the first-ever availability of the national census online in 2006). Despite a common platform, leveraging it across traditionally separate entities in order to integrate service offerings is a more complex undertaking. The main barrier is getting departments to work together in sharing information and combining authority in order to realize more 'citizen-centric' processes. The vertical structures of separate departments serving individual ministers largely translate into autonomy over interoperability: "Silos continue to reign" (Coe, 2004, p. 18). Such is the context that drove the creation of Service Canada in 2005, a new government-wide vehicle for integrated service delivery both online and via other delivery channels as well (Roy, 2006b).

CONVENIENCE, COMPLEXITY, AND ACCOUNTABILITY

With respect to service delivery, it is not uncommon to hear project champions both inside and outside of government insist that "the citizen does not care about how governments are organized internally—and how they process information and undertake decisions, their only—or perhaps primary concern is getting good service" (i.e., the end result of a service encounter). Such a viewpoint is analogous in some respects to online, citizen-centric banking where the typical customer accesses his or her entire portfolio of products and services through an integrated portal, caring little about the organizational architecture that facilitates this one-stop, integrative experience.

In terms of security, a similar sentiment would be that the primary concern of the citizen lies with safety and the prevention of harmful or disruptive acts—with far less attention accorded how government ensures such an outcome. In both cases of service and security, it is the outcome that weighs more heavily than process. In short, understanding how government is organized is deemed as relatively unimportant to the public—a sentiment reflected in the first part of the following passage from the Australian context (but not out of step with the logic employed by many governments around the world):

To accommodate citizens' increasing expectations for e-government to simplify interactions with government and to hide the complexity of the bureaucracy needed to manage the complex policy issues of our time, integrated services that cross agency and jurisdictional boundaries are necessary. (Barrett, 2002a; National Office for the Information Economy, 2002)

To protect the autonomy of governments at different levels and to maintain the democratic principle of allowing people to elect representatives in line with their view of delivery of representational capacity, these integrated services will be agglomerations of individually crafted components found in many jurisdictions and even in the private sector. (Balmer, 1981; Barnet, 2002a)

To coordinate the operation of these integrated services in some equitably governed approach will require creation of organizations with unique ownership structures, novel governance structures, and subject to innovative accountability regimes. (Barrett, 2002a; Turner, 2004, p. 136)

The latter part of this quote is instructive in seeking a balance between the need to hide bureaucracy in a transactional, service-oriented manner while at the same time addressing the separate and overlapping democratic accountabilities at play (in this case across different levels of government, but the point also applies in equal measure to separate ministerial units within a single government). Indeed, here is where there are important and consequential distinctions between government and business in terms of the expecta-

tions and actions of customers and citizens—and the accountability requirements that result. In the private sector, the conditions of competition and choice that define a customer's connection to any private firm (or an investor as well) are more conducive to performance-based accountability than is the case in government where democratic citizenship implies a more multi-faceted relationship between the public and governing bodies.

The ability of citizens to hold their governments accountable in a democratic context depends on more than the transactional encounters with the public sector as a service provider. Not only is information the lifeblood of accountability, but the notion of accountability carries an important learning component in terms of generating capacities for social learning and collective judgment that underpin a government's ability to itself deal with increasingly complex and multi-faceted policy problems (Paquet, 2000; Juillet & Paquet, 2002). In other words, a government's ability to address complexity depends on the public's capacity to appreciate it—whereas a misleading or overly simplistic presentation of how government is actually exercising its duties is therefore detrimental to both public confidence and collective learning.

SECRECY AND INTEROPERABILITY

A sophisticated and reliable digital infrastructure is a necessary precursor to such government-wide action, and as such, interoperability has become a guiding principle in such efforts. Although often viewed in a technical or digital manner (i.e., computers, networks, and databases being able to communicate with one another), in any organizational environment the human and managerial layers to such connectedness are as complex, if not more so (Allen et al., 2005; Scholl, 2005). Moreover, in a public sector environment—with a host of managerial and political boundaries separating units both within and between governments—such complexity is further heightened. Finally, in terms of a holistic or systemic view of security within a jurisdiction such as a country, interoperability across sectors (notably, the private sector) also becomes an important element (Dutta & McCrohan, 2002). For instance, the U.S. strategy for cyber-security relies heavily on public–private sector cooperation, a bolstered priority but one that remains perilously under-recognized for some (Worthen, 2005).

Central to not only cyber-security efforts but also much of the homeland security apparatus are information flows and identities. With respect to information, the challenge is not generating more of it but rather making sense of it (and creating knowledge as a result[6]). Accordingly, an important tool in homeland security is data mining that, much like the term implies, involves digitally and virtually trolling through massive amounts of information gathered in raw form, and then analyzed for meaningful patterns or events (Sirmakessis, 2004). Cyber-security and information management systems are thus not only crucial to gathering and processing information, but also safeguarding it against accidental or malicious threats. Even prior to 9/11, concern had been growing about the accelerating costs of technical breakdowns from viruses, hacking, and the like. The problem is now viewed as central to national security as the potential for electronic threats against critical infrastructure components that include information holdings, defense operations, and energy and environmental management systems that all rely increasingly on computer systems and connectivity (Denning, 2003).

Some industry estimates point to homeland security spending levels in the United States to surpass $180 billion by 2008, a figure that includes all levels of government and the private sector (and an amount that nearly equals the total annual budget of the Government of Canada).[7] Such massive injections of public funds face growing questions about the extent to which managerial accountability and oversight capacities are up to the challenge of deploying these resources in a responsible and effective fashion. Difficulties that plague the U.S. Department of Homeland Security are a case in point: the department has been unable to fulfill its role in effectively consolidating and coordinating the formation and usage of terrorist watch lists from its various sub-units, a deficiency ascribed by department officials to an absence of resources and sufficiently developed infrastructure for doing so.[8]

A key issue in such an environment is an absence of sufficient openness on the part of public authorities (Reid, 2004). U.S. government watchers claim that over the past four years, in particular, the culture of secrecy has been significantly reinforced at the expense of transparency and public accountability.[9] The following explains another related dimension to

the concern that secrecy is becoming the norm in security matters, due in part to covert activity, but also the extraordinary level of complexities that permeate an increasingly ubiquitous and invisible infrastructure extending across the realms of both government and commercial activities:

Law enforcement and intelligence services don't need to design their own surveillance systems from scratch. They only have to reach out to the companies that already track us so well, while promising better service, security, efficiency, and perhaps most of all, convenience. It takes less and less effort each year to know what each of us is about.... More than ever before, the details of our lives are no longer our own. They belong to the companies that collect them and the government agencies that...demand them in the name of keeping us safe. (O'Harrow, 2005, p. 300)

Such concerns tie together the focus on capacities to gather and make use of information and the concept of individual identity. Both are interdependent by virtue of the fact that in order to learn anything specific about an individual or group of individuals, there must be reliable identifiers. The existence and reliability of such identifiers thus become critical enablers of the functioning of the system as a whole—and as such, the notion of identity is a central tenant of domestic security efforts—as well as the digitization of such efforts (Heymann, 2002).

A holistic response by the Government of Canada came in 2004 via Canada's first ever National Security Policy, which featured a more integrated framework: anti-terrorism, policing, border control, and cyber-security are the purview of a single minister. The U.S. Department of Homeland Security served as inspiration for Canada's Department of Public Safety and Emergency Preparedness Canada (PSEPC):

(PSEPC) was created to secure the safety of Canadians while maintaining the benefits of an open society. It integrates under one minister the core activities of the previous Department of the Solicitor General, the Office of Critical Infrastructure Protection and Emergency Preparedness and the National Crime Prevention Center.[10]

Cyber-security and informational strategies have been greatly bolstered: indicative of new approaches is the Advance Passenger Information/Passenger Name Record (API/PNR) program, designed "to protect Canadians by helping to identify high-risk, would-be travelers":

The Canada Border Services Agency (CBSA) is authorized to collect and retain information on travellers and to keep it for customs purposes under section 107.1 of the Customs Act. API is basic data that identifies a traveller and is collected at the time of check-in.[11]

While the Canadian government points to 9/11 as reason enough for such measures, four important concerns have been presented by critics (Roy, 2005b):

i.   infringement on the privacy rights of Canadians;
ii.   the secrecy surrounding government operations managing such initiatives (and by extension the related information sources);
iii.   the potential for 'function creep', where information gathered by one part of government for one purpose (in this case anti-terrorism) invariably finds its way into other processes tied to other purposes; and
iv.   the possibility for errors or mishaps due to mismanagement of information and identities in particular.

The interplay of these four sets of concerns has shaped much of the debate. For example, although the first point is partially mitigated by a variety of legislative safeguards addressing privacy concerns, as well as the independent Privacy Commissioner (reporting to Parliament rather than the government), these same commissioners are often among the most active critics of government action, underscoring problems associated with secrecy, function creep, and identity management (Loukidelis, 2004; Posner, 2006).[12] The potential for error and mismanagement within the security apparatus is also a prevalent theme of the most recent auditor general findings (Auditor General of Canada, 2003, 2004, 2005).

This need for a more explicit form of collaboration and connectedness across countries underscores the fluid nature of identity and privacy for individuals, as well as challenges to traditional notions of sovereignty and power for nations (Bennett & Raab, 2003; Hayden, 2005). Whereas recent decades have witnessed at-

tempts to expand an ideology of individual freedom, mobility, and commerce beyond national borders, the present environment also features steps by national governments to monitor and, if necessary, curtail human and commercial mobility. Security and mobility thus become co-evolving agendas that carry at least the potential for tension and conflict, notably in the efforts of any one country to configure its border in terms of its own interests as well as its inter-related interests with other countries, particularly those in close geographic proximity (Salter, 2004).

Such is the new context of Canada-U.S. relations within which 'smart border technologies', border controls and more technologically sophisticated identification schemes, and heightened pressures for information sharing and coordinated bilateral action have exerted a significant influence on the Canadian federal government during the past few years (Roy, 2005b).

CONCLUSION: A NEW CONSERVATIVE BALANCE?

With the arrival in Canada of a conservative minority government to power in January 2005 (led by Prime Minister Stephen Harper), there is at the least the potential for a recasting of political priorities and actions, and an alternative set of mechanisms to be designed to pursue them (the first change in political parties controlling government since 1993). The conservative agenda may be examined through three of the most significant and inter-related themes discussed in the preceding sections: the security architecture, accountability and openness, and Canada-U.S. relations.

With respect to the architecture of security, the conservatives had little to say (as was the case with all parties) on the intricacies of security as a basis for service delivery, but they proved to be bullish on plans to expand security efforts tied to national defense, sovereignty, and public safety. Along with new military spending, Harper's party promised to bolster resources to the Canada Border Services Agency (CBSA) and to create a new foreign intelligence unit to focus on covert action and intelligence gathering.

While indications are that the new government intends to continue with the expanded emphasis on security underway since 2001, there are important differences that may emerge in the managing of information and decision making within this governance architecture. For example, the centerpiece of the campaign and the first legislative action in 2006 is the Federal Accountability Act, designed to increase transparency and oversight in most all aspects of government decision making. Furthermore, the government has promised to proceed with a planned review of access to information laws and how they can be strengthened.

What will be important to watch is the extent to which this emphasis on openness and strengthened accountability extends into the realm of security or rather stops short. The CBSA is a case in point: criticized by Senate members and others for being overly secretive in its operations (often refusing to divulge performance-related information pertaining to its activities on national security grounds), the conservative platform promises to bolster this agency's resources but says little as to whether its governance will be altered. Similarly, the conservatives have said little as to their intentions regarding a proposed Parliamentary Committee on National Security, a pending and much delayed effort to foster stronger democratic monitoring and awareness of the greatly expanded security apparatus of the past few years.[13]

Along with political platforms the findings from two judicial inquiries also represent an important variable. The first, the Gomery Commission, created in the aftermath of the so-called federal sponsorship scandal stemming from corrupt contracting practices between the Liberal Party and advertising companies in Quebec in the aftermath of the 1995 provincial referendum on sovereignty, concluded its efforts on February 1, 2006. A major factor in the demise of the previous government, the thrust of this commission has been to reinforce conservative directions for openness and accountability, both politically and within the public service. The result is likely to be at least a modest reduction in secrecy in many aspects of federal operations, particularly with regard to financial and program management. As noted, the extension of this reduction into the epicenter of government secrecy—security and public safety—remains to be seen.

Perhaps the most important influence on this latter question is the second judicial inquiry set to report later in 2006. The Arar Commission, established to investigate the deportation of a Syrian-born Canadian, Maher Arar, from the United States to Syria, where he was held and tortured for more than one year, carries implications for information management and accountability both domestically and bilaterally (i.e.,

appropriate levels and mechanisms of cooperation with U.S. authorities). The commission itself has faced resistance from the previous government during its hearings regarding the public release of various information sources deemed overly sensitive, and it has been far less publicly visible and galvanizing than that of Gomery. Nonetheless, its findings are likely to strengthen the case for openness and oversight in the realm of security, and the conservatives will face important decisions in terms of their response and the impacts on the public's trust in public sector governance and information management.

The final thematic dimension then is Canada–U.S. relations and whether the conservatives are likely to embrace closer ties with the U.S. on key matters of trade, defense, and security. Regarding the latter realm of security, there is pressure from the private sector in Canada to more aggressively pursue what may be termed a form of political interoperability via more integrated governance mechanisms (despite little evidence that such an agenda would gather traction in Washington[14]). There is some tension here between the common conservative orientations of President Bush and Prime Minister Harper (and the feeling in both countries that relations have deteriorated in recent years under Liberal rule, a dynamic not limited to Canada of course) and the latter's calls for the bolstering of Canadian defense forces and more assertions of Canadian sovereignty (particularly in the Arctic where Canadian claims are resisted by the U.S. and, indeed, many other countries).

On the whole, however, there is little reason to expect a departure from the trend of this decade of U.S.-led security efforts shaping Canadian policy and governmental organization. While the previous government pursued continental alignment and interoperability in a largely reactionary manner, often disconnected from the more contentious political discourse of trade disputes and sovereignty assertions, the conservative government will need to reconcile both continental and domestic pressures in balancing openness and democratic accountability with ongoing pressures for secrecy that are prevalent in the realm of security.

REFERENCES

Allen, B.A., Paquet, G., Juillet, L. & Roy, J. (2005). E-government as collaborative governance: Structural, accountability and cultural reform. In M. Khosrow-Pour (Ed.), *Practicing e-government: A global perspective* (pp. 1-15). Hershey: Idea Group.

Auditor General of Canada. (2003). *Information technology: Government online.* Ottawa: Government of Canada.

Auditor General of Canada. (2004). *National security in Canada—the 2001 anti-terrorism initiative.* Ottawa: Government of Canada.

Auditor General of Canada. (2005). *Passport services.* Ottawa: Government of Canada.

Bennett, C.J., & Raab, C. (2003). *The governance of privacy.* Burlington: Ashgate.

Coe, A. (2004). *Government online in Canada: Innovation and accountability in 21st century government.* Cambridge: Kennedy School of Government.

Curtin, G., Sommer, M.H., & Vis-Sommer, V. (Eds.). (2003). *The world of e-government.* New York: Haworth Press.

Denning, D. (2003). *Information technology and security.* In M. Brown (Ed.), *Grave new world—security challenges in the 21st century.* Washington, DC: Georgetown University Press.

Dutta, A., & McCrohan, K. (2002). Management's role in information security in a cyber economy. *California Management Review, 45*(1), 67-87.

Fountain, J.E. (2001). *Building the virtual state: Information technology and institutional change.* Washington, DC: Brookings Institution Press.

Hayden, P. (2005). *Cosmopolitan global politics.* Burlington: Ashgate.

Heeks, R. (Ed.). (1999). *Reinventing government in the information age—international practice in IT-enabled public sector reform.* London: Routledge.

Heymann, P.B. (2002). Dealing with terrorism: An overview. *International Security, 26*(3), 24-38.

Juillet, L., & Paquet, G. (2002). *The neurotic state. How Ottawa spends 2002-2003: The security aftermath and national priorities* (pp. 69-87). Don Mills: Oxford University Press.

Loukidelis, D. (2004). *Identity, privacy, security—can technology really reconcile them? An address by BC's Privacy Commissioner.* Victoria: Office of the Privacy Commissioner.

O'Harrow, R. (2004). *No place to hide.* New York: The Free Press.

Open the Government. (2005, April). *Secrecy report card—an update.* Retrieved from *www.openthegovernment.org*

Paquet, G. (2000). The new governance, subsidiarity and the strategic state. *Proceedings of the OECD Forum for the Future Conference on 21st Century Governance: Power in the Global Knowledge Economy and Society,* Hannover, Germany.

Pastor, R. (2003). *North America's second decade.* Retrieved from *http://www.foreignaffairs.org*

Posner, R.A. (2006). *Remaking domestic intelligence.* Stanford: Hoover Institution Press.

Reid, J. (2004). Holding governments accountable by strengthening access to information laws and information management practices. In L. Oliver & L. Sanders (Eds.), *E-government reconsidered: Renewal of governance for the knowledge age.* Regina: Canadian Plains Research Center.

Roy, J. (2005a). Services, security, transparency and trust: Government online or governance renewal in Canada? *International Journal of E-Government Research, 1*(1), 48-58.

Roy, J. (2005b). Security, sovereignty and continental interoperability: Canada's elusive balance. *Social Science Computer Review, 22*(2), 1-17.

Roy, J. (2006a). *E-government in Canada: Transformation for the digital age.* Ottawa: University of Ottawa Press.

Roy, J. (2006b). E-service delivery and new governance capacities: 'Service Canada' as a case study. *International Journal of Services Technology and Management.*

Salter, M. (2004). Passports, mobility and security: How smart can the border be? *International Studies Perspective, 5,* 71-91.

Scholl, H. (2005). Motives, strategic approach, objectives and focal points in e-government-induced change. *International Journal of E-Government Research, 1*(1), 59-78.

Sirmakessis, S. (2004). *Text mining and its applications.* Heidelberg: Springer.

Turner, T. (2004). Accountability in cross-tier e-government integration. In J. Halligan & T. Moore (Eds.), *Future challenges for e-government.* Canberra: Government of Australia.

Worthen, B. (2005). The sky really is falling. *CIO Magazine,* (October 1).

KEY TERMS

Data Mining: Digitally and virtually trolling through massive amounts of information gathered in raw form, and then analyzing the information for meaningful patterns or events.

E-Government: The usage of new policy tools and organizational processes involving digital technologies in order to improve public sector capacities.

Function Creep: The deployment of information strategies and computer systems by governments for one purpose that extends to other, unintended or unannounced purposes and objectives.

Governance: Mechanism of coordinating resources, making decisions, and structuring accountability.

Identity Management: Policies and technologies that enable authenticated identities to be verified in order to confirm and enable access or transactions between individuals and organizations.

Interoperability: The ability of different information and computer systems to exchange data and enable communication and coordination across different organizations or sub-systems within an organization in order to participate in shared governance systems.

Smart Border: The usage of new technologies to improve cross-border flows of people and commerce while also bolstering security capacities aimed at criminal and terrorist activities.

ENDNOTES

[1] The results of such surveys are summarized in the annual reports for the GOL exercise (http://www.tbs-sct.gc.ca/organisation/ciob-ddpi_e.asp).

[2] www.canada.gc.ca

[3] There are three main sub-selections from the main portal: Canadians, non-Canadians, and businesses, the logic being that the sorts of information and services required by online visitors generally falls into one of these three camps.

[4] n its 2005 GOL Annual Report, the Government of Canada reports that over 40% of individual tax returns were filed online in 2003 (a level expected to increase to over 50% by 2005) and more than 90% of federal job applications are now received online.

[5] http://www.pwgsc.gc.ca/text/factsheets/secure_channel-e.html

[6] Indeed, many scholars distinguish between information and knowledge management, underscoring the latter when organizations refine and make use of information to facilitate learning and the pursuit of specific objectives. Accordingly, knowledge management is a useful prism to examine and understand many aspects of defense, intelligence, and homeland security (Desouza & Vanapalli, 2005). While acknowledging to the distinction and its relevance, this article will not pursue it, referring exclusively to information as all forms of data inside and outside of governments.

[7] This estimate was reported by 'GlobalSecurity.org', an American observatory and research group devoted to security, defense, and intelligence matters.

[8] Main findings of an August 2004 Report by the Office of the Inspector General (OIG-04-31). The report underscores the challenges of deploying information technologies in a uniquely large and fluid organizational context (similar concerns have been raised by the Canadian Auditor General with respect to Canadian authorities: see the section on "Secrecy and Interoperability"). It also noteworthy here that mismanagement and weak comptrollership are charges made regularly by critics of the Pentagon (both inside and outside of Congress), the point being that it is hardly unusual to witness large bureaucracies facing

operational difficulties with such huge amounts of dollars (and DHS faces the additional pressures of an accelerated and politically charged formation period).

9   In 1999, for example, 126,809,769 pages of government information were declassified. By 2004, this number had dropped to 28,413,690 (Open the Government, 2005).

10   The minister is also responsible for a portfolio of six agencies: Canada Border Services Agency, Canada Firearms Center, Canadian Security Intelligence Service, Correctional Service of Canada, National Parole Board, and the Royal Canadian Mounted Policy.

11   http://www.cbsa-asfc.gc.ca/newsroom/factsheets/2004/0124passenger-e.html

12   The Privacy Commissioner of BC has voiced his concern against surveillance and data-mining efforts, underlining 'function creep' as a serious threat (Loukidelis, 2004). He also underscores problems of secrecy and complexity that impede public accountability and that raise the prospect of unintended consequences.

13   Such a committee would not have oversight powers in an American Congressional sense, but it would mark the first time in the Canadian Parliamentary model that elected officials (other than cabinet ministers) are brought under the purview of national security. In one of the many contentious issues debated over the past three years, such a committee would seemingly report to Parliament indirectly via the Prime Minister, and its members would face stiff secrecy and confidentiality requirements regarding their ability to receive and subsequently disclose information provided by security authorities.

14   Still, proponents of this direction—inspired by the work of Pastor (2003) and others—point to modest steps in recent times such as the trilateral vision endorsed by prominent representatives of Canada, the U.S., and Mexico. and released by the Council of Foreign Relations (at a time chosen in part to coincide with the North American Leaders Summit in Waco, Texas, in March 2005). From this summit, North American leaders agreed to form the Security and Prosperity Partnership of North American (www.spp.gov).

Security Model for Educational Satellite Networks

Sanjay Jasola
Indira Gandhi National Open University, New Delhi

Ramesh C. Sharma
Indira Gandhi National Open University, New Delhi

INTRODUCTION

Education has been the greatest tool for human resources development. The advances in information and communication technology has brought out a paradigm shift in the educational sector by making it more accessible, relevant, qualitative, and equitable for the masses. The use of satellite technology like INTELSAT, PEACESAT, and ATS in education has enhanced the opportunities for learners to acquire new skills (Moore & Kearsley, 1996). Both on-campus and distance mode students can be benefited by it. The satellite technology can serve a large geographical area. It allows audio and video signals uplinked from a station to be received to any number of downlink earth stations (Willis, 1995). Oliver (1994) reported that the transmission costs do not increase with the increase in the number of downlink stations. Satellite Instructional Television Experiment (SITE), one of the India's early experiments conducted during 1975 to 1976, produced and transmitted 150 different science programs of 10 to 12 minutes duration, offering them to more than 2,330 villages in six geographical clusters. According to Shrestha (1997) and Govindaraju and Banerjee (1999), this experiment demonstrates the effectiveness of satellite communication for educational purposes.

EduSat is the first exclusive educational satellite of India (*www.edusatindia.org* and *www.ignou.ac.in*), especially designed to provide satellite- based education through the audio-visual medium by employing DTH (direct-to-home) quality broadcast (*www.edusatindia.org*). A complete nationwide coverage is ensured through multiple regional beams. There are five Ku-band transponders with spot beams covering northern, northeastern, eastern, southern, and western regions of India. The entire Indian mainland is covered through the footprint of one national beam of a Ku-band transponder and six channels through extended C-band transponders. A two-way video communication system, Space Collaboration System (SCS), is being used as a cooperative distance education project between Japan, China, and Thailand (Tanigawa, Ileura, Anzai, & Kaneko, 2002). A Direct Broadcast Satellite (DBS) is being used extensively in the United States by the learners to receive educational programs at home or offices through a small inexpensive satellite dish, which soon would take over video broadcasting and narrowcasting (Moore & Kearsley, 2005). The University of the South Pacific also offers distance education to its 12 member countries through its own satellite communication network (USPNet) (see http://www.usp.ac.fj). USPNet is used for audio conferencing among various campuses, and video broadcast of live or pre-recorded lectures.

RELATED RESEARCH

The EduSat network operates under several different operating systems, a variety of Web-based and client/server applications, and other components from several vendors. This heterogeneous network introduces a high level of complexity when it comes to management and security issues. This complexity makes it impossible to effectively secure an entire networking environment with a single component such as a firewall. Such situation calls for a total information security solution, which includes policy and procedure, access control, user authentication, encryption, and content security. By focusing a security solution on only an individual component, such as access control or an encryption method, one risks leaving holes in the security shield that can be exploited by a hacker (Cheswick & Bellovin, 2000). The EduSat network is mainly utilized as the data transport mechanism, so one can expect various attacks mounted from the underlying infrastructure. The attacks may not necessarily be aimed at the network, but also at the resources attached to the network and the information contained within. These attacks can be of various forms and impact corporate information resources in a variety of ways. The typical points of network vulnerabilities are weak administrative and user passwords, modem connections, system back doors, poor user adherence to security policy, and poorly configured firewalls and Web hosts. The corruption or compromise of data is accomplished in a variety of ways. Corporate data can be damaged, destroyed, and/or stolen when not properly protected. These attacks do not always originate from outside of the trusted environment. The different types of attacks that satellite-based information systems are subjected to are: social engineering, viruses/trojan horses, denial of service (DoS), IP spoofing, worm, replay attack, and theft of information (Oppliger, 1997).

Skinnemoen et al. (2004) proposed a consolidated approach for IP over satellite networks based on open standard DVB-RCS (Digital Video Broadcasting–Return Channel via Satellite). Cruickshank et al. (2005) offered measures for securing multicast in DVB-RCS satellite systems. The overview of the VIP-TEN project architecture and VoIP measurement campaign over the EuroSkyWay test-bed have been presented by Cruickshank et al. (2001). Togel et al. (2005) deployed IP telephony over satellite links and QoS as the enabling technology for the combination of data and voice service. The level of service quality achieved on LAN and satellite links by using QoS mechanisms (available, off–the–shelf routers and switches) has been discussed in Feltrin et al. (2003). Nguyen et al. (2001) reported the performance results of laboratory experiments for VoIP over satellite under different link and traffic conditions. A security system for satellite networks was developed by Cruickshank (1996). Noubir and Von Allmen (1999) have also discussed security issues in Internet protocols over satellite links.

OVERVIEW OF THE SECURITY MODEL

The implementation of a security model within the EduSat network has been achieved in the following, step-by-step manner:

1. **Development of an IT Security Policy:** The development of an IT security policy is carried

out in three steps. First, the security level required and appropriate for the company is determined. The IT Security Committee (ITSC) is established with the task of attaining and maintaining the desired level of security. The ITSC then prepares the Internal Security Standards (ISSs).

2. **Elaboration of the Internal Security Standards:** In order to implement security targets, security standards are compiled based on a detailed risk analysis for applications requiring high-level protection and the use of standard security guidelines.

3. **Implementation of the IT Security Standards:** By defining priorities, designating responsible staff, and planning the realization of objectives, the ISS are implemented according to plan.

4. **Training and Awareness:** A training concept is developed in order to prepare all levels of the organization, from management to the end users, to increase their awareness of the security guidelines, to provide the necessary explanations regarding correct IT usage, and to ensure adherence to these guidelines.

5. **Ongoing Security Management:** The IT security process does not end when ISSs have been implemented, but requires periodical controls, which, in case of changes, also provide for the updating of the system security concept. The reactions to any incidents relevant to security are also monitored in order to limit damage and avoid repetition.

IMPLEMENTING THE IT SECURITY PROCESS

The first step in development of an information security model is to establish a high-level security policy. A security policy establishes the rules or protocol under which the entire organization or company will be required to operate. The protocols established in an organization's security policy are incorporated into the daily habits of every employee. The policy is backed up by an ISO 17799-based standards or procedures document that specifies the access control requirements for information and other assets throughout the organization. A typical security standards document will include information like: host and network marking requirements, host security control requirements, network security control requirements, monitoring and alert management, Internet and intranet access, authorization and access controls, data backup and restoration, encryption technology, move/add/change management, auditing functions, physical security, and accountability and responsibility. There are many hardware and software components that make up a comprehensive security model. These components or sub-systems will vary in size, capacity, processing power, and traffic throughput. The categories of security sub-systems and the core technologies are: firewalls (Chapman & Zwicky, 1995), encryption standards (McMahon, 1998), certificate authorities, authentication mechanisms, remote access services, intrusion detection/response, and logging/audit.

The action plan previously summarized is described in detail below. This detailed framework is followed to achieve proper implementation.

Development of an IT Security Policy

The development of an IT security policy took place in three steps. First, the appropriate security level for the organization was determined. Then the ITSC was established with the task of attaining and maintaining this security level. The team then developed the IT security policy of the organization.

Determining the Security Level

It is not possible to achieve 100% security either in everyday life or in security (Anonymous, 1997). Security is viewed as a cost-benefit factor (www.gocsi.com). The value of securing an object must not exceed the value

of the object itself. Each resource in an organization needs a value associated with it. This value will determine the amount of security, if any, applied to the resource. This is where the cost-benefit analysis plays a critical role. The effort and resources expended to secure an item should not exceed the value of the item. Determining the value of an object can be difficult, but assigning an object to one of the following four value categories can be helpful, as shown in Table 1.

Creation of the IT Security Committee

The tasks required to attain and maintain the IT security level desired are controlled and coordinated by one body in the company. This body is described as the "ITSC." The most important aspects for the establishment of the ITSC are:

- The overall responsibility for the correct and reliable fulfillment of tasks (and thus IT security) rests with the management.
- The responsibility for IT security at the various hosts/workstations are delegated in precisely the same manner as the responsibility for the original task.
- The results of the above are set down in an IT security policy document. When initiating the IT security process, it is important that management emphasizes the importance of security throughout the organization. The security policy describes the level of security that the organization is aiming at and how this safety level affects the tasks and duties of the organization. All members of staff are made aware of the fact that commitment, co-

Table 1. Value categories

Value	Definition
Unclassified	Distribution of this material is not limited. This includes any information cleared for release to the public. Data on public Internet servers shall be unclassified. Unclassified systems are not specifically restricted by this security doctrine.
Confidential	Disclosure of this information could cause measurable damage to the organization as a whole. Confidential material should be safeguarded at all times, but trusted employees are permitted to access confidential information.
Secret	Disclosure of this information would cause serious damage to the organization as a whole. This includes trade secrets or information that if released to competitors could cause the loss.
Top Secret	Disclosure of this information would cause grave and irreparable harm to the organization as a whole. This includes legal documents, high-level strategies, and proprietary secrets upon which the organization is based.

operation, and responsibility are expected of them with regard to the fulfillment of tasks in general, but also with regard to security. The IT security policy document addresses the significance of IT security, the importance of IT for the completion of business, the desired level of security of the organization, the security targets for the IT users, a report on the establishment of the ITSC, appointment of the information security officer, and the explanation of the responsibility of the staff for IT security. This document successfully fulfills its function, when it is known throughout the entire organization. Every person is made aware of it. Equally important is that management makes clear that it fully supports this document and the goals it contains.

Preparing the Security Concepts and Guidelines Document

In order to be able to implement these security goals defined in the security policy, an analysis of the risks is made to meet the particular requirements of the organization. This assessment concentrates on finding ways to reduce all risks as quickly and cost effectively as possible. No matter how small a risk may appear to be, it is always advisable to have a detailed analysis for it and not to treat any serious risk superficially. The following strategy is used in the EduSat network to find the right balance between these extremes.

Starting with the IT systems, the applications are identified. After determining the protection requirement of the IT applications and information, the protection requirement of the IT systems (on which these IT applications and information are processed) is determined. This protection requirement states how important it is to protect the system from damage. If this potential damage is acceptable, it is recommended to use Standard Security Guidelines (SSGs) for this system. If major damage is feared, however, the risks are investigated in detail using a risk analysis and are subsequently reduced. This procedure, which combines the benefits of SSG and risk analysis, allows effective and appropriate Internal Security Standards to be selected in a timesaving and inexpensive manner. At the same time, it is possible to adequately protect the systems, which require a high degree of protection. A risk will remain after implementation of the selected ISS, as 100% security can never be attained. After the

remaining risk has been determined, it is the task of the management to decide whether this risk is acceptable. If not, further SSGs must be defined which then reduce the remaining risk to an acceptable level.

Implementation of the Internal Security Standards

After all Internal Security Standards for protection against the known risks have been identified, a plan for the implementation of these ISSs is drawn up. This plan contains all short, medium, and long-term actions required for the implementation of the selected ISS. This plan contains a list of the security standards to be implemented for each system, the related costs in the form of investments, labor, training and so forth. This also includes the priorities; a budget and a timeframe; a list of the actions, projects, and so forth required for the implementation of the measures; monitoring possibilities such as specific allocation of responsibilities and resources; and definition of control mechanisms for the implementation. In addition, most Internal Security Standards require a suitable organization environment in order to be fully effective (Peltier, 2000). The information security officer is, in general, responsible for preparing the implementation plans within the organization.

Training and Awareness Measures

The training and security awareness program affects all areas of the organization, from senior academics to end users. This program explains the IT security policy in the organization and ensures that the rules and regulations regarding security are understood. Understanding and motivation are essential to the fulfillment of IT security goals. End user training makes or mars a network security implementation. If the end user is not properly trained and informed on the corporate security structure, it would be easy to compromise the network via a social attack. An uninformed and untrained end user can negate all of the electronic security measures in place. The aim of this training program is to ensure that all employees are aware of the importance of IT applications and information, and that a loss of confidentiality, integrity, or accessibility can have serious consequences for both the institution and employees. The training and awareness courses are repeated at regular intervals in order to refresh existing knowledge and to inform new employees. Further, all new, promoted, or transferred employees are trained in security to the extent required by the position held. The most important aspect of this training and awareness program, however, is that it is planned and implemented in good time. Training and Internal Security Standards are not particularly effective if they are implemented years after these measures have been introduced.

Ongoing Security Management

This is an often-overlooked important facet of security. ISS not implemented or out-of-date, passwords left on the screen, and open firewall ports are all common occurrences. It is thus necessary to check whether the ISSs are in place, whether they are adhered to, whether they fulfill the requirements during current operation, and whether they are still relevant or should be altered after changes have taken place. Incidents relating to security are required to be treated correctly. The information security officer is responsible for coordinating these ongoing security management activities throughout the organization.

LAYERED SECURITY MODEL

There are three layers in the EduSat network which have been implemented for ensuring security. The layered model ensures that the systems are protected using multiple security strategies so that in case of failure of one strategy, the other can protect the system and data.

Level 1 Security Actions

This layer is like the four walls and the roof of a secure house. It includes firewalls, routers, proxy servers, the application servers, Web servers, and mail servers. While traffic is regulated at the perimeter depending on the needs of the organization, the applications utilizing the traffic run on different application/Web servers, which in turn run on operating systems. An abuse of operating system privileges can potentially compromise network security. Users with access to the underlying operating system can jeopardize the availability and integrity of the firewall and expose critical

network resources to both internal and external security threats. Hardening this layer protects the network from a number of internal threats. Vulnerabilities exist in operating systems, Web servers, proxy servers, mail servers and application servers that need patches/service packs/hotfixes to fill those holes. Some of the general practices that have been implemented are:

- Placed the servers and communication equipment in a secure room.
- Given restricted access to server/communication room.
- Using server consoles are avoided as much as possible.
- Disabled CD-ROM or floppy disk boot.
- Online warnings have been implemented to inform each user of the rules for access to an organization's systems. Without such warnings, internal and external attackers can often avoid prosecution even if they are caught.
- A protective net of filters have been established to detect and eradicate viruses—covering workstations (PCs), servers, and gateways. Ensure that virus signatures are kept up to date.
- Back-ups are taken regularly so that files can be restored from those backups.
- Logging for important system-level events and for services and proxies are enabled, and set up a log archiving facility. Systems without effective logging are blind and make it difficult to learn what happened during an attack, or even whether an attack actually was successful.
- System audits are performed to learn who is using the system, to assess the existence of open ports for outsiders to use, and to review several other security-related factors about the system.
- The information security officer or his/her designate runs password-cracking software to identify easy-to-guess passwords. Weak passwords allow attackers to appear as "authorized" users. That allows them to test weaknesses until they find ways to take control of those systems.
- The network is scanned to create and maintain a complete map of systems to which users are connected.
- Intrusion detection is implemented for the important servers to enable immediate response to unauthorized access.

- An incident response team has been identified and the procedures to be used to respond to various types of attacks are established.

Level 2 Security Operations

Once the perimeter defense is tightened and the OS fine-tuned, there is a need to look at another threat from the internal workstations connected to the network. A national survey showed that 70-80% of attacks are internal, that is, from within the organization's internal network (Carnegie Mellon CERT Coordination Center, n.d.). However, having only this strategy is not enough to protect any network and valuable information. One of the common attacks on this layer is the DoS (Denial of Service) attack, which involves flooding the point of connection to the outside world with unproductive traffic. This brings communications with the Internet to a standstill. Some of the common DoS attacks on routers are Smurf, Syn, Ack, and Rst attacks. There is a need to have host security for two reasons: to protect against someone trying to attack from within the network and to protect the data stored on a workstation from someone coming in through the firewall. Some of the key implementations done at this layer are listed below:

- User access policy is formulated and implemented.
- The patches/hotfixes are regularly updated for the workstation operating system and applications.
- The network resources access is restricted from workstations. Only what is a "MUST REQUIRED" is assigned.
- Anti-virus software is installed and updated regularly on all the workstations.
- Workstation data is included in daily nightly backups.
- Modems are not allowed on workstations.
- Only one user is allowed to login on each workstation.
- Maximum logging is enabled for workstations.
- A personal firewall is installed on all workstations.
- Faulty or old hard disk drives are removed and crashed when not using them.
- Access control lists (ACLs) are set on critical files, directories, and routers.

- The latest applicable patches are implemented. Unnecessary services are removed and operating system settings on each host are tightened.

Level 3 Security Operations

ISO makes a significant difference in improving security by implementing the actions of Level 1 and Level 2 operations. However, this can be thwarted partially or completely by security breaches caused by one or a combination of factors involving people who use those computers and networks. Level 3 operations are designed to help reduce the chance that such security breaches will occur. These actions are focused on overcoming organizational impediments to security and may be more difficult to implement than those in Level 1 and Level 2. There is an acute need for Level 3 security actions. Banking executives and senior military officials with experience analyzing the causes of multiple successful attacks have demonstrated the strongest support for Level 3 operations:

- Configuration management (which controls the introduction of new systems to the network) are implemented.
- A regular network mapping and scanning has been implemented to ensure compliance with new system introduction controls.
- Specific programs are deployed to reduce the chance that newly deployed applications introduce unexpected vulnerabilities.
- Security awareness education programs are launched to help users know what to do in case they encounter a potential security breach and how users can avoid unsafe computing.
- Encryption has been implemented to avoid disclosure of sensitive information traveling over the network.

CONCLUSION

Security in the EduSat network cannot be achieved by merely implementing various security systems, tools, or products. However, security failures are less likely through the implementation of security policy, process, procedure, and product(s). Multiple layers of defense have been applied to design a fail-safe security system for this network. The idea behind multi-layered defense security in EduSat is to manage the security risk with multiple defensive strategies, so that if one layer of defense turns out to be inadequate, another layer of defense will, ideally, prevent a full breach. It is believed that, at a minimum, managers must apply a range of security perimeter defenses so that EduSat network resources are not exposed to external attacks. It has also been ensured that the security system is not limited by the weakest link of the security layer.

REFERENCES

Anonymous. (1997). *Maximum security: A hacker's guide to protecting your Internet SITE and network.* Sams.net Publishing.

Carnegie Mellon CERT Coordination Center. (n.d.). Retrieved from http://www.cert.org/nav/index_red.html

Chapman, D.B., & Zwicky, E.D. (1995). *Building Internet firewalls.* O'Reilly & Associates.

Cheswick, W.R., & Bellovin, S.M. (2000). *Firewalls and Internet security, repelling the wily hacker.* Boston: Addison-Wesley.

Cruickshank, H. et al. (2001). Analysis of IP voice conferencing over EuroSkyWay Satellite system. *IEEE Proceedings of Communication, 148*(4), 202-206.

Cruickshank, H., Howarth, M.P., Iyengar, S., Sun, Z., & Claverotte, L. (2005). Securing multicast in DVB-RCS satellite systems. *IEEE Wireless Communications, 12*(5), 38-45.

Cruickshank, H.S. (1996, May 13-15). A security system for satellite networks. *Proceedings of the 5th International Conference on Satellite Systems for Mobile Communications and Navigation, 1996.*

Feltrin, E. et al. (2003). An IP based satellite network for distance learning. *Proceedings of the IEEE International Conference on Information Technology: Research and Education* (pp. 416-420).

Govindaraju, P., & Banerjee, I. (1999). A retrospective view of the countrywide classroom in India. *Journal of Educational Media, 24*(2), 103-116.

McMahon, P. (1998, December 6-11). PKI discussion. *Proceedings of the 14th Annual ACSA Conference,* Phoenix, AZ.

Moore, M., & Kearsley, G. (1996). *Distance education: A systems view.* Belmont, CA: Wadsworth.

Moore, M., & Kearsley, G. (2005). *Distance education: A systems view.* Belmont, CA: Wadsworth.

Nguyen, T. et al. (2001). Voice over IP service and performance in satellite networks. *IEEE Communications Magazine,* 164-171.

Noubir, G., & Von Allmen, L. (1999, September 19-22). Security issues in Internet protocols over satellite links. *Proceedings of the 50th IEEE VTS* (vol. 5, pp. 2726-2730).

Oppliger, R. (1997). *Internet and intranet security.* Boston/London: Artech House.

Oliver, E.L. (1994). Video tools for distance education. In B. Willis (Ed.), *Distance education: Strategies and tools.* Englewood Cliffs, NJ: Educational Technology.

Peltier, T.R. (2000). *Information system security policies and procedures: A practitioners' reference.* New York: PHI.

Shrestha, G. (1997, March). *A review of case studies related to distance education in developing countries.* Retrieved from http://www.undp.org/info21/public/review/pb-revke.html

Skinnemoen, H. et al. (2004). Interactive IP network via satellite DVB-RCS. *IEEE Journal on Selected Areas in Communications, 22,* 508-517.

Tanigawa, T., Ileura, T., Anzai, M., & Kaneko, I. (2002). Development of distance learning system by using satellite communication network. *System and computer in Japan, 33*(8), 41-50.

Togel, R. et al. (2005). Deploying IP telephony over satellite networks. *Proceedings of the International Conference on IEEE* (pp. 624-628).

Willis, B. (1995). *Distance education at a glance.* College of Engineering, Engineering Outreach, University of Idaho, USA. Retrieved from http://www.uidaho.edu/eo/distglan.html#index

KEY TERMS

Corporate Information Resources: Essential components of corporate information resources include various databases, servers, IT infrastructures, and so forth.

Data Transport Mechanism: Refers to the use of various protocols for communication of data (voice, video, text) over the Internet. The most commonly used protocol suite is TCP/IP.

EduSat: The first exclusive satellite of India for serving the educational sector which is put into the geo-stationary orbit. It is specially configured to meet the growing demand for an interactive satellite-based distance education system in India through audio-visual medium, employing direct-to-home (DTH) quality broadcast.

Firewall: A device or system that enforces an access control policy between two networks. In principle, the firewall provides two basic services: (1) blocks undesirable traffic, and (2) permits desirable traffic.

Social Engineering: A technique used by attackers to gain system access or information by exploiting the basic human instinct to be helpful. In most cases, social engineering exploits are successful because the targeted enterprise lacks an awareness program to educate employees of their security-related duties and responsibilities.

Total Information Security System: A comprehensive set of processes, protocols, IT-infrastructure, skilled and trained manpower, and so forth required to ensure protection from physical and logical threat.

S

Security of Communication and Quantum Technology

Gregory Paperin
Monash University, Australia

INTRODUCTION

In this article we aim to analyze some of the advances in security of communication since this discipline evolved and to pinpoint the main problems. We then introduce a modern attempt to solve some of these problems, in particular the key distribution problem, by using the theory of quantum mechanics to construct a communication system that automatically detects eavesdropping. We examine some of the implications of quantum mechanics relevant to this field and then introduce a selection of communication protocols based on them. Finally we examine how secure these protocols are and identify their potential weaknesses.

BACKGROUND

Traditional Cryptography and the Key Distribution Problem

Ever since people began to use remote communication systems, they have been concerned with the security of the messages they send. Two main problems were recognized thousands of years ago and still remain the main problems in the field of communication security:

- How do we make sure that only authorized recipients will read and understand a message?
- How do we verify the authenticity of a message—that is, how do we check that the sender is really the person he or she claims to be and that the message has not been altered on the way?

Since ancient times two types of approaches have attempted to solve these problems:

- make the communication channel so secure that the message cannot be interrupted before reaching the authorized recipient (secure channel); and

- encode the message in a way such that even if the message is intercepted, no unauthorized person can read and understand it (encryption).

A combination of these two methods is usually the most promising. But how can this be achieved?

Historians report tricks that ancient Romans used to encode their messages (e.g., Cesar Cipher) (ArticSoft, 2003; Singh, 1999)—for example the use of a table to substitute letters for other letters. Only someone possessing such a table could decipher the message.

In 1466, Leon Battista Alberti invented and published the first poly-alphabetic cipher, which was not as liable to statistical analysis as simple substitution ciphers. This class of ciphers was not broken until the 1800s. The most famous cipher of this type is Vigenere, a variation of which is still today considered to be the only absolutely secure encoding method. Unfortunately it requires a key as long as the message, which can be used only once and is therefore hardly practical. Alberti also wrote extensively on the state of the art in ciphers, putting cryptography on a proper scientific foundation for the first time. (New Order, 2003).

These and similar approaches rely on the sender and the receiver having exclusive knowledge of the key used to encode and decode the message. If someone else were to get a hold of this information, he or she could interrupt and read the message or even forge one. This constitutes the key distribution problem: how can we securely let the authorized recipients (or senders) know the cipher key without allowing it to become public?

Usually, the encryption key needs only be communicated once. After that, many messages can be sent securely using that key. This lowers the probability of successful eavesdropping, but does not remove it.

During World War II the German army used an encryption device called Enigma. This electromechanical device consisted of a complicated system of rotors and included a plug board allowing the user of Enigma to swap any letter for any other letter. The use of this

Figure 1. A classical crypto-communication system: Alice, the sender, encrypts the plaintext P into the cipher text C using a secret key K, which she shares only with Bob, the authorized receiver, and sends C over an otherwise insecure channel, on which Eve is eavesdropping. Bob receives C and uses K to decrypt it to P. A secure channel is required for Alice and Bob to agree on K. (Lomonaco, 2002).

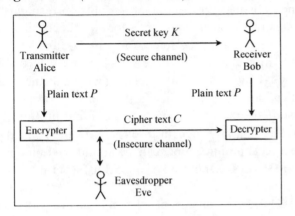

plug board increased the number of combinations of Enigma settings by a factor of 1015, which made a statistical analysis or a brute force attack (trying all possible keys) extremely hard. However, knowledge of the general encryption principle allowed British mathematicians, led by Alan Turing, eventually to crack the code.

Public Key Cryptography

With the appearance of modern communication technologies, the demand for secure communication increased. In the 1970s a new technique was devised to overcome some of the problems with key distribution. This new approach is known as Asymmetric-Key or Public-key cryptology.

The main idea of this approach is that there are now two keys: one to encrypt and another to decrypt the message. These keys are distinct, and it is infeasible to derive one from the other. The method constitutes a good attempt to solve the key distribution problem: for example, when a secret agent needs to send a message to his base, the base can broadcast the encryption key over a non-secure channel. Even if the enemy first interrupts the key and then the message sent back by the agent, the enemy will not be able to decrypt the message because the decryption key is kept secret.

An advantage of this system is that the algorithm used can be (and usually is) very well known to everyone—it does not provide any help in deciphering the text. Without the private decryption key, the message cannot be decoded.

However, how does the base know that the message was indeed sent by a trusted agent? To achieve such security the agent needs a second, private key, which is used to encrypt the message again. The problem of communicating that second key to the agent persists.

The algorithms used in modern public-key crypto-technology are based on the RSA algorithm (named after its inventors Rivest, Shamir, & Adelman, 1978), which is based on the prime factorization problem: it is computationally very intensive to factorize a very large number, if its only factors are two very large primes.

In RSA, one of two very large primes p and q is used as the private key and p • q is used as a public key. When p and q are sufficiently large (a few hundred digits), it will take the most efficient algorithm known today, running on the fastest supercomputer, many years to factorize p • q. By then, the secret information will be of no use.

There are, however, two major problems with this approach:

- The message may remain sensitive for a longer period of time and the sender may not want it decoded by unauthorized people even after many years.
- Currently, there is no known efficient factorization algorithm. However, there is no mathematical proof that such an algorithm exists. If such an algorithm was developed, all modern RSA-based encryption algorithms would become useless overnight.

This situation is not satisfactory in the long term. In particular, recent advances in quantum computing encourage scientists to look for alternatives to common RSA, since there is a known algorithm for a quantum computer to factorize large numbers efficiently. Once such machine has been built; it will be the end of conventional RSA-based approaches to encryption.

Interestingly, the same theory that promises to break RSA offers the basis for the technology that is set to provide a new level of communications security in the future.

Figure 2. A public key crypto-communication system: Alice looks up Bob's public encryption key (e.g., in a public key directory). She uses that key to encrypt the plaintext P to cipher text C. She then sends C over an insecure channel. Bob receives C and uses his private decryption key to transfer C back to P (Lomonaco, 2002).

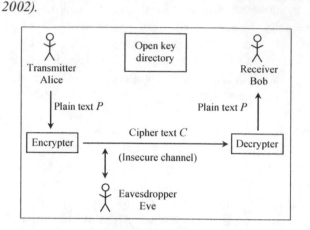

The Theory of Quantum Physics

Quantum mechanics is a theory in physics that deals with the behavior of matter and light on the atomic and subatomic scale. It attempts to describe and account for the properties of molecules and atoms and their constituents—elementary particles.

Three results of quantum theory are particularly important for encryption: entanglement, Heisenberg's Uncertainty Principle, and superposition.

Quantum entanglement is a quantum mechanical phenomenon in which the quantum states of two or more objects have to be described with reference to each other, even though the individual objects may be spatially separated. This leads to correlations between observable physical properties of systems that are stronger than any classical correlations. As a result, measurements performed on one system may be interpreted as "influencing" other systems entangled with it (Zeilinger, 1998; Einstein, Podolsky, & Rosen, 1935).

The Heisenberg Uncertainty Principle states that one cannot simultaneously know both the position and the velocity of a given object to arbitrary precision. Furthermore, it precisely quantifies the imprecision (Encyclopedia Britannica, 2006).

Quantum superposition occurs when an object simultaneously "possesses" two or more values for an observable quantity (e.g., horizontal and vertical polarization). Any observable quantity corresponds to an "eigenstate," and the linear combination of two or more eigenstates results in quantum superposition of two or more values of the quantity. If the quantity is measured, the projection postulate states that the state will randomly collapse onto one of the values in the superposition. Under certain circumstances, quanta obey the Heisenberg Uncertainty Principle, and a distinct state of one observable corresponds to a superposition of many states for the other observable (Zeilinger, 1998; Nielsen & Chuang, 2000).

Unfortunately, we have no space to even briefly discuss these fascinating phenomena and their implications, such as Young's two slit experiments. A good general introduction can be found in Zeilinger (1998), and an excellent discussion in the context of secure communication can be found in Lomonaco (2002). For a deeper analysis, see Einstein et al.'s (1935) seminal text.

These phenomena provide the theoretical background for various communication protocols, which have an extremely desirable property: they automatically detect eavesdropping.

Quantum Communication

Traditional crypto-techniques use mathematical approaches to protect transmissions from being decoded by eavesdroppers, whereas quantum cryptography uses the laws of physics. This science is very young; at present, it does not attempt to encode and transmit entire communications. It rather aims to provide a secure channel to communicate a short message, for example a key, which can then be used to encrypt and transmit information over a common channel, thereby solving the key distribution problem.

In fact, today's quantum cryptographic techniques do not even attempt to guarantee that the eavesdropper will not get a hold of the information; what they try to provide is secure knowledge about whether the message was interrupted. If communication partners know that their key has been intercepted by an eavesdropper, they can simply not use it.

There are various types of such quantum cryptosystems. Ekert (1995) classifies them as follows:

- cryptosystems with encoding based on two non-commuting observables proposed by Wiesner (1983) and by Bennett and Brassard (1984;

Figure 3. A quantum cryptographic communication system: The system consists of two communication channels. One is a classical public communication channel, the other is a secure quantum channel. Alice uses the quantum channel to tell Bob a secure encryption key K. Then Alice uses K to encrypt a message and send it to Bob over the public channel. Bob then uses K to decrypt the message to clear text and replies in the same way (Lomonaco, 2002).

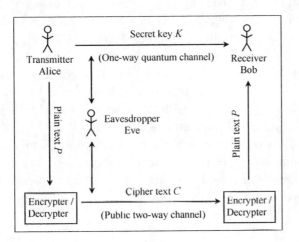

Bennett, Bessette, Brassard, Salvail, & Smolin, 1992);

- cryptosystems with encoding built upon quantum entanglement and the Bell Theorem proposed by Ekert (1991; Ekert, Rarity, Tepster, & Palma, 1992); and
- cryptosystems with encoding based on two non-orthogonal state vectors proposed by Bennett (1992).

The first type is the most widely used, and several experimental systems have been built using the BB84 and the B92 protocols based on this idea.

A sender will send photons in one of four polarizations—0°, 45°, 90°, or 135°—and a recipient measures the polarization of the received photons. According to the laws of quantum mechanics, the receiving apparatus can distinguish between the perpendicular polarizations (0° and 90°), or it can be quickly reconfigured to differentiate between the diagonal polarizations (45° and 135°). Importantly, the recipient cannot distinguish both types at the same time. The key is distributed in several steps. First, the sender chooses one of the four polarizations at random and sends photons. The recipient chooses a random measurement setup for

Figure 4a. Photon polarisation filtering. The bit-value represented by a photon is the oscillation direction of its field, i.e. its polarisation. Without loss of generality, the communicating parties agree that 1 is represented by photons with a polarisation of 0° or 45° and 0 is represented by photons with a polarisation of 90° or 135°.

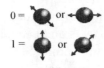

Figure 4b. Photon polarisation filtering. One filter can be used to distinguish between the upright polarised photons and another filter can be used to distinguish between diagonally polarised photons. When a photon passes through an appropriate filter its polarisation does not change.

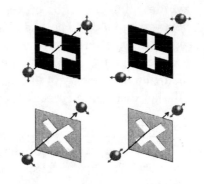

Figure 4c. Photon polarisation filtering. When a photon passes through an incorrect filter, its polarisation is randomly modified to one of the directions set by the filter.

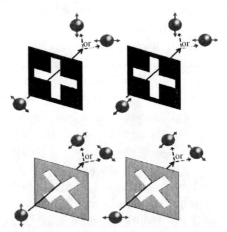

each incoming photon: either rectilinear or diagonal. The recipient records the measurement results and keeps them secret. At the next stage the recipient communicates the types of measurement it used to the sender over a public channel, while keeping the results secret. The sender tells the receiver for which of the measurements the correct setup was used. Then the sender and the receiver keep the results for which the correct measurement setup was used. These results are translated into 0s and 1s and become the key (Ekert, 1995; BB84 Quantum Coding Scheme, n.d.).

An eavesdropper necessarily introduces errors into such a transmission because he or she does not know the polarization type of each photon, and quantum mechanics does not allow them to acquire sharp values of two non-commuting observables (here upright and diagonal polarizations). The two legitimate users of the channel can test for eavesdropping by revealing a subset of the key and by checking the error rate (Ekert, 1995).

While eavesdropping cannot be prevented in this way, it will never go unnoticed, because even the most subtle and sophisticated effort to tap the channel will be detected. Whenever the communicating parties are not satisfied with the security of the channel, they can perform the key distribution process again (Ekert, 1995).

Systems based on quantum entanglement work somewhat differently. A sequence of correlated particle pairs is generated, and each party detects one member of each pair (e.g., a pair of Einstein-Podolsky-Rosen photons, created when fusing a positron and an electron; the polarizations of the photons are measured). An eavesdropper on this communication needs to detect a particle and then to resend it in order to remain unnoticed. But the act of detection of one particle of a pair will destroy its quantum correlation with the second particle. This can be detected by the two parties without revealing their own measurement results by communication over an open channel (Ekert, 1995).

The first quantum communication system developed at the IBM Thomas J. Watson Research Center used the BB84 protocol. It transmitted over a length of just 30 cm at a rate of 10 bits/s, but provided a proof of concept (Bennett & Brassard, 1984; Bennett et al., 1992). Since then, however, the quality of optical components has advanced, allowing for larger systems. A polarization-based system has been successfully employed over a distance of 1 km (Muller, Breguet, & Gisin, 1993),

quantum entanglement has been tested over 4 km (Tapster, Rarity, & Owens, 1994), while single-photon interference fringes have been produced in transmissions over a 10 km-long fiber optic cable (Townsend, Rarity, & Tapster, 1993; Ekert, 1995).

The first quantum communication products have already been commercialized. The company MagiQ runs a commercial quantum communication system in New York City, and the firm ID Quantique runs one in Geneva. Users of the systems include military and intelligence agencies, financial companies, and other firms that require the highest levels of security.

While these communication links are point-to-point connections, an actual quantum network, called the DARPA Quantum Network, is currently being developed at BBN Technologies of Cambridge, Massachusetts (Anderson & Kendall, 2003).

As companies become more concerned with communication security, these technologies will be developed further and are likely to become commonplace in the future.

DISCUSSION

The marketers of quantum networks speak of 100% security and absolutely unbreakable technology, protected by the laws of physics. But are quantum nets really perfectly secure?

Over time, the science of cryptography has learned one lesson for sure: the more trust you put in your security system, the easier it is to compromise.

The model on the basis of which quantum communication networks are developed is indeed unbreakable. Or more precisely, the theoretical model is indeed theoretically unbreakable. A real system that is engineered on the basis of such a theory will be a more or less good approximation to the model. How good and therefore how secure this approximation is depends on the state of the art of the engineering technologies used.

Let us see how the evil eavesdropper Eve can possibly interfere with the technology to achieve her malicious task.

In cryptosystems based on two non-commuting observables (such as BB84), the detection of eavesdropping is theoretically guaranteed because the quantum state of a particle (polarization of a photon) cannot be measured by an eavesdropper without altering it. This means, however, that a bit must be carried by one single photon; unfortunately, it is extremely difficult to realize this in practice. Normally, several (or even several thousand) photons will be sent in a burst to communicate one bit. Eve can divert a fraction of these without affecting the others and perform the same measurements as the receiver.

Further theoretically possible attacks target the technology of the devices used for photon sending and receiving. When Eve knows the two possible polarization angles, she can use a high-energy pulse to overload the corresponding receiver, possibly unnoticed by the communicating parties. This gives Eve the knowledge that only photons of the other polarization angle are received properly.

Yet another possibility for Eve is to send photon pulses to the sender's laser and use its reflection properties to detect the quantum state of the information-carrying photons (Anderson & Kendall, 2003).

All these (and other) possibilities are hypothetical; no one has applied them yet. The engineers of quantum communication networks are aware of them, which means that they will be working to minimize the possibilities of them happening. Nevertheless, they exist and demonstrate that the 100% security promise is not realistic.

And even if one could really build an absolutely secure comm-channel, would it provide for a fully secure communication? The biggest risk factor in security has always been, and remains, the human factor. What use is a key communicated over an absolutely secure channel if you let someone look over your shoulder when reading the private message? The majority of security problems in corporate IT systems are caused by negligence of staff or because the hackers were able to get a hold of sensitive information via some non-electronic channel, such as beguilement, bribery, or physical break-in.

CONCLUSION

Quantum communication technology is a new and important advance in the technology of secure communications; it has the potential to revolutionize cryptology in a way similar to the public-key technology that came before it. Quantum channels attempt to solve one of the biggest problems in cryptology: the key distribution problem.

However, there is nothing magical about it and, in common with any other technology, it cannot offer perfectly secure communication. Human factors will always be the weakest link in any security system, and only high and constant awareness of this can offer genuine security.

The future will show whether quantum communication technology will manage to evolve to a level where it can replace common copper and fiber channels, so that a whole new quantum internet can physically evolve.

REFERENCES

Anderson, K.M. (2003). The secret is out. New Scientist, 180(2423), 24.

ArticSoft. (2003, February). Introduction to encryption. Retrieved June 22, 2006, from http://www.articsoft.com/wp_explaining_encryption.htm

BB84 Quantum Coding Scheme. (n.d.). Retrieved June 22, 2006, from http://www.cki.au.dk/experiment/qrypto/doc/QuCrypt/bb84coding.html

B92 Quantum Coding Scheme. (n.d.). Retrieved June 22, 2006, from http://www.cki.au.dk/experiment/qrypto/doc/QuCrypt/b92coding.html

Bennett, C.H., Bessette, F., Brassard, G., Salvail, L., & Smolin, J. (1992). Experimental quantum cryptography. Journal of Cryptography, 5, 3.

Bennett, C.H. (1992). Physical Review Letters, 68, 3121.

Bennett, C.H., & Brassard, G. (1984). Proceedings of the IEEE International Conference on Computers, Systems and Signal Processing. New York: IEEE.

Einstein, A., Podolsky, B., & Rosen, N. (1935). Can a quantum mechanical description of physical reality be considered complete? Physical Review, 47, 777.

Ekert, A.K. (1991). Physical Review Letters, 67, 66.

Ekert, A.K. (1995, March). What is quantum cryptography. Retrieved June 22, 2006, from http://www.qubit.org/library/intros/crypt.html

Ekert, A.K., Rarity, J.G., Tapster, P.R., & Palma, G.M. (1992). Physical Review Letters, 69, 1293.

Encyclopedia Britannica. (2006). Uncertainty principle. Retrieved August 2, 2006, from http://www.britannica.com/eb/article-9381497

Lomonaco, S.J. Jr. (2002). A talk on quantum cryptography, or how Alice outwits Eve. American Mathematical Society Proceedings of Symposia in Applied Mathematics (vol. 58, pp. 237-264).

Muller, A., Breguet, J., & Gisin, N. (1993). Europhys. Lett., 23, 383.

New Order. (2003, October). History of Encryption. Retrieved June 22, 2006, from http://neworder.box.sk/newsread.php?newsid=9257

Nielsen, M., & Chuang, I. (2000). Quantum computation and quantum information. Cambridge University Press.

Rivest, R., Shamir, A., & Adleman, L. (1978). A method for obtaining digital signatures and public-key cryptosystems. Communications of the ACM, 21(2), 120-126. (Previously released as an MIT "Technical Memo" in April 1977).

Singh, S. (1999). The code book. New York: Doubleday.

Tapster, P.R., Rarity, J.G., & Owens, P.C.M. (1994). Physical Review Letters, 73, 1923.

Townsend, P.D., Rarity, J.G., & Tapster, P.R. (1993). Electron. Lett., 29, 1291.

Wiesner, S. (1983). Special Interest Group on Algorithms and Computation Theory News, 15, 78.

Zeilinger, A. (1998). Fundamentals of quantum information. Physics World, (March). Retrieved August 2, 2006, from http://physicsweb.org/articles/world/11/3/9/1

KEY TERMS

Cryptography: A discipline that deals with security of information, in particular with encryption, decryption, and authentication. Also referred to as cryptology.

Decryption: The act of converting a previously encrypted message back to its original form.

Eavesdropping: The intercepting or altering of communicated information by an unintended (possibly malicious) party.

Encryption: The act of obscuring the information contained in a message in order to make it inapprehensible for someone without special knowledge, such as for instance a decryption key.

Key Distribution Problem: The collective term for the issues involved in securely communicating a cipher key intended for encryption or decryption of messages to the authorized recipients (or senders) without allowing it to become public.

Public Key Cryptography: A form of cryptography that allows two users to communicate securely without relying on a shared secret key. This is usually done by using two keys, one of which is public and the other private to one of the users. Also referred to as asymmetric key cryptography.

Quantum Communication: Secure communication based on the results of quantum physics and mechanics.

Quantum Entanglement: A quantum mechanical phenomenon in which the quantum states of two or more objects have to be described with reference to each other. This can lead to strong correlations between the physical properties of some remote systems. As a result, measurements performed on one system may be interpreted as influencing other systems.

Quantum Mechanics: A branch of theoretical physics that describes the properties and interactions of sub-atomic particles. Together with relativity theory, quantum theory provides the modern mathematical basis for most of natural science. Also referred to as quantum physics.

Quantum Superposition: Is said to occur when an object simultaneously possesses two or more values for an observable quantity. If the quantity is measured, it will randomly collapse onto one of the values in the superposition.

Secure Channel: A communication channel by which information can be transmitted without any risk of interception or tampering.

Security of Communication: A collective term for issues involved in preventing unauthorized parties from gaining access to remotely communicated information and in ensuring that such information is authentic.

Security Protection for Critical Infrastructure

M. J. Warren
Deakin University, Australia

T. B. Busuttil
Deakin University, Australia

INTRODUCTION

Understanding and managing information infrastructure (II) security risks is a priority to most organizations dealing with information technology and information warfare (IW) scenarios today (Libicki, 2000). Traditional security risk analysis (SRA) was well suited to these tasks within the paradigm of computer security, where the focus was on securing tangible items such as computing and communications equipment (NCS, 1996; Cramer, 1998). With the growth of information interchange and reliance on information infrastructure, the ability to understand where vulnerabilities lie within an organization, regardless of size, has become extremely difficult (NIPC, 1996). To place a value on the information that is owned and used by an organization is virtually an impossible task. The suitability of risk analysis to assist in managing IW and information infrastructure-related security risks is unqualified, however studies have been undertaken to build frameworks and methodologies for modeling information warfare attacks (Molander, Riddile, & Wilson, 1996; Johnson, 1997; Hutchinson & Warren, 2001) which will assist greatly in applying risk analysis concepts and methodologies to the burgeoning information technology security paradigm, information warfare.

Risk analysis provides a basis for evaluating vulnerabilities of information systems and was attractive because the need for countermeasures could be justified.

Development

The problem is that traditional risk analysis methods are not able to deal with the complexities An exception to this is the development of RAND Corporation's "Day Of...Day After...Day Before..." approach (Molander et al., 1996). This approach to impact modeling allows the analyst to take a three-step look at how IW can be perceived and therefore possibly countered. The proposed first step is to look at what occurs on the "Day Of..." the IW attack and to fully understand what is happening to all stakeholders involved in the system being reviewed. We must then look at "Step Two—The Day After..." and "Step Three—The Day Before..." which will allow us to see exactly what has happened, is happening, and what will happen, within the scenario being reviewed, in an easy-to-understand format.. Other research in this field (Shedden, Ruighaver, & Ahmad, 2006; Koh, Ruighaver, Maynard, & Ahmad, 2005) is exploring the possibility of extending the existing security risk analysis paradigm to deal with IW security issues. This research relates to the new development of a new SRA method (Busuttil & Warren, 2002a) with a view toward an SRA methodology for organizational information infrastructure (OII).

SRA AND INFORMATION INFRASTRUCTURE PROTECTION

The major characteristics of IW which set it apart from information security (IS) are the need to deal with:

- scalability
- flexibility
- difficulty in cost evaluation of threats, vulnerabilities, and attacks

The methods offered to deal with these shortfalls are offered in research which forms a basis for these further investigations (Busuttil & Warren, 2002a). One of the major advantages of LTMs are the ability to build security into information systems in an adaptable manner (Baskerville, 1993). It is also important to build security in across the breadth and depth of the organiza-

Table 1. Infrastructure-level notations (Busuttil & Warren, 2002a)

Infrastructure Level	Notation
Global Information Infrastructure	GII
National Information Infrastructure	NII
Organizational Information Infrastructure	OII
Personal Information Infrastructure	PII

tion, as focusing on one major area to secure can often be a downfall of organizations (Cramer, 1997).

The proposal of the idea of a fourth generation of SRA model comes about as a result of the lack of suitability of the aforementioned SRA methodologies to information warfare (Busuttil & Warren, 2002a) and the infrastructure level scalability issues discussed earlier. The notation of different levels of infrastructure is shown in Table 1.

CASE STUDY: APPLICATION OF CONCEPTUAL MODEL TO REAL-LIFE SCENARIO

This case study shows the application of Layered Logical Transformation Models (LLTMs) to an organization. The organization we will focus on is the Australian Internet service provider, Alphalink. The reasons for the selection of Alphalink are that it relies on the NII for business continuity while also providing connection infrastructure for its customers' PII. Alphalink runs its business within an organizational infrastructure and relies on the national and global II to provide the underlying communications and computing support necessary for it to conduct business. Alphalink should not do anything to actively compromise its connections to the NII/GII or the actual NII/GII. Customers of Alphalink rely on a dependable method of connection to Alphalink's OII, while they should also be able to ensure that they do not actively attempt to compromise the connection to Alphalink's OII or the actual OII. The following list shows the five major principles that need to be upheld (Busuttil & Warren, 2002a):

1. Alphalink can expect a certain level of service from the level of infrastructure above.
2. Alphalink should do all it can to ensure that the links between itself and any higher-level infrastructure entities are secure.
3. Alphalink should focus on securing itself to the best of its abilities in four major categories, defending against:
   - high-level infrastructure attacks,
   - internal attacks,
   - low-level infrastructure attacks, and
   - partnership attacks.
4. Alphalink must ensure that the connection to the lower infrastructure level is not compromised and should also expect a degree of care to be exercised by the user.
5. Alphalink should ensure that the integrity of lower-level infrastructure components is upheld during any interaction with customers and should also expect users to maintain II entities.

The conceptual diagram of this case study application, including references to the implied steps and the level of hierarchy they must take place within, is shown in Figure 1.

Figure 1. Alphalink's application of the LLTM concept

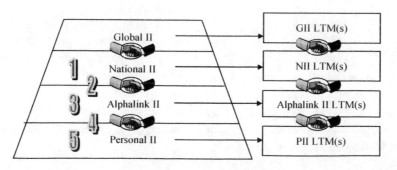

INFORMATION INFRASTRUCTURE SECURITY RISK ANALYSIS METHODOLOGY

When building an information security system using logical transformation models, there are a number of steps that need to be followed. Firstly, a system implementation participation group representing a large cross-section of the involved system users should undertake the approach, as this will assist in the exposition of infrastructure definitions, vulnerabilities, and countermeasures. For each defined piece of the information infrastructure, the following information needs to be stored:

- infrastructure definitions
- an infrastructure vulnerability assessment on each infrastructure level

Once a vulnerability assessment has been completed, the group can then attempt to map the vulnerabilities to areas of infrastructure and organizational responsibility so as to get an overall understanding of the problems that face the organization undertaking this risk analysis approach. The following formal steps are required for completing fourth-generation security risk analysis (see Figure 2):

1. Form system implementation participation group
2. Define infrastructure
3. Complete vulnerability assessment on each infrastructure level
4. Derive countermeasures based on findings from steps 2 and 3

Step 1 should be completed once at the beginning of the lifecycle of the risk analysis process. Step 2 should be completed once for each piece of infrastructure that is introduced to the overall system. Steps 3 and 4 should be completed once at the beginning of the analysis to cover all the parts that exist at this time within the infrastructure system, and should be updated regularly for both new and previously integrated infrastructure entities. A formal description of each of the aforementioned steps follows.

(1) Form System Implementation Participation Group

The first step in the fourth-generation SRA methodology, layered logical transformation modeling, was originally to construct a committee with a wide cross-section of understanding regarding the current computing environment within the organization in which the risk analysis is being undertaken. This committee was designed to encompass people from all levels of the organization (e.g., management to clerks) and also different areas of expertise (e.g., computing to accounting). The reason for this diversity to be inherent within the panel undertaking the analysis is that the organization is looking for all information infra-

Figure 2. OII SRA methodology: Process map

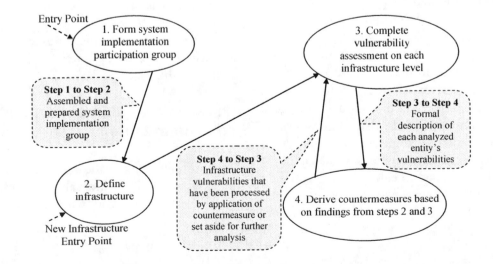

611

Table 2. Basic infrastructure definition

Classification	Explanation
Entity	Web server
Connections	Internet connection via
Security	Firewall, well-configured security options
Past Problems	DDOS attack
Past Problems Solution	Reconfigured and updated Web-based security

structure security risks, and the wider the net is cast, the more likely each ensuing step will be completed to an efficient level.

The concept of bringing people's concerns to the discussion table or at least voicing opinions is believed to be an important step in constructing systems that are efficient. However, the major goals of forming a committee are often not met if a leader champions the group with strong views toward an issue or with a preconceived and/or stubborn approach to the process (Davey, 2002). In view of this situation, a more effective approach to the first step of the methodology is to accept representative views in electronic form, and allow computing technology and a system operator to take the form of a trusted third party that offers pre-programmed cataloging and indexing of the problems and formulates them in a way so as to allow easy understanding of where the problem lies, who is affected, and also when and how the problem occurs or has occurred in the past. This approach offers two major advantages over the original committee-based approach. Firstly it allows issues to be raised in an unfettered manner by the system implementation participation group, and secondly the results are stored in an easy-to-read-and-recall environment that can be access controlled. This method of system development has been characterized by the Joint Application Development (JAD) methodology originally employed in the early 1970s by IBM as a way of designing systems that fit requirements of all the users. JAD required a number of participants from all areas within the project scope as well as outsiders to discuss and document the system requirements, while also communicating with those who would ultimately use, implement, and maintain the system (Hoffer, George, & Valacich, 2002). It was originally designed to cater to the creation of computing and information systems. The creation and implementation of a security policy is similar as there

is a final goal and an ongoing, sign-posted, evolutionary process to achieve this goal.

These points all lead toward the implementation of a system that involves canvassing a wide cross-section of views from throughout and also from outside of the organization undertaking the risk analysis. There is also evidence to suggest that a trusted outside party should be in charge of the process, as opposed to allowing an insider with a vested interest in a particular area of the organization to control the RA process.

(2) Define Infrastructure

This step requires the committee to classify what sort of II it is dependent on. In reference to the case study, Alphalink makes use of an organizational II that administers personal IIs while being reliant on a national II. At this stage the system boundaries (Vidalis & Blyth, 2002) should be mapped so as to understand where different LTMs are required for different layers of II. The total OII should be broken down into sections that can be defined, classified, and analyzed separately. This definition of infrastructure entities may include a mapping to the infrastructure, including its interfaces to other infrastructure within and outside of the organization, as well as the current security measures currently in place. Previous security incidents (if any) and the relevant countermeasures taken (if any) would also assist in the further steps in the model. A basic example of this step is shown in Table 2.

(3) Complete Vulnerability Assessment on Infrastructure Levels

The third step requires the completion of a vulnerability assessment. The vulnerability assessment should include a thorough rundown of likely vulnerabilities within the organization as a whole and also any known vulnerabilities within its connection scope to particular entities within the OII. A method of vulnerability assessment within the scope of electronic payment systems (EPSs), named 'Threat Assessment Model for EPS' (TAME) (O'Mahony, Peirce, & Tewari, 1997) shows a loosely coupled decision loop that allows for on-the-fly adjustment to system threats and inputs and outputs (Vidalis & Blyth, 2002). The steps involved in this system are useful, however it is important to know where an organization is in the security process. The TAME system also focuses greatly on assessing threat which takes impetus away from finding vulnerabilities within the organization. Concentration on threat as opposed to vulnerability can cause security weaknesses to go unnoticed as there may be a threat that can never be prepared for. If the organization attempts to keep vulnerabilities to a minimum, then it is not overly important to know the nature of the threat agent (Malone, 2002).

The new methodology takes into account the following contiguous stages (Busuttil & Warren, 2005):

- assessment scope,
- scenario construction and modeling,
- vulnerability analysis, and
- evaluation.

These stages consist of a number of steps that should be completed in turn so as to be easier to follow and keep track of. The concepts covered in the new methodology are similar to those discussed in the TAME system.

Table 3 lists the steps involved at each stage of the TAME methodology that are being used in the new methodology.

(4) Derive Countermeasures

The final step in this security risk analysis is to derive countermeasures for the vulnerabilities that were identified in the vulnerability assessment. These countermeasures should attempt to solve the security problem being faced while also attempting to maintain a reasonable degree of subjective cost benefit. The derivation of countermeasures can be done in many ways:

- applying bug fixes,
- updating security policy,
- informing and training staff,
- installing new software and hardware solutions, and
- deleting unrequired associations.

The formal presentation of these countermeasures should be delivered as shown in Table 4 for each vulnerability.

Table 3. Steps in new methodology as derived from TAME methodology (Vidalis & Blyth, 2002)

Stages	Sub-Steps
Assessment Scope	Business Analysis
	Stakeholder Identification
	System Boundaries Identification
Scenario Construction and Modeling	Scenario Generation
	System Modeling
	Asset Identification
Vulnerability Analysis	Vulnerability Type Identification and Selection
	Vulnerability Complexity Analysis
Evaluation	Stakeholder Evaluation
	Vulnerability Statement Generation

Table 4. Basic example of a countermeasures table

Vulnerability	Countermeasure
Apache Server security hole	Install firewall and configure correctly to assist in the stopping of DOS attacks

CONCLUSION

The major direction of this research at the current point is to derive a step-wise methodology that can be put into place to allow the SRA process to be undertaken. An aside to this would also be the creation of an information infrastructure notation language perhaps, due to the nature of infrastructure and the dependencies therein, based on object modeling theory. These two products would allow for a more easily workable and hence more efficient final methodology. Further to this manual risk analysis format would be the development of a computer-based system that would catalog all the information and become the basis for the implementation of the OII SRA methodology.

The OII SRA methodology is a move toward dealing with the scalability issues that have in the past meant that RA was not immediately adaptable to information warfare and other information infrastructure protection requirements. This methodology would prove to be helpful to organizations with mid-level infrastructure such as an organizational information infrastructure if undertaken in solitude, however the true benefits of this methodology would be seen if it was put into practice by higher-level infrastructure stakeholders. This uptake by higher-level infrastructure would lead to higher dependability and reliability being built into the infrastructure system from the outset. Information warfare needs a unique security methodology that is useful at dealing with all the previous concerns that computer security and information security dealt with, along with the ability to be adaptable and scalable also. When researching existing methodologies, logical transformation models proved to be a suitable method for coping with adaptability issues. The scalability issues are dealt with through the application of multiple layers of LTMs. Cost evaluation has been found to be an outdated function when analyzing IW risks; LTMs have the added feature of being solution oriented and independent of any cost evaluation procedures. This methodology is fairly flexible but has a format that will be easily transferable from a formal rule set to a computer-based methodology.

REFERENCES

Baskerville, R. (1993). Information systems security design methods: Implications for information systems development. *ACM Computing Surveys, 25*(4), 375-414.

Busuttil, T.B., & Warren, M.J. (2002a). A conceptual approach to information warfare security risk analysis. *Proceedings of the 2nd European Conference on Information Warfare,* London.

Busuttil, T.B., & Warren, M.J. (2002b). A formalisation of an information infrastructure security risk analysis approach. *Proceedings of the 3rd Australian Information Warfare & Security Conference 2002,* Perth, Australia.

Busuttil, T.B., & Warren, M.J. (2005). An Australian risk analysis approach for critical information infrastructure protection. *Proceedings of the 4th European Conference on Information Warfare and Security,* Glamorgan, Wales.

Cramer, M.L. (1997). Measuring the value of information. *Proceedings of NCSA InfoWarCon 97.*

Cramer, M.L. (1998). Information warfare: A consequence of the information revolution. In A.L. Porter & W.H. Read (Eds.), *The information revolution: Current and future consequences.* Ablex.

Davey, J. (2002). Comment made at 'information warfare' workshop. *Proceedings of the 3rd Australian Information Warfare & Security Conference,* Perth, Australia.

Hoffer, J.A., George, J.F., & Valacich, J.S. (2002). *Modern systems analysis and design.* Englewood Cliffs, NJ: Prentice Hall.

Hutchinson, W., & Warren, M.J. (2001). *Information warfare—corporate attack and defence in a digital world.* Oxford, UK: Butterworth-Heinemann.

Johnson, L.S. (1997). Toward a functional model of information warfare. *Studies in Intelligence, 1*(1).

Koh, K., Ruighaver, A.B., Maynard, S.B., & Ahmad, A. (2005, September 30). Security governance: Its impact on security culture. *Proceedings of the 3rd Australian Information Security Management Conference,* Perth, Australia.

Libicki, M. (2000). *The future of information security* (p. 10). Institute for National Strategic Studies.

Malone, J. (2002). Comment made at 'information warfare' workshop. *Proceedings of the 3rd Australian Information Warfare & Security Conference,* Perth, Australia.

Molander, R.C., Riddile, A.S., & Wilson, P.A. (1996). *Strategic information warfare: A new face of war.* Washington, DC: RAND Corporation.

NCS. (1996). *Risk assessment: A nation's information at risk.* Arlington, VA: National Communications System.

NIPC. (1996). *Critical infrastructures.* National Infrastructure Protection Center.

O'Mahony, D., Peirce, M., & Tewari, H. (1997). *Electronic payment systems.* Artech House.

Shedden, P., Ruighaver, A.B., & Ahmad, A. (2006, April 19-20). Risk management standards—the perception of ease of use. *Proceedings of the 5th Security Conference,* Las Vegas, NV.

Vidalis, S., & Blyth, A. (2002). Understanding and developing a threat assessment model. *Proceedings of the 2nd European Conference on Information Warfare,* London.

KEY TERMS

S

Hacker: One who uses programming skills to gain illegal access to a computer network or file.

Internet: An interconnected system of networks that connects computers around the world via the TCP/IP protocol.

Risk: The possibility of suffering harm or loss; danger.

Security: Something that gives or assures safety as: (a) measures adopted by a government to prevent espionage, sabotage, or attack; or (b) measures adopted by a business or homeowner to prevent a crime.

Threat: An indication of impending danger or harm.

Vulnerability: Susceptible to attack.

Spyware

Thomas F. Stafford
University of Memphis, USA

INTRODUCTION

There is a potent threat to computer security represented by the emerging class of applications commonly known as "spyware," designed to remotely monitor and report on user activity. The threat manifests itself indirectly, unlike hacker intrusions and many virus infections. These remote monitoring applications record and transmit information on computer user behaviors to third parties, who then utilize monitored customer data for marketing segmentation and targeting, or for more nefarious violations of user computer security. Most spyware is legal, having typically been installed during free software downloads online. Some spyware is illegal, having been remotely installed by bots on visited Web sites, and can remotely monitor for illegitimate purposes such as keystroke logging and password theft and account access. Spyware is often defended by its sponsors as a means of more effectively targeting the Internet experience to users, but users typically find the costs of this purportedly customer-centric monitoring process objectionable in terms of subsequent advertising distraction and system resource monopolization.

WHAT IS SPYWARE?

Spyware is a term loosely used to characterize an emerging class of remote monitoring applications designed to run on user computers and report aspects of user computer behavior across Internet connections back to a remote third party (Stafford & Urbaczewski, 2004). It is estimated that as much as 90% of home computers (Farrow, 2003; Schmidt & Arnett, 2005) and small-to-medium-sized business computers (Zhang, 2005) are infected with spyware, and it is not unheard of for computers to come directly from the manufacturer with spyware applications already installed (Levine, 2004; Thompson, 2003).

Spyware, in the specific form known as adware, typically acts to track Internet use and subsequently

target pop-up advertising to user computers (Fox, 2005), though far more nefarious uses have been observed such as keystroke logging, password theft, and commandeering user system resources for external use, which typically are performed by surreptitiously installed "backdoor" versions of Trojan horse applications (Volkmer, 2004). Trojan horses, often simply called "Trojans," are surreptitiously installed applications, often arriving hidden in parts of seemingly legitimate files such as e-mail attachments that later activate in order to capture and report user activity data.

Aside from the privacy and security issues of remote third-party monitoring of individual user computers, there is the not-inconsiderable issue of spyware as a resource-hungry application that consumes noticeable amounts of computing resources while running as an ever-present background application on PCs (Stafford & Urbaczewski, 2004). Unexpected and sudden degradations in system performance are often the first clear symptoms of spyware, as they attach system resources at the expense of legitimate applications. As difficult as it can be to detect spyware running on your machine, these applications can be tougher to clean. Typical spyware removal war stories include subsequent failures of user Internet connections, since some applications alter the Winsock stack (Foster, 2002).

The Winsock "stack" in Microsoft operating systems is an interface and supporting program that handles input/output requests for Internet applications (Whatis. com, 2006). The name "Winsock" is derived from its adaptation by Microsoft of the Berkeley Unix sockets interface, which serves to connect with and exchange data between two program processes, in this case between OS-supported user applications such as browsers and the TCP/IP protocol stack that permits computers to communication in data packets across the Internet. Since spyware applications are specifically designed to commandeer Internet communication procedures, the Winsock stack is typically implicated in infestations, and removal very often damages the operating system functionality for Internet communication.

WHERE DOES SPYWARE COME FROM?

The typical cause of spyware infestations on user computers is a free Internet download of a software application (Taylor, 2002). Spyware applications typically come bundled in downloads of popular freeware applications, such as peer-to-peer file sharing applications as well as specific accessory applications such as Bonzi Buddy, Comet Cursor, Xupiter Toolbar, and Bargains.exe (Coggrave, 2003). Many applications that users find cosmetically appealing as addition to their computer interface include graphic cursors and related animated applications, and various "effort-saving" toolbars typically represented as shopping aids or news sources. Many of these "cosmetic" applications come packaged with remote monitoring applications; indeed, even legitimate versions of such applications, such as the Google and Yahoo Toolbars, are capable of collecting information on user Internet activity and transmitting it to the sponsoring organization. In some cases, this user monitoring process is represented by the provider as a means to tailor the tool to individual preferences, and users are sometimes permitted to opt out of remote monitoring during installation. In other cases, the user installs a pretty graphic on the computer and also ends up unwittingly installing a bundled adware product that will produce noticeable increases in pop-up activity upon activation.

Among the "bundling" vectors that can provide spyware—aside from P2P file sharing applications, cosmetic applications, and shopping agents—are certain e-mail and instant messaging programs; some illegal spyware applications will even install themselves unbidden during Web site visits, which is known as a "drive-by download" (Stafford & Urbaczewski, 2004). The method frequently used to avoid prosecution for illegal installation of spyware applications involves bundling spyware with licensed commercial applications, including an affirmative installation statement in the license agreement that comes with the associated and sought after user application (Schultz, 2003).

The reason that free software downloads online often serve as a vector for remote monitoring applications is due to an emerging revenue model for supporting the provision of "free" software (cf., Gibson, 2005; Klang, 2003). Developers essentially seek to recoup their expense in creating freeware applications by selling bundling rights to sponsors of remote monitoring applications who desire greater access to information about Internet user behaviors. As noted above, users are routinely provided with a disclosure of this bundling of remote monitoring applications as part of a download in the typical "clickwrap" licensing agreement for freeware, but many users do not pay adequate attention to the licensing provisions of applications that they agree to download for free (Stafford & Urbaczewski, 2004). Since nothing of value is ever truly free, the effective exchange transaction users enter into for "free" downloads involves the (often unwitting) exchange of personal information and loss of online privacy to third parties on the Internet via remote monitoring applications that are installed on their computers (Stafford, 2005).

EMERGING TRENDS IN SPYWARE THREATS

The Gartner Group expects that spyware will become the tool of choice for identity theft in the near future (Radcliff, 2004). Remote applications that monitor user keystrokes and account access can serve to capture passwords, PIN numbers, and associated account information such that third parties would be in a position to fraudulently represent themselves using stolen user and account information for identity theft purposes. Hence, it may be expected that the illegal hacker community will continue to develop remote monitoring applications that will typically install themselves surreptitiously and illegally on user computers.

Aside from the widespread trend of seeking to install surreptitious monitoring and display applications on user computers, a frequent hacker community spyware threat has been in the form of "dialers," which cause computer modems to automatically engage in the dialing of overseas or toll-linked phone numbers in order to incur financial charges for the user. "Web bugs," which are single-pixel GIF-format files downloaded with Web pages, also have become quite popular for both illicit and legitimate monitoring purposes, serving essentially the same purposes as cookies by providing 'loggable' download events to document user actions and histories.

Businesses find vast utility in the ability to monitor computer users for marketing segmentation purposes (Foster, 2002), but businesses also find remote monitoring applications useful for providing an agent on customer computers for purposes of checking for upgrades and for promoting new software features (Anon, 2004). An example of this sort of usage is found in the Kodak company's inclusion of BackWeb Lite as part of its digital camera imaging software application; BackWeb is one of the remote monitoring applications that popular spyware detection and removal applications routinely identify in computer sweeps, but Kodak specially adapted a version of BackWeb to automate its software upgrade process and for purposes of "pushing" certain camera-related promotions and upgrades out to consumers (Stafford & Urbaczewski, 2004).

Commercial uses of monitoring software can be viewed as a legitimate systems management process in business, and include applications such as Net-Nanny, Cybersitter, and WinWhatWhere, which are installed by a concerned third party on a user's computer for monitoring purposes. Practical examples of the legitimate use of such applications might include employers monitoring company computer and network usage, or parents keeping watch on their children's computer use. Even so, legitimate remote monitoring applications that are not well written tend to interfere with computer functionality (Anon, 2004), since most spyware applications tend to make a lot of registry entries (Radcliff, 2004). While the spyware can be removed, the registry alterations typically have to be done manually and can be tedious.

Sometimes spyware-like applications are used for product activation purposes, as is the case with software sold by Quicken, Microsoft, and Macromedia (Stafford & Urbaczewski, 2004). Along with simple product activation, these applications can be used to urge product registration and collect information about the application user for the software vendor or coder. Microsoft's practice of occasionally causing Internet Explorer browsers to redirect displays to the Microsoft update site, rather than the user-selected homepage, is a limited example of a practice that would otherwise be known as "browser hijacking," were the Microsoft redirect not permitted under the company's licensing agreement with the user. In browser hijacks, homepage displays are redirected to some external party's desired setting. In the Microsoft case, this is a legitimate use, since it involves notification about browser security updates, but extreme examples of browser hijacking include "scumware," where Web site content is changed by the spyware application by linking Web page keywords to third-party sites. Users find themselves forced to view pages they have not selected when these applications are operating on their computers; this can be inconvenient, and even offensive, depending on the sort of Web page the redirect process has targeted for user viewing.

While businesses often have legitimate reasons for monitoring computer user behavior on the corporate campus, this does not mean that businesses are not prey to the illegitimate and nefarious forms of spyware described here as threats typical to consumer users. To the extent that computer users in business environments contract illegitimate and illegal spyware infestations on company computers, businesses may face even more critical threats, since the collection of passwords, account information, and authorization procedures can have a more serious impact in environments where more than just a household income or a home computer is at risk.

WHAT CAN BE DONE ABOUT SPYWARE?

Several pieces of legislation protect computer users from spyware attacks. For example, unauthorized third-party spyware installations are typically considered in contravention of federal wiretapping statutes (Farrow, 2003), and the Department of Justice considers unauthorized spyware installations to be a felony offense (Stafford & Urbaczewski, 2004). In addition, a number of legislative initiatives in the United States have made their way into law (Poston, Stafford, & Hennington, 2005), including recent initiatives aimed at regulating spyware beyond national borders (Tech Law Journal, 2006).

In terms of user actions against spyware, awareness of the threat is the first step to remediation of the security breach potentially implied by a spyware installation; many have argued that simple education initiatives designed to persuade users to be aware of the threat and to closely inspect clickwrap licensing agreements can be the solution to the promulgation of spyware (Hu & Dinev, 2005; Zhang, 2005). Unfortunately, despite widespread recognition and awareness of the existence of spyware as a computer security problem, very few users actually take concrete action to protect their individual systems (Hu & Dinev, 2005; Poston et al., 2005).

As a response to the threat of spyware, coupled with seeming user apathy about taking steps to protect themselves (e.g., Zhang, 2005), key companies in the Internet arena such as America Online and Microsoft have begun to offer spyware screening as part of their service to users (Poston et el., 2005). Entrepreneurs are also offering a host of spyware-countering applications as both paid and free applications.

EMERGING TRENDS TO COMBAT SPYWARE

Based on the growing recognition of spyware as a computer security threat, the Federal Trade Commission (FTC) has issued definitions of spyware for regulatory purposes, and subsequent acts of Congress have sought to codify this in law (Poston et al., 2005). The Safeguard Against Privacy Invasion Act (SAPIA) defines spyware not only in existential terms, but also delineates what might constitute the user provision of consent to receive spyware, while the Software Principles Yielding Better Levels of Consumer Knowledge Act (SPYBLOCK) enacts a legal requirement for vendors and providers of software programs to demonstrate purposeful installation by users (Urbach & Kibel, 2004; Volkmer, 2004; Stafford & Urbaczewski 2004).

On the business front, anti-spyware products are now frequently included with popular antivirus software applications (Hu & Dinev, 2005; Stafford & Urbaczewski, 2004). Free applications to combat spyware also exist and are widely available (Beith, 2005), including well-known applications such as Lavasoft's Adaware (*http://www.lavasoftusa.com/software/adaware*), Computer Associate's Pest Patrol (*http://www.pestpatrol.com*), and the popular shareware application, Spybot Search & Destroy (*http://www.safer-networking.org*). These applications, when installed on user computers and regularly updated with new detection files, operate very much like antivirus applications. Users instantiate a sweep of their computer systems and receive a report of detected threats. Threats subsequently detected can both be removed and blocked from future reinstallation with leading anti-spyware applications.

Some anti-spyware applications have options that work very much like operating system firewall utilities. They serve to detect and block, either automatically or manually with a user notification, the execution of active program content downloaded from Internet sources. Firewalls, now included as operating system options in many Microsoft-equipped computers, can serve as protection against spyware by detecting and alerting users to application attempts to utilize Internet connections. However, to the extent that many spyware applications ride "on top of" or use legitimate applications for Internet communication, such as the Winsock Stack on Microsoft operating systems, firewalls can only serve as partial protection from the full range of threats that spyware applications represent.

The key to secure computing is an informed computer user; there are multiple solutions and they are readily available, but users must take the first active step to access protection and make use of it. Unfortunately, many users either are unaware of or unconcerned about the security threat that spyware represents (Poston et al., 2005; Zhang, 2005). Whether users will find protection from proactive business initiatives to provide security through Internet service accounts, as is currently offered by America Online and other Internet service providers, or whether users will actively seek their own solutions is an open question. Sadly, the issue is only likely to be resolved after spyware takes an even greater toll on user computer resources and computer security in the future.

CONCLUSION

Spyware is a class of remote monitoring applications designed to survey and report across the Internet to third parties about computer user behavior. This remote monitoring process has not only legal and legitimate uses, but increasingly illegal and illegitimate uses across the computing milieu. Regardless of the intent of the spyware application author, provider, or user, in most cases computer security is reduced and even dangerously compromised by the process of third-party surveillance of computers and user behavior.

As was seen with the proliferation of computer viruses in the prior decade, there is a learning curve related to the recognition of and remediation of computer security threats. It appears we are only now in the middle of the learning curve related to the security threats presented by spyware.

REFERENCES

Anonymous. (2004). Spyware: Spycatcher. *New Media Age,* (January 8), 25.

Beith, M. (2005). Spyware vs. anti-spyware. *Newsweek,* (January 1), 30.

Coggrave, F. (2003). How to tackle the spyware threat. *Computer Weekly,* (November 18), 30.

Farrow, R. (2003). Is your desktop being wiretapped? *Network Magazine, 18*(8), 52.

Foster, E. (2002). The spy who loves you. *Infoworld, 24*(20), 60.

Fox, S. (2005). *Spyware.* Retrieved August 30, 2006, from http://www.pewinternet.org/PPF/r/160/report_display.asp

Gibson, S. (2005). Spyware was inevitable. *Communications of the ACM, 48*(8) 37-39.

Hu, Q., & Dinev, T. (2005). Is spyware an Internet nuisance or public menace? *Communications of the ACM, 48*(8) 61-66.

Klang, M. (2003). Spyware: Paying for software with our privacy. *International Review of Law, Computers & Technology, 17*(3), 313-322.

Levine, J.R. (2003). *Written comments of Dr. John R. Levine.* Retrieved September 5, 2006, from http://commerce.senate.gov/pdf/levine032304.pdf

Poston, R., Stafford, T.F., & Hennington, A. (2005). Spyware: The view from the [online] street. *Communications of the ACM, 48*(8), 96-99.

Radcliff, D. (2004). Spyware. *Network World, 21*(4), 51.

Schultz, E. (2003). Pandora's box: Spyware, adware, autoexecution, and NGSCB. *Computers & Security, 22*(5), 366.

Schmidt, M.B., & Arnett, K.P. (2005). Spyware: A little knowledge is a wonderful thing. *Communications of the ACM, 48*(8), 67-70.

Stafford, T.F. (2005). Spyware. *Communications of the ACM, 48*(8), 34-36.

Stafford, T.F., & Urbaczewski, A. (2004). Spyware: The ghost in the machine. *Communications of the Association for Information Systems, 14,* 291-306.

Taylor, C. (2002). What spies beneath. *Time, 160*(15), 106.

Tech Law Journal. (2006). *Senate subcommittee holds hearing on spyware.*

Retrieved October 2006 from http://www.techlawjournal.com/home/newsbriefs/2005/10a.asp

Thompson, R. (2003). *Cybersecurity & consumer data: What's at risk for the consumer?* Testimony before the U.S. House of Representatives Subcommittee on Commerce, Trade, and Consumer Protection. Retrieved August 30, 2006, from http://www.iwar.org.uk/comsec/resources/consumer-risk/Thompson1799.htm

Urbach, R.R., & Kibel, G.A. (2004). Adware/spyware: An update regarding pending litigation and legislation. *Intellectual Property & Technology Law Journal, 16*(7), 12-16.

Volkmer, C.J. (2004). Should adware and spyware prompt Congressional action? *Journal of Internet Law, 7*(11), 1-8.

Whatis.com. (2006). *Winsock 2.* Retrieved October 2006 from http://searchwinit.techtarget.com/sDefinition/0,290660,sid1_gci213376,00.html

Zhang, X. (2005). What do consumers really know about spyware? *Communications of the ACM, 48*(8) 44-48.

KEY TERMS

Adware: Tracks user Web behavior and targets specific pop-up ads based on the behavior profile.

Backdoor: A variety of Trojan horse that allows full remote access and control to an outside third party. These typically present as remote control programs like Back Orifice or SMTP engines used as covert relays to send e-mail spam.

Browser Hijacker: Changes the default Web page settings on browsers without user permission. May even make registry changes to prevent users from regaining their default settings.

Dialer: Program that uses a PC modem to dial expensive toll numbers resulting in unauthorized charges to the user. These often access 900 numbers, 10-10-xxx access codes, and overseas connections.

Drive-by Download: Surveillance application that installs itself on a computer without consent. These applications are clearly illegal, not utilizing even basic clickwrap license provisions.

Keystroke Logger: A type of Trojan that captures keystrokes and records them to a remotely accessed file. These are often used to capture credit card numbers, passwords, and other information used for identity theft.

Scumware: A type of application that changes Web site content by linking Web page keywords to third-party sites.

Spyware: A general term used to describe any application that reports on computer usage to a remote server.

Trojan: A type of illegal spyware that gives access to monitor and control a PC to an outsider.

Web Bug: A 1-pixel graphic or cookie that is placed on a user computer by a Web site and is then subsequently used to track user computing behavior. These often come hidden in an HTML-formatted mail message, typically to identify to the sender if the message has been read or not.

S

Sustainable Information Society

Ralf Isenmann
University of Bremen, Germany

INTRODUCTION

As a development goal, a sustainable information society is emerging at present, with the aims of sustainability and an information society as its converging elements. This article introduces the conceptual elements of sustainability and the information society, while bringing to the surface underlying normative issues. Further, a series of opportunities is presented on how to develop towards such a promising approach. Finally, examples of using information and communication technologies (ICTs) from the 'Memorandum Sustainable Information Society' are discussed. That publication was recently released by a working group of the German Society for Informatics. The memorandum provides a valuable source of the role modern ICT is playing on the road to a forward-looking society which is based on increasing use of ICT on the one hand, while at the same time it meets the fundamental sustainability criteria of human, social, and ecological comparability on the other hand.

SUSTAINABILITY: FROM AN ENVIRONMENTAL AND DEVELOPMENT POLICY TERM TO THE GOAL FOR A LONG-TERM LIVEABLE FUTURE

Sustainable development has its roots in environmental and development policy. As such, sustainable development mirrors the efforts of the international community to meet the recent social, economic, and environmental challenges we are facing today, for example, among others, population development, food, health protection, combating poverty, and global environmental problems (Jorissen et al., 1999).

Although the idea and concept had a number of predecessors in the 1970s (Harborth, 1993), the term "sustainable development" first became popular in the wake of the so-called "Brundtland report" of the World Commission for Environment and Development in Stockholm in 1987 (Hauff, 1987). This conference was initiated under the banner of the United Nations (UN) and guided by the Norwegian prime minister Gro Harlem Brundtland. International leading experts prepared a comprehensive program of recommendations for the above mentioned global problems. The "Brundtland report" was a turning point of the environment and development policy at that time, in that the assumption of industrialization in developing countries seemed no longer tenable without a profound rethink of the lifestyles and consumption levels in industrialized countries.

The "Brundtland report" created the foundation for the current understanding of sustainable development. In a nutshell, sustainable development aims to create economic living conditions that enable all the Earth's population to satisfy their needs today, without compromising the ability of future generations to satisfy theirs. This brings two concepts of justice into play (Eckardt, 2005): firstly, *intra*generational responsibility concerning all humans alive today, and secondly, *inter*generational responsibility for the relationship between today's and future generations. Sustainable development must be regarded as a normative concept in the sense that it reposes on the two ideas of justice mentioned above: though there is no formulation of an explicit goal, sustainable development promotes a vision or a "regulative idea" in the sense of Immanuel Kant, on how all human beings could lead a decent life today and in the future. Furthermore, it discusses the minimum conditions that *should* be respected for this aim.

Sustainable development was included in the United Nations' action program for the 21st century, the so-called "Agenda 21," at the Conference for Environment and Development 1992 in Rio de Janeiro to serve as an orientation for subsequent measures regarding social and economic aspects such as population dynamics, reduction of poverty, health preservation, conservation and management of natural resources, and stakeholder dialogues. Since then, sustainable development is regarded as the unifying aim for a long-term globally livable future. The Summit for Sustainable Development at Johannesburg 2002, the "Rio+10 Conference," confirmed the global standing of the aim of sustainable development.

Sustainable development does contain a *regulatory* dimension as well: any decision making at local, regional, national, or global levels must be implemented in such a way that any costs are not borne by uninvolved parties, future generations, or nature. In other words, the three criteria of environmental integrity, social justice, and economic quality should always be respected (Zwierlein & Isenmann, 1995), and by all social actors, be it individual persons as well as groups or institutions (e.g., families, universities, companies, or countries). This regulative idea underscores the processual character of sustainable development, that is to say, providing guidance, but not an explicit goal.

In Germany, the roots of the concept of sustainable development are believed to come from ideas of 18th century forest management, whereas the concept's etymological origins can be traced back much further, to the 12th century (Grober, 2002). Two-hundred-and-fifty years ago, revenues of forest owners collapsed when more and more forests were cleared. This led to the insight of only cutting as many trees in the future as would be newly planted. Thus, by respecting an economic principle of conservation of capital, forest revenues were stabilized for long-term benefit.

Not just the concept of sustainable development, but also its current interpretations have its roots in forest management (Ott & Döring, 2004). *Strong* sustainability stipulates living solely off the interest of natural capital. The latter must be preserved in its total amount, non-renewable resources should not be utilized and renewables only to the extent of their regeneration rates. On the other hand, adherents of *weak* sustainability want to keep constant the sum of natural and human capital only, allowing therefore substitution of natural by human capital.

THE TWO GLOBAL TRENDS OF SUSTAINABILITY AND INFORMATION SOCIETY

The development towards an information society is the second global trend influencing our modern industrial society in its combination of technical progress, economic growth, and social change (Müller-Merbach, 1998, p. 6):

- *Technical progress* is marked by innovations, especially in information and communication technologies. Digitalizing, miniaturizing, development of user interfaces, and system integration progress rapidly and lead to the amalgamation of computer technology, telecommunications, consumer electronics, and new media. The resulting applications become examples of "pervasive computing" (its consequences are discussed in Hilty, Som, & Köhler, 2004; Hilty et al., 2005a).

- The industrial sectors of ICT and multimedia, among them chip manufacturers, hardware and software developers, and information service providers, can be counted among the biggest growth sectors worldwide. They are an important part of future *economic growth.*

- Use of modern ICT and information services lead not only to changes in the way work is organized and carried out, they exert a strong influence on social models of consumption, individual lifestyles, leisure pursuits, and accelerate *social change.*

The UN world summits on the information society, in Geneva in 2003 and in Tunis in 2005, can be taken as proof of the strong political interest in this phenomenon touching the entire human society.

Rapid ICT development contributes to technical progress in many domains. ICTs facilitate professional work and can render daily life more pleasant in many ways. Further, ICTs can provide unique opportunities for sustainable development (cf. resources of the Technical Committee on Computer Science in Environmental Protection, 2006; further: Hilty, Seifert, & Treibert, 2005b; Waage, Shah, & Girshick, 2003; Rautenstrauch & Patig, 2001), for example, helping to dematerialize economic processes and therefore reduce material and energy throughput (Teitscheid, 2002).

However, increasing use of ICTs does not automatically contribute towards sustainable development (Schauer, 2000, 2003). Its rapid progress and ubiquitous use create new problems for individuals, society, and nature. Thus, we need an ethical understanding of its promises and risks on the one hand and a political implication on the other hand in order to render our developing information society (Woesler, 2005) compatible with the aim of sustainability.

Electronic waste, high consumption of resources for the manufacturing of PCs, and the consumption of energy by the Internet are only a handful of indicators (cf. *Journal of Industrial Ecology,* 2002; von Geibler, Kuhndt, & Türk, 2005) for the danger of accelerating unsustainability brought about by the development of an information society. There is a need to discuss and develop integrative approaches, for example contributions from informatics (Rolf, 1998; Hilty & Ruddy, 2000; Möller & Bornemann, 2005), social sciences (Grossmann et al., 2002; Orwat & Grunwald, 2005), economics (Schneidewind, Truscheit, & Steingräber, 2000), and administration (Deutscher Bundestag, 1998; Forum Information Society, 1998; Angrick, 2002; Radermacher, van Dijk, & Pestel, 2000) in order to bring together in a systematic manner policy discussions on information society and on sustainable development.

Doing so might enable humanity to benefit from the opportunities ICTs can offer for a sustainable information society, while managing the associated risks (opportunities and risks are discussed, e.g., by Radermacher et al., 2000; Hilty et al., 2004, 2005a).

AN ETHICAL FOUNDATION FOR A SUSTAINABLE INFORMATION SOCIETY

Ethics as a theory of moral acts asks the question of how *individuals* may lead their lives successfully (Spaemann, 1989). With regards to its aim, ethics can be seen as a way of reaching a state of happiness via a path of virtue. Ethics is thus a manner of cultivating oneself. A pursuit of a successful and happy life, however, must include an interest in others, humans and non-humans, in the *social* and *natural* world surrounding the individual. Ethics then becomes a question of justice, benevolence, and assuming responsibility

(Spaemann, 1993). We can regard ethics as an attempt to evaluate our moral experience in a normative manner. Table 1 provides an overview of the domain.

The responsibility of an ethical actor consists of justifying and legitimizing his or her decisions to act or not act vis-à-vis third parties that are subjected to a decision's consequences. Here, an "ethical gap"—an incapacity to see an act's moral dimension—manifests itself the very moment when power differences come into play. This "Einstein dilemma" dates back to the great physicist deploring our mastery of perfect (technological) means, but utilizing them without being able to provide a clear aim. In other words, there is an imbalance between sophisticated technico-economic *applied knowledge* and still quite rudimentary *ethical knowledge* providing an orientation for the first (Mittelstraß, 1992). We could say that "we are technical giants and ethical dwarves at the same time" (Zwierlein & Isenmann, 1995, p. 38).

Normative aspects such as questions of power and of justice play a decisive role in the development of an information society as well (Zwierlein, 1998; an up-to-date overview is provided by the *International Journal of Information Ethics,* 2004; Capurro, Wiegerling, & Brellochs, 1995). The traditional ethical questions arising from the development of ICT such as data protection, security, freedom of opinion, and intellectual property rights are complemented by new themes: digital divide (Capurro, Scheule, & Hausmanninger, 2004), gender issues (World Bank, 2004), rebound effects (Binswanger, 2001), and cultural diversity (Beckett, 2004), among others.

The information society's political vision (cf. e.g., BMWA, 2002, 2003) has normative implications as well (Isenmann, 2001), in the creation of specific re-

Table 1. Ethics—An overview

	Ethics: Comprehensive theory of practice (moral actions)	
Focus	Individual: Human	Community: Fellow human being, creature
Issue	Good life	Justice
Objective	Happiness	Benevolence
Approach	Virtue	Responsibility
Effects	Personal (inner world): What makes an actor good?	Social (civilization), ecological (nature): What makes an action good?
Criterion	Human compatibility	Social and ecological compatibility

search funding programs that tie up funds that are no longer available for other competing types of projects. The normative perspective becomes clear when the central question of "what kind of technology do we need for living in what kind of world?" is tackled in the development of an information society, taking into account the consequences of ICT for humans, society, and nature.

ICT as a technical means is in need of a normative orientation (Mittelstraß, 1992) and an understanding of technological decision making (Rohbeck, 1993). As such, modern ICT would be conceived and used in adequation with computer power and human reason, the title of an important book by Joseph Weizenbaum (1976). Any ethical reflection, however, must remain powerless if it is considered only as a means of resolving a crisis, as Schefe (2001) warns. A much more fruitful implication of ethics in research, science, and teaching places it at the heart of a prevention strategy (cf. e.g., Behrendt, Hilty, & Erdmann, 2003), as the philosopher Hans Jonas (1984) suggested in his book, *The Imperative of Responsibility: In Search of an Ethics for the Technological Age.*

Mere appeals to an idealistic conscience are bound to fail, though. The consideration of specific professional ethics (Hausmanninger, 2003), ethical guidelines for ICT-related associations (Berleur, Ducenoy, & Whitehouse, 1999; Gesellschaft für Informatik, 2004), and codes of conduct for ICT professions (Berleur & Brunnstein, 1996; Schefe, 1995; Wedekind, 1987) needs to be complemented by a discussion of how a sustainable information society can become real. The memorandum of the association "Nachhaltige Informationsgesellschaft" (Sustainable Information Society) is a good example of a document working for the creation of a coherent set of policy measures for that goal.

THE MEMORANDUM "SUSTAINABLE INFORMATION SOCIETY"

The professional association "Nachhaltige Informationsgesellschaft" (Sustainable Information Society) was created as a working group of the German Society for Informatics in the year 2000 by Michael Paetau, Bonn, and Lorenz M. Hilty, St. Gallen. Its aim is to combine research and policy making on the two global trends of sustainable development and on the information soci-

ety. The association's members are of the opinion that the development of an information society is strongly influenced by modern ICTs, unfortunately without due respect to sustainability criteria.

The "Memorandum Nachhaltige Informationsgesellschaft" ("A Sustainable Information Society Doesn't Come About by Itself"), published in 2004, provides a synthesis of the association's work so far. It aims to clarify the contribution ICT can make towards sustainable development (Dompke et al., 2004). First of all, the opportunities and risks of ICT development are considered with respect to sustainable development. This *inventory* forms a basis for practical recommendations and "good practice" examples for selected domains. The role of this memorandum is to push the envelope further and to consolidate the existing dialogue. The document is addressed to members of the scientific community, including teachers and students in all kinds of educational establishments, as well as to political and corporate decision makers.

We present here a two-dimensional grid of criteria for showing the complex relationships between ICTs and sustainability: these comprise the fundamental criteria for sustainable development set against three different levels of impact of ICT development.

The fundamental sustainability criteria comprise the following three dimensions:

- **Human Compatibility:** Individuals should not suffer damages from development. Their personal dignity must be respected.
- **Social Compatibility:** Relationships of people with one another and the resulting society should not be infringed. Individual participation in our communities needs to be protected and supported.
- **Ecological Compatibility:** The natural environment must not be irreversibly damaged, and our life support systems must be protected.

These three criteria reflect the fundamental relationships of humans with their surrounding environment (Isenmann, 2001). They are an expression of the ethical implications (cf. Table 1) and cover the major themes of sustainable development. The three perspectives include the widely discussed three categories of economic, environmental, and social development—the "three pillars of sustainable development" (cf. e.g., Deutscher Bundestag, 1998).

The impact of ICT on individuals, society, and nature is classified according to three different perspectives:

1. **effects of ICT provision**, e.g., use of resources and energy in the manufacturing, use and disposal of ICT hardware;
2. **effects of ICT use**, e.g., energy savings from process optimization or commuter traffic reduction as a result of telecommunication; and
3. **systemic effects**, e.g., rebound effects as a reaction to efficiency gains, changes of economic structures, institutions, and consequences for individual lifestyles.

The combination of the three sustainability criteria and the three levels of ICT impact results in a 3x3 matrix. The memorandum discusses all nine fields, in the form of a description of the *status quo* and practical recommendations for attaining a sustainable information society.

For the domain of *ICT provision,* covering all measures for the creation and maintenance of ICT infrastructure, the three main recommendations are:

- All aspects of ICT provision should be scrutinized with regard to their impact on *human working conditions* (human compatibility).
- Evaluating the quality of ICT provision should include social factors, among them *free access* to make use of the opportunities they offer (social compatibility).
- Lastly, ICT must be manufactured, used, and disposed in a manner that respects *ecological criteria* (ecological compatibility).

The *use of ICT* concerns all aspects of social life, ICT at the workplace, as well as for household use and entertainment. The following three recommendations apply:

- ICT use should always promote the *users' autonomy,* and technical dependence must be avoided that degrades people into objects of ICT (human compatibility).
- A democratic and mature use of ICT requires users to be adequately competent not just in the technical use of ICT, but also in the *critical reflection on their usefulness* (social compatibility).

Figure 1. Roadmap of a sustainable information society

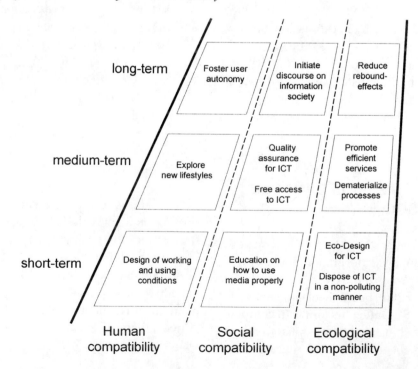

- The development of resource-efficient ICT-based services (replacing products) is an important part of good ICT use. The necessary production processes need to be *dematerialized* (ecological compatibility).

Apart from the direct effects of provision and use, ICT leads to a number of *secondary effects* separated in space and time from the first. The following three recommendations need to be considered:

- Research must be undertaken on the *new lifestyles* brought about by ICT, so that changes in human behavior are better understood (human compatibility).
- A *societal discourse* on the information society needs to be established and institutionalized, comprising a critical discussion on the aims and development paths (social compatibility).
- Lastly, *rebound effects* must be neutralized so that the achieved efficiency gains and possible resource savings are not offset by other, wasteful ways of using ICT (ecological compatibility).

From a perspective of short-term, medium-term, and long-term measures to be taken, we can classify the above recommendations into a framework of priorities with respect to their importance and time requirements (Möhrle & Isenmann, 2005). This matrix describes activities that must be tackled immediately or in the short term, others that have a more medium-term timeframe, and lastly long-term aims (see Figure 1).

Such a matrix, resembling a roadmap, can provide a concise overview of important milestones on the way towards a sustainable information society.

CONCLUSION

Can we create a sustainable path towards an information society? Even if we leave our personal convictions aside for the moment, we can see clearly that ICTs do not just bring about new opportunities, but also new problems. Whether in a prudent or in an optimistic way, we need to be able to manage those opportunities and risks of ICTs. On the one hand, fears need to be taken seriously and accepted as indicators for risk, without giving in to pessimism and panic (Röglin, 1994). On the other hand, the opportunities that ICTs offer merit exploitation and not a categorical refusal.

According to the first World Summit on the Information Society held in 2003 in Geneva, the potential for synergy of sustainable development and an information society has not yet been recognized: the lack of "digital visions" is deplored (von Damm & Schallaböck, 2004). An essential requirement for a sustainable information society, however, must be an ethical consideration of relevant criteria, an appropriate scale for ICT application, and their implementation. An ethics for a sustainable information society will be based on compatibility with individuals, communities, and nature. Modern ICT, a powerful development vector for technological progress, economic growth, and social change, will play a key role in the development towards a sustainable information society. Only if the discourse on information society is combined with the discourse on sustainability will it be possible to avoid negative effects of ICT on humans, society, and nature. The challenge consists of winning the hearts and minds of ICT experts and decision makers for sustainable development.

REFERENCES

Angrick, M. (2002). Das Internet— Antwort Auf Die Frage Nach Information und Nachhaltigkeit. In G. Altner (Eds.), *Jahrbuch ökologie 2003* (pp. 124-130). München: Beck.

Beckett, R. (2004). Communication ethics and the Internet: Intercultural and localizing influencers. *International Journal of Information Ethics, 2,* 1-8.

Behrendt, S., Hilty, L.M., & Erdmann, L. (2003). Nachhaltigkeit und Vorsorge—Anforderungen der Digitalisierung an das Politische System. *Aus Politik Und Zeitgeschichte, B*(42), 13-20.

Berleur, J., & Brunnstein, K. (Eds.). (1996). *A handbook prepared by the International Federation for Information Processing (IFIP) Ethics Task Group.* London: Chapman & Hall.

Berleur, J., Ducenoy, P., & Whitehouse, D. (Eds.). (1999). *Ethics and the governance of the Internet—to promote discussion inside the International Federation for Information Processing (IFIP) National Societies.*

Laxenburg: IFIP. Retrieved March 12, 2005, from http://www.info.fundp.ac.be/~jbl/IFIP/cadresIFIP.html

Binswanger, M. (2001). Technological progress and sustainable development: What about the rebound effect? *Ecological Economics, 36,* 119-132.

BMWA (Bundesministerium für Wirtschaft und Arbeit). (2003). Aktionsprogramm der Bundesregierung. In Bundesministerium für Bildung und Forschung (BMBF) (Eds.), *Informationsgesellschaft Deutschland 2006.* Berlin: BMWA, BMBF.

BMWA (Bundesministerium für Wirtschaft und Arbeit). (2002). Innovation und Arbeitsplätze in der Informationsgesellschaft des 21. Jahrhunderts. Fortschrittsbericht zum 6. Aktionsprogramm der Bundesregierung. In Bundesministerium für Bildung und Forschung (BMBF) (Eds.), *Informationsgesellschaft Deutschland.* Berlin: BMWA, BMBF.

Capurro, R., Scheule, R., & Hausmanninger, T. (Eds.). (2004). *Vernetzt gespalten. Der Digital Divide in ethischer Perspektive.* München: Fink.

Capurro, R., Wiegerling, K., & Brellochs, A. (Eds.). (1995). *Informationsethik. Schriften zur Informations-Swirtschaft, band 18.* Konstanz: UVK Universitätsverlag Konstanz.

Deutscher Bundestag. (1998). *Final report of the 13th German Bundestag's Enquete Commission on the protection of humanity and the environment: Objectives and general conditions of sustainable development.* Bonn: Economica.

Dompke, M. et al. (2004). *Memorandum nachhaltige Informationsgesellschaft.* Stuttgart: Fraunhofer IRB. Retrieved January 24, 2005, from http://www.giani-memorandum.de

Eckardt, F. (2005). *Das Prinzip Nachhaltigkeit. Generationengerechtigkeit und globale Gerechtigkeit.* München: Beck.

Forum Information Society. (1998). *Challenges 2025: On the way to a sustainable world-wide information society.* Ulm: Research Institute for Applied Knowledge (FAW). Retrieved February 6, 2001, from http://europa.eu.int/ISPO/policy/isf/documents/decla.../Challenges-2025-Declaration.htm

Gesellschaft für Informatik (GI). (2004). *Ethische Leitlinien der Gesellschaft für Informatik. Ausgear-beitet vom Arbeitskreis: Informatik und Ethik.* Bonn: GI. Retrieved February 4, 2005, from http://www.gi-ev.de/verein/struktur/ethische_leitlinien.shtml

Grober, U. (2002). Modewort mit tiefen Wurzeln—kleine Begriffsgeschichte von "Sustainability" und "Nachhaltigkeit." In G. Altner et al. (Eds.), *Jahrbuch Ökologie 2003* (pp. 167-175). München: Beck.

Grossmann, W.D. et al. (2002). Sozial- und umweltfreundliche Informationsgesellschaft. In I. Balzer & M. Wächter (Eds.), *Sozial-ökologische Forschung. Ergebnisse der Sondierungsprojekte aus dem BMBF-förderschwerpunkt* (pp. 261-280). München: Oekom.

Harborth, H.J. (1993). *Dauerhafte Entwicklung statt globaler Selbstzerstörung. Eine Einführung in das Konzept des "sustainable development* (2nd ed.). Berlin: Edition Sigma.

Hauff, V. (Ed.). (1987). *Unsere gemeinsame Zukunft—der Brundtland-Bericht der Weltkommission für Umwelt und Entwicklung.* Greven: Eggenkamp.

Hausmanninger, T. (Ed.). (2003). *Handeln im Netz. Bereichsethiken und Jugendschutz im Internet.* München: Fink.

Hilty, L.M. et al. (2005a). *The precautionary principle in the information society—effects of pervasive computing on health and environment* (2nd rev. ed). Bern: Swiss Center for Technology Assessment (TA-SWISS), TA46e/2005, and the Scientific Technology Options Assessment at the European Parliament, STOA 125 EN. Retrieved March 6, 2006, from http://www.ta-swiss.ch/www-support/reportlists/publicationsinfosoc_d.htm

Hilty, L.M., & Ruddy, T.F. (2000). Towards a sustainable information society. *Informatik, 4,* 2-9.

Hilty, L.M., Seifert, E.K., & Treibert, R. (Eds.). (2005b). *Information systems for sustainable development.* Hershey, PA: Idea Group.

Hilty, L.M., Som, C., & Köhler, A. (2004). Assessing the human, social, and environmental risks of pervasive computing. *Human and Ecological Risk Assessment, 10*(5), 853-874.

International Journal of Information Ethics. (2004, February). Retrieved January 5, 2005, from http://www.ijie.org

Isenmann, R. (2001). Basic ethical framework. Guidance for environmental informatics towards a sustainable information society. In L.M. Hilty & P.W. Gilgen (Eds.), *Sustainability in the information society* (pp. 127-134). Marburg: Metropolis.

Jonas, H. (1984). *The imperative of responsibility: In search of an ethics for the technological age*. Chicago: University of Chicago Press.

Jorissen, J. et al. (1999). *Ein integratives Konzept nachhaltiger Entwicklung. Wissenschaftliche Berichte FZKA 6393*. Karlsruhe: Forschungszentrum Karlsruhe. Technik und Umwelt.

Journal of Industrial Ecology. (2002). Special issue on e-commerce, the Internet, and the environment. *Journal of Industrial Ecology, 6*(2).

Mittelstraß, J. (1992). *Leonardo-Welt: Über Wissenschaft, Forschung und Verantwortung*. Frankfurt am Main: Suhrkamp.

Möhrle, M.G., & Isenmann, R. (Eds.). (2005). *Technologie-Roadmapping. Zukunftsstrategien für Technologieunternehmen* (2nd ed.). Berlin: Springer.

Möller, A., & Bornemann, B. (2005). Kyoto ist anderswo. Zwischen Interdisziplinarität und Nachhaltigkeit. *Informatik Spektrum, 28*(1), 15-23.

Müller-Merbach, H. (1998). Der Dreiklang—technischer Fortschritt, wirtschaftliches Wachstum, gesellschaftlicher Wandel. *Technologie & Management, 37*(3), 6-9.

Orwat, C., & Grunwald, A. (2005). Information und Kommunikationstechnologien und nachhaltige Entwicklung. In S. Mappus (Ed.), *Erde 2.0—technologische Innovationen als Chance für eine nachhaltige Entwicklung?* (pp. 243-273). Berlin: Springer-Verlag.

Ott, K., & Döring, R. (2004). *Theorie und Praxis starker Nachhaltigkeit*. Marburg: Metropolis.

Radermacher, F.J., van Dijk, J.A., & Pestel, R. (2000). The European way: Towards a global information society. In K. Tochtermann & W.-F. Riekert (Eds.), *Hypermedia im Umweltschutz* (pp. 23-32). Marburg: Metropolis.

Rautenstrauch, C., & Patig, S. (Eds.). (2001). *Environmental information systems in industry and administration*. Hershey, PA: Idea Group.

Röglin, H.-C. (1994). *Technikängste und wie man damit umgeht*. Düsseldorf: VDI-Verlag.

Rohbeck, J. (1993). *Technologische Urteilskraft: Zu einer ethik technischen Handelns*. Frankfurt am Main: Suhrkamp.

Rolf, A. (1998). Herausforderungen für die Wirtschaftsinformatik. *Informatik-Spektrum, 21*(5), 259-264.

Schauer, T. (2000). *Lifestyles, future technologies and sustainable development*. Ulm: Research Institute for Applied Knowledge Processing (FAW).

Schauer, T. (2000). *The sustainable information society—visions and risks*. Ulm: Universitätsverlag Ulm.

Schefe, P. (1995). Philosophische Ethik und Informatik. *Ethica, 3*(4), 381-397.

Schefe, P. (2001). Ohnmacht der Ethik? Über professionelle Ethik als Immunisierungsstrategie. *Informatik-Spektrum, 24*(3), 154-162.

Schneidewind, U., Truscheit, A., & Steingräber, G. (Eds.). (2000). *Nachhaltige Informationsgesellschaft. Analyse und Gestaltungsmöglichkeiten aus Management und institutioneller Sicht*. Marburg: Metropolis

Spaemann, R. (1989). *Basic moral concepts* (trans. T.J. Armstrong). London/ New York: Routledge.

Spaemann, R. (1993). *Glück und Wohlwollen. Versuch über Ethik* (3rd ed.). Stuttgart: Klett-Cotta.

Technical Committee (TC) 4.6.1 "Computer Science in Environmental Protection" of the German Computer Society. (2006). *Information about the TC*. Retrieved February 24, 2006, from http://www.iai.fzk.de/Fachgruppe/GI/welcome.eng.html

Teitscheid, P. (2002). *Nachhaltige Produkt und Dienstleistungsstrategien in der informationsgesellschaft*. Berlin: Erich Schmidt.

von Damm, T., & Schallaböck, J. (2004). *Fehlende digitale Visionen—Bilanz des ersten Teils des Weltgipfels zur Informationsgesellschaft*. Bonn: Forum Umwelt & Entwicklung, Berlin: Deutscher Naturschutzring (DNR) und Perspektiven Globaler Politik (Per Global).

von Geibler, J., Kuhndt, M., & Türk, V. (2005). Virtual networking without a backpack? Resource consumption of information technologies. In L.M. Hilty, E.K. Seifert, & R. Treibert (Eds.), *Information systems for sustainable development* (pp. 109-126). Hershey: Idea Group.

Waage, S., Shah, R., & Girshick, S. (2003). Information technology and sustainability: Enabling the future. *International Journal of Corporate Sustainability, 10*(4), 281-296.

Wedekind, H. (1987). Gibt es eine Ethik der Informatik. Zur Verantwortung des Informatikers. *Informatik-Spektrum, 10*(6), 324-328.

Weizenbaum, J. (1976). *Computer power and human reason: From judgment to calculation.* New York: W.H. Freeman & Company.

Woesler, M. (2005). *Ethik der Informationsgesellschaft. Privatheit und Datenschutz. Nachhaltigkeit, Humans-, Sozial-und Naturverträglichkeit, Interessen und Wertekonflikte, Urheber und Menschenrechte.* Berlin: European University Press.

World Bank. (2004). *Engendering information & communication technologies. Challenges & opportunities for gender-equitable development.* Washington, DC: World Bank.

Zwierlein, E. (1998). Digitale Zukunft. Philosophische Reflexionen zur Verantwortung im Informationszeitalter. In E. Zwierlein & R. Isenmann (Eds.), *Virtuelle Welten und Teleworking. Herausforderungen–chan-Cen–Risiken* (pp. 5-13). Aachen: Shaker.

Zwierlein, E., & Isenmann, R. (1995). *Ökologischer Strukturwandel und Kreislaufökonomie. Wege zu einer umweltorientierten Materialwirtschaft.* Idstein: Schulz-Kirchner.

KEY TERMS

Ecological Compatibility: A fundamental sustainability criterion emphasizing that nature must not be irreversibly damaged, and its life support systems must be protected.

Ethics: The theory of moral acts dealing with how individuals may lead their lives successfully. The aim of ethics is the way of reaching a state of happiness, via a path of virtue. As a pursuit of a successful and happy life, ethics includes an interest in the social and natural world surrounding the individual. In total, ethics is an attempt to evaluate the moral experience in a normative manner.

Human Compatibility: A fundamental sustainability criterion stressing that individuals should not suffer damages from development. Their personal dignity must be respected.

Information Society: An approach of a post-industrial society characterized through the rapid progress and ubiquitous use of information and communication technologies in many domains, be it lifestyle, private consumption and industrial production of good and services, professional work, or governmental affairs and administration.

Social Compatibility: A fundamental sustainability criterion highlighting that relationships of people with one another and the resulting society should not be infringed upon. Individual participation in our communities needs to be protected and supported.

Sustainability Criteria: The fundamental requirements that must be taken into account for any decision making to approach sustainability. The fundamental sustainability criteria comprise the three dimensions of human compatibility, social compatibility, and ecological compatibility. These dimensions include the widely used "three pillars" of sustainable development.

Sustainability: A normative concept with the aim to create economic living conditions that enable all the earth's population to satisfy their needs today, without compromising the ability of future generations to satisfy theirs (short form of sustainable development).

Sustainable Information Society: A development goal with the aims of sustainability and an information society as its converging elements. As a concept it brings together in a systematic manner the policy approaches on information society and sustainable development, finally to benefit from the opportunities ICTs can offer for sustainable development, while also managing the associated risks.

Taxonomy of Computer and Information Ethics

Sabah S. Al-Fedaghi
Kuwait University, Kuwait

INTRODUCTION

Computer ethics, information ethics, personal informa-tion ethics, privacy ethics, and many other terms that juxtapose the terms "ethics," "privacy," and "informa-tion" call for a uniform treatment to understand the topography of these topics. This article presents the taxonomy of the ethical landscape in terms of catego-ries that serve to differentiate among privacy-related discourses in ordinary ethics, information ethics, and personal information ethics. The taxonomy is applied to distinguish between different forms of privacy intrusion on personal information.

THE ETHICAL LANDSCAPE

Our objective is to present a taxonomy of the ethical landscape. Such a venture is first motivated by a more modest problem. Al-Fedaghi (2007) claims that there are several types of privacy intrusion in personal in-formation ethics (PIE). Also, it is claimed that there is a difference between the act of intruding on a person and intruding on that person's personal information. Al-Fedaghi (2007) investigated these types of privacy intrusion in the context of Floridi's case of "the husband who reads the diary of his wife without her permission" (Floridi, 1998). Still, it is not clear how these types of intrusions are related to ordinary ethics, information ethics (IE), and PIE. Even if the wife's dairy is blank, there is a sense of privacy intrusion. If we are to accept the PIE thesis that such an intrusion is non-PIE intru-sion, how does it relate to privacy? In general, we may ask: what is the nature of privacy that does not involve personal information? To answer such a question, we have to look at the topology of different ethics and then position each ethical setting accordingly. Upon surveying the ethical landscape, we find a disarray of terms that do not suit our purpose.

There are many assertions regarding the domain of different ethics. Computer ethics (CE) is said to be unique in terms of providing answers to new ethical situations, since traditional ethics does not apply to these cyber-situations (Moor, 1985). Information eth-ics means different things, such as computer ethics, business ethics, medical ethics, and so forth (Floridi, 2005). Floridi (1998) proposed to base IE on the concept of information, as its basic phenomenon is recognized to have an intrinsic moral value. Floridi and Sanders (2004) extended the ethical discourse of IE to include the analysis of the artificial agent's morality "in order to understand a range of new moral problems not only in computer ethics but also in ethics in general, especially in the case of distributed morality." Al-Fedaghi (2007) proposed to adapt Floridi's notion of the moral value of information to personal information such that personal information ethics recognizes personal information itself as having an intrinsic moral value.

Other types of ethics that are related to information and privacy may be referred to as "privacy ethics," "ethics of privacy," "ethics of information," "ethics of information privacy," "ethics of informational privacy," "privacy-based ethics," and so forth. According to Duncan (1994): "We need to be (1) guided by an *ethics of information*, and (2) cognizant of special problems raised by computer and communications technology.... lack of relevant ethical guidance suggests the need for a new framework for consideration of privacy and information issues." This terminology that juxtaposes the terms "ethics," "privacy," and "information" raises the issue of the connection among these terms.

To deal with this problem, Al-Fedaghi (2007) proposed an agent-patient model as a foundation for the taxonomy of ethics. Different types of agents and patients are identified, utilizing the notions of person/ non-person, identifiability, informational ontology, and privacy-relatedness. Accordingly, the taxonomy reveals 70 kinds of ethical categories.

TAXONOMY OF ETHICS

The taxonomy of ethical landscape is built utilizing categories that juxtapose humans, human-based systems, machines, hybrid systems formed by digital agents, artificial agents, and so forth. It answers the question: "What discourses are possible for certain types of (moral) ethical agents and patients?" It is a system that formalizes knowledge in the domain of ethics and provides a better understanding of the rationality of ethics, taking into consideration the informational/non-informational ontology of the participants and the privacy-relatedness of the category. The resultant ethical categories can facilitate the making of ethical decisions. In ethics as in law, "better understanding of the law depends upon a sound taxonomy of the law" (Geoffrey, 2004).

The Al-Fedaghi classification of types of ethics uses a model that includes the basic elements of ethical categories: agent, patient. An "ethical category" is a discerned ethical situation that includes a "typified" moral agent and a patient, according to the following:

person, human-based entity, or non-human entity. Furthermore, patients are segregated according to informational and normal ontologies and according to the privacy-relatedness of the category. The types (e.g., person) and property (identifiable) of agents and patients, and their ontology (e.g., informational) and the privacy-relatedness of the discourse (e.g., anonymity) are factors that determine what we call an *ethical category*.

Building on this classification, we categorize person agenthood into identifiable persons (e.g., *John ought to tell the truth*) and non-identifiable persons (e.g., *A person should not murder another person*). The latter type is in contrast to non-identifiable human-based agents, as in *The government ought to protect the environment,* or identifiable human-based agents, as in *The USA ought to join the Kyoto accord.* The person-patients also are divided into identifiable and non-identifiable patients.

Additionally, patients are further classified according to their ontology: ordinary or informational. Ordinary ontology refers to the usual physical and

Table 1. Taxonomy of ethics according to agents and patients

			Ontology of Patient	Privacy-Related	AGENT				
					Person		Human-Based		Non-Human
					Identifiable	Non-Identifiable	Identifiable	Non-Identifiable	
PATIENT	Person	Identifiable	Ordinary	P	1	2	3	4	5
				N	6	7	8	9	10
			Information	P	11	12	13	14	15
				N	16	17	18	19	20
		Non-Identifiable	Ordinary	P	21	22	23	24	25
				N	26	27	28	29	30
			Information	P	31	32	33	34	35
				N	36	37	38	39	40
	Human-Based		Ordinary	-	41	42	43	44	45
			Information	-	46	47	48	49	50
	Non-Human		Ordinary	-	51	52	53	54	55
			Information	-	56	57	58	59	60
	Personal Information		Information	P	61	62	63	64	65
				N	66	67	68	69	70

P: Privacy-related situation with respect to the patient

N: Non-privacy-related situation with respect to the patient

"-": Indicates irrelevancy, since privacy is defined to be applied only to humans

non-physical ethical entities. Informational ontology refers to the ontology of Floridi's IE infosphere where everything is a "packet of information." IE implicitly assumes that such an ontological principle is applied only to patients.

The final taxonomy is shown in Table 1, which includes 70 ethical categories numbered from 1 to 70. We will refer to category i as Ci. We next describe different ethical categories given in this table.

ETHICAL CATEGORIES

First, we will explain the ethical categories C1, C6, C11, and C16. As shown in Table 2, these types of ethical categories include identifiable persons, categorized according to the ontology of the patient and privacy-relatedness of the discourse. We separate privacy-based ethics from other types of ethics that involve non-privacy-related acts (e.g., murder). Also, we separate ethics through specifying the ontology: IE normative principles (e.g., *entropy is bad*) from *ordinary* normative principles (e.g., *bad because anonymity encourages crimes*).

Categories Involving an Identifiable Person as Patient

These categories include categories C1 through C20. We will discuss C1, C6, C11, and C16 in that order; we also will take the opportunity to explain their relationship with the other categories to the left of them in Table 1.

C1 (Patient: Person, Identifiable, Ordinary Ontology, Privacy-Related Category)

Figure 1 represents an ethical category that includes an agent type who is an identifiable person who acts on a patient type who also is an identifiable person. We assume that some ethical value is associated with the act.

In this example, the patient's ontology is ordinary, in contrast to informational in the sense of the IE of informational ontology. The ethical category reflects a statement such as *Alice ought not to ridicule John while he is strolling downtown wearing red pants.* This category involves privacy-related discourse since we assume that the ridicule is triggered by the sight of John having taken the liberty in choosing to wear his clothes in a public setting.

This privacy-related category (row C1 is labeled "P" in Table 1) is not in the domain of personal information ethics, as will be discussed further later. The act (ridiculing) is directed towards the patient himself and does not involve his personal information. It is a type of "passive privacy" where the person has privacy because "others leave him/her alone." "Privacy" here means freedom "from" being subjected to others' activities with regard to private *affairs* (not information).

To illustrate the relationship between categories, we jump two positions to the right of C1 in Table 1 to C3, where the agent is a human-based entity (e.g., organization) and the ethical category is still a privacy-related category (row labeled with "P"). A possible statement in C3 is *The New York Times ought not to publish that John's cause of death was drug overdose.* The New York Times (a human-based organization) is the agent and John (a human) is the patient. Here we can see the benefit of distinguishing between C1 and C3. The same act can be right in one category and wrong in another category. In C1, *Doctor Alice ought to tell her patient Jim (who told her that he is a drug addict) that John's cause of death was drug overdose.* The difference (*ought not to publish* vs. *ought to tell*) is that in C3, the agent is a human-based entity while the agent in C1 is an *identifiable* person (hence, her profession is known and professional ethics requires

Table 2. C1, C6, C11, and C16 classified according to ontology and privacy

		Privacy	
		Related	Non-Related
Ontology	Ordinary	C1	C6
	Informational	C11	C16

such an act). We will discuss this issue further later. If we move one position to the right in Table 1, the human-based entity is non-identifiable, hence includes such a statement as *A newspaper ought not to publish that John's cause of death was drug overdose.*

C6 (Person, Identifiable, Ordinary Ontology, Non-Privacy-Related Category)

Consider the ethical statement: *Jim's act of murdering John is wrong because God says it is wrong.* The ethical category here is concerned with an identifiable person with ordinary ontology and non-privacy-based matters (row labeled "N" in Table 1). The moral judgment is based on ordinary ontology and reasons that usually are given by different classical ethical theories. As in C1, C6 is a case of ordinary ethics (e.g., deontological) where the agent is a person and the patient is a person. If we say *Jim's act of murdering is wrong*, then such a statement may fall into several categories because the agent is not specified. It can be in:

C2 or C16: If the patient is known.
C26 or C36: If the patient is an unknown person.
C41 or C46: If the patient is a group of people (e.g., Al Capone killing a group of people in the St. Valentine's Day Massacre).
C51 and C56: If the patient is a robot (!).

In this scenario, categories C1, C11, C21, and C31 are excluded because "murdering" is not a privacy-related event. Further categories can be formed if the statement is *Murdering is wrong*, where we move on to categories that involve different types of agents. The reader may now see a general picture of generalization and specification as we move down or to the right of Table 1. For example, *Any person ought not to murder another person* is in categories C27 (ordinary ontology—hence, ordinary ethics) or C37 (informational ontology—hence, IE).

C11 (Patient: Person, Identifiable, Informational Ontology, Privacy-Related Category)

This type of category is a privacy-related category and a sub-class of Floridi's IE where the patient is a person. Consider the statement *Alice ought not to ridicule John while he is strolling downtown wearing red pants*, discussed in C1, where the moral justification is based on ordinary ontology such as *Alice's act is bad because she should not interfere with the liberty of a person in selecting his clothing as long as he has not violated the law.* Privacy in C1 is based on liberty. On the other hand in the context of category C11, the patient is considered—according to the IE thesis—as a "packet of information." The following justification may be introduced: The act is wrong because the person, as an information entity, has the right to be different. Information is *a difference that makes a difference* (Gregory Bateson), and entropy is the condition of no difference.

C16 (Patient: Person, Identifiable, Informational Ontology, Non-Privacy-Related Category)

Consider the C16 ethical statement *Jim ought not to assassinate John because John is an informational entity.* In this case, John is an identified patient in a non-privacy-related act. According to Floridi's IE, everything is a "packet of information," hence the base for ethical judgment is different from ordinary ethics. To the right of C16, we see category C17 in Table 1, where the agent is an unidentified person and the ethical category is a non-privacy-related category, as in *A person ought not to assassinate John because he is an informational entity.* If we move three positions down to C37 (non-identifiable agent and patient), we find the statement *A person ought not to assassinate another person because every person is an informational entity.*

If we look to the right of C17, in category C19, we can find the statement *The government ought not to assassinate John because John is an informational entity.* If we move four positions below C46, we find C50, which corresponds to *The government ought not to assassinate a person because he/she is an informational entity.* We can see here that the ethical judgment may differ depending on the type of ethics. For example, *A person ought to shoot any murderer* (C27) seems to be wrong, while *A government ought to hang any murderer* (C39) seems to be right.

Categories Involving a Non-Identifiable Person as a Patient

Categories C21 through C36 are similar to C1 through C16, except that the patient is not a particular person because of the absence of his/her identity.

C21 (Patient: Person, Unidentifiable, Ordinary Ontology, Privacy-Related Category)

An example of statements in C21 is: *It is bad that John published the name of the public figure, who was a relative of a man arrested by the police.* If we generalize these statements, as in C19, we have: *It is bad that a journalist published the name of the public figure, who was a relative of a man arrested by police.*

C26 (Patient: Person, Unidentifiable, Ordinary Ontology, Non-privacy-Related Category)

An example in C26 is: *John's murdering of a stranger is wrong because religion says it is bad.* Notice that the judgment that *John's murdering of a stranger is wrong* is in C26 or C36, depending on whether the justification is based on informational or ordinary ontology.

C31 (Patient: Person, Unidentifiable, Informational Ontology, Privacy-Related Category)

An example of a statement in C31 is: *John ought not to spy on the private affairs of another person because this increases information entropy in our infosphere.* This can be generalized in C32 to *Any person ought not to spy on the private affairs of another person because this increases information entropy in our infosphere,* which in turn can be generalized in C34 to *The government agency ought not to spy on private affairs of a person because this increases information entropy in our infosphere.*

C36 (Patient: Person, Unidentifiable, Informational Ontology, Non-Privacy-Related Category)

An example of a statement in C36 is: *The television host John ought not to show an exotic suicide scene of an unidentified man because it may cause "copycat" suicides, hence destroying informational entities.*

Categories Involving Human-Based Entity as a Patient

These categories include mainly C41-50. Again, we categorize agents according to their (hypothetical) ontology—informational and ordinary ontology—to accommodate Floridi's information ethics, which counts every entity as an informational entity. We claim that our method of distinguishing between these types of categories contributes to clarifying several ethical issues.

Example: Stanley (1998) gives the following argument as an example of the wrong usage of inductive generalization:

1. Murder is wrong
2. Genocide is not murder
3. Therefore, genocide is not wrong

Stanley (1998) uses the distinction between *Murder is wrong* in "fact" and *Murder is wrong* by "`defini-tion`" to refute such an argument. In our taxonomy, we can avoid this type of argument by identifying the type of ethical category related to each statement. Identifying the exact category in Table 1 would fix the meaning of the statements.

Let us ignore the type of agent and concentrate on the type of patient. *Murder* in statement (1) needs a patient to identify the relevant category. Genocide is a description of an act on *people of a certain race* (human-based categories C41-C45), hence to make statements (1) and (2) patient-compatible, (1) should be written as (4) *Murdering people of a certain race is wrong.*

Similarly, statement (2) *Genocide is not murder,* as a declarative version of the same ethical discourse, needs a patient:

- If we know that *genocide* is *murdering people of a certain race,* then (2) should be written as the contradictory statement (5) *Murdering people of a certain race is not murder.*

- Assume that we do not know that *genocide* is *murdering* people of a certain race. In the absence of any specific meaning of *genocide,* statement (2) should be written as (6) *Acting on people of a certain race is not murder.* We cannot say in (3) *Genocide is not wrong* because we cannot say *Acting on people of a certain race is not wrong.* Statement (4) is an example of such an act that is wrong.

Thus, we have avoided Stanley's argument by mapping the given statement to the "right" ethical category.

Categories Involving a Non-Human as a Patient

These ethical categories include C51 through C60. We do not distinguish between "privacy-related" and "non-privacy-related" discourses here because we assume that the notion of privacy does not apply to non-human entities. A good case that represents the ethical category C57 is the case of a boy who acts as on a dumping-ground. The boy is playing in a dumping-ground with many old abandoned cars and entertains himself by breaking their windscreens. According to information ethics, "the boy's behaviour is a case of blameworthy vandalism: [because] he is not respecting the objects for what they are, and his game is only increasing the level of entropy in the dumping-ground, pointlessly" (Floridi, 1998).

In this scenario, the patient (a dumping-ground) is a non-human entity that is viewed as an informational entity. Each category in C51-60 can be classified according to different kinds of non-human patients such as living systems (e.g., bioengineering ethics, which is concerned with "The Ethics of the Stem Cell").

From the taxonomy in Table 1, it is apparent that the ethical controversy over embryo research is a conflict regarding the "correct" category to be applied.

PERSONAL INFORMATION AS PATIENT

At this stage we can analyze our modest problem: the claim that there are several types of privacy intrusion (Al-Fedaghi, 2007). Categories C61 through C70 concern the domain of personal information ethics. Personal information is not human, nor a human-based entity that refers to human organizations. It is also not a non-human entity because it is a "constitutive part of me-hood." Notice that non-personal information is a non-human entity.

We discuss next the differences between C61-C65, which are privacy-related categories that correspond to the row labeled "P," and C66-C70, which are non-privacy-related categories that correspond to the row labeled "N." Personal information may be acted on in a private or non-private setting. The usual references to persons, such as *President Bush announced cuts in the budget,* are personal information in the strict sense of being a linguistic assertion that refers to an identified person. Nevertheless, this statement is not understood in a privacy-related sense. Public news and public reporting that embed an identifiable person are certainly not privacy-related events, even though they contain personal information in the strict sense of the definition given by Al-Fedaghi (2007). These types of personal information are in the domain of C66 through C70. These categories represent acts "on" personal information without the significance of privacy. The sensitivity of personal information may be the factor between placing personal information in C61-C65 or C66-C70. In current U.S. law, there is a sense of this difference in the significance of acts "on" personal information where even if it is disclosed publicly, the tort for public disclosure of private facts limits the liability to defendants who spread personal information in a highly offensive manner.

Not only the act, but also the type of personal information is a factor in distinguishing between applying C61-C66 or C66-C70. Consider the uproar over Kerry's bringing up Cheney's daughter's sexual preferences during the 2004 presidential debate. Supposing that he had been asked about the role of his family in his campaign and he had answered:

All politicians are helped by their families in their campaigns: Laura Bush campaigns for her husband, and Cheney's daughter campaigns for her father.

Notice that this latter statement is in C66 and refers to the same individual *Cheney's daughter,* while Kerry's actual statement in C61 has privacy significance.

CONCLUSION

The taxonomy of normal ethics, IE, and PIE uncover interesting relationships among ethical categories classified according to the agent-patient relationship, taking into consideration the types of agents and patients, their ontology, and their privacy-relatedness. The resultant classification can be applied in many fields such as different ethical and legal analyses.

REFERENCES

Al-Fedaghi, S. (2007). Personal information ethics. In M. Quigley (Ed.), *Encyclopedia of information ethics and security.* Hershey, PA: Information Science Reference.

Duncan, G.T. (1994.October 7-9). Ethics, mediating of disputes, and protecting privacy on the information highway. *Proceedings of the AAAS Conference on Ethical, Legal and Technological Aspects of Network Use and Abuse.* Retrieved from http://www.aaas.org/spp/egii/opeds/DUNCAN.HTM

Floridi, L. (1998, March 25-27). Information ethics: On the philosophical foundation of computer ethics. *Proceedings of the 4th International Conference on Ethical Issues of Information Technology* (ETHICOMP98), Erasmus University, The Netherlands.

Floridi, L. (2005). Information ethics, its nature and scope. In J. van den Hoven & J. Weckert (Eds.), *Moral philosophy and information technology.* Cambridge: Cambridge University Press.

Floridi, L., & Sanders, J.W. (2004). On the morality of artificial agents. *Minds and Machines, 14*(3), 349-379.

Geoffrey, S. (2004). English private law: Old and new thinking in the taxonomy debate. *Oxford Journal of Legal Studies, 24,* 335-362.

Moor, J. (1985). What is computer ethics? *Metaphilosophy, 16*(4), 266-279.

Stanley, M. (1998, August 10-15). The geometry of ethics. *Proceedings of the 20th World Congress of Philosophy,* Boston. Retrieved from http://www.bu.edu/wcp/Papers/TEth/TEthStan.htm

KEY TERMS

Ethical Agent: One who performs an act that has an ethical dimension.

Ethical Category: A discerned ethical situation that includes an ethical agent and an ethical patient typified according to being a person, an organization, or a non-human entity.

Ethical Patient: A recipient of an act that has an ethical dimension.

Information Ethics: A field of applied ethics that addresses issues related to information creation, processing, gathering, and disclosure.

Personal Information: Information that has referents signifying individuals.

Personal Information Ethics: A field of applied ethics that addresses issues related to personal information creation, processing, gathering, and disclosure.

Personal Information Privacy: A property of a state of affairs that involves an act on personal information.

Personal Information Security: An area of information security that addresses personal information.

Proprietor of Personal Information: The person whom a piece of personal information refers to.

Tools for Representing and Processing Narratives

Ephraim Nissan
Goldsmiths College, University of London, UK

INTRODUCTION

Narratives describe and link events. Narratives are pervasive. The representation of the handling of a project or life experiences are narratives (i.e., it is we that draw the links). Some suggest that Web sites should be designed considering visits as narratives. In research in museology, it has become popular to consider visiting a museum as a narrative. Narrative is stressed in some approaches to diagnosis (including in knowledge acquisition for intelligent systems). It stands to reason that handling narratives should loom large in information processing, or at the very least in artificial intelligence (AI). In fact, after the 1980s (during the "AI Winter"), AI retreated from a concern with narratives. However, narrative has leaked since then into other domains of computing, such as human interface design and multimedia (e.g., in tools for assisting in the editing of videos). Computational or computer tools for handling crime analysis and legal evidence need be aware of legal scholars' work on legal narratives and how to apply argumentation to their reconstruction. Ethical arguments are applied in a narrative context. Consider computer crime events: hypothetical reconstruction constructs possible narratives to match what actually happened. We focus on AI tools for analyzing or generating narratives. We also devote a section of this article to organizational storytelling, which sometimes uses databases of stories.

BACKGROUND: A CONCISE HISTORY OF THE DOMAIN

Roger Schank's *conceptual-dependency* approach to the automatic understanding of narratives is goal driven. It is based on a set of basic notions of action or thought, and in analysis it proceeds in a bottom-up fashion. Characters have a hierarchy of goals. To achieve a goal they select a plan, which itself sets some goal or goals. Schank's several books include Schank and Abelson (1977) and Schank (1986). A high level of sophistication was already achieved by conceptual-dependency theory practitioners by the early 1980s, for example in Michael Dyer's BORIS system (Dyer, 1983). Robert Wilensky (1983) introduced a detailed classification of characters' goals. Tools like BORIS parse and make sense of a narrative in a bottom-up fashion. Ethics in BORIS concerns breach of contract (e.g., adultery).

Schank's school appeared to supersede the *story-grammar* approach (Frisch & Perlis, 1981; Garnham, 1983), which is top-down and rooted in structuralism. Story grammars remain central to narratology as practiced in folklore studies. Following the appearance in 1958 of an English translation of Vladimir Propp' seminal work (Propp, 1928), in turn Dundes (1962-1975) and Jones (1979) became the foundation of the structural narratological study of folktales.

Also consider Maria Nowakowska's cluster of mathematical theories from the 1970s: her motivational calculus (Nowakowska, 1984, ch. 6), theory of actions (ch. 9), theory of dialogues (ch. 7), and theory of multimedia units for verbal and nonverbal communication (Nowakowska, 1986, ch. 3).

SOME OLDER HISTORY

In the late 1970s and early 1980s, Roger Schank's research group at Yale University "quickly became focused on understanding narratives. In a series of programs, they developed a theory of the knowledge structures necessary to understand narratives" (Mateas & Sengers, 2003, p. 2). "[T]hese early narrative systems fell out of favor" as "[t]hey were intensely knowledge-based" and therefore were difficult to be made more general (p. 2). "Except for occasional exceptions continuing in the Yale tradition, such as Mueller's model of daydreaming [(Mueller, 1990)] and Turner's

MINSTREL model of storytelling [(Turner, 1994)], sustained work on narrative disappeared from AI" (p. 3). Mueller's bibliography and portal on story processing programs (Mueller, 2005) shows that few, yet important contributions to the field kept being made throughout the 1990s. Whatever remained of narrative processing was marginalized within AI, while awareness of the importance of handling narratives surfaced sometimes in other areas of computer science (hypertext design and human-computer interface design).

Proceedings continued to appear, for example, of the *1995 AAAI Spring Symposium on Interactive Story Systems*. The MIT Media Lab's Narrative Intelligence Reading Group, active during in the 1990s, continues as an e-list. CMU's OZ interactive fiction project is influential; GLINDA fits in OZ (Kantrowitz, 1990). Story generation models include Okada and Endo (1992) and Smith and Witten (1991).

Schubert and Kwang (1989) discussed an episodic knowledge representation for narrative texts. Within Stuart Shapiro's long-lived SNePS project in knowledge-representation, consider Shapiro and Rapaport (1995) about narrative understanding. Zarri (1998) developed knowledge-representation tools, applied to narrative reports.

Several systems of interest to narrative processing were specifically concerned with explanation, such as Leake's ACCEPTER (Leake 1992, 1994)—Leake also worked on SWALE (Schank 1986)—Kass's TWEAKER/ABE (1994), and Hobbs' TACITUS (Hobbs, Stickel, Appelt, & Martin, 1993). Connectionist approaches to narrative processing include St. John's Story Gestalt model (1992), Langston, Trabasso, and Magliano (1999), and UCLA's ROBIN and DISCERN projects (Miikkulainen, 1993). Schrodt, Davis, and Weddle (1994) reported about KEDS, a program that processes event data from a Reuters data source and answers queries about news events. Hayes, Knecht, and Cellio (1988) reported about a news story categorization system. Janet Kolodner's CYRUS, applying case-based reasoning, answered queries about the travels and meetings of U.S. Secretary of State Cyrus Vance (Kolodner, 1984).

SOME RECENT WORK

AI research into the processing of narratives, active in the 1980s, declined in the 1990s, until the current comeback. See Mateas and Sengers's edited book (2003) and Bringsjord and Ferrucci on BRUTUS (2000), Mueller (2004), Halpin, Moore, and Robertson (2004), Green et al. (2004), Pérez y Pérez & Sharples (2001), Liu and Singh (2002), and Szilas and Rety (2004). Lang (ch. 12 in Mateas & Sengers, 2003) augments the story grammar approach with a treatment of goals rooted in Schank's school; Lang's system generates folktale-like stories. The 1990s saw steady progress in the field of automatic summarization as applied to reports (narrative or otherwise); see Nissan (2003a).

Introducing MAKEBELIEVE, their interactive story-generation agent, Liu and Singh (2002) claimed: "We picked story generation because we feel it is a classic AI problem that can be approached with a creative use of commonsense knowledge. Compared to problem solving or question answering, story generation is a 'softer' problem where there is no wrong solution per se, and that solution is evaluated subjectively."

MEXICA produces frameworks for short stories (Pérez y Pérez & Sharples, 2001). It combines engagement (which comprises generation) and reflection, during which, for example, it "evaluates the novelty and interestingness of the story in progress." MEXICA goes beyond "those models of computerized story-telling based on traditional problem-solving techniques where explicit goals drive the generation of stories": generation in MEXICA is done "avoiding the use of explicit goals or story-structure information" (Pérez y Pérez & Sharples, 2001), thus committing to neither goal-driven narrative processing, nor story grammars.

In COLUMBUS (unimplemented), Nissan (2002a) showed how, making a hierarchy of goals explicit, these are either character's goals or goals of the narration (which may, e.g., resort to mock-explanation). The given humorous literary text is in the genre of pastiche, and intertextuality (allusions to texts from the literary canon) plays a major role; the model captures this, just as it captures the mock-explanatory strategy of the narrator. A formal representation for narratives, which captures concepts such as beliefs, goals, purposeful action, perceptions, communication, testimony, deception, physical possession and ownership, various modes of holding or assuming an identity, and so forth, very much in debt to Schank's conceptual-dependency theory, was applied by Nissan (e.g., 2003b) to the analysis of various narratives. Nissan (2002b) analyzed Pirandello's play *Henry IV*. The application in Nissan, Hall, Lobina, and de la Motte (2004) is to policy-making analysis.

VIRTUAL ENVIRONMENTS, EMBODIED AGENTS, AND NARRATIVE

In virtual environments with animated characters, it is useful to have formal representations for feeding a narrative and instructing the characters. Some models of agent behavior are merely reactive; other models (from cognitive robotics) also endow agents with some cognitive abilities, enabling them to display reactive, as well as deliberative and social behavior. Chen, Bechkoum, and Clapworthy (2001) described an extended event calculus for a cognitive model of agents, reconciling the autonomy of the agent with agent instructability on the part of the user. That architecture also includes an emotion synthesizer. On embodied agents, see, for example, Trappl and Petta (1997), Dechau et al. (2001), and Nijholt (2002). Sometimes agents need reason about their own or another agent's body, like in a sample narrative analyzed in Nissan's TIMUR project (ongoing).

NARRATIVES OF BEHAVIOR: DECEPTION

The relations between the beliefs, goals, and actions of characters are very important. So is the manner in which these affect communication. For computer modeling of trust and deception in societies of artificial agents, see Castelfranchi and Tan (2002). IMP (Jameson, 1983) gave misleading information while avoiding outright lies. IMP may try to mislead on purpose, without actually lying. A dialog system, it impersonates a realtor, trying to rent moderately priced furnished rooms on the Hamburg market.

IMP tries to convey a good impression about the goods, and about itself as well. It would not volunteer damaging information, unless a direct, specific relevant question is made. IMP has a goal of maintaining a neutral image of itself and an impression of completeness for its own answers; on occasion, it reportedly simulated insulted surprise if an intervening question by the customer seems to imply (by detailed questioning) that IMP is concealing information. By the early

2000s, models emerged of agents' deliberately deceptive communication conveying false content.

PARTISAN GOALS AND BIAS

AI even produced tools that relate to narratives with a bias. Jaime Carbonell's POLITICS (1981) modeled U.S. hawkish vs. dovish thinking on international politics. PAULINE generated partisan reports on given events (Hovy, 1993). *Terminal Time* (Domike, Mateas, & Vanouse, 2003) generates a cookie-cutter documentary (this is a form of historical documentary that is dominant in popular media today). The program combines audiovisual segments in order to describe historical events in a way shaped by ideological rhetoric. Feedback from audiences is used in order to determine and reinforce the bias. This is related to: (a) interactive television (Blair & Meyer, 1997); and (b) tools for automating the editing of video representations.

ALIBI (Kuflik, Nissan, & Puni 1991) is a computer program that impersonates an accused person, and either seeks exoneration or admits to an account of the events, only involving a lesser liability than in the accusation. On computational approaches to legal narratives (e.g., Schum, 2001), see "Legal Evidence—Tools from Artificial Intelligence for Handling It."

ANTI-STORY IN ORGANIZATIONAL STORYTELLING

Organizational storytelling has been a fashionable narrative approach in management studies since the 1990s, being applied within the field of knowledge management. Connell (20005) is an encyclopedia entry. Several books exist; see for example Denning (2000) and Brown, Denning, Groh, and Prusak (2004). Within knowledge management, the application of organizational storytelling envisages storing the narratives in databases; retrieval is, unambitiously, by indexing.

Here are a few story types:

A springboard story is a story that enables a leap in understanding by the audience so as to grasp how an organization or community or complex system may change. A springboard story has an impact...through catalyzing understanding. It enables listeners to visualize from a story in one context what is involved in a large-scale transformation in an analogous context.... Anti-stories aim at undermining the original story." (Denning, 2004)

There are ethical concerns with eliciting stories from staff, for example, stories of failure. Staff may be anxious that employers' reassurances about the exercise are not to be trusted, and that stories disclosed verbally, or even stored in an archive, will someday be used against the employee.

RECOMMENDED APPROACH

AI's concern in the 1990s with well-defined problems was unfortunately accompanied by shying away from sustained engagement with further strengthening of AI's achievements in the *treatment of narratives*. The resurgence of that field within computing (not just AI) is to be applauded. Multimedia research will need to pay close attention. Tools for the cultural heritage (e.g., museums) need to engage narratives, and some projects strive to do so.

The emergence of tools for handling reasoning on legal evidence brought together legal narratives and tools for argumentation, and this trend should be pursued forcefully. Interface design and research into the usability of computer products need to focus on users' narratives of use. Project management can benefit from narrative approaches. Incorporating some narrative intelligence into a variety of computer tools can ultimately produce more useful tools, less "dumb" when serving their users.

FUTURE TRENDS AND CONCLUSION

AI's renewed engagement with narratives is termed narrative intelligence. Some old partitions have come down: within computing, interface design, not just AI, engages narratives; goal-driven and story-grammar approaches to analysis are being combined. Narrative processing was a major casualty of the "AI Winter" after the 1980s. Yet, also subsymbolic computation suffered a major crisis before its triumphant comeback. Likewise, computational linguistics and its subfield, machine translation, both suffered a nearly fatal setback after initial hopes from the 1950s and 1960s, yet since the 1980s they have been vindicated.

Narrative approaches permeate the social and human sciences. Social computing is on the rise. Information technology can only ignore engagement with narratives at its own peril, or rather that of its customers' satisfaction. Expectations from computing are ever higher. Remaining unable to handle narratives weights down ITC's ability to meet the challenge.

REFERENCES

Blair, D., & Meyer, T. (1997). Tools for an interactive virtual cinema. In R. Trappl & P. Petta (Eds.), *Creating personalities for synthetic actors*. Heidelberg: Springer-Verlag.

Bringsjord, S., & Ferrucci, D.A. (2000). *Artificial intelligence and literary creativity*. Mahwah, NJ: Lawrence Erlbaum.

Brown, J.S., Denning, S., Groh, K., & Prusak, L. (2005). *Storytelling in organizations*. Oxford: Butterworth-Heinemann.

Carbonell, J. (1981). POLITICS (ch. 11); Micro POLITICS (ch. 12). In R.G. Schank & C.K. Riesbeck (Eds.), *Inside computer understanding* (pp. 259-307, 308-317). Hillsdale, NJ: Lawrence Erlbaum.

Castelfranchi, C., & Tan, Y. (2002). *Trust and deception in virtual societies*. Dordrecht: Kluwer.

Chen, L., Bechkoum, K., & Clapworthy, G. (2001). A logical approach to high-level agent control. *Proceedings of the 5th International Conference on Autonomous Agents* (pp. 1-8), Montreal.

Connell, N.A.D. (2005). Organizational storytelling as a knowledge management medium. In D. Schwartz (Ed.), *Encyclopedia of knowledge management*. Hershey, PA: Idea Group.

Dechau, J., Finke, M., Gerfelder, N., Ide, R., Kirste, T., & Spierling, U. (2001). The telebuddy. *Computers and Graphics, 25*(4), 601-608.

Denning, S. (2000). *The springboard*. London: Butterworth-Heinemann.

Denning, S. (2004). *What are the main types of stories and narratives?* Retrieved from http://www.stevedenning.com/Main_types_story.html

de Rosis, F., Castelfranchi, C., & Carofliglio, V. (2000) On various sources of uncertainty in modeling suspicion and how to treat them. *Proceedings of the Workshop on Deception, Fraud and Trust in Agent Societies,* at the *Autonomous Agents 2000 Conference* (pp. 61-72).

Domike, S., Mateas, M., & Vanouse, P. (2003). The recombinant history apparatus presents *Terminal Time.* In M. Mateas & P. Sengers (Eds.), *Narrative intelligence* (pp. 155-173). Amsterdam: Benjamins.

Dundes, A. (1975). From etic to emic units in the structural study of folklore. In A. Dundes (Ed.), *Analytic essays in folklore* (pp. 61-72). The Hague: Mouton.

Dyer, M.G. (1983). *In-depth understanding.* Cambridge, MA: MIT Press.

Frisch, A.M., & Perlis, D. (1981). A re-evaluation of story grammars. *Cognitive Science, 5*(1), 79-86.

Garnham, A. (1983). What's wrong with story grammars? *Cognition, 15,* 145-154.

Green, N.L., Carenini, G., Kerpedjiev, S., Mattis, J., Moore, J.D., & Roth, S.F. (2004). AutoBrief. *International Journal of Human-Computer Studies, 61*(1), 32-70.

Halpin, H., Moore, J.D., & Robertson, J. (2004, October 15). Towards automated story analysis using participatory design. *Proceedings of the 1st ACM Workshop on Story Representation, Mechanism, and Context,* at the *12th ACM International Conference on Multimedia,* New York.

Hayes, P.J., Knecht, L.E., & Cellio, M.J. (1988). A news story categorization system. *Proceedings of the 2nd ACL Conference on Applied Natural Language Processing* (pp. 9-17).

Hobbs, J.R., Stickel, M.E., Appelt, D.E., & Martin, P. (1993). Interpretation as abduction. In F.C.N. Pereira & B.J. Grosz (Eds.), *Natural language processing* (pp. 69-142). Cambridge, MA: MIT Press.

Hovy, E.H. (1993). Automated discourse generation using discourse structure relations. *Artificial Intelligence, 63*(1/2), 341-385.

Jameson, A. (1983). Impression monitoring in evaluation-oriented dialog. *Proceedings of IJCAI'83* (vol. 2, pp. 616-620), Karlsruhe.

Jones, S.S. (1979). The pitfalls of Snow White scholarship. *Journal of American Folklore, 90,* 69-73.

Kantrowitz, M. (1990, July). *GLINDA.* Technical Report CMU-CS-90-158, Computer Science, Carnegie Mellon University, USA.

Kass, A.M. (1994). Tweaker: Adapting old explanations to new situations. In R.C. Schank, A. Kass, & C.K. Riesbeck (Eds.), *Inside case-base explanation* (pp. 263-295). Hillsdale, NJ: Lawrence Erlbaum.

Kolodner, J.L. (1984). *Retrieval and organizational strategies in conceptual memory.* Hillsdale, NJ: Lawrence Erlbaum.

Kraus, S. (1996). An overview of incentive contracting. *Artificial Intelligence, 83*(2), 297-346.

Kuflik, T., Nissan, E., & Puni, G. (1991). Finding excuses with ALIBI. *Computers and Artificial Intelligence, 10*(4), 297-325.

Langston, M.C., Trabasso, T., & Magliano, J.P. (1999). A connectionist model of narrative comprehension. In A. Ram & K. Moorman (Eds.), *Understanding language understanding* (pp. 181-226). Cambridge, MA: MIT Press.

Leake, D.B. (1992). *Evaluating explanations.* Hillsdale, NJ: Lawrence Erlbaum.

Leake, D.B. (1994). Accepter: Evaluating explanations. In R.C. Schank, A. Kass, & C.K. Riesbeck (Eds.), *Inside case-base explanation* (pp. 167-206). Hillsdale, NJ: Lawrence Erlbaum.

Liu, H., & Singh, P. (2002). MAKEBELIEVE. *Proceedings of the 18th National Conference on Artificial Intelligence* (pp. 957-958).

Mateas, M., & Sengers, P. (Eds.). (2003a). *Narrative intelligence.* Amsterdam: Benjamins.

Miikkulainen, R. (1993). *Subsymbolic natural language processing.* Cambridge, MA: MIT Press.

Mueller, E. (1990). *Daydreaming in humans and machines.* Norwood, NJ: Ablex.

Mueller, E.T. (2004). Understanding script-based stories using commonsense reasoning. *Cognitive Systems Research, 5*(4), 307-340.

Mueller, E.T. (2004). *Story understanding resources.* Retrieved from http://xenia.media.mit.edu/~mueller/storyund/storyres.html

Nijholt, A. (2002). Embodied agents: A new impetus for humor research. *Proceedings of the 12th Twente Workshop on Language Technology* (pp. 101-112).

Nissan, E. (2002a). The COLUMBUS model (two parts). *International Journal of Computing Anticipatory Systems, 12,* 105-120, 121-136.

Nissan, E. (2002b). A formalism for misapprehended identities. *Proceedings of the 20th Twente Workshop on Language Technology* (pp. 113-123).

Nissan, E. (2003a). Review of I. Mani, *Automatic Summarization* (Amsterdam: Benjamins, 2001). *Cybernetics and Systems, 34*(4/5), 559-569.

Nissan, E. (2003b). Identification and doing without it, parts I to IV. *Cybernetics and Systems, 34*(4/5), 317-358, 359-380; *34*(6/7), 467-500, 501-530.

Nissan, E., Hall, D., Lobina, E., & de la Motte, R. (2004). A formalism for a case study in the WaterTime project. *Applied Artificial Intelligence, 18*(3/4), 367-389.

Nowakowaska, M. (1984). *Theories of research* (2 vols.). Seaside, CA: Intersystems.

Nowakowaska, M. (1986). *Cognitive sciences.* Orlando, FL: Academic.

Okada, N., & Endo, T. (1992). Story generation based on dynamics of the mind. *Computational Intelligence, 8*(1), 123-160.

Pérez y Pérez, R., & Sharples, M. (2001). MEXICA. *Journal of Experimental and Theoretical Artificial Intelligence, 13*(2), 119-139.

Propp, V. (1928). *Morfologija skazki.* Leningrad, 1928. English: *Morphology of the folktale.* Bloomington: Indiana University, 1958.

Savage, T. (2000). Artificial motives. *Connection Science, 12*(3), 211-277.

Schank, R.C. (1986). *Explanation patterns.* Hillsdale, NJ: Lawrence Erlbaum.

Schank, R.C., & Abelson, R. (1977). *Scripts, plans, goals, and understanding.* Hillsdale, NJ: Lawrence Erlbaum.

Schrodt, P.A., Davis, S.G., & Weddle, J.L. (1994). Political science: KEDS. *Social Science Computer Review, 12*(4), 561-587.

Schubert, L.K., & Kwang, C.H. (1989). An episodic knowledge representation for narrative texts. *Proceedings of the 1st International Conference on Principles of Knowledge Representation and Reasoning* (KR89) (pp. 444-458), Toronto. San Francisco: Morgan Kaufmann.

Schum, D.A. (2001). Evidence marshaling for imaginative fact investigation. *Artificial Intelligence and Law, 9*(2/3), 165-188.

Shapiro, S.C., & Rapaport, W.J. (1995). An introduction to a computational reader of narratives. In J.F. Duchan, G.A. Bruder, & L.E. Hewitt (Eds.), *Deixis in narrative* (pp. 79-105). Hillsdale, NJ: Lawrence Erlbaum.

Smith, T.C., & Witten, I.H. (1991). A planning mechanism for generating story text. *Literary and Linguistic Computing, 6*(2), 119-126.

St. John, M.F. (1992). The story gestalt. *Cognitive Science, 16*(2), 271-306.

Szilas, N., & Rety, J.-H. (2004, October). Minimal structure for stories. *Proceedings of the 1st ACM Workshop on Story Representation, Mechanism, and Context,* at the *12th ACM International Conference on Multimedia* (pp. 25-32).

Trappl, R., & Petta, P. (Eds.). (1997). *Creating personalities for synthetic actors.* Heidelberg: Springer-Verlag.

Turner, S.R. (1994). *The creative process.* Mahwah, NJ: Lawrence Erlbaum.

Wilensky, R. (1983). *Planning and understanding.* Reading, MA: Addison-Wesley.

Zarri, G.P. (1998). Representation of temporal knowledge in events. *Information and Communications Technology Law, 7*(3), 213-241.

T

KEY TERMS

Automated Summarization: The generation of meaningful abstracts, by computer (Nissan 2003a).

Conceptual Dependency: Goal-driven, script-based processing of narratives.

Event Data Coding: For news flow automated analysis: the shallow narratives processing of masses of text (Schrodts et al., 1994).

Multi-Paragraph Text In-Depth Understanding: Sophisticated analysis of short, yet articulate narratives; for example, in BORIS (Dyer 1983).

Narrative Intelligence: A descriptor in use in the 2000s. Narrative as processed not only in AI, but also elsewhere in computing (interfaces, browsers, even visits to real or virtual museums).

News Story Categorization: Very shallow processing of news items, by guessing from keywords what they are about (e.g., Hayes et al., 1988).

Partisan Reports: Biased perspectives on events, in describing them or answering questions.

Story Generation: Producing narrative text as output: for example, explanations, or fables.

Story Grammar: A top-down, structuralist analysis of narratives, typically folktales.

Traditional Knowledge and Intellectual Property

Ulia Popova-Gosart
Lauravetlan Information and Education Network of Indigenous
Peoples of Russian Federation (LIENIP) and University of California in Los Angeles, USA

INTRODUCTION

During the past two decades, the search for an appropriate mechanism to protect 'traditional knowledge' has been a subject of discourse among international law and policies agents, actors of global trade, academia, environmentalists, and the indigenous-rights activists. Within the framework of international law, the discussion went into two main directions: protection of knowledge products, and protection of rights over knowledge resources as a part of a movement to preserve vitality and diversity of indigenous cultures.

Western intellectual property (IP) has been a prime mechanism for the development of legal solutions for the protection of traditional knowledge. As pertinent to the issues of indigenous peoples, the concept, the legal instrument, and the goal of intellectual property are discussed today in relation to human rights, preservation of biodiversity, indigenous cultures, religious freedom, indigenous survival, and innovation in law.

BACKGROUND

Intellectual Property: Conceptual Framework

The World Intellectual Property Organization (WIPO) refers to intellectual property as legal rights resulting from intellectual activity (WIPO, 2004). The concept is defined further by the Convention Establishing the World Property Organization (1967) and includes rights relating to artistic, literary, and scientific works; inventions; industrial designs; performances, broadcasts, and sound recordings; trademarks; scientific discoveries; protection against unfair competition; and other rights resulting from intellectual activities on the scientific, artistic, literary, and industrial levels.

The essence of the IP concept reflects a necessity of creation of the state-sponsored monopoly of ideas. The next main reason for existence of intellectual property is economic: the state guarantees an inventor profit by providing her or him with the right of ownership to stimulate, as believed, innovation/development. To answer a need to regulate both social and economic aspects of IP, most legal structures work under utilitarian perspective, where intellectual property provides a balance between the need for knowledge invention and its dissemination and open access (Maskus, 2000; Boyle, 1997).

The main categories of intellectual property are *copyrights (and related rights)* and *industrial property.*

The development of rights of ownership over knowledge stems primarily from eighteenth-century European philosophy about social progress, and is directly linked to the rise of industrial capitalism and the nation state. The most prominent historical evidence of this process, considered to be the genesis of the current copyright law, is the 1709 *Stature of Ann,* generally served to benefit publishers in early eighteenth-century England (Woodmansee & Jaszi, 1994). The major forces which allowed development of the IP concept are those that influenced major shifts in Western culture and philosophical thought:

- **Mid-1400s–18th Century**—The Print Revolution: A consequent need to consign ownership over published works -> development of a concept of authorship. **Consequence:** Author is an *original creator,* rather than a producer of a work -> a work of mind/creativity is a product and property of its creator.
- **18th–20th Centuries:** Development of science and growth of its influence in the society -> reductionism is a leading mode to evaluate knowledge. **Consequence:** Disappearance of book culture.

• **Mid-20ᵗʰ Century–Today:** Invention of information technology. **Consequence:** Knowledge as information; information as a central resource of global economy.

The two treaties that establish the base of international IP law are the *Berne Convention for the Protection of Literary and Artistic Works* (adopted in 1888) and the *Paris Convention for the Protection of Industrial Property* (1883). The third most significant document is considered to be the *TRIP* agreement (1986), which reflects an international effort to strengthen and upgrade global norms for the IP protection today.[1] Under the TRIP agreement the functional areas of the IP under protection include copyrights, trademarks, and geographic indications, patents, integrated circuits, and trade secrets.

The international forum for discourses toward development of IP as related to the issues of traditional knowledge on a global level is the World Intellectual Property Organization's Intergovernmental Committee on Intellectual Property and Genetic Resources, Traditional Knowledge and Folklore (IGC), created in 2000.

Traditional Knowledge: Conceptual Framework

The concept of traditional knowledge (also referred to as indigenous, native, and aboriginal knowledge) in respect to developments of legal structures to define rights over knowledge of indigenous communities stems primarily from the definition of "folklore," first used in the 1980s, and developed by WIPO and UNESCO.[2] "Folklore" referred to art forms, created by individuals or groups, tradition-based, group-oriented, which adequately expressed cultural and social identity and reflected the expectations of a community (expressed as language, literature, rituals, dance and music, mythology, crafts, architecture, and other art forms). The term later implied inferiority of indigenous cultures (Carpenter, 2004). The further developments resulted in the broader definition and a term, *traditional knowledge.*

Today traditional knowledge is described as a holistic concept, which embodies expressions of culture, folklore, and science. It is developed, sustained, and transmitted between generations, and presents means for defining the cultural/spiritual identity of a group or of a person. The concept includes the knowledge

derived from plants and animals to allow norms of the copyright law, patent law, and biodiversity rights standards to be applied to description and evaluation of traditional knowledge expressions and products (Daes, 1993; Blakeney, 1999; Simpson, 1997; UNPFII, 2005; WIPO, 2005).

In parallel to the developments in the spheres of international law and human rights, attempts to define distinct characteristics of traditional knowledge came from academia.[3] Efforts to describe the essence of knowledge of indigenous peoples on the base of differences within the accepted Western modes of scientific knowledge ended with the notion of absence of any universal criteria to be used to distinguish both entities (Agrawal, 2002).

Finally, from the perspectives of indigenous scholars, traditional knowledge appeared in professional literature as "living knowledge" (Urion, 1999) and consisted of physical, emotional, mental, and spiritual components. Since it comes from the Creator, it is understood as sacred; since it provides means for living and connects all living things, it is viewed as an expression of life itself. Contrary to Western scientific paradigms of knowledge evaluation, which validate certain types of data and exclude others, indigenous scholars see all experiences and all data to be relevant to all things, viewing indigenous knowledge systems as an interrelated net between all forms of existence (Stewart-Harawira, 2005).

Awareness that traditional knowledge constitutes and safeguards the foundations of indigenous cultures influences the global movement to seek protection of knowledge of indigenous communities as a part of the world heritage. A major part of this movement—the struggle of indigenous peoples to protect their cultures—is centered around concerns over misappropriation of traditional knowledge, the preservation of biodiversity, use and endorsement of knowledge for development, and outside pressures exercised on marginalized groups (Commission on Intellectual Property Rights, 2002).

DISCUSSION

The Western intellectual property system—the prime instrument for protection of rights over knowledge in the global economy—has been a conceptual framework for development of a mechanism to protect traditional knowledge.[4]

The review of literature on the subject reveals that during the past two decades the discourse over traditional knowledge protection with the means of IP went into the two main directions. Some (Posey, 1994) underline that the protection today must be directed toward exclusively traditional knowledge products; others (WSIS, 2003; UNESCO, 2005) insist that the law will also protect the environments of knowledge creation, and thus support vitality and future development of the indigenous cultures.

The concept of IP refers to protection of "creations of the mind" (WIPO, 2006) or intellectual products understood as property. Since IP legal statutes are directed to control knowledge and protect it from damage in the arena of the information market, within the IP frame, traditional knowledge can only be understood as a commodity, and used and protected as such.

IP legal agreements, however, provide a trial ground for development of international and national law for the protection of rights over traditional knowledge. The political character of these developments provides time and possibilities to better the existing IP mechanism. The law will work to further construct a conceptual apparatus over control of knowledge assets, by defining boundaries over access to knowledge and benefit-sharing means from the knowledge products.

The developments in international law to protect knowledge of indigenous peoples can also be regarded as a movement to protect creation of cultural/intellectual products (as opposed to ownership) by indigenous communities. A dialog over preservation of diverse cultures and protection of indigenous communities from political/cultural domination is the framework for these developments, as well as a movement for protection of emerging rights of indigenous peoples.

Thus, the subject of traditional knowledge protection falls into several distinctive areas, which range from an economic and legal sphere to the human rights, within a legal international framework as the prime vehicle to protect cultural heritage of indigenous communities.

PROTECTION OF TRADITIONAL KNOWLEDGE PRODUCTS

Practical application of an IP mechanism to a traditional setting reveals the main difficulty of incomparability of traditional knowledge to the technical norms of IP.

Under IP convention, knowledge can be protected only when expressed in material form. In the indigenous communities, knowledge is often conveyed in oral form and/or in the form of actions or movements. To assign authorship over these types of knowledge is impossible, unless knowledge is transformed out of its intangible state into a legally appropriate form—the process which causes traditional knowledge in part or entirely lose its characteristics as indigenous. Creation of indigenous databases to catalog specific elements of traditional knowledge and the "best practices" is the most famous evidence of this difficulty. The newly created, IP-protected forms of knowledge bore little or no relevance to the needs of the communities which developed and held traditional knowledge (Agrawal, 2002). Moreover, creation of indigenous databases brought a threat and a reality for the knowledge of indigenous peoples to become a part of public domain, the least protected information sphere today. Indigenous rights activists underline that becoming a part of public domain not only causes traditional knowledge to lose its distinctive cultural elements, but also undermines the knowledge authenticity[5] (WSIS, 2003; Brown, 2003).

The second difficulty is naming a legal personality on the base of whom the IP could be held. Communal organizational structure of most of the indigenous communities lacks a natural or corporate entity to assign rights over knowledge to. Indigenous people, as a rule, view their knowledge as a collective property and the source of their belonging and identity, rather than of economic wealth. Protection of knowledge is an individual as well as a collective responsibility realized through the net of relationships, rather than via implementation of legal norms. Thus, the issue of authorship also becomes problematic.

Finally, a problem of knowledge authenticity: traditional knowledge is historically collected information, which is centuries old. Under IP standards, traditional knowledge cannot be considered an original, new type of knowledge, but rather the intellectual commons that must be freely available for all.

These difficulties do not mean, though, that the essence of IP is an exclusively Western phenomenon; rather it is the modern IP system that is not an adequate means to protect collectively held knowledge. The logic of IP, which recognizes a legal system of compensation and licensure, is applicable to the indigenous cultures, even though they lack a legal mechanism to support it (Riley, 2004; Brown, 2003).

IP must be used as the only available instrument to protect access and sources of traditional knowledge, and compensate the communities.[6] It is more so, since lack of legal means for traditional knowledge protection often results in different versions of this knowledge to be shaped into a copyrighted cultural form and used by non-indigenous agents to generate profits. Biopiracy is among the most notorious examples of this threat (Shiva, 1997).

The use of trademarks and certificates of origin proved to be one of the most effective ways to protect indigenous cultural products today. Trademarks as symbolic representations of identity of its makers act to indicate authenticity of the products simultaneously protecting them from other companies (tempted to confuse buyers by using the same trademark). Indigenous-to-indigenous joint ventures would provide sources to develop such products and distribute them. Though causing some tension between the artistic freedom and bureaucratic control, use of trademarks as cultural attributes of indigenous communities is also a way to draw attention to the indigenous cultures, thus building a respect to the indigenous communities on the way to cultural diversity (Posey, 1996; Riley, 2004; Brown, 2003).

Protection of Traditional Knowledge Rights

Protection of the traditional knowledge rights, on the other hand, is a fundamental question of a search for an appropriate legal basis for the indigenous peoples to own their knowledge, and protect and control its use.

In the face of the emerging global information society, the issue of traditional knowledge rights protection takes a form of movement to protect integrity of indigenous cultures and world cultural diversity, as well as to ensure survival of indigenous communities in the new information environments (UNESCO, 2001, 2005). The discourse over protection of traditional knowledge rights is conducted through the dialog over protection of human rights,[7] religious freedom, environments, and cultural heritage, within the framework of international law.

The main difficulty in applying a Western IP system to protect knowledge of indigenous peoples is the system's inability to secure "collective" (ILO, 1989, or

"neighboring" (UNESCO/WIPO, 1985) rights over knowledge and their relationship to it. The existing IP system is based on the belief that an individual, not a group, owns the knowledge property, which he or she can exploit for profit and exclude others from using. Not only is the knowledge-commodity idea for the most part alien to holders of traditional knowledge, but the concept of exclusivity of knowledge right is also unacceptable to traditional worldviews.

Attempts to characterize intellectual property from the view of indigenous scholars imply that recognition of the core value of traditional knowledge through the utilitarian logic of the IP norms may be impossible (Riley, 2004). In many respects, only indigenous peoples can determine value of their knowledge, which includes spiritual, emotional, and religious aspects, impossible to measure and be compensated for. While regimes and knowledge protection protocols exist in the indigenous communities, their meaning is not derived solely from functioning of a social order in the community, but it is also a result of existence of certain beliefs and relationships among the people.

Among the solutions to develop legal norms to protect TK, the main one suggests using the combining approach as a starting point. Such an approach would incorporate[8]:

- recognition and inclusion of indigenous knowledge protection mechanisms and customary laws to the current IP system, and creation of *sue generis* instruments (Oguamanam, 2004; Almeida, 2005)[9]
- recognition and employment of systems of compensation and benefit sharing within the framework of the international law, and use of the prior informed consent principle[10] (DESA, 2005)
- repression of unfair competition

Complicated mechanisms of international law well address the unique problems inherent to the nature of knowledge of indigenous peoples (see Appendix 1). However, the current instruments of international law are still insufficient to address the problem of traditional knowledge protection in full. Moreover, the laws are frequently not implemented and remain only a theoretical tool rather than an instrument for actions.[11]

Experts also indicate that as long as the context of the market is proposed as a solution for the multilateral treaties implementation on a global scale, the dialog on the traditional knowledge protection conducted among member states and research institutions will be limited to protection of only economically valued knowledge (Gibson, 2004).

Finally, access to the laws, including legal education among indigenous population, is drastically limited, which makes interpretation of international laws concerning IP as well as intricacies of the world IP system on the local and national level increasingly difficult.

At the same time some worry that development of indigenous-oriented IP regimes will hurt IP laws by turning them into instruments to protect cultural integrity (while it is still not clear if these developments will benefit the indigenous communities) (Brown, 2003). What is clear, though, is that for as long as indigenous rightful owners of knowledge will be excluded from gaining benefits from that knowledge, IP will not gain much support.

One must note also that the international arena is frequently not the immediate traditional knowledge holders, but the governments, academia, and at times indigenous elite, whose involvement in the decision over the fate of knowledge at times has no approval from or even participation of the representatives of indigenous communities. For as long as the traditional knowledge holders remain recipients of the Western lawmakers, tolerance toward diversity will be difficult, if not impossible, to achieve.

In the meantime the core of the problem remains protection of access to knowledge. Scientific studies done on the indigenous territories and published in the West are still mostly perceived as free of obligation, even if traditional knowledge was an essential part of the research findings (Bannister, 2004). Indigenous communities remain among the most vulnerable parts of world population, with the low educational opportunities and access to information and technology.

Currently, most of them are left with only one method of protection: silence.

FUTURE TRENDS

Knowledge of indigenous peoples will be a considerable part of the future, discovered as the modern source of the wealth, developed over thousands of years. The sole fact that the knowledge, a few decades ago assessed as superstitious, is influencing global economy,

provokes major challenge and provides grounds for expectations.

However, it is preliminary to hope that this will cause rights of indigenous peoples to be respected and recognized in light of the hegemony of the global information market.

Expanding of IP rights in the global economy for the past two decades brought generation of profits for a few, rather than social good for many. It caused the free flow of knowledge from developing countries to become IP-protected, profit-generating cultural forms of the developed world. Indigenous communities are not the only communities whose knowledge depositories are threatened under the existing IP regime. Marginalized communities of the Third World, especially in the rural areas, are also under threat for as long as members of the dominating society perceive them as underdeveloped and with whom the benefits are not shared.

The clear definition of the terms and boundaries of IP application are still up in the air, and the access to the law for the most part is limited to the indigenous as well as marginalized communities. These difficulties will influence the problems of IP application to stay or even worsen.

The subject of protection of traditional knowledge is wide, interconnected with many disciplines, and has a worldwide resonance. It is directly related to cultural changes in the world of the past century, technological revolution, transformation of social institutions, and radical changes in political and social life. It is directed to recognize partial failure of the scientific rationalism to support representation of reality and be an official mode of knowledge. It touches the very substance of human societies and gives hope for the renaissance of human values in the Western world.

CONCLUSION

A weapon is an enemy even to its owner. (Turkish proverb)

In this article, which only generally discussed the topic of protection of traditional knowledge, the term "knowledge" was used in a limited fashion: it described qualities of an entity, possible to be located, measured, and presented as a specific type of evidence, a fact, a raw material, or an intellectual asset. However, by following this "exclusionary" logic, one could not avoid the two main questions:

- What alternatives can one present to evaluate knowledge?
- Who "owns" knowledge?

Knowledge belongs to an intellectual domain of life. It may be described as a source of human capacity for survival, compared to the Aristotle's regenerating power of nature to constantly evolve through the shapes of the world (and human thoughts). Knowledge may also be presented as an entity, consisting of a variety of parts and bits as different as theories placed upon their evaluation from which knowledge will always be independent. Any attempt to evaluate/define knowledge objectifies it, while it is not an object found in reality, but rather a reality itself.

Knowledge production (as much as genetic making of animals and plants) can be seen as the most profitable enterprise of the global economy; however, unlike mechanical reproduction of goods, knowledge can never be made; it is as much a possibility as it is an act and a result of creation.

The tension between the concept of knowledge as a whole and the knowledge systems that the world actually possesses well describes the shortages of the existing IP system. While the IP legal logic sets norms over knowledge access, use, and control, its rationality cannot grasp the complexity of interrelationships that compose the reality of knowledge.

Any ideology placed upon knowledge recreates it in the light of its own beliefs: if the market has knowledge as an asset, intellectual products produced by this market not only justify the reasons to validate knowledge as such, but also are evidence of the society's acceptance of market ideology as dominant. Knowledge as an independent source of wealth, on the other hand, is a relatively new phenomenon: history indicates that knowledge-commodity is a historically contingent, socially constructed concept.

In many ways IP reflects an attempt of humans to reconcile with the power of technology. An "apotheosis of human reason" (Brown, 2003, p. 53), IP is the construct that transfers the laws of economy to life, dissolving life into an autonomous, mechanically self-reproducing set.[12]

The subject of knowledge protection—traditional and Western alike—is the fundamental theme of human survival with technology, not a narrow issue assigned to legal and political actors.

One must beg the question here: Do we, in the West, live in a spiritually rich and culturally diverse society, which contributes to development of knowledge as the manifestation of the common spirit of humanity? Or, following the logic of our laws, do we actually see ourselves (without much acknowledgment) as objects of trade, as our thoughts and bodies can be easily turned into commodities by the laws which we ourselves created?

REFERENCES

Agrawal, A. (2002). Indigenous knowledge and the politics of classification. *International Social Science Journal, 54*(173), 287-297.

Almeida, E. (2005, September 21-23). Some aspects on intergrading indigenous perspectives into works on traditional knowledge. *Proceedings of the UNPFII International Workshop on Traditional Knowledge,* Panama City. Retrieved from http://www.un.org/esa/socdev/unpfii/documents/workshop_TK_almeida.pdf

Bannister, K. (2004). Indigenous knowledge and traditional plant resources of the Secwepemc (Shuswap) nation. In M. Riley (Ed.), *Indigenous intellectual property rights: Legal obstacles and innovative solutions* (pp. 279-308). Walnut Creek, CA: AltaMira Press.

Blakeney, M. (1999, November 9). Intellectual property in the dreamtime—protecting the cultural creativity of indigenous peoples. *Proceedings of the Oxford Intellectual Property Research Center Research Seminar, Part 1.* Retrieved from http://www.oipirc.ox.ac.uk/EJWP1999.html

Boyle, J. (1997). *Shamans, software & spleen: Law & the construction of the information society.* Cambridge, MA: Harvard University Press.

Brown, M. (2003). *Who owns native culture?* Cambridge, MA: Harvard University Press.

Commission on Intellectual Property Rights. (2002). *Integrating intellectual property rights, and development policy, executive summary.* Retrieved from http://www.iprcommission.org/graphic/documents/final_report.htm

Daes, E. (1993). *Study on the protection of the cultural and intellectual property of indigenous peoples.* UN ESCOR Document E/CN.4/Sub.2/1993/28.

DESA. (2005, January 17-19). Contribution of the convention on biological diversity and the principle of prior and informed consent. *Proceedings of the UN International Workshop on Free, Prior and Informed Consent and Indigenous Peoples,* New York. Retrieved from http://www.un.org/esa/socdev/unpfii/documents/FPIC_%202005_CBD.doc

Dutfield, G. (2004, October 24-27). What is biopiracy? *Proceedings of the International Expert Workshop on Access to Genetic Resources and Benefit Sharing, Cuernavaca, Mexico. Retrieved from* http://www.canmexworkshop.com/documents/papers/I.3.pdf

Gibson, J. (2004). Traditional knowledge and the international context for protection. *SCRIPT, 48.* Retrieved form http://www.law.ed.ac.uk/ahrb/script-ed/docs/TK.asp

Guerrero, M. (2004). Biocolonialism and isolates of historic interest. In M. Riley (Ed.), *Indigenous intellectual property rights: Legal obstacles and innovative solutions* (pp. 251-277). Walnut Creek, CA: AltaMira Press.

ILO. (1989). *International Labor Organization convention concerning indigenous and tribal peoples in independent countries.* Retrieved from http://www.unhchr.ch/html/menu3/b/62.htm

International Bureau of WIPO. (2004). *WIPO intellectual property handbook. Policy, law and use.* WIPO Publication No. 489(E). Geneva: WIPO. Retrieved from http://www.wipo.int/about-ip/en/iprm/index.htm

Maskus, K. (2000). *Intellectual property rights in the global economy.* Washington, DC: Institute for International Economics.

Moran, K. (2004). Benefit sharing. In M. Riley (Ed.), *Indigenous intellectual property rights: Legal obstacles and innovative solutions* (pp. 153-172). Walnut Creek, CA: AltaMira Press.

Oguamanam, C. (2004). Localizing intellectual property in the globalisation epoch: The integration of indigenous knowledge. *Indiana Journal of Global Legal Studies, 11*(2), 135-169.

Posey, D. (1994). International agreements and intellectual property right protection for indigenous peoples. In T. Greaves (Ed.), *Intellectual property rights for indigenous peoples: A sourcebook* (pp. 223-251). Oklahoma City, OK: Society for Applied Anthropology.

Posey, D. (1996). Protecting indigenous peoples' rights to biodiversity. *Environment, 38*(8), 6-17.

Posey, D. (1999). Safeguarding traditional resource rights of indigenous peoples. In V. Nazarea (Ed.), *Ethnoecology: Situated knowledge/located lives* (pp. 217-229). Tucson: University of Arizona Press.

Posey, D., & Dutfiled, G. (1996). *Beyond intellectual property: Toward traditional resource rights for indigenous peoples ad local communities.* Ottawa: International Development Research Center.

Riley, M. (Ed.). (2004). *Indigenous intellectual property rights: Legal obstacles and innovative solutions.* Walnut Creek, CA: AltaMira Press.

Shiva, V. (1997). *Biopiracy: The plunder of nature and knowledge.* Boston: South End Press.

Simpson, T. (1997). *Indigenous heritage and self-determination: The cultural and intellectual property rights of indigenous peoples.* Copenhagen: IWGIA.

Sinjela, M., & Ramcharan, R. (2005). Protecting traditional knowledge and traditional medicine of indigenous peoples through intellectual property rights: Issues, challenges and strategies. *International Journal on Minority and Group Rights, 12,* 1-24.

Stewart-Harawira, M. (2005). *The indigenous new responses to imperial globalization order.* London/New York: Zed Books.

UNESCO. (2001). *UNESCO universal declaration on cultural diversity.* Retrieved from http://europa.eu.int/comm/avpolicy/extern/gats2000/decl_en.pdf

UNESCO. (2005). *Convention on the protection and promotion of the diversity of cultural expressions.* Retrieved from http://unesdoc.unesco.org/images/0014/001429/142919e.pdf

UNESCO/WIPO. (1985). *Model provisions for national laws on the protection of expressions of folklore against illicit exploitation and other prejudicial actions.*

UNPFII. (2005, September 21-23). *Report of the technical workshop on indigenous traditional knowledge, Panama City.* Retrieved from http://www.un.org/esa/socdev/unpfii/documents/workshop_TK_report.pdf

University of Sussex, Institute of Development Studies. (1979). *IDS bulletin.* Brighton, England: Institute of Development Studies.

Urion, C. (1999). Recording first nations traditional knowledge. *Unpublished papers of the U'mista Cultural Society.*

WIPO. (2005, September 21-23). Information note by the secretariat of the WIPO. *Proceedings of the UNPFII International Workshop on Traditional Knowledge, Panama City.* Retrieved from http://www.un.org/esa/socdev/unpfii/documents/workshop_TK_WIPO.pdf

WIPO. (2006). Retrieved February 6, 2006, from http://www.wipo.int/about-ip/en/

Woodmansee, M., & Jaszi, P. (Eds.). (1994). *Construction of authorship: Textual appropriation in law and literature.* Durham, NC: Duke University Press.

WSIS. (2003). *Indigenous position paper for the world summit on the information society.* Retrieved from http://www.unige.ch/iued/wsis/DEVDOT/02511.HTM

KEY TERMS

Biodiversity: Quality/state of having a variety of life forms in their natural environments.

Biopiracy: Unauthorized appropriation of medical knowledge, knowledge of medical plants and seeds (biomedical knowledge) of indigenous communities by foreign entities (including governments, corporations, and academia) mostly by the application of patens. Also used to mark the site of conflict over benefits of biodevisity between developed (Western) and developing worlds.

Copyright: One of the two main categories of intellectual property to provide exclusivity of the right to publish, sell, and distribute a work of art (literary, musical, or artistic) or science.

Industrial Property: One of the two main categories of intellectual property to provide exclusivity of the right to use industrial designs and inventions (patents, trademarks, integrated circuits, and trade secrets).

Intellectual Property: Legal rights resulting from intellectual activity.

Knowledge Asset: Knowledge understood as property and measured by putting a value on individual skills and people's collective capability to influence conditions of the knowledge market (includes, inter alia, computer systems of an organization and people's embedded intelligence).

Traditional Knowledge: A holistic entity to embody traditional cultural/folklore expressions, practices, and skills, developed, sustained, and transmitted between generations, and to present means for cultural/spiritual identity. Includes knowledge derived from plants and animals as a major part of interaction between a community and its natural environment, as well as knowledge of physical environments (ecological knowledge).

World Intellectual Property Organization (WIPO): An intergovernmental agency of the United Nations system, with the mission to promote dissemination, use, and protection of the intellectual products to stimulate creativity and protect economic and moral interests of creators for the progress of humankind. Established in 1967 in Stockholm, WIPO currently counts 182 Member States to direct and monitor its activities.

APPENDIX 1

Standards for the protection of traditional knowledge through *protection of human rights* are defined by the following documents:

- Universal Declaration of Human Rights (UDHR), Articles 7, 17, 27
- International Covenant of Economical, Social and Cultural Rights (ICESCR), Article 15
- Convention on Biological Diversity (CBD), Article 8(j)
- International Labor Organization Convention No. 169, Articles 2, 13, 15

- Draft Declaration on Rights of Indigenous Peoples, Articles 12, 18, 19, 29 (E/CN.4/Sub.2/1992/28)
- UNESCO's 1989 Recommendation on the Protection and Safeguarding of Folklore and Traditional Knowledge
- Agenda 21, Chapter 26
- The Mattatua Declaration (1993)

Standards to ensure traditional knowledge rights through *the land property laws* include the following documents:

- The Charter of the Indigenous-Tribal Peoples of the Tropical Forests, Articles 14, 15, 40, 42
- The Indigenous Peoples' Earth Charter, Articles 10, 97, 104
- The Declaration of Principles of the World Council of Indigenous Peoples, Articles 3, 7, 10, 11, 12, 13, 18
- International Labor Organization Convention 169 (ILO), Article 4 (Section 1), 13

DISCUSSION FORUMS

The principle location in which representatives of the indigenous communities can interact with nation-states is the Working Group on Indigenous Populations (created in 1981 by the UN Economic and Social Council, ECOSOC).

The forum to influence the directions of national and international law to recognize the needs of indigenous populations is the Permanent Forum of Indigenous Issues (established in 2000).

ENDNOTES

[1] For the list of the main treaties in the field of IP, please refer to Sinjela and Ramcharan (2005).

[2] *Model Provisions for National Laws on the Protection of Expressions of Folklore Against Illicit Exploitation and Other Prejudicial Actions* (1985) is the document where the definition appeared first. See the works of the Group of Experts on the Protection of Expressions of Folklore by Intellectual Property and the resulting documents for further uses.

[3] For the first major scholarly contribution in understanding the traditional knowledge by the Western academy, see the *IDS Bulletin* (Institute of Development Studies, 1979). Works of Brokensha, Warren, Brush, Richards, and Chambers among others have been crucial in recognizing the worth of indigenous peoples' knowledge resources, helping to create greater awareness of the indigenous issues among policymakers and scholars.

[4] Also, an IP-related system of plant breeders' rights can be used to protect *plant varieties*. See the *International Convention for the Protection of New Varieties of Plants* (1961) and the works of the Union for the Protection of New Varieties of Plants (Geneva, Switzerland).

[5] The fact that indigenous cultures are not immune from the influences of the outside world, and are prone to what some experts call "hybridization" or mixing of various elements of outside cultures into their own, makes some experts link development of legal means to protect traditional knowledge to the protection of public domain (Brown, 2003). The response of indigenous activists to these proposals is highly negative: they stress that comparison of knowledge of indigenous peoples with the public domain not only distorts the understanding of what knowledge means for the indigenous peoples, but also causes the world to see traditional knowledge as a property of no one and treat it as such, or with no respect. (WSIS, 2003).

[6] Ways to protect confidential information, for example, can be applicable to the protection of traditional knowledge as a subject to customary law restrictions. Also, "moral-rights" can be used as a measure to prevent degrading use of cultural expressions of indigenous peoples, while contemporary art and music of indigenous communities are subject to copyright protection (WIPO, 2005).

[7] Article 27 of the *Universal Declaration of Human Rights* underlines the right to benefit from protection of interests resulting from authorship of scientific, literary, or artistic production, thus making a direct link between human- and IP-related rights.

[8] Also employment of legal instruments for the protection of land, to which the indigenous people

[9] have reciprocal relationships, is discussed as one of the possible solutions (Riley, 2004).

[9] For examples of *sue generis* initiatives, see Sinjela and Ramcharan (2005).

[10] For a case study and practical examples, see Moran (2004).

[11] Many difficulties exist with implementation of international laws on the national level. Nation-states, which ratify the international standards, hold the status of sovereign entities. They have the right to choose the priorities of legal issues within their citizenry and decide to ignore the issues, concerning protection of intellectual property of indigenous peoples. The prime reasons for ignoring the issue include de-evaluation of traditional knowledge in the past; difficulties associated with management of indigenous communities, including luck of funds and the fear of running into larger problems (as demands for sovereignty); and legal difficulties associated with implementation of international law. Moreover, as national laws take precedence over community laws, legal traditions/customs of indigenous communities, as a rule, are not recognized (Riley, 2004). As IP rights are "territorial" in scope, conclusion of international agreements is often necessary for the rights to become applicable on the national and international levels.

[12] The Human Genome Project, for example, is directed to interpret genetic data (material) into a text, which can later be edited and copyrighted, thus turning the human body into a commodity upon which ownership can be placed. As is pertinent to indigenous peoples, there is a second Human Genome Diversity Project, called by one scholar "invisible genocide" (Guerrero, 2004, p. 251).

Universal Internet Access under an Ethical Lens

Alessandro Arbore
Bocconi University, Italy

INTRODUCTION

Universal service is a long-standing tradition of telecommunications policy, designed to ensure that all citizens have access to affordable, quality telecommunications services regardless of geographic location and socioeconomic status. The origins of it are usually traced to the U.S. 1934 Communications Act and, also within the European Union, this principle was made explicit since the very first documents on the issue, as in the Green Book of 1995 or, even before, in the Council Resolution (93/C213/01) accepting the Commission guidelines for the liberalization of voice telecommunications (COM(93)159).

In Europe, as in the U.S. with the 1996 Telecommunications Reform,[1] it is currently recognized as a dynamic nature of universal service. According to the 1996 act, in particular, the FCC is in charge of defining it and making it *evolve consistently with technological progress* (s. 254(c)(1)). This innovative approach is followed by the European Union as well ((EC) No 34/96). The recent implementation of this principle in western countries, however, has been controversial, giving us the starting point for a broader discussion.[2]

Among other things, in fact, critics have charged that the definitions of what constitutes universal service have not been adequately addressed: a critical question is whether Internet access should become part of a universal service application, which means to take on the obligation to make Internet access to every citizen possible at affordable rates and have its costs subsidized through universal service funding.

The aim of this article is to frame the question within an ethical background able to steer our judgment and root our evaluation into some solid moral argument. The contribution will try to show different ethical perspectives to approach the debate. As a final remark, while for *developing* countries the real issue today remains "Internet access," for *developed* countries the reader should interpret the problem of "Internet access" as "Broadband Internet access": *mutatis mutandis,* all the considerations made remain valid in both contexts.

UNIVERSAL INTERNET ACCESS: DISCUSSION

As anticipated above, it is important to understand what one means by universal access to the Internet. If Internet access as universal service means to guarantee the minimal technical conditions of the national telephone network to access the Internet, then such access is in fact already becoming available universally, even for broadband services. Likewise, if we require the presence of supply in every area so to have potential access countrywide, this condition has already been achieved by the private industry. However, these basic definitions are intuitively too narrow to be consistent with what is discussed above. So, if "universal Internet access" is to be something more, then what? Should we guarantee the provision of the service at affordable conditions? Should we guarantee some equipment as well? More widely, should we guarantee that every person, independently from her status or skills, could access the Internet?

From this last statement, two different levels of the problem emerge: an economical level and an attitudinal one. Even if the two should have the same logical standing, the debate seems to be excessively focused on the economic barriers. In this article we consider the idea of universal access to the Internet as embedded in both dimensions:

a. universal access as the transfer of resources to the poor in order to provide them with the minimum tangible assets to access the Internet, and
b. universal access as the transfer of knowledge and skills to the new "techno-illiterate" in order to

provide them with the minimum intangible assets to access the Internet.

How do we discern whether the provision of telecommunications universal service should include goal A or goal B or both? And which would be the minimum level of tangible or intangible assets to grant? Our aim cannot be limited to understand if A or B is simply desirable. It seems easy to agree that both A and B are desirable. However, in the presence of scarce resources, the policy debate centers on prioritizing needs: "How important is Internet access in an area without safe water?" (Pruett & Deane, 1998).

Instead of giving a deterministic answer, in the following pages we will frame the issue within different ethical backgrounds, trying to provide a more complete picture of the problem. Specifically, policies A and B will be commented on according to three important theoretical frameworks: the rights theories, the utilitarian theories, and the theory of justice.

The Human Rights Approach

The extension of traditional universal service might be justified if we proved that certain services are basic human rights.

The claim of the right to Internet access could be argued—first—by analogy from traditional telephone services, postal services, and universal education.

When referring to traditional telephone service, "the entitlement argument asserts that in a modern society telephonic communication, like education, basic medical care, and postal service, is an inherent attribute of citizenship....*No one...should be denied the participation in the life of the community* that the telephone provides" (Pool, 1984, p. 115). This argument also gained some legal force. For example, the Montana Supreme Court ruled in a 1987 case that the lack of a telephone is a significant "barrier to employment" (cited in Hadden, 1991). In our times, these considerations appear extendible to Internet access. It is because, no doubt, an increasing part of community life is moving into the so-called cyberspace. An early study conducted by RAND, for example, noted how the lack of an e-mail address could quickly become a new barrier to employment (Anderson, Bikson, Law, & Mitchell, 1995).

By providing asynchronous written communication, the basic features of e-mail services are analogous to those of postal services. Yet, they are extremely faster (almost real-time delivery), more flexible (it is possible to access one's e-mail from different locations), and in general, more convenient (especially if the same message must be sent to multiple addresses). Not surprisingly, its diffusion is becoming widespread. Therefore, in the same way we recognized in the past the postal services as a universal right, we might recognize today the right to a universal e-mail address.

Similar appeals can be found for universal education. In the mid-1800s the masthead of the Working Man's Advocate read: "All children are entitled to equal education; all adults to equal privileges" (Binder, 1974, p. 33, cited in Sawhney, 1995). The argument here was that universal education is a *necessary requirement for modern life*. This resembles the way in which the skills to access the Internet are becoming more and more necessary *to have comparable opportunities in modern life*.

A complementary way to claim the right to Internet access is by deriving it from a superior right which it implements. Assemblywoman Gwen Moore, for example, adopted this strategy in California (Jacobson, 1989). Her argument was grounded in a broad interpretation of the "free speech" clause by the California Supreme Court. The rationale is that if the freedom to communicate is a fundamental right, then access to the means of communication must also be a fundamental right. Without Internet access, one cannot be a part of the telecommunicating community.

It is important to notice, however, that we should not make confusion between negative rights (the legitimate right of being free to access the Internet if I want to) and positive rights (the right—still to be proved—to receive any support so that I can access the Internet).

According to this first ethical perspective, then, it is possible to conclude that:

a. A positive right for Internet access—deducted by analogy—is plausible, even if not necessarily a *home* access: it could be a public access to the internet, like in schools or libraries. Concerning the availability of e-mail addresses for everyone, it is interesting to note how the private entrepreneurship already overcame this issue by providing free accounts. Referring to the negative right for Internet access, a constant reduction of technical barriers to broadband Internet access is clearly desirable. In developed and developing countries, indeed, both technological (especially wireless) and competitive dynamics are steering the investments right in this direction.

b. Conceptually, once a right for Internet access has been recognized, there should be no distinction between economical and attitudinal barriers: both of them should be removed. This would mean, for example, to think at training and supporting points, maybe in the same public places where Internet access is granted. Moreover, this way of thinking advocates for a compulsory computer science education. Indeed, also in this case, policy makers and educational institutions are already moving in such a direction.

The Utilitarian Approach

A different perspective to consider our issue comes from the utilitarian theories, started with Bentham (1789/1948). The basic idea behind the utilitarian argument is that the provision of Internet services on a universal basis could make it possible for the social system as a whole to function more efficiently. If the overall social benefits of universal Internet access would outweigh its costs, then it should be adopted.

At the utilitarian end, then, is efficiency. The Internet provides a fast, reliable, and efficient means of conveying information and interacting with persons (interaction through the medium) or with machines (interaction with the medium) (Hoffman, Novak, & Venkatesh, 1996). This modifies the way the production is organized as well as the context in which exchanges are arranged. For these reasons, the Internet is deemed to be a powerful instrument to achieve commercial and economic benefits, contributing to increased market efficiency and increased economic competitiveness.

Indeed, a fundamental point to discuss the utilitarian rational for a universal Internet access is a basic characteristic that the Internet shares with other communications services: call and network externalities are an important determinant of demand. Call externalities arise because a communication between two parties is typically initiated by one party, whose decision is guided by its private benefit. But benefits (which in some cases could be negative) are conferred (or inflicted) on the other party too. In this case an individual's decision about using a communications service may not be consistent with maximum social welfare because the individual benefits of decision makers do not coincide

with social benefits. Similarly, network externalities arise because the individual's decision to join a network is typically guided only by the benefit that one can receive by communicating with others on the network. This private benefit differs from the social benefit, which includes the benefits others receive from being able to communicate with the individual in question. The traditional view is that these externalities will result in networks that are too small in comparison to the optimal (social welfare maximizing) network (Mitchell & Vogelsang, 1991).

The bottom line is: considering that each additional Internet user increases the value of the entire network and considering that a wide use of the Internet could turn in many advantages for other industries as well, the overall benefit to the system is likely to be higher than the cost of subsidizing the service to those portions of the population that cannot afford the service (or do not have the necessary skills).[3]

What about the distinctions between policies A and B? In the utilitarian perspective, the only rule to share our financial resources would be to consider if higher benefits are retrieved for a dollar spent to provide access to a poor person (a) or to an unskilled person (b). The same logic would govern the decision about the scope of the two policies. For example, considering A, should we provide to the poor free Internet access, or a modem as well, or a terminal? We would grant the poor with an additional dollar to access the Internet until: (1) this cost is lower or equal to the additional benefit to the society (considering the private benefit to the poor plus the social benefit to all the other users); and (2) such additional benefit is higher than the additional benefit that the society would retrieve if the dollar were spent for policy B, as well as for other concurrent policies. *Mutatis mutandis,* the same would be for B.

It is important to underline two points: first, while this reasoning is straightforward from a theoretical point of view, the actual identification and monetarization of costs and benefit may be a very complex task or, according to some criticisms, even a non-realistic goal. It is also true, however, that CBA (cost-benefit analysis) techniques are getting more and more sophisticated and reliable. The second caveat is more conceptual than practical: this approach is focused especially on efficiency and not on equity, while universal service has equity and not efficiency goals. A CBA analysis, nonetheless, may be extremely useful to evaluate the actual costs of similar policies and to discern the best alternative to reach our equity goals (so-called cost-effectiveness analysis).

The Social Contract Approach and the Theory of Justice

The third perspective that we propose to consider the problem is a neocontractual approach. Philosophical and ethical discussions on the subject of information society often underline the notion of *information poverty,* which is risky tied to the notion of economic poverty. Within the framework in point, the objective of a universal Internet access would be to avoid a new stratification between "information rich" and "information poor."

In theory, it is argued, the means to handle information are becoming more available and democratic. In practice, however, there is the danger that new information elitism may arise to further disenfranchise poor people.[4] Of course, as observed in these pages, information poverty in the Internet era is not only a problem of low socioeconomic classes. People with higher incomes may lack the necessary computer skills, or they may lack the appropriate information retrieval skills. In addition, people may not understand the sheer volume of information possible. "Too much information can be a form of information poverty, especially if it drives people away from communicating or listening to useful information" (Sweetland, 1993, p. 9).

'Information poverty' provides the right context to frame a famous quote by James Madison:

A popular government, without popular information, or the means of acquiring it, is but a prologue to a farce or a tragedy, or perhaps both. Knowledge will forever govern ignorance and people who mean to be their own governors must arm themselves with the power knowledge gives. (1865, p. 276)

In this perspective, it is interesting to note that *information poverty exists as a relative condition.* Not to be able to retrieve information from the Internet (for economic or attitudinal reasons) becomes a problem when part of the population is able to. According to Internet statistics, well-educated, not aged, not poor citizens have a privileged position to access informa-

tion, the raw material potentially able to improve their knowledge, alias power. The aim of this section is to deal with the issue of universal Internet access *by asking if such a situation would be consistent with a hypothetical agreement between rational persons in an original position of equality.*[5]

This perspective is that of Johan Rawls' (1971) theory of justice, a theory elaborated within the ethical approach of the social contract. The root idea behind the social contract theories is that any set of rules will be fair and just if persons agree to abide by these rules (Rogerson, 1991). The agreement can be merely hypothetical: we can specify morally binding social principles by requiring that the principles are ones to which all reasonable persons would consent, if given the chance. Rawls explains that in the original position (a substitute for the Lockean state of nature), "[t]he principles of justice are chosen behind a veil of ignorance. This ensure[s] that no one is advantaged or disadvantaged in the choice of principles by the outcome of natural chance or the contingency of social circumstances" (p. 505).

Moving back to our issue, it seems reasonable that a rational person in the original position would agree on the principle that the society should equalize at least *the opportunities* of its citizens.

A way to grant equal opportunities is to act "on the upstream," by *granting equal access to the sources* of knowledge and, therefore, to the privileges that knowledge gives. And, of course, a privileged access to the new information media could be considered a privileged source of knowledge, alias power, in Madison's words. In other words, to act on the upstream implies that equal access opportunities to the Internet—with its *mare magnum* of contents—should be granted.

Going deeper, it is plausible to argue that in Rawls' "original position," the problem of material poverty would probably find higher standing than that of information poverty: a war on information poverty would be logically legitimized only as a means to fight material poverty, if more effective than other means. As we could expect, in fact, the framework suggested by Rawls seems to advocate for a support to universal Internet access only in the measure that it could lead to a more egalitarian society, and only after that human dignity is guaranteed to everybody.

CONCLUSION

The aim of this article was to frame the problem of universal Internet access and to exemplify how the issue can be observed from different ethical perspectives.

The main points suggested in this article are not the only possible ones. However, once that the main goal has been reassessed, it is possible to sum up some of the considerations that have emerged.

Generically, a universal access to the Internet (maybe a broadband access) is probably coherent with all the approaches examined here. The scope of such a policy, however, is not easy to limit. First, the current competitive, technological, and demand dynamics seems to be able to grant, alone, a mere availability of technical access. A public intervention could be limited to support access to the Internet from public spots. In addition, a voucher for poorer people could be the subject for a specific cost-benefit analysis: we urge the necessity of this kind of information to support the current debate. Any subsidy, however, should be strictly related to the income status of a citizen, and not—as for current universal service provisions—on geographic averaging.

In considering a support for people having only attitudinal barriers for accessing the Internet, the perspectives illustrated here provides less converging insights. If we consider Internet assess as a right, then economic barriers and attitudinal barriers should have the same standing and should be opportunely removed. If the utilitarian perspective is preferred, then we should prioritize the removal of those barriers granting higher efficiency recovery. Finally, if we embrace the neo-contractual approach, a war to attitudinal barriers might not be considered a priority.

In conclusion, this article would like to underline how important is to make always explicit—maybe to ourselves first—the normative background on which we base any legitimate contribution to the debate on universal Internet access. This would certainly help the dialectic.

REFERENCES

Anderson, R.H., Bikson, T.K., Law, S.A., & Mitchell, B.M. (1995). *Universal access to e-mail: Feasibility and societal implications.* RAND Report.

Arrow, K. (1964). *Social choice and individual values.* New York: John Wiley & Sons.

Barker, E. (1962). *The politics of Aristotele.* Oxford University Press.

Bentham, J. (1948). *An introduction to the principles of morals and legislation.* New York, Hafner (originally published in 1789).

Binder, F.M. (1974). *The age of common school.* New York: John Wiley & Sons.

Bosah, E. (1998). *Cyberghetto or cybertopia? Race, class, and gender on the Internet.* Westport, CT: Praeger.

Brock, G.W. (1994). *The telecommunications policy for the information age.* Cambridge, MA: Harvard University Press.

Di Maggio, P., Hargittai, E., Celeste, C., & Shafer, S. (2004). Digital inequality: From unequal access to differentiated use. In K. Neckerman (Ed.), *Social inequality* (pp. 355-400). New York: Russell Sage Foundation.

Ditzion, S. (1947). *Arsenal of a democratic culture* (p. 99). American Library Association. Cited in Sawhney, H. (1994). Universal service: Prosaic motives and great ideals. *Journal of Broadcasting & Electronic Media, 38*(Fall), ref. 27, 209.

FCC (Federal Communication Commission). (1997). *Report & order in the matter of federal-state joint board on universal service.* CC Docket No. 96-45.

Hadden, S. (1991). Technologies of universal service. In *Annual review, 1991: Universal telephone service: Ready for the 21st Century?* Nashville, TN: Institute for Information Studies.

Hahn, F., & Hollis, M. (1979). *Philosophy and economic theory.* New York: Oxford University Press.

Hoffman, D.L., Novak, T.P. & Venkatesh, A. (2004). Has the Internet become indispensable? *Communications of the ACM, 47*(7), 37-42.

Jacobson, R. (1989). *An open approach to information policy making: A case study of the Moore Universal Telephone Service Act.* Ablex.

Kahin, B., & Keller. J. (1995). *Public access to the Internet* (pp. 34-45). Boston: MIT Press.

U

Katz, J.E., & Aspden, P. (1997). A nation of strangers? *Communications of the ACM, 40*(12), 81-86.

Katz, J.E., & Rice, R.E. (2002). *Social consequences of Internet use: Access, involvement and interaction.* Cambridge, MA: MIT Press.

Madison, J. (1865). Letter to W.T. Barry, August 4, 1822. From "Letters and Other Writings of James Madison," third volume. Published by order of Congress.

Mossberger, K., Tolgert, C., & Stansbury, M. (2003). *Virtual inequality: Beyond the digital divide.* Washington, DC: Georgetown University Press.

Mueller, M. (1996). *Universal service: Interconnection, competition, and monopoly in the making of the American telephone system.* Cambridge, MA: MIT Press.

Mueller, M. (1997). Universal service and the new telecommunications act: Mythology made law. *Communications of the ACM, 40*(March), 185.

Norris, P. (2001). *Digital divide: Civic engagement, information poverty, and the Internet worldwide.* Cambridge: Cambridge University Press.

Pool, I.S. (1984). Competition and universal service: Can we get there from here? In H.M. Shoosan (Ed.), *Disconnecting bell: The impact of the AT&T divestiture.* Pergamon.

Pourciau, L.J. (1999). *Ethics and electronic information in the twenty-first century.* West Lafayette, IN: Purdue University Press.

Pruett, D., & Deane, J. (1998). The Internet and poverty. *Panos Media Briefing, 28*(April).

Rawls, J. (1971). *A theory of justice.* Cambridge, MA: Harvard University Press.

Rawls, J. (1979). *The concept of justice in political economy.* In F. Hahn & M. Hollis (Eds.), *Philosophy and economic theory.* New York: Oxford University Press.

Roberts, H.H. (2000). Developing new rules for new markets. *Journal of the Academy of Marketing Science, 28*(1).

Rogerson, K.E. (1991). *Ethical theory.* Holt, Rinehart and Winston.

Rousseau, J.J. (1947). *The social contract* (edited by C. Frankel). New York: Hafner (originally published in 1762).

Sawhney, H. (1994). Universal service: Prosaic motives and great ideals. *Journal of Broadcasting & Electronic Media, 38*(Fall).

Sweetland, J.H. (1993). Information poverty—let me count the way. *Database, 16*(4).

Tarjanne, P. (1996, October 25). The Internet: Enabling whom, when and where? *Proceedings of the United Nations University INTECH Seminar,* Maastricht, The Netherlands.

Turkle, S. (1996). Virtuality and its discontents: Searching for community in cyberspace. *The American Prospect, 24,* 50-57.

Warschauer, M. (2003). *Technology and social inclusion: Rethinking the digital divide.* Cambridge, MA: MIT Press.

Warschauer, M. (2003). Demystifying the digital divide. *Scientific American,* (August), 42-47.

Wilson, J.Q. (1974). The politics of regulation. In J.W. McKie (Ed.), *Social responsibility and the business predicament.* Bookings.

KEY TERMS

Digital Divide: The growing gap of opportunities between information reach and information poor (see also "information poverty"). It can refer to persons, countries, or institutions (e.g., a digital divide between large companies and small and medium enterprises).

Information Apartheid: See *Information Poverty.*

Information Poverty: The condition of persons or institutions unable to retrieve the benefits of our current information society because of their inability to access new media, such as the Internet. Such inability may be caused by economic as well as by attitudinal barriers. See also *Techno-Illiterate* and *Digital Divide.*

Internet Access: Refers to the possibility to connect to the public Internet and the World Wide Web. For private users, this is generally achieved through an Internet service provider (ISP), mainly via the traditional public telecommunications network (either through a dial-up narrowband connection or an ADSL broadband connection) or via a CATV network, where available (cable-modem broadband connection). Larger business and institutional users are generally connected to the Internet in a direct, permanent way, by leasing the necessary bandwidth from a telecommunications provider (e.g., T1 lines in the U.S. or E1 lines in Europe); the access, then, is distributed internally through a wired or wireless LAN.

Techno-Illiterate: People unconfident with new technologies or even ignoring how to use them, especially information and communication technologies (ICTs). This may be a cause for *Information Poverty*.

Universal Internet Access: A proposal for taking on the obligation to make Internet access to every citizen possible at affordable rates and have its finances subsidized through universal service funding. Currently, Internet access is not part of universal service applications, neither in the United States nor in Europe.

Universal Service: A long-standing tradition of telecommunications policies in western countries, designed to ensure that all citizens have access to affordable, quality telecommunications services regardless of geographic location and socioeconomic status. The origins of universal service policy are usually traced to the U.S. Communications Act of 1934.

ENDNOTES

[1] Public Law No. 104-104, 110 Status 56. Codified at 47 U.S.C. § 254(b).

[2] For the U.S., see FCC (1997). For the EU, the implementation is left to the different National Regulatory Authorities (NRAs).

[3] Also in this case we can find an analogy with universal education: "Where every individual thought and deed affected the social mechanism of the whole, it become[s] the interest of the whole to provide the necessary education for its part" (Ditzion, 1947).

[4] Representative Edward Markey, for instance, coined the expression "informational apartheid" (Luncheon Speaker at Broadcasting and Cale Magazine Telecommunications Forum, September 27, 1995).

[5] By hypothesis, in the original position "no one knows his place in society, his class position or social status, nor does any one know his fortune in the distribution of natural assets and abilities, his intelligence, strength, and the like" (Rawls, 1971, p. 137).

Key Term Index

DARPA, 315

NASA, 315

Index